P9-BJR-689

Nineteenth-Century Literature Criticism

Topics Volume

Guide to Gale Literary Criticism Series

For criticism on	Consult these Gale series
Authors now living or who died after December 31, 1959	*CONTEMPORARY LITERARY CRITICISM (CLC)*
Authors who died between 1900 and 1959	*TWENTIETH-CENTURY LITERARY CRITICISM (TCLC)*
Authors who died between 1800 and 1899	*NINETEENTH-CENTURY LITERATURE CRITICISM (NCLC)*
Authors who died between 1400 and 1799	*LITERATURE CRITICISM FROM 1400 TO 1800 (LC)* *SHAKESPEAREAN CRITICISM (SC)*
Authors who died before 1400	*CLASSICAL AND MEDIEVAL LITERATURE CRITICISM (CMLC)*
Authors of books for children and young adults	*CHILDREN'S LITERATURE REVIEW (CLR)*
Dramatists	*DRAMA CRITICISM (DC)*
Poets	*POETRY CRITICISM (PC)*
Short story writers	*SHORT STORY CRITICISM (SSC)*
Black writers of the past two hundred years	*BLACK LITERATURE CRITICISM (BLC)*
Hispanic writers of the late nineteenth and twentieth centuries	*HISPANIC LITERATURE CRITICISM (HLC)*
Native North American writers and orators of the eighteenth, nineteenth, and twentieth centuries	*NATIVE NORTH AMERICAN LITERATURE (NNAL)*
Major authors from the Renaissance to the present	*WORLD LITERATURE CRITICISM, 1500 TO THE PRESENT (WLC)*

ISSN 0732-1864

Volume 72

Nineteenth-Century Literature Criticism

Topics Volume

Excerpts from Criticism of Various Topics in Nineteenth-Century Literature, including Literary and Critical Movements, Prominent Themes and Genres, Anniversary Celebrations, and Surveys of National Literatures

Janet Witalec
Editor

GALE
DETROIT • LONDON

STAFF

Janet Witalec, *Editor*
Denise Evans, Daniel G. Marowski, *Contributing Editors*
Suzanne Dewsbury, Ira Mark Milne, *Associate Editors*
Craig Hutchison, *Assistant Editor*
Aarti D. Stephens, *Managing Editor*

Susan M. Trosky, *Permissions Manager*
Kimberly F. Smilay, *Permissions Specialist*
Steve Cusack, Kelly A. Quin, *Permissions Associates*
Sandra K. Gore, *Permissions Assistant*

Victoria B. Cariappa, *Research Manager*
Gary Oudersluys, *Research Specialist*
Tamara C. Nott, Tracie A. Richardson, Cheryl Warnock, *Research Associates*
Corrine Stocker, Research Assistant

Mary Beth Trimper, *Production Director*
Deborah L. Milliken, *Production Assistant*

Christine O'Bryan, *Desktop Publisher*
Randy Bassett, *Image Database Supervisor*
Robert Duncan, Michael Logusz, *Imaging Specialists*
Pamela A. Reed, *Imaging Coordinator*

This book is printed on acid-free paper that meets the minimum requirements of American National Standard for Information Sciences—Permanence Paper for Printed Library Materials, ANSI Z39.48-1984.

Library of Congress Catalog Card Number 84-643008
ISBN 0-7876-2420-9
ISSN 0732-1864
Printed in the United States of America

10 9 8 7 6 5 4 3 2 1

Contents

Preface

Since its inception in 1981, *Nineteenth-Century Literature Criticism* has been a valuable resource for students and librarians seeking critical commentary on writers of this transitional period in world history. Designated an "Outstanding Reference Source" by the American Library Association with the publication of its first volume, *NCLC* has since been purchased by over 6,000 school, public, and university libraries. The series has covered more than 300 authors representing 29 nationalities and over 17,000 titles. No other reference source has surveyed the critical reaction to nineteenth-century authors and literature as thoroughly as *NCLC.*

Scope of the Series

NCLC is designed to introduce students and advanced readers to the authors of the nineteenth century, and to the most significant interpretations of these authors' works. The great poets, novelists, short story writers, playwrights, and philosophers of this period are frequently studied in high school and college literature courses. By organizing and reprinting commentary written on these authors, *NCLC* helps students develop valuable insight into literary history, promotes a better understanding of the texts, and sparks ideas for papers and assignments. Each entry in *NCLC* presents a comprehensive survey of an author's career or an individual work of literature and provides the user with a multiplicity of interpretations and assessments. Such variety allows students to pursue their own interests; furthermore, it fosters an awareness that literature is dynamic and responsive to many different opinions.

Every fourth volume of *NCLC* is devoted to literary topics that cannot be covered under the author approach used in the rest of the series. Such topics include literary movements, prominent themes in nineteenth-century literature, literary reaction to political and historical events, significant eras in literary history, prominent literary anniversaries, and the literatures of cultures that are often overlooked by English-speaking readers.

NCLC continues the survey of criticism of world literature begun by Gale's *Contemporary Literary Criticism (CLC)* and *Twentieth-Century Literary Criticism (TCLC),* both of which excerpt and reprint commentary on authors of the twentieth century. For additional information about *TCLC, CLC,* and Gale's other criticism series, users should consult the Guide to Gale Literary Criticism Series preceding the title page in this volume.

Coverage

Each volume of *NCLC* is carefully compiled to present:

- criticism of authors, or literary topics, representing a variety of genres and nationalities
- both major and lesser-known writers and literary works of the period
- 4-8 authors or 4-6 topics per volume
- individual entries that survey critical response to an author's work or a topic in literary history, including early criticism to reflect initial reactions, later criticism to represent any rise or decline in reputation, and current retrospective analyses.

Organization

An author entry consists of the following elements: author heading, biographical and critical introduction, list of principal works, excerpts of criticism (each preceded by a bibliographic citation and an annotation), and a bibliography of further reading.

- The **Author Heading** consists of the name under which the author most commonly wrote, followed by birth and death dates. If an author wrote consistently under a pseudonym, the pseudonym will be listed in the author heading and the real name given in parentheses on the first line of the biographical and critical introduction. Also located at the beginning of the introduction to the author entry are any name variations under which an author wrote, including transliterated forms for an author whose language uses a nonroman alphabet.

- The **Biographical and Critical Introduction** outlines the author's life and career, as well as the critical issues surrounding his or her work. References are provided to past volumes of *NCLC* in which further information about the author may be found.

- Most *NCLC* entries include a **Portrait** of the author. Many entries also contain reproductions of materials pertinent to an author's career, including manuscript pages, title pages, dust jackets, letters, and drawings, as well as photographs of important people, places, and events in an author's life.

- The list of **Principal Works** is chronological by date of first publication and identifies the genre of each work. In the case of foreign authors with both foreign-language publications and English translations, the English-language version is given in brackets. Unless otherwise indicated, dramas are dated by first performance, not first publication.

- **Criticism** in each author entry is arranged chronologically to provide a perspective on changes in critical evaluation over the years. All titles of works by the author featured in the entry are printed in boldface type to enable the user to easily locate discussion of particular works. Also for purposes of easier identification, the critic's name and the publication date of the essay are given at the beginning of each piece of criticism. Unsigned criticism is preceded by the title of the journal in which it appeared. Publication information (such as publisher names and book prices) and some parenthetical numerical references (such as page and line references to specific editions of works) have been deleted at the editors' discretion to provide smoother reading of the text. Footnotes that appear with previously published pieces of criticism are reprinted at the end of each essay or excerpt. In the case of excerpted criticism, only those footnotes that pertain to the excerpted text are included.

- A complete **Bibliographic Citation** provides original publication information for each piece of criticism.

- Critical excerpts are prefaced by **Annotations** providing the reader with a summary of the critical intent of the piece. Also included, when appropriate, is information about the critic's reputation, individual approach to literary criticism, and particular expertise in an author's works, as well as information about the relative importance of the critical excerpt. In some cases, the annotations cross-reference excerpts by critics who discuss each other's commentary.

- An annotated list of **Further Reading** appearing at the end of each entry suggests secondary sources on the author. In some cases it includes essays for which the editors could not obtain reprint rights.

Cumulative Indexes

- Each volume of *NCLC* contains a cumulative **Author Index** listing all authors who have appeared in Gale's Literary Criticism Series, along with cross-references to such biographical series as *Contemporary Authors* and *Dictionary of Literary Biography.* Useful for locating authors within the various series, this index is particularly valuable for those authors who are identified with a certain period but who, because of their death dates, are placed in another, or for those authors whose careers span two periods. For example, Fyodor Dostoevsky is found in *NCLC,* yet Leo Tolstoy, another major nineteenth-century Russian novelist, is found in *TCLC* because he died after 1899.

- Each *NCLC* volume includes a cumulative **Nationality Index** which lists all authors who have appeared in *NCLC,* arranged alphabetically under their respective nationalities.

- Each new volume in Gale's Literary Criticism Series includes a cumulative **Topic Index**, which lists all literary topics treated in *NCLC, TCLC, LC 1400-1800,* and the *CLC* Yearbook.

- Each new volume of *NCLC,* with the exception of the Topics volumes, contains a **Title Index** listing the titles of all literary works discussed in the volume. In response to numerous suggestions from librarians, Gale has also produced a **Special Paperbound Edition** of the *NCLC* title index. This annual cumulation lists all titles discussed in the series since its inception. Additional copies of the index are available on request. Librarians and patrons have welcomed this separate index: it saves shelf space, is easy to use, and is recyclable upon receipt of the following year's cumulation. Titles discussed in the Topics volume entries are not included in the *NCLC* cumulative index.

Citing *Nineteenth-Century Literature Criticism*

When writing papers, students who quote directly from any volume in Gale's Literary Criticism Series may use the following general forms to footnote reprinted criticism. The first example pertains to material drawn from periodicals, the second to material reprinted from books:

[1]T.S. Eliot, "John Donne," *The Nation and Athenaeum,* 33 (9 June 1923), 321-32; excerpted and reprinted in *Literature Criticism from 1400-1800,* Vol. 10, ed. James E. Person, Jr. (Detroit: Gale Research, 1989), pp. 28-9.

[2]Clara G. Stillman, *Samuel Butler: A Mid-Victorian Modern* (Viking Press, 1932); excerpted and reprinted in *Twentieth-Century Literary Criticism,* Vol. 33, ed. Paula Kepos (Detroit: Gale Research, 1989), pp. 43-5.

Suggestions Are Welcome

In response to suggestions, several features have been added to *NCLC* since the series began, including annotations to excerpted criticism, a cumulative index to authors in all Gale literary criticism series, entries devoted to criticism on a single work by a major author, more illustrations, and a title index listing all literary works discussed in the series.

Readers who wish to suggest authors, single works, or topics to appear in future volumes, or who have other suggestions, are cordially invited to write: The Editors, *Nineteenth-Century Literature Criticism,* The Gale Group, 27500 Drake Rd., Farmington Hills, MI 48331-3535; call toll-free at 1-800-347-GALE.

Acknowledgments

The editors wish to thank the copyright holders of the excerpted criticism included in this volume and the permissions managers of many book and magazine publishing companies for assisting us in securing reproduction rights. We are also grateful to the staffs of the Detroit Public Library, the Library of Congress, the University of Detroit Mercy Library, Wayne State University Purdy/Kresge Library Complex, and the University of Michigan Libraries for making their resources available to us. Following is a list of the copyright holders who have granted us permission to reproduce material in this volume of *NCLC*. Every effort has been made to trace copyright, but if omissions have been made, please let us know.

COPYRIGHTED EXCERPTS IN *NCLC*, VOLUME 72, WERE REPRODUCED FROM THE FOLLOWING PERIODICALS:

America, v. 112, May 1, 1965. © 1965. All rights reserved. Reproduced with permission of America Press, Inc.,106 West 56th Street, New York, NY 10019.—***Anglican and Episcopal History/Historical Magazine of the Protestant Episcopal Church***, v. XXXIII, March, 1964; v. XLVIII, June, 1979. Copyright 1964, 1979, The Historical Society of the Episcopal Church. Both reproduced by permission.—***Faith & Reason: The Journal of Christendom College***, v. III, Summer, 1977. © Christendom Educational Corporation 1997. Reproduced by permission of The Christendom College Press.—***French Studies***, v. II, July, 1957. Reproduced by permission.—***Studies in the Novel***, v. 26, Fall, 1994. Copyright © 1994 by North Texas State University. Reproduced by permission.—***The Yale Review***, v. 66, Autumn, 1976. Copyright © 1976 by Yale University. Reproduced by permission of Blackwell Publishers.

COPYRIGHTED EXCERPTS IN *NCLC*, VOLUME 72, WERE REPRODUCED FROM THE FOLLOWING BOOKS:

Abrams, Meyer H. From ***The Mirror and the Lamp: Romantic Theory and the Critical Tradition***. Oxford University Press, 1953. Copyright 1953 by Oxford University Press, Inc. Renewed 1981 by Meyer Howard Abrams. Reproduced by permission of Oxford University Press, Inc.—Borsch, Frederick H. From "Ye Shall Be Holy: Reflections on the Spirituality of the Oxford Movement" in ***Tradition Renewed: The Oxford Movement Conference Papers***. Edited by Geoffrey Rowell. Pickwick Publications, 1986. Introduction and this collection Copyright © 1986 Geoffrey Rowell. © 1984 Frederick H. Borsch. All rights reserved. Reproduced by permission.—Brendon, Piers. From ***Hurrell Froude and The Oxford Movement***. Paul Elek, 1974. Copyright © 1974 Piers Brendon. All rights reserved. Reproduced by permission of the author.—Chadwick, Owen. From "'Lead, Kindly Light'" in ***The Spirit of The Oxford Movement: Tractarian Essays***. Cambridge University Press, 1990. © Cambridge University Press, 1990. Reproduced with the permission of Cambridge University Press and the author.—Chapman, Raymond. From ***Faith and Revolt: Studies in the Literary Influence of the Oxford Movement***. Weidenfeld and Nicolson, 1970. © 1970 Raymond Chapman. All rights reserved. Reproduced by permission.—Charvet, P. E. From ***A Literary History of France: Volume IV, The Nineteenth Century: 1789-1870.*** Ernest Benn, Barnes and Noble Books, 1967. Copyright © 1967 by P. E. Charvet. Reproduced by permission.—Cheyette, Bryan. From "The Other Self: Anglo-Jewish Fiction and the Representation of Jews in England, 1875-1905" in ***The Making of Modern Anglo-Jewry***. Edited by David Cesarani. Basil Blackwell, 1990. Copyright © Basil Blackwell Ltd. 1990. All rights reserved. Reproduced by permission.—Denomme, Robert T. From ***The French Parnassian Poets***. Southern Illinois University Press, 1972. Copyright © 1972 by Southern Illinois University Press. All rights reserved. Reproduced by permission of the publisher.—Fisch, Harold. From ***The Dual Image: The Figure of the Jew in English and American Literature***. KTAV Publishing House, Inc., 1971. © Copyright 1971 World Jewish Congress British Section. Reproduced by permission.—Hunt, Herbert J. From ***The Epic in Nineteenth-Century France***. Basil Blackwell, 1941.—Ince, W. N. From ***Heredia***. The Anthlone Press, 1979. Copyright © 1979 W. N. Ince. Reproduced by permission.—Lambropoulos, Vassilis. From "Violence and the Liberal Imagination: The Representation of Hellenism in Matthew Arnold" in ***The Violence of Representation: Literature and The History of Violence***. Edited by Nancy Armstrong and Leonard Tennenhouse. Routledge, 1989. © 1989 Nancy Armstrong and Leonard Tennenhouse. All rights reserved. Reproduced by permission of Routledge.—Lapati, Americo D. From ***John Henry Newman***. Twayne Publishers, Inc., 1972. Copyright © 1972 by Twayne Publishers, Inc. All rights reserved. Reproduced by permission of Twayne Publishers, Inc., an imprint of Simon & Schuster Macmillan.—Maison, Margaret M. From ***The Victorian Vision: Studies in the Religious Novel***. Sheed & Ward, 1961. Copyright (c) Margaret M. Maison, 1961. Reproduced by permission of Sheed & Ward, an Apostolate of Priests of the Sacred Heart.—Modder, Montagu Frank. From a conclusion to ***The Jew in the Literature of England: To the End of the 19th Century***. Meridian Books, 1960. Copyright 1939, renewed 1967 by The Jewish Publication Society of America. Reproduced by permission of the Jewish Publication Society.—Mordecai, Rachel. From "The Correspondence, 1815" in ***The Education of the Heart: The Correspondence of Rachel Mordecai Lazarus and Maria Edgeworth***. Edited by Edgar E. MacDonald. The University of North Carolina Press, 1977. Copyright © 1977 by The University of North Carolina Press. All rights reserved. Reproduced by permission of the publisher.—Naman, Anne Aresty. From ***The Jew in the Victorian Novel: Some Relationships Between Prejudice and Art***. AMS Press, Inc., 1980. Copyright © 1980 by AMS Press, Inc. All rights reserved. Reproduced by permission.—Nockles, Peter. From "Oxford, Tract 90 and the Bishops" in ***John Henry Newman: Reason, Rhetoric and Romanticism***. Edited by David Nicholls and Fergus Kerr, OP. The Bristol Press, 1991. © David Nichollas and Fergus Kerr, OP, 1991. Reproduced by permission of Gerald Duckworth & Co. Ltd.—Nockles, Peter. From "The Oxford Movement: Historical Background 1780-1833" in ***Tradition Renewed: The Oxford Movement Conference Papers***. Edited by Geoffrey Rowell. Pickwick Publications, 1986. Introduction and this collection Copyright © 1986 Geoffrey Rowell. © 1986 Peter Nockles. All rights reserved. Reproduced by permission.—Ragussis, Michael. From ***Figures of Conversion: 'The Jewish Question' & English National Identity***. Duke University Press, 1995. © 1995 Duke University Press. All rights reserved. Reproduced by permission.—Reed, John Shelton. From ***Glorious Battle: The Cultural Politics of Victorian Anglo-Catholicism***. Vanderbilt University Press, 1996. Copyright © 1996 by Vanderbilt University Press. All rights reserved. Reproduced by permission.—Rosenberg, Edgar. From ***From Shylock To Svengali: Jewish Stereotypes in English Fiction***. Stanford University Press, 1960. © 1960 by The Board of Trustees of the Leland Stanford Junior University. All rights reserved. Reproduced with the permission of the publishers, Stanford University Press.—Svaglic, Martin J. From an introduction to ***Apologia Pro Vita Sua: Being A History of His Religious Opinions***. By John Henry Cardinal Newman. Edited by Martin J. Svaglic. Oxford University Press, 1967. © Oxford University Press 1967. Reproduced by permission of Oxford University Press, Inc.—Tillotson, Geoffrey. From ***Mid-Victorian Studies***. By Geoffrey and Kathleen Tillotson. The Athlone Press, 1965. © G. and K. Tillotson, 1965. Reproduced by permission.

PHOTOGRAPHS AND ILLUSTRATIONS APPEARING IN *NCLC,* VOLUME 72, WERE RECEIVED FROM THE FOLLOWING SOURCES:

A title page for *Children of the Ghetto* by Israel Zangwill, London, William Heinemann, 1892 edition, photograph. The Department of Rare Books and Special Collections, The University of Michigan Library. Reproduced by permission.—A title page for *Daniel Deronda* by George Eliot, New York, Harper & Brothers, Publisher, 1876 edition, photograph. The Department of Rare Books and Special Collections, The University of Michigan Library. Reproduced by permission.—A title page for *Émaux et Camées* by Théophile Gautier, Paris, 1888 edition, photograph. The Department of Rare Books and Special Collections, The University of Michigan Library. Reproduced by permission.—A title page for *Le Parnasse Contemporain: Recueil de vers nouveaux* by Alphonse Lemerre, Éditeur, Paris, 1876 edition, photograph. The Department of Rare Books and Special Collections, The University of Michigan Library. Reproduced by permission.—A title page for *Reuben Sachs: A Sketch* by Amy Levy, Macmillan and Co. and New York, 1888 edition, photograph. The Department of Rare Books and Special Collections, The University of Michigan Library. Reproduced by permission.—Eliot, George, drawing. The Library of Congress.—Keble, John, engraving. Archive Photos, Inc. Reproduced by Permission.—Levy, Amy, photograph. From an illustration in The Complete Novels and Selected Writings of Amy Levy 1861-1889. Edited by Melvyn New. University Press of Florida, 1993.—Newman, John Henry, Cardinal, photograph. Corbis-Bettmann/Hulton-Deutsch Collection. Reproduced by permission.—Oriel College, Oxford (chapel windows and square Gothic tower behind), 1813, aquatint by Philip de Bay. Historical Picture Archive/ Corbis. Reproduced by permission.—Pusey, Edward Bouverie, engraving. Corbis-Bettmann. Reproduced by permission.—Zangwill, Israel, photograph. Hulton-Deutsch Collection/Corbis-Bettmann. Reproduced by permission.

The Oxford Movement

INTRODUCTION

A revival of Roman Catholic doctrine within the Anglican Church in the first half of the nineteenth century, the Oxford Movement has been understood as a reaction against the conventional understanding of religion in Victorian Britain, governmental involvement in ecclesiastical life, the increasing secularism that accompanied the rising importance of economic structures, and the rationalist thought that sprang from the Enlightenment. Calling for a return to the beliefs of early Christianity, the leaders of the Oxford Movement emphasized religious dogma, the centrality of faith, and its practice in daily life. Although the Oxford Movement remained a minority faction within Anglicanism, and many of its members eventually left the national Church, its challenges to complacent spirituality—its commitment to a more fervent, mindful, and almost ascetic engagement with the divine, and stringent protections of religious life from the authority of the state—spurred intense intellectual controversy and contributed to the reform of the Anglican Church.

The official beginning of the Oxford Movement is marked by John Keble's Oxford Assize Sermon (published as "National Apostasy") on July 14, 1833, which focused on the problem of spiritual apathy as well as the diminishing power of the Church. Richard Hurrell Froude, Robert Wilberforce, and Isaac Williams, all students of Keble, would form the earliest core of the Oxford Movement. Two other major figures also taught at Oxford, in Oriel College: John Henry Newman, the most well-known leader of the Oxford Movement, and Edward Bouverie Pusey, who only later joined the group and would succeed Newman as leader after Newman's 1845 conversion to Catholicism. All of these men saw the Anglican Church as undergoing a period of crisis and resolved to take action to rejuvenate its authority through sermons and religious tracts. A series of printed pamphlets, called *Tracts for the Times* (1833-41), attracted attention both within and outside Oxford, and its writers would come to be known as Tractarians. These works engendered a great deal of controversy within the Church, and the leaders of the Oxford Movement gained increasing influence at the University.

A common charge leveled against the Tractarians was their Papist leanings, manifested by their attachment to Christian dogma, their alertness to heretical beliefs and practices, and their claim of apostolic priesthood (implying authority exceeding that of the state). In staunchly anti-Catholic England, this was an eventually crippling accusation. The posthumous publication of Froude's letters and journals, *Remains of the Late Reverend Richard Hurrell Froude* (1838), caused further controversy and popular hostility towards the Oxford Movement. The revivalist excitement generated by the Tractarians' publications and sermons, however, also spread to the United States and the Continent. Over the entire course of the Oxford Movement, its proponents were forced to reiterate their loyalty to Anglicanism, with an insistence that grew sharper with Newman's decision to convert to Catholicism and the younger leaders' deep criticisms of the Anglican Church. Immediately before his conversion, Newman wrote the last and most famous of the Tracts, Tract 90 (February 1841), on the significance of the Thirty-Nine Articles of the Anglican Church, which he claimed do not reject Catholic tradition but do establish some distance from it. Newman wrote the tract in order to argue against those within the Oxford Movement whom he considered excessively enthusiastic about the Romanization of the Anglican Church. The Anglican response to Newman's Tract 90 was dramatic and harsh, and Newman soon left the Movement. In 1844 W. G. Ward wrote *The Ideal of a Christian Church, considered in comparison with Existing Practice*, in which he argued openly for the supremacy of Roman doctrine. The leaders of the Oxford Movement swifly condemned the work and acted to distance their position from that of Ward. With increasing secessions to Rome and attacks from moderate Anglicanism, the Tractarians were forced to reform their movement throughout the remainder of the nineteenth century. Under Pusey's leadership, which succeeded that of Newman, the Oxford Movement moved into increasing mysticism and ritualism, as well as continuing doctrinal orthodoxy. "Puseyism," as it came to be known, was deeply unpopular among Anglicans, who were profoundly suspicious of extremist faiths of all varieties. Tractarianism impacted the Anglican Church in a more subtle way by challenging the secularist leanings of Victorian England and by re-establishing, as Raymond Chapman claims, "a more Catholic interpretation of [the Church of England's] functions."

The evolution of the Oxford Movement, as an intellectual controversy, was displayed in literature as well as in religious and political journals of the time. Not only were the early leaders of the movement articulate and impassioned authors—Newman is particularly noted in this regard—but the ideas spawned by the movement inspired such novelists and poets as Matthew Arnold, Anthony Trollope, and Charles Kingsley. Newman's clarity of style and religious faith impelled not only his many sermons, letters, and essays, but his two novels as well: *Loss and Gain* (1848) and *Callista* (1856). Both novels traced crises of faith that were in part drawn from Newman's own experiences, and presented staunchly Catholic and somewhat ascetic resolutions to these crises.

The Oxford Movement was deeply conservative in its attempts to revive the Catholic roots of the Anglican Church. Its emphasis on the importance of faith entailed, relative to other major political and religious causes of the period, a disregard of social reform as an explicit, defining feature. As such, some critics underscore the link between the Tractarians and the medieval Church, in its monasticism, greater authority, and adherence to the early beliefs and practices of Christianity. Although most scholars agree that the Oxford Movement failed to attain popular support within the Anglican Church and after its brief heyday devolved into extreme ritualism that existed on the periphery of Anglicanism, Tractarianism successfully challenged the disintegration of Church authority and the unreflective growth of secularism in Britain. Many recent authors claim that the Oxford Movement prefigured issues that confront current religious institutions, and generated impassioned and articulate responses to the central conflicts of nineteenth-century thought.

REPRESENTATIVE WORKS

Tracts for the Times (essays) 1833-41

Richard Hurrell Froude
Remains 2 vols. (letters, journals) (edited by John Henry Newman and John Keble) 1838-9

John Keble
National Apostasy Considered in a Sermon Preached in St. Mary's, Oxford Before His Majesty's Judge of Assize, on Sunday, July 14, 1833 (lecture) 1833
Lyra Apostolica (lectures) 1836

John Henry Newman
Loss and Gain: The Story of a Convert (novel) 1848
Callista: A Sketch of the Third Century (novel) 1856
Apologia pro Vita Sua (nonfiction) 1864
Certain Difficulties Felt by Anglicans in Catholic Teaching Considered: In a Letter Addressed to the Rev. E. B. Pusey, D. D., on occasion of his Eirenicon of 1864 (letter) 1876
Letters and Correspondence of John Henry Newman During his Life in the English Church 2 vols. (letters) (edited by Anne Mozley) 1891

William G. Ward
The Ideal of a Christian Church (nonfiction) 1844

OVERVIEWS

Charles Frederick Harrold (essay date 1950)

SOURCE: "The Oxford Movement: A Reconsideration," in *The Representation of Victorian Literature,* edited by Joseph E. Baker, Princeton University Press, 1950, pp. 33-56.

[*In the following essay, Harrold contends that the primary goal of the Oxford Movement was a rejuvenation of the "apostolic conception of Christianity," a radical reaction against European secularism and liberalism.*]

In our present years of crisis it is appropriate to reconsider a movement which in itself was the product of a crisis, and which looked backward and forward to a series of culminating forces which give the word "modern" a meaning at once hopeful and ominous. For the Oxford Movement was not merely the work of what someone has called "a band of Oxford parsons," but an event—a continuing event—which has especial significance for anyone contemplating the fateful years of 1789, 1830, 1848, 1870, 1914, and 1939.

In the framework of this historical perspective, it is no longer possible to follow the traditional accounts of Tractarianism as largely an "aspect of the Romantic Revival,"[1] or as a religious form of early nineteenth-century obscurantist Toryism, or as the expression of a weak-minded hunger for dogma. It would be idle to deny that the Oxford Movement shared with the great Romantics their sense of the mysterious depths in nature and in man, or their appreciation of the value of the past. It is unforgettable, too, that in the wretched England of Chartism, "The Song of the Shirt," *Sybil,* and *Hard Times,* Newman and his cohorts attacked such earnest and admirable reformers as Mackintosh, Brougham, and Shaftesbury for permitting the plight of the Victorian masses to blind them to the importance of the "Apostolical Succession" and "the prophetical office of the Church." It is true, again, that the Newmanites frankly preached the necessity of dogma, though in a far different spirit from that attributed to them by readers ignorant alike of dogma and of the true nature of religion.

We shall find it profitable to consider the Oxford Movement in terms less temporal and controversial, regarding it, rather, as a part of a vast European effort to retrieve and to warn. Unfortunately, most of the literature resulting from the movement has suffered from the difficulty and the remoteness of its language. The "educated" man of today no longer understands the highly specialized theological traditions of his own culture. Now that religious education has gone the way of theological education—becoming the possession of the expert—the average person is simply a religious illiterate. Newman and Keble and Pusey speak to him in a dead language, about ideas of which he has never heard, on premises which seem to him preposterous, and for purposes which strike him as fantastic and superstitious. Yet at the core of the Tractarian teaching, there lay a set of intelligible convictions which have relevance not only to "the stupid nineteenth century" but also to the "highly informed" twentieth century.

Originally, of course, the Oxford leaders were concerned with problems which demanded an immediate solution: the assertion of the spiritual independence of the church from the state; opposition to the rationalism of the "Noetic" group (Whately, Arnold, Hampden) in Oriel College;[2] a search for a firmer foundation than current theology for the Catholic tradition latent in Anglicanism; and a recovery of the tradition of piety, spirituality, and authority, as found in the English divines of the seventeenth century (Hooker, Andrewes, Vaughan, Ken) and in the great Church Fathers of the fourth and fifth centuries. The determination of the Tractarians, in the fourth decade of the nineteenth century, was boldly to realize the primitive "apostolic" conception of Christianity, and to apply it uncompromisingly to modern conditions. This was at once the great strength of the movement and the great obstacle to its acceptance. Yet in the degree that it brought itself into collision with the main spirit of its own time, it remains today a continuing power against the forces which have largely produced the world crisis of the twentieth century. Its very radicalism—a religious radicalism more explosive in its potentialities than any conceivable secular radicalism—throws into sharp relief some of the basic ills of modern society.

One is therefore justified in asking precisely in what respects a movement so theological can throw light on our own time, on the problems of economic injustice, social dissolution, competing political ideologies, and atomic warfare. The light will often be indirect, as we shall see. But a close study of the Tractarian point of view may convince some of us that, as Nicholas Berdyaev pointed out,[3] we have reached the bitter end of Renaissance secularism, in the increasing dehumanization of man, in the loss of spiritually organic social unity, in the vast and barbarous conflict which comes from the exploitation of nature rather than in a sacramental use of it in the service of the human spirit. A kind of "liberalism" had "burst out in infidel fury at the French Revolution," and so naturalized itself in England that even Greville regarded it in 1830 as "the spirit of the times . . . a movement no longer to be arrested,"[4] and which "believed that rational intelligence, education, and civilization would cure all the evils and sorrows of mankind."[5] This is not to say, of course, that the splendid gains of nineteenth-century liberal culture are to be denied reality. We shall see that it was not liberalism in the deepest sense that the Tractarians opposed, but a secular liberalism which looked to a millennium based on the spirit-denying, Philistine proposition that to make men perfect is no part of mankind's objective, but to make imperfect men comfortable.[6] We shall see that the Tractarians attacked liberalism, and its bourgeois world, because for them it meant the ultimate victory of secularism. They had a dim premonition, based on a profound knowledge of religion and human nature, that secularism would destroy the last remnants of organic social order. They could not foresee the specific shape of things to come, but from the general nature of their teachings, we may draw the conclusion that the *total* secularization of life leads to the depersonalization of man in the triumphant despotic state.

II

The Oxford Movement was not of course an isolated phenomenon. As is well known, it was a part of the general European reaction against the spirit of the *Aufklärung* and of the French Revolution. It was indeed a part of the English effort in the early nineteenth century to re-enter the circle of European life. At bottom, it was, as Guido De Ruggiero has pointed out, "an expression of the same universalistic attitude which inspired . . . the Radicals, economists, and Liberals."[7] This effort to break down the isolation imposed by the pride of past generations of Englishmen, this tendency to Europeanize itself, forms one of the most striking characteristics of Victorianism. In the field of religion, the Oxford leaders, in thus reaching out for contact with what they regarded as the central tradition of continental Christianity, shared the general recoil of the conservative spirit against revolutionary liberalism. This reaction was far from being as simple as is sometimes believed: it was at once religious, intellectual, and political. Everywhere, whether in France, in the work of Chateaubriand, De Maistre, De Bonald, and Lammenais, or in Germany, in the labors of Görres, Friedrich von Schlegel, or Novalis, the spiritually conservative mind—sensing the mystery of loyalty, imagination, the soul—looked with distrust upon the dangerously facile intellectual statements of eighteenth-century revolutionism—the "rights" of man, and of reason; the contractual nature of society; the ideals of liberty, equality, and fraternity.[8] It sought, on the contrary, to resuscitate the sense of corporate and organic order, with authority (the rights of God and of governors) as the only true basis of such order, and with a concrete and total conception of man's nature to oppose the abstract, fragmented view of man as a rational animal. To such a mind, valuable as is liberty, advantageous as is equality, Christian as is fraternity, there was one fatal flaw in the revolutionary program: it was conceived in terms of human self-sufficiency, in terms of rebellion to divine authority. To such a mind, European Christendom for the past three hundred years had been progressively apostate to authority. No genuine reform could be effected without the humbling of human pride before an authority transcending the instabilities of human nature. This seemed to have been proved by three centuries of change. "The literary revolt of the fifteenth century, the religious revolt of the sixteenth, the philosophical systems of the seventeenth, the political revolution of the eighteenth, were all parts of a whole, successive steps in the dread argument that had been fulfilling itself in history."[9]

In England, where the revolution had been won gradually, and was at last legally and peacefully accomplished, there was less need of the swift and politically militant counter-reformation which occurred in France; it could afford to be more personal and religious in character. The Oxford Movement was not concerned with rehabilitating the old hierocratic doctrine of political authority as resting upon the spiritual authority of a divine institution. It was, however, concerned with discovering an authority capable of resisting that mild, persuasive, "reasonable" "Liberalism" which, in England, was the equivalent for the violent but less insidious Gallican "Revolution."[10] It was not merely interested in defeating the Whigs' intentions of disestablishing the church (of which there was really little danger in 1833), or in asserting the essence of the church to lie in the doctrine of Apostolical Succession or of the three-fold ministry of bishops, priests, and deacons. There were other and less ecclesiastical objectives, and it is these which have especial relevance for us today.

The Oxford leaders were as acutely aware as were Coleridge and Carlyle (and Burke before them) that the new secularism, founded in eighteenth-century empirical skepticism, and developed in modern materialistic industrialism, was to be the supreme enemy of man's spiritual identity. Once the revolutionary democracy of 1789 came into functional service with the machine and the laissez-faire market, the time was ripe for social dissolution and the progressive emptying of man's meaning for himself as an individual. All truly final authority—transcending the never-ending contingent authorities of nature and man—would yield to competing secularisms, and men would find themselves isolated in the mechanical meshes of an atomic social "order." This was the nightmare of Coleridge, Carlyle, Maurice, Ruskin, Arnold, and all those Victorians who failed to be quickened or comforted by the gospel according to Lord Bacon and Jeremy Bentham, or by their evangelists Macaulay, Brougham, Peel, and John Stuart Mill. Many took heart at Carlyle's oft-reiterated affirmation, "There is a Godlike in human affairs. . . . Man is still Man,"[11] and not a "Patent Digester" or "Motive-grinder"[12] and social order is a "mystic, miraculous, unfathomable Union"[13] of men in the bonds of spirit, not a contractual "partnership-agreement in a trade of pepper and coffee, calico or tobacco . . . to be taken up for a little temporary interest."[14] The seat of authority for man and society must be sought in a sphere transcending the mechanisms of logic, on a plane where man's spiritual wholeness will be inviolable. By 1870, many could feel, with Ruskin, that when confronted by the "dry-featured dwarfish caricatures" of men,[15] one's own contemporaries, one had the eerie sensation of talking to specters: "in our modern life . . . you not only cannot tell what a man is, but sometimes you cannot tell whether he *is,* at all!—whether you have indeed to do with a spirit, or only with an echo."[16] Most popular "advanced" religious thought of the day followed Coleridge, or Carlyle, or Thomas Erskine of Linlathen, or Maurice. These sought to rehabilitate man's spirit by pointing to the universality of genuine spiritual *experience,* hoping somehow, by means of it, to divinize history and nature. Whether in the transcendental idealism of Coleridge, in the "natural supernaturalism" of Carlyle, or in the Christian-Platonic doctrine of the *logos* in Julius Charles Hare, Erskine, or Maurice, there was persistent hope in seeing in "God's universe a symbol of the Godlike . . . [in] Immensity a Temple . . . [and in] Man's History, and Men's History [biography] a perpetual Evangel."[17] This was the century-long hope, the creation of what amounted to little more than a new "nature myth." It was eventually to vanish in the rose-colored mist of Victorian pantheism, leaving behind it the iron god of Mammonism, worshiped by those who had divinized nature just enough to sanctify labor, money, and property.

The Tractarians, on the other hand, protected by the Pauline and Augustinian emphasis on "the transcendence of the supernatural order and the incommensurability of Nature and Grace,"[18] felt none of the seductions of nature, but instead saw in the Church, as divinely established, an instrument which alone could provide a principle of order beyond the reach of "the all-corroding, all-dissolving skepticism" of the intellect where it is permitted unrestricted freedom in dealing with man's nature or with the character of the world. For the Tractarians, nothing but a divinely authoritative religion could cope with the unique predicament of man, that of being fated to live in two different orders: in his own "existence," which is always personal although full of super-personal values, and in the objective world, which is always non-personal and quite indifferent to human values. If man defined himself solely in terms of the second order, he would end by denying his own essence. All the religious sanctions for the power which had held society in an organic unity would collapse, and with the fall of religious authority, a new and remorseless authority would take its place: the Caesarism of the all-embracing secularist state.

One of the first stages in the triumph of the secularist spirit was the enthronement of the middle class. Thus, long before there rose threat of "the Man versus the State,"[19] the Tractarians could easily see—what was celebrated by Macaulay, denounced by Carlyle, and satirized by Matthew Arnold—the "bourgeoization" of standards and values. On religious grounds alone this was highly repugnant to men like Newman. The still popular theological utilitarianism of William Paley—"doing good to mankind . . . for the sake of everlasting happiness"[20]—was but the counterpart of that cruder utilitarianism of the reformers which organized society for the making of money and disorganized it for anything else. It smiled upon the principle that the secular rules of the market justified the merchant in using for his own benefit whatever gifts had been bestowed upon him. As one critic has already noted, it might well have taken for its motto those words from Tyndale's translation of the Bible which R. H. Tawney has placed at the head of his account of the Puritan-Capitalist movement: "And the Lorde was with Joseph, and he was a luckie felowe."[21] This spirit of adjustment of religion to worldly success—one of the least admirable aspects of the "Victorian compromise"—was especially hateful to the Tractarians, for whom, as we shall see, all things have properly a sacramental value. They could easily foresee that condition in England which later, in the 1860's, Bishop Creighton saw in Oxford, after the defeat of Newman and the advent of Mill's *Logic* as the dominating influence there: "At the close of the 'sixties it seemed to us at Oxford almost incredible that a young don of any intellectual reputation for modernity should be on the Christian side."[22] The triumph of "modernity"—liberalism, secularism, mechanical civilization—inevitably nourished the conception of religion as at best merely an investment, and at least as a moral and emotional stimulant. Under the influence of the middle-class spirit, the English Church had drunk deeply of the temper, ideas, and laws of an ambitious and advancing civilization; it had become respectable, comfortable, sensible, temperate, liberal; it had laid its blessing on what Dean Church designated as "triumphant Macaulayism."[23] And to the Tractarians, as to Carlyle, the outlook was inexpressibly dreary as the "Gospel of Mammonism" surrendered humanity to the tender mercies of industrialism.

It was precisely in the social dissolution resulting from an advancing industrialism that the Oxford men saw one of the greatest threats to that high organic idea of society which Burke had held, and which Coleridge, Southey, and Carlyle were keeping alive in the mind of many an enlightened conservative. In fact, as we shall see, the Toryism of the Tractarians was not that of the "two-bottle orthodox . . . the thoroughgoing Toryism and traditionary Church-of-England-ism" which Newman found in the colleges and convocation of Oxford;[24] it was, instead, a spiritual Toryism which opposed endorsing remedies for reform derived solely from a philosophy fundamentally individualist and secular. Its aim was, in fact, twofold: "Tractarianism not only brought Industrialism under the condemnation of the Church. It set itself also to recover a right doctrine of 'the World,' in opposition to the Evangelical identification of it with 'some particular set of persons, or pleasures, or occupations,'"[25] and in opposition to the economic liberals' conception of it as a mere quarry for exploitation. It hoped to retrive the seventeenth-century conception of the church and state as organically one, when, in Coleridgean terms, "the National Church was no mere State-institute" but rather the "State itself in its intensest federal union, . . . the guardian and representative of all personal individuality."[26] In the 1840's, it was this lost organic unity and humanity which was disturbing all classes. It was by no means an accident that the authors of the *Communist Manifesto,* in 1848, deplored in the language of *Past and Present* the modern "nexus between men" as being nothing but "callous 'cash payment.'" Marx and Engels lamented in almost Romantic terms the fact that the bourgeoisie had "put an end to all feudal, patriarchal, idyllic relations" among men, "those feudal ties that bound man to his natural superiors." The rapacious mercantile class had "drowned the most heavenly ecstasies of religious fervor, of chivalrous enthusiasm, of philistine sentimentalism, in the icy waters of egoistical calculation."[27] This is the language not only of nineteenth-century Marxians but also of Burke and Cobbett. Something incommensurable with money was vanishing from the world.

It was partly to redeem men from such despair of the supersensible that Newman emphasized the sacramental character of the world. Though Newman himself seldom speaks of nature in definitely sacramental terms—the Calvinist in him never died, and "the whole world lieth in wickedness"[28]—nevertheless there are innumerable passages in his works where the notion is clearly present:[29] the Christian will of course "see God in all things," but he will more specifically "see Christ revealed to his soul amid the ordinary actions of the day, as by a sort of sacrament."[30] All objects and events are at once profane and sacred, finite instrumentalities for the realization of divine ends, ends which alone can give meaning to the groping significance of nature's symbols. To seek a meaning solely among the symbols, to seek a humane ideology among economic or political secularisms, is to follow false gods, to cut man from man, and frustrate tragically the fierce longing of man to solve his social and individual problem. For by some strange fact of his constitution, man continually discovers that "so long as the economic [or political] operation is conceived as the human end, no truly humane ideology can be evolved. The strange but characterizing feature of humanity is that the principle of its true socialization cannot be discovered within earthly horizons, and must be sought in a transcendent sphere. It is only when work is governed by the sacramental idea of realization of spiritual ends through visible means, that a distinctly *human* co-operation emerges."[31] The lost sense of the spiritually organic unity of society, which Carlyle sought to revive through transcendentalism, the Tractarians sought to revive through "sacramentalizing" the world and restoring man to his dual citizenship in the two orders of nature and spirit.

It was Tractarian sacramentalism which, when applied to social order, gave rise to the superficial belief that the Oxford Movement was, after all, merely the religious aspect of the hidebound Toryism of Eldon and Wellington. But the official Toryism dominant in Newman's early career was just as secular at heart as was the Liberalism which the Newmanites opposed, and had not even the humanitarianism and the moralism which were at least two undeniably redeeming characteristics of the best Liberals. If we are to call Newman a Tory, then his Toryism was of a singularly revolutionary kind, with its emphasis upon the divine issues of social order, the supernatural value of every man, and the sacramental relation of the world to the spirit of man. "In so far as the Oxford Movement was Tory, its Toryism was not that of the defenders of vested interests, the 'Conservatives' who aroused Hurrell Froude's scorn, but that of Southey and Coleridge and the young Disraeli who were among the first to denounce the injustices of the Industrial Revolution."[32] Indeed, for a time in 1833, Newman seems to have moved astonishingly close to Radicalism, noting how, at least historically, "the people were the fulcrum of the Church's power."[33] And in more specifically social terms, not only Newman but also Pusey and Keble were able to rise above the barriers of cultural and intellectual inequality in their personal attitudes toward poor and humble folk.[34] While the Tractarians never cast their thought in the mold of social science, and never familiarized themselves with contemporary economic problems, the fact remains that they boldly criticized existing social conditions, condemned injustice and oppression, and clearly asserted the radical conflict between the aims of industrial capitalism and the aims of the Christian religion. Thus we find Pusey denouncing the prevailing idolatries: "Covetousness . . . is the very end and aim of what men do, the ground of their undertakings, to keep and enlarge their wealth. . . . In our eager haste to heap more comfort to ourselves, we beat down the wages of the poor, in order to cheapen or multiply our own indulgence."[35] And it is Newman who lashes out at the money-hungry middle class in his famous sermons at St. Mary's, in which he flagellates the early Victorians for their "avarice, fortune-getting, amassing of capital."[36] In the sermons of the Tractarians there are unmistakable hints that they heard the ominous rumblings of world-wide disaster. "The kingdoms of this world," said Pusey in his *Christianity without a Cross,* are "retaining an outward civilization, [but] they are fast decaying and becoming uncivilized."[37]

The Tractarian opposition to Liberalism as a method of regulating the economic process rested, one should add, on what in their own day, as in ours, provoked the opposition of innumerable intelligent readers: namely, on the very limited value which they placed upon the historical spirit. It is because the Oxford Movement has long been dealt with through an overworked historical sense that it has so often been seen in a false light. To account for the movement solely in terms of historical cause and effect is to fall into the very secular fallacy which they saw overtaking their contemporaries. It is to judge an absolute standpoint from a relativist point of view: valid only to a certain degree, but fatally missing the essence of the thing judged. For it must always be remembered that when we are dealing with a movement based upon theological propositions, the essence of the movement will transcend the limits of historical definition. Like the fundamentals of metaphysical truth, the basic dogmas of theology do not change. And it is on this vantage ground that the Tractarians were able to overcome that "historicism" which Etienne Gilson has shown to have vexed the minds of later nineteenth-century historians,[38] that imprisonment in historical relativity which prevented any genuine solution of real problems, because the only leverage for dealing with nature and history must be found outside the circle of cause and effect. Put into social terms, this means that Tractarianism naturally finds no help for man's deepest needs in the state. The state is not concerned with life, but only with the ordering of life, with organization and control. The real friend of life, the only true source of spiritual power, is to be found ultimately in religion. Men like Keble, Newman, and Pusey had no need to be reminded, as most of us do, that all genuine forms of religion—contemplation, sacrifice, unselfish action—are a turning away from the external, centrifugal, non-vital activity to the heart of life, to sources of power inaccessible by the crude hand of secular or civil authority. The Oxford leaders were relatively indifferent to the claims of the new "historical spirit" because they felt that it dealt, after all, with "fallen" human nature, which needs something supra-historical: a new principle of life which would reveal the inadequacy of human knowledge and human civilization, and heal and restore them. The Tractarians were no more indifferent to the Corn Laws than were the early Christians to Roman slavery; they were no more eager to destroy the Victorian secular civilization around them than were the early Christians to destroy the Roman empire. They were not social idealists. On the other hand, they were blessed with a sophistication far more profound and far more profitable than that of the hard-headed social reformer: a religious sophistication, by which they realized man's dilemma more intensely than the most fervid secular idealist, since they saw it as an inner, "inherited" burden of evil which could never be lifted by any political or economic program, but which required, for its eradication, a turning to a frame of reference transcending the flux of history.

We should now be able to understand the grounds on which the Tractarians distrusted "Liberalism." To them the word "Liberalism" referred to a twofold modern movement, at once intellectual and political. In 1833, it was the intellectual aspect of the movement which disturbed them; Newman has defined it clearly in the *Apologia* as "the exercise of thought upon matters, in which, from the constitution of the human mind, thought cannot be brought to any successful issue. . . . Among such matters are first principles of whatever kind; and of these the most sacred and momentous are especially to be reckoned the truths of Revelation."[39] The application of what Newman calls "liberal" reason to philosophy and theology results in positivism, in the scientism of popular thought, in the de-supernaturalism of the "social Christianity" of Protestantism, and in the general absorption of religion into the secularized culture of the modern world. The political side of Liberalism laid less claim on Newman's attention, but it represented the outer or practical manifestation of the same spirit. It has been conveniently summed up by Matthew Arnold, in *Culture and Anarchy,* as "middle-class liberalism, which had for the cardinal points of its belief the Reform Bill of 1832, and local self-government, in politics; in the social sphere, free trade, unrestricted competition, and the making of large industrial fortunes; in the religious sphere, the Dissidence of Dissent and the Protestantism of the Protestant religion."[40] Liberalism in either sense represented the effort of man to solve the problem of life "without the aid of Christianity."[41]

It was the conviction of the Tractarians—as of many other religious Victorians—that nineteenth-century Liberalism could be but a temporary phenomenon, a transition between a Christian culture and one that is completely secularized. It was plain to them that European culture had already ceased to be Christian in the eighteenth century, and that while it retained the inherited moral standards and values of a Christian civilization, it succeeded only in erecting a quasi-religious substitute for faith. For the time being, it was living on the spiritual capital inherited from historic Christianity; as soon as this was exhausted, something else must come to take its place. Once society were really launched on the path of secularization, it could find in Liberalism only a half-way house; it must go on to the bitter end: some form of "state-ism"—what the twentieth century was to know as "totalitarianism." The Tractarians could have no knowledge of the exact forms which secular Liberalism would take, but there is an inner logic in any secularism, a logic which can easily enough be seen in the programs against which the Oxford leaders fought. For if we believe, with the secularists, that the Kingdom of Heaven can be established by political and economic programs, then we have no right to object to the claims of the state to embrace the whole of life in order to produce and distribute its secular goods, even though it demands—as it logically will in time—the absolute submission of the individual will and conscience. The realization of this fact drove the religious conscience of the Victorian age to disapprove of unrestricted liberal doctrine. Not only the Tractarians, but also Maurice, Coleridge, Carlyle, Ruskin, and Arnold were outspoken in their distrust of mass-democracy and economic individualism. The universal expectation of a liberal millennium[42] was scoffed at by Carlyle in his social writings, in which he gave Europe two hundred years in which to learn, painfully, that the worship of Mammon must end in some form of power-leadership.

For Newman the very word "progress" was merely a "slang term."[43] For him "the progress of the species" meant greater and greater loss of spiritual nourishment for mankind. He was not unaware of the possibility of a proletarian revolution; as the masses were increasingly deluded with the expectation of the fruits of secularism, and at the same time bored and angered by the spiritual vacuity of their lives, a new barbarism would generate from within the very heart of civilization. "Who are to be the Goths and Vandals who are to destroy modern civilization?" asked one of Newman's friends in 1871; and answered, with Newman's approval, "The lowest class, which is the most numerous, and is infidel, will rise up from the depths of the modern cities, and will be the new scourges of God." "This great prophecy," adds Newman, "is first fulfilled in Paris [of the Commune]—our turn may come a century hence."[44]

III

Such words make any reconsideration of the Oxford Movement a study in the implications which it has for our own time. Making allowances for what the Oxford leaders did not say, or did not intend to say, it is possible nevertheless to draw up some very pertinent conclusions based on the general tendency of their thought. Of these, perhaps the most notable at present is the fact that the secularism which they feared and fought has attained precisely the proportions which could have been predicted at the time when Newman wrote his first tracts. It is not too much to say that in the apparently beneficial soil of secular Liberalism, there lay the seeds of totalitarianism, whether in form of Fascism or Communism, or in the form of national mobilization by democratic nations for that "total warfare" which is the natural offspring of nineteenth-century middle-class industrialism.

The debacle of civilization is not merely a failure in leadership, as Carlyle had maintained; it has been a failure of *spiritual* leadership. For generations, religion has steadily retreated into man's inner life; it has left social and economic life to the state and to a civilization becoming secularized. Losing its hold on social life, religion loses its hold on life altogether. By the end of the nineteenth century, it could no longer be said of any nation that "Christianity was the law of the land." Never before in the history of the world had civilization become so completely secularized as was that of the late-Victorian and Edwardian periods. Soon the new secularism was to cease being content to dominate the outer world, leaving man's inner life—his loyalties, his enthusiasms, his imagination, his capacity for sacrifice—to religion. Within a generation it was to begin claiming the whole man. New and bastard religions were to arise, appealing to man's mystical instincts, in the name of "Race," or of "the State," or of "the Proletariat." These show a phenomenon new in history: the "Kingdom of Anti-Christ" fully equipped with political form and substance, standing over against the Christian church as a *counter-church,* with its own dogmas, moral standards, hierarchy, and militant will to world conquest.

All this may seem a far cry from Newman's original grievance against Lord Grey and his Reforming Whigs of 1830, but there is an unbroken continuity underlying the advances and retreats of Liberalism from those early years to the present. Political liberalism, such as Gladstone's, is now dead.[45] But the secularism on which it fed has crowded out that spiritual authority which once was sovereign over all temporalities. Even in the democracies it threatens to erect a new "church," what has been called the "omnicompetent State," which will mold the mind and guide the life of its citizens from the cradle to the grave, developing a kind of democratic *étatisme* which, while being less arbitrary and inhumane than Communism or Fascism, will make just as large a claim on the individual and demand an equally whole-hearted spiritual allegiance. Both in war and in peace, it will continue to differ from the "police-state" of the nineteenth-century Liberals, but will become "a nurse, and a schoolmaster and an employer and an officer—in short, an earthly providence, an all-powerful, omnipotent human god—and a very jealous god at that."[46] This will be the logical outcome of setting up the City of Man as an end in itself. Men will have forgotten that even the pagans knew that social order rested on a center not its own, i.e., on a divine center. Men have always felt that civilization did not exist merely for the gratification of needs and desires, but that it ought to be a sacred order resting on what Plato called "the divine Law."[47]

That the Oxford Movement is so frequently seen in only its narrower aspects—in relation to theology, church history, and the problem of belief—is no doubt owing to the scarcity of studies dealing with its larger implications. As we have already noted, it was a part of a wide European movement in search of a true principle of authority or sovereignty. Various writers have touched upon the Tractarians' relation with France, notably in the work of Fairbairn, Knox, and Laski,[48] but we need a full treatment of it as a separate subject. If, as Knox says, "the religious Romantics of France were indirect, but far from insignificant factors in the development of the Oxford Movement,"[49] then it would be well to know precisely how such works as Lammenais' *Essai sur l'indifférence* and *Des progrès de la révolution* affected Newman and Hurrell Froude. Much remains to be discovered about Newman's correspondence in 1837 with the French Abbé, M. Jager, about the Roman Catholic influence on many Englishmen when England opened her doors to refugee clergy, monks, and nuns in 1789-1790, about the surprising similarities between the early issues of Lacordaire and Montalembert's new journal, *L'Avenir,* and the first *Tracts for the Times,* about the "secret" efforts of Bloxam and Ambrose Philipps de Lisle, even before the publication of Tract XC (1841), to make the Oxford Movement a means of uniting the Church of England with the Church of Rome. Little as has been written on the Oxford Movement and France, still less has been written on the Oxford Movement and Germany. The best study we have is L. A. Willoughby's,[50] which surveys the affinities of two points of view, leaving detailed treatment for other students. Here the relations are indeed tenuous, real German echoes of Newman coming only late in the century, from Ignatius Döllinger, the Modernist.[51]

The relation of the Tractarian Movement to the social and intellectual changes of the nineteenth and twentieth centuries has received considerable attention, but special studies still remain to be done. The general work in this field has been carried on, for the most part, by clergymen;[52] but students of Victorian literature have an equal interest in the subject inasmuch as the Oxford Movement was both the background and the material for much Victorian prose and poetry. It remains to be proved "how little [the Movement] touched [the] characteristic and creative minds" of the period.[53] It is true, as Storr has said, that "none of the greater poets of the nineteenth century yielded themselves to its spell. Tennyson and Browning show no sympathy with Anglo-Catholicism."[54] Yet just what impact it made on such men, as well as on Clough, William Morris, Swinburne, and various minor poets, makes an interesting speculation. The often-noted parallels between elements in Coleridge's thought and that of the Tractarians still remain to be systematically examined. If Carlyle's acerb observation be true, that from Coleridge's "Cloud-Juno" came "spectral Puseyisms, monstrous illusory Hybrids,"[55] then there is room for a definite statement of just how that "seminal mind" affected, not Newman himself, but the atmosphere in which the Oxford Movement generated its power. The degree in which the movement found expression and opposition in Victorian fiction has already been well indicated by Joseph E. Baker;[56] but there still remain the wider fictional backgrounds which throw the movement into sharper focus. According to T. S. Eliot, three distinct stages can be traced in the attitude of Victorian novelists toward Christianity. In the first "the Faith is taken for granted, but omitted from their picture of life; in the second it is contested or worried about; in the third (which was reached with the present generation) it is treated as an anachronism."[57] Scott, Thackeray, and Dickens show considerable interest in religion, but are somewhat unfair to nonconformity and evangelicalism. Later in the century, Kingsley's *Alton Locke* conveys, perhaps unintentionally, a rather vulgar and materialistic account of nonconformity. It is the women novelists, George Eliot and Mrs. Gaskell, who give a juster picture of the religious life of Victorian England. By the end of the century, Hardy, Meredith, and Butler reflect the moral and spiritual conflict around them; religion has become a problem. How accurate such generalizations as these may prove to be, can be shown only by special studies. The varieties of Victorian religion, as seen through Victorian fiction, are still to receive adequate treatment.

In any reconsideration of the Oxford Movement, whether on its theological, intellectual, or literary side, it is no longer sufficient to think of it as a backwater in the onward rush of nineteenth-century enlightenment. It had its own center, its own motive-power, and its significant place among those articulations of modern uneasiness which now may be seen as more prophetic than even the Victorians could have believed. Perhaps its greatest significance for a time of crisis, such as ours, is to remind us that man is so constituted that even in his idealism, if such idealism is turned to his own glorification, he gravitates toward materialism and boredom and destruction. The great idealisms of the nineteenth-century Liberals resulted, strangely enough, in the crass acquisitiveness of capitalism, and led onward to the vast and anonymous savagery of mechanized wars. Thus, with all their intellectual limitations, and in spite of the technical objectives at which they aimed, the great Tractarians remain, in the general grounds of their thought, singularly prophetic of much that astounds us in the wreck of our modern world.

Notes

[1] The true relation between Tractarianism and Romanticism has been ably stated by Yngve Brilioth, in *The Anglican Revival* (London, 1925, 1933), pp. 57-58, 71: "The Oxford Movement . . . can only to a small extent be explained by the literary currents of the age. It was prepared for by these, and appropriated some of their thoughts; but it was not evoked by them, nor can it . . . be classified only as part of the Romantic Movement." A more recent, and very cogent, account concludes that in the light of history, and by any accurate use of words, "the core of the Revival is a faith which stands in eternal opposition to the Romantic spirit"—Hoxie N. Fairchild, "Romanticism and the Religious Revival in England," *Journal of the History of Ideas,* II (1941), 330-338.

[2] Mark Pattison has maintained that the Oxford Movement, far from reacting against the Noetics, was in fact an outgrowth of their teachings; the Oriel school "implanted the germ" (see Pattison's review of T. Mozley's *Reminiscences* in *The Academy,* July 1, 1882, quoted by S. L. Ollard in *A Short History of the Oxford Movement,* London, 1915, p. 15). However, we have Newman's word that, in 1828-29, he came sharply to resist his own Noetic tendency "to prefer intellectual excellence to moral"—*Apologia,* ed. Wilfrid Ward (London, 1913), p. 116.

[3] *The End of Our Time* (London, 1933), Chapter 1; also the same author's *The Fate of Man in the Modern World* (London, 1935), pp. 9, 26-27, 113, etc.

[4] See *sub ann.* 1830 (August 31), *Leaves from the Greville Diary,* ed. Philip Morrell (London, 1929), pp. 109-110.

[5] Ollard, *op. cit.,* p. 9. See also, for a satire on the superficial progressivism of the time, Thomas Love Peacock, *Crotchet Castle,* Chapter II, "The March of Mind."

[6] Utilitarian secularism found its great prophet, for many early Victorians, in Lord Bacon, rather than in Bentham or James Mill. Macaulay represents this more theoretical "liberalism," and founds his own middle-class philosophy upon the "two words which form the key to the Baconian doctrine, Utility and Progress. . . . To make men perfect was no part of Bacon's plan. His humble aim was to make imperfect men comfortable." See Macaulay's essay on *Lord Bacon.*

[7] *The History of European Liberalism,* translated by R. G. Collingwood (London, 1927), pp. 121-122.

[8] The revival of French Catholicism, in theocratic Ultramontanism, was of course heralded by Chateaubriand's *Génie du Christianisme* (1802), which was so successful as to lead De Maistre to formulate his hierocratic doctrine of papal authority as the guarantee of royal power (*Du Pape,* 1819). De Bonald had already ascribed sole sovereignty to God, who transmits it to the pope and thence to the king (*Théorie du pouvoir politique et religieux dans la société civile,* 1796). Lammenais, hoping to "ensoul" the liberal gains in France, gathered about him such ardent disciples as Lacordaire, Montalembert, and Maurice de Guérin, and molded a whole generation with his famous *Essai sur l'indifférence en matière de reli-*

gion (1817-21), which argued for authoritarian religion as the basis of social order. The German reaction may be observed in Joseph von Görres' *Christliche Mystik* (1836-42), in Novalis' *Die Christenheit oder Europa* (1799), and in F. von Schlegel's *Geschichte der alten und neuen Literatur* (1815).

[9] A. M. Fairbairn, *Catholicism: Roman and Anglican* (London, 1899), p. 101.

[10] *Ibid.*, p. 112.

[11] "Characteristics," *Collected Works*, Centenary Ed. (London, 1896-99), XXVIII, 42.

[12] *Sartor Resartus*, ed. C. F. Harrold (New York, 1937), pp. 210, 160, 162, etc.

[13] "Characteristics," p. 11.

[14] Burke's words, quoted here, are a satirical statement of the secular-utilitarian concept of society as held by eighteenth-century left-wing Whigs and French Jacobins (*Reflections on the Revolution in France*, London, 1790, p. 143).

[15] On the despiritualizing of man in the Victorian epoch, much stimulating thought will be found in H. V. Routh's *Money, Morals, and Manners as Revealed in Modern Literature* (London, 1935); see also his better known *Towards the Twentieth Century* (London, 1937).

[16] *Lectures on Art*, in *Works* (London, 1904), p. 94.

[17] *Sartor Resartus*, pp. 253-254. The appeal to "experience," as the basis of religious evidence, in the thought of Coleridge, Carlyle, Erskine, and Maurice, had already been made in Germany by Kant and Schleiermacher. However, in men like Hare, Maurice, and Erskine, man and nature are redeemed from finitude by "a continual inflowing of the Logos"; thus the spiritual unity and authority which they sought really comes from the neo-Platonic element in Christianity, as expressed in the Fourth Gospel. See Vernon F. Storr, *The Development of English Theology in the Nineteenth Century: 1800-1860* (London, 1913), pp. 337-356; and L. E. Elliott-Binns, *Religion in the Victorian Era* (London, 1936), pp. 131-152.

[18] Christopher Dawson, *The Spirit of the Oxford Movement* (New York, 1933), p. X.

[19] See Herbert Spencer, *Man versus the State* (London, 1884) for a late-Victorian secularist realization of the dilemma produced by the conflicting authorities of the individual and society when neither has any longer a spiritual significance.

[20] *Moral and Political Philosophy* (London, 1785), Book I, Chapter 7.

[21] See William George Peck, *The Social Implications of the Oxford Movement* (New York, 1933), p. 102; and Tawney, *Religion and the Rise of Capitalism* (London, 1926), Chapter 4.

[22] *Life and Letters of Mandell Creighton*, I, 75, quoted in Elliott-Binns, *op. cit.*, p. 323.

[23] *Life of R. W. Church*, p. 27, quoted by Ruth Kenyon in "The Social Aspect of the Catholic Revival," *Northern Catholicism: Centenary Studies in the Oxford and Parallel Movements*, ed. N. P. Williams and Charles Harris (London, 1933), p. 377.

[24] *Apologia*, ed. Wilfrid Ward, pp. 117, 494.

[25] Ruth Kenyon, in *Northern Catholicism*, p. 379, quoting from Newman's "The World Our Enemy," in *Parochial Sermons*, VII, iii. See also Newman's sermon on "Doing Glory to God in Pursuits of the World," in *Parochial Sermons*, VIII, xi.

[26] *Aids to Reflection* (London, 1859), p. 238: "For the Church is the shrine of morality: and in morality alone the citizen asserts and reclaims his personal independence, his integrity."

[27] Karl Marx and Friedrich Engels, *Manifesto of the Communist Party* (Chicago: Charles H. Kerr and Co., n.d.), p. 15.

[28] *Parochial Sermons*, VII, 31.

[29] On the sacramentalism of Newman's general philosophy, see C. F. Harrold, "Newman and the Alexandrian Platonists," *Modern Philology*, XXXVII, 283-288.

[30] *Parochial Sermons*, VIII, 158, 165. See also *The Idea of a University*, Discourse v, final paragraph.

[31] W. G. Peck, *op. cit.*, p. 197.

[32] Christopher Dawson, *The Spirit of the Oxford Movement*, p. xi. See also Southey's dialogues on society, *Sir Thomas More*, and Macaulay's brilliant but superficial reply in his review-essay on Southey's volume.

[33] "If we look into history, whether in the age of the Apostles, St. Ambrose's, or St. Becket's, still the people were the fulcrum of the Church's power," wrote Newman in 1833, on returning from the Mediterranean full of hatred for the reforming Whigs and the inert Tories. "Expect on your return to England to see us all cautious, long-headed, unfeeling, unflinching Radicals." *Letters and Correspondence*, ed. Anne Mozley (London, 1891), L, 454; also p. 450.

[34] See Peck, *op. cit.*, pp. 62-63, for Isaac Williams' astonishment at John Keble's affection and reverence for the humble folk of his parish.

[35] Quoted from the sermons on "The Danger of Riches" and "The Sin of Judas," in Peck, pp. 66-67.

[36] Quoted by R. W. Church, *The Oxford Movement* (London, 1892), p. 140.

[37] Peck, p. 69.

[38] *The Unity of Philosophical Experience* (New York, 1937), p. 319.

[39] *Apologia,* ed. W. Ward, p. 483. For Newman's complete definition and illustration of "Liberalism," see the Note, on pp. 491-502.

[40] *Culture and Anarchy,* ed. J. Dover Wilson (Cambridge, 1935), p. 62.

[41] Newman, in his famous *Biglietto* speech, on attaining the cardinalate, in 1879, summed up the subject as follows: "Liberalism in religion is the doctrine that there is no positive truth in religion, but that one creed is as good as another. . . . It is inconsistent with any recognition of any religion, as *true.* It teaches that all are to be tolerated, for all are matters of opinion. Revealed religion is not a truth, but a sentiment and a taste; . . . and it is the right of each individual to make it say just what strikes his fancy. . . . It is as impertinent to think about a man's religion as about his sources of income or his management of his family. Religion is in no sense the bond of society. . . . Hitherto, it has been considered that religion alone, with its supernatural sanctions, was strong enough to secure submission of the masses of our population to law and order; now the Philosophers and Politicians are bent on satisfying this problem without the aid of Christianity. Instead of the Church's authority and teaching, they would substitute first of all a universal and thoroughly secular education, calculated to bring home to every individual that to be orderly, industrious, and sober is his personal interest. . . . It would provide the broad fundamental ethical truths, of justice, benevolence, veracity, and the like; proved experience; . . . natural laws . . . in society, in social matters, whether physical or psychological . . . in government, trade, finance, sanitary experiments, and the intercourse of nations. As to Religion, it is a private luxury, which a man may have if he will; but which of course he must pay for, and which he must not obtrude upon others, or indulge in to their annoyance." Wilfrid Ward, *Life of Newman* (London, 1912), II, 460-461.

[42] For a picture of the heyday of liberal optimism (1831-32), in which "every clique, every sect, almost every middle-class family believed that . . . every question could be solved instantly and forever by the triumph of right—that is, of themselves," See Thomas Mozley, *Reminiscences: Chiefly of Oriel College and the Oxford Movement* (London, 1882), I, 272-275.

[43] Ward, *Life of Newman,* II, 81.

[44] The friend was F. M. Capes, editor of *The Rambler.* See Ward, II, 344. For a glimpse of the spread of rationalism and atheism among the Victorian working classes, see Amy Cruse, *The Victorians and Their Reading* (New York, 1935), pp. 122-123: "When the youth comes out of the hall [of the Socialists], he has a printed paper in his hand, a leaflet issued by the Society of Rational Pioneers, Leeds. It is headed, *Twenty-five Reasons for Being an Atheist.*"

[45] See George Dangerfield's *The Strange Death of Liberal England* (London, 1935).

[46] On the possibilities of the triumph of the god-State, even in the Western democracies, see Christopher Dawson, *Religion and the Modern State* (New York, 1940), Chapter 6, "Religion and Politics," especially pp. 105-110.

[47] "To that Law," says Plato, "he who would be happy holds fast and follows it in all humility and order; but he who is lifted up with pride or money or honor or beauty, who has a soul hot with folly and youth and insolence, and thinks that he has no need of a guide or ruler, but is able of himself to be the guide of others, he, I say, is deserted of God; and being thus deserted, he takes to himself others who are like him, and jumps about, throwing all things into confusion, and many think he is a great man. But in a short time he pays the penalty of justice and is utterly destroyed and his family and state with him" (*Laws,* IV, 716).

[48] A. M. Fairbairn, *op. cit.,* pp. 96-110, 128 n., etc.; E. A. Knox, *The Tractarian Movement: 1833-1845, a Study of the Oxford Movement as a Phase of the Religious Revival in Western Europe in the Second Quarter of the Nineteenth Century* (London, 1933), Chapter 3, "Oxford and France"; Harold J. Laski, *Studies in the Problem of Sovereignty* (New Haven, 1917), Chapter 3, "The Political Theory of the Oxford Movement," and Chapter 4, "The Political Theory of the Catholic Revival."

[49] Knox, pp. 45-46.

[50] "On Some German Affinities with the Oxford Movement," *MLR,* XXIX (1934), 52 ff.

[51] See Ward, *Life of Newman,* I, 438-446, 479, etc.; also II, 375, 379-380, 466. See also C. Broicher, "Anglikanische Kirche und deutsche Philosophie," *Preussischer Jahrbücher,* CXLII (1910), 205-233, 457-498.

[52] The best work of this kind is by William George Peck, *The Social Implications of the Oxford Movement,* the Hale Lectures, 1933 (New York, 1933). He makes profitable use of the labors of C. C. J. Webb, G. C. Binyon, V. A. Demant, Ruth Kenyon, M. B. Reckitt, and P. E. T. Widdrington, listed in his bibliography, pp. 333-337. See also Christopher Dawson, *The Spirit of the Oxford Movement* (New York, 1933).

[53] Fairbairn, *op. cit.,* p. 312, also pp. 313-315.

[54] V. F. Storr, *op. cit.,* p. 272.

[55] *Life of Sterling,* Centenary Ed. of *Works,* pp. 61-62. Broicher, *op. cit.,* is a good example of how one may overstate the similarities between the ideas of Newman and those of Coleridge (pp. 469-471, 473-484).

[56] *The Novel and the Oxford Movement* (Princeton, 1932).

[57] See L. E. Elliott-Binns, *Religion in the Victorian Era,* p. 343, paraphrasing from T. S. Eliot's chapter on "Religion and Literature," in *Faith that Illuminates,* p. 39.

Americo D. Lapati (essay date 1972)

SOURCE: "The Oxford Movement," in *John Henry Newman,* Twayne Publishers, Inc., 1972, pp. 30-53.

[*In the essay that follows, Lapati chronicles Newman's involvement in the Oxford Movement from 1833 until his conversion to Catholicism in 1845.*]

When Newman returned to England in the summer of 1833, he found evidence justifying his fears for the future of the Anglican Church. The eminent Oxford professor, Thomas Arnold, had written: "The Church, as it now stands, no human power can save."[1] The liberal Whig party was now in power; for generations the Established Church had allied itself with the conservative Tory power. The Anglican bishops, as members of the House of Lords, had offended the common people by voting against the Reform Bill of 1832, which sought the extension of the franchise; the Irish sees had already been suppressed by Parliament; and a group known as the Erastians were attempting to influence the Whigs with the view of Thomas Hobbes that the state, not the church or the Bible, ought to be the final authority about religious belief. Disestablishment of the church was certainly passing from the realm of the possible to the probable.

The Anglican Church itself appeared ineffective in counteracting the tide running against her. Most of the intellectuals belonged to the liberal side. Its clergy "had become, for the most part, amiable and respectable gentlemen, who were satisfied to read Morning and Afternoon Service on a Sunday, and to dislike Dissenters."[2] The bishops, having been appointed by Tory prime ministers for many years, were regarded as agents of a defunct Tory government and were known for their practice of nepotism and political patronage.[3] Moreover, the liberal cause was aided by the liberal spirit rampant on Continental Europe. The French Revolution had canonized liberal secularistic ideas, and the July Revolution of 1830 in France, which Newman regarded as "the triumph of irreligion,"[4] had popularized the new watchwords of "progress," "reason," "disestablishment"; Auguste Comte's Positivism challenged the traditional methods of studying God, religion, and society; and German theologians were even employing a new historical methodology that startled everyone in their application of it to the Bible. The desire of workers to share the gains of the Industrial Revolution with capitalists made many more concerned with acquiring the riches of the earth rather than aiming at a heavenly goal. True, there were Romanticists in England who called for an emphasis upon man's spiritual depths instead of upon material satisfaction; but they were weak voices in the wilderness. Thomas Carlyle has aptly termed the period as one "destitute of faith and terrified at skepticism."[5]

I Beginnings of the Oxford Movement

On July 14, 1833, five days after Newman's return to England, John Keble preached at Oxford his famous Assis Sermon, published under the title of "National Apostasy." Keble condemned the liberalism of the age and feared that its triumph could divide greatly between one's duties toward the church and the state. He pleaded for "resignation" on the part of devoted members of the church. Although Newman and Froude preferred action, Newman regarded the day as the start of a religious movement.[6] The clarion call was sounded; the Oxford Movement began. As a reform movement within the Church of England, it sought to demonstrate the continuity between the primitive church of the Fathers and the Anglican Church of the nineteenth century and to stem the tide of rationalism and liberalism which could undermine her doctrine and authority.

For the purpose of concerted action, a meeting was held from July 25 to 29. An Association of Friends of the Church was proposed, but only petitions to clergy and laity urging the support of the Established Church emerged. Froude attended the meeting, as did Hugh James Rose, a Cambridge man and editor of the *British Magazine,* which had published Newman's Mediterranean verses; but Newman did not attend, largely because he disliked the valuable time lost at meetings by too much talk and argument. "No great work was done by a system," he later commented on this decision, "whereas systems rise out of individual exertions."[7] When differences as to courses of action arose at the meeting, Newman felt all the more justified in individual effort.

Newman began to make visits and to write letters to clergymen and friends. Whether these were members of the High Church or the Low Church did not matter; his main intent was to unite all who were opposed to the liberal cause. Most of these attempts appeared unsatisfactory to Newman, but he was assured that a trend of popular opinion was slowly turning toward the church. He also inaugurated a series of letters to a newspaper, *The Record,* in which he dealt primarily with church reform and discipline, as based on Scripture and as applied in the context of the day. The series terminated with the sixth letter, which dealt with temperance societies. The editor feared a possible controversy on the topic, which he felt undesirable; and so this other effort came to an end.[8]

Newman, who now saw the need for more deliberate action, issued on September 9, 1833, three tracts, the beginning of a series to which others, notably Froude and Pusey, also contributed and which was published as *Tracts for the Times.* Friends and ex-pupils were enlisted to distribute these leaflets; even the shy Newman engaged in their hand-to-hand distribution; for he was "becoming perfectly ferocious in the cause."[9] Tract 1, a four-page leaflet, was entitled "Thoughts on the Ministerial Commission" and was addressed to the clergy. Writing anonymously, Newman boldly warned: "Should the Government and the country so far forget their God as to cast off the Church, to deprive it of its temporal honours and substance, *on what* will you rest the claim of respect and attention which you make upon your flocks? Hitherto you have been upheld by your birth and education, your wealth, your connexions; should these secular advantages cease, on what must Christ's ministers depend?" Newman answered his own question: "Christ has not left His Church without claim of its own upon the attention of men. . . . Hard Master He cannot be, to bid us oppose the world, yet give us no credentials for so doing." And Newman emphasized the real ground of authority, too often neglected—"our apostolical descent."[10]

A total of ninety tracts were issued from September, 1833, to February, 1841, of which Newman wrote twenty-nine[11] Every aspect of religion and of the Anglican Church was examined in these leaflets: church government and administration, doctrine, moral teachings, worship, ecclesiastical history. Repeatedly emphasis was laid upon the doctrine of apostolic succession with its basis in Sacred Scripture and in the teachings of the Fathers of the Church. The tracts were always unsigned. With the exception of the "Tract on Baptism" to which Edward B. Pusey added his initials, thus causing the group to become known as the Puseyites. The name of Pusey added prestige to the

John Keble (1792-1866)

movement since he was a professor and canon of Christ Church, Oxford. The writers of the tracts were also referred to as Tractarians because of the manner in which they released their views.

Many of the ideas contained in John Keble's *The Christian Year,* published in 1827, were revived in the Tracts. Newman's friendship with Keble had begun in 1828, although he had known him as a student at Oriel and had always admired his reputation as an outstanding scholar. Keble had been the teacher of Froude, who was largely instrumental in having Newman and Keble discuss their common leanings in theology. Newman's belief in the importance of authority in religious matters, an appreciation of the sacramental system as "the doctrine that material phenomena are both types and the instruments of real things unseen," and his new insight into Butler's doctrine of probability as "living power of faith and love" are attributed to Keble's influence.[12]

In 1836, Newman began to edit an English translation of patristic writings to be known as the "Library of the Fathers." He also became editor of the *British Critic,* which became the official organ of the Oxford Movement. With Pusey, Newman led in that same year a successful fight against the appointment of Renn Dickson Hampden as a professor at Oxford. Hampden, a liberal, was appointed by the Whig government; but opposition was so great that a committee was formed to investigate Hampden. Newman and Pusey, assigned to the committee, convinced its members to reject the appointment of Hampden—a victory for the conservative Oxford group.

The power of the pulpit was also a powerful force that Newman employed during the Tractarian days. His famous four o'clock Sunday afternoon sermons at St. Mary's, Oxford, drew crowds. His sermons, not marked by elaborate argumentation, were "plain, direct, unornamented, clothed in English that was only pure and lucid, free from any faults of taste, strong in their flexibility and perfect command, . . . in their piercing and large insight into character."[13] He did not repeat views in the *Tracts* but chose a wide range of topics: "The Individuality of the Soul," "The Invisible World," "The Ventures of Faith," "Warfare the Condition of Victory," "The Cross of Christ the Measure of the World," "The Church a Home for the Lonely." His appeal was primarily to the heart and not to the mind. "After hearing these sermons," observed a listener, "you might come away still not believing the tenets peculiar to the High Church system; but you would be harder than most men, if you did not feel more than ever ashamed of coarseness, selfishness, worldliness, if you did not feel the things of faith brought closer to the soul." As a result, even "those who by early education and conviction were kept aloof from the peculiar tenets of High Churchmen could not but acknowledge the moral quickening which resulted from the movement, and the marvelous character of him who was the soul of it."[14] When published, these sermons "put all other sermons out of the market."[15]

II The Via Media

While Newman wrote his tracts, preached his sermons, and delved more thoroughly into the Church Fathers for a vision of the primitive church, he began the formulation of a theory called the *Via Media*. Opponents of the Oxford Movement charged it with "Popery" and declared that it would eventually lead to Roman Catholicism. To disavow such a leaning, Newman responded in lectures delivered at St. Mary's; and these he later recast for publication in 1837 as *The Prophetical Office of the Church, Viewed Relatively to Romanism and Popular Protestantism;*[16] and in this work his *Via Media* theory first appeared. Since the title seemed negative, he felt it necessary to give definite shape and character to the content. Newman enumerated the many points of agreement between the Anglican Church and the Roman Church; indeed, he insisted that the Catholic Church in all lands had been one from the first for many centuries. But, in the course of time, Rome had made many superstitious additions to the original body of divine truths; Protestantism, on the other hand, had capriciously subtracted. The Anglican Church stood in the safe, middle way between these extreme positions; it had remained faithful to the original apostolic church; and its presentation of unblemished divine truth throughout the centuries made it the true church.

More specifically, in *The Prophetical Office* Newman dealt with the problem of religious authority. Roman Catholicism, he argued, went to one extreme in her doctrine of infallibility by often neglecting and even overriding the consent of the Fathers as necessary historical evidence for belief: "We have her own avowal that the Fathers ought to be followed, and again that she does not follow them."[17] Furthermore, Newman also noted a contradiction in the notion of infallibility and the limitations of human knowledge. Protestantism went to the extreme of private judgment, which Newman characterized as an absurdity since man always needed to rely on some form of authority and rarely ever acted solely on private judgment.[18] The Anglican Church, in opposition to these extremes, pursued a *via media* between authoritarianism and anarchic individualism, thereby conforming to the early church, which claimed authority but not infallibility. Thus, the Anglican Church promoted a spirit of intellectual freedom without encroachment upon the mind; yet it curbed that freedom when a tendency to lose restraint arose. Newman had not discarded his earlier view of the Pope as anti-Christ; however, despite many unacceptable doctrines, the Roman Church still maintained a connection with the ancient church. But he saw no hope as yet for his union with or submission to Rome.

Lectures on Justification, published in 1838, sought to find a middle way between Roman Catholics and Lutherans on the topic of worthiness for salvation.[19] The Catholics emphasized a mingling of faith and love that resulted in "good works." The Lutherans held to justification by the power of faith alone; no form of good works or penance would be needed. Roman Catholics placed too much reliance on man's actions; Lutherans, on God. Newman upheld justification by baptism, which elevates man from a state of nature to a state of grace and which thereby opens to man a supernatural faith and gives him power to act meritoriously.[20]

An article, "Prospects of the Anglican Church," in the *British Critic* of April, 1839, showed another development of Newman's *Via Media*.[21] After presenting a résumé of the efforts of the Tractarians to 1839 and after classifying their movement more as a "spirit afloat" reacting to the dry and superficial character of religious teaching and literature and clamoring for a deeper religious philosophy, Newman presented his alternatives: either the *Via Media* of Anglicanism or Roman

Catholicism. In his *Lectures on Justification,* he concluded that Luther had placed "Christians in bondage to their works and observances; released them by his doctrine of faith; and left them in bondage to their feelings."[22] Now, he concluded, "The spirit of Luther is dead; but Hildebrand and Loyola are alive." With the extreme position of Protestatism rejected, Newman asked: "Would you rather have your sons and daughters members of the Church of England or the Church of Rome?"[23]

While this question was still in his mind, Newman continued his study of the early church. His special topic was now the Monophysite or Eutychian heresy. Eutyches[24] had rejected the teaching of the Council of Chalcedon in 451 that Christ possessed both a divine and a human nature; he and his followers, called Monophysites, claimed only a divine nature for Christ and considered his humanity as only an appearance. In studying the different factions of this controversy over Christ's nature, Newman noted a similarity of the *via media* position of the Anglican Church in the nineteenth century to that of the Monophysites of the fifth century. Both argued from the Fathers of the Church and were supported by civil powers; and the *via media* of the fifth century was a heretical position. This led Newman to ponder: "My stronghold was Antiquity; now here, in the middle of the fifth century, I found, as it seemed to me, Christendom of the sixteenth and the nineteenth centuries reflected. I saw my face in that mirror, and I was a Monophysite. The Church of the *Via Media* was in the position of the Oriental Communion, Rome was where she now is; and Protestants were the Eutychians."[25] The tenability of Anglicanism now came into doubt.

Before even concluding his study of the Monophysites, a friend, Robert Williams, drew Newman's attention to an article entitled "Anglican Claim" in the *Dublin Review* by Nicholas Wiseman, a Roman Catholic. Wiseman contended that the Donatists of the fourth century and the Anglicans maintained similar positions. Donatism fell into schism by refusing submission to the authority of the Pope. A quotation of St. Augustine as applied to the Donatists impressed Newman: *Securus judicat orbis terrarum,* "the whole world judges right." Donatism then and Anglicanism now stand against the whole church. "By those great words of the ancient Father, interpreting and summing up the long and varied course of ecclesiastical history," Newman later wrote, "the theory of the *Via Media* was absolutely pulverized."[26]

III Indecision and Doubt

But Newman was still in no position to embrace the Church of Rome. In the *British Critic* of January, 1840, he conceded that Rome had the strong point of universality; the Church of England, however, had "primitiveness," since Rome had made many additions to the apostolic faith. "While Rome, though not deferring to the Fathers, recognizes them, and England, not deferring to the large body of the Church, recognizes it, both Rome and England have a point to clear up."[27] Later, he wrote more strongly: "If the Note of schism, on the one hand, lies against England, an antagonist disgrace lies upon Rome, the Note of idolatry." The duty of Anglicans, he felt, was to initiate ways of "how to comport themselves towards the Church of Rome, while she is what she is."[28]

With an ardent concern to free the Anglican Church from the condemnation of schism and to demonstrate her unyielding loyalty to the original apostolic church, Newman threw himself into a study of the Thirty-nine Articles drawn up by the Church of England in the sixteenth century. He concentrated on what appeared to him as the all-conclusive problem: how can the Church of England win back its "Catholic" character? The answer to this question was found in "Remarks on Certain Passages in the Thirty-nine Articles" (Tract 90).

Many Anglicans conceded that their Creeds and *Book of Common Prayer* were capable of a Roman Catholic interpretation—but not the Articles, which were distinctly Protestant. Newman, who wished to extend a Roman Catholic interpretation to the Articles, argued that the Articles were not directed to the teachings of the early church and to the formal dogmas of the Roman Catholic Church as set forth in her general councils, including the Council of Trent in the sixteenth century, which had preceded the formulation of the Articles. But the Articles did condemn many popular beliefs and usages which steadily had crept in through the centuries and which Rome did sanction; these he termed "dominant errors." The Articles were also directed against the political supremacy of the Pope and not against the Church of Rome; and Newman found nothing in apostolic teaching which granted the Pope authority over the whole church. He did concede, however, that, although the Pope's supremacy was not a matter of faith, it was an expedient ecclesiastical arrangement and a long-standing custom. The Oath of Supremacy enjoined on Englishmen by Henry VIII prevented a foreign prelate from having jurisdiction on anyone in England. Anglicans, therefore, freed themselves only from the Pope's jurisdiction but not from the Church Catholic. "We find ourselves, as a Church, under the King now, and we obey him; we were under the Pope formerly, and we obeyed him."[29] Newman thus felt that he had absolved the Anglican Church of schism and had demonstrated her "Catholic" character.

Tract 90 had been issued on February 27, 1841. Without seeking any defense or explanation from Newman, protests and demonstrations were made in the halls and classrooms of Oxford and from the pulpits of the

Anglican Church. Throughout England, Newman was denounced as a traitor to the Church of England and as an advocate of popery and Romanism. He betrayed his allegiance to the Articles which he had sworn to uphold when he had entered Oxford as a student and when he had been ordained to the Anglican ministry. Feelings of mistrust grew. Tract 90 was branded as "evasive hypocrisy," and one prominent churchman's remark was often quoted: "I should be sorry to trust the author of that Tract with my purse."[30] Newman had failed, therefore, to convince his fellow Anglicans; he was not able to have them follow the continuity of his own logic as it had been unfolding itself since the beginning of the Oxford Movement. In the eyes of many in England, he was "a subtleminded ecclesiastical hairsplitter and special pleader."[31] Anglicans of the twentieth century, reflecting earlier opinion, have labeled Tract 90 as "a very melancholy document" with "a certain double dealing," showing "how a really great man can become little in a false and ambiguous situation,"[32] and as a "culmination of sophistries" which "falsify history."[33]

At first, Newman reacted quite calmly to the charges made against him, or almost as if he had anticipated the stir. In a letter to his friend Bowden, he wrote: "Do not think all this will pain me. You see no *doctrine* is censured, and my shoulders shall manage to bear the charge. If you knew all, or when you know, you will see that I have asserted a great principle, and I ought to suffer for it."[34] And to a former pupil, Frederick Rogers, he wrote: "I am now in my right place, which I have long wished to be in, which I did not know how to attain, and which has been brought about without my intention. . . . I cannot anticipate what will be the result of it in this place or elsewhere as regards *myself.* Somehow I do not fear for the *cause.*"[35]

Newman, however, underestimated the extent and the depth of opinion against his having written Tract 90. The bishops of the Anglican Church, alarmed by the many protesting letters they were receiving, urged Newman's ecclesiastical superior, Bishop Bagot, to take action. Bagot sought advice from the Archbishop of Canterbury, who deemed desirable the immediate discontinuance of the Tracts. But Newman was requested by Bagot not only to discontinue the Tracts but also to withdraw Tract 90. If Newman had heeded Bagot's decision, his acceptance would have implied that he had received an official censure and that he would have to sacrifice his principles. Newman, caught in an ecclesiastical web, told Pusey that "if it was condemned as to doctrine, I should feel I had no business in his diocese. I should not be signing the articles in the sense he meant them to be signed."[36] Bagot, who respected Newman's position, effected a compromise: Tract 90 would not be censured and could remain in print if Newman discontinued the Tracts and if he would no longer write about the Articles; furthermore, Newman was to send to his bishop a letter, to be made public, stating his repudiation of the Church of Rome.[37] Bishop Bagot accepted the letter as satisfactory since Newman had written: "I think that to belong to the Catholic Church is the first of all privileges here below, as involving in it heavenly privileges, and . . . I consider the Church over which you preside the Catholic Church in this country."[38] For the moment, at least, the turmoil subsided.

Since 1839, Newman had been contemplating the leaving of St. Mary's, Oxford, to live at Littlemore, several miles away, where he had built a church. A number of reasons led to this consideration: he doubted having any pastoral influence over his Oxford parishioners, with whom he admitted having no personal acquaintance; he felt guilty about using St. Mary's as a university office to give prestige to his ideas rather than for the performance of its intended parochial duties; and he also feared that his sermons were disposing the congregation towards Rome. At Keble's advice, however, he decided to continue at St. Mary's; but his trips to Littlemore became more frequent; and, on the publication of Tract 90 in February, 1841, he was taking steps toward his eventual withdrawal from St. Mary's, Oxford. He spent the summer of 1841 at Littlemore "without any harass or anxiety" on his mind, "determined to put aside controversy," and to translate St. Athanasius.[39]

But anxiety and controversy were Newman's lot. The Anglican bishops, fully aware of the impact of Tract 90, began leveling charges at Newman. A determined movement to discredit him became evident when seven bishops had condemned him by the end of 1841 and twenty-four by 1844. At first, Newman planned a protest; but he felt tied by the cords of ecclesiastical obedience and gave up the thought in despair.[40] On the affair of the Jerusalem bishopric, however, Newman did not give up. A Protestant English bishopric was to be set up in Jerusalem; the bishop was to be consecrated by the Anglican archbishop; and he would rule the Lutheran and Calvinist congregations of the East.

Newman, who considered this act as the granting of status to Protestantism in the East, wrote against the scheme in the July, 1841, issue of the *British Critic;* and he asserted that, while the Anglican Church was censuring him for avowing an approach to the Roman Church, "it actually was courting an intercommunion with Protestant Prussia and the heresy of the Orientals." He also denounced the move as a political stunt of cooperating with the Prussians to offset the influence in Jerusalem of France and Russia, which had established themselves as protectors of the Roman Catholics and of the Orthodox. On November 11, 1841, Newman formally protested to his own bishop and to the Archbishop of Canterbury, but without success; this episode brought Newman "on to the beginning of the end."[41]

In January, 1842, another disappointment followed when John Keble retired from Oxford and his position as Professor of Poetry became vacant. A follower of Newman, Isaac Williams, was considered by many to be the best qualified candidate; but Williams was defeated for the post, presumably on the grounds of his adherence to the Tractarian movement, although he clearly demonstrated no sympathy towards Rome. As an indication of loss of prestige and influence at Oxford, Newman established permanent residence at Littlemore on April 19, 1842. He would minister to his Littlemore parishioners, and his curate to the Oxford members of his congregation. Furthermore, he considered retirement from Oxford expedient in such a period of controversy.

The charges of the Anglican bishops persisted while Newman was at Littlemore. Newspapers circulated all sorts of rumors as to the purpose of his retreat to Littlemore; and "insidious," "sly," "dishonest" were used to describe him. He was even accused of "rearing . . . a nest of Papists."[42] When his attention was called to the descriptions being circulated about Newman and his companions at Littlemore, Bishop Bagot regarded an inquiry necessary; and he requested from Newman an explanation of the reports that he had established an Anglo-Catholic monastery approaching the monastic orders of the Roman Catholic Church. When Newman replied to this and other topics of "incessant interpretation," he denied any erection of a monastery, but he upheld his right to devote himself to a life of greater religious regularity and to more intense personal prayer.[43]

The year 1843 became an eventful one for Newman, for his formal retraction of all he had said against the Church of Rome was published in February in the *Oxford Conservative Journal* with the expected reaction on the part of his opponents; he was branded with the charge of duplicity. In May, Pusey preached a sermon on "The Holy Eucharist a Comfort to the Penitent." Despite Pusey's careful adherence to Anglican doctrine, Oxford's officials suspended him from preaching at the university. Pusey's previous defense of Tract 90 was a sufficient "guilt by association" in the minds of Oxford. In August, the occasion for resigning from St. Mary's took place when William Lockhart, a follower of Newman at Littlemore, joined the Roman Catholic Church and was admitted into one of her monastic orders. When newspapers publicized the conversion and critical letters poured into Littlemore, Newman, convinced that he could no longer maintain a position of leadership and influence while retaining his official post in the Anglican Church, presented his resignation on September 18 as Vicar of St. Mary's to Bishop Bagot.

On September 25, Newman delivered his last sermon as an Anglican, "The Parting of Friends." A hearer noted "the faltering voice, the long pauses, the perceptible and hardly successful efforts at restraining himself, together with the deep interest of the subject which were almost overpowering," as Newman bade farewell to friends, parishioners, and associates at St. Mary's and Oxford.[44] He expressed regret at leaving the church of his birth but, at the same time, found her wanting in adherence to divine truth. He urged everyone present to pray "that in all things he may know God's will, and at all times he may be ready to fulfill it."[45]

Newman retired in quiet seclusion to live a quasi-monastic discipline at Littlemore. Without his leadership, many of his followers became unrestrained in emphasizing the most Roman interpretation of the Oxford Movement; and, by 1845, their influence as a party of reform within the Anglican Church became minimal. Newman's retirement marked an end to any participation on his part in the Oxford Movement.[46] Instead, Newman began a period of intensive prayer and study. Many Anglicans were expecting an immediate announcement of his conversion to Roman Catholicism, but Newman was not yet ready for such a step; his mind was too unsettled. Many followers were looking to him for direction; but his own soul and mind became his only concern. "How could I in any sense," he deliberated, "direct others, who had to be guided in so momentous a matter myself?"[47]

A few of Newman's followers had gone over to the Church of Rome. A year after resigning from the Anglican priesthood, Newman explained the unsettled state of his mind and the difficulty which confronted it in reference to choosing Roman Catholicism:

> I had been deceived once; how could I be sure that I was not deceived a second time? I thought myself right then; how was I to be certain that I was now? How many years had I thought myself sure of what I now rejected? how could I ever again have confidence in myself? As in 1840 I listened to the rising doubt in favour of Rome, now I listened to the waning doubt in favour of the Anglican Church. To be certain is to know that one knows; what inward test had I, that I should not change again, after I had become a Catholic? I had still apprehension of this, although I thought a time would come, when it would depart.[48]

Many factors contributed to Newman's hesitation in his acceptance of Roman Catholicism. He would have to forsake the church of his birth, which he had so staunchly defended against the liberals. Many friends and colleagues at Oxford, the associations of many years, would no longer be his. Members of his family, especially his sisters, noting a possible trend towards Rome, pleaded with him against taking such a drastic step. He knew what and whom he was to leave; he did not know what and whom he was to join. He had had little contact with members of the Roman Catholic clergy and faith. He had been brought up in a tradition of prejudice towards Roman Catholics, who, for many years in Great Britain, had been ostracized from political and social life. He had been to Rome on his Mediterranean trip and remembered her as a "city under a curse." Religious conversions require more than logic; reason too frequently finds itself entangled in emotions. Prayer and study were regarded all the more as necessary means to Newman's searching mind and soul.

IV Essay on Development

Towards the end of 1844, Newman resolved to write down the results of his study at Littlemore in a work that he entitled *An Essay on the Development of Christian Doctrine.* While reviewing the thoughts of his projected thesis, he was confronted by a dilemma of his own making. He had been an exponent of the static view of the church—a view which held that Christian truth was known completely by the church at its very beginning and that, therefore, antiquity was the chief note of the true church. But he had now become influenced by a more dynamic view which claimed that, although all truth had been given to the church upon its establishment, subsequent thought and reflection produces clarification and a better understanding of Christ's teachings. The fact of heresies, even in early Christianity, proved necessary the action of the church in issuing decrees of belief for the purpose of avoiding misinterpretation of Christian teaching. Delving farther into the Fathers of the Church and early Christianity demonstrated to Newman that the growth or development of Christian doctrine was an idea that clearly existed in theological thought and that St. Irenaeus, Origen, St. Basil, St. Jerome, and St. Gregory Nazianzen had subscribed at least implicitly to the view.[49]

In his introduction to the *Essay on Development,* Newman insisted that Christianity had to be viewed as a historical fact and that throughout its eighteen hundred years of existence certain apparent inconsistencies and changes in doctrine and worship have occurred. He regarded any inquiry as to the mode and meaning of these apparent inconsistencies and charges as justified; and, since he himself had been beset by the problem, he directed the *Essay* toward its solution.[50] Concerning the doctrine and worship of Christianity, he mantained that the history of eighteen hundred years ought to make us consider

> that the increase and expansion of the Christian Creed and Ritual, and the variations which have attended the process in the case of individual writers and Churches, are the necessary attendants on any philosophy or polity which takes possession of the intellect and heart, and has had any wide or extended dominion; that, from the nature of the human mind, time is necessary for the full comprehension and prefection of great ideas; and that the highest and most wonderful truths, though communicated to the world once for all by inspired teachers, could not be comprehended all at once by the recipients, but, as being received and transmitted by minds not inspired and through media which were human, have required only the longer time and deeper thought for their full elucidation. This may be called *The Theory of Development of Doctrine.*[51]

As Newman sought to substantiate his theory of development, he emphasized the natural function of the human mind as being always engaged in passing judgment on what it comes to know: "We allow nothing to stand by itself: we compare, contrast, abstract, generalize, connect, adjust, classify; and we view all our knowledge in the associations with which these processes have invested it."[52] Such mental activity would not be peculiar to religious ideas alone: mathematical, physical, political, historical, ethical, metaphysical ideas would also be subject to the mind's scrutiny.[53] All ideas characterized as "living" have generated "a general agitation of thought, and an action of mind upon mind."[54] So has been the historical development of such doctrines as "the divine right of kings," "the rights of man," political constitutions, the philosophies of great men.

Since Christianity is a universal religion and is not bound to one locale or period of history, it must be able to accommodate itself towards the world in which it finds itself: its different persons and circumstances of any place or time. All Christian sects have appealed to Scripture, but with varying interpretations of the texts, and even as to the authority to interpret them. The unsystematic structure and figurative style of Scripture have required constant study and examination in the light of changing times—an argument for the development of Christian doctrine as based on Scripture. And Newman emphasized that, "in an age in which reason, as it is called, is the standard of truth and right, it is abundantly evident to any one . . . that, if things are left to themselves, every individual will have his own view of them, and take his own course."[55] To maintain unity and continuity in Christian doctrine throughout all periods of history postulates some supreme power to control the mind and to compel agreement.

By this reasoning Newman concluded in favor of the role of infallibility claimed by the Roman Catholic Church against private interpretation of the Scriptures as advocated by Protestantism: "If Christianity is both social and dogmatic, and intended for all ages, it must humanly speaking have an infallible expounder. Else you will secure unity of form at the loss of unity of doctrine, or unity of doctrine at the loss of form; you will have to choose between comprehension of opinions and a resolution into parties, between latitudinarian and sectarian error."[56] If St. Athanasius or St. Ambrose were to come to life, they would undoubtedly recognize the Roman Catholic Church, and not any other Christian denomination, as the expounder of Christ's doctrine today. Allowance would have to be made for changes of words to explain doctrine; emphasis in argumentation would have to be accommodated to existing circumstances—but these are of the essence of development of doctrine.

Newman had resolved the most pressing difficulty in his mind regarding the acceptance of the Church of Rome: had Rome adhered to or swayed from primitive Christianity? And he concluded that "of all existing systems, the present communion of Rome is the nearest approximation in fact to the Church of the Fathers."[57] Newman, moreover, presented not only a conclusion; he documented it with the results of his serious study in which he contrasted the teachings of Roman Catholicism in the nineteenth century with those of the early Christian Church.

He chose the following doctrines to illustrate a genuine development from earlier and simpler forms: the Canon of the New Testament, the doctrines of Original Sin and Infant Baptism, Communion in One Kind, the Divine Nature of Christ, the Incarnation, the dignity of the Blessed Virgin and the Saints, and Papal Supremacy. With proofs taken from the texts of Scripture, the opinions of Church Fathers, and the practice of the early church, he demonstrated how these doctrines had developed throughout the church's history into their form in the nineteenth-century Church of Rome.[58] Intimate connection and oneness of past and present in doctrine afforded Roman Catholicism, in Newman's mind, "undeniably the historical continuation of the religious system, which bore the name of Catholic in the eighteenth century, in the seventeenth, in the sixteenth, and so back in every preceding century, till we arrive at the first;—undeniably the successor, the representative, the heir of the religion of Cyprian, Basil, Ambrose, and Augustine. . . . Modern Catholicism is nothing else but simply the legitimate growth and complement, that is, the natural and necessary development, of the doctrine of the early Church, and that its divine authority is included in the divinity of Christianity."[59]

But the fact and necessity of development comprise only a part of Newman's efforts in this treatise; for the process by which religious ideas genuinely develop forms an even greater section of his study. In the course of time, an idea may not become a development; it may become a corruption. Development denotes life; "corruption, on the contrary, is the breaking up of life, preparing to its termination."[60] Newman distinguishes seven "notes," or tests, to judge development or corruption of doctrine. *Preservation of type* is the first test offered, and it is based on the analogy of physical growth. Animals remain within their species throughout their lives. Birds do not become fish; the child does not generate into the brute. Continuity of species is maintained. Ideas also develop with subsequent thought and reflection; they take on new meaning in the crucible of experience. As Christians reflected upon and sought to apply Christ's doctrine to their everyday lives, their faith took on new dimensions without undergoing radical change.[61] Newman details the history of the church in the first six centuries with all the problems attendant upon an organization seeking the fullest possible growth in order to fulfill the aims of its founder. Whether viewed "in its age" or "in its youth," the organization has maintained identity. In her growth and development, "such a religion [the Roman Catholic Church] is not unlike the Christianity of the fifth and sixth centuries."[62]

Religious doctrines also evolve from principles. The sciences of mathematics and physics, by analogy, have developed basic permanent principles from which, in the course of study and experimentation, much new knowledge has been derived. Although principles are largely general and abstract, their application leads to the discovery of many new facts. As a second test, *continuity of principles* causes religious doctrine to grow and develop: Christ enunciated the basic permanent principles; His church enlarges upon them as they are applied to future generations.[63] And so the Church of Rome—faithful to Christ's principles, as the supremacy of faith over reason, the preference of the mystical to the literal interpretation of Scripture, the necessity to defend and to transmit defined doctrine—has stood firm, especially against heresies; has maintained the principles and has put them in vigorous operation.[64]

For the third test, *power of assimilation,* Newman again makes use of the analogy of physical growth: life grows by absorbing or assimilating into its own substance external materials, as is done in the matter of food. In the intellectual order, many an ideas has resulted from a similar process.[65] In seeking to attract converts, yet desiring to have them feel "at home" in a newly adopted religious faith, the church has frequently employed many customs and usages of pagan rites, such as incense, candles, festival days. Rather than obliterate, the Church has "Christianized" them.[66]

Logical sequence, the fourth test, occasions development simply by affirming any progress of the mind from one judgment to another. If the original teaching is correct, doctrines logically deduced from it represent logical conclusions.[67] To demonstrate this test in the church's history, Newman confines himself to examples of doctrine which consider sin after baptism. The necessity of remitting sin after baptism and of rendering possible reconciliation with God was given serious thought in the early church. In her desire to fulfill Christ's hope for the salvation of sinners and to carry out its authority of "binding and loosing," the church adopted systems of penances and satisfaction for sin.[68]

The fifth test, *anticipation of its future,* considers that an idea that has life has the power to develop under favorable circumstances with the passage of time. The development of a doctrine, therefore, may be vague and slow; but the workings of logical minds will eventually bring a doctrine to its fullest development.[69] Such would be the case, Newman asserts, with doctrines relating to relics, to the cult of saints and angels, and to the Blessed Virgin.[70]

The words of Christ, "I have come not to destroy, but to fulfill," provide the basis for the sixth test: *conservative action upon its past.* Although an idea may have developed with time, "a true development . . . may be described as one which is conservative of the course of antecedent developments being really those antecedents and something besides them: it is an addition which illustrates, not obscures, corroborates, not corrects, the body of thought from which it proceeds."[71] Heresies, Newman points out, have made it necessary for the church to reaffirm previously declared doctrine, as, for example, in the Incarnation, the Trinity, and the Blessed Virgin; but it did so with the purpose of clarification and of placing proper emphasis of various aspects of the specific doctrines.[72]

The seventh and final test is *chronic vigour:* duration or long standing characterizes the faithful development of an idea. Heresies or corruptions of doctrine are short-lived, as are the peculiarities of a country, the customs of a race, or the temporary response to the changing tides of opinion; they cannot maintain their vigor with the passage of time and with divergent cultures.[73] An examination of Roman Catholic doctrines in themselves and in comparison with other religious faiths leads Newman to conclude:

> After violent exertion men are exhausted and fall asleep; they awake the same as before, refreshed by the temporary cessation of their activity; and such has been the slumber and such the restoration of the Church. She pauses in her course, and almost suspends her functions; she rises again, and she is herself once more; all things are in their place and ready for action. Doctrine is where it was, and usage, and precedence, and principle, and policy; there may be changes, but they are consolidations or adaptations; all is unequivocal and determinate, with an identity which there is no disputing.[74]

Since Newman presented a developmental theory in 1845, both critics and friends have attributed his view to the influence of nineteenth-century thought.[75] Comte, Condorcet, and Kant viewed humanity as a developing organism; the French Revolution had called for the progressive improvement of mankind, and Hegel had popularized the notion of progress in his philosophy of history. Moreover, Spencer in the field of sociology emphasized the need of man to adjust to a constantly changing environment; indeed, crities have even associated Newman with Darwinian evolution: "We cannot but see on every page of the *Development* Darwin's advancing shadow."[76] Since Newman repeatedly employed the analogy of organic development, his doctrine has been interpreted in biological terms; one critic calls the process of development *epigenesis;* another refers to it as "homogeneous evolution."[77] But the *Origin of the Species* was not published until 1859; and, after its publication, Newman gave no indication of accepting Darwin's thesis in the physiological order, least of all in matters of revealed religion.[78]

Newman had resolved to write the essay on doctrinal development with the purpose of clearing his own mind of the rising doubts in favor of the Roman Catholic Church. At the beginning of writing the essay he acknowledged, "If, at the end of it, my convictions in favour of the Roman Church were not weaker, of taking the necessary steps for admission into her fold."[79] As he progressed in its writing and as his difficulties were gradually resolved, he ceased to speak of "the Roman Catholics"; and he called them "Catholics." "Before I got to the end, I resolved to be received."[80]

Although the essay on doctrine achieved for Newman a justification of the claims of Roman Catholicism, not all Roman Catholics accepted his thesis. Two Jesuit theologians in Rome admitted the principle of development, but they claimed that Newman had carried the principle too far.[81] Newman's American friends wrote of the poor reception of the book by American bishops, who characterized it as "half Catholicism half infidelity."[82] Orestes Brownson, himself a convert, charged Newman with lack of adequate understanding of the Catholic Church and declared that in the essay he reasoned as a Protestant: "This elaborate essay belongs to his past life; let it go with all that Protestantism he abjured before he was permitted to put on the livery of Christ. It belongs not to his Catholic life, and is only accidentally connected with it. . . . The essay he will write hereafter, out of the fulness of his Catholic heart, will breathe a different tone, and fetch another echo."[83] Brownson, who had a static view of Christianity, maintained that the original creed was complete: new definitions of doctrine represented not a subsequent "apprehension and understanding of the sacred deposit of faith committed to her charge" (as Newman asserted), but formulations occasioned by new heresies: "The Church has no natural history, for she is not in the order of nature, but of grace."[84]

Catholic theologians, however, have also indicated that the idea of the development of dogma had existed long before Newman in the writings of the Fathers of the Church and in theological thought.[85] Newman may not have been the originator of the idea, but he has been its ablest expounder. Bishop John J. Wright of Pittsburgh, in speaking of Vatican Council II's role in the updating of Catholic doctrine, echoed Newman's thought: "New Testament verses are the seeds of doctrine. With each popping out of a branch, with each flowering of a leaf, you have a new branch and a new leaf. But each branch and each leaf is in the pattern of the original seed."[86]

V Conversion

Convinced of the truth of Roman Catholicism, Newman's conversion was only a matter of time and circumstance. Two of his companions at Littlemore, Ambrose St. John and John D. Dalgairns, had already joined the Church of Rome. Father Dominic, a missionary in the Congregation of the Passion, planned to visit Dalgairns at Littlemore on October 8, 1845. Newman had submitted his letter of resignation as Fellow of Oriel on October 3, and two days later he noted in his diary that he was making immediate preparation for admittance to Roman Catholicism. With the knowledge of Father Dominic's impending visit, he wrote to Henry Wilberforce that he would ask the missionary priest to receive him into the Church of Rome.[87] On the evening of October 8, Newman was received, with two companions, Frederick Bowles and Richard Stanton.

Upon his conversion Newman's plans for the future were unsettled. Father Dominic suggested that he and his companions visit Bishop Nicholas Wiseman at Oscott and receive the sacrament of confirmation. Newman, who had already met Wiseman as rector of the English College in Rome in 1833, offered Wiseman a copy of his *Essay on Development* for approval. Wiseman felt that the book should be published unchanged or without theological censorship in the hope that it would present a more effective plea for Roman Catholicism. Knowing of the new converts' desire to remain together and also of their unsettled minds as to their next course of action, Wiseman proposed that they move to Old Oscott College in a "Littlemore continued." The converts accepted the offer, and Newman named their house Maryvale.

The secluded life of Littlemore was resumed at Maryvale. Newman declined an offer to write an account of his reasons for joining the Roman Church; he deemed it inopportune to engage in controversy. Moreover, he suggested that the *Essay on Development* had already made his position clear.[88] Instead, Newman preferred to delve into a more thorough study of the ways and traditions of his newly chosen faith and to help his associates prepare for the possible reception of Holy Orders. Although hesitant upon his conversion about being ordained a Roman Catholic priest, Newman decided to take the step. But what work was he to do, and should it be under a bishop of a diocese or in a religious congregation of priests? Father Dominic hoped that the converts would be preachers and missionaries. Bishop Wiseman considered the founding of a school of divinity for preparing future priests—a work for which Newman had had experience as a teacher at Oxford and for which he had demonstrated a wealth of theological knowledge and history in the *Essay on Development.* Since Newman could not make a decision, he expressed the desire to go to Rome and, as his companions felt, have Rome decide for him.[89]

In September, 1846, Newman and St. John left for Rome. They first spent four or five weeks at Milan, where they admired the churches and the art of the city. After a similar study of Rome, they resided at the College of Propaganda, a seminary founded in the seventeenth century for training young men of every nationality for missionary work. When Newman discussed with many in Rome the possibilities of his future work,[90] the objections he heard expressed against his *Essay on Development* dissuaded him from founding any divinity school. Having a natural bent towards community life, but for one without too many monastic restrictions, Newman took a liking for the Oratorians, a congregation founded by St. Philip Neri in the sixteenth century.[91] Pope Pius IX approved wholeheartedly of Newman's wishes; and, after Newman's required training period was completed in Rome, the Pope would concur with the hope of Newman and the converts to establish themselves as members of this congregation of priests in England.[92] The Pope appointed the Oratorian Father Carlo Rossi to supervise their training and granted them the use of a wing of the Monastery of Santa Croce for their home in Rome. Newman was ordained a Roman Catholic priest on May 30, 1847.

While in Rome, Newman also found time to write. He directed his energies to a novel about religious conversion: *Loss and Gain: the Story of a Convert,* which was published in 1848 upon his return to England. *Loss and Gain* was occasioned by the success in England in the summer of 1847 of a novel, whose author was not identified, *From Oxford to Rome,* which pretended to portray the inside picture of the "defection" of the Oxford converts to Roman Catholicism. Newman considered the book as "wantonly and preposterously fanciful." Rather than honor the book by a formal critique of its contents, he deemed it more suitable to answer by writing his novel, one "drawn up with a stricter regard to truth and probability, and with at least some personal knowledge of Oxford, and some perception of the various aspects of the religious phenomenon, which the work in question handled so rudely and so unskilfully."[93]

Newman claimed that *Loss and Gain* was an imaginary tale and that neither the principal characters nor the history of any individual mind among the converts was delineated: only "free use has been made of sayings and doings which were characteristic of the time and place in which the scene is laid."[94] Despite the unintended suggestion to the reader of real individuals, there is an obvious identification of the characters in the novel with Newman's own religious development and experiences at Oxford. Charles Reding, the main character, bears a striking resemblance to Newman. Reding, the son of an old-fashioned Anglican clergyman, is sent to Oxford, where he becomes confused as a result of the conflicting views expressed about religious matters. He begins to question the Thirty-nine Articles and even becomes interested in Roman Catholicism, to the displeasure of the university authorities. Excessive preoccupation with religious uncertainties causes his failure in his first attempt at examinations. However, since Reding has every desire to remain in the Anglican Church, he spends considerable time reading and studying more about his faith, while also seeking advice from learned Anglican theologians. But these efforts prove fruitless. To the sorrow of family and friends, Reding, who feels in conscience that he must leave the church of his birth, goes to London to be received into the Church of Rome by a Passionist priest.

Reding and Newman, moreover, possessed many of the same personality traits. Both were shy and sensitive, which led to their being misunderstood and to a feeling of isolation. Both were able to overcome their scholastic failure. They were lovers of music, not given over to socializing, and were inclined from youth to a life of celibacy. Both refrained from accepting Roman Catholicism until all reasonable doubt was cleared from their minds.

As a novelist, Newman lacks dramatic quality. The elements of conflict and suspense are superficial since the reader is never held in abeyance as to the next development of the action. In his evaluation of *Loss and Gain,* Baker points out how the novel "reflects merely intellectual steps along the way to conversion, not emotional reaction of man on man."[95] The characters in the novel are classified as "caricatures" and as "shadowy outlines"[96] and as hardly recognizable if met in real life.[97] Yet Newman's novels are still reprinted and read. Besides their historical and biographical value, they contain many humorous, eloquent, and satirical passages.

Newman spent the remainder of 1847 in Rome and in visiting Oratorian establishments and shrines in various cities of Italy. Several conferences with the Pope were used to determine his future work in England, for which Newman set sail on December 6.

Notes

[1] J. P. Stanley, *Life of Thomas Arnold, D.D.* (London, 1904), p. 278.

[2] S. L. Ollard, *A Short History of the Oxford Movement* (London, 1915), p. 17.

[3] D. C. Somervell, *English Thought in the Nineteenth Century* (New York, 1929), p. 17.

[4] A. Mozley, *Letters [and Correspondence of John Henry Newman During His Life in the English Church, with a Brief Autobiography.* (London, 1891)], I, 233.

[5] See Thomas Carlyle's essay on "Sir Walter Scott," *Collected Works,* Vol. IV of *Critical and Miscellaneous Essays* (London, 1896-1899), p. 49.

[6] *Apologia [pro Vite Sue* (London, 1864)], p. 23.

[7] *Ibid.,* pp. 27-28.

[8] *Ibid.,* p. 28.

[9] Meriol Trevor, *Newman* (New York, 1962), I, 148.

[10] *Tracts for the Times* (London, 1833-41), I, 1-2.

[11] Of the tracts, Newman was the author of nos. 1, 2, 3, 6, 7, 8, 10, 11, 15, 19, 20, 21, 33, 34, 38, 40, 41, 45, 47, 71, 73, 75, 76, 79, 82, 83, 85, 88, and 90.

[12] *Apologia,* pp. 11-15. See also Sylvester P. Juergens, *Newman on the Psychology of Faith in the Individual* (New York, 1928), pp. 72, 167, 176.

[13] R. W. Church, [*The Oxford Movement* (Hemden, Conn., 1966)], pp. 129-30.

[14] Quoted from W. Ward, [*The Life of John Henry Cardinal Newman* (London, 1913)], I, 66.

[15] Thomas Mozley, *Reminiscences Chiefly of Oriel College and the Oxford Movement* (London, 1882), I, 313.

[16] This work was later published as the first volume of the *Via Media* (London, 1877).

[17] *Via Media* [(London, 1877)], I, 79.

[18] *Ibid.,* 137.

[19] *Lectures on Justification* (London, 1838).

[20] Yngve Brilioth feels that these lectures "form perhaps the chief theological document of the Oxford Movement." See *The Anglican Revival* (London, 1933), p. 282.

[21] See *Apologia,* pp. 62-69.

[22] *Justification,* p. 340.

[23] *Apologia,* p. 68.

[24] Eutyches was an abbot of an important monastery during the mid-400s in the outskirts of Constantinople; he is considered the father of Monophysitism.

[25] *Apologia,* p. 76.

[26] *Ibid.,* p. 78.

[27] *Ibid.,* p. 74.

[28] *Ibid.,* p. 75.

[29] *Tracts,* V, 79.

[30] Church, *Oxford,* pp. 298-99.

[31] [C. F.] Harrold, [*John Henry Newman* (New York, 1945)], p. 43.

[32] Brilioth, *Revival,* p. 155.

[33] E. A. Knox, *The Tractarian Movement: 1833-1845* (New York, 1933), p. 255.

[34] Quoted from Trevor, *Newman,* I, 244.

[35] *Ibid.,* pp. 244-45.

[36] *Ibid.,* p. 246.

[37] *Via Media,* II, 6.

[38] Trevor, *Newman,* I, 246.

[39] *Apologia,* pp. 89-91.

[40] *Ibid.,* p. 93.

[41] *Ibid.,* pp. 93-97.

[42] *Ibid.,* pp. 114-15.

[43] *Ibid.,* pp. 115-17.

[44] Quoted from Trevor, *Newman,* I, 303.

[45] *Ibid.,* p. 304.

[46] For further developments and the revival of the Oxford Movement, see Brilioth, *Revival;* Church, *Oxford;* L. E. Elliott-Binns, *Religion in the Victorian Era* (London, 1936); Knox, *Tractarian;* Shane Leslie, *The Oxford Movement* (Milwaukee, 1933); J. Lewis May, *The Oxford Movement* (London, 1933); J. H. Overton, *The English Church in the Nineteenth Century* (London, 1894); W. J. S. Simpson, *The History of the Anglo-Catholic Revival from 1845* (London, 1932); Vernon F. Storr, *The Development of English Theology in the Ninetenth Century: 1800-1860* (London, 1913); C. C. J. Webb, *Religious Thought in the Oxford Movement* (New York, 1928).

[47] *Apologia,* p. 145.

[48] *Ibid.,* pp. 151-52.

[49] Juergens, *Newman,* p. 265.

[50] Newman first published the work in 1845, but the *Essay* in this study is examined from the 1878 edition, since this is the form in which Newman desired it to be judged. See Cross, *Newman,* p. 179. For a comparative study of the 1845 and 1878 editions, see Harrold, *Newman,* pp. 394-95.

[51] *An Essay on the Development of Christian Doctrine* (London, 1878), pp. 29-30.

[52] *Ibid.,* p. 33.

[53] *Ibid.,* pp. 41-53.

[54] *Ibid.,* p. 37.

[55] *Ibid.,* pp. 89-90.

[56] *Ibid.,* p. 90.

[57] *Ibid.,* p. 97.

[58] *Ibid.,* pp. 122-65.

[59] *Ibid.,* p. 169.

[60] *Ibid.,* p. 170.

[61] *Ibid.,* pp. 171-78.

[62] *Ibid.,* p. 322.

[63] *Ibid.,* pp. 178-85.

[64] *Ibid.,* pp. 323-54.

[65] *Ibid.,* pp. 185-89.

[66] *Ibid.,* pp. 355-83.

[67] *Ibid.,* pp. 189-95.

[68] *Ibid.,* pp. 383-99.

[69] *Ibid.,* pp. 195-99.

[70] *Ibid.,* pp. 400-18.

[71] *Ibid.,* p. 200.

[72] *Ibid.,* pp. 419-36.

[73] *Ibid.*, pp. 199-206.

[74] *Ibid.*, p. 444.

[75] Wilfrid Ward, *Problems and Persons* (London, 1903), p. 9; Guitton, *Philosophie,* pp. 54, 137-40.

[76] [William F.] Barry, *Newman* [(New York, 1905)], p. 278.

[77] *Ibid.*, p. 280.

[78] R. Blennerhassett, "Some Recollections of Cardinal Newman," *Living Age,* XIII (1901), 796.

[79] *Apologia,* p. 152.

[80] *Ibid.*, p. 156.

[81] W. Ward, *Newman,* I, 161. While he was preparing for the Roman Catholic priesthood in Rome, Newman had the opportunity to discuss his theory on development with a number of outstanding theologians; see *ibid.*, pp. 184-87.

[82] *Ibid.*, p. 160.

[83] Orestes A. Brownson, "Newman's Development of Christian Doctrine," *Brownson's Works* (Detroit, 1882-87), XIV, 27.

[84] *Ibid.*, p. 25.

[85] Juergens, *Newman,* p. 265; F. Marin-Sola, *L'évolution homogène du dogme catholique* (Paris, 1924), II, 127; Edmond D. Benard, *A Preface to Newman's Theology* (St. Louis, 1945), pp. 84, 96.

[86] Quoted from Lee E. Dirks, *Religion in Action* (Silver Spring, Md.), p. 13.

[87] Newman to Robert Wilberforce, October 7, 1845, in W. Ward, *Newman,* I, 92-93.

[88] Newman to Spencer Northcote, February, 1846, in *ibid.*, pp. 121-22.

[89] *Ibid.*, pp. 125-26.

[90] *Ibid.*, pp. 157-69.

[91] Newman to J. D. Dalgairns, January 15, 1847, in *ibid.*, p. 176.

[92] Ambrose St. John to J. D. Dalgairns and Newman to J. D. Dalgairns, February 24, 1847, in *ibid.*, pp. 181-82.

[93] *Loss and Gain: the Story of a Convert* (London, 1848), p. ix.

[94] *Ibid.*, p. vii.

[95] Joseph E. Baker, *The Novel and the Oxford Movement* (Princeton, N.J., 1932), pp. 62, 64.

[96] Harrold, *Newman,* p. 288.

[97] Joseph J. Reilly, *Newman as a Man of Letters* (New York, 1925), p. 95.

BACKGROUND OF THE MOVEMENT

Raymond Chapman (essay date 1970)

SOURCE: "The Background of the Movement," in *Faith and Revolt: Studies in the Literary Influence of the Oxford Movement,* Weidenfeld and Nicolson, 1970, pp. 9-29.

[*In the following essay, Chapman contends that the Oxford Movement emerged in an environment of intense religious controversy between Anglicanism and Roman Catholicism in England.*]

The temptation to contain human complexities in simple images is nowhere stronger than in matters of religion. The churchgoing Victorian, puritan and fundamentalist, is an image that has resisted the revaluation of nineteenth-century society more successfully than most. In popular estimation that society existed in an age of faith, to be viewed with nostalgia, contempt or indifference according to the presuppositions of the modern observer. The image may contain as much truth and as much error as most generalizations. The religious temper of the Victorians showed itself in protest and revolt as well as in acceptance.

That religion penetrated the thinking of the age in many of its aspects is not in question. The Victorians were openly concerned about religion. The previous century, chastened by memory of religious strife at home and awareness of worse overseas, had played a quieter note. To be 'enthusiastic' was an offence against that politer mode of conformity where

> To rest, the cushion and soft dean invite,
> Who never mentions Hell to ears polite.[1]

Yet the enthusiasts like Wesley and Whitefield brought a resurgence of faith to their own age and passed on its legacy to the next. They were an offence to those for whom reason was more worthy than passion, for whom the areas of agreement were to be broadened and those of dispute minimized or ignored.

Both the enthusiast and the latitudinarian found new voices in the nineteenth century: so did many others who previously had lingered inarticulately on the fringes of society. There were heard objections to Christianity stronger and more wide-spread than before, but these too often had an essentially religious temper. Most of the great doubters and agnostics believed that basic values had been betrayed by formalized religion and they sought rather to assert those values on a new basis than radically to change them. They reacted with distaste to the cruder manifestations of anti-Christian feeling which accompanied Continental scepticism. Like the eponymous hero of *Robert Elsmere,* one in retreat from the orthodox position could be hurt when his new associates mocked the faith which he had left. To understand at all, it is necessary to enter into the belief that religion matters, in all its shades and affiliations. It is a hard exercise for the modern humanist who has dismissed religion as irrelevant, as hard perhaps for the modern Christian who can accept as commonplace the issues which were bitterly fought over not so long ago.

No date, no accession, no publication, can mark a decisive break between one age and the next. Theological ferment increased but older attitudes lingered. The young Queen reacted against the slack morality of Regency years but also retained the distrust of extremes in religion. Guided in the early years of her reign by Melbourne, to whom studied moderation was a creed, she was never at ease with the stronger manifestations of that piety for which her own household became the exemplar. Both temperament and the demands of her position kept her from favouring any but the moderate; Evangelicals and Anglo-Catholics alike roused her distrust. Many of her subjects felt the same and, like Kingsley's old squire, would curse the Methodists, 'under which name he used to include every species of religious earnestness, from Quakerism to that of Mr Newman'.[2]

Other men, including Kingsley himself, could rather rejoice in the excitement that was being aroused by religion. A multiplicity of new ideas and practices might bewilder the old, but large-scale production was pleasing to those who found their age a challenge. The idea of progress, with Britain in the lead, demanded experiment before the ideal was attained:

> What a chaos of noble materials is here—all confused, it is true, polarized, jarring, and chaotic—here bigotry, there self-will, superstition, sheer Atheism often, but only waiting for the one inspiring Spirit to organize, and unite and consecrate this chaos into the noblest polity the world ever saw realized![3]

Beyond conformity or enthusiasm, the objector could be socially as well as personally insecure. An agnostic's little girl would remember all her life the feeling of deprivation at not going to Sunday School with other children, and the castaways of the Oxford Movement would keep up the practice of family prayers long after their own orthodox belief had gone.[4]

In public as well as family life religion was a strong preoccupation. One can scarcely conceive a modern newspaper editor keeping a list of the London clergy with notes on their theological tendencies.[5] Or a popular novelist, and one for whom popularity was studied, taking for granted his readers' interest in religious affairs as part of the social background:

> The story was thoroughly English. There was a little fox-hunting and a little tuft-hunting, some Christian virtue and some Christian cant. There was no heroism and no villainy. There was much Church, but more love-making.[6]

Something more has to be realized if we would enter fully into the mind of that age. It was not only the basic acceptance of Christianity that mattered, for two men might each profess to believe every word in the Bible yet consider the other utterly wrong on matters of interpretation. Although the ecumenical spirit was slowly emerging by the end of the century, we have come so much farther in the last generation that we may have a mental block about the *odium theologicum* which raged in the Tractarians as strongly as in their bitter opponents. Goodwill in one section of the community and indifferentism in another are both disabilities in studying the importance of denominations. For the divisions of religious allegiance were social as well as religious. To change was to affect cultural life, reading and leisure, to be largely severed from one's past, often to lose the comfort of family and friends when they were most needed. Conversion could not remain a private affair: it involved the whole of a man's immediate circle and, for a man of Newman's position, the whole of society. Even one whose profession was not the Church but the Law could set down for his own consideration among reasons for not becoming a Roman Catholic, 'hesitation at separating myself from every relative I have'.[7]

We shall meet a great deal of the hostility to Rome in what follows and we have to accept its reality at the time. One of the things which brought the Oxford Movement into public concern was the fact that it made secession a living possibility. By raising questions about authority and true catholicity, it developed Papal claims from a distant horror to one near at hand. The fear and antagonism were, of course, old enough. Folk memories of Marian persecutions and Elizabethan plots, kept alive by a secular as well as an ecclesiastical anathema on Guy Fawkes',[8] mingled with the consideration that the Pope was a foreign potentate whom no trueborn Englishman could serve. The few Roman Catholic families at the beginning of the nineteenth century tended to keep to themselves, thankful if they could escape the penalties which the law still laid on the practice of their faith, a handful in infidel territory where no hierarchy was established.

Catholic emancipation came in 1829, largely as a political move to assuage the growing discontent in Ireland after the Union of 1800 had denied hopes of national independence. The chief immediate beneficiaries were the English Roman Catholics who were now admitted to full citizenship in most respects. Political measures did not bring a change of heart, as Victorian reformers were to learn in other fields. The emergence of Roman Catholics into the full light of day made it possible to accept them as reasonable human beings. There was still suspicion of their clergy and bitter hostility to the idea of a Protestant seeking the Roman yoke. To be a crypto-Papist was a terrible thing, an accusation that could be levelled with deadly effect by religious opponents. It was even, however improbably, alleged of the Prince Consort when he was suffering from general unpopularity in the country.[9] To some extent, emancipation led to an exacerbation of anti-Roman feeling, particularly when some of the younger generation began to look for closer links with Italy and to urge the establishment of a territorial hierarchy.

Hostility became hysterical when a significant number of lay and clerical converts moved to Roman Catholicism around the middle of the century. Hitherto the Papists had been virtually confined to old families which had passed on the faith, foreign denizens and immigrants, and the growing number of Irish settlers. Now it seemed that thoughtful and devout men could pass from one allegiance to another. They did so at the cost of personal anguish as well as private hostilities and public obloquy. The problem of ultimate religious authority gave to the Oxford Movement a deep vein of tragedy. There was a special tension for men who had been brought up to see religious attachments as the simple polarities of good and evil.

For the majority of Englishmen there was little desire either to understand or to accommodate the differences between Protestants and Romanists. General sympathy would be with the kind of parson who 'did not want to be reconciled to the Church of Rome; he wanted to make all Roman Catholics turn Protestants, and could never understand why they would not do so'.[10] Proximity and the real possibility of secession led to more fear, as Newman could point out to a 'zealous Catholic layman' in 1841:

> Suspicion and distrust are the main causes at present of the separation between us, and the nearest approaches in doctrine will but increase the hostility, which, alas, our people feel towards yours, while these causes continue.[11]

Newman, alone of the writers of *Tracts for the Times,* went over; those who remained suffered the charge of being dishonest or stupid tools of Rome. The fever did not abate until the century was nearly over; it ranged from the almost lovable mania of Borrow with his gibes at 'old Mumbo-Jumbo' to the tolerant amusement of Sydney Smith who could sympathize with the wrongs suffered by Irish Catholics yet sneer at their 'bargains for shirts and toe-nails of deceased saints—surplices and trencher-caps blessed by the Pope'.[12] At all levels it betokened more fear than theological dispute, the need for a national scapegoat, and the 'dogged hatred of Popery which lies inarticulate and confused, but deep and firm, in the heart of the English people'.[13]

'Frustrate the machinations of Popery, whether within or without the Church' was the prayer of an Evangelical family in 1849.[14] For them the meaning of 'the Church' was as unequivocal as it had been for Fielding's chaplain: 'When I speak of religion, I mean the Christian religion; and not only the Christian religion, but the Protestant religion; and not only the Protestant religion, but the Church of England.'[15] Yet the power of that Church over the nation as a whole was declining, until by the middle of the century not more than half the churchgoing population was at an Anglican place of worship.[16]

The Protestant dissenters had often been mocked for their apparent excesses or despised for their narrowness, but they had escaped the smear of potential disloyalty to the Crown which had stuck to Roman Catholics. They abounded in those virtues of industry, sobriety and honesty to which the age paid homage. The repeal of the Test and Corporation Acts in 1828 lifted from them most of the civil disabilities from which they had in theory suffered, although for many years there had been an annual indemnification of offences against those laws. Also there were many Protestant dissenters who found no difficulty in assenting to the Articles and appearing at Anglican services so long as they were free also to hear more congenial preaching. The Methodists indeed scarcely regarded themselves as a separated body and felt, as Wesley had done, that they were a special part of the Church of England. As time went on, however, the Methodists tended to produce new sects which would emphasize their differences from the Establishment.

The older dissenting groups held themselves more apart. Baptists and Congregationalists were for the most part socially and educationally poor; their belief in each local church as a self-governing entity hindered progress until they formed national unions. For the early part of the century they lived and worshipped within the constrictions memorably depicted by Mark Rutherford. Yet there was fervour and deep consolation as well, and great names of the past to be recalled with pride.

Further out theologically were the Unitarians, drawn partly from seceders from the Church of England but also from the English Presbyterians rejected in 1662. Despite their Socinian denial of the divinity of Christ and the Trinity, they were generally regarded as reasonable dissenters. Only the theologically perceptive were inclined to put them outside the orthodox pale, and even these did not class them as dangerously as Papists. A moderate High Churchman could write to a young man applying for a post in a Unitarian-sponsored hostel:

> I do not see that this employment need bring you into hurtful intimacy with Unitarians. There is no reason why we should not know Unitarians. I have been well acquainted with some myself.[17]

Unitarianism collected some of the drifters-through from orthodoxy to agnosticism. Francis Newman was disappointed at their credulity when he first came among them but he defended them against prejudices which were excluding their writings as rigorously as the Roman Index.[18] Their intellectual status declined, but it was something to have been associated with names like Hazlitt, Gaskell and Martineau.

As the old sects grew more moderate and hence more respectable, new movements foreshadowed a crop of wilder unorthodoxies later in the century. Edward Irving achieved a spectacular success in the thirties when he claimed special revelation to found the 'Catholic Apostolic Church' and to ordain a new ministry in preparation for the Parousia. Carriages blocked the approach to his church in Hatton Garden as the fashionable world came to hear the 'speaking with tongues' which unfortunately produced no clear interpretation. The movement survived into the present century and was a precursor of the conflicting claims of Theosophy, Christian Science, Mormonism and the spiritualism which fascinated Elizabeth Barrett Browning, drove her husband to wrathful satire and even drew a leading Catholic layman to 'spirit rappings' in the course of which he talked with a 'Buddhist spirit in misery'.[19]

These excesses came later, but they grew from a period in which the Church of England, though still entrenched, was heavily embattled. The clergy were disposed to feel secure in their own position in face of dissent or infidelity, but the more intelligent were coming to realize that complacency was ill-founded. Their Church had emerged from conflict and controversy in the sixteenth and seventeenth centuries. Its long reign with the full protection of the State was drawing to a close: there were challenges which struck at the roots of its being and which were to bring great gains out of seeming loss.

The gloomy picture of the spiritual state of the Church of England just before the Oxford Movement began has been too strongly drawn, particularly by apologists of that movement. The worst was over by the time the Tractarians became articulate about the situation. One may compare the evils of industrialism, which were still bad but past their worst when they became matter for the polemical novel. The Oxford Movement was the principal but not the sole element in the Anglican revival. Both the support which it won and the opposition which it aroused were the products of a situation in which religion mattered. Men like Newman, Keble and Pusey were serious Christians disputing with other serious Christians. The lack of fervour in the Church of their young days was the result of the deliberate distrust of enthusiasm as much as of slack indifference. The Oxford Movement was a deeply religious movement in a religious age.

Nevertheless, the criticisms of the Church, from inside and from outside, had some basis. The case against was put strongly by J. A. Froude, who had grown up in a clerical household, became involved with the Tractarians and eventually cut away from his Anglican allegiance. His diatribe is in a tone which many others adopted, and it is not totally unjust. Froude understood the tensions and pressures better than most men, though he wrote out of a personal suffering in which the bad examples seemed to outdo the good.

> What a sight must this age of ours have been to an earnest believing man like Newman, who had an eye to see it, and an ear to hear its voices? A foolish Church, chattering, parrot-like, old notes, of which it had forgot the meaning; a clergy who not only thought not at all, but whose heavy ignorance, from long unreality, clung about them like a garment, and who mistook their fool's cap and bells for a crown of wisdom, and the music of the spheres; selfishness alike recognized practically as the rule of conduct, and faith in God, in man, in virtue, exchanged for faith in the belly, in fortunes, carriages, lazy sofas, and cushioned pews; Bentham politics and Paley religion; all the thought deserving to be called thought, the flowing tide of Germany, and the philosophy of Hume and Gibbon; all the spiritual feeling, the light froth of the Wesleyans and Evangelicals; and the only real stern life to be found anywhere in a strong resolved and haughty independence, heaving and rolling under the chaff-spread surface. How was it likely to fare with the clergy gentlemen and the Church turned respectable, in the struggle with enemies like these?[20]

Here are themes and words that will come up often in our exploration—the clergy rich, time-serving, ignorant; the easy accommodation of utilitarian secularism; the threats of new German rationalism and old British scepticism; the shallow emotionalism of the Evangelical section. How valid, as a total concept, was the attack on a 'foolish Church'?

Although the diversities within were not yet fully developed or strongly marked by outward practice, the

Church of England was not monolithic. In the early years of the Oxford Movement she seemed to be 'a bundle of religious systems without number'.[21] For the majority there was no problem in falling in with the requirements of the Book of Common Prayer as interpreted in the most Protestant sense. The emphasis in public worship was on preaching rather than on sacrament. Celebrations of Holy Communion were infrequent and without ceremony: usually four times a year though sometimes more often. There is evidence, however, that 'Sacrament Sunday' brought a large congregation in many parishes and that the attitude was reverent on the part of both priest and people. The simplicity of form was compensated by that decency and orderliness which are fundamental concepts in Anglicanism.

There is evidence of the other extreme too, of instances of pluralism whereby a man could hold more than one benefice and draw the main revenues for the cost of an underpaid curate too overwhelmed by financial worry to give much pastoral care. Then, as always, the Church had her scandals as well as her saints. The significance of what happened in Oxford from 1833 does not rest ultimately on either extreme. It depends largely on the fact that the Anglican clergy, good, bad or unfortunate, were almost all united in their acceptance of the Church of England as a Church established by law. The ultimate protector and the supreme legislator was the Crown. The Church had the right to tithe and to oversee the flock, with the concomitant duty to obey enactments legally made.

Some clergymen took their duties more seriously than others; few indeed thought of themselves as priests in the Apostolic order, endowed with spiritual powers and obligations which might conflict with their role in the established system. Not all had sought ordination simply as a means of earning a living, but few indeed had seen it as a sacramental seal on a divine calling. How could it be so understood when there were no theological colleges, when the examination of ordinands was rudimentary or non-existent? Consider the clergy of Jane Austen, men not shown as generally contemptible: Mr Collins is an unusually nasty piece of work. Yet they inspire little respect beyond that given to their social position. Edmund Bertram is at some trouble to explain that he has chosen to be a clergyman and is not entering on the profession purely for family reasons, although Miss Crawford is unconvinced and sees him as 'fit for something better'.[22]

To regard the Church as a part of the national system, a profession within which both the privileges and the obligations of the national law operated, was to take a 'Low' view. Neither 'High' nor 'Low' in regard to churchmanship had the connotations of doctrine and practice which were later associated with them. The general, conformist view of the Church of England was Low; its opponents sometimes called it Erastian. The belief that the Church should be subject to the ordinances of the State might find philosophical justification in Selden and Hobbes, with pragmatic approval in a general desire for lawful order and a distrust of sects.

The High Churchman counted himself an equally loyal citizen but was more inclined to stress the rights of the Church as an abiding institution which the State had not created. He looked with some favour on the example of the non-jurors who had been deprived for refusing the Oath of Allegiance to William III. Without being greatly exercised by any residual Stuart claims, he found strength in the Caroline divines who had promulgated a theory of the Church within which Anglicanism had an honourable identity and who had regarded their ministry as something more than a Crown licence to preach.

However, High Church was a comprehensive and sometimes vague description. It could include those whose main claim to it was the Tory resistance to Whig encroachments on ecclesiastical privilege but who were otherwise content with the standard practice of the State Church. The more theologically minded of the High wing could nevertheless hold that their priesthood was within the Apostolic Succession on which Newman based the appeal of the first of the *Tracts for the Times*. This doctrine appeared, for instance, in Daubeny's *Guide to the Church* (1798) and Van Mildert's Bampton Lectures (1814). The group known as the Hackney Phalanx or the Clapton Sect, led by Joshua Watson, took a view that foreshadowed the early Tracts, though those who lived to see it were mostly repelled by the Romeward movement of Newman and others. A High Doctrine of the Church as a divine society rather than a department of State was held by believers as distant from the Tractarians and from one another as the Evangelicals and the Noetics.

The Whig Low Churchmen in fact did not have things all their own way even before 1833; and theological principles were intertwined with politics in the years leading up to the new movement. The fact that many High Churchmen accepted views expressed in Laudian days inclined them towards a Catholic interpretation of their churchmanship, with an opposition to Rome that was bigoted but better reasoned than other Protestants could produce. When the increasing challenge of secular control became urgent, the underlying theological principles were emphasized and brought into public controversy. Hurrell Froude and John Keble both grew up in clerical families where traditional High Church principles were held, and on this basis, different though they were in temperament, built a structure that altered the face of their beloved but threatened Church.

High and Low alike, the clergy were not well placed in public esteem. The wealth and temporal assets of the higher dignitaries had grown and were emphasized by the poverty not only of the lay working class but of many of the ordinary priests; though some of the parochial incumbents were rich men. The bishops were members of the House of Lords, where their presence seemed to symbolize the radical view that clergymen in general were State hirelings, the oppressive allies of the landowning class. When John Sterling described the parson as 'a black dragoon in every parish'[23] he may have provoked laughter among his contemporaries at Cambridge but he said something that many in the nation would approve. The muttering became a roar of fury when the bishops, with only two exceptions, voted against the first Reform Bill. 'It was not safe for a clergyman to appear in the streets,' Sydney Smith recalled when the crisis was past.[24] In Bristol the Bishop's palace was burnt; a dead cat was thrown at the Archbishop of Canterbury in his coach; stones and insults were hurled even at humbler members of the clergy. The popular dislike of anything that emphasized the special position of the priesthood was another cause of hostility to the Tractarians in the years to come.

For Churchmen did not cease to be targets for hostility when the Reform Act was eventually passed. The new Parliament of 1832 was indeed much less reformed than some had hoped and others had feared; but it was in a reforming mood. There had been a taste of what could be done through the legislative process, and the reactionary attitude of the majority of the clerical Establishment was not forgotten. A series of attacks on ecclesiastical privilege began.

The Church from which issued the *Tracts for the Times* was a Church under fire. In 1832 Lord Henley, Peel's Evangelical brother-in-law, produced his *Plan of Church Reform.* He proposed, among other things, the redistribution of revenue by reducing cathedral and collegiate establishments, the removal of the few remaining disabilities on dissenters and the formation of a commission to manage Church income and property. The Ecclesiastical Commission was set up after the report of the Ecclesiastical Duties and Revenues Committee which investigated the matter in 1835 and 1836.

Thus the Church of England was dragged protesting into the new age, to undergo the typical nineteenth-century process of agitation followed by inquiry, report and legislation. Various legal measures were passed which reduced the huge gaps between the highest and the lowest clerical incomes, rooted out the worst cases of pluralism and produced better parochial stipends at the expense of some rich prebends. What inequality remained can be seen in the pages of Trollope two decades later.

At the same time the native Irish got a certain oblique revenge for centuries of suffering. The Anglican Church in Ireland was in a peculiarly vulnerable position once the Whig attacks had begun in earnest. She had the status and privileges of establishment while numbering only a small fraction of the population as her flock. Closer scrutiny of the anomaly came as more intelligent Englishmen turned their interest towards Ireland—some from a simple love of justice, others from curiosity about a country where Roman Catholic dominance in faith could be observed without leaving the British Isles. The retreat from orthodoxy of both Francis Newman and J. A. Froude was hastened by their experiences in Ireland.

The Irish Catholics, mostly poor and ignorant through little fault of their own, were valuable to those who looked for any stick with which to beat Papistry. The fact of Protestant control over the government and economics of the country was conveniently ignored. Yet the contrast between the wretched state of the peasants and the comparative wealth of the English Church in their land was not always seen complacently:

> The revenue of the Irish Roman Catholic Church is made of halfpence, potatoes, rags, bones and fragments of old clothes; and those Irish old clothes. They worship often in hovels, or in the open air, from the *want* of any place of worship. Their religion is the religion of three-fourths of the population! Not far off, in a well-windowed and well-roofed house, is a well-paid Protestant clergyman, preaching to stools and hassocks, and crying in the wilderness; near him the clerk, near him the sexton, near him the sexton's wife—furious against the errors of Popery, and willing to lay down their lives for the great truths established at the Diet of Augsburg.[25]

The questioning which these contrasts caused brought the whole idea of Establishment in consideration. Was the Irish parson preaching to stools and hassocks so much worse than the English one who seldom preached in his parish at all? A beneficed clergyman, a prebendary, a bishop, could defy almost any attempt to remove them for inadequate performance of duties. The age was not so tolerant of sinecures as the previous one had been.

Some clergy too were beginning to wonder if the link with the State was entirely beneficial to the Church. The whittling down of temporal power gave new importance to the indelible nature of priesthood. What had sustained the despised Romanists through the penal centuries? Could a Church in fact be stronger, holier, more spiritual, without the hand of Government poised to crush as well as to protect? Questions like these were being asked in Oxford and elsewhere.

While many of the reformers were loyal churchmen seeking to improve a corrupt situation, others saw in legislation the means of undermining the Church of

England. She seemed 'ripe for dissolution'[26] in the view of Jeremy Bentham, who carried most of his disciples with him in the opinion that traditional religious institutions were outworn, useless, an offence against efficiency and the general tidying of society. He struck a blow against the older universities, Oxford in particular, when he helped to found the new University College in London which soon became 'the monument, totem and temple of the forward-looking, anti-classical, non-Anglican reformers'.[27]

Open atheism was still unfashionable even in the House of Commons, as Bradlaugh was later to discover. Already, however, objections were being more freely voiced against the assumptions of Christianity rather than against this or that Church. As the most powerful institution, the Church of England was the most sharply attacked. The attackers came in many shapes and colours, united only in the belief held by James Mill that the '*ne plus ultra* of wickedness . . . was embodied in what is commonly presented to mankind as the creed of Christianity'.[28] Many of those in the rationalist line of Locke and Hume had kept up a cynical outward conformity while established religion was accepted with little question and were now emboldened to more open dissent. Others had adopted one of the several varieties of Deism—a creed as productive of sects as the Trinitarian orthodoxy which affronted it—ranging from belief in moral government of the present world to vague postulation of a withdrawn First Mover. The Industrial Revolution had brought sufferings that produced a tough anti-clerical pragmatism in men like Robert Owen. There was the moral objection, voiced by Paine and echoed in the next generation, against the faith that seemed to depend on fear of 'a God who kept a hell prison-house'.[29] There was the challenge, as yet slight but steadily growing, of a more confident and mechanistic science. And, still little known outside the company of a few theologians like the young Professor Pusey, there were the probings of German rationalist criticism.

With such challenges and uncertainties it was no wonder that many Anglicans felt that anxiety about the future which was to haunt them and their successors all through the century. Not only the disenchanted believed that the Church of England had barely escaped alive: fifty years later, Newman's brother-in-law looked back to the time just before the Oxford Movement began, when:

> Every party, every interest, political or religious, in this country was pushing its claim to universal acceptance, with the single exception of the Church of England, which was folding its robes to die with what dignity it could.[30]

Yet it was not a question of loyalty or opposition to a moribund institution. The attacks showed that there was less indifferent religious acquiescence that there had been fifty years earlier. On the more positive side, the Evangelical revival had changed the appearance of Christianity for many people.

The Evangelical view was not the dominant Victorian mode of faith; nor was it totally opposed from the start to the Oxford Movement; nor was it confined to a single denomination. It was general in the nonconformist churches but had substantial support in the Church of England. Methodism had started as an attempt to evangelize the Church of England, but Wesley had been excluded from some Anglican pulpits for his Arminian view that the benefit of Christ's redemption was freely available to all. Strict Evangelicals, both churchmen and dissenters, followed Whitefield in the austere Calvinist belief that some individuals were elected to salvation and that for them alone Christ had died.

A change of religious temper came over the country towards the end of the eighteenth century. There was a new seriousness, caused partly by the Napoleonic threat and the concomitant domestic troubles, which prepared the way for the earnest Victorian agnostic as well as for the Anglo-Catholic revival. Fear of atheism, militant and destructive in the pattern of the Jacobins, made a link between dissenters and Anglicans. Divines of all churches sprang to the defence of Christianity with the learned publication of 'evidences' to assert the inalienable truth of their faith. Yet the Evangelical revival was, unlike the Oxford Movement, never primarily a clerical matter. Indeed, it did little to exalt the position of the clergy, and some of the most influential Evangelicals like Wilberforce and Shaftesbury were laymen.

The Evangelical emphasis was on personal salvation by acceptance of Christ's saving power. After conviction of sin and a realization that unaided human nature was in a state of total depravity, there should be repentance, a humble acknowledgement of justification in Christ, followed by assurance of pardon and of perseverance to final salvation. This encounter between Christ and the individual soul could be mediated by no person or institution, though preaching could open the heart to conversion. Sacraments were effective not for any power inherent in them or in their minister but as tokens of what Christ had done and commanded. Salvation could be merited by no works: the insistence on faith alone brought a danger of antinomianism to the weaker brethren. The great philanthropists of the movement, and the lives of humbler men and women too, proved that the Evangelical could be active in love. The highly individualist doctrine put emphasis on self-improvement and duties of thrifty activity which accorded well with the temper of the age—and perhaps helped to form that temper. A sense of social responsibility soon developed. Nevertheless, there was a danger that spirituality would neglect the intellectual demands on human nature and 'leave it a fallow field for all unsightly weeds to flourish in'.[31]

It is not to be supposed that the whole nation experienced an Evangelical conversion. Many people were repelled by the negative side of the movement—its puritanism, its exclusionist attitude, its tendency to self-congratulation and smugness. The Evangelicals were strong sabbatarians, and what they gave humanely by keeping Sunday as a day of rest they took away by making it a day of gloom. They could seem reactionary enemies of the working man who had no other chance for recreation but who found the doors closed and the chance of travel restricted.

To oppose sabbatarianism became a proof of opposition to the whole Evangelical principle. Francis Newman as a boy was upset when his father commanded him to copy a letter on Sunday and his refusal was supported by his elder brother. J. A. Froude recalled how people had worried themselves about what was or was not permissible on Sunday—letters could be read but not written, serious books were accepted, but not novels or newspapers. Places of entertainment were closed; London museums and art galleries did not open on Sundays until 1896.

Another Evangelical feature was the support of missions. The establishment of new missionary bodies helped to shake the old Anglican societies from their torpor and consequently to produce a period of unedifying sectarian squabbling in the mission field. In contrast, an early blow for ecumenism was struck by the Evangelical British and Foreign Bible Society with its dual secretariat of an Anglican and a dissenter. The opposition could find in attention to heathens abroad yet another sign of indifference to sufferings at home, an image immortalized by Dickens in the chaotic state of Mrs Jellaby's family. Yet missionizing at home was active and often criticized. Exeter Hall in the Strand was a centre of Evangelical preaching, in which Irish clergy and laymen played a prominent part. Their natural eloquence, applied to militant Protestantism through their minority position at home, gained them fame or notoriety. One of the few points on which Kingsley and Newman were ever in agreement appears in their attitude to the characters of O'Blareaway in *Yeast* and O'Niggins of the Roman Priest Conversion Branch of the Tract Society in *Loss and Gain.*

The greatest influence of the Evangelicals in institutional religion was exercised when their spiritual fervour had waned and the observation could be made that: 'Preached in the pulpits of fashionable chapels, this religion proved to be no more exacting than its "High and Dry" rival.'[32] Their very success had tended to make them static within the framework of specific organizations. They were probably at their strongest as a national pressure-group between 1850 and 1860, when the Evangelical Summer was Archbishop of Canterbury and Palmerston was the political leader. The divisions in the Anglican Church following the Oxford Movement, and the excesses which marked some aspects of that movement in the second generation helped to bring new respect for Evangelicals. The assertion of the Protestant position and the desire for firmer links with nonconformity were natural for those who feared that the alternative was a further drift to Rome. By 1870, Matthew Arnold marked the decline:

> The Evangelical clergy no longer recruits itself with success, no longer lays hold on such promising subjects as formerly. It is losing the future and feels that it is losing it. Its signs of a vigorous life, its gaiety and audacity, are confined to its older members, too powerful to lose their own vigour, but without successors to whom to transmit it.[33]

Though they might be influential, the Evangelicals were never widely popular. They came to see themselves as the divine answer to Puseyism, but they were deplored by many staunch English Protestants who continued to regard as dangerous all extremes in religion. Broad Churchmen like Kingsley who hated Roman and Anglo-Catholics were equally scathing about Evangelicals. Frances Trollope painted a bitter picture of an Evangelical clergyman in *The Vicar of Wrexhill* (1837). Her son, though as we have seen not very theologically penetrating, found Evangelicalism a blanket condemnation for the Proudies and Slopes. Dickens brought out humbug and cant in Evangelical terms with Stiggins and Chadband. No major novelist of the period had a good word to say for the extreme Evangelical.

The novelists expressed what was widely felt: 'the British public feared Puseyites and despised Evangelicals.'[34] There was a general assumption, almost as potent as the folk-myths about Roman Catholics, that the Evangelical discourse masked hypocrisy, complacency and greed. The nature of their profession made it easy to accuse the Evangelicals of spiritual selfishness. At Oxford their stock was very low by 1830 and they could easily be discounted as holding no firm theological position.[35] Yet the Oxford Movement owed much to those who cared enough about religion to be unpopular for its sake and who provided a climate of moral seriousness in which other emphases could grow. The Evangelical spirit was highly susceptible to abuse by charlatans, but it also produced some of the noblest Victorians. It is worth remembering that Pusey once said: 'I love the Evangelicals because they love our Lord.'[36]

Despite the gloom of some of her adherents and the exultation of her opponents, there was still life in the Church of England when the Oxford Movement began. The strength to fight back against the growth of infidelity was provided by Evangelical fervour and by the

High Church assurance of a city not built with hands. The backward longing for the days of Caroline Anglican ascendancy could produce something more than nostalgia, and Romantic enthusiasm for the Middle Ages brought an exaggerated but encouraging notion of a society in which faith was universal and the Church powerful. Although the Romantic Revival was to be blamed for the trappings of later Anglo-Catholic extremists, it had also helped to bring new religious orientations. Borrow could sneer at Scott's effect on 'Charlie over the waterism' and his glorification of Stuart legitimism. Newman never ceased to look on Scott's novels as an anticipation of some aspects of the movement:

> The general need . . . of something deeper and more attractive than what had offered itself elsewhere, may be considered to have led to his popularity; and by means of his popularity he reacted on his readers, stimulating their mental thirst, feeding their hopes, setting before them visions, which, when once seen, are not easily forgotten.[37]

The older Romantic poets had their place in the genesis of the movement, though the younger generation were regarded as sadly fallen into disbelief and immorality. Wordsworth's late rediscovery of loyalty to the Church of England could not fail to be encouraging to those like Keble who regarded his poetry with admiration amounting almost to reverence. Wordsworth was not a systematic thinker; he found in the Church a means of particularizing, with all the associations of dignity and tradition, the more general and mystical spirituality of his earlier years.

Coleridge was intellectually tougher and his influence was correspondingly more widespread. Through Maurice he became a source of Broad Church inspiration which reached its height after the first impetus of the Oxford Movement was over. But on that movement too he had his effect, most of all perhaps through his insistence on the absolute need of the individual for faith rather than the production of reasoned 'evidences'. His respect for historical development and his concept of a universal, supernatural Church as distinct from the national 'clerisy' that might not necessarily be Christian, all gave backing to the anti-Erastian school. Here was the doctrine of a Church which had neither been created by the State nor could be changed by it in a moment of time.[38]

A more political warrant for High Church claims came from the new Toryism, derived again partly from Coleridge and from Burke, which offered more respect to the Established Church in a reuniting of ancient national strands against the divisive force of Whiggery and mercantilism. The relationship between Church and State was forcing itself on the attention of all thinking men in those years. Some saw the answer in the kind of syncretism which Arnold proposed in his *Principles of Church Reform* (1833), a truly Christian State whose national Church should comprehend all believers except Socinians, Quakers and (of course) Roman Catholics. The leaders of the Oxford Movement saw in this proposal the confirmation of some of their worst fears.

From fears as well as from hopes there grew a revival which changed the face of the Church of England and touched in some way all who retained any concern with the Christian faith. Anglicans found themselves members of a Church with claims more lofty than the old 'High and Dry' adherents had ever thought to make; Roman Catholics, in the euphoria that followed Emancipation and then the restoration of the hierarchy, were compelled to defend their claim to unique catholicity; Protestants of all denominations had to think harder about the positive nature of their protest and the distinctiveness of their confessions.

There were gains and there were losses, for individuals and for Churches. For many who stood firm there grew a new vision, of something scarcely to be recognized in the Church of their youth. Thus it appeared to one who, guided by a leader of the early movement, claimed for herself neither sanctity nor heroism:

> It spoke of the glorious company to which they belonged: of the Angels at their side; of the Saints made perfect, who were their brethren; of the whole Catholic Church praying with them and for them; of the Comforter within their hearts; of the Brother who is touched with a feeling of our infirmities; of the Father whose hand is ever over us. Dreary and dark the world around might be, but the path of the righteous would only be a shining light, shining more and more unto the perfect day.[39]

How different from the attitude of Mr Harding, that kindly and respected old clergyman, who 'performs afternoon service every Sunday, and administers the Sacrament once in every three months'.[40] The tensions between those views of the Church of England made the Oxford Movement necessary and inevitable.

Notes

[1] Pope, Epistle IV of *Moral Essays* ('To Richard Boyle, Earl of Burlington'), ll. 149-50.

[2] Charles Kingsley, *Yeast* (1850); (all references to Eversley edn, London, 1902), pp. 124-5.

[3] Ibid., ch. 17, p. 345.

[4] I. Stock, *William Hale White* (London, 1956), p. 63; F. L. Mulhauser, ed., *The Correspondence of Arthur*

Hugh Clough (Oxford, 1957), p. 515; W. H. Dunn, *James Anthony Froude* (Oxford, 1961) p. 196.

[5] R. B. Martin, *The Dust of Combat* (London, 1959), p. 34.

[6] Anthony Trollope, *Autobiography* (1883), ch. 8, referring to *Framley Parsonage.*

[7] E. Bellasis, *Memorials of Mr Serjeant Bellasis* (1893), p. 78.

[8] The Gunpowder Plot, or rather its detection, was commemorated by a special service in the Book of Common Prayer until 1859.

[9] O. Chadwick, *The Victorian Church* (London, 1966), p. 162.

[10] Samuel Butler, *The Way of All Flesh* (1903), ch. 28.

[11] *Apologia Pro Vita Sua* (1864); (all references to Fontana edn, London, 1959), p. 241.

[12] *The Wit and Wisdom of Sydney Smith* (1886), p. 121.

[13] Charles Kingsley, *Two Years Ago* (1857), ch. 2; (all references to New Century edn, London, 1908), p. 67.

[14] Bellasis, op. cit., p. 19.

[15] Henry Fielding, *Tom Jones* (1749), bk 3, ch. 3.

[16] The 1851 census gave a total of 7,261,915 in attendance at some place of worship on 30 March in that year, of whom 3,773,474 were at a Church of England service.

[17] Hawkins of Oriel to A. H. Clough; F. L. Mulhauser, op. cit., p. 237.

[18] Francis Newman, *Phases of Faith* (1850); (all references to 1881 edn), p. 15.

[19] F. L. Mulhauser, op. cit., p. 461.

[20] J. A. Froude, *The Nemesis of Faith* (1849), pp. 152-3.

[21] T. B. Macaulay, 'Gladstone on Church and State', review article in *Edinburgh Review* (April 1839).

[22] *Mansfield Park* (1814), ch. 9.

[23] The words, spoken in a debate at Cambridge, 'ruffled the young imagination with stormy laughter' (Carlyle, *Life of John Sterling* (1851), ch. 4).

[24] *Works* (1850 edn), p. 625.

[25] *The Wit and Wisdom of Sydney Smith* (1886), pp. 135-6.

[26] N. Sykes, *The English Religious Tradition* (London, 1953), p. 74.

[27] C. R. Woodring, *Victorian Samplers* (Lawrence, Kansas, 1952), p. 127.

[28] J. S .Mill, *Autobiography* (1873), ch. 2.

[29] J. A. Froude, op. cit., p. 17.

[30] T. Mozley, *Reminiscences, Chiefly of Oriel College and the Oxford Movement* (1882), vol. I, p. 273.

[31] A. P. Stanley, *Life and Correspondence of Thomas Arnold;* (all references to eighth edn, 1858), vol. I, p. 255.

[32] R. W. Church, *The Oxford Movement* (1891), p. 12.

[33] Preface to *St Paul and Protestantism* (1870).

[34] O. Chadwick, op. cit., p. 446.

[35] T. Mozley, op. cit., vol. I, pp. 23-4; cf. *Apologia,* p. 173.

[36] S. L. Ollard, *A Short History of the Oxford Movement* (London, 1915), p. 141.

[37] *Apologia,* p. 168.

[38] 'Coleridge . . . had taken the simple but all-important step of viewing the Church in its spiritual character as first and foremost and above all things, essentially a religious society of divine institution, not dependent on the creation or will of man, or on the privileges and honours which man might think fit to assign to it; and he had undoubtedly familiarized the minds of many with this way of regarding it, however imperfect, or cloudy, or unpractical they might find the development of his ideas, and his deductions from them' (Church, op. cit., p. 129).

[39] Charlotte M. Yonge, *The Castle Builders* (1854), ch. 15; (all references to 1885 edn), p. 187.

[40] Anthony Trollope, *The Warden* (1855), ch. 21; (all references to World's Classics edn, London, 1961), p. 262.

John Griffin (essay date 1979)

SOURCE: "John Keble: A Report from the Devil's Advocate," in *Historical Magazine of the Protestant Episcopal Church,* Vol. XLVIII, No. 2, June, 1979, pp. 219-38.

[*In the following essay, Griffin argues that Keble's high status in Christian scholarship is somewhat inflated, given his inconsistent positions and cautious activism; however, Griffin also notes that Keble was not the egotistical and rigid figure depicted by his critics.*]

The start of what has been called the "informal beatification"[1] of John Keble began with the sermons that were delivered at his grave[2] and has continued down to the most recent studies on his life, work, and the poetry. Keble's biographers all agree that he was worthy of the title saint, and have used such a title to describe him. Keble was and is a Catholic saint.[3]

Keble was the author of the best-selling volume, *The Christian Year* (1827) and a brilliant student at Oxford with every promise of a comfortable, academic career, but he turned his back on the prospects of either a literary or academic career for the sake of a humble ministry at his parish in Hursley. According to Newman, Keble was the author of the Oxford Movement,[4] the most controversial episode in the history of the English Church; but he never affected the least singularity in any of his doctrinal teachings. His life was always characterized by a saintly, "self-effacing" deference to eccelesiastical and patristic authority.[5]

Part of the rationale behind the repeated claims for Keble's sanctity is to be found in the above, especially his thirty-year ministry to the lower classes of Hursley. But the most important aspect of the claims for his sanctity is to be found in his loyalty to the Church of England.[6] In the words of one Anglican scholar:

> If the Anglican Communion had not embalmed her power to canonize, John Keble would be the first of the latter-day saints to adorn her Kalender. He never despaired when days were darkest and his calm continuance in the Church of England is a lasting rebuke to those who faint and fall away when all seems lost.[7]

Other scholars have found the central aspect of Keble's sanctity in the simplicity and purity of his life. E. R. Norman has recently written of Keble's "luminous presence":

> Keble's importance is as a saint, not as a poet or critic. He inspired others because they saw in his simplicity a luminous presence removed frrom the normal expectations of human personality.[8]

Historians of the Oxford Movement have supplemented Norman's judgment. According to Owen Chadwick, Keble represented the "moral" and "pastoral" basis of the Oxford Movement.[9]

In addition to Keble's loyalty to the Church of England, his simplicity of character, and his thirty-year ministry to the "humblest of his parishioners,"[10] there were further elements in his character and life that confirm the designation of saint. In the years after Newman's move to Rome, Keble did his best to retain others in the English church, an awesome task if we remember the harsh treatment that was given to the Anglo-Catholics by the various statesmen and bishops of the mid-Victorian period. The basic argument that underscored his "perfect confidence"[11] in the Catholic claims of the English church was his belief that God placed men in the religion where, in all probability, they were to find their salvation. Thoughts of leaving the English church ought to be put aside, he said, in the same way that one put aside temptations to adultery or murder.[12]

A further aspect of Keble's sanctity is to be found in his role as a courageous confessor of Catholic doctrine and devotion. According to Anglican scholars, there was nothing new in the doctrinal ideology of 1833 and beyond,[13] but doctrines like the Real Presence and Apostolic Succession had become "less and less prominent"[14] in the eighteenth century. Keble's task as a confessor or witness for those doctrines was to call men back to their Anglo-Catholic inheritance of the seventeenth century, an inheritance that he learned from his father:

> . . . when Newman and Froude were all enthusiasm for some item of Catholic faith or practice, which had burst upon them with the force of a new revelation, Keble would nod approval and remark in tones of highest commendation, 'Yes, that is exactly what my father taught me.'[15]

The remarks in the above suggest a direct quotation that I have not been able to trace to its source, and the comments have been repeated by recent scholars with the implication that if Keble's doctrines of 1833 were new and not learned from his father, it would tell against his claims to either sanctity or confessorship. No one can profess doctrines that are new to himself or his church and be rewarded as a saint in that church; Keble scholars have therefore insisted that his teachings were ancestral in their origin.[16] Keble believed, said another scholar, that

> . . . the Catholic Church was really one, in spite of minor and external differences in no way affecting the faith of the Creeds, was . . . the corner-stone of the entire fabric of Keble's thought.[17]

Keble's teaching, moreover, was the basic teaching of the English and the primitive church.[18] The doctrines of 1833 were the "fundamental ideas" of his life,[19] and he did no more than pass on to his generation those ideas that he had learned from his father.

The claims, then, for Keble's sanctity and his role as a confessor of English Catholic doctrines are intimately related to the repeated assertion that his teachings were an authentic part of the Anglo-Catholic teachings of the Church of England and of his own background. His confession of doctrine was not only a personal expression or a witness for himself. Keble's life-long confession of Anglo-Catholic doctrines was a witness to the truths of Anglicanism.

In this essay I will challenge all of the above commentary on Keble's life and work. I have no scandal to report of Keble's private life, but I do think that his biographers and Anglican scholars have tended to repeat one another rather than to examine his published texts and private correspondence with any kind of detachment. It will be shown that Keble, in fact, was a liberal (anti-dogmatic), Protestant clergyman until he was nearly forty. My argument does not tell directly against the beatification process, but it does raise the question as to whether he can be justly regarded as a Catholic saint, the claim that scholars make for him. As a part of this argument, I will challenge the idea that he regarded the doctrinal differences between Rome and Canterbury as "minor," or that he was in any sense an ecumenical thinker.[20] I will question one basic theme of his Anglican biographers—that Keble possessed a "perfect confidence" in the Church of England. Religious difficulties are the destiny of every Christian, but Keble's multiple difficulties suggest a state of mind that cannot easily be distinguished from doubt itself. These difficulties, taken as a whole, do seriously challenge the assertion of his saintliness; and they contradict altogether the idea that Keble might be regarded as a confessor of the Anglican faith. Finally, I will suggest that Keble was frequently unfair towards persons with whom he disagreed, especially the converts of 1845 and beyond. Far from behaving towards the converts with "extraordinary generosity,"[21] as one scholar has suggested, Keble was not unwilling to slander those who went over. The greatest objection of all to the claims for Keble's canonization is to be found in the enormous inconsistency of his views and statements, and I will direct a major portion of this essay in documenting those inconsistencies. It is a gross oversimplification to describe Keble as a saint and confessor of the English church, for his attitude towards that church and its doctrines changed frequently throughout his life.

II—Early Life

One of the most dramatic changes in Keble's life is to be found in the different versions of the Eucharistic sacrifice. In one of the final poems in *The Christian Year,* "The Gunpowder Treason," there is a stanza that appears to negate the Anglican notion that Keble, because of his high-church background, believed in the doctrine of the Real Presence:

O Come to our Communion Feast,
  There present in the heart,
Not in the hands, the eternal Priest
  Will his true self impart.

In the edition published shortly after Keble's death, the third line was changed to read, "as in the hands." A candid reader might ask, which of the two versions did Keble learn from his father and why was Keble so long in making the change if, as scholars tell us, he believed from the very first in the doctrine of the Real Presence? As we will see in a later section of this paper, Keble may never have accepted the doctrine of the Real Presence.

Until quite recently we had no way of knowing what were the religious beliefs and teachings of John Keble's father. A few years ago, however, a collection of his sermons was placed on a permanent loan basis in the Lambeth Palace Library. There are ten sermons in the collection; each was delivered many, many times over a long span of time, and the careful dating of each of the sermons suggests that Keble's father was far from energetic in the discharge of his clerical duties. None of the sermons contains even a remote hint of a high-church doctrine, and there are direct attacks on doctrines which the Oxford Movement later espoused, namely the doctrines of the Real Presence, Purgatory, and the idea of Tradition as a teaching instrument of the church. The Bible alone was the standard of faith to Keble's father, and apart from a series of attacks on Methodists and Catholics, there is no real affirmation of any kind of belief in the sermons.[22]

John Keble did reflect his father's anti-dogmatic Protestantism until he was forty years old (1832). The lengthy correspondence with a variety of friends and the pre-*Apostasy* sermons are void of any ideas or doctrines that might be called high-church. As late as 1832 Keble was challenging some of the doctrinal ideas of a friend on the subject of the Eucharist for their tendency to "turn good young Protestants in to Papists." In this same letter he praised the early reformers (Ridley and Co.) as the "noble martyrs" of the church and its authority on doctrinal matters. He vigorously attacked his friend's hint that "every Layman [was] wrong who turned Protestant in the 16th century." At the very end of the letter he noted that he was writing in the presence of his father.[23]

Keble's biographers have also failed to notice his long friendship with Dr. Thomas Arnold. The friendship with Arnold existed ten years before Keble had met Froude and Newman, and it must have been intellectual, as well as social, in character, for Arnold later asked Keble to be the godfather to his first son, Matthew. When the Oxford Movement was underway, that friendship was given up. Arnold, as well as numerous others in the Keble circle, insisted that it was Keble who changed in

1833. Keble's oldest and closest friend passed over with embarrassment the period of *National Apostasy* in his *Memoir,* as if to suggest that that period of Keble's life was a change from his earlier and later views.[24]

It might be further argued that Keble's early theological liberalism exceeded even that of his father or Thomas Arnold. Keble broke off a promising career with the *Quarterly Review* because of its attacks on some deists:

> I write to Rennell by Tomorrow's post. . . . I do not at all like the Spirit + Stile [sic] of it on certain subjects. In the last number for instance the virulence of abuse against some Socinians.[25]

Keble's early liberalism does not tell against the case of his sanctification, but it does suggest that his various biographers who have gone over the manuscript correspondence have either neglected or glossed this material. His early sanctity, at least, was a Protestant sanctity, and the doctrines of 1833 were as new to him as to his Protestant audience.

III—Keble and the Oxford Movement

Modern scholars have attacked Newman for his portrait of Keble as the "true and primary" author of the revival of 1833 and his sermon, *National Apostasy,* as its beginning.[26] I have argued elsewhere for Newman's accuracy on this matter, and might briefly review those findings. Keble was a political radical in 1833, and the Oxford Movement, in its origin, was an attempt to foster a break in the alliance of church and state.[27] Keble and his younger friends believed that the erastianism of 1833 was a moral evil. In a letter of 1833 Keble expressed his belief that only the erastian clergy of the day would endure the alliance under its existing terms.[28] The alternative to the state-church was the "apostolic church in these realms."[29]

In his much discussed sermon, *National Apostasy,* Keble had set forth the means by which the church could break with the government, knowing that such a break would mean poverty for the clergy. In another letter of 1833 Keble told Newman that spoliation of the church would be generally "wholesome," for it would teach churchmen that they could no longer rely on the state to protect them.[30] The lesson of *National Apostasy* was that the leaders of the church should give in to the popular demands for disestablishment and "let them [the people] have their own way."[31]

As early as 1827 Keble had expressed the idea that it would be better for the church if it were completely independent from the state. He seems to have had in mind an independent Protestant sect when he wrote to Coleridge in that year:

> Nor has there been any moment in my memory when the Church of England, *as an establishment,* seemed in so much jeopardy. . . . I really think that matters are in a train to give either us or the next generation an opportunity of practicing your lessons and St. Paul's teaching on non-resistance and acquiescence. . . . [32]

In the years after 1827, Keble's radicalism took on a more militant character. By the time of *National Apostasy* he was enthusiastic about the pending break in the alliance. The most striking of Keble's many radical letters from 1833 was one that Keble sent to Newman shortly after *National Apostasy* was published. The letter might be quoted at length for the insight it provides into the original revival:

> I think my mind is made up thus far, that I cannot take the Oath of Supremacy in the sense which the Legislature clearly now puts upon it. I cannot accept any curacy or office in the Church of England . . . if the reaction does not amount to a retraction of the anti-church *principle,* I think we ought to be prepared to sacrifice any or all our endowments sooner than sanction. 'Take every pound, shilling, and penny, only let us make our own bishops, and be governed by our own laws.[33]

We should notice that the above letter was sent from Keble to Newman. In later years Keble told Isaac Williams that he had been "carried away" by Pusey's and Newman's excitements in 1833.[34]

In little more than a year Keble gave up the radicalism of 1833, in particular his enthusiasm for clerical poverty and independence from the state. In a letter of 1834, after a highly secular analysis of the advantages of a good living, Keble told one friend that if he liked such a living, he "would take it."[35] In November of 1835 he preached a sermon ("Church and King") on the kinds of endowment that the state owed to the church. The state should provide for the church in the most handsome way possible, "whatever else appears to be neglected."[36] The sermon, with its insistence on the necessity of the alliance and the importance of the benefits that derived from that alliance, directly contradicts the message of *National Apostasy* and the radical correspondence of 1833.

Keble may have recognized the inconsistency of his position in 1835 with that of 1833, for he was curiously silent on his marriage of 1835 and his appointment to the living at Hursley in his frequent letters to Newman from this period. The marriage itself might also be seen as an abandonment of some of his earlier ideas on the subject of celibacy. As late as December, 1834, he had expressed the wish that the state, through disestablishment, would remove "all temptations to marry."[37] The ideal of celibacy is posited in several of the poems in *The Christian Year,* and in his private correspondence Keble urged the idea that celibacy represented a higher moral state than the married life.[38] Keble, moreover, had been a part of the Newman-Froude discussions on the need for a celibate clergy once disestablishment had taken place and the connections with the upper-classes dissolved, for it was at Keble's request that Newman wrote the most radical of all the early *Tracts* (#10, "Heads of a Week-Day Lecture") in which the results of disestablishment were discussed in detail.[39] And, finally, there was the radical letter to Newman (cited above) in which Keble had pledged himself not to accept any "curacy or office" in the church under the existing erastian system.

Keble's acceptance of Hursley, therefore, did not mean the advance of Tractarian principles to the countryside; nor should we assume, with Chadwick, that Keble represented the "pastoral" side of the Oxford Movement because of his long residence there. The original ideal of 1833 had been an itinerant ministry, like that of the Dissenters and Roman Catholics,—one that was completely independent of the upper-classes who controlled such livings and one that was identified with the laity in poverty. Each of the early Tractarians had agreed that major reasons for the chronic unpopularity of the church were its gentlemen-clergy and its connection with the aristocracy.

Hursley, it should be noted, is a beautiful place. These scholars who have praised Keble for taking up such a residence appear never to have seen it. Hursley was a handsome living by any standard, and, as we will see, it provided not merely a physical beauty that could scarcely be rivaled by any place in England. Hursley gave Keble an intellectual independence that he exercised all his life.

Keble once admitted to a change in some of the principles of 1833. In 1854 he mentioned to Isaac Williams that he regarded the "great Oxford Movement" as no more than a "sort of parenthesis" in his life. The remarks are worth quoting in full:

> About a year ago, when staying at Hursley, I remember John Keble saying, 'I look upon my time with Newman and Pusey as a sort of parenthesis in my life; and I have now returned again to my old views such as I had before. At the time of the great Oxford Movement, when I used to go up to you at Oxford, Pusey and Newman were full of the wonderful progress and success of the movement—whereas I had always been taught that the truth *must* be unpopular and despised, and to make confession for it was all that one could do.'[40]

The remarks confirm my argument that Keble had changed his mind about some of the basic principles of 1833. The remarks also suggest an attitude towards Christian truth that is at very least dangerous, for Keble, in the above and in other places, suggests that the "truth" of the Anglican Church or any church could be known but to very few. There is also a sense in which the remarks are simply not true. In a passage following the above, Keble remarked that he had been "carried away" by Pusey and Newman. The radical letters went from Keble to his younger friends and to others outside the Apostolic circle. Pusey was not really a part of the Oxford Movement until 1835, and he seems never to have heard of its fundamental radicalism.[41]

In the next section I will explore what kind of witness Keble provided for the truths of Anglicanism. I will challenge the idea that his confession was either reliable or heroic. I will also question the recurrent idea that he regarded the differences that separated Rome from Canterbury as minor. Victorian England has been justly celebrated for its anti-romanism, and Keble was among the foremost spokesman of that creed.

IV—Keble as Confessor

Various scholars have praised Keble for his extensive efforts to keep persons loyal to the Church of England in the years after Newman's move.[42] Indeed, the task of keeping persons in the church was to Keble the most important problem facing the church in the years after 1845. Even after the appointment of Hampden to an episcopal see in 1848 and the Gorham decision in 1850, Keble insisted that retaining persons in the Church of England was the greatest task of the moment:

> I have only one regret [he told Pusey] about not speaking the other day. I wish I had said something about people not going to the Oratory + c., with itching ears; for I observed when Mr. Darling spoke of it there was a rather a titter about the room, and I think it is the worst sign of the day.[43]

There were several devices that Keble used to retain persons, but the most common of these devices was to encourage persons who might be looking towards Rome as a solution to the erastian question to recommend that they dismiss such thoughts as one would dismiss thoughts of impurity. In his "Preface" to *Sermons* (1848) he urged that no one should become a Roman Catholic without "overwhelming evidence" that was "almost miraculous" in character. No one should follow this own private judgment in such a matter of choosing religion, for it was probable that God had placed men in the religion where they were to find their salvation. Staying in the Church of England and being content with what "you have" was the "safest way."[44] Such arguments do tell against moving to Rome, but they also tell against the act of conversion itself, and even the act of faith which Keble ten years earlier had defined as a "venture" into the unknown.[45] The

"Preface" is poor apologetics, and the argument of following the "safest way" tends to qualify the image of Keble as a militant confessor of Anglicanism.

The "Preface" contains one of the few public expressions of a device that Keble used with increasing frequency after 1845 in his efforts to prevent massive conversions: the slan der of converts. The "Preface" charges those who had gone over with restlessness and pride in their failure to follow the judgment and guidance of others, namely Keble's judgment and guidance.

The private correspondence is filled with even more striking instances of Keble's habitual slander of the converts. Henry Wilberforce, while under the influence of Keble, said to Newman that Keble regarded all the converts, save Newman, as "beacons"; that is, moral warnings in themselves not to follow their example. Newman himself did not escape the general slur on the moral character of the converts. The letters to Coleridge have numerous references to Newman's restlessness,[46] and Keble charged Newman with having been a disloyal Anglican for the five years preceding his conversion.[47] Keble's most notable contribution to the general process of slandering Newman was to hint that his mind was unsound when he became a Catholic.[48] It was perhaps no accident that Keble's closest friend, John T. Coleridge, lectured Newman at the end of the Achilli trial on his degradation since becoming a Catholic.[49] Keble did nothing, moreover, to contradict the frequent attacks on Newman's character in the Anglo-Catholic press, though he was in active correspondence with the various Anglo-Catholic journals.

Notwithstanding the attacks on the converts and the earnest pleadings for Anglicans to remain loyal to the Church of England, it should be noted that Keble's record of success was not that great. Manning, Hope-Scott, the two Wilberforces (Henry and Robert), and Thomas Allies had all been a part of the Keble circle or under his influence.

The denunciation of public sinners is of course not an argument against Keble's sanctity and his place as a confessor for the Church of England. The great saints of antiquity would have approved of the process. But there was one vital ingredient lacking in his attacks on the converts and the idea of converting to Rome: intellectual conviction in the position he was up-holding. The vague attacks on the morals of the converts alone suggests an interior weakness, for that is the oldest rhetorical device in the history of speech. But there is even better evidence to reject the invariably repeated assertion that Keble felt a "perfect confidence" in himself and in the national church.

The fact that Newman felt obliged to edit heavily many of Keble's letters to him from 1843 on should have warned scholars from any assertion about his confidence in the Church of England, and it might have been better for Keble's reputation if others had followed Newman's example. G. Battiscombe has indirectly professed to have read the whole of Keble's correspondence of 1845 and beyond, and she wrote:

> When he [Newman] says that Keble was so profoundly affected by the trouble of the time he is unconsciously transferring his own emotions to his friend. . . . There is no evidence to be found either in his letters to Newman or in the rest of his correspondence which can be made to show that he was especially depressed at this period.[50]

Battiscombe, however, missed the point of Newman's work as an editor: it was because Newman had carefully blacked out the offending passages that there "is no evidence to be found . . . in his letters to Newman." And there is a great deal of evidence in the letters to Coleridge.

Keble's second volume of poetry, the *Lyra Innocentium,* he told Coleridge, was written to overcome the "desolation" he (Keble) felt at the prospect of Newman's move. When the news of the conversion came, he told Coleridge that he was physically ill. Shortly after Newman's move, he told Coleridge:

> I have made up my mind that such as I must expect to pass the time in doubt + perplexity, I don't feel as if I should have the courage to read N's book. . . . I have a sensation as if I should shrink from his writings for a very long time.[51]

Newman became "practically dead" in Keble's words, and the estrangement continued for twenty more years, though Keble professed on enduring friendship to Newman after he had gone.

The above comments on "N's book" became the rule for Keble, and I think it can be seriously doubted whether he ever read any of Newman's Catholic works, save the *Apologia.* He briefly mentioned, by way of dismissal, Newman's *Essay* as a "pretty theory."[52] It appears that Keble was unhappy with the *Apologia,* for the letter in which the work is discussed by Keble is missing from the Coleridge Collection, and it is the only letter that is missing. Keble, thus, attacked the converts and the Catholic Church without really being able to defend his own religion, except that it was probable that God placed men in the religion where they were to remain and that conversion would cause a scandal.[53]

There is even better evidence than the above to point out Keble's diminished confidence in himself and in the Church of England. Public mention of the Catholic claims of the Church of England was kept to an absolute minimum in his published work of 1846 and beyond. Even in his pastoral "letters" of 1850, there is no use of words like *Catholic* or *Apostolic* to describe the Church of England; indeed, Keble argued that the church was founded by Henry VIII and that the Gorham Trial was a violation of ecclesiastical laws put into force in the sixteenth century. He also encouraged others to be cautious in their assertions of the Catholic Claims of the English church. Discussing Pusey's projected pamphlet, he told Coleridge, "I am sure that with caution one may give a very Catholic view on the subject."[54]

In his *Memoir* Coleridge noted that there had been a controversy between himself and Keble on the question of one of the poems in *The Lyra Innocentium.*[55] The poem under discussion was the "Mother out of Sight," a poem in praise of Mary. Coleridge gave an extended explanation of why the poem was omitted from the volume, but he did not cite any of Keble's most revealing letters on this subject. Coleridge noted that no one in the Keble circle entertained any high veneration of Mary, a remark that tells against Keble as a spokesman or confessor of seventeenth century high-church Anglicanism. The more important reason for not including the poem in the collection was Coleridge's belief that the poem was too Catholic for Anglican readers. Keble capitulated, and agreed to leave the poem out. In his letter of capitulation, he told Coleridge that his giving in on this matter meant a denial of his "priestly function."[56] In another letter on this subject, he told Coleridge:

> I should not be candid, if I were not to own to you that as far as I can remember + understand myself, no one thing has served to me to tell so much against our Church, as your scruples + those of the Dysons, on . . . the B. Virgin.[57]

The word *scruple* does not quite describe the Dyson attitude towards the Blessed Virgin. In the relevant correspondence, the Dysons had denied that Mary was in any sense at all unique in the Christian tradition. But my argument in the above is that Keble's beliefs, in many areas of doctrine, were completely his own and that he was the very opposite of a militant confessor of those beliefs.

In other letters of this period he professed his suspicions about the Church of England and his role in that church. In a letter of June, 1845, for example, he wrote:

> . . . it makes me even sadder than I was before, as shewing how very very far even the purest specimens of the English Church are from *the whole Church* everywhere else.[58]

And in another letter he described himself as in the role of "the blind leading the blind"[59] in describing his role as an advisor to others who were experiencing difficulties of belief in the Catholic claims of the Church of England. Keble's difficulties, nevertheless, did not prevent him from continuously attacking either the converts or the Roman Church.

Keble's method with prospective converts suggests a process that is the very opposite of confessorship and witness for the truths of Anglicanism. In the "Preface" to his *Sermons,* as we have seen, he recommended that persons turn away from all theological controversy and be content with what they have. Charlotte Yonge mentioned in her biographical comments on Keble in his last twenty years that he opposed all theological questioning and that his advice to persons was that they ignore troublesome matters as a way of settling their minds.[60] He did express (several times) his fears that the Catholics were gaining the upper-hand in the controversies over the Catholic claims of the English church,[61] but he, nevertheless, criticized those who would not remain as "restless." Even in the letters cited by G. Battiscombe (the most ardent of Keble's hagiographers) there is an open advocacy of ignoring difficult problems and attacks on those who had gone over.[62] In a letter to Pusey, Keble gave an instance of his method and success with the Bishop of Brechin:

> . . . our friend had been with me since Friday evening . . . we had some more talk; all confirming me in the impression that it is a longing for rest rather than intellectual conviction that Rome is right which is working on him. I hope he was a little more comfortable when he left us . . . promising to do as I desired him; which was to treat the haunting thought as simply a distress. . . . I also begged him to think of the terrible consequence of such moves.[63]

This method of dealing with religious dfficulties, while possibly pious in itself, is not characteristic of either saintliness or witness.

There is one further example of Keble's pronounced opposition to the idea of inquiry and witness, his response to the Denison Trial. Contrary to the numerous historians who have asserted that Keble believed in and promulgated the doctrine of the Real Presence, it can be argued that there is little evidence to suggest that Keble ever believed in that doctrine. Charlotte Yonge lists the doctrine as one of Keble's major objections to the Roman Church,[64] and in the preliminaries to the Denison trial of the doctrine we find Keble dissenting from the views of both Pusey and Denison on the question of Christ's presence in the Eucharist.[65] Most important, however, was his (Keble's) vigorous opposition to Denison's promulgation of the doctrine and his ending up in a civil court over his teachings on the Eucharist. The lesson of the Gorham trial was that the clergy should do all in their power to stay away from any confrontation with the civil authority:

> The good young clergymen [he wrote to Coleridge] of the last 5 or 6 years have not for the most part realized the Gorham Decision nor its effects on us all, but hangs like a dead weight over us. This will make them aware of it.[66]

Keble's argument was that Denison's belief about the Eucharist was pretty much his own business, as long as he did not end up in a court of law. It should be noted that in Keble's letters to Coleridge, who served on the Privy Council that tried Denison, there is a denial of Denison's version.[67] Keble may have been indirectly responsible for the verdict that was given against Denison, but the idea of confession, whether Denison's or Keble's, is destroyed by Keble's on-going resistance to raising doctrinal questions in the years after Newman's move.

V—Keble and the Bishops

The theological basis of the original Oxford Movement was the doctrine of Apostolic Succession and its corollary that the bishops were to be respected and obeyed completely in all religious questions. In his work of 1833 Keble continuously put forward that idea that the apostolicals should do nothing that is not "sanctioned episcopally."[68] In *National Apostasy* and in his first contribution to the *Tracts for the Times* he had argued that the bishops were the authority in the Church of England and that they should be followed as such. But when the various bishops came out against the Oxford Movement, Keble and his group responded by coming out against the bishops.

In the years after Newman's move to Rome, Keble was a constant thorn in the side of various bishops. His private correspondence has frequent references to a sharply changed attitude towards the set of men that he had once encouraged others to look upon as the voice of ecclesiastical authority. Anglican scholars have praised Keble and Pusey for their resistance to the bishops without noticing the profound change in the ecclesiology of the Anglo-Catholics and the marked inconsistency of Keble. Equally important, we should notice that the fiery letters to Wilberforce and other bishops go a great length to qualifying the description of Keble as "self-effacing" and humble. In a letter, for example, to the Bishop of Oxford (S. Wilberforce), Keble virtually denied to him any kind of religious authority:

> I wholly dispute and challenge the legal right of any Bishop or Synod of Bishops to limit the discretion of English priests, as to whom they shall admit or move to Confession in the way not claimed.[69]

The letter is but a brief portion of a long letter in which Keble questioned Wilberforce's "legal" rights to control Pusey, and yet Keble somewhat inconsistently expressed the suggestion that Pusey might abandon the practice of editing continental manuals for confession.[70] (Keble did not practice confession on a routine basis because of his patron's prohibition of it.)[71]

Wilberforce was not the only bishop to incur Keble's wrath. When the Bishop of Winchester took a public position against the Anglo-Catholics, Keble wrote to him:

> I never supposed, when the "Movement," as it is called, began (or rather drew attention to itself) that its success was to be a test of its propriety. The principles of it seemed to me then, and now seem to me, equally true and right, whether two or three acknowledge them, or two or three million. It seems to me also that if Rome has claims upon us now, she had just the same claims then, and would have had the Movement been ever so successful . . . the truth might perhaps be held by a remnant only.[72]

The bishops, Keble argued, were simply misguided in their apprehensions about the progress of many "Puseyites" to Rome. The bishops, taken as a whole, did their best to drive the Anglo-Catholics out of the church, and their fears that the logical result of Pusey's teaching was to lead men to Rome was really not answered by Keble. Wilberforce had every reason to fear the influence of Keble and Pusey on the younger generation, for he had lost several relatives to Rome. It might be briefly noted that Keble's staying influence on the younger generation and his friends in itself would challenge the idea that he was a saint or that his teaching was representative of Anglicanism. Several of Keble's closest friends went over, and the reason for their conversion was invariably the question of church authority, a question not answered in Keble's repeated blandishments that they look away from the erastian issues of 1850 and beyond.

It should also be noticed that Keble was not above narrowing the truths of Catholicism to a "remnant" of "two or three," a dangerous process in itself and a direct contradiction of his earlier statement that "tens of thousands" were awaiting the apostolic truths that would come from the episcopacy.[73]

In his later years, Pusey boasted that he had "never trusted the bishops," and in one of his last recorded statements of such an attitude he included John Keble as an exponent of the same idea:

> Dear J.H.N. said to me one day at Littlemore, 'Pusey, we have leant on the Bishops, and they have given way under us.' Dear J.K. and I never did lean on the Bishops, but on the Church.[74]

Pusey's statement was certainly well-founded if we concentrate on the period of Keble's life after Newman's conversion. But if the state and the bishops were not the final authorities in the Church of England, the question might be asked, who was? The letter to the Bishop of Winchester and the comments to Isaac Williams suggest that Keble was not afraid to narrow the exponents of Catholic orthodoxy to a "remnant only." In the following section, I will argue that Keble was the major representative of that remnant.

VI—Keble and Private Judgment

In his essay on the Oxford Movement, James Antony Froude described the "high authority"[75] that Keble exercised over many of the other Anglo-Catholics; and while Froude's portrait of Keble was generally negative, his comments on Keble's authority is confirmed by Anglican scholars. Liddon wrote of Keble's influence,

> When all else had been said and done, people would wait and see what came from Hursley before making up their minds as to the path of duty.[76]

The "path of duty," as Liddon knew when he wrote of Keble's life, was to remain in the Church of England, but his remarks suggests that Keble occupied a higher place of spiritual authority than even the bishops, who would have welcomed the departure for Rome of the Anglo-Catholics.

In this final section I will suggest the most trenchant of the various charges that I have made against Keble as a saint and confessor of the Church of England. I will argue that Keble, far from being "loyal" to the English church in any critical sense, was in fact loyal to himself. Part of my argument is simply a following out of a logical process by which Keble denied spiritual authority to those with whom he disagreed: bishops, fellow Anglicans, whether Protestant or Anglo-Catholic, and of course the state in its various representatives the Prime Minister, the Queen, or the Privy Council.

While denying the exercise of private judgment to those who were seeking a resolution to the question of spiritual authority in the Church of England,[77] Keble invoked such a privilege for himself. In a letter of 1850, written shortly after the Gorham Decision, Keble gave among his many reasons for not becoming a Catholic, the Catholic Church's alleged denial of the privilege of private judgment, a "responsibility that cannot be evaded."[78]

The best instance of Keble's assertion of the rights of his own private judgment in determining orthodoxy came at the end of the Gorham Trial. When the trial had been concluded and the doctrine of Baptismal Regeneration declared to be an "open question" by the Privy Council, Keble remarked, "If the Church of England were to fail, it should still be found in my parish." This version is from Purcell's *Life of Manning* and should be quoted in full:

> We agreed to a string of propositions deducing that, by the Gorham Judgment, the Church of England had forfeited its authority as a divine teacher. The next time we met, Pusey and Keble were there. They refused this; and got it changed to 'If the Church of England shall accept this Judgment it would forfeit its authority as a divine teacher.' This amendment was accepted because it did not say whether the Church of England had or had not de facto accepted the Judgment. Hope said: 'I suppose we are all agreed that if the Church of England does not undo this we must join the Church of Rome. This made an outcry; and I think it was then that Keble said: 'If the Church of England were to fail, it should be found in my parish.'[79]

The statement has caused some embarrassment among Keble scholars with its suggestion that a single individual was able to become the chief exponent of Catholic orthodoxy in the English world. G. Battiscombe has given a pious explanation of the statement by suggesting that when Keble spoke of the church, he meant his parishioners at Hursley.[80] David Newsome used an earlier letter to Robert Wilberforce in which Aristotle's *Politics* was invoked by Keble to the effect that the health of an institution was not to be measured by its parts.[81] The Battiscombe analysis begs the question, and the second does not really fit if we remember that Aristotle was, after all, not talking about religion.

I would suggest again, that Keble meant literally what he said. The remark has an internal logic to it that does not readily allow any other interpretation. Rome was emphatically out because of its doctrines of Papal Infallibility and Transsubstantiation and its "worship of the B.V.M,"[82] as well as its corrupting influence on those who had joined it. English Protestants were out because they endorsed the Gorham decision. The bishops were out because they had been appointed by a Protestant Prime Minister, and some of Keble's fellow Anglo-Catholics were out because of their views on other doctrines. The laity were never a part of Keble's ecclesiastical views. The end result of the process of eliminating other candidates for spiritual authority was to narrow the list down to the vicar of Hursley.

VII—Summary

The argument of this paper has not been so much against Keble's moral character as against his biographers who have exposed themselves by claiming too much for Keble's character. Consistency is not perhaps a moral virtue, but it is one of the distinguishing features of most of the great Catholic saints and confessors, and certainly Keble's invocation for himself of the doctrine of what theologians call "invincible ignorance"[83] tells against the repeated Anglican claim that he was a saint and confessor of the English Church. The clue to Keble's life is to be found in a phrase, or its derivative, that occurs with some regularity in his prose, *the safe way.* In 1831 he had argued that the safest way for the government was to assert itself with force against the threat of massive rebellion;[84] in 1833 the safest way was for the church to allow itself to be disestablished,[85] and from that time on there is a series of religious and political—the two can scarcely be distinguished sometimes in Keble's controversial prose—changes that defy any close analysis, except that it was always a great sin to leave the Church of England.

The above material, however, is not without its positive side. Far from being the narrow-minded clergyman that has come down to us in some of the biographies, Keble's mind changed frequently. Newman's judgment, from the time that he first knew Keble until his death in 1866, is closer to the truth: "You did not know where to find him."[86]

Notes

[1] D. Morse-Boycott, *They Shine Like Stars* (London, 1947), 35.

[2] E. Churton, "The Powers of Holy Ministrelsy," (Oxford, 1866) in Keble Collection, Bodleian, Oxford.

[3] A. Clifton-Kelway, *The Story of the Anglo-Catholic Revival* (London, 1933), viii; G. Battiscombe, *John Keble: A Study in Limitations* (New York, 1963), xvii, 353-4; W. Lock, *John Keble* (London, 1893), *in passim;* K. Ingram, *John Keble* (London, 1933), 183; E. Wood, *John Keble* (London, 1909), 11.

[4] John H. Newman, *Apologia* (Everyman ed.; London, 1921), 56.

[5] O. Chadwick, *The Mind of the Oxford Movement* (London, 1960), 31.

[6] G. Battiscombe, *John Keble,* 265.

[7] D. Morse-Boycott, *They Shine Like Stars,* 174.

[8] E. Norman, "John Keble," *Times Literary Supplement* (Feb. 25, 1977), 211.

[9] O. Chadwick, *The Mind of the Oxford Movement,* 30ff; also C. Dawson, *The Spirit of the Oxford Movement* (London, 1933), 6.

[10] K. Ingram, *John Keble,* 183.

[11] *Ibid.,* 122.

[12] John Keble, "Preface," *Sermons, Academical and Occasional* (London, 1848), vii.

[13] F. Cross, *The Oxford Movement and the Seventeenth Century* (London, 1933), 11.

[14] A. Clifton-Kelway, *The Story of The Anglo-Catholic Revival,* 1.

[15] G. Battiscombe, *John Keble,* 11.

[16] R. Chapman, *Faith and Revolt* (London, 1970), 30; T. Parker, "The Rediscovery of the Fathers in the Seventeenth Century Anglican Tradition," in *Newman: A Portrait Restored,* edited by J. Coulson and T. Allchin (London, 1967), 6.

[17] M. McGreevy, "John Keble on the Anglican Church and the Church Catholic," *Heythrop Journal,* V (1964), 27.

[18] M. McGreevy, "John Keble on the Anglican Church and the Church Catholic," 28.

[19] B. Martin, *John Keble, Priest, Poet and Professor* (London, 1976), 11.

[20] M. McGreevy, "John Keble's Way to Christian Unity," *One in Christ* I (1965), 53-61.

[21] T. Allchin, "The Via Media," in *Newman: A Portrait Restored* (London, 1967), 78.

[22] John Keble [Senior] Sermons in Williams Deposit, #Three, Manuscript Collection, Lambeth Palace Library, no pagination; dates of delivery are found on reverse side of last page of each sermon.

[23] Ms. letter J. Keble to A. Perceval (May, 1832), Pusey House, Oxford.

[24] J. T. Coleridge, *A Memoir of the Rev. John Keble* (5th ed.; London, 1880), 218.

[25] Ms. letter, J. Keble to J. Coleridge (Jan. 24, 1816), Coleridge Collection (3 vols.) Bodleian, Oxford, I; hereafter CC.

[26] Newman, *Apologia,* ed. cit., 56.

[27] J. Griffin, "John Keble: Radical," *Anglican Theological Review,* XLIII (1971), 167-173; J. Griffin, "The Meaning of *National Apostasy,*" *Faith and Reason,* II (1976), 19-33.

[28] Ms. letter, Keble to B. Holmes (Aug. 1833) in Keble Collection, Keble College, Oxford; cited in Griffin, "John Keble: Radical," 172.

[29] J. Keble, "National Apostasy," in *The Oxford Movement,* edited by E. Fairweather (Oxford, 1964), 46.

[30] Ms. letter, J. Keble to J. Newman (July, 1833), Correspondence Public, Birmingham Oratory, Birmingham.

[31] J. Keble, "National Apostasy," Fairweather ed., 44.

[32] Ms. letter, J. Keble to J. Coleridge (June, 1827), CC, II.

[33] In *Letters and Correspondence of John Henry Newman,* edited by Ann Mozley (2 vols.; London, 1891) I, 484.

[34] Isaac Williams, *Autobiography,* edited by G. Prevost (London, 1892), 118.

[35] Ms. letter, J. Keble to Mrs. Pruen (1834), Keble College, Oxford.

[36] J. Keble, "Church and King," in *Sermons, Academical and Occasional* (2nd ed.; Oxford, 1848), 131.

[37] Ms. letter, J. Keble to J. Coleridge (Dec. 3, 1834), CC, II.

[38] Ms. letter, J. Keble to J. Coleridge (Aug. 10, 1825), CC, II.

[39] J. Griffin, "The Social Implications of the Oxford Movement," *Historical Magazine of the Protestant Episcopal Church,* XLIV (1975), 163ff.

[40] Isaac Williams, *Autobiography,* ed. cit., 119.

[41] J. Griffin, "Dr. Pusey and the Oxford Movement," *HMPEC,* 42 (1973), 137-153.

[42] E. Norman, "John Keble," *TLS* (Feb. 25, 1977), 211; G. Battiscombe, *John Keble,* 265; D. Newsome, *The Parting of Friends* (London, 1966) 390ff.

[43] Ms. letter, J. Keble to Pusey (Oct. 18, 1850), Pusey House, Oxford.

[44] J. Keble, "Preface," *Sermons,* vii, ff.

[45] J. Keble, "Preface," *Remains of R. H. Froude,* Part II (London, 1839) I, xx.

[46] Ms. letter Keble to Coleridge (Sept. 8, 1846), CC, II: "Pusey I trust is in a way to mend . . . I suppose J.H.N.'s visit was a part of the same temperament w[h] has taken him from us: his love too keen for his patience." This comment was Keble's way of explaining Newman's visit to Pusey when Pusey professed to be dying. Newman spent 24 hours on the top of coach in his efforts to see Pusey before his death.

[47] See J. Griffin, "The Anglican Response to Newman's Conversation," *Faith and Reason,* III (1977), 23. Keble's statement contradicts an earlier statement to J. Watson (March 30, 1841): "I do not believe anything in the world would drive him to such a thing—much less into Romanism; the dangers of w[h] + its evil he seems to see more clearly + work against more steadily than any person I ever knew." *Keble to J. Watson, 1836-1847, No. 67, Keble College, Oxford.* Keble's comments on Newman violate his pledge of friendship to Newman when he was made aware that Newman had gone over to Rome.

[48] *Letters of J. B. Mozley,* edited A. Mozley (London, 1888), 170.

[49] Cf. J. Griffin, "The Anglican Response to Newman's Conversion," 25ff.

[50] G. Battiscombe, *John Keble,* 234.

[51] Ms. letter, Keble to Coleridge (Oct. 16, 1845) CC, II.

[52] Ms. letter, Keble to Mrs. Armstrong (Jan. 12, 1863), Keble College, Oxford.

[53] See below note 63.

[54] Ms. letter, Keble to Coleridge (Jan. 22, 1846), CC.

[55] *A Memoir of the Rev. John Keble,* ed. cit., 218ff.

[56] Ms. letter, Keble to Coleridge (Jan. 1846), CC.

[57] Ms. letter, Keble to Coleridge (Feb. 1846), CC.

[58] Ms. letter, Keble to Coleridge (June, 1845), CC.

[59] Ms. letter, Keble to Coleridge (June, 1845), CC.

[60] C. Yonge, *'Musings' on the 'Christian Year'* (London, 1870), xiiff.

[61] Ms. letter, Keble to Coleridge (Aug. 5, 1842), CC.

[62] G. Battiscombe, *John Keble,* 280.

[63] Ms. letter, Keble to Pusey (June 14, 1864) Pusey House, Oxford.

[64] C. Yonge, *'Mustings' on the 'Christian Year'* (London, 1871), xxii.

[65] Ms. letter, Keble to Coleridge (June 19, 1854), CC, II.

[66] Ms. letter, Keble to Coleridge (Dec. 5, 1854), CC, II.

[67] Ms. letter, Keble to Coleridge (June 19, 1854), CC, II.

[68] Ms. letter, J. Keble to J. Newman (July, 1833), Correspondence Public, Birmingham Oratory.

[69] H. Liddon, *Life of E. B. Pusey* (4 vols.; London, 1898) III, 316; see also A. Ashwell, *Life of Samuel Wilberforce* (3 vols.; London, 1881) II, 93-96.

[70] Cf. H. Liddon, *Life of E. B. Pusey,* III, 316.

[71] Cf. J. Coleridge, *A Memoir of the Rev. John Keble,* 315-16.

[72] Ms. letter, Keble to the Bishop of Winchester (Feb. 1850), CC, II.

[73] J. Keble, "Advertisement," to *National Apostasy,* Fairweather ed., 49.

[74] Liddon, *Life of E. B. Pusey,* IV, 231.

[75] J. A. Froude, "The Oxford Counter-Reformation," in *Short Studies on Great Subjects* (9th series; London, 1883), 189.

[76] Quoted in G. Battiscombe, *John Keble,* 354.

[77] J. Keble, "Preface," to *Sermons, Academical and Occasional,* viii, ff.

[78] Quoted in A. Clarke, *The Oxford Movement and After* (London, 1932), 217.

[79] E. Purcell, *Life of Cardinal Manning* (2 vols.; London, 1896) I, 528-9.

[80] G. Battiscombe, *John Keble,* 303.

[81] D. Newsome, *The Parting of Friends,* 394.

[82] Ms. letter, J. Keble to Coleridge (Oct. 1850), CC.

[83] H. Liddon, *Life of E. B. Pusey,* IV, 257-8.

[84] J. Keble, "On the Dangers of Sympathizing with Rebellion," in *Sermons, Academical and Occasional,* 120ff.

[85] J. Keble, "National Apostasy," in *Sermons, Academical and Occasional;* or Fairweather edition.

[86] Newman to H. Woodgate (Oct. 18, 1873) in *Letters and Diaries of John Henry Newman,* edited by C. S. Dessain and T. Gornall (Oxford, 1974) XXVI, 375.

Peter Nockles (essay date 1986)

SOURCE: "The Oxford Movement: Historical Background 1780-1833," in *Tradition Renewed: The Oxford Movement Conference Papers,* edited by Geoffrey Rowell, Pickwick Publications, 1986, pp. 24-50.

[*In the essay that follows, Nockles emphasizes that the Oxford Movement is best understood in its historical context and claims that Tractarian spirituality had deep continuities with earlier Church revival movements.*]

The passage of time is normally conducive to the attainment of a balanced and objective historical perspective. However the commemoration of great historical events can be a powerful barrier against it, and in this respect the Oxford Movement has proved no exception. For the celebration of the centenary in 1933 was productive of some glaring historical misconceptions, partly, be it noted, out of the very focusing of the participants on what happened in 1833 and the years following. For while on the one hand outright enemies of the Catholic tradition in Anglicanism, such as Bishop Knox, berated the movement as innovatory and alien to the true Protestant spirit of the Church of England as bequeathed by the Reformers and Elizabethan settlement,[1] on the other the hagiography which Dean Church, Pusey's biographer, Liddon, and Canon Ollard had firmly established was carried to new lengths. What both had in common was their propagation of the view that 1833 was *the* magic year that marked a radical, if not revolutionary break from what had gone before in English church history. Shane Leslie epitomised this historical treatment of the movement when he described it as having been 'born out of fallow and dust'.[2] The older high church tradition in Anglicanism that remained alive throughout the so-called 'tunnel-period' of the mid-eighteenth century was too often either ignored or derided. When its existence was recognised it was found to be theologically ambiguous, Erastian, 'high and dry'—a favourite epithet—worldly, and in matters of ritual and spirituality cold and dull, when judged by the apparently higher standards later set by the Catholic revival after 1833. Although the Swedish historian Archbishop Brilioth, in his work, *The Anglican Revival,* published in 1925, sought to question some of these presuppositions and to exonerate the pre-Tractarian Church of England from some of the standard aspersions made against it, his more sympathetic understanding of the older high churchmanship was not echoed by many. Even he dwelt heavily on the supposed sterility of that older tradition, in contrast with what he termed the 'Neo-Anglicanism' of the Oxford Movement.[3] At best, the old high church tradition was treated as a mere backcloth or background to what followed after 1833.[4] For instance, Canon C. P. S. Clarke, the first contributor in 1933 to the volume of centenary studies of the movement, called *Northern Catholicism,* set the tone by brushing aside Brilioth's portrait of the older high church tradition as too flattering, and rested content with the aphorism of a Scottish geologist, Hugh Miller, whom he quoted as having 'compared the pre-Tractarian High Churchmen to bulbs in a drawer, and the post-Tractarian High Churchmen to the same bulbs after they were planted out and were in flower'.[5] Such an assumption needs some questioning. Not only was there genuine high church continuity in the late eighteenth century but an actual high church revival—to use Miller's analogy, a real 'flowering of the bulbs' in the forty to fifty years immediately prior to 1833; a revival, one might add, which in origin dated from the accession of George III, but which was also a fruit of the general conservative reaction against the French Revolution. At the centre of this revival were the leaders and associates of the so-called 'Hackney Phalanx', Joshua Watson, Henry Handley Norris, Thomas Sikes, John Hume Spry, William van Mildert and Christopher Wordsworth, to which Nancy Murray has drawn attention,[6] and like-minded allies such as Charles Daubeny. They are commonly referred to and given due recognition in the histories of the movement, but rarely without at least the underlying hint that their teaching was in some ways defective, their temper over-rigid and narrow. It was these apparent negative qualities in them that led the Tractarians, with their enormous sensitivity to what they called ethos, to dub both them and their successors in the era of the movement, such as Edward Churton, William Palmer of Worcester and R. W. Jelf, as 'Zs'[7] or conservative churchmen.

It is time to look at some of these figures anew, and thereby to set the Oxford Movement more firmly within the context and perspective of the rich and varied high church tradition which they represented in their day. One of the most revealing entries in the manuscript diaries of Joshua Watson's niece Mary is that the leader of the 'Phalanx' was by the early 1840s expressing extreme disquiet at what he called 'the inclination to make a great era of the year 1833'. Indeed Mary Watson records her uncle as repeatedly saying in his latter years, 'I am only solicitous to get rid of all the history of the agitation'.[8] Watson's concern was shared by many old high churchmen of the younger generation who went far in support of the movement in its early stages. For instance, Benjamin Harrison, appointed chaplain to the Archbishop of Canterbury in 1838 but the actual author of No. 49 of the *Tracts for the Times,* by 1843 was complaining of the widespread 'notion, which it is most desirable to get rid of, of church principles being altogether a creation of the last ten years'. He felt that what was then wanted was 'to have the "Tracts", if possible, forgotten—merged, at least, in the view of Christian Faith, and the Christian church, and the long course of eventful history and warfare which they have passed through'. Harrison wished that thinking men would but 'look a little deeper than the opinions and efforts of any individuals, or combination of individuals, ten years ago, as the source and spring of the late movement'.[9] Other old high churchmen reiterated the point with telling insistence. In 1840, in a work ostensibly written in defence of the Tractarians, the reactor of Leigh, Essex, James Beaven, argued that their real influence had been 'very much overrated, both by friends and foes'.[10] Perhaps still more striking though, was the testimony of Edward Churton, rector of Crayke, who in 1846 tried to temper the zeal of his Tractarian-minded friend William Gresley, by impressing upon him the example of another Oxford-inspired high church movement, that of the so-called 'Hutchinsonians' of the previous century. The Hutchinsonians comprised the high church followers of the mystical theories of the Hebraist John Hutchinson,[11] led by George Horne, President of Magdalen College and later Bishop of Norwich, William Jones, vicar of Nayland, and the layman William Stevens. They were the natural predecessors of the 'Hackney Phalanx'. It was natural for Churton to invoke their name to the Tractarians, in order to press the idea of continuity and to detract from Tractarian assumptions of novelty and thereby alleviate the growing anxieties of the original 'Phalanx'. As he told Gresley:

> The value of the labours of Bishop Horne, Jones of Nayland and their friends, will not be forgotten by any faithful historian of the church of the eighteenth century . . . I want you to refer to such good men's names . . . not only as a matter of justice but because I believe nothing will tend more to make what you are now doing more acceptable to my good old friends . . . Nothing is more important in my mind, than to show that Anglicanism, as it is now called, is not a new party, but has come down to us in regular descent from the Reformation, from Hooker to Andrewes, Andrewes to Laud, Bramhall, and Hammond, thence to Pearson and Jeremy Taylor, thence to Bishop Bull, thence to Hickes and Robert Nelson, Leslie and other names . . . After the succession of George III these principles were again enquired for, and Horne and Jones answered to the call. Horne and Jones have their disciples still living. Tell the world this.[12]

If we look at the three main themes or facets of Tractarianism—the doctrine of the church, its apostolicity, unity, independence and relation to the State; the rule of faith, role of tradition and the Fathers; and finally, spirituality and its different elements, along with sacramentalism and the symbolic significance of rite and ceremony—we can find ample evidence of renewal and resurgence in each, within the high church tradition in the forty or fifty years preceding the dawn of the movement. Of all the doctrines inculcated by the early Tractarians, none was given greater prominence than that of the apostolical succession, constitution, order and spiritual independence of the Church Catholic. As is well known, in the face of the Whig-Erastian reforms and constitutional changes of the early 1830s they urged the clergy of the Church of England, in the words of No. 1 of the *Tracts for the Times,* to rely only on their 'apostolic descent', and not merely worldly position. They assumed in doing this that they were rousing discussion, in the words of the Advertisement to the second volume of the Tracts, 'on points which had long remained undisturbed'.[13] However the evidence from the previous half-century shows just how mistaken they were in this assumption. Much too much reliance has been placed upon Bishop Blomfield's supposed and oft-quoted remark, apparently made to Joshua Watson on the eve of the Oxford Movement, to the effect that the number of clergy who still believed in the doctrine of the apostolical succession could be counted on two hands.[14] Moreover one should be equally sceptical about the validity of Gladstone's contention in the famous article in the *Foreign and Colonial Review* in 1843, that few bishops and archdeacons in their pre-Tractarian era ever touched upon this subject in their charges and sermons.[15] Significantly the old high churchmen or so-called 'Zs' resented these assumptions about the period which most of them had lived through, and in private correspondence with their Tractarian friends went to enormous lengths to refute them. For instance, in May 1836 one of the old high churchmen most sympathetic to the new movement, Hugh James Rose, after perusing No. 71 of the *Tracts for the Times,* wrote to Newman, its author: 'I wish that you had somewhat more represented the Apostolic Succession as a regular, undoubted doctrine, held undoubtingly by all true churchmen, and only a little neglected—than as a thing to which we were to recur as a sort of ancient novelty—a truth now first recovered.'[16]

The charges of the bishops relating to the movement, which were delivered in the years 1841 to 1843, were especially insistent upon this point. The leaders and followers of the movement at the time, and many later historians, were able to perceive little more than a blind and negative Protestant spirit of condemnation in those charges.[17] I do not propose to demonstrate the weakness of this view here, but suffice to say that there were many contemporaries who recognised in those charges positive statements of classical high church teaching, and a generous anxiety to uphold what was good and true in the movement, and in conformity with the old high church tradition. A good source in this respect is an interesting work entitled *Testimonies to Church Principles selected from Episcopal Charges and Sermons,* published in 1843, which found the great bulk of them to be much more in accord with the Tractarians than their Evangelical opponents.[18] Even the extreme Tractarian Frederick Oakeley was prepared to admit, early in 1843, that 'the general tenor of the charges delivered during the past year has been in a most unprecedented degree in favour of catholic views'.[19] Certainly many Evangelicals were critical of the bishops for being too lenient. For instance, Archdeacon Browne could complain to C. P. Golightly in 1843: 'What an afflicting consideration it is that no measures are taken by the bench of bishops collectively for arresting the progress of either [Tractarianism or Popery]. What indeed is to be expected, when the Primate has a Puseyite for his chaplain, and the calumniator of Foxe for his librarian.'[20]

Moreover the Evangelical divine William Goode made the point still more strongly, when he complained that the 'culpable apathy or worse, of the heads of the church in this matter is making our church an object of wonder and I might almost say derision to the whole of Protestant Europe and America'.[21]

All this is not surprising, considering that many of these bishops in their earlier years had themselves been closely linked with the 'Hackney Phalanx', and what William Molesworth aptly described as the 'Canterbury party' of Establishment high churchmen centred around the court and government circles in the 1810s and 1820s.[22] None the less this background made them keen to play down the significance of what happened in 1833 and afterwards. The attitude of Christopher Bethell, Bishop of Bangor, who as a member of the 'Phalanx' had been raised to the bishopric of Exeter in the 1800s, was a case in point. As one who in his charges in that period had emphasised the doctrines of the Church and succession, Bethell had every right to complain of the Tractarians in his charge of 1843, that:

> Some of their encomiasts have spoken of them as truths which had been forgotten and lost to the church till they were rescued from oblivion by the authors of the Tracts. It may be allowed that they were kept much in the background but they never ceased to be held and avowed . . . in illustration of this, we need only refer to the writings of Archdeacon Daubeny, and Mr Jones of Nayland, whose works on the church were widely circulated, and received with great approbation.[23]

In fact we may cite among many others William Stevens's *Constitution of the Catholic Church* (1784), Daubeny's *Guide to the Church* (1798) and Sikes's *Parochial Communion* (1812), as examples. Another instance illustrative of their real priorities was the especial concern of Horne, Jones, Stevens and Daubeny, for the disestablished and recently persecuted Episcopal Church in Scotland. Not only did they give generous aid but they were active, along with another high churchman, Bishop Horsley, in persuading parliament finally to repeal the major disabilities on Scottish episcopacy in 1792.[24] Both the Hutchinsonians and the leaders of the 'Phalanx' valued Establishment but still insisted that, in the end, it was only a most valuable appendage. They were sensitive to charges of Erastianism levelled against the Church of England of their day. For instance, in a letter to Joshua Watson in 1815 Christopher Wordsworth actually complained that there was too much stress in SPCK publications on the Church as an Establishment.[25] Significantly in his memoir of Bishop Horne, first published in 1795, Jones of Nayland laid particular stress on his part in the restoration of the Scottish Episcopal Church to favour:

> In order to show not only that the bishops of Scotland are true Christian bishops, but that the bishops of England, from the part they kindly took in the affair, do little deserve the clamour which some have raised against them, as if they were so dazzled by their temporalities, as to lose sight of their spiritual character, and bury the christian bishop in the peer of parliament.[26]

The essential anti-Erastianism of these old high churchmen deserves emphasising, since from what the Tractarians themselves, and then later writers in the Catholic tradition, have assumed, they have been made to appear tainted in this respect.[27] The Tractarians felt that they were actually substituting what they called 'apostolicity' for what had passed as high churchmanship, but was really 'high establishmentism'[27] or Erastianism—Z-ism in Froude's vocabulary. The Zs, they assumed, were prepared to compromise the spiritual integrity and independence of the Church in order to preserve its mere temporal well-being, the trappings and privileges of Church Establishment. Seeking inspiration not only in the nonjurors but in St Ambrose and St Athanasius and even Hildebrand and Becket, the Tractarians found it, in William Copeland's words, 'a relief to contrast' those figures with 'the cold heartedness and semi-infidel conservatism of many of the maintainers of our so-called happy establishment'.[28] Indeed John Mason Neale even went so far as to claim that the old high church tradition, even its pure Laudian form, was infused by what he termed a 'fearful Erastianism'.[29] Yet the Tractarians and their successors have tended to pose a false dichotomy between zeal for the inherent spiritual rights of the Church and a loyal and hearty belief in Establishment and the positive role of the State, especially the crown, in matters ecclesiastical. The two co-existed quite happily, side by side, in old high church teaching. The royal supremacy was viewed in a positive light, as a reflection of the monarch's sacral and quasi-religious character as 'Defender of the Faith', whose duty was laid down in the coronation oath to watch over and protect the Church as a 'nursing father', not imperious tyrant.[30] The non-established Episcopal Church in America and especially one of its leading figures, John Henry Hobart, are usually seen as potent forces of inspiration for the Tractarians. However, unlike the Tractarians, old high churchmen were not always impressed by the example of that church[31] and they reacted angrily to Bishop Hobart's strictures on Church-State relations in England in 1826.[32] Watson, for instance, was apt to refer disparagingly to the 'pseudo-anti-erastianism of America'.[33] Disestablishment played into the hands of ultra-Protestants and republicans. Thus, they would disagree with those Tractarians who ascribed all the evils they faced in the 1830s to the tyranny of State laws. As Edward Churton reminded William Copeland in 1840:

> The religion of Ultra-Protestantism is essentially a religion against all ordinances, whether of Pope, Prelate, or Caesar, and the man who adopts it, calls history an old almanac, and writes the year of his own conversion or first formation of a system as the year one of Christianity. It is not the result of an Establishment, but pride of reason and spiritual wickedness and rebellion.[34]

Thus in a real sense prelate and Caesar, church and king, stood or fell together, and of course, the lessons of the French Revolution seemed to provide exclusive proof for the axiom. Yet for all their strictures on 'Z' attitudes the early Tractarians themselves were in fact remarkably in accord with this more political facet of old high churchmanship. Virtually to a man, they were high Tories,[35] and ardent royalists—W. G. Ward causing great offence by his irreverence to the memory of the 'Royal Martyr'[36] Charles I. For it was devotion to the principles enshrined in the coronation oath, almost as much as to the notion of 'apostolical descent' that was at stake for the Tractarians in 1833.[37] It was only later that the view developed that the origin of the movement had no connection with the political changes of the time.[38]

Above all we should recognise, as Edward Norman has reminded us, 'that it was the interdependence of church and state, and not the dependence of the church upon the state' that underlay the old high church position.[39] In fact so interchangeable did the two often appear that there is no doubt that the very term 'Establishment' was often used as much to denote the actual episcopal regimen and spiritual constitution as the merely temporal framework of the Church. Therefore we should not be surprised to find startling assertions of Church independence in even those pre-Tractarian high churchmen who had the worst reputation for being merely Establishment-minded, 'high and dry' and worldly. Godfrey Faussett, Lady Margaret Professor of Divinity in the University of Oxford, and the author of a bitter attack on the Tractarians in a notorious sermon called *The Revival of Popery,* preached from the university pulpit in 1838, appeared to 'apostolicals' as a prime case in point, the personification of the pampered aristocrat in ecclesiastical dress. The Tractarians much disliked Faussett's ethos, and in an article in the *British Critic* in 1841 Thomas Mozley made a scurrilous parody of him[40] which caused widespread offence and embarrassed Keble and Newman. However there was much more to Faussett than the Tractarians, and especially Newman who wrote a famous reply to his *Revival of Popery* sermon, realised. At that time Faussett had over thirty years of writings in defence and propagation of high church principles behind him—writings which reveal him to have been no mere Erastian, political churchman. In his Bampton Lectures of 1820 Faussett maintained that the union of Church and State was a union of independent powers on the principles of federal, not incorporating, union. Certainly his ideal was that of Hooker and the Elizabethan settlement, not that of the later nonjurors, as it was for the Tractarians, but he was not complacent or prepared to temporise.[41] He frankly castigated the practical deviations from the Elizabethan ideal that had occurred, such as the silencing of Convocation since 1717, the persecution of the Scottish Church and establishment of presbyterianism in Scotland, and the prolonged failure to send bishops to America. He complained of 'the listless apathy, the blind security, and latitudinarian spirit of these alarming times', and lamented 'a complete confusion of ideas between the church as a society of divine institution, and the church as a political establishment, or rather, perhaps a disposition to consider the church, so far as its outward polity is concerned, as left altogether to human discretion'.[42] Clearly the utilitarian arguments for Establishment of Warburton, William Paley and their school were abhorrent to him.

On the question of apostolical succession Faussett was especially explicit. Even Newman's apparently radical suggestion in No. 41 of the *Tracts for the Times,* that the Thirty-Nine Articles be amended to include an explicit statement of the doctrine,[43] had been prefigured by Faussett in these lectures.[44] Moreover John Hume Spry, rector of Marylebone and also considered to be very 'high and dry', made the same call in his own Bampton Lectures for 1816, entitled *Christian Unity Doctrinally and Historically Considered.* Like works such as Daubeny's *Guide* and Sikes's *Parochial Communion,* it contained an explicit enunciation of the classic high Anglican 'branch theory',[45] by which catholicity was made dependent on a strict adherence of the churches to episcopal order and succession, and as a result of which Protestant dissenters were effectively 'unchurched' while Rome as well as the Orthodox were deemed true in foundation, if corrupt in practice. In fact all the evidence suggests that the late 1810s and 1820s witnessed a steady growth in popularity and acceptance of the doctrines of the Church, a point actually insisted upon by a writer in the high church periodical journal, the *Christian Remembrancer,* in 1821.[46] Two other works that had particular influence were Joshua Watson's brother, Archdeacon John James Watson's *Divine Commission and Perpetuity of the Christian Priesthood* (1816)—a work which owed much in spirit to that of the nonjuror George Hickes's *Christian Priesthood* of 1712—and John Oxlee's *Three sermons . . . on the Power, Origin and Succession of the Christian Hierarchy* (1821). The kinship of Watson's work to Tractarian publications on the same theme in the 1830s was such that it was republished in 1839, precisely because, as Joshua Watson told Henry Handley Norris, 'the 30 years which have crossed over our heads since its delivery would save it from the prejudice of being only the product of the current controversy'.[47] However the writings of the obscure rector of Scrawton, Yorkshire, John Oxlee, reveal him as a still more remarkable precursor of the movement on the same theme. This was so, not simply because of his almost monotonous emphasis on apostolic succession and endeavours to prove in table form what he described as 'a continued and uninterrupted list of Christian bishops from the blessed Apostles, Peter, Paul, and John, down to the present prelates of Canterbury, York and London'.[48] This in itself could be dry, uninspiring work. What is striking about Oxlee and a whole number of other pre-Tractarian high churchmen is another more imaginative, out-going, truly Catholic dimension, not often fully recognised.

It was to be a familiar criticism of old high churchmen by the later Tractarians that, holding the apostolical succession in only a negative sense and failing to draw out its consequences, they were incorrigibly insular. They were considered only to value the doctrine as a weapon in the Anglican armoury against Rome, to glory too much in the isolation of the English Church from the Continent, and to be infected by what John Mason Neale described as a 'Donatist temper'.[49] It is true that to a great extent the old high churchmen's very sense of kinship with Rome on account of a common apostolical heritage through the channel of episcopal order, led them to emphasise Rome's supposed doctrinal and practical 'corruptions', and thereby shield the Church of England from the charge of schism at the time of the Reformation.[50] Some of them, such as Thomas Burgess, Bishop of Salisbury, seemed to fit Neale's description and wrote lengthy treatises asserting the apparent original independence from Rome, of primitive, apostolically ordered British churches.[51] Nevertheless it was hard for even the most anti-Romanist of pre-Tractarian high churchmen entirely to overlook or deny the fact that the English Church had depended on Rome for many centuries,[52] both for the reconversion of England by Roman missionaries in Anglo-Saxon times, and above all for the lineal transmission of her apostolic succession. There were many strikingly candid admissions of indebtedness to Rome. Thus John Oxlee looked forward to a reunion of Christendom on the basis of a mutual intercommunion of episcopally constituted 'branch' churches, once Rome had been shorn of her supposed later 'corruptions' and had returned to her original 'pure' state. Oxlee's readiness to commend what he called 'the glorious episcopate of Gregory the Great' and 'the venerable see of Rome',[53] made him rejoice that the Church of England had derived her orders through such a source, and poured scorn on Protestant cavils at the fact. Stephen Hyde Cassan made the point more forcefully in an aside in his *Lives of the Bishop of Winchester,* published in 1827:

She [Rome] is our Mother-Church, in as much as it is through her, and through her alone, as a connecting link that we can, with any degree of certainty, derive the right of administering the word of God and the sacraments. Those who would thus disclaim our Romish parentage seem to forget that the further they remove us, in the superabundance of their zeal, from the Roman Catholic Church, the lower they sink us, and the nearer they cause us to approach to the degraded and precarious position of Dissenters.[54]

However perhaps the most remarkable figure of all was Samuel Wix, rector of St Bartholomew-the-Less, London. In his significantly entitled *Christian Union without the Abuses of Popery,* published in 1820, Wix maintained that 'no solid objection prevails against the Church of England attempting an union with the Church of Rome, since the Church of Rome is acknowledged by the Church of England to be a true apostolical church'.[55] Wix even went so far as to predate the very argument employed by Newman in 1841, in Tract 90, when Newman had sought to distinguish between the so-called practical corruptions of the popular Roman religious system, which both labelled 'popery', and the more 'catholic' or 'primitive' official teaching of the Roman Church as enshrined in the Council of Trent. Newman sought to justify this position by appealing to the authority of Charles Lloyd, Bishop of Oxford, from whom he and other future Tractarians first imbibed Catholic Anglican principles in the 1820s.[56] In fact Newman's views were more closely anticipated by Wix rather than Lloyd. For both argued that Rome in her official teaching actually disowned this supposed popular system. What mattered was that many of these later corruptions such as the invocation of saints and communion under one kind, were not always *'de fide'* matters anyway. As long as they could simply be dismissed as 'things indifferent' on the Anglican principle of adiaphora, then here was a basis for reconciliation.[57] Clearly from all this the concept of the 'via media' as formulated by Newman in his *Prophetical Office of the Church,* by which the Church of England was firmly detached from the level of the Protestant churches of the Continent, and defined as at least as far removed from Geneva as from Rome, was very much a living reality for high churchmen in the half-century prior to the movement. Henry Handley Norris made this point quite as uncompromisingly as any of the Tractarians, as early as 1812, when he wrote:

If names had any weight, I much more highly prize the title of a Catholic than that of a Protestant, which later appellation I am by no means fond of, as it confounds one with those from whom Christianity, I verily believe, has suffered more outrages than from the papists themselves. The distinguishing title of a member of the Church of England is a Reformed Catholic—and this places him in a central situation from which the Papist and the larger portion of that mixed multitude known by the name of protestant diverge, in opposite directions indeed but to equal distances.[58]

Another important aspect of the way in which the high church tradition prefigured Tractarianism in the half-century preceding 1833 was in its deference to antiquity, and especially the writings of the early Fathers, as either testimonies to fundamental doctrines or as standards of faith and practice. No. 78 of the *Tracts for the Times* was devoted to a *'catenae patrum'* of Anglican divines who had upheld the so-called Vincentian rule—*'quod semper, quod ubique, et quod ab omnibus'*—the principle formulated by Vincent of Lérins in the fifth century. High churchmen had long appealed to this rule for a Catholic consent of Fathers and councils as the basis of Catholic truth. Unlike ultra-Protestants, they did not rest content with the testimony of Scripture alone. In Tract 78, in Keble's famous Visitation sermon of 1836, *Primitive Tradition recognised in Holy Scripture,* and in Newman's controversy with the Abbé Jager between 1834 and 1836, due acknowledgement was made to the Caroline divines and nonjurors for their witness to this rule. However the witness of high churchmen of the previous half-century was almost entirely overlooked. Works which did uphold it in that period included Kett's Bampton Lectures (1793), Daubeny's *Guide* (1798), Van Mildert's Boyle Lectures (1804), Martin Routh's *Reliquae Sacrae* (1814), Oxlee's *Christian Priesthood* (1816), Spry's Bampton Lectures (1816), Archdeacon Pott's *Grounds and Principles of the Church of England* (1824) and Bishop Kaye's *Ecclesiastical History of the Second and Third Centuries* (1826).

However there were two vitally important works to which the Tractarians did acknowledge their debt—Bishop Jebb's sermon, published in 1815, entitled *The Peculiar Character of the Church of England as distinguished from other branches of the Reformation, and from the modern Church of Rome;*[59] and the later Provost of Oriel Edward Hawkins's sermon of 1819, *The Use and Importance of Unauthoritative Tradition.* Many of Hawkins's latitudinarian friends such as Whately and Arnold were dismayed and embarrassed by the use which the Tractarians were to make of this sermon in the 1830s. For instance, in 1835 Thomas Arnold complained that Hawkins's sermon had 'served the cause of schism and error',[60] while in 1836 he told Whately that Hawkins had 'contributed to their mischief by his unhappy sermon on Tradition'.[61] Hawkins was sensitive to these criticisms, and complained to Whately in 1836, 'Keble has published a very puerile sermon on Primitive Tradition, which makes me more desirous of following your advice and rewriting "unauthoritative Tradition"'.[62] Yet though

Hawkins might try to retract or shift his ground his influence on Newman, as Louis Bouyer has shown, remained profound. Significantly Newman defended his view of the *'disciplina arcani'*, the idea of a secret tradition within the bosom of the Church, which he first formulated in his *Arians of the Fourth Century* in 1832[63] by direct reference both to the writings of Bishop Kaye,[64] and to Hawkins's sermon on Tradition.[65] Moreover he was able to go to the same source in order to defend the *'argumentum ad hominem'* which he employed in No. 85 of the *Tracts for the Times,*[66] to justify such doctrines as the Trinity on the basis of tradition alone, on the grounds that they were not clear from the text of Scripture only.[67]

Yet perhaps surprisingly it was in its character as a primarily religious, spiritual movement that Tractarianism owed its greatest debt to the high churchmanship of the preceding half-century. Following the verdict of the Tractarians themselves many later writers have taken for granted a massive degeneration from the ideal of primitive holiness after the revolution and Hanoverian succession, even within the ranks of the high church party.[68] Brilioth drew heavily on the testimony of Bishop Jebb and his lifelong friend and correspondent Alexander Knox, who both had strong formative influences on the movement, and were both very un-'Z'-like in the almost Evangelical warmth and feeling of their piety. In comparison the men of the 'Phalanx' and their associates seemed very 'high and dry'. It was Brilioth's contention, after showing the comparison, that:

> the weakness of that kind of High Churchmanship which was preached by Daubeny and his likes, and its inability to win the ear of the age, rested perhaps not least on the fact that they so entirely cut themselves off from the spiritual well which streamed forth from the Evangelical revival of the eighteenth century.[69]

There was a certain truth in this; a deep seated prejudice against any so-called 'enthusiasm' in matters spiritual was responsible for some lowering of the religious temperature among many old high churchmen. Yet the charge of worldliness and coldness has been overplayed, and Brilioth's estimate is in need of distinct modification. The Hutchinsonians, George Horne especially, retained an almost Evangelical warmth of religious expression in devotion, but perhaps more surprisingly even Daubeny, whom Brilioth described as clinging to 'a narrow ecclesiasticism',[70] was no exception in this respect. One of his first actions on becoming a prebend of Salisbury in 1784 was to transcribe Bishop Andrewes's Morning Prayer for daily use.[71] Moreover his aids to devotion read like a catalogue of the richest treasures of Caroline and nonjuring spirituality—Jeremy Taylor's *Holy Living and Holy Dying,* Bishop Wilson's *Sacra Privata,* Bishop Ken's *Manual for Winchester Scholars.*[72] In fact it was Brilioth's main source for his verdict—Knox and Jebb—that needs scrutiny. On his visits to England the famous Bishop of Limerick recorded his favourable impression of Henry Handley Norris, but also his criticisms of him and the 'Phalanx' as a whole, Sikes and Spry especially, for rigidity and dryness,[73] but it was Daubeny who attracted his severest strictures. However the attitude of Alexander Jolly, the Scottish episcopalian Bishop of Moray, towards Knox and Jebb's criticism of Daubeny and the 'Phalanx' is most revealing. After sorting through Jolly's papers after his death in 1838 James Walker, Bishop of Edinburgh, wrote to Henry Handley Norris, to reassure him just how much Jolly had disapproved of Knox and Jebb's criticisms of Daubeny as contained in their recently published *Thirty Years Correspondence.*[74] Another high churchman of an apparently similar dry mould, Daubeny's diocesan Thomas Burgess, Bishop of Salisbury, has been similarly misunderstood. He was much more than a narrow 'high and dry' anti-Roman polemicist. According to Burgess's biographer James Harford, when the future Bishop of Salisbury had been rector of Winston, Co. Durham, his spiritual reflections 'were chiefly written in the blank leaves and in the margins of some of his favourite devotional writers, among whom may be enumerated Bishop Wilson's "Sacra Privata" . . . Payne's Thomas à Kempis, Nelson's "Practice of True Devotion", Law's "Serious Call"'.[75]

It is the influence of William Law, the nonjuror's *Serious Call* (1728) on old high churchmen, that provides an important piece of evidence to their continued adherence to the ascetic element in spirituality which was especially to characterise the Oxford Movement. It was not the Tractarians who first rediscovered Law, as is often supposed. For instance, George Horne moulded his spirituality on Law's ascetic example,[76] while it was Thomas Rennell, Dean of Winchester 1805-40 and a leading member of the 'Hackney Phalanx', who first introduced the young W. F. Hook to Law's *Serious Call,* while Hook was a curate on the Isle of Wight in the early 1820s.[77] Examples of the value set upon fasting and celibacy can repeatedly be found. Both Horne and William Stevens frequently referred to the latter in their writings, as a worthy spiritual ideal.[78] We can even find surprisingly favourable views of at least the original monastic ideal. Certainly there were some robustly Protestant, 'high and dry' denunciations of it in any form, notably from Robert Southey in his *Book of the Church* of 1824. Thus Southey attacked monasticism even in what he termed 'its first stage, when it had nothing useful or ornamental to compensate for its preposterous austerities'. He poured scorn on those pilgrims of the early Church who went 'to behold and reverence, like a living idol, a maniac in Syria, who, under that burning climate, passed his life upon the top of a lofty column, and tied with the goguecs of India in the folly and perseverence with which he inflicted voluntary tortures upon himself'.[79] Yet even Southey advocated religious sisterhoods in the Church of England, and 'the first Anglican convent was established as his posthumous memorial'.[80] Clearly there was a tension between medievalism and anti-catholicism in Southey. However, more typical of the better type of old churchman was Edward Churton's love of Anglo-Saxon saints such as Bede and Alcuin.[81] Churton condemned what he called Southey's 'absurd vulgar trash about St Dunstan' and for following 'no system of distinguishing between the age of credulity and the age of imposture'.[82] Churton was quite prepared to defend the ideal of early monasticism. He wrote:

> It is impossible for a serious mind to suppose that a rule of life so early introduced into the Christian church, so approved by the most eminent Fathers and confessors of those early times, and so long kept up in almost every christian country, can have been allowed without some providential purpose.[83]

Moreover both Watson and Norris were favourably disposed towards the Tractarian plan for the revival of sisterhoods. Watson was even sympathetic to a revival of monasticism itself. As Charles Marriott told Newman, after staying at the home of Watson's sister-in-law at Daventry: 'I was desirous to know what he thought of the monastic life . . . I found the good old man . . . spoke decidedly in favour of some institution of the kind. I told him what you were doing at Littlemore, and he seemed to like the notion of it much.'[84]

Another characteristic theme of Tractarian spirituality was of course that spirit of awe and reserve in sacred matters, borne out of a reaction to the apparently profane over-familiarity of popular protestantism. Newman seized upon the concept of the *'disciplina arcani'* in the Fathers, according to which there had to be reserve or restraint in the communication of religious knowledge, so as to avoid a situation whereby 'pearls' might be 'cast before swine'.[85] As is well known, the notion was given full expression in No. 80 of the *Tracts for the Times:* Isaac Williams, *On Reserve in Communicating Religious Knowledge.* The Tractarians, especially Keble, recognised a debt to Bishop Butler on this,[86] but it is wrong to assume that they were the first to rediscover it. The Hutchinsonians had all witnessed to it, in practice as well as theory. There were some at the time who realised that this was so. For instance, in 1846 at the time when the Tractarian position on this question was widely assumed to be novel William Teale, in a memoir of Jones of Nayland, with somewhat heavy irony cited Jones as an example of the fact 'that English churchmen had condemned the irreverent admixture of things sacred and profane long before some late assailants of the same offences against decorum and religious feeling were born to denounce them to the world as the results of the English Reformation'.[87] Particularly striking was the precise way in which the central argument of Tract 80 was prefigured by Daubeny in a charge which he delivered to the clergy of Salisbury archdeaconry in 1824, when he attacked what he called 'the unreserved and indiscriminate application of strong evangelic language to Christians who might be in the infancy of their growth' and therefore could not 'be supposed to have attained in any degree to that stage of spiritual proficiency, to which that language originally belonged'.[88] Moreover this ethos of reserve was central to the spiritual make-up of the 'Hackney Phalanx'. It lay at the root of their opposition to propagate the Scriptures without any comment or guidance among the unlearned, and thus determined their resistance to the activities of the British and Foreign Bible Society in the thirty years prior to the movement. It was thus indicative of Newman's new adherence to the high church camp when in 1829 he formally cut his links with that organisation. Certainly Newman, Keble or Williams in the mature stage of Tractarianism could not have bettered the reasons given by Henry Handley Norris for his opposition to the Bible Society, in a letter to his friend Ralph Churton, the father of Edward, in 1813. Scripture, he wrote:

> is not in the purpose of God, the instrument of conversion—but the repository of divine knowledge for the perfecting of those already converted. I mean that it is the children's bread and not to be cast to dogs . . . the Scriptures are not a self-sufficient means of grace and salvation but co-ordinate only with the appointed ministry who must superintend the cultivation of the Divine word in order to procure for it the blessing of increase from the Almighty.[89]

Another important element in Tractarian religion, wholeheartedly embraced by old high churchmen of the preceding years, was its anti-rationalist emphasis. It needs to be recognised that a depreciation of the eighteenth-century cult of unaided human reason and perfectibility, a rejection of mere moralism and utilitarianism as the basis of faith and conduct, as exemplified in the writings of William Paley, was as much a feature of the Hutchinsonians and Hackney Phalanx as of the Oxford Movement. Froude's Essay on Rationalism, published in his *Remains,* and a famous university sermon of Newman's of 1830 on the subject, set the characteristic Tractarian tone of emphasis on childlike humility and reverence for truth. As such they are usually regarded as complementary to, and the true successors of, those eighteenth-century Evangelicals who assailed the standard moralism and evidential theology of the day, a theology to which not only outright latitudinarians but the so-called 'high and dry' apparently subscribed. It is often forgotten that the Hutchinsonians and the 'Phalanx' also joined forces with Evangelicals, in asserting the absolute supremacy of faith over verifiable external evidence. In short, they were quite as antagonistic to Paleyism as Evangelicals and Tractarians alike. As George Horne put it:

> Reason can no more find out, without the help of Revelation, the original state and constitution of man, the changes that have happened in his nature, and the counsels of God, that have taken place in consequence of these changes . . . than she can prove metaphysically, that William the Conqueror vanquished Harold, at Hastings, in Sussex.[90]

Significantly the two most lasting products of the high church revival of the 1790s—the foundation by Horne and Jones of the periodical *British Critic* in 1792, and the Society for the Reformation of Principles in 1795, with its series of publications entitled *The Scholar Armed against the errors of the times*—both had as their original leading aim the reversal of the rational spirit of the age. It is interesting to note that the Tractarian William Copeland, in his *Narrative of the Oxford Movement,* specifically acknowledged the close affinity of the *Scholar Armed* in its aims and spirit with the *Tracts for the Times.*[91]

The final aspect of Tractarian spirituality which the older high churchmen foreshadowed was an emphasis on the importance of mysticism, allegory and typology, and what might be called the sacramental principle of the symbolism of rites and ceremonies. This aspect of Tractarian teaching, as is well known, found expression in Pusey's unpublished lectures of 1836, on types and prophecies, and in Keble's No. 89 of the *Tracts for the Times, On the Mysticism of the Fathers.* At its root lay a consciousness that not only was man's reason and his ability to glimpse into the spiritual and even visible creation necessarily limited, but that for the man of faith there was another method of perceiving spiritual truth. This method lay through the typological principle which Keble defined in a well-known phrase, 'as the doctrine that material phenomenon are both the types and the instruments of things unseen'.[92] The Tractarians found this principle to have been employed by Hooker[93] and later Bishop Butler,[94] but overlooked the contribution of the Hutchinsonians and members of the 'Phalanx' such as Van Mildert. It was given perhaps its fullest expression in a course of lectures given by Jones of Nayland preached in Nayland parish church in 1786, entitled *On the Figurative Language of Holy Scripture.* Like Pusey in his lectures in 1836, Jones of Nayland argued that the language of Scripture consisted not merely in words themselves but 'signs or figures taken from visible things'.[95] To explain his meaning, he demonstrated that religious rites and ceremonies were far more than 'things indifferent' as some held, but divinely-ordained visible signs of 'things unseen':

> Priests and singers in our church wear a white linen garment as a sign of purity, and to give them a nearer alliance to the company of heaven. Chanting by responses . . . was intended to imitate the choir of angels, which cry out to one another with alternate adoration. The primitive christians turned towards the east, in their worship, to signify their respect to the true Light of the World. They set up candles as a sign of their illumination by the Gospel; and evergreens are still placed there at Christmas, to remind us that a new and perpetual spring of immortality is restored to us, even in the middle of winter, by the coming of Jesus Christ.[96]

This theoretical sacramentalism was reflected in the attention to ritual and ceremonial practice by old high churchmen. In his university sermon of 1830 on the subject Newman argued that Christians 'must receive the Gospel literally on their knees, and in a temper altogether different from that critical and argumentative spirit which sitting and listening engender'.[97] Accordingly he always made a point of kneeling or bowing to the altar in St Mary's for long periods,[98] a practice which George Home and then Dr Routh observed in Magdalen Chapel.[99] Thomas Sanders had made precisely the same point as Newman in a sermon before the University of Oxford in St Mary's in 1801. Sanders condemned the modern practice of congregations sitting when they should kneel, arguing, like Newman was to, that it was 'essentially necessary that our outward deportment should indicate humility, and correspond with the inward disposition of the soul'.[100] It was this same conviction that led many old high churchmen to state their preference for the spirit of Roman Catholic rather than Presbyterian worshippers. For instance, Daubeny, after a tour of the Continent in 1788, lamented that the Swiss Reformed were not what he called 'kneeling Christians', but rather, 'peripatetic Christians'.[101] Thus it is not surprising that high churchmen should have become actively engaged in a movement towards ritual and ceremonial renewal and restoration, long before the ecclesiological arm or ally of the Oxford Movement, the Cambridge Camden Society, took up this cause in the 1840s. Both Watson and Norris had for long been involved in just such a cause, the former being responsible for restoring the print of the communion office in the Book of Common Prayer to large bold type.[102] Watson's own career and experiences made him most impatient of the assumption of Tractarians and ecclesiologists that all was cold and dead in ritual before their own emergence. As he put it, in the early 1840s at the time of the so-called ritual controversy, 'much of the evil we now deprecate arises from those who are now agitators not having seen the church in her beauty in their own early days'.[103] He was especially critical of the Camden Society for their attitude in this respect—'the impertinence of these Camdenians', he wrote, 'is perfectly unendurable . . . they would almost seem to take to themselves the language of the prophetess, and say that the highways were unoccupied, and the people wandered in byways, until the Camdenians arose, masters in Israel'.[104]

In conclusion, the degree of high church continuity throughout the half-century prior to the movement has been seriously underestimated, and the extent to which the Tractarians owed a direct debt to the high Anglican tradition upheld by their precursors, for too long overlooked. It was a debt which Pusey warmly acknowledged when he wrote to Joshua Watson in the summer of 1839 after a visit to the venerable old high churchmen at Brighton. Pusey told Watson, 'how cheering' it was:

> to be recognised by you as carrying on the same torch which we had received from yourself, and those of your generation, who had remained faithful to the old teaching. We seemed no longer separated by the chasm from the old times and old paths to which we wished to lead people back; the links which united us to those of old seemed restored.[105]

None the less there were important differences in both temper and teaching, between the new and old high churchmen. The differences were evident as early as 1833, and Keble implicity recognised them when in that very year he informed Newman that, in the manner of Burke's pamphlet with regard to differences among the Whigs in the 1790s, he was planning 'an Appeal from the New to the Old Churchmen, or some such thing'.[106] These differences widened and deepened as the years passed. Only Watson's generosity of spirit prevented him from spelling them out more clearly to his Tractarian friends. Above all the older men of Hackney lamented a spirit of youthful impatience with, and even growing insubordination towards, episcopal authority.[107] They sighed over their apparent want of discretion, practical sense and sound judgment. As Edward Churton told William Copeland in 1841, 'I love them, but how is it possible to keep them, when their conduct tomorrow may contradict the defence you have made for them today?'[108] In particular the old high churchmen regretted that the Tractarians, for all their sincere professions that they were but following in 'the old paths', had not been better grounded in the older tradition. As a writer in the *Christian Remembrancer,* a periodical which reflected the older standpoint, put it in 1841:

> The leading minds among these writers had not the advantage of being trained themselves in the Anglo-Catholic school; they had to grope for their principles, as men suddenly beset by nightly robbers catch at such weapons as the moment allows . . . Their sentiments therefore had not been worked out by a previous development of the English system, but were taken up by persons who came rather as allies than as subjects to the defence of the church.[109]

Joshua Watson made the same point himself, complaining in private that the Tractarians 'begin to fight before they scarcely know the weapons wherewith they should arm themselves'.[110] In consequence he felt that they did less than justice to the vigour and achievements of the high church tradition in the previous century,[111] while Hugh James Rose was especially critical of Newman's contention in the introduction to his *Lectures on the prophetical office of the Church,* that Anglicanism had never had a wide influence historically while both Romanism and dissent had.[112] The old high churchmen as a whole insisted that the Tractarians exaggerated not only the extent of decay in the past but the evils of the present condition of the Church. Significantly Churton later told William Gresley how fond Watson was of quoting, against the Tractarians, Hooker's dictum: 'He who goes about to persuade the young that they are ill-governed, shall never want hearers.'[113] Essentially, because they came to similar views but by very different routes, the Tractarians were never likely to rest content with the careful bounds and limits observed by the old high churchmen. Moreover the fact that so many of them had been reared in an alien religious tradition in itself caused them to misunderstand the high church tradition, and led them to pervert it to some extent. In the end, what Churton called a 'practical "beau ideal" of catholicity'[114] that was to be strived after, was substituted for what old high churchmen were content to respect as the concrete and living catholicism of the Church of England as she already was. However the question of the full extent to which the Oxford Movement in its mature and later phases came to diverge from the old high church tradition is beyond our scope here. Yet that which we have touched upon, and especially the alarm and response of the bishops, many of whom, such as Christopher Bethell, had been associated with the 'Hackney Phalanx', leaves us justified in at least posing the question as to whether in the final analysis this later divergence was not to prove as significant as the broad continuity we have outlined.

For if the evidence of Joshua Watson from the manuscript diary of his niece Mary, and the testimony of others in the 'Phalanx' is anything to go by, then George Tavard was absolutely right when he maintained that the most powerful theological opposition to the movement actually came from those who had always professed what had hitherto passed as high churchmanship, and not 'from the Evangelicals, who were far too far from it to be able to understand it, or from the latitudinarians, who were not equipped to treat it as anything but as crypto-Romanism'.[115] Thus whereas in its basic themes and temper this chapter shows the movement to have been clearly the heir of a rich and varied pedigree of high Anglicanism, this always needs to be qualified by the reflection that its later growth and development was by no means always on the lines that older adherents of that tradition would have considered sound or legitimate. In the end we must agree with George Ayliffe Poole, friend of W. F. Hook and an old high churchman who keenly supported the movement in its early stages. For Poole, with the advent of the Oxford Movement, 'a modification of High Churchmen arose, which we are obliged to recognise as another party'.[116] For all the debt that movement owed the high Anglican tradition, Tractarianism and the Anglicanism of that tradition were not identical.

Notes

[1] E. A. Knox, *The Tractarian Movement, 1833-1845: a study of the Oxford Movement, as a phase of the religious revival in western Europe in the second quarter of the nineteenth century* (London 1933), ch. 18.

[2] S. Leslie, *The Oxford Movement* (London 1933). See also S. Ollard, *The Anglo-Catholic Revival* (London 1925); F. L. Cross, *The Oxford Movement and the Seventeenth Century* (London 1933); C. B. Moss, *The Orthodox Revival, 1833-1933* (London n.d.); H. L. Stewart, *A Century of Anglo-Catholicism* (London 1929); D. Morse-Boycott, *The Secret Story of the Oxford Movement* (London 1933); T. H. Whitton, *The Necessity of Catholic Reunion* (London 1933).

[3] See Yngve Brilioth, *The Anglican Revival: Studies in the Oxford Movement* (London 1925), ch. 2 and 4.

[4] See for example, F. W. Cornish, *The English Church in the Nineteenth Century,* 2 vols (London 1910), I, pp. 62-76; G. Worley, *The Catholic Revival of the Nineteenth Century* (London 1894), ch. 2; G. Wakeling, *The Oxford Church Movement: sketches and recollections* (London 1895); J. H. Moorman, 'Forerunners of the Oxford Movement', *Theology,* 25 (1933), pp. 6-11; B. Reardon, *From Coleridge to Gore: a century of religious thought* (London 1971), pp. 31-41.

[5] Quoted by C. P. S. Clarke, 'The Genesis of the Movement', in N. P. Williams and C. Harris, *Northern Catholicism: centenary studies in the Oxford and parallel movements* (London 1933), p. 8.

[6] N. Murray, 'The Influence of the French Revolution on the Church of England and its Rivals, 1789-1802' (unpublished D. Phil. thesis, Univ. Oxford 1975). The term 'Hackney Phalanx' was used to denote the large and rather amorphous group of pre-Tractarian high churchmen, based in, or linked to, the metropolis of London, which was particularly active in the years, c. 1805 until c. 1835. The 'Hackney Phalanx' took its name from the vicar (afterwards rector) of Hackney, Archdeacon John James Watson, elder brother of Joshua Watson, its unofficial leader, and from the rector of South Hackney, Watson's close friend, Henry Handley Norris.

[7] Hurrell Froude first used the slang epithet 'Z' to describe conservative or old high churchmen, while Evangelicals were labelled 'Xs' and the Tractarians or 'apostolicals' were termed 'Ys'. cf. *Remains of the Late Reverend Richard Hurrell Froude,* MA [Part I], 2 vols (London 1838), I, p. 429.

[8] Quoted in A. Webster, *Joshua Watson: the story of a layman* (London 1954), p. 29.

[9] B. Harrison to W. E. Gladstone, 16 November 1843, MS Add. 44204 ff. 114-15. Gladstone MSS (British Library). Typical of the Tractarian attitude which Harrison deplored was Manning's remark to Newman in 1843, 'that the church has passed under a fearful influence for 150 years is sadly true; but surely the last ten years have dispelled much, and brought the living church back again?' H. E. Manning to J. H. Newman, 23 October 1843, Manning MSS V, 26 (Bodleian).

[10] J. Beaven, *A Calm Exposure of the Unfairness of the 'General Reply to all Objections' of 'Ancient Christianity'* (London 1840), p. 37.

[11] For an account of Hutchinsonianism, see E. Churton, *Memoir of Joshua Watson,* 2 vols, (Oxford 1861), I, pp. 39ff. cf. R. Spearman, *Life of John Hutchinson prefixed to A Supplement to the Works of John Hutchinson Esq.* (London 1765), pp. i-xiv.

[12] E. Churton to W. Gresley, 25 May 1846, Pusey MSS (Pusey House).

[13] *Tracts for the Times,* II, p. ii.

[14] W. Copeland to T. Bowdler, 6 December 1841. Copeland MSS (Pusey House). cf. W. Copeland, MS, 'Narrative of the Oxford Movement' (n.pl. n.d.), Copeland MSS (Pusey House). Newman helped to give credence to the alleged remark. See John Henry Newman, *Apologia Pro Vita Sua* (London 1864), p. 94.

[15] Draft of Gladstone's article, 'Present Aspect of the Church', in *Foreign and Colonial Review* (1843), MS Add. 44360 f. 250, Gladstone MSS (British Library).

[16] H. J. Rose to J. H. Newman, 9 May 1836, in J. W. Burgon, *Lives of Twelve Good Men* (London 1889), p. 108.

[17] See Newman's comment about 'the growing consensus of the episcopal bench against catholic truth', J. H. Newman to E. B. Pusey, 24 August 1842, Pusey MSS (Pusey House). cf. J. H. Newman to H. A. Woodgate, 8 November 1841, MS Eng. Lett. d. 102 f. 103 (Bodleian). See Keble's comment on the bishops: 'I see few signs of good information among them', J. Keble to J. T. Coleridge, 24 November 1841, MS Eng. Lett. d. 134 f. 37 (Bodleian).

[18] *Testimonies to Church Principles, selected from Episcopal Charges and Sermons* (London 1843), p. 5.

[19] *British Critic,* 33 (January 1843), p. 274.

[20] J. H. Browne to C. P. Golightly, 9 June 1842, MS 1804 f. 106, Golightly MSS (Lambeth Palace).

[21] W. Goode to C. P. Golightly, 29 May 1843, MS 1804 f.108, Golightly MSS (Lambeth Palace).

[22] W. N. Molesworth, *History of the Church of England from 1660* (London 1882), p. 317.

[23] C. Bethell, *A Charge to the Clergy of the Diocese of Bangor* (London 1843), pp. 15-16.

[24] W. Stevens to J. Boucher, 11 September 1793, B/3/38 Boucher MSS, Locker-Lampson Coll. (East Sussex County Record Office, Lewes).

[25] C. Wordsworth, *Annals of my Early Life 1806-1846* (London 1891), p. 330. cf. E. Churton, *Memoir of Joshua Watson* (1861), I, pp. 130-1.

[26] W. Jones, *Memoirs of the Life, Studies, and Writings of the Rt. Rev. George Horne,* DD (London 1795), p. 22.

[27] In 'Home Thoughts from Abroad', first published in *British Magazine,* Newman argued that the 'element of high-churchmanship (as that word has common been understood) seems about to retreat again into the depths of the Christian temper, and apostolicity is to be elicited instead, in greater measure . . . high churchmanship looking at the matter historically—will be regarded as a temporary stage of a course . . . I give up high-churchmanship'. *British Magazine,* 9 (March 1836), p. 358. Newman later came to identify the Anglican system per se, as Erastian: John Henry Newman, *Certain Difficulties Felt by Anglicans in Catholic Teaching Considered* (London 1850), p. 112.

[28] W. J. Copeland to M. A. Copeland, 3 May 1836, Copeland MSS (Pusey House).

[29] J. M. Neale, 'The Laudian Reformation Compared with that of the Nineteenth Century', in *Lectures Principally on the Church Difficulties of the Present Time* (London 1852), p. 172.

[30] For a classic statement of this high church interpretation of the supremacy, see J. Reeves, *Considerations on the Coronation Oath to maintain the Protestant Reformed Religion and the Settlement of the Church of England* (London 1801), p. 22.

[31] G. D. Faussett, *The Alliance of Church and State Explained and Vindicated* (Oxford 1834), p. 11. cf. S. Wilberforce, *A History of the Protestant Episcopal Church in America* (London 1844).

[32] H. J. Rose to H. H. Norris, 4 November 1826, Norris MSS (Bodleian). W. F. Hook, staunch old high church friend of the Tractarians and admirer of the American church, also dissociated himself from Bishop Hobart's criticisms. See J. McVicar, ed., *The Early and Professional Years of Bishop Hobart . . . with a Preface Containing a History of the Church in America, by W. F. Hook* (Oxford 1838), p. iii. For Hobart's strictures, see J. H. Hobart, *The United States of America Compared with Some European Countries, Particularly England; in a Discourse Delivered in Trinity Church, in the City of New York, October 1825, with an Introduction and Notes* (London 1826), pp. 19-35.

[33] M. Watson, MS, 'Reminiscences', J. Watson to C. Wordsworth (jun.), 7 September 1852, f.348 Watson MSS (Torquay). For Watson's attempt to convert Hobart to the old high Anglican ideal of Establishment, see E. Churton, *Memoir of Joshua Watson,* II, p. 155.

[34] E. Churton to W. J. Copeland, 30 May 1840, Churton MSS (Sutton Coldfield).

[35] For evidence of the high, divine-right, 'Jacobite' Toryism of the early Tractarians, see especially Edward Bouverie Pusey, *Patience and Confidence the Strength of the Church: a Sermon preached on the fifth of November, before the University of Oxford at St Mary's* (Oxford 1837). Even prior to Pusey's sermon, the moderate Evangelical *Christian Observer* was accusing the Tractarians of wishing 'to restore the doctrines and practices of Laud and Sacheverell'. Among these doctrines the old Tory notions of non-resistance and passive obedience were listed as figuring prominently: *Christian Observer,* 37 (September 1837), p. 586. In similar vein, Thomas Arnold referred to the Tractarians as 'Church Tories' in the mould of the 'high flyers' of the reign of Queen Anne: T. Arnold, 'The Oxford Malignants', *Edinburgh Review,* 63 (April 1836), p. 235. On this politically Tory aspect of early Tractarianism, see Peter Nockles, 'Pusey and the Question of Church and State', in Perry Butler, ed., *Pusey Rediscovered* (London 1983), pp. 275-82.

[36] W. Ward, *William George Ward and the Oxford Movement* (London 1889), p. 214. Newman went to great lengths to keep what for high churchmen was a special day of observance, King Charles the Martyr's day, on 30 January. The entry in his diary for 30 January 1836 reads: 'The martyrdom. Tried to find church open in vain'! T. Gornall (ed.), *The Letters and Diaries of John Henry Newman* (London 1981), V, p. 216. The cult of the 'Royal Martyr' in high church Anglicanism was manifested as late as 1879, with Charles Phillimore's edition of the Royal 'Martyrology', *Eikon Bazilikeh: the Portraiture of his Sacred Majestie in his Solitudes and*

Sufferings, first published in 1648, and claimed by high churchmen to have been the spiritual manual of Charles I himself, while imprisoned by the Parliamentarians in the Isle of Wight.

[37] See Newman's declaration in a letter to the *British Magazine* in 1834: 'If it be said that the act of settlement secures to the people certain liberties, I reply that the coronation oath has secured to the church its liberties also to the utter annulment of all former precedents of tyranny—and that we stand by that oath as our law as well as our sovereign's sanction and acknowledgement of it, and that any power in the state that innovates on the spirit of that oath tyrannises over us.' T. Gornall, ed., *Letters and Diaries of J. H. Newman*, V, p. 164.

[38] See Copeland's comment to Pusey in 1864: 'The political element, the reform bill, had not any effect in producing the "Tracts for the Times".' W. Copeland to E. B. Pusey, 30 October 1864, Pusey MSS (Pusey House). For discussion of this point, see Peter Nockles, 'Pusey and the Question of Church and State', pp. 257-61.

[39] E. R. Norman, *Church and Society in England, 1770-1970: an historical study* (London 1976), p. 22.

[40] 'The Oxford Margaret Professor', *British Critic*, 30 (July 1841), pp. 214-43. cf. E. A. Knox, *The Tractarian Movement*, pp. 302-3.

[41] G. D. Faussett, *The Claims of the Established Church to Exclusive Attachment and Support, and the Dangers which Menace her from Schism and Indifference*, Bampton Lectures (Oxford 1820), p. 313.

[42] ibid. p. 316.

[43] John Henry Newman, Tract 41, *Via Media II*, pp. 3-4.

[44] Faussett, *The Claims of the Established Church*, pp. 9-12.

[45] J. H. Spry, *Christian Unity Doctrinally and Historically Considered*, Bampton Lectures for 1816 (Oxford 1817), p. 189.

[46] *Christian Remembrancer*, 3 (March 1821), p. 157.

[47] J. Watson to H. H. Norris, n.d., Norris MSS (Bodleian Library). cf. J. J. Watson, *The Divine Commission and Perpetuity of the Christian Priesthood as Considered in a Charge to the Clergy of the Archdeaconry of St Albans at his Primary Visitation . . . in . . . 1816*, reprinted (London 1839).

[48] J. Oxlee, *A Sermon, in which all Due and Lawful Claim of the Protestant Dissenters to any Part of the Christian Ministry is Further Disproved and Rejected* (York 1821), p. 71.

[49] J. M. Neale, 'The Laudian Reformation Compared with that of the Nineteenth Century', in *Lectures on Church Difficulties*, pp. 181-3.

[50] As Ralph Churton explained, 'this charge, unfounded, as it is, can only be refuted by showing . . . that the points which compelled us to separate from the Church of Rome, were matters not merely wrong, but highly sinful'. R. Churton, *An Answer to a Letter from Francis Eyre of Warkworth* (London 1796), p. 12.

[51] See especially T. Burgess, *Tracts on the Origin and Independence of the Ancient British Church, on the Supremacy of the Pope, and the Inconsistency of all Foreign Jurisdiction with the British Constitution, and on the Differences between the Churches of England and Rome* (London 1815).

[52] Bishop Burgess does appear to have been a notable exception, as Bishop Kaye's comment to W. F. Hook in 1842 makes clear: 'it is well for you that Bishop Burgess is not alive. You would otherwise be called to strict account for setting forth Augustine, as the founder under God, of the Church of England'. J. Kaye to W. F. Hook, 22 January 1842, No. 15 Hook MSS (Bucklebury-Coatalen).

[53] J. Oxlee, *Three Letters addressed to Mr C. Wellbeloved, Tutor of the Unitarian College, York; Being Occasioned by his Epistolatory Attack on a Late Visitation Charge of the Ven. and Rev. Francis Wrangham,* MA, *Archdeacon of Cleveland* (York 1824), pp. 42-3.

[54] S. H. Cassan, *Lives of the Bishops of Winchester*, 2 vols (London 1827), II, p. 16.

[55] S. Wix, *Christian Union without the Abuses of Popery: a Letter to the Rt. Rev. The Lord Bishop of St David's, in reply to his Lordship's Letter entitled 'Popery Incapable of Union with a Protestant Church'* (London 1820), pp. 16-17. cf. B. and M. Pawley, *Rome and Canterbury through Four Centuries* (London 1974), pp. 110-11.

[56] J. H. Newman, *A Letter Addressed to the Rev. R. W. Jelf in Explanation of No. 90 in a Series called the 'Tracts for the Times' by the Author* (Oxford 1841), pp. 8-12. On Bishop Lloyd as a formative influence in the origins of the Oxford Movement, especially by instilling knowledge of the Roman breviary, see F. Oakeley, *Historical Notes on the Tractarian Movement* (London 1865), pp. 12-14. cf. id. 'Catholicism Fifty Years Ago', *Contemporary Review* (June 1879), p. 469. See also W. J.

Baker, *Beyond Port and Prejudice: Charles Lloyd of Oxford, 1784-1829* (Orono, Maine 1981), pp. 214-15.

[57] S. Wix, *Reflections Concerning the Expediency of a Council of the Church of England and the Church of Rome Being Holden, with a View to Accommodate Religious Differences, and to Promote the Unity of Religion in the Bond of Peace* (London 1818), p. 13.

[58] H. H. Norris to R. Churton, 30 September 1812, Churton MSS (Sutton Coldfield).

[59] Francis Huyshe republished the sermon as *A Tract for All Times, but Most Eminently for the Present* (London 1839).

[60] T. Arnold to E. Hawkins, 4 November 1835, in A. P. Stanley, *Life and Correspondence of Thomas Arnold*, DD, 2 vols (London 1845), p. 17.

[61] T. Arnold to R. Whately, 4 May 1836, in ibid. II, p. 34.

[62] R. Whately to E. Hawkins, 11 September 1836, Hawkins MSS (Oriel College).

[63] J. H. Newman, *The Arians of the Fourth Century* (London 1833), pp. 147-9.

[64] See Newman's defence of the principle to Hugh James Rose: 'I have no reason to change my mind about it - and that the Bishop of Lincoln [Kaye] grants that Clement holds it.' J. H. Newman to H. J. Rose, 15 December 1836, in Gornall, ed., *Letters and Diaries of J. H. Newman*, V, p. 178.

[65] J. H. Newman to J. E. Tyler, 5 March 1836, Newman MSS, No. 84 (Birmingham Oratory).

[66] John Henry Newman, Tract 85, *Lectures on the Scripture Proofs of the Doctrines of the Church*, p. 5.

[67] E. Hawkins, *Dissertation Upon the Use and Importance of Unauthoritative Tradition* (Oxford 1819), p. 64.

[68] cf. C. J. Abbey and J. H. Overton, *English Church in the Eighteenth Century* (London 1878), I, p. 136.

[69] Brilioth, *The Anglican Revival*, p. 45.

[70] ibid.

[71] C. Daubeny, *A Guide to the Church in Several Discourses . . . to Which is Prefixed Some Account of the Author's Life and Writings* (London 1830), p. xi.

[72] ibid. p. lxvi.

[73] J. Jebb to C. A. Ogilvie, 16 June 1820, MS Eng. Lett. d.123 f.141 (Bodleian). cf. C. Forster, ed., *Thirty Years' Correspondence between John Jebb and Alexander Knox*, 2nd edn, 2 vols (London 1836), II, p. 4.

[74] Bishop J. Walker to H. H. Norris, 25 September 1839, Norris MSS (Bodleian).

[75] J. S. Harford, *Life of Thomas Burgess* (London 1840), p. 182.

[76] W. Jones, *Memoirs of George Horne* DD, p. 22.

[77] Quoted in W. R. Stephens, *Life and Letters of Walter Farquhar Hook*, 2 vols (London 1878), I, p. 97. cf. *Catalogue of the Extensive and Valuable Library of the Late Thomas Rennell* DD, *Dean of Winchester* (London 1840), p. viii.

[78] W. Jones, *Memoirs of George Horne* DD, p. 44.

[79] R. Southey, *Book of the Church*, 2 vols (London 1824), I, p. 16. For similar anti-ascetic attitudes among pre-Tractarian high churchmen, see G. Nott's Bampton Lectures for 1802, *Religious Enthusiasm* (Oxford 1803), pp. 339-40. cf. R. Polwheele, ed., *The Enthusiasm of Methodists and Papists Compared*, new edn of Bishop Lavington's 1749 work (London 1833). See Hook's explanation of his high church mother's view of the movement, to Pusey: 'She has the old notions of the last century, considers all you are doing as enthusiasm', W. F. Hook to E. B. Pusey, 10 October 1840, Pusey MSS (Pusey House).

[80] S. Gilley, 'Nationality and Liberty, Protestant and Catholic: Robert Southey's "Book of the Church" ', in S. Mews, ed., *Religion and National Identity*, Studies in Church History, XVIII (Oxford 1982), p. 420. For Southey's advocacy of Church of England nunneries and celibacy of the clergy, see R. Southey, *Sir Thomas More; or Colloquies on the Progress and Prospects of Society*, 2 vols (London 1829), I, pp. 93, 154-5, 339-40; II, pp. 37, 228.

[81] E. Churton to W. Gresley, 10 May 1842, Pusey MSS (Pusey House).

[82] E. Churton to W. Gresley, 7 April 1840, Pusey MSS (Pusey House).

[83] E. Churton, *Biography of the Early Church* (London 1840), p. vi.

[84] C. Marriott to J. H. Newman, 10 January 1842, Ollard MSS (Pusey House).

[85] Newman, *Arians of the Fourth Century*, pp. 149-52. As Copeland explained, 'People have got to learn that true piety lies too deep to be always in the tongue, and

is too sublime to be talked about.' W. Copeland to M. A. Copeland, 4 November 1836, Copeland MSS (Pusey House).

[86] W. Copeland, MS, 'Narrative of the Oxford Movement', Copeland MSS (Pusey House).

[87] W. Teale, 'William Jones', in *Lives of English Divines* (London 1846), p. 363.

[88] C. Daubeny, *A Charge Delivered to the Clergy of the Archdeaconry of Sarum* (London 1824), p. 8.

[89] H. H. Norris to R. Churton, 4 March 1813, Churton MSS (Sutton Coldfield).

[90] G. Horne, *An apology for Certain Gentlemen in the University of Oxford, Aspersed, in a Late Anonymous Pamphlet* (Oxford 1756), p. 14. cf. G. Watson, *A Seasonable Admonition to the Church of England: a sermon preached before the University of Oxford at St Mary's* (Oxford 1751), p. 14. Edward Churton's view of the impact of Horne's sermons and writings at Oxford is significant: 'Bishop Horne, long before he was bishop, had as much influence on the minds of the young men at Oxford, as ever Newman or Pusey have lately had', and was 'attacked much in the same way by the high and dry or latitudinarian party', E. Churton to W. Gresley, 25 May 1846, Pusey MSS (Pusey House).

[91] W. Copeland, MS, 'Narrative of the Oxford Movement', Copeland MSS (Pusey House).

[92] Quoted in J. Coulson, *Newman and the Common Tradition: a study in the language of Church and society* (London 1970), p. 58.

[93] J. Keble, ed., *Works of. . . Richard Hooker,* 3rd edn, 3 vols (Oxford 1845), I, pp. xci-xcii.

[94] See Newman's remark to Sir James Stephen, how Butler's 'wonderfully gifted intellect caught the idea which had actually been the rule of the primitive church, of teaching the more sacred truths by rites and ceremonies'. J. H. Newman to J. Stephen, 16 March 1835, MS Add. 7349 f.138. (Cambridge Univ. Lib.).

[95] W. Jones, *A Course of Lectures on the Figurative Language of Holy Scripture and the Interpretation of it from Scripture Itself, Delivered in the Parish Church of Nayland in Suffolk, in the Year 1786* (London 1786), p. 9.

[96] ibid. pp. 318-19. cf. T. Wilson, *Ornaments of Churches Considered: A Sermon Preached Before the University of Oxford, at St Mary's* (Oxford 1761), p. 97. Another late-eighteenth century 'Hutchinsonian' high churchman, the American loyalist Jonathan Boucher, likewise stressed the 'peculiar sacredness of places of worship', and was highly critical of latitudinarianism, indifferentism or mere utilitarianism, on the subject, *Anti-Jacobin Review,* 2 (March 1799), p. 411.

[97] J. H. Newman, *Parochial and Plain Sermons* (London 1879), p. 28.

[98] For evidence of this, see E. B. Pusey to Bishop R. Bagot, 26 September 1837, Pusey MSS (Pusey House). cf. P. Maurice, *The Popery of Oxford Confronted, Disavowed and Repudiated* (London 1837).

[99] R. D. Middleton, *Magdalen Studies* (London 1936), p. 15.

[100] T. Sanders, *A Practical Sermon on the Nature of Public Worship* (Oxford 1801), pp. 11-12.

[101] C. Daubeny, *A Guide to the Church,* p. xviii.

[102] W. Copeland, MS, 'Narrative of the Oxford Movement', Copeland MSS (Pusey House).

[103] E. Churton, *Memoir of Joshua Watson,* I, pp. 139-40; II, p. 131. For instance, an American churchman, Philander Chase, noted on a visit to Manchester in 1823, 'Prayers are read and the psalms chanted every day in the Old Cathedral Church', *Bishop Chase's Reminiscences,* 2 vols (Boston 1848), I, p. 218. Magdalen College Chapel under George Horne also set a high ceremonial standard. See R. D. Middleton, *Newman and Bloxam* (London 1947), p. 26; and H. Best, *Four Years in France* (London 1826).

[104] Quoted in E. Churton, *Memoir of Joshua Watson,* II, pp. 201-2.

[105] E. B. Pusey to J. Watson, 30 October 1839, Pusey MSS (Pusey House). cf. E. B. Pusey to J. H. Newman, 11 September 1839, Pusey MSS (Pusey House); and E. B. Pusey, *A Letter to Richard, Lord Bishop of Oxford, on the Tendency to Romanism of Doctrines held now as of old in the English Church* (Oxford 1839).

[106] J. Keble to J. H. Newman, 8 August 1833, in I. Ker and T. Gornall, eds., *Letters and Diaries of J. H. Newman,* IV, p. 23.

[107] See Churton's comment, 'The Church at large will think, as I feel more than half inclined to think myself, that the principles of the juniors at Oxford has destroyed all natural respect for the aged and honourable.' E. Churton to E. B. Pusey, 9 December 1841, Pusey MSS (Pusey House).

[108] E. Churton to W. J. Copeland, 10 August 1841, Churton MSS (Sutton Coldfield).

[109] *Christian Remembrancer,* 3 (April 1841), p. 426. See Thomas Mozley's comment in 1841, that those who joined the movement were 'not what was called high church some thirty years since', *British Critic,* 30 (July 1841), p. 226.

[110] M. Watson, MS, 'Reminiscences', f.166, '16 May 1845', Watson MSS (Torquay).

[111] E. Churton, *Memoir of Joshua Watson,* II, p. 169.

[112] H. J. Rose to H. E. Manning, 20 March 1837, V, No. 40, Manning MSS (Bodleian).

[113] E. Churton to W. Gresley, 5 June 1846, Pusey MSS (Pusey House).

[114] E. Churton to J. C. Crosthwaite, 13 April 1842, MS Eng. Misc. e.117 f.135, Crosthwaite MSS (Bodleian).

[115] G. H. Tavard, *The Quest for Catholicity: a study in Anglicanism* (London 1963), p. 173.

[116] G. A. Poole, *The Present State of Parties in the Church of England,* 2nd edn (London 1842), p. 11.

THE OXFORD MOVEMENT AND EDUCATION

Timothy Corcoran, S. J. (essay date 1926)

SOURCE: "Liberal Studies and Moral Aims: A Critical Survey of Newman's Position," in *Thought,* Vol. 1, No. 1, June, 1926, pp. 54-71.

[In the following essay, Corcoran examines Newman's late essay "Discourses on University Education," an elaboration of the methods and goals of liberal education, which "must not be 'burdened' or 'implicated' with virtue or religion."]

I

Seventy-five years have elapsed since, in the interval between the Falls of 1851 and 1852, John Henry Newman composed, delivered publicly, and issued in book form his "Discourses on University Education."

Rare indeed are those treatises in English, setting forth a theory of education, which can be praised as being not only sustained expositions of constructive thought, but also choice models of that high dignity of style and mastery of expression befitting an arduous synthesis of intellectual principles. Such a union of matter and form is found in Plato and Quintilian, writers on education during the Classical Period. It is found again in Sadolet, Vives, and Muretus, during that reversion to classical ideals in education which was so marked a characteristic of Renaissance culture. It was not the possession of Milton or Locke, or of any other English writer, until in the middle of the last century Newman composed in England, and delivered in Dublin, his "Discourses on the Scope and Nature of University Education, addressed to the Catholics of Dublin." The weekly parts into which these "Discourses" were divided were in the early winter of 1852 published in that city; were recast and condensed some seven years later; and are now entitled "The Idea of a University, Defined and Illustrated." Within the past twenty-five years the influence of Newman's method of stating his views on education, no less than that of his views in themselves, has become widespread. Sir A. Quiller-Couch, at Cambridge, has directed special attention to this one work of Newman, and he has had notable echoes in America. Even the London *Times,* when in December, 1915, it declared itself, characteristically, in the words:

> Newman has not been accepted as a great educational writer, except by Roman Catholics of the intellectual type. We understand that there is one British University in which teachers-in-training read his work as a "set book," but that is a Catholic University,

yet subjoined the excellent advice:

> We venture to urge the the re-reading of Newman's work for its educational stimulus as well as for its literary style.

On both these issues, indeed, "The Idea of a University" will most amply repay reflective study. To trace that "idea" through the preface and the nine discourses to which the original ten (the weekly addresses delivered in Dublin in the spring and summer of 1852) are now reduced, and to expound it in its recurrent forms, is a splendid intellectual exercise. In no section of the "Discourses" is there a finer sample of Newman's superb power than in the three devoted to the definition and illustration of his concept of liberal education. *Knowledge Its Own End, Knowledge Viewed in Relation to Learning, Knowledge Viewed in Relation to Professional Skill* form a unit in themselves, with a specific aim and a clear-cut result in the field of thought—an aim and a result summarized in the first of the three titles, and so furnishing a line of solution for the problems raised in the two sequels. The definition of Newman's "idea" is always recurrent, but always presents a new facet or aspect of its content. Illustration is varied, cumulative, superbly suasive throughout these three discourses on knowledge. Newman was not mistaken in his choice of a definitive title. He excelled in defining and illustrating his "idea," and both aspects of his literary art will richly reward the keenest analytical examination.

Oriel College, Oxford University, Oxfordshire, England

That his idea of liberal knowledge, declared in his own words to be "the scope of a university," was fully open to critical investigation, Newman himself was conscious. Three separate strands of evidence as to his state of mind on this dominant issue, all falling within the years 1851-1854, may be here adduced in a summary form. He wrote his *Introductory* in the autumn of 1851, and in it affirmed that he was about to expound an idea which he had really lived at Oxford, and which was absolutely unaltered since. "The views. . . . have grown into my whole system of thought, and are, as it were, part of myself. Many changes has my mind gone through; here it has known no variation or vacillation of opinion." He was going, as he declared in writing to himself, to "import into Ireland: . . . Oxford. . . . in its principles, ways, methods, and arguments." He claimed that these Oxford principles were consonant with the idea of a Catholic university which it was his mission to organize and direct; for

> the principles, which I can now set forth under the sanction of the Catholic Church, were my profession at that early period of my life. . . . They did but take greater hold upon me as I. . . . approached in sentiment and desire to Catholicism; and my sense of their truth has been increased with the experience of every year since I have been brought within its pale.

But he was quite conscious that his concept of university education, the Oxford concept, was open to critical review; this avowal he made immediately after the avowal of the unchanged state of his mind.

> The principles I would maintain on the subject of Liberal Education, although those, as I believe, of the Catholic Church, are such as may be gained by the mere experience of life. . . . they are dictated by that human prudence and wisdom which is attainable where grace is quite away. . . . They may be held by Protestants as well as by Catholics; they may. . . . be taught by Protestants to Catholics.

This "true Philosophy of Education," whose principles are "those of the Catholic Church," might, he declared, "be understood better and held more firmly, by Protestants than by ourselves," possibly just because it is a philosophy "founded on truths in the natural order." The views here advanced amount to an assertion that the philosophy of education which was lived, elaborated, and maintained at Oxford in the generation before the year 1845, three centuries after Oxford had quitted the fold of Catholic education and Catholic truth, yet embodied "the principles of the Catholic Church on the subject of Liberal Education." The strength of this assertion, too, is obviously not unconnected with the view that this "true philosophy of education" is just a natural science. On both these issues, and on many matters of fact implicit in them, there was evidently room for critical discussion.

That Newman soon had cause to realize this, is made clear by a remarkable *Introduction,* which in the Dublin edition of 1852 was apparently intended to be placed between the *Preface* (of twenty-five pages) and the first or *Introductory Discourse* actually delivered. That *Introduction* was of scarcely one page in length; it is found in one copy alone, as far as can be ascertained, of that first edition of the "Discourses;" and it has at its conclusion the following clause: "(*To the binder of the volume.* Cancel this introduction.)" The binder failed to do so in one instance, which enables the contents of that one page to be cited here:

> As misconceptions may arise with regard to some of the points treated in the following pages, in consequence of the impossibility of introducing at once all the safeguards and explanations which they respectively require, the Author would observe,
>
> 1. That he is treating here of the object of a University in the *abstract* and in its *idea;* 2. that, as such, its object is *knowledge,* as such; 3. but that a *Catholic* University will, in all its regulations and appointments, and in its routine, distinctly recognise Catholicism; and 4. that for its integrity, though not for its essence, it ought to be invested with a *coercive* power, enforcing order, discipline, and religious and moral behaviour on its subjects.

Some of the phrases of this cancelled introduction (those under clauses 1, 2, especially), were later on inserted incidentally in the recast English edition, in scattered places. The impression which this page leaves is fairly clear. Discussion had arisen in the months of the summer and early autumn of 1852 as to the compatibility of the Oxford idea of liberal knowledge and the Oxford philosophy of education, as affirmed in the *Preface* and expounded in ten "Discourses," with the Catholic concept of a Catholic university. The *Preface,* though specially written later than the "Discourses"—issued every week in parts, while being delivered at the Dublin Rotunda—was for a while at least felt by Newman not to have removed all grounds for a critical attitude towards his declaration of principles.

That there were evident grounds for such a critical attitude was realized by Newman himself when he came to examine the commission to organize the Catholic University of Ireland issued by Pope Pius IX by his Brief *Optime noscitis,* dated March 20, 1854. In this fully explicit letter of direction, the Holy See declared its surprise that the Catholic University had not been constituted, and referred to the apostolic confirmation of the decrees of the National Synod of 1850 on its establishment and to the subsequent apostolic letters issued on May 3, 1852, to the same effect. A meeting of the Irish episcopate was now directed to be held under the presidency of the Apostolic Delegate, Archbishop Cullen, at Dublin, with its primary business defined as the making of speedy arrangements for the erection and opening of "this Catholic University." The exceptionally important Brief concludes with a fully explicit definition of what "this Catholic University" must be, in its aims, spirit, and methods of education. Here is affirmed "The Idea of a University" as conceived by the Holy See, and directed to be realized forthwith in Ireland. The organizing assembly, writes Pope Pius IX to the bishops of Ireland, is to be the place where

> Episcopal solicitude will prompt the taking of timely measures to ensure that the university will fully correspond to the dignity and the inviolate character of the name of Catholic which adorns it. It will be the task of the Bishops to exert the most watchful care in providing that our Divine religion will be the soul of the entire academic education. Therefore, let the holy fear and reverence of God be cherished and developed, the deposit of Faith be kept intact; let all branches of science expand in the closest alliance with religion, all types of study be enlightened by the bright rays of Catholic truth, and the educative force of sound teaching be rigorously maintained. Whatever is uttered from the supreme See of St. Peter, Prince of the Apostles, the entirely safe haven for the whole Catholic communion, the mother and mistress of all churches, is to be believed and received as Catholic. Whatever differs from that teaching is to be vigorously and unflinchingly rejected. Let all errors and all novelties from secular sources be repelled and cast out. Let the professors of the university show themselves in all ways models of well-doing, in their teaching and in their integrity and dignity of life. They should have nothing more at heart than to fashion with all care the minds of young men to the practice of religion, to uprightness of conduct, and all virtuous dealing; and to educate them zealously in letters and sciences according to the mind of the Church Catholic, the pillar and the guarantee of truth.

The Brief concludes by mention of the previous choice of Dr. Newman as rector of the new university; and in approving of it, with mention of his conspicuous personal qualities and knowledge and religious zeal, expressed the Pope's will that he should enter on the duties of his office.

On the concluding section of this important letter expressing the aims and requirements of the Holy See in erecting the Catholic University of Ireland, Newman would appear to have pondered deeply. The official "Life of John Henry Cardinal Newman" by Wilfrid Ward (I., 368), gives us a brief but sufficient extract from Newman's personal records, to let us see that the writer of "The Idea of a University" gave marked attention to the profound distinction between what one may call the "Oxford idea" and the Roman and Catholic concept of the scope, nature, and aims of the university which Newman was now about to administer. His notes run as follows. (Here, as elsewhere in quotations, the italics have been added by the present writer.)

> *"Divina nostra religio tanquam anima totius litterariae institutionis;"* that is, the form. *"Omnes disciplinae"* are to go forward in the most strict league with religion; that is, with the assumption of Catholic doctrine in their intrinsic treatment; and the professors are directly to mould, *"totis viribus,"* the youth to piety and virtue, and to guard them, in literature and science, in conformity with the Church's teaching. *I wrote on a different idea my "Discourses on University Education" in 1852.*

The traditional character of the idea of a university so finely and so amply expressed in the concluding section of the Roman letter of 1854 will be obvious to all students of education who are conversant with the creative age of European universities, that is, from the twelfth century to the close of the fifteenth. This concept was fully maintained in the Renaissance as well as in the Middle Ages; it was characteristic of Newman's own University of Oxford in the epoch of its European influence and of its academic greatness. At that time its faculty of arts issued into and was knit closely to its great professional faculties: like every European university, its function was to produce trained professional workers for expert service in Church and State. When the religious revolt came, and when Oxford accepted the injunction of the Tudors to abandon all teaching of canon law, the organized study of theology and of all the other professional sciences wilted and died away. The same decay affected the major or scientific studies of the faculty of arts. The four advanced sections of the traditional seven liberal arts, the pure and the applied sciences, also became atrophied; they had been the natural route from language studies into professional studies. Newman provides in his seventh discourse, on *Knowledge Viewed in Relation to Professional Skill,* his list of university subjects fitted for giving "real exercise [to] the judgment," a "rule of selection by which the different parts of learning may be classed for our purpose." It does not contain any exact or applied science, nor any professional subject. He was, indeed, as he expressly declared, ousting them from their historic position in European universities. "I am arguing, and I shall argue, against Professional or Scientific Knowledge as the sufficient end of a University education." What he had set himself to do was to formulate a philosophy of education that would afford a justification of the actual academic position of Oxford in his own times. There it had come to pass that the preliminary or language section of the historic faculty of arts (all the later branches and all the subsequent professional schools having perished in decay) had assumed to itself the entire functions and scope of a university. That fragment called for a philosophy of self-justification, and this new philosophy of education was superbly formulated by Newman in the discourses on his idea of a university. If the citadel of his university could be defended, it would have been defended by his mighty pen. His argument was rigorous, coherent, unflinching in its assertions and in its avowals; with admirable fearlessness he traced out all its consequences. But the consequences were startling indeed; and when he read the enunciation of the only true "idea of a university" in the clear and decisive utterances of the Holy See, he found himself confronted with the traditional doctrine of Christian Europe, and realized that he himself, two years before, had formulated "a different idea," the Oxford philosophy of liberal education, new in the world of European culture, and by no means true.

II

What was this philosophy of education, this justification of Oxford to itself, which proved divergent from the broad current of cultural tradition? It may be briefly set forth in Newman's own terms, both as to its originating postulates and as to its explicit consequences. It is set out by Newman in the three discourses on the nature of liberal knowledge, which are the intellectual core and seed-bed of his whole work on the scope and nature of a university.

"Knowledge *which is its own end* I call Liberal Knowledge; I educate for it: I make it *the scope of a University.*" "That alone is liberal knowledge which stands on its own pretensions, which is independent of sequel, expects no complement." A game of cricket is bodily exercise, and is "liberal;" a treatise on surgery is intellectual, and has no "liberal" quality, because it is professional. Commerce "affords scope for the highest and most diversified powers of mind," but is not liberal at all. "The highest pursuits lose the specific character [of being] liberal when they minister to something beyond them;" the very nobility of their end makes them the farther from being "liberal." "Theology, if represented by the catechism, loses the particular attribute" of being liberal; to keep that attribute, it must remain in the speculative order, must be its own end, must not be useful or yield fruit. Applied in the catechism, or used "for the purpose of the pulpit," it ceases to be liberal, just "as a labourer's hand loses its delicateness." No wonder, then, that if students at a university "use physical sciences for the purpose of fruit," if they apply chemistry or physiology to medicine, for instance, their studies cease to be liberal, just as when theological science is used for preaching or for teaching Christian truth. It is of the essence of liberal knowledge that it be "its own end;" it must serve no other end, however intellectually or morally great, under penalty of "losing its specific character" of being "liberal." This liberal knowledge, "self-sufficient and complete" in itself, is "the scope of a University;" and, having "its end in itself, it has its use in itself also."

That use must be strictly "in itself": otherwise it ceases to be "liberal;" it is denatured, if the word may be borrowed from an applied science. It must not externate itself in work or results, under the same annihilating penalty. Hence it is strictly static, connoting a finished and completed "state of mind," "majestically calm," characterized by a "philosophical repose" which "is almost the repose of faith." A liberal education is to produce "a habit of mind which lasts through life, of which the attributes are freedom, equitableness, calmness, moderation, and wisdom"—attributes which do not include any element of work, service, or external action. Such is the scope of a university. No wonder that it excludes any "process of training by which the intellect is *formed or sacrificed* to some specific *profession,* or *study,* or *science,*" as Newman affirms. No wonder that the advancement of learning itself, in Newman's "The Idea of a University," has a cold welcome indeed. Its presence must be tolerated in deference to an unenlightened public opinion outside: but it must be made to realize that it is quite out of place; it comes too close to the concept of "professional" to be "liberal"—"the scope of a university." "Nor am I banishing, far from it, the possessors of deep and multifarious learning from my ideal University; *they adorn it in the eyes of men;* I do but say that *they constitute no type of the results at which it aims.*" As if such a statement were not an absolute decree of banishment in the academic order!

Yet this rigorous limitation of the scope of a university is only the basis and starting-point for another tremendous and far-reaching limitation established in Newman's idea of a university and philosophy of education. Had his concept reached its term in the doctrine set out above, and had he not given his principles their ultimate issue, the divergence between Newman's idea and the concept of the whole European tradition of education would not have struck himself so forcibly when he read the apostolic letter of March, 1854. His philosophy of education would remain an interesting mental plea for that Oxford of 1850 where, as Professor Adamson shows on contemporary evidence in his chapters in the "Cambridge History of English Literature" (reprinted August, 1925), out of over 1500 students, modern history could claim eight; chemistry, five and a half; botany, six; medicine, none; Arabic, Sanscrit, Anglo-Saxon, none; and the multitude, of one mind, were students of *litterae humaniores,* that liberal knowledge which is "its own end." But there is more. Newman was unflinching in facing the consequences of his own enunciation of what "Knowledge Its Own End" necessarily involved, not in the natural content and aims of liberal knowledge alone, but as to the far more serious issue of moral education.

Liberal education, to be "its own end. . . . self-sufficient and complete," to be able to "have its use in itself" and thereby "have its end in itself also," has to face squarely the issue of its relation to moral education. "Education is a high word: it is *commonly* spoken of in connection with religion and virtue," is a sentence which meets us in the sixth section of the discourse on *Knowledge Its Own End;* and the adverb is an advance signal. This common apprehension must be dissipated as regards liberal knowledge, the scope of a university. "For all its friends, or its enemies, may say, *I insist upon it, that it is as real a mistake to burden it with virtue or religion,* as with the mechanical arts." A far-reaching statement, this: it is so worded in the definitive English edition of the "Discourses," while in the first or Dublin edition of 1852 the concluding words are: "it is as real a mistake to *implicate* it with virtue or religion, as with the arts." The sense is substantially the same; both the metaphors are full of meaning. An entanglement, an extrinsic, imposed load—such is virtue, such is religion, in relation to a liberal education in its essence. Liberal knowledge is "an object as intelligible as the cultivation of virtue, while, at the same time, it is absolutely distinct from it." Knowledge is one thing, virtue is another;" liberal knowledge, the scope of a university, "however enlightened, gives *no* influential motives, *no* vivifying principles." It does its work in making "the gentleman," Newman declares; and "the gentleman, with a candid, equitable, dispassionate mind, a noble and courteous bearing in the *conduct of life,*" may quite at the same time, and as stated in the same sentence, be "profligate, heartless." The whole passage in the initial discourse on knowledge deserves the most careful study. Within even single sentences of the argument, the student will see the grounds on which many exponents of Newman's mind can base their contention that he was an anti-intellectualist; while others can adduce his reiterated declaration that "Liberal Education is *simply* the cultivation of *the intellect as such,* and its object is nothing more or less than intellectual excellence," as proof of the opposite view.

The results of this remarkable attempt to sever the intellectual from the moral elements in the one process which is called education may be observed also in a long passage of the second discourse on liberal knowledge. In it Newman affirms that the Oxford of the period 1750-1800, "which had no professors, or examinations at all, but merely brought a number of young men together for three or four years, and then sent them away," gave "discipline of the intellect," could "train, mould, enlarge the mind." He goes on to vouch that the public schools of England, similarly circumstanced, did the same; that "these Universities and scholastic institutions, with miserable deformities on the side of morals, and a heathen code of ethics, can boast of men conspicuous for great natural virtues, habits of business, cultivated tastes, accomplishments." How is this? Expressly setting aside "moral and religious considerations," as his special philosophy of education, already set out above, would assist him to do, he argues that "the conversation of all is a series of lectures to each, and they gain for themselves new ideas, and distinct *principles for judging and acting.*" "The youthful community will embody a specific idea, will administer a code of conduct, and will furnish principles of thought and action." "Here, then, *is real teaching, whatever be its standards and principles, true or false, it at least tends to the cultivation of the intellect.*" Words could not be found to make it more clear how fully the severance of the intellectual and the moral in education is made by this philosophy of education. It is equally evident, from the definite and concrete instances adduced and described in conclusive terms, that this severance was not limited to the realm of the "bare idea," or to "the abstract"; but that "real education," sundered from any consideration of the truth or falsity of its standards and principles, irrespective of "moral and religious considerations," could be and was and is an actual fact. Because it "tends to cultivate the intellect," whatever its morality or immorality, it can fully claim the noble title—that "high word," Education—as really its own, and its intrinsic right. It certainly can not be said that, on this line of thought, Newman failed to carry his philosophy of education to its ultimate issues in the real as well as in the ideal order.

The logical consequence of this doctrine of severance can be clearly traced in many passages of the "Discourses." "(Liberal) knowledge is a state or condition of mind;" it is static; it must not do any work, save in a strictly internal way. "Knowledge, indeed, when exalted into a scientific form, is also power"—"but that is a further consideration, with which I am not concerned." It must not be called wisdom: for the word wisdom "has a direct relation to conduct and to human life," and a university "professes to exercise the mind neither in art nor in duty;" it regards "research and system as ends in themselves, distinct from effects and works of any kind." And so on; the doctrine of severance, the rigid limitation of liberal education so as to be concerned with intellectual excellence, neither more nor less, is everywhere adduced. We are here far indeed from the European tradition voiced from the Eternal City in 1854 and in all the preceding ages—the doctrine, not of the severance of liberal education from the concepts of work and duty, but of the unity of the whole of humanity in the exercise of all its powers, expressly directed to moral and religious, no less than to intellectual ends.

The philosophical compatibility of all these ends in the actual as well as in the speculative order needs no demonstration here. It is well known to all students of ethical theory that this interrelation of multiple ends, intellectual and moral, can and ought to be effected; and that all of them can be conjointly impressed on action and on thought without any sacrifice or destruction of their individual completeness. The liberal character of scientific research in physical science, or of the surgeon's skill, is in no way lost by their being applied to national service or to individual welfare. Science does not lose its intrinsic character because it is applied to promote moral instruction or civic efficiency. It is in the realm of ends that Newman constructed this Philosophy of Severance and applied it to education in his "Discourses" of 1852. Speculative theology is liberal; it loses its liberalness if it is used for the purposes of the pulpit; it becomes a mere "art, or a business making use of Theology." The liberal and the useful are utterly distinct, and can not co-exist, "for the plain reason that one idea is not another idea." The highest pursuits lose this character of being liberal "when they minister to something beyond them;" and losing it, they find themselves quite outside the scope of a university. For one moment, in the first discourse on knowledge, he would appear to have contemplated the possible fusion of these aims. "The same person," he says, "may cultivate it [knowledge] in both ways [the liberal and the useful] at once." But the withdrawal of attention is immediate, when he proceeds to reflect that "this again is a matter foreign to my subject." In other words, such a fusion of ends, moral and intellectual, can not be contemplated in his idea of a university; for "Knowledge is one thing, Virtue is another," and liberal knowledge must not be "burdened" or "implicated" with virtue or religion. The practical consequences of any acceptance of this Philosophy of Severance as to the unitary process of education need not be dwelt on here. It is obvious that they could not be limited to one area of time or place—to university education in England, for instance. Admit such a concept, and it would have far-reaching effects in secondary and in primary education as well; effects that well deserve to be pondered over by students of Newman's theory as to the scope of the university.

III

The final topic connected with that theory or philosophy of education that can be alluded to in this brief examination now emerges. The scope of a university having been thus delimited, and its strictly intellectual and self-sufficient nature dissevered from all relation to, or influence on, moral results or any other, the query presents itself as to whether on the principles so laid down there could be a Catholic university at all? More especially, could there be a Catholic university in the sense of that great tradition so fully and authoritatively set forth in the apostolic letter of March, 1854, on the Catholic University of Ireland? Incidental phrases in the "Discourses" make it clear that Newman held this to be capable of realization in the actual order. "I say a University, taken in its *bare idea,* and *before we view it as an instrument of the Church,* has this object and mission: it contemplates neither moral impression nor mechanical production; its function is intellectual culture; it has done its work when it has done as much as this." The same idea recurs elsewhere in his text. The fact, however, is, that Newman's "bare idea" of a university intrinsically repels all possibility of the university's becoming an instrument of the Church at all, save at the cost of a transformation or annihilation of what he defines to be the scope of a university. That scope is liberal knowledge; and liberal knowledge, as he says, must lose its liberalness when it ministers to something beyond itself, when it is used, even by the Church. The fate of theology itself, highest of all liberal sciences when in the speculative order, is fully and fearlessly described by Newman as an illustration of his decisive policy with ideas. If applied to catechetical instruction or to the purposes of the pulpit, it is denatured, deliberalized; "it does lose the particular attribute I am illustrating: for Theology thus exercised is an art or a business making use of Theology." It alters its intrinsic nature; it "forfeits its rank," in his own phrase. It is no longer "simple knowledge," no longer liberal; and being no longer liberal, it is by definition outside the scope of a university. The conclusion seems inevitable, that if the Church "makes use of a university," it does so by transmuting the very nature of the studies done there, so that they are no longer within the true ambit of university studies at all.

This consideration is evidently one of great moment and of high seriousness. From it Newman endeavored to escape, in the introductory paragraph cited above as having been prepared for the Dublin edition of 1852 but afterwards canceled. The effort to find admission for the action of the Church and for the action of moral education—as an *integral,* not as an *essential* element—is not successful. The idea of the university formulated by Newman rejects, by its intrinsic constitution, those integrating characteristics which he would affix to it as an afterthought. For virtue and religion have been told in explicit terms that they would be a "burden" to liberal knowledge, the scope of a university, whose function is to be "simply the cultivation of the intellect as such." And were liberal knowledge to imagine it could aid religion or virtue, it would be utterly mistaken; any such effort would be "an encroachment on a province not its own, as the political economist who should maintain that his science educated him for diplomacy." The very illustration he uses might well have made Newman pause. But he insists that liberal knowledge, "however enlightened, however profound," can not effect connection with moral training: "it gives *no* command over the passions, *no* influential motives, no vivifying principles. Liberal education makes not the Catholic, but the gentleman."

Nor is this all. The route of escape from the same urgent difficulty, created by the very essence of his defined idea of a university and by his teaching that liberal knowledge, at the peril of its existence, must be and remain its own end, self-sufficient and complete, expecting no complement—that route of escape, sought for in the transient *Introduction* prepared later in the year 1852, was already cut off by the very first sentences of his first discourse on the *Scope and Nature of a University.* The destructive clause comes at the end of that opening paragraph, which must be given in full:

The view which these Discourses take of a University is of the following kind: that it is a place of *teaching* universal *knowledge.* This implies that its object is, on the one hand, *intellectual* not *moral;* and, on the other hand, that is is the diffusion and extension of knowledge rather than the advancement. If its object were scientific and philosophical discovery, I do not see why a University should have students; *if religious training, I do not see how it can be the seat of literature and science.*

The striking assertion of Newman in this sweeping clause is obviously quite divergent from the traditional concept enunciated in the letter of directions from the Holy See two years later. It was not without grounds that Newman said in his first Discourse: "I am investigating in the abstract, and am determining what is in itself right and true. For the moment, so to say, I know nothing of history. I have no concern with the past." Such an attitude in determining the scope and nature of university education has its palpable risks, and they made themselves felt with effect. The effect was that he missed the large view, that of the broader stream of university life and aims in the Europe of the Middle Ages and the Renaissance, and based his whole philosophy of education on a theory which expressly derived from, and sought to justify and vindicate, the Oxford which had quite strayed from the policies and aims of its age of greatness. It is not surprising that, having written on the idea of a university so as to "import into Ireland the principles, ways, methods, and arguments," of that Oxford of which he affirms that it had "grown into my whole system of thought," and which was, he said, "part of myself," a living experience as to which, despite many other changes in mind, he had undergone "no variation or vacillation of opinion," he found and admitted that his idea of a university had been quite different from that so clearly and authoritatively expressed by the See of Peter.

The definitive English edition of his "Idea" of 1852, issued after Newman had withdrawn from Ireland in 1857-58, shows that he had abated none of his views. But when at work in the Catholic University of Ireland, 1854-1857, he certainly carried out in main aims and in constructive practice the purposes of the Holy See and the needed practical called for by the situation in the Ireland of the day. He would probably have done more, had he been less closely connected with advisers having claims on his attention, based on the Oxford that he had lived in, the Oxford that he largely and generously tried to set aside in his years of initiation and organization at Dublin. For the valuable pioneer work he then planned and strove to carry out, Newman has never received a tithe of the credit due to him, either in Ireland or elsewhere. His official biographer did not show all his worth in the chapters on the Irish period published fifteen years ago. Much fuller justice has been done him, five years later, in an important official notice published within the United States. To its significance and to the value of the services to which it pays tribute, it will be a pleasure to recur on a future occasion.

William T. Noon (essay date 1965)

SOURCE: "Newman's 'Apologia'—1965: A Testament with a Special Meaning for all Christians in These Ecumenical Days," in *America,* Vol. 112, No. 18, May 1, 1965, pp. 631-36.

[*In the essay that follows, Noon characterizes Newman's* Apologia *as a "history of his religious opinions" and contends that this pioneering work stands as part of a Christian tradition of self-reflection.*]

There may be an appropriateness, during this seventh centenary of Dante's birth, in saluting John Henry Newman's *Apologia pro Vita Sua,* now in the 100th year after its appearance as a book. Both Dante and Newman are first-class Christian citizens and witnesses. Across the "dark backward and abysm of time," both continue to hold the attention of almost all who are now trying to live Christian lives of the imagination and the mind. Newman, especially, speaks our own language. And he speaks it, as it were, in the diaspora—long after Dante's ideal of an earthly Christian commonwealth has for most of us faded away.

Even before the *Apologia*'s centenary year, the life and thought of Newman were receiving increased attention. Meriol Trevor's two-volume biography, *The Pillar of the Cloud* and *Light in Winter* (Doubleday. 1962, 1963), is one of many recent valuable tellings of the Newman story. It is this biography that—after the *Apologia* itself—has most arrestingly captured the attention of 20th-century minds. Various paperback anthologies, too—for example, Fr. Vincent Blehl's *The Essential Newman* (Mentor)—and various editions of Newman's sermons and other writings, and many essays in criticism, are appearing here and in England with accelerating frequency. (Fr. Blehl, director of Fordham University's new Center of Newman Studies, has been collaborating with Newman scholars from around the world on the new and complete re-edition of all Newman's letters being prepared by the Newman Oratory of Birmingham, England. A widely attended symposium on the *Apologia* took place at the Fordham University center on October 12, 1963.)

Jean Guitton, capable Augustinian scholar and first of the lay observers at Vatican II, has said that among modern thinkers Newman is closest peer to St. Augustine, and Eric Przywara calls him *Augustinus redivivus.* In James Joyce's *Ulysses,* in the long chapter of parodies (from before *Beowulf* on through *Ulysses* itself), Newman's prose style is the only one to go unparodied. "I have read him a great deal," Joyce told Jacques Mercanton, "and in the 'Oxen of the Sun' . . . where all the authors are parodied, Newman alone is rendered pure, in the grave beauty of his style." As James Atherton has admirably shown, echoes of Newman are sounded almost everywhere in Joyce, variously orchestrated from almost all Newman's published works.

The *Apologia* came into being in a rather curious way. It grew out of Charles Kingsley's review of James Anthony Froude's *History of England,* volumes 7 and 8. In this piece, Kingsley asserted by way of incidental premise: "Truth, for its own sake, has never been a virtue with the Roman clergy. Fr. Newman informs us that it need not, and on the whole ought not to be." The review first came to Newman's attention in December, 1863, and appeared in *Macmillan's Magazine* for January, 1864. A published correspondence between Newman and Kingsley followed. As a kind of impetuous finale (so he thought) to this correspondence, Kingsley in exasperation composed a free-wheeling pamphlet, "What, Then, Does Dr. Newman Mean?" It was in answer to this pamphet that Newman's *Apologia* was written. The work first appeared in pamphlet form on successive Tuesdays, from April 21 to June 2, 1864. (On June 16, two weeks after publication of the seventh pamphlet, Newman issued another, entitled: "Answer in Detail to Mr. Kingsley's Accusations." This is sometimes included in, sometimes omitted from, editions of the *Apologia.*)

In the letters Kingsley exchanged with Newman, and especially in his pamphlet, which came in to Newman on Palm Sunday, March 20, 1864, Kingsley (who had never met Newman) asserted that Newman's religious views were impossible to pin down. There had been so many tergiversations in Newman's different religious positions, so many unpredictable fluctuations of his views, that it was difficult if not impossible—so Kingsley felt and proclaimed—to tell what Newman might mean at any time, in any utterance, or to distinguish in his writings between the silliness, the equivocations and the inconsistencies of his ever changing religious points of view.

Several of Newman's most highly respected friends, notably his non-Catholic friends, advised him not to trouble himself about what they called Kingsley's "trash." Newman, however, took counsel with himself. After prayer, he decided to answer Kingsley's stinging pamphlet. He would write a history of his religious opinions, and he would call it *Apologia pro Vita Sua.* This title does not, to be sure, signify an "apology" in the usual English sense, that is, an "excuse," nor even a self-"defense." By a special irony, these English senses of the title would, of course, in the circumstances be overheard. But Newman wanted to make himself responsible for a record—a narrative, as true as he could tell, a history as faithful as he could reconstruct—of the different spiritual crises in his life and of his consequent changes of mind.

In writing the *Apologia,* Newman is a man caught, as it were, in the middle, looking two ways at once: back through the haze at the past as now he tries to relive it, then around him now in his present much troubled position.

As for the past time, the lost time, the once happy, later sad time that he is now trying to understand, "a darkness it emphatically was." Newman's life in the Catholic Church had been no crown, no bed of roses. His *Apologia* was as much motivated by the earnest wish of his faith to dispel the cloud that highly placed Catholics suspended over his head as it was by the wish to account, if he might, for Kingsley's hostile public references to his many changes of mind. (His tenaciously held presumption in charity that these Catholic adversaries of his were acting in good conscience made their actions all the more mysterious, even horrible to endure. Msgr. George Talbot, for example, a chamberlain of Pius IX and a kind of chargé d'affaires for English Catholic Church matters at the Vatican, described Newman as "the most dangerous man in England." There were those in England itself who wanted to see Newman "crushed.")

This undertaking of 1864 was for Newman, in a literal sense, an almost back-breaking chore. He was now 63 years old. His principal and most dramatic religious crisis, his going away from Oxford and his reception into the Church of Rome, had taken place twenty or more years before. In the space of ten weeks, he had to write to old friends involved in his crises, for records, known, lost or forgotten. He was obliged, as he says, to *relive* these old "crises of the heart and head." In spite of his lack of leisure, he was obliged to endure, as he also says in the *Apologia,* "the ripping up of old griefs," to practice on himself a "cruel operation" so as to make a public statement that others might believe.

Although he was the most painstaking and scrupulous of stylists, prone ever to revise and re-revise almost endlessly all that he wrote, he was now obliged to meet weekly deadlines of composition and publication, to correct at once galleys and final proofs, to attend simultaneously to the countless harassing details of week-by-week publication. And every word that he wrote, every name, every date, would be subjected to intense and not always friendly scrutiny.

Newman composed the *Apologia* in longhand, and much of it standing up at a kind of lectern-desk—562 pages in ten weeks. Walter E. Houghton, who has written the best book of all on its prose, *The Art of Newman's "Apologia"* (1945), notes that different "states of mind" rather than methods of thought are the prevailing dialectic of Newman's argument. This kind of record is always better expressed by the voices of living speech than by a rigorous advancing logic.

The *Apologia* at once caught on, both with the public and with scholars, best of all with his old Anglican friends. Three times—1865, 1869 and 1873—Newman himself made some revisions, alterations, omissions and reshufflings in the textual presentation of the *Apologia.* (As time went on and the various new editions of this story appeared, Charles Kingsley's peevish attacks on him tended to fade out of Newman's text. When Kingsley died, in 1876, Newman offered Mass for the repose of his soul.) Others have often edited or re-edited the text—perhaps most notably, in 1913, Wilfred Ward, son of W. G. Ward, one-time editor of the *Dublin Review* and an old Catholic-convert adversary and former friend of Newman himself. Fr. Philip Hughes, in our own day, has made the original text of Newman's pamphlets available in his 1956 Image Book edition of the *Apologia.*

Any man's story of the secret life of his soul soon turns into a highly personal and emotion-laden account—especially when this life of the soul is the only important part of his life story that the autobiographer chooses to tell. The heart tends to take precedence over the head. In Newman's own case, the drama of how he came to the Church of Rome had, moreover, been played out excitingly and in the limelight nearly two decades before. Now, in 1864, as he had to arrange the scenes and compose the verbal score, he vividly relived his personal drama of that earlier time. Such dramas of the head and heart may come to a kind of completion, or stasis, but they never really end.

As the sixth part of the *Apologia* moves to its sad-glad climax, Newman quotes from old letters to old friends: "Littlemore, October 8, 1845. I am expecting this night Father Dominic, the Passionist." And from another letter: "How lonely I am."

Fr. Dominic Barberi is the Italian Passionist, "Dominic of the Mother of God," C.P., a missionary at the time in England, who received Newman into the Catholic Church. He was recently beatified by Pope Paul VI, in St. Peter's Basilica, on October 27, 1963. Fr. Dominic was in England at the time of the excitement of the Oxford Movement. Early he showed himself sympathetic to its leaders and its aims, which were in general the recovery of a lost Catholic inheritance for the Church of England. Not a sentimental man, he nevertheless felt shame for some of his fellow Christians, especially his English ones, for what he conceived to be their unfeeling views of this Oxford Movement—Tractarianism so-called. He himself never for a moment doubted Newman's intelligence and good will, never questioned his faith. He much respected the high sense of duty that Newman ardently felt toward his own Church of England, and he could understand Newman's loneliness now at the end, at Littlemore "simply by myself."

Newman, in the *Apologia* and elsewhere, has special relevance in these ecumenical days of renewal under Vatican II. He was a man of his own times, but yet how far ahead of his times! No hint of disrespect need be inferred if one notices that the Fathers of our present Church Council appear, occasionally, to be just now catching up with Newman's thought and practice. Four characteristic areas of Newman's thinking enforce this conclusion.

1. The theology of the act of faith as it is now presented by most highly respected Catholic theologians owes very much in its inspiration and analysis to Newman's *An Essay in Aid of a Grammar of Assent* (1870). This is the book on which Newman's Jesuit friend, Fr. Thomas Harper, and other prevailing Catholic theologians passed most severe strictures when it was first published. (Fr. Harper was himself a convert to Catholicism—1852—and like Newman had received Anglican orders. His massive censures, a classic instance of "overkill," on the *Grammar of Assent* troubled Newman more than Fr. Harper ever knew.)

2. The idea of the development of Christian doctrine, now a highly privileged one in all theological circles, is a subject on which Newman wrote a famous essay in 1845, as he made his way to Rome. This *Essay on the Development of Christian Doctrine* concludes with Simeon's prayer, now Newman's own: " . . . a light of revelation for the Gentiles, and the glory of your people Israel." Time is short, eternity is long: *Nunc dimittis, Domine.*

3. Newman's pioneering theological ideas on consulting the laity are now almost universally taken for granted by way of premises in Catholic theological discussions of this subject. His *On Consulting the Faithful in Matters of Doctrine* was first presented as an article in the *Rambler* (1859), some five years before the *Apologia* appeared. It has recently (1962) been re-issued in book form. At the time of its first appearance, this article caused much hard feeling. Catholics in high places and in low viewed it with much suspicion and some bitterness. It was delated to Rome, and as a consequence Newman was for a long time under a cloud at the Vatican. Except for Msgr. Joseph C. Fenton's predictably disenchanting comments, or strictures, on the recent book version of Newman's essay on consulting the faithful, this reissue has been widely welcomed. (Msgr. Fenton has often asserted in the pages of the *American Ecclesiastical Review* that "Newman has been idolized rather than studied." For nearly ten years, maybe longer, he has been talking down "the Newman cult," "the Newman legend," "Newman idolatry," and here in America anyway he has been trying to correct what he calls this Catholic "folk custom." But very good minds, Catholic and non-Catholic, continue to pay close attention to whatever Newman says. His essay on consulting the faithful goes a long way toward defining what the actual "role" of the laity in matters theological might be in practice, not just in platitude. Newman wanted the layman to take a supporting part in the Catholic drama, not simply to work off-screen or as—in John Cogley's phrase—a kind of "Hollywood extra.")

4. With the ever accelerating rate of attendance of Catholic undergraduates at non-Catholic colleges, Newman's ideas on university education are again coming to the fore. A recent comment in *America* (3/13/65, p. 345) noted that it is now predicted that by 1985 there will be "2.4 million Catholic students . . . attending secular colleges and universities," that is, 80 per cent of all Catholic students who are attending college at all. So it is understandable why Newman's ideas on university education, in general, and on Catholics attending non-Catholic universities, in particular, should now be coming up for rethinking, new accommodations and over-all re-evaluations.

Newman never thought of himself, nor does he ever allow others to think of him, as a post-Christian man. In the concluding section of his *Apologia*, he is made sorrowful by the appalling vision of "atheism in one shape or another" that he sees. But he does not back away from this vision, "the intensity of the evil which has possession of mankind." Face it he must, and face it he does in the strength of his God-given faith.

"Ten thousand difficulties do not make one doubt," says Newman near the start of this same concluding section. This part, a "General Answer to Mr. Kingsley," is also, according to the 1865 book version of the *Apologia,* sometimes simply called "The Position of My Mind Since 1845"—that is, since Newman became a Catholic. "Ten thousand difficulties"—this many and more might easily have come to mind for Newman in 1864. By that time, he had been for nearly twenty years a Catholic. Now in 1965, in our own present position, why not ten thousand welcomes to the *Apologia?* After a hundred years, the "grave beauty" of this one man's record of a most human and most searching experience has not at all gone out of date.

RELIGIOUS RESPONSES

Kenneth M. Peck (essay date 1964)

SOURCE: "The Oxford Controversy in America: 1839," in *Historical Magazine of the Protestant Episcopal Church,* Vol. XXXIII, No. 1, March, 1964, pp. 49-63.

[*In the following essay, Peck discusses the significance of the Oxford Movement in the United States, which, as he argues, was largely isolated to the religious leadership, in contrast to the widespread controversy in Britain.*]

Some difficulty is encountered ascertaining exactly when the Oxford Movement made its appearance in this country. The problem is confused by two factors. First, the Hobartian High Church party emphasized the sacramental life of the Church and the apostolic ministry which were also two important emphases of the Oxford Movement. *The Episcopal Recorder* remarked that the erroneous teachings of the Oxford divines were present in this country prior to their appearance at Oxford.[1] When Bishop McIlvaine of Ohio warned of the private character of opinions which do more than affirm "the Apostolic origin of Episcopacy *as a fact*"[2] or when Bishop Chase of Illinois warned against "extremes" between "apostolic order" and "evangelical doctrine,"[3] the implied criticism is applicable to either the older Hobartian High Church party or the Oxford Movement. Second, the influx of Irish Roman Catholics which was a feature of this decade gives rise to a double interpretation of the cry of "popery." This accusation was used frequently by Protestants against the Episcopal Church;[4] however, during the thirties there was a surge of anti-Roman sentiment in this country which was a result of the great influx of Roman Catholics.[5] Consequently, when Bishop McIlvaine, just returned from a visit to the universities of England where he undoubtedly encountered the Oxford Movement, complained of the arrival of "popery" from Great Britain,[6] he may have had reference either to the Oxford theology or the Irish immigration. By January 1838, the movement had received sufficient attention in this country to merit an attack upon its Eucharistic teaching in the *Princeton Review.* The irony of the attack was that the very passage of the *Tracts* which it chose to denounce was merely a translation, without proper citation, of the *Princeton Review's* own beloved *Institutes* of John Calvin, a fact which the High Churchmen were quick to point out.[7] Late in 1839, the editor of *The Churchman* stated that for "several years" it had republished portions of the *Tracts,* but that they had aroused no interest.[8] The editor also observed that *The Episcopal Recorder* had "first sounded the alarm" against their danger.[9] In these years prior to 1839, however, very little space was devoted either *pro or con* to the Oxford Movement. The first extensive attack specifically directed against the movement in the Episcopal press seems to have been in the form of a reprint from the London *Christian Observer* of a review of "A Layman's Essays on the Church."[10] Apparently the Oxford Movement was primarily known in this country only to those who had been in England or had occasion to read English periodicals. The editor of *The Churchman,* reading a few of these *Tracts* and finding them sympathetic to that paper's High Church preferences, published some of them.[11]

The first big year of the controversy in the periodical press was 1839. From the first *The Episcopal Recorder* kept up a steady barrage. In January the editor spoke eloquently against the revival of "'the stinking puddles' of human tradition" which go "at every step upon the heels of popery."[12] The next month he was astonished

> at the bold strides toward thorough conformity to the false doctrines of the Romish Church. . . . The extracts which . . . [we republish in this issue] are alarming indeed.
>
> They renounce the names of Protestants and Protestantism. They introduce the worship of the Virgin Mary and the saints. They propose prayers for the dead.[13]

Later, Episcopalians who leaned toward Rome were accused of betraying the Episcopal Church, of being false sons of the Church, and of being "mere excrescences upon our ecclesiastical body."[14] By March, *The Episcopal Recorder* had heard reports that Newman had had a number of "secret conferences" with the Pope's private secretary in Rome and demanded an explanation of the purposes of these conferences.[15] Meanwhile, *The Southern Churchman* was feeling a little uneasy about the controversy. In March the editor refused to publish any correspondence on the Oxford Movement, either *pro* or *con,* lest it lead to "profitless discussion."[16] Two weeks later, both sides were accused of "a vein of conceit and a pride of logical acumen."[17] In the same issue a letter was published which praised *The Southern Churchman* for its silence, criticized those who had attacked the *Tracts* on the grounds that such attack would inevitably lead to their defense as a whole, and accused the critics of distorting the statements of the *Tracts.*[18] About the same time the *Gambier Observer* in an article signed "Cramner" (probably by Bishop McIlvaine) violently denounced the Oxford Movement as "putrid meat" and severely criticized *The Churchman* and *Banner of the Cross.*[19]

This attack had been provoked by the sympathetic attitude of the editor of *The Churchman* toward the Tractarians. As early as February *The Churchman* had carried some of Dr. Walter Farquhar Hook's remarks on the *Tracts* while at the same time adding an editorial disclaimer to some of his opinions.[20] The next month the extent of this disclaimer was made more specific. The editor felt the *Tracts*

> transcended those limits within which the best sons of the Church of England . . . have restrained their views. . . . We have yet seen enough to awaken our apprehensions, that on . . . fundamental questions . . . the Oxford divines are in danger of effacing those lines which broadly discriminate us from Rome and Geneva.[21]

In spite of the reservation concerning the orthodoxy of the *Tracts, The Churchman* felt that they were valuable antidotes for the erosion of the traditional theological position of the Church which was being effected by the strong stream of American evangelicalism and ought to be republished in this country.[22] This desire to republish the *Tracts* was the occasion for the famous "Cranmer" attack. The *Banner of the Cross* was even more enthusiastic about the *Tracts.* While holding reservations about the *"peculiar views"* of the *Tracts* and their mode of argument in some cases, that newspaper held that they maintain

> scriptural principles, divine institutions, and primitive practices. . . . The current charge of an inclination to Popery, much less, of a desire to lead others to Popery, has not the slightest foundation, but *exactly and altogether the reverse*—there being, as can easily be shown, no living writers who possess in a greater degree either the will or the power to conduct the controversy with Rome to a triumphant issue.[23]

The "Cranmer" attack realized the worst fears of *The Southern Churchman,* for *The Churchman* replied quiet heatedly. *The Churchman* held that although the errors of Newman should not be accepted, yet the *Tracts* ought not to be suppressed on that account but rather used for "aids and incitements to investigation." The *Gambier Observer* was accused of popery by their proscription of the *Tracts* in their own "Index Expurgatorius." The editor suggested that the works of both Newman and Bishop McIlvaine be published side by side in the confidence "that the 'poison' of the one . . . would find its antidote in the . . . other."[24] Furthermore, the unqualified judgment that the *Tracts* had on occasion strayed from the bounds of Anglican orthodoxy began to be modified by uncertainty that the *Tracts* actually had gone beyond the limits of Anglican doctrine.[25] At the same time "Cultor" observed

> I know not a more signal instance in which enemies have conferred a special favor than in the case of the far-famed Oxford divines. Their enemies have been the making of them in this country. But for the hue-and-cry which they have raised, it is probable that the Oxford Tracts would hardly have been known among us.[26]

Meanwhile, a proposed American edition of the Oxford *Tracts* had run into trouble. The proposal had been to turn the proceeds of the publication over to General Theological Seminary, which prompted one of the trustees of that seminary to have the edition suppressed. *The Churchman* sadly commented, "With all her [America's] boast of free institutions, she is virtually subjected, even in religion, to the tyranny of a majority."[27] This prompted two other trustees to write to *The Churchman* condemning the trustee who had caused the suppression of the *Tracts;*[28] however the plan was not revived. Although General Seminary was not to get the profits, the republication of the *Tracts* and related writings was continued through private subscriptions.[29] In announcing the proposed publication of a sermon expressing the Oxford theology, *The Churchman* took a dig at Bishop Moore of Virginia, who had asked his convention to condemn the *Tracts,* by observing, "If our ecclesiastical conventions are to anathematize those excellent productions for 'heresy,' it is at least desirable that their members be furnished with a copy."[30] The first of these reprints of the *Tracts* and Oxford writings appeared on July 30, 1839.[31]

The debate calmed down somewhat in the latter part of 1839, except for *The Episcopal Recorder,* which published such polemic as that of "Warburton," who, after a long listing of Oxford errors, adds

> I cannot positively assert that these Oxford divines are the disguised friends and secret emissaries of Rome, because it is not given to human perspicacity to penetrate the veil that conceals the heart of man; but I do assert with confidence, and an entire conviction of the truth of the proposition, that if a band of Jesuits were associated at Oxford for the express purpose of reviving in England all the popish superstitions, and were in constant correspondence to this end with the pope and his conclave at Rome, their united counsels could not have devised a wiser plan to accomplish that object than that which is pursued by these Oxford divines.[32]

While *The Episcopal Recorder* raged hot on the issue, *The Southern Churchman* attempted to remain silent, probably in the hope that if ignored the Oxford *Tracts* would lose their interest. Meanwhile, *The Churchman* tried to show the value which the *Tracts* might have on the American scene and to point out the dangers of the evangelical tendencies of American Christianity. One of the more ironic articles of the period appeared in *The Episcopal Recorder.* Dr. Isaac Taylor had written a book, *Ancient Christianity and the Doctrine of the Oxford Tracts,* showing the unreliable and unevangelical character of the Church fathers. The appearance of the book led the editor to remark:

> We rejoice to inform our readers, that the indications around us, are of a stopping of the plague. Even some who were at first deceived by the errors of these writers are now understanding them. And the whole question will settle down. . . . Unless some new fact demands their notice, we shall consider the subject a settled and finished one.[33]

From this cursory examination of the initial stage of the controversy over the Oxford *Tracts* in 1839, some difficulty is encountered coming to an understanding of their appeal in this country on one hand and of the opposition to them on the other. At least two factors must be considered: (1) the peculiar situation of the Episcopal Church in the United States; and, (2) the general character of the whole of American religious life.

The decimation of the Episcopal Church at the time of the American Revolution and its subsequent lethargy have been standard themes of Church histories.[34] During the American Revolution, in spite of the many leading Episcopalian revolutionaries, the Tory connections of the Church, especially in New England where Bishop Seabury himself had been known for his loyalist sentiments, was a direct source of suspicion toward the Church.[35] Furthermore, with the exception of the Methodists, every major denomination in America had sought refuge in the colonies from the Church of England.[36] Thus the *Chronicles of the Church* observed

> one of the first things implanted in the minds of the children, of the first settlers of New England, was, *hostility to the Episcopal Church.* And the seed thus early sown, sprung up, and produced a most abundant crop. In short, from the first moment that Episcopacy made its appearance in New England, it was regarded as a deadly enemy, and a most unrelenting foe. Prejudice and hatred were the feelings with which it was regarded; persecution, fines, and imprisonment, the lot of its professors. To join the Episcopal Church, in those days, was to renounce the friendship and good opinion of all former friends, with the certain knowledge, that hereafter they would be regarded only as hypocrites in religion, and enemies to the state.[37]

Furthermore, the presence of bishops, vestments, a ritual, etc. did give the undiscriminating the impression of a Romanizing tendency.

> It is not known to every one that after the departure of our Bishop from the country parishes, the ears of the clergy are assailed by one and another remark; almost every act performed by him and he himself, is associated with popery. . . . It has come to such a pass, that Episcopalians can scarcely do any thing, without having it labelled "Popery." . . . If a preference is given our church by prominent individuals of the place, immediately the report goes forth, "that is a popish church;" "we have never seen the shadow of an argument for observing Christmas as a holy festival. It is a relic of popery." Robes, gowns, surplices and Prayer-books are all popish.[38]

This charge of "popery" was not an idle one in a period of rapidly increasing Irish immigration and the resultant rise in anti-Roman sentiments, often expressed in violence. The connection with the Church of England, the former Tory sentiments of many of the clergy, and the external appearance of Romanism all combined to give the Episcopal Church a distinctly un-American hue.

The dominant motif of American religious life at this time was revivalistic, with extreme emphasis placed upon the experience of conversion. "A Layman of the Church" wrote to *The Churchman* reporting the proceedings concerning two candidates for membership in congregational churches as being typical. In the first the candidate was denied admission solely on the grounds that he could not "tell *when* and *where* he was converted," that is, that he was "sensible" that his "whole soul" had "been at any time changed," and that he "felt" that he was "really a new creature." In the second case the candidate, a woman of local notoriety, was admitted solely because of her description of how she had hated religion, but by chance had gone to a revival meeting where she was converted in a very emotional manner.[39] *The Episcopal Recorder* found fault with those

> who find in their external connection with, and participation of the privileges of the Christian Church, in the fact that they have been baptized into the name of Jesus, and perhaps have carried out their profession into a submission to his other institutions, a warrant for neglecting to address to their hearts the searching inquiry, "Have I been born of God?" Have I experienced the quickening influences of his Holy Spirit? Have I become inwardly as well as outwardly a "new man" in Christ Jesus?[40]

A corollary to the second awakening seems to have been the non-denominational societies. Those who had the revival experience gave expression to their conversion in societies formed for specific purposes apart from denominational structures. These covered the field from Bible societies, tract societies, the Y.M.C.A., missionary societies, to temperance and abolitionist societies.[41] Against this background, the evangelical party generally supported both the revivalistic motif and the non-denominational societies. Basically, the evangelicals desired to retain the basic order of the Church and its ritual, both interpreted liberally, while entering into the mainstream of American religious life. On the other hand, the High Churchmen saw in revivalism and non-denominational societies the danger of the distinctive character of the Church being eroded away into what some Anglo-Catholics call "pan-Protestantism."

However, the desire of the High Churchmen to adhere to the traditional forms and structures of the Church must not be regarded as entirely foreign to the American scene. Their concerns coincided with those who belonged to the conservative parties of every major—and many minor—denominations on the American scene. As a result Old School Presbyterians (e.g., Samuel Miller), Dutch Reformed (e.g., John W. Nevin), Congregationalists (e.g., Horace Bushnell), and even the Southern Baptist Old Landmarkers could agree with High Church Bishop Hobart on the "subjective" dangers of revivalism.[42] Possibly a similar connection is to be found in Bishop Francis Patrick Kendrick's battle against Trusteeism in the Roman Catholic Church.[43] During the period under consideration the struggles over Episcopalian participation in non-denominational societies had lapsed into a state of "peaceful co-existence" in which the evangelicals participated with these societies and the High Churchmen abstained. However, in the preceding decade, under the leadership of Bishops Hobart and Moore, the issue was more lively. Bishop Moore was the president of the Virginia branch of the American Bible Society, while Bishop Hobart was fighting to keep Churchmen out of such societies.[44] The key issue in 1839 was over the matter of revivalism.

The evangelicals were the supporters of a modified form of revivalism in the Episcopal Church. *The Episcopal Recorder* observed that, "Much as revivals are made the occasions . . . of doubt and opposition among the lukewarm professors of the Gospel, we are still unshaken in our conviction that they are the work of God."[45] They felt keenly the call to minister to infidels. "Thousands and millions of our race are dying in their sins. . . . Our great work is to try to save some of these!"[46] Because of this concern, the evangelicals thought that the peculiarities of the Episcopal Church must take a secondary role to the "doctrine" of the Church, that is, justification by faith alone.[47] Thus the important factor in religion was the individual's experience of God's grace.[48] The High Church emphasis upon the sacramental life of the Church with its corollary idea of "growth in grace" seemed to be part of "the popish doctrine of justification in part by works,"[49] because, rather than relying upon a "spontaneous" experience of God's grace, sacramentalism required the "work" of participating in that sacramental life in order to obtain the experience of God's grace. The two candidates who were applying for admission to the congregational churches serve as excellent examples. In the case of the man, the evidence pointed toward a slow process of growth in grace which made it impossible for him to say "*when* and *where*" he had been converted; whereas the woman had had the required "spontaneous" experience of God's grace.[50] This tendency of the High Church emphasis upon the sacramental life to result in a different kind of religious experience led *The Episcopal Recorder* to remark that the "great object" of the sacraments

> is to pacify the claims of an awakened conscience, to supply its wants, and to remove its fears. To accomplish this, . . . [some] impose and endure a burden of penances, and multiply rites and forms of outward worship, and thus is produced the shape of Popery. . . . [This is only an] effort to satisfy an awakened conscience without submitting the heart to God. . . . True religion brings the whole case to Christ, and finds in him, its ample and adequate remedy.[51]

The capacity of the forms of worship to sooth the conscience, thus lessening the possibility of revivalistic religious experience, was seen by the evangelicals as a perversion of the Christian religion. However, it should not be concluded from this attitude that the evangelicals were ready to throw out the episcopacy and Prayer-book. They held "that ardent zeal and experimental godliness are in no wise inconsistent with an intelligent and firm support of our admirable Liturgy and Apostolic ministry."[52] Rather, this zeal gave life to these outward forms. While holding to these forms, the evangelicals felt that to emphasize them in an exclusive manner hindered the work of the Church.

> We simply affirm the apostolic origin of Episcopacy as a fact, and say that our Church as a necessary consequence has determined that there shall be no other ministry permitted within her bounds, while we carefully avoid the extreme of denouncing all communions destitute of the Episcopacy, as having departed from the essentials of the Christian faith . . . and are without valid sacraments.[53]

To do so, they felt, would only stir up "evil passions" and "provoke bitterness."[54]

The High Churchmen felt that the attitude of the evangelicals must ultimately lead to the loss of the distinctive characteristics of the Episcopal Church—the episcopacy and the liturgy. Carried to its logical conclusion, it seemed, the evangelicals must eventually abandon every aspect of the Church which was different from the emerging patterns of American Christianity. Not only High Church Anglicans challenged this pattern, but Lutherans, Reformed, and Presbyterians as well. The resultant emphasis upon the individual in revivalism led to a "subjectivism" which must be balanced against the "'objective' aspects of Christianity which lie outside of and above the individual." Such "objective" Christianity is to be found in the historic Church, the sacraments, the creeds, etc. Although the specific doctrinal emphasis in each denomination differed, the general principle is equally applicable in each.[55] From this counterstream in American Christianity came "the decline of nondenominational unity" and the rise of denominationalism, which may have opened the possibility of a later and deeper theological unity.[56]

Commenting on the evangelical criticism of the Oxford *Tracts* and their dangers, the editor of *The Churchman* stated that he had "greatly mistaken the character of our age and country if it is in danger of any errors which have a leading to Rome. The tendency is all the other way."[57] The individualism of the day was about to destroy historic Christianity; in spite of the teaching of the Church and the Bible itself, "'I think so,' 'My conscience tells me so,' is the conclusion of all argument."[58] "Anticeptic" quotes "Tract 73" with some satisfaction:

> "There is a widely spread, though variously admitted school of doctrine among us . . . which intends and professes peculiar piety, as directing its attention to the *heart itself,* not to any thing external to us whether creed, actions, or rituals. I do not hesitate to assert that this doctrine is based upon error, that it is really a specious form of trusting man rather than GOD . . . and that it tends to Socinianism."[59]

The editor of *The Churchman* finds in the Oxford *Tracts* a remedy for "the practical Antinomianism, the lawless independence, the familiar and often contemptuous freedom with holy things," that characterized much of American religiosity. The *Tracts* have aimed to replace "the meagre piety which feeds without thriving on sentiments and abstractions" with a

> substantial faith, which, instead of living on its own consciousness, or evaporating in "frames" and "experiences," makes itself seen and felt in *good works,* in prayers and fastings, in almsgiving and self-denial, in conformity to the ordinances of the Church and obedience to the precepts of the Gospel.[60]

Episcopalians, a "Churchman" observes, must associate with those who hold the peculiarities of various individuals such as Luther, Calvin, and Arminius; to avoid adopting some of these views has proved impossible. As a result some Churchmen "in their desire to promote peace . . . are willing to obtain it even by keeping out of sight all that may offend the scruples of those who esteem our claims absurd."[61] As a result there was a desire of High Churchmen to maintain the distinctive features of the Episcopal Church in order to prevent the Church's amalgamation into the vague American religiosity. The Oxford *Tracts* appealed to American High Churchmen in so far as they gave undergirding to the desire for distinctiveness. The reservations which the editor of *The Churchman* had toward Newman's theology significantly had to do with a tendency to efface "those lines which broadly discriminate us from Rome and Geneva, and . . . which has formed . . . [our] distinctive character and glory."[62] It is important to notice that he includes Newman's leanings toward *Calvinism* as well as the Church of Rome in his censure. "A Churchman" writes in the same vein:

> The safety of the Church, as well as her hope of extension, is confirmed only by drawing with distinctness the line which separates her teachings from heterodoxy. No portion of what she transmits should be altered or concealed to gratify the captiousness of others. The charity, (falsely so called,) which leads to the purchase of peace by the sacrifice of principle should not be her characteristic. Her present position is rather one of indecision—a halting between opinions. Let her be just to herself, and confide in the promise of her omniscent Head, that the gates of hell shall not prevail against her.[63]

This attitude of the High Churchmen begins to take on more meaning when seen in its proper context. In the preceding decade the New School Presbyterians had been cooperating with the Congregationalists in western missionary work through the non-denominational missionary societies. This had led to a tendency to merge the Calvinism of traditional Presbyterianism into the revivalistic Puritanism (which was also derived from Calvin) of the Congregational leaders such as Timothy Dwight and Lyman Beecher. This development led to a controversy between the orthodox Old School and the New School culminating in a schism in 1837, thereby greatly reducing the missionary effectiveness of the Presbyterians on the frontier.[64] Although the argument of the High Churchmen threatened the Episcopal Church with a similar schism, the alternative seemed to be a continual drift into the revivalistic-Puritanism of the day. Rather than this loss of identity, they hoped to be able to remain united as well as retain their distinctive Anglican traditions.

One more factor ought to be mentioned regarding the relationship of High Churchmanship to the revivalistic-Puritanism of this period. Revivals had been extremely intense in some areas, especially in New England and upstate New York—so much so that this area was called the "burnt-over" district. In these areas there was a particularly strong reaction to the "subjective" aspects of revivalism. High Churchmen were able to capitalize on this reaction, so that this "burnt-over" area became one of the strongest centers of later Anglo-Catholicism.[65] An American denomination produced by the same reaction in the same district was the Mormons. The Church of Jesus Christ of the Latter-day Saints was a highly theocratic society closely regulated in its spiritual, economic, and social life by its bishops.[66] The Book of Mormon provided the Mormons with a direct source of divine authority, and its centralized hierarchy provided an "objective" source of organization.[67] While there may be a tendency to assume that the Church of Jesus Christ of the Latter-day Saints is evangelicalism gone berserk, it is more properly seen as a part of the churchly reaction to evangelicalism with its strong emphasis upon the doctrine of the Church and "objective" rather than "subjective" religion. The parallels with High Church Anglicanism ought not to be ignored. The appeal to Catholic Truth, the emphasis upon strong episcopal government, the exclusionist attitude toward those who are not within the orthodox fold of the Church and the attempt to bring the whole realm of the lives of Churchmen under the direct supervision of the Church all have parallels in such a denomination as the Mormons. To be sure, this *sectarian* attitude was not explicit in the High Churchmen of the thirties, but certainly such attitudes became characteristic of later Anglo-Catholicism.

The controversy over the Oxford *Tracts* in the late thirties had its roots in the long-standing tensions between the evangelical and High Church parties in the Episcopal Church. In fact, the first appearance of the *Tracts* in this country seems to have been due to their adoption by High Churchmen as expressing in a particularly scholarly way those particular doctrines which they had long cherished. What was at first a qualified approval of the teaching of the Oxford divines became, in the heat of evangelical attacks, progressively less qualified. These attacks were brought about by the concern of the evangelicals lest the emphasis upon the episcopacy and liturgy by the High Churchmen would hinder the missionary expansion of the Church by arousing the suspicions of Americans that the Episcopal Church was un-American. This un-Americanism seems to have been the meaning behind the charge of "popery." In so far as the tenets of the High Church party did go against the dominant themes of American religious life—revivalism and non-denominational societies—it was un-American. However, the High Church party was the Episcopal counter-part to the conservative forces in all American denominations. This general movement in American religious life, although differing in particulars, shared in the common emphasis upon traditional forms and practices as true "objective" Christianity in opposition to the "subjective" emphasis of revivalism. Particularly significant in this respect are the parallels which later appeared between Anglo-Catholicism and the Church of Jesus Christ of the Latter-day Saints.

When the appearance of the Oxford Movement on the American scene is seen as a part of a more general development of American religiosity, a further extension of the ground suggests itself. Surely the emphases of revivalism have a number of profound relationships with the dominant Jacksonian democracy of the day.[68] Likewise, the churchly reaction to this revivalism had parallels with the federal unionism of Daniel Webster.[69] If such connections can be sustained in further research, the panic of 1837 resulting from Jackson's bank policies might be seen as contributing to the appeal of High Church conservatism, especially in commercial New England. Winthrop Hudson, although developing the opposite thesis, suggests that rationalism in religion, which among High Churchmen in the thirties was seen as a product of revivalism[70] was associated in the minds of many with the excesses of the French Revolution.[71] If this thesis is correct, then another connection between the High Church party and contemporary conservative fears of the dangers of Jacksonian democracy, which may have seemed to some to threaten America with the excesses already seen in the French Revolution, possibly may be demonstrated. These are only a few suggestions for possible further historical studies in the area of the parties within the Episcopal Church which has, to date, been sadly neglected.

Notes

[1] *Episcopal Recorder* (Philadelphia), February 2, 1839.

[2] *Journal of the Proceedings of the Nineteenth Annual Convention of the Protestant Episcopal Church in the Diocese of Ohio* (Gambier, Ohio: Western Protestant Press, 1839), pp. 10-11.

[3] *Journal of the Third Annual Convention of the Protestant Episcopal Church in the Diocese of Illinois* (Peoria: S. H. Davis, Printer, 1837), p. 9.

[4] Clowes Chorley, *Men and Movements in the Episcopal Church* (Hamden, Connecticut: Archon Books, 1961), pp. 134-35. *Episcopal Recorder,* February 2, 1839.

[5] H. Shelton Smith, Robert T. Handy, Lefferts A. Lotescher, *American Christianity: An Historical Interpretation with Representative Documents,* II, (New York: Charles Scribner's Sons, 1963), pp. 5-6.

[6] *Journal of the Proceedings of the Eighteenth Annual Convention of the Protestant Episcopal Church in the Diocese of Ohio* (Gambier, Ohio: Western Protestant Press, 1835), p. 13.

[7] *Churchman* (New York), August 31, 1839.

[8] *Ibid.,* November 30, 1839. In 1835 selections had been published on primitive episcopacy; and in 1836 "Richard Nelson" was reprinted. The first controversial note was in 1837 over some of Newman's practices, but not the Tracts. (George E. DeMille, *The*

Catholic Movement in the American Episcopal Church [2d ed. rev.; Philadelphia: Church Historical Society, 1950], pp. 41-42.)

[9] *Churchman,* November 30, 1839.

[10] *Southern Churchman* (Richmond), November 30, 1838.

[11] DeMille, *op. cit.,* p. 41.

[12] *Episcopal Recorder,* January 19, 1839.

[13] *Ibid.,* February 9, 1839.

[14] *Ibid.,* February 16, 1839.

[15] *Ibid.,* March 30, 1839.

[16] *Southern Churchman,* March 1, 1839.

[17] *Ibid.,* March 15, 1839.

[18] *Ibid.*

[19] *Episcopal Recorder,* April 6, 1839, and *Churchman,* April 13, 1839, quoting *Gambier Observer* (Gambier, Ohio).

[20] *Churchman,* February 9, 1839.

[21] *Ibid.,* March 2, 1839.

[22] *Ibid.*

[23] *Ibid.,* March 16, 1839, quoting *Banner of the Cross* (Philadelphia).

[24] *Churchman,* April 13, 1839.

[25] *Ibid.,* April 20, 1839.

[26] *Ibid.*

[27] *Ibid.*

[28] *Ibid.,* April 27, 1839, and May 4, 1839.

[29] Members of the University of Oxford [John Henry Newman, et al.], *Tracts for the Times* (3 vols.; 2d ed.; New York: Charles Henry, 1839-40). Apparently the American edition which should have run around five volumes was never completed.

[30] *Churchman,* June 1, 1839. For the bishop's remarks see *Journal of the Protestant Episcopal Church in the Diocese of Virginia* (Richmond: The Southern Churchman, 1839), p. 10.

[31] *Churchman,* July 27, 1839.

[32] *Episcopal Recorder,* October 19, 1839. Cf. *Churchman,* November 16, 1839.

[33] *Episcopal Recorder,* November 23, 1839.

[34] E.g.: James Thayer Addison, *The Episcopal Church in the United States: 1789-1931* (New York: Charles Scribner's Sons, 1951), pp. 51-87. Chorely, *op. cit.,* pp. 27-30. DeMille, *op. cit.,* pp. 1-8. William Wilson Manross, *A History of the American Episcopal Church* (2d ed. rev.; New York: Morehouse-Gorham Co., 1950) pp. 172-314.

[35] Addison, *op. cit.,* pp. 51-53.

[36] Clifton E. Olmstead, *History of Religion in the United States* (Englewood Cliffs, N. J.: Prentice-Hall, Inc., 1960), pp. 62-91, 144-54.

[37] *Churchman,* November 16, 1839, quoting *Chronicles of the Church.*

[38] *Episcopal Recorder,* February 2, 1839.

[39] *Churchman,* August 31, 1839.

[40] *Episcopal Recorder,* September 7, 1839.

[41] Smith, *op. cit.,* pp. 10-19.

[42] *Ibid.,* pp. 70-71.

[43] *Ibid.,* pp. 84-86.

[44] Addison, *op. cit.,* pp. 101 and 111.

[45] *Episcopal Recorder,* August 17, 1839.

[46] *Ibid.,* February 2, 1839.

[47] E.g., *Ibid.*

[48] *Ibid.,* September 7, 1839.

[49] *Ibid.,* October 12, 1839.

[50] *Churchman,* August 31, 1839, Cf., *supra,* p. 55.

[51] *Episcopal Recorder,* July 20, 1839.

[52] *Ibid.,* August 17, 1839.

[53] *Ibid.,* February 9, 1839.

[54] *Ibid.*

[55] Smith, *op. cit.,* pp. 67-68.

[56] *Ibid.,* p. 74.

[57] *Churchman,* March 2, 1839.

[58] *Ibid.,* November 16, 1839.

[59] *Ibid.,* April 27, 1839, quoting Members of the University of Oxford, "On the Introduction of Rationalistic Principles into Religion," *op. cit.,* vol. III, p. 125.

[60] *Churchman,* June 29, 1839.

[61] *Ibid.,* June 22, 1839.

[62] *Ibid.,* March 2, 1839.

[63] *Ibid.,* June 22, 1839.

[64] Smith, *op. cit.,* pp. 12-16, 28-29, 88-90. Olmstead, *op. cit.,* p. 270.

[65] Cf., *Churchman,* August 31, 1838.

[66] Smith, *op. cit.,* p. 72.

[67] *Ibid.,* pp. 80-81.

[68] *Ibid.,* pp. 17-18.

[69] *Ibid.,* p. 74.

[70] *Churchman,* August 31, 1839.

[71] Winthrop S. Hudson, *The Great Tradition of the American Churches* (Harper Torchbook ed.; New York: Harper and Row, Publishers, 1963) p. 67. Hudson is developing the thesis that the revivalism of Lyman Beecher was in part due to his reaction to the "liberal" disestablishment of the Congregational Church in Connecticut.

Martin J. Svaglic (essay date 1967)

SOURCE: In an introduction to *"Apologia Pro Vita Sua": Being A History of His Religious Opinions, by John Henry Cardinal Newman,* edited by Martin J. Svaglic, Oxford University Press, 1967, pp. xxxvii-lix.

[*In the excerpt that follows, Svaglic introduces Newman's* Apologia *by locating the work in the larger context of Newman's conversion and his intellectual conflict with Charles Kingsley.*]

That Newman could write, in less than three months, the many-sided account of his spiritual history which is the *Apologia,* then the longest and still the most varied of his works, is an extraordinary testimony to his powers of concentration. It becomes more understandable, however, as we realize that the *Apologia,* like Kingsley's attack, was due to no sudden impulse but was rather the product of many years of reflection on various personal attacks and the desirability or possibility of answering them; on the nature of persuasion; on the essentials of good biography; and above all on the previous life of one who had felt since his Evangelical youth that, as life was primarily a series of transactions between God and the individual soul, the contemplation of things past afforded him the best opportunity of tracing God's hand at work, until the places and friends he so deeply loved had assumed the importance of actors in a divinely conceived drama. 'Let us humbly and reverently attempt to trace His guiding hand in the years which we have hitherto lived', he had long ago urged in a sermon called 'Remembrance of Past Mercies'. And as Jacob 'delighted lovingly to trace, and gratefully to acknowledge, what had been given, leaving the future to itself', so Newman, as we have seen, was in the years of his sorrow making the *Apologia* possible by 'living in memory rather than in hope, counting times, recording seasons, keeping days; having his history by heart, and his past life in his hand'.[2]

He directed the *Apologia* not to Kingsley, whom he considered beyond persuasion, but to the English public at large, which he knew shared many of Kingsley's views. Kingsley's pamphlet had 'poisoned the wells' against him by casting so much doubt on his character and by implication on his patriotism that no detailed answer to each of the charges would have any real chance to penetrate minds already so hardened against him, even if such minds were capable of following the subtleties of complex theological and ethical problems. Yet Newman had no perplexity as to the method of answering Kingsley, not because he wished to write an autobiography for its own sake, but because he never doubted the truth of what Aristotle's *Rhetoric* and his own experience had taught him: that in persuasion, personal influence was of the first and utmost importance since, except in mathematical science, conviction depended not on the intellect alone but on the right state of mind and heart which made successful reasoning possible. And the heart is 'commonly reached, not through the reason, but through the imagination, by means of direct impressions, by the testimony of facts and events, by history, by description. Persons influence us, voices melt us, looks subdue us, deeds inflame us.'[3] In the writings of the Fathers of the Church, in Scripture itself, 'dogma and proof' were 'at the same time hagiography'.[4] Newman would subdue his readers and make them believe he was an honest Englishman, not so much by argument, at least at first, as by giving them his living mind in action: by giving them himself.

He would keep for the last chapter direct answers to Kingsley's charges against himself and the Roman clergy he had been made to represent; there, those who wished to examine them might do so in at least a more open, perhaps now a sympathetic, frame of mind.[5] In the story itself there would be no special pleading for Roman Catholicism, he assured the Anglican friends whose aid he rather hesitantly appealed for: 'I have no idea whatever of giving any *point* to what I am writing,' he told Church, 'but that I did not act dishonestly.'[6] To Rogers he wrote:

> I sincerely wish only to state facts, and may truly say that it, and nothing else, has been my object. So far as my character is connected with the fact of my conversion I have wished to do a service to Catholicism,—but in no other way. I say this because my friends here think that the upshot of the whole tells *against* Anglicanism; but I am clear that I have no such intention, and cannot at all divine what people generally will say about me. I say all this in fairness,—it is what has made me delicate in applying to Anglican friends.[7]

One of Newman's greatest handicaps was his own temperament, whose natural reserve had been strongly accentuated by the quest for sanctity which inspired the Oxford Movement and made anything in the nature of self-display abhorrent. 'When you see part of my publication', he confessed to Keble, 'you will wonder how I could ever get myself to write it. Well, I could not, except under some very great stimulus. I do not think I could write it, if I delayed it a month.'[8] Lack of easily accessible material and shortness of time increased his difficulty. There was an abundance of documents to be consulted—no strictly autobiographical notes, it is true, as we are told in the preface to the *Apologia,* but letters he had received from his earliest years, many copies of those he had sent, annotated and illustrated classroom journals, personal notebooks sometimes in Latin when dealing with religious and moral problems, study notes at Oxford, a journal begun in 1821.[9] Yet, though these are today all classified and available to students in the Oratory at Birmingham (and many of them have been published in the volume called *Autobiographical Writings*), in March 1864 they were only in process of being put into order; and, as we have seen, Newman had not got beyond 1836. Most of his own early books he had last read when revising the proof sheets. Friends like Church and Rogers and Keble had to be asked for letters he had sent them—'that kind of literature which more than any other represents the abundance of the heart'[10]—as well as for criticism and advice. Above all there was the necessity which his own common sense told him and his publisher Longman never let him forget: the account had to be relatively brief, or it would not be read; and it had to be done at once, while public interest was at its height, if it was to be done at all. 'Under these circumstances', Newman wrote,

> my sketch will of course be incomplete. I now for the first time contemplate my course as a whole; it is a first essay, but it will contain, I trust, no serious or substantial mistake, and so far will answer the purpose for which I write it. I purpose to set nothing down in it as certain, for which I have not a clear memory, or some written memorial, or the corroboration of some friend. There are witnesses enough up and down the country to verify, or correct, or complete it; and letters moreover of my own in abundance, unless they have been destroyed.[11]

Newman began to write soon after the appearance of Kingsley's pamphlet, certainly before the end of March. He considered for a time a series of lectures like the *Difficulties of Anglicans,* which Ambrose St. John had urged, but soon gave up the idea of a lecture platform as incongruous with the nature of the revelations he would have to make. He resolved instead to publish his story at his own expense in a series of weekly pamphlets. Longmans hesitated at first but then agreed that the novelty of the method would help to attract attention. Accordingly, the *Apologia* first appeared in seven pamphlets published on Thursdays between April 21 and June 2, 1864, with an eighth, an appendix called *Answer in Detail to Mr. Kingsley's Accusations,* appearing two weeks later on June 16.[12] Newman allowed the interval, not merely because the eighth part was longer than the others and required more time, but because he wished to consider any reply Kingsley might have made in the meantime. His failure to do so Newman considered a great tactical error.

The fact is that on medical advice Mrs. Kingsley saw to it that her run-down and overworked husband, already in a high state of tension, did not read the *Apologia* until it was complete. Then, though he had earlier hinted at 'such a revanche as will make [Newman] wince, if any English common sense is left in him, which I doubt',[13] Kingsley decided to let the whole thing drop and 'retired . . . into silence, with a reputation permanently damaged'.[14]

The first two of Newman's pamphlets were called 'Mr. Kingsley's Method of Disputation' and 'True Mode of Meeting Mr. Kingsley'. Pamphlets III-VI (1865 edition, Chapters I to IV) were known as 'History of My Religious Opinions'. Part VII was called 'General Answer to Mr. Kingsley'. According to the account given to Wilfrid Ward by Fr. Ignatius Dudley Ryder, who succeeded Newman as Superior of the Birmingham Oratory, Newman found the 'effort of writing the weekly parts . . . overpowering. On such occasions he wrote through the night, and he has been found with his head in his hands crying like a child over the, to him, well-nigh impossibly painful task of public confession.'[15]

Newman first sketched the general plan of the work, with the principal heads of narrative and argument, and fixed it in large letters to the wall opposite his desk. He did his writing on large sheets of paper folded down the middle. Each page he divided in two and wrote on both sides, on the recto leaving the right-hand column free for his many additions and corrections, and on the verso doing the reverse so that when the sheets were unfolded, the text occupied the centre in two columns.[16] Scattered throughout the manuscript are pages not divided but written across.

Most of the manuscripts of Newman's published works have disappeared, possibly having been disposed of by printer or publisher, though this seems strange when one considers how careful Newman invariably was in keeping even the smallest records of his life. Much of the manuscript of the *Apologia* has survived, however, perhaps because what the printer received was not most of what remains at the Birmingham Oratory but a copy of this manuscript made by Newman's sometime secretary and future literary executor, Fr. William Neville.

The manuscript at the Oratory consists of the first four parts, more than half of Part VI, and several sections and scattered pages of Part VII. There are also fragments of Part V and of Part VIII. Part VI differs from most of the rest in that the pages are not divided into columns and are written on one side only. The writing, much clearer than elsewhere, is probably Fr. Neville's, whose script closely resembled Newman's. At the top of the first page of VI is written in pencil *'copy'* and 'Part 6 copy of 6th'. At the top of the page where it breaks off (1864 ed., p. 321), the same unknown hand has written 'This makes the whole of Part 6', an obvious error unless it means all that has survived of that part.

The manuscript of Part VI and a few other pages are signed occasionally in the margins with the names 'Edwards' and 'Yeowall'. If, as seems possible, these are the names of printers at the London firm of Gilbert and Rivington, which printed the *Apologia,* then these signed pages may be the only part of the final manuscript which survives. In any event, much of the present manuscript is so heavily corrected and revised as to be virtually illegible from time to time, even to those familiar with Newman's script; and it is hard to see how the most hardened printers could have worked with it. Furthermore, the manuscript differs frequently, sometimes extensively, from what actually appeared in the pamphlets of 1864. Surviving scraps show that Newman heavily revised his galley proof, sometimes at the suggestion of friends like Copeland and Keble, who received copies of it. The present edition of the *Apologia* supplies in the notes the more significant of the passages in the original manuscript which Newman later cancelled.

It was on April 10 that he began the stretches of prolonged labour he has described so vividly in letters to intimate friends. 'During the writing and reading of my Part 3', he confessed to Rogers on April 22, 'I could not get on from beginning to end for crying.'[17] On May 2 he wrote to Hope-Scott:

> I never have been in such stress of brain and such pain of heart,—and I have both trials together. Say some good prayers for me. I have been writing without interruption of Sundays since Easter Monday—five weeks—and I have at least three weeks more of the same work to come. I have been constantly in tears, and constantly crying out with distress. I am sure I never could say what I am saying in cold blood, or if I waited a month. . . . [18]

One day, we learn from his diary, he worked uninterruptedly for sixteen hours on Part III and once for twenty-two on Part V. As he began in Part III to tell his own story and the details piled up, he had twice to enlarge his original plan, which called for a 'History of My Religious Opinions' first in Parts III and IV, then in III, IV, and V, and finally in the four parts from III to VI.[19] This change of plan during the course of composition may account in part for a certain confusion in the chronology of the chapters: e.g. the fact that Tract 90 is treated at the end of Part IV (to 1839), although it did not appear until 1841. However, this confusion is more apparent than real and may be explained better on thematic grounds. Tract 90 grew out of speculations that long antedated 1841, and it is part of the general case for Anglo-Catholicism that is the main subject of Part IV (1865, Ch. II).

When it was all over and peace of mind was again possible, and with the acclaim his story had received reinforcing the artist's satisfaction in a work well done, Newman could look back on his ordeal with almost childlike wonder and exhilaration. 'I never had such a time of it', he wrote to a Dominican nun. 'When I was in Oxford I have twice written a pamphlet in a night, and once in a day, but now I had writing and printing upon me at once; but with so much suffering, such profuse crying, such long spells of work . . . that it is a prodigious, awful marvel that I have got through it and that I am not simply knocked up by it.'[20] His success was a providential sign that there was still a work in the world for him to do. Henceforward he would be heard with respect and considerable sympathy. The *Apologia* meant the start of a new and final period of literary activity.

Rarely has any prophecy been more quickly fulfilled than Newman's assurance that he would vanquish, not his accuser, but his judges. Before the last part of the *Apologia* was in print, the reviews began to come in; and in spite of certain qualifications and some dissenting opinions (one or two pamphlets in Kingsley's favour appeared, and there were those who agreed with the view that T. H. Huxley expressed much later: 'That man is the slipperiest sophist I have ever met with. Kingsley was entirely right about him'[21]), most critics in the influential journals of opinion agreed that Newman had unquestionably won his point and proved himself an honest man.[22]

R. H. Hutton again led the way with two articles in the *Spectator* of June 4 and June 11. He admitted that for those neither far enough away to judge by his writings alone nor close enough to be his confidants, Newman's behaviour during the years of his uncertainty might have seemed perplexing, even to the extent of shaking one's trust in his simplicity of purpose. Yet he repeated his original view 'that there was absolutely no justification for Mr. Kingsley's rash accusation' and contended that 'it would be mere dullness of nature not to recognize freely the whole truthfulness and almost childlike candour of the autobiographic sketch now before us', which was the work of a 'great and noble mind', one 'incapable . . . of insincerity'.[23]

On June 16 *The Times* devoted three columns to the *Apologia,* affirming that 'every candid reader will acquit Dr. Newman of any dishonest intentions in his relations towards the English Church during his abode in her', a transition state being a very trying period: 'It is a situation which involves many tender considerations, and nice estimates, and intricate comparisons of conflicting duties; but it is a situation which a person may be in without dishonesty, and which he may carry out without dishonesty; and Dr. Newman may claim with perfect right a decisive verdict in his favour on this question.' Perhaps the most perceptive of the critic's observations was that

> . . . the accuracy and minuteness with which Dr. Newman registers all the different fluctuations of the theological barometer and conducts a doctrinal transmutation through all its stages, noting its rises and falls, its pauses and advances, till it reaches its destined completeness, unconsciously reveal in the *Apologia* an undertaking which, though doubtless accompanied with much to harass and distress, has been in some respects not other than a labour of love to him.[24]

On June 25 the *Saturday Review,* which had already castigated Kingsley, introduced its review of the *Apologia* with the remark that a

> loose and offhand, and, we may venture to add, an unjustifiable imputation, cast on Dr. Newman by a popular writer more remarkable for vigorous writing than vigorous thought, has produced one of the most interesting works of the present literary age. Dr. Newman is one of the finest masters of language; his logical powers are almost unequalled, and, in one way or other, he has influenced the course of English thought more perhaps than any of his contemporaries.

It spoke of his task as to account for 'what vulgar minds will always brand as an act of desertion'. The complexity of his mind meant that it is 'not given to the gentlemen who write in religious newspapers, or to the ordinary run of pious Christians, to understand Dr. Newman; and to say that a man is receiving Protestant pay while he is teaching Popish doctrine saves thought, and gives an opportunity for coarse-minded piety to violate the ninth commandment'. The *Apologia* as a whole it found chiefly useful not as a vindication of the author's sincerity and pureness of motive, 'for such was not required', but as 'a curious and most interesting chapter in psychology', and as 'a valuable contribution from the most trustworthy source to the inner history of the Church of England in very momentous times', the cold facts of a William Palmer having 'at last been invested with life, and described with the energy of a master, by the one original genius who has risen above the heavy clouds and fog of the Tractarian flats'. It reaffirmed that there was 'the stamp of truth in every word which Newman utters about himself', and that he was 'thoroughly and implicitly to be believed'. Newman had anatomized himself with 'dignity and pathos': the 'lofty egotism' of the work was 'inseparable perhaps from the occasion'.[25]

Of the monthly and quarterly magazines, we may take *Blackwood's,* the *Edinburgh Review,* and the *Quarterly* as examples. The first, though finding the dialectical duel 'not in any sense of the term an agreeable spectacle', devoted much of its space to an attack on Kingsley, 'entirely and wantonly the aggressor', for endangering 'higher interests than the personal reputation of a rash man'. It lamented the 'strange confusion of ideas from which, let him discuss what topic he may, Mr. Kingsley seems incapable of extricating himself'. As for Newman, it expressed the opinion that he showed a far greater yearning for truth than Mr. Kingsley in any of his works: 'We believe him to be now, and always to have been, a thoroughly honest man. We do not distrust one word of all that he has written about himself.' Kingsley was only 'a misguided clever man', but Newman was 'a fallen angel'.[26]

The *Edinburgh Review,* in an article on Whately's *Miscellaneous Remains from the Commonplace Book,* was inclined to think Whately right in holding that there was too much 'reserve' and 'economy' in the conduct of the Oxford Movement, but spoke of the *Apologia* as a 'most engaging record . . . now in the hands of every one'; and of Newman as a 'great leader of men', and of the 'honest allegiance to truth' of 'a man of honour'.[27]

Most pointed of all the reviews and in the long run perhaps the most influential was that by Samuel Wilberforce in the *Quarterly.* The writer, son of the Evangelical abolitionist and himself the Bishop of

Oxford, had seen his three brothers and many of his old friends go over to Rome since Newman's conversion; his own faith in Anglicanism remained unshaken, however, and in his review he attempted to show that nothing in Newman's process of change was an argument in favour of following him. He is gentle to Kingsley, not anxious to give more than 'bare justice' to Newman, and holds that 'this strange narrative' offers 'abundant reason . . . for the widely-diffused impression of that being true which it is so pleasant to find unfounded'. Nevertheless, he is quite definite about Newman's success. These pages, he says, were meant to exhibit to Newman's countrymen

> . . . the whole secret of his moral and spiritual anatomy; they were intended to prove that he was altogether free from that foul and disgraceful taint of innate dishonesty, the unspoken suspicion of which in so many quarters had so long troubled him; the open utterance of which, from the lips of a popular and respectable writer, was so absolutely intolerable to him. From that imputation it is but bare justice to say he does thoroughly clear himself. The post-mortem examination of his life is complete; the hand which guided the dissecting-knife has trembled nowhere, nor shrunk from any incision. All lies perfectly open, and the foul taint is nowhere.[28]

Early in the controversy Kingsley's own master and friend, F. D. Maurice, who judged men more by the nature of their search than by the views they held, expressed the opinion that (despite 'all apparent evidence') 'Newman loves the truth in his heart of hearts, and more now than when he was an Anglican'.[29]

And how did Kingsley feel about all this? Hutton had written: ' . . . we can scarcely conceive that Mr. Kingsley himself can read this apology without the profoundest personal conviction of the stedfast uprightness and true simplicity of Dr. Newman's theological career.'[30] He was very wrong. Kingsley was still convinced that Newman was alternately a knave and a fool, but he was now more prudent than to pursue the matter further. On June 8, 1864, he wrote to Alexander Macmillan a letter 'so deplorable in taste', says one of his biographers, 'that if it had not already been made public one could wish to leave it unnoticed'.[31]

> Here is my ultimatum on the Newman question, which please shew (privately) to any one and every one you like, including Mr. Hutton.
>
> I have determined to take no notice whatever of Dr. Newman's apology.
>
> 1. I have nothing to retract, apologize for, explain. Deliberately, after 20 years of thought, I struck as hard as I could. Deliberately I shall strike again, if it so please me, though not one literary man in England approved. I know too well of what I am talking.
>
> 2. I cannot trust—I can only smile at—the autobiography of a man who (beginning with Newman's light, learning, and genius) ends in believing that he believes in the Infallibility of the Church, and in the Immaculate Conception. If I am to bandy words, it must be with sane persons.
>
> 3. I cannot be [?] weak enough to put myself a second time, by any fresh act of courtesy, into the power of one who, like a treacherous ape, lifts to you meek and suppliant eyes, till he thinks he has you within his reach, and then springs, gibbering and biting, at your face.

He goes on in this vein, ending with a wish that 'poor dear Thackeray' were alive:

> He knew what I know, and would have taken a tone about this matter, which would have astonished too many literary men. He was too true a liberal to pat lies and bigotry on the back.
>
> Give my really kind regards to Mr. Hutton, for whom I have a sincere respect.[32]

There were, of course, various objections to Newman's position as outlined in the *Apologia*. The reaction of Catholics, best indicated by the letters Newman later incorporated in the text, was immensely favourable, on the whole, but with some reservations.[33] It was hardly to be expected, however, that a group of Protestant writers in nineteenth-century England should applaud Newman's choice of creed as well as his honesty in making it. At least some indication of their views may be given here, though it will necessarily be inadequate.

Like many critics of Newman to this day, the reviewers generally attributed his conversion to faulty premisses logically carried out, to various psychological factors more or less determining his conclusions, or to both. Thus to Hutton (who in later years moved closer to Newman's thought), all Newman's 'premises of thought were Roman Catholic from the beginning'; his logic, as displayed in the *Apologia,* registered 'the *rate*' rather than 'the track' of his advance; and, except for the relation of God to the soul, all the other great theses of Newman's theology 'seem to us to recommend themselves less as self-demonstrating, than as parts of a great system which is given on a high authority, and which he finds perfectly adapted to cope with the naturalism and anarchy of what he calls Liberal thought'. Newman's was 'the mind of a great reactionary, recoiling upon the strongest defences it can find against the decomposing power of modern thought, instead of throwing itself on that power of faith which is really greatest only in alliance with perfect freedom'.[34]

The fact that Anglo-Catholicism, at least as a coordinated theory, was still relatively undeveloped when

Newman wrote the *Apologia*, may help to account for the agreement of *Blackwood's*, *The Times*, and the *Saturday Review* that Newman's theory of the Church was not only individual but even highly visionary from the start. Both the *Saturday Review* and *The Times* likened Newman in some respects to an Irvingite, and though the latter admitted that 'his course of change was from the first in one direction, and . . . exhibits a unity and consistency', still it felt compelled to state that the *Apologia* 'has not diminished our idea of the extraordinary wildness and visionariness of the task which he imposed upon himself and the object he fixed upon in this undertaking of Church reformation as he understood and conceived it'. Characterizing as obsolete Newman's 'fundamental idea of the theological necessity of going ahead, absolute logical development in one direction, &c.', *The Times* held that such an attitude had long been changed for 'a larger basis of judgment'.[35]

Blackwood's agreed that Newman had built up a theology of his own, to which Evangelicals and liberals were expected to subscribe, and was therefore wrong because his principles were 'indefensible *ab initio*', however perfectly they might agree with one another.[36] The *Saturday Review*, looking askance at the influence of the Alexandrian Platonists and at Newman's 'mysterious view' of two and two only luminously self-evident beings, felt there was truth in the opinion that Newman had never really understood the Church of England, and spoke of his religious system as a 'piecing here and patching there'.[37]

From Bishop Wilberforce, a moderate Anglo-Catholic and not likely therefore to regard Newman's conception of the Church as visionary or obsolete nor his logic as flawless, came an interpretation almost wholly psychological. Newman's 'defection' was due to the 'peculiarities of the individual'. His mind was eminently subjective and, though honest, had no engrossing affection for abstract truth. In fact, so feeble was Newman's hold on any truth external to himself by comparison with his conception of what was passing within himself 'that the external truth was always liable to corrections which would make its essential elements harmonize with what was occurring within his own intellectual or spiritual being'. From such a condition came both an 'inexhaustible mutability in his view on all subjects' and 'a continually recurring temptation to entire scepticism as to everything external to himself'. Wilberforce saw no logical connexion between the various steps outlined in the *Apologia:* 'It was not that argument was weighed against argument: there was argument nowhere. The leaning to Rome was from the bias of his own mind, not from the strength of her cause; that bias was counteracted only by personal inclination, which a change in the atmosphere around him might at any moment reverse.' This change came with the outburst against Tract 90, which had a decisive effect on 'that sensitive, ill-understood soul', already marked by 'a noble and mounting ambition . . . struggling within him'. From that time on, '[h]is heart . . . began to eat itself'.[38] In this important review are anticipated such later interpretations of Newman as those of A. M. Fairbairn, F. L. Cross, and Walter E. Houghton.

One other note in Wilberforce's essay deserves attention, for as we have seen, it reflects a strain in English thought which has by no means disappeared: i.e. that granting Kingsley's mistakes and Newman's honesty, there still remains the question whether, as Mrs. Kingsley put it, 'the Roman Catholic priesthood are encouraged or discouraged to pursue "Truth for its own sake"'. Kingsley himself, according to his wife, always felt 'that the general position which he had taken up against the policy of the Roman Catholic Church, remained unshaken'; and in his funeral sermon for Kingsley, Dean Stanley, endorsing his view, implied that the Roman Church substituted authority for truth.[39] Wilberforce expressed the opinion that truthfulness was more likely to be found among Anglicans than among Catholics. And a biographer of Kingsley has written: 'Nor is it true, though Mrs. Kingsley has affirmed it, that "the main point of issue was the question whether the Roman Catholic priesthood are encouraged to pursue truth for its own sake", and not the personal integrity of Newman, though the former question, if really discussed on its merits, would have been far more fruitful.'[40]

With the public at large, however, the *Apologia* probably accomplished its aim even in regard to this matter. It was a triumph not only for Newman but for the Roman Church in general. As Hutton wrote in 1890, it was 'a book which, I venture to say, has done more to break down the English distrust of Roman Catholics, and to bring about a hearty good fellowship between them and the members of other Churches, than all the rest of the religious literature of our time put together'.[41]

The *Apologia* appeared first, as we have seen, in the form of eight pamphlets. These were later corrected for minor errors and then published in book form. In this form there are three principal versions:

1. The first edition: *Apologia Pro Vita Sua: Being A Reply to a Pamphlet Entitled 'What, Then, Does Dr. Newman Mean?'* (London: Longman, Green, Longman, Roberts, and Green, 1864). This consists of the first seven pamphlets or 'parts' consecutively paged and a separately paged appendix including the eighth pamphlet, 'Answer in Detail to Mr. Kingsley's Accusations'; notes giving the Latin, French, and Italian originals of various passages translated in the preceding section; a list of Newman's works; and a postscript containing Bishop Ullathorne's testimonial letter. (430+127 pp.)

Parts I and II and the original Appendix, in which Kingsley's charges were refuted as 'blots' and numbered presumably after the Articles to a total of thirty-nine, are reprinted in Appendix C of the present edition. It should be noted that there are at least two issues of the first edition which differ very slightly in minor wording from what might be called the standard version of the 1864 text. One of these was known to Wilfrid Ward, who supplied the variant readings in his 1913 edition of the *Apologia.* Another, differing only slightly from Ward's variant issue, is in the Newberry Library, Chicago. The variant readings of both issues are supplied in the present edition. Like Wilfrid Ward, I am unable to account for these variants but would surmise that they represent wording changed early, at Newman's direction, during the printing of the original pamphlets. Some of these early pamphlets must have remained to be bound up with the rest in book form. If this theory is correct, it is possible that there are still other variant issues of the first edition.

2. The second edition: *History of My Religious Opinions* (London: Longman, Green, Longman, Roberts, and Green, 1865). It consists of a brief Preface replacing the polemical Parts I and II of the first edition; five chapters (Parts III-VII, slightly revised) which form the heart of the *Apologia;* a series of Notes numbered A to G which represent a recasting of the 'Answer in Detail' so as to eliminate all reference to Kingsley, plus two new Notes: A and B, 'Liberalism' and 'Series of Saints' Lives of 1843-44', as well as a partially new one: D, 'Ecclesiastical Miracles'. There is also a section of 'Supplemental Matter', including a chronological list of the letters and papers quoted, a list of Newman's works, Bishop Ullathorne's letter, and the letters from the various groups of clergy and laity. (xxiv+379 pp.)

3. The definitive text: *Apologia Pro Vita Sua: Being a History of his Religious Opinions,* on which the present edition is based. This version, which reached its final form *c.* 1886, about four years before Newman's death, differs from the second edition only slightly in the main body of the text and is printed from the same plates. The original title returned in 1873, the title of the second edition (with 'My' changed to 'his') being used for a subtitle. The Preface was enlarged in 1869 by the addition of extracts from Parts I and II, and there were some sixty small textual changes made in various impressions after 1865, only a few of them at all significant. The principal difference is the series of 'Additional Notes' supplied by Newman between 1869 and 1879. (xxviii+395 pp.)[42]

The second edition of the *Apologia* was reprinted, usually in runs of 500 or 750 copies each, in 1869 (twice), 1873, 1874, 1875, 1876, 1878, 1879 (twice), 1881, 1882, 1883, 1885 (when Longmans acquired the copyright from Newman and the stereotype plates from Rivington), and almost yearly thereafter for many years. After 1885 Newman was paid in advance a royalty of one-fourth the retail price (6*s.*) on each new impression: e.g. £56. 5*s.* on a run of 750 copies. Previously he had paid Longmans a 10 per cent. commission on sales.[43] Newman retained the right to make small additions to and corrections in the text without charge. The last significant one he made concerned hell, which he tried to make 'less terrible' (p. 19) to the 'reason' in 1864, to the 'intellect' in 1865, and finally to the 'imagination' *c.* 1886. Save for insignificant changes in punctuation, the present edition gives all the variant readings.[44] If the first variant listed is undated, it is the reading of the 1864 edition. If the variant is dated, e.g. 64-78, it means that this is the reading in all impressions before that of 1879. As it has proved impossible thus far to assemble all the impressions in which Newman could have made his various small changes after 1865, these dates may in a few cases be only close approximations rather than exact.

The material dropped in the second edition is almost entirely concerned with Kingsley, who is no longer ever mentioned by name and is alluded to only when necessary as 'my accuser' or 'a popular writer' or included in the group of 'my accusers'. The duel with Kingsley had served its purpose in winning Newman a hearing; Newman had nothing against Kingsley personally; and the sharp thrusts, especially of Part I and of the Appendix, had pained some readers. Accordingly, Newman dropped such remarks as 'Mr. Kingsley's word of honour is about as valuable as in the jester's opinion was the Christian charity of Rowena' and 'I am in a train of thought higher and more serene than any which slanders can disturb. Away with you, Mr. Kingsley, and fly into space.' The last chapter, 'General Answer to Mr. Kingsley', became 'Position of My Mind Since 1845'.

From the 'thirty-nine blot' Appendix, which as we have seen he completely recast, Newman eliminated even his answer to what the Kingsleys always regarded as a serious objection:

> Then he says that I committed an economy in placing in my original title-page, that the question between him and me, was whether 'Dr. Newman teaches that Truth is no virtue'. It was a 'wisdom of the serpentine type', since I did not add, 'for its own sake'. Now observe: First, as to the matter of fact, in the course of my Letters, which have that Title-page, I printed the words 'for its own sake', *five* times over. Next, pray, what kind of a virtue is that, which is *not* done for its own sake? So this, after all, is the Writer's idea of virtue! a something that is done for the sake of something *else;* a sort of expedience. He is honest, it seems, simply *because* honesty is 'the best policy', and on that score it is that he thinks himself virtuous. Why, 'for its own sake' enters into the very idea or definition of a

virtue. Defend me from such virtuous men, as this Writer would inflict upon us! Blot thirty-six.

It is easy enough to understand why some of Newman's readers had found such passages less than edifying.

There is no doubt that the *Apologia* of 1865 is a clearer and more effective book than its predecessor. There is no very substantial difference between them, to be sure: almost half the roughly nine hundred changes in the main body of the text are in punctuation; and the rest are often so slight in nature and subtle in effect as almost to preclude formal analysis. Yet slight as most of the changes are, anyone interested in the nuances of style will find much of interest and value in the process whereby a great writer, always given to the most painstaking revisions and now no longer pressed for time, made what had already been acclaimed a masterpiece into the clearer, more vivid, and dramatic story of a still more appealing human being.[45]

The history of Newman's reputation parallels the intellectual development of the modern world. At the turn of the last century, when rationalism still predominated, it was customary to praise Newman for his style and charm and to pass over, if not to deplore, his thought. A verdict like Saintsbury's that he was 'one of the greatest masters of quietly exquisite prose that the world has ever seen'[46] was commonly rendered innocuous by a warning like Hugh Walker's that 'his brilliant logic had no sound foundation in reason' and that he was 'a conspicuous, though personally blameless and most attractive, specimen of the class of those who sink "from the van and the freemen" back "to the rear and the slaves"'.[47]

Half a century later, in a world more apt to turn for guidance to a Freud, a Kierkegaard, or a Sartre than to T. H. Huxley or John Stuart Mill, such judgements had come to seem as shallow as they were rare. Today we are witnessing the fulfilment of Dean Church's prophecy that Newman was 'a great writer, of whose genius and religious feeling Englishmen will one day be even prouder than they are now'.[48]

Almost inevitably, of course, judgements of Newman and the *Apologia* continue to be coloured to some degree by the religious or ideological bent of the judges. Ever since the appearance of Geoffrey Faber's *Oxford Apostles* in 1933, for instance, one strain in the writing on Newman has implied that the subconscious motives evident in the feminine traits of his character and the power of his attraction to Hurrell Froude are of far greater significance in his development than Newman himself or a pre-Freudian age could be expected to realize. Anglo-Catholics and some Protestants, though respecting and even venerating Newman, are likely to account for his secession more or less in terms of his sensitivity to criticism, to a feeling of what a sympathetic and scholarly biographer, F. L. Cross, has called *ressentiment* at the treatment he received in the affair of Tract 90. Roman Catholic writers stress the rational grounds for his change of creed.

If one accepts Newman's own view that 'my one paramount reason for contemplating a change is my deep, unvarying conviction that our Church is in schism, and that my salvation depends on my joining the Church of Rome',[49] as the present writer does, for the evidence of Newman's letters and later life seems to bear it out, there is no denying that many influences converged to bring him to this frame of mind. As he himself said, 'things are wonderfully linked together', and it is precisely Newman's recognition of the multiplicity of influences that combine in every significant human decision which makes the *Apologia* an unusually sophisticated book for its age. At any rate, it seems clear enough today that Newman was almost as much influenced by the 'bright and beautiful' Hurrell Froude as Tennyson, say, was by Hallam—though the Freudians are too apt to forget that like Tennyson, Newman had a well-attested masculine as well as a feminine side to his character. And though he himself said more than once that he was 'not conscious of resentment, or disgust, at any thing that has happened to me',[50] he also recognized that 'it has been the recent speeches and acts of authorities, who had so long been tolerant of Protestant error, which has given to inquiry and to theory its force and its edge'.[51]

Still, he puts the decisive stress on 'inquiry' and 'theory', wishing to be guided by his reason and conscience, he says, and not by his feelings. And he gives us a clue to his development that has not yet been followed up in the detail it requires: a feeling that 'the reasons for which I believe as much as our system teaches, *must* lead me to believe more, and that not to believe more is to fall back into scepticism'.[52] Given the Anglo-Catholic premisses Newman had come to accept before 1833, a temperament deferential to authority, and an intellect unusually responsive to argument from analogy and what he called antecedent probability—it was analogy that led him to the theory of development—is there anything really surprising or 'illogical' in a decision for Rome, let alone so surprising as to warrant the assumption that the compelling motives of a convert always scrupulously introspective were other than those he adduces? Perhaps Newman could have made clearer in the *Apologia* the process by which in the years from 1843 to 1845 theory or opinion gradually became certitude; but he would have thought it beyond the power of the mind to know or words to register more fully than he has done, 'when it is, that the scales in the balance of opinion begin to turn, and what was a greater probability in behalf of a belief becomes a positive doubt against it'.[53] And here again, as the critic of the *Saturday Review* recognized, he seems more sophisticated than those who expect more.

But of course such matters are incapable of final resolution in this world. The important thing is that it is far easier now for the unbeliever to see the *Apologia* as George Eliot saw it long ago: 'as the revelation of a life—how different in form from one's own, yet with how close a fellowship in its needs and burthens—I mean spiritual needs and burthens'.[54] And once he begins to read Newman, he is likely to respond to him less like Hugh Walker and more like Lionel Trilling: 'the challenge that he offers to one's assumptions is so lively and so real, his sense of the world is so subtle and coherent, and his psychological perception is so complex and shrewd that any reader who takes pleasure in endangering his own fixed ideas must be grateful for the exhilaration that Newman can give'.[55]

As for the believer, the striving of an ecumenical age toward 'a deeper understanding of the grounds of faith and the nature of religious experience' has made it easier for men of all creeds to recognize the justice of Basil Willey's verdict: 'It is because Newman contributed so largely to the deepening of that understanding that we may claim for him a place, not amongst the reactionaries or obscurantists, but among the light bearers of the nineteenth century.'[56]

For this Newman, who as another Protestant scholar has written, 'remains, and will always remain, an abiding force for all men of intellect and imagination',[57] the reader must look especially to the moving sermons, Anglican and Catholic; to the profound speculations on faith and reason which begin with the *University Sermons* and culminate in *A Grammar of Assent;* to the influential but too commonly unread *Development of Christian Doctrine;* and to that epitome of Christian humanism, *The Idea of a University*. To this perennial Newman, the *Apologia* is an admirable introduction, being the quintessence of his thought. It suffers, however, from being tied to the events, figures, and terminology of a theological history, both ancient and modern, which had already grown obscure by 1864 and has become infinitely more so since the virtual eclipse of theology in the educational world.

If the *Apologia* needed annotation in 1864, as William Longman implied to Newman, it needs it all the more today if the book is to be more than another widely acknowledged but largely unread classic. It is the hope of the present editor that the notes here provided—in Newman's own words when possible—may lead the reader to what Newman himself would have considered a real and not merely a notional knowledge of his remarkable odyssey. The more one thinks of the task that Newman set himself in his *Apologia*—to chart in all its complexity the spiritual evolution of a gifted and sensitive human being—the easier it becomes to understand how he could say of it without exaggeration: 'I have done various bold things in my life: this is the boldest.'[58]

Notes

[2] *Parochial and Plain Sermons,* v. 84, 80, and 82.

[3] *Discussions and Arguments,* p. 293.

[4] *Historical Sketches,* ii. 223. The very title of Newman's story, *Apologia pro Vita Sua,* links it to the Fathers, who produced works with similar titles. Newman's own favourite, Athanasius, that untiring defender of orthodoxy whose name became a rallying cry in nineteenth-century England, wrote an *Apologia de Fuga Sua.* (The title of Coleridge's poem 'Apologia pro Vita Sua' was apparently an editorial one, given to it in 1907. See *The Complete Poetical Works of Samuel Taylor Coleridge,* ed. E. H. Coleridge [2 vols., Oxford, 1912], i. 345.)

[5] The *Apologia* is not an autobiography nor even a complete spiritual autobiography of the years between 1801 and 1845. It is primarily a work of rhetoric. For a discussion which space does not permit here of how Newman put it together, the materials he used and the dramatic framework into which he cast them, see Martin J. Svaglic, 'The Structure of Newman's *Apologia*', in *Victorian Literature: Modern Essays in Criticism,* ed. Austin Wright (New York, 1961), pp. 225-37, reprinted from *PMLA,* lxvi (1951), 138-48. See also Walter E. Houghton, *The Art of Newman's 'Apologia'* (New Haven and London, 1945).

[6] [Wilfrid] Ward, [*The Life of John Henry Cardinal Newman* (2 vols., London, 1912)], ii. 21.

[7] Ibid., p. 24.

[8] Ibid., p. 22.

[9] For some of the information that follows, I am indebted to a valuable article by Henry Tristram, 'Note au bas d'un grand texte', *La France franciscaine. Recherches de théologie, philosophie, histoire,* iiie *série,* xxii (1939), 35-48.

[10] *Historical Sketches,* ii. 219.

[11] *Apologia,* Appendix C, p. 407.

[12] And not on June 25, as Ward says (*Life,* ii. 28).

[13] Quoted from a letter to his curate Frederick Stapleton by M. F. Thorp, *Charles Kingsley,* p. 159.

[14] Guy Kendall, *Charles Kingsley and His Ideas,* p. 157. This is perhaps overstated, as Kingsley's career, at least, does not appear to have suffered any damage from the episode. In 1873 he was made Canon of Westminster.

[15] Ward, *Life,* ii. 23.

[16] See Tristram, 'Note au bas d'un grand texte', p. 36.

[17] Ward, *Life,* ii. 19.

[18] Ward, *Life,* ii. 25.

[19] Tristram, 'Note au bas d'un grand texte', pp. 42-44.

[20] Ward, *Life,* ii. 30-31.

[21] From a letter of May 30, 1889, to Sir James Hooker. *Life and Letters of Thomas Henry Huxley* (2 vols., London, 1900), ii. 226. The principal reviewer to make this charge was James Fitzjames Stephen, brother of Leslie, whose similar views have already been referred to. In *Fraser's Magazine,* lxx (1864), pp. 265-303, Fitzjames Stephen argued that though Newman was personally honest, he had 'been brought to accept superstition by sophistry' and that the 'misapprehension of the nature of probability' vitiated his argument.

On the other hand, the *Westminster Review* held that Newman not only clearly bested Kingsley in the polemic but, though wrong in his ultimate conclusion, was logical and consistent in his progress; whereas Kingsley and similar compromisers between 'freedom and authority' were themselves guilty of sophistry. (N.S. xxvi. [1864], 137-51 and 357-77.) These are important reviews, but the nature of their argument makes brief summary impracticable.

[22] The response of the denominational journals varied pretty much according to their attitude toward Catholic theology and Rome. See V. F. Blehl, S.J., 'Early Criticism of the *Apologia*', in *Newman's 'Apologia': A Classic Reconsidered,* pp. 47-63.

[23] *The Spectator,* xxxvii (1864); 655 and 683.

[24] *The Times,* Thursday, June 16, 1864, p. 12.

[25] *The Saturday Review,* xvii (1864), 785 and 786.

[26] *Blackwood's Edinburgh Magazine,* xcvi (1864), 292, 299, 308.

[27] *The Edinburgh Review,* cxx (1864), 378 and 382.

[28] *The Quarterly Review,* cxvi (1864), 544.

[29] In a letter to Dean Stanley, Apr. 19, 1864. See *The Life of Frederick Denison Maurice,* ed. Frederick Maurice (2 vols., London, 1884), ii. 478-9.

[30] *Spectator,* xxxvii (1864), 655.

[31] Kendall, p. 157. The letter was first published by Mrs. Thorp in her *Charles Kingsley* (1937).

[32] [Margaret Farrend Thorp], *Charles Kingsley* [(Princeton, N.J., and London, 1937)], p. 160.

[33] Thus, the future Cardinal Vaughan read it with a mixture of pain and pleasure, the 'egotism' of the book 'disgusting him', the 'satire and contempt appealing to one's bad nature, unfortunately'. Manning, who said the book was like 'a voice from the dead', was annoyed at the parts of the work that he rightly sensed were directed against views and attitudes like his own. See Dom Cuthbert Butler, *The Life and Times of Bishop Ullathorne* (2 vols., London, 1926), i. 332; and Edward Kelly, S.J., 'The *Apologia* and the Ultramontanes', in *Newman's 'Apologia': A Classic Reconsidered,* pp. 26-46.

[34] *Spectator,* xxxvii. 655 and 683. But compare these remarks with his essay 'Newman and Tennyson', *Brief Literary Criticisms* (London, 1906), pp. 192-200.

[35] Thursday, June 16, 1864, p. 12.

[36] *Blackwood's Edinburgh Magazine,* xcvi. 306 and 308.

[37] xvii. 786.

[38] *The Quarterly Review,* cxvi. 546 ff., *passim.* In a letter of May 10, 1864, W. J. Copeland called Newman's attention to perhaps the earliest of the interpretations based on the theory of Newman's 'oversensitive mind': in the *English Churchman* of Oct. 16, 1845, reprinted with editorial comment in the *British Magazine* for November of that year, pp. 530-1 and 537. Copeland's concern was with the rather confusing letter's charge that Newman was, without dishonesty, 'in heart and intention, while nominally with us . . . during the last four years a member of the Roman Communion'. (MS. *Apologia* Letters, Birmingham Oratory.)

[39] See *Life and Works of Charles Kingsley* [(19 vols., London, 1902)], iii. 198-9.

[40] Kendall, *Charles Kingsley and His Ideas,* p. 156. The question, both about Newman and the Roman clergy, seems to have been raised most commonly by historians. Well before Kingsley's charge, Acton doubted that Newman believed in truth for its own sake.

See Joseph L. Altholz, 'Newman and History', *Victorian Studies,* vii (Mar. 1964), 285-94. The author acknowledges in a footnote that 'Recent historians would not accept as norms Acton's ideals of scientific history and absolute truth', but maintains nevertheless that 'his viewpoint supplies a useful angle of approach for a critique of his contemporary, Newman'. We are then told that 'Newman quailed before the massive impartiality and dangerous independence of scientific history' and that his 'commitment to religion was too profound to allow him to submit to the *rival discipline* of history'. (292-4. Italics mine.) But see Owen Chadwick, *From Bossuet to Newman: The Idea of Doctrinal Development* (Cambridge, 1957), *passim*, esp. pp. 193-5; Günter Biemer, 'B. G. Niebuhr and J. H. Newman', *Newman Studien,* vi (1964), 39-54; and the letter of J. Derek Holmes in *Victorian Studies,* viii (1965), 271-7.

[41] Richard Holt Hutton, *Cardinal Newman* (London, 1891), p. 230.

[42] A 'Letter to the Very Rev. Canon Flanagan' was added to the 1904 sixpenny edition by Newman's literary executor, Fr. William Neville. It is not reprinted in the present edition.

[43] The record of these transactions is partially preserved at the Birmingham Oratory in the correspondence of Newman with Longman and with the printing firm of Rivington. There is nothing about the revisions themselves, when they were made or why, except for Longman's concurrence—and perhaps initial suggestion—that the second edition be recast in a permanent literary, less polemical form. (Most of the records at Longmans were destroyed in the air raids of the Second World War.)

Another record in the Oratory files indicates that there were new impressions of the *Apologia* every year from 1865 to 1890, but this is not borne out by the Longman correspondence or by the sales figures for the book, which are given by Martin J. Svaglic in 'Newman's *Apologia:* Introduction, Notes, and Commentary', an unpublished doctoral dissertation (University of Chicago, 1949), pp. 211-13. It may be, however, that Longmans dated anew every year the stock sent out of any given impression.

[44] Wilfrid Ward's Oxford edition of 1913 included the first two editions but only a few of the changes subsequent to 1865. Ward's ingenious method of combining the two editions in the body of the text, with the aid of round and square brackets, proved distracting for many readers and so has not been followed in the present edition.

[45] For a discussion of these matters, see Martin J. Svaglic, 'The Revision of Newman's *Apologia', Modern Philology,* 1 (1952), 43-49.

[46] George Saintsbury, *A History of English Prose Rhythm* (London, 1912), p. 388.

[47] Hugh Walker, *The Age of Tennyson* (London, 1909), pp. 152-3.

[48] R. W. Church, *Occasional Papers* (2 vols., London, 1897), ii. 415.

[49] *Apologia,* p. 206.

[50] Ibid., p. 206.

[51] Ibid., p. 136.

[52] Ibid., p. 207.

[53] Ibid., p. 195.

[54] *The Letters of George Eliot,* [ed. Gordon S. Height (7 vols., New Haven and London, 1954-57)], iv. 159.

[55] *The Nation,* clxii (Feb. 2, 1946), 132. Cf. John Holloway, *The Victorian Sage* (London, 1953), p. 158.

[56] *Nineteenth Century Studies* (London, 1949), p. 90.

[57] Charles Frederick Harrold, ed., *A Newman Treasury* (London, 1945), p. 30.

[58] *Apologia.* p. 91.

Piers Brendon (essay date 1974)

SOURCE: "Froude's Remains," in *Hurrell Froude and The Oxford Movement,* Paul Elek, 1974, pp. 180-97.

[*In the following essay, Brendon argues that the figure of Hurrell Froude reflects the controversy, passion, and piety that characterizes the Tractarian Movement as a whole, particularly as manifested in his* Remains *and the uproar surrounding its publication.*]

Froude's *Remains* constituted a stumbling-block to High Churchmen: to Evangelicals it was not so much foolishness as down-right heresy. Its effect in both cases was to divide. It pushed the Oxford Movement towards a new radicalism, which may have been acceptable to the leadership and to Young Turks like Ward and Oakeley, but was very far from being palatable to a considerable number of its more staid followers. Establishment men like Edward Churton, the biographer of Joshua Watson, were deeply shocked by the *Remains.* Churton told Pusey that 'there are sentences and even pages of that book which I could wish almost to have lost my right hand sooner than seen published.'[1] Moreover, the *Remains* decisively demonstrated the essential Tractarian animus against Low Churchmen, who regarded the Reformation as the *clou* of the Church of England. Until 1838 many Evangelicals, especially those of the *Christian Observer* school, might have been prepared to sink theological differences with the devout men of Oxford in a common defence of the Church against liberalism.[2] After the publication of the *Remains* the *Christian Observer* pronounced, 'The battle of the Reformation must be fought once more.'[3]

The book, especially the first volume which consisted largely of Froude's letters to friends and extracts from his private journal (the other three volumes contained more orthodox and less out-spoken sermons and essays), was abundant posthumous fulfilment of his wish to be an ecclesiastical agitator. It polarised opinion. It was an anti-eirenicon *par excellence.* The book, indeed, out-raged so many readers, with its revelations of the close counsels of the Movement and, more shocking, of the intimate details of Froude's spiritual life, that commentators at the time and historians subsequently questioned the probity of the editors' motives as well as the soundness of their judgement. Why did Newman and Keble publish the *Remains?*[4]

The first point to be emphasised is that they had a very shrewd idea of the kind of impact the book would make. They had no misapprehensions about the nature of its contents and few illusions about the antagonism which would be aroused. From the very first Newman regarded Froude's essays, particularly that on Rationalism, as being 'strong in doctrine', and thought of the publication of his sermons as a necessary ballast to them. These 'would conciliate readers to his essays etc. as showing that he was not a mere ingenious writer, but was serious-minded'.[5] However, Newman was not inhibited by the possibility of protests—'As to rationalists and peculiars clamouring at it, if they did, yet one's knowledge how utterly he would despise such clamours, would make me feel no pain at subjecting him to them.'

By July 1837 Newman was advocating the publication of extracts from Froude's letters in spite of the 'very bold things said' in them. It was the ideal way, whatever the disapprobation, to 'kindle enthusiasm' and to 'show what he was in himself', and Newman was now 'determined any how that the book will be a somewhat romantic one'.[6] In August Newman first read Froude's private Journal and was deeply impressed by its tone of sanctity. It seems that he persuaded Keble that it was their duty to run the risk of publishing it. There is more than a hint of lingering doubt in Keble's comment on Newman's transcription of passages to be included in the *Remains.*

> It being once determined to publish the Journal at all, I do not see that we can be wrong in giving the details of it, startling at first sight as it is to one's mind to think of seeing them in print . . . You may *omit* without scruple as far as I am concerned.[7]

If Froude's letters to Newman are anything to judge by, it is remarkable how much (especially minutiae) was included—undoubtedly by Newman, worried as he was by time's winnowing of memories. The dots in the *Remains* do not conceal nearly as much as nervous contemporaries suspected.

Newman recognised that it was the Journal which would come in for the most unstinting disapproval, but he was intent on showing that the key to Froude's linguistic code was to be found in his personality, which the Journal so nakedly revealed. By reference to Froude's personality his apparent sins of terminological omission and commission could be 'economised' and approximated to the Tractarian doctrinal norm. Newman accurately forecast that Froude would be criticised for not referring to Christ in his Journal and for seeming to lay more emphasis on his own efforts at self-sanctification than on the doctrine of the Atonement. But he and Keble knew Froude to be the true embodiment of Tractarianism and believed that others would come to know him as such through the Journal. The editors found it necessary to labour the point, both in the *Remains* and elsewhere, that they sanctioned and esteemed the whole Froude, embarrassing lacunae, extravagant vocabulary and all. Newman, for instance, aimed to clear Froude 'from the charge of rash affection'[8] by justifying his aggressive remarks on one of the Protestant Reformers, Bishop Jewell, in a long footnote. More generally, Keble chided Perceval about his letter to the *Irish Ecclesiastical Journal*[9]

> which may tend to lessen the authority of his [Froude's] sayings, the later of them: whereas I really think that he wrote more and more calmly as his days shortened: e.g. the Remarks on Arnold are in a perfectly subdued tone, and you yourself have observed on the modification of his views on Romanism.[10]

But for the forthright sponsorship of the cautious Keble and the sibylline Newman, Froude's *Remains* could have been easily dismissed as the aberration of a wild young man. The editors' imprimatur stamped his pronouncements as the official apologia of the Movement.

Newman told Keble that Froude's writings 'contain very deep truths and valuable remarks so as to demand publication in themselves—and useful hints too for the Christian's practice'.[11] The numerous subsidiary arguments in favour of publication which Newman mustered mainly emphasised the heuristic value of the *Remains.* Newman offered Rogers[12] and Keble an array of differing reasons, calculated to appeal to each of them respectively, and perhaps indicative of his own uneasiness. To the latter he wrote,

> These Thoughts will show people what is the real use of such memoranda, and what is the true character of them, not to ascertain our spiritual state in God's sight, but only by way of improving ourselves, discovering our faults etc.

> They show *how* a person may indulge *metaphysical* speculations to the utmost extent and yet be *practical.* It might be a good lesson to various Cambridge men and others . . .

> His profound Church views, as brought out in the Becket Papers, have sometimes seemed to me as a sort of gracious reward for his denying himself that vulgar originality which is rationalistic.[13]

The importance of the practical, on which Keble particularly insisted, was an integral part of the Tractarian message. Newman believed that if Froude could be made to instruct, as it were *in propria persona,* his doctrinal lessons would be illustrated with unforgettable impact.

These reasons for preserving Froude the man as well as Froude the evangelist all point to the fundamental but subterranean motive for the publication in Newman's intensely totemistic mind. Corresponding to his personal desire, previously noticed, to erect a permanent memorial to his friend, impervious to the obliteration of time, Newman felt a public need to forge a distinctive iconography for the Movement. It lacked a labarum, an identificatory symbol, a magnetic focus—a martyr or a saint perhaps. Two years before Froude's death Newman had had a powerful premonition, almost an apocalyptic vision, that Froude was mysteriously ordained to some remarkable religious achievement.

> It is quite impossible that, some way or other, you are not destined to be the instrument of God's purposes. Though I saw the earth cleave, and you fall in, or Heaven open and a chariot appear, I should say just the same . . . You might be of use in the central elemental fire; you might be of use in the depths of the sea.[14]

As Newman studied Froude's papers, as he mused 'upon one who had the most angelic mind of any person I ever fell in with—the most unearthly, the most gifted'[15] it came to him that he had in his hand a sacred text, the testimony of the first Tractarian saint, the revelation of one of God's 'Angels in disguise'.[16] Never mind that the manifestation was flawed and incomplete: Newman recognised, as Tom Mozley put it, that 'a fragment is the very emblem of preciousness.'[17] By consecrating Froude's symbolic relics as an Apostolical shrine, Newman believed he was implementing the divine plan both for his friend and for the Movement. He exclaimed to his friend J. W. Bowden,

> What a marvel it is! but I really do think that a fresh instrument of influence is being opened to us in these Papers. They do certainly portray a saint. They bring out, in the most natural way, an [ethos] as different from what is now set up as perfection as the East from the West.[18]

Thus, the editors knew that the *Remains* was strong meat. They rightly calculated on the volume and nature of the opposition—though they were perhaps somewhat ingenuous in anticipating such things as serious criticisms of the principle of asceticism rather than easy sneers at particular instances of its practice. They were willing to endure discord and vilification of themselves and their friend both because they considered that Froude represented the true, uncompromising spirit of the Movement and because they believed that wide unacceptability was the best guarantee of truth. Newman brought Keble to feel that Froude's death and the discovery of his rich documentary heritage had been a providential provision, that it was their duty, even their fate, to eschew reserve and give pre-eminence to Froude as Tractarian standard-bearer. 'Frittering away . . . his legacy'[19] would not only be a gross betrayal, it would contravene the celestial design.

The editors were clearly acting with the best intentions and from the highest motives throughout. The controversy over their wisdom, or lack of it, in publishing the *Remains* is more difficult to settle. Obviously the book reveals much that is jejune and callow in Froude. Equally apparent is the authenticity and candour of the account of his spiritual striving and the rich suggestiveness of his theological writing. Similarly, though many contemporaries, among them Newman's sister Harriett, condemned the publication as a shocking example of 'bad taste'[20] and a flagrant 'breach of confidence',[21] the student of the period can only be thankful that this unique record of religious development and Tractarian history has been preserved. The very qualities of the *Remains* which offended fastidious contemporaries constitute its chief merits for the historian. It is precisely the raw immediacy, the unpremeditated urgency of the book which are its main credentials. From the practical point of view it is at least arguable (indeed, it was argued by Arnold himself) that the *Remains* jolted the Movement forward in the direction in which Newman and Keble wanted it to go, that the dedication of those committed to the advance more than compensated for the alienation of moderate support, and that extreme High Churchmen were presented with a notable prophet.

What impact did the *Remains* have? The question is an interesting and important one. For the answer to it illuminates both the Delphic possibilities of Froude's life and thought as portrayed in the book as well as the extraordinary heterogeneity of Anglican beliefs. Fissiparousness has always been one tendency latent in Anglican eclecticism. The *Remains,* as Yngve Brilioth has said, was a wedge which split the Tractarian block.[22]

The embryonic right wing of the Movement, the extreme High Church Tractarians, embraced Froude's *Remains* with the same enthusiasm that Newman had evinced on first seeing his papers—they were not only 'very valuable', they were 'so perfect'[23] that they could be regarded as constituting a kind of rubric. The ebullient theological controversialist W. G. Ward read the *Remains* in 1838 and told Pusey, 'From that time . . . began my inclination to see truth where I trust it is.'[24] His friend Frederick Oakeley, also a Fellow of Balliol, testified from his own experience 'to the exceeding practical value of the "Journal"', and added that 'in more than one instance within the author's knowledge, the study of this portion of Mr. Froude's Remains is felt to have been blessed in a very remarkable manner.'[25] The distinguished barrister J. R. Hope learnt habits of self-discipline from Froude and transcribed extracts from the *Remains* into a small notebook for devotional use.[26] The hymn writer Frederick Faber was romantically entranced by the 'rough rude music' emanating from the *Remains* and the 'eccentric feats of chivalry' with which its pages were studded.[27] No doubt such Tractarians as T. W. Allies, William Lockhart and J. D. Dalgairns (all of whom seceded to Rome) read the *Remains* with the same kind of 'exceeding interest and pleasure'[28] as did H. E. Manning—though he, keeping (as he was to do when Cardinal) a weather eye on the Church hierarchy, preserved a rigorous orthodoxy about the Reformation[29] which the wavering Faber, for example, was far from exhibiting at the time.[30] It is not too much to say that the electric suggestiveness of the *Remains* charged the extreme High Church movement with its initial life.

Froude's personal example of holiness, his romantic vision of the medieval Church, his corresponding denigration of the Reformation, his ambitions to 'unprotestantize' the Church—all these things inspired the secessionist wing of the Tractarian Movement. Ward and others of his ilk were willing to rack Froude's principles to their logical breaking point. Whether they actually snapped and their integrity was essentially violated is an almost infinitely debatable question. Newman himself was not prepared to call a halt to the expansions of Froude's epigones. Later, Oakeley tried to work out a precise calculus of where Froude's beliefs would have led him had he lived.[31] It is singularly inconclusive. What can be definitely stated, however, is that Froude's *Remains* was enormously important in changing the climate of Tractarian opinion, in moving its whole axis to the right. Edward Churton, who so lamented the publication, is a reliable witness. He wrote to a friend in 1839,

> It is most extraordinary how opinions change. In my early days I used to be a kind of marked man among my acquaintance for High Church bigotry and extravagance; nobody agreed with me. Now I find myself so fairly out done, that I am unable to follow the flights of many who are advocating the same views. But I really know no difference in myself.[32]

To High Churchmen of the Ward/Oakeley school (including the uneasily acquiescent Newman) Froude's shade seemed to point from the *Remains* imperiously in the direction of Rome.

The secessionist interpretation of the *Remains* was firmly denied by those Tractarians, the followers of Keble and Pusey, who stayed within the Anglican communion to form the core of the Anglo-Catholic party. These can be distinguished from the members of the old High and Dry school—Joshua Watson, H. H. Norris, Edward Churton, William Gresley, J. T. Coleridge, Palmer of Worcester, Hook, Gladstone and so on—by the fact that the latter deplored the publication in more or less strong terms. Of course, High and Dry (like Evangelical) is a loose denomination and the groups merged into one another, with men like Isaac Williams, A. P. Perceval, H. J. Rose, T. Keble (John's brother) and George Cornish holding the middle ground. Thus, for example, Keble recorded that,

> George Cornish and the clergymen round him do not pretend entirely to approve, but it is evident they are on their way to good principles, and that the book has been no check to them whatever: and with regard to the beauty and interest of it, I have found no one who speaks more feelingly. He is especially struck by the Paper on the Liturgies.[33]

Neutrality was not easy. If the *Remains* can be regarded as a litmus paper test on different sections of the Church of England, almost all reactions were strongly positive or negative. In the early stages of the Movement, according to Copeland, 'the older party in London were slightly jealous of what they considered the overforward action and dangerous outspokenness of the younger in Oxford.'[34] The *Remains* transmuted their jealousy into indignation. Its publication, in Roundell Palmer's view, meant that at last 'the departure from the original "Anglican" position of the *Tracts for the Times* became manifest.'[35] To follow Froude in attempting to restore Anglicanism to Apostolicity without straying into Roman Catholicity was a task to which only a few could dedicate themselves.

Keble led the way. He had no regrets about the publication and he became the guardian of Froude's heritage within the Established Church. As time went on, and Newman's allegiance to the Church of England became less reliable, it was Keble's stamp of approval which seemed to guarantee that the *Remains* was Anglican property. In comparison, Pusey's underwriting seemed somewhat half-hearted. He '"swallowed Froude's Remains," as [Newman] said, "with a gulp"', but he could only stomach it, in Copeland's opinion, because he was 'very chivalrous and sanguine'.[36] In other words, his apology for Froude was like so much else in his life, an act of homage to Newman. Thus within the Church of England it was not from Pusey but from Keble and his disciples that the most unembarrassed advocacy of the *Remains* came.

The most intellectually distinguished member of this group, which included men like Frederic Rogers, Tom Mozley, W. J. Copeland, R. W. Church and Charles Marriott, was J. B. Mozley. He was an able theologian who eventually became Regius Professor of Divinity at Oxford. As a clever young under-graduate at Oriel, Mozley had been fascinated by Froude, filling his letters home with eulogistic references to him.[37] In the 1840s Mozley succeeded in producing the best defence of his friend as the author of an impeccable Anglo-Catholic encyclical. In two articles in the *Christian Remembrancer*[38] Mozley set Froude up as the great practical exponent of the *Via Media*. It may have been, as Professor Owen Chadwick claims, that 'affection led Newman to exaggerate Froude's gifts.'[39] It is less easy to dismiss Mozley's high estimate as hyperbolical partiality.

Mozley's verdict was generally accepted by Anglo-Catholics. They believed Froude to have been a man of original genius and zealous piety. Living on borrowed time he had had to condense his thought into ironic gnomes and unpalatable aphorisms. Mozley, Rogers and Church, particularly, anchored themselves to the secure High Anglicanism which they believed Froude had professed. The subsequent adoption by these three men of various more liberal Anglo-Catholic views provides an interesting parallel to the liberal Roman Catholicism which Newman later espoused. Dean Church, indeed, who knew Froude only through the *Remains* (but well enough thus to be impressed by his resemblance to Pascal[40] and to be influenced by his anti-Erastianism) has been dignified by the description 'The Anglican Response to Newman'.[41] Such a title merely serves to enhance the overwhelming stature of Newman. It would be less portentous and perhaps more convincing to claim Church, Mozley and Rogers as the nucleus of (the phrase, it will be remembered, was Mozley's) 'the Democratical High Church School' founded by Froude.[42]

The main body of the High and Dry school, for whom orthodoxy and decorum were themselves forms of piety, probably felt more sorrow and anger about the *Remains* than any other group. There seemed to be only two possibilities. Either the book was a sinister confirmation of the Romish tendencies to which the enemies of the Movement had been animadverting—in which case it was disastrous. Or alternatively it was a gross act of provocation amounting almost to a betrayal of principles—in which case it gave needless ammunition to the foe. Whatever the truth, publication of the close details of Froude's spiritual life was an unforgivable breach of propriety and of confidence. For the editors to sanction it was, in Robert Southey's words, 'a deplorable example of mistaken zeal'.[43]

Sir J. T. Coleridge's vigorous remonstrations with Archdeacon Froude illustrate the prevalent mood of the High and Drys. He regretted the publication of the Journal as unnecessarily laying bare 'the self-tormenting anatomy of his [Froude's] thoughts and feelings, and which he would never have committed to paper if he had dreamt of it meeting the public eye'. He then commented on some of the letters and continued,

> On public grounds unless I am much mistaken, this volume is objectionable, because it will very seriously prejudice the success of what I hope and did unhesitatingly believe to be the *good* cause, which Keble and Mr. Newman have at heart to advance . . . I can conceive nothing so likely to prejudice its advancement as this unfavourable disclosure.[44]

Though he later came to think that the *Remains* was capable of 'instructing and improving', Coleridge maintained his opinion about the unwisdom of its publication and argued that it contributed markedly to the accumulation of bitterness which greeted Tract 90.[45] Coleridge was a man of overwhelming discretion whose judgements were never lightly bestowed. His condemnation was authoritative. It was a conclusive demonstration that the eponymous High and Drys would never be swept away by inundations of Oxonian enthusiasm.

This is not to say, however, that the High and Drys were a completely homogeneous group or that in their hostility to the *Remains* they were all entirely impervious to its influence. Edward Churton adopted one or two of Froude's ideas, for example.[46] But generally the reactions of High and Dry Churchmen to the *Remains* closely corresponded to those of J. T. Coleridge. As much as the book itself they deplored the prefatory endorsement. They longed for, as the High Church reviewer William Sewell put it, 'such an explanation as would exonerate the editors from the unfavourable conclusions which are naturally drawn from it'.[47] They could not disguise their anguish and vexation at the practical damage the book might do, yet they were loth to pronounce immediate anathemas for fear of inculpating Tractarian principles and practices of which they did approve. Thus, like William Palmer, Joshua Watson said nothing, though the *Remains* undoubtedly constituted one of the 'rude shocks' which he experienced at the hands of the Oxford leaders during the late 1830s.[48] W. F. Hook, Vicar of Leeds, was privately convinced that the *Remains* would 'keep back Church principles for fifty years or more'.[49] Publicly the attacked those who condemned the *Remains,* while asserting that he himself dissented from many of Froude's opinions, notably those on the Reformation,[50] to which all Froude's critics repeatedly returned. Even the High Churchmen William Gresley and Sewell, who believed that if the *Remains* was 'thoroughly studied, much of the paradox will vanish',[51] agreed with Hook that Froude's strictures on the Reformers were rash and intemperate.

But in spite of their protests the High and Drys could never, after the publication of the *Remains,* look on the Reformation in quite the same light again. However much they argued that it was a restoration and not a reconstruction, men like Gresley were forced to admit that the Reformers had committed acts of 'irreverence and insubordination' which had positively endangered the Church.[52] Froude's ideal was a radical Church founded on Catholic truth. His achievement was to draw dramatic attention to the incongruity of a conservative Church resting, partially at least, on a revolutionary base. It is understandable that the High and Drys, so steeped in conservatism, resented having their attention drawn to the latent existence of subversive principles within the pregnant body of Christian ideology—to which Froude was so assiduously playing midwife.

The reactions of the various types of High Churchmen to Froude's *Remains* are obviously of the greatest importance because they were all more or less influenced by the book. Many had connections with Oxford and thus had intimations of what the *Remains* might contain. If they were swayed by Froude it was often because they were predisposed to accept on trust the offerings of the Tractarian leaders. Protestant sections of the Church were less impressed by the book's antecedents. They had not generally been immunised by contact with Newman, Keble or Froude and were immediately laid low with amazement and repugnance. Copeland explained that

> no-one who might be brought into relation with them could fail to be sensible of the charm which they were beginning to exercise both separately and collectively on those immediately around them. Subjects were rising to the surface which brought out in conversation the genius and depth of the men themselves and scope for the many pointed sayings of Hurrell Froude, which while they gained currency by repetition from mouth to mouth at the time . . . [did not see light in print until 1838 and] came like a thunderclap upon those who were by that time only too ready to find cause for astonishment and indignation.[53]

The ecclesiastical hierarchy, the large body of Latitudinarian clergy, Low Churchmen and their Evangelical allies responded to the *Remains* in a predictable and pejorative fashion.

For the bishops the *Remains* was the first solid confirmation of the papistical leanings of the Tractarians. Even the moderate Archbishop of Canterbury, William Howley, 'mentioned particularly the publication of Froude's Remains as one chief point which he regretted' about the Movement.[54] Others were more outspoken. The Evangelical Bishop of Ossory, Dr J. T. O'Brien, considered that the *Remains* produced, particularly by its attachment of Froude's ideas to his personality, a 'strong and extensive effect' and that it first signalled the Movement's 'real direction', i.e. towards Rome.[55] His Charge of 1842 was described by Gladstone as 'the heaviest blow that has ever been aimed at Tractarian theology'.[56] In general the prelates were unaccustomed to the task of weighing casuistical distinctions between Catholicism and Popery. It was enough that 'those who sit in the Reformers' seat are traducing the Reformation'[57] and they condemned the *Remains* accordingly. Other Churchmen were not slow to do likewise.

The indiscriminate cry of Popery was also raised by the Low Church periodical press. The moderate Evangelical *Christian Observer* now became raucously hostile to the Oxford Movement. The Protestant *Church of England Quarterly Review* thought that the *Remains* was quite overtly instilling Romanism. 'If words have meaning the author desired the subversion of our existing institutions.'[58] The extreme Evangelical *Christian Examiner* was glad that the Oxford heresiarchs had finally declared themselves. It referred to the 'more-than-semi-Popery of Mr. Froude' and claimed that there was a distinct absence of proof that he had ever been 'converted to God'.[59] Even secular journals were infected with the panic. In an article entitled 'Treason within the Church', *Fraser's Magazine* claimed it as self-evident that Froude was '*more than half* a Papist'.[60] And the *Eclectic Review* implied that the 'Froudeites' would inevitably 'fly to the infallibility of Rome'.[61] Such written fears were tame beside the wild rumours which circulated from mouth to mouth, about the habits and intentions of the Tractarian leaders, after the publication of the *Remains.* Pusey reported one of the apocryphal stories to Newman about his family's excesses in self-mortification and added, 'The gossiping of the Peculiars seems to be tremendous.'[62] This was encouraged by the occasional deliberate lie promulgated by unscrupulous opponents of the Oxford Movement. Pusey gave Bagot, the Bishop of Oxford, an example—

> an Exeter Radical paper which was shown me this morning, which had strung together in the form of extracts from "Froude's Remains" a set of sentences which nowhere occur in them, at the same time repeating all the false assertions as to the Chapel at Littlemore [i.e. concerning clandestine Roman Catholic practices], coupled with Mr. Newman's name.[63]

English hysteria at the incursions of Rome, latent throughout the nineteenth century, needed only slight encouragement to break out in epidemic proportions.

Oxford itself was particularly susceptible to the contagion. Among others the Margaret Professor of Divinity, Dr Godfrey Faussett, attacked the *Remains*. (Newman was quick to fly to his friend's defence and he made effective propaganda out of Fausset's sermon, entitled *The Revival of Popery,* in a long, clever pamphlet rebutting the professor's charges.) C. P. Golightly and his friends began to canvass their scheme for a Martyrs' Memorial in the autumn of 1838. Some of them, according to Pusey, openly avowed it as 'a counter-movement against Froude's "Remains" . . . It was intended to set the Reformers against the Fathers, and to set up certain views which some people identify with the Reformers against those of the ancient Church.'[64] Strong episcopal pressure was applied on the Tractarian leaders to subscribe to the Memorial and thus to kill the canard of Romanism. They did not succumb to this pressure. The Martyrs' Memorial was a local and specific assertion of the principles of Protestantism, just as the Parker Society, founded in 1844 with the object of re-publishing 'the entire mass of the printed works of the leading divines of our reformed church',[65] was a national and general one. Froude's trumpet had given a certain sound and Oxford and England were taking the *Christian Observer's* advice and preparing to fight the battle of the Reformation once again.

What doctrinal song the *Remains* really sang or what ideological name Froude would have assumed had he lived, though puzzling questions, are not beyond all conjecture. Indeed, contemporaries and subsequent commentators have often done more than conjecture—they have dogmatised. This is understandable because the problem is, in a certain sense, much more than a hypothetical one, a futile though intriguing 'might have been' of history. It relates not only to the progress of important minds within the Oxford Movement but also to the theological drift of the Movement as a whole. To give a convincing account of what Froude's destination would have been is a very significant step in calculating the true direction and nature of the Movement. The *Remains* is, as Canon Ollard said, 'the quarry to which every Protestant controversialist has gone for stones to throw at the Oxford Movement'.[66] From the *Christian Guardian* in 1838, which concluded that had Froude 'lived a little longer, he would have found it necessary to recede from the English Church',[67] to W. Walsh in 1897, who described Froude as 'the most advanced Romanizer of the new party',[68] Protestants excavated the *Remains* for their most damning evidence that Froude and his friends had been bound for Rome from the very first. But the book is also a quarry which both Anglo-Catholics and Roman Catholics have mined for their own propagandist purposes. As usual, didactic history reveals more of the historians than of their subject, but their contrasting perspectives on Froude do manage to throw some of the complexities of the Oxford Movement into sharp relief.

Newman himself contributed greatly to the controversy. From both the personal and the religious points of view it was of vital importance to him to feel that he was Froude's heir when he seceded in 1845. He believed then, as he told Keble, that Froude had played a crucial part 'in setting my face in that special direction which has led me to my present inestimable gain'.[69] He repeated afterwards that Froude 'would now be, or be coming, on my side'.[70] Newman saw his life as a process of organic growth in which each part was integral to the whole. For Newman to accept that Froude did not contribute positively to his final religious position would have involved, as it were, the amputation of part of his psyche. Moreover, in the few years after 1845, when there still seemed a chance that a section of the Church of England might follow him to Rome, Newman though it right once again to exploit Froude's potential for propaganda in his *Difficulties Felt by Anglicans.*[71] The implication was plain. If the man whom Newman designated (wrongly, as has already been suggested) as 'the author of the Movement'[72] would have become a Roman Catholic, what was retarding his followers?

Many Roman Catholics, at the time and subsequently, were convinced that the Oxford Movement was God's chosen instrument to restore the English Church to her true mother. Nicholas Wiseman had devoted his life to this hope ever since the visit that Newman and Froude had paid him in 1833.[73] Froude's *Remains* seemed to him a sign that the great body of Tractarians were, in the words of Greville, 'very nearly ripe and ready for reunion with Rome'.[74] He maintained that Froude would undoubtedly have arrived at the right answer had he been vouchsafed a longer search. 'He is another instance of that same mysterious Providence, which guided a Grotius and a Leibnitz to the threshold of truth, but allowed them not the time to step within it, into the hallowed precincts of God's visible Church.'[75] Frederick Oakeley, though he shared Wiseman's motives, offered a much more cautious and detailed analysis. Having balanced the obvious pro-Roman and anti-Roman statements in the *Remains* against each other, he summed up: taking all in all, 'the Church would more easily have conquered his prejudices than the Establishment retained his allegiance.'[76] Many Roman Catholic historians have been unable to resist the temptation of echoing the faith of Newman, Wiseman and Oakeley. Froude's own biographer stated that the Tractarian seceders were his true heirs and implied that he would have preceded Newman to Rome.[77] Others have taken the same line.[78] Corresponding not to objectively verifiable evidence but to the beliefs of a group, it constitutes a kind of retroactive prophecy, or more simply, a myth.

Anglican commentators have been equally busy propagating the counter-myth in an effort to legitimise Froude, and through him the Oxford Movement, as part of their own religious tradition. Many have followed the doctrinaire opinion of Keble and Prevost, supported by Isaac Williams and Tom Mozley, that Froude 'could not have joined the Church of Rome'.[79] They emphasise, with Deans Church and Burgon, that Froude had no 'intention of joining' Rome, that his Anglican 'allegiance never wavered',[80] and that he was 'to the last a faithful adherent of the Church of England'.[81] They contend, like Tom's brother J. B. Mozley, that Froude was truly at home in the tradition of his father and Keble, whereas the ex-Evangelical Newman was a stranger, pausing merely on a longer pilgrimage.[82] From A. E. Abbott, who stressed in 1892 the 'points on which Froude's mind was settled while Newman's was still in flux',[83] to R. D. Middleton who stated (1950) that 'Froude most certainly had no Romeward tendencies',[84] the Anglican faith has been maintained.

An entirely different construction was put on his views by one who was in a unique position to judge—his brother William. His principles of thought were based on the mental training he had received from Hurrell. William firmly believed that these principles had been 'legitimately developed', though he admitted them 'to be at variance with Hurrell's direct teaching'.[85] William was led to his conclusions partly by his scientific work (he found Brunel's methods and opinions remarkably supplemental to Hurrell's) and partly by a revulsion at the party denunciations which the Oxford Movement had engendered. He wrote to Hawkins in 1855,

> I now look back with wonder, and not without humiliation, at the heat and vehemence with which I joined in the fray, conscious as I ought to have been that I was taking part in a movement, not which my own judgement imperiously drove me into, but which the exigencies of partisan warfare seemed to require.[86]

By about this time William had abandoned dogmatic religion altogether, in favour of agnosticism and scepticism. Probability really had become his guide to life. He was prepared to act on it and to cultivate right conduct, but he thought that no accumulation of probabilities could create certainties of the kind Newman accepted.[87] Doubts were 'to be cherished as sacredly as beliefs'. Hurrell's mind was in a considerable number of respects 'in a state of transition' and William found many reasons for believing that he would 'have arrived at the same conclusions as those at which I have arrived'.[88] However, the last word on Hurrell's putative faith must be given not to his brother William but to Anthony. Historian by profession and euhemerist by determination, Anthony entered the inevitable and convincing verdict of non-proven. He added the charming rider that if by any chance Hurrell had succumbed to the lure of Rome 'the Pope would have found him an unmanageable subject.'[89]

Hurrell Froude continues to attract or repel, to fascinate or disgust, partly because his ambiguities are legion. He eludes definition, he conforms to no formula, he cannot be confidently fitted into any pattern. He remains in many respects the Protean enigma he appeared to contemporaries, a bundle of paradoxes searching for resolution. He was a High Churchman who espoused the enthusiasm which was normally the prerogative of the Evangelicals, a Catholic whe reverenced Rome but hated Trent, a Christian without compassion for slaves. He was a High and Dry Tory who evolved a democratic theory of Church government, an academic historian who dredged revolutionary practical ideas from the Middle Ages, a theological innovator who had no turn for theology as such. He was a well-born intellectual who disliked society as much as 'the aristocracy of talent',[90] a Romantic who believed in self-discipline, a scientist who depreciated reason. He was an outspoken practitioner of reserve, an introverted agitator. He was a man of unsurpassed vitality who was being consumed by tuberculosis. He was a sectarian whose life and work enriched many outside his own sect. Above all, he was a rash, unformed youth, pitted with many flaws and faults, who inspired his own distinguished tutor, profoundly influenced one of the greatest men of the nineteenth century and was integral to the etiology and development of the Oxford Movement. The aim of this study has been to expose as well as to elucidate these paradoxes, to sharpen and define Froude's angularities. It will be clear that if there was any single overweening force in Froude which resolved, unified and transcended these paradoxes it was that of piety. What is best described as the duty of holiness was the source of Froude's ethos, of his zealous, chivalric, self-sacrificing nature.

Froude bequeathed much to the Oxford Movement and in some ways its subsequent history can be seen as a reflection of the ambiguities of his legacy. The Tractarians continued to feel the lure of Rome but for the most part they baulked at Trent and, clinging to their own brand of Catholicism, refused to follow Newman when he seceded in 1845. Both before and after that great caesura in the progress of the Movement they remained a combative sectarian group. They frequently resorted to ecclesiastical agitation (for example, over the Jerusalem Bishopric, Hampden, Gorham, *Essays and Reviews,* ritualism) to propagate their theological views and to evolve an independent role for the Church in a pluralistic and increasingly democratic society, thus provoking the hostility of the conservative Establishment as well as many sections of the public. Yet more and more they concentrated on practical ameliorative endeavours the evangelisation of large industrial towns, the founding of Anglican monastic orders, the revival of worship, especially its sacramental side, the diffusion of devout and high principled ministers through the parishes of England. The Tractarians drew men to their faith by appealing to their imaginative and aesthetic capacities as well as to their intellectual and moral ones. They released the Church's hidden reserves of spiritual energy and quickened the religious life of the Victorian era. Holiness was the chief resource of regeneration. Hurrell Froude's lifelong quest for it, revealed in such self-denying detail in the *Remains,* was his most inspiring gift to the Oxford Movement. With all its imperfections his was a heroic piety. From beyond the grave it spoke eloquently to the men of his own age; its echoes linger still.

Notes

[1] Pusey House MSS., 21 September 1838.

[2] D. Voll, *Catholic Evangelicalism* (1963), 30.

[3] *The Christian Observer Conducted by members of the Established Church,* XXXVIII (August 1838), 507.

[4] A more detailed and comprehensive answer to this question is to be found in P. Brendon, 'Newman, Keble and Froude's *Remains', English Historical Review,* LXXXVII. No. 345 (October 1972), 697-716.

[5] Oratory, Box 65, Newman to Keble, 18 April 1836.

[6] ibid., Newman to Keble, 16 July 1837.

[7] Pusey House MSS., Keble to Newman, 31 August 1837.

[8] Oratory, Box 65, Newman to Keble, 26 February 1839.

[9] A. P. Perceval, *A Letter . . . in the 'Irish Ecclesiastical Journal'* (1841), 41-2.

[10] Pusey House MSS., 7 January 1841.

[11] Oratory, Box 65, 30 June 1837.

[12] A. Mozley, *Letters and Correspondence of Newman,* II. 237.

[13] Oratory, Box 65, 30 June 1837.

[14] A. Mozley, *Letters and Correspondence of Newman,* II. 75.

[15] Trevor, *The Pillar of the Cloud,* 182.

[16] Newman, *Parochial Sermons,* IV. 248. Sermon XIV, 23 October 1836. From the context it seems almost certain that Newman was thinking of Froude in the impressive passage from which this quotation comes.

[17] *British Critic,* XXVII (April 1840), 397.

[18] Oratory, Box 18, 6 October 1837.

[19] Oratory, Box 26, Newman to J. F. Christie, 26 June 1836.

[20] D. Mozley, *Newman Family Letters,* 73.

[21] This was Golightly's charge. Oratory, Box 10, Rogers to Newman, 20 March 1838.

[22] Brilioth, *The Anglican Revival,* 142.

[23] Oratory F.P., Newman to Archdeacon Froude, 30 March 1836.

[24] W. Ward, *Ward and the Oxford Movement,* 81.

[25] F. Oakeley, *Sermons Preached chiefly in the Chapel Royal at Whitehall* (Oxford, 1839), xxiv.

[26] R. Ornsby, *Memoirs of James Robert Hope-Scott of Abbotsford D.C.L., Q.C.* (1884), I. 192.

[27] F. W. Faber, *The Cherwell Water-Lily and Other Poems* (1840), 157.

[28] E. S. Purcell, *Life of Cardinal Manning* (1895), I. 228.

[29] See e.g. H. E. Manning, *The Rule of Faith* (1838), 49.

[30] See Chapman, *Father Faber,* 38 ff; F. W. Faber, *The Reformation and the Duty of Keeping to its Principles* (1838).

[31] Oakeley, *Notes on the Tractarian Movement,* 29-31.

[32] Pusey House MSS., E. Churton to W. Gresley, 20 September 1839.

[33] ibid., Keble to Newman, 7 August 1838.

[34] Copeland, 'History of the Oxford Movement'.

[35] R. Palmer, Earl of Selborne, *Memorials Part I. Family and Personal, 1766-1865* (1896), I. 259.

[36] Pusey House MSS., Pusey to Bagot, 12 November 1839. Note in the margin over the initials W.J.C.

[37] J. B. Mozley, *Essays Historical and Theological,* I. xxix and xxviii.

[38] *Christian Remembrance,* XIII (October 1844) and XI (January 1846).

[39] Chadwick, *The Victorian Church,* I. 172.

[40] M. C. Church (ed.), *Life and Letters of Dean Church* (1895), 315.

[41] B. A. Smith, *Dean Church: The Anglican Response to Newman.*

[42] J. B. Mozley, *Essays Historical and Theological,* I. xix.

[43] C. C. Southey (ed.), *The Life and Correspondence of the Late Robert Southey* (1850), VI. 371.

[44] Keble F.C., Quoted by Archdeacon Froude to Keble, 26 February 1838.

[45] Coleridge, *Memoir of Keble,* I. 253.

[46] See e.g. Pusey House MSS., Churton to Pusey, 26 May 1843.

[47] *Quarterly Review,* LXIII (March 1839), 552.

[48] Churton, *Memoir of Joshua Watson,* II. 143.

[49] British Museum, Add. MSS. 44213/19, Hook to Gladstone, 22 January 1839.

[50] W. F. Hook, *A Call to Union on the Principles of the English Reformation* (1838), 167.

[51] *Quarterly Review,* LXIII. 567.

[52] W. Gresley, *Anglo-Catholicism* (1844), 84 ff.

[53] Copeland, 'History of the Oxford Movement'.

[54] Liddon, *Life of Pusey,* II. 43.

[55] J. T. O'Brien, *A Charge . . . 1842* (3rd edn, 1843), 145 and 138.

[56] Lathbury, *Correspondence of Gladstone,* I. 287.

[57] J. B. Summer, *A Charge . . . 1838* (1838), 2.

[58] *The Church of England Quarterly Review,* V (January 1839), 220 and 228.

[59] *The Christian Examiner,* III (July 1838), 386, 383 and 391.

[60] *Fraser's Magazine,* XVIII (August 1838), 194.

[61] *The Eclectic Review,* IV (November 1838), 551.

[62] Pusey House MSS., 22 August 1838.

[63] ibid., 12 November 1838.

[64] Liddon, *Life of Pusey,* II. 68.

[65] H. Gough, *A General Index to the Publications of the Parker Society* (Cambridge, 1855), ii.

[66] S. L. Ollard, *A Short History of the Oxford Movement* (1915), 58.

[67] *Christian Guardian,* XXX (November 1838), 434.

[68] W. Walsh, *The Secret History of the Oxford Movement* (1897), 5.

[69] Dessain, *Letters and Diaries of Newman,* XI. 34.

[70] ibid., XI. 102 and XVI. 65.

[71] Newman, *Difficulties Felt by Anglicans,* 86, 87 and 94.

[72] ibid., 32.

[73] W. Ward, *The Life and Times of Cardinal Wiseman* (1897), I. 119.

[74] P. W. Wilson (ed.), *The Greville Diary* (1927), II. 305.

[75] *Dublin Review,* VI (Dublin, May 1839), 435.

[76] F. Oakeley, *Notes on the Tractarian Movement,* 33.

[77] Guiney, *Hurrell Froude,* 226-7.

[78] e.g. S. O'Faolain, *Newman's Way* (1952), 238; Trevor, *The Pillar of the Cloud,* 216; Dawson, *The Spirit of the Oxford Movement,* 100-1.

[79] Prevost, *Autobiography of Isaac Williams,* 84; T. Mozley, *Reminiscences,* I. 441.

[80] Church, *The Oxford Movement,* 51 and 54.

[81] Burgon, *Twelve Good Men,* 90.

[82] *Christian Remembrancer,* XI (January 1846), 186.

[83] Abbott, *The Anglican Career of Newman,* I. 171.

[84] R. D. Middleton, *Newman at Oxford: His Religious Development* (Oxford, 1950), 66.

[85] Harper, *Cardinal Newman and William Froude,* 118-19.

[86] Oriel College MSS. 66, 8 August 1855.

[87] W. Ward, *The Life of John Henry Cardinal Newman* (1912), II. 588.

[88] Harper, *Cardinal Newman and William Froude,* 119 ff. Newman did not agree, of course; yet his own words to Mrs Froude on 3 April 1844 seem to support William. Of Hurrell Newman wrote, 'He went by no theory; he was bent on defending no system, he was no Advocate, laughed at economies, merely investigated—and in consequence, and just in the same proportion, did not attack the Church of Rome and disliked attacks on it.' ibid., 39.

[89] Dunn, *James Anthony Froude,* I. 17.

[90] W. Ward, *Life of Newman,* II. 333.

John R. Griffin (essay date 1977)

SOURCE: "The Anglican Responce to Newman's Conversion," in *Faith & Reason: The Journal of Christendom College,* Vol. III, No. 2, Summer, 1977, pp. 17-33.

[*In the essay that follows, Griffin claims that Newman's 1845 conversion to Catholicism generated a series of attacks on and misrepresentations of his thought by Anglican scholars, which remain dominant in some critical interpretations.*]

> I have only one regret about not speaking the other day. I wish I had said something about people not going to the Oratory, &c., with itching ears; for I observed that when Mr. Darling spoke of it there was rather a titter about the room, and I think it is the worst sign of the day.

(John Keble to Edward Pusey, October 18, 1850)

Historians of the Oxford Movement in its post 1845 period have failed to notice any changes in the Movement in the years after Newman's conversion.[1] One slight modification to the idea that the Movement was unchanged has been added recently by certain scholars who suggest that there was something ecumenical about the revival in its second generation. In the words of a recent ecumenist:

> Henceforth the Anglo-Catholic movement was to be marked by a quality of openness towards Rome. . . . Newman received much abuse and misrepresentation at this time; but not from Keble or Pusey.[2]

The argument of the above is founded on an excellent Ph.D. thesis by Greenfield and I must first express my own gratitude to the author for allowing me to read it. At the same time, I cannot agree with Dr. Greenfield when he writes:

> This refusal to take a positive stand against the Roman Church was the counterpart of Keble's position of neutrality towards Rome.[3]

In what follows, I will argue that those who remained in the Church of England during the second half of the nineteenth century were intensely critical of Rome and of Newman (and all converts), and used every device to prevent others from following the example of Newman. My essay is mainly concerned with the response of Keble, Pusey, Marriott, and James Mozley (Newman's brother-in-law) to Newman, who bore the major thrust of the slander concerning moral character and sanity, but the "response" that I will be describing was applied to all converts, and is still used by Anglo-Catholic historians of the Movement and biographers of Pusey and Keble. It was imperative that Keble, Pusey and the others discredit Newman's move or at least minimize its significance for themselves; and the same principle is at work in the Anglican scholarship of this century. It consists of praising those who were loyal to the Church of England and who argued its cause and attacking those who left. It is the various attacks on those who left that is the concern of this paper.

I. The Early Response Re-evaluated: Pusey

The Anglican response was readied for the "thunderbolt"[4] of Newman's conversion several months before he left, at a time when Newman was in friendly correspondence with and giving in exact detail the reason for his move to Dr. Pusey. Pusey did not tell the truth when he gave as the basic reason for Newman's conversion Newman's "sensitivity", and no man knew better than Pusey that it was not the truth. Still, it was essential that an anti-Newman platform be constructed.

At least two historians, Allchin and Greenfield, have quoted extensively Pusey's "Letter" to John Keble in the *English Churchman* of October 20, 1845. The evidence of Pusey's correspondence suggests that the Letter was prepared several months in advance of the event. If it was prepared in advance, some of its "unselfish"[5] element is lost or at least suspect, but what might be documented here is Pusey's attempt to minimize the significance of Newman's conversion.

Pusey was the first to suggest that something be done to diminish the impact of Newman's conversion. Pusey and Keble expressed the hope that Newman would go to the continent to make his profession of faith.[6] Manning, Isaac Williams, Marriott, Pusey and several other high-churchmen conferred on the subject. The Manning correspondence of these years is marked "confidential", and it appears that Manning asked Williams for a meeting in London to discuss what should be done about the pending event. Manning asked Williams to tell him all that he knew about the Newman affair and anything that Newman might have told him (Williams).[7] The image of the future Cardinal that comes through these letters is not a pleasant one; and when scholars, like D. Newsome, profess their inability to understand why people prefer Newman to Manning,[8] they might look at this correspondence for their answer. Manning's *Charge of 1845,* in addition, does nothing to enhance his reputation for fairness or accuracy on the Newman question.[9]

Meetings between Williams and Manning were arranged in London, but we have no knowledge of what was decided. All that we know is that Williams was apparently frightened by some of the measures proposed by Manning and determined, following Keble's advice, to do nothing.[10] The Manning plan or declaration was given up, and he, along with Williams, T. Keble, and Marriott, adopted a partial silence in response to the early converts. Marriott seems to have been the most disturbed among this group, and he coped with the event by adopting a useful piece of slander put forward by James Mozley—Newman had never been a true Anglican.[11]

It remained for Pusey to take the active role in accounting for Newman's conversion and the Letter to John Keble was his first public contribution to the cause. Allchin's description of the Letter as reflecting "an extraordinary generosity of spirit"[12] seems to me exactly wrong. Pusey wrote of what he was intending in the work:

> I am hoping that people may come to think that he has a special mission and call and so that it may not be looked upon as an example to all who have learnt of him, but it will be, I fear, a most fearful rent, draining our Church of so much of her strength.[13]

This is a fair measure of his achievement, even in the excerpts given by Allchin. Pusey attempted to minimize the event and its implications by a seemingly complimentary set of remarks about Newman's solitary genius. Newman was a "great instrument of God" and "our Church has not known how to employ him." The conclusion of the Letter partly contradicts some of the earlier comments:

> He seems then to me not so much gone from us, as transplanted into another part of the Vineyard, where the full energies of his powerful mind can be employed, which here they were not.[14]

The *English Churchman* [*EC*] rightly understood the meaning of the Pusey comments, and used this later against Newman.[15]

With one of the other converts, Pusey was much more open in his criticism. When F. Oakeley's conversion was an accomplished fact, Pusey published another long letter in the *EC*. Again the textual evidence suggests that it was written before the conversion took place. The "Letter" was reprinted with Pusey's permission and it is hard to find any other reason for the letter or its reprinting except that of keeping people from Rome and discrediting converts.

The Letter is in Pusey's worst style and, inadvertently, destructive of the Anglo-Catholic version of church history. Twice, Pusey dated the history of the Church of England from the last "three hundred years", that is, Henry VIII whom the Anglo-Catholics denounced as warmly as their Catholic brethren, if they ventured to discuss him at all. The Letter is not widely known, and therefore a long excerpt is given:

> As far as I can see, you seem to me more drawn by sympathy towards the Roman Church than by any feeling of duty. But love for the Roman church should not make us forget all the blessings which God has given us in our own, and our duties to her. But love for the Roman Church . . . is no reason why we should leave that Church in which God has placed us. The question is not, whether she has high gifts, but whether we have the Presence of Christ. Since we have, (which cannot be doubted) then we are safe where we are, and we should labour . . . in that part of the vineyard where we have been called . . . no truths abroad, no contradictions at home, are any grounds whatever for abandoning the Church in which God has placed us. . . . There is, I suppose, hardly any Protestant leaders in Germany altogether sound in essential articles of Faith. In England our course has been upward. The life of our Church has been tried in every way that it can be tried; and now, after three centuries, it has a more vigorous life than ever. . . . Of us, it seems to be said, 'They bring forth more fruit in their age, that they may show how true the Lord our strength is'. . . . It is certain that we have life. [I recommend] . . . general confession. If you know of no other to receive it, I am sure that the Rev._____ would. You could say that I commended you to him . . . divide your life into stated periods . . . carrying on warfare against your sins.[16]

We should remind ourselves that these comments on Oakeley's going to confession and how he should examine his conscience (the longest part of the Letter) were published. It might be doubted whether anyone should write such a letter for publication, and Pusey really did not know Oakeley that well. At the same time, there was a certain brilliance of strategy in the approach used by Pusey: Oakeley and anyone else who might be thinking of Rome were guilty of some moral turpitude that only a confessor could root out. We should also remember that the *Letters from Dr. Pusey on the Case of Mr. Oakeley* was published after Oakeley had gone over. It is not drawing too much from Pusey's Letter to suggest that he must have regarded the Catholic Church and its attractions as a special matter for confession.

This idea that the thought of leaving the religion of one's birth for Rome reflected some kind of moral weakness became a dominant theme in the Anglican response to Newman. God placed men in the Church of England because that was where they were to find their salvation. To change religion was to reject one's duty. There was an excellent reason for one of Pusey's closest friends (Dodsworth) to note the strong anti-Romanism of Dr. Pusey in several of his letters.[17] What is relevant is that Pusey's vigorous anti-Romanism developed only after Newman's departure.

There is a final element in both letters that might be noted. Pusey wrote glowingly of the renaissance of religious ideals during this period. This optimistic note is perhaps the one reason why persons have always described Pusey as "sanguine". My reservations on the matter derive from Pusey's private letters where one finds no such optimism about the Church of England and a great deal of just the opposite.

In addition to the above ideas that Pusey put forward to keep his friends in the Church of England there is one other device that, so far as I have been able to discover, none of the others used, the vow of obedience to himself. Dodsworth, a close friend of Pusey and a convert of 1850, may have had some intimation of the device, for he complained several times of Pusey's fastening some of the women to himself.[18] Whether the idea came first from Pusey or the women who took the vows of obedience, Pusey did accept such vows and on occasion at least insisted upon them.[19]

II. A Rising Attack: Keble and Other Voices

Keble was less prominent in this struggle than Pusey, but he did make several contributions to the Anglican response that go beyond even those of Pusey. Keble pledged his lasting friendship to Newman when the latter was about to take the final step to Rome, but when the move was known he broke off all communication with him (and everyone else who went over). S. Bellasis noted one example of this method at work when Keble remarked on a gesture of hostility by one of his friends: "That is exactly the way to treat those fellows."[20]

Keble made a habit of staying away from people whom he disliked or with whom he disagreed, but I suggest that the above is part of the new anti-Romanism developed as a response to those who went over. Accordingly, I find no evidence for the "neutrality towards Rome", of which Dr. Greenfield writes, but a great deal of evidence for increased contempt, fear, and even hatred of Rome in the years from 1845 until the end of his life.

Going over to Rome meant the abandonment of one's moral duty to remain in the religion of one's birth; and it emphatically meant the giving up of any kind of friendship with John Keble. R. Wilberforce noted that the only thing that kept him so long in the Church of England was Keble. The Keble-Wilberforce correspondence suggests that Keble used every kind of device to keep him, including a great deal of brow-beating and reasoning that defies logical analysis. Wilberforce was wrong to look upon any of the evils in the Church of England,[21] including that great problem of erastianism. Keble failed with Wilberforce, but it was not for a lack of effort. With some of the other potential converts he was more successful. In 1864 he wrote to Pusey of his experiences with the Bishop of Brechlin:

> . . . our friend had been with me since Friday evening . . . we had some more talk; all confirming me in the impression that it is a longing for rest rather than intellectual conviction that Rome is right which is working on him. I hope he was a little more comfortable when he left us . . . promising to do as I desired him; which was to treat the haunting thought as simply a distress . . . casting it as he would any other on Him. . . . I also begged him to think of the terrible consequence of such moves.[22]

Such was his general practice with those who might be looking towards Rome as a solution to their problems. On the strength of the Pusey-Keble and Keble-Wilberforce correspondence alone, it can be argued that the anti-Roman element of the Oxford Movement was much stronger in the years after 1845 than before. Indeed, the most consistent theme among the high-church group was that it was wrong to forsake one's duty in the national church. What is especially relevant is not the anti-romanism of this period, but the use of malicious devices to keep persons from going over. For Keble and Pusey especially these dvices might have been left to the more violent Protestants and high-churchmen because neither Pusey nor Keble had enough confidence in his own position to advise others.

The campaign against the Catholic Church and individual converts went beyond even the level described above. Keble referred to the converts as a "beacon"[23], that is, a moral warning to others not to follow in their steps. He hinted with some regularity that Newman's sanity was questionable,[24] and on one occasion added a direct piece of slander about Newman's early loyalty to the Church of England:

> The next is confidential. I think I once told you that N's expression to me was that he has *for some* years, 5, I think now, had a strong intellectual conviction "that the R.C. System + Xtianity are convertible terms." This seems to settle the point as to the extent of his adherence.[25]

The remark cannot be true if any of the Newman-Keble correspondence or the Newman letters to other friends have any truth at all.[26]

Keble's one public contribution to the controversy was his "Preface" to a second edition of his *Sermons* (1848). The Preface is a useful guide to Keble's approach to Rome and the question of converts, but its mode of argument is so weak that it defies analysis. The basic theme of his argument was that any thought of leaving "Mother Church"[27] should be dismissed as one would rid himself of temptations of impurity or murder. A good churchman was obliged not to believe any evil in his church, including erastianism, in the same way that a dutiful child ought not to believe anything evil of his parents without overwhelming evidence. Keble made certain moral charges against those who had left the Church of England (restlessness) and compared the Roman attitudes towards the Church of England unfavorably with Anglican attitudes towards Rome. There is, finally, an appeal to the sentiments of the reader not to abandon the religion of his birth. The most probable explanation of a man's birth in England and baptism in the Church of England was that was where God intended him to find his salvation.

Much more could be used to illustrate the deepening hostility of Pusey and Keble to the Catholic Church and those who went over, but it might be useful to pass on to some of the less well-known Anglo-Catholics of that time. We might remember that all of the men that I will discuss in the following were close friends of Keble and Pusey. The first is A. P. Perceval (one of the founders of the Oxford Movement) who attacked Newman in a pamphlet of 1846, *Results of an Ecclesiastical Tour.*

> . . . none of Mr. Newman's worshippers, whose blind adulation helped to turn a brain, voluntarily and deliberately weakened and exposed to the temptations of satan by excessive fasting . . . neither he nor his flatterers (for they do not deserve to be called friends) can blame me [for this attack]. (70)

Perceval continued his attack on Newman's theory of development and the "modern Roman Mariolatrists". Greenfield has made a distinction between the above attitude and that of Keble and Pusey, but much of the above can be found in the correspondence and published writings of both men; in particular the suggestions about Newman's insanity and the standard Protestant fare about "mariolatry" might be traced to Keble.

Another high-churchman who joined in the attack on Newman was J. B. Mozley, co-editor of the high-church journal, the *Christian Remembrancer* [*CR*], and Newman's brother-in-law. When Newman's conversion was known, W. Scott, the other co-editor of the *CR,* wrote to him: "It is expected of us to take a line about Newman, and We Cannot Avoid It."[28] Mozley commented on the line that he took on Newman's conversion:

> I am here at C.R. work—just seeing through the press the most disagreeable article I have ever had to write—one namely on Newman's secession. It was absolutely necessary to notice the fact and it fell to me to do it . . . the fact is not to be avoided that a new relation is begun between Newman and the English Church, and somebody must be the person to express that new relation.[29]

Mozley's article was, from the Anglican point of view, a brilliant stroke. It was entitled *The Recent Schism. Schism* became the standard word for the act of conversion and its implications ought not be forgotten by the modern reader, nor should Mozley's use of the word *secession* in the above letter. What Mozley attempted to do was to discredit anything that Newman might say about the Church of England, for Newman, according to the Mozley version, had never been a real Anglican. Newman had never married, never engaged in parish work; his attachment to the Church of England had been purely intellectual. He was like a pilgrim travelling through the Church of England but never at rest in it.[30]

The third personality in this brief survey is John Taylor Coleridge, intimate and life-long friend of Keble. Coleridge of course was the recipient of Keble's slanderous letters about Newman and the other converts; in 1850, at the end of the Achilli trial, he demonstrated how well he had learned his lessons from Keble and the others. When Newman was judged to be technically guilty of libel against Achilli . . . and a fine of one hundred pounds levied, he read Newman a lengthy "sermon" on his moral deterioration as a convert, the basic theme of the Anglican response.[31] Those who went over to Rome went to pieces, intellectually and morally. The Coleridge "jobation" was described by another convert, who had suffered from the same kind of attack, as a "Puseyite sermon".[32] The designation was just. Pusey, Keble and all the other prominent Anglo-Catholics contributed to the legend that men who went over deteriorated, and most of them suggested that the process had begun before the conversion—that was why they went in the first place. The hard-core Protestantism and Erastianism of the Church of England had nothing to do with the question.

III. The Anglo-Catholic Press

The Anglo-Catholic press, in particular *The English Churchman, The Christian Remembrancer,* and the *Guardian,* took up the question of converts. It should be remembered that *The English Churchman (EC)* was the major vehicle for Pusey's frequent letters. *The English Churchman* is the paper that will be studied the most closely in what follows, partly because it is the least known of the three journals and partly because it is the most honest of the three. Its articles were much briefer than those of the *CR* or *Guardian* and they lacked the contrived rhetoric of the others.

The English Churchman criticized every hint of Protestantism in the English Church as "ultra-Protestant", but it joined hands with the Protestant press in its rigorous condemnation of Catholics, the Catholic Church, and those who left the Church of England. The later remarks of Kingsley on Newman and the Catholic Church were almost pallid compared to the weekly installments of the *Churchman*. Again, it might be noted that there is nothing new in the various charges against converts. The difference is one of tone, and in certain instances it appears that the charges were taken directly from Keble, Pusey and the prominent Anglo-Catholics. The following is but one example of the use that was made of Pusey's Letter to John Keble:

> With regard to Mr. Newman, all who know him seem to agree in describing him as a man of exquisitely sensitive feeling;—who can tell then, how much even his mighty intellect may have been swayed by feelings keenly wounded. . . . Dr. Pusey indeed, who tells us that for 22 years he has had the opportunities of watching the operations of his mind, put wounded feelings prominently forward as an explanation of the phenomenum of his act of schism. . . . If then it would be shown that feeling has had a share in enducing these . . . men to fall into schism, it would surely be a great source of comfort for us to reflect, that where a obvious known infirmity was a party to the decision, the result arrived at was . . . probably erroneous.[33]

Pusey was responsible for the legend that it was Newman's sensitivity that led him to Rome and not intellectual conviction, and again no one could have known as well as Pusey the inaccuracy of the charge.

Other issues of the *Churchman* amplified the idea that there was something insane about those who went over. In 1850, for example, a dissenter named Gorham was declared to be less of a heretic than Newman and Catholics who honored the "Holy Virgin".[34] The Gorham decision, which seemed to illustrate the erastianism of the Church of England, actually contributed to an increase in converts to Rome during the succeeding year, but the *Churchman* would not allow that there was any reason for men to examine their position in the national church. All who went over went over because of some "crochet or fancy".[35] They became schismatics and had been morally deficient even before their conversions:

> . . . their conduct, for some time previous to their secession, had been palpably and deliberately inconsistent with an honest and faithful discharge of their duties toward the Church.[36]

In addition, the "perverts" who seceded were routinely described as dishonest. In 1850 it was recommended by the *Churchman* that potential converts be retained in some "quiet asylum",[37] an idea that was written into The Ecclesiastical Titles Bill of 1850.

What might be observed from the above is that there is nothing new in any of the charges against converts that cannot be found in, or at least traced to, leading Anglo-Catholics. The one exception might be the idea of retaining men or women in some quiet place, although this writer believes that even that measure may have been prompted or at least supported by some of the leaders. Philpotts, one of the principal advocates of the Bill, was an intimate friend of Pusey.

An extensive review of *The Christian Remembrancer* and the *Guardian* would require a single volume on this topic alone, but there are certain aspects of the response that are fairly easy to discern. The first is kindred to the above, the personal attack on converts, especially Newman. These attacks were complemented by harsh reviews of books by any of the converts, especially those of Newman. It should be added that none of the journals would review Newman's books unless it was inescapable, as with *On the Development of Christian Doctrine* or *Apologia Pro Vita Sua*. There was even a refusal to accept advertisements for Newman's books, a decision that was only overcome when Newman's publisher threatened to cancel all advertisements. The few reviews which were written about the *Development* were harsh and, though it is not to my purpose, ignorant. Newman expressed his disbelief once that men (and friends) like J. Mozley, F. Rogers, and others could have written so ignorantly. There was a curious growth of anti-Catholicism in many of the essays in the *Christian Remembrancer*. One striking example was the "Achilli Trial" of 1851. Achilli was one of several apostate priests who came to England as a result of his Protestant association. Newman attacked him in 1851 as a liar and a rapist, and was sued by Achilli. This essay, written before a biased and unsubstantiated judgment against Newman was given, attacked the Catholic Church, claiming that Rome knew of Achilli's sexual conduct and yet promoted him. Celibacy, moreover, was blamed as the root cause of Achilli's problems. No mention was made of Newman's innocence in the charges against Achilli. In fact, this essay included only the barest mention of Newman, concentrating rather on portraying Achilli as a man victimized by the discipline of the Catholic Church and promoted by the Roman Curia presumably because it sanctioned Achilli's activities.

There were other essays in the *Remembrancer* that seem to have had no other purpose than to raise some kind of slanderous question about the Catholic Church; and again the approach to Catholicism used by the high-church journals, filled as they were with all the standard Protestant lore on the laxity of the Catholic Church, Mariolatry, and the deterioration of converts, resembles that of the militant Protestant press.

There are other parts of this response that I have not mentioned, but one final example of the recurrent charge against the morals of those who went over might be given. In 1878 Dr. Littledale, one of the prominent Ritualists, wrote:

> Our general experience is that conversion to Rome involves, in a large majority of instances, sudden, serious, and permanent intellectual and moral deterioration, especially as to the quality of truthfulness.[38]

A friend of Newman, G. Ryder, answered Littledale and faulted him for giving no evidence for a serious charge. Littledale's method, however, was the accepted way. J. M. Todd, another convert, had mentioned as a solemn fact "the deterioration of converts" to which Newman responded: "This deterioration lies in becoming a Catholic (which is of course a begging of the question)."[39] Other elements in the response that I have not mentioned include the recurrent rumors that Newman was about to return to the Church of England because he was miserable in his new religion. This legend was repeated even after Newman's *Apologia* was published.[40]

The above stories about Newman and his fellow converts are but a very brief survey of the Anglican response to Newman and could be amplified to fill out several volumes. I suggest again that there was nothing ecumenical about the revival in the period after 1845 and, as I have argued, there was little that reflects the basic rudiments of charity in the conduct, writings, and letters of Keble, Pusey, and those who remained. Of course the first Oxford Movement had been anti-Roman, but the traditional Protestant arguments about the morals of Catholics had never been used. It was the task of the Anglo-Catholics to refurbish those arguments.

20th Century Scholarship: A Continuing Myth

In a very brief conclusion I would like to illustrate the same kind of response in twentieth century Anglican scholarship. I believe very strongly that the started intentions of Keble, Pusey, and the others are at work in these numerous studies.

The idea of elaborate praise for those who remained in the Church of England as "loyal" is a major facet of the response. It was with good reason that a learned historian of the Church of England complained of the "mounds of Hagiography" that have been written about the personalities in the Oxford Movement. Biographers of Keble and Pusey and historians of the Oxford Movement do freely refer to both men and their disciples as "saints".

Another aspect of this response that might be noted briefly is the unwillingness of historians of the Oxford Movement to discuss the questions of erastianism or even use the word itself. The question and the word are usually ignored. One might blame Dean Church's seminal account of the Oxford Movement for this phenomenon. Church barely used the word erastian, and avoided all of Newman's controversial writings in writings his *Oxford Movement,* especially Newman's *Difficulties,* even though he did expand his "memoir" to include scholarly references from other high-church Tories who, like Church, feared disestablishment as the greatest evil that could befall the Church of England.

Other historians of the Movement have been expressly critical of Newman. Overton, citing the Mozley essay, wrote that Newman had never been a true Anglican.[41] S. L. Ollard made much of the sensitive Newman, and criticized those who left in (*ca.*) 1850 for their panic.[42] He concluded his book with the boast that only one of three had left the Church of England,[43] a remark extremely misleading in itself and, from an historical point of view, false. That Anglican biographers and historians have been tough and even judgmental, without evidence, on Newman and his fellow converts, and laudatory of those who remained, again without checking their evidence, can be illustrated as long as one has patience to read.[44] There is, however, one particularly fine example in F. L. Cross' *John Henry Newman,* written for "The Tractarian Series", and published alongside biographies of Keble, Pusey and others in 1933. Cross' book is very different from the studies on Keble and Pusey, which were highly complimentary and even hagiographic. The biographers of Keble and Pusey had no difficulty in calling their subjects "saints". In contrast, Cross' portrait of Newman is that of a vengeful egotist, a man of "resentiment".[45] In Cross' view, Newman's conversion of 1845 was the result of his frustrated ego. There was no intellectual conviction behind it. As if more were needed, Cross attacked the work in which Newman discussed the reasons for his conversion. The *Apologia* was "fundamentally misleading", and Cross' argument was apparently made stronger by attacking one of the supposedly weak elements in it: its account of *National Apostasy.*[46]

A second work that has been even more pernicious than that of Cross was G. Faber's *The Oxford Apostles* (1933). Under the cloak of "modern knowledge", Faber presented a picture of Newman as a tortured and sensitive egotist whose move to Rome came partly because of his lack of manliness. Faber enhanced his portrait of Newman by making much of the pledge of virginity that Froude and Newman had discussed. The work has been shown up as ignorant and based on a (deliberate?) misconstruction; but the legend has held on. If modern knowledge tells us much, it warns us of persons who find homosexuality everywhere.[47]

There are other works of more recent vintage that manifest the same spirit as the above and the earlier response to Newman that formed the substance of this paper. It seems that Newman and all who went over, from the Anglican point of view, must be discredited. My complaint here has mainly been against the prejudicial history of the Oxford Movement, which may be understandable since it is based on tradition. Nevertheless, the first element in Newman's life and work that a serious student will notice is consistency. Thus Newman's work as an Anglican was based on a misconception that the state-church alliance was no more than a "happy anomaly",[48] and when he learned of his error, he took corrective steps.

With those who had known Newman during his Anglican years, it is less easy to be forgiving. I have argued that his friends, E. B. Pusey, John Keble, James Mozley, and the others, deliberately set out to discredit him in order to retain persons in the Church of England. Even this, though I believe it involved lying about Newman, is understandable but for one point. The faith of Keble and Pusey in the system they professed was far too shaky for them to attempt to advise others. Keble described himself once as in the role of "the blind leading the blind."[49] Pusey in many places admitted that the Oxford ideal was not working, in spite of the professed optimism in his published Letters.

It should also be remembered that those who went over to Rome suffered a complete alienation from their friends, the risk of slanderous attacks and estrangement even from relatives. There is one thing more. Those who went over, almost to a man, underwent severe financial reverses. Those who remained "loyal" to the Church of England, whatever may have been their relationship to bishops and laity,[50] were at least spared that.

Notes

[1] *Cf.* Clarke, *The Oxford Movement and After* (1933); Sparrow-Simpson, *The History of the Anglo-Catholic Revival from 1845* (1932); Ollard, *A Short History of the Oxford Movement* (1915); Thereau-Dangin, *The English Catholic Revival in the Nineteenth Century* (1932); *Northern Catholicism* (1933); and every other volume that has been written on the second generation of the Oxford Movement as well as the major lives of Keble, Pusey and the prominent Anglo-Catholics.

[2] Allchin, *The Via-Media, An Anglican Revaluation* in *Newman: A Portrait Restored* (pb. 1965), 68.

[3] *The Attitude of the Tractarians to the Roman Catholic Church (1833-1850* (D. Phil. thesis, Oxford, 1956, 2 vols.), I, 477-8.

[4] Keble's recurrent description of the event; *cf.* ms, letter to Pusey (Oct. 21, 1845), Pusey House, Oxford; hereafter referred to as PH.

[5] Liddon, *Life of E. B. Pusey* (4 vols.; 1898), II, 463; Liddon did not cite the relevant letters to Pusey during this period.

[6] Ms. letter Keble to Pusey (June 20, 1845); the idea was originally Manning's and Coleridge's according to Pusey.

[7] Ms. letter to Williams (Nov. 7, 1844) in Williams Deposit, No. 3, Lambeth Palace Library; hereafter referred to as LP.

[8] *Newmania* in *Journal of Theological Studies,* XIV, Pt. II, 420ff.

[9] Quoted in E.S. Purchell, *Life of Cardinal Manning* (2 vols.; 1898) I, 305ff.

[10] Ms. letter to Pusey (May? 1845), in Williams Deposit, No. 3, LP.

[11] Ms. letter to Pusey (Jan. 4, 1846); before the article, Marriott admitted to "severe agitation" because of Newman's *Essay; cf.* letter to Pusey (Nov. 30, 1845), PH.

[12] Allchin, 78; in addition, there is no evidence for Allchin's remark on Pusey's "deep conviction of God's continuing purpose for the Church of England," 78, and very much evidence in the opposite direction; *cf.* ms. letters to Manning of 1845-6, esp. Jan. 1845; Jan. 22, 1845.

[13] Ms. letter to Keble (April 27, 1845), PH.

[14] *Letter to the English Churchman* (Oct. 21, 1845); see also Liddon,II,460-3.

[15] See below, n. 32.

[16] *Letter from Dr. Pusey on the case of Mr. Oakeley,* in *English Churchman* (Oct. 30, 1845); the advertisement to the pamphlet reprint reads, "written in August . . . reprinted with his permission . . . in the hope that a more extensive circulation of it may . . . be useful to the Church."

[17] *Cf.* ms. letters Dodsworth to Pusey, esp. Nov. 28, 1846, PH.

[18] Ms. letter to Pusey (June 18, 1846), PH.

[19] For citations of this material see Griffin, *Dr. Pusey and the Oxford Movement* in *HMPEC* (1973); and *Satiric Elements in Newman's Apologia* in *Revue de l'Universite D'Ottawa* (1974).

[20] *Memorial of S. Bellasis* (1923), 56 and *in passim.*

[21] Some of the relevant correspondence between Keble and Wilberforce is printed in Newsome, *The Parting of Friends* (1966), 394ff.

[22] Ms. letter to Pusey (June 14, 1864), PH.

[23] *Letters and Sermons of J.H. Newman,* ed. Dessain (1961).

[24] *Cf. Letters of J.B. Mozley* (1888), 170 and other letters of Keble to Pusey (1845), PH.

[25] Ms. letter to J. Coleridge (June 14, 1845) in Coleridge Collection, Vol. II, Bodleian, Oxford.

[26] *E.g.,* Newman's letter to R. Westmacott (April, 1841): "I have no thought whatever of going over to Rome, or letting others."—in Manuscript collection, Yale U.; all of Newman's letters of this year reflect a similar attitude.

[27] *Cf., Preface* of *Sermons* (1848 ed.), IV.

[28] *Letters of J.B. Mozley,* 172.

[29] *Ibid.,* 173.

[30] *The Recent Schism* in *CR* (1846), XI.

[31] The "sermon" was reprinted in *The English Churchman* (1850), 85, with a brief editorial: "Dr. Newman has assuredly violated every precept of good taste, of gentlemanly feeling, and of common decency, by his language with respect to the Church he abandoned."; p.87: "Achilli had his ground of complaint and a real one against Rome."

[32] J. M. Capes (who had suffered under the same kind of attacks) to Newman in *Letters and Diaries* (1963) XIII, 285.

[33] *English Churchman* (Feb. 26, 1846).

[34] *English Churchman* (Feb. 28, 1850), 138-9; Gorham denied Baptismal Regeneration and won the case against his bishop in a civil court.

[35] *Ibid.* (April 4, 1830), 218.

[36] *Ibid.* (April 11, 1850), 394.

[37] *Ibid.* (Sep. 18, 1845), 598.

[38] *Why Ritualists do not become Roman Catholics* in *Contemporary Review* (Nov. 1878), 819.

[39] *Letters and Diaries of John H. Newman,* ed. Dessain (1963), XIII, 39.

[40] *Cf.* E. Husband, *What then will Dr. Newman Do* (1870); the *Letters and Diaries* contain more than twenty references to this recurrent legend and Newman's persistent denial of it.

[41] *The Anglican Revival* (1915), 47.

[42] *A Short History . . .* (1915), 113ff.

[43] Ollard, 273.

[44] For a brief survey, see Abbott, *The Anglican Career of Cardinal Newman* (1892); Williams, *Autobiography* (1892); Grafton, *A Journey Godward* (1910); Donaldson, *Five Great Oxford Leaders* (1905); Morse-Boycot, *They Shine Like Stars* (1947); Weatherby, *Cardinal Newman and his Age* (1973), 235ff; B.A. Smith, *Dean Church: The Anglican Response to Newman* (1958) contains little that might be construed as an attack on Newman's moral character or reliability as an historian of the Oxford Movement and it has provided me with a title for this paper, but Smith suggests nothing in Church's life or writings that might be regarded as a "response" to Newman.

[45] Cross, 70 and *in passim.*

[46] *Ibid.,* 162; Cross' reading of the "myth" of *National Apostasy* was the direct object of attack in my *The Meaning of National Apostasy* in *Faith & Reason,* II (1976).

[47] It would appear that Keble had ideas about celibacy himself and believed for a brief period at least that the state should remove "all temptations to marry. . . . "; ms. letter to Coleridge (Dec. 3, 1834). Coleridge Collection, I, Bodleian, Oxford.

[48] *Cf.* Griffin, *The Radical Phase of the Oxford Movement* in *JEH* (1976).

[49] Ms. letter to Coleridge (June 1844), Taylor Collection, Bodleian.

[50] The laity and bishops attacked the Puseyites at frequent intervals; this is one reason why I think the word "loyal" cannot be applied to Keble and Pusey; *cf.* Griffin, *The Oxford Movement: A Revision* (1977).

Frederick H. Borsch (essay date 1984)

SOURCE: "Ye Shall Be Holy: Reflections on the Spirituality of the Oxford Movement," in *Tradition*

Renewed: The Oxford Movement Conference Papers, edited by Geoffrey Rowell, Pickwick Publications, 1986, pp. 64-77.

[*In the essay that follows, Borsch describes the most significant tenets espoused by the Oxford Movement—primarily their emphasis on moral seriousness, adherence to traditional dogma, and authenticity of faith.*]

> We know two things of the Angels—that they cry Holy, Holy, Holy, and that they do God's bidding.[1]

Seeking better to understand and appreciate the spirituality of the Oxford Movement and its first leaders we become quickly implicated in the complexities of their personalities as well as of the sociological and intellectual currents which helped to shape the movement. Especially is this true if we define spirituality sufficiently broadly, so as to be inclusive of not only conscious acts of prayer, meditation and devotion, but of the whole human effort to live lives that seek to realise and be faithful to God's purposes in creation. 'Spirituality', John Macquarrie maintains, 'is the process of becoming a person in the fullest sense.'[2] That breadth of vision for the life of the Spirit—the sense that all life must be consecrated to God and offered for his glory, we soon come to recognise as the guiding force in the lives of Newman, Keble, Pusey and many of their companions and followers.

This inclusive view makes more difficult, however, the task of trying to sort out predominant influences and strains of thought and practice. We are forced, first of all, to realise how distinctive were the personalities of the Oxford Movement leaders and how much their individual circumstances and motivations varied. Whatever else brought these men together into a good measure of common cause, it was not some obvious similarity of temperament or character. Moreover each personality was intricate in its own right. Newman continues to defy biographers and other commentators who wish to establish his personality type. But it is also becoming increasingly clear that the caricatures of Keble as the self-effacing equanimous parson and Pusey as the doctrinaire devotionalist distort more than inform the complexities of their lives. Nor do their better known followers, men like Richard Hurrell Froude and Isaac Williams, readily match up in terms of personality or background with Keble, Pusey or Newman.

In turning from the personalities to the sociological and intellectual context, we again find a number of strands. In order to explain the character of the Oxford Movement different analysts have stressed the background of Newman in evangelicalism and the response of the leaders of Tractarianism to the Evangelicals' piety and view of the Church, the continuing power of the older high church tradition's view of Catholic England (with an important strand coming from the nonjurors), that tradition's devotional practice leading from Lancelot Andrewes through William Law, the Romantic movement (with all its complexities and contradictions), the influence of the Oriel Noetics and a reaction to some of that group's liberalisms, a desire to prove that faith and reason are not incompatible coupled with a sometimes fierce rejection of the dominance of rationalism in faith issues, and the writings of a number of early Christian teachers. These and other factors have been seen as having critical influence on the formation and direction of the Oxford Movement and its spirituality.

Certainly it is also important to recognise that, in their different ways (Newman's urban middle-class background was hardly the same as Keble's intimate connections with the country squirearchy), the leaders of the movement were all sufficiently affiliated with the established upper socio-economic groups of the time so that the attitudes and emotionalism associated with the piety of at least many of the Evangelicals were regarded with grave suspicion. While the Oxford Movement leaders could certainly be emotionally demonstrative in their personal lives and make use of strong sentiment and feeling in their poetry, prayers and homiletic appeals, they were cautious about the role of excitement or overt passion in religious practice and especially as a basis for a way of demonstrating religious conviction. Since they were also distrustful of the rationalism, which they regarded as a corrosive force in contemporary religion, they found themselves on a narrow course—guarding against both an excess of emotion and of intellectualism in religion. Yet they were men with well-trained minds and passionate feelings. Much of the force of their preaching and writing may indeed issue from this tension of powerful emotion constrained by the strength of the intelligence of men who were at the same time not convinced that intellectual effort led to God, and who thus could not satisfy their longing in the exercise of reason alone.

Part of the interest that the Tractarians continue to hold for us may lie just here. In their suspicion of either too much emotionalism or reason in the practice and understanding of religion, they anticipate aspects of the dilemma of contemporary men and women of faith. Newman in particular, with his fear of the road opened by Hume, his belief that all the rational discussion of the 'evidences' of religion had not made one new disciple, and his strong if uninformed distrust of the new German theology and historical criticism, still held reason to be a way of expositing and partially confirming faith. But it was not its instigator. Undirected by faith's commitment, reason easily led away from God. Undisciplined emotion and feeling were still more unreliable. Newman, whose sermons could enthral with their intensity of passionate feeling suppressed in a web of delicate argumentation, yet found in neither emotion nor intellect a path to the confirmation of faith and relationship with God that were his life's preoccupations. Still God and the transcendent world of divine realities seemed so tantalisingly near. With the different emphases of their temperaments this dilemma was also experienced by Keble and Pusey.

How then could God be known and made known in the world?

Owen Chadwick looks to find a dominant strain in the diversity of the lives of the Tractarians and comes at least close to identifying a primary means they all chose to bring them nearer God. 'It would be too sharp a dissection,' he writes, 'but not therefore without its truth to say that Newman represented the moral and intellectual force of the Movement, Keble the moral and pastoral, Pusey the moral and devotional.'[3] The common element in their religious quest is their concern for the authenticity of discipleship manifested in the moral life. Moreover it is the will to be disciples, to seek sanctification and holiness through the following of conscience which leads individuals to God. 'Conscience, not logical reason—the ethical judgment rather than the argumentative judgment—is for all these Tractarians the chief road to religious knowledge.'[4]

This emphasis on conscience was inherited from Bishop Joseph Butler whose *The Analogy of Religion, Natural and Revealed, to the Constitution and Course of Nature,* the appended *Of the Nature of Virtue,* and *Fifteen Sermons,* were textbooks for Newman, Keble and others. Their understanding of the relationship between the natural and supernatural worlds and the sacramentalism of nature was strongly influenced by the bishop, but his teaching about the compelling authority of conscience may have had an even greater effect upon their epistemology and spirituality.

Butler was concerned to refute Thomas Hobbes's argument that self-interest could be a proper moral guide. Butler wanted to believe that true self-love and the dictates of conscience would one day be seen to be in harmony, but in the present human condition conscience must be regarded as the supreme authority calling forth an obedience which did not consider the consequences for self. True benevolence and love of one's neighbour were strictly disinterested. The Tractarian leaders also believed that conscience was from God and that obedience to conscience led to the sense of God's nearness and presence. Faith was kept on the right course by dutifulness. It was those who were pure of heart who could see God.[5] 'It is holiness,' maintained Newman, 'or dutifulness, or the new creation, or the spiritual mind, however we word it, which is the quickening and illuminating principle of true Faith, giving it eyes, hands, and feet.'[6]

> . . . [R]eal Faith [Newman held was] a reaching forward, yet not of excitement or of passion—a moving forward in the twilight, yet not without clue or direction . . . kept in the narrow path of truth by the Law of dutifulness which inhabits it, the Light of heaven which animates and guides it . . . it takes its character from the moral state of the agent. It is perfected, not by mental cultivation, but by obedience.[7]

The obedient conscience is not the only guide to religious truth but it certainly is critical.

Similarly Pusey preached that 'Scripture gives us but one rule, one test, one way of attaining the truth, i.e. whether we are keeping God's commandments or no, whether we are conformed to this world, or whether we are by the renewing of our mind, being transformed into his image.'[8] As he did at other times, Isaac Williams put the thought more directly, while stressing the theme of self-denial which was so central to Tractarian morality and spirituality: 'Actions of self-denial dispose the heart to prayer, prayer to the love of God, and the love of God to the knowledge of Him.'[9] These words come from Williams's Tract 80, the first part of his controversial essay, 'On Reserve in Communicating Religious Knowledge', which held that certain religious teachings could not and should not be imparted until persons were in the right moral state.

The reverse corollary was, of course, also true. 'One thing only deafens us to the voice of God, untunes all, sets us out of harmony with all . . . ' taught Pusey, 'sin.'[10] The remedy was a disciplined, obedient life. So Keble instructed Thomas Arnold that he could best cure himself from doubt not by 'reading and controversy, but by diet and regimen, i.e. holy living'.[11] Similarly Newman in his sermon 'Obedience the Remedy for Religious Perplexity' advised, 'To all those who are perplexed in any way soever, who wish for light but cannot find it, one precept must be given—OBEY. It is obedience which brings a man into the right path, it is obedience keeps him there and strengthens him in it.'[12] Repeatedly in their sermons Newman, Keble and Pusey stressed the necessity of obedience to conscience and moral living in even the smallest details of life. 'Whoso is faithful in little, is faithful also in much' (Luke 16:10) was a favourite text. 'Is not holiness', Newman asked rhetorically in his sermon 'Holiness Necessary for Future Blessedness', 'the result of many patient repeated efforts after obedience, gradually working on us, and first modifying and then changing our hearts?'[13] Only by means of such conscientious living could God's presence and the reality of the transcendent realm be realised.

As an epistemology such an approach to religious truth may seem somewhat naive and to leave much to be desired. By seeking to prove in life the reality it has already assumed—to interpret life on the basis of prejudgments of faith—the approach fully partakes of what today we call the hermeneutical circle. The believer-interpreter stands within the world of faith as a participant and has no platform outside that world view from which it might be objectively criticised.

Again however the Tractarians may be seen to be our precursors, for a century and a half of philosophy, science and theology later it has become more clear that there is no escaping the circle. All knowing results from expectations and prejudgments about what is to be known.[14]

This awareness need not lead to sheer relativism and the setting aside of all discrimination and critical judgment, for we can still ask about consistency and whether what is being believed can be authentically lived. Verification becomes at least partially dependent on how one lives. If, for instance, I believe that God is trustworthy, am I able to live in such a fashion as to show that I depend on that trust? If I believe that there is a God who desires to share his will with humanity through prayer, do I pray? Does such prayer give to my life a deeper awareness of the divine reality and strengthen me to live a life of sanctification? Does my belief make me different in these ways from those who do not believe? Am I willing to make the sacrifices and undergo the disciplines that are evidences of faith?

Now we begin to feel the dynamics of the moral seriousness and *earnestness* (a word often used to describe the Oxford leaders) which impelled the Tractarians and powered their spirituality. What was most dangerous to faith—most likely to disprove its claims—was inauthentic Christian living. But if they could begin to live lives of sanctification—if their lives could evidence the differences in purity and charity that Christianity was supposed to make—then at least the authenticity if not the truth of Christian believing could be seen. The value that Newman placed upon celibacy (knowing it was not for everyone, he still severely tested his relationships with Keble and Henry Wilberforce in his displeasure at their marriages), and Pusey, for instance, on fasting, lay especially here. Austerity and rigour of discipline were signs of complete commitment. 'Try yourself daily in little deeds to prove that your faith is more than a deceit,' preached Newman in his 1833 sermon 'Self-Denial: the Test of Religious Earnestness'. And again, 'A rigorous self-denial is a chief duty, nay, that it may be considered the test whether we are Christ's disciples, whether we are living in a mere dream, which we mistake for Christian faith and obedience, or are really and truly awake, alive, living in the day, on our road heavenward.'[15] The importance of alms-giving, though properly unostentatious, still had to be thoughtfully stressed. Keble and Newman ran the dangers of scrupulosity in the care with which they exercised their pastoral and parochial responsibilities. It is hard to overemphasise the effects of these life styles (what they called then 'ethos' upon others, especially its attractiveness for the young men of Oxford. Here was holy living. Here was 'singleness of purpose' (another favourite Tractarian phrase). Here was no *cheap grace,* no mere formalism—not just respectability or moralism posing as true religion, but instead fully committed authentic Christianity. With respect to Christian zeal no Tractarian need stand in the shade of any Evangelical!

Of course, the Tractarians did not offer their way of life as a definitive argument for the authenticity of their faith. In addition to all else it would have seemed immodest to suggest that one could so establish Christianity's truth claims through our own life, and the Oxford leaders had a keen sensitivity to the dangers of public piety. They were caught in the dilemma of those who wish to let their lights shine but for God's glory, not their own—to evidence the virtues of faith, among which is humility. They would also have recognised better than most how open such an argument was to the attacks of logic. 'The Oxford men', Chadwick writes, 'did not affirm, that which helps men to be saints must be true. But they had much sympathy with the proposition, and would probably have agreed that it contained more than a seed of truth.'[16] It is the thesis of this essay that in their daily living—as a motivation for their spirituality—this seed had taken deep root in the lives of the Tractarians.

Such a motivation could lead to a high level of hypocrisy if our primary audience were other men and women. The Tractarians however had a far more difficult audience to convince with their moral argument for the validity of Christian faith: they were acting the parts of Christian disciples for themselves. In the first and last analysis it was their own doubts that had to be overcome by the power of Christian believing for holy living. Because their backgrounds and personalities were different, this heavy responsibility bent their lives in particular ways, but we can still discern the similar shape of the burden of their earnestness and their developed capacities for introspection. Pusey grew steadily more determined to find no pleasure in this world which might distract his vision from the transcendent—a determination which at times had been taken to extremes by the enthusiasms of Hurrell Froude. Keble was generally more willing to see God present in nature and some of life's simple pleasures while yet experiencing not infrequent depressions because of what he regarded as his failures. This sense of heavy responsibility is most evident in the emphases we find among them all on conscience as the best guide to God's purposes, on the duties of Christian discipleship and the role of obedience. Through such obedience others would see again the vital nature of Christian faith. Isaac Williams summed up the task of evangelism with these words:

> If people were now asked what was the most powerful means of advancing the course of religion in the world, we should be told that it was eloquence of speech or preaching . . . Whereas, if we were to judge from Holy Scripture of what were the best means of promoting Christianity in the world, we should say obedience; and if we were asked the second, we should say obedience; and if we were to be asked the third, we should say obedience.[17]

As has happened before and since with those seeking so seriously to lead lives of Christian discipleship, what they sadly came to know as their chief obstacle to holy living was sin. It could not be ignored or minimised. Indeed perhaps nothing proved the validity of the Christian way more than the strength of the obstacle it must overcome. Superficial and unexamined human life does not even begin to understand this. Rigorous honesty, obedient perseverance, self-denial and severity of discipline are the weapons in a fierce battle. The arena is the human will.

Of course human beings do not struggle unaided. In one sense the whole point of the contest is to show forth the power of the grace of God. All the Oxford men, Keble especially in his poetry and Newman in his sermons, knew how to express their joy in the experience of that gracefulness. Yet here also is that paradox known by so many Christians beginning with St Paul: 'Work out your own salvation with fear and trembling: for God is at work in you, both to will and to work for his own good pleasure' (Phil. 2:12-13). Keble, having imbibed from infancy his understanding of God's grace working through the Church and sacraments, may have had a somewhat easier time dealing with the problem of the role of the human will in interaction with God's grace than did Newman, although Newman certainly came to stress the graceful presence of Christ in the Eucharist and the importance for believers of experiencing that relationship. Pusey's sacramental mysticism sometimes drew near to ecstasy as he used biblical imagery to tell of dying and rising with Christ in baptism and continuing in relationship with that body of Christ through the Eucharist. His words point beyond themselves to his faith in that mystery by which God penetrates into this physical world and then draws his faithful ones into his divine life.

Yet there has to be this faithfulness. Christians can cut themselves off from the grace of the sacraments and therefore must be exhorted to their reception. The true efficaciousness of the sacraments was only realised as disciples entered upon the imitation of the way of the cross, for which suffering the sacraments were also types—the chalice and baptism of tribulation and passion. Such dying to the world in order to be reborn to the risen life of Christ required, as we have seen, self-denial and disciplined obedience.

Newman, with his defensive attitude towards Lutheran teachings and the strong influence of Calvinism on his early life, can be seen wrestling with this paradox of grace both in theory and practice. A number of his most carefully constructed sermons are balanced on the horns of the dilemma. The issues have rarely been argued more delicately than in his *Lectures on Justification.* Eugene Fairweather calls these discourses 'the most important attempt to find the theological expression of [the Oxford Movement's] piety',[18] for they focus on these critical questions regarding God's grace and the human will. Unaided sinful humanity cannot even begin to do God's bidding. Only God's grace can offer justification and the life of righteousness, and that grace is given through the Church in the sacraments of baptism and especially Holy Communion. Yet individuals must accept the sacraments and are called to obedience in order to show forth the light of grace by holy living. '[S]uch co-operation is the condition, not of our acceptance, or pardon, but of the continuance of that sacred Presence which is our true righteousness.'[19]

We must not expect, however, some sudden outward moral change, but there begins an inner transformation as when a light enlightens a room.[20] It is then 'our blessedness to have our glory swallowed up in Christ's glory, and to consider our works and our holiness, to avail merely as securities for the continuance of that glory . . . as tokens that His grace is not in vain.'[21] Newman explicitly rejects both what he understands to be the Lutheran teaching of justification by faith alone and the Roman justification by obedience, especially when either is held exclusively.[22] In his thought the doctrine of justification becomes one of sanctification through sacramental grace and, viewed in the right way, 'to believe and to obey be but different characteristics of one and the same state of mind'.[23]

Still, why is it that some accept this way of life and others do not? At some fundamental level Newman's Calvinistic background may have continued to whisper to him that it must be a matter of divine choosing. God enables some to accept grace. Yet Newman seems also to have experienced the classical Calvinistic *angst:* one can only know election by God's grace if one manifests that grace and not just to others but to oneself. Therefore one must show forth and experience within oneself the obedience and character of God's chosen. As with many Christians before and since, the doctrine of grace appreciated theologically becomes difficult fully to accept in daily life. The grace may be a gift, but the individual must take a great measure of responsibility for being receptive to that gift. Again God becomes real to those who will commit themselves to live out their faith in God's reality.

This concern with grace was also orchestrated by the Oxford men into that more complex symphony which in some ways soothed but in other ways heightened their personal difficulty, for God's grace did not act just through individuals. It moved through history and especially in the life of the Christian community. (Here more than anywhere else the Tractarians differed from the Evangelicals who stressed individual salvation and the personal holiness of an invisible gathering of disciples.)[24] 'Speak to all the congregation of the children of Israel, and say unto them, ye shall be holy: for I the Lord your God am holy', reads the text (Lev. 19:2). The appeal and the challenge were to the visible church as the body of Christ and the new Israel to show forth by its obedience the power of God's grace and holiness.

The music is now more intricate but the fundamental counterpoint can still be heard. Is it God's grace or human effort which makes the Church holy? Perhaps it must be some dance of both, at least theologically speaking, but surely it is God's grace which has to lead while the Church must regularly be urged and chastised to respond to God's call. Since it is a matter of God's grace and the Church's holiness, the will to show forth this spiritual character cannot come from without the Church—from society-at-large or the State. Reform, however much needed, can only come from within the Church. In this context Keble's Assize Sermon is preached.

The Church is not primarily a human institution. However lethargic and even corrupt the Church may appear it is divine in origin and is the theatre for the drama of God's special acts of grace. The apostolic succession is a vital doctrine ensuring this continuity of divine purpose, and so the Church of England was not to be viewed as some part-Protestant and part-Catholic quasi-political entity produced in reformation conflict. It is more than a *via media.* It is a living extension of the ancient Church. It is God's Church.

Keble and Newman could differ on the political steps that should be taken to help maintain the divine character of the Church. Newman still hoped for a 'Churched-England' while Keble recognised that separation was likely the only answer. But they were one in believing that State interference, however well intended, and the mixing in Church affairs by Roman Catholics and dissenters were, at the least, a threat to their view of a Church whose true leadership reached back through the centuries to the authority and purpose of the Son of God. They were also largely at one in their vision of what the Church ought to be. The clarification of that vision and exhortation in the hope that it might become practice were the purposes of the Tracts.

In his 'Advertisement' or preface to the publication of the first collection of the Tracts, Newman set forth their intent while also sketching the circumstances they were trying to improve: 'The neglect of the daily service, the desecration of festivals, the Eucharist scantily administered, insubordination permitted in all ranks of the Church'.[25] Two of the Tracts (25 and 26) were reprints of the seventeenth-century Bishop William Beveridge's sermons on the importance and value of the daily service and frequent communion. Fasting, together with other forms of austerity and ascetical practice, and auricular confession were important not only for their benefits but as signs that this was a church in continuity with both the early church and its developing life through the centuries. Excommunication had its purpose in maintaining the necessary authority and discipline of the body of Christ. And all this was to be carried out through a devoted, dignified and meticulous pastoral care. St Mary's and then even more evidently Littlemore were testing and training grounds. In quite different circumstances Keble's Hursley was meant to be the ideal apostolic parish. Among a group of friends concerned about the course of Church events, Keble is reported to have exclaimed, 'If the Church of England were to fail altogether yet it would be found in my parish.'[26] Generations of clergy were to be enlightened by this vision, and, in time, the concern with incarnating God's love through pastoral care would become a wellspring for social action ministries and spirituality expressed through them.

Much of the Tractarian's faith in how God would accomplish this renewed Church centred around the sacraments. In a mystical, sometimes almost quasi-physical manner, the Eucharist, which was the sacramental channel between the divine and creaturely worlds, was seen as the focus of God's grace. This was above all how Christians came into contact with the living God. For Keble much of the importance of the apostolic succession lay in its guarantee of the validity of the Eucharist.[27] Froude, who often took his friends' concerns two steps further, was ready to urge the benefits of daily communion.

In all this however little effort was made to call attention to these practices in terms of their outward performance. The Tractarian clergy celebrated the sacraments, said the offices, preached and went about their pastoral duties with restraint and a minimum of ceremonial. It was as if to call attention to their outward form might detract from the inner grace which was all important. Theirs was not a this-worldly religion. The divine services and sacraments pointed not to themselves but beyond to the more important and lasting world. As we have noted, for Pusey especially it was important to seek to die to things of this world in order to realise the reality of the divine. 'The less we live for things outward, the stronger burns our inward life. The more we live to things unseen, the less hold will this world of sense have over us.'[28] It would be left to another generation to give a more incarnate character to their reverent sacramentalism through church decoration, ritual and devotional acts.

Yet while in their priestly offices and personal lives the Oxford leaders remained distrustful of display, the almost magnetic energy produced by so much passionate intensity held under control by a restraining simplicity of life was a source of powerful attraction. To many who gathered about them it made them appear to glow with an inner light. They seemed to make the unseen world real. They stood close to the holy God.

Yet what if, after all their exhortation and effort to bring people to God's grace, the Church, which is meant to be at least a penetration of the invisible world into what is seen, appears no holier? Might it then not be God's chosen way of grace? In response to such doubts one can appeal to the Church's holiness in the past and the connection of the present Church with that past—stressing the signs and means of continuity while conversely disparaging the importance of the abrupt changes of the reformation. One can realistically recognise that the Church must remain imperfect in an imperfect world while still calling for a new holiness of life for the present-day Church modelled on and developing from the earlier Christianity.

But what if the Church seems largely deaf to those challenges, and the signs of apostolicity and continuity appear dim at best? Newman can ameliorate the doubt and pain of his individual dilemma about salvation by projecting it on to the screen of the Church as a historical and present-day institution. There secure grace might be known and the response of holiness be thought of more corporately. Yet if there remain doubts as to whether that grace is genuinely manifested in a particular church and might instead be found in another, then the pain is experienced again in a different form. As Newman drew closer to Roman catholicism, the question of the signs of the Church's holiness and saintliness became more and more important to him. He pondered as he edited and worked during this period on the *Lives of the English Saints.* While W. G. Ward's views are hardly a reliable guide for Newman's, the contention in Ward's *Ideal of a Christian Church* (1844) that the Church of Rome better carried forward and exemplified saintliness than did the Anglican Church was clearly a potent factor in Newman's agonised thinking.

We began this chapter with the understanding that the spirituality of the Oxford Movement can only be viewed as a complex development. No one theme can fully characterise it. No one cause can fully explain it. We have, however, seen how the hope that God's grace could be realised through individual and corporate holiness in such a manner as to evidence the authenticity of Christian faith served as an important dynamic at the heart of the movement. We have also recognised the ways in which the search of the Oxford leaders for authentic Christian living, as a response to the rising tides of relativism, the scientific method and historical criticism, anticipated many of the concerns about the bases for faith which were also to be problems for later Christians. The Tractarians too lived among circumstances which created for them the clangour of *cognitive dissonance,*[29] that is a sharp want of harmony between many of the truth claims of Christianity and the apparent realities of the world and the Church.

To the extent that their best response to religious uncertainty was to try so to live as to affirm 'that which helps men to be saints must be true', we, with them, can be aware of some of the unsatisfactory aspects of that answer. Yet we can also recognise that this response is far from insignificant. In a number of areas of human experience we can only know what may be true by attempting rigorously to live as if it is true. That is no simple tautology but rather part of the awareness of the hermeneutical circle of the interpretation of life which everyone must enter in order to know at all. 'I have more understanding than the aged, *because* [his emphasis] I keep thy commandments' (Ps. 119:100) is the text for Newman's sermon, 'Inward Witness to the Truth of the Gospel'. 'By obeying the commands of Scripture, we learn that these commands really come from God; by trying we make proof; by doing we come to know.'[30]

The Bible taught the Oxford Movement's leaders that holiness of life is the pathway to the Lord's presence. 'Follow peace with all men and holiness, without which no man shall see the Lord' (Heb. 12:14) served as the text for one of Pusey's first formative sermons.[31] Holiness and its disciplines brought the gift of the vision of God's otherwise invisible kingdom. The Tractarians also realised, better than some who lived before and after them, that Christian experience is meant to take on its true depth and colour in forms of community. Anselm's 'I believe that I may understand' had for them become 'we will seek holiness that we my believe'.

What is rightly to be remembered in the life of the Church is how earnestly and sacrificially the Oxford leaders invested themselves in that way of exploration and, with all their frailties and insecurities, sought to show forth what they believed to be the action of God's grace in their lives through authentic Christian spirituality. In retrospect their appeal to the Church's authority and many of their ecclesiastical and doctrinal teachings had little lasting effect on the Church. A different world view was coming into being even as they wrote and preached, and a new order of response was needed to meet the challenges of science and relativism and to the inspiration of the Bible. Events soon superseded their kind of conservatism with respect to biblical interpretation and their metaphysical perspective. Even their appeals to the teaching and practice of the ancient Church have had to be fully re-evaluated. Many Christians of the later nineteenth and twentieth centuries have been searching for spiritualities which seek to experience God through the world rather than by transcending the material creation. They have been looking for a sense of authority which arises through the activity of the Spirit, from within the ongoing body of the Church rather than being seen only in a hierarchical manner. Yet the responses of the Oxford leaders to the challenges of their times in terms of single-hearted discipline, sacrifice and devotion, their sense of God's sacramental presence and their basic theological awareness that the authenticity of Christian faith had to be tested through serious commitment in the examples of their lives together with their call of a church to holiness—these deeply rooted themselves in many hearts and imaginations, sending up shoots to bear fruit in subsequent generations.

Notes

[1] John Henry Newman, *Parochial and Plain Sermons,* new edn, 8 vols (London 1878), VIII, pp. 264-5.

[2] John Macquarrie, *Paths in Spirituality* (New York 1972), p. 47.

[3] Owen Chadwick, ed., *The Mind of the Oxford Movement* (London 1960), p. 48.

[4] Chadwick, *Mind,* p. 36. See also Yngve Brilioth, *The Anglican Revival: studies in the Oxford Movement* (London 1925), esp. pp. 210-79.

[5] John Keble, Tract 89, *On the Mysticism Attributed to the Early Fathers of the Church,* p. 135. Here Keble speaks of the moral means of repentance, devotion and self-denial necessary for a right reading of Scripture.

[6] John Henry Newman, *Sermons Chiefly on the Theory of Religious Belief, Preached before the University of Oxford* (London 1843), p. 228.

[7] ibid. pp. 243-4.

[8] Edward Bouverie Pusey, *Parochial Sermons,* rev. edn, 3 vols (London 1878), III, p. 202. See also Newman's sermon 'Faith and Obedience' on the text, 'If thou wilt enter into life, keep the commandments' (Matt. 19:17), *Parochial and Plain Sermons,* III, pp. 84-97.

[9] Isaac Williams, Tract 80, *On Reserve in Communicating Religious Knowledge,* pp. 40-1.

[10] Edward Bouverie Pusey, *Sermons during the season from Advent to Whitsuntide* (London 1848), p. 280.

[11] Quoted by Georgian Battiscombe, *John Keble: a study in limitations* (London 1963), p. 63.

[12] Newman, *Parochial and Plain Sermons,* I, p. 267.

[13] ibid. pp. 12-13.

[14] See, for example, the discussions by A. C. Thiselton, *The Two Horizons: New Testament Hermeneutics and Philosophical Description with Special Reference to Heidegger, Bultmann, Gadamer and Wittgenstein* (Grand Rapids, Michigan, and Exeter 1980), pp. 16-19, 103-14 *passim.*

[15] Newman, *Parochial and Plain Sermons,* I, pp. 65-82.

[16] Chadwick, *Mind,* p. 12.

[17] Isaac Williams, Tract 87, *On Reserve in Communicating Religious Knowledge* (conclusion), p. 82. See also Newman, *Parochial Sermons,* I, p. 12.

[18] E. R. Fairweather, ed., *The Oxford Movement* (New York and Oxford 1964), p. 215.

[19] John Henry Newman, 'Righteousness Viewed as a Gift and a Quality', Lecture VIII, in *Lectures on the Doctrine of Justification* (London 1838), p. 214.

[20] ibid., 'The Characteristics of the Gift of Righteousness', Lecture VII, p. 196.

[21] ibid., Lecture VIII, p. 231.

[22] cf. ibid., Lecture I, pp. 1-31.

[23] id., *Parochial and Plain Sermons,* III, p. 95.

[24] See J. E. Linnan, 'The Search for Absolute Holiness: a study of Newman's evangelical period', *Ampleforth Journal,* 73 (1968), pp. 161-74, who illustrates from Newman's first sermons strong parallels with the Evangelicals' call to personal holiness.

[25] John Henry Newman, 'Advertisement', in *Tracts for the Times,* I, p. iv.

[26] See Battiscombe, *John Keble,* p. 303.

[27] See M. R. O'Connell, *The Oxford Conspirators: a history of the Oxford Movement 1833-45* (London 1959), p. 213.

[28] Pusey, *Sermons from Advent to Whitsuntide,* pp. 299-300.

[29] On cognitive dissonance, cf. L. Festinger, in L. Festinger, H. W. Riechen and S. Schachter, *When*

Prophecy Fails: a social and psychological study of a modern group that predicted the destruction of the world (New York 1956); and L. Festinger, *A Theory of Cognitive Dissonance* (California 1957).

[30] Newman, *Parochial and Plain Sermons,* VIII, pp. 112-13.

[31] See O'Connell, *Oxford Conspirators,* p. 99.

John Shelton Reed (essay date 1996)

SOURCE: "The Seeds of Ritualism," in *Glorious Battle: The Cultural Politics of Victorian Anglo-Catholicism*, Vanderbilt University Press, 1996, pp. 3-28.

[*In the following essay, Reed assesses the impact of Tractarianism on Anglo-Catholicism in nineteenth-century Britain.*]

The Church of England at the end of the nineteenth century was a very different institution from what it had been seventy or eighty years before.[1] Of course England was a different place, and many of the changes in the Church simply reflected that. The nation's population had more than doubled between the 1830s and the 1880s; that of London had nearly trebled. Hundreds of new churches had been built in an attempt to keep up with the growing urban and suburban population, and the numbers of clergymen and churchgoers had also greatly increased—if not as fast as the population.

The new clergymen struck many observers as more earnest, more hard working, more professional than their predecessors, and more of them had received theological training, in the new theological colleges founded during the period. Some of the worst abuses of patronage and plurality had been eliminated, and if anticlericalism was still widespread, it was at least less violent than it had been in 1830. The Church of England was a leaner, more efficient institution than ever before. The concentration of population in the cities and improved transportation in the countryside meant that clergymen could gather more often, and they did, in ruridecanal conferences, diocesan synods, annual church congresses, and meetings of innumerable groups for special purposes. The convocations of Canterbury and York had begun to meet again, giving the clergy of the Church a greater voice in its government, and the decennial Lambeth Conference had even begun to gather Anglicans from around the world.

Disturbingly, however, each of these improvements seemed to be matched by other, less encouraging changes. The proportion of the population actually attending Anglican churches—or any churches, for that matter—had declined steadily throughout the century. Particularly in the working-class areas of English cities, attendance had reached levels that contemporary observers thought alarmingly low. Some people did not much care for the new sort of clergymen, either, and pointed out that fewer had university degrees or were, in a word, gentlemen. Whether as cause or effect, the social standing of the clergy was markedly lower at the end of the century than it had been at the beginning.

Disestablishment was still a threat, and the Church had lost its monopoly in education. More and more, it seemed, decisions were being made without reference to the Church or the Church's law—decisions about social services, about divorce and remarriage, even about who could be buried in Anglican graveyards. Religious censuses had revealed what everyone already feared, that as many as half of English churchgoers were to be found in congregations other than those of the Church of England. Particularly in the cities, the parish system had pretty well broken down. Many parishioners stayed home on Sundays; others went to Dissenting or Roman Catholic churches; still others crossed parish boundaries to attend Anglican services more to their taste than those offered by their parish churches.

And by the end of the century there were many varieties of Anglican worship to choose from. (Some believed that this was an improvement, but many disagreed.) An ecclesiastical Rip Van Winkle roused from a seventy-year sleep in the 1890s would have noticed few changes in the Church of England more startling at first glance than those in the conduct of public worship. It would not have been immediately evident that those changes were bound up, one way or another, with all of the other changes in the Church, but they were.

Varieties of Anglican Worship

Suppose that our sleeper awoke to find himself in London, at Oxford Circus, on a Sunday morning.[2] Within a few blocks he would find a bewildering array of services ranging from some almost identical to those he had known seventy years before to some that he would not recognize as Anglican at all.

If he walked north along Regent Street, for instance, he would immediately enter the parish of All Souls, Langham Place. Soon he would come to the church itself, a fine neoclassical building dating from 1824, where he would find a service very much like what he was accustomed to. Most of the congregation would be seated in their family pews, rented by the year, and he would be directed by the verger to one of the "open" (i.e., public) seats at the rear of the church. The members of the choir, in their Sunday best, would also be in the back of the church.

The service would be the Prayer Book office of morning prayer, with a sermon. It would be read by the rector, in a white surplice with his M.A. hood; to preach the sermon, he would change to a black Genevan gown. Accompanied by Miss Bloomer on the organ, the congregation would sing hymns from the *Hymnal Companion;* some would be new to him, but neither they nor the sermon would contain any novel doctrine (although he might find both somewhat "methodistical" by the standards of the 1830s). He would not be surprised to learn that there were to be two services of evening prayer that same day, the second with another sermon. If it happened to be a communion Sunday, the service of Holy Communion would follow morning prayer. The minister, wearing his surplice and hood, would read the Prayer of Consecration standing to the left of the communion table, sideways to the congregation, as the Prayer Book directed.

The observer would notice a few changes. Even at morning prayer, there would be a collection, or "offertory." And he would be startled to learn that there was a communion service every Sunday—if not after morning prayer, then early in the morning, in the afternoon, or after evening prayer. He would also find more weekday services than he was used to: morning prayer on Wednesdays, Fridays, and saints' days; evening prayer on Wednesdays. But, all things considered, he would not be alarmed by what he encountered at All Souls.

If he turned south from Oxford Circus, though, he would enter the parish of St. John the Baptist. A left turn on Argyll Place would take him in a couple of blocks to the church, a small, recently constructed Gothic Revival building on Great Marlborough Street. Entering, he would find all but fifty of the 460 seats open to the public, and he could probably sit where he pleased. Morning prayer would begin early, at 10:30, to allow a service of Holy Communion to follow.

The service would begin with a procession from the back of the church: the choir, in surplices, would take their place in the chancel, at the front of the church. The ministers (there would probably be more than one) would also wear surplices, but with brightly colored embroidered stoles rather than academic hoods. The visual focus of the church would be the communion table rather than the pulpit; it would be decorated with an embroidered frontal, flowers, and candles, and would bear little resemblance to the plain wooden table to which the visitor was accustomed. The psalms and canticles would be sung, not read, with a rather florid setting, and some of the hymns in *Hymns Ancient and Modern* might sound strangely "Romish" (for example, number 97: "Faithful Cross, above all other"). The sermon might puzzle the visitor, too: it might deal with some point of ecclesiastical history or symbolism. He would notice that the preacher did not change to his black gown for the sermon.

When morning prayer ended and the communion service began, he would probably be struck by the celebrant's reading the Prayer of Consecration with his back to the congregation. He would certainly be startled to learn that there had already been an early communion service that morning, and that there was another every Thursday, as well as on holy days.

Our observer would recognize the words of the *Book of Common Prayer,* but few of the accompaniments would be familiar unless he had extensive experience in Anglican cathedrals. He would certainly be more struck by the changes than by the continuities. He might or might not be disturbed to learn that what he saw was becoming typical of Church of England services.

But if he walked a little farther down Regent Street to the next parish, St. Thomas, he would almost certainly be shocked. If he knew something of the Roman Catholic Mass, he would recognize what he saw at St. Thomas's Church, although he might wonder why the words were those of the Anglican prayer book. If he knew nothing of Catholicism he would be mystified.

The interior of the seventeenth-century building, redone in the 1860s by William Butterfield, would be filled with light and shadow and vivid color. Ornamental banding, encaustic tile, banks of flowers, many candles, embroidery, stained glass—all would contribute to an overwhelming impression, only heightened when the church was seen through the haze of incense, which would be liberally burned in procession and during the Mass that followed. With the thurifer in procession would come a surpliced choir, acolytes, and a number of priests, one of them (the preacher) wearing what our visitor might just possibly recognize as a cope, the others in gorgeous vestments of a sort nowhere to be found in the Church of England of the 1830s.

There would be no reserved pews. Some of the music would be Gregorian, and the Prayer Book communion service would be read with a great deal of crossing, bowing, and genuflecting. Not only would the congregation engage in mysterious signs of devotion from time to time, but some of them would be very strange-looking folk—especially some women dressed in the habits of sisters.

The sermon might be especially striking; if our visitor knew his history, he might observe that it was as if the Reformation had never taken place. The announcements would be equally strange, dealing with the activities of a number of parish guilds and perhaps exhorting the congregation to avail themselves of the opportunity for confession and absolution.

During the celebration of Holy Communion, the celebrant would face the altar, his back to the congregation, flanked by two other oddly vested clergymen. Some of the prayers would be virtually inaudible, and they would be punctuated by long intervals in which the celebrant appeared to be praying privately. After the consecration, the celebrant would himself consume the consecrated elements: probably our visitor would not be given the opportunity to receive communion. If he asked, he would be told that those who wished to do so had come to one of two earlier celebrations. There was a celebration every morning at St. Thomas's, two on Thursdays and saints' days, and five on great festivals.

Here, in a stroll of less than half a mile down Regent Street, on any Sunday in the 1890s, our observer could witness a range of Anglican worship that he would probably refuse to believe possible. At All Souls, an austere Evangelical service not very different from what he would have seen in most English parish churches sixty years before. At St. John the Baptist, a lavishly decorated choral service reminiscent, perhaps, of cathedral services early in the century, but increasingly representative of "normal," middle-of-the-road parochial worship. At St. Thomas, Regent Street, a High Mass almost indistinguishable save in language from that of any well-to-do Roman Catholic church of the period. The same contrasts could be seen in many other neighborhoods of London, in most large cities of the nation, and in many smaller ones.

What had happened while our observer slept? The answer is that a movement called "Anglo-Catholicism" had sprung up and, despite reversals, had flourished. St. Thomas was among the churches in the vanguard of that movement; they showed how far it had come since its beginnings. The worship at St. John the Baptist looked like Anglo-Catholic worship of an earlier day, but it was not an Anglo-Catholic church. It illustrated, rather, how much the great central body of Anglican practice had been influenced by the movement. Even All Souls, Langham Place, had been influenced by Anglo-Catholicism, although in a reactive way. Its weekday services and weekly communion had been Anglo-Catholic innovations, but Evangelicals alarmed at their rivals' success had adopted those practices in self-defense.

In short, the Anglo-Catholics had not only won their right to toleration within the Church of England, they had by their example and success influenced the practice and attitudes of all parts of the Church. How had this come about?

The history of the Anglo-Catholic movement in the nineteenth-century Church of England comes in two parts, one relatively well known, the other largely forgotten, even by Anglo-Catholics. The first part, the story of the Oxford Movement, is told in John Henry Newman's *Apologia pro Vita Sua,* and it has often been told since, largely in the terms that Newman laid down: as the story of his vision, his discouragement, his spiritual crisis, and his conversion to Roman Catholicism. But the history of the movement after Newman's secession has been much less thoroughly described.[3] In serious histories of Victorian Britain, even in most serious histories of Victorian religion, the heroes and mock-heroes of the second, "Ritualist" phase of the Anglo-Catholic revival are usually relegated to a becoming obscurity. The movement's most important political ally, Gladstone, and its most effective political adversary, Disraeli, are remembered for many things but seldom for their opinions on Anglo-Catholicism. Its most significant clerical ally, "Soapy Sam" Wilberforce, bishop of Oxford and then of Winchester, is probably remembered today, if at all, for coming off second-best to T. H. Huxley in an exchange concerning the theory of evolution.

Although some historians are now beginning to put this situation right, for a picture of the movement in the second half of the nineteenth century we still must turn to dusty Victorian and Edwardian biographies and memoirs, to hagiographies compiled to mark this or that centenary, or to little-read novels by authors like Shane Leslie and Compton Mackenzie.

Foremost among the several reasons for the relative neglect of the movement's later period, I suspect, is one that is almost purely aesthetic. The story of the Oxford Movement is so compelling, so dramatically complete, that the rest comes as an anticlimax. To demonstrate that (and also to show that many of the later movement's characteristics and problems were present almost from the start) it may be appropriate briefly to recount what happened in Oxford in the years 1833-1845.[4]

Tracts for the Times

On July 14, 1883, John Keble preached a sermon on "National Apostasy" in the church of St. Mary the Virgin, Oxford. John Henry Newman later identified that sermon as the beginning of the Oxford Movement, and subsequent historians have generally followed his lead. On its face, the sermon protested parliamentary interference in the affairs of the Church, specifically a proposal by the Whig government to suppress some bishoprics of the Church of Ireland. Keble's point was not that the bishoprics were needed (they assuredly were not), but rather that Parliament was an assembly of laymen (including non-Anglican laymen) and had no business ordering the affairs of the Church as if it were merely a branch of government like the postal service.

Of course the movement did not spring up full-blown from that single sermon. But its message fell on fertile ground. Many churchmen were concerned about growing popular hostility to the Establishment, expressed not only in acts of Parliament but in the actions of mobs like those that stoned the carriage of the bishop of Bath and Wells, burned the bishop's palace in Bristol, and on Guy Fawkes Day in 1831 burned the bishop of Exeter himself, in effigy, after the bishops voted in the House of Lords against the First Reform Bill. In part, the movement was a reaction against lethargy and negligence in the Church (often overstated, to be sure, by sympathetic historians); in part it was merely an amplification and mobilization of the already-existing High Church tradition that Keble's poems in *The Christian Year* exemplified.[5] But even if Keble's sermon did nothing more than focus Newman's attention, it can serve as a convenient marker for the start of a dramatic twelve years.

The course of the movement in its Oxford home began with excitement and success. A series of ninety *Tracts for the Times* was begun shortly after Keble's sermon, with a tract by Newman defending the spiritual independence of the Church under bishops standing in the apostolic succession. Other tracts followed, arguing the case for orthodoxy in other respects.[6] The publication of the *Tracts* and Newman's sermons in St. Mary's won adherents to the cause, both enthusiastic undergraduates and distinguished High Church divines, notably E. B. Pusey, professor of Hebrew and fellow of Christ Church, who soon became identified as a leader of the movement, with Newman and Keble. Newman's brilliance, Keble's manifest holiness, Pusey's scholarship—all were put to the service of an exalted vision of the English Church and its ministry, a vision with obvious appeal to young men destined for that ministry and more subtle but no less potent attractions for others. Within a year of Keble's sermon, a declaration of "deep attachment to the apostolical doctrine and liturgy and polity of the Church of England" was drawn up, signed by seven thousand clergymen, and presented to the archbishop of Canterbury.[7]

But almost from the beginning the Tractarians (as they came to be known) faced external opposition. As long as the movement remained a donnish affair, its opposition was theologically based, but it was no less fierce for that. Three months after the first tracts appeared, the *Record,* an Evangelical newspaper, denounced the series and its writers for Romanism. This accusation would be incessant, and soon it would be made by others besides extreme Low Churchmen.

Also virtually from the beginning, there was internal division on matters of both policy and substance. On the one hand, the younger men—like Newman, Keble, and their friend Hurrell Froude—wanted to take a stand on principle and to make a commotion, not fearing even disestablishment if it came to that (Keble would have welcomed it). On the other hand was the group that Froude called the Z's, conservative High Churchmen like William Palmer and Hugh James Rose who valued Establishment and disliked enthusiasm, even in its support.[8] This group was responsible for the moderate tone of the declaration delivered to the archbishop, and was dubious at first about the *Tracts.*

Soon there followed what the conservatives saw as a series of disastrous blunders, feeding the suspicions of the movement's Evangelical opponents, alienating many potential supporters, and contributing to a growing impression in many quarters that the Tractarians were dishonest, disloyal, and too clever by half. In 1836 the Tractarians opposed the Prime Minister's appointment of Dr. Hampden, a divine of doubtful orthodoxy, as Regius Professor of Divinity. The protest was as much against the way in which such appointments were made as against Hampden's teaching, and the Tractarians had a legitimate point, but they succeeded only in denying the new professor the right to help select university preachers and laid the groundwork for future troubles by persuading many in Oxford, and elsewhere, that they were spiteful bigots.

In the Hampden controversy, the Tractarians had acted in concert with Evangelicals, but that uneasy alliance was soon shattered irreparably. When their beloved friend Hurrell Froude died of tuberculosis in 1836, Newman and Keble undertook to edit his letters and journals, and published them as a memorial in 1838. Opinions differ about whether this was an act of staggering innocence or a conscious attempt to polarize opinion, but even a sympathetic historian has observed that "to describe [the book's] publication as indiscreet is far too weak an expression."[9] Most readers would have found the harrowing self-discipline, spiritual minutiae, and anguished scruples revealed in the diaries unsettling enough, but what really confirmed Low Churchmen's worst suspicions were Froude's exuberant attacks on the English Reformers. One example sums it up: "Really, I hate the Reformation and the Reformers more and more."[10]

Thomas Arnold remarked of Froude's *Remains* that its "predominant character" was its "extraordinary impudence."[11] An indirect result of its publication was the erection of the Martyrs' Memorial in Oxford, to honor the Reformers, and a direct result was greatly heightened suspicion of a movement led by men who could publish such a work without dissociating themselves from it.

The next year saw another cause for suspicion. Isaac Williams, Keble's student and, for a time, Newman's curate, published Tract 80, "On Reserve in Communicating Religious Knowledge." Williams's argument for teaching religious truths only after adequate preparation was unremarkable, if not unexceptionable; taken out of context, however, he could be seen as arguing for practices that some Protestants liked to call Jesuitical. To the charge of disloyalty was added that of dishonesty, and Williams paid for his own lack of "reserve"; denounced by several bishops (including the bishop of Gloucester, who had apparently read only his title), he was denied the Professorship of Poetry at Oxford in 1842.

After 1838 the uneasiness that conservatives in the movement felt toward those who shared Froude's opinions or his temperament was exacerbated by the presence and activities of a number of unabashed Romanizers, such men as W. G. Ward, Frederick Oakeley, and F. W. Faber (all of them later to become Roman Catholics). In 1841, Newman's probably hopeless attempt to reconcile this group to the Church of England led to the disaster of Tract 90, in which he attempted to show that the Church's Thirty-Nine Articles were not incompatible with the formulations of the Council of Trent. This was the last straw for many churchmen, while for Hampden's friends and others it was the ammunition they had been waiting for. Four Oxford tutors, including the future Archbishop Tait, protested; the powerful Heads of Houses at the university, almost without exception, condemned the tract; one bishop allowed that he would not want to trust its author with his purse; and Newman, apparently bewildered by the firestorm he had provoked, agreed to put a stop to the *Tracts,* at the bishop of Oxford's request.

Edward Pusey (1800-1882)

The movement's enemies were now in the ascendant. In 1843, without a hearing, an explanation, or the opportunity for a defense, Pusey was condemned for one of his sermons by an ad hoc committee of his enemies appointed by the vice-chancellor of the university, and he was suspended from preaching for two years. Pusey by all accounts accepted this punishment with humaility and an absence of bitterness, but the message was not lost on his fellow Tractarians.

The year before, Newman had withdrawn from his rooms in college and retired to Littlemore, a village in the parish of his church of St. Mary's. Disturbed and unsettled by the response to Tract 90, as well as by his study of the Arian heresy (wherein he detected analogies to the Church of England) and by plans affot for cooperation between Anglicans and Protestants (Lutherans) in the Holy Land, he converted some sheds into the semblance of a monastic establishment where, with some friends, he kept a schedule of worship and study.

In February of 1843 Newman preached his last sermon before the university. In September, after Pusey's condemnation in June, he resigned the living of St. Mary's. On September 25 he preached his last sermon as an Anglican, at Littlemore. The subject, "The Parting of Friends," was occasioned by the secession to the Roman communion of one of the young men of Littlemore, but its words left no room for doubt about what was to follow.

One blow remained. In the summer of 1844 W. G. Ward published *The Ideal of a Christian Church,* in which he made it plain that in his view only the Roman Catholic Church met that ideal, yet that he gloried in the "most joyful, most wonderful, most unexpected sight" that he and other English churchmen could believe everything that Roman Catholics believed, without being censured for it.[12] This provocation, surely intended, led the Heads of Houses to summon a meeting of Convocation. In February 1845 Oxford graduates gathered from all over England in the Sheldonian Theatre, solemnly condemned Ward's book (by a two to one vote), stripped him of his Oxford degrees (by a closer vote), and were prevented from condemning Tract 90 and, by implication, its author only by the proctors' exercise of their statutory veto. The drama of the occasion was somewhat undermined by the undergraduates who threw snowballs at the vice-chancellor as he entered the theater, and by the fact that Ward's witty defense of himself evoked what one observer called "one of the historical laughs of the world."[13]

But the condemnation of Ward and the knowledge that only a procedural stratagem had saved Newman from a like condemnation was no laughing matter at Littlemore. Newman was clinging to Anglicanism by a thread, and it was now apparent to him not only that his hopes for the Church of England were in vain but that there was no place for him in it. The steady flow of secessions continued, but still Newman hesitated. His friends watched breathlessly as the summer passed. On October 3, Newman resigned his fellowship at Oriel. Five days later a Roman Catholic priest, Father Dominic, came to Littlemore to receive Newman into the Church of Rome.

And there the story often ends. It is a great tale, when told well: early, heady success and excitement; internal division and growing opposition; the first reversals, then disaster piled on disaster; Newman's retreat to Littlemore, the hushed anticipation of his conversion, his seclusion (reminiscent of Gethsemane); the inevitable calling in of the Passionist father to receive the great man's submission. At that point the Oxford Movement, properly speaking, was over. Disgraced in Oxford, its enemies' suspicions wholly confirmed, abandoned by its greatest spokesman and by the many lesser figures who preceded and followed him—the curtain should fall, or we risk bathos.

The "Subtractarians"

Respect for the drama is surely one reason for the general neglect of the Anglo-Catholic revival's later history. But there is another. As one historian has written, rightly, "This second phase of the Oxford Movement compares, on the whole, unfavourably, at least in intellectual and spiritual interest, with its predecessor."[14] The post-Tractarians or (as they have been called fondly, but with full awareness of the implications) "subtractarians" were many things: pastors, organization-builders, hymn-writers, ecclesiologists, controversialists, and vestry-room lawyers.[15] But until the emergence of "Catholic modernism" at the end of the century, few who propelled the movement after 1845 were thinkers whose thought still commands attention.[16]

In 1874, one partisan, responding to the charge that "no men of genius or mark" were connected with the movement, simply granted the point and observed that Jesus' early disciples were an undistinguished lot as well; besides, he said, this lack was "one of many indications that the work is *not* from man."[17] If so, the Lord's ways were as mysterious as usual, because some of the movement's most conspicuous adherents lacked not just genius but common sense, and a few were clearly unhinged. At times one gets the sense that twentieth-century Anglo-Catholics who know of these figures at all find them a little embarrassing, a clutch of monomaniacal Uncle Tobies lurking in the family tree.

It is easy to forget that the Oxford Movement had its silly side, too—to forget, for example, J. B. Morris, who irritated Newman by arguing in a sermon at St. Mary's that the brute creation should fast and who, Mark Pattison recalled, "passed his whole time up the tower of Exeter College, reading the Fathers and cutting jokes upon 'our step-mother, the Church of England.'"[18] But the leaders of the Oxford Movement were so patently un-silly, such imposing moral and intellectual presences, that the high jinks of lesser figures pale into insignificance, at least in retrospect.

The post-Tractarians, in contrast, could not be said to have had leaders. The only two who could have claimed that role were Pusey and Keble, and neither was willing to accept it. Not only was there no dominant figure to color the entire movement by force of personality or intellect, there was no one in a position to check the excesses of the more zealous partisans, or to expel from the movement those who eventually went too far. The result was that side by side with the movement's authentic saints walked some of the most colorful eccentrics of the age, and the story is complicated by the fact that some of the eccentrics had their saintly qualities, and some of the saints their eccentricities.[19]

Anglo-Catholics can take pride, for example, in a number of great slum priests, men of holy lives, who gave themselves in selfless service to the poor of Victorian cities.[20] But what is one to make of that other slum priest, the Reverend Dr. F. G. Lee of All Saints, Lambeth, who obtained bishop's orders from a mysterious source (allegedly on the high seas, to avoid jurisdictional difficulties), proclaimed himself pro-provincial of Canterbury, and went about secretly reordaining clergymen who had come to doubt the validity of Anglican orders?[21]

One can likewise admire many of the pioneers in the reestablishment of Anglican religious orders. Priscilla Lydia Sellon's iron will prevailed in the face of bitter prejudice against both her religion and her sex, and enabled her to found and to direct what became the Society of the Most Holy Trinity.[22] W. J. Butler was an exemplary parish priest as vicar of Wantage and combined his parochial duties with the oversight of the Community of St. Mary the Virgin, his foundation.[23] The delightful John Mason Neale annoyed his bishop and sometimes his friends by his immoderate enthusiasm for "the good old times of England," but that enthusiasm led him to establish the Society of St. Margaret, and to guide its early history, while pursuing the scholarship that made him perhaps Anglicanism's greatest hymn-writer and translator.[24] R. M. Benson's founding of the Society of St. John the Evangelist (the

Cowley Fathers), the great preaching order of the Anglican Communion, is also an edifying and relatively well-known story.[25]

But these communities have survived to a respectable middle age. Less stable founders produced less stable communities, and there were many of these as well. For instance, J. L. Lyne, who preferred to be known as "Father Ignatius," set out single-handedly to revive the Benedictine Order in the Church of England, and was said by some of his admirers to have raised a young woman from the dead with a relic of the True Cross—conduct, Sir Shane Leslie remarked, thought by some to be uncalled-for in an Anglican curate.[26] Most Anglo-Catholics were so sympathetic to Lyne's aims that they kept their misgivings about this and other excesses to themselves, and the movement may have suffered in consequence.

Lyne's co-worker in the monastic revival, Father George Nugee, was less quixotic, but almost as odd. Quietly removed by Bishop Wilberforce from his family living in Hampshire on charges of "impropriety and immorality (especially but not exclusively with a person called Sister Agatha)," Nugee retired to South London and founded St. Austin's Priory, which one historian has called "a residential club for religious eccentrics."[27] No less an aesthete than Walter Pater was delighted by the gorgeous services at the priory: one of Nugee's proteges, Richard Jackson, a young clergyman and amateur painter also known as "Brother à Becket," was the original for Pater's portrait of Marius the Epicurean.[28]

Dean Church and Canon Liddon of St. Paul's Cathedral, Benjamin Webb of St. Andrew's, Wells Street, and scores if not hundreds of other clergymen in parishes across England maintained a sober Tractarian emphasis on loyalty to the Church of England and decency and order in worship, but others embraced ceremonial and decorative extravagances hard to defend as the result of obedience to the Church's law.[29] Sometimes these excesses seem to have been calculated to offend the movement's enemies; sometimes they achieved the same result out of thoughtless exuberance—as in the case of the Reverend John Purchas of Brighton, brought to trial in an ecclesiastical court on thirty-five counts of ceremonial irregularity, including hanging a stuffed dove over the altar at Whitsuntide.[30]

In Christina Rossetti the movement nurtured a remarkable poet, but the aesthetic impulse elsewhere produced wackier results, as at the hands of the Reverend Sabine Barin-Gould, author of "Onward, Christian Soldiers" and collector of ghost stories, who thundered against Protestantism from his remote vicarage and forbade his daughters to read the novels he wrote or to mention the Reformation in his presence.[31] Even quainter was Baring-Gould's fellow poet, Parson Hawker, vicar of Morwenstow in Cornwall for forty-one years.[32] Hawker designed his own yellow vestment (a copy, he said, of St. Padarn's) and paced his parish in a purple cassock, a blue jersey, high wading boots, and an assortment of headgear that included a pink cap resembling a fez. Hawker kept a pet pig that followed him like a dog, he believed that pixies were the souls of unbaptized children, and he paid his parishioners ten shillings for every washed-up corpse that they brought him, unrobbed, for proper burial.

Obviously, these flamboyant characters were hardly representative. Few contributed to building the movement's institutional base; they were not leaders or even reliable followers, and none was an intellectual figure of much account. Some of their allies found them an embarrassment at the time, and others perhaps should have. Still, they were as much of a presence in the movement as the responsible, earnest, and quiet folk, and there is a sense in which they should be taken as seriously. They belong in the movement's history not just for the sake of comprehensiveness, but because they helped to shape the popular response to Anglo-Catholicism as much as the others, and possibly more.

The Question of Continuity

Perhaps it is not surprising that it has suited some friends of Anglo-Catholicism to emphasize the movement's early years, discreetly passing over its later, Ritualist phase. Other historians have gone further still, arguing (like some of the movement's opponents at the time) that the later developments were a perversion of the earlier movement, or even a new and quite distinct phenomenon. Just after the turn of the century, Archbishop Davidson, testifying before the Royal Commission on Ecclesiastical Discipline, quoted liberally from Newman, Pusey, and Keble to show that they were relatively indifferent to "ritual" practices compared to those who claimed to be their successors, and Davidson was neither the first nor the last to distinguish invidiously between the intellectual and devotional contribution of the Oxford Movement, on the one hand, and the ceremonial froth it stirred up later, on the other.[33]

But even if Ritualism could be shown to be an alien or irrelevant growth, somehow grafted onto a serious movement by lesser men of a later generation, that would not be grounds for dismissing it as unworthy of serious attention. In any case, some recent historians have agreed with the Ritualists' own argument, that their program was a natural and inevitable result of Tractarian ideas planted in new and different circumstances.[34]

Certainly, as its name implies, the Oxford Movement was largely an academic affair; more than that, it was largely a clerical movement, and its concerns and its style reflected that fact. Its appeal was not wholly to the intellect—Keble's poetry, Newman's sermons, Pusey's personal example of sanctity and scholarship were persuasive in other ways—but as long as the movement was confined to Oxford common rooms and the studies of rural vicarages, its principal mode of expression was verbal (as its other label, "Tractarian," makes plain). When the movement went out from Oxford into the parishes and sought a lay following, however, it necessarily underwent some changes. In two respects, later developments in the movement were clearly in line with the wishes of the founders: both the establishment of religious orders and the revival of the practice of "auricular confession" had the explicit sanction of the movement's surviving leaders. As Archbishop Davidson's testimony shows, what sometimes unsettled, puzzled, or displeased the Tractarian elders who survived to the last third of the century was the growth and development of the Ritualists' distinctive ceremonial and decorative practices.

But even in this respect, those who have argued great discontinuity between the Oxford Movement and the Ritualists have overstated the case. Aside from the Ritualists' own denial, there are two answers to the charge that Ritualism departed from the ideals of the original Tractarians. One is to show that Newman, Pusey, and Keble themselves were sympathetic to ritual "advance," although with qualifications that the Ritualists did not share: any discontinuity, then, reflects the dropping of the qualifications, not the emphasis on ritual itself. The other response is to show that, from the first, lesser figures in the movement attached considerable importance to various controversial practices, as expressions of the doctrines they were absorbing.

Ritualism and the Leaders of the Oxford Movement

When comparing the attitudes of the Tractarians to those of the Ritualists, however, we must keep in mind that the meaning of the disputed practices changed as time passed. In the 1840s and 1850s services were disrupted in a number of places when clergymen followed the Prayer Book directions and preached in surplices rather than black gowns. Forty years later, that was the practice in nearly all except the most extreme Evangelical churches in London and was unexceptionable almost everywhere else in England. By then Protestant demonstrators were protesting, among other things, the distinctively Roman Catholic service of "Creeping to the Cross" on Good Friday. While Newman was still at Littlemore and still an Anglican, an altar cross and candles were as provocative as incense and images would be fifty years later. So in arguing, for instance, that Pusey would not have approved of incense in the 1840s (or for that matter in the 1870s), we should not lose sight of the fact that some of the things he very much wanted to introduce in the 1840s were as offensive to contemporary Low Churchmen as some of the things he later opposed as unnecessarily offensive. Pusey's views had not changed, but the times had, and his views were no longer so radical.

Of the three acknowledged leaders of the Oxford Movement the one least uneasy about the proto-Ritualists in the movement was probably Newman, less because he shared their enthusiasms than because he was not temperamentally opposed to controversy and did not oppose their activities on grounds of prudence. True, he referred to them as the "gilt-gingerbread school," and he was quite conservative in his own practice as long as he remained an Anglican. Pusey said, for example, that Newman always consecrated at the north end of the altar (sideways to the congregation), as the Prayer Book directed, unlike most Anglo-Catholics, who took the so-called eastward position (facing the altar, back to the congregation), which they held to be that of a sacrificing priest.[35] Still, Newman placed candles on the altar and mixed water and wine in the chalice at St. Mary's, both innovations that would later become the grounds for controversy elsewhere. And he did not object when his curate at Littlemore introduced a stone cross behind the altar, a crimson Bible and glided wooden candlesticks on it, a credence table, litany desk, and wooden alms dish—decorations that produced an "indescribable horror" in Peter Maurice, chaplain of New College and author of *Popery in Oxford.* When Newman heard rumors that candles burned night and day at Littlemore and that his surplice was adorned with "a rich illuminated cross," he seems to have been more amused than alarmed.

No, Newman was not hostile to ceremonial and decorative innovation; he seems simply not to have been very interested in the subject. As Thomas Mozley observed, "Newman never went into architecture," and he criticized those like the ecclesiologists of the Cambridge Camden Society, who, he feared, were "making a fair outside, while within are dead men's bones." He added that "we shall do nothing until we have a severer religion."[36] His real interests lay elsewhere: in the grand project of editing the *Lives of the Saints,* for instance.

But if Newman was not a major innovator in the ornamentation of churches and ministers, some of the early distinguishing marks of the Tractarians may owe themselves to his example. At St. Mary's in 1834 he began daily morning prayer (as directed by a widely ignored Prayer Book rubric), and he instituted an early communion service on Sundays four years later. Until churchmen of other persuasions followed suit in later decades, such "multiplication of services" was almost a party badge for Anglo-Catholics. Newman read the daily office kneeling on the altar step, facing east, a practice that tended to accompany the restoration of the daily services, according to S. L. Ollard. (In 1835, Hurrell Froude wrote that it "seems to be striking all apostolicals [his preferred name for the less conservative adherents of the movement] at once," but it does not seem to have persisted.) Newman also used a small hand-held prayer book rather than the volume on the reading desk, a custom taken up by his young admirers, although the only reason for Newman's practice was that he was nearsighted. When Newman retired to Littlemore, he and the young men who joined him there were not surrounded by material beauty, but they did keep a schedule of prayer (basically the monastic hours) that would have been called Ritualistic a few years later. By that time, however, Newman had joined a communion where Ritualism was not at all controversial.

Although some of the Oxford Movement firebrands grumbled about Newman's timidity, there is little in his behavior or his writings to suggest that he was afraid of controversy, and certainly he was less cautious than other leaders of the movement.[37] He felt that the controversy stirred up by the *Tracts* could only be a good thing, since it at least drew attention to them. He called them "a dose of volatile salts, pungent but restorative." Of one of his poems he said, "Moderate and well-judging men will be shocked by it." At the Oxford Movement's high point he must have shared the opinions of his friend Froude: "Church principles, forced on people's notice, must work for good."[38] The young Newman would not have abandoned the Ritualists in their troubles on grounds of prudence alone.

It is idle to speculate about the possible development of Newman's views had he remained an Anglican, but he would probably have been sympathetic to the Ritualist impulse. While still a Church of England clergyman he wrote to his friend Manning: "You must make the Church more suitable to the needs of the heart. . . . Give us more services, more vestments and decorations in worship; . . . give us the signs of an apostle, the pledges that the Spouse of Christ is among us."[39] And after his conversion he offered this description of his former Church before the Oxford Movement:

> a ritual dashed upon the ground, and broken piecemeal; . . . vestments chucked off, lights quenched, jewels stolen, the pomp and circumstances [*sic*] of worship annihilated; a dreariness which could be felt, and which seemed the token of an incipient Socinianism, forcing itself upon the eye, the ear, the nostrils of the worshipper; a smell of dust and damp, not of incense; a sound of ministers preaching Catholic prayers, and parish clerks droning out Catholic canticles; the royal arms for the crucifix; huge ugly boxes of wood, sacred to preachers, frowning on the congregation in the place of the mysterious altar; and long cathedral aisles unused, railed off, like the tombs (as they were) of what had been and was not.[40]

Many who stayed within the Anglican communion felt the same, and believed that there was only one course of action to be taken. Grant their premise, and no logician as astute as Newman could have quarreled with their conclusion.

Rather more to the point, however, are the views of Keble and Pusey, who stayed in the Church of England and witnessed the development of Ritualism from positions (undesired, to some extent) of leadership. Archbishop Davidson summarized Keble's position:

> He never himself adopted vestments or other ritual usages of the kind. He continued to deprecate the practice of non-communicating attendance [on the grounds of primitive practice], and he strongly disapproved of any insistence upon a rule of fasting reception [on the grounds that it made things difficult for the aged and infirm and those who could not come to early services]. On the other hand, he was, on large principles, in favor of all that gave increased dignity to, and implied a deeper reverence for, the Holy Communion. And in this way he was constantly quoted by the younger school, who thought that their ritual usages were implicitly sanctioned by his teaching, though not part of his own practice.[41]

This summary seems fair enough. Keble believed that the so-called Ornaments Rubric of the Prayer Book, which stipulated that "such Ornaments of the Church, and of the Ministers thereof at all times of their Ministration, shall be retained, and be in use, as . . . in the Second Year of the Reign of King Edward the Sixth," sanctioned most pre-Reformation ceremonial and usages. He believed that the neglect of that rubric was "a real blemish in our ecclesiastical practice [and] a contradiction to our theory." He thought that charity and pastoral considerations dictated a temporary inconsistency: "The time and manner of regaining the old paths must, under our circumstances, be a question of equity and charity, not of strict law alone." But, he added, "I, for one, rejoice whenever and wherever I see that kind of revival successfully and tranquilly accomplished."[42]

It would be wrong to say that Keble saw the usages for which the Ritualists were to fight as unimportant, but he did not see them as important enough to fight for, or about. It seems unlikely that he ever accepted the Ritualists' argument that their ceremonial served an evangelistic function, first to draw people to church, then to instruct them in doctrine. It may be that his position of vicar of a village church, with an established tradition of churchgoing, colored his views; if he had been serving an East End slum church with no established congregation to upset, his opinions and practice might have been different. As it was, Keble's role in the ritual disputes that he lived to see was that of the pastor, urging charity, compromise, moderation, seeing the other side's point of view. He apparently did not always accept the Ritualists' claim that attacks on ritual were simply disguised attacks on doctrine—and, indeed, in a parish like his they almost certainly would not have been. But when he was convinced that doctrine was at stake, he was as forthright a partisan as anyone could ask.

The only Tractarian leader who stayed an Anglican and lived long enough to witness Ritualism full-blown was E. B. Pusey, and by the 1870s he was thoroughly put out with some of those who were seen as his successors, although he, too, stood by them loyally when persuaded that doctrinal questions were at issue.[43] "I have a thorough mistrust of the Ultra Ritualist body," he wrote in 1873. "[I] fear that the Ritualists and the old Tractarians differ both in principle and in object." The next year, he and his friend Liddon wrote the Ritualistic vicar of St. Alban's, Holborn, to ask whether some of "the exaggerated ceremonial and ill-considered language, which are sometimes to be found among (so-called) 'Ritualists'" could not be tempered, for political purposes. And in 1875 Pusey wrote: "There has been, and is, a good deal of infallibilism outside the Vatican decree. The whole extreme Ritualist party is practically infallibilist. 'We will not retreat because we are certainly right.' And so they must lay the whole blame on their opponents' hostility, as they think, to truth. Yet very much of their practice has no relation to the truth, or only so far as it makes the Eucharistic Service gorgeous."

These and many other quotations reveal that Pusey was out of sympathy with those who claimed to be his followers in the 1870s. And this was not a new development. In 1860, when rioters at St. George's-in-the-East were protesting the vicar's introduction of "Puseyite" practices, Pusey wrote Bishop Tait of London: "In regard to my 'friends,' perhaps I regret the acts to which your Lordship alludes, as deeply as you do. I am in this strange position, that my name is made a by-word for that with which I never had any sympathy, that which the writers of the tracts, with whom in early days I was associated, always deprecated; any innovations in the way of conducting the service, anything of ritualism, or especially any revival of disused vestments." If Pusey's report of what he and the writers of the *Tracts* "always deprecated" is correct, that would seem to settle the matter.

But was that his earlier view? Archbishop Davidson argued that it was and based his argument primarily on an exchange of correspondence between Pusey and the Reverend J. F. Russell in 1839, a correspondence that requires closer examination, particularly in the light of Pusey's own experience a short time after with the church he endowed in Leeds, St. Saviour's.

In his letters to Russell, Pusey certainly did attempt to discourage Russell and his friends from some practices they had adopted and were contemplating: "You will not mind my freely saying to you that I cannot hear without much anxiety of some practices of some friends of yours, e.g., the hanging a room with black velvet during Lent." Pusey gave several reasons for restraint, including prudence. Concerning a proposal that, on a given day, all Tractarian clergymen should reassume the eucharistic vestments, he wrote: "At present we have the surplice for a token of purity, and the scarf as an emblem of Christ's yoke. But beyond this I should deprecate anything which could serve as the badge of a party; at present, much as the opposed party speaks of it, they can find nothing; but the agreement to adopt a dress which would be peculiar would furnish them with what they want." Moreover, he argued, the change would be undesirable in itself: "Hardly anything, perhaps, has given so much handle as this subject of dresses; it has deterred many, made many think the questions at hand to be about outward things only, given occasion to scoffing, and disquieted many sober people."

A case could be made that Pusey simply did not regard such matters as important; certainly time and again he displayed an ignorance that, in anyone else, would have produced the suspicion that he was joking. "Please do tell me what a cope is," he is reported to have said one day to J. R. Bloxam.[44] In 1851 he wrote to a clergyman who was having trouble for (among other things) taking the eastward position for the Prayer of Consecration, "I was not ritualist enough to know till the other day that the act of turning had any special meaning in the consecration" and almost twenty-five years later he wrote of Charles Lowder's insistence on censing persons and things that "to the mass of the English people (and among them to me) it is an un-understood rite. Three different explanations of it have been given me by ritualists. As it does not concern me, I have not looked into books."

But in his letters, and especially in his practice, Pusey made a distinction among the disputed ornaments and usages that suggests that his attitude was more complicated than simple disapproval of disturbing innovations. He was especially opposed to those, like vestments, that had any tendency to exalt the person of the minister. He suspected the Ritualists of self-will, a characteristic that he greatly distrusted in others as in himself. This man who was later to set himself a course of penitential discipline harrowing even to contemplate, who wore a hair shirt until his death, vowed never to smile except at children, regarded himself as "scarred all over and seamed with sin, so that I am a monster to myself," and longed for "the discipline" (flagellation) that his poor health forbade—this man had little patience with those who, he thought, sought "occasion for distinction by the very means of Church practices" or made "an idol of self, while seeming to honour God and the Church."[45] To Russell he wrote that he had heard men aruge that others should take up new practices at once, "for a few years hence they would be so common that there would be no distinction in them, or something to this effect." Such seeking after glory was wrong: "It is tricking up an idol, and that idol, self: not serving God. I must pain you by so writing, and I am sorry to do so; but I really feel I cannot write strongly enough, if by any means that veil could be torn off your friends' eyes and they taught to act . . . reverently and soberly, not amuse themselves (for it is nothing better) with holy things."

That Pusey's letters to Russell were written shortly after the death of his beloved wife lends a poignant ambiguity to his words, "the garment of mourning was fitter for us than one of gladness." One might speculate that his wife's death affected Pusey's opinions on this subject. Certainly he had been a good deal more tolerant the year before. When Pusey's assistant lecturer in Hebrew began to wear an embroidered stole in his duties at St. Thomas's, Oxford, and the bishop wrote Pusey for an explanation, he replied that the stole was "very narrow" and the embroidered crosses "very unpretending," and that he had warned the young man "not to let his attention be distracted by these things from others of more moment," but "it seemed a very safe way for the exuberance of youth to vent itself in."[46]

Pusey apparently viewed his wife's death as punishment for his sins and was afterwards less willing to make allowances for youthful exuberance. "It seems beginning at the wrong end for the ministers to deck their own persons," he wrote Russell. "Our own plain dresses are more in keeping with the state of the Church, which is one of humiliation. It does not seem in character to revive gorgeous or even in any degree handsome dresses in a day of reproach and rebuke and blasphemy; these are not holiday times." Pusey wore eucharistic vestments himself only much later, and then rarely, in churches where their use was customary.[47]

But when a decoration was clearly for God's glory and not the minister's, Pusey could be as enthusiastic and (surely unintentionally) as provocative as any Ritualist. His advice to Russell was to do without vestments for the time. "As far as externals will contribute to greater reverence, it were far better and far more influential to begin with that which is furthest removed from self. . . . It were better far to begin with painted windows, rich altar cloths or Communion plate."

St. Saviour's, Leeds

Six years later, however, Pusey's attempt to follow his own advice led to the tragicomic events surrounding the consecration of St. Saviour's, Leeds.[48] The story is worth retelling, since it illustrates that Pusey was far from indifferent to the "externals" of worship. It also shows that beginning with painted windows, altar cloths, and communion plate—although it might avoid the spiritual dangers Pusey saw—did nothing to forestall the movement's enemies. And since Pusey's concern for externals led him in this case into painful conflict with a bishop, perhaps we can understand why he did not encourage others, later.

After his wife's death, Pusey, who viewed himself as a penitent, resolved to devote his private means to the building of a church. He wrote his friend W. F. Hook, the High Church vicar of Leeds, "I know a person who wishes in such degree as he may, if he lives, to make up a broken vow." He wrote that this "friend" wished to build a church in Leeds, the only condition being that it should display the inscription, "YE WHO ENTER THIS HOLY PLACE, PRAY FOR THE SINNER WHO BUILT IT." Hook accepted the offer, and plans went forward to build the church in one of the squalid slums of Leeds, an area housing approximately eleven thousand souls, in the shadow of the Black Dog Mill. Pusey desired that the church should be beautiful and edifying, and also that it should be served by a "college" of celibate clergymen living in community nearby. Both parts of his plan would involve him in difficulties.

Throughout the early 1840s Pusey, acting as "agent" of the donor, involved himself in planning the new church and recruiting its clergy. Apparently a plan to transport a building from Portugal (where the established church had just been dissolved and lovely old buildings could be picked up at bargain prices) was considered and rejected. Instead, Pusey chose a plan submitted by a student of the noted Gothic Revival architect (and convert to Roman Catholicism) A. W. N. Pugin, a plan true to Pugin's teachings about the importance of medieval principles in church architecture. Pusey's own wish, embodied in the design of the church and its furnishings, was that everywhere the worshipper looked, he should see the cross: the church itself was to be cruciform, and every window and fitting was to be embellished with the cross. It would be named Holy Cross Church.

For help with the windows and furnishings, Pusey turned to the Cambridge Camden Society, a newly formed group of Catholic-minded amateur church archaeologists and historians who were trying to rediscover and restore pre-Reformation patterns of church design and decoration. We shall return to this society in the next chapter, but because it is sometimes credited with independently raising the aesthetic issues that characterized Ritualism, it is important to note that Pusey turned to them voluntarily for advice and that the cooperation was, for the most part, an easy one. (The Camdenians were distressed that Pusey insisted on erecting the Ten Commandments at the front of the church, but he was determined to follow current practice in that respect.[49])

Meanwhile Pusey was interviewing candidates for the clergy of the church, making what use he could of the "old boy" network of Anglo-Catholic clergy, which was only beginning to be established. Among those considered were Keble's curate at his church in Hursley and the Reverend G. R. Prynne, later to become vicar of St. Peter's, Plymouth. Prynne was thought unsuitable because he would not promise that he would not marry.

Troubles began almost immediately, first with the bishop, then with Pusey's friend Hook, the vicar of Leeds. The bishop objected to the name Holy Cross Church. The Church of England, he said, did not accept the legend of the discovery of the Holy Cross, and it could not risk implying that it did. Reluctantly, Pusey changed the name to St. Saviour's. (In 1850, incidentally, Pusey laid the cornerstone for St. Saviour's Home, Osnaburgh Street, London, on Holy Cross Day, with the understanding that the words St. Saviour's were "code" for Holy Cross.[50]) The college arrangement of curates and vicar was too monastic, the bishop said (although, as Sabine Baring-Gould pointed out later, every college at Cambridge and Oxford was operated on similar lines); the plans for the vicarage made no provisions for housing a wife and children; Pusey's plan to allow the college to elect a successor on the death of the vicar was unacceptable; the institution must be called a community rather than a college (an obscure objection); the covered walk connecting the vicarage to the church was too much like a cloister and could not be permitted. Pusey yielded on all of these points. Anticipating trouble because of a recent dispute in Cambridge, Pusey took legal opinion on whether he could install a stone altar, or at any rate an altar with a stone slab set into it: he was told that the altar must be wooden and movable.

A west window had been designed for the church, incorporating an illustration of the Holy Face of Jesus, copied from the Cirencester parish church. The bishop rejected the plan as "Romish." A new plan was produced, approved, and executed, but shortly before the scheduled consecration of the church someone complained to the bishop that it showed a crowned Virgin and that angels were shown catching the blood of Christ in chalices. The bishop of Ripon was unimpressed by the argument that the seals of his brother bishops of Lincoln and Salisbury incorporated crowned Virgins, and the offending panels had to be replaced with plain glass for the consecration service. The altar linen also proved to be unacceptable, since it covered only the mensa rather than the entire table.

But the saddest conflict was over a set of communion plate. In 1844 Pusey's daughter Lucy, dying of tuberculosis at the age of fifteen, had expressed a wish that her jewelry and her inheritance should go to make up a set of plate, and the Camden Society's design for a chalice pleased her very much. After her death, her brother, sister, and friends saw to the completion of the service as a memorial. The six pieces incorporated over two hundred precious stones, including diamonds, rubies, pearls, and emeralds. Pusey himself had the plate inscribed, in Latin, "Have Mercy, Lord, on Lucy Maria." As the clergy were lining up for the procession into the church at its consecration service, Bishop Longley refused to go ahead if the plate were used: the inscription was a prayer for the dead (implying belief in Purgatory). One who was present when the gift was refused never forgot the sadness in Pusey's face.

But one more matter remained to be resolved. The bishop noticed the inscription over the west door, asking prayers for the donor of the building. He demanded that it come down, but relented when he was assured that the donor was still living and that he would be informed if the donor died while he was bishop. At last the troubled church, Pusey's self-denying and anonymous gift, was consecrated.

Its history, off to such a difficult start, was not to be easy. In keeping with Pusey's views, the ornaments of the clergy were relatively sedate; black scarves were replaced by white stoles at Christmas in 1849, but it was not until 1859 at the earliest that eucharistic vestments were introduced and the altar adorned with a cross and lighted candles. On the other hand, daily celebration of Holy Communion was begun during the 1849 cholera epidemic and continued more or less regularly after that. (At the same time, and apparently with the bishop's permission, the Catholic practice of reserving the Sacrament was introduced, ostensibly so it could be administered to the sick.) A community of laymen grew up around the clergy of St. Saviour's, and a new building was added to house the overflow from the clergy house. Although the clergy displayed sartorial restraint within the church, about 1850 they and these laymen began to wear cassocks and birettas as their ordinary dress—a development with which Pusey could hardly have been pleased.

These and other practices led the church's many critics to keep up a running chorus of complaints to the bishop. The atmosphere of distrust made any innovation suspect. Dr. Hook, for example, had no objection to splendid worship—he himself introduced choral services at the Leeds parish church. But he did take a less sanguine view than his friend Pusey of what he saw as "Romanism" at St. Saviour's, and he came to believe that the "hornet's nest" (as he called it) was more trouble than it was worth. In later years he joined those who complained to the bishop about the clergy's taking the eastward position, keeping the monastic schedule of prayer, carrying lighted candles in procession at baptism, and placing a cross over the chancel screen.

One practice was especially objectionable in itself, and it also somehow stood for all of the other objectionable developments. As Keble reported to Pusey, after an interview with Hook in 1848: "He did not specify any evil practice, so that, as far as it can be seen, his alarm resolves itself into an attack on the principle of private confession and absolution. I was, as you may suppose, delighted with St. Saviour's, and with the kind and earnest people there: surely they and their work will be blest." But Hook's suspicions were not entirely unfounded. Nine of the first fifteen clergymen associated with St. Saviour's became Roman Catholics, although it is impossible to say how much the attitude of the Diocese of Ripon had to do with this statistic.[51]

The point of all these details is simply that Pusey's distinction between ornaments of the minister and ornaments of the church, important to him though it may have been, was not one that the movement's opponents made. Those who were simply conservative and opposed to unsettling innovations opposed the two sorts indiscriminately. Those who disliked "Puseyism," for whatever reason, saw both sorts of change (rightly) as marks of that faction. And those whose real opposition was to the doctrines and the extra-liturgical practices of the clergy of St. Saviour's viewed any innovation of theirs with deep suspicion.

Moreover, the distinction did not convince many of the movement's adherents, especially those who did not share Pusey's deep conviction of personal unworthiness. "What sense is there—" John Mason Neale wrote a few years later, "what sense can there be—in rejoicing that His inanimate creature, the altar, should be vested in the richest apparel; if you would forbid His not only animate, but especially consecrated, creature, the Priest, to wear any but the simplest vestments?"[52] At the very least, the same ecclesiological considerations that made it appropriate or even mandatory to ornament churches in pre-Reformation splendor applied to the dress of ministers. Pusey had conceded the propriety of a jewelled chalice: why should the priest who elevated that chalice be restricted to the mundane black and white of surplice and scarf?

Of the three early leaders of the movement, then, none could be said to have been a proto-Ritualist. Newman, perhaps the likeliest candidate by temperament, was more concerned with other things, and in any case removed himself from the controversy in 1845. Keble sympathized with the Ritualists, but also with laymen who were bewildered or annoyed by changes in familiar and beloved patterns of worship: he lacked the Ritualists' burning conviction that their changes were important, although he welcomed them when they were brought about happily. Pusey, at least after the death of his wife, was suspicious of the Ritualists' motives, but he too welcomed the changes they introduced when convinced of the humility of the innovators. None of the three could have objected in principle to the Ritualists' arguments for their changes, although each might have argued countervailing considerations in any particular case. And certainly none could have objected to the doctrines that motivated the Ritualists—for where, after all, had those doctrines been learned?

The "Gilt-Gingerbread School"

When the Ritualists claimed, as they did, that their ceremonial and decorative practices were somehow the natural expression of Catholic doctrine, they could certainly have made at least an empirical case for that argument. From a very early stage of the Oxford Movement, Tractarian doctrine often did lead to the revival of pre-Reformation usages or the adoption of contemporary Roman Catholic practice. We saw that Pusey as early as the 1830s was warning his followers about their innovations, and old-fashioned High Churchmen who had originally supported the movement found a good deal to be alarmed about as it progressed. Much of what concerned them was more serious than ceremonial or decorative exuberance, but they did object from time to time to such things as a curate in "a short surplice edged with lace and a stole with crosses, looking as like a Roman priest as possible" (the words are Hook's, in a letter to Pusey).[53] When Pusey's assistant lecturer took to wearing a "very narrow" stole (and Pusey, as we saw, defended him to the bishop of Oxford), a canon of Durham warned the clergy under his supervision against such practices, and the bishop of Oxford ventured in his charge of 1838, "I do not think it likely we shall hear of a repetition of this or of similar indiscretions." But, as S. L. Ollard pointed out, there was already a shop in Leicester where stoles could be purchased.[54]

Oddly enough, the groundwork for these developments and for the later revival of eucharistic vestments had been laid by one of the most conservative adherents of the Oxford Movement. The year before Keble's Assize sermon, William Palmer of Worcester College (who was later to urge that the *Tracts* should be approved by a committee and who grew very uneasy about the Romanizing tendencies of the movement) published *Origines Liturgicae*. In that work he described and illustrated the alb, chasuble, and stole, and asserted that the Ornaments Rubric ordered their use.

Palmer seems to have intended his book to be a work of liturgical archaeology, certainly not a guide for immediate application, but the book was undoubtedly read and assimilated by J. R. Bloxam, Fellow of Magdalen and Newman's curate at Littlemore from 1837 to 1840.[55] Bloxam was responsible for the decorations at Littlemore that horrified the chaplain of New College, and he was described some years later as "the father or grandfather of all ritualistics." In the late 1830s he wore a black silk stole over his surplice at Littlemore and in chapel at Magdalen, and another Fellow of Magdalen also wore a stole, crossed over his shoulder because he was only a deacon. The *Quarterly Review* and the *British Magazine* saw fit to comment.

Magdalen became something of a center for these activities as other Fellows followed Bloxam's lead. One of them, who doubled as rector of a parish in Lincolnshire, had by 1842 converted a tomb to make a stone altar and placed a cross and candles upon it. He had also begun to wear a maniple when celebrating Holy Communion and had painted the ceiling of the sanctuary blue, with gold stars. In 1839 another Fellow, who served a proprietary chapel, vested his choir in cassocks and surplices.[56]

This last innovator, R. W. Sibthorpe, was the first notable Tractarian convert to Roman Catholicism, "poping" (as it was later to be called) in 1841. He seems to have been unusually susceptible to conversion: he soon returned to the Church of England, went back to Roman Catholicism some years later, and was buried as an Anglican in 1879.[57] (Sibthorpe once compared the Church of England to "a stiff, cross, unattractive old maid by the side of a most fascinating adulteress."[58])

The tendency to ceremonial extremism seems to have been most marked among those given to doctrinal extremism—that is, to Romanizers like Sibthorpe. For some of these men the appeal to contemporary Roman Catholic usage was explicit, and not because it was "Catholic" (that is, medieval) but because it was Roman. W. G. Ward (or "Ideal" Ward, as he was called after the controversy over his *Ideal of a Christian Church*) was another one of these; yet another was F. W. Faber.

Faber wrote the life of St. Wilfrid in Newman's series of *Lives of the English Saints,* and his account of the seventh-century bishop of York who brought the Celtic Church of England into conformity with Roman practice was filled with little lessons for those disposed to seek them.[59] In Lindisfarne, "in the very stronghold of Scottish usages," the young Wilfrid grew uneasy. "Whether he had fallen upon some old books, or from whatever cause, he began to suspect that there was a more perfect way of serving God; that there were ancient traditions of Catholic customs which it was most dangerous to slight, and yet which were utterly neglected." Eventually, Wilfrid understood that "the one thing to do was to go to Rome, and learn under the shadow of St. Peter's chair the more perfect way." Faber observed that "to look Romeward is a Catholic instinct, seemingly implanted in us for the safety of the faith." For any readers who missed the point, Faber added that Wilfrid went first to the archbishop of Canterbury, "St. Honorious, a man who is described as particularly skilled in ecclesiastical matters. . . . But it was short of Rome." After Wilfrid learned the more perfect way in Rome, he introduced it to the British Church.

Feber's book concluded, oddly enough, with some pages critical of the ceremonial revival then taking place—a revival that had the effect, after all, of approximating Church of England practice to that of Rome—and an appeal to the young "who require some field for their zeal" to consider "the pursuit of Holy Virginity." These passages, so foreign to the burden of the preceding two hundred pages, were quoted against the Ritualists in a pamphlet of 1882 and attributed to Newman himself, and they may well have been added by him, as editor of the *Lives,* or at his suggestion.[60]

In any case, Faber did not himself stop at Canterbury, but not surprisingly went with Wilfrid, and Newman, to Rome. So did most of the other early Romanizers, and in fact there was a more or less constant trickle of converts from that wing of the Anglo-Catholic movement where "Roman fever" was endemic. From time to time, whenever the Church of England committed itself to what Anglo-Catholics regarded as some new and egregiously "Protestant" error, the trickle became a torrent, but a steadily increasing number of Anglicans were directed by their Catholic instincts to look Romeward for their liturgical models. And the more of them who did so, the less necessary it was for anyone actually to become Roman Catholic in order to find "the more perfect way."

True, there were other, less theological tributaries to the current of the ceremonial revival. Even without the Oxford Movement and the *Tracts* there would have been elaboration of the interiors of churches and of the services conducted in them. It could not have been otherwise, given Victorian taste, which would also have guaranteed a backward look to "antique" models. As early as 1823, well before Newman came to understand Keble, A. P. De Lisle, later a great friend of Bloxam's but then a dreamy fourteen-year-old, persuaded the vicar of his Leicestershire parish church to wear a cope and donated a French-style altar to the church, with a black wooden altar cross (the bishop of Peterborough ordered that it be removed).[61] Pugin, although he had become a Roman Catholic in 1834, was explicating his Gothic Revival architectural principles to an audience that included some grudgingly admiring Anglicans as early as 1836, and there were many other, lesser-known enthusiasts for reviving Gothic architecture, if not Gothic religion. The Cambridge Camden Society's more than seven hundred members included two archbishops, sixteen bishops, thirty-one peers and M.P.s, and sixteen architects. As Owen Chadwick has observed, a society with that membership was not Tractarian, and it consulted happily with both High and Low Church builders and restorers until its leaders' identification with Anglo-Catholicism led to its breaking up and re-formation as the Ecclesiological Society.[62]

But from early in the course of the Oxford Movement, the impulse to restore old churches and to build new ones on old models became identified in the public mind and in fact with Tractarianism. So did the impulse to ornament the ministers of those churches in pre-Reformation style, to restore the worship of the Church to old patterns, to reintroduce old practices like sacramental confession and old institutions like religious orders, to revitalize or (in some cases) to reintroduce old beliefs and doctrines—apostolic succession of bishops, the real presence of Christ in the Eucharist, the invocation of saints, Purgatory. All of this, as both the movement's opponents and its uneasy allies feared, was latent in the movement in its earliest years.

Only a few of the movement's adherents embraced full-blown "Anglo-Romanism," but those who did not found it extraordinarily difficult to criticize those who did, on any grounds other than those of prudence. When, years later, Pusey criticized some of the Ritualists for going too far down this path, Archdeacon Denison (no Ritualist himself, but a sympathizer) is said to have remarked: "If Pusey did not foresee how the fire would burn, he should not have lighted it."[63] Certainly the evidence was all around him from the first days of the movement.

Notes

[1] Owen Chadwick's masterful two-volume *The Victorian Church.* (London: Adam & Charles Black: 1971, Part I, 3d ed.; and 1972, Part II, 2d ed.) examines the changes. Also valuable is Desmond Bowen, *The Idea of the Victorian Church: A Study of the Church of England, 1833-1889* (Montreal: McGill University Press, 1968); S. C. Carpenter's earlier treatment, *Church and People, 1789-1889: A History of the Church of England from William Wilberforce to "Lux Mundi"* (London: SPCK, 1933); and M. A. Crowther, *Church Embattled: Religious Controversy in Mid-Victorian England* (Newton Abbot, Devon: David & Charles, 1970). Roger Lloyd provides useful material on the Victorian Church as background in *The Church of England, 1900-1965* (London: SCM Press, 1966).

[2] The information in the following paragraphs is from *Mackeson's Guide to the Churches of London and its Suburbs for 1894-5* (London: Metzler, 1866 *et seq.*). This annual publication by Charles Mackeson will be cited hereafter as *Mackeson's,* with the date.

[3] Nigel Yates, *The Oxford Movement and Anglican Ritualism,* General Series 105 (London: Historical Association, 1983), offers a short, recent survey. Geoffrey Rowell, *The Vision Glorious: Themes and Personalities of the Catholic Revival in Anglicanism* (Oxford: Oxford University Press, 1983), is also useful. Other recent works have treated specific aspects of the movement, conflicts in particular locales, or the life and work of individual figures. See especially the Oxford Prophets series, which includes, for instance, Peter Cobb, *Doctor Pusey* (London: Church Literature Association, 1983); Roger Greenacre, *Lord Halifax* (London: Church Literature Association, 1983); and John Newton, *Edward King* (London: Church Literature Association, 1983). There has, however, been no recent general history like those published to mark the Oxford Movement centenary (e.g., W. J. Sparrow Simpson, *The History of the Anglo-Catholic Revival from 1845* [London: George Allen & Unwin, 1932]; Herbert Leslie Stewart, *A Century of Anglo-Catholicism* [London: J. M. Dent & Sons, 1929]; T. Dilworth-Harrison, *Every Man's Story of the Oxford Movement* [London: Mowbray, 1932]). W. S. F. Pickering's recent *Anglo-Catholicism: A Study in Religious Ambiguity* (London: Routledge, 1989) is a valuable treatment of the movement in the twentieth century.

[4] Histories of the Oxford Movement that treat it as finished after Newman's secession begin with his own *Apologia pro Vita Sua,* first published serially in 1864. Any listing would also have to include R. W. Church's influential *The Oxford Movement: Twelve Years, 1833-1845,* 3d ed. (London: Macmillan, 1892). E. A. Knox, *The Tractarian Movement, 1833-1845,* 2d ed. (London: Putnam, 1934), and Geoffrey Faber, *Oxford Apostles: A Character Study of the Oxford Movement* (New York: Charles Scribner's Sons, 1934), give us inter-war Evangelical and modernist views, respectively, and a good recent history is Marvin R. O'Connell, *The Oxford Conspirators: A History of the Oxford Movement, 1833-45* (London: Macmillan, 1969), but all three follow the dramaturgical conventions laid down by Newman and Church. One "standard" history that violates this convention is S. L. Ollard's charming *Short History of the Oxford Movement,* 2d ed., ed. A. M. Allchin (1932; reprint, London: Faith Press, 1963), which does devote 98 of its 188 pages to the post-Newman movement. My brief account here borrows heavily from Ollard and from Chadwick, *Victorian Church,* 1:64-211. A recent study critical of the Newman-centered account is George William Herring, "Tractarianism to Ritualism: A Study of Some Aspects of Tractarianism Outside Oxford, From the Time of Newman's Conversion in 1845, Until the First Ritual Commission in 1867" (D. Phil. thesis, Oxford University, 1984), which shows

that many Tractarians outside Newman's circle greeted his secession with relief (24-35).

[5] On this tradition in Anglicanism, see George H. Tavard, *The Quest for Catholicity: A Study in Anglicanism* (New York: Herder & Herder, 1964), and Richard Sharp, "New Perspectives on the High Church Tradition: Historical Background, 1730-1780," in *Tradition Renewed: The Oxford Movement Conference Papers,* ed. Geoffrey Rowell (London: Darton, Longman & Todd, 1986). On its particular relation to the Oxford Movement, see Peter Nockles, "The Oxford Movement: Historical Background, 1730-1780," in *Tradition Renewed: The Oxford Movement Conference Papers,* ed. Geoffrey Rowell (London: Darton, Longman & Todd, 1986).

[6] Selections, with a useful introduction, can be found in Owen Chadwick, ed., *The Mind of the Oxford Movement* (Stanford, Calif.: Stanford University Press, 1961). Representative documents with helpful commentary can also be found in Elizabeth Jay, ed., *The Evangelical and Oxford Movements* (Cambridge: Cambridge University Press, 1983), and in Eugene R. Fairweather, ed., *The Oxford Movement* (New York: Oxford University Press, 1964).

[7] Chadwick, *Victorian Church,* 1:75-77. His characterization of the address is quoted from p. 76.

[8] On the difficult relationship of these men to Tractarianism, see Peter Nockles, "Continuity and Change in Anglican High Churchmanship in Britain, 1792-1850" (D. Phil. thesis, Oxford University, 1982), 429-528, 602-35 (recently published, much revised, as *The Oxford Movement in Context: Anglican High Churchmanship, 1760-1857* [Cambridge: Cambridge University Press, 1994]); and Reginald H. Fuller, "The Classical High Church Reaction to the Tractarians," in *Tradition Renewed: The Oxford Movement Conference Papers,* ed. Geoffrey Rowell (London: Darton, Longman & Todd, 1986). On their particular uneasiness with the movement's sympathy for Rome, see Robert H. Greenfield, "Attitude of the Tractarians to the Roman Catholic Church, 1833-1850" (D. Phil. thesis, Oxford University, 1956).

[9] Ollard, *Short History,* 53. Piers Brendon, "Newman, Keble and Froude's *Remains,*" *English Historical Review* 87 (October 1972): 697-716, makes a strong case that the editors expected a hostile response and may even have intended to alienate the movement's merely lukewarm supporters. Certainly neither ever conceded that the publication was a mistake.

[10] Quoted in Ollard, *Short History,* 54.

[11] Quoted in Raymond Chapman, *Faith and Revolt: Studies in the Literary Influence of the Oxford Movement* (London: Weidenfeld & Nicolson, 1970), 47.

[12] Quoted in Church, *Oxford Movement,* 374.

[13] J. B. Mozley, quoted in Ollard, *Short History,* 79.

[14] J. Lewis May, *The Oxford Movement: Its History and its Future, A Layman's Estimate* (New York: Dial, 1933), vii.

[15] "Subtractarians" is Athelstan Riley's coinage, according to J. G. Lockhart, *Charles Lindley, Viscount Halifax* (London: Centenary, 1935), 1:92.

[16] Many have made this point. See, for instance, Yates, *Oxford Movement and Anglican Ritualism,* 21; May, *Oxford Movement,* vii. Marcus Donovan, *After the Tractarians,* (London: Philip Allan, 1933), 29, also notes the accusation but is less ready to admit its truth.

[17] John B. Dykes, *Eucharistic Truth and Ritual: A Letter to the Right Reverend the Lord Bishop of Durham* [etc.], 2d ed. (1874; PH 1631).

[18] This faction (which included W. G. Ward) is described in C. P. S. Clarke, "The Genesis of the Movement" in *Northern Catholicism: Centenary Studies in the Oxford and Parallel Movements,* ed. N. P. Williams and Charles Harris (New York: Macmillan, 1933), 23-26 (quotation from 25). See also C. P. S. Clarke, *The Oxford Movement and After* (London: Mowbray, 1932), 88-97.

[19] For sketches of a number of these figures see, for example, B. C. Boulter, *The Anglican Reformers* (London: Philip Allan, 1933), or Desmond Morse-Boycott, *Lead, Kindly Light: Studies of the Saints and Heroes of the Oxford Movement* (London: Centenary, 1932).

[20] See below, chapter 8.

[21] Henry R. T. Brandreth, *Dr. Lee of Lambeth: A Chapter in Parenthesis in the History of the Oxford Movement* (London: SPCK, 1951).

[22] Thomas Jay Williams, *Priscilla Lydia Sellon: The Restorer after Three Centuries of the Religious Life in the English Church* (London: SPCK, 1950); Peter F. Anson, *The Call of the Cloister: Religious Communities and Kindred Bodies in the Anglican Communion* (London: SPCK, 1955), 259-79.

[23] Anson, *Call of the Cloister,* 244-51.

[24] A. G. Lough, *The Influence of John Mason Neale* (London: SPCK, 1962); Anson, *Call of the Cloister,* 337-47.

[25] M. V. Woodgate, *Father Benson, Founder of the Cowley Fathers* (London: Geoffrey Bles, 1953); Anson, *Call of the Cloister,* 75-83.

[26] The comment is from Shane Leslie's *The Oxford Movement, 1833 to 1933* (London: Burns Oates &

Washbourne, 1933), 126. This account, by an Anglo-Irish novelist and convert to Roman Catholicism, is not the most reliable history of the movement, but it is certainly the most amusing. On Father Ignatius, see Peter Anson, *Building Up the Waste Places: The Revival of Monastic Life on Medieval Lines in the Post-Reformation Church of England* (Leighton Buzzard: Faith Press, 1973), and *Call of the Cloister,* 419-24. Beatrice de Bertouch, *The Life of Father Ignatius, O.S.B., The Monk of Llanthony* (London: Methuen, 1904), is a remarkable work by a charmingly uncritical admirer, but Donald Attwater, *Father Ignatius of Llanthony: A Victorian* (London: Cassell, 1931), is more reliable, and Arthur Calder-Marshall, *The Enthusiast: An Enquiry into the Life, Beliefs and Character of The Rev. Joseph Leycester Lyne alias Fr. Ignatius, O.S.B., Abbot of Elm Hill, Norwich, and Llanthony, Wales* (London: Faber & Faber, 1962), is probably the last word on the subject.

[27] Wilberforce's correspondence with Nugee has only recently come to light, and the charge should probably be regarded as not proven. See Nigel Yates, *Ritual Conflict at Farlington and Wymering,* Portsmouth Papers no. 28 (Portsmouth: Portsmouth City Council, 1978), 11-21 (correspondence discussed, 15; Peter Anson quoted, 17). See also Anson, *Call of the Cloister,* 90-103.

[28] Thomas Wright, *The Life of Walter Pater,* 2 vols. (London: Everett, 1907), 2:31-48 (photograph of Jackson as Brother à Becket opposite 52).

[29] On the dean of St. Paul's, see B. A. Smith, *Dean Church: The Anglican Response to Newman* (London: Oxford University Press, 1958).

[30] So far as I can determine, Purchas has not been the subject of a biography. Omitted even from compilations of short, admiring biographical sketches, he is a rare bird indeed among Victorian ecclesiastical celebrities.

[31] Chapman, *Faith and Revolt,* examines the literary impact of Anglo-Catholicism; Rossetti is treated, 170-97. William Purcell, *Onward Christian Soldier* (London: Longmans, Green, 1957) and Bickford H. C. Dickinson, *Sabine Baring-Gould: Squarson, Writer and Folklorist, 1834-1924* (Newton Abbot, Devon: David & Charles, 1970), are recent biographies of the squire and parson ("squarson") of Lew Trenchard.

[32] Piers Brendon, *Hawker of Morwenstow: Portrait of a Victorian Eccentric* (London: Jonathan Cape, 1975).

[33] Royal Commission on Ecclesiastical Discipline, *Report of the Royal Commission on Ecclesiastical Discipline* and *Minutes of Evidence Taken before the Royal Commission on Ecclesiastical Discipline,* 3 vols. (London: H.M.S.O., 1906), 2:340-74. (Hereafter, this source will be cited as *Minutes of Evidence.*) A recent argument for discontinuity is Herring, "Tractarianism to Ritualism."

[34] See, for example, Yates, *Oxford Movement,* especially 21-23.

[35] Information on Newman's practice from Ollard, *Short History,* 116-18.

[36] Mozley and Newman quoted in James F. White, *The Cambridge Movement: The Ecclesiologists and the Gothic Revival* (Cambridge: Cambridge University Press, 1962), 21-24. White says that Newman's decision to build the chapel at Littlemore in Gothic style seems to have been "almost accidental."

[37] On criticism of Newman's "timidity," see Clarke, *Oxford Movement and After,* 94.

[38] Newman and Froude quoted in Clarke, "Genesis of the Movement," 15-16.

[39] Quoted in P. T. Marsh, *The Victorian Church in Decline: Archbishop Tait and the Church of England, 1868-1882* (London: Routledge & Kegan Paul, 1969), 112-13.

[40] Quoted in E. A. Down, "Pastoral Ideals and Methods of the Movement: The Tractarian Tradition," in *Northern Catholicism: Centenary Studies in the Oxford and Parallel Movements* ed. N. P. Williams and Charles Harris (New York: Macmillan, 1933), 265.

[41] *Minutes of Evidence,* 2:343.

[42] Quoted in *Minutes of Evidence,* 2:343.

[43] The following quotations from Pusey and this summary of his views are from *Minutes of Evidence,* 2:343-46, unless otherwise indicated. See also Leonard Prestige, *Pusey,* new ed. (1933; reprint, London: Mowbray, 1982), especially 142-59.

[44] This story sounds unlikely on its face, but it is given in Clarke, "Genesis of the Movement," 26.

[45] On Pusey's self-mortification, see Faber, *Oxford Apostles,* 399-400.

[46] Quoted in Ollard, *Short History,* 120. Chadwick suggests that Maria Pusey's death left her husband a changed man (*Victorian Church,* 1:198), but David Forrester argues, in "Dr. Pusey's Marriage," *Ampleforth Journal* 77 (1973): 33-47, that Pusey's conviction of his own depravity dates from as early as 1835—that is, practically from the beginning of his association with the movement.

[47] Carpenter, *Church and People,* 213.

[48] The following account of the early history of St. Saviour's is adapted from Stephen Savage and Christopher Tyne, *The Labours of Years: The Story of St. Saviour's and St. Hilda's, Leeds* (Cowley: Bocardo & Church Army. Press, n.d.), 266-89; and Nigel Yates, *The Oxford Movement and Parish Life: St Saviour's, Leeds, 1839-1929,* Borthwick Papers no. 48 (York: University of York, Borthwick Institute of Historical Research, 1975), and *Leeds and the Oxford Movement: A Study of "High Church" Activity in the Rural Deaneries of Allerton, Armley, Headingley and Whitkirk in the Diocese of Ripon, 1836-1934,* Publications of the Thoresby Society, vol. 55, no. 121 (Leeds: Thoresby Society, 1975). For an early account by the church's senior curate, see George Peirce Grantham, *A History of Saint Saviour's, Leeds* (1872; PH 13499).

[49] White, *Cambridge Movement,* 22.

[50] Thomas Jay Williams and Allan Walter Campbell, *The Park Village Sisterhood* (London: SPCK, 1965), 73-74.

[51] Carpenter, *Church and People,* 178.

[52] J. M. Neale, *Extreme Men. A Letter to A. J. B. Beresford Hope* (1865; PH 6002).

[53] Quoted in Clarke, "Genesis of the Movement," 27.

[54] Ollard, *Short History,* 121.

[55] Ibid., 117-19.

[56] Ibid., 123.

[57] Ibid., 77n. Pauline A. Adams, "Converts to the Roman Catholic Church in England, *circa* 1830-1870" (B.Litt. thesis, Oxford University, 1977), 178-80, offers several other examples of back and forth conversion. She concludes that Tractarian converts were of greater symbolic than numerical importance; see especially 9-29.

[58] Quoted in Clarke, *Oxford Movement and After,* 84-85.

[59] [F. W. Faber], *St. Wilfrid, Bishop of York* (James Toovey, 1844), 3-5, 204-8.

[60] The attribution to Newman is in *Animadversions by Distinguished Divines and Others, on the False Position of the Ritualistic Clergy in the Church of England* (London: Hamilton, Adams, 1882).

[61] Ollard, *Short History,* 115-16.

[62] Chadwick, *Victorian Church,* 1:213.

[63] Quoted in Boulter, *Anglican Reformers,* 60.

LITERARY ASPECTS

Joseph Ellis Baker (essay date 1932)

SOURCE: "Newman as Novelist," in *The Novel and The Oxford Movement*, Princeton University Press, 1932, pp. 54-68.

[*In the following essay, Baker discusses Newman's novels,* Loss and Gain *and* Callista *as partly autobiographical reflections on spiritual faith as an "inner drama."*]

John Henry Newman wrote two novels, both portraying a development of mind somewhat similar to his own,—a development which, for him, culminated in one of the most important events in the history of the Church since the Reformation, his conversion to Rome. Since fiction is freer than history, some of Newman's spiritual experiences are suggested here that are not set forth in the *Apologia. Loss and Gain* appeared in 1848, only three years after his conversion, and it reflects immediately the Oxford phase of the Movement. In the summer of 1847, some tale directed against the converts to the Catholic faith had been sent to Newman. "Its contents were as wantonly and preposterously fanciful, as they were injurious to those whose motives and actions it professed to represent; but a formal criticism . . . seemed . . . out of place. The suitable answer lay rather in the publication of a second tale; drawn up with a stricter regard to truth and probability, and with at least some personal knowledge of Oxford, and some perception of the various aspects of the religious phenomenon, which the work in question handled so rudely and unskilfully."[1] The result was *Loss and Gain: The Story of a Convert,* a realistic novel of contemporary life in form largely argumentative dialogue. It is austerely barren of the pleasures of plot. Charles Reding, son of an old-fashioned clergyman of the Church of England, goes to Oxford and becomes interested in Catholicism. Suspected of being more Roman than is strictly true at the time, he is sent home from college. Because of the distractions of religious uncertainity, he fails in the examination for honours. He even postpones taking his B.A. because of conscientious difficulties in subscribing to the Articles. The conviction that Rome is the only true Church grows on him. At last, after various sects try to win him, he joins the Church of Rome.

In the early spring of the same year that *Loss and Gain* was published, Newman also began what was to be-

come the sub-plot of *Callista: A Sketch of the Third Century,* writing then parts of chapters I, IV, and V, and sketching the character and fortunes of Juba.[2] A year later, in a letter of February 28, 1849, he says, speaking of historical work:

> What I should like would be to bring out the [*ēthos*] of the Heathen from St. Paul's day down to St. Gregory, when under the process, or in the sight of the phenomenon, of conversion; what conversion *was* in those times, and what the position of a Christian in that world of sin, what the sophistries of philosophy viewed as realities influencing men. But besides the great difficulty of finding time, I don't think I could do it from History. I despair of finding facts enough—as if an imaginary tale could alone embody the conclusions to which existing facts *lead.*[3]

Evidently the general idea of what became the main plot of *Callista* was beginning to take shape in his mind. He did nothing more with this story for six years. In July, 1855, he suddenly resumed it and completed it in a few months.[4] It appeared in 1856. Kingsley's *Hypatia,* published three years before, had offended the more Catholic party in the Church of England with its tolerance of pagan thought and its attack on monasticism among the early Christians.[5] The purpose of Newman's novel is the opposite, that is, "to imagine and express, from a Catholic point of view, the feelings and mutual relations of Christians and heathens at the period to which it belongs."[6] This, too, is a story of conversion, and hence its basis in the author's own experience lay in the period when he was yet an Anglican. It is something of a historical romance, something of a saint's life, something of a psychological study, and, though less so than *Loss and Gain,* something of a series of arguments. Agellius, a Christian, loves Callista, a Greek girl who works for his uncle. Though a pagan, she is interested in hearing about Christianity. Since a plague of locusts is ascribed to the presence of the Christians, a mob rises against them. In its wild fury it captures Callista at the hut of Agellius. In prison, she finally joins the Church, and becomes a martyr and saint. Her body works miracles, for instance curing of his madness Juba, brother of Agellius, who had been under the evil influence of their mother, the witch Gurta.

Although the advertisement of 1848 states specifically that *Loss and Gain* is not the history of any individual mind among the recent converts,[7] we now know enough of Newman's life to show that he has drawn largely upon his own experience, even to many details. The hero, like the author, was retiring and over-sensitive, and in his first years at college he was much alone.[8] Like Newman, he stood for honours and failed.[9] Mr. Reilley points out that both were impatient of party men and "mere talkers," expressed a love of Gregorian music, and that "the 'Father Dominic', a Passionist born in Italy, who received Reding into the Church, was the same" in name and antecedents as he who received Newman himself.[10] We may add that both felt from boyhood that they should remain celibate.[11] Both delayed their entrance into the Catholic Church for a long time to be sure that they were not deluded. And Reding's estrangement from Sheffield is paralleled by Newman's from Frederic Rogers, long his most intimate friend. Like Reding and Sheffield, they had roomed on the same staircase at Oxford.[12] On the other hand, it seems to have been an event in the life of another, a Mr. Morris, that suggested the incident in which Charles is sent home from college because of coming into conflict with his college authority over his belief in the Intercession of the Saints. Like Mr. Morris, Reding in the novel draws a distinction between Intercession and Invocation.[13] But Reding is not Newman, and the Oxford Movement in which he is taking part has been sketched with the central figure omitted. There is a passing reference to the preaching at St. Mary's,[14] but we miss entirely the politics, parties, combat, leadership, action of corporate bodies, and attempts to influence public opinion, which are part of the Movement. The author's gaze is turned inward upon the development of an individual soul.

As we might expect from so skillful a controversialist as Newman, his novels are largely devoted to presenting Catholic doctrines and portraying Catholic practices. That he wished some of the discussions in *Loss and Gain* to be received as serious explanations of his views is indicated by a passage in a letter written thirty-one years later: "And now I go on to the relation of the will to assent . . . as to which . . . I have not made my doctrine quite clear to you in the passage in Loss and Gain."[15] He then analyzes in detail the passage in question. Sometimes Newman embodies his ideas in concrete events. Baptism suddenly produced in Callista a serenity different from anything she had ever before the power of conceiving.[16] But more often he pushes the story aside and presents his arguments directly, putting them into the mouth of a figure who seldom exists as anything more than a mouth from which comes forth theory. Occasionally he rejects even this ghost of narrative and speaks out from the page *in propria persona,*—as when he opens a chapter by arguing that, "There is no . . . inconsistency in a person first using his private judgment [to reach Catholicism] and then denouncing its use,"[17] or when he defends dogma by saying that unless there is one center on which the mind sits men will be inconsistent, but real liberty consists in being subject to truth.[18] Now that Newman has left the Anglican Church, it is interesting to see how he answers the thesis of his own Tract 90, which caused the series to be stopped: The argument is that the Articles may be given a Catholic interpretation. Charles' reply is that the English Church *might* have adopted this interpretation, but did not.[19] Among the other subjects dealt with in the novels are the Apostolic Succession, Mass, Vestments, Confession, the Supremacy of Rome, Devotion to the Blessed Virgin.

Newman's chief opponent, Kingsley, preaching a Christianity that considered physical well-being a valuable aid to a Christian life, had prefaced *Hypatia* with an attack on asceticism. Newman takes the other side. When Callista's health is injured by the heat of the prison and she loses her former beauty, he tells us that rudiments of a diviner loveliness were taking its place.[20] And Charles Reding says, "the idea of an apostle, unmarried, pure, in fast and nakedness, at length a martyr, is a higher idea than that of one of the old Israelites sitting under his vine and fig-tree, full of temporal goods, and surrounded by sons and grandsons."[21] Charles says he fancied that fasting, abstinence, and celibacy might be taken as a make-up for sin.[22] When Callista asked to be made a Christian, there was an "utter disappearance of that majesty of mien . . . a gift, so beautiful, so unsuitable to fallen man. . . . She had lost every vestige of what the world worships under the titles of proper pride and self-respect."[23] Proud liberty of intellect is denounced. We are shown the fate of Juba, brother of the hero, who, for his free-thinking, is punished with madness, being possessed with an evil spirit. Against his will, Juba falls on his knees before an idol of Pan, laps up the blood of sacrifice, and among other horrible things spouts a chorus of Greek, a language he had never heard before.[24] But even while yet a maniac, he has changed for the better, we are told, for his expression of pride is gone.[25] The sign of the cross he cannot resist in spite of manifest antagonism. At last, after Callista's death, he is forced to touch the feet of her corpse. The evil spirit goes out, leaving him an idiot.[26] Newman's direct argument for belief in miracles is much more plausible than this concrete illustration.[27] But this part of the tale is one of the most interesting of the Catholic attacks upon the scepticism of Victorian science, and one of the strangest fruits of a strange imagination. The nineteenth century, for all its Medievalizing, seldom came nearer to producing something that might really have been written during the Middle Ages, for this incident is surrounded with no atmosphere of romantic distance. And whatever the faults of Newman as an historical novelist, we cannot accuse him of being out of sympathy with his subject. Indeed, his mind preferred to dwell in centuries earlier than the Medieval. It was to the writers of the first Christian centuries that he went for guidance. "The Fathers," he said, "made me a Catholic."[28] Indeed, he himself seems to belong with the early Christians. Was not the decaying empire of pagan culture destroyed by just such penetrating dogmatism and subtle patience, sacrificing every measurable and worldly good, nay, even every liberty of the private judgment, in grim obedience to an intuition of God? I suspect that modern scepticism does not fully know the deep strength of its foe, this power of faith, that it has taken up weapons against so lightly.

The problem of the relation between an author's religious convictions and his artistic technique has been somewhat neglected by literary scholarship. We have in Newman excellent examples of this connection. His belief in miracles permits him to use, with serious intent, certain devices which, in some writers, would seem merely unreal coincidence or romantic accident. He tells us that the plague of locusts was sent from God because of the iniquity of the inhabitants of Sicca. The "natural and direct interpretation was, 'Do penance, and be converted.'"[29] We have already mentioned how he disposes of the arguments of scepticism by delivering the sceptic to an evil spirit. But, in spite of this and other colorful materials in the historical romance, a certain tepidness of treatment keeps it from giving the delight expected. His heart was not in this sort of thing. Who was he to set himself telling of narrow escapes and love affairs, or describing the appearance of a mob or of a witch—this austere mystic? He had no interest in the externals of things. "I wish I lived as much in the unseen world," he said, "as I think I do not live in this."[30]

The plots of the two novels reflect Newman's asceticism. *Loss and Gain* is as devoid of a love story as is any biography of its author. To the conversion story of his later romance, he adds the fact that Agellius is in love with Callista. That is as far as it goes. When she, not yet a Christian, rebukes her lover for courting her instead of trying to convert her, he is shocked at his own conduct and bitterly repentant.[31] The novel ends not in a marriage but in death. All the emotional ecstasy that would ordinarily be lavished upon sexual love is devoted to the divine. As Callista was put on the rack, "She spoke her last word, 'For Thee, my Lord and Love, for Thee! . . . Accept me, O my Love, upon this bed of pain! And come to me, O my Love, make haste and come!'"[32] When Chione (the slave), and Agellius spoke of their Master, they blushed.[33]

If the author does not succeed in giving us the thrill of adventure and the feeling of a colorful historical background in *Callista,* nor the political aspect of the Oxford Movement in *Loss and Gain,* it must be remembered that in both novels Newman is chiefly interested in the inner drama of a change in faith. The belief that the most important event in life is not any measurable success nor even human failure, but the attainment of a certain subjective attitude, assent, communion with the true Church, this belief makes itself manifest in the choice of incident and the management of each story, and is present in the climax. This concentration upon one character and one action gives excellent unity of structure. On the other hand, it does permit *dialogue* that is quite undramatic, that reflects merely intellectual steps along the way to conversion, not emotional reaction of man on man.

But the most important influence of Newman's religious beliefs upon his technique grows out of his conviction that the progress of a soul is ultimately not due to its surroundings nor to the individual himself, but to God.[34] The novel of Hardy and of Zola, under the sway of "scientific" determinism, was to become a study of the influence of environment upon character. Newman in each of his novels gives us a plot based upon the opposite assumption, a picture of a character acting in a certain way *in spite of* heredity, environment, and self-interest. He considered his own conversion the result of a call, or "an election of grace."[35] Before coming to his final decision, he had held aloof from Roman Catholics. Similarly, the hero in *Loss and Gain,* up to the time when he decides he must join their Church, does not know any Roman Catholics.[36] It is not even the writings of the early Fathers which make Reding a Catholic, as it was in Newman's own case. In the *Apologia,* the author has told us what books caused him to doubt the validity of Anglicanism. But doubt occurs to Charles without such preparation.[37] Charles, we are told, could not escape the destiny of being one of the elect of God.[38] A naturalistic novel, as a study in mundane cause and effect, makes the background a part of the story, almost one of the actors, that could not be removed without breaking a link in the sequence of events. Newman's supernaturalism allows him to write without achieving that intimate fusion of setting and plot. We feel that the subjective study has been worked out first, then the frame fitted rather awkwardly around it. The social and physical world never emerges into convincing reality. In his youth, Newman had "thought life might be a dream, or I an Angel, and all this world a deception, my fellow-angels by a playful device concealing themselves from me, and deceiving me with the semblance of a material world."[39] In his novels, action and setting are hardly more than coating for the pill. He seems to pull up his conversion-story at certain intervals, as if to say, "Now I must stop the argument and describe the scenery or let the characters drink another cup of tea."

It is interesting to compare Newman to Eliot, who, chronologically and philosophically, lies between him and the naturalists. Her position is not merely that of determinism.[40] Protestant in her origins, she emphasizes the moral responsibility of the individual. She attempts to penetrate to the ultimate motives that cause the will to swerve from duty, and soberly analyzes the consequences of deeds. Newman, vividly conscious of being in the hand of God, shows us not the consequences of acts of will, but the stages in the path along which the soul is led by a divine power quite independent of time, place, circumstance, and personal inclination. Of course, this is not to say that Newman denies free will. It is open to the soul to decide for itself whether it will or will not follow the light which God has granted, but the important thing is the act of grace, not the act of will. Newman's chief characters do not exhibit a conflict of desire and duty. They are eager to obey if only they may learn what is right. They are full of hope, for nothing can prevent the interposition of a personal Deity, actually a *deus ex machina.* There is no real conflict, no real suspense, in these plots. From the first, we can see what is coming. And yet we miss the feeling of inevitability which an irresistible impersonal cause or Fate would give us.

In short, with the novel of psychological study, as we pass from Newman through Eliot to Hardy we pass from supernaturalism, in which a man's fate is offered him by benevolent Providence; through a form of moral Protestantism in which men owe their fate largely to their own actions, and then to Naturalism, in which fate is determined by circumstances. Hence the setting was to become more and more important. Trollope and Eliot, writing later than Newman, gave with artistic care the local color that would be perceived by the normal human consciousness, not yet the background as discovered by the mystic or scientist. But with Egdon Heath, of *The Return of the Native,* or the social milieu of Zola's *Débâcle,* the setting becomes the real center of interest. Second only to background for increasing importance is the past of the individual; in Eliot, Trollope, (and Yonge), the individual's earlier deeds; in Hardy even his heredity.

The divine influence which guides Callista is not merely conscience, but a voice from a Personality outside herself.[41] Nevertheless, conscience is on the side of the Creator,[42] Who has planted in us, the *Apologia* says, certain sentiments of right and wrong. Both Callista and Charles Reding seem to know what they ought to believe before they believe it, a complex psychological condition which may perhaps help us to understand Newman's own development. Callista's "was not a change which involved contrariety, but one which expanded itself in (as it were) concentric circles." Every day was the child of the preceding, yet "had she been asked . . . where was her principle and consistency, what was her logic, or whether she acted on reason, or on impulse, or on feeling, or in fancy, or in passion, she would have been reduced to silence."[43] Hence her strange rebuke, while she is yet pagan, to her lover for not preaching Christianity to her. When she first read the Gospel, she found that here was that towards which her intellect tended, though that intellect could only approve, not originate.[44] Charles Reding, having a notion that celibacy is better than married life, when he sees that Catholicism justifies his thoughts and explains his feeling, finds this a direct argument for Catholicism.[45] "Conviction," says Charles, "is the eyesight of the mind, not a conclusion from premises; God works it, and His works are slow."[46] But Charles seems to know as well as his author where he is going. And so does the reader.

The creation of characters is probably the ultimate test of an author's breadth and humanity. When Newman gives us prototypes of himself, they are real enough. But if we compare his characters, say with those of the Colloquies of Erasmus (who are also figures created for the presentation of Catholic arguments), we are tempted to conclude that Newman's sympathy was confined within the bounds of his dogma. It is not that Catholic thinking itself involves meagerness of sympathy for *la perduta gente.* Newman loved to repeat that for him there were but two beings of any consequence, God and himself.[47] To those of his creatures who are neither Romanist nor High Anglican, he is absurdly unjust, seeming to assume that the lost soul knows at heart the truth of Catholic doctrine but through sinful stubbornness refuses to admit it. Juba is not only sceptical, he is also superstitious. He uses amulets against scorpions, and stands for intellectual freedom. When a priest claims him "as one of my children" Juba winces, but says scornfully, "You are mistaken there father; speak to those who own you. I am a free man."[48] Of these hostile portraits, the most interesting are those in which Newman, with cold scorn, angles a puppet to typify ridiculously some opinion he dislikes. In *Loss and Gain,* there is a cutting satire in designating the Evangelicals present at a tea as No. 1, No. 2, No. 3.[49] But he makes most sport with the representatives of absurd cults who, just before Reding joins the Catholic Church, try to win him to their own religions. There is Dr. Kitchens with his book "Spiritual Elixer," of which the "operation is mild and pleasurable" and acts in a few hours.[50] A young lady tells him that some of them are organizing a religious body. He asks their tenets.

> "Here, too," she replied, "there is much still to be done; the tenets are not fixed either, that is, they are but sketched; and we shall prize your suggestions much. Nay, you will, of course, have the opportunity, as you would have the right, to nominate any doctrine to which you may be especially inclined."
>
> Charles did not know how to answer to so liberal an offer.[51]

Considered merely as a story, *Callista* shows a marked improvement over the earlier novel, for it has more plot, more suspense, more emotion, more action. On the other hand, *Loss and Gain,* dealing as it does with contemporary experience, leaves an impression of deeper sincerity. Its casual flow of argument, its England and its Oxford and its mild clerical life seem very near reality. But not on such an esthetic basis would Newman have us judge his books. The novelists of the 'forties had more serious purposes in mind. Anne Mozley tells us that "The ethos, as Mr. Newman calls it, of a book came always foremost in his critical estimation."[52] He writes in 1837 that he misses something in Jane Austen. "What vile creatures her parsons are! She has not a dream of the high Catholic [*ēthos*].'[53] And when he came to write novels himself ten years later his first concern, as I have shown, was to paint souls moved by Catholic ideals. He was using fiction to convey dramatically moral insight into values that may make character and determine conduct. Besides esthetic and ethical interest, Newman's novels have unusual historical and biographical value. He calls *Loss and Gain* "A Tale, which . . . is a more intelligible and exact representation of the thoughts, sentiments, and aspirations . . ." prevailing then at Oxford "than was to be found in the pamphlets, charges, sermons, reviews, and story-books of the day."[54] We see what it meant to turn the back on one's family and the high wordly position of an English clergyman, to join the despised Catholics.[55] As long as men turn to literature for serious knowledge of human character, of social history, and of the ideals that have moulded conduct, these novels will always be documents of some value. I have treated them at such length because of their earnest portrayal—with a delicate insight into rare states of mind—of a profound and very important change of belief, a Protestant's conversion to Rome, by the one who, of all men with literary power in the nineteenth century, had best knowledge of that experience. These novels are built upon that portion of Newman's life which is the central fact in the history of Romanism and of Anglo-Catholicism in modern England.

Notes

[1] Advertisement to the Sixth Edition, 1874, p. ix.

[2] Postscript (after Advertisement), pp. vii-viii.

[3] Letter to Frederick Capes, quoted in Ward, *Life of . . . Newman,* I, 245.

[4] Postscript, *Callista,* p. viii.

[5] *Charles Kingsley, His Letters and Memories of his Life,* ed. by his wife, I, 366; II, 179.

[6] *Callista,* Advertisement, p. vii.

[7] P. vii.

[8] *Loss and Gain,* Part I, Ch. i, p. 3; *Apologia,* Ch. I, 118.

[9] *Loss and Gain,* II, xxi, 335; *Letters and Correspondence,* I, 46.

[10] Reilley, J. J., *Newman as a Man of Letters,* 82.

[11] *Apologia,* I, 110-111; *Loss and Gain,* II, iv, 192; Cf. also III, ii, 349, a passage of which a Freudian might make much.

[12] Thureau-Dangin, *op. cit.,* I, 262-263.

[13] *Loss and Gain,* II, x, 234-241; *Correspondence of John Henry Newman with John Keble and Others,* 229-230.

[14] *Loss and Gain,* II, iii, 184; see also *Correspondence . . . with John Keble and Others,* 200-201 where "Smith" of *Loss and Gain,* II, 120, is associated with Newman.

[15] Unfinished letter to William Froude, Rome, April 29, 1879, quoted in Ward, *Life of . . . Newman,* Appendices, II, p. 591.

[16] *Callista,* XXXI, 348.

[17] *Loss and Gain,* II, vi.

[18] *Ibid.,* I, iii, 17-18.

[19] *Ibid.,* I, xv, 132-135.

[20] *Callista,* XXVIII, 307-308.

[21] *Loss and Gain,* II, v, 196-197.

[22] *Ibid.,* II, v, 200.

[23] *Callista,* XXXI, 345.

[24] *Ibid.,* XXIV, 271.

[25] *Ibid.,* XXXI, 349.

[26] *Ibid.,* XXXVI, 380-381.

[27] See *Apologia,* Note B, p. 401.

[28] Newman, *Certain Difficulties felt by Anglicans,* 24.

[29] *Callista,* XVI, 178-179. Cf. the way the Anglo-Catholic novelist William Sewell kills off a Jesuitical-Chartist villain in *Hawkstone,* II, xxiii, 337: "It was an accident—such an accident as Providence usually employs in executing his justest vengeance!"

[30] *Letters and Correspondence,* II, 279.

[31] *Callista,* XI, XII.

[32] *Ibid.,* XXXIV, 369.

[33] *Ibid.,* XIX, 221.

[34] *Ibid.,* XIX, 223; *Loss and Gain,* II, vi, 204-205.

[35] See letter quoted by W. S. Lilly in "Anglicanism Old and New," *Dublin Review,* CXXXVIII, Jan. 1906, p. 174. Cf. *Apologia* I, 110.

[36] III, v, 370; and III, ix, 417.

[37] *Loss and Gain,* I, xi, 92.

[38] That is, of becoming a Catholic. *Ibid.,* II, vi, 206.

[39] *Apologia,* I, 106.

[40] Cf. Letters to the Hon. Mrs. Ponsonby, Dec. 10, 1874, and Aug. 19, 1875, in J. W. Cross, *George Eliot's Life,* III, 176f. and 188f.

[41] *Callista,* XXVIII, 314; cf. XXVII, 293.

[42] Cf. as to Juba, *ibid.,* XIV, 165.

[43] *Callista,* XXVII, 291-292.

[44] *Ibid.,* XXIX, 326.

[45] *Loss and Gain,* II, vi, 204-205.

[46] *Ibid.,* II, xvii, 294.

[47] Thureau-Dangin, *op. cit.,* III, 95.

[48] *Callista,* XIV, 163.

[49] I, xvii, 146-154.

[50] *Loss and Gain,* III, viii, 409.

[51] *Ibid.,* III, vii, 396.

[52] *Letters and Correspondence,* II, 224, note 1.

[53] *Ibid.,* II, 224, Letter to Mrs. John Mozley, Jan. 19, 1837.

[54] Dedication, p. vi.

[55] *Loss and Gain,* III, v, 370.

Works Cited

FICTION

Newman, John Henry, *Callista: A Sketch of the Third Century,* 1856. References are to ed. 1873

Loss and Gain: The Story of a Convert, 1848. References are to sixth ed., 1874

Sewell, William, *Hawkstone; a Tale of and for England in 184-,* 1845. References are to sixth American ed., N.Y., 1848

NON-FICTION, ORIGINAL SOURCES

Newman, John Henry, *Apologia Pro Vita Sua,* The Two Versions of 1864 and 1865 Preceded by Newman's and Kingsley's Pamphlets. With an Introduction by Wilfred Ward, 1913. (Unless otherwise indicated, references are to 1865 version.)

Certain Difficulties Felt by Anglicans in Catholic Teaching Considered: In a Letter Addressed to the Rev. E. B. Pusey, D.D., on occasion of his Eirenicon of 1864 (etc.) 1876

Correspondence of John Henry Newman with John Keble and Others, 1839-1845, 1917

Difficulties Felt by Anglicans in Catholic Teaching Considered. Fourth ed. (1872)

An Essay in Aid of a Grammar of Assent, 1870

Letters and Correspondence of John Henry Newman During his Life in the English Church. Ed. by Anne Mozley (including autobiographical memoir down to 1832), 1891

SECONDARY AUTHORITIES, GENERAL

Thureau-Dangin, Paul, *La Renaissance Catholique en Angleterre au XIXe Siècle,* Paris, 1899-1906. Translated unreliably as: *The English Catholic Revival in the Nineteenth Century.* "Revised and Re-edited from a Translation by the late William Wilberforce," 1914. This is more flattering to smug susceptibilities than the French original, and is perhaps better adapted to advance the Catholic cause in England. E.g., the original says that in the slums of London there

BIOGRAPHICAL STUDIES

Eliot

George Eliot's Life as related in her Letters and Journals arranged and edited by her husband, J. W. Cross, N.Y., 1885

Kingsley

Charles Kingsley, His Letters, and Memories of his Life, edited by his wife, second ed., 1877

Newman

Lilly, W. S., "Anglicanism old and new," *The Dublin Review,* CXXXVIII, cclxxvi, Jan., 1906

Reilley, Joseph J., *Newman as a Man of Letters,* N.Y., 1925

Ward, Wilfred Philip, *The Life of John Henry Cardinal Newman,* 1912

M. H. Abrams (essay date 1953)

SOURCE: "Poetry as Catharsis: John Keble and Others," in *The Mirror and the Lamp: Romantic Theory and the Critical Tradition*, Oxford University Press, 1953, pp. 138-48.

[*In the essay that follows, Abrams examines John Keble's* Lectures on Poetry, *in which he links the cathartic function of poetry to primitive instincts, in a prefiguration of psychoanalytic interpretations of the role of literature in human existence.*]

Latent in the term 'expression' is the notion of something that is forced out by a pressure from within. The alternative metaphor, 'overflow,' by suggesting the fluid nature of feeling, also involves a question in regard to the hydrodynamics of the poetic process. It was to be expected that some romantic critics should find the impulse to composition in the pressure of pent-up feeling, or in the urgency of unfulfilled desires. And naturally enough, Aristotle's description of the cathartic effect of tragedy upon the pity and fear of its auditors was generalized to include all emotions in all forms of poetry, and silently shifted to denote the healing expenditure of feeling in the poet himself.

That emotions exert a kind of psychic pressure, and that their suppression is morbid and their verbal expression a therapeutic measure, had long been a maxim in folk-psychology. 'Give sorrow words,' Malcolm counseled Macduff,

> the grief that does not speak
> Whispers the o'er fraught heart and bids it
> break.

The Elizabethan critic, George Puttenham, applied this concept to explain one kind of lyric, the 'forme of poetical lamentations,' as an homeopathic remedy by which the poet plays physician to his auditors, 'making the very greef it selfe (in part) cure of the disease.'[45] In the latter part of the eighteenth century, poets began to testify that, in their experience, diverse kinds of literary composition served them as a personal therapy. Burns wrote in 1787 that 'my Passions . . . raged like so many devils, till they got vent in rhyme; and then conning over my verses, like a spell, soothed all into quiet.'[46] To reassure George and Georgiana Keats against taking fright at his wooing of easeful death in the sonnet, 'Why did I laugh tonight?' Keats wrote them that after composing the poem, 'I went to bed, and enjoyed an uninterrupted Sleep. Sane I went to bed and sane I arose.'[47] Byron declared that 'it comes over me in a kind of rage every now and then . . . and then, if I don't write to empty my mind, I go mad.' He did not hesitate to extend his private experience to poets in general. Poetry

> is the lava of the imagination whose eruption prevents an earthquake. They say poets never or rarely go mad . . . but are generally so near it that I cannot help thinking rhyme is so far useful in anticipating and preventing the disorder.[48]

Related to this view is the concept that the compulsion to poetry lies in the disproportion between man's desires, or man's ideals, and the world of reality. Aristotle, defining poetry as imitation, had attributed its origin merely to the human instinct for mimicry, and for taking delight in the imitations of others.[49] Longinus, on the other hand, set current the suggestion that writers who achieve sublimity are activated by the fact that 'not even the entire universe suffices for the thought and contemplation within the reach of the human mind . . . '[50] The most important document in this development was Francis Bacon's *Advancement of Learning.* The use of 'fained historie,' or narrative and dramatic fiction, 'hath been to give some shadowe of satisfaction to the minde of Man in those points wherein the Nature of things doth denie it.' That the poet has the power to reform nature, delivering a golden for a brazen world, had been a commonplace of Renaissance criticism. What Bacon added to this concept was a theory of the dynamics of the idealizing process, in the compelling desires of man for 'a more ample Greatness, a more exact Goodnesse, and a more absolute varietie then can bee found in the Nature of things.' These desires remould the shadows of things when reality proves recalcitrant:

> And therefore [Poesie] was ever thought to have some participation of divinesse, because it doth raise and erect the Minde, by submitting the shewes of things to the desires of the Mind, whereas reason doth buckle and bowe the Minde unto the Nature of things.[51]

Some eighteenth-century critics tended to merge the statements of Longinus and Bacon into a single doctrine. As Richard Hurd said, 'fiction,' which is essential to poetry, is to be ascribed to 'something in the mind of man, sublime and elevated, which prompts it to overlook all obvious and familiar appearances, and to feign to itself other and more extraordinary . . . '[52] In this period, however, all theories of this kind were strictly qualified. The desires that may validly shape the matter of poetry are those common to all men, and are restricted to the noble modes of aggrandizing, beautifying, moralizing, and multiplying the variety of given nature. In one fashion, indeed, men of this age conceived the imagination to picture the fictional satisfactions for all kinds of desires, whether general or personal, noble or ignominious—in the activity they sometimes called castle-building, and we call wishful thinking. Dr. Johnson, for one, was acutely aware of the immense disproportion between what a man wants and what he is likely to get, and of the strength of the impulse to make up the difference in phantasy; this observation is the theme of many of his best writings in verse and prose. 'The Dangerous Prevalence of Imagination,' he says, exhibits itself in revery, when a man 'must find pleasure in his own thoughts, and must conceive himself what he is not; for who is pleased with what he is?'

> He then expatiates in boundless futurity, and culls from all imaginable conditions that which for the present moment he should most desire, amuses his desires with impossible enjoyments, and confers upon his pride unattainable dominion.[53]

Johnson, of course, had no intention of applying his analysis of the imagination in wish-fulfillment to the valid play of this faculty in poetry. In that province, its function is to exemplify truth in an imaginative instance, for 'poetry is the art of uniting pleasure with truth, by calling imagination to the help of reason.'[54] To find a conflation of the sources of art and the daydream we must look ahead to certain critics of the romantic generation.

William Hazlitt defined poetry in general as 'the natural impression of any object or event . . . exciting an involuntary movement of imagination and passion, and producing, by sympathy, a certain modulation of the voice, or sounds, expressing it.' It is 'the language of the imagination and the passions,' or alternatively, it is 'natural imagery or feeling, combined with passion and fancy.'[55] Tragedy, no less expressive than the lyric, is 'the most impassioned species' of poetry. And in the narrative form, Dante 'interests by exciting our sympathy with the emotion by which he is himself possessed'; his great power 'is in combining internal feelings with external objects.'[56]

One of Hazlitt's contributions to the expressive theory of poetry stems from his persistent interest in the impulsions, the inner forces which compel human action, including the creation of poetry. A salient aspect of the romantic era in general was the sharpened 'Inner Sense,' as Coleridge called it, for the goings-on of the mind, and a new power, by those poets and critics who are 'accustomed to watch the flux and reflux of their inmost nature, to venture at times into the twilight realms of consciousness.'[57] Coleridge himself had no equal as a microscopic analyst of the interplay of sensation, thought, and feeling in the immediate cross-section, or 'fact of mind.' Hazlitt differed from Coleridge in that his psychological occupation was less with the nuances of a mental event than with its springs and motives, and particularly, with the secret motives, hidden from the world, and sometimes from the agent himself.

Hazlitt's chief complaint against the current psychology of rationalism and of hedonistic calculus was its failure to take into account the complex urgencies underlying behavior. Bentham, he said, 'has not allowed for the wind.' 'We are the creatures of imagination, passion, and self-will more than of reason or even of self-interest.'[58] In his own theory, Hazlitt, who had set out in his youth to be a philosopher, amalgamated Hobbes's principle that the power-drive is the prime human motive with La Rochefoucauld's readiness to look for the Ego hidden behind the curtain. His paper 'On Depth and Superficiality,' published in *The Plain Speaker,* may be recommended as a demonstration. In it Hazlitt lays bare 'the intricate folds and delicate involutions of our self-love'; points to the hunger for 'power,' or 'down-right love of pain and mischief for the interest it excites,' as 'the root of all the evil, and the original sin of human nature'; and adumbrates the mental mechanisms of suppression and hidden conflict in describing the 'obscure and intricate way' in which 'unconscious impressions necessarily give a colour to, and re-act upon our conscious ones.'[59] In his essay 'On Dreams,' we find a neat epitome of the Freudian concepts of the repression of unwelcome desires, and the partial release of unconscious thought in sleep.

> We may sometimes discover our tacit, and almost unconscious sentiments, with respect to persons and things in the same way. We are not hypocrites in our sleep. The curb is taken off from our passions, and our imagination wanders at will. When awake, we check these rising thoughts, and fancy we have them not. In dreams, when we are off our guard, they return securely and unbidden . . . Infants cannot disguise their thoughts from others; and in sleep we reveal the secret to ourselves.[60]

In numerous passages, Hazlitt surrenders the poetic imagination, like the imagination of the dreamer, to the motive power of unrealized desires. In the essay 'On Poetry in General,' into which he crammed all the odds and ends of his poetic speculation, he makes the point that

> if poetry is a dream, the business of life is much the same. If it is a fiction, made up of what we wish things to be, and fancy that they are, because we wish them so, there is no other nor better reality.

Hazlitt then characteristically misquotes from memory Bacon's explanation of poetry as 'conforming the shows of things to the desires of the soul,' and interprets this doctrine in a way that eliminates the earlier restriction of poetry to the desires for more grandeur, variety, and morality than the real world affords. 'We shape things according to our wishes and fancies, without poetry; but poetry is the most emphatical language that can be found for those creations of the mind "which ecstasy is very cunning in." '[61] Elsewhere he writes that 'poets live in an ideal world, where they make everything out according to their wishes and fancies.' He even suggests that one impulse to art is the need to compensate for a physical defect. Thus Byron's 'miss-shapen feet' contributed to his genius; they 'made him write verses in revenge.'

> There is no knowing the effect of such sort of things, of defects we wish to balance. Do you suppose we owe nothing to Pope's deformity? He said to himself, 'If my person be crooked, my verses shall be strait.'[62]

To this theory, that at least some literature is a form of *Wunschbild,* Hazlitt adds the doctrine that it provides an emotional catharsis for its author. Rousseau had already confessed that *La Nouvelle Héloïse* originated in the compulsive daydreams in which he compensated for his frustrations as a lover,[63] and Goethe was soon to describe in *Dichtung und Wahrheit* how his youthful despairs and disappointments had transformed themselves into *Die Leiden des jungen Werthers,* which he wrote in four weeks 'almost unconsciously, like a somnambulist.' 'I felt, as if after a general confession, once more happy and free, and justified in beginning a new life.'[64] Hazlitt himself, in his complex and tangled personality, was strongly subject to the impulse for public confession. In his *Liber Amoris,* he poured out the humiliating details of his unrequited passion for the coquettish daughter of his lodging-house keeper, not, as in *Werther or The New Héloïse,* transformed into fiction, but under the sole and readily penetrated disguise of anonymity.[65] Why, Hazlitt asks in his essay 'On Poetry in General,' are we 'as prone to make a torment of our fears, as to luxuriate in our hopes of good?' The answer is, 'Because we cannot help it. The sense of power is as strong a principle in the mind as the love of pleasure.' Under the heading of 'the sense of power,' Hazlitt elaborates the concept, which has since become a familiar element in expressive theories, of the capacity of art to master, by objectifying, the chaotic press of emotion. 'This is equally the origin of wit and fancy, of comedy and tragedy, of the sublime and pathetic.' In all these forms, the motive is the relief that attends upon our identifying and making conscious, and, therefore, manageable, the importunity of unarticulated feelings and desires.

> The imagination, by thus embodying and turning them to shape, gives an obvious relief to the indistinct and importunate cravings of the will.—We do not wish the thing to be so; but we wish it to appear such as it is. For knowledge is conscious power; and the mind is no longer, in this case, the dupe, though it may be the victim of vice or folly.[66]

Hazlitt's exposition of 'the sense of power' may have contributed to De Quincey's well-known distinction between 'the literature of power' and 'the literature of knowledge' which he substituted for Wordsworth's distinction between 'poetry' and 'matter of fact, or science.' In the third of his *Letters to a Young Man* (1823), in which he first expanded upon his thesis, De Quincey gave credit to Wordsworth himself for this, 'as for most of the sound criticism of poetry.'[67] But De Quincey's description of the communication of power as the occasion on which one is 'made to feel vividly, and with a vital consciousness, emotions which . . . had previously lain unawakened, and hardly within the dawn of consciousness' suggests, rather, Hazlitt's 'On Poetry in General,' published only five years before. Under the influence of the traditional theory of rhetoric, in which De Quincey prided himself on being adept, he based the initial antithesis between the literature of knowledge and that of power on the relation of utterance to hearer: 'The function of the first is—to *teach;* the function of the second is—to *move;* the first is a rudder; the second, an oar or a sail.'[68] In his essay on 'Style,' however, De Quincey substituted for this distinction the German antithesis between subjective and objective writing, and described the discrimination and objectification of feeling as a process in the writer himself. In his characteristic eddyings and dallyings with the subject, De Quincey (whose reputation as a critical theorist is over-inflated) succeeds in muddying the already turbid distinction. Subjective writing turns out to include the extraordinary combination of theology, geometry, metaphysics, and 'meditative poetry'; while the natural sciences are classed with Homeric poetry as forms of objective writing. But De Quincey's analysis of the nature of literary subjectivity is worth quoting:

> In very many subjective exercises . . . the problem before the writer is to project his own inner mind; to bring out consciously what yet lurks by involution in many unanalysed feelings; in short, to pass through a prism and radiate into distinct elements what previously had been even to himself but dim and confused ideas inter-mixed with each other . . . Detention or conscious arrest is given to the evanescent, external projection to what is internal, outline to what is fluxionary, and body to what is vague . . . [69]

De Quincey allows for the existence of an objective kind of poetry; and Hazlitt, although he gives an important role to personal desires in shaping the poetic design, insists that the terminal product must be particularized and concrete, and holds that the intensity of the poet's emotional response is a condition for his grasping and realizing the essential qualities and sensuous particulars of the world without. He also joins this theory to a denunciation of contemporary poets (including Wordsworth and Byron) who depart from tradition in writing about themselves rather than about other men and things, and so express personal moods and feelings without finding for them, as we might now say, an objective correlative:

> The great fault of a modern school of poetry is, that it is an experiment to reduce poetry to a mere effusion of natural sensibility; or what is worse, to divest it both of imaginary splendour and human passion, to surround the meanest objects with the morbid feelings and devouring egotism of the writers' own minds. Milton and Shakespeare did not so understand poetry.[70]

One writer of the romantic period, however, made no distinction between objective and subjective poetry, or between expression and self-expression. Everything, in fact, that earlier critics had conjectured about the emotional dynamics and therapeutic function of poetic composition was but a prelude to the amplification given this theme in the criticism of the Reverend John Keble.

Keble revised and published in 1844, under the title *De poeticae vi medica,* the lectures he had delivered from the Chair of Poetry at Oxford between the years 1832-41. The lectures were delivered in Latin, according to the tradition that persisted until the incumbency of Matthew Arnold, and their somewhat bravura quality is emphasized by the lecturer's device of setting off a lyric of Robert Burns from its Latin context by translating it into Theocritan Greek. Keble dedicated his book, in terms most laudatory, to William Wordsworth. In addition to his many echoes of Wordsworth's criticism in detail, his basic theory is in considerable part a single-minded exploitation of Wordsworth's principle of poetry as the spontaneous overflow of feeling; although this principle is joined by Keble to ideas from quite different sources, and interpreted in a way Wordsworth had never intended. The book has received remarkably scant attention, even after its translation into English by E. K. Francis in 1912. Yet, if we take into account the authoritative position from which they were voiced, Keble's *Lectures* must surely be regarded as, under their pious and diffident surface, the most sensationally radical criticism of their time. They broach views of the source, the function, and the effect of literature, and of the methods by which literature is appropriately read and criticized, which, when they occur in the writings of critics schooled by Freud, are still reckoned to be the most subversive to the established values and principles of literary criticism.

Keble's most compendious statement of his position is the definition of poetry he proposed in a review of Lockhart's *Life of Scott,* written while he was in the process of delivering his Oxford lectures.

> Poetry is the indirect expression in words, most appropriately in metrical words, of some overpowering

> emotion, or ruling taste, or feeling, the direct indulgence whereof is somehow repressed.[71]

In his *Lectures on Poetry,* he supports this position by pointing to the origin of poetry in the passionate outcries of savages, and validates this speculation, in the cavalier fashion of eighteenth-century primitivists, by quoting instances of 'primitive' song indiscriminately from the Hebrew, Old Norse, Lappish, Polynesian, and North American Indian, all having their origin in 'the desire to relieve thoughts that could not be controlled.'[72] All the arts, including music, sculpture, and architecture, are linked by expressing feeling in diverse media; thus, 'the poetry of painting simply consists in the apt expression of the artist's own feeling . . . '[73]

From the same point of departure, that poetry 'gives healing relief to secret mental emotion,' Keble goes on, in a way that 'has occurred to no one, as far as I know,' to reorder drastically the poetic kinds. First, he distinguishes between the class of primary poets 'who, spontaneously moved by impulse, resort to composition for relief and solace of a burdened or over-wrought mind,' and the worthy but lowly class of secondary poets who 'imitate the ideas, the expression, and the measures of the former.' Within the province of primary poetry, 'it will follow that there will be as many and as many kinds of poems as there are emotions of the human mind.'[74]

By this stroke of logic, Keble hurls down the structure of the genres which, with relatively minor modifications and exceptions, had endured as a corner-stone of criticism from Aristotle through the neo-classic period. For the mimetic and pragmatic differentiations based on the subjects imitated, the means and manner of imitation, and the kind of effects to be achieved in the audience, he substitutes a simple classification based on the mental dispositions and emotions which a poem expresses. This classification, he tells us, is adapted from Quintilian's rhetorical distinction between *pathos* and *ethos. Ethos,* as Keble interprets it, is a matter of long-term character traits; *pathos* is a passing impulse of feeling, short, intense, and overpowering.[75] Under the expression of *pathos,* Keble groups the traditional forms of lyric, elegy, and some modes of satire; under the rubric of *ethos* he includes the epic, dramatic, and narrative forms (produced by poets who by nature are 'fond of action'), as well as georgics and eclogues (produced by those dominated by a love for 'restful things, the country, or quiet pursuits'). And as the emotional lyric forms had most exercised eighteenth-century critics who attempted to demonstrate that all poetry is imitation, so now tragedy and epic, the extended presentations of men in action, prove least amenable, Keble admits, to his attempt to ground poetry in 'the surging unrest of a passionate spirit.' His solution depends mainly on showing that these expanded forms are projected equivalents of *ethos,* or the deep-rooted and persistent sentiments and needs that compose the poet's permanent character.

> We see, therefore, that there is nothing irrational in the contention that even an Epic may serve the purpose of the most fervid poet and soothe deep-rooted and vital yearning.
>
> . . . [Such poems] reflect the character of a lifetime, and tastes which have become familiar to the mind by long association.[76]

The thesis that poetry is the imagined fulfillment of ungratified personal desire—which had appeared as an erratic but recurrent suggestion in what De Quincey described as the 'abrupt, insulated, capricious and . . . non-sequacious' course of Hazlitt's criticism[77]—is at the heart of Keble's poetic theory. The play of poetic imagination, he says, 'paints all things in the hues which the mind itself desires.' Nothing, in fact, is felt to be 'touched with poetic feeling' which 'does not by some refined consolation appease a yearning desire which for the present is denied satisfaction.'[78] And for Keble, very much as for Byron, poetry, in the last analysis, is a release of the affects in words, affording relief from threatening inner pressures. In place of Byron's volcano, however, Keble introduces the less spectacular mechanical analogy (modeled, he says, on the ancient notion that poetic inspiration is a form of insanity) of 'a safety-valve, preserving men from actual madness.'[79]

Keble's chief importance, historically considered, is in his thesis that there is a conflict of motives in poetic creation, and in his view that poetry is, therefore, not a direct, but a disguised form of self-expression. This concept, as Keble says, 'is the very pivot on which our whole theory turns.'[80] The impulse to express one's emotions is 'repressed,' in Keble's term, 'by an instinctive delicacy which recoils from exposing them openly, as feeling that they never can meet with full sympathy.'[81] There ensues a conflict in poets between the need for relief on the one side, and the 'noble and natural' requirements of reticence and shame on the other; a conflict which threatens 'their mental balance.' Poetry is a divinely bestowed medicine because, by means of 'those indirect methods best known to poets,' it is able to satisfy opposed motives by giving 'healing relief to secret mental emotion, yet without detriment to modest reserve.' It is, therefore, 'the art which under certain veils and disguises . . . reveals the fervent emotions of the mind.'[82]

It may seem odd that this radical, proto-Freudian theory, which conceives literature as disguised wish-fulfillment, serving the artist as a way back from incipient neurosis, should come out of the doubly conservative environment of High-Anglicanism and the Oxford Chair of Poetry. But the very fact that

Keble was more a theologian than a critic goes far to explain the nature of his poetics. Ideas, which in theology have become matter of course and inert, may become alive and drastically innovative when transferred—as Keble patently transferred them—into the alien soil of aesthetics. Keble himself gives us the clue to the source of his formulas, in his frequent allusions to poetry as something near allied to religion, almost a sacrament. He compares the motive for veiled self-expression in poetry to the instinct that made the Fathers of the Church take every care 'lest opponents and mockers should attain knowledge of sacramental mysteries and the keywords of the faith';[83] and his basic concept of veiled self-revelation had its roots in a well-established theological opinion in regard to the nature of God. Various religious observances also suggest Keble's view of the poetic function. There is, for example, the parallel with the healing relief of prayer, and also with the disburdening of guilt in the privacy of the confessional—as a leader in the Oxford Movement, Keble frequently regretted that in the Anglican Church, auricular confession was voluntary rather than the rule.[84] The parallelism between the poetic theories of Keble and Freud may be taken as one more evidence of the extent to which psychoanalysis is a secularized version of religious doctrine and ritual.[85]

Keble's consonance with Freud extends to his analysis of the psychology of the reader. Those who fasten upon certain poems with enthusiasm, he says, 'believe themselves to have lighted, at last, upon a unique mental solace.' And 'the peculiar delight which some men feel in some poetry will be found, if analyzed, mainly to depend'—not 'on the subject, or the skill of creating it'—but 'on the sympathy they feel for the character of the author, indirectly made known to them through his verses.'[86] Here is further evidence of how completely traditional poetics gets reversed by such an uncompromising commitment to the view that poetry is self-expression. To enjoy literature is to reachieve the catharsis of its creator; the question of taste reduces mainly to the congruence of one's emotional needs with those of a particular writer; when the reader looks at the work, what he finds is a veiled reflection of its author. It will not be a surprise when we find, later on, that according to Keble, the chief task of practical criticism is to reconstruct in detail, from the traces left in a poem, the sentiments and temperament of the poet who wrote it.

Notes

. . .[45] *Elizabethan Critical Essays,* ed. G. G. Smith (Oxford, 1904), II, 49. Puttenham explains this effect on the auditor by analogy with homeopathy in medicine, 'as the *Paracelsians,* who cure *similia similibus,* making one dolour to expell another . . . ' (ibid. p. 50). Cf. Milton's homeopathic analysis of tragic purgation in his preface to *Samson Agonistes.*

[46] Letter to Moore, 2 Aug. 1787, *The Letters of Robert Burns,* ed. J. De Lancey Ferguson (Oxford, 1931), I, 112.

[47] 19 Mar. 1819, *The Letters of John Keats,* p. 318.

[48] *Letters and Journals,* V, 215 (2 Jan. 1821); III, 405 (10 Nov. 1813).

[49] *Poetics* 4. 1448^b.

[50] *On the Sublime,* trans. W. Rhys Roberts, XXXV, 2-3.

[51] *Advancement of Learning,* Bk. II, in *Critical Essays of the Seventeenth Century,* ed. Spingarn, I, 6; cf. *De augmentis scientiarum,* Bk. II, Chap. xiii.

[52] 'On the Idea of Universal Poetry,' *Works,* II, 8-9. Addison, in *Spectator* No. 418, explains that it is the part of a poet to mend and perfect nature 'because the mind of man requires something more perfect in matter than what it finds there.' See also Reynolds, Discourse XIII, *Works,* II, 78; and John Aikin, *Essay on Song-Writing,* 1772 (new ed.; London, 1810), pp. 5-6.

[53] *Rasselas,* Chap. XLIII, *Works,* III, 419-21.

[54] 'Life of Milton,' *Lives of the Poets* (ed. Hill), I, 170. The special and lowly exception is the prose romance; see *Idler* No. 24.

[55] 'On Poetry in General,' *Complete Works,* V, I, 4, 11.

[56] Ibid. pp. 5, 17-18.

[57] *Biographia* I, 172-3; II, 120.

[58] *Complete Works,* XI, 8; XX, 47, 43. See also ibid. II, 113, and XII, 250-51; and Elizabeth Schneider, *The Aesthetics of William Hazlitt* (Philadelphia, 1933), p. 93.

[59] Ibid. XII, 348-53.

[60] Ibid. XII, 23. De Quincey, a greater expert in dreams, gives this even more startling capsule version of the theory of conflict, waking amnesia, and the compulsive repetition by each individual of the guilty, archetypal dream-myth of the human race: 'In dreams, perhaps under some secret conflict of the midnight sleeper, lighted up to the consciousness at the time, but darkened to the memory as soon as all is finished, each several child of our mysterious race completes for himself the treason of the aboriginal fall' ('The English Coach,' *Collected Writings,* XIII, 304; the passage came

to my attention by its quotation in Harry Levin's *James Joyce,* Norfolk, Conn., 1941, p. 158). German theorists, Novalis and J. P. Richter most notably, had earlier brooded over the mysterious and guilty self opened up to us in our dreams; see Chap. VIII.

[61] *Complete Works,* V, 3.

[62] Ibid. IV, 151-2; XI, 308; cf. IV, 58.

[63] *Confessions,* Book IX.

[64] *The Autobiography of Goethe,* trans. John Oxenford (Bohn ed., 1903), I, 511.

[65] See P. P. Howe, *The Life of William Hazlitt* (London, 1922), pp. 349-50.

[66] 'On Poetry in General,' *Complete Works,* V, 7-8. Croce gives a terse summary of the more recent form of this doctrine (*The Essence of Aesthetic,* trans. Douglas Ainslie, London, 1921, p. 21): 'By elaborating his impressions, man *frees* himself from them. By objectifying them, he removes them from him and makes himself their superior.' For an expanded version, see Yrjö Hirn, *Origins of Art* (London, 1900), pp. 102ff.

[67] *Collected Writings,* X, 48n. Cf. Essay Supplementary to the Preface (1815), *Wordsworth's Literary Criticism,* p. 198: 'Every great poet . . . has to call forth and to communicate *power.*'

[68] 'The Poetry of Pope' (1848), ibid. XI, 54-5.

[69] Ibid. X, 219-27. On romantic discussions of subjective and objective, see Chap. IX, sect. iii.

[70] 'On Shakespeare and Milton,' *Complete Works,* V, 53.

[71] Review of *Life of Scott* (1838), in *Occasional Papers and Reviews* (Oxford, 1877), p. 6.

[72] *Lectures on Poetry,* trans. E. K. Francis, I, 19-20; 59-66.

[73] Ibid. I, 42-7.

[74] Ibid. I, 22, 53-4, 87-8. Relevant to the effect of the expressive point of view on the theory of genres is Wordsworth's attempt, in his 1815 Preface, to rationalize the curious classification of his poems in that volume, on the basis of 'the powers of mind predominant in the production of them.' See also Markham L. Peacock, Jr., *The Critical Opinions of William Wordsworth* (Baltimore, 1950), pp. 111-12.

[75] Ibid. I, 88-9; see Quintilian, *Institutes* VI. ii.

[76] Ibid. I, 92, 86, 90.

[77] De Quincey, 'Charles Lamb,' *Collected Writings,* V, 231-2.

[78] *Lectures on Poetry,* I, 21-2, 25-6.

[79] Ibid. I, 22, 55-6. Cf. 'Review of Lockhart,' *Occasional Papers,* p. 24: 'The epic, therefore, or any other form, may act, as was said, like a safety-valve to a full mind . . . '

[80] Ibid. I, 73.

[81] 'Review of Lockhart,' *Occasional Papers,* p. 11.

[82] *Lectures on Poetry,* I, 20-22, 47.

[83] Ibid. I, 13, 74.

[84] J. T. Coleridge, *Memoir of the Reverend John Keble* (4th ed.; Oxford, 1874), pp. 302, 313. Keble himself, as a religious poet, was almost morbidly sensitive to the self-exposure involved in publication. See Walter Lock, *John Keble* (3d ed.; London, 1893), p. 57.

[85] For a comment on the connection between Keble's theory of poetry and religion, see Cardinal Newman, 'John Keble' (1846), *Essays Critical and Historical,* II, 442-3.

[86] *Lectures on Poetry,* I, 56 (cf. p. 66); *Occasional Papers,* pp. 24-5. . . .

Margaret M. Maison (essay date 1961)

SOURCE: "Prigs, Pews and Penitents: Early Tractarian Fiction," in *The Victorian Vision: Studies in the Religious Novel*, Sheed & Ward, 1961, pp. 11-30.

[*In the following essay, Maison surveys the Anglican novels of the Victorian period, with particular consideration of Tractarian fiction.*]

If England escaped the horrors of a revolution in the Victorian age her National Church did not. The history of the Church of England during this time is a stirring record of warfare, struggle, persecution, agonized secession and fiercest conflict, differences of religious belief causing hostilities not merely confined to verbal clashes, lawsuits and imprisonments but extending to the level of actual physical fighting. Witness the state of St. Barnabas' Church, Pimlico, in 1851:

> During the whole of that memorable year it was held only as a beleaguered city is held by armed men against the violence of enemies who battered

the doors, shouted through the windows, hissed in the aisles, and tried to storm the chancel gates.

The Anglican Church had indeed awakened from her eighteenth-century slumbers to become a real Church Militant. It was unfortunate, however, that so much of her war was internal, that the enemy was within as well as without, and that, in addition to the attacks of scientists and biblical critics, rationalists and agnostics, the hostilities of Dissent and the audacities of "papal aggression", she had to contend with innumerable battles among her own ranks. The three principal groups in the Church of England, High, Low and Broad, were frequently at daggers drawn, and controversy raged throughout most of Queen Victoria's reign, the ritualism that marked the second phase of the Oxford Movement causing even greater uproars and the growth of religious liberalism provoking the increasing wrath of its opponents as the century progressed. High attacked Low and Broad, Low and Broad attacked High, Broad attacked Low, Low attacked Broad, confusions within the parties themselves making matters worse, for each group had its moderates, its extremists and various divergences, giving every appearance of a reign of anarchy within the one Church. Here is an attempt at clerical classification made by the Rev. W. J. Conybeare in his essay on "Church Parties" (1853). He gives:

Low Church: Normal type ("Evangelical"), Exaggerated type ("Recordite"), Stagnant type ("Low and Slow")

High Church: Normal type ("Anglican"), Exaggerated type ("Tractarian"), Stagnant type ("High and Dry")

Broad Church: Normal type (Subdivided into "theoretical" and "anti-theoretical"), Exaggerated type ("Concealed infidels"), Stagnant type ("Concealed infidels").

Passions ran high, causing many broken hearts and homes, and the unhappy verdict of the Rev. Thomas Mozley, Newman's brother-in-law, gives us a vivid glimpse of the chaotic situation. He wrote in his reminiscences:

The Church of England was one vast arena of controversy. Ten thousand popes—the lay popes ten times more arrogant, unreasonable and bitter than the clerical, and the female popes a hundred times worse than either—laid down the law and demanded instant obedience.

Any survey of the Anglican novels of this period must take into account this state of division and warfare within the Church of England, for the majority of religious stories of the time not only reflect these passionate controversies but are actually inspired by them, and innumerable "lay popes", "clerical popes" and "female popes" all took up their pens to join in the War of the Novels and to lay down their religious laws through the medium of fiction.

Early Tractarian fiction shows something of this heady mixture of idealism and aggression. Tracts for the times were followed by tales for the times and early efforts to reach the public by pious allegory were quickly ousted by "red-hot Puseyite stories" and "Oxford Movement tales", which flourished considerably in the eighteen-forties and fifties and were enthusiastically welcomed by keen Tractarians.

Today, however, even the most devout High Anglican would survey these novels with a more critical eye. Their faults are glaring. Crude in technique, clumsy in construction, they are deficient in plot, characterization and entertainment value. In general they conform to two set patterns and describe two imaginary types of lives—either the history of the chastened penitent or the life and opinions of a kind of propaganda prig. "Whether we like it or not," wrote Elizabeth Sewell, "we all by our lives preach a sermon, either of warning or example." Early Tractarian novels are chiefly concerned with these lives of warning and example. There are countless stories of those who go astray, especially in the quagmires of ignorance, Dissent, Liberalism and Socialism (all devilish snares for unwary Victorian churchmen) and who, often in the last chapter, learn the error of their ways and return to the bosom of the Church, usually only to die there. Equally plentiful are stories of men, women and children who, absorbing the truth of church doctrine, develop into founts of wisdom, model clergymen, zealous schoolmasters, exemplary farmers, dutiful wives and mothers and ideal citizens. In the first type the novel is a cautionary tale, in the second, a mere manual for instruction, a sort of glorified Church Catechism. Both, in the early years of Tractarian fiction, are brimful of sermons. Not content with letting the lives of their characters preach the messages of warning or example, the authors often burst out *in propria persona,* fulminating against Evangelicals or pews or poaching, or the dangers of rebellious intellect and private judgement.

Such prigs, penitents and "preachments" abound in the novels of the Rev. William Gresley. He and his friend, the Rev. Francis Edward Paget, another country clergyman, are, according to *Fraser's Magazine,* the "acknowledged fathers" of Tractarian fiction, and Gresley in particular holds up for us the first fictional models of Puseyite virtue and reveals the "most awful and perilous position" of those separated from Tractarian truth. In his two early novels, *Portrait of an English Churchman* (1838) and *Charles Lever* (1841), he draws his typical saint and sinner and sets the stock patterns for succeeding novelists to copy.

His English Churchman is a clergyman called Herbert who combines "deep thought" with "youthful ardour" and "practical piety". He explains his religion in detail, expounds the *via media,* condemns the ungodliness of daily newspapers and London life, gives sound advice to unsettled Oxford students—*"Shun the agreeable infidel and the accomplished profligate"*—and lashes out unmercifully at Dissenters, while advising churchmen never to lose their tempers in argument.

Herbert is the first of a long line of "new High" clerical heroes, all smug, colourless and encyclopaedic in their religious conversations. There is another in Gresley's *Bernard Leslie: or, a Tale of the Last Ten Years* (1842). (Tractarian writers frequently used alternative titles, a common practice in popular fiction of the time.) Bernard Leslie circulates an enormously long pamphlet on the dangers of Dissent, rebukes the Liberal parish doctor and reforms an eccentric curate who, with tonsure and cassock, is going a little too far in reviving the "superstitions of Romanism". (Exaggerated forms of ritualism received short shrift from Tractarian novelists of this decade.) Herbert is celibate, but Bernard Leslie gets married, the author treating the subject rather gingerly, but nevertheless defending married clergy. (It is interesting to notice how clerical writers of the period generally fight shy of marriage and its preliminaries in their novels. Paget tells us in the course of one of his stories that he "would not write an episode on lovemaking for any consideration" and therefore has to leave it all to "the reader's discretion and imagination". But those religious novelists brave enough to get their characters to the altar have a golden opportunity for preaching which they seldom miss.) Bernard Leslie finally restores the dilapidated parish church, thus fulfilling one of the cherished dreams of all Tractarians of that time.

Even more goody-goody are the heroes of Robert Armitage's novels. In his *Dr. Hookwell; or, the Anglo-Catholic Family* (1842)—one of the first novels to employ the new term "Anglo-Catholic"—we meet the reverend doctor, a man of "mighty intellect and superior disposition", who holds forth to an eager circle of listeners on almost every aspect of Tractarian worship "Anglo-Catholicism", he tells them, "is not a novelty on the earth but a good old Protestant way." His opinions occupy three massive volumes—such novels as these could hardly be accused of frivolity and lack of seriousness!

A similar mine of information is Ernest Singleton, the clerical hero of Armitage's novel of that name (1848), who discourses on a bewildering variety of topics from capital punishment to the intelligence of tortoises. Unlike so many early Tractarians who, holding the "branch theory," turned eastward to the Orthodox communions, Ernest looks westward to the new world and is anxious to promote more cordial relations between the Church of England and her "daughter" Church in America. His biography is nauseatingly exemplary and the modern reader soon tires of the unbearably overemphasized moral of the importance of being Ernest.

Nor can we feel much sympathy or admiration for the model English citizen in Gresley's *Clement Walton* (1840), a paragon of insularity, who daily blesses the providence of God in supplying England with a "pure reformed Communion", "a healthy branch of the true Church". Such heroes as these, all pompous, didactic and faultless, are merely mouthpieces through which their authors voice their own prejudices and predilections. They all talk too much, either in monologue or disputation, and, like Samuel Wilberforce, the bishop who used to prepare "launchers" (suitable conversational openings calculated to lead to the discussion of some vital matter), they are all made to introduce subjects of talk as a mere peg on which to hang their authors' religious opinions.

The lives of the penitents are slightly more colourful, and in describing the temptations into which their erring heroes are led the authors have more scope both for narrative and for imaginative writing, although they are somewhat hampered by early Victorian moral and literary conventions, as Gresley's *Charles Lever* shows. Charles is the victim of Satanic influences, a Dissenting father and a Latitudinarian schoolmaster who teaches him "a sort of general religion". (Gresley here quotes the delightful story of the French tutor who asked his pupils' father: *"Mais, monsieur, quelle religion faut-il enseigner à vos enfants? J'en connais toutes."*) Poor Charles inevitably becomes a Liberal, then a Socialist and then apparently something too dreadful to mention. "We must here draw a veil over some portion of our hero's life", says the author discreetly. However, after seeing a savage mob in action, Charles becomes ill and contrite, and finally, as a "sincere penitent" he supports the tottering steps of his aged mother to church for the daily prayers that the vicar, "a most zealous Church-restorer", has instituted. Charles, of course, is a more puppet, but the book is an interesting social document, revealing and analysing as it does the various Tractarian anathemas—Dissent, Liberalism, Socialism, Chartism—and emphasizing the dire consequences of disobedience to established authority.

Liberalism and Chartism are also responsible for the downfall of Luke Sharp, in Paget's novel of that name (1845), who ends up deported and dying in the Convicts' Hospital, Norfolk Island, realizing too late that "*knowledge without religion* is POISON and DEATH." (Paget has a weakness for italics and capital letters to adorn his tales and point out his colossal morals.)

Dissent brings ruin to another foolish character, Eleanor in *Enthusiasm not Religion* by M. A. C.—(1848), an amazing novel written by a Tractarian teenager. Her heroine Eleanor finds church dull and escapes to meeting-houses, enjoying the delights of Nonconformist "enthusiasm" and the "sweet, warm, impassioned prayers" of Dissenting ministers. She soon becomes disillusioned however, especially when a friend of hers becomes "a raging maniac" through her disobedience to the Church. "Thus awfully has the Omnipotent avenged His outraged Laws", declares the young author triumphantly. (Madness was a favourite punishment for rebellious spirits in early Tractarian fiction; Ernest Singleton's friend dares to dabble in mesmerism and eventually reaches the padded cells of Hanwell Asylum, while the ungovernable Caleb in Paget's *Caleb Kniveton* (1833) ends his days as the village idiot.) Eleanor then renounces her "religious dissipations" and is "restored to Church fellowship".

There are many silly stories among the religious novels of this period, but in spite of all the false notes struck and the generally low level of literary composition these early tales have their value, not only by virtue of their interesting revelations of the political, social and economic implications of Tractarianism but also on account of their clearly-emphasized concepts of belief and behaviour and the ideals they hold up for ordinary people in search of a creed and a code. The saving of souls is after all a primary concern of these religious novelists and the fundamental question "What must I do to be saved?" is answered in detail through the medium of the narrative.

Some of the best answers are given in the novels of the Rev. William Heygate who specialized in tales of struggling penitents striving to fulfil the ideals of good churchmanship. In his *William Blake; or, the English Farmer* (1848) we see the penitent's programme: frequent Communion, daily prayers at church, private religious reading (it's not enough for a farmer just to know his catechism, we are told), regular self-examination (William "continually asked himself why he had said and done his last words and acts"), self-denial, self-sacrifice, strict obedience to the local vicar by virtue of his apostolic succession, generous almsgiving and charitable help for the poor. (The poor are frequently with us in early Tractarian fiction and their welfare is to be achieved by the paternal care and charity of the more fortunate since, as Gresley assures us in his novel *Colton Green* (1846), God has placed men "in their respective stations in order to make trial of their spirits, until the number of his elect be accomplished: the poor, in the patient endurance of their allotted toil, in soberness, obedience and faith—the rich and the influential, in the charitable provision which they afford their poor dependent brethren for knowing and doing the will of Him Who made them".) William sells his corn at a reasonably low price, even after hard winters, for to do otherwise would imply "a distrust of God's providence". He forms a night school to teach his labourers Church principles as well as the three R's and pays his men on Fridays instead of Saturdays to avoid "Saturday night drinking" and "Sunday shopping". Yet William is no Puritan and believes in enjoying himself with games, amusements and social relaxations on Sunday. (The campaign for Brighter Sundays was very strong among Tractarians, who, accusing the Puritans of turning the Sabbath into "a dismal cheerless day of austerity and gloom", advocated all manner of "festivities", "lawful enjoyments" and "innocent mirth" after morning service.) William's recreations, however, do not include shooting, for, as an act of self-denial, he has renounced his favourite sport for a year. Similarly Godfrey, the penitent undergraduate in another of Heygate's novels, gives up riding and shooting in favour of "the simplest pleasures". His gun, we are told, "lay in its case month after month".

Whereas men penitents are usually required to moderate their field sports, the women, in fiction at least, are continually being exhorted to moderate their finery. William's wife learns to dress in "a humble and retiring manner", for as the author reminds us "the great temptation and snare to young women of the present day is vanity in dress". Tractarian clergymen made great attacks on female finery. Pusey, it will be remembered, once referred in a sermon to a £60 dress that he had seen in an Oxford-Street shop window and expressed horror that "one Christian lady was to wear as one of her manifold exterior dresses what would have removed the gnawings of hunger of some 7,000 members of Christ". Such dresses were not only a cause of extravagance and vanity but were also, as Heygate noticed, impediments to devotion since they induced ladies "not to kneel or not to go to Church at all in bad weather". It is significant that "Father Ignatius", that extraordinary "free-lance" Anglican monk (described by his admiring female biographer as one of the most "stupendous results" of the "Tractarian upheaval"), had a special changing room fitted up near his church where women removed the steel hoops of their crinolines and "in the church itself every woman looked as if she had just had the steam roller over her".

The importance of churchgoing and receiving frequent Communion is emphasized in almost every story. To explain the sacramental way of life to the uninitiated is, of course, one of the chief aims of all early Tractarian fiction. It continually hammers home the lessons of sacramental grace and all the prigs preach what all the penitents come to learn—the value of the two sacraments of the Anglican Church.

The sacrament of baptism is particularly stressed; indeed, descriptions of christenings with ten-page sermons attached were a commonplace feature of Tractarian fiction long before the famous Gorham case focused nation-wide attention on the doctrine of baptismal regeneration. *The Times* of that period regarded this doctrine as "a mass of indigestible rubbish which none but a theological ostrich could swallow", and novelists eventually dropped prolix explanations of this controversial issue in favour of more exciting stories of unbaptized adults dying in agony on desert islands. (Kind friends from the shipwreck, remembering the sound advice of their local vicar at home, dip their fingers in seawater, perform the necessary rites and all is well.)

Penance, of course, was not considered as a sacrament and the practice of auricular confession was not emphasized in the fiction of the time, being regarded by early Tractarians as a purely voluntary affair. Lady Georgiana Fullerton however, before seceding to Rome, wrote a fantastically melodramatic murder story called *Ellen Middleton* (1844) showing the necessity for confession. This created a *furore* and was praised by Gladstone for its "tremendous moral". Usually, however, it was only in later and frequently hostile novels that all the more sensational possibilities of the practice of confession were fully exploited.

Since so many of the Tractarian doctrines were highly controversial and liable to the wildest misunderstandings, education in Church principles was regarded as an urgent duty, and several novelists touch on the problems of education: how to instruct ignorant Anglicans as well as how to reach the vast heathen populations of the new manufacturing districts. Some novelists even advocate sending a kind of squad of worker-priests to the industrial areas. Gresley's story *Church-Clavering* (1843) gives the fullest details of contemporary Tractarian views on schooling. Education without religion is madness, compulsory State education is a shocking and disgraceful "foreign system", Church schools should be organized through the existing diocesan and parochial systems, and the leading textbook should be the Catechism, as "there cannot be a more beautiful practical model for the instruction of children than the Church Catechism".

Education in church behaviour would appear to be another necessity for, if we are to believe the novelists, sleeping, yawning, refusing to kneel, lolling, whispering, laughing, "spitting in a filthy manner", and dashing out of church at the end like unbridled horses were all common habits of Anglican congregations of the eighteen-forties. Gresley declares that Roman Catholics and even Turks put Anglicans to shame in the matter of reverent behaviour in places of worship.

The state of the churches, of course, was partly responsible for this laxity, and the subject of church restoration inspired some of the liveliest Tractarian novels of the period. The pew was a particular grievance. J. M. Neale's paper to the Cambridge Camden Society on the history of pews, prefaced by twenty-four good reasons for getting rid of those abominations, soon fired the imaginations of the novelists. Paget, in his *St. Antholin's; or, Old Churches and New* (1841), gives us an entertaining tale on the subject. St. Antholin's is in a sadly unreformed state. An archdeacon, visiting the church, asks the churchwarden:

> "Why, what in the world is this, Mr. Ouzel?"
>
> "This, Sir, is Mrs. Clutterbuck's pew."
>
> "Pew!" exclaimed Dr. Sharpe, "I thought it was her *bed.* Why, it is all curtains and pillows. Take care if you please, Mr. Church-warden, that no pews are built in this fashion for the time to come. Churches are houses of prayer, not bedchambers."

Later in the story part of the church falls down and a cheapjack architect, an expert in "Gothic pigeon-houses", supervises rebuilding with "snug easy pews" and a huge stove in the centre aisle. This horror is fortunately burned down and an unknown benefactress gives six thousand pounds for a new church "on condition there are to be no pews". Paget devoted the profits from this novel to church restoration and in the following year produced another anti-pew propaganda tale, *Milford Malvoisin; or, Pews and Pew-holders.* This story, with its "wooden hero", is equally effective and contains plenty of intelligent comedy and satire—rare and refreshing qualities in early Tractarian fiction.

F. A. Paley, secretary of the Camden Society, was also moved to write a novel revealing the scandalous state of church interiors. In his book *The Church Restorers* (1844) he describes the Squire's pew thus:

> It was a very large enclosure, occupying a space fully capable of accommodating at least twenty-five persons on open seats. It was carpeted, curtained round, and furnished with a mahogany drawing-room table and a set of cane chairs. There were two easy chairs, with footstools, placed by a brazen stove on one side, which was duly furnished with fire-irons, grate and coal-scuttle. Elegant bound bibles and prayer-books lay upon the table, and costly velvet cushions with fringes and tassels lay on the ground for the use of the occupants if at any time disposed to kneel.

The altar is "a discarded dressing-table belonging to the Rectory", often used as a scaffold for white-washing or a table for parish meetings, the pulpit is in front of the altar and close to it is a huge "black cast-iron stove, of Birmingham-gothic design". Fortunately the rector's son, an ecclesiologist, soon puts things right and restores open benches and a fixed stone altar. After reading the evidences of

Paget and Paley one can well understand the Tractarians' *cri de coeur:* "Our houses of prayer are a shame and a reproach to us."

Restoration of lands to the Church is also recommended in several novels. Characters become conscience-stricken about their ill-gotten wealth derived from the robberies of the Reformation and hasten to give it back, not to the Catholics, but to the Tractarians. In J. M. Neale's *Ayton Priory* (1843) a rich colonel, realizing that his estates were originally taken from the monks at the Reformation, hands them back to the "Anglo-Catholicks" and helps with the "re-establishment" of a monastery.

The monastic aspects of Tractarian activity, and indeed the "Catholicizing" tendency of the entire movement, seemed, of course, to Protestant England to be nothing short of "rank Popery", and an account of the Romeward trend of High Anglicanism, one of the most controversial themes of Victorian religious fiction, must be reserved for a special chapter of its own. Meanwhile we shall see how some of the early Tractarian ideals are used and developed in the less theological but more domestic type of religious novels written by three Anglican ladies of the Victorian age.

Works Cited

Armitage, Robert, *Doctor Hookwell; or, The Anglo-Catholic Family,* 1842.

———*Ernest Singleton,* 1848.

Conybeare, William J., *Perversion; or, The Causes and Consequences of Infidelity,* 1856.

Fullerton, Lady Georgiana, *Ellen Middleton,* 1844.

———*Grantley Manor,* 1847.

———*Lady-Bird,* 1853.

———*Seven Stories,* 1855.

———*Laurentia: A Tale of Japan,* 1861.

———*Constance Sherwood,* 1865.

———*Mrs. Gerald's Niece,* 1869.

Gresley, William, *Portrait of an English Churchman,* 1838.

———*Clement Walton; or, The English Citizen,* 1840.

———*Charles Lever; or, The Man of the Nineteenth Century,* 1841.

———*Bernard Leslie; or, a Tale of the Last Ten Years,* 1842.

———*Church-Clavering; or, The Schoolmaster,* 1843.

———*Colton Green, a Tale of the Black Country,* 1846.

———*Frank's First Trip to the Continent,* 1845.

———*Bernard Leslie, Second Part,* 1859.

Heygate, William E., *Godfrey Davenant, a Tale of School Life,* 1847.

———*William Blake, or The English Farmer,* 1848.

———*Godfrey Davenant at College,* 1849.

———*Ellen Meyrick,* 1851.

Neale, John M., *Ayton Priory,* 1843.

Paget, Francis E., *Caleb Kniveton, The Incendiary,* Oxford 1833.

———*St. Antholin's; or, Old Churches and New. A Tale for the Times,* 1841.

———*Milford Malvoisin; or Pews and Pewholders,* 1842.

———*The Warden of Berkingholt, or Rich and Poor,* Oxford, 1843.

———*Luke Sharp, or Knowledge without Religion,* 1845.

———*Lucretia; or The Heroine of the Nineteenth Century,* 1868.

Paley, Frederick A., *The Church Restorers,* 1844.

Sewell, Elizabeth M., *Amy Herbert,* 1844.

———*Gertrude,* 1845.

———*Margaret Percival,* 1847.

———*The Experience of Life, or, Aunt Sarah,* 1852.

———*Cleve Hall,* 1855.

———*Ivors,* 1856.

———*Ursula, a Tale of Country Life,* 1858.

———*A Glimpse of the World,* 1863.

———*The Journal of a Home Life,* 1889.

Geoffrey Tillotson (essay date 1965)

SOURCE: "Newman The Writer," in *Mid-Victorian Studies*, by Geoffrey and Kathleen Tillotson, The Athlone Press, 1965, pp. 239-58.

[*In the essay that follows, Tillotson contends that Newman has been undervalued for his literary abilities—his clarity, attention to detail, and use of imagery.*]

When a great author writes mainly 'prose of thinking' there is the danger that his writing may come to belong too much to its special field and too little to literature as a whole. Pusey, let us say, was a theologian; his writings are prose of thinking; but the literary critic, for reasons I shall imply later in speaking of Newman, is quite willing to leave both him and his writings to theologians and ecclesiastical historians. With Newman, however, it must always be different. Some of his works are very much read. I recall that when books were scarce in the late war a bookseller in central London told me that, if he had had them, he could have sold two copies of the *Apologia* daily. And there can be few educated people who do not honour *The Idea of a University*.[1] Both those books are of general interest: they are of as much interest to the secular-minded as to the religious. But if we read much further it is because we are interested in the 'ecclesiastical' matter Newman usually treats of (by 'ecclesiastical' I mean pertaining to the doctrines, character and material being of the Roman and English churches): we go to him as we go to Pusey or his modern equivalent, and should feel equally profited if his writings had been written by Pusey. This sort of reader seeks first his matter and no doubt loves it the more because it comes to him as, say, meaning does in a sung service. Or alternatively we may read on because we like great literature, and know that Newman's writings never cease to deal with the general matters literature likes to deal with. I grant that the reader who mixes these two interests is the best sort of reader for Newman. The perfect reader is one whose mind is as like his as possible—as much that of a sensuous poet as it is that of a thinker and worshipper. The case for meeting an author with what, comparatively speaking, is identity of mind has been much discussed in recent times. It was well urged by Coleridge on behalf of George Herbert:

> G. Herbert is a true poet, but a poet *sui generis*, the merits of whose poems will never be felt without a sympathy with the mind and character of the man. To appreciate this volume [*The Temple*], it is not enough that the reader possesses a cultivated judgment, classical taste, or even poetic sensibility, unless he be likewise a *Christian*, and both a devout and a *devotional* Christian. But even this will not quite suffice. He must be an affectionate and dutiful child of the Church, and from habit, conviction and a constitutional predisposition to ceremoniousness, in piety as in manners, find her forms and ordinances aids of religion, not sources of formality; for religion is the element in which he lives, and the region in which he moves.[2]

This desideratum applies also to readers of Newman. The ideal reader for a writer who is a great writer, and who writes mainly about the ecclesiastical, must be both a literary critic and a believer, and both of them at a high intensity. In practice we find few readers to fill this bill. Writers on Newman tend to be disproportionately one thing or the other. They proceed as by a division of labour, which is the consequence no doubt of a cleavage of ordinary human minds into species—one sort of mind deals best with a certain thing, another sort with some other thing. Among these species the ecclesiastical exists at a remove from the others. The literary critic can take on historians (say Gibbon) and politicians (say Burke) and art critics (say Ruskin) more comfortably than he can take on Newman. And the reverse is true. The ecclesiastical writer is usually far from being the literary critic. An interesting example of this separation exists in one of the best papers ever written on Newman—the late Father Henry Tristram's 'On Reading Newman',[3] which purports to do nothing more than give the reader a sense of whereabouts amid Newman's many writings, but does a great deal more than that. Tristram was one of the most devoted, learned and wise of Newman scholars—there is no one yet to fill the gap he has left—but I cannot help feeling that his interest in Newman's Catholicism depressed Newman for him as a writer. In that essay he makes one misvaluation, as it seems to me, which strikes at Newman's literary credentials. I shall concern myself with it later on.

2

Everybody agrees that Newman had many dazzling gifts. He was a distinguished holder of several public offices. He was a priest and so looked up to as an example in point of piety, learning, and morality, a preacher, an instructor, a confidant and a counsellor, and his parish—to judge by his postbag—represented the whole of intellectual England. He was Fellow and Tutor of a college, the most intellectually distinguished in the Oxford of his day. He was one of the moving spirits of a great rebellion of thought. He was the centre of at least one informal and one formal fraternity. He founded and directed a school for boys. He edited magazines. He was a fashionable lecturer. He was head of a newly founded university. He became a Cardinal. And while holding all these offices he continued to be a prolific and much-read writer, unmatched for virtuosity: Polonius would have enjoyed listing the kinds—the controversial writings, tracts, poems, dialogues, essays, histories, open letters, biographies, autobiographies, lectures, treatises, novels, sermons, editorial prefacings, and annotations. In a word he was one of the supreme geniuses of nineteenth-century England.

And a supremely literary genius. If we were to take upon ourselves the boldness of arranging his gifts in order of greatness, that for writing would, I think, come out near the top. There will always be a variety of views about his character and personality; as a leader of men he has had his dubious admirers; but to the literary critic he must always appear a writer among those whom it is 'vain to blame and useless to praise'. And so completely did his pen express his self, his affairs and his whole mental life—for so it seems—that his writings survive as a permanent medium for all of them in all their fullness.

He himself did not encourage people to detach his literary gift from what it served and to rank it so high. 'I am hard-hearted', he wrote in 1848, 'towards the mere literary ethos, for there is nothing I despise and detest more.'[4] It was a thing often said in the age of Victoria. He would not have cared to be a poet as Keats had been a poet, or, much as he admired the Waverley novels, a novelist as Scott had been a novelist. He must have despised what he came to see of the movement of 'art for art's sake', which in revolt against the use, or over-use, of literature for the sake of practical matters grew strong in the latter half of the nineteenth century. Few of his writings are created without reference to contemporary affairs—the sort of contemporary affairs to which newspapers like *The Times* and the *Guardian* give their best attention. By the time he had many works to look back on he saw them as so much a part of the big public interests of their time as to fall into the category of things prompted by occasions. In the Advertisement before the *Lectures and Essays on University Subjects,* 1859, he noted (in the third person) that 'It has been the fortune of the author through life, that the Volumes which he has published have grown for the most part out of the duties which lay upon him, or the circumstances of the moment.' And again, in 1874:

> What I have written has been for the most part what may be called official, works done in some office I held or engagement I had made—all my Sermons are such, my Lectures on the Prophetical Office, on Justification, my Essays in the *British Critic,* and translation of St. Athanasius—or has been from some especial call, or invitation, or necessity, or emergency, as my Arians, Anglican Difficulties, 'Apologia' or Tales. The Essay on Assent is nearly the only exception. And I *cannot* write without such a *stimulus.* I feel to myself going out of the way, or impertinent, and I write neither with spirit nor with point.[5]

Many great works have been prompted by occasions and in the nineteenth century there was a higher proportion of them than in the eighteenth century and perhaps also the seventeenth century; but no nineteenth-century author wrote so high a proportion of them as Newman.

All these self-descriptions are perfectly satisfactory, but on one level only. They ignore what, if I read him rightly, has much importance—the necessity which drove him not only to write so much and to write so clearly but to write so beautifully. To judge by results, if by no other evidence, he was born to be a writer—just as Dickens was, and Thackeray, and the Brontës, and Tennyson, and Ruskin (who believed he was born to be a painter)[6]. Newman began as a born writer should—by copying the styles of the writers he admired: 'At the age of fourteen a sort of passion for writing seems to have possessed him.'[7] And

> There are many boyish anticipations or buddings of his after thoughts noted down at about this date [1817]. On reading these later in life, Dr. Newman is severe on his early style:
>
> The unpleasant style in which it is written arises from my habit as a boy, *to compose.* I seldom wrote without an eye to style, and since my taste was bad my style was bad. I wrote in style as another might write in verse, or sing instead of speaking, or dance instead of walking.[8]

And if this is true, we must not take his insistence on occasions for more than it is worth. In the essay I have already named, Tristram drew from the documents the following conclusion: 'whatever [Newman] was . . . he certainly was not a writer, a man of letters, *de son métier.* He only became such incidentally, as it were, in implementing his vocation as a priest, whether in his Anglican or in his Catholic days'.[9] This fails to allow that Newman became a printed author before he became a priest—it was as an undergraduate that he helped produce *St Bartholomew's Eve.* And I shall have something to say later that bears on the word 'incidentally'. Those are small points, but Tristram, I think, soon went wrong more thoroughly: he believed that when Newman had his pen in his hand he was working against the grain, and so gives the impression that in less provoking times he would have written little or nothing. 'He had no joy in writing, as such'—that was Tristram's view, and he based it on the much corrected state of Newman's manuscripts, and on his describing the painful production of the books as 'mental childbearing'.

Of his corrections Newman speaks on several occasions, as, for instance, in a letter of 1838:

> My book on Justification has taken incredible time. I am quite worn out with correcting. I do really think that every correction I make is for the better, and that I am not wasting time in an over-fastidious way, or even making it worse than it was; but I can only say this—openings for correction are inexhaustible.

I write, I write again: I write a third time in the course of six months. Then I take the third: I literally fill the paper with corrections, so that another person could not read it. I then write it out fair for the printer. I put it by; I take it up; I begin to correct again: it will not do. Alterations multiply, pages are re-written, little lines sneak in and crawl about. The whole page is disfigured; I write again; I cannot count how many times this process is repeated.[10]

Nor did the correcting end with the printing of the manuscripts. However satisfactory a manuscript had seemed its printed form always prompted further revisions for the second edition and for each successive one. The remarks I have just quoted are perhaps recalled a quarter of a century later in a letter to E. G. Ward—the most important of all the documents on this matter:

I suspect your psychological facts [Ward had sent him two of his publications], e.g. you speak at p. 26 of the 'keen and constant pleasure which intellectual processes afford.' I am far from denying there is a pleasure, and one providentially assigned, as pleasant flavour to food; but, if you mean that 'keen and constant pleasure' attends ordinarily on intellectual processes, well, let them say so, who feel it. My own personal experience is the other way. It is one of my sayings, (so continually do I feel it) that the composition of a volume is like gestation and childbirth. I do not think that I ever thought out a question, or wrote my thoughts, without great pain, pain reaching to the body as well as to the mind. It has made me feel practically, that labour *'in sudore vultus sui,'* is the lot of man, and that ignorance is truly one of his four wounds. It has been emphatically a *penance;* and in consequence I have hardly written anything, unless I was *called* to do it, e.g. I had to provide a sermon weekly for the pulpit, & c. I recollect a friend asked me, soon after writing my volume on Justification, whether it was not interesting to write, and my answer was to the effect that 'it was the painful relieving of an irritation,' as a man might go to a dentist, not for 'keen and constant pleasure,' but with the mingled satisfaction and distress of being rid of pain *by* pain. When I wrote the Arians six years earlier, I was so exhausted at length, that for some days as it approached finishing, I could scarce keep from fainting. The exercise which most nearly has approached to pleasure, has been the finding parallel passages to passages in St. Athanasius, or writing verses, processes which have not much of active intellect in them. I might say a great deal more on this subject; but I have said enough as giving the testimony of at least one person.

What I feel, others may feel. Others again may feel *neither* your pleasure *nor* my pain. At all events, I think you must not take for *granted,* what all men do not recognize to be true.

What has been my own motive cause in writing may be that of others,—the sight of a truth, and the desire to show it to others. Juvenal says, 'Facit indignatio versus.' I do not feel this in the case of verse; I do, in the case of prose.

I am far from denying of course, that, if one thinks one has done a thing well, one may be tempted to be pleased at it. But here it is the *work* effected not the *process* that pleases. 'When the shore is won at last, Who will count the billows passed?' Our Lord says, 'When she is delivered of the child, she remembereth not the anguish, *because,* &c.' Of course she may idolize her child, for the very reason that it has cost her pain, but pain never can be 'keen and constant pleasure'; and she never would bear a child for the sake of the childbirth.

Not at all denying, then, that there is a class of minds such as your own, Sir W. Hamilton's, Lord Brougham's, and the Academics, to whom exercises of intellect are simply 'keen and constant pleasure', I cannot think it is more than one class.[11]

It is clear from these accounts that Newman was pleased at least with the results of his labours, as were his readers, even though one of them drew an unacceptable inference as to the 'interestingness' of the process. As to its pleasure Newman was not conclusive: he granted that intellectual processes have a pleasure to them as pleasant as flavours are in food, but he also found in them pain. Not all pain, however, is painful and nothing else, and Newman's must have been qualified into some sort of pleasure by the warmth of his application, and his persisting prospect of success.[12] The labour of writing he might liken to battling with billows, but there are some swimmers who are confident that they can gain the shore. And though it was on the completion of the process that Newman spoke pleasantly of 'little lines [that] sneak in and crawl about', the timing may not be significant, for it is obvious that he enjoyed the use of the pen as a deft instrument. His handwriting had a rapid economy not without elegance,[13] even when modified under stress; and the business of making lines sneak and crawl accommodatingly cannot but please in some sort. We may contrast Shelley. He believed that 'when composition begins, inspiration is already on the decline',[14] and accordingly his manuscripts are without trace of pleasure—Trelawny describes that of 'Ariel to Miranda . . .' as like 'a sketch for a marsh overgrown with bulrushes, and the blots for wild ducks'.[15] Newman is another matter. I cannot but compare him with Pope, whose handwriting was aesthetically similar to his, and who explained his numerous and constant corrections by 'I corrected because it was as pleasant to me to correct as to write'[16]—an airy account, but airy merely because in accord with Addisonian manners. Only one valid inference can finally, I think, be drawn from the evidence of fact and comment—namely that Newman did not belong to the less common of the two classes of writers distinguished by him, the writers whose words came right straight off, but to the class of inky strugglers. And so the presence or absence of correction has at bottom nothing to do with the presence or absence of joy. For him composition in all its fulness was the only means of making inspiration profitable to great numbers of men—or fully profitable even to himself. Without the aid of words in their concretest and most exacting form, he could not come by his sense as a thing established in the shades of meaning he was so well gifted to discriminate. He had no choice but to *work* at expression, but then he was never one to jib at work.

Nor, finally, do we lack external evidence that pains could sometimes be joyful to the point of hilarity—as they were for Cowper when he wrote 'John Gilpin':

> The author's enjoyment of this task is illustrated by an anecdote told by Mr. Kegan Paul in his 'Biographical Sketches': 'A friend, also a convert, related not long since how, in the winter of 1847, he was a very constant visitor to Dr Newman and was puzzled at finding him so frequently laughing to himself over the manuscript on which he was then engaged, till he said: "You do not know what I have been doing. Poor Burns, the late High Church publisher, a convert like ourselves, has got into difficulties, owing to his change of faith and I am going to give him this manuscript [that of *Loss and Gain*] to see if it may not help him a little out of them".'[17]

Evidently no laughter issued from the writer of *Lectures on Justification,* but I do not think we need go to the other extreme and believe with Tristram that Newman found 'no joy in writing, as such'. Some pleasure must also have come from one of the objects that the corrections had in view. They were not solely intellectual. If they had been only that, the achievement of clarity and order would have been enough. Newman's labours sought also sensuousness, both of music and colour. These are objects of poetical composition and we have Newman's word for it that for him their pursuit 'most nearly . . . approached to pleasure'.

3

Nor must we take 'occasions' in too strict a sense. Many were invited. If you take orders you expect to have to deliver sermons. If you become a Fellow of an Oxford college and are also (as you had to be at that time) in orders, you may expect to be asked to preach before the University. If you become eminent in a cause, people on both sides will look to you for guidance or for 'a statement'. Many occasions Newman consciously laid himself open for. Of the rest several were potent only because he allowed them to be. The occasion for his writing *The Tamworth Reading Room* was the report of the speech delivered by a politician in his faraway constituency when opening a library for working men. The occasion for *Who's to Blame?* was less pointed still—Newman wrote it because, like the rest of England, he had read about the conduct of the Crimean War. Even the *Apologia* sprang from a *chosen* occasion—there had been many taunts against him before he chose to reply to Kingsley's. The same is true even of the novel, *Loss and Gain*—there had been many novels about religious converts before Miss Harris's *From Oxford to Rome.* And when he wrote without the sort of stimulus he had in mind, which in varying degrees we can call public, he did not step outside his usual matter—the undergraduate poem is on a religious subject, the *Dream of Gerontius* deals with a theme he had treated in the sermons, the *Grammar of Assent* follows on from the university sermons. In other words, both when he is free and when he is called, he writes on a matter one and the same. He is not a writer who wants to write on one matter but is obliged by duties to write on another. Even if his so-called occasions had not cropped up, we should have had writings, in the main, similar to those we have. Do not therefore let us take his speaking of occasions too seriously.

There was, I think, a psychological reason for his appeal to occasions. Newman subscribed to a then rather old-fashioned conception of the gentleman. We know how charming were his social manners on almost all of the thousands of recorded occasions. In his writings Matthew Arnold found the same 'delicacy' and 'urbanity'. His written words are often beautifully apologetic if he fears that there will be offence or crudity in some point or other he is driven to make. Alternative to this humility and charm there is of course fierceness and sharpness; but that comes from between the cracks. The man and writer when, as almost invariably, he lived up to his ideal for himself, was extremely polite. We can see him as wanting to write under certain conditions, one of which was the psychological or social condition of having an occasion that could be agreed to be public enough to allow him not to seem obtrusive: in the passage quoted above he speaks of his need not to feel 'impertinent'. But again we should note that his required easiness on that score is represented as a literary requirement also. Unless he felt welcome to write, the product would lack the prized literary virtues of 'spirit' and 'point'.

As final reason there was his strong need to feel assured that when he spoke he would be speaking to men. How strong that need was can be illustrated by one of the most remarkable passages he ever wrote, a passage that is one of the additions made from time to time to the manuscript account of his tour in Sicily. The particular addition was made at Littlemore in 1840, when he was taking to his 'deathbed' as an Anglican:[18] 'The thought keeps pressing on me, while I write this, what am I writing it for? . . . '

In any man's life there must be several 'spots of time' when thoughts like these are thought, but few, if any, when they are written down. Newman provided this exception, and a hundred like it, because he was a man who found writing a solace in itself, and also because, for as profound a reason, he longed to have readers—at some near point of time for preference, but if not that, at a later. I think we can discern in much of the writing, public and private, his strong need to achieve communication. This need accounts for the clarity of everything he wrote. Of the millions of his written sentences there can be few which do not convey what they were meant to convey. But along with the need for light went the need for sweetness—or, at times, sharpness. He wished to communicate something definite and to communicate it personally. The motto he chose for his cardinalate was *cor ad cor loquitur*—heart speaks to heart. For many reasons his words had often to be written words, and as means of expression written words have notorious limitations, especially where they are speaking the matters of the heart. Communication of the most piercing kind comes usually by other even more primitive means. 'Voices melt us, looks subdue us, deeds inflame us'[19]—that names three other powerful means. In his sermons he could rely on two of them in addition to words, and he relied on them to some purpose, for we have many accounts of the thrilling experience of hearing and seeing him preach. His lectures, too, availed themselves of the means of words, voice and look. When writings were written only for cold print Newman used many arts to suggest the completer range of medium. His printed words carry as much personal force as any words ever have. They take on as much of tones, looks, and gestures as possible. For us who never heard his voice, the print seems to speak, and the famous face looks out from the page.

4

Newman loved the means of communication and the art of making the most of them. We are fortunate that it was so, for he might not have cared. In the *Apologia* he speaks of his 'mistrust of the reality of material phenomena' and his 'rest[ing] in the thought of two and two only supreme and luminously self-evident beings, myself and my Creator'.[20] The words he designed for his tombstone spoke the same 'fact': 'JOHANNES HENRICUS NEWMAN/ EX UMBRIS ET IMAGINIBUS/ IN VERITATEM/ DIE———A.S. 18[ ]/ REQUIESCAT IN PACE.' Feeling the things of the world to be shadows, he might have been haunted by their insubstantiality to the point of neglecting the material a writer must use. We recall the Scotch-Calvinist gardener in *The Newcomes* who handled the melons and pineapples 'provisionally, and until the end of the world'.[21] In his writings, however Newman handled earthly things *as if* they were real, as if he were as sure of them as he was of himself and his Creator. In his writings he seems as thoroughly at home among things as Chaucer or Shakespeare or Pope or Dickens. He speaks—if we add his unpublished to his published writings—with complete freedom: in the manuscript text of his account of the Sicilian tour he refers to piles and Epsom salts. There is nothing particularly literary in the mere possessing of this freedom, but it helps to produce the keen effects a piece of writing is the better for. Newman is constantly keen, however, not just because of his free speech but because his mind is sensuous, and therefore ready with the imagery which the sensuous mind contributes freely to thinking and feeling. He was sensitive enough as a physical organism to be sharply aware of the finger-tips of his Sicilian servant when applying vinegar to his nose, and he was agile enough of mind to connect the sensation with one stored in his memory—he writes of them as 'great bullet-tips'. Everywhere in his writings is the proof of this sensitiveness of sense and this prehensile agility of mind. It is the most obvious of the proofs that he is a poet. And it serves him very well as a philosopher. He is often dealing with abstract matter and dealing with it for the benefit of as many readers as he can gather. So that none shall turn aside because of too great an abstraction, he uses much imagery. He 'remembereth that we are dust'. His very account of thinking is as of a physical process.[22]

Finally, it is by virtue of much of his matter that Newman stands square with our great writers. He writes often about what literature most prefers to deal with. His constant attention to the 'scope and nature' of Christianity enfolds an attention as close to quotidian affairs. He is as alert to the trivial round as Wordsworth of Hardy; as alert as Matthew Arnold to those urgent public matters of the day—e.g. cholera, mesmerism, the goldfields—which pitilessly exact from journalists their 'nutshell truths for the breakfast table';[23] as alert as a novelist to the personal characteristics of everybody he met. And since he is often the philosopher, there is much attention to another prime concern of literature—the nature of man. Though his hope is always to shame the nature in man and to divert his natural religion into Christianity, he does not scamp his study of all that we are by unaided nature.

Co-extensive with the consideration of all these things proceeds his untiring introspection. There were several reasons for that activity, one of which was his frank love of particulars. The nearest source of these lay in his own field of body, mind and spirit, each of which seemed to him as important as the others because making an equal contribution to a whole. In *Loss and Gain* we hear that 'a man's moral self . . . is concentrated in each moment of his life; it lives in the tips of his fingers, and the spring of his insteps'.[24] Or there is the mixed account of his leaving Littlemore in 1846: 'I am burning and packing *pari passu* reading and disposing, passing from a metaphysical MS. to a lump of resin or a penwiper.'[25] And in another letter written a little later: 'I quite tore myself away, and could not help kissing my bed, and mantelpiece, and other parts of the house. I have been most happy there, though in a state of suspense.'[26] When in the *Apologia* he recalls how the Anglican Church looked to him after leaving it, he seems to be looking at it with physical as well as mental eyes:

> I have been bringing out my mind in this Volume on every subject which has come before me; and therefore I am bound to state plainly what I feel and have felt, since I was a Catholic, about the Anglican Church. I said, in a former page, that on my conversion, I was not conscious of any change in me of thought or feeling, as regards matters of doctrine; this, however, was not the case as regards some matters of fact, and, unwilling as I am to give offence to religious Anglicans, I am bound to confess that I felt a great change in my view of the Church of England. I cannot tell how soon there came on me,—but very soon,—an extreme astonishment that I had ever imagined it to be a portion of the Catholic Church. For the first time, I looked at it from without, and (as I should myself say) saw it as it was. Forthwith I could not get myself to see in it any thing else, than what I had so long fearfully suspected, from as far back as 1836,—a mere national institution. As if my eyes were suddenly opened, so I saw it—spontaneously, apart from any definite act of reason or any argument; and so I have seen it ever since. I suppose, the main cause of this lay in the contrast which was presented to me by the Catholic Church. Then I recognized at once a reality which was quite a new thing with me. Then I was sensible that I was not making for myself a Church by an effort of thought; I needed not to make an act of faith in her; I had not painfully to force myself into a position, but my mind fell back upon itself in relaxation and in peace, and I gazed at her almost passively as a great objective fact. I looked at her;—at her rites, her ceremonial, and her percepts; and I said, "This *is* a religion;" and then, when I looked back upon the poor Anglican Church, for which I had laboured so hard, and upon all that appertained to it, and thought of our various attempts to dress it up doctrinally and esthetically, it seemed to me to be the veriest of nonentities. Vanity of vanities, all is vanity! How can I make a record of what passed within me, without seeming to be satirical?[27]

And to take a last random instance from the mass, there is the letter of 1862 which he addressed to the *Globe* newspaper in an attempt to silence once for all the reports that he was returning to the English Church, and in which he seems to be spewing it and all its works out of his mouth:

> Therefore, in order to give them full satisfaction, if I can, I do hereby profess 'ex animo' with an absolute internal assent and consent, that Protestantism is the dreariest of possible religions; that the thought of the Anglican service makes me shiver, and the thought of the Thirty-nine Articles makes me shudder. Return to the Church of England! No! 'The net is broken and we are delivered.' I should be a consummate fool (to use a mild term) if in my old age I left 'the land flowing with milk and honey' for the city of confusion and the house of bondage.[28]

He ejects the Anglican Church as if he has it in his system, and his life up to the secession shows us he had. That was why he was so unconscionably long a-dying as an Anglican. He drew all things into himself,[29] so that even an external thing like a logical demonstration or a history issues from him as personal as a love letter. This unusual characteristic was soon seized on by his contemporaries: when the *Quarterly Review* began its sixty-page-long review of that book of his which had so much general interest for its own time and ours[30]—the *Essay on the Development of Christian Doctrine*—it recognized that here was a book that was more than a book:

> Our business is with Mr. Newman's book, not with Mr. Newman himself . . . It will, however, be impossible altogether to separate the examination of his work from what Mr. Coleridge would have called the psychological study of his mind—so completely is the one the reflexion, dare we use the word, the transfiguration of one into the other.[31]

As we should expect, he does not always rest content with the colouring his mind has given to his matter—he often lingers to describe the pigmentation and how he felt during its process. A frequent effect in his writings is that his thinking is progressing alongside a diary of the experience of the thinking for 'the whole man'.[32] This 'whole man' contained for him the unconscious, or what we should call the subconscious. If he reproduced on paper the light in his mind, he also reproduced the darkness with which it coexisted, and he looked at the darkness as hard as at the light. Instances are everywhere in the correspondence and in the *Apologia*.

Because of all this, Newman is one of the shining demonstrations that the style is the man. His personality exists as clearly in his style as in his choice of matter—or, rather, in his choice of just that shade and aspect of his matter. And since he constantly gives us consideration of the thing as well as the thing itself, it was to be expected that he should offer an account of the personality of style. I quote it at length because it is one of the most luminous things he wrote, confirming his belief that 'simplicity . . . is the attribute of genius':[33]

Here then, in the first place, I observe, Gentlemen, that, Literature, from the derivation of the word, implies writing, not speaking; this, however, arises from the circumstance of the copiousness, variety, and public circulation of the matters of which it consists. What is spoken cannot outrun the range of the speaker's voice, and perishes in the uttering. When words are in demand to express a long course of thought, when they have to be conveyed to the ends of the earth, or perpetuated for the benefit of posterity, they must be written down, that is, reduced to the shape of literature; still, properly speaking, the terms, by which we denote this characteristic gift of man, belong to its exhibition by means of the voice, not of handwriting. It addresses itself, in its primary idea, to the ear, not to the eye. We call it the power of speech, we call it language, that is, the use of the tongue; and, even when we write, we still keep in mind what was its original instrument, for we use freely such terms in our books as saying, speaking, telling, talking, calling; we use the terms phraseology and diction; as if we were still addressing ourselves to the ear.

Now I insist on this, because it shows that speech, and therefore literature, which is its permanent record, is essentially a personal work. It is not some production or result, attained by the partnership of several persons, or by machinery, or by any natural process, but in its very idea it proceeds, and must proceed, from some one given individual. Two persons cannot be the authors of the sounds which strike our ear; and, as they cannot be speaking one and the same speech, neither can they be writing one and the same lecture or discourse—which must certainly belong to some one person or other, and is the expression of that one person's ideas and feelings,—ideas and feelings personal to himself, though others may have parallel and similar ones,—proper to himself, in the same sense as his voice, his air, his countenance, his carriage, and his action, are personal. In other words, Literature expresses, not objective truth, as it is called, but subjective; not things, but thoughts.

. . . Literature is the personal use or exercise of language. That that is so, is further proved from the fact that one author uses it so differently from another. Language itself in its very origination would seem to be traceable to individuals. The peculiarities have given it its character. We are often able in fact to trace particular phrases or idioms to individuals; we know the history of their rise. Slang surely, as it is called, comes of, and breathes of the personal. The connection between the force of words in particular languages and the habits and sentiments of the nations speaking them, has often been pointed out. And, while the many use language, as they find it, the man of genius uses it indeed, but subjects it withal to his own purposes, and moulds it according to his own peculiarities. The throng and succession of ideas, thoughts, feelings, imaginations, aspirations, which pass within him, the abstractions, the juxtapositions, the comparisons, the discriminations, the conceptions, which are so original in him, his views of external things, his judgments upon life, manners, and history, the exercises of his wit, of his humour, of his depth, of his sagacity,—he images forth all these innumerable and incessant creations, the very pulsation and throbbing of his intellect,—he gives utterance to them all,—in a corresponding language, which is as multiform as this inward mental action itself and analogous to it, the faithful expression of his intense personality, attending on his own inward world of thought as its very shadow: so that we might as well say that one man's shadow is another's, as that the style of a really gifted mind can belong to any but himself. It follows him about *as* a shadow. His thought and feeling are personal, and so his language is personal.[34]

Constantly exemplifying this theme, Newman is among the most fascinating writers of English. If the declared aim of his use of English was clarity, the result is not colourless transparency. Art is supposed either to hide or show itself, but there are countless degrees of the concealment and exhibition. The art of Newman's writing is never wholly hidden. It comes near to being so in the 'plain' and 'parochial' sermons, where, as I have said, it was designed to receive the added arts of the voice and general presence of the preacher. Elsewhere in his writings the art is usually less concealed. In the Tracts it is sometimes noticeably abrupt, and deliberately so—Thomas Mozley said that among the Tractarians only Newman 'could write a tract', giving as explanation that only he had read enough of them himself.[35] But, just as the variety of his art is obvious, so, by and large, it is triumphant. And, in accordance with that Newmanian law, he tells us how he made it so. I have already quoted the material evidence of his care and given some of his own accounts of his corrections. The thing written was expression achieved, imperfect at first and then more perfect. What guiding principle was at work is suggested in Newman's definition—one of the best we have—of style, which he called 'a thinking out into language',[36] a process that was almost palpable for him: 'Besides re-writing, every part has to be worked out and defined as in moulding a statue.'[37] As usual, Newman speaks his difficult matter so clearly because his experience of it has been his own, and being that, has been of extreme vividness.

5

In consequence of all this, the case for regarding Newman as supremely literary as well as supremely 'ecclesiastical' is inescapable. One of the points I wish to make is that Newman is always literary, even, all things considered, when he is most narrowly ecclesiastical. How well he caught himself—all the more truly because from an unusual angle—in a letter of 1850:

> You must undeceive Miss A. B. about me, though I suppose she uses words in a general sense. I have nothing of a saint about me as every one knows, and it is a severe (and salutary) mortification to be thought next door to one. I may have a high view of many things, but it is the consequence of education and a peculiar cast of intellect—but this is very different from *being* what I admire. I have no tendency to be a saint—it is a sad thing to say so. Saints are not literary men, they do not love the classics, they do not write Tales.[38]

In quoting that I feel compunction at taking him when, comparatively, he is off his guard. So strongly does he recoil from the ascribed saintliness that he opposes to it the most secular self-description, imputing to himself the literary ethos he had said he was 'hard-hearted' against. Offered as proof of his weakness, the description is of strength in a different department. And with it goes a remark, which again one feels some compunction in overhearing—it occurs late in those sincerest of sincere documents, the letters he sent to Keble during the long period of his secession: 'My great fault is doing things in a mere literary way from the love of the work, without the thought of God's glory.'[39] It happens that under obedience to chronology Wilfrid Ward passes directly from the letter repudiating saintliness to the *Lectures on Certain Difficulties felt by Anglicans,* with which, after some hesitation, Newman met the occasion of the Gorham judgment.[40] Merely as a matter of course he describes the lectures as 'brilliantly witty'. Yes, they are accurately that, and the ease with which he can be brilliantly witty seals him of the tribe of the Henry Jameses and Oscar Wildes as certainly as the capacity to write on ecclesiastical matters seals him of the tribe of the Puseys and W. G. Wards. And he had other gifts as literary, like that which made George Eliot find *The Present Position of Catholics* 'full of clever satire and description',[41] or like that which made Pater praise his *Idea of a University* as showing 'the perfect handling of a theory'.[42]

Notes

[1] As originally printed the sentence ran ' . . . who have not read *The Idea of a University*', but the guess there made has proved to be badly out. Even though the idea of a university has been much in the air of recent years, I have not seen the book much referred to. My present guess is made on p. 272 below, where I say more vaguely that Newman's writings 'speak, and will go on doing so, to the cultivated'. Evidently they do not speak to all the cultivated. When reviewing the selection which my essay introduced Mr Raymond Mortimer contested the truth of my original guess. He thought that if I enquired of my Birkbeck colleagues I should find among them few readers of *The Idea.* For forty years I have been mistaking the implications of what I read as a boy in the excellent pages of Quiller-Couch: in ch. ii of his *Art of Writing* he recommended *The Idea* so warmly to his Cambridge audience that I assumed that his recommendation had been taken by the tens of thousands, Cambridge men and others, who admired his criticism as I did (and still do). Quiller-Couch was wrong in thinking that the lectures that made up *The Idea* are 'fragmentary'. They were designed as a conspectus of knowledge. Most of the 'cultivated' who read them to-day have to make allowances. They find Newman's calm assumption that theology can be shown to be the queen of the sciences a delusion. For most of the cultivated theology is only admissible, if at all, as a part of philosophy, and then mainly because of its historical interest. They see how wrong is the notion that a university exists to teach rather than to teach and research—they will prefer to require university teachers to research so that their research can improve their teaching both in accuracy and brightness. Quiller-Couch was recommending the book for reasons other than the soundness of its schemes of thinking, and those reasons still hold good. To put it briefly, the book is a pleasure to read because of the way it is written and because of its brilliant fragments of truth, whether you are a Catholic or an atheist, a scientist or a humanist, a Russian or an Englishman.

[2] *Coleridge's Miscellaneous Criticism,* ed. T. M. Raysor, 1936, p. 244.

[3] Contributed to *John Henry Newman: Centenary Essays,* 1945, pp. 223-41.

[4] Quoted by Tristram, op. cit., p. 224.

[5] Wilfrid Ward, *The Life of John Henry Cardinal Newman based on his Private Journals and Correspondence,* 1912, ii, 400.

[6] Augustine Birrell, *Frederick Locker-Lampson,* 1920, p. 109.

[7] *Letters,* i, 19.

[8] *Letters,* i, 25. See also the letter to John Hayes, 13 April 1869, reprinted in *Newman: Prose and Poetry,* Reynard Library, 1957, pp. 802 f.

[9] op. cit., pp. 223 f.

[10] *Letters,* ii, 250.

[11] Ward's *Life,* i, 637 f.

[12] Cf. the letter written after the success of the lectures in the University at Dublin: 'I have been prospered here in my lectures beyond my most sanguine expectations . . . my good Lord has never left

me, nor failed me in my whole life' (Fr McGrath, *Newman's University,* 1951, p. 161).

[13] Cf. Charles Reding in *Loss and Gain,* Reynard Library *Newman,* p. 321: 'I know persons . . . who believe that handwriting is an indication of calling and character.'

[14] *Defence of Poetry,* para. 10 from the end.

[15] *Recollections of the Last Days of Shelley and Byron,* ed. E. Dowden, 1923, p. 50.

[16] Preface to *Works* 1717, para. 6.

[17] Ward's *Life,* i, 191.

[18] I quote the passage below, p. 262.

[19] See Reynard Library *Newman,* p. 101.

[20] See id., p. 581 [Ward's edn., p. 108].

[21] Thackeray, *The Newcomes,* ch. iii.

[22] See Reynard Library *Newman,* pp. 559 f.

[23] See Reynard Library *Newman,* p. 363.

[24] See id., pp. 321 f.; cf. the bullet-tips, p. 251, above.

[25] Ward's *Life,* i, 115. For Newman's editing of this passage see below, p. 272.

[26] id., i, 117.

[27] *Apologia,* Ward's edn., pp. 393 f.

[28] Ward's *Life,* i, 581.

[29] Cf. Leslie Stephen's masterly review of the *Essay in Aid of a Grammar of Assent,* collected in *An Agnostic's Apology,* 1893, pp. 205 ff.

[30] See the letter of 1878 from Mark Pattison to Newman, quoted in my *Criticism and the Nineteenth Century,* 1951, p. 200; and A. N. Whitehead's *Adventures of Ideas,* 1933, p. vii, which records a debt to Gibbon's *Decline and Fall* and Newman's *Essay on Development* et al., for his 'general way of looking at [his] historical topic'.

[31] *Quarterly Review,* lxxvii (1845-6), p. 405.

[32] See Reynard Library *Newman,* p. 704.

[33] In the lecture 'Literature' in *Lectures and Essays on University Subjects,* 1859, p. 50.

[34] *Lectures and Essays on University Subjects,* 1859, pp. 35 ff.

[35] *Reminiscences chiefly of Oriel College and the Oxford Movement,* 1882, i, 312.

[36] In the lecture 'Literature' in *Lectures and Essays on University Subjects,* 1859, p. 41.

[37] *Correspondence of John Henry Newman with John Keble and Others 1839-45,* p. 382.

[38] Ward's *Life,* i, 229 f.

[39] *Correspondence,* p. 245.

[40] Namely, to use Ward's concise words, the 'celebrated decision of the Privy Council . . . overruling the refusal of the Bishop of Exeter (confirmed by the Court of Arches) to institute Mr. G. C. Gorham to the vicarage of Brampford Speke on the ground that he denied the doctrine of baptismal regeneration' (i, 230).

[41] *George Eliot Letters,* i, 372. Another letter records the stages of her interest in the *Apologia:* 'I have been reading Newman's *Apologia pro Vita Suâ,* with such absorbing interest that I found it impossible to forsake the book until I had finished it. I don't know whether the affair between him and Kingsley has interested you, or whether you have shared at all my view of it. I have been made so indignant by Kingsley's mixture of arrogance, coarse impertinence and unscrupulousness with real intellectual *in*competence, that my first interest in Newman's answer arose from a wish to see what I consider thoroughly vicious writing thoroughly castigated. But the Apology now mainly affects me as the revelation of a life—how different in form from one's own, yet with how close a fellowship in its needs and burthens—I mean spiritual needs and burthens' (iv, 158 f.). Another letter remarks that the *Apologia* has 'breathed much life into her', and that she 'would like to make an expedition to Birmingham for [the] sole end' of 'seeing and hearing Newman' (iv, 160).

[42] *Appreciations,* 1889, p. 14. Father McGrath argues against the unqualified acceptance of this praise, op. cit., p. 292. In 1852 at least Newman was greatly pleased with the work in its first printed form (see Reynard Library *Newman,* p. 354).

Owen Chadwick (essay date 1990)

SOURCE: "'Lead, Kindly Light'," in *The Spirit of The Oxford Movement: Tractarian Essays,* edited by Richard Fisher, Cambridge University Press, 1990, pp. 86-98.

[*In the following essay, Chadwick evaluates Newman's devotional poetry, in its reflection of the theological principles of the Oxford Movement.*]

THE PILLAR OF THE CLOUD.

LEAD, kindly light, amid the encircling gloom
Lead Thou me on!
The night is dark, and I am far from home—
Lead Thou me on!
Keep Thou my feet; I do not ask to see
The distant scene—one step enough for me.

I was not ever thus, nor pray'd that Thou
Shouldst lead me on.
I loved to choose and see my path, but now
Lead Thou me on!
I loved the garish day, and, spite of fears,
Pride ruled my will: remember not past years.

So long Thy power hath blest me, sure it still
Will lead me on,
O'er moor and fen, o'er crag and torrent, till
The night is gone;
And with the morn those angel faces smile
Which I have loved long since, and lost awhile.

At Sea, June 16, 1833

Afterwards a title was given to the poem or hymn: 'The Pillar of the Cloud'. Newman first gave it, perhaps more as a text or motto than a title, when he reprinted the poem in *Occasional Verses* (1868). It is a very inappropriate title. A pillar of cloud led the Israelites by day, a pillar of fire by night. The author of the hymn is in dusk. The original had no title but 'Faith'. The first table of contents described it correctly as 'Light in Darkness'. That table of contents placed it under the general heading of 'Faith'.

Newman had written verse from time to time since 1819. At the end of 1832 he began to write systematically. When in December 1832 he set off with the two Froudes for the Mediterranean, the leisure and the absence of books allowed him to try his hand at verses almost regularly; sometimes day after day. He already had a purpose beyond the expression of a poetic instinct. In that November he suggested to the editor of the *British Magazine,* Hugh James Rose, that he should print a series, under the name *Lyra apostolica.* The object would be to assert truths 'with greater freedom, and clearness, than in the *Christian Year*' of John Keble. He told his friend Rogers (1 December 1832) that stirring times bring out poets, and that he hoped by this poetry to create 'a quasi-political engine'.

By the time he got back to England he had quite a collection. It was enough to feed the *British Magazine* with verse till the end of 1836, with the help of friends, especially Keble. In the collected edition of *Lyra apostolica* there are 179 poems; 109 are by Newman and 46 by Keble. It was almost entirely a Newman-Keble collection, and Newman predominated.

In Rome, March 1833, he talked with Froude of the verses as having a purpose. To his friend Rogers he justified the time spent on versification: 'Ten thousand obvious ideas become impressive when put into metrical shape; and many of them we should not dare to utter except metrically, for thus the responsibility is (as it were) shoved off of oneself and one speaks *hos paidizon* (as if playfully), though serious. I am so convinced of the use of it, particularly in time of excitement, that I have begun to practise myself, which I never did before.' To his sister he called the verses 'my follies' (*The Letters and Diaries of John Henry Newman,* edited at the Birmingham Oratory, 3/236 and 132ff.—hereafter *LD*).

After being near death from fever in Sicily, he set off for England again from Palcrmo in June 1833. He sailed in an orange boat on 13 June. The *Apologia* does not quite say, but has been commonly understood as saying, that 'Lead, Kindly Light' was written as the ship lay becalmed in the straits of Bonifacio between Sardinia and Corsica. Newman's diary shows that he must have written it while the ship was becalmed before it entered the straits. For the poem is dated 16 June. The diary shows that they came in sight of Sardinia on 17 June and were through the straits on 22 June. A letter to Capes of August 1850 described it as written 'in the sun off Sardinia' and mentioned the cool translucent lazy wave. So the dusk of the poem was mental.

The editor of the *British Magazine* grew nervous of the political freedom of the verses which he was being asked to print as *Lyra apostolica.* This nervousness caused Newman further to express what he thought his verse intended to do. 'What is the *Lyra Apostolica* but a ballad? It was undertaken with a view of catching people when unguarded' (to Bowden, 17 November 1833, *LD,* 4/109: Bowden contributed six poems to *Lyra;* his muse was pedestrian; he was a very close friend of Newman). But when in 1836 Newman collected the verses in a single volume, the devotional idea predominated over the political, as was proved by the discussion over the format. Both Newman and the publisher wanted the volume to look like the *Christian Year* of Keble—same type, same size of page, same appearance. That is, they conceived it as a continuation of a devotional book, probably aimed at the same kind of reader (see *LD,* 5/334-5).

He continued to be very modest about his verse and intention. 'My object was *not* poetry but to bring out *ideas.* Thus my harshness, as you justly call it, (if nothing else) was part of a *theory.* I felt it absurd to set up for a poet' (to F. W. Faber, 1 February 1850, *LD,* 11/401).

Lyra apostolica came to three editions by 1838, and was evidently being used by a few hundred people as a devotional manual. Its authors were still anonymous, though now they were distinguished by Greek letters. Scott Holland would later call it 'the song book of English Catholicity, in its most militant and defiant mood' (in his introduction to the 1901 edition of *Lyra apostolica*).

Newman arranged that Samuel Wilberforce should review the book in the *British Critic*. This review appeared in the number for January 1837 (167ff.) and may have helped to make readers aware of the volume, but disappointed Newman. Wilberforce said that the disturbed times had led many members of the Church of England to study Catholic antiquity; and 'even as they have read, the spirit of poetry has come down upon them'. He said that the inspirations of *Lyra* had drawn from purer and holier fountains than those which nourished Methodist and Evangelical hymnody. He criticized the anonymous Newman for obscurity, and for something constrained and inharmonious. Miss Keble afterwards said to Isaac Williams, another contributor to *Lyra* (nine poems), as Williams recorded in his autobiography (written 1851, published 1893) that this criticism by Wilberforce was bad for Newman because it discouraged him from using his natural vein of poetry. We have no reason to think that Miss Keble knew much about Newman's feelings.

The Evangelical *Christian Observer* of 1837 (460ff.) reviewed *Lyra* as 'a chequered book'; with much sunlight and much shade; much admirable, much dangerous; the Church as primary, religion as subordinate. It talks of tradition, and the power of the priestly office, and prayers for the dead. The reviewer selected Delta (who was Newman) and said that he had more poetic tendency in his thought than poetic power. The reviewer said that the authors were ponderous and gloomy; that they trod the religious path painfully; and that every word was expressive of toil.

This was the first sign of what was to become the main attack upon 'Lead, Kindly Light'. It was sad. It had not the confidence of faith. It had not the sense of free grace. It was the soul struggling. The true Christian ought not to be in a world of gloom and twilight.

Earlier in life Newman wrote an essay on the nature of poetry (*Essays and Sketches,* 1 (1948), ed. C. F. Harrold, 55-82). Most of this meditation was nothing to do with the lyrics or semi-lyrics which he now attempted. But some of the phrases sound with an authentic ring—poetry 'provides a solace for the mind broken by the disappointments and sufferings of actual life; and becomes, moreover, the utterance of the inward emotions of a right moral feeling, seeking a purity and a truth which this world will not give'. 'With Christians, a poetical view of things is a duty—we are bid to colour all things with hues of faith, to see a divine meaning in every event . . . '

Some of the poetic influences can be discerned. Blake meant nothing, Byron nothing, Wordsworth (strangely) not a lot. Scott's poetry he loved, but it was of a different type from these lyrics. For this *lyra* we may think of three especial models in the general background of Newman's aesthetic sensibility: Crabbe, whom he often cited; Cowper, whom he knew well from his Evangelical days; and John Keble, for whom he felt at that time so profound an admiration. His own contributions to the *Lyra* have a truer vein of poetry than those which Keble contributed. In the 1901 edition of *Lyra* H. C. Beeching attributed the qualities of simplicity and directness partly to natural simplicity, partly to Newman's early study of Greek tragedy and its choruses; and Beeching was a sensitive and expert critic of English poetry.

The devotional poetry of *The Christian Year* by Keble began quickly to be incorporated into hymn books for the use of congregations. *Lyra apostolica,* though less used and less generally suitable, naturally came under similar consideration for use in hymnody. Surprisingly early someone saw, what Newman never dreamed of and for long afterwards refused to accept, that the three personal stanzas from the coast of Sardinia would make a singable hymn. As early as 1845 (!) Dr Horatius Bonar, a Scottish Presbyterian, put it into the *Bible Hymn Book.* So far as we yet know he did not bother to seek the permission of the author, whose name was still unknown to the public. And it is improbable that he sought any leave, because he altered the first line:

> Lead, Saviour, lead amid the encircling gloom.

And Dr Bonar was the first to realize that congregations would never have heard the word *garish* in the couplet

> I loved the garish day, and, spite of fears
> Pride ruled my will: remember not past years.

Congregations would not know the word, even though it came in Shakespeare's *Romeo and Juliet* and was the kind of word used by literary men when they were being literary. Dr Bonar changed it to

> I loved the glare of day,

which was not so good and did not have the nuance of the original. Dr Bonar's rewording was followed by a series of other attempts to cope with the word *garish.* (Julian traced several of these variants in his *Dictionary of Hymnology,* rev. edn (1907), 1/669.)

Here were two desires to amend the stanzas; first by making its beginning, and so its whole, more evidently

Christian, and therefore by putting Lord or Saviour where stood the kindly light; and secondly by getting rid of the unknown word. The Americans found particular difficulty. Henry Ward Beecher's *Plymouth Collection* (1855) began

> Send, kindly light.

In 1860 an American book of the Protestant Episcopal Church, *Hymns for Church and Home,* coped with these two 'difficulties' in its own way. It began:

> Send Lord thy light amid the encircling
> gloom.

And it did better than Dr Bonar with *garish,* though not perfectly:

> I loved day's dazzling light.

But the Americans had a new difficulty. All the poem was personal, but the last stanza was the most personal. They wanted to Christianize Newman's portrait of the soul trudging over the moors and mountains and marsh:

> So long thy power hath blest me, sure it still
> will lead me on
> O'er moor and fen, o'er crag and torrent, till
> The night is gone.

The American Episcopalians produced the lowest bathos ever perpetrated upon this private poem in the effort to make it a congregational hymn:

> So long thy power hath bless'd me, surely still
> 'T will lead me on
> Through dreary hours, through pain and
> sorrow, till
> The night is gone.

So far as is known, no one asked Newman's permission for any of this piracy.

However, by now the identity of the author was clear. In 1853 Newman, as Rector of the University of Dublin, collected his own verses, including those in the *Lyra apostolica,* and published them at Dublin as *Verses on Religious Subjects.*

Anglican hymn books in England at first rejected it as unsuitable. They may also have been influenced by the controversial repute of the author, who had left their Church amid much publicity. Even the first two editions of *Hymns Ancient and Modern* (1860 and 1861), which was intended to be the Tractarian hymn book, and which soon conquered the Church of England, did not contain it. And yet when Newman wrote his religious autobiography during the first months of 1864, he described the circumstances in which the poem was written, and said

> Then it was that I wrote the lines, *Lead kindly light,* which have since become well known.

If they were well known, they were not well known to everyone under that name, which so many books altered.

The Church hymn books objected to the poem because it could be sung by Unitarians. It was not theological enough for churchmen. The Unitarian *Hymns of the Spirit,* published that same year in Boston, Massachusetts, included 'Lead, Kindly Light', under that beginning; though the garish day was day's dazzling light and the moor and fen turned into dreary doubts. Hymn books, there was no doubt, could be a trial to a poet.

In 1870 one of the Evangelical collectors in the Church of England tried to remedy the situation.

Edward Henry Bickersteth was admired by many Victorians as a religious poet. In 1866 he published an epic poem, on the lines of Dante or Milton, describing a visit under guidance to the world of the spirits. It was entitled *Yesterday, Today and For Ever.* Princess Alexandra read parts of the poem to her husband the Prince of Wales in his near-mortal illness.

In 1870 Bickersteth published *The Hymnal Companion to the Book of Common Prayer,* which became the hymn book of the Evangelicals and more than the Evangelicals.

Naturally he wanted something more assured in faith than the stanzas which Newman wrote. He therefore added a fourth stanza:

> Meantime along the narrow rugged path
> Thyself hast trod
> Lead, Saviour, lead me home in childlike
> faith,
> Home to my God,
> To rest for ever after earthly strife
> In the calm light of everlasting life.

In the printing he added the stanza as though it was part of the same poem.

Four years later someone wrote to Newman to point out that a verse was added to his poem. On 17 June 1874 Newman wrote a humble letter to the publisher, Sampson Low and Co. ('I beg your pardon if this letter is grounded in any mistake'). He said that he did not doubt that he had given leave for the poem to be inserted into the collection, and readily, but an addition? 'It is not that the verse is not both in sentiment and in language graceful and good, but I think you will see at once how unwilling an author must be to subject himself to the inconvenience of that being ascribed to him which is not his own.'

The publishers passed this letter to Bickersteth, who explained to Newman that he had added a verse; that this verse was a great comfort in mortal illness to his daughter Alice Frances; and that he would add a note in the next edition to show that he had added a verse to Newman's poem. He told Newman that the verses as they stood did not make it a hymn, and therefore he added his verse; as if (he did not say this) he needed to Christianize Newman.

Newman's reply (20 June 1874) was a model of forbearance. He had every ground for severity.

> I agree with you that these verses are not a hymn, nor are they suitable for singing, and it is this which at once surprises and gratifies me, and makes me thankful that, in spite of their having no claim to be used as a hymn, they have made their way into so many collections.

He thanked the bishop for sending him a beautiful memoir of his daughter. Never did Newman write a kinder letter.

Three days later Bickersteth sent Newman a copy of his poem *Yesterday, Today and for Ever* (8th edn, 1873). Newman acknowledged it with thanks on 11 July. The poem had 435 pages, of which 140 were cut by Newman or one of the other fathers of the Oratory at Birmingham (*LD,* 27/80, 88).

For Newman it was all very inconvenient. From all over the country, even from America, correspondents wrote to ask him whether the fourth stanza was his. In 1878 Bickersteth published a new edition in which he showed that the fourth stanza was by a different author from the first three. He did not get rid of the stanza altogether till after a protest by one of Newman's colleagues and in the 1890 edition, when he relegated the extra stanza to an appendix. Newman's letters of denial to correspondents grew steadily stronger. In March 1881 he allowed the editor of another collection to print it, but only on condition that it was printed unaltered. 'No one likes interpolations in what he has written' (*LD,* 29/351). To Talbot, the Warden of Keble College, he wryly pointed out that this business of interpolation was a crime which Protestants usually attributed to Catholics. That month he assigned the copyright in *Lyra apostolica* to Keble College. Talbot (11 April 1881) undertook that so long as the copyright existed the poems must be printed as written (*LD,* 29/359).

In extenuation of those who amended his poem, Newman was always one for amending his own poems. He was a great tinkerer with his texts in second or third editions. In 1868 he introduced the doctrine of purgatory into the poem 'Rest' in *Lyra apostolica,* with devastating bathos. He wisely removed it six years later. But he never touched 'Lead, Kindly Light'; unless we count a playing, not for the better, with the title of the poem.

The poem, in its original form, was now in *Hymns Ancient and Modern,* the hymn book of high churchmen, and in a corrupt but more obviously Christian form in the hymn book of Evangelical churchmen. It began to be so well known that it was used devotionally at death-beds. When Queen Victoria's son the Duke of Albany was dying, the Queen quoted all the last stanza, though not quite correctly (*LD,* 30/387). Perhaps the Queen had met the stanza in one of its 'corrupt' forms. In 1876 came the first of several renderings into Latin. Soon there were several translations into Welsh. It was the favourite hymn of the Archbishop of Canterbury, A. C. Tait (P. T. Marsh, *The Victorian Church in Decline,* 3n).

In the original text the poem was not suitable for funerals. It was an act of faith by someone near the start of a journey. The three stanzas had none of the feeling of a Nunc Dimittis. Bickersteth's fourth stanza made the poem into a hymn perfect for use at funerals, a very strong act of faith in life after death. As an act of faith for funerals it caught people's sentiment all over England. It grew so familiar as a hymn at funerals that it continued to be used at funerals even after the fourth stanza was no longer added. The angel faces of the last couplet, understood in a particular way, were enough to keep people's love of it as a hymn of departing. There were those who felt the loss of Bickersteth's additional verse to be a religious loss (see *Notes and Queries* (1880), 1, 480).

In January 1884 Newman's friend R. H. Hutton, the editor of the *Spectator,* lectured to an audience of nearly 300 working men. When he referred to 'Lead, Kindly Light', there was a 'perfect thunder of applause' (*LD,* 30/294). The hymn had become national. Newman himself must have been one of the minority of Englishmen who never heard it sung (*Guardian* (1890), 1377). A majority of hymn books still omitted it as unsuitable. Some said it was too vague and weak a way to address God. But these books were not the popular editions.

In 1879-80 the hymn was so well known that public discussion arose over the meaning of the last lines:

> And with the morn those angel faces smile
> Which I have loved long since, and lost
> awhile.

When *Lyra apostolica* first appeared, William Greenhill went to Newman's friend and colleague Charles Marriott and asked what this meant. Marriott suggested that the couplet touched on the idea that infants have a more intimate communion with the unseen world; for Newman had talked of this sensitivity in the little child in one of his parochial sermons (*PS*, 2/ 63-5):

> There is in the infant soul in the first years of its regenerate state, a discernment of the unseen world in the things that are seen and realization of what is Soverign and Adorable . . . he has this one great gift, that he seems lately to have come from God's Presence.

But when in 1879 Newman was asked what the couplet meant, he refused to answer. He appealed to the doctrine of John Keble, that poets are not bound to give a sense to what they have written.

> There must be a statute of limitations for writers of verse, or it would be quite a tyranny if, in an art which is the expression not of truth, but of imagination and sentiment, one were obliged to be ready for examination on the transient states of mind which come upon one when homesick, or seasick, or in any other way sensitive or excited. (*LD*, 29.11)

With Newman's permission Greenhill sent to the *Guardian* this refusal to explain (printed 25 February 1880).

The wording of the refusal was remarkable. Somebody said that here for many years he had been valuing the verse as a true poetic expression of sincere religious feeling, and now the author tells him that it could be the mere result of depression caused by seasickness (see *Notes and Queries* (1880), 1, 232).

The refusal, and the wording of the refusal, left the field open to speculators. Was Newman running down his own poem because it was an Anglican poem and its author was not now an Anglican? Was this a man who now professed the doctrine of purgatory and must try to discredit non-Catholic words hardly compatible with a doctrine of purgatory (see *Notes and Queries* (1880), 2, 52)? Were the words to be suspect as the doubts of a man worrying whether to become a Roman Catholic? Did it make the poem suspect as a hymn, because it showed that its author had for the moment lost the qualities of faith and assurance? At Clevedon in Somerset they put their own interpretation into a stained glass window: an angel bears two babies to heaven, with Newman's couplet beneath, so that the meaning would be a hope in reunion with the departed. Other interpretations were profferred. Someone said *angel* in *angel faces* was only an adjective meaning good, and had nothing to do with angels. (Debate in *Notes and Queries* (3 April, 8 May, 12 June, 7 August, 1880), summarized Julian, 1/668). Though Newman refused to say, we must think Marriott's understanding to be correct.

We may take as an example of the objectors to 'Lead, Kindly Light' a booklet on *Our Church Hymnody* (1881) by the editor of the *Anglican Psalter Noted*, John Heywood. The words of hymns were becoming subjective, and too emotional. Such hymns dealt with the aspirations of a few individuals rather than the experience of Christians. Their use in a congregation therefore turns an act of devotion into a sham. 'Lead, Kindly Light' tells of a struggle which, it is to be hoped, few will have to undergo. Its proper use is by individuals, in particular circumstances of suffering. Used by a congregation, it becomes 'meaningless'.

As with all hymns a large part of the enchantment in congregational use was the tune. The tune came into the head of J. B. Dykes while he was walking in the Strand. When he got back to Durham he started writing it out, and published it in Barry's *Psalms and Hymns* (1867). Thence it was revised and taken into the appendix of the new edition of *Hymns Ancient and Modern* (1868). In 1886 two of the Oratorian fathers in Birmingham played over to Newman the tune by Dykes, which he had never heard before. 'He seemed rather surprised at its very quiet, hymn-like, quality' (E. Bellasis, *Cardinal Newman as Musician* (1892), 38).

The tune was the cause of as much argument as the words. During the time when the hymn was more usually the property of non-Anglicans, it was given various tunes, of which one survived into English hymn books, that by the Scot Charles Purday. Dykes's tune did not at first capture the field, though in 1874 he went to St Paul's Cathedral and heard it sung as the first hymn. It was abused as sentimental and even unworthy. People even talked of the 'licence' creeping into church music. Arthur Sullivan refused to have Dykes's tune for his *Church Hymns* of 1874 and composed his own, which has survived in some books. Robert Bridges could not bear Dykes's tune and composed his own for the *Yattendon Hymnal.* To this day some hymn books will only allow Dykes as an alternative tune.

But whether, as some said, the words were perfectly unsuitable to a mixed congregation, none of whom knew what they meant; or whether, as some said, the tune was sentimental and tasteless in the context, the union of Newman's words with Dykes's tune had captured the affection of the people of England.[1] For it had faith. That faith might be hesitant. But hesitant faith was what so many souls felt themselves to possess. When Newman was very ill during the year before he died, he asked the Oratorians that he might hear the hymn 'Eternal Years', a strong hymn by Faber on the assurance of hope and faith. They brought a harmonium to the passage between his two rooms. One father played, another sang, and a third knelt by his side saying words. Then Newman said:

> Some people have liked my Lead, kindly light, and it is the voice of one in darkness asking for help from our Lord. But this (Eternal Years) is quite different; this is one with full light rejoicing in suffering with our Lord, so that mine compares unfavourably with it. This is what those who like Lead, kindly light have got to come to - they have to learn it. (Bellasis, *Cardinal Newman as Musician,* 38)

Newman was wrong about himself and his hymn. It was the wrongness of his modesty. His poem had never been intended as a hymn, and to the end he thought it unsuitable as a hymn. He never regarded it as true poetry. Earlier critics said that it was sad. But when it was taken to the heart of the English people, it was found that a people's consciousness had more judgment than the critics.

Notes

[1] Two exegetical commentaries on the hymn were published: J. S. Zelie, *The Book of the Kindly Light* (1910); Isaac Hartill, *Lead, Kindly Light: an Exposition* (1925). See also A. H. Jenkins, 'The Meaning of the Lyra Apostolica and the Genesis of "Lead, Kindly Light" ', in *International Cardinal-Newman Studies,* XII (1988), 117ff.; and Gordon Wakefield, *Kindly Light* (1984).

Peter Nockles (essay date 1991)

SOURCE: "Oxford, Tract 90 and the Bishops," in *John Henry Newman: Reason, Rhetoric and Romanticism*, edited by David Nicholls and Fergus Kerr, OP, The Bristol Press, 1991, pp. 28-87.

[*In the essay that follows, Nockles discusses the Anglican response to the publication of Newman's* Tract 90, *which marked a crucial episode in Newman's conversion to Catholicism and in the popular attitude toward Tractarianism.*]

For many, the claim of John Henry Newman to fame and greatness rests on that period of his Anglican career when he was the acknowledged inspiration and leader of a well-known High Church revival of religious life and thought within the Church of England which emanated from within the University of Oxford during the period 1833 to 1845. This revival was known, due to its place of origin, as the Oxford Movement, or Tractarianism after the series called 'Tracts for the Times' which the Movement's leaders, Keble, Froude and Pusey as well as Newman, produced as a medium for the dissemination of its teaching and influence. It was a movement which was to leave an indelible mark on the faith and practice of the Church of England. Although he was to secede to the Church of Rome in 1845, Newman's role in the profound impact of the Oxford Movement on the Church of England was crucial. Any reconsideration or reappraisal of Newman cannot afford to overlook this vital portion of his life when for at least twelve years he was virtually centre-stage in the history of the Church of England, and when the history of Oxford University almost becomes his own personal religious history. Above all, such a reappraisal cannot avoid focusing on the climactic episode in the history of the Oxford Movement and Newman's Anglican career—the controversy surrounding his notorious Tract 90, the last in the series 'Tracts for the Times'. The impact of Tract 90 can scarcely be over-estimated. According to a contemporary observer, 'with perhaps, the exception of Burke's *Reflections on the Revolution in France,* no pamphlet ever created a sensation so wide, so deep, so enduring'.[1] In fact, within a fortnight of its publication in January 1841, 2,500 copies of Tract 90 had been sold.[2] London as well as Oxford was stirred up, and the newspapers were full of the ensuing row. Clearly, there are good grounds for a consideration of Tract 90 as a key element in any re-evaluation of Newman's thought, his personality and his place in religious history.

The wider story of Newman and Oxford has been often told, and little more than an outline as a necessary background to understanding the Tract 90 controversy and what Newman was striving to achieve, need be repeated here. Yet, something of a reconsideration is necessary, precisely because of the distorting lens that has been provided by an almost inevitable concentration on the Oxford Movement as viewed through Newman's eyes. One reason for the pervasiveness and influence of the Newmanite perspective is easy to discern. A rich and fertile quarry for historians has been provided by that magnificent personal literary record of his religious odyssey, which Newman has left posterity, in his *Apologia pro Vita Sua,* first published in 1864. The result has been that an historiography has grown up, that focuses almost exclusively on Newman, with lesser attention devoted to other Tractarian leaders. The Movement has come to be viewed through Newman's eyes, its opponents judged from his point of view. For instance, Newman has been allowed to set the very dates of both the dawn and apparent conclusion of the Oxford Movement—the Assize Sermon by Keble on 14 July 1833,[3] and the condemnation of W.G. Ward by the Oxford Heads of Houses in February 1845, respectively. In fact, a good case can be made out for predating the origin of the Movement back to 1829 with the University's rejection of Sir Robert Peel as its MP in protest at Catholic Emancipation.[4] At the same time, the fact that Newman was removed effectively from any further direct part in the Tractarian controversy in 1845 is not sufficient ground for considering that that in itself marked the end of the Oxford Movement.

In a real sense then, it seems that our historical understanding of the Oxford Movement has come to be coloured and shaped by the personal drama of Newman's peculiar religious odyssey. It has been essentially as a landmark in the unfolding of this religious journey that the merits of Tract 90 and the official Anglican reaction to it have been viewed and judged. The result has been the gradual emergence of a distinctive historiography of the Movement in many ways moulded by Newman's immediate followers such as Dean Church, the author of a classic and highly influential historical account. In this historiography, the official negative reaction to Tract 90 has pride of place as the cathartic, bitter experience that broke Newman's supposedly meek spirit and made his position in the Church of England intolerable. Newman and those of his followers who seceded with him to the Church of Rome, were portrayed as innocent victims of an 'anti-Catholic' vendetta or persecution, led by Anglican bishops, whom we are informed, should have known better. As Church put it, the authorities 'treated as absurd, mischievous, and at length traitorous, an effort, than which nothing could be more sincere'.[5] Yet, there is another side to this story which must be examined. Some have recently begun to question various aspects of the account given by Newman in the *Apologia*. Attention has been drawn to what has been called Newman's 'subjectivism' in his portrayal of his dealings with the Anglican authorities.[6] However, there is now room for a wider revision of some long accepted viewpoints.

In his famous *Lectures on Anglican Difficulties* published in 1850, Newman was to argue that the whole direction of the Oxford Movement ever since its formal inauguration in 1833 had always inevitably pointed in the direction of the Church of Rome.[7] Thus, the ultimate submission of Newman and some of his followers to Rome in 1845 and subsequent years, could plausibly be presented as the Movement's true and fitting fulfilment. Yet, as Christopher Dawson once argued, this view was not shared by any other leader of the Movement, with the possible exception of Hurrell Froude,[8] whose early death in 1836 makes what might have been his final outlook a matter for mere conjecture. Pusey and Keble certainly did not view the destiny of the Oxford Movement in these terms, still less that large, amorphous mass of Anglican High Churchmen who rallied to the Movement in 1833 and retained varying degrees of sympathy with it for a number of years. For these, so-called 'old High Churchmen', not only Newman's eventual secession, but the twists and turns of the Oxford Movement under his leadership from 1838 onwards and certainly after Tract 90, would be tantamount to a betrayal of what they conceived to have been the original principles of 1833. For such early supporters of the Movement, these principles were none other than those traditional High Church Anglican principles which the Church of England had never ceased to uphold, albeit at times haltingly and ambivalently. These principles had flourished in the seventeenth century. They had been expressed in the writings of the Caroline Divines and early Nonjurors. Moreover, contrary to the view of many historians, and not least the Tractarians themselves, these same principles had continued to be upheld by numerous eighteenth- and early nineteenth-century Churchmen, variously described and classified as old High Church or Orthodox.[9]

Of course, when the Oxford Movement commenced, Newman along with Keble and then Pusey, insisted that they intended but to restate and follow out these traditional Anglican High Church principles. Yet, change and flux were always latent in Newman's approach. Behind the façade of the initial apparent unanimity among conservative Churchmen in 1833 against the perceived liberal threat posed by Whig expropriation of Church property and Erastian interference in matters spiritual, there lay concealed intrinsic inner differences that time would widen and expose. Any definition of the Oxford Movement must take into account the fact that it was not a static phenomenon, but rather, one which developed and underwent modifications in response to the flux of ideas and changing circumstances. The party of 1845 was manifestly not the party of 1833. There was to be a definite evolution of theological principles. In this evolution, Tract 90 was indeed to prove a landmark.

The Oxford Movement increasingly was to diverge, especially from 1841 and Tract 90 onwards, from the classic High Anglican tradition to which the University of Oxford had remained broadly loyal since the seventeenth century. Of course, a theological consensus was provided by a common belief in such doctrines as the Apostolical Succession, Baptismal Regeneration and the Eucharistic Sacrifice. However, on questions as fundamental as the rule of faith, the merits of the Reformation and attitude to the Church of Rome, and the relationship between Church and State, the Tractarians would come to differ markedly from the bulk of High Churchmen who at first tended to support the Movement but who eventually, albeit often reluctantly, came to express their unease and disagreement. An awareness of this divergence is vital for a true understanding of the history of the Oxford Movement and its relationship to the older High Church traditions in the Church of England, as I have made clear elsewhere.[10] Moreover, it is a conclusion supported by some recent scholarship. For my view that the Tractarians came to challenge, then shatter, the doctrinal consensus of earlier High Church Anglicanism, seeming to dis-

Cardinal John Henry Newman (1801-1890)

solve the Church of England into its constituent parts as never before, has been corroborated by the recent work of Paul Avis.[11] It is then in the historical context of the revolutionary potential and impetus of the Oxford Movement and of its breach as well as elements of continuity with pre-Tractarian *High* Churchmanship, that Newman's Tract 90 and the response elicited to it, needs to be set.

For a period, it was simply the need for all conservative forces in Church and State to unite in the face of what then seemed like a common enemy, that helps explain the wide early appeal of the Movement at Oxford.[12] Clearly, the times were ripe for the message of the early numbers of the 'Tracts for the Times'. In a period of apparent danger to the Church, the unfettered but simple High Church message they conveyed struck a chord with many who would soon be disillusioned when the immediate external danger to the Church relaxed and ebbed away. Moreover, many High Churchmen would continue to sympathise with, if not support, the Movement, out of what was to prove to be a quite mistaken notion of its essentially conservative tendency. An example of this type of support was represented by that important group which in 1833 actually formed one wing of the original Movement and which formed an association in defence of the Church. Signatures were collected, the Archbishop of Canterbury and the King were petitioned. Stalwarts of this group included such learned but lesser known Oxford figures as William Palmer of Worcester College, Charles Ogilvie of Balliol College and Vaughan Thomas of Corpus Christi College. In Hurrell Froude's idiosyncratic parlance, Churchmen such as Palmer, for all their detestation of liberalism and dissent and for all their rigid High Churchmanship, were nonetheless what he called 'Z's'.[13] By the epithet 'Z', Froude referred to a conservative, protestant High Churchmanship, which he sharply distinguished from Tractarianism. For the Tractarians proper, Froude claimed the title of 'Apostolicals' and the code label, 'Y's'. This, in turn, marked them out from the 'X's' represented by 'ultra-Protestants' or Evangelicals. A follower and later annalist of the Oxford Movement, William Copeland, rightly argued that it was 'extremely important to keep the Movement, which was from within, as clear as possible from the external circumstances, with which it came into contact'. As Copeland pointed out, 'Froude certainly had as much dreaded the calm of the church, as Palmer was frightened at the storm raised against it.'[14] Almost from the start, Palmer was nervous about the publication of the Tracts as potentially prejudicial to the Movement's acceptance, and he repeatedly advised caution and recommended a committee of revision to avoid 'unguarded expressions'.[15] In their turn, Newman, Froude and Keble grew increasingly impatient with Palmer's cautious line. Froude counselled that the Tractarians should 'throw the 'Z's' overboard'.[16]

Newman and his followers certainly were happy to avail themselves of the tacit support of the 'Z's' in the early phase of the Movement. In particular, they owed much to the moral support of one 'Z' who went further than many in collaboration, Hugh James Rose. Yet, even Rose was suspected of being a 'mere conservative' at heart, by Froude. Froude kept up pressure on Newman to maintain his distance, and to set the Movement on a more dynamic course. Froude succeeded. The always uneasy coalition between the two elements in the original Movement was doomed to break down, with differences becoming ever more apparent. These differences were as much psychological as theological. They consisted in what Newman described as 'the principle of personality'. For Newman, 'Z's' such as Palmer lacked,

> any insight into the force of personal influence and congeniality of thought in carrying out a religious theory, a condition which Froude and I considered essential to any true success in the stand which had to be made against liberalism.[17]

Significantly, Newman considered that Palmer had too many establishment connections among 'high church dignitaries, archdeacons, London rectors, and the like'.[18] In contrast, the Tractarians prided themselves on their relative freedom from ties of high office in the Church that might have inhibited their room for manoeuvre. In Oxford itself, the Tractarians tended to represent the grass-roots feelings of younger members of the University as opposed to 'men of rank and station'. Part of their moral strength and religious influence derived from their sense of detachment from the University of the seniors as represented by that close-knit but aloof oligarchy, the Heads of Houses. The dealings of the Tractarian leaders with the Heads confirmed them in their wariness of committees of what Newman disparagingly called 'sound, safe men'. Of the utmost significance in this context, was Newman's later avowal in the *Apologia,* that 'deliverance is wrought not by the many, but by the few, not by bodies but by persons'.[19] In fact, Newman insisted on the intensely personal medium of much of the Movement's growing influence among the junior ranks of the University in the years after 1833. Although no longer himself a tutor at Oriel after 1830, Newman rightly stressed the extent to which the spread of ideas and principles was fostered through the agency of the pedagogical relationship between college tutor and pupil as personalised by himself and his followers.[20]

It was these factors of temperament, ethos and circumstance, that help explain the almost total want of fixedness in the Movement. It was a lack of direction which Newman readily admitted and was almost proud of. As he later put it, 'I was not the person to take the lead of a party; I never was, from first to last, more than a leading member of a school'.[21] Even more candidly, he later confessed that 'the Movement, viewed with relation to myself, was but a floating opinion; it was not a power. It never would have been a power, if it had remained in my hands'. He freely applied to himself what was said by St Gregory Nazianzen, 'I could'st a people raise, but could not rule'.[22] Yet there was an attempt here to evade responsibility, and something akin to false modesty. The Movement was a power because of Newman's advocacy. He may not have sought leadership but it was thrust upon him. Followers hung on his every word, even imitating his very gait and gestures. 'Credo in Newmannum' was to become the watchword of a whole generation of undergraduates and younger MAs.[23] Newman could not have been altogether unconscious of the immense power which he exercised through personal friendship and discipleship, moral example and, above all, through the spiritual impact of his preaching in St Mary's.[24] At times, he acted in a way that showed that he was conscious of this power and force to mould and influence. What the younger members of the University who were vulnerable to Newman's spell required was guidance and direction. In his sermons, he certainly inculcated the ideal of holiness but the limits and parameters of Anglican teaching Newman seemed almost constitutionally incapable of providing.

Traditional High Churchmen knew where they stood. However, their essentially static theological position not unnaturally had less appeal to the younger Oxford generation than the more inspirational vision of catholicity provided by Newman. Yet, at the same time they were drawn down a path to which there was no obvious end or object in view. Moreover, High Churchmen and others on whose support the Movement relied in the early stages, were provoked rather than always conciliated or put at ease. Much blame can be laid on Newman here. His behaviour seemed designed to narrow rather than broaden the confines of support and would ultimately confer an essentially 'party', extraneous and sectarian character on the Oxford Movement. As Newman later candidly admitted,

> it came to pass at that time, that there was a double aspect in my bearing towards others . . . My behaviour had a mixture in it both of fierceness and of sport; and on this account, I dare say, it gave offence to many; nor am I here defending it.

Newman enlarged further on what he meant, admitting that,

> I was not unwilling to draw an opponent on step by step to the brink of some intellectual absurdity, and to leave him to get back as he could. I was not unwilling to play with a man, who asked me impertinent questions. I was reckless of the gossip which was circulated about me; and, when I might easily have set it right, did not deign to do so. Also I used irony in conversation, when matter-of-fact men would not see what I meant . . . This kind of behaviour was a sort of habit with me.[25]

It would seem that friends and early supporters such as the 'Z' Palmer of Worcester were almost as much victims of this 'fierce' behaviour as open opponents such as the editor of the evangelical *Christian Observer* and the 'high and dry' Margaret Professor of Divinity, Godfrey Faussett.[26] A later, albeit hostile reviewer of Newman's *Apologia* was not altogether unfair in suggesting that in such behaviour there was perhaps more 'of the "knowledge" that "puffeth up" than of the "charity" which "edifieth" '.[27]

Newman's almost arrogant self-confidence in his mature Anglican years perhaps inevitably came to blight his judgment. Again, in the *Apologia* many years later, Newman was prepared to admit almost as much. As he then explained,

> This absolute confidence in my cause, which led me to the imprudence or wantonness which I have been instancing, also laid me open, not unfairly, to the opposite charge of fierceness in certain steps which I took, or words which I published.[28]

Newman had in mind instances of extravagant and highly coloured language as in *Lyra Apostolica,* when he maintained that before learning to love, we must 'learn to hate'.[29] However, one of the more glaring instances of seemingly misguided steps that he took as a consequence of this self-confidence, was one which he never admitted to having been rash or mistaken. This was the decision to publish the *Remains* of Richard Hurrell Froude in 1838.

The controversial publication of Froude's *Remains* represented a landmark and turning-point in the history of the Oxford Movement. The publication provoked bitter reaction, and exposed latent, hither-to largely hidden differences between the traditional High Churchmen and Tractarians. Prior to this, there had existed a degree of outward unison between Tractarians, traditional High Churchmen and many conservative Evangelicals, exemplified by the triple alliance forged at Oxford in February 1836 to protest against the Whig government's appointment of the allegedly heterodox, Renn Dickson Hampden to the Regius Professorship of Divinity. The publication of Froude's *Remains* dashed this tentative alliance apart, and brought into the open the first rumblings of official disapproval of the Movement. It was probably inevitable that the revelations of Froude's unguarded and sometimes immature railings against the English Reformers and Reformation, should have provoked widespread offence. Many High Churchmen no less than Evangelicals were outraged.[30] As editors of the *Remains,* Newman and Keble were responsible. Why had they allowed the publication of such controversial matter? It might have been thought that the storm raised would have made them realise that publication had proved a grave mistake. Yet, far from being apologetic or contrite over the furore and regretting the potential damage done to the progress of the Movement, Newman rejoiced in what he felt was the blow struck for Catholic principles by the publication. As Piers Brendon has aptly put it, Newman almost welcomed the hostile reaction from High Churchmen and Evangelicals, as conclusive proof of his 'theorem that wide unacceptability was the best test of truth'.[31] Yet, at the same time, Newman displayed inconsistency. For when Godfrey Faussett bitterly assailed the Tractarians on the basis of Froude's *Remains* from the pulpit of St Mary's in May 1838, Newman's reaction was fierce and indignant. Newman responded with a lengthy point by point rebuttal of Faussett's critique and produced a theological apologia for the Movement.[32] Newman deliberately helped fuel the controversy, and gave Faussett a handle, for in his own reply, Faussett was able to cite a series of reputable High Church authorities apparently supportive of part of his argument.[33] In short, the waters had been muddied, and those old High Churchmen most sympathetic to the Movement were given reasons for distancing themselves. Newman had forfeited the moral high ground.

The apparent bravado that Newman had first evinced on the publication of the *Remains* was no less in contrast with his complete over-reaction to the first very mild episcopal hints from his diocesan, Bishop Bagot, that all was not right with the Movement. In his charge delivered in 1838 Bagot was highly laudatory of the Tractarian endeavour. This commendation was only slightly offset by the Bishop's suggestion that there might have been language used in some of the tracts that could be misconstrued and points raised that could benefit by clarification or correction.[34] The Bishop was quite clear that he found no fault of substance. However, Newman appeared to be quite thrown off guard. He was inclined to exaggerate the very modest degree of criticism that had been made. The contradiction in Newman's conduct was well delineated by Abbott. For as Abbott observed, at this time Newman wished,

> to use extreme language, which will, he knows, make many people call him a Papist; yet he is angry with the people who call him so. He trades on the chance that the silence of the Bishops may imply a sanction of his principles; yet he is irritated when they refuse to give him this tacit sanction.[35]

There was the same, somewhat disingenuous double aspect to Newman's response to the first expressions of disquiet by the Oxford Heads of Houses. Newman appeared to cultivate a certain ambiguity over the status and relation of the Movement to the University, designed to capitalise on the link when circumstances favoured, but to disavow it when it might prove disadvantageous.

Of course, Oxford University *qua* university was not formally responsible for the Oxford Movement, either in its achievements or failures. I have explored the exact nature and degree of the relationship elsewhere.[36] The sense of Tractarian detachment has been noted above, but alongside this attitude went a close identification with what Tractarians considered historic ethos as well as privileges of the University. The leaders of the Movement not only aimed to preserve this historic, traditional Oxford, but contrary to what its liberal critics may have thought, had a clear, definite vision and ideal of the University. In Dean Church's words, the University was 'the fulcrum from which the theological revival hoped to move the Church'.[37] The Tractarian orchestration of the campaigns against the admission of Dissenters, in defence of the traditional mode of subscription to Articles by all undergraduates as well as MAs, and against Hampden's appointment, in the mid-1830s, was motivated and infused by devotion to this ideal.

Yet, try as they might, the Tractarians had no claim or mandate to speak for the University as a whole. By the late 1830s, the Tractarians could claim no monopoly of moral or religious earnestness in the University. The latitudinarian Dr Arnold arguably had done as much as Newman to leaven the University with a higher moral and religious tone than existed for generations. Moreover, Newman's stress on the 'monastic' character of the collegiate system and call for a restoration of the 'spirit of our founders',[38] was not only highly unpalatable to the liberal reforming party at Oxford but presented potentially destabilising implications in the eyes of many High Churchmen who were content with the mere *status quo.* The bulk of the Oxford Heads inclined to the latter position, somewhat reluctantly following the Tractarian lead in the stand against admission of Dissenters and the appointment of Hampden, but fearful of the radical direction and implications of the Movement. It was inevitable that they should come to resent Newman's tendency to appear to speak on behalf of the University in some sort of official capacity. The rising external hostility to Tractarianism began to run off on the University as a whole, and parents began to prefer the sister university, Cambridge, as a safer haven for their sons.[39]

When questions began to be asked in Parliament identifying the whole University with what was said and done by the leaders of the Movement,[40] the Heads not unnaturally felt it was time to make a stand. The spectre of a parliamentary visitation of the University was already on the horizon. Newman, who was always emphasising the University aspect of the Movement was in no real position to complain, but complain he did. As Abbott declared, Newman,

> makes much of the name of the University and of the deference paid to Oxford, and of the consequent authority reflected on the 'Oxford' Tracts and 'Oxford' principles: and yet we shall find him aggrieved at an attempt on the part of the University authorities to dissipate this popular delusion.[41]

The attempt here alluded to was the formal judgment of the Oxford Heads in March 1841 condemning the 'modes of interpretation' of the Thirty-Nine Articles suggested in Tract 90, which followed the initial letter of protest to the editor of the Tract by four Senior Tutors. It was a protest which brought the controversy surrounding the Movement to a climactic head and crisis. It brought Newman face to face with the raw reality of the undercurrent of hostility to the Movement that had been smouldering since 1838. Tract 90 touched a nerve, and Newman was to pay for it.

The official protest as well as popular reaction to Tract 90 can only be fully appreciated against a background of the growing theological divergence of Newman from even the Movement's avowed original starting-point. Up until 1839, as he later confessed, Newman remained secure and confident in his Anglicanism. Yet, even in the *via media* phase of Newman's religious history, one can sense that Newman's concept of Anglicanism was nebulous and somewhat theoretical. Much to his friend Rose's chagrin, Newman insisted on arguing in his classic treatise, the *Prophetical Office of the Church* published in 1837, that Anglicanism had never, even in the seventeenth century, been fully 'realised'.[42] At the same time, Newman did honestly throw himself into the spirit and writings of the great Anglican divines as well as the early Fathers.[43] In truth, it was not the case that his commitment to the ideal of Caroline Anglicanism, was always half-hearted, shallow or insincere, as some critics like Abbott maintained. Viewed in retrospect, Newman's *via media* phase seems but a temporary staging-post in his overall religious odyssey, but at the time it was held and propounded with a conviction, passion and 'fierceness' which could not have been excelled.

It is not then the genuineness of Newman's commitment to historic Anglicanism for a time that should be doubted, but the basis on which that commitment was erected and the manner in which it increasingly came to be expressed. Newman tried to erect a dogmatic edifice on a structure not designed to support it. The key perhaps to Newman's eventual loss of faith in High Anglicanism, lay in his misconceived desire to systematise and harmonise a body of divinity that was essentially unsystematic and varied, if not sometimes discordant. He conceived of the *via media* as but a 'paper theory', lacking in substance and only existing in outline. He sought to make it 'professed, acted on and maintained on a large sphere of action'. As Newman put it, 'we too have a vast inheritance, but no inventory of our treasures. All is given us in profusion; it remains for us to catalogue, sort, distribute, select, harmonise and complete'.[44] Yet, the dangers of such an approach were only too obvious to the Movement's critics and even erstwhile friends. As Abbott not unfairly deduced, in the *Prophetical Office,*

> substitute 'pick and choose' for 'discriminate and select', and we have Newman himself here gravely proposing that he and a group of Oxford friends of his should set up that which he regarded as an abomination of desolation, that portentous impiety called 'Private Judgment', by sitting in a Commission of Inquiry into the great Divines of the Anglican Church.[45]

In essence, Newman had an 'idea of catholicism', and was yet unsure whither it might lead. In contrast, the old High Churchmen were on no such voyage of discovery. As Rose cautioned Newman,

> We know exactly what the Truth is. We are going on no voyage of discovery. We know exactly the extent of the shore. There is a creek here, and a bay there,—all laid down in the charts; but not often entered or re-surveyed. We know all this beforehand, and therefore can lay down our plans, and not, (as I think), feel any uncertainty where we are going, or feel it necessary or advisable to spread our sails, and take our chance of finding a new Atlantis.[46]

Newman could never accept such limitations. He wanted the Church of England literally to represent the Church of antiquity in fullness of doctrine and devotion, ceremonial and ritual, if it were to compete with the Church of Rome on an equal basis. However, it can be said that Caroline divinity and the many different facets of the High Church tradition which Newman sought to blend, harmonise and complete, could never have fulfilled this expectation. Newman was seeking the impossible.

The somewhat tentative, albeit sincere, nature of Newman's advocacy of the *via media* arguably always rendered him vulnerable to external challenge. During the summer of 1839, eighteen months prior to Tract 90, Newman's faith in Anglican catholicity had been dealt its first blow and his first doubts were sown. Newman was unsettled by an article by Nicholas Wiseman in the Roman Catholic *Dublin Review* in which the Church of England's relation to the Church of Rome was likened to that of the Donatists with the early Catholic Church. As Newman put it in a well-known passage in the *Apologia,* with Wiseman's application of the words of St Augustine, 'securus judicat orbis terrarum', 'the theory of the *via media* was absolutely pulverised'.[47] Newman remained convinced of Anglicanism's conformity with antiquity, but the doubts raised about her catholicity were not easily shaken off. He continued to seek to prove the catholicity of Anglicanism, as in a famous article entitled 'The Catholicity of the English Church', in the *British Critic* in 1840, but he increasingly felt that the Thirty-Nine Articles were perceived at least by some of his younger followers as a major stumbling block. This question mark being raised over the Articles might seem ironic given the vigour of Newman's rebuttal of the liberal campaign to relax the terms of subscription at Oxford in the mid-1830s. However, it was the principle of subscription, and the apparent submission of intellect and reason to a test of doctrinal authority involved, on which the Tractarians had laid stress. As to the actual terms of the Articles themselves, Newman had confided as early as 1835, that he was 'no friend to them'.[48] Implicitly, he appeared to perceive the Articles as Protestant and a potential obstacle to the fuller development of Catholic views which he envisaged. Tract 90 was an attempt to come to terms with and overcome this apparent obstacle. Newman freely admitted that it represented an experiment, an 'experimentum crucis'.[49] The formulation of the Tract can be said to have been a consequence of the breakdown of his earlier confidence in Anglicanism. Without the doubts in 1839, it probably would never have been written.

In much of the historiography of the Movement, emphasis is laid upon the apparent unreasonableness and unfairness of the reaction to Tract 90, with the response of the Heads being particularly censured. Thus, according to Dean Church, the resolution of the Heads criticising the Tract, 'was an ungenerous and stupid blunder, such as men make, when they think or are told that "something must be done", and do not know what'.[50] Yet, the reality seems to show otherwise. The mood in Oxford was more favourable to the action of the Heads than the Tractarians assumed. As one Oxford resident put it, 'the general feeling is that some interference was absolutely required and that the Heads of Houses have done perfectly right in putting forth their protest'.[51] In fact, a policy of universal proscription against the Tractarians, as desired by zealots like C.P. Golightly, manifestly was eschewed by the University authorities. Indeed, there were some bitter complaints that the Heads had not acted sooner, and that their declaration of 15 March 1841 against Tract 90 had not been applied to the whole series of the *Tracts for the Times.*[52] Moreover, it can be argued that the action of the Heads in 1841 and the arguments by which they defended it, were precisely in accord with the type of exercise of the University authorities' religious function as enshrined in the statutes, which in any other circumstances, as when employed against Hampden in 1836, the Tractarians themselves would have welcomed. By the statutes, the authorities had a duty to ensure that the hitherto received meaning of subscription was adhered to, and to repudiate evasions or quibbles likely to unsettle, as Vice-Chancellor Philip Wynter put it, 'the minds of our younger members'.[53] Regardless of any theological errors, High Churchmen at Oxford who in the mid-1830s had defended the high religious theory of subscription alongside the Tractarians, now felt that the very ecclesiastical conception of the University which they both had upheld against liberals, was being undermined by Tract 90. It was on this ground that a High Churchman like Robert Scott, Fellow of Balliol, defended the course taken by the Heads. As Scott told his colleague A. C. Tait, one of the signatories of the Letter of the Four Tutors,

> There was undoubtedly a cause why the University, which exists on the condition of teaching—i.e. affixing a sense to—these Articles, should protest against their

> having a no-sense-at-all peremptorily fixed upon them. This publication struck a blow at the very mission of the University; and therefore the interference could never at another time have been so well timed.[54]

In short, if it really was the duty of tutors to instruct undergraduates in the Articles—and this all the pamphlets in defence of Oxford's system of subscription at matriculation in 1834-5, and not least those penned by Tractarians had taken for granted—then it could not be a matter for indifference to the Heads, in what sense those Articles were going to be subscribed and their meaning conveyed.

Much of the historiography of the Movement has also emphasised the apparent modesty of Newman's aim in Tract 90. This aim was explained as an attempt to show that while the *Prayer Book* was acknowledged as Catholic, the Articles though the 'offspring of an uncatholic age' were capable or 'patient' of a Catholic meaning.[55] At the same time, Newman's conduct is portrayed as meek and patient, and he is commended for the perfect simplicity and honesty with which he undertook his task.[56] Yet, the evidence suggests that Newman's task was rather more ambitious than is often assumed, while his approach and mode of treating opposition is somewhat less than open or simple. For in effect, in Tract 90, Newman was putting the Church of England on a trial of his own devising. Tract 90 may have been intended as a peace offering, but as Paul Avis has recently aptly put it, it was 'a peace offering to the Church of England—delivered with a slap in the face'.[57]

It was not so much the principle of Tract 90, the attempt to demonstrate the compatibility of the Thirty-Nine Articles with Catholic truths, however defined, that would most concern critics. After all, there were at least some historical precedents, albeit ill-fated, for such an exercise. One such precedent was that made by Christopher Davenport in 1634. Another was undertaken by a little known pre-Tractarian High Churchman, Samuel Wix in 1818.[58] What prompted the most disquiet was the execution of the Tract, and its reasoning. Newman's meaning was unclear. Ambiguity abounded. Newman claimed to be arguing that only what he called the 'dominant errors' or 'the actual popular beliefs and usages sanctioned by Rome in the countries in communion with it' rather than 'the Catholic teaching of early centuries' was condemned in the Articles.[59] However, Newman attempted to distinguish the so-called 'dominant errors' or popular abuses, from the formal dogmas of Rome as enshrined in the Council of Trent, and thus representing 'official' teaching. Newman insisted that some of these dogmas were condemned in the Articles, but that some were not. In general it was only the abuses and popular interpretations that were repudiated in the Articles. Here was rich ground for confusion and misunderstanding. The distinctions drawn between these categories, like the categories themselves, appeared to some to be as vague as they were arbitrary. Where was the clear principle for sifting the wheat of Catholic teaching from the chaff of 'dominant errors', critics asked? Such critics felt that there was an almost conscious and deliberate straining of hitherto accepted doctrinal limits, in the Tract. It is true that earlier in the century orthodox and evangelical Churchmen had disputed the meaning of certain Articles, notably Article 17 covering election and free will. Moreover, pleas for latitude in the interpretation of such disputed Articles had been made by High Churchmen since the days of Laud. What Newman was pleading for, was for something new, a latitude or elasticity in the interpretation of Articles that bore on the Church of Rome whose meaning and terms had hitherto been accepted as clearly and unequivocally Protestant by High Churchmen and Evangelicals alike.[60]

What did Newman mean by 'Catholic'? The term became overworked by the Tractarians but was rarely satisfactorily defined. Newman's admittedly biased and embittered brother, Francis, later argued that in Tract 90 his use of three epithets, 'Roman', 'Catholic' and 'Papal' enabled him 'to play his own game on simple minds'.[61] Even Liddon felt that Newman's use of the phrase 'doctrine of the Old Church'[62] with which he sought to render the Articles compatible, was an ambiguous expression, open to misunderstanding. Certainly, there was more than a suspicion that by 'Catholic', Newman meant not only the teaching of the early Church alone but also part of the official teaching of the Church of Rome as enshrined in the Tridentine decrees, which High Churchmen had always insisted that the Thirty-Nine Articles authoritatively condemned. In this context, Newman's assertion that the Articles were 'not uncatholic', though they were 'the offspring of an uncatholic age' could scarcely be welcomed as a concession by traditional High Churchmen. In what sense was the age of the Reformation 'uncatholic'? Was it because the authority of the papacy had been rejected? Many already feared that Newman was working, albeit perhaps unconsciously, towards this viewpoint. As one High Church critic complained,

> What does our author mean by an 'uncatholic age', or by what rule does he measure his catholicity? Surely he leaves his readers the option of measuring catholicity by simple subjection to the Papacy; for we cannot find any other proof of the uncatholicity of England in the day when her Articles were delivered, than a determination not to submit any longer to the usurped tyranny of the Pope.'[63]

The difference between Newman's proposed *rapprochement* with Rome and that pursued by individual divines like Samuel Wix in an earlier period was clear. The latter took for granted that the creed of Pius IV which Anglicans accused Rome of having added to the

Faith, would have to be abandoned as a precondition of any reconciliation between the two Churches. The Church of Rome thereby would be back in the state of the primitive Church in possessing the three creeds,

> and the Church of England, continuing to hold those three ancient Creeds, could then dispense with all her negative articles, which are the subject of inquiry in the Tract before us.

In complete contrast, Newman in Tract 90 regarded the Council of Trent as not only the real point of reference or contact, but almost as the actual basis around which the two Churches might be brought closer together. The Tract did envisage a softening down of the Articles, 'so as to no longer hinder any of us taking them in a Catholic, or—if the author of the Tract had spoken more correctly—a Popish sense'.[64]

The principle of selecting and harmonising which Newman had applied to the *Prophetical Office,* was taken a stage further in Tract 90. Many baulked at some of the logical distinctions which Newman attempted to draw between, for instance, Romish 'Masses' and 'the Mass'. Certainly, the use of the plural in the text of the Article enabled Newman 'to turn topsy-turvy a plain meaning'.[65] Moreover, some considered that the citations which Newman made of particular Anglican divines apparently holding particular tenets often condemned as 'Romish', bordered on the far-fetched, if not sophistical. As Abbott later complained, Newman,

> seemed to assume that every opinion, however extreme in the direction of Rome, that had been once expressed by any one High Church Bishop or Divine, and had not been authoritatively censured, at once became part of justifiable Anglican doctrine.[66]

An example of Newman's method, was in his treatment of Articles 20 and 21 on Church Authority and General Councils respectively. These Articles were hardly supportive of Tractarian claims. The definition of the Church seemed inadequate, while Article 21 in contradiction of Tractarian argument, stated that General Councils could err. Some nimble reasoning was needed to bridge this gap, and this Newman provided. Newman was able to offset the letter of these Articles by selective statements from Anglican divines apparently more in accord with a 'Catholic' position. Yet, while Newman cited Henry Hammond on the infallibility of General Councils, no authority was given. Moreover, statements of Hammond suggesting that General Councils were fallible were conveniently ignored.[67]

Other instances of Newman's selectivity and one-sidedness were noted by critics of Tract 90. For instance, while at one moment Newman would repudiate the teaching enshrined in the Book of Homilies as Protestant and a 'yoke of worse than Egyptian bondage', at another, in order to evade the literal meaning of the Articles, he would refer 'to the Homilies to show that more Catholic notions were held at the time'. It was a case of following the line of least resistance to finding official authority or precedent for the particular Catholic notion he happened to be advocating. To many, it appeared worse that disingenuous. In particular, by attempting, as it were, to 'correct' ambiguities in the Articles by reference to the Homilies for which on other occasions he had shown little respect, Newman seemed to be guilty of imposing 'on the construction of the Articles, documents [i.e. the Homilies] which he does not recognise himself'.[68] By such logical twists and turns, Newman might appear to adhere to the letter of a particular portion of the Anglican formularies, but in practice he was going against the overall spirit underpinning the whole. As a leading Oxford critic of Tract 90 tellingly remarked,

> I do think, (to borrow Mr. Newman's illustration), that the Articles are not a heap of stones but a building, and that he who induces himself by thirty-nine quibbles to assent to them piecemeal, and then denies them as a whole, is guilty of the most hateful verbal sophistry and mental reservation.[69]

The straightforwardness and fairness of Newman's interpretation of other particular Articles was called in to question by many who were otherwise sympathetic to the Movement. One such critic, cited above, especially complained of a false distinction drawn between 'Romish' and 'Tridentine'[70] that seemed to pervade the whole edifice of argument in the Tract. The essence of Newman's argument seemed to be that on such and such a particular doctrine, the Articles actually 'by anticipation' approved of the Tridentine position and merely condemned a corrupt, albeit popular, 'Romish' version of that sound doctrine. By such an argument, even a modified version of the worship of images could be supported. High Church critics of this reasoning felt that Newman was throwing dust in the eyes of his readers. To highlight what was deemed to be the sophistical nature of the argument, using an interesting analogy, the above critic witheringly maintained,

> By this fanciful mode of reasoning a sinner may justify any sin or species of vice, if only he comfort himself by merely saying, 'Not every view of this sin or this vice is condemned, but only the one as practised in such or such a place'; for vice has its changes and fashions as well as doctrines. In the New Testament epistles we find sins marked out by name, and mentioned as peculiar to the church to which the apostle wrote. Well, how easily any sinner of another church might have remained at ease in the indulgence of sin, by saying, 'Not every sin of this nature is condemned, but the Corinthian

or the Galatian view'. And so they might all have gone on in their sins, if only they did not adopt the precise opinions or mode of indulgence in that sin as practised in other places. We never met more extraordinary reasoning; it is mere trifling; it is perversion of reason.[71]

This critic went on to complain about what he regarded as the no less specious reasoning and unsatisfactory language which Newman adopted apparently to escape the force of the grammatical sense of Article 38—'The Bishop of Rome hath no jurisdiction in this realm of England'. Certainly, the critic had reason to consider Newman's extrapolation of the Article rather lame. For Newman, it was sufficient to state that 'we find ourselves, as a church, under the king now, and we obey him; we were under the Pope formerly, and we obeyed him'. For one who frankly confessed to an admiration for the political doctrines of passive obedience and even sacral kingship enshrined in the Homilies, this did seem to be placing the basis of loyalty and allegiance on too low and utilitarian grounds.[72]

Was Newman aware that by his reasoning alone he gave ground for much offence in the Tract? It would appear so. Newman himself appeared to reveal an element of self-conscious cynicism in the method he adopted, when he admitted in the *Apologia* that,

> Every Creed has texts in its favour, and again texts which run counter to it: and this is generally confessed. And this is what I felt keenly;—how had I done worse in Tract 90 than Anglicans, Wesleyans, and Calvinists did daily in their sermons and publications? . . . why was I to be dishonest and they immaculate?[73]

This was hardly taking the moral high ground, and such admissions go some way to blunting the force of the complaints by himself, his friends and followers, that the hostile reaction to Tract 90 was entirely unfair and undeserved. As in the furore over Froude's *Remains,* there surfaced an element of provoking verbal sparring with opponents that did not seem designed to conciliate, disarm or win over. Pertinent here was Newman's admission in the *Apologia* about his conduct and frame of mind at this critical turning-point in the Movement's history;

> 'Two can play at that game', was often in my mouth, when men of Protestant sentiments, appealed to the articles, homilies, or Reformers; in the sense that if they had a right to speak loud, I had both the liberty and the means of giving them tit for tat.[74]

There was a widespread perception of an undutiful tone permeating the Introduction to the Tract, with its references to 'ambiguous formularies' and to 'stammering lips', and with the Church of England described as 'in bondage'.[75] Objections to tone and language far outweighed complaints over the substance of the Tract from this quarter. Gladstone expressed a common view when he later maintained that, 'there never was an uproar, and there never were censures, which were more attributable to the manner and language of a publication as contrasted with its substance'.[76]

Yet, for some of the older High Church school, the apparently disrespectful language and way of viewing the Church of England it implied, was but symptomatic of a deeper flaw and malaise in Newman's evolving theory of Catholicism. Joshua Watson, the acknowledged leader of the standard bearers of this older school, the so-called 'Hackney Phalanx' always retained a warm regard for Newman and Pusey, who in turn looked up to him as something of an oracle in his generation.[77] What he thought of Tract 90 could not lightly be dismissed. Characteristically, Watson avoided outward criticism, but privately, according to his biographer, Edward Churton, Watson 'felt very acutely the wrongfulness of the words in the Introduction to No. 90, and expressed his grief'.[78] What Watson, quite as much as Protestant High Churchmen like Godfrey Faussett who indulged in public rebuke, disliked was the apparent arraignment by Newman of the living, existing Catholicism enshrined in the Church of England's formularies, on the bar of a preconceived, theoretical and nebulous concept of what was 'primitive'.

Newman's friend and erstwhile ally, Palmer of Worcester, was no less convinced of an implicit animus against the Church as she was, running throughout the Tract. It is interesting to see how Palmer took account of this, when one compares the relevant section of the first and second editions of his *Treatise on the Church of Christ,* published in 1838 and 1842 respectively. In the 1838 edition of the *Treatise,* Palmer had simply stated as one of the rules of interpretation of the Thirty-Nine Articles, that they were to be understood in 'the sense most conformable to Scripture and to Catholic Tradition, which she [the Church] acknowledges to be her guides'.[79] Clearly, four years later, Palmer felt that he had to be more precise, in the light of Tractarian assumptions as to what constituted 'Catholic Tradition'. Thus, in the enlarged 1842 edition, in the wake of Tract 90, Palmer added a highly significant note of caution, explaining just what he meant by interpreting the Articles in the 'most catholic sense'. In an added passage clearly aimed at the principle of Tract 90, Palmer now made clear that,

> the rule of interpreting the Articles in the most catholic sense, is one which must not be vaguely and indiscriminately applied to all the Articles, as if we were at liberty to affix to them whatever meaning seems to us most consistent with Scripture or with Tradition. The principle thus applied would lead to a most dangerous tampering with the authorised formularies of the church; would open the way for

> evasions of their most evident meaning, and thus render them wholly useless as tests of belief or persuasion.

On the contrary, such a rule of interpretation could only apply to,

> particular cases where a legitimate doubt of the meaning of any Article exists, and where it cannot be solved either by the language of other parts of the Articles, or of other formularies of the church.[80]

Moreover, it was a similar objection that prompted the discriminating critique of Tract 90 undertaken by an Irish High Churchman, Charles Elrington. Elrington made quite clear that he did not disagree with Newman's basic premise that the Thirty-Nine Articles should be 'interpreted according to the teaching of the Church Catholic'. His complaint was simply that, in practice as expounded by Newman, this amounted to interpreting the Articles 'according to the view each has of the teaching of the Church Catholic'.[81]

Old High Churchmen tended to feel placed in an invidious and vulnerable position as a consequence of Tract 90. They feared that the broader cause in favour of 'Church principles' was endangered by the course that Newman was taking. They were alarmed, and not without reason, at the prospect of a Low Church backlash against such principles. Thus, the Movement of 1833 seemed as if it would now weaken rather than bolster the traditional High Churchmanship which they represented. Several in the group of younger, so-called 'Z's such as Palmer of Worcester felt most threatened, as they were bound by ties of personal allegiance and that network of 'spiritual amicitia' which Newman tended to foster. It is these personal ties which help to explain Palmer's extraordinarily favourable public reception of Tract 90, which contrasted not only with that of Watson and the older generation, but with his own private misgivings, given lucid theological expression in the subtle and judicious revisions to the relevant portion of the *Treatise* as described above. It is striking that a time when the Tract was attracting widespread public opprobium, Palmer stood by Newman, and wrote him a generous letter, full of comfort, sympathy and encouragement. In it, Palmer declared that he had 'no hesitation in expressing an opinion that' Tract 90 was 'the most valuable of the series of Tracts that has come under my observation'.[82] The evidence suggests that this letter was written to anchor Newman in his attachment to the Church of England. Certainly, the sentiments did not reflect Palmer's true attitude. According to James Mozley, 'Palmer sent this letter quite spontaneously, and it does him great credit, especially as he and Newman were rather on cool terms some time ago'.[83] However, it was Edward Churton who provides evidence as to Palmer's real alarm, albeit hidden from public view. Churton confided to Arthur Perceval in December 1841 that he had received,

> a painfully interesting letter from my friend William Palmer, a good true hearted Irishman, with whose opinions and yours on the later proceedings of the Tracts, I have the happiness almost entirely to agree. He condemns No. 90, as Mr. Joshua Watson and all good churchmen of my acquaintance do.[84]

The same conflict between personal loyalty and private disapprobation was evident in the attitude of another 'Z', W. F. Hook. As Hook explained, 'I had intended to answer Tract 90 and had begun to do so, but I would not attack my friends when they had fallen'.[85] No little personal sacrifice was involved, evident in Hook's avowal to Gladstone, that 'I sacrificed my own character rather than give' up 'the good men at Oxford', 'on the publication of Tract 90'.[86] Clearly, Newman had no grounds for complaint of lack of support, understanding or loyalty from those who had perhaps the most to lose in any vigorous Low Church backlash against the Movement which Tract 90 seemed likely to provoke.

Newman showed little concern for the predicament in which Tract 90 placed erstwhile supporters like Palmer, Hook and Churton. He could only insist that he had never written Tract 90 with them in mind. Newman had avowedly composed Tract 90 in order to help settle the growing doubts about Anglicanism held by a substantial portion of his younger followers who seemed to be drifting in the direction of the Church of Rome. Newman became aware of this 'Romanising' undercurrent to the Movement from 1840 onwards. He was aware of the possibility of secessions in a way which Palmer of Worcester could not yet have comprehended. As Newman confided to his friend, John Bowden, at this time, 'the danger of a lapse into Romanism, I think gets greater daily. I expect to hear of victims. Again I fear I see more clearly that we are waking up to a schism in our Church'.[87] In short, it cannot be said that Newman did not have his eyes open. Moreover, if Newman's aim in writing Tract 90 partly was to check the 'Romanising' trend, from the Anglican viewpoint his aims could be commended as laudable. Yet, whatever his intentions, the result of Tract 90 was to be a strengthening rather than weakening of the Romeward trend among Newman's followers. Why was this so?

In the first instance, Tract 90 soon came to be perceived more as a concession to, or compromise with, an existing Romanising spirit than an effective braking operation. Roman Catholic controversialists encouraged the popular impression that Newman was playing into the hands of Rome by appearing to argue that the Thirty-Nine Articles were reconcilable with the decrees of

Trent. The feeling was that Newman was aiding and abetting, albeit unintentionally, the work of Roman Catholic priests in England.[88] Moreover, some of the specific argument in Tract 90 had flaws which were readily capitalised upon by Roman Catholic writers. In particular, a contradiction with Newman's earlier position in regard to the Council of Trent became apparent. Earlier, Newman had argued that the corruptions of Romanism only became formalised and made binding at Trent.[89] Even Hurrell Froude had described Roman Catholics as 'wretched Tridentines'.[90] Tract 90 involved something of a *volte-face* in Newman's attitude. The formal, 'official' Tridentine position was now deemed worthy of accommodation with the Articles, and contrasted favourably with a pre-Tridentine, corrupt, popular Romanism which was deemed to have been the real object of repudiation by the Articles. In his own response to Tract 90, the Roman Catholic, Wiseman, was able to taunt and tease Newman over this. Wiseman's jibe, which strongly paralleled a similar observation from the High Churchman, Faussett, was designed to hit home. With some justice, Wiseman complained that Newman had hitherto blamed Roman Catholics for adhering to the decrees of Trent, 'yet you now blame us for departure from them. Why not suspect your judgments, if you find that they vary?'[91]

Newman's professed aim of halting the drift towards Rome might have succeeded in the months after Tract 90's publication if Newman and the Tractarian leaders had sat quiet and bided their time. This was the earnest hope of the High Churchmen, and they did all they could to calm the situation and assuage popular fears. . . .

Conclusions: Loss and Gain

It has become clear that Tract 90 was the pivotal episode in Newman's Oxford and Anglican career, and the one on which his final journey into the Church of Rome partly hinged. Much more could have been said about the theological merits both in favour and against the arguments and content of the Tract itself. However, this is ground that has been well covered in innumerable theological studies. Certainly, the impression should not be given that in the long-term, Newman necessarily 'lost' the theological argument. Not only is that issue not central to our study, but the answer ultimately depends on one's particular theological or denominational standpoint. Nonetheless, viewed strictly historically, Newman ultimately 'won' the argument in the limited sense that his principle of 'catholic' interpretation of the Articles gradually came to win widespread acceptance within the Church of England.

This wider acceptance was already evident by the mid-1860s when Pusey published his *Historical Preface.* It became axiomatic for Anglican Churchmen to maintain that Newman's method of interpretation was no more 'forced' or any less 'natural' than that preferred by Evangelicals on the one hand or by Broad Churchmen on the other.[161] In fact, the growing theological polarisation characteristic of the post-Tractarian Church of England and emergence of more rigid Church party divisions, helped Newman's view to triumph as a tenable option. Catholic 'latitude' became acceptable, as the so-called 'liberal Catholicism' emerged. Distinct as it was from the rising liberal Protestantism, 'liberal Catholicism' flourished in the climate of greater theological pluralism in the Church, once the initial 'Oxford controversy' had died down.

Ironically it was to be the long-term success of Newman's view that the Articles were compatible with 'catholic' teaching that enabled subsequent generations of Anglo-Catholics to rest at greater ease than they otherwise might in the Church of England, and to refrain from following Newman's example in seceding to Rome. In short, Newman's Tract 90 was more successful in the very long term than Newman had the patience to foresee at the time. The sense of resentment felt by Tractarians like Copeland who remained Anglicans, at the authorities' treatment of Newman, was sharpened by this very consciousness of later success and fulfilment.

Yet, while later Anglo-Catholics benefited from the gradual growth in tolerance of different shades of theological opinion in the Church of England, including the principle of Tract 90 itself, it cannot be said that Newman the Roman Catholic could have welcomed this belated trend. It came twenty years too late, and probably succeeded then in putting the brake on potential conversions to Rome which Newman had evidently envisaged in the early 1840s. Moreover, while his view of the Articles had benefited from support from the younger generation of liberals at Oxford such as A. P. Stanley, with Stanley and Jowett defending Tract 90 on latitudinarian principles in the mid-1840s, this was always in part a source of embarrassment for Newman. Tactical support from Oxford liberals might be one thing, but Newman and above all, Pusey, remained adamant that rationalism was the great evil of the day. Newman, and Pusey in his *Historical Preface,* stressed that the claim to 'catholic latitude' as proposed in Tract 90 could not be applied to the fundamental Catholic doctrinal verities of the 'faith once delivered to the saints'.[162] Therefore, they were adamant that the principles of Tract 90 could in no way support a general latitudinarianism in regard to creeds and tests, and did not discountenance the principle of subscription which the Tractarians had stoutly defended against the Oxford liberals in the mid-1830s.

However, this did not prevent a much later generation of Anglo-Catholic commentators from anachronistically appealing to a doctrinal liberalism and relativism in ridiculing the Protestant High Church opponents of

Newman's arguments for 'elasticity' in interpreting the Articles in the 1840s, which in other circumstances they would have been the first to disavow. Moreover, the Tractarian reluctance to submit to or obey the dictates of episcopal authority in the early 1840s, was to leave an unhappy legacy to later Anglo-Catholicism which was to carry resistance to such authority to ever greater lengths. In fact, many contemporary opponents of the Movement had cause to note the apparent contradiction between the theoretical exaltation of episcopal authority by the Tractarians, and at the same time, a practical evasion, if not repudiation of that authority if exercised in what leaders of the Movement deemed to be defiance of true Catholic principles.[163] Ultimately Newman was perhaps more sensitive to this apparent contradiction than many of his followers, especially those who remained in the Church of England. It was probably a factor in his decision to retire once and for all from the public Anglican arena in 1843. Certainly, the cynical view that developed among many of those who did not take Newman's honest step was less creditable—this was the argument that 'some among us may . . . have been unfaithful both to our duties and to our knowledge of Scripture and Antiquity, by aggrandizing the Episcopate in the tacit depression of the Presbyterate'.[164] It seemed too coincidental that it was only when he was at the receiving end of episcopal authority that these first doubts should have been raised.

At the heart of our discussion, though, has not been the respective theological 'pros' and 'cons' of Tract 90, or the issue of who 'won' or who 'lost' ultimately. The central question, and one of perennial fascination, has been what the Tract 90 episode reveals about the Anglican Newman's personality and human leadership, and above all, his place in the history of the Oxford Movement. Our study has brought to light some slight flaws in Newman's personality and psyche. These flaws need to be set alongside Newman's undoubted literary genius and his moral and spiritual heroism. Nothing that has been argued here could or should detract from Newman's holiness of life, the quality of his preaching and ability to inspire and enthuse a whole generation of young men with religious fervour and a sense of mission. The positive, dynamic aspect of Newman's religious odyssey, the drama and poetry as well as negative features should never be forgotten. In this context, while the reaction to Tract 90 was a trial for Newman and helped to undermine his confidence in Anglicanism, it should not be argued that Newman became a Roman Catholic simply in recoil from this defeat, or from any mere display of wounded pride. Of course, his grounds for conversion were much deeper and more positive than this. In short, Newman's later jocular refrain, 'Oxford made us Catholics' does not represent the whole truth. One must not overlook the deeply spiritual motivation at the heart of Newman's religious quest. The search for holiness and the mark of sanctity as a formal note of the true Church became an abiding concern after 1842.[165] Ultimately, Newman became a Roman Catholic because he could no longer be sure of his own salvation outside her communion.

Newman was a great religious teacher and moral exemplar in his generation. At the same time, it is unfortunate that many have been almost blind in overlooking, ignoring or denying some of the weaknesses and flaws that the Tract 90 episode revealed in the Anglican Newman. At the time, and not only to avowed enemies, these flaws were more apparent than later hagiography has allowed. Sometimes, it is true, there were personal reasons for some of the animus against him. There were those such as Richard Whately who had befriended the young Newman at Oxford and to whom Newman owed much, but between whom misunderstanding arose and a parting of the ways. It may seem harsh to suggest that Newman had a martyr-complex, but he could exaggerate the extent to which people were against him, as the way he reacted to the Bishops' charges proved. Newman was conscious that many thought him devious. He later recalled that for a time, nearly the whole world thought that at Oxford he had deliberately pursued a policy characterised by deep design and conscious duplicity.[166] Yet, was there not some basis to such criticism? Certainly, there were those even in sympathy with him who could accuse him of over-subtlety, and of literary or verbal sleights of hand. Typical of an instinctive reaction to Tract 90 aroused even among natural allies, was that of a Yorkshire High Churchman, Miller of Scarborough. Commenting on Miller's tract against No. 90, Edward Churton, himself resident in Yorkshire, concluded that Tract 90,

> has certainly given some, who were well disposed to us, an impression that Newman is not an honest man . . . It do think, with all respect for him, and great admiration of all that he has written, that his mind, which is a mind of great subtlety, played him a trick, and made him write what our Yorkshire common sense . . . cannot digest.[167]

Examples of such an impression being inspired are very numerous, and it is nearly always Tract 90 that was cited as the most glaring instance of the manifestation of this apparent trait in the Anglican Newman. As Gladstone put it, shortly after Newman's death in 1890, 'Tract 90 opened a joint in Newman's armour, it showed that in his wonderful genius there was a distinct flaw—a strong sophistical element'.[168] Moreover, liberals such as Jowett, Huxley, Henry Sidgwick and Lord Acton, all alluded to an element of sophistry and even habitual untruthfulness in Newman's writings and argument.[169] Many felt there was an often unconscious sceptical tendency in his remorseless logical applications. As the historian, G. M. Young has remarked of him,

> He is always skimming along the verge of a logical catastrophe, and always relying on his dialectic agility to save himself from falling: always exposing what seems to be an unguarded spot and always revealing a new line of defence when the unwary assailant has reached it.[170]

Yet, Newman knew what he was doing. One can say that his method of argument was not to everybody's taste, and that it could repel as many as it might attract. Less subtle minds could all too easily misunderstand him and mistake his drift. Nonetheless, the grosser charge of deliberate dishonesty which Newman's harshest and least fair critics such as Abbott and his own embittered brother, Francis, freely raised, deserves to be discounted. The *Apologia* itself, for many, laid such a charge conclusively to rest. For even a hostile reviewer of the *Apologia* admitted that Newman had indeed,

> convincingly established his own personal truthfulness. Whatever in his cause or in his teaching may have seemed inconsistent with personal sincerity, we now see must be attributed to the very difficult circumstances in which he was placed, which at a certain period rendered a policy of reserve the only one possible for him.[171]

Nevertheless, even the *Apologia,* while settling some of the question marks over Newman's mental integrity in his favour, at the same time threw up some new doubts as to Newman's selectivity and interpretation of events surrounding the Oxford Movement which have become all too apparent in this essay. We have remarked upon his unfair dealing with opponents, to which he himself admitted in the *Apologia.* A glaring instance, for which he did not apologise, was his apparent misrepresentation of Hampden's position in his polemical *Elucidations* published in 1836. There was also a one-sided selectivity about many of the 'catenae patrum' which Newman constructed for various numbers of the *Tracts for the Times.* Certainly, there is ample room for faulting what has been called Newman's 'subjectivism', and the *Apologia* itself abounded in fresh instances of this. It was Julius Hare who accused the Anglican Newman, in the context of the latter's hostile view of Martin Luther, 'of a practice which has been gaining upon him, that of substituting the creations of his own mind for the realities of history'.[172] If this was true of Newman's portrayal of Luther and Lutheranism, the same can be applied to Newman's own, inevitably very personal, view of the history of the Oxford Movement and Tract 90.

Factual errors and mistatements can readily be detected in Newman's version of the Oxford events. We have seen that Newman could be unfair and perhaps mistaken in his estimate of the real principles and motives of the Anglican Bishops in the early 1840s. However, a specific, glaring instance of unfairness in the *Apologia* was Newman's somewhat ungracious as well as mistaken notice of Bishop Blomfield. In a travesty of Blomfield's real position, Newman accused Blomfield of having, 'for years engaged in diluting the high orthodoxy of the church by the introduction of the Evangelical body into places of influence and trust'.[173] Yet, this was the same Bishop who was linked to the 'Hackney Phalanx', had well demonstrated his High Church credentials at Chester,[174] and who as Bishop of London had himself been often accused of Tractarianism, not least on account of his influential episcopal charge in 1842. That charge was itself denounced for being Tractarian in inspiration,[175] and was reputed to have been instrumental in drawing more than one Low Churchman over into the Tractarian camp.[176]

Other instances of Newman's inaccuracies could be multiplied. Yet, there was probably far more of self-deception than deliberate distortion in them.[177] Given the nature, background, and real purpose of Newman's *Apologia* perhaps this should not surprise us. As Newman once candidly explained, he had a much better memory for what he called 'anxieties and deliverances' than actual outer facts and circumstances.[178] Thus, the latter perhaps could sometimes unconsciously be sacrificed or subordinated for an overall effect conveyed in the unfolding of the human and moral drama involved in the delineation of the 'anxieties and deliverances'. In a sense perhaps both elements—factual blemishes alongside the dramatic, heroic account—were inseparable in Newman's portrayal of events in which he had been so intimately involved. Thus, the *Apologia* deserves to be considered much more as autobiography than a full or authoritative history and elucidation of the *Tracts for the Times.*[179]

Newman was always at his strongest and most winningly persuasive when he was able to utilise the true religious passion which was always the great moral strength of the Oxford Movement and which gave it such a dynamic edge over the older, more prosaic High Churchmanship. It was a moral strength infused with Romanticism, and it was the combination of the two that explains the almost secret power which enabled the Movement to capture the hearts as well as the minds of the younger Oxford generation. This authentic voice of the Movement was much more evident in works such as the reply to Faussett and in the *Letter to Jelf* than in Tract 90 itself, with its logical nit-pickings.

The greatness of the *Apologia* lay in its recapturing of the religious passion integral to Newman's leadership of the Movement. It would be churlish to allow quibbles, albeit important, over its accuracy to overshadow our appreciation of this. In the last analysis, it is fitting that it should be through the medium of such a great literary work of art and chronicle of such a religious odyssey, that the full drama of the Movement and especially Tract 90 should be conveyed to us, even if that very medium can be shown to have been an often one-sided and distorting lens. For the revelation of Newman's flaws of intellect and even to an extent of character, cannot detract from his towering moral strength or status in the religious annals of nineteenth-century England. The Oxford Anglican Newman was a flawed genius, but a genius, nevertheless.

Notes

[1] The term 'Tractarian', defined as applicable to those who were 'the authors, editors and approvers of the *Tracts for the Times'*, appears to have been first coined by the Master of the Temple, Christopher Benson. See C. Benson, *Discourses upon Tradition and Episcopacy* (London, 1839), p. 101; cf. *British Critic* XXVI (October, 1839), p. 508.

[2] J. B. Marsden, *History of Christian Churches and Sects* (London, 1865), p. 40; M. C. Church (ed.), *Life and Letters of Dean Church,* R. W. Church to F. Rogers, 14 March 1841 (London, 1895), p. 33. For full publishing data on Tract 90, see R. Imberg, *Tracts for the Times: a complete survey of all the editions* (Lund University, 1987), p. 133.

[3] J. H. Newman, *Apologia pro Vita Sua; being a reply to a pamphlet entitled 'what then, does Dr. Newman mean?'* (London, 1864), p. 100. For the argument against accepting Newman's view, see F. L. Cross *John Henry Newman* (London, 1933), Appendix IV, 'The myth of July 14, 1833' pp. 162-3. The so-called old High Churchmen resented the later tendency to make too much of 1833 and thus impute too much specifically to the Oxford Movement in the wider Church revival. This was the view of the acknowledged leader of a dominant grouping among the pre-Tractarian High Churchmen, the 'Hackney Phalanx', Joshua Watson. See A. Webster, *Joshua Watson: the story of a layman* (London, 1954), p. 29. Cf. B. Harrison to W. E. Gladstone, 16 November 1843, Gladstone MSS, British Library, MS Add. 44204ff. pp. 114-15.

[4] According to his former friend and one-time Fellow of Oriel, the renegade Spanish priest, Blanco White, Newman's sudden shift into union with the anti-Catholic Emancipation party against Robert Peel in 1829, represented, 'the first manifestation of the mental revolution . . . from which we have those very strange productions, entitled, Tracts for the Times'. J. H. Thom (ed.), *The life of the Rev. Joseph Blanco White, written by himself, with portions of his correspondence* (London, 1845) III, p. 131.

[5] R. W. Church, *The Oxford Movement: twelve years* (London, 1892), p. 251.

[6] T. Gornall, 'Newman's lapses into subjectivity', *Heythrop Journal* XXIII (1982), pp. 46-7.

[7] See J. H. Newman, *Certain difficulties felt by Anglicans in Catholic teaching considered: in twelve lectures addressed in 1850 to the party of the religious movement of 1833* (London, 1850).

[8] C. Dawson, *The Spirit of the Oxford Movement,* Fourth impression (London, 1945), chap. 2.

[9] See P. Nockles, 'The Oxford Movement: historical background, 1780-1833', in G. Rowell (ed.), *Tradition renewed: the Oxford Movement conference papers* (London, 1986), pp. 24-50.

[10] P. Nockles, 'Continuity and change in Anglican High Churchmanship in Britain, 1790-1850', Oxford D.Phil thesis, 1982 (to be published in revised form by CUP, *c.*1991).

[11] P. Avis, *Anglicanism and the Christian Church: theological resources in historical perspective* (Edinburgh, 1989), p. 158.

[12] J. Garbett, *Dr. Pusey and the University of Oxford* (Oxford, 1843), p. 8. cf. *Christian Remembrancer* I (April, 1841), pp. 425-6. Cf. G. V. Cox, *Recollections of Oxford* (London, 1870), p. 289. The comment on the Tractarians by the then Vice-Chancellor of the University, the High Churchman, A. T. Gilbert, Principal of Brasenose, is pertinent here;—'At first rise, and for some succeeding years, they were looked upon not unfavourably by many of all ranks in the church', A. T. Gilbert to Duke of Wellington, 26 December 1839, Wellington MSS, 2/250/64, Southampton University Library.

[13] *Remains of the late Richard Hurrell Froude M.A.* [Part I] Vol. I (London, 1838), p. 429. For convenience, the so-called 'old High Churchmen' or 'Z's' will be simply referred to in our text as High Churchmen, only the epithet 'traditional' being added where deemed appropriate. Such 'High Churchmen' are to be distinguished from unreserved and active adherents of the Oxford Movement, who will be described as 'Tractarian', though it is recognised that, as with all such labels, the distinctions were often less than clear-cut.

[14] W. J. Copeland to the Warden of Keble (Talbot), 22 September 1879, Keble MSS, Keble College Library, Oxford.

[15] W. Palmer to J. H. Newman, August 1843, Newman MSS, No. 50, Birmingham Oratory Library.

[16] A. Mozley, *Letters and correspondence of John Henry Newman during his life in the English Church* (London, 1891), I, p. 484. R. H. Froude to J. H. Newman, 17 November 1833, cf. *Letters and Diaries of John Henry Newman* IV (London, 1981), pp. 98-9, J. H. Newman to J. W. Bowden, 13 November 1833.

[17] J. H. Newman, *Apologia*, p. 108.

[18] *Apologia*, p. 109.

[19] *Apologia*, pp. 107-8.

[20] A. Dwight Culler, *The imperial intellect: a study of Newman's educational ideal* (New Haven, 1955), p. 67, cf. H. Tristram (ed.), *John Henry Newman: autobiographical writings* (London, 1956), p. 90, also cf. F. Oakeley, *Historical notes on the Tractarian Movement* (London, 1865), p. 180.

[21] *Apologia*, p. 132.

[22] *Apologia*, pp. 133-4.

[23] Testimonies to Newman's influence over undergraduates are numerous. The complaint of the Whig and anti-Tractarian Warden of New College, Philip Shuttleworth in 1836, can be taken as representative;—'Our undergraduates I fear are much bitten by the self-mortifying spirit of Newman and Pusey', P. Shuttleworth, 19 June 1841 (copy) Bodleian Library, Oxford, MS Eng. Hist. *c*.1033, f. 230. However, a contemporary American observer insisted that it was the MAs who were the most susceptible to Tractarian influence. See C.A. Bristed, *Five years in an English University* (New York, 1873), p. 82. By 1845, it was estimated that among the resident members of Convocation in Oxford, the Tractarians had a majority of nearly four to one J. Bateman, *Tractarianism as described in prophecy. A word to the wise on the Oxford crisis* (London, 1845), p. 43; cf. M. Ward, *The yong Mr. Newman* (London, 1948), p. 321; cf. D. Newsome, *The parting of friends: a study of the Wilberforces and Henry Manning* (London, 1966), pp. 63-9.

[24] J. C. Shairp, *Studies in poetry and philosophy* (London, 1868), p. 273, cf. J. C. Shairp, *John Keble* (London, 1866), p. 17. Cf. K. Lake, *Memorials of W.C. Lake* (London, 1901), pp. 49-50. Cf. A. I. Dasent, *John Thadeus Delane: editor of* The Times, *in his life and correspondence* (London, 1908) I, 20. Cf. W. Lockhart, *Cardinal Newman: reminiscences of fifty years since* (London, 1891), pp. 5-6. Cf. C. E. Mallet, *A History of the University of Oxford* (London, 1927) III, pp. 241-3.

[25] *Apologia*, pp. 114-15.

[26] Faussett was to be the victim of a satirical, if not scurrilous Tractarian caricature, painted by Thomas Mozley. See *British Critic* XXX [T. Mozley], 'The Oxford Margaret Professor' (July 1841), pp. 241-3. Cf. T. Mozley, *Reminiscences chiefly of Oriel College and the Oxford Movement* (London, 1882) II, p. 245. Faussett had long been honoured by Tractarians with the facetious nickname, 'Il Dottore Falsetto'. G. Tracey (ed.), *The Letters and Diaries of John Henry Newman* VI (London, 1984), p. 324.

[27] *London Quarterly Review* XXIII, 'Mr. Kingsley and Dr. Newman' No. XLV (October, 1864), p. 147.

[28] *Apologia*, p. 116.

[29] *Apologia*, p. 117.

[30] Samuel Wilberforce wrote of 'the mischievous delirium of publishing Froude's unguarded thoughts to a morbidly sensitive and unsympathetic age as this . . . that work has put back Church principles for fifty years'. Bodleian Library MS Wilberforce d.38, f. 130. Cf. A. R. Ashwell, *Life of the Rt. Rev. Samuel Wilberforce* I (London, 1880), p. 112, H.J. Rose to J. Watson, January 1838. Cf. W. F. Hook to W. E. Gladstone, 22 January 1839 Gladstone MSS B.L. MS Add. 44213f.19.

[31] P. Brendon, 'Newman, Keble, and Froude's "Remains"', *English Historical Review* LXXXVII No. CCCXLV (October, 1972), p. 706. Newman's justification to Churton, of the decision to publish the 'Remains', is characteristically revealing;—'I have never repented publishing them one single moment . . . I do dislike uncommonly to keep things in, and seem to be playing a double part'. G. Tracey (ed.), *Letters and Diaries* VI, p. 325, J. H. Newman to E. Churton, 3 October 1838. Cf. G. Tracey (ed.), *Letters and Diaries* VI, pp. 118-19, J. H. Newman to J. Keble, 21 August 1837.

[32] J. H. Newman, *A letter to the Rev. Godfrey Faussett D.D. Margaret Professor of Divinity, on certain points of faith and practice* (Oxford, 1838).

[33] G. Faussett, *The revival of popery: a sermon preached before the University of Oxford at St. Mary's . . . May 1838* third edition (Oxford, 1838), pp. vii-viii.

[34] R. Bagot, *A charge delivered to the clergy of the diocese of Oxford* (Oxford, 1838), pp. 20-1. In private correspondence with Newman and Pusey, Bagot relentlessly stressed his continued sympathy with the apparent aims of the Movement at that date, and urged them not to be disheartened by hs charge. See Pusey MSS Pusey House Library (P.H.L.) Oxford, R. Bagot to E. B. Pusey, 12 September 1838, cf. Pusey MSS P.H.L. Oxford, R. Bagot to J.H. Newman, 20 August 1838.

[35] E. A. Abbott, *The Anglican career of Cardinal Newman* (London, 1892) II, p. 95.

[36] P. B. Nockles, 'The great disruption: the University and the Oxford Movement' in M. Brock (ed.), *History of the University of Oxford* Vol. VI (to be published, 1991/2). Cf. W. R. Ward, *Victorian Oxford* (London, 1965) chap. 6.

[37] R. W. Church, *Oxford Movement,* p. 154.

[38] For further discussion of Newman's Oxford 'idea of a university', see A. Dwight Culler, *The imperial intellect,* chap. 3, pp. 96-120. For an example of Newman's romanticised, medievalist conception of a revived 'monastic' Oxford, see [J. H. Newman], 'Memorials of Oxford', *British Critic* XXIV (July 1838), pp. 133-44. Cf. [J. R. Hope-Scott], 'The statutes of Magdalen College', *British Critic* XXVI (January 1840), pp. 367-96 and R. Ormsby, *Memoirs of James Robert Hope-Scott of Abbotsford* (London, 1884) I, chap. 10.

[39] *A letter of remonstrance, addressed to an undergraduate of the University of Oxford, concerning the tenets of Dr. Pusey and Mr. Newman* (Oxford, 1840), p. 20. Cf. [E. Fry] *The listener in Oxford* (London, 1839), p. 22.

[40] M. C. Church (ed.), *The life and letters of Dean Church,* R.W. Church to F. Rogers, 14 March 1841 (London, 1895), p. 28.

[41] Abbott, pp. 95-6.

[42] J. H. Newman, *Lectures on the prophetical office of the Church viewed relatively to Romanism and popular Protestantism* (London, 1837), p. 20. In the second edition, the sentence, 'the Via Media has never existed' to which Rose so strongly objected, was altered to, 'the Via Media viewed as an integral system has scarcely had existence'.

[43] T. Parker, 'The rediscovery of the Fathers in the seventeenth century Anglican tradition', J. Coulson and A. M. Allchin (eds), *The rediscovery of Newman: an Oxford symposium* (London, 1967), p. 41.

[44] J. H. Newman, *Lectures on the prophetical office,* p. 30.

[45] Abbott, p. 81. It must be said that Newman was never an uncritical admirer of Caroline divinity, so that to 'pick' and 'choose' would become a necessity for him. For instance, see Newman's comment to Churton as early as 1837;-'How come [Jeremy] Taylor to be so liberal in his Liberty of Prophesying? And how far is Hammond tinctured as regards the Sacraments with Grotianism?' G. Tracey (ed.), *Letters and Diaries* VI, p. 41. J. H. Newman to E. Churton, 14 March 1837. See Note 98, for evidence of the application of this selective method in Tract 90.

[46] J. W. Burgon, *Lives of twelve good men* I (London, 1889), p. 219, H. J. Rose to J. H. Newman, 13 May 1836.

[47] *Apologia,* p. 212.

[48] Newman had gone so far as to refer to the Articles in private, as countenancing 'a vile Protestantism'. T. Gornall (ed.), *Letters and Diaries of John Henry Newman* V (Oxford, 1981), p. 70, J. H. Newman to R. H. Froude, 13 May 1835.

[49] *Apologia,* p. 232.

[50] R. W. Church, p. 292.

[51] Lambeth Palace Library Longley Papers I, f. 205, J. R. Hall to C. T. Longley, 23 March 1841.

[52] (R. Whately), *The controversy between Tract No. XC and the Oxford tutors* (London, 1841), pp. 10-11.

[53] P.H.L., Oxford. Pusey MSS, MS 'Memoir of Dr. Wynter' (1845). Joshua Watson's guarded support for the action of the Oxford Heads in 1841, and later, in 1845, is significant;—'The cards were dealt to them; and if they had refused to play, they had surely failed in their duty to the University as "custodes judiciae academicae". Nothing could release the body from their obligation to protect those entrusted to their charge from looking upon the bonds of subscription as a mere rope of sand.' E. Churton, *Memoir of Joshua Watson* (London, 1861) II, p. 152.

[54] Lambeth Palace Library Tait Papers 77, f. 34. R. Scott to A. C. Tait, April 1841. Cf. J. Jordan, *A second appeal to the Rt. Rev. the Lord Bishop of Oxford* (Oxford, 1841).

[55] [J. H. Newman], 'Remarks on certain passages in the Thirty-Nine Articles', *Tracts for the Times* No. 90, second edition (London, 1841), p. 4.

[56] R. W. Church, p. 281.

[57] P. Avis, *Anglicanism,* p. 226.

[58] See S. Wix, *Reflections concerning the expediency of a Council of the Church of England and the Church of Rome* (London, 1818), p. 13. Cf. G. Tavard, *The quest for Catholicity: a study in Anglicanism* (London, 1963), pp. 149-50.

[59] *Apologia,* pp. 159-60.

[60] As Godfrey Faussett inconveniently pointed out, 'unfortunately for his object, the very questions he feels interested in leaving open, are for the most part precisely those which our Reformers were especially careful to close'. G. Faussett, *The Thirty-Nine Articles considered* (Oxford, 1841), p. 17.

[61] F. W. Newman, *Contributions chiefly to the early history of the late Cardinal Newman,* second edition (London, 1891), p. 97.

[62] H. P. Liddon, *The life of Edward Bouverie Pusey* II, fourth edition (London, 1894), pp. 162-3. As Brilioth tellingly puts it, 'here already occurs a shadow, which falls ever thicker over the path of progressive Anglo-Catholicism right down to the present day, the absence of any clear content in the idolised formula of catholicity'. Y. Brilioth, *The Anglican revival: studies in the Oxford Movement* (London, 1925), p. 155. Cf. G. Tavard, chap. 7.

[63] J. R. Page, *The position of the Church of England in the catholic world suggested by a perusal of No. XC of the 'Tracts for the Times'* (London, 1844), p. 47.

[64] Page, p. 10, nonetheless for all the ambiguity of his language, it cannot be maintained that Newman was formally advocating reunion at this stage. O. Chadwick, *The mind of the Oxford Movement* (London, 1960), p. 55.

[65] Brilioth, p. 154. Newman himself later was dissatisfied with his own reasoning on the subject of Article 31, the 'sacrifice of Masses'. This is significant in that it was to be the only portion of Tract 90 over which he ever came to express the slightest regret. See *Correspondence of John Henry Newman with John Keble and others . . . 1839-1845. Edited at the Birmingham Oratory* (London, 1917), p. 76.

[66] Abbott, p. 247. Bishop Knox later argued that Newman's assumption that the Articles supported a 'Catholic' as opposed to 'Protestant' position, 'finds no support in the Articles except by insisting on what the Articles do not say. Tract XC is a supreme example of the argument "ex silentio", the most unsafe of all historical or theological arguments'. E. A. Knox, *The Tractarian Movement, 1833-1845* (London, 1933) p. 260.

[67] Abbott, p. 250.

[68] R. Lowe, *Observations suggested by 'A few more words in support of No. 90'* (Oxford, 1841), pp. 20-1.

[69] Lowe, p. 18.

[70] Page, p. 198.

[71] Page, p. 199.

[72] Page, pp. 226-7, cf. W. Sewell, *A letter to the Rev. E. B. Pusey on the publication of No. 90 of the Tracts for the Times* (Oxford, 1841).

[73] *Apologia,* p. 171.

[74] *Apologia,* p. 182.

[75] [J. H. Newman], 'Remarks' Tract 90 first edition (London, 1841), p. 4. In the second edition, 'stammering lips' was altered to, 'through the medium of indeterminate statements'. [J. H. Newman], 'Remarks' Tract 90 second edition (London, 1841), p. 4. See R. Imberg *Tracts for the Times: a complete survey,* pp. 163-4.

[76] W. E. Gladstone, *Correspondence on Church and Religion* D. C. Lathbury (ed.) I (London, 1910), p. 281.

[77] P.H.L., Pusey MSS, E. B. Pusey to J. Watson, 30 October 1839. Cf. P.H.L., Pusey MSS, E. B. Pusey to J. H. Newman, 11 September 1839.

[78] Churton MSS, Sutton Coldfield, E. Churton to W. J. Copeland, 28 February 1860.

[79] W. Palmer, *A treatise on the Church of Christ* first edition (London, 1838) I, p. 204.

[80] Palmer, *Treatise* third edition (London, 1842), II, p. 214.

[81] C. R. Elrington, *Subscription to the XXXIX Articles* (Dublin, 1842), p. 15, cf. H. Phillpotts, *A Charge to the clergy of the diocese of Exeter* (London, 1842) p. 28.

[82] P.H.L., Pusey MSS, W. Palmer to J. H. Newman, 9 August 1841.

[83] A. Mozley (ed.), *Letters of the Rev. J.B. Mozley* (London, 1885), p. 113, J. B. Mozley to A. Mozley, 13 March 1841. Cf. L.P.L. Williams Deposit 9/36; I. Williams to J. Keble, 22 March 1841. Cf. National Library of Scotland, Edinburgh, Hope-Scott MSS, MS 3668 pp. 173f. F. Rogers to J. R. Hope, 28 April 1841. However, Owen Chadwick has suggested another explanation. See O. Chadwick, *Mind of the Oxford Movement,* p. 54.

[84] P.H.L., Pusey MSS, E. Churton to A. P. Perceval, 20 December 1841.

[85] Birmingham Oratory Library, 'Tract 90 Correspondence', W. F. Hook to W. G. Ward, 20 March 1841.

[86] W. R. Stephens, *The life and letters of Walter Farquhar Hook* (London, 1878) II, p. 136. W. F. Hook to W. E. Gladstone, 11 December 1841. Gladstone likewise ini-

tially accepted the Tract 'with surprising equanimity'. P. Butler, *Gladstone, Church, State and Tractarianism: a study of his religious ideas and attitudes, 1809-1859* (Oxford, 1982), p. 174.

[87] Mozley, *Letters* II, p. 297. J. H. Newman to J. W. Bowden, January 1840. Cf. Birmingham Oratory Library Newman MSS, J. H. Newman to H. A. Woodgate, 3 March 1839.

[88] E. Thompson, *A triumph of Christianity* (London, 1841), p. 20.

[89] *Tracts for the Times,* No. XV (Oxford, 1834), p. 10. Cf. R. Imberg, *In Quest of Authority* (Lund, 1987), p. 96 and Imberg, *Complete Survey,* pp. 149-50.

[90] Quoted in N. Wiseman, *A letter respectfully addressed to the Rev. J. H. Newman, upon some passages in his letter to the Rev. Dr. Jelf* (London, 1841), pp. 29-30.

[91] Wiseman, p. 30; cf. Imberg, *In Quest,* p. 131. . . .

[161] Cross, pp. 127-8.

[162] *Tract XC With a historical preface by Pusey,* p. xliii, cf. F. L. Cross, p. 113.

[163] William Goode pointed out to Bishop Bagot that by the way in which they had conducted themselves, the Tractarians had not put into practice their professed principle 'of doing nothing without the Bishop'. 'For did they consult your Lordship when they originated the Tracts for the Times, and commenced that "mighty movement", which they now tell the Bishops is too late to check, however much they may wish to do so?' W. Goode, *Some difficulties,* p. 17, cf. W. S. Bricknell, *The judgment of the Bishops upon Tractarian theology* (Oxford, 1845). Appendix G 'Tractarian reverence for Episcopacy', pp. 695-7. For further discussion of Tractarian/Anglo-Catholic practical defiance of episcopal authority, see J. R. Griffin, *The Oxford Movement: a revision* (Edinburgh, 1989), pp. 270-4. Newman's own explanation of the apparent contradiction, is interesting: 'the more implicit the reverence one pays to a Bishop, the more keen will be one's perception of heresy in him', *Apologia,* p. 275, cf. Imberg, *In Quest of Authority,* pp. 181-7.

[164] *English Churchman* I, No. 56 (1843), pp. 56-7.

[165] J. H. Newman, *A letter to the Rt. Rev. Father in God, Richard, Lord Bishop of Oxford* (Oxford, 1841), p. 45.

[166] *Apologia,* pp. 30-1, 41-2. In fact, such a charge was confined to Newman's more extreme Protestant opponents. For instance, see S. Minton, *An exposure of the inconsistencies, fictions and fallacies of Dr. Newman's lectures at Birmingham* (London, 1851), p. 8.

[167] Churton MSS, Sutton Coldfield, (priv.), E. Churton to W. J. Copeland, 11 February 1842.

[168] Quoted in Cross, p. 127.

[169] Avis, p. 233.

[170] T. Vargish, *Newman: the contemplation of mind* (Oxford, 1970), p. 19.

[171] *London Quarterly Review* XXIII, No. XLV, 'Mr. Kingsley and Dr. Newman' (October, 1864), p. 116.

[172] Quoted in Avis, *Anglicanism,* p. 256.

[173] *Apologia,* p. 94.

[174] Bodleian Library, Norris MSS, MS Eng. Lett. cf. 789. C. J. Blomfield to H. H. Norris, 2 September 1824, cf. E. Churton, *Memoirs of Joshua Watson* I, pp. 249-50.

[175] *The Bishop's Charge, not as it was, but as it should have been. By a Protestant* (London, 1843), cf. J. T. Holloway, *The reply, Baptismal Regeneration and Sacramental Justification not the doctrine of the English Church* (London, 1842).

[176] F. Bennett, *The story of W.J.E. Bennett* (London, 1909), pp. 38-9, cf. W. J. E. Bennett, *A farewell address to his parishioners* (London, 1861), pp. 4-23.

[177] Even one of the most bigoted and intemperate of Newman's later critics conceded, 'it is evident, on every page, that Dr. Newman has deceived himself before deceiving his readers'. Pastor Chiniquy, *The Perversion of Dr. Newman to the Church of Rome* (London, 1883), p. 21.

[178] W. E. Houghton, *The art of Newman's Apologia* (London, 1945), p. 22.

[179] *London Quarterly Review* XXIII, 'Mr. Kingsley and Dr. Newman', p. 129.

POLITICAL IMPLICATIONS

Thomas Arnold (essay date 1836)

SOURCE: "The Oxford Malignants and Dr. Hampden," in *The Edinburgh Review,* Vol. LXIII, No. CXXVII, April, 1836, pp. 225-39.

[*The father of English man of letters Matthew Arnold, Thomas Arnold was a distinguished scholar of classical literature and Christian doctrine. In the following essay, he defends the Bampton Lectures of Dr. Hampden, who criticized the perpetuation of Catholic traditions within the Anglican Church, against the accusations of "rationalism" by the proponents of the Oxford Movement. This essay, deemed excessively pro-Catholic by the critic's peers upon its publication, nearly cost Arnold his position as Master of Rugby School.*]

Dr Hampden, the present Regius Professor of Divinity in the University of Oxford, after having obtained as a young man the highest academical distinctions, was appointed, in the year 1832, to preach what are called the 'Bampton Lectures.' These consist of a course of eight sermons, preached before the University every year on some point of Christian theology; and when the preacher is a man of any ability or reputation, the sermons, from their elaborate character, and from being delivered during a period of several weeks, always attract considerable attention. In the following year, Dr Hampden was appointed by Lord Grenville, Principal of St Mary's Hall; and, in 1834, he was elected Professor of Moral Philosophy,—the electors being the Vice-chancellor and Proctors for the time, the Dean of Christ Church, and the Presidents of Magdalen and St John's Colleges; and one of the qualifications required in the Professor by the statutes being, that he should be *sinceritate fidei commendatus*. The Dean of Christ Church, Dr Gaisford, and the Presidents of Magdalen and St John's, Drs Routh and Dynter, held their present situations in the year 1834, and elected Dr Hampden to the professorship. The 'Purity of his Faith' received also, on the same occasion, the sanction of Dr Rowley's approbation, the Master of University College, who was, in 1834, as he still is, the Vice-chancellor of the University.

A career so marked at every period by academical honours, pointed out Dr Hampden as one of the most distinguished members of his University; and when the King's Government selected him to fill the important office of Regius Professor of Divinity, upon no other recommendation than that of his high public and academical character, it might have been supposed that their choice would have been received by the University, not with satisfaction merely, but with gratitude. The Government had, in a manner, believed the University's testimonial; and had attached so much weight to it as to be thereby influenced in the disposal of a piece of preferment not more lucrative than honourable.

But instead of peace there came a whirlwind. A numerous party in the University first took upon themselves, with characteristic modesty, to petition his Majesty to rescind his own appointment; and when this application was treated with due contempt, the baffled petitioners, or rather conspirators, commenced one of the most extraordinary courses of agitation ever yet witnessed even in the annals of party malignity.

As a first step, they met in the common room of Corpus Christi College, and named a committee to conduct their business. The committee drew up a declaration, which was submitted to the whole body of the conspirators, and then published, with a long list of names subscribed to it. The declaration contained a protest against Dr Hampden's appointment: it charged him with having 'contradicted the doctrinal truths which 'he was pledged to maintain;' and with having 'asserted principles which necessarily tend to subvert, not only the authority of the Church, but the whole fabric and reality of Christian truth.' By way of scholium on this declaration, the committee annexed to it an extract from their own report, in which they explained the mischievous principles ascribed to Dr Hampden as no other than what they call the 'Philosophy of Rationalism.' 'It is the theory of rationalism,' they say '(as set forth systematically in the Bampton Lectures of 1832, and still more recently asserted in lectures addressed to students), which is to be considered the root of all the errors of Dr Hampden's system.'

We feel, that in this last quotation, we are drawing somewhat largely upon the confidence of our readers. We can indeed, to speak plainly, forgive them if they mistrust us. It is monstrous, it is almost incredible, that a charge of 'mischievous principles' should be founded upon Dr Hampden's Bampton Lectures of 1832; and not only this, but that these mischievous principles should be described as 'SET FORTH SYSTEMATICALLY!' Mischievous principles, SET FORTH SYSTEMATICALLY, in a course of eight sermons preached successively in the University pulpit, before the Vice-chancellor and all the Dignitaries and Tutors of the University,—and no proceedings instituted, no censure passed, no accusation made,—but, on the contrary, the preacher subsequently receiving from the University the highest degree in divinity—that degree which is virtually a professorship of theology—the University's commission to give lectures to its students in every branch of that faculty—receiving again the office of Head of a Hall—and, lastly, the Professorship of Moral Philosophy! Such was the University of Oxford's censure upon eight sermons full of 'SYSTEMATIC MISCHIEF,'—preached in her own church,—and in the presence of her highest authorities! And this statement comes, not from an enemy, not from a rival;—it is no dissenting slander; no *Edinburgh Review* calcumny;—but it is given out to the world from the very heart of Oxford herself; and subscribed with the names of five of her most devoted sons, who have known her long and well, who cannot misrepresent her in ignorance, who would not slander her in malice!

But the marvel is greater still. This charge against Dr Hampden's Bampton Lectures, made by five individuals, has been adopted and sanctioned by seventy-six others—all of them masters of arts at the least—all describing themselves as persons 'engaged or interested in the religious instruction of the University.' All the five accusers, and an immense majority of the seventy-six sanctioners of the accusation, were exactly as much engaged and interested in the religious instruction of the University, in 1832, as they are now, in 1836. A reference to the Oxford calendar of 1832 will prove this at once to those to whom it is not notorious. Was there ever an accusation involving its unhappy promoters in such a dilemma of infamy? Compromisers of mischievous principles in 1832, 1833, 1834, and 1835,—or slanderers of a good and most Christian man in 1836—disqualified for the office of religious instructors, upon their own showing, by four years of either dulness or indifference, during which they could not understand, or did not notice, what was 'mischievous'—or else by one month of audacious and unprincipled calumny! We leave it to the nation to decide for which of these merits it will continue to respect and confide in the greater part of the eighty-one graduates, fellows, and tutors who have signed the declaration against Dr Hampden.

Still, here is a phenomenon which requires explanation. What new circumstances have either enlightened the ignorance of these persons, or awakened their slanders? Whence this hurricane after so profound but, it seems, so treacherous a calm? Dr Hampden, in 1834, published a pamphlet, entitled 'Observations on Religious Dissent, with particular reference to the use of Religious Tests in the University;' and, in 1835, he was a strenuous advocate for the measure, which had received, it is said, the sanction of the Duke of Wellington, the Chancellor of the University; namely, the substituting of a Declaration of Agreement with the doctrines of the Church, so far as the declarant's knowledge went, in the place of the unqualified subscription to the Thirty-nine Articles, now required of every young man who enters at Oxford. It was natural that these acts should throw a new light on all that Dr Hampden had formerly written; nor can we be surprised that the eighty-one graduates, &c. should have partaken in this sudden illumination.

We return, however, to our narrative. The Corpus new Political Union petitioned the Board of Heads of Colleges and Halls, to propose to Convocation two measures:—one, an address from the University to the Bishops, requesting them not to require from candidates for orders the usual certificate of having attended the lectures of the Regius Professor of Divinity, but to be satisfied with attendance on the lectures of the Margaret Professor of Divinity, Dr Fawcett;—the other, a statute to be passed by the University itself, depriving the actual Regius Professor of his voice in the nomination of the select preachers, and also in the cognizance of any alleged heretical preaching. But the Heads of Houses refused to bring forward either of these measures before the Convocation.

Undismayed by this check, the unionists, by dint of sheer importunity and agitation, prevailed upon the Board to depart from their former resolution, and to propose the second of the two measures to Convocation,—the address to the Bishops being tacitly relinquished. Accordingly, notice was officially given, that on the 22d day of March a Convocation would be held for the consideration of the proposed statute. This precious bill of attainder states, in its preamble, that the University has no confidence in its Regius Professor of Divinity, in consequence of the manner in which he has treated theological subjects, in his published writings; and then, an enactment follows, divesting the said Professor of the powers which we have mentioned a little above, and which are attached to his office.

It were waste of time to comment on this proceeding: it were idle to dwell on the utter confusion which it exhibits of the simplest principles of good government—on the attempt to substitute the vote of a factious majority for the sober judgment of a court of justice—to put a vague charge of 'having forfeited the confidence of the University' in the place of the definite, intelligible, and tangible accusation of 'having preached doctrine contrary to the Articles of the Church.' For the Church of England, like every other society, is not without a legal check upon the conduct of its ministers. If a clergyman's preaching be at variance with the tenets of the Church, the Bishop of his diocese may take cognizance of it; or if the alleged offence be committed in Oxford, the University statutes have provided that the vice-chancellor, with the assistance of six doctors of divinity, shall enquire into the truth of the charge, and pass sentence accordingly. If Dr Hampden had really published any thing in opposition to the Articles of the Church of England, there was a ready way of substantiating the charge, and obtaining a censure upon him, from a competent authority. But the course of truth and honesty was not suited to the eighty-one conspirators. They thought that they had a secure majority in Convocation, which would vote for any thing that they proposed to it. A *vote,* they knew, might give them what they could never dare to hope from a *verdict.* If Justice were to decide upon the case, they were sure to be disgracefully defeated; if Faction could be made the judge, they had a reasonable prospect of success.

Mean time, a charge that dared not abide the decision of a legal tribunal, was to be supported by evidence worthy of itself. A pamphlet was published, entitled 'Elucidations of Dr Hampden's Theological statements,' consisting of a number of quotations from his works, classed in such an order, and separated in such a manner from the context, as might best serve the compiler's purposes. This was followed by another and more elaborate production, which we have noticed at the head of this article, in which a number of propositions on different points of theology are professedly selected from Dr Hampden's works, and contrasted with the Articles of the Church of England—a selection made precisely in the same spirit, and conducted with the same honesty, as the famous selection of articles from Wycliff's works, which had the honour of being condemned by the Council of Constance.

We have before us a copy of the 'Elucidations,' in which the *omissions* in the pretended quotations there given from Dr Hampden's works have been carefully noted down; and these omissions happen so unluckily to fall upon passages which would have altered the whole tone and character of the quotation, that there is no possibility of acquitting the compiler of deliberate dishonesty. For instance, that person, in order to 'elucidate,' which, in his language means 'to misrepresent,' Dr Hampden's Doctrine on the Trinity, begins a quotation with this sentence: 'No one can be more convinced than I am, that there is a real mystery of God revealed in the Christian dispensation; and that no sclieme of Unitarianism can solve the whole of the phenomena which Scripture records. But I am also as fully sensible, that there is a mystery attached to the subject, which is not a mystery of God;' and then follows the explanation of this last clause, for which the passage has been selected. The appearance, therefore, to the reader of the 'Elncidations' is necessarily this, that Dr Hampden, after one prefatory sentence expressing, for decency's sake, his belief that there was *a mystery* connected with the divine nature, goes on with great satisfaction to dispute, or undervalue the peculiar view of this mystery entertained by the Chnrch of England. Accordingly, the pretended elucidator observes, in his introduction to this chapter of his work, that 'Dr Hampden holds that there is *some* mystery in the divine nature; but what that mystery is, or that it is the very mystery which the Catholic doctrine of the Trinity expresses, is, he considers, net revealed.' A grave charge undoubtedly against a member and a minister of the Church of England, which professes its belief in the especial doctrine of the Trinity! But what shall we say to this elucidator, when we find that this serious charge rests only on his own direct falsification of what Dr Hampden has written? For the quotation which we have copied is preceded by about a page and a half, in which Dr Hampden has been at great pains to distinguish between the doctrine of the Trinity itself, and the technical language in which it has been expressed in the writings of theologians; and to urge that it is only this language which has thrown a difficulty in the way of receiving the doctrine;—'causing,' he says, 'the wisdom of God to be received as the foolishness of man.' And then the paragraph with which the elucidator's quotation begins, begins in reality with the following sentence, which alone is sufficient to refute the whole charge founded upon its deliberate suppression. 'The truth itself, of the Trinitarian doctrine, emerges from these mists of human speculation, like the bold naked land on which an atmosphere of fog has for a while rested, and then been dispersed.' It is apparent enough that the atmosphere of fog, of which Dr Hampden speaks, has rested without being dispersed, upon the understanding or conscience of the 'elucidator.'

This same falsehood, for it deserves no lighter name, runs through all the second pamphlet, the preface to which is actually signed with the name of Dr Pusey. The technical language in which scriptural truths have been expressed is carefully confounded with the truths themselves. Dr Hampden as carefully distinguishes them; repeating over and over again his firm belief that the scriptural truths are such in substance as the Church of England represents them—but agreeing with many of other good and sound divines, in regarding the language in which they are conveyed in theological writings, as perplexing; and as not setting forth the truth in the same practical manner as it is to be found in the scripture. Now, if a minister of the Church of England did not believe that her articles expressed substantially the truth, as it is in the scripture, he would undoubtedly be guilty of great inconsistency in subscribing them; but to account *historically* for the origin of the technical language of those articles,—and to separate it from the divine truth intended to be expressed by it, is neither inconsistent with the faith of an orthodox Christian, nor with the subscriptions signed by a clergyman of the Church of England.

With a natural and pardonable earnestness, yet paying, we think, far too great deference to charges so worthless in themselves, and known to proceed from authors whose censure was to be coveted by every good Christian minister, Dr Hampden's friends were at the pains of publishing 'statements of Christian doctrine,' extracted also from his works; and containing a series of passages on every important point in theology, so full, so clear, so entirely in unison with the doctrines of the Church, and expressed with such intense earnestness of sincerity, that it might seem beyond the power of the very spirit of calumny itself to affix a charge of heresy on their author. It is very important also to observe, that these passages are extracted in great proportion from a published volume of Dr Hampden's parochial sermons;—a work which his calumniators took good care not to notice. Now, it is manifest, that the real nature of a man's religious views and feelings is to be collected most perfectly from his general pastoral preaching to his own congregation; and not from a set of sermons preached on a particular subject, and when that subject is in itself of an abstract and unimpassioned character. The subject of Dr Hampden's

Bampton Lectures was the influence of the Scholastic Philosophy on Christianity; his business therefore was less to enforce the original truths of the gospel, than to condemn the corruptions of them; his statements were of necessity negative rather than positive; confuting error rather than inculcating truth. To quote, therefore, exclusively from such a work, even had the quotations been fairly made, was to give an utterly inadequate and unjust view of Dr Hampden's character as an instructor in positive Christianity.

In the midst of all this ferment, the day arrived on which Dr Hampden was to deliver his inaugural Lecture. As might have been expected, an immense crowd of hearers attended it. It was a trying moment; for as the Professor looked round upon his audience, he saw the well-known faces of his persecutors, who had already shown abundantly that they were of those who make a man an offender for a word, and who were come to his lecture not to be convinced, not to be softened, not to listen and to judge with fairness and truth; but to lay hold upon every expression, to misunderstand or misrepresent his matter, and to pervert his tone and manner;—ready to call conciliation cowardice, and firmness pride. Yet from this fiery ordeal Dr Hampden came forth nobly triumphant. It was touching to observe the subdued emotion of his countenance, and the unquelled and unexcited dignity of his voice:—it was beautiful to mark how he had triumphed over opposite temptations,—how meekly and patiently he laboured to remove misunderstanding,—how honestly he abstained from one word of unworthy compromise,—yet how heroically he forbore from every expression of resentment or contempt towards the faction of his unworthy calumniators. We cannot resist the pleasure of copying the concluding passage of this most Christian address.

> 'I appeal from an excited spirit to a spirit of soberness and candour; I demand not to be tried by the conclusions of an adverse school, but by the calm and gentle reason of men disposed to give me credit for no less love of the truth and the faith than themselves, and who will openly contend with me by argument, not by censure and intimidation, and the array of hostile numbers: "Non tam bene cum rebus humanis agitur," says an ancient philosopher, "ut meliora pluribus placeant; argumentum pessimi, turba est." And a far greater than the philosopher has said:—"Woe unto you when all men shall speak well of you."—"Blessed are ye when men shall revile you and persecute you, and shall say all manner of evil against you falsely for my sake."—"If any man will come after me, let him deny himself, and take up his cross and follow me." These words are my comfort; I trust he who spoke them will enable me to proceed on my way without repining at the suffering through which he has required that I should pass;—and without relaxation of spirit in his work under the painfulness of the counteraction against which it must be done. I am at all times ready to meet fair and free discussion, but to misrepresentation, and clamour, and violence, with God's help I will never yield. I pray God to forgive those who may have employed such weapons against me, and to turn their hearts, and to grant them more of that mind which was in Christ Jesus.
>
> 'It is a great grief to me, I acknowledge, to know that there are any whose honest though mistaken zeal I may have offended. Such are, I trust, open to conviction and kinder feelings; I should, however, unless experience had furnished ample instances of it, wonder that Christian zeal should in any individual have carried him to proceedings destructive of Christian purity and peace. A sense of Christian duty and the kind feelings of the heart will never, I believe, be found apart from each other, and least of all, in doing "the work of the Lord."
>
> 'After all, however, I appear not here as a functionary of the University, or of the Church alone, but as the servant of a Master in Heaven by whose judgment I must stand or fall. For let me say it with that humility which becomes me in applying to myself such sacred words: "With me it is a very small thing that I should be judged of you or of man's judgment; yea, I judge not mine own self. For I know nothing by myself; yet am I not hereby justified: but he that judgeth me is the Lord. Therefore judge nothing before the time, until the Lord come, who both will bring to light the hidden things of darkness, and will make manifest the counself of the hearts; and then shall every man have praise of God." '

This might have been thought irresistible; but faction and fanaticism combined are proof against any impression of truth or goodness. The conspirators actually adjourned their meetings from Corpus common room to Mr Baxter's Printing office; there, with the press before them, they issued with unabated zeal their placards, and circulars, and elucidations, and statements,—all designed to fanaticise their partisans amongst the country clergy, whom they had summoned up to Oxford to secure their expected triumph in the Convocation on the 22d of March.

There is no reason to doubt that their arts would have been successful; but the exemplary firmness of the Proctors saved the University, for a time at least, from the deep disgrace in which the party would have involved it. By the constitution of Oxford, if two Proctors are agreed, they can interpose a *veto* upon any measure brought forward by the Heads of Houses; and thus prevent it from being submitted at all to the votes of the Convocation. On the 19th of March the Proctors gave official notice of their intention to negative the statute. The factious and fanatical party, deceived by the unscrupulous falsehoods of the Tory Newspapers, still expected that there would be a division, and crowded up to Oxford. When the 22d of March arrived, they found out their error:—the Convocation was held, and the Proctors, as they had declared they would do, put their negative on the statute in the usual form. The conspirators and their country disciples consoled themselves by fresh placards, and by a meeting in Brazenose Hall, where they had the pleasure of listening to speeches from Lord Kenyon, Lord Encombe, Mr A. Trevor, and Dr Pusey.

Thus the persecution rests for the present. But it will be renewed, in all probability, early in the next term, when new Proctors will have come into office. Mean while, we may be thought to have given undue importance to these Oxford squabbles; and to have unwisely gratified the vanity of a few obscure fanatics by noticing them in this Journal. The *individuals,* indeed, are sufficiently insignificant;—nor shall we, by naming them, confer on them that notoriety for which nature has not designed them. But the *party,* unworthy as it is, is yet strong enough to be mischievous. Always defeated in the end, it has yet always impeded the progress of good, and in some degree marred its triumph;—so it did at the Revolution of 1688,—so it did at the Reformation.

The common language, which describes history to be philosophy teaching by examples, is an ambiguous expression of a great but ill-understood truth. No man would go to history for lessons of private morality: we have other far better and readier means of learning these. But what history does furnish, when read aright, is a mirror to reflect the true character of existing parties, and so, to determine our judgment in taking part with one or another. It gives us this true mirror when we have learned, in the parties and revolutions of past times, to separate what is accidental and particular from what is essential and universal—to fix first the true standard of all political enterprise, and then to judge of parties, whatever may be their subordinate resemblances or differences, by their attachment or opposition to this one great end. Thus we find, that the zealous worshipper of the saints and apostles, in the sixteenth century, was the real moral successor of their persecutors in the first; and thus the fanatic who now spreads the no-popery war-cry, is the genuine representative of those very Papists of the sixteenth century, whose names he is overwhelming with obloquy.

This is consoling, because it shows that the world has on the whole advanced;—that the heresy of one period becomes the orthodox faith of another;—and that that which great and good men taught at the price of their blood, obtains in the end so sure a triumph, that even the low and the wicked are obliged to do it homage, and make use of its name to exclude that further development of truth which is indeed its own genuine child. Thus, even the Tories of our days profess to admire the Revolution of 1688; but whilst exalting the individual of the race, as it were, who has done his appointed work, and has nearly lived out his generation, they would fain see his lineage become extinct for ever, and no heir born in due season to continue and improve what he had begun. For it is false to say that the reform, or the truth, of a later age undoes or despises the reforms and the truths which have preceded them. They do not destroy, but complete;—holding in honour, loving, and using the reforms and the truths achieved and discovered by their fathers,—but deeming it the worthiest tribute to their fathers' memory to imitate their example, by farther reforming and developing some farther truth, as they did.

But on the character of no party does history throw so full and clear a light as on the High Church party of the Church of England—the party of the Oxford conspirators. Unlike the political Tories, who are only analogously like the Tories of the Revolution, by being as much in the rear of the existing generation as the old Tories were in the rear of theirs, these Church Tories have stirred neither actually nor relatively; they are the very Nonjurors and High Church clergy of King William's, and Anne's, and George the First's reign, reproduced, with scarcely a shade of difference. Now, as then, this party is made up of two elements; of the Hophni and Phinehas school, on the one hand—the mere low worldly clergy, careless and grossly ignorant,—ministers not of the Gospel but of the aristocracy, who belong to Christianity only from the accident of its being established by law; and of the formalist Judaizing fanatics, on the other hand, who have ever been the peculiar disgrace of the Church of England; for these High Church fanatics have imbibed, even of fanaticism itself, nothing but the folly and the virulence. Other fanatics have persecuted, like the Romanists, in order to uphold a magnificent system, which, striking its roots deep, and stretching its branches wide, exercises a vast influence over the moral condition of man, and may almost excuse some extravagance of zeal in its behalf. Others again have been fanatics for freedom, and for what they deemed the due authority of God's own word. They were violent against human ceremonies—they despised learning—they cast away the delicacies, and almost the humanities of society, for the sake of asserting two great principles, noble even in their exaggeration,—entire freedom towards man, and entire devotion towards God. But the fanaticism of the English High Churchman has been the fanaticism of mere foolery. A dress, a ritual, a name, a ceremony;—a technical phraseology;—the superstition of a priesthood, without its power;—the form of Episcopal government, without the substance;—a system imperfect and paralysed, not independent, not sovereign,—afraid to cast off the subjection against which it is perpetually murmuring. Such are the objects of High Church fanaticism—objects so pitiful, that, if gained ever so completely, they would make no man the wiser or the better,—they would lead to no good, intellectual, moral, or spiritual—to no effect, social or religious, except to the changing of sense into silliness, and holiness of heart and life into formality and hypocrisy.

Once, however, and once only, in the history of Christianity, do we find a heresy—for never was that term more justly applied—so degraded and low principled as this. We must pass over the times of Romanists—we must go back to the very beginning of the Christian Church, and there, in the Jews and Judaizers of the New Testament, we find the only exact resemblance to the High Churchman of Oxford. In the zealots of circumcision and the ceremonies of the law,—in the slanderers and persecutors of St Paul—the doters upon old wives' fables and endless genealogies—the men of 'soft words and fair speeches,'—of a 'voluntary humility,' all the time that they were calumniating and opposing the Gospel and its great apostle;—in the malignant fanatics who, to the number of more than forty, formed a conspiracy to assassinate Paul, because he had denied the necessity of ceremonies to salvation—the men of 'mint, and anise, and cummin,' who cared not for judgment, mercy, and truth—the enemies and revilers of the holiest names which earth reverences, and who are condemned, in the most emphatic language, by that authority which all Christians acknowledge as divine;—in these, and in these alone, can the party which has headed the late Oxford conspiracy find their perfect prototype.

But we may not press this farther *now*. Most true and complete as is the parallel, and most instructive as it is, towards setting a mark upon these revived Judaizers, to warn all Christians against their spirit and their practice, yet it would lead us into matter, and thoughts, and feelings too deep to find a place here. We turn to a comparison less solemn—to a period and a country less remote—to the events of scarcely more than a century ago—to the spirit and the proceedings of the High Church party under the Liberal Government that followed the Revolution. The tricks that have been now attempted to be played in the Convocation of the University were then played in the Convocation of the Clergy. There, we find the bigot Dr Jane, who defeated the attempt of King William's Government to effect a union between the Church and the Dissenters, by the parrot-like repetition of *Nolumus leges Angliæ mutari.* There we find Burnet's *Exposition of the Articles* condemned by the lower House of Convocation, on grounds similar to those now urged by the Oxford conspirators against the writings of Dr Hampden; namely, 'that it allowed a diversity of opinions, which the Articles were framed to avoid; that it contained many passages contrary to the true meaning of the Articles, and to other received doctrines of our Church; and that some things in it were of dangerous consequence to the Church, and derogated from the honour of the Reformation.' Such was the sentence passed by the High Churchmen of the last century, upon a book which is now universally received as a correct statement of the doctrines of the Church, and which is commonly recommended by the Bishops as a companion to the theological studies of candidates for orders! Again, the rancorous slanders of the High Churchmen against names amongst the most revered in the annals of the Church, may sufficiently console Dr Hampden for the same slanders now vented against himself. The Irish nonjuror Lesley, in an anonymous pamphlet, professing to be written by 'A true son of the Church,' and published in 1695, writes thus of Archbishop Tillotson:—'His politics are Leviathan, and his religion is latitudinarian, which is none; that is, nothing that is positive, but against every thing that is positive in other religions. . . . He is owned by the atheistical wits of all England as their true primate and apostle. They glory and rejoice in him, and make their public boasts of him. He leads them not only the length of Socinianism (they are but slender beaux who have got no further than that), but to call in question all revelation, to turn Genesis, &c., into a mere romance—to ridicule the whole, as Blount, Gildon, and others of the doctor's disciples have done in print.' Lesley goes on to call Tillotson's principles 'diabolical,' and says that he had by them 'deeply poisoned' the nation.[1] And another nonjuror, Hickes, a man, like one or two of the Oxford conspirators, much vaunted by his party for the pretended holiness of his life, because he used a sentimental style of excessive religious feeling in his prayers and other compositions, found his religion perfectly compatible with falsehood and malignity; for he was privy to the writing of this wicked libel, and recommended it, hoping that it might see the light before the publication of his own discourses upon Dr Burnet and Dr Tillotson.[2] These men, whose intellectual powers were so low, that Johnson himself, in spite of all his prejudices in their favour, declared, 'that with one exception, he never knew a nonjuror who could reason,' appear to have exactly reversed the precept of St Paul, which bids us 'in malice to be children, but in understanding to be men.'

But the Government held on its way in spite of the clamours, the constant libels, and the occasional treasons of the High Church clergy. It continued to advance real Christians, like Burnet and Tillotson, to such important stations in the Church as fell vacant. The higher elergy were thus gradually purified; and of the lower, the Hophni and Phinehas party, seeing which way promotion came, composed their outward bearing accordingly, while the more fanatical party died out in their own folly. Then came a period in which the spirit of the Heads of the Clergy was indeed an honour to the Church of England—the period marked by the names of Wake, of Butler, of the apostolical Bishop Wilson, and of Secker—men firm and earnest in the faith of the Church of England; but in whom faith ministered to holiness and to charity, because it was the faith of Christians, and not of Judaizers.

Yet the experience of the last century affords, in one respect, a warning by which we hope that the Liberal Government of the present day will not fail to profit. The poisonous plant of Judaism was cut down or withered away; but the root was left in the ground; and thus, when its season returned, it sprung up again, and is now again growing rankly. In other words, Oxford was allowed to retain its exclusive character—opinions and prejudices of one sort only found admission to it—it stood aloof from the great mass of the intelligence of the nation, neither influencing it, nor influenced by it. The consequences were doubly injurious: Oxford, on the one hand, lived wholly in the past, and that past continually viewed amiss; whilst the active part of the nation, finding one of its great seats of education thus incompetent to discharge its duties, could but supply its place imperfectly by other means. Men's views became too exclusively practical and utilitarian—they lived too entirely in the present; and thus learning decayed, and a narrowmindedness of another sort began to prevail, equally injurious to that lofty wisdom, which, by ever looking at the present through the past, learns thus, and thus only, to provide aright for it and for the future. We are satisfied that there is a spirit, in an ancient and magnificent University like Oxford, far too valuable to be quietly suffered to taint and spoil itself, by refusing the wholesome combination of elements of a different species. If Oxford be left alone, and a substitute for it be sought in a new University, both will suffer, for both will remain more or less sectarian;—the High Church fanaticism will become more and more inveterate, while it will be met by extremes of another sort, not more respectable or profitable.

One word more in conclusion. We have used the language of severe condemnation in speaking of the late proceedings at Oxford, and of the party which originated them. We should be most unwilling to speak harshly of any mere differences of opinion, utterly false and mischievous as we hold the views of the High Church party to be; yet, if it were merely an *intellectual error,* it should be confuted, indeed, firmly and plainly, but still, with all tenderness to the persons of those who held it. But the attack on Dr Hampden bears upon it the character, not of error, but of *moral wickedness.* When men break through the charities and decencies of life, to run down a good and pious individual—when they raise a cry against him which they know will arouse the worst passions, and be re-echoed by their baser followers with a violence to shame even themselves—when they appeal not to any legal and competent tribunal, but to the votes of an assembly where party spirit is notoriously virulent—when they garble the writings of their intended victim, wholly neglecting such as would palpably refute their charge, and so detaching the passages which they quote from the context, and keeping out of sight the writer's general object, as to produce an impression unfair and false—above all, when refusing to give credit to a good man's solemn declarations, they labour as far as in them lies to ruin his character,—to say nothing of the acute pain occasioned to a noble mind by being insulted with such suspicions,—in such a proceeding we see nothing of Christian zeal, but much of the mingled fraud, and baseness, and cruelty, of fanatical persecution. And, for such persecution, the plea of conscience is not admissable; it can only be a conscience so blinded by wilful neglect of the highest truth, or so corrupted by the habitual indulgence of evil passions, that it rather aggravates than excuses the guilt of those whom it misleads.

Notes

[1] Birch, Life of Tillotson, p. 297, 2d ed. 1753.

[2] Birch, *ubi supra.*

John L. Morrison (essay date 1959)

SOURCE: "The Oxford Movement and the British Periodicles," in *The Catholic Historical Review,* Vol. XLV, No. 2, July, 1959, pp. 137-60.

[*In the essay that follows, Morrison examines the political conservatism of the Oxford Movement, which called for strong protection of the Church against government intervention and the renewed sanctity of the Anglican Church; he traces the changes in public opinion of the movement by reviewing journals and periodicals of the time.*]

Periods of political reform are often marked by reactionary movements in religion. As the liberals take control of the legislative processes, Toryism retreats within the sanctuary where religion not infrequently becomes the tortoise shell of the conservatives. Safely ensconced, their defensive needs narrow to the requirement that they not be drawn out by the demands of the State. They seek to formulate a system which justifies and sustains a maximum of independence from secular control. Historically, they become attracted to a romanticized past in which incidents like Henry IV's submission at Canossa loom as a kind of *beau idéal.* Intellectually, they fashion arguments to support Gelasius' classic doctrine of the two swords. The Tractarian or Oxford Movement, coinciding as it did with England's Reform Age, 1832-1867, educed just such tactics. Tractarian theology, from this standpoint, was not exclusively a religious issue. It could instead be interpreted as the doctrinal imperative of an anti-Erastian polity. The informed British public usually took this view of the matter. Englishmen who discussed the Oxford doctrines found themselves interested in the impact of Tractarian thought upon Church-State relations and political theory. For most, this constituted the chief attraction of the Oxford Movement.

The founders of the Oxford Movement, led by John Keble, can all be classified as strong Tories whose initial purpose, at least, was to protect the Church from the encroachments of the State.[1] The movement began with the suppression by the British reformers of ten Irish bishoprics. Their action provoked Keble's assize sermon on "National Apostasy," which called for resistance to the invasion of the Church's rights.[2] Responding to Keble's call, a small band of theologians united in this hour of peril to save the Church "by reviving together with the doctrine of apostolical succession what we may term the ecclesiastical spirit, 'the mind of the Church.'"[3] As their little group labored at comparatively isolated Oxford, issuing the *Tracts for the Times,* preaching, and propagandizing among the clergy, a fierce controversy raged outside over the Irish Church Bill. The leading British journals entered the lists in this and succeeding struggles. In so doing, they provided a partisan commentary on the development of the Oxford Movement. More than that, they supplied an answer to the neglected question of what the Oxford Movement meant to factions not directly involved in it.

A relatively new phenomenon at the time, the British periodicals furnish the historian with an excellent sampling of public opinion. Displaying considerable gusto and intellectual vigor, they were at the height of their influence in this era. Francis Jeffrey had established the *Edinburgh Review* in 1802 as his contribution to the Whig cause. The Tories had countered with *Blackwood's Magazine* (1817) and the more moderate *Quarterly Review* (1809). Later the utilitarians obtained a voice in the *Westminster Review* (1824), while the Non-conformist bastion was defended by the *British Quarterly Review* (1845). Each journal thus represented a major political force operative in nineteenth-century England. Its political allegiance was, in turn, determined by its adherence to a particular philosophical outlook, economic interest, and social class. A periodical's policy toward events in the religious field effectively reflected these loyalties and indicated the extent to which they were affected by ecclesiastical trends.[4]

Sharing as it did the Tractarians' apprehensions about the government's religious program, *Blackwood's Magazine* was the first to give attention to the protests emanating from Oxford. This aggressively Tory journal discerned in the Irish Church Bill an attack upon all the established interests—nobility, throne, and landed estates. It angrily charged that the bill was spawned from the lowest depths of Jacobinism. The measure, it said, gave "damning confirmation to all that has been asserted respecting the dominion of the mob."[5] The Church had been singled out for destruction, the magazine continued, because its teachings constituted the principal defense of the established order. Sweep away that barrier and the rest—destruction of society, the constitution, and all the other symbols of conservatism—would be easy.[6] To forestall such horrors, *Blackwood's* echoed the Tractarian demand that the Church assert its integrity and demonstrate that it was not "a mere engine of State policy, . . . a mere State religion—a mere thing created by an act of Parliament."[7]

Up to this point Toryism, as exemplified by *Blackwood's,* went right along with the thinking of the Oxford reformers. Farther than this it refused to go. *Blackwood's* balked because its approach was fundamentally distinct from that of the Tractarians. Keble, Newman, and the Puseyites were motivated by religious zeal; they feared for the sanctity of their Church. The Tories' position rested on economic foundations; they feared for the sanctity of their property. It was not the elimination of the bishoprics that alarmed *Blackwood's,* but the "sacrilegious appropriation" of property involved in the financial provisions of the Church Bill. The magazine argued that if the government had the right to dispose of the bishops' lands at its own discretion, then it had an equal right to seize the lands of every nobleman and gentleman. Shuddering in dismay at the prospect, the Tory journal declared that the government's principle had dangerous tendencies. What happened to the Church seemed a portent of what might happen next to the gentry.[8]

In view of this outlook *Blackwood's,* although concurring with the Tractarians' diagnosis of the disease, could not agree with the strong anti-Erastian remedy concocted at Oxford. In its place the Tories offered a more cautious theory of the Establishment. An established church is a necessity for a State which professes to be Christian, the Tory argument ran. Since Church and State must be mutually dependent on each other, the point at which the actions of the more aggressive partner, the State, begin to infringe upon the welfare of the Church may be taken as the utmost limit of the State's rights. Applying this semi-Erastian conception to England, *Blackwood's* concluded that the State has the power to reform the Church, but may not adopt any measure tending to its harm or destruction. Similarly, the State is duty-bound to aid in projects which the Church adjudges essential to her well being.[9]

In contrast to the Oxford program, *Blackwood's* plan was inherently incapable of defending the Establishment against governmental encroachment. It was, of course, intended to be a counsel of moderation, but a scheme so filled with flaws could only produce an abject Tory retreat. Three criticisms seem in order.

According to *Blackwood's,* the State was to have the right of reforming the Church. The Church Bill was such a reform. Who was to say otherwise? Who was to decide when reform became destruction? With the Tory tide ebbing, the bishops unwilling to speak, perhaps, for fear of losing their livings, and the Puseyites rejected, who could better decide than the State itself, the representative of the people? And the people approved of the Church Bill. Secondly, *Blackwood's* case was historically weak. In accepting the association of Church and State, the whole record of political interference in religious affairs, from Henry VIII's confiscation of monastic property to the Irish Church Bill's confiscation of the bishops' lands, was accepted by implication. Finally, *Blackwood's* was guilty of illogically asking the Church to unite with a State whose governors, it said, were political Jacobins and enemies of religion.

Upon analysis it is apparent that the Tory mouthpiece preferred to rely on a historically shopworn bromide rather than accept the Puseyite program. A seemingly natural alliance with the Oxford forces was rejected, even at the risk of disaster to the Tory cause. The reason for this Tory aversion to Tractarianism, which can be found not only in *Blackwood's* but in all the British press, helps to explain the relatively minuscule influence of the Puseyites. The Tractarians were clearly headed toward the Roman Catholic faith. The prospect of a victory for Rome so repelled all English factions, on nationalistic if not theological grounds, as to override all other considerations. A fictional satire in *Blackwood's* expressed this British distaste for Romanism most forcefully. The story played expertly upon popular misconceptions of the Tractarians, their supposed hypocrisy, deception. Jesuitical tactics, and Roman sympathies. The villain of the piece was a cunning Tractarian priest who had taken orders in the Roman Church but retained his curacy in the Anglican. The victim was a moderate High Church minister who was being forced by his parishioners, especially the young ladies, to introduce Tractarian ritual. The priest, who had been representing himself as an orthdox Anglican, was called in to stem the tide. He proceeded to ingratiate himself with minister and parish, abolishing all that hinted of Puseyism. When his control was secure, however, he set out to achieve his real aim. He began to advocate ritualism, declaring that the form was more important than the spirit: "Go through the ceremonies, sir—the feeling in time will come . . . kneel when you have no devotion, bend yourself to decrees and ordinances when you have no humility and no faith; and, entering on that course with the scoff of Voltaire, you will emerge from it with the sanctity of Vincent de Paul."[10] He encouraged belief in miracles which were ridiculous frauds and slowly let his Roman ideas be known. By the time the local minister realized what was happening, his flock was securely within the Tractarian fold.[11] Such tales as this afford valuable insight into popular anti-Tractarian prejudices which formed a part of English opinion on the Oxford Movement.

British journals realized the Tractarians' Romeward drift early in the Oxford Movement. After 1838, e.g., *Blackwood's* railed incessantly against the "Progress of Popery."[12] The *Edinburgh Review,* on behalf of the Whigs, hinted at Romish tendencies as early as 1836 when it reviewed John Henry Newman's *History of the Arians.*[13] In July, 1838, the review made its charge specific in an article entitled "Oxford Catholicism." Rome and Oxford, said the Whig organ, concur in demanding submission to human authority, in elevating external acts of devotion above spiritual feeling, and in substituting imagination and sense experience in areas reserved to the intellect. "In what," therefore, they asked, "does the modern creed of Oxford differ from the ancient faith of Rome?"[14] In 1841 the *Edinburgh Review* accused the Tractarians of excusing the faults of Rome while severely censuring those of the Anglican Church. Their adoption of the spirit and general content of Roman doctrines, the journal alleged, made them "enemies of all that distinguishes the Protestant creed!"[15] Subsequently, the review greeted the appearance of Newman's celebrated Tract Ninety as an attempt on his part to hold back a major emigration to Rome. His *via media,* with its Catholic interpretation of the Thirty-Nine Articles, was upbraided as a desperate expedient for holding Oxfordites who were convinced they belonged in the Roman fold. It would not work, said the journal, for the *via media* was nothing but "the old Roman Road uncovered and made passable."[16] The final judgment of the *Edinburgh Review* amounted to a sentence of journalistic excommunication against the Newman forces: "Their doctrines may be right, but they are not those of the English Church."[17]

The conversion of Newman to the Roman Catholic faith in 1845 confirmed, of course, all these suspicions and occasioned no surprise. The newly founded magazine of the Non-conformists, the *British Quarterly Review,* interpreted Newman's departure as proof that "Puseyism is popery—nothing less."[18] Scattering its fire recklessly, the review assailed the Oxford Movement as a treacherous attack on Protestantism, the Reformation, the Bible, and justification by faith. Its disciples really belonged in Rome, where, according to the Non-conformist journal, their slanders and misrepresentations of Protestantism would be properly appreciated.[19]

Despite these initial shotgun tactics, the *British Quarterly Review* soon settled down to a more sober evaluation of the Oxford Movement. In retrospect, the magazine found that it had no quarrel with the Tractarians' original purpose, reinvigoration of the Anglican Church. In its opinion, however, the method which had been employed at Oxford, revival of the claims of the priesthood through apostolic succession, had led to fatal results. It had involved tracing a line of descent through the Roman Church, an institution which everyone, Tractarians included, had identified with Antichrist. Newman had escaped this dilemma by establishing an independent succession within the English Church. Thus the *via media* had been born, and the Anglicans presented to the world as the One, Holy, Apostolic, Catholic Church.[20] The *British Quarterly Review* did not find such historical sleight of hand very impressive. The *via media,* it said, became nothing but a floating island between the solid rocks of Catholicism and Protestantism. When the seas were troubled, men would desert the island for the safety of the rocks.[21]

Continuing its historical review of the Oxford Movement, the Non-conformist journal asserted that the Tractarians, deluded by their own arguments, had tried to mold the English Church to the new image. They had revived many of the beliefs discarded in the Reformation: clerical celibacy, purgatory, transubstantiation, miracles, confession, and veneration of relics. Liturgy and ritual, lamented the review, had usurped the place of the Bible, while the Redeemer had been pushed into the background by the concept of an infallible Church. Tractarian methods had soon become increasingly Jesuitical. Novels, e.g., had been used to propagate doctrines which they had dared not express openly. By 1845 their theological progress toward Rome had been consummated. Many Tractarians had become Catholics, the review noted, but some retained their livings in the English Church and worked secretly as agents for the cause of Rome.[22] The Oxford Movement had, therefore, eventuated, in the opinion of the *British Quarterly Review,* in "a system of priestly power to sway the destinies of two worlds."[23]

It would appear from this review that the Catholic philosophy of the Newmanites, for which their adherence to Rome was merely a repulsive symbol, was the primary cause of Non-conformist opposition to the Oxford Movement. Tractarian hostility to Protestant doctrine, and incidentally to the *Weltanschauung* growing out of that doctrine, were the offending features. Unfortunately, the *British Quarterly Review* offered no extended analysis of the subject to clarify its philosophical and political implications.

To the Nonconformists, Newman's flight to Rome may simply have excited their anti-Catholic animus, but to the *Quarterly Review,* spokesman for the more moderate, less aristocratic Tory faction, it posed singular problems. Less hidebound conservatives than those represented by *Blackwood's,* the *Quarterly's* constituents were profoundly disturbed by the strange new weapon forged by the Tractarians. Their High Church sentiments as well as their political prejudices led them to embrace the Oxford Movement as a reassertion of orthodoxy. Its ritualism, mysticism, and doctrinal absolutism appealed to their conservative spirit. Consequently, until the dreaded specter of Romanism repelled them, their journal undertook a sympathetic defense of the Puseyites. The result was a revealing exposition of the social implications of Tractarian theology.

It is a conservative habit to lament the lapses of the current generation. The *Quarterly* was no exception. The present age, it asserted, "has waded far into disorder, . . . low materialistic views, rationalism, . . . and self-indulgence."[24] The country was going to the devil—the devil in this case being that combination of dissenters, utilitarians, and liberals responsible for the reform bills. Afflicted with such leadership Englishmen, especially the commoners, were tempted to "insubordination" and neglected the "principles of order and discipline." Formerly the Church, in co-operation with the State, had been able to provide the moral cement which bound society together. Now with the government behaving like an enemy and conqueror, the Church was itself in danger of succumbing to the forces of disruption. If the Tory version of the good society were to be saved, the Church's vigor must be restored. The *Quarterly* thereupon proceeded to compound a prescription of Catholic principles, reverence for antiquity, and episcopal authority as an antidote for the Erastian poison.[25]

As the *Quarterly* saw it, then, the Oxford Movement promised to be a second Reformation. The original Protestant Revolt, it believed, had restored the pristine purity of the Catholic faith after it had been corrupted by the See of Rome. Catholicism had been rescued from Popery. Now the Church was being menaced by "Ultra Protestants," and it must combat the "Popery of Dissent."[26] Both Reformations, said the *Quarterly,* assumed that the essence of the English Church was its Catholicism. Rome had distorted, the liberals had rejected its exclusively Catholic nature. They had encrusted the faith with doctrinal changes, subjected the institution to illicit authority. Reform meant that the Church must scour off this noxious incrustation and reaffirm its divine commission. On this basis the review reasoned that the Church's salvation lay, not in Roman reaction or liberal innovation, but in the restoration of Catholicism.[27]

In the Tory mind, as mirrored in the *Quarterly Review,* Catholicism was equated with those religious practices which encouraged respect for the powers that be. Tractarian theology was supposed to culminate in the virtue of obedience. The first step toward this socially desirable goal was to revive the authority of the Church itself. Doctrines designed to exalt the

Church's stature, independent of the State, were, therefore, treated sympathetically by the Tory journal. Apostolic succession, which derived clerical authority from Christ Himself, was defended as an established Anglican tradition. The administration of sacraments, which placed in the priest's hands the instruments of grace, was warmly approved.[28] If such beliefs produced a highly formal, heavily ritualized style of worship, so much the better. Ceremony appealed to the physical senses and to simple imagination, the review observed. These being the qualities attributed to the people, ritual would satisfy their appetites and divert them from dangerous individualistic thoughts.[29]

Elevation of the office of the clergy was expected to produce one result of particular merit in Tory eyes. It would encourage respect for all other offices, from the king down to the lowliest justice of the peace. A modified version of divine right would prevail, in which the official derived his powers ultimately from God. Surely, the journal thought, the people would revere their divinely sustained governors. They would not refuse to render "obedience to His appointment, whose authority he hath."[30] Entertaining such hopes, the *Quarterly Review* did not allow aversion to Rome to obscure the value of the Oxford Movement. Naturally the journal disavowed the spread of "superstitious and Roman doctrines,"[31] but even after Newman's conversion it tried to retain the Tractarians within the Anglican fold. Its attitude toward the schism was moderate, conciliatory, and grief stricken: "We must also contend that the transition of individuals to the Roman communion should be regarded as the greatest public calamity by all those who are anxious for the prevalence of truly sound and Catholic sentiments within the Church herself. . . . "[32]

The Tory defense just examined was not particularly strong. It blandly assumed the identity of Catholicity and spiritual truth, and of Anglicanism and Catholicism. Since these were the very points at issue, the *Quarterly* was bound to stumble over every rock strewn along the *via media*. But its argument was sensible, for it applied the Oxford techniques to the politico-religious needs of the conservative cause. A powerful Church would command respect and obedience from the commoners, who were otherwise prone to stray into the dissenters' ranks. If the masses were inured to spiritual obedience, they were less likely to prove unruly in secular affairs. Church discipline led to political discipline—that in brief seemed to be one of the most compelling attractions of the Oxford Movement for the Tories. Not even the scandal of Romanism could make them renounce such a wholesome advantage. By holding fast and tenaciously riding out the storm of Newmanism, they managed to salvage a good deal. The Tractarians were forced to compromise theologically, and the Roman elements in their system were carefully winnowed out. As a result the Oxford Movement and the High Church merged into something distinct from either, modern Anglo-Catholicism. Later, when it was all over, the *Quarterly* would take pride in what the Tory absorption of Puseyism had wrought. A new Catholic faith, spiritually vital, socially comfortable, was ritualistically reflecting the conservative milieu:

> Look at the new-built and restored churches of the land; look at the multiplication of schools; the greater exactness of ritual observance; the higher standard of clerical life, service, and devotion; the more frequent celebrations; the cathedrals open; the loving sisterhoods labouring, under episcopal sanction, with the meek, active saintliness of the Church's purest time; look—above all, perhaps—at the raised tone of devotion and doctrine amongst us, and see in all these that the movement did not die.[33]

If conservatives found much to interest them in the fortunes of the Tractarians, the liberal forces found themselves even more vitally concerned. The voice of the Whigs, the *Edinburgh Review,* surpassed all other English journals in the amount of attention devoted to the Oxford Movement. Allowances being made for the pungent, partisan style of criticism which was common at the time, its discussions were serious attempts to grapple with the theological problems that had been raised. Much of its analysis was penetrating in its insight into the strengths and weaknesses of the Tractarians. There was a good understanding of the aims of Puseyism and a fair struggle against the methods employed. There was, above all, a clear conflict of basic philosophies, a conflict which reveals to some extent the effects of the Oxford Movement on middle class Protestantism.

In the beginning Lord Jeffrey's review did not regard the Oxford Movement as a serious challenge to its philosophical assumptions. Advised by Dr. Thomas Arnold, of Rugby fame, it dismissed the "Oxford Malignants" as a group of formalizing Judaizers creating a stir over worthless objects: "a dress, a ritual, a name, a ceremony;—a technical phraseology;—the superstition of a priesthood, without its power;—the form of Episcopal government, without the substance. . . ."[34] Nevertheless, the journal appreciated that important questions of institutional reform had been raised by the Irish Church Bill. These problems might involve practical politics rather than theological truth, but they would help determine the Church-State relationship within which doctrinal matters could be decided. The Whig organ was much concerned with the Tractarian position from this point of view.

The *Edinburgh Review* took the position that the Church Bill generally achieved the good of the Church. The question was one of fact, not of principle. The condition of the Irish Establishment was so intolerable as to require immediate action. Size, the proportion of clergy to communicants, was the great defect of the Irish Church. Not only did this burden the Irish financially, but it was harmful to the spiritual efficiency of the Church. Although great difficulties were involved, the Church Bill removed these admitted defects, the latter through suppression of bishoprics, the former through tithe relief. The long range effects would be the renovation of the Irish Church and improved relations with the Irish Nonconformists.[35]

Realizing, however, that the Tory argument rested fundamentally on economic interest and social fear, the Whig review went beyond a mere appeal to expediency. The immediate issue, it reasoned, was State control over Church property; the underlying principle was the sanctity of all property. But, the Whigs contended, the Church was not a corporation at all in a legal sense, and so could hold no property. Clerical holdings, in land or otherwise, must be considered as public property, the revenues from which the State has assigned to the clergy in return for the performance of public duties. Since public property exists only for the benefit of the community, it cannot be alienated from the State, which retains at all times the power of disposal. The power of the State to dispense property so as to best benefit the civil and religious interests of the nation was absolute and unconditional. It included both the transfer of property from one parish to another, and the reappropriation of property from religious to secular purposes.[36]

This theory accomplished the Whigs' aims. It enabled them to argue that appropriation of Church property had nothing to do in principle with individual or corporate private property. It reconciled friends of the Church to the measure by assuring them that its welfare was the sole motive for and result of the Church Bill. It permitted the practical isolation of the Irish from the English Church question. However, had the Tories cared to debate the issue on the higher ground occupied by the Whigs, they might have made some embarrassing inquiries. The corporate status of the Church, e.g., had not been definitively determined in law. By taking such a controverted point for granted, the *Edinburgh* articles reached the very conclusion which was contended, the right of the State to interfere with the Church. At a time when the Tractarians were loudly protesting that they would brook no intervention in religious affairs, the *Edinburgh Review* smugly stated that Parliament's power over the Church was absolute. By constructing a defense dependent in every particular on a disputed premise, it only convinced the Tractarians of the Church's danger. They were prodded into fighting fire with fire, one revolutionary principle, Erastianism, with another, apostolic succession. Keble's group was stimulated, not silenced, by the liberal theory. Excessive reliance on expediency might also have been charged against the Whigs. If Parliament could remove property as it saw fit, there was nothing to prevent a gradual alteration of the Church's status. Even though the liberals now considered an Anglican Establishment to be expedient, they made no secret of the fact that their ideal was State support of all religions. Should the inroads represented by the Church Bill continue, the obstacles to the realization of this ideal would be reduced. The fate of the Establishment under this theory was highly uncertain.

Implicit in the Whig argument was a conception of the Church diametrically opposed to that of the Tractarians. The *Edinburgh Review* refused to recognize the idea of a visible Catholic Church, the existence of which was essential in Tractarian theology. It declined also to identify the Church with its clergy, doctrine, or ceremony. If, indeed, there was such an entity as the Church beyond the parish unit, its essence lay in the communicants, and its unity derived from their common religious worship. Moreover, the review was willing to embrace within the meaning of "common worship" the greatest possible divergence in doctrinal opinion and the most complete freedom of inquiry into religious questions.[37] It was attacking, in other words, the very elements which constituted the core of the Oxford Movement: the Church as a divine institution, the supremacy of authority over private judgment, and the dogma of apostolic succession.

Since its appeal to expediency led unavoidably to a fundamental difference in principle, the *Edinburgh Review* was certain to attempt a more basic analysis as the Oxford Movement developed. By 1843 it reported with some alarm that Puseyism was being insidiously diffused "in periodical publications of all sorts and sizes—in Reviews, Magazines, and Newspapers, in flimsy Pamphlets and bulky Volumes, in letters, in dialogues, in tales and novels, in poetry, in congenial fiction and perverted history, in every form of typography, and in every species of composition. . . ."[38] Under these circumstances Tractarian doctrines no longer seemed self-refuting. Once it had seemed sufficient to allege that Puseyism contradicted liberal beliefs, but now it appeared that the superiority of liberal values must be demonstrated. Attack was considered the best defense. By demolishing Tractarian theology, the Whigs would be able to contrast the ruined edifice of their opponents with their own shining, solid fortress of enlightened faith.

The *Edinburgh Review* placed itself in a good position for a fair tilt with the champions of Oxford. Unlike many who, from religious left and right, tried to sully the character of the Puseyites, the Whig journal realistically recognized that the Tractarians were men of high abilities and lofty sentiments, sincere, self-denying, virtuous leaders who were inspired by a "Divine command to recall their country to a piety more profound and masculine, more meek and contemplative."[39] Their integrity had impressed others and had allowed them to play an ever greater role in the lives of clergy and laity. It would be well to concede, said the *Edinburgh Review,* that: "They are not mere antiquarians. . . . They are men of our own times—holding opinions which sway the tone and temper of many a mind at this day; and wielding an influence whose centre is perhaps to be placed in our universities, but whose circumference is wide enough to enclose the remotest corners of the land."[40]

Having no temptation, therefore, to indulge in personalities or insinuate base motives, the Whig journal managed to confine its remarks to the ideology of the Oxford Movement. In making this approach it acted on the premise that the anti-Erastian policy of the Tractarians flowed necessarily from their fundamental theological tenets. Given Tractarian assumptions about the nature of the Church, opposition to the Irish Church Bill and other Whig measures followed with perfect logic. Better than the other British periodicals, the *Edinburgh Review* appreciated that no defense of the government would be adequate which did not grapple with the roots of Tractarian theology. Particular laws were matters of the moment. What counted was the intellectual frame of reference out of which the State's religious bills were formulated. If, therefore, the Whig program was to be secured as the basis for England's future progress, the Whig philosophy must be vindicated and the fallacies of Tractarian thought exposed. Political duels, the *Edinburgh Review* reasoned, could be fought most advantageously in the theological field.[41]

With this groundwork laid, the Whig journal proceeded to an acute, critical analysis of the Tractarian argument. According to the review, the Oxford Movement was, above all, an ethical movement. Its whole system was built on the belief that man's highest perfection lay in the habitual obedience of his will to the divine law of good, i.e., to morality. The Tractarians understood, however, that in practice right and wrong were apt to intermingle. In fact, the mixture of good and evil was so complex and so subtle that in most cases they could not be distinguished by human reason. But if unaided reason lacked the power to separate right from wrong, a power which was indispensable to human life, then it must be sought elsewhere. The Tractarians, said the *Edinburgh Review,* maintained that it could be possessed only by a divine agency, which is the Church. Thus from a practical point of view, the Newman group arrived at an institutional imperative, exaltation of Church authority in the interest of morality.[42] Subsequent Tractarian claims were nothing but props for an authoritarian institution. The *Edinburgh Review* pictured this distrust of human abilities as the motivating force behind the Oxford Movement. The Tractarian mind, said the journal, could rest easy only when it had secured divine assistance for human frailty. The confidence of inspiration rather than the challenge of investigation was its lodestar. Correctly enough, the review regarded this as a rejection of the two great advances of the modern era, the Enlightenment and the Reformation. Most Englishmen, it was certain, still preferred the private judgment encouraged by the Reformation and the independent inquiry fostered by the Age of Reason to the comfort of authority. The British people knew that good habits could not be created by suppressing the logical faculties, that zeal was not a substitute for conviction, and that morality was not just a matter of form. These truths, the *Edinburgh Review* believed, were sufficient to shatter any pseudo-divine house of glass.[43] The journal admitted that, for those who desired it, there was an authority which claimed inspired infallibility in faith and morals. But that authority was to be found in the Roman Church, not the Anglican. Tractarian doctrines could be held consistently within the framework of Roman Catholic theology, where they did not repudiate Britain's development during the preceding three centuries. The Tractarians have renounced history, said the journal; now they should sever their ties with the English Church.[44]

In the remaining controversy, the *Edinburgh Review* returned constantly to its final conclusion: that Tractarian theology failed because it tried to uphold Roman Catholic doctrines in a Protestant Church. The useless attempt only injured the Church and did violence to the consciences of the Tractarians themselves. For the sake of the Establishment, the review demanded that the Church authorities refuse to tolerate Puseyism. For the sake of consistency, it urged Newman and Pusey to enter the Roman Church.[45]

The *Edinburgh Review's* analysis of the Oxford Movement had so far explained why the Tractarians desired an authoritarian Church. The magazine next discussed the doctrinal means by which such an institution could be established. In its judgment, the Tractarians relied chiefly on three concepts: emphasis on the fathers of the Church, the spirit of Catholicism, and the dogma of apostolic succession. The first, acting as it did as the foundation for the other two, received the most intensive treatment from the review.

The Tractarians were true reactionaries, said the Whig journal, and their attachment to the Church Fathers proved it. Disavowing the present Establishment, they had searched the past for the kind of Church they wanted. They found what they were looking for in patristic theology. The fathers, who had preached the superiority of the City of God over the State, as represented by the old Roman Empire, seemed to be writing for the nineteenth century. St. Augustine made good sense to a Tractarian. Consequently, the Puseyites had revived the authority of the patristic authors. They collected certain "scattered notions" of the great Anglican divines to prove that perfected Christianity could be best studied in the Church of the patristic age. While not denying the divinely inspired character of the Bible, they revered the fathers as a source of revelation equal if not superior to Scripture. Private interpretation of the Bible, they contended, should be constrained within the bounds set by the fathers and directed by the guideposts of tradition. By these means, commented the *Edinburgh Review*, the Tractarians had surrounded their ideal of an independent, sacerdotal Church with the aura of antiquity and the discipline of custom.[46]

The *Edinburgh Review* was not so ready to dethrone the Scriptures as the sole rule of faith. It was prepared to contend that the patristics were unreliable and less than inspired. What were the views of the fathers, the review inquired? There were insuperable difficulties in the way of finding an answer. The patristic manuscripts were disfigured by forgeries and interpolations; there was no agreement as to which documents were genuine; their works were voluminous and written in a dead language; and they contained errors, obscurities, and contradictions. The inevitable result was a fruitless, arid battle of citations:

> The Romanist brings forward a citation:—'you are to consider the rhetorical mode of reasoning of these venerable men,' exclaims the Protestant. The Protestant countercites—'you are not to forget,' says the Romanist, 'that it was said in the heat of controversy, when it is so natural to deal in unlimited propositions.' The Romanist is ready with another; 'the writing is not genuine—most probably a forgery,' shouts the Protestant. . . . To a fourth it is said, 'it is an interpolation of the Greeks.' To a fifth, 'it was foisted in by the Latins.' To a sixth, 'the passage is corrupt; there are five different readings, and twice as many renderings.' To a seventh, 'it is a contradiction only in appearance. . . .' To an eighth, '. . . you are to consider the *reserve* of the early Church.' To a ninth, 'true, that the passage says so, but here is another from the same author, directly in the teeth of it;' and so on forever. . . . Babel itself is but a faint image of this 'confusion of tongues.'[47]

Still other objections against the fathers were urged by the *Edinburgh Review*. They had lived in a superstitious and relatively ignorant age, from which they had naturally imbibed many false notions. They had been intellectually surrounded by and infected with polytheism, paganism, and Oriental religions. Some of their doctrines, consequently, were foreign to the spirit of the Bible. Still other beliefs, such as monasticism, hagiolatry, and miracles, could not be reconciled with the Anglican system. Further problems were discovered by the Whig magazine in the celebrated rule of Vincent of Lerins—tradition is that which has been believed everywhere, always, and by all. This rule, said the journal, was either an absurdity, since it was impossible to employ without limitations, or a nullity, since it required qualifications that destroyed its utility as a guide. Thus, carried along by the cumulative force of its own criticisms, the review confidently concluded that patristic literature was generally worthless, that it was not divinely inspired, and that it represented a corruption rather than a development of scriptural doctrine. The fathers, some of whom were learned for their day, should be judged and respected on the same basis as other mortals. Nothing, said the journal, could be more ridiculous than the extravagant claims which have made demigods out of them.[48] The folly of the Tractarians in elevating them to such a high station manifestly suggested the Newmanites' desperate plight. They could not just publish their personal opinions, that would be presumptuous; they needed a historical foundation for their theology. Tradition, first principles of the Church, patristic teaching—all these titles were intended to dignify the ideas of Newman and Pusey. But the Whigs were not to be hoodwinked; they had seen through the mask of tradition which disguised the *ex cathedra* pronouncements of the Tractarians.[49]

The *Edinburgh Review* wasted little time in disposing of the other Tractarian doctrines. Apostolic succession, according to the review, was a palpable absurdity, destitute of historical proof and offensive to Christian charity. Historically, the Reformation had made the validity of Anglican orders under apostolic succession an impossible proposition. How, the journal inquired, could the Tractarians escape from the obvious dilemma? "If error in essentials is sufficient to invalidate Orders, we ask—had the Romish Church so erred when you separated from her? If she had, her own Orders were invalid, and she could not transmit yours. If she had not, as you all affirm that nothing but heresy in fundamentals can justify *separation,* you are schismatics, and your own Orders are invalid."[50] Of even greater concern to the *Edinburgh Review* was the twofold offense of apostolic succession against charity and holiness. No sensible gifts were bestowed upon the recipient at ordination; he was not made wiser, purer, or given miraculous power. Yet this concept presumed to confer spiritual functions upon the ordained without the slightest regard for his fitness. A minister might not be moral, might not even be a Christian, yet if he were in the correct line of succession his orders were legitimate. Contrariwise, the clerical claims of the non-episcopal minister with surpassing piety and learning were coldly rejected. A doctrine so contrary to the spirit of the New Testament could not be accepted, said the Whig review.[51]

Adoption by the Tractarians of the trappings of Catholicism also antagonized the *Edinburgh Review*. It charged that Oxford Catholicism produced bitter controversies over trifles like the use of the surplice and of wax candles. More fundamentally, the journal accused the Tractarians of reviving the Roman conception of the sacraments. In denouncing their sacramental notions, the review relied on customary Protestant arguments. The spirit of the Gospel and the evidence of the senses, it stated, were offended by the Tractarian rites. All logic was defined when baptism was wasted on infants. If the sacrament effected regeneration, why not postpone it until late in life and remove the terrible doubt of salvation? Decency was outraged when burial rites were denied to those who neglected to fulfill to the letter the forms of Tractarian baptism. Similar objections could be raised against other sacraments, the review assured its readers. But enough had been said to demonstrate that vague, anti-social, irrational sacramental mysteries were unacceptable.[52]

Having confuted to its satisfaction the major tenets of Puseyism, there was little for the *Edinburgh Review* to do but sit back and await the impending collapse of the Oxford Movement. It perceived already the signs of disintegration. The one, visible Church of the Tractarians was no closer to reality than ever. With Catholics and Protestants still hostile, "It would sadly perplex any ordinary understanding to comprehend how many communities can be one, which are not only hostile, but mutually excommunicate."[58] In the face of this failure, the Puseyites were growing more vain and intolerant, the *Edinburgh Review* continued. They now denied credentials as ministers of Christ to the entire Nonconformist clergy of England. They no longer distinguished in their reckless condemnation between those who refused to obey Christ's commands and those who disagreed on what His commands were. Their educational system was falling apart too, as a result of their determination to block all avenues of understanding except the Bible and Church tradition. Every effort to increase the activities of the natural sciences, history, and the liberal arts met with their resistance. They neglected knowledge for obedience, investigation for blind adoration.[54] Jubilantly, the *Edinburgh Review* predicted that the movement would soon end in "a vigorous reaction which will give the doctrines and principles of the Reformation a revived hold on the public mind and the Biblical and Protestant elements in the English Church their legitimate expansion."[55]

The repudiation of Puseyism which the *Edinburgh Review* had begun on religious grounds was completed by the *Westminster Review* on philosophical grounds. Relatively intent on its own utilitarian mission, the *Westminster Review* had devoted little space to the Tractarians. Not until 1850 did their theology come under its scrutiny, and then the magazine's reaction was entirely predictable in the light of the well known anti-Catholic, secularistic bias of the utilitarian school. Most of the review's statements rehearsed familiar refrains. The Oxford Movement was foreign to the spirit of the times, the magazine argued. The Tractarians were antiquarians who deserted rather than solved modern problems. They were characterized by "learned selfishness and aristocratic apathy." Their concept of an authoritarian Church was Romanist, formalist, and illogical.[56] Attacking their principle of reserve in communicating religious truth, their sacerdotal system, and their reliance on the fathers, the review alleged that they had substituted a gospel of fear and mystery for the gospel of love and understanding. They had constructed a religion of manuscripts and mysticism in which the laity were given neither function nor emotional satisfaction.[57]

Primarily, however, the *Westminster Review* interpreted the Oxford Movement as an anti-Erastian reaction, a search for a theology which could sustain the Church as a supernatural corporation free from the control of any secular agency. The Tractarians wished to reap the temporal benefits of an Establishment in which one party was "an independent, self-governing, immutable body, exempt from constitutional restraints, and shielded from those changes which the progress of knowledge and the vicissitudes of thought introduce everywhere else."[58] Such a Church, thought the review, could never be accepted by the people or by the State. The people would not accept it because it was hostile to their liberty, foreign to their genius, and contrary to their diverse religious beliefs. The State must reject it because it would mean political servility.[59] The *Westminster Review* hastened to describe the type of Church which would be acceptable. In its Establishment, the State would have the power to decide on theological questions. Not being theologians, the politicians would employ one criterion in defining doctrine, public opinion, and desire one object, moral efficiency. Such a Church would permit the utmost latitude of opinion. It would bring doctrinal beliefs up to date with philosophic and scientific advances. And it would place its faith in the laity rather than the clergy.[60] In contrast to an Establishment isolated from society and intellectually stagnant, the utilitarian journal looked for its lay-centered Church to win new laurels for progressive religion: "English orthodoxy has always been found on the side of resistance. . . . It is to our laity, and to that part especially which has little ostensible religious character, that every victory over bigoted intolerance is due."[61]

The attitude of the *Westminster Review* toward the Oxford Movement was a good measure of the distance between philosophical radicalism and religious reaction in the Reform Age. Equally notable, the review centered its discussion around the problem of Church-State relations. This was chiefly a political question, but the utilitarian magazine's concentration upon the political rather than the spiritual importance of the Oxford Movement was typical. All of the British periodicals tended to share with the *Westminster Review* a concern for the secular implications of Tractarian thought. By contrast, nowhere in the journals was the customary version of the Oxford Movement reflected extensively. Usually, the movement has been presented by Catholic historians as a vehicle for the career of Cardinal Newman, and by Protestant writers as the story of spiritual rebirth within the Anglican Church. Viewed internally, as Tractarians saw themselves and as their Anglican brethren responded to Puseyism, the traditional picture is valid and valuable. The spiritual odyssey of a famous churchman and the revitalization of a great institution are matters of considerable historical moment. But study of the British magazines suggests that this approach to the Oxford Movement is too limited. Viewed externally, as political and intellectual factions saw the Tractarians, it was the political implications of their theology which seemed paramount. Certainly, many individual members of these factions must have had strong spiritual feelings about Puseyism. Personally they may have cared little about its practical effects. But their personal emotions were not the concern of the group to which they belonged. To the organized faction as such, the impact of Tractarian thought on the status and political fortunes of the party was the dominant interest.

The Tories disagreed on the merits of Puseyism as a support for their position. The *Quarterly Review* used the Catholic elements in the Oxford Movement to entrench themselves behind the wall of clerical authority and to encourage respect for their leadership in local government. On the other hand, *Blackwood's* attached so much significance to the temporalities of the Church that it lost sight of the spiritual strength which Tractarian ideology offered to its cause. *Blackwood's* believed that in defending Church property it had fastened upon the heart of the matter. Any defense which ignored the economic question seemed foolish if not dangerous. To its consequently obscured vision, the Tractarians were childish men who had deceived themselves into thinking that they were restoring the purity of the Church. The magazine advised its readers to "leave those pompous triflers to their obscure squabbles; and add something manly, honest, and rational to the national defense of Christianity."[62]

By concentrating on Tractarian theology, the *Edinburgh Review* departed, to some extent, from the usual practice among the journals. Yet the difference was one of degree, not kind. At bottom, the Whig journal too was interested in the political aspects of the Oxford Movement. Its Tractarian studies, however, were not focused on politics directly, but were oriented toward the philosophical bases of political disputes. It was this theoretical approach to political realities which made the Whig articles the most penetrating description of the Oxford Movement. The *Edinburgh Review,* in its disdain for Romanism, its staunch support of the Reformation and the Enlightenment, and its demolition of the anti-Erastian concept, spoke for the Reform Age. Its dismissal of religious conservatism typified the optimistic, progressive temper of the times. Nevertheless, the journal had been forced to contend strenuously with this conservative spirit. By raising a serious challenge, the Tractarians had caused the Whigs to think about the first principles upon which they were providing leadership to England. As an intellectual stimulus to the often torpid politician, the Oxford Movement was, therefore, a success. It did not materially alter England's political development, but it did require that the liberal statesmen, taking Newman's advice, "Should strive afresh against their foe, Should strive and should prevail."[63]

Notes

[1] Descriptive sketches of the Oxford reformers are available in R. W. Church, *The Oxford Movement, Twelve Years, 1833-1845* (London, 1861), pp. 23-91. Church and other authorities, notably George M. Trevelyan, *British History in the Nineteenth Century and After, 1782-1919* (New edition, London, 1937), p. 281, maintain that the Oxford reformers had little interest in political affairs. The point is debatable. For a contrary view, cf. Alvan S. Ryan, "The Development of Newman's Political Thought," *Review of Politics,* VII (April, 1945), 211: "It is no exaggeration to say that the Movement was as much concerned with politics as with religion, for from its inception the central question was that of the relation between Church and State."

[2] Church, *Oxford Movement,* p. 4.

[3] Elie Halévy, *A History of the English People,* translated by E. I. Watkin and D. A. Baker (3 vols., New York, 1924-1928), III, 151.

[4] For a study of the British magazines, cf. Walter J. Graham, *English Literary Periodicals* (New York, 1930), pp. 251-254, 275-280.

[5] "The Progress of the Movement," *Blackwood's Magazine,* XXXIII (April, 1833), 651. Henceforth this journal will be cited as *Blackwood's.* With rare exceptions, all articles in the British journals were anonymous and represented the editorial policy of the magazine.

[6] *Ibid.*, pp. 654-655.

[7] *Ibid,* pp. 664-665.

[8] *Ibid.*, pp. 653-655. It should be noted that the Tractarians were also worried about the State's financial weapon, although they were concerned about the Church, not the gentry. Quoting Lacordaire's remarks to the French bishops, Richard Hurrell Froude had pointed out that: "Une seule chose leur est possible; le retranchement de votre budget." Quoted in Ryan, "Development of Newman's Thought," *Review of Politics,* VII (April, 1945), 215. In his *Apologia* Newman had condemned the proposition that: "The Civil Power may dispose of Church property without sacrilege." John Henry Newman, *Apologia Pro Vita Sua* (London, 1900), p. 296.

[9] "A Letter to the King on the Irish Church Bill," *Blackwood's,* XXXIII (May, 1833), 724-725, 727; "Moneypenny on Church Extension," *Blackwood's,* XLII (September, 1837), 380-381, 383.

[10] "Letters to the Rev. Charles Fustian," *Blackwood's,* LXV (June, 1849), 692.

[11] *Ibid.*, pp. 679-696.

[12] "The Progress of Popery," *Blackwood's,* XLIV (October, 1838), 494-507.

[13] "Newman's History of the Arians," *Edinburgh Review,* LXIII (April, 1836), 53. Henceforth this journal will be cited as *E. R.*

[14] "Oxford Catholicism—The Lives of Whitfield and Froude," *E. R.*, LXVII (July, 1838), 531.

[15] "Tracts for the Times—Number Ninety," *E. R.*, LXXIII (April, 1841), 272.

[16] *Ibid.*, 275, 286; "Puseyism, or the Oxford Tractarian School," *E. R.*, LXXVII (April, 1843), 504.

[17] "Tracts for the Times," *E. R.*, LXXIII (April, 1841), 273.

[18] "Tractarian Theology. Ward's Ideal of a Christian Church," *British Quarterly Review,* I (February, 1845), 39. Henceforth this journal will be cited as *B. Q. R.*

[19] *Ibid.*, pp. 43, 56, 77-78.

[20] "Churchmen on the Church," *B. Q. R.*, XLI (January, 1865), 82-83.

[21] "Tractarian Novels," *B. Q. R.*, VIII (August, 1848), 211.

[22] *Ibid.*, pp. 203-204, 212, 226; "English Thought and the English Church," *B. Q. R.*, XXXVII (April, 1863), 473.

[23] "Tractarian Novels," *B. Q. R.*, VIII (August, 1848), 232.

[24] "Oxford Theology," *Quarterly Review,* LXIII (March, 1839), 538. Henceforth this journal will be cited as *Q. R.*

[25] *Ibid.*, 559-560; "The Universities," *Q. R.*, LIX (October, 1837), 483; "Memorials of Oxford," *Q. R.*, LXI (January, 1838), 226-228.

[26] *Ibid.*, p. 227.

[27] *Ibid.*, pp. 227-228; "The Universities," *Q. R.*, LIX (October, 1837), 483.

[28] "Oxford Theology," *Q. R.*, LXIII (March, 1839), 538-539.

[29] "The Cathedral Establishments," *Q. R.*, LVIII (February, 1837), 224.

[30] "Oxford Theology," *Q. R.*, LXIII (March, 1839), 538-539.

[31] "Rubrics and Ritual of the Church of England," *Q. R.*, LXXII (May, 1843), 236-237, 276.

[32] "Ward's Ideal of a Christian Church," *Q. R.*, LXXV (December, 1844), 193.

[33] "Dr. Newman's Apologia," *Q. R.*, CXVI (October, 1864), 542.

[34] "The Oxford Malignants and Dr. Hampden," *E. R.*, LXIII (April, 1836), 235.

[35] "First Session of the Reformed Parliament," *E. R.*, LVIII (October, 1833), 203-204; "Ireland," *E. R.*, LVII (April, 1833), 275.

[36] "Abolition of Church Rates," *E. R.*, LXV (July, 1837), 187; "Tory Proceedings—State of Parties," *E. R.*, LIX (July, 1834), 512-514; "Appropriation of Church Property—Irish Catholic Clergy," *E. R.*, LX (January, 1835), 485, 490-495.

[37] *Ibid.*, 485; "Tory Proceedings," *E. R.*, LIX (July, 1834), 512-514.

[38] "Puseyism," *E. R.*, LXXVII (April, 1843), 506.

[39] "Oxford Catholicism," *E. R.*, LXVII (July, 1838), 524.

[40] "History of Arians," *E. R.*, LXIII (April, 1836), 44.

[41] "Tracts for the Times," *E. R.*, LXXIII (April, 1841), 271.

[42] "History of Arians," *E. R.*, LXIII (April 1836), 45-46.

[43] *Ibid.*, 45; "Oxford Catholicism," *E. R.*, LXVII (July, 1838), 525; "The Right of Private Judgment," *E. R.*, LXXVI (January, 1843), 382-419.

[44] "Puseyism," *E. R.*, LXXVII (April, 1843), 528; "Recent Developments of Puseyism," *E. R.*, LXXX (October, 1844), 371-372.

[45] *Ibid.*, pp. 369, 371-372.

[46] "Puseyism," *E. R.*, LXXVII (April, 1843), 504-505.

[47] *Ibid.*, p. 530.

[48] *Ibid.*, pp. 530-535, 543-545. At the risk of suggesting a thought not entertained by the *Edinburgh Review*, it might be noted that this vigorous assault on the fathers may have been motivated, in part, by the journal's realization that Church tradition and political conservatism were closely allied. Ryan, "Development of Newman's Thought," *Review of Politics*, VII (April, 1945), 223-224, points out that Newman adopted Burke's traditionalist view of the British constitution.

[49] "Puseyism," *E. R.*, LXXVII (April, 1843), 528.

[50] *Ibid.*, pp. 513-514.

[51] *Ibid.*, pp. 511-518.

[52] *Ibid.*, pp. 511-523; "Recent Developments," *E. R.*, LXXX (October, 1844), 369.

[53] "Puseyism," *E. R.*, LXXVII (April, 1843), 524.

[54] "Dr. Pusey's Sermon on the Fifth of November," *E. R.*, LXVI (January, 1838), 404-405, 415; "The Late Dr. Arnold," *E. R.*, LXXVI (January, 1843), 375-377. Maisie Ward, *Young Mr. Newman* (New York, 1948), p. 115, explains charges of vanity and intolerance made against the Puseyites: "For the Liberal the only fundamental was personal liberty—for the Tractarian the question at issue was what God had said and what God had meant. Safeguarding this divine Word they grew fierce—and the Liberals realised so little what the fierceness was about that they took it as personal: as the result of pique, annoyance or sheer personal prejudice."

[55] "Recent Developments," *E. R.*, LXXX (October, 1844), 374-375.

[56] "Early Christianity, Its Creed and Heresies," *Westminster Review*, LIX (April, 1853), 564-565; hereafter this magazine is cited as *W. R.*

[57] "The Church of England," *W. R.*, LIII (April, 1850), 96, 101-102; "Early Christianity," *W. R.*, LIX (April, 1853), 564-565.

[58] "Church of England," *W. R.*, LIII (April, 1850), 95.

[59] "The Battle of the Churches," *W. R.*, LIV (January, 1851), 234.

[60] "Church of England," *W. R.*, LIII (April, 1850), 89, 93, 113-114. The contrast with Tractarian opinion is marked here. Thus Newman, *Apologia*, p. 296, condemns the proposition that: "The Civil Power has the right of ecclesiastical jurisdiction and administration. Therefore, e. g. Parliament may impose articles of faith on the Church. . . ."

[61] "The Religious Weakness of Protestantism," *W. R.*, LXIX (January, 1858), 75.

[62] "The World We Live In," *Blackwood's*, XLIII (January, 1838), 80.

[63] John Henry Newman, "The Dream of Gerontius," in *Verses on Various Occasions* (London, 1903), p. 363.

FURTHER READING

Abercrombie, Nigel. "Some Directions of the Oxford Movement." *The Dublin Review* 193, No. 386 (July 1933): 74-84.

Provides a general introduction to the Oxford Movement and its influence on intellectual history since the nineteenth century.

Brendon, Piers. "Newman, Keble, and Froude's *Remains*." *The English Historical Review* 345 (October 1972): 697-716.

Compares the two major texts of the Oxford Movement—Newman's *Tract 90* and Froude's *Remains*.

Butler, Perry. *Gladstone: Church, State, and Tractarianism. A Study of His Religious Attitudes, 1809-1859*. Oxford: Clarendon Press, 1982, 246 p.

Charts William Gladstone's involvement in the Oxford Movement and its role in his political and intellectual development.

Chadwick, Owen. "Introduction." In *The Mind of the Oxford Movement*, edited by Owen Chadwick, pp. 11-64. Stanford: Stanford University Press, 1960.

Introduces the primary texts of the Oxford Movement by giving a general overview of the major figures and their significance.

Dawson, Christopher. *The Spirit of the Oxford Movement*. London: Sheed & Ward, 1933, 144 p.

Discusses the significance of the Oxford Movement for religious history.

Delaura, David S. "Matthew Arnold and John Henry Newman: The Oxford Sentiment and the Religion of the Future." *Texas Studies in Literature and Language* 6, No. 1 (Spring 1964): 573-702.

Traces the influence of Newman on Matthew Arnold's intellectual ideals and spiritual beliefs.

Faber, Geoffrey. *Oxford Apostles: A Character Study of the Oxford Movement.* London: Faber & Faber, 1933, 467 p.

Studies the figure of Newman through a primarily psychological perspective.

Griffin, John R. *The Oxford Movement: A Revision*. Edinburgh: Pentland Press, 1984, 100 p.

Examines the issue of erastianism—the question of church authority—in the Tractarian Movement.

May, J. Lewis. *The Oxford Movement: Its History and Its Future: A Layman's Estimate*. London: John Lane, The Bodley Head, 1933, 301 p.

Contends that the Oxford Movement's emphasis upon the spiritual over the secular serves as a major guide for the institution of Christianity in the twentieth century.

McGreevy, Michael A. "John Keble on the Anglican Church and the Church Catholic." *The Heythrop Journal* 5, No. 1 (January 1964): 27-35.

Considers Keble's views on the relationship of Anglicanism to Catholicism, and his figurative understanding of the role of the Church.

Newsome, David. "Newman and Oxford." In *Newman: A Man for Our Time*, edited by David Brown, pp. 35-51. London: SPCK, 1990.

Recounts the influence of the Anglican Oxford University on the development of Newman's thought.

O'Connell, Marvin R. *The Oxford Conspirators: A History of the Oxford Movement 1833-45*. London: Macmillan, 1969, 468 p.

Provides a general overview of the first and most controversial years of the Oxford Movement.

Ollard, S. L. *A Short History of the Oxford Movement*. London: A R. Mowbray & Co., 1915, 283 p.

An early chronicle of the development of the Oxford Movement.

Weil, Louis. "The Tractarian Liturgical Inheritance Reassessed." In *Tradition Renewed: The Oxford Movement Conference Papers*, edited by Geoffrey Rowell, pp. 110-19. Allison Park, Penn.: Pickwick Publications, 1986.

Emphasizes the significance of the Tractarian recovery of traditional Catholic sacramental doctrines.

Willey, Basil. "Newman and the Oxford Movement." In *Nineteenth Century Studies: Coleridge to Matthew Arnold*, pp. 73-101. New York: Columbia University Press, 1949.

Relates the search for spiritual foundations manifested in the revivalism of the Oxford Movement to the general development of nineteenth-century English thought.

The Parnassian Movement

INTRODUCTION

The Parnassian Movement comprised a group of young poets writing in mid-nineteenth century France. Taking their name from the Greek mountain sacred to Apollo and the Muses, the Parnassians, while displaying considerable breadth of subject matter and style, were characterized by their concern for craftsmanship, objectivity, and lasting beauty. Critics, describing the movement as the poetic workshop of the mid-century, recognize the importance of the Parnassians in developing the artistic voices that emerged in reaction to Romanticism and laid the groundwork for the Symbolist and Decadent poetic traditions. While Charles-Marie-René Leconte de Lisle is recognized as the leading figure of the Parnassian movement, it also included the work of Théodore de Banville, Henry Cazalis, François Coppée, Anatole France, Théophile Gautier, José-Maria de Heredia, Sully Prudhomme, Paul Verlaine, and Charles Baudelaire.

Identified by such names as *Les Stylistes*, *Les Formistes*, and *Les Impassibles*, the poets became known as the Parnassians following the publication in 1866 of *Le Parnasse contemporain: recueil de vers nouveaux* (*The Contemporary Parnassus: An Anthology of New Verse*). The publication, produced by Alphonse Lemerre and collected in collaboration with Catulle Mendès and Louis-Xavier de Ricard, includes the verse of thirty-seven poets whose work was drawn from the literary salons of Mendès, Ricard, Leconte de Lisle, and Nina de Villars. The collection granted important critical and public exposure to its poets, and was successful enough to warrant publication of subsequent volumes in 1871 and 1876. As the centerpiece of the movement, the three volumes of *Le Parnasse contemporain* are considered, claims critic Aaron Schaffer, to "represent a phenomenon of the utmost importance in the history French lyric poetry." Together, they comprise the work of ninety-nine poets and contain, according to Schaffer, "representative verses of virtually every poet of any significance in the third quarter of the century."

While Lemerre, Mendès, and Ricard are generally credited with bringing the Parnassians together, critics point to Théophile Gautier as the intellectual and artistic progenitor of the movement. His plea in 1832 for "art for art's sake," a decided reaction against the social Romanticism which was popular at the time, called for a recognition of art independent of any moral, social, or scientific consideration. This ideal, later adopted as a principal tenet of the Parnassian movement, was developed from the aesthetic writings of Immanuel Kant, Georg Wilhelm Friedrich Hegel, and Friedrich Schiller, and put into practice in his two-volume collection of poetry, *Emaux et camées* (*Enamels and Cameos*), first published in 1852. Gautier's concern with preserving the autonomy of art was not only a reaction against the predilections of Romanticism, but was also, according to critic Robert T. Denommé, an attempt "to encourage and ensure the practice of poetic expression in a society predominantly concerned with more immediately useful values." And, otherwise lacking a definitive theory or doctrine, it was this theme under which the Parnassian poets united.

Better understood as sharing an artistic attitude rather than a specific technique, the poets of the Parnassian movement rejected the emphasis on subjective expression and unrestrained imagination which characterized the Romantic period. Disenchanted with the values which dominated mid-century France, the Parnassians conceived their poetry as a way to divorce themselves from social context. Instead of concerning themselves with social or political considerations, they advocated perfection of form, language, and pictorial imagery. Eschewing all which fell outside the "art for art's sake" ideal inherited from Gautier, the Parnassians attempted to create a lasting art which transcended both the attitudes and predispositions of the artist as well as the reality of the times in which it was produced. Often linked to the idea of scientific positivism, the Parnassian movement advocated form as an inseparable part of content, and sought to restore art to its original purity, stripping away all other considerations. "The world of beauty," claimed Leconte de Lisle, "the only objective of Art, comprises in itself an infinite which can have no possible contact with any type of inferior conception." The search for a lasting beauty led the Parnassians, and Leconte de Lisle in particular, to the culture and art of ancient Greece. Denommé writes, "De Lisle's conception of Hellenism constituted one of the principal cornerstones . . . of Parnassianism. The antiquarianism he advocated gave fuller dimension to such notions as antiutilitarianism, impersonalism, scientific orientation and the idealization of beauty which eventually became part and parcel of the outlook of the major Parnassian poets."

While English-language criticism and translations of Parnassian poetry remain limited, the movement is recognized as having played an important role in the development of French poetry. Its reaction against Romanticism and championing of the "art for art's sake" doctrine not only protected art from the disapproving tenor of mid-century France, but allowed for the development of the Symbolist and Decadent poetic movements which would come to dominate French literature in the following years. And while the movement produced few poets of lasting renown, its significant influence has been recognized by artist and critic alike.

REPRESENTATIVE WORKS

Louise Ackermann
Premières poésies 1860, published in 1874
Poésies philosophiques 1874

Théodore de Banville
Les Exilés 1867
Petit Traité de versification française (prose) 1872

Louis Bouilhet
Festons et astragales 1857
Dernières chansons 1872

Henry Cazalis (Jean Lahor)
Vita tristis 1865
l'Illusion 1875

François Coppée
Oeuvres de François Coppée, Poésies, vols. 1-3 1864-78

Léon Dierx
Poèmes et poésis 1864
Les Lèvres closes 1867

Anatole France
Idylles et légendes 1870

Théophile Gautier
Emaux et camées 1852

Albert Glatigny
Les Vignes folles 1860
Les Flèches d'or 1864

José-Maria de Heredia
Les Trophées 1893

Alphonse Lemerre, publisher
Le Parnasse contemporain: recueil de vers nouveaux, 3 vols. [collaboration of several poets] 1866, 1871, 1876

Leconte de Lisle
Poèmes antiques 1852
Poèmes et poésies 1855
Poèmes barbares 1862
Les Poètes contemporains (essays) 1864

Catulle Mendès
Soirs moroses 1868
Poésies de Catuule Mendès première série, 1871
Contes épiques 1872

Sully Prudhomme
Les Èpreuves 1866

Louis-Xavier de Ricard
Ciel, rue et foyer 1865

Louis de Ronchaud
Poèmes de la Mort 1886

Armand Sylvestre
Poésies 1860-74
Poésies 1872-78

Paul Verlaine
Poèmes saturniens 1867

OVERVIEWS

Aaron Schaffer (essay date 1929)

SOURCE: "Parnassus in France," in *Parnassus in France: Currents and Cross-Currents in Nineteenth-Century French Lyric Poetry,* University of Texas Press, Austin, 1929, pp. 46-71.

[*In the following excerpt, Schaffer provides an overview and history of the Parnassian movement, focusing on the poets and poetry featured in the three volumes of* Le Parnasse contemporain.]

Romanticism had freed literature of the fetters that had so long shackled it, and now men no longer blushed to pour out their souls in verse and to give these verses to be read by others. In the hands of Lamartine, Hugo, Vigny, and Musset, lyric poetry again became in France one of the dominant *genres;* in those of Gautier it became a "thing of beauty" rather than of passion or of metaphysical contemplation. The stage was set for an efflorescence of lyric poetry such as France has seldom known; this efflorescence we are now prepared to study in its successive stages and to follow to its decline.

Gautier's *Emaux et camées* was published in 1852; fourteen years later the first *Parnasse contemporain: Recueil de vers nouveaux* issued from the press. The three intervening lustra were marked by epoch-making achievements in the realm of French literature: Leconte de Lisle's *Poèmes antiques* appeared in 1852, as did *la Dame aux Camélias* of Dumas fils; the year 1857 saw the publication of Flaubert's *Madame Bovary,* Baudelaire's *les Fleurs du mal,* and Théodore de Banville's *Odes funambulesques.* In the field of the novel and the drama, the pendulum swung from the extreme of Romanticism to that of Realism, a swing that was the resultant of numerous forces: the unprecedented advances made in the various sciences, the rise to power of the moneyed *bourgeoisie* with its emphasis upon the value of physical possessions as opposed to artistic creations; briefly, the positivism of which Auguste Comte and Herbert Spencer were the philosophical mouthpieces. Poetry, though recognizing the encroachment of the materialistic spirit and in a measure succumbing to it, was yet determined to maintain its independence; and it was the Parnassian group that stood forth as the defenders of Erato in her "struggle for existence." Let us, then, acquaint ourselves with the history of *le Parnasse contemporain.*

In the year 1859, there came up to Paris from Bordeaux a Jewish banker, Tibulle Mendès, his Catholic wife, and an eighteen-year-old son who very appropriately bore the name of Catulle. This young man enjoyed a most liberal allowance, which he seemed eager to squander, for he soon hit upon the idea—hardly an original one for provincials in Paris—of founding a review. He was not slow in carrying out his idea and the result was what he himself has styled "le premier des journaux parnassiens."[1] The periodical flaunted the name of *la Revue fantaisiste,* and it specialized in printing the poems, sketches and fantasies of a group of young writers who were distinguished "par la témérité des opinions et par l'impertinence aussi de l'attitude." The review was interested in only two things, "la Poésie et la Joie." It was favored with the high patronage of Gautier, Banville, and Baudelaire, and some of its contributors later carved their names in large letters upon the history of French poetry. At the *bureau* of *la Revue fantaisiste,* there would gather of an afternoon, Banville, Charles Asselineau, Philoxène Boyer, Baudelaire, Albert Glatigny, and numerous others. One of the contributors to the *Revue* was a young musician who was struggling bitterly for recognition and whose *Tannhäuser* had been hissed off the stage of the *Opéra* in Paris—Richard Wagner. "Presque tous les poètes d'alors vinrent à *la Revue fantaisiste,*" Mendès tells us, and he claims the credit for having helped to bring to light such talents as Villiers de l'Isle-Adam, Sully Prudhomme, and Léon Cladel. A one-act play of his own, *le Roman d'une nuit,* which Mendès published in his review, brought the author-editor a fine of five hundred francs and one month's imprisonment on the charge of "immorality." The fine was too heavy for the purse of *la Revue fantaisiste,* the strings of which had apparently been cut by Mendès' father, who was at first none too sympathetic towards his son's literary bohemianism, and the periodical expired. It was succeeded, as mouthpiece of some of its contributors, by such journals as *la Revue française* and *la Revue du progrès,* short-lived and otherwise unimportant, while the better-known *Revue de Paris* printed the verses of such of the future Parnassians as Heredia, Verlaine, Cladel, and others.

During these early years of the sixties, a group of poets, among whom were Banville, Sully Prudhomme, Léon Dierx, Heredia, and Armand Silvestre, had been meeting regularly, every Saturday, at the home of Leconte de Lisle in the boulevard des Invalides. Simultaneously, Mendès, in his handsome apartment in the rue de Douai, was conducting his own *salon,* with such poets as Coppée, Léon Valade, and Albert Mérat, as his guests. The two groups were brought together by the Hellenist Louis Ménard, and placed themselves at once under the tutelage of Leconte de Lisle. The meetings of this amalgated *cénacle* were devoted to free discussions of philosophy, æsthetics, and especially literature; in the words of Emile Zola, the group "se cloîtrait dans un coin pour faire de la poésie une véritable religion."[2] Not infrequently, one of the assembled poets would read a composition of his own. Leconte de Lisle was a severe judge, but he was appreciative of any type of genius, provided it was animated by "la vénération de l'art, le dédain des succès faciles." It was in this group that the idea of *le Parnasse contemporain* originated.

Another element had to be assimilated, however, before Parnassus could definitely be transported to Paris. The members of the Leconte de Lisle-Mendès band, impecunious poets who were rich in nothing but leisure, gathered also, at more or less regular intervals, at the home of Théodore de Banville and at the *salons* of the poetess, Mme. Nina de Callias, the princess Mathilde, and the Marquise de Ricard.[3] The last-named, a woman of culture and intelligence, had a son, Louix-Xavier de Ricard, who, like Mendès, was casting his generous allowance into the insatiable maw of a review of which he was, of course, the editor—a handsomely made up and consequently expensive weekly entitled *l'Art,* the second of the "journaux parnassiens." Mendès, foreseeing the early demise of this periodical, prevailed upon Ricard to convert it into a magazine devoted exclusively to poetry, to be edited jointly by the two men.

The result was *le Parnasse contemporain: Recueil de vers nouveaux.*[4] Mendès takes the credit (though others have disputed it) for the coining of the name, the idea for which he received from collections of verse like Théophile de Viau's *le Parnasse satirique.* Five issues of the new review appeared at irregular intervals in 1865, and it would soon have gone the way of most literary periodicals had not the group been introduced by a rather erratic violinist, Ernest Boutier, to Alphonse Lemerre who undertook its publication. Lemerre's offices in the passage Choiseul at once became the rendezvous of the contributors to the review, who had almost spontaneously come to be known as the *Parnassiens,*[5] and who filled the room which had been assigned to them by the publisher with their boisterous criticisms and recitations of their verses. In a series of triolets called "l'Entresol du Parnasse," Gabriel Marc,[6] a cousin and disciple of Théodore de Banville, brings together, in Lemerre's shop, Leconte de Lisle, Banville, Mendès, Heredia, Theuriet, Coppée, Glatigny, Sully Prudhomme, Valade, Mérat, Dierx, d'Hervilly, Armand Renaud, Cazalis, Lafenestre, and Armand Silvestre. These men, and a score of others, were the authors of the poems selected by Mendès and Ricard for the eighteen numbers of the review, which were, in 1866, bound and issued as a single volume bearing the name of the periodical. And thus was achieved the transmigration of Mount Parnassus.

Alphonse Lemerre was, apparently, a shrewd business man. It is difficult to suppose that, in offering to assume the costs and responsibility of the publication of *le Parnasse contemporain,* he did so merely as a Maecenas to a group of struggling poets whose work might otherwise never have been seen in print.[7] Be that as it may, *le Parnasse contemporain* evidently proved a sound financial investment. For, three years later, in 1869, Lemerre prepared for publication a second *Parnasse contemporain: Recueil de vers nouveaux,* containing characteristic verses of no less than fifty-six poets, among whom were practically all of the original thirty-seven. Mendès and Ricard had very little hand in the editing of this volume, which was assembled under the direction of Banville, and the actual publication of which was delayed until 1871, though the title-page bears the date of 1869; this *Recueil* was less representative of the Parnassians than had been its predecessor.[8] Lemerre, by this time, was also the official publisher of the members of the group, whose individual volumes he was bringing out in rapid succession. These ventures must have brought the entrepreneur ample returns; for, in 1876, he issued *le Parnasse contemparain: Recueil de vers nouveaux,* number three. The poets honored by inclusion now counted sixty-three; the comparative homogeneity of the first collection had entirely disappeared, and, though most of the Leconte de Lisle-Banville-Ricard enthusiasts were to be found within the covers of the third *Recueil,* they were now rubbing shoulders with numerous interlopers, some of whom were outspokenly hostile to the Leconte de Lislean and Banvillean æsthetics. In a word, the once proud *Parnasse contemporain* had degenerated into a mere anthology. There was no fourth *Recueil.*

From the foregoing, it is evident that the three volumes of *le Parnasse contemporain* represent a phenomenon of the utmost importance in the history of French lyric poetry. In its pages are to be found representative verses of virtually every poet of any significance in the third quarter of the century, with the single exception of Victor Hugo. That Hugo is not to be found between its covers may have been due, at least in part, to the fact that, at the time of the preparation of the first two *Recueils,* he was still enjoying his exile on the island of Guernsey, and that, in 1876, when the third *Recueil* appeared, the editors feared to approach him on the subject of inclusion in a mere anthology. Be that as it may, if Hugo was not actually a collaborator of the *Parnasse contemporain,* his spirit undoubtedly hovered over those who were responsible for its inception. Champions of the cultivation of art in an age rapidly growing more and more materialistic, the original Parnassians thought with veneration of the great rebel of the Romantic *cénacle.* And, with Hugo ever in mind, they sounded the call to all the poets of the day who truly worshipped at the altar of poesy to rally about the standard. The call was answered by a host of men and women, most of them overflowing with the enthusiasm of youth, and some of them to take their places, before long, in the very forefront of contemporaneous poetry. Many of the poems which were printed in the *Parnasse* had previously, to be sure, appeared in volumes published by their authors; but an even greater number here saw the light of day in print for the first time. Not a few of the younger Parnassians may be said to have made their literary *début* in the pages of the *Parnasse,* to have been "brought out" by one or another of the three *Recueils.*

A warning must be sounded at this point, however, against the error into which many critics and literary historians have fallen, largely through inadequate acquaintance with the actual contents of the three *Recueils.* These writers are constantly speaking of the "Parnassian school" and its "doctrine," and passing judgments which indicate that they look upon the Parnassians as an entity after the fashion of the sixteenth-century *Pléiade.* Nothing could be farther from the truth; . . . the heterogeneity of the group [can be seen] from the points of view of influence, native endowment, temperament, philosophy of life, and literary technique. Let us, for the moment, listen to Catulle Mendès on the subject. Mendès begins the first of the four lectures which he delivered in Brussels on the theme of the "légende du *Parnasse contemporain*" with the assertion that the Parnassians had not given themselves this name but had been thus dubbed by adverse critics after the publication of their first collection of "vers nouveaux." Even before the appearance of the 1866 *Recueil,* the group had been honored with several sobriquets: because of their concern with style and external form, they had been called by some *les Stylistes,* by others *les Formistes;* as a result of their connection with the *Revue fantaisiste,* they had been named *les Fantaisistes;* and a poem from the pen of Glatigny, entitled "l'Impassible," earned them, Mendès claims, the nickname of *les Impassibles.*[9] As a matter of fact, the poets of the French Parnassus were generally considered "grotesques", and it was not long before the word "Parnassien" became a term of denigration in the mouth of the *bourgeois.* Mendès then insists, with all the conviction at his command, that the Parnassians were merely a "groupe" and not an "école." "Attirés," he says, "les uns vers les autres par leur commun amour de l'art, unis dans le respect des maîtres et dans une égale foi en l'avenir, ils ne prétendaient en aucune façon s'engager à suivre une voie unique. . . . Aucun mot d'ordre, aucun chef, toutes les personnalités absolument libres."[10] Some of the poets were interested in antiquity—religious, historical, or mythological—others in the various aspects of contemporaneous life. The motto of the group might have been: "Fais ce que tu pourras, pourvu que tu le fasses avec un religieux respect de la langue et du rhythme." And in another account of the aims and achievements of the Parnassians,[11] Mendès sums up this diversity of outlook and of technique in the following sentence: "Je ne pense pas qu'à aucune époque d'aucune littérature des poètes du même moment aient été à la fois plus unis de cœur et plus différents par l'idée et par l'expression." The *Parnasse contemporain* was not to be the organ of any one group, but was intended to be, and was, eclectic in its nature; it proposed to serve the same function for poetry that the *Salon* does for painting.[12]

Before entering upon our study of the contents of the three volumes of the *Parnasse contemporain,* we may do well to cite the opinions of two writers who were, by temperament, diametrically opposed to the Parnassians—Henri-Frédéric Amiel and Emile Zola. Amiel, the Swiss professor who might have been one of the foremost literary critics of his day if his overmastering self-consciousness had not lamed his mind and his hand whenever he set out to write for publication and whose undeniable talents were to be revealed only in his posthumously published *Journal intime,* was himself a poet, but one whose aspirations, as he himself sadly confessed, far exceeded his gifts. His reactions to the Parnassians were definitely hostile; on December 9, 1877, a year after the publication of the third *Parnasse contemporain,* he made the following pronuciamento in his diary:[13]

> Les Parnassiens sculptent des urnes d'agate et d'onyx, mais que contiennent ces urnes? de la cendre. Ce qui manque, c'est le sentiment vrai, c'est le sérieux, c'est la sincérité et le pathétique, c'est l'âme et la vie morale. Je m'efforce en vain d'aimer cette manière d'entendre la poésie. Le talent est prestigieux, mais le fond est vide. L'imagination veut tout remplacer. On trouve des métaphores, des rimes, de la musique, de la couleur; on ne trouve pas l'homme. Cette poésie factice peut enchanter à vingt ans; mais qu'en peut-on faire à cinquante? Elle me fait songer à Pergame, à Alexandrie, aux époques de la décadence, où la beauté de la forme cachait l'indigence de la pensée et l'épuisement du cœur. J'éprouve avec intensité la répugnance que cette poétique inspire aux braves gens. On dirait qu'elle n'a souci de plaire qu'aux blasés, aux raffinés, aux corrompus, et qu'elle ignore la vie saine, les mœurs régulières, les affections pures, le travail rangé, l'honnêteté et le devoir. C'est une affectation, et parce que c'est une affectation, l'école est frappée de stérilité. Le lecteur désire dans le poète mieux qu'un saltimbanque de la rime et un piqueur de vers; il veut trouver en lui un peintre de la vie, un être qui pense, qui aime, qui a de la conscience, de la passion, du repentir.

Zola, the self-professed founder and law-giver of the Naturalist school, had much the same fault to find with the Parnassians, but stressed their "uselessness" more than their "unmorality."[14] He first crucifies Gautier as the inventor of the theory of "l'art pour l'art." All of Gautier's written and spoken work, says Zola,

> a été une gymnastique étourdissante sur le terrain du paradoxe. Il écrivait comme on peint, avec le seul souci des lignes et des couleurs. . . . Il a poussé du premier coup le romantisme à la perfection classique. . . . Le romantisme se fige dans l'art pour l'art qui est sa forme classique. . . . Dès qu'une littérature ne vit plus que par les mots, elle meurt. Avec Gautier, le romantisme . . . en est à sa phase parfaite, . . . qui annonce l'écroulement. Il n'y a plus d'idée dessous, plus de base humaine, plus de logique ni de vérité. L'école n'aura bientôt qu'à se faisander avec les Parnassiens et à mourir de sa belle mort. . . . C'est un romantisme . . . devenant dogmatique, se glaçant pour imposer une formule de beauté parfaite et éternelle. . . . La versification ainsi entendue devient un art délicat, très compliquée et très charmant, qui se suffit à lui-même en dehors de l'idée.

Zola was indignant over the fact that the Parnassians stopped up their eyes and their ears "pour ne pas être troublés par le milieu vivant qui les entourait. . . . Tous reconnaissaient la souveraineté de la forme, tous juraient de bannir les émotions humaines de leurs œuvres. . . . Il fallait être sculptural, sidéral, se placer en dehors des temps et de l'histoire, mettre son génie à trouver des rimes riches et à aligner des hémistiches aussi durs et aussi éclatants que le diamant." But, like Amiel, Zola is compelled to admit the surpassing wizardry of the Parnassians as artists. "Jamais, à aucune époque," he finds himself avowing, "on n'a rimé avec une largeur plus grande. La langue française, sous leurs doigts, a été travaillée comme une matière précieuse." Ironically enough, Mendès, the historiographer of the French Parnassus, returned Zola's compliment by declaring that the Médan group[15] were Parnassians and that *Nana* was "la création d'un poète"[16] rather than the depiction of a phase of life as seen by a Naturalist.

The very enemies, thus, of the Parnassians were compelled to make grudging admission of the fact that, whatever else they may have done or neglected to do, they were, for the most part, animated by an exceedingly lofty ideal. This ideal, borrowed from Gautier

Théophile Gautier (1811-1872)

and practiced assiduously by the leaders of the group, may be styled, for our purposes, Parnassianism; it was never formulated into a "doctrine," and it represented an attitude rather than a technique. In its broadest sense, it was, briefly stated, a constant striving after perfection of form, with the elimination, as far as was humanly possible, of the personal element; only the first half of this definition, however, might be said to hold true for all the Parnassians, for the Baudelairean wing of the group, at least, was as introspective, in its own peculiar way, as were ever the most rabid of the Romanticists. Preoccupation with form and objectivity was not confined to the Parnassians, properly so called; they were manifest in the works of the great novelists and dramatists of the period, in those, for instance, of Flaubert and Alexandre Dumas fils. The critic Brunetière, therefore, states, with some show of justice, that, if the birth of Parnassianism at all bears dating, the year to which this event might best be attributed would be 1857, which saw the publication of *Madame Bovary, les Fleurs du mal,* Dumas' *la Question d'argent,* and the first edition of the complete works of both Leconte de Lisle and of Théodore de Banville.[17] The grouping of the names of these two poets and of Baudelaire is most significant for our purpose; for it was under their guidance and inspiration that the new generation was attempting the difficult task of clambering beyond the foothills of Parnassus. Describing this tripartite influence, Gautier asserts that some of the Parnassians imitated the "sérénité impassible" of Leconte de Lisle, others the "ampleur harmonique" of Banville, and still others the "âpre concentration" of Baudelaire, "chacun," however, "avoc son accent propre qui se mêle à la note empruntée."[18] The Parnassians' concern for form was so intense as frequently to degenerate into a maniac clownery and more than occasionally to make for banality, if not even for nullity, of content. By their mass effort, the group lent to the theory of "art for art's sake" appropriated from Gautier a dignity it might otherwise have lacked. For those who think, with Brunetière[19] that form is the chief justification of poetry, the Parnassians performed a signal service in the cause of French lyric verse; but the groups who denominated themselves Symbolists and Decadents, "transfuges du *Parnasse contemporain,*" rebelled violently against this form-idolatry and "ont revendiqué l'ancienne liberté du poète."[20] Thus, the Parnassians found themselves before long in the position of revolutionaries who have substituted their autocracy for the one they have been at such pains to annihilate, and whose despotism, equal to that of the deposed tyrants, hastens their own overthrow.

Hardly had the first issues of *le Parnasse contemporain* appeared than an outburst of violent carpings was leveled at the heads of its collaborators. The irascible Barbey d'Aurevilly was one of the bitterest of the critics; in a series of "Médaillonets" contributed to *le Nain jaune* during the month of November, 1866, he fired a fusillade at each of the thirty-seven poets of the group.[21] The attack at times took on the guise of burlesque. Thus, a band of young poets—either because they had not been invited to contribute to *le Parnasse contemporain* or for more genuinely artistic reasons—composed, early in December, 1866, a collection of parodies under the general title of *le Parnassiculet contemporain.*[22] This otherwise totally unimportant volume almost provoked a duel between the leader of the hostile group, Paul Arène, and Catulle Mendès, and called forth replies in kind from various Parnassians. In April, 1867, there appeared, for example, a periodical called *la Gazette rimée,* published by Lemerre, a satirical review, the expenses of which were borne by one of the lesser Parnassians, Robert Luzarche, and the principal contributors to which were Paul Verlaine and Anatole France. Other periodicals created to defend the group against its vilifiers were *la Parodie,* which dragged out a brief existence in 1869; *la Renaissance littéraire et artistique,* issued at about the same time; *la Revue du monde nouveau,* in 1874; *le Siècle littéraire,* in 1875, and, in the same year, perhaps the most important of all, *la République des lettres.* The greater number of the contributors to these periodicals were Parnassians; and *la République des lettres,* owned and directed by

Catulle Mendès, the original "fantaisiste," enjoyed comparative success, as it lasted for three years. With his usual sympathy for youthful writers, irrespective of literary leanings, Mendès published in this review not only the poems of his colleagues, but the compositions of such men as the members of Zola's Médan group, æsthetically the very antipodes of the Parnassians. Thus, Maupassant, Huysmans, Léon Hennique, and Paul Alexis appeared in its pages; and, most surprising of all, when the periodical which was printing Zola's *l'Assommoir* in instalments suspended its publication because of the furor it was creating, Mendès, realizing the true merits of the work, welcomed the Naturalist leader into his fold and carried the novel to its completion in *la République des lettres.* In this way, Mendès confuted the charge (made, among numerous others, by Zola himself) that the Parnassians were a closed corporation; moreover, as early as 1871, the same enterprising lover of the arts had inaugurated a series of "matinées de poésie ancienne et moderne" in the *théâtre de l'Ambigu,* the prime purpose of which was to acquaint the populace of Paris with the poetic strivings of these so-called impassible artists. By 1880, the Parnassians had earned an almost legendary position in the history of mid-nineteenth-century French literature; but the rumblings of revolt that had been faintly making themselves heard were soon to burst forth in the Symbolist-Decadent reaction which, for the next two decades, almost completely crowded their literary progenitors off the stage of French lyric poetry.

We are now prepared to offer ourselves a bird's-eye view of the contents of the three volumes of *le Parnasse contemporain.* The first *Recueil,* as we have seen, was published in 1866 and contained the contributions of thirty-seven poets. That the work was undertaken under the ægis of Gautier is demonstrated by the fact that the volume opens with a group of five poems from his pen. The attachment of the Parnassians to the Romanticists is evidenced by the inclusion of two members of the earlier Romantic *cénacle,* Emile Deschamps, one of the founders of *la Muse française,* and his brother Antoni. Arsène Houssaye, a hanger-on of Romanticism in the days of its decline and for seven years director of the Comédie française, is represented by a far larger group of poems than his talents deserved. With the publications of compositions of these four poets, the Parnassians seemed to feel that they had fulfilled their obligations to the parent body, for the overwhelming majority of the contributors were young men and women, many of them in their early twenties in 1866. Most of these budding geniuses went to school to one or another of the three poets whose names have already been linked, Leconte de Lisle, Banville, and Baudelaire; these men and their immediate disciples play so important a rôle in the development of French lyric poetry of the latter half of the nineteenth century that they merit consideration in independent chapters. Banville, who follows Gautier in the *Recueil,* is represented by only one poem, "l'Exil des Dieux," an elegy on the disappearance of the pagan gods and all that their names connote, which may be regarded as the keynote of the volume. Time and again, the strain of sadness and of ennui, of hatred for the *bourgeois* and his new gods, is to be heard in the verses of the Parnassians. Aphrodite, as spokesman for the gods in Banville's poem, laments:[23]

> . . . Nous errons vaincus parmi les fondrières.
>
> . . . . .
>
> Homme, vil meurtrier des dieux, es-tu
> content?
>
> . . . . .
>
> Tout est dit. Ne va plus boire la poésie
> Dans l'eau vive! les dieux enivrés d'ambroisie
> S'en vont et meurent, mais tu vas agoniser.
> Ce doux enivrement des êtres, ce baiser
> Des choses, qui toujours voltigeaient sur tes
> lèvres,
> Ce grand courant de joie et d'amour, tu t'en
> sèvres!

Then follow five sonnets by José-Maria de Heredia, the last of which, "Prométhée," echoes Banville's plaint in the words, "car il n'est plus de Dieux."[24] Heredia's master, Leconte de Lisle, appears next, with a group of nine characteristic poems, in the last of which, "la Dernière vision," the poet prognosticates the end of mankind and of all its illusions:

> Et ce sera la Nuit aveugle, la grande Ombre
> Informe, dans son vide et sa stérilité,
> L'abîme pacifique où gît la vanité
> De ce qui fut le temps, et l'espace, et le
> nombre.[25]

The Leconte de Lislean ideal is most succinctly expressed, in this volume, by a sonnet called "Nirvana," the first of a series of five "Sonnets mystiques" by Louis Ménard who, it will be later shown, had pronounced literary and philosophical affiliations with the master. The sonnet bears quoting in its entirety.[26]

> L'universel désir guette comme une proie
> Le troupeau des vivants; tous viennent tour à
> tour
> A sa flamme brûler leurs ailes, comme autour
> D'une lampe l'essaim des phalènes tournoie.
>
> Heureux qui, sans regrets, sans espoir, sans
> amour,
> Tranquille et connaissant le fond de toute joie,
> Marche en paix dans la droite et véritable
> voie,
> Dédaigneux de la vie et des plaisirs d'un jour!

Néant divin, je suis plein du dégoût des
choses;
Las de l'illusion et des métempsycoses,
J'implore ton sommeil sans rêve; absorbe-moi,

Lien des trois mondes, source et fin des
existences,
Seul vrai, seul immobile au sein des
apparences,
Tout est dans toi, tout sort de toi, tout rentre
en toi!

The remaining sonnets of Ménard reveal the same weariness with life. "Thébaïde" concludes with the statement that the poet has found, in place of "le ciel rêvé dans l'âpre solitude," only "la morne impuissance et l'incurable ennui."[27] And again, in "la Sirène":

Mais moi, je ne sais pas pourquoi j'ai voulu
naître;
J'ai mal fait, je me suis trompé, je devrais
bien
M'en aller de ce monde où je n'espère rien.[28]

This ennui is, of course, a heritage of the Romantic era and is to be observed in the verses of a goodly majority of the Parnassians. One of the youngest of them, François Coppée, who was later, because of his predilection for subjects drawn from the life of the "submerged tenth" to earn for himself the title of "le poète des humbles," voices the same languorous boredom in the four poems by which he is represented in the *Recueil.*

The third of the triumvirs who held sway over the younger Parnassians, Charles Baudelaire, is represented in the first *Parnasse contemporain* by a group of no less than fifteen poems printed under the caption of *Nouvelles fleurs du mal.* The first of these is an "Epigraphe pour un livre condamné" in which the "peaceful and bucolic reader" is urged: "Jette ce livre saturnien, Orgiaque et mélancolique." The poet whose *Fleurs du mal* had stirred up a scandal similar to that of *Madame Bovary* appeals: "Lis-moi pour apprendre à m'aimer" and closes with the cry: "Plains-moi . . . sinon, je te maudis."[29] All the poems are marked by the magic workmanship of their creator and the temptation is almost overpowering to quote freely from them, inasmuch as they exemplify Baudelaire's individual peculiarities. In "Madrigal triste," the poet, with his characteristic perversity, pictures a love strikingly different from that of a Lamartine or a Musset.

Je t'aime surtout quand la joie
S'enfuit de ton front terrassé;
Quand ton coeur dans l'horreur se noie;
Quand sur ton présent se déploie
Le nuage affreux du passé.[30]

As long as she will not have felt "l'étreinte de l'irrésistible Dégoût," his love will be unable to declare: "Je suis ton égale, ô mon Roi." In "Recueillement," the poet bids his grief be calm: "Entends, ma chère, entends la douce Nuit qui marche";[31] and in "le Gouffre," he paints the "multiform nightmare of fear" which pervades all of life:

En haut, en bas, partout, la profondeur, la
grève,
Le silence, l'espace affreux et captivant.

J'ai peur du sommeil comme on a peur d'un
grand trou,
Tout plein de vague horreur, menant on ne
sait où."[32]

Here we have the Romantic longing known as the "mal du siècle" turned inside out and its hollow nothingness exposed.

Sully Prudhomme, one of the most important of the poets for whom the *Parnasse contemporain* was the "jumping-off point," contributed to the *Recueil* three poems, the first of which, "les Ecuries d'Augias," shows him already preoccupied with the questions of justice and truth. A sonnet, "le Doute," also reveals the metaphysical penchant which was to make of him the philosophical poet of his day:

La blanche Vérité dort au fond d'un grand
puits.
Plus d'un fuit cet abîme ou n'y prend jamais
garde;
Moi, par un sombre amour, tout seul je m'y
hasarde,
J'y descends à travers la plus noire des nuits.

Et j'entraîne le câble aussi loin que je puis;
Or, je l'ai déroulé jusqu'au bout, je regarde,
Et, les bras étendus, la prunelle hagarde,
J'oscille sans rien voir ni rencontrer d'appuis.

Elle est là cependant, je l'entends qui respire,
Mais, pendule éternel que sa présence attire,
Je passe et je repasse et tâte l'ombre en vain.

Ne pourrai-je allonger cette corde flottante,
Ou remonter au jour dont la gaîté me tente,
Et dois-je dans l'horreur me balancer sans
fin?[33]

Another sonnet well worth citing is that with which Paul Verlaine opens a group of seven short poems. The æsthetics of the Leconte de Lisle Parnassians, whom Verlaine was soon to abandon to become the follower of Baudelaire and the divinity of the Decadents, is to be found succinctly stated in "Vers dorés":

L'art ne veut point de pleurs et ne transige
pas,
Voilà ma poétique en deux mots: elle est faite

De beaucoup de mépris pour l'homme et de
combats
Contre l'amour criard et contre l'ennui bête.

Je sais qu'il faut souffrir pour monter à ce
faîte
Et que la côte est rude à regarder d'en bas.
Je le sais, et je sais aussi que maint poète
A trop étroit les reins ou les poumons trop
gras.

Aussi ceux-là sont grands, en dépit de l'envie,
Qui, dans l'âpre bataille ayant vaincu la vie
Et s'étant affranchi du joug des passions,

Tandis que le rêveur végète comme un arbre
Et que s'agitent—tas plaintif—les nations,
Se recueillent dans un égoïsme de marbre.[34]

The Baudelairean heritage is manifest in such poems as "Cauchemar" and "Dans les bois," where the poet trembles "à la façon d'un lâche," and the very brooks "font un bruit d'assassins."[35] "Mon rêve familier" paints the unknown woman whom the poet might love:

Son regard est pareil au regard des statues,
Et pour sa voix lointaine et calme et grave,
elle a
L'inflexion des voix chères qui se sont tues.[36]

This same statuesqueness is masterfully achieved in a brief water-scape, "Marine". . . .

In a group of nine poems, Stéphane Mallarmé, the second of the outstanding disciples of Baudelaire, gives voice to a long cry of sterility and hopelessness. In "le Sonneur," the poet declares that he is weary unto death:

J'ai beau tirer le câble à sonner l'idéal,

. . . . .

Mais, un jour, fatigué d'avoir enfin tiré,
O Satan, j'ôterai la pierre et me pendrai.[37]

"L'Azur" opens with a stanza in the same strain;

De l'éternel Azur la sereine ironie
Accable, belle indolemment comme les fleurs,
Le poète impuissant qui maudit son génie
A travers le désert stérile des Douleurs.[38]

Life is ineffably wearisome. "La chair est triste, hélas! et j'ai lu tous les livres," begins "Brise marine,"[39] and in the "Epilogue" to his group of contributions, the poet threatens to break with his past:

Je veux délaisser l'art vorace d'un pays
Cruel . . . .[40]

[The score] or more remaining contributors to the first *Parnasse contemporain* need not retain our attention much longer. . . . For the present, a word will suffice on the subject of a few of those whose names appear in the table of contents of the *Parnasse contemporain* and who merit at least passing attention. That the editors of the first *Recueil,* Catulle Mendès and Louis-Xavier de Ricard, were better organizers than poets is evident from the verses which they included as most characteristic of their talents. The very names of Mendès' contributions—"le Mystère du lotus," "Dialogue d'Yama et d'Yami," "l'Enfant Krichna," and "Kamadéva"—testify amply to the fact that the ebullient Catulle was paying Leconte de Lisle his usual compliment of imitation. The only point worthy of note in Ricard's nine poems is his use of a verse-form which he calls "sonnet estrambote" and which has three, instead of the usual two, tercets rhyming *aab ccb ddb* or *aab cbc bdd.* A poet of real power . . . is Léon Dierx, represented in the first *Recueil* by six poems. Finally, Auguste Villiers de l'Isle-Adam, later to become celebrated as the author of *Contes cruels* and other works in prose, began as a Parnassian, with three poems in the first *Recueil.* The collection is brought to a close with sonnets by seventeen poets including, in addition to virtually all those mentioned thus far in this chapter, Léon Valade, Albert Mérat, and Henri Cazalis, who also wrote under the pseudonym of Jean Lahor.

Let us now cast a rapid glance over the second and third volumes of the *Parnasse contemporain* in order to note their most significant features. It is the second *Recueil* that contains the sonnet called "l'Impassible". . . . This poem was written in 1866, too late for inclusion in the first *Parnasse* and is here quoted because of its possible connection with the point raised by Mendès as to why the Parnassians were also sometimes called *les Impassibles*":

La Satiété dort au fond de vos grands yeux;
En eux, plus de désir, plus d'amour, plus
d'envie;
Ils ont bu la lumière, ils ont tari la vie,
Comme une mer profonde où s'absorbent les
cieux.

Sous leur bleu sombre, on lit le vaste ennui
des Dieux,
Pour qui toute chimère est d'avance assouvie,
Et qui, sachant l'effet dont la cause est suivie,
Mélangent au présent l'avenir déjà vieux.

L'infini s'est fondu dans vos larges prunelles,
Et, devant ce miroir qui ne réfléchit rien,
L'Amour découragé s'assoit, fermant ses ailes.

Vous, cependant, avec un calme olympien,
Comme la Mnémosyne, à son socle accoudée,
Vous poursuivez, rêveuse, une impossible
idée.[41]

Mendès, it will be remembered, declares that it is to Albert Glatigny's "l'Impassible" that the group owed this particular one of its many nicknames. Now Glatigny's poem has as little reference to a band of poets as does Gautier's sonnet, both clearly depicting the *hetaira* who has been disenchanted in her search for the ideal lover. As a matter of fact, there is little need to look to either of these poems for the origin of this sobriquet of the Parnassians, inasmuch as the adjective "impassible" had been applied to Leconte de Lisle soon after the appearance of his *Poèmes antiques* in 1852, and the epithet might readily have been transferred from the master to his disciples.

In this connection, it is of interest that Glatigny's "l'Impassible" was not published in any of the three *Recueils,* although four poems from his pen are included in the second *Parnasse.* This unusual personage, a strolling actor by profession and a poet by avocation, is the subject of the larger part of the first *conférence* of Mendès' *Légende,* in which the pseudo-historian exaggeratedly dates the birth of Parnassianism from his meeting with Glatigny in Paris in about 1860. Some attention will be given the picturesque career of this barnstorming histrion in our study of Théodore de Banville and his followers.

Leconte de Lisle and Banville are, of course, both to be found between the covers of the second and third *Recueils;* but the name of Baudelaire, who had come to his pitiful end in 1867, is not included. Leconte de Lisle is represented by a biblical poem, "Kaïn,"[42] in the 1869 collection, and in that of 1876 by "Hiéronymus,"[43] the first part of what was to be an epic poem, in three parts, to be known as *l'Epopée du moine.* Banville's contribution to the second *Recueil* was a group of ten "ballades joyeuses"[44] and to the third a bouquet of "rondels composés à la manière de Charles d'Orléans." Heredia's sole attempt at a poem *de longue haleine,* an epic of the conquest of Peru and its gold by Pizarro, entitled "la Détresse d'Atahuallpa" never advanced beyond the prologue "les Conquérants de l'or," which is to be found in the second *Parnasse;* and in the third there is a group of twenty-five sonnets from the hand of this master sonnetteer.[45] Another truncated composition in the second *Recueil* is Mallarmé's dramatic poem, *Hérodiade,* which he styles "fragment d'une étude scénique d'un Poème de Hérodiade."

Among the poets whose names appear for the first time in the second *Recueil* is a group of no less than five women: Nina de Callias, Louisa Siefert, Mme. Auguste Penquer, Mme. Blanchecotte,[46] and Louise Colet, more celebrated as the mistress of Flaubert than in her own right. But by far the most noteworthy of the *débutants* of this volume is Anatole France. In his early twenties at the time of the publication of the original *Parnasse,* France was carried away by the love of antiquity that animated the Leconte de Lisle *cénacle,* and the second *Recueil* contains two poems of his in the Biblical strain, while the third published the first part of his neo-pagan *les Noces corinthiennes.*[47] Anatole France, however, could not long endure the shackles of poetry, and he soon passed into the fields of fiction and criticism in which he won the laurels that made him universally recognized as the supreme French *prosateur* of his day.

Of the minor poets of the Parnassian group, at least four should be mentioned here: Léon Cladel, whom Mendès styles "un des plus grands lyriques du siècle,"[48] Armand Silvestre, Albert Mérat and Léon Valade. The two last-named were inseparable friends who shared Mendès' enforced poverty when the banker's dissatisfaction with his son's bohemian dilletantism had compelled him to endure the privations of the Latin Quarter garret, and they had later been presented by him to Leconte de Lisle and his disciples. Mérat earned for himself some slight renown as the poet of the environs of Paris, and it is these that he celebrates in a group of seven poems published in the second *Parnasse* under the name of *Hors des murs.* The contributions of Valade to the three *Recueils* are in the lofty strain of the poet conscious of the dignity of his calling and thirsty for a share in the universal beauty.

A word about a few of the contributors to one or another of the three *Recueils* who did not, properly speaking, belong in the fold, and we shall have concluded this rather dreary catalogue. Victor de Laprade (1812-1883) was a somewhat windily pompous poet whose cultivation of antiquity made him, in a sense, a predecessor of Leconte de Lisle, though he was never actually a member of the Parnassian group. Mme. Louise Ackermann (1813-1890) enjoyed some consideration as a philosophical poet. Paul Bourget, the foremost present-day exponent of the psychological novel in France, began as a poet, disciple of Anatole France and Leconte de Lisle. The celebrated critic, Sainte-Beuve, who entirely disclaimed poetry after the severance of his relations with the Romanticists (about 1840), has somehow or other crept into the second *Recueil* with one poem. Auguste Barbier (1805-1882), whose volume of political verse, *les Iambes* (1831) brought him momentary glory, was all but rescued from oblivion by the same *Recueil;* and Paul de Musset, shining in the light reflected by his brother, is represented in the anthology, as is Jean Aicard, later to become a staid member of the French Academy. Finally, Eugène Manuel and Armand Renaud, poets of the people like Coppée, are given places in the seats of the mighty.

The three volumes of the *Parnasse contemporain,* thus, are a rather amorphous congeries of verses from the pens of a varied assortment of lyric poets of every degree of endowment, from Gautier and Leconte de Lisle down to the veriest poetaster. It is significant, indeed, that the contributors to the third *Recueil* are listed in alphabetical order; this volume, at least, was looked upon as a mere anthology, whereas the other two collections had been edited with some view to presenting the work of poets animated largely by similar artistic ideals. What, then, is the importance of the three *Recueils?* Briefly, they may be said to offer us a cross-section of French lyric poety of the third quarter of the last century which would scarcely be obtainable in any other manner. Here we see the *genre* in divers stages of growth, from the feeble Romanticism of the brothers Deschamps through the great neo-Romantics, the Parnassians properly so called, to the horde of poets who received at their hands their first training in the difficult task of Pegasus-taming and then, in many instances, turned their steeds along the new paths of Symbolism and Decadence. The *Parnasse contemporain* permits us, as it were, a glimpse into the poetic workshop of the middle of the century; here we see poets who have "arrived" extracting from previously-published volumes compositions to serve as stimulus to their disciples; here we observe the neophytes making their first faltering steps up the steep slopes of Parnassus. Many of the poems in the three *Recueils* are intrinsically precious, many others are worthless; all are representative. In keeping alive the flame of poetry at a time when scientific positivism was making its most serious inroads into art, *le Parnasse contemporain* performed an invaluable service, and is consequently, despite its obvious shortcomings, deserving of a generous chapter in any history of French lyric poetry. Virtually every poet of the succeeding generation underwent, positively or negatively, the influence of the Parnassians, just as the dramatists who followed Scribe had all to reckon with that "carpenter of plays." Even the vers-librists, paradoxical though this may seem, are in their debt, if not for their technique, at least for their susceptibility to form and line and color in the manifestations of the objective world and for their feeling for the *nuances* of words. . . .

Notes

[1] Mendès: *la Légende du Parnasse contemporain,* deuxième conference, from which the quotations on the following pages are taken, execpt where otherwise noted.

[2] *Documents littéraires* (Paris, Charpentier, 1881, chapter on "les Poètes contemporains").

[3] For a discussion of the Parnassian *salons,* vide the present author's article, "The Parnassians at Play," which is to appear in the *Romanic Review* early in 1930.

[4] Paris, Lemerre, 1866.

[5] The authorship of this name has been attributed to Jules Barbey d'Aurevilly who, in a series of articles called "Médaillonets" (printed in *le Nain jaune* in November, 1866) bitterly attacked the thirty-seven contributors to *le Parnasse contemporain.*

[6] A contributor to the second and third series of the *Parnasse.* The "Entresol du Parnasse" was written in 1870 and published in Marc's volume, *Sonnets parisiens* (1875).

[7] *Cf.* on this point, Remy de Gourmont: *Promenades littéraires,* vol. V (Paris, Mercure de France, 1913, p. 49).

[8] In the *Nouvelles littéraires* for October 10, 1925, Marcel Coulon publishes an interesting letter, hitherto "inédite," from Arthur Rimbaud to Banville, dated May 24, 1870. Rimbaud, then only fifteen years old and later to become the boon companion of Verlaine and the deity of the Symbolists, sent Banville three poems with the following request: "Si ces vers trouvaient place au *Parnasse contemporain?*—Je ne suis pas connu, qu'importe?" Rimbaud had been encouraged in this request by the fact that the *Parnasse* contained poems not only by the masters, but also by poets of second and third rank, and some even by totally unknown writers. But Rimbaud's contributions were not included in the second *Parnasse contemporain.*

[9] Contained in *les Vignes folles (Poésies complètes,* Paris, Lemerre, 1879, p. 43). Mendès incorrectly states that this poem was dedicated to Gautier, whereas it was actually inscribed to Baudelaire. Mendès' error may have arisen from the fact that Gautier, too, was the author of a sonnet called "l'Impassible," which will be quoted and discussed later in this chapter.

[10] *Op. cit.,* pp. 19 et seq.

[11] *Le Mouvement poétique français de 1867 à 1900* (Paris, Fasquelle, 1903, p. 114).

[12] Vide J. Huret: *Enquête sur l'évolution littéraire* (Paris, Charpentier, 1891, p. 289).

[13] Vol. II, pp. 243-44.

[14] *Documents littéraires*—vide the chapter on Gautier and that on "les Poètes contemporains."

[15] Which met weekly during the winter at Zola's home in Paris and in summer at his country-home at Médan, on the Seine, not far from Versailles, and included Guy de Maupassant, J. K. Huysmans, Léon Hennique, Paul Alexis, and Henri Céard. In 1880, this group published a volume of stories under the caption of *les Soirées de Médan.* Maupassant's contribution, "Boule de suif," was easily the best story of the volume and the success enjoyed by this, his first published fictional effort, set him on the path which was to lead him to the heights of fame.

[16] *Legende,* p. 146.

[17] *Histoire et littérature* (Paris, Lévy, 1885—essay on *"le Parnasse contemporain,"* vol. II, pp. 207-33).

[18] *Le Progrès de la poésie française depuis 1830,* which forms a *suite* to his *Histoire du Romantisme* (Paris, Fasquelle, 1911). Gautier also adds, as a fourth pattern for imitation, the "farouche grandeur de la dernière manière d'Hugo." Modesty forbade any mention of the group's indebtedness to his own poetry.

[19] *Loc. cit.*

[20] *Nouvelles questions de critique* (Paris, Lévy, 1898—essay on "le Mouvement littéraire au XIXe siècle," p. 310).

[21] He had, in the same journal, in 1864, executed, in a similar manner, the members of the French Academy in a series of *Médaillons de l'Académie française.* . . . Some of the facts of this paragraph are taken from M. Ibrovac's exhaustive work on José-Maria de Heredia (Paris, *les Presses françaises,* 1923).

[22] Paris, *Librairie centrale,* 1867. No less a personage than Alphonse Daudet, then twenty-six, collaborated in the composition of this series of parodies.

[23] *Parnasse contemporain,* vol. I, pp. 10-11.

[24] *Ibid.,* p. 16.

[25] *Ibid.,* p. 32.

[26] *Ibid.,* p. 33.

[27] *Ibid.,* p. 34.

[28] *Ibid.,* p. 35.

[29] *Ibid.,* p. 65.

[30] *Ibid.,* p. 67.

[31] *Ibid.,* p. 78.

[32] *Ibid.,* p. 79.

[33] *Ibid.,* p. 97.

[34] *Ibid.,* p. 137.

[35] *Ibid.,* pp. 138-39.

[36] *Ibid.,* p. 144.

[37] *Ibid.,* p. 163.

[38] *Ibid.,* p. 165.

[39] *Ibid.,* p. 168.

[40] *Ibid.,* p. 170.

[41] *Parnasse contemporain,* vol. II, p. 261.

[42] Spelled "Qaïn" in the edition of the *Poèmes barbares* (1862), in which it was first published.

[43] Never completed. It was included under the name "Hiéronymus" in the *Poèmes tragiques* (1884).

[44] Included in *Trente-six ballades joyeuses* (1875).

[45] The fragment and the sonnets were later published in *les Trophées* (1893).

[46] Mme. Blanchecotte and one Mélanie Bourotte (who is represented in the third *Recueil)* were disciples of the erratic poet, Thalès Bernard, whose exaggerated self-esteem made him an enemy of Leconte de Lisle and kept him out of the Parnassian group. The two poetesses were humorously dubbed "Cotte et Rotte."

[47] Published in its entirety, by Lemerre, in 1876. It had been preceded in 1873, by a volume entitled *Poèmes dorés.*

[48] Vide J. Huret, *op. cit.,* p. 299.

The pressure of the new Realistic forces, particularly as regards science and the objective attitude towards history and nature, impinges on poetry in the work of the Parnassians. The activity of these poets was brought to a focus in the collection called *Le Parnasse contemporain* (1866, 1869 f.) which gave its name to the school. The group started with diverse talents and aims, but with a common desire for faultless artistic workmanship. Some of the early founders (Catulle Mendès, Glatigny, etc.,) never made a profound mark; others began as Parnassians and ended as something else. This was the case with Sully Prudhomme, François Coppée and Verlaine. The term "Parnassiens" came to connote an Olympian calm, which these young writers affected; they were averse to Romantic storm, stress and subjectivism; for similar reasons they were also known as "les Impassibles." For a time they all submitted to the influence of a strong chieftain who gave direction and body to the movement.

William A. Nitze and E. Preston Dargan, in A History of French Literature: From the Earliest Times to the Present, *revised edition, Henry Holt and Company, 1927.*

P. E. Charvet (essay date 1967)

SOURCE: "The Parnassians and Heredia," in *A Literary History of France,* Vol. IV: *The Nineteenth Century, 1789-1870,* Ernest Benn Limited, and Barnes and Noble Inc., 1967, pp. 344-7.

[*In the following except, Charvet outlines a brief history of the Parnassian movement, discussing, in particular, the work of José-Maria de Heredia.*]

Three efforts at least were made in the early 1860's to build a new literary school round a critical review: Catulle Mendès launched the *Revue fantaisiste* in February 1861; it survived till November. Louis Xavier de Rizard founded the *Revue du progrès moral, littéraire, scientifique* in March 1863; its title at least reflects the new intellectual orientation, the desire to harness literature to social progress and science; it lasted a year. Another review, *L'Art,* owed its short existence (November 1865-January 1866) to the same founder.

The sense of a certain community of attitudes promoted by these 'ephemera' was also promoted by what may be regarded as the first 'Naturalist' play—though the term had not yet been coined—*Henriette Maréchal.* The performances, which faintly echoed the 'battle of Hernani', brought the partisans of the new ideas closer together, but in the absence of public interest and funds to establish on a firm basis a critical review as a rallying ground, the idea of a volume of contemporary poetry was born in the mind of the publisher Lemerre. Though lacking the character of an aggressive literary manifesto, *Le Parnasse contemporain, recueil de vers nouveaux* (1866) has given its name to a generation rather than a school of poets; amongst the contributors—some forty in all—figured poets as diverse as Baudelaire and Heredia, Mallarmé and Verlaine. The watchwords were craftsmanship, plasticity, objectivity; at least they could share their admiration for a trinity of poets—Gautier, Leconte de Lisle, Banville, and their dislike of much Romantic poetry, especially the sentimentalism of Lamartine and Musset.

Of all the poets who contributed to the *Parnasse contemporain* the most representative is José Maria de Heredia (1842-1905). By 1866 he was already the acknowledged master of the sonnet; *Les Trophées* (1893) contains the full collection of 118 sonnets, composed with splendid craftsmanship over the previous thirty years, 'Romancero', a ballad in Romantic vein on the 'Cid', and a minor epic, 'Les Conquérants de l'or', saga of Pizarro, the Spanish Conquistador.

With this apparently modest baggage Heredia has an assured place in French literature, showing thereby with [Mallarmé], though only remotely of his persuasion, that concentration and quality are more important than the dispersal and quantity that come from the outpourings of Romantic emotion.

The sonnet form is usually associated with love poetry—Petrarch, Ronsard, Du Bellay, Shakespeare. Heredia's own master, Leconte de Lisle, uses the sonnet only rarely; his themes—e.g. the legends of primitive peoples on man's origins, the horrors of modern materialism and more generally of this life, the peace of Nirvana, the cruelties of nature in exotic climes—seemed too copious a draught for so small a vessel, designed to contain only the fragrant essence of love or some other lyrical mood; the few sonnets in *Poèmes Barbares* suggest that he chose the sonnet when passion—love, hatred, contempt—welled up in him and needed to be communicated in a discreetly personal but not dispassionate form: e.g. 'Le Colibri', 'Les Montreurs', 'Le Voeu suprême', 'Aux Modernes'.

Heredia's most successful sonnets, in contrast, have no appeal to the emotions. The ephemeral nature of things admittedly recurs often:

> La vie O Sextius est brève. Hâtons-nous
> De vivre . . .
>
> ('A Sextius')

> Tout meurt . . .
> Les roses et les lys n'ont pas de lendemain
>
> ('Sur le livre des Amours')

> Le temps passe. Tout meurt. Le marbre même s'use
>
> ('Médaille Antique')

But even if this theme represents the poet's own pessimism, its purpose in the sonnets concerned is not to reveal his mood, it is to evoke the ethos or fit into the picture of a period: Rome, the Renaissance, Sicily. In none of the sonnets concerned is the reader allowed to dwell on the idea of the fugacity of things and give it personal lyrical importance by an inward look on himself. This is particularly true in the last case where the attention is at once fastened on history and concrete details:

> Agrigente n'est plus qu'une ombre, et Syracuse
> Dort sous le bleu linceul de son ciel indulgent.

In short, Heredia as a good Parnassian transposes emotion from a personal to an aesthetic key. This is well brought out by comparing his sonnet 'Soir de Bataille', with Leconte de Lisle's poem 'Le Soir d'une Bataille'. The slight difference in the title has its importance; Leconte de Lisle's battle has substantival and therefore greater force than the adjectival force of Heredia's. From the outset therefore we are warned that Leconte de Lisle is going to evoke the horrific aftermath of a specific battle and make a direct impact on the reader's emotion, whereas Heredia intends to take advantage of battle effects in general, to make an aesthetic impact. The absence in Heredia's title of the definite article reinforces this impression, by giving it general significance, which in its turn seems to remove the horror from close proximity to our personal experience.

These impressions are confirmed by the contents of the poems themselves. Leconte de Lisle's, a modern battle, something close to the reader's experience therefore, or at any rate only a short remove from it by imagination, the whole ending on a political note—the value of the sacrifice in the name of liberty; Heredia's, on the other hand, far removed in time. We can therefore imagine the scene with as little personal emotion as though we were watching it through a telescope on the moon; distance in space or time transforms emotion into intellectual interest or curiosity. Here, perhaps, lies the explanation why Heredia's evocations of past situations come no nearer to us than the Renaissance. He then veers to the East—distance in space. Any attempt to capture the spirit of the modern age might have meant a departure from the objectivity Heredia cultivated. Only in the last section, 'La Nature et le Rêve', does the poet allow a personal element to creep in, but this section which, save in the pen pictures of Brittany, lacks a theme like those that give unity to each of the other sections, is not the most characteristic or satisfying of *Les Trophées*.

At their best Heredia's sonnets are like microcosms of a given age or civilization; references that invoke the reader's own framework of knowledge:

> La terre maternelle et douce aux anciens
> Dieux.
>
> ('L'Oubli')

Vivid sensuous impressions:

> Le ciel vert, au couchant, de pourpre et d'or
> se frange
>
> ('Le Prisonnier')

rhythms that create the desired image:

> La houle s'enfle, court, se dresse comme un
> mur
> Et déferle . . .
>
> ('Le Bain')

and above all the technique Heredia made all his own—the last line that releases the reader's imagination from the narrow confines of the sonnet and gives the miniature the dimensions of a large canvas. Examples of this abound, but the classic case occurs in 'Antoine et Cléopâtre':

> Et sur elle courbé, l'ardent Imperator
> Vit dans ses larges yeux étoilés de point d'or
> Toute une mer immense où fuyaient des
> galères.

Here two factors combine to produce a maximum effect: the physical images conveyed by the lines and the knowledge the framework provides. The qualifying phrase—'étoilès de point d'or'—retains our attention for a moment longer on Cleopatra's eyes and then they, like a 'fading' on the films, merge into the vast horizon of the sea; but what strengthens the impact of the latter is our realization that the allusion is to Actium, seen as in a convex mirror endowed with the magic power of reflecting the future; references, sensuous impressions, skilful techniques all are tightly packed within the narrow confines of Heredia's sonnets, like 'Le combat des Titans au pommeau d'une dague'.

When the *Parnasse Contemporain* was published the intention was to follow it up with other similar collections. A second volume appeared in 1871, a third in 1876. By then the character, in so far as it existed, of the first volume had disappeared. Time had revealed that the three collections were no more than anthologies, and that Parnassianism, since affecting the form rather than the substance of poetry, could cover a diversity of attitudes; there are the poets who, with Heredia, followed closely in the line of Leconte de Lisle: Louis Bouilhet (1828-69), the friend of Flaubert, Léon Dierx (1838-1912)—a native of Réunion like the master—Catulle Mendès (1842-1909); though scholar, painter, teacher and even scientist more than poet, Louis Ménard (1822-1901) belongs to this group by his enthusiastic Hellenism; Sully Prudhomme (1839-1907) veers towards philosophic Parnassianism, as does Madame Ackermann (1813-90); François Coppée (1842-1908) found a fruitful and successful vein of poetic inspiration in the virtues of the humble poor; Albert Glatigny (1839-73) remained in the strict obedience of Théodore de Banville.

With all their skills and contemporary successes their originality was not strong enough to ensure their literary survival, except as names or anthology poets. Not even the Nobel Prize for literature (1907) and 'Le Vase brisé' has saved Sully Prudhomme. Time soon betrays the facile or the derivative, in poetry perhaps even more quickly than in any other art form. To read these poets nowadays is to be overcome with a paralyzing sense of sameness and boredom. . . .

Robert T. Denommé (essay date 1972)

SOURCE: "From Art for Art's Sake to Parnassianism," in *The French Parnassian Poets,* Southern Illinois University Press, and Feffer and Simons, Inc., 1972, pp. 1-37.

[*In the following essay, Denommé offers a history and overview of the Parnassian movement, showing its development in reaction to Romanticism and its emergence out of the "art for art's sake" movement led by Théophile Gautier.*]

As significant literary currents of the nineteenth century, Art for Art's Sake and Parnassianism rose in open reaction to the types of social and utilitarian Romanticism that came to dominate the two decades of the July Monarchy. Just as the earliest Romanticists sought the freedom of literary expression from the constraint and rigidity of lingering neoclassical formulas during the years immediately following the French Revolution, the most forceful exponents of Art for Art's Sake and Parnassianism advocated the liberation of art from the kind of didacticism that tended to render it subservient to specific causes and programs during the reigns of Louis-Philippe and Louis-Napoleon from 1830 to 1870.

Despite a mutually articulated goal of autonomy in literature and other notable resemblances in attitude, Art for Art's Sake and Parnassianism underscored sufficiently distinguishing features that precluded their assimilation into any single prevailing literary movement. In their reaction to lyrical expression during the 1830s and 1840s, the leading proponents of Art for Art's Sake attempted a redefinition of Romanticism by suggesting a change of emphasis from the highly imaginative recreation of ideal truth to the more accurate observation and objective reproduction of concrete reality. It is no exaggeration to say that Art for Art's Sake pleaded for considerably more than the expurgation of all forms of partisanship from literature; it encouraged the supplantation of the emotional and sentimental appeal in lyricism by a more disciplined aesthetic preoccupation.

The leading advocates of Parnassianism staunchly upheld the main tenets of the practitioners of Art for Art's Sake, in large measure, because they concurred with their own ambitious designs for the reform and renewal of the rhetoric of the French lyric. Doubtless impressed by some of the positivist currents dominating the 1850s and 1860s, the most prominent Parnassian poets supported an alliance with scientific methodology in order that the observation of external reality might be achieved with the calm deliberation of the scholar rather than with the enervating passion of the unpredictable lyricist. Whatever differences of opinion and interpretation may have ultimately separated the proponents of Art for Art's Sake from their congeners in Parnassianism, these two literary attitudes contributed significantly to the transformation of French Romanticism from a philosophical conception of life to a considerably more genuine literary doctrine.

To a large degree, the reforms of Art for Art's Sake and Parnassianism managed to counterbalance the mysterious inner reality which preoccupied Romanticism with the more critical appreciation of external reality which concerned such distinguished poets as Théophile Gautier and Leconte de Lisle.

It would be erroneous to assume that the growing encroachment of industry, economics, and politics upon Romantic literature passed unnoticed or went uncriticized until the publication of Gautier's celebrated manifesto on Art for Art's Sake in the preface to *Albertus* in 1832. Such divergent public personalities as the socialist thinker, Proudhon, and the literary critic, Sainte-Beuve, warned of the degeneracy of literary expression through the increasing collaboration between art and commerce.[1] Along with such lesser-known figures as Gustave Planche and Saint-René Taillandier, literary and social commentators during the opening years of the July Monarchy, Sainte-Beuve voiced his dismay over the casual manner in which increasing numbers of writers had so blatantly compromised their talents to satisfy and flatter the questionable artistic trends of a rapidly expanding industrialized bourgeoisie. To complicate matters, such notable ideological groups as the Saint-Simonians and the Fourierists, to mention but the most prominent, vigorously enlisted the aid of writers to further the cause of the transformation of France into a highly contrived social and political utopia.

The overwhelming majority of writers in the 1830s and 1840s either endorsed and campaigned tirelessly in behalf of the various ideological aspirations of what became known as social Romanticism or quietly consented to the practice of popular literature for the sake of swift personal recognition and financial gain. As early as 1830, it had grown increasingly evident that both the social Romanticists and the so-called industrial artists had placed the autonomy of "pure" literature in serious jeopardy.

When Gautier's dramatic plea for Art for Art's Sake appeared in 1832, it was contemptuously dismissed as the ranting supplication of a bohemian whose irresponsibility prevented him from adjusting his poetic vision to the pragmatic sights of a regime conspicuously confident of the nature of its social mission. Gautier's critics in 1832 curiously echoed the characteristic objection of Charles de Rémusat in the *Globe* of 1825: "Man was not created so that he might merely sing, believe, and love without any specific purpose or objective."[2] Gautier's preface to *Albertus* nevertheless constituted the first significant thrust in defense of *le romantisme artiste* at precisely the moment when most cultural programs were undergoing drastic pragmatic revisions under the impulse of the Industrial Revolution.

The theory of Art for Art's Sake, as Théophile Gautier understood it in 1832, rested upon a conception of ideal beauty rooted at least partially in attitudes projected at various intervals by such eighteenth-century German aestheticians as Kant, Hegel, and Schiller. All advocated, with deliberate forcefulness, a philosophy of art which underscored complete independence from any moral, social, or scientific consideration. Their respective ideas on the idealization of beauty, based largely upon imaginative and abstract interpretations of reality, made their way into France at least casually if not systematically in the treatises and lectures of such critics of French Romanticism as Madame de Staël, Victor Cousin, and Théodore Jouffroy.

Specific reference to the theory of ideal beauty appeared as early as 1813 in Book Two of Madame de Staël's *De l'Allemagne* [*Concerning Germany*] where credit is ascribed to the German archaeologist, Wincklemann, for having developed the principles of idealization in the arts as residing in the imagination rather than outside the mind of the artist.[3] In a subsequent allusion to the theory of ideal beauty, Madame de Staël translates her familiarity with the Kantian doctrine on the independence of art and comments: "The Germans do not consider, as we ordinarily do, that the imitation of nature constitutes the primary objective of art; it is the idealization of beauty which appears to them to be at the root of all literary and artistic masterpieces."[4]

Shortly after his return from Germany in 1817, Victor Cousin endorsed the Kantian distinction on the autonomy of art and elaborated upon Wincklemann's conception of ideal beauty in a protracted series of lectures in 1818 which were subsequently published in book form as *Du Vrai, du beau et du bien* [*Concerning truth, beauty, and morality*] in 1836. Much of the thrust behind Cousin's hypothesis on the nature of ideal beauty constituted hardly more than a well-presented paraphrase of Quatremère de Quincy's *Essais sur l'idéal* [*Essays concerning idealism*] which came under heated academic debate and discussion in 1805.[5] In the seventh lesson of his treatise, for example, Cousin summarizes the major theses of Wincklemann and de Quincy when he points out that the essence of beauty does not reside in the artful imitation of nature, and that the object of the artist's contemplation should be the ideal rather than the realist interpretation of nature in all of its contingencies.[6]

In a similar fashion, Théodore Jouffroy argued in 1825 that the concepts of beauty and utility represented a contradiction in terms, and that the very notion of art excluded all predetermined causes and objectives.[7] What is particularly noteworthy about the passages under discussion is their uniform defense of the function of the imagination in art and literature. The implicit and explicit rejection of the principle of utility by Madame de Staël, Victor Cousin, and Théodore Jouffroy would win the predictable endorsement of both the proponents of Art for Art's Sake and Parnassianism, but the importance ascribed to the role of the imagination would only gain the cautious approval of such practitioners of Art for Art as Théophile Gautier and the gentle yet firm admonition of the more scientifically oriented Parnassians as Leconte de Lisle.

Even the most casual examination of the early theoretical pronouncements of prominent exponents of social Romanticism discloses some startling resemblances in disposition with what will become known as Art for Art's Sake or literary bohemianism after 1832. Consideration of Victor Hugo's wavering attitude between noncommitment and commitment in literature during the 1820s and 1830s, for example, brings into sharper perspective the nature of the ideological principles which divided the advocates of the two literary stances in question. In his several pleas in behalf of the priorities of literary expression over the inhibition of rigid classical formulas, Hugo came astonishingly close to proclaiming the gratuity of art.

The 1826 preface[8] to *Odes et Ballades,* which argued against the lack of any apparent aesthetic justification for the classical rule on the separation of the *genres,* brought Hugo closer to the position of Théophile Gautier. The preface to the *Orientales* in 1829 brought him virtually to the brink of declaring complete autonomy for the poet, and provoked the obvious displeasure of Pierre Leroux and Hippolyte Carnot, the cofounders of the *Revue encyclopédique,* who admonished Hugo for advocating and writing verse of little or no consequence with relation to the predicaments of modern man.[9] Hugo's flirtation with Art for Art's Sake reached its apogee in 1830, ironically at the very moment when French Romanticism scored its first major victory over the lingering yet stubborn supporters of neoclassicism. *Hernani* accomplishes significantly more than project the portrait of a fatalistic individual; the drama asserts the notion of a gratuitous freedom with the kind of boldness rarely encountered before in French literature. When Hugo's protagonist, Hernani, declares to Doña Sol "I am propelled by a force that goes," the dramatist proclaims through the admission of his character that poetic freedom excludes any commitment to a preconceived or predetermined cause. It remains a fact that the poetic hero of Hugo's drama remains conspicuously faithful to the uninhibited impulses of his own imagination by rejecting all forms of temporary or practical relationships.

Such potential disciples as Alfred de Musset and Théophile Gautier were quick to register their disappointment in the discernible shift in tone and mood of Hugo's literary conception after 1830. The change of emphasis in the poet's attitude may be detected in the publication of a curious preface which Hugo was prompted to write after an official ban had been placed on his drama, *Le Roi s'amuse* [*The king is enjoying himself*], in November of 1832 by the July Monarchy, ostensibly on the grounds of immorality. The essay is naturally divisible in two parts because of the unexpected turn of the polemical arguments half way through the preface.

The treatise begins, predictably, with a virulent attack on the spirit of repression that ordered the play banned, and by the poet's solemn resolve to struggle in behalf of the establishment of freedom of expression in the theatre. The fact of the matter was that the opening arguments in favor of a liberated theatre gave familiar indications of disintegrating into a sequel to the *Préface à Cromwell* [*Preface to Cromwell*] of 1829. The sudden jolt in Hugo's plea occurs when he openly questions his attitude of detachment from political, social, and moral considerations in literature. The tenor of the rest of the essay is one of acquiescence and resignation: "The poet has his own task to perform; he knows what he must do, and nothing must deter him from fulfilling his obligation. At the moment, he has acquired a political responsibility which he did not seek but which he accepts willingly." It is no small irony that Hugo's admittedly reluctant subversion of art to political designs occurred at precisely the moment when he meant to protest the political interference which resulted in the ban placed on *Le Roi s'amuse*.

If it is true that 1832 marked the beginnings of Hugo's allegiance to the conception of a utilitarian literature, the same year also signaled the start of Théophile Gautier's almost relentless campaign in behalf of an aesthetics of Art for Art's Sake in France. After the July Revolution of 1830, the Saint-Simonians and the Fourierists had succeeded in luring the majority of the leading Romanticists from their respective *cénacles* and drawing rooms into the public arena of political and ideological activism. The preface to *Albertus* pointed to the literary crossroads at which Victor Hugo and Théophile Gautier had arrived. Gautier's prefatory treatise constitutes a rather convincing argument for autonomy in art, and issues a scathing denunciation of the degrading compromises to which the social Romanticists had subjected literature with their propaganda:

> What cause does art serve? It serves the cause of beauty. Isn't that enough? Like the flowers, like perfume, like the birds, like all that man has been unable to deprave and subvert to meet his own ends. . . .
>
> . . . Art is freedom, luxury, efflorescence; it's the blossoming of the soul in idleness. Painting, sculpture, music serve no purpose whatsoever, yet who would dare think of doing away with them?[10]

The advocacy of the independence and gratuity of art and literature is made to rest on a principle which Gautier reveals with quasi-aphoristic force: "Generally, when something becomes useful, it ceases to be beautiful."[11]

The 1835 preface to *Mademoiselle de Maupin* reinforced with still more vehemence the thesis on the autonomy of art advanced some three years earlier in the introductory essay to *Albertus*. Both the preface to *Mademoiselle de Maupin* and the novel itself unveil in particularly revealing terms the nature of the aesthetic code devised by Gautier and the reason that motivated its adoption. The prefatory essay translates with sharp humor and characteristic vividness his belief that art is not a generative force for what may be considered good or useful but that it is solely an instrument of beauty. Listen to his categorical dismissal of utilitarianism in art: "Only that which cannot serve a purpose may be considered truly beautiful. Everything that is useful is ugly, for usefulness expresses human needs, and they are base and debilitating. The most useful rooms in a house are the latrines."[12]

The fiction itself appends the conception of plasticity to the notion of autonomy in art and tends to equate it with the manifestation of ideal beauty. To a significant degree, Gautier embodies the aesthetic stance of his protagonist, D'Albert, whose sensory and emotional satisfaction are gratified through the contemplation of idealized beauty. For Gautier and D'Albert, an identification is made between the conception of beauty and the visual forms that are emphasized by the artist: "Three things please me: gold, marble and the crimson dyes of the Ancients: flashes of light, solidity of form, color. My dreams are made of such stuff, and all the castles of my dreams are constructed with these materials."[13] The importance ascribed to the concrete and plastic interpretations of art in *Mademoiselle de Maupin* were destined to receive fuller elaboration in the collection of poems Gautier published in 1852 and 1857, *Emaux et Camées* [*Enamels and Cameos*].

The probable explanation of Gautier's complete rejection of the more personal aspects of Romanticism during the mid-1830s may be found in the frenetically fanciful effusions of his first poems, collected and published in 1830. His early poetry betrays a near-obsessive concern with the ephemeral and fragile nature of human life. The personal distress he experienced through the more metaphysical interpretations of existence infused him with a sense of inadequacy and dejection which he attempted with dogged determination to dispel.

The great chasm that existed between human aspiration and limited achievement, and his intense consciousness of life's transitoriness eventually induced him to retreat behind a mask of impassibility before the urgent immediacies of everyday situations in order to gain a measure of the mental tranquility which he urgently sought. Gautier elected to withdraw from the immediacy of the contingencies of daily existence and learned to stifle or control his own emotions and reactions so that he might avoid the expenditure of energy upon matters of little or dated significance. To achieve his aim, he steeped himself in the conception of hellenic serenity which permeated the bucolic verse of André Chénier.

He eventually evolved the kind of poetic disposition which, although somewhat inclined toward immobility, would allow him to obtain at least the quiet illusion of permanence from a world bereft of such values. The fact of the matter was that Gautier's aesthetic attitude, stripped of all utilitarian concern, corresponded to his deep-seated interest in painting and the plastic arts since it emphasized the sensory reproduction and idealization of reality. In his search for ideal beauty through the observation of external nature, he concluded that the work of art constituted the only lasting value in an otherwise overwhelmingly valueless world. Through the creation of works of lasting beauty, the artist could convince himself of the continuity and the perpetuation of human aspirations that somehow rendered his otherwise heterogeneous view of man's predicament considerably more homogeneous.

The contemplation of the artistic legacy bequeathed modern man by the ancient epochs and civilizations provided Gautier with the most ideal means by which he could achieve the type of remoteness from the pragmatic concerns of the contemporary situation that his new aesthetic code required. The artistic expression of Greek Antiquity, for example, afforded him the splendid opportunity of viewing its masterpieces with the kind of emotional detachment which he so eagerly sought.

With its emphasis on the material and pagan aspects of civilization, the artistic accomplishments of classical Antiquity reinforced Gautier's own marked preference and propensity for the visual and plastic conception of literary expression. The search for the hard and durable forms that would ensure the survival of poetic expression had already received the attention of such French Romanticists as Vigny in his "Bouteille à la mer" [*Bottle in the sea*].[14] Gautier's celebrated program poem, "L'Art," published in the 1857 edition[15] of *Emaux et camées,* proclaimed the exultant answer to the riddle with its exclamation that the eventual triumph of matter over the thwarted dreams and aspirations of the human mind could be realized through the work of art.

More than merely the plea for the artist to practice the care and control advocated by such classical reformers as Malherbe and Boileau, "L'Art" bespeaks behind the mask of its apparent formula for objectivity the kind of personal drama that lends the poem its own emotional strain and detectable lyrical dimension. "L'Art" emerges as something considerably more than a carefully reasoned argument in favor of tightly controlled formal structures; it releases in ostensibly measured terms the publicly objective solution to a private, a personal dilemma:

> Tout passe.—L'art robuste
> Seul à l'éternité,
> Le buste
> Survit à la cité,
>
> Et la médaille austère
> Que trouve un laboureur
> Sous terre
> Révèle un empereur.
>
> Les dieux eux-mêmes meurent.
> Mais les vers souverains
> Demeurent
> Plus forts que les airains.
>
> ["Everything dies. Only the robust art lives forever: only the bust outlives the city. And the austere medallion which a ploughman discovers beneath the earth discloses the portrait of an emperor. The gods themselves die. But poems possess a sovereignty that remains stronger than that of bronzes."]

The poem's ready recourse to the material substratum of Antiquity and the advocacy of a calm and pondered approach to artistic expression would receive the enthusiastic endorsement of the latter Parnassian poets as well as of the proponents of Art for Art's Sake.

Despite its predominant emphasis upon the necessity to observe the concrete manifestations of nature, Gautier's aesthetic attitude categorically rejected the view that art should aim at the mathematically precise rendering or reproduction of that reality. Rather, the kind of realistic expression that was sought was that begotten by the imaginative interpretation of observed facts. Art, then, was not the simple translation of any factually observed reality but rather its idealization. His *Histoire du Romantisme* [*History of Romanticism*] reminds the poet of his obligation to transform his vision of the external world through the various forms, shades and colors at his disposal so that individual readers might be encouraged to articulate the dreams and the ideas that remain partially rooted and locked in such observations.[16]

Gautier openly railed at those artists who sought to mirror reality without any kind of intervention by dismissing their so-called realistic portraitures as cheap and valueless copy. The validity of artistic expression, he maintained, rested in its efficacity to detect and seize upon characteristic human traits, and to remove them from the ugly limitations of particularized contexts in order to transform them into statements of lasting beauty. Art is superior to nature, since beauty is something intrinsic to the poet or artist's creativity. In the "Salon de 1837," Gautier explains the creative genius of the painter, Cabat, in the following manner: "The model is hideous, yet the portrait has charm: how can that be? It is simply that art is something more beautiful, more powerful than nature; nature is stupid; it is not conscious of itself . . . it's something that is cheerless and colorless: it needs a creative soul to endow it with animation."[17] Since art emerges as something essentially superior to nature, it also asserts its independence from the social and moral constructions of specific men at given times and places.

The very concept of ideal beauty carried in its train strong suggestions of the rare, the sacred, and the mystical which appealed not only to Gautier but also to such a congener in Art for Art's Sake and Parnassianism as Leconte de Lisle. Anticipating the positivist framework of the 1850s and 1860s, Gautier found it convenient to replace the metaphysical postulates upon which rested the principal beliefs of the major Western religions with an aesthetic creed whose foundations were cemented in concrete reality.

Just as the later Positivists appended a mystique of progress to their scientific orientation, the practitioners of Art for Art's Sake or literary Realism made a religion out of beauty and art. What both Baudelaire and Leconte de Lisle call sacred objects and inaccessible eternal essences in their respective poems, "Hymne à la beauté" [*Hymn to beauty*] and "Hypatie," Flaubert referred to a kind of mysticism and a refuge in a letter to Louise Colet, dated 14 August 1853: "Humanity despises us [artists]; we shall not serve its cause and we shall despise humanity because it seeks to wound us. Let us love one another in Art as the mystics love one another in God, and let everything fade before this love."

The great majority of the adepts of Art for Art's Sake and Parnassianism subscribed to the idea that art was absolute, an end in itself, and that the beauty which emanated from a work of art constituted something divine. Yet all remained mindful of the fact that the cult of beauty to which they had submitted their art was linked to the visible world rather than to the invisible one of their metaphysical counterparts in social Romanticism.

It would be a serious error to conclude that Gautier's aesthetic pronouncements in the prefaces to *Albertus* and *Mademoiselle de Maupin* elicited the kind of enthusiastic endorsement that made of Art for Art's Sake a major literary attitude during Louis-Philippe's July Monarchy. Gautier's conception of the autonomy of literature instigated instead the condemnation of virtually every significant partisan of social Romanticism. The Saint-Simonians dismissed his thesis with the categorical assertion that the only justification of art rests in its social function and in its contribution to the progress of civilization.

Liberal Catholics joined forces with such republican and socialist reformers as Louis Blanc and Proudhon to denounce Art for Art's Sake as the expression of a dangerous egotistical individualism. Scores of editorial comments in such notable journals as *Le Globe, L'Avenir,* the *Revue encyclopédique,* and *Revue républicaine* underscored the nefarious consequences implicit in an aesthetic code that concerned itself primarily with the purely descriptive portraiture of past civilizations.

In his *Esquisse d'une philosophie* [*Outline for a philosophy*] of 1840, Lamennais, with characteristic verve, argued quite simply: "Art is nothing less than the external form of ideas, the expression of religious dogma and of the dominant social principles of a given epoch. No form of art may exist within a vacuum; Art for Art's Sake is an absurdity."[18] Lamennais articulates, to a significant degree, the mood and temper of the July Monarchy that stirred thinkers and writers to commit themselves to the more pressing problems of social reform and revolution. Even such stalwart supporters of Parnassianism in the 1850s and 1860s as Leconte de Lisle, Louis Ménard, and Louis Bouihlet infused their writings with social and political propaganda in the years immediately preceding and following the Revolution of 1848. In short, Art for Art's Sake had succeeded in securing only the uncertain adherence of a small group of sympathizers during the regime of Louis-Philippe. The bitter disillusionment experienced by a great number of socially active thinkers and writers in 1851 inspired the kind of interest and enthusiasm in Art for Art's Sake that made of it a major literary reaction during the first decade of Louis-Napoleon's Second Empire.

With the suppression of freedom of the press and the elimination of universal suffrage during the opening years of the Second Empire, the most adamant republican and socialist advocates of reform were either quickly disorganized and exiled or deported. For socially committed poets like Hugo, determined to unleash their prophetic deprecations upon a repressive regime, only one choice was open to them: that of exile from their native France.

If the government of Louis-Napoleon openly encouraged useful and moral art, it also unwittingly favored the blossoming of Art for Art's Sake in the 1850s. The Second Empire tolerated with some condescension the aesthetic attitude of Art for Art's Sake only because it affirmed complete disassociation from all political as well as moral and social considerations. The truth of the matter, however, was that no literary or artistic stance enjoyed complete freedom from governmental interference and control.

The official condemnation of Flaubert's *Madame Bovary* and Baudelaire's *Les Fleurs du Mul* [*The flowers of evil*] in 1857, on the charges of outrage against public morality, served as a vivid reminder of the kind of censorship which was imposed. Nevertheless, the publication of such significant volumes as the *Emaux et Camées* of Gautier and the *Poèmes antiques* [*Ancient poems*] of Leconte de Lisle in 1852 as well as the fiction and poetry of Flaubert and Baudelaire constitutes sufficient justification for labelling Art for Art's Sake a major literary attitude of the 1850s. For lack of any more cohesive doctrine than the bold assertion of autonomy and independence from any outside influence, the principles underlying its aesthetic code came under the fairly steady attacks of both its enemies and of some of its own practitioners. In his 1852 essay on the poetry of Pierre Dupont,[19] Baudelaire questions the philosophy of noninvolvement in Art for Art's Sake: "The childish utopia of the school of Art for Art's Sake, in excluding ethical considerations and very frequently even passion, was necessarily sterile." Baudelaire's position with reference to the theory and practice of a purely autonomous literature is one both of sympathy and exasperation. Such poems in his *Fleurs du Mal* such as "La Beauté" [*Beauty*] and "Hymne à la beauté" are unquestionable endorsements of the formal and the philosophical principles of Art for Art's Sake. His 1859 appraisal of Gautier's art is nothing less than a panegyric of praise for autonomy in literature and a scathing denunciation of the concept of utility.[20] Yet, his study on "L'Ecole païenne" [*The pagan school*] in *L'Art romantique* unveiled again serious reservations which he entertained concerning the curtailment of personal expression in art and poetry.

The answer to Baudelaire's wavering position with respect to Art for Art's Sake is contained in his own poetry. While he espoused the cause of stricter forms in literary expression, he felt intimidated or limited by the heavy insistence upon a less personal and more plastic or concrete interpretation of reality. His increasing reliance upon unrestricted metaphors and images to convey the subjective allusiveness of musical sounds in his verse points to the development of future French Symbolism rather than to the orthodox expression of Art for Art's Sake or Parnassianism.

There existed few centers in the 1850s and early 1860s where the adept practitioners of the new literary aesthetic could rally to voice their common aims and iron out their respective differences of opinion. The most important of these rallying points was certainly the drawing room of Madame de Sabatier, dubbed "la présidente" by Gautier, where such writers as Flaubert, Gautier, Baudelaire, and Bouihlet met on consecutive Sundays in 1863 in order to read and discuss one another's works. The only major literary journal of note to recognize the merits of Art for Art's Sake in the 1850s was *L'Artiste,* whose direction and editorship Gautier assumed in 1856. The "Introduction," published in the 14 December 1856 issue, articulated the policy of autonomy in art and literature in the most explicit terms yet.

> We believe in the complete independence of art; art, for us, is not the means but the end. In our estimation, any artist who considers accomplishing something other than the beautiful in his work is not an artist at all. We have never understood the attitude that divorces ideas from their forms. A pleasing form is a pleasing idea, for what good is a form that expresses nothing?

The example of Gautier's sustained adherence to the principle of aesthetic autonomy during the years in which Art for Art's Sake remained overshadowed by social Romanticism through the first decade of the Second Empire records the history of the movement from its virtual inception to its eventual confrontation with Parnassianism in the mid-1860s. The differences which ultimately distinguished Art for Art's Sake from Parnassianism resulted from slight yet discernible shifts in emphasis and direction rather than from any serious divergence in orientation and ideology.

The very choice of the word, Parnassian, to describe fundamentally the continued practice of Art for Art's Sake in French poetry at first proved to be almost as controversial as it was arbitrary. An obscure poet, Marty-Laveaux, suggested the term to the editor, Alphonse Lemerre, who had agreed to publish a collection of poems, the majority of which shared a certain spiritual affinity with Art for Art's Sake, and for which anthology he eagerly sought a title. Leconte de

Lisle voiced his bitter objection over the designation of Parnassian as entirely inappropriate and utterly absurd in the proposed context, yet the codirectors of the project, Catulle Mendès and Xavier de Ricard, ignored the objection,[21] and had the word incorporated into the title page in 1866, as, *Le Parnasse contemporain: recueil de vers nouveaux* [*The contemporary Parnassus: an anthology of new verse*].

The *Parnasse contemporain* of 1866 marked the first of three collections of poems claiming at least some vague allegiance to the attitude of Art for Art's Sake. The two remaining volumes appeared in 1871 and 1876 respectively. Taken compositely, the *Parnasse contemporain* affords the opportunity of surveying the poetry of some one hundred poets in the ten-year span from 1866 to 1876. Despite the conspicuous absence of any specific theory or doctrine, the *Parnasse contemporain* suggests, at least implicitly if not explicitly, a decided reaction to the exaggerated emotionalism and sentimentalism marring the French Romantic lyric. The one hundred poets represented in the anthologies are more urgently united in the solidarity of their artistic endeavor than they are in any specifically rigid attitude or school of thought. A partial listing of the wide range of poets most frequently encountered in the three volumes reveals the generous latitude in poetical outlook that motivated the organizers of the project. Such obviously prone practitioners of the plastic conception of Art for Art's Sake as Leconte de Lisle, Sully Prudhomme, and José-Maria de Heredia are interspersed with the more appropriately drawn exponents of Symbolism such as Baudelaire, Verlaine, and Mallarmé.[22]

LE

PARNASSE

CONTEMPORAIN

Recueil de vers nouveaux

(1876)

PARIS

ALPHONSE LEMERRE, ÉDITEUR

27-31, PASSAGE CHOISEUL, 27-31

If it could be convincingly argued that the *Parnasse contemporain* failed to advance any noticeably evolved aesthetic statement in behalf of a plastic Parnassianism that distinguished it significantly from the kind of Art for Art's Sake published in the 1850s, it might be equally maintained that no such theoretical purpose motivated the undertaking of Lemerre, Mendès, and Ricard. Indeed, Mendès spoke in unmistakably clear terms on the matter: "Parnassianism was born from the need to react to the license present in the poetry of Murger, Charles Bataille, Amédée Roland. . . . The Parnassian group is neither based on any theory nor on any aesthetic code."[23] While Mendès's assertion may strike us as debatable on several accounts, the defensive thrust behind his declaration betrays a sense of discomfort over the precarious state of poetry during the age of Positivism in France.

The various literary drawing rooms of such varied patrons as Nina de Villars, Madame de Ricard, Catulle Mendès, and Leconte de Lisle during the 1860s were constituted primarily to assert the need for autonomy in art, and to encourage and ensure the practice of poetic expression in a society predominantly concerned with more immediately useful values. Despite its claims at objectivity and its scientific orientation, the poetry of Art for Art's Sake and Parnassianism failed to enlist the interest and enthusiasm of any significantly substantial reading public. From 1851 to 1866, the editors of such prestigious firms as Michel Lévy, Charpentier, and Hetzel refused to consider any kind of poetry for publication. In their struggle against the contemptuous indifference of potential readers and the hostility of editors, the Parnassian poets understandably encouraged the interest which the well-known publisher, Alphonse Lemerre, had expressed over their plight. An admirer of the verse of Leconte de Lisle and Heredia, Lemerre invited the poets to read and discuss their poems at his bookstore at the passage Choiseul.

Eventually, Lemerre suggested to Xavier de Ricard that he abandon the directorship of his financially troubled journal, *L'Art,* to edit the series of poetry collections that was destined to be associated with the cause of Parnassianism. The appearance of the three instalments of the *Parnasse contemporain* represented, then, a considerable psychological victory for the poets whose verse purported no more than to celebrate formal beauty at a time when such poetry was being dismissed as gratuitous in favor of literary works that blatantly exploited scientific methodology for material ends. The rich variety in form as well as in thematic development rescued the *Parnasse contemporain* from any exclusive identification with any sectarian aesthetic philosophy. Public reaction to the three collections proved to be moderately successful. More important still, the poets in question benefited from both the public and critical exposure afforded them by the series.

Despite the absence of any theoretical argument in favor of Art for Art's Sake in the *Parnasse contemporain,* critics of the concept of autonomy in art nevertheless voiced their antipathy in a series of essays and parodies which, in some cases, served to elicit interest in the poets under attack. The succession of articles appearing in *Le Nain jaune* [*The yellow dwarf*] from 27 October to 14 November 1866 under the signature of Barbey d'Aurevilly constituted the most sustained virulent attack upon the literary current detectable in the first volume of the collection.

In general, Barbey reproaches the poets of the *Parnasse contemporain* for their conspicuous lack of belief and conviction, patently labeling them as dimunitive imitators: ". . . this bunch of monkeys who think they're men and who parade while beating their own drums on the stretched ass skins of the *Parnasse contemporain* . . . they're nothing more than poetical baboons and wistiti!" Barbey's burlesque, *Les Trente-sept médaillonets du Parnasse* [*The thirty-seven small medallions of Parnassus*], an obvious allusion to the thirty-seven poets represented in the 1866 edition, hardly succeeds as effective caricature since the portraits of such adherents of Parnassianism as Leconte de Lisle and Banville, for example, are difficult to distinguish.

An equally ambitious attack upon the attitudes manifest in Lemerre's anthologies was that undertaken by Alphonse Daudet and Paul Arène in the amusing pamphlet called, *Le Parnassiculet contemporain* [*The low-browed contemporary Parnassus*] in 1866 and 1872. The collaborators of this diverting spoof on such well-known personalities as Louis Ménard, Leconte de Lisle, and Heredia display considerable talent in protesting mostly the effrontery behind the conception of the anthologies: the arrogant supposition that only the included poets give the complete picture of French poetic expression. Paul Arène, by far the most successful contributor, wrote a thoroughly entertaining playlet entitled, *Gaël-Imar au grand pied* [*Big-footed Gaël-Imar*], an effective parody of Leconte de Lisle's manner with Scandinavian legend, and by far the most consistently amusing feature in the *Parnassiculet.* Whatever negative image it may have hoped to suggest, the critical reaction to Lemerre's anthologies underscored the growing influence which the poets of Art for Art's Sake had finally managed to exert on the French literary scene.

Despite the frequently biased accounts that detract from the credibility of Catulle Mendès's history of the literary movement during the 1860s, *La Légende du Parnasse contemporain* did corroborate the widely held assumption that the theoretical bases of Art for Art's Sake evolved somewhat loosely from the discussions in which its leading advocates participated at Alphonse Lemerre's bookstore at the passage Choiseul as well as in the several drawing rooms and literary workshops already mentioned. Under the official and effective leadership of Leconte de Lisle, the poets, increasingly referred to as Parnassians, sought to define the principles and attitudes that explained their common aesthetic outlook. The literary code of the Parnassian poets of the 1850s and 1860s is most easily deciphered in the program poems of its major practitioners and in the prefatory essays to Leconte de Lisle's collections of poems.[24] The purely technical aspects of Parnassianism are conveniently expressed in handbook form as *Petit Traité de poésie française* [*Introductory treatise on French poetry*], published by Théodore de Banville in 1872.

It is just as logical as it is ironic that the concepts of objectivity and ideal beauty that infiltrated the poetics of Parnassianism so thoroughly and effectively should be rooted in personal interpretations of man's predicament. Lyricism, the fusion of reason and feeling, purports to convey such personal reactions to human experience. However well disguised in the cloak of formal objectivity, the truly effective poetical expression of Parnassianism sought to infuse outwardly passive attitudes with a discernible, though controlled, personal dimension. Much maligned and misinterpreted by their detractors on the count of so-called impassibility, the leading Parnassian poets waged an almost relentless if somewhat unsuccessful battle to rid themselves of a charge they considered totally unjustified.

The designation resulted most probably from the obvious misreading of either Gautier or Glatigny's sonnets, "L'Impassible," in the 1871 edition of the *Parnasse contemporain.* Leconte de Lisle's abrupt reply to Jules Huret's query on impassibility and Parnassianism, subsequently recorded in the *Enquête sur l'évolution littéraire,* reveals the extent to which the term exasperated him: "When will they ever tire of that stupid story? Imagine, an impassive poet! I suppose that when one doesn't reveal how he buttons his trousers or divulge every aspect of his love life, one is called an impassive poet? The whole thing is stupid!"

In rejecting the excessive effusion of Romanticism, the Parnassians vowed to champion a tightly constructed and more impersonal lyricism steeped in the ready observation of concrete reality rather than in any carelessly devised and vaguely defined metaphysical attitude. In a probable allusion to Musset's parable of the pelican in "La Nuit de mai" [*Night in May*], Leconte de Lisle's sonnet, "Les Montreurs" [*The Showmen*], published in *Les Poèmes barbares* of 1862, decried the shameless practice of public personal confession in poetry as a prostitution of art. If "Les Montreurs" relegates such poets and such avowals to the barbaric tradition, the sonnet also succeeds admirably in defining the kind of tempered lyrical expression that was sought by the Parnassians. The two tercets conclude Leconte de Lisle's denunciation in the kind of impassioned language that blends ideas with personal feelings and conviction.

> Dans mon orgueil muet, dans ma tombe sans gloire,
> Dussé-je m'engloutir pour l'éternité noire,
> Je ne te vendrai pas mon ivresse ou mon mal,
>
> Je ne liverai pas ma vie à tes huées,
> Je ne danserai pas sur ton tréteau banal
> Avec tes histrions et tes prostituées.
>
> ["Even if it meant my disappearance into the black abyss of eternity, in my muted pride and from my anonymous grave, I would not divulge my ecstasy or my disappointment to you. I refuse to disclose my private life to your public's clamor. I refuse to dance on your tawdry stage with your clowns and prostitutes."]

The aesthetic philosophy to which the majority of Parnassian poets subscribed underlined the vast differences in personal outlook that distinguished them from the most prominent social Romantic poets. The latter proceeded to write their poems on the supposition that an accord between the individual and exterior nature could be achieved through the various conflicting cosmogonic explanations more replete with inspiration and emotion than with reason and factual observation. Social Romanticism was the poetry of the limitless possibilities of man. The Parnassians found the basis for their expression in the sober and precise observation of nature and history and tended to project the limitations of human design and accomplishment in the kind of verse which tacitly suggested a pondered and quiet resignation to such limits.

The fact of the matter was that the Parnassian objection to the preposterous claims of social Romanticism came, for the most part, on the heels of the failure of the 1848 Revolution and the attendant fiasco of the shortlived Second Republic. Thus, the majority of Parnassian poets tended to judge the unlimited optimism of Romantic aspiration from the optic of a recent historical event as well as from the obvious sense of disillusionment they experienced as a result of such a drastic event. The quasi-metaphysical tinge and the detectable tone of anticipation present in the writings of Baudelaire, Leconte de Lisle, and Louis Ménard in 1848, for example, constitute fairly indisputable evidence that these future partisans of Art for Art's Sake and Parnassianism shared in the enthusiasm that infused social Romanticism during the last years of the July Monarchy.

From the perspective of the ensuing Second Empire, the Parnassians countered the hopeful aspirations of a prior Romanticism with a sober, if not pessimistic, appraisal of the human predicament that resulted from their close observation of fact and reality. If social Romanticism proclaimed an inspired mystique of progress and energy, Parnassianism voiced a discouraging conviction of the futility of effort in modern times. The claims of social Romanticism surfaced in an undisguised individualism and subjectivity; the assertions of Parnassianism resulted from the methodical control of significantly more objective observation of external nature. The difference divorcing Romanticism from Parnassianism, then, was one of method or approach rather than one of ideological attitude. The latter emerged the result or the consequence of the methodology employed.

Leconte de Lisle's preface to the *Poèmes antiques* of 1852 issued an unmistakable reprimand to the Romanticists whose lyrical expression displayed the woeful lack of any kind of method or cohesiveness, and concluded somewhat caustically: " . . . you were incapable of mouthing anything else but your own inanity." From the vantage point of the aftermath of the 1848 Revolution, Leconte de Lisle defines the shift in orientation and methodology that will rescue poetry from its ridiculous presumption. The definition that he advances betrays the personal sense of frustration and futility which he feels when confronted by the contemporary situation of 1852.

> In these uncertain times, the most sensible and reasonable minds stop to consult one another. The others do not even know where they come from or where they are going: in their haste and blindness, they subscribe to whatever feverish agitation they encounter. Only the former are conscious of the transitory character of their age and of the fatal demands it may make on them. We are a generation of scholars; the spontaneous world of instinct, so abundantly in evidence during our youth, has been withdrawn from us: such is the irreparable fact. Poetry, expressed as an art form, will no longer preoccupy itself with heroic deeds nor will it inspire men to social action because the power of its sacred language has been diminished. As in every period of literary decadence, in the desperate hope of discovering some latent form of heroism or some remnant of virtue, poetry has become reduced to expressing only petty personal impressions punctuated by an arbitrary use of neologisms. In short, poetry has become enslaved to the caprice of personal taste, and it is no longer fit to teach man.

Leconte de Lisle's essay has the thrust of a virtual manifesto advocating the complete reform of poetic expression. It is replete with allusions to such notions as antiquarianism, antimodernism, impersonalism, antiutilitarianism and scientific orientation which eventually worked their way into the fabric of the Parnassian aesthetic. Considerably more than a prospectus on the impersonalized verse that he attempted to achieve in the *Poèmes antiques,* the introductory article constitutes a summation of the type of indoctrination which gradually infiltrated the minds of eager disciples who frequented the literary workshop of Leconte de Lisle on the boulevard des Invalides.

By the sheer aggressiveness of its tone, the preface to the *Poèmes antiques* may be construed as a categorical breach with social Romanticism. In general, the essay received the approbation of the sympathizers of Art for Art's Sake. In a letter to Louise Colet, however, Flaubert took exception both to Leconte de Lisle's advocacy of a return to the study and emulation of Greek antiquity, and to his heavy insistence upon formal perfection: " . . . we must not attempt a return to Hellenism but rather content ourselves to borrowing its methods and procedures. There are more things to art than well-written lines and polished surfaces."[25] In the epigram to his study of six French poets, *Les Poètes contemporains,* collected and published in the posthumous volume, *Derniers poèmes,* Leconte de Lisle articulated the principle that crowned his entire aesthetic outlook: "The world of beauty, the only objective of Art, comprises in itself an infinite which can have no possible contact with any type of inferior conception."

It was the nineteenth-century critic, Jules Lemaître, who most accurately defined Leconte de Lisle's Greek antiquarianism as the union of the two strongest sentiments that came to dominate his life and work: the love of plastic beauty and a sense of disenchantment with contemporary existence.[26] De Lisle's ultimate disillusionment with the vaguely prophetic Fourierism to which he had subscribed as well as the personal dissatisfaction he experienced emotionally brought him to the brink of complete disgust and exasperation as early as 1845. What he lacked was precisely the sense of purpose, direction and cohesion that he had so urgently sought. He found it gradually in the formulation of the conclusion that happiness resided in the love and cult of an imperishable beauty that was conceived as impersonally as possible.

The concept of permanence, alien to the world which in its everyday activity underscored the transitoriness of existence, became associated with the concrete manifestations bequeathed by past civilizations. Whatever corroboration Leconte de Lisle may have required for his thesis, it was more than abundantly supplied in the person and thought of Louis Ménard, Hellenist philologist and ardent champion of Greek art and stoical philosophy. His *Prométhée délivré* [*Prometheus unchained*] and *Rêveries d'un païen mystique* [*Musings of a mystical pagan*] preached the superiority of pagan Greek polytheism over Christianity because it encouraged the harmonious union of religion with philosophy and poetry, and thus achieved a measure of success in satisfying the most pressing requirements of man's aspirations.

In Leconte de Lisle's view, this doctrine corresponded closely to his own interpretation of reality, and as early as 1846, under the friendly tutelage of Louis Ménard, he began in earnest his study of the Greek language and civilization. Both Leconte de Lisle and Louis Ménard figured prominently in the subsequent literary movement that favored a revival of the contemplation and imitation of Greek antiquity. De Lisle's conception of Hellenism constituted one of the principal cornerstones upon which he constructed the most important part of the aesthetic code of Parnassianism. The antiquarianism he advocated gave fuller dimension to such notions as antiutilitarianism, impersonalism, scientific orientation and the idealization of beauty which eventually became part and parcel of the outlook of the major Parnassian poets.

In large measure, the preface to *Poèmes et poésies* of 1855 may be construed as Leconte de Lisle's attempt to justify the Hellenism which served to detach him from Romanticism and to set him in opposition to Hugo. In an obvious reply to Flaubert's objection to his stated preference for Antiquity over modernism, de Lisle makes no effort to disguise his contempt for the latter: "I would like to think—and may I be forgiven for making this monstrous comparison—that the work of Homer will be significantly more appreciated in the history of humanity than the work of Blanqui." Leconte de Lisle's return to antiquarianism constituted more than a refuge or retreat from which he could indulge in the quiet contemplation of perfection in art, it also provided him with the vantage point he needed to vent his disgust for the ugliness and neobarbarianism of a disdainful nineteenth century. The utilitarian spirit of Comte's evolved Positivism, for all of its scientific pretensions, has created a world devoid of poetry. He unleashes all of his venom against the heresy of didacticism in art and literature.

> The various hymns and odes inspired by the discoveries of steam and electric telegraphy only stir my most mediocre sentiments, and all these didactic periphrases which have nothing to do with art tend to convince me that poets are becoming more and more useless to modern societies. Doubtless, poets have suffered in every age, but even in the most unfavorable times, in exile or in madness, the merit of their genius remained undisputed and incontestable. But the moment is rapidly drawing near when they shall

> be forced to cease writing to avoid their own intellectual demise. I am thoroughly convinced that such will soon be the inevitable plight of all those who refuse to prostitute the nature of their vocation for the benefit of the monstrous alliance between poetry and industry. It is because of the natural repulsion which we experience for that which destroys us that I loathe the times in which I live.

De Lisle equates modernism with barbarianism and decries the utilitarian exigencies which have stripped humanity of its sense of the ideal. He would replace modernism with Greek antiquity, restore the Greek temples and resurrect the menagerie of Greek gods because he may attest to their survival in the lasting beauty bequeathed them by their sculptors and poets. The alliance between sculpture and poetry, taken up again by Théophile Gautier in his manifesto poem, "L' Art," in 1857, best ensures the idea of an enduring and permanent work of art.

The adoption of the cult of Hellenism by such poets as Leconte de Lisle, Louis Ménard, Théodore de Banville, Sully Prudhomme, and Heredia exposed through indirection the pessimistic attitude that punctuated their aesthetic philosophy. Their common stance is that of rejection of the aspirations and values which dominated the era in which they lived. The subject matter and the themes associated with past cultures afforded the Parnassians the perfect opportunity of divorcing themselves officially from the social and historical contexts of the day with precisely the kind of detachment they desired. The poetic and artistic exploitation of antiquarianism catapulted them psychologically into an ambience far removed from the practical contingencies of their own, and favored the pursuit of ideals more attuned with their personal aspirations. Their consequent idealization of Antiquity provides an implicit though nonetheless eloquent contrast with the pettiness of modern times. The particular manner in which they approached ancient art and civilization endowed their poetry with the kind of exoticism that rescued them ultimately from succumbing to feelings of abject despair. Their antiquarianism, then, constituted a refuge and a retreat from the crass considerations of a modern society bereft of any meaningful idealism. To a significant degree, the various interpretations of Antiquity infused Parnassian poetry with a decidedly personal and lyrical flavor.

The Parnassian preference for essentially static civilizations over modernism projects a profound sense of pessimism into their verse which is frequently more than readily discernible. The 1850s signal the beginning of literary decadence and of social degeneracy since purely dated issues, rooted in the relativity of pragmatic principles, have succeeded in dominating French institutions at the noticeably painful exclusion of all idealism. In a sonnet composed for its inclusion in the *Poèmes barbares,* Leconte de Lisle denounces the preoccupations of his contemporaries in unmistakable terms. "Aux Modernes" [*To the moderns*] effectively uses the kind of visual imagery that appeals vividly to the imagination in a blunt condemnation of modern man's empty vision of existence:

> Votre cervelle est vide autant que votre sein,
> Et vous avez souillé ce misérable monde
> D'un sang si corrompu, d'un souffle si malsain,
> Que la mort germe seule en cette boue immonde.
>
> Hommes, tueurs de Dieux, les temps ne sont pas loin
> Où, sur un grand tas d'or vautrés dans quelque coin,
> Ayant rongé le sol nourricier jusqu'aux roches,
>
> Ne sachant faire rien ni des jours ni des nuits,
> Noyés dans le néant des suprêmes ennuis,
> Vous mourrez bêtement en emplissant vos poches.
>
> ["Your brain is as empty as your breast, and you have contaminated this wretched world with blood so depraved and a climate that is so unhealthy, that only death germinates from this unspeakably filthy mire. Men, killers of gods, the time is not far off when, sprawled out in some corner on huge mounds of gold, having corroded even the rocks of the earth that fostered you, and not knowing what to do with your days and nights, drowned in the nothingness of a colossal boredom, you shall die stupidly while stuffing your pockets."]

De Lisle's ominous predictions of the consequences of a mindlessly utilitarian society are invested with the kind of prophetic tone that penetrated the Parnassians's rejection of contemporary civilization.

The striking contrast between the splendors kindled by the imagination and the painful limits imposed by reality led the Romantic poets to articulate their dilemma over man's predicament in terms that frequently betrayed the pretension of personally evolved cosmogonic explanations. There are many instances in Romantic poetry which point to an intimate alliance with metaphysics. For the most part, Romantic optimism stemmed from the intuitively founded conviction that the poet, serving as intermediary between God and man, could successfully resolve the cosmic enigma of human destiny, and enlighten man spiritually and socially through his diligent guidance and leadership. Social Romantic expression took frequent recourse in the vague and ethereal qualities of language that was more ideally suited to translate the crystallized *rêveries* of the poets in question.

Parnassianism, on the other hand, chose to approach the same dilemma of the ideal and the real through the projection of an attitude that made specific reference to systematic study and the factual observation of the external forms of reality. The recorded efforts of man in past civilizations to find the answer to the riddle of the human enigma convinced the Parnassian poets of its insolubility. In a manner reminiscent of Senancour's protagonist, *Obermann,* they concluded that the understanding of the essence of human nature would never be achieved, and adopted an attitude that resembled stoicism. Since man could not aspire to the realization of any metaphysical knowledge in human existence, he would find solace in the observation and contemplation of the surfaces and appearances of a world that manifested itself in purely plastic and material terms. From such a confrontation with the external features of nature, the Parnassian poets hoped to extract an appreciation of the ideal and the beautiful. The positive and material aspect of their poetry proceeds logically from an emphatic interest in the outward aspects of reality. The philosophical implication in their stance echoes the following line from Baudelaire's "L'Amour du mensonge" [*The love of the lie*], inserted in the 1861 edition of the *Fleurs du Mal:* "Masque ou décor, salut! J'adore ta beauté." ["Mask or prop, I hail you! I love your beauty."]

In their common resolve to eschew the arbitrariness and the pretentiousness of the social Romanticists, the Parnassian poets publicized their intention to establish poetry upon the more objective foundation of a scholarly representation of beauty in art. Leconte de Lisle's preface to the *Poètes contemporains* in 1864 described the poet's procedure as follows: "He perceives things immediately and much further, much higher, much more profoundly than anyone else because he contemplates the ideal through visible beauty, and contains and enshrines it in his own precise language."

The poet's task, then, was to seek out the manifestations of a lasting beauty residing in the concrete reality which he observed, and to transpose his sense of beauty in verse that tended, for the most part, toward the descriptive. The Parnassian poet meticulously avoided the arrangement of ideas with a view to prove a point, and attempted to mask his personal stance with objectivity. The ideals which he sought to impart were those most closely identifiable with the material texture of the universe rather than with any spiritual value which he may have personally derived from the suppositions of metaphysical considerations.

It may be safely said that both the Parnassians and the Positivists, in their admitted preference for the kind of evidence which resulted from factual observation, asserted the supremacy of a material world. Such a view, of course, tended to predispose them toward materialistic interpretations of the human predicament but did not rule out the possibility of their private subscription to a spiritually oriented explication of man. Like the Positivists, the Parnassian poets excluded the realm of the spiritual from their preoccupations because it could be neither controlled nor verified by factual observation.

It is not altogether accurate to assume that the Parnassian poets refrained completely from imparting certain points of view and from infusing their verse with an almost mystical declaration of faith in their own aesthetic principle. The truth of the matter was that their rejection of the paradoxical Romantic explanation of man's enigma—that his quest for unity is achieved in the duality of matter and spirit—led them directly to their conception of the cult of idealized beauty. The quest for an ideal transcending the contingencies of nature and daily existence became entangled in the unfounded dogmas of a personally inspired religion for the Romanticists.

The Parnassian poets in their desire to link the ideal with the real associated their quest with art. The cult of idealized beauty in art rescued them from the deteriorating aspects of a pessimism that stifled both life and action, and inspired them to seek a partial solution to man's dilemma in art. What the Parnassians actually meant by their avowed cult of the beautiful may be deciphered in Leconte de Lisle's poem, "La Vénus de Milo," inspired in large measure by Théodore de Banville's "A la Muse grecque" [*To the Greek muse*], and published in the 1852 edition of the *Poèmes antiques:*

> Du bonheur impassible ô symbole adorable,
> Calme comme la Mer en sa sérénité,
> Nul sanglot n'a brisé ton sein inaltérable,
> Jamais les pleurs humains n'ont terni ta
> beauté.
>
> . . . . .
>
> Iles, séjour des Dieux! Hellas, mère sacrée!
> Oh! que ne suis-je né dans le saint Archipel,
> Aux siècles glorieux où la Terre inspirée
> Voyait le Ciel descendre à son premier appel!
>
> ["Oh adorable symbol of impassive Beauty, as calm as the sea in its serenity, no sob has disturbed your unalterable breast, and never have human tears tarnished your beauty. Islands, sojourn of the gods! Hellas, sacred mother! Oh, why could I not have been born in the holy Archipelago during that glorious era when an inspired earth could see the heavens descend at its first appeal."]

These stanzas constitute more than a mere visual celebration of the virginal purity and harmony which the contemplation of the statue of Venus of Milo inspires in the poet. The qualifying adjectives, which follow one another in fairly rapid succession, *impassive, calm* and *inalterable,* emphasize the Parnassian conception of ideal beauty while they also convey the poet's impression of the superiority of Greek antiquity. The beauty of Venus escapes the disfigurement of time and passion, and carries in its train the suggestion of permanence, the artist's material embodiment of the notion of eternity in a lasting work of art. De Lisle's admiration for ancient Greece is punctuated by a nostalgic regret for not having known Antiquity first-hand. The poem conjures the contemporary reader, obsessed with a preoccupation for the spiritual, to suspend his religious interpretation of humanity sufficiently long to appreciate the impassive happiness derived from the contemplation of such idealized beauty.

Both by their theoretical pronouncements and by their poetic practice, the Parnassians enabled the materialization of art to become increasingly more erudite and systematic. Like the plastic arts, their poetry attempted to represent external reality without too many subjective rearrangements to illustrate a purely personal reaction or point of view. Only representational art was pure and durable for it sought the reproduction of those characteristic qualities in nature which successfully managed to elude the fate reserved the banal and quickly dated theses of utilitarian works. In representational art, the writer's poetic imagination made willing reference to fact and experience in order to capture the salient features of reality and to avoid insistence on any given subjective viewpoint.

Such art, buttressed by truth, infused itself with a sense of vitality that enhanced the chances for its survival. If it may be said that the leading Parnassians sought the corroboration of science and experience, it should also be underlined that they campaigned just as vigorously to keep their poetry intact from any subservience to science. What interested them was the methodology of science which they sought to implement in various fashions in their own poetry. Because the reigning "Scientism" and the Positivist spirit of the time lent itself so readily to the designs of an officially sanctioned utilitarianism, such practitioners of an allegedly pure and untainted art as the Parnassian poets voiced their suspicion of science, and distinguished between a disinterested scientific method and pragmatic science.[27]

In his essay on Théophile Gautier in the *Art romantique,* Baudelaire pointed out the consequences reserved for literature if any strict alliance was made with science and ethics: "At the risk of its failure and demise, poetry cannot become assimilated to science or to morality." As the most influential proponent of Parnassianism, Leconte de Lisle underscored the common denominators between art and science with respect to morality and encouraged a cautions *rapprochement* between poetry and scientific method. What Leconte de Lisle sought in the *rapprochement* which he urged was the achievement of a more precise conception of reality through the critical faculties sharpened by a controlled, scientific approach to poetry. The scientific or scholarly approach to lyricism would endow poetry with a more universally identifiable picture of reality by keeping in check, but not squelching, the important role played by the imagination in works of art.

The most successful poetry of the Parnassian movement achieves such an objective. Parnassian art, then, aimed at translating the artist's own predispositions within the contained limits which objectivity and impersonality imposed in its expression. Théodore de Banville in his *Petit Traité de poésie française* [*Introductory treatise on French poetry*], published in 1872, fathoms the objectives of Parnassian poetry as follows: "Your poetry will express your mind and heart, and we will see clearly reflected your vices, your failings and weaknesses. You will perhaps manage to deceive some men, but your hypocrisy will never succeed in fooling the Muse."

The poet's mission is to restore art to its original purity. The Parnassian poets took from science its method in order to rejuvenate art and proclaim its ideal which had for so long been obscured by purely dated and pragmatic considerations. The aesthetic code to which the majority of French Parnassians subscribed did not outlaw all form of action from poetic expression. The Parnassian creed warned its practitioners, however, of the dangers and risks engendered in close involvement with present issues. It favored the scholarly study of past civilizations and traditions so that the inevitable laws upon which rest the future of mankind might be divulged through lasting works of art. Parnassianism sought to remind poets of the veritable aims of their art. Leconte de Lisle explained this ambition in the preface to the *Poèmes antiques:*

> Art and science, separated for so long by divergent intellectual reactions, must aim to link themselves close together. Art has expressed the primitive revelation of the ideal contained in exterior reality, while science has calmly analyzed the poetic claim in order to expose it more clearly. But art has lost its intuitive spontaneity, or rather, it has exhausted it. It is now for science to infuse art with a renewed appreciation of its forgotten traditions so that it may be enabled to crystallize them in appropriate formal expression.

It was precisely the mutual *rapprochement* advocated between art and science, and detectable in the poetic practice of its leading exponents that ultimately distinguished Parnassianism from the kind of Art for Art's Sake that is best characterized in French poetry by Théophile Gautier.

The flexibility and the freedom with which the Parnassian poets evolved their aesthetic code prevented their discussions on art from disintegrating into a mere laboratory or workshop with the obvious objective of grinding out the theoretical aspects for set verse forms. The only attempt to impose official doctrine on the art of versification proved unsuccessful. Théodore de Banville's *Petit Traité de poésie française,* published only in 1872, constituted little more than a handbook on versification that remained ignored by the Parnassian poets except for Glatigny.

The truth of the matter was that the various poets exercised their right to develop the kind of verse form that suited their disposition, the only rule enforced for each one being "that each verse must show that it has been well thought out and chiseled." An examination of the poetry of the major collections of Banville, Prudhomme, de Lisle, and Heredia shows that Parnassian verse forms run the gamut from Romantic looseness to the classical regularity sought by de Lisle.

The Franco-Prussian War and the ensuing Commune of 1871 brought about the decline of Parnassianism and its eventual dispersion. The urgent sense of struggle for personal and national existence pervaded the movement with principles that proved incompatible with its avowed aesthetic attitude. Many of the poems written by such diverse figures as Banville, Gautier, Prudhomme, and de Lisle during 1871 are little more than calls to patriotic action.

The fall of Sedan and the subsequent siege of Paris only served to reinforce, however, de Lisle's political disdain and contemptuous regard for the times in which he lived. De Lisle and Heredia, notably, would continue to publish verse that conformed to the code that had been evolved during the 1860s. Other poets like Théodore de Banville, for example, defected from the aesthetic of Parnassianism for personal and ideological reasons. It may be safely concluded that both Art for Art's Sake and Parnassianism rose in idealistic reaction to the social Romanticism of the 1830s. The formal reforms instituted by Art for Art's Sake and Parnassianism were destined to survive in the Symbolist verse that dominated French poetry after the Franco-Prussian War.

Notes

[1] Albert Cassagne, *La Théorie de l'art pour l'art en France chez les derniers romantiques et les premiers réalistes* (Paris; Lucien Dorbon, 1905), pp. 21-24.

[2] Charles de Rémusat in the 12 March 1825 issue of *Le Globe.*

[3] Madame de Staël, *De l'Allemagne* (n.p. [London], 1813), vol. 2, p. 6.

[4] Ibid., vol. 3, p. 9.

[5] Although Quatremère de Quincy published his *Essais sur l'idéal* in 1836, his theories on the autonomy of literature were known as early as 1805 because of his open debates with Emeric David, the defender of the traditional realist aesthetic.

[6] *Du Vrai, du beau et du bien,* Essay 7 in the 1836 edition. It is interesting to compare this edition with the subsequent versions of 1846 and 1858, for example, where certain moral restrictions are inserted. These are likely accounted by the fact that Victor Cousin was appointed Minister of Public Education in 1840 and came under heavy attack by the clergy.

[7] Théodore Jouffroy, *Cours d'esthétique* (1826), Essay 4. The *Cours d'esthétique* is essentially a revision of Jouffroy's lectures at the Ecole Normale. Sainte-Beuve attended these lectures. See Cassagne, *La Théorie de l'art pour l'art,* p. 41.

[8] There were actually four different prefaces written for the *Odes et ballades:* 1822, 1824, 1826 and 1828. My quotation is from the preface of 1826.

[9] See "Adresse aux artistes" in the November-December 1831 issue of *La Revue encyclopédique.* The journal had been founded only the previous September.

[10] Théophile Gautier, *Préface à Albertus,* 1832.

[11] Ibid.

[12] See Louise B. Dillingham, *The Creative Imagination of Théophile Gautier* (Bryn Mawr, Pa.: Bryn Mawr College, 1927), pp. 25-26. Gautier gradually drew back from his closest friendly associations and confined his affections in so far as possible to the least exacting objects: his family and his animals.

[13] Théophile Gautier, *Mademoiselle de Maupin* (Paris: Garnier, 1966), p. 231.

[14] See my study, *Nineteenth-Century French Romantic Poets* (Carbondale: Southern Illinois University Press, 1969), pp. 81-82 for a fuller discussion of the problem.

[15] "L'Art" was first published in *L'Artiste* on 13 September 1857 under the title, "A M. Théodore de Banville, réponse à son odelette."

[16] Théophile Gautier, *Histoire du Romantisme* (Paris: Charpentier, 1884), p. 216.

[17] Théophile Gautier, "Salon de 1837" in the 24 March 1837 issue of *La Presse.*

[18] Félicité de Lamennais, *Esquisse d'une philosophie,* ed. Chesnaie (n.p. [Paris], 1841), vol. 8, pp. iii, 133-34.

[19] Charles Baudelaire, "Pierre Dupont" in *L'Art romantique* (Paris: Garnier, 1962), p. 556.

[20] Ibid., pp. 659-86. Especially: "La poésie, pour peu qu'on veuille descendre en soi-même, interroger son âme, rappeler ses souvenirs d'enthousiasme, n'a pas d'autre but qu'Elle-même."

[21] See Edmond Lepelletier, *Paul Verlaine: sa vie, son oeuvre* (Paris: Mercure de France, 1907), pp. 188-89. Paul Souriau, in *Histoire du Parnasse* (Paris: Spes, 1929), p. 251, suggests that Mendès and Ricard sought to diminish Leconte de Lisle's influence by ignoring his objection to the title of the collection.

[22] The following fourteen poets published in each of the three issues of the *Parnasse contemporain:* Banville, Cazalis, Coppée, Dierx, des Essarts, Heredia, Leconte de Lisle, André Lemoyne, Catulle Mendès, Mérat, Xavier de Ricard, Antoine Renaud, Sully Prudhomme, and Valade. The *Parnasse contemporain* attracted the attention of other poets not usually associated with the movement. Rimbaud, for example, read the Parnassian journal assiduously and hoped to have such poems as "Credo in unam" and "Sensation" published in the 1871 issue. He wrote to Théodore de Banville in this respect but was informed that he applied too late for inclusion. See Wallace Fowlie, *Rimbaud: A Critical Study* (Chicago; University of Chicago Press, 1965), pp. 10-13.

[23] Interview published by Jules Huret in *Enquête sur l'évolution littéraire* (Paris: Charpentier, 1891), pp. 288-89.

[24] The prefaces to the *Poèmes antiques,* the *Poèmes barbares* and the *Poèmes tragiques* have been grouped and are published together in the posthumous volume that includes the *Derniers poèmes* in 1894.

[25] Gustave Flaubert, *Correspondence,* vol. 2 (Paris: Charpentier, 1899), pp. 199-200.

[26] Jules Lemaître, *Les Contemporains,* vol. 2 (Paris: Lecène et Oudin, 1885), p. 45.

[27] See Cassagne, *La Théorie de l'art pour l'art,* pp. 267-68 for a fuller treatment of the question.

Alvin Harms writing about Théodore de Banville:

Within the group of poets known as Parnassians, Banville's role has perhaps been overrated. Although he was one of the older members, he was constantly overshadowed by Leconte de Lisle, who was as domineering as Banville was mild-mannered. He was not assertive and self-promoting and did not always receive the credit he deserved. It is unfortunately so often forgotten, for example, that the ideas in Gautier's famous "L'Art" come from a poem by Banville to which "L'Art" is merely a reply. As a poet he incorporated some of the ideas of the Parnassians. Though he wrote with ease, he was a strong believer in the importance of craftsmanship. He shared with many of his colleagues a dislike for his own age and an admiration for Greek antiquity. He lacked the erudition of Leconte de Lisle and Heredia and his talent was not in the realm of epic poetry. His wit and humor stood out in noticeable contrast to the gravity of some of the Parnassians. On the other hand, he was one of the most faithful adherents of the doctrine of art for art's sake.

Alvin Harms, in Théodore de Banville, *Twayne Publishers, 1983.*

W. N. Ince (essay date 1979)

SOURCE: "Jose-Maria de Heredia," in *Heredia,* The Athlone Press, 1979, pp. 1-27.

[*In the following excerpt, Ince provides a brief survey of the themes and styles which characterized the Parnassian movement.*]

Le Parnasse contemporain, recueil de vers nouveaux was not to make its first appearance until 1866 but the tastes and tendencies that were eventually to achieve prominence through that publication were taking shape many years earlier in various reviews and gatherings of poets. The first, and very short-lived, of these publications worth our notice was the *Revue fantaisiste,* begun in 1861 by Catulle Mendès. This enthusiastic poet of eighteen years was encouraged by older and greater poets like Gautier, Baudelaire and Banville; many of those who were to become *Parnassiens,* like Albert Glatigny, Sully Prudhomme or Louis Bouilhet, contributed poems to it. The *Revue française,* founded in 1861 by Adolphe Amat, eschewed politics and encouraged young writers eager to publish; some of its contributors were inherited from the defunct *Revue fantaisiste,* like Mendès himself and Glatigny, but there were others whose names became better known as the Parnassian movement was formed: Georges Lafenestre, Léon Dierx, Emmanuel des Essarts and Heredia himself, who published there in 1863 five sonnets—'Le Triomphe d'Iacchos', 'Pan', the diptych 'Le Lis' and 'Vœu'—which he later stigmatized as *libertins,* that is, irregular, and four of which he excluded from *Les Trophées* in 1893.[8] In 1864, it was the turn of the *Revue de Paris* to publish three of Heredia's sonnets, one new, 'La Mort de l'aigle', and two—'L'Héliotrope' and 'Mer montante'—which had already appeared, as has been noted, in the yearbooks of *La Conférence La Bruyère.* Other contributors were Gautier, Banville, Emmanuel des Essarts, Louis Bouilhet and Léon Cladel. Another publication of some importance in these early years was the *Revue du progrès,* founded in 1863 by

Louis-Xavier de Ricard, which published, pseudonymously, Verlaine's first poems. Ricard and Mendès were leaders of a sort and entertained their young poet friends in their own homes and took them to each other's: Mendès received on Wednesdays, Ricard—or perhaps more properly, his mother, la marquise de Ricard—on Fridays. These meetings of enthusiastic young artists were lively, sometimes noisy, as they discussed and recited poetry, often intoxicated enough by their commitment to poetry to need no stronger drink than tea. Another salon, gayer still and more extravagant than those of Mendès and Ricard, was Nina de Villard's, where open table was kept for all comers and Madame Villard's musical talents were regularly required. But all these gatherings were eclipsed by the crucial, culminating reception of the week, on Saturdays, at Leconte de Lisle's small flat on the fifth floor at 8 Boulevard des Invalides. Up the narrow stairway that led to this sanctum there climbed many of the poets who were to be associated with the new poetic movement: Mendès, Banville, Ménard, Coppée, Villiers de l'Isle-Adam, Dierx, Silvestre, Prudhomme, Lafenestre and Heredia. Though the conversation could be animated in Leconte de Lisle's salon and the tone heated, not least when Leconte de Lisle himself was delivering some energetic diatribe, the young disciples regarded with unanimous veneration the Master who by the force of his example in his *Poèmes antiques* (1852) and *Poèmes barbares* (1862), as well as by the force of his teaching and presence in his salon, represented for them all a summit of poetic achievement. Of all these young poets, Heredia was to become by far the closest friend of the Master and perhaps the nearest to him in the artistic aims he was to embody in *Les Trophées*. In 1894, by then a member of the Académie française which he was representing at the funeral service of Leconte de Lisle, Heredia looked back over three decades of close friendship and collaboration to sum up the older poet's influence:

> Illustre avant d'être célèbre, il n'a pas cherché le succès, il a conquis la gloire. L'influence de son noble génie fut salutaire. Durant trente années il fut, pour les jeunes poètes, un éducateur, un modèle incomparable. Il avait l'âme tendre et fière, un esprit profond et charmant. Tous ceux qui l'ont connu, l'aimaient autant qu'ils le vénéraient. Il a été pour nous le vrai maître, un maître amical et fraternel.[9]

The events immediately preceding the appearance in 1866 of *Le Parnasse contemporain, recueil de vers nouveaux* are now as legendary as the formation of the *Pléiade* in the sixteenth century or, in the nineteenth, the triumph of Romantic drama at the *bataille d'Hernani*. Alphonse Lemerre was the owner of a bookshop at 47 passage Choiseul, whose principal clients were buyers of prayerbooks and other works suitable for pious people. Lemerre was thinking of bringing out an edition of the poets of the Pléiade when he was asked to publish the poems of Xavier de Ricard (*Ciel, rue et foyer,* 1865) and later of other young poets. In the early days, publication was at the poets' expense! Lemerre also took over the journal *L'Art* which had been started elsewhere by the same Xavier de Ricard. The young poets who had assembled in the premises where *L'Art* had been first published transferred themselves to Lemerre's bookshop in the passage Choiseul and they were joined there by others at what became, from 1865, regular daily meetings. The noise and long-haired appearance of these young men risked disturbing more sedate customers; Lemerre was led therefore to give his young poets a back-room on the mezzanine floor, reached by a spiral staircase. This was to be the much celebrated *Entresol du Parnasse,* an area sometimes so crowded that late-comers had to sit on the stairs, where from four to seven every afternoon the future Parnassians recited their own poems and others' and passionately discussed all aspects of poetry. The mood was serious and light-hearted by turns, usually good-tempered and sometimes uproarious. The memoirs written later in the century about these golden days of the 1860s often mention the ebullient presence of the young Heredia, impeccably dressed—unlike some of his companions—and usually very much to the fore and in the thick of discussion and activity. Many of the regular attenders at Lemerre's *entresol* were poets who also frequented the salons of Mendès, Ricard, Villard and Leconte de Lisle. Gabriel Marc's poem 'L'Entresol du Parnasse' became a much quoted evocation of the figures seen at Lemerre's, of whom the most notable were Dierx, Armand Renaud, Coppée, Glatigny, Sully Prudhomme, Henry Cazalis, Armand Silvestre, Mendès, Emmanuel des Essarts, Anatole France, Xavier de Ricard and Heredia. José-Maria's presence was well captured:

> Tout tremble: c'est Heredia
> A la voix farouche et vibrante,
> Qu'en vain Barbey parodia.[10]
> Tout tremble: c'est Heredia,
> Heredia qu'incendia
> Un rayon de mil huit cent trente![11]
> Tout tremble: c'est Heredia
> A la voix farouche et vibrante.
> (*Sonnets parisiens,* 1875)

Older members, with settled reputations, such as Leconte de Lisle, Gautier and Banville, also joined the young zealots.

The term *Parnassien* was not of course to be applied to these poets until 1866 and later; it was at first a rather derisive label, coined from the title, *Le Parnasse contemporain* (which seems to have owed its name to *Le Parnasse satyrique* of the seventeenth-century poet, Théophile de Viau), but it was soon adopted by the poets themselves. Some later denied that they formed a school or movement. *Groupe* was the most cohesive term that, for instance, Catulle Mendès would allow to describe them, in his *Légende du 'Parnasse contemporain'* (1884). At the Saturday meetings in his salon, Leconte de Lisle gave much advice that was respectfully absorbed and often observed by his neophytes; he heard and corrected poems that were submitted to his judgement. But there were no interdictions and there was no party line. Each Parnassian poet was free to develop his own talent and express what was unique to him. Thus Leconte de Lisle's own poetry usually has a philosophic background, a high seriousness and a contained impersonal strength of feeling which stamp it as quite different from the poetry of Théodore de Banville, equally enamoured of ancient Greece but mostly lighter in tone and more playfully experimental than that of the Master. What united this group of poets was a certain number of attitudes and tendencies. A new generation is often best defined by its opposition to its predecessors or at least by its differences. The poet who received the scantest respect from the Parnassians was Alfred de Musset (though not all despised him and Heredia himself respected his work). Musset and, to some extent, Lamartine represented for our poets an over-personalized, insipid, sentimental *vague à l'âme* which offended their desire for more objective, controlled and compact writing. The sonnet was to become a favoured verse-form because more than any other it aided and patently embodied this ideal. In his poem 'A Ronsard' (*Les Vignes folles,* 1860), the young Albert Glatigny spoke for many when he conveyed his disgust for the sentimental, formless poetry which had been produced by some Romantic poets and which, following the example of Musset and Lamartine, was still popular in the middle of the nineteenth century:

> Moi, que tout ce pathos ennuie
> A l'égal de la froide pluie,
> Je veux, rimeur aventureux,
> Lire encor, Muse inviolée,
> Quelque belle strophe étoilée
> Au rythme doux et savoureux;
>
> Un fier sonnet, rubis, topaze,
> Ciselé de même qu'un vase
> De Benvenuto Cellini.

Distaste for effusiveness or even for too directly personal revelation was allied with a rejection of what were thought to be the facile values of the man-in-the-street and of the contemporary society that could not appreciate good art in any form. The Latin poet Horace's theme of *odi profanum vulgus* was given its most proud and fiercely contemptuous expression by Leconte de Lisle in, significantly, a sonnet:

> Tel qu'un morne animal, meurtri, plein de poussière,
> La chaîne au cou, hurlant au chaud soleil d'été,
> Promène qui voudra son cœur ensanglanté
> Sur ton pavé cynique, ô plèbe carnassière!
>
> Pour mettre un feu stérile en ton œil hébété,
> Pour mendier ton rire ou ta pitié grossière,
> Déchire qui voudra la robe de lumière
> De la pudeur divine et de la volupté.
>
> Dans mon orgueil muet, dans ma tombe sans gloire,
> Dussé-je m'engloutir pour l'éternité noire,
> Je ne te vendrai pas mon ivresse ou mon mal,
>
> Je ne livrerai pas ma vie à tes huées,
> Je ne danserai pas sur ton tréteau banal
> Avec tes histrions et tes prostituées.

'Les Montreurs' (*Poèmes antiques,* 1852)

The Parnassian poets were to achieve fame and good sales of their poems before the end of the 1860s but they were never truly popular, particularly in the early days of the decade, and they were proud to be in this position; it mirrored their ambition to purify their art, to give it the dignity and even isolation which, in their eyes, it necessarily entailed. 'L'idéal du vrai poète a été et sera toujours le contraire de celui du public', wrote Léon Dierx in the preface to his collection of poems *Les Lèvres closes* (1871).

The preoccupation of the Parnassians with what is vaguely called 'form' is a major factor for our understanding of them. Before the term *Parnassien* became consecrated by usage, other short-lived labels crystallized this aspect of their endeavours: as well as *impassibles* they were called *stylistes* and *formistes.* In negative terms, their concern for form is a reaction against what they saw as loose, careless, flabby writing by earlier poets. For the Parnassians, *forme* was not just a secondary consideration, a way of describing the means whereby a poet communicated the more important *fond* or ideas he had. Ideas as such were not the particular domain of poetry. Form was as important as content, form was indeed a part of content: the inseparability of *forme* and *fond* was their way of purifying poetry of its more prosaic elements. For them, the best poet was the subtle, conscious manipulator of language. So-called 'inspired' composition risked degenerating into flatulent, over-sincere prolixity. In practice, considerations of form for many Parnassians therefore involved the need for careful, ordered composition, French that was correct as well as being lyrical, good rhymes, preferably 'rich', and language that was both evocative and precise. The *mot juste* becomes both a kind of rallying-cry and a widespread practice—the practice never stronger than in Heredia himself. All these aspirations of Parnassian poetry are brilliantly summed up by the young Verlaine in the first flush of his enthusiasm for the ideals he shares (and which

he will not fully exemplify even in his early poetry and will later quite abandon):

> Ah! l'Inspiration superbe et souveraine,
> L'Egérie aux regards lumineux et profonds,
> Le Genium commode et l'Erato soudaine,
> L'Ange des vieux tableaux avec des ors au fond [. . .]
>
> La Colombe, le Saint-Esprit, le saint délire,
> Les Troubles opportuns, les Transports complaisants,
> Gabriel et son luth, Apollon et sa lyre,
> Ah! l'Inspiration, on l'invoque à seize ans!
>
> Ce qu'il nous faut à nous, les Suprêmes Poètes
> Qui vénérons les Dieux et qui n'y croyons pas,
> A nous dont nul rayon n'auréola les têtes,
> Dont nulle Béatrix n'a dirigé les pas,
>
> A nous qui ciselons les mots comme des coupes
> Et qui faisons des vers émus trés froidement,
> A nous qu'on ne voit point les soirs aller par groupes
> Harmonieux au bord des *lacs* et nous pâmant,[12]
>
> Ce qu'il nous faut, à nous, c'est, aux lueurs des lampes,
> La science conquise et le sommeil dompté,
> C'est le front dans les mains du vieux Faust des estampes,
> C'est l'Obstination et c'est la Volonté! [. . .]
>
> Libre à nos Inspirés, cœurs qu'une œillade enflamme,
> D'abandonner leur être aux vents comme un bouleau:
> Pauvres gens! l'Art n'est pas d'éparpiller son âme;
> Est-elle en marbre, ou non, la Vénus de Milo?
>
> Nous donc, sculptons avec le ciseau des Pensées
> Le bloc vierge du Beau, Paros immaculé,
> Et faisons-en surgir sous nos mains empressées
> Quelque pure statue au péplos étoilé [. . .]
>
> (from 'Epilogue', in *Poèmes saturniens,* 1866)

But poets, even Parnassian poets, do not live by form alone, still less by pronouncements about it, however eloquent and well turned. If we look at the themes of the Parnassians' poems, we are struck by their fondness for all manifestations of beauty and particularly for pictorial effects as well as for those arts which make a predominantly visual appeal. Poets are repeatedly seen as emulating the painter or sculptor. The images used by Verlaine in the stanzas just quoted of the poet 'chiselling' and 'sculpting' words and ideas are typical and directly descended from Gautier's famous poem 'L'Art' in the 1858 edition of *Emaux et camées* where the peremptory injunction to the poet is

> Sculpte, lime, cisèle;
> Que ton rêve flottant
> Se scelle
> Dans le bloc résistant!

The *transposition d'art*—expression of one art's aims or ideals in the medium of another—was the most striking representation of this aesthetic ideal and most successfully exploited by Gautier and Heredia. The Parnassian poets tend in their poetry to turn away from contemporary society, disgusted by its ugliness and stupid materialism, disheartened by its naïve, muddled and self-seeking politics. Many turn to the past, to an imagined age, especially that of classical Greece, when beauty and harmony were duly honoured by both artists and society. Leconte de Lisle's *Poèmes antiques*

(1852) gave powerful impetus to this tendency, but, though the most important, Leconte de Lisle was only one of many.

I have suggested that the Parnassians can perhaps be best understood, at least initially, in the light of their opposition to certain Romantic poets such as Musset and Lamartine and to those poets—and they were legion—who wrote in their manner without their genius. But no creation comes *ex nihilo,* poetic or other, and the Parnassians can just as cogently be seen as continuing and extending the example set by other Romantic poets, since the term Romanticism covers diverse poets and emphases. To some extent, Hugo influenced every poet in the nineteenth century, if only by his liberating example in the field of vocabulary, rhythm and versification. The Hugo who was to influence the Parnassians was not the humanitarian idealist and visionary but the author of *Les Orientales* (1829), those vivid verbal pictures of the languor and implicit ferocity of the East in poems that were in the 1830s to be a dazzling revelation to poets then young, like Leconte de Lisle, for their striking imagery and rhythms—author, too, of the first series of *La Légende des siècles* (1859), epic scenes from man's spiritual and historical evolution. Théophile Gautier, 'le bon Théo', was to die in 1872 but however diminished by the 1860s in terms of his personal presence, he attended the meetings of the young Parnassians and encouraged their efforts; his past writings both as poet, above all in *Emaux et camées* (1852), and as prose-writer and theorist of *l'art pour l'art* which he propounded in the 1830s—cf. his seminal preface to his novel *Mademoiselle de Maupin* (1835)—formed a direct link with the principles and practice of the new poets. Gautier was a bridge between Romanticism and *Le Parnasse.* In 1856, in *L'Artiste,*[13] Gautier is enunciating ideas that recall the preface to *Mademoiselle de Maupin.* They are Parnassian *avant la lettre* and very much foreshadow what Heredia will accomplish in many sonnets:

> Après avoir vu, notre plus grand plaisir a été de transporter dans notre art à nous nos monuments, fresques, tableaux, statues, bas-reliefs, au risque souvent de forcer la langue et de changer le dictionnaire en palette [. . .] L'art pour nous n'est pas le moyen, mais le but [. . .] Une belle forme est une belle idée, car que serait-ce qu'une belle forme qui n'exprimerait rien.

Before the end of the 1840s there had begun a strong revival of Hellenic and Roman values in both the theatre and poetry, of which noteworthy examples were: Edgar Quinet's verse drama *Prométhée* (1838), Ponsard's classical tragedy *Lucrèce* (1843) and his short comedy *Horace et Lydie* (1850), Augier's plays *La Ciguë* (1844) and *Le Joueur de flûte* (1845), the prose poem by Maurice de Guérin *Le Centaure* (1840) and Victor de Laprade's narrative poem *Psyché* (1841). Théodore de Banville's poems *Les Cariatides* (1842) helped to diffuse the Grecian ideal that was to be more magnificently displayed in Leconte de Lisle's *Poèmes antiques* (1852). And behind the work of poets and writers lay the philosophic, historical, archaeological and other scientific researches into the past that would cause Hippolye Taine, for example, and, later, Paul Bourget, to celebrate the marriage of science and art. The immediate predecessors in poetry or theatre exemplified traits that were in some degree to be characteristic of all the Parnassians: impersonality, compact, well-planned composition, correctness if not perfection of form, exoticism, return to much earlier or classical times and a general fusion of art and historical interest.

Such, in brief outline, was the background and context for all the poets who assembled in the *Entresol du Parnasse* at Lemerre's bookshop. The first *livraison* of the *Parnasse contemporain* appeared on 3 March 1866. Seventeen more instalments were to appear between then and June. Later in 1866 the eighteen instalments were published together in book form. The direction of the enterprise was in the hands of Catulle Mendès and Xavier de Ricard, and this included decisions concerning the contributors, of whom there were thirty-seven, ranging from the older Gautier, Banville, Leconte de Lisle and Baudelaire to some twenty relatively young poets like Verlaine, Mallarmé, Coppée and, with several sonnets, Heredia. A measure of Heredia's growing stature was that he served on the committee in charge of the second *Parnasse contemporain,* due to appear in 1869 but, owing to the Franco-Prussian war, not published until 1871; it was here that Heredia published the epic poem that was to be included in the edition of *Les Trophées* in 1893: 'La Détresse d'Atahuallpa. Prologue: Les Conquérants de l'or.' This prologue was as far as he got. The full poem was never completed. Heredia also served on the committee responsible for the third and last *Parnasse contemporain* of 1876, in which he published twenty-five 'sonnets héroïques'. The decade between the first and third *Parnasse contemporain* thus saw the emergence of Heredia as a leading Parnassian poet and a recognized master of the sonnet form, and of sonnets that by theme and style, with all the influences that were at work on him, bore his individual mark. . . .

Notes

. . . . .

[8] See Heredia's preface to the *Voyage en Patagonie* (Hachette, 1901) by the comte Henry de la Vaulx where he recalls that

> quelques jeunes hommes se rencontraient deux ou trois fois la semaine dans un petit rez-de-chaussée

obscur et bas de la rue d'Amsterdam. C'était le bureau de rédaction de *La Revue française* [. . .] C'est là dans ce lieu sans lumière, que, pour la première fois, j'entendis le beau poète Armand Silvestre réciter ses premiers *Sonnets païens,* magnifiques et voluptueux. Jules Clarétie y fit ses premières armes de plume. Quant à moi, je confesse y avoir publié quelques médiocres sonnets, mal venus et mal bâtis, à rimes incorrectement entrecroisées, dont Théophile Gautier, avec sa bonhomie gouailleuse, paternelle et magistrale, daigna me dire: '—Comment! Si jeune, et tu fais déjà des sonnets *libertins!*'—Et c'est pourquoi je n'en fis et je n'en ferai plus jamais de tels.

[9] 'Discours prononcé le 21 juillet 1894 aux funérailles de Leconte de Lisle', Institut de France, Académie française, Firmin-Didot, 1894, p. 8. Cf. Mendès: 'La seule discipline qu'il imposât,—c'était la bonne,—consistait dans la vénération de l'art, dans le dédain des succès faciles. Il était le bon conseiller des probités littéraires; sans gêner jamais l'élan personnel de nos aspirations divines, il fut, il est encore notre conscience poétique elle-même [. . .] Il condamne ou absout et nous sommes soumis' (*La Légende du 'Parnasse contemporain',* Bruxelles, Brancart, 1884, p. 226). Cf. also Maurice Barrès: 'C'était une sorte de prêtre, qui dénonçait le siècle au nom du Beau éternel' ('Discours de réception à L'Académie française', Firmin-Didot, 1907, p. 12).

[10] It was Barbey d'Aurevilly's scathing comments, in November 1866 in the *Nain jaune,* which did much to bring the Parnassian poets to the attention of a wide public.

[11] Heredia is seen as recapturing some of the militant glory of the literary battles fought by the Romantics at the end of the 1820s.

[12] A dig at Lamartine's famous poem 'Le Lac' (*Méditations poétiques,* 1820).

[13] Quoted by U.-V. Châtclain, 'José-Maria de Heredia, sa vie et son milieu', *Cahiers des études littéraires françaises,* fascicule no. 2, undated, p. 6.

PARNASSIANS AND EPIC FORM

Herbert J. Hunt (essay date 1941)

SOURCE: "The General Contribution of *Le Parnasse,*" in *The Epic in Nineteenth-Century France: A Study in Heroic and Humanitarian Poetry from Les Martyrs to Les Siècles Morts,* Basil Blackwell, 1941, pp. 367-401.

[*In the following excerpt, Hunt details the contributions of several Parnassian poets to the development of the epic form in nineteenth-century French literature.*]

There are few indeed among both greater and lesser Parnassians who did not at some time or other try their hand at pastiche epic. In fact, we might reasonably call it the characteristic form of a large group of poets whose set purpose it was to eschew the more fluid kinds of composition as too readily lending themselves to sentimental laxity and personal self-abandon. As a compensation for the self-restraint imposed upon them by the choice of episodic narratives, even when they conceived of them as a vehicle for elegy or for philosophic meditation, the poets enjoyed full liberty to exercise their ingenuity in the achievement of descriptive effects, to indulge their taste for local colour in setting scenes, for sculptural evocation in placing characters, for the technique of enumeration and suspension in unfolding action, and for dramatic sensation or epigrammatic surprise in preparing dénouements and establishing, by subtle hint or clearly-drawn inference, the equation between the symbolic fiction devised and the idea which was at once its first and final cause. Such had been, from Vigny onwards, the recognized formula for this genre whose character can be almost as rigidly specified as the modern verse-fable invented by La Fontaine, and which we might well define as the *epic parable.*

The only considerable variation this form allows is that of size and concision, since the term we have suggested may be used to cover a whole range of poems from the sonnet or epigram favoured by Jean Lahor or Louise Ackermann to the lengthy story—we might almost say verse-romance—exemplified in Coppée's *Justicier,* Mendès' *Hespérus* and Léon Dierx' *Souré-ha.* Many poets of this generation even follow the lead given by Leconte de Lisle in *Hélène* and *les Érinnyes,* and effect a transition from the epic to the dramatic form. We have already cited Édouard Grenier's *Prométhée délivré,* which falls into this category. To it we could well add Arthur de Gobineau's *Samson,*[1] Anatole France's *Noces Corinthiennes,*[2] and Louis de Ronchaud's *Poèmes de la Mort.*[3] Indeed, so closely are some of these poems associated with the poetic tradition we have been considering that it is difficult to leave them out of account altogether, even though they deviate widely from the accepted form. Further than that we cannot go: the dramatic cycle of Charles Grandmougin,[4] for instance, can have no place in this work, however much it may illustrate the continued prestige enjoyed by biblical and classical myths down to the end of the century—the interest it evokes being almost solely dramatic. Even without such works, which could scarcely be forced into the category of 'little epics,' there is still an overwhelming wealth of material to examine. One feature alone justifies pieces of such diverse inspiration being thus segregated in a chapter to themselves: their authors' lack either of co-ordinating ideas or of a sense of unity and continuity in the march of historical events—the failure in fact of each poet concerned to bind his compositions together so as to make of them a 'legend of the ages.' They represent, so to speak, the by-products or waste material left over from the nineteenth century's efforts at epic fabrication.

At first sight it might seem unjust to deny to the authors of certain collections the honour of having in a modest way followed the example of Victor Hugo and Leconte de Lisle and strung together a loosely-connected series of historical pageants. What for example of Léon Dierx, whose *Poèmes et Poésies* (1864) and *Lèvres Closes* (1867) present quite a miscellany of scenes from the past, and whose skill in the 'little epic' is scarcely inferior to that of his master Leconte de Lisle? What of Louis-Xavier de Ricard, whose *Ciel, Rue et Foyer* (1865) reflects some of the ideas to be found in Quinet's *Génie des Religions?* What of Catulle Mendès, whose *Pagode* gave added lustre to the first *Parnasse Contemporain,* whose *Soleil de Minuit* stands out in strong relief among the heterogeneous poems contributed to the third *Parnasse,* who moreover dedicated to Léon Dierx and published in 1872 a sheaf of *'Contes épiques'* in which the first hero is Lucifer and the last Garibaldi? What of François Coppée, with his twenty-three *Récits épiques* of 1878 which open with the Creation and end with the War of 1870, with his numerous series of versestories depicting modern heroism and self-devotion?[5] And why not add Jean Lahor to the list, since we read in the preface to the fifth edition of *l'Illusion*[6] that

> l'évolution de sa pensée ou de son âme était justement celle de l'âme ou de la pensée aryenne, qui, partie du panthéisme, puis du pessimisme et du nihilisme hindous, avait, après bien des voyages, abouti au stoïcisme des admirables Pensées de Marc-Aurèle?

Might we not well expect that the poet's thought would project itself into those remote ages and translate into pictorial objectivity the spiritual odyssey of the races he admires?

Unfortunately the claim of none of these men will bear closer investigation. If we take Léon Dierx' two collections of verse, four-fifths of the poems are purely lyrical, which only leaves us a slender supply of nine poems as material for a legend of history. These nine have their own special value, but though they demand attention they cannot by any stretch of the imagination be held to make up a historical mosaic. Mendès' poems are at best 'anecdotes épiques,' as M. Souriau aptly styles them,[7] nor do those of Coppée deserve a more ambitious title. As for Jean Lahor, his *Chants Panthéistes, la Gloire du Néant, Heures Sombres* and *Vers stoïciens,* collected to form the final and definitive editions of *l'Illusion,* in no way fulfil the promise of the sentence just quoted, in no way show the history of Aryan speculation. He has remained content to consign his own philosophy to short poems or sonnets whose complexion is usually lyrical or metaphysical. As befits a historian of Hindu literature, he turns almost invariably to the East to find symbols for his ideas, but with rare exceptions what I have already referred to (when studying Leconte de Lisle) as the *static* conception prevails in his work. His other poetic productions are mere translations.[8] Dierx and Lahor are interesting, profound, and often original. Mendès and Coppée on the other hand are picturesque narrators, though born plagiarists. And all the other poets whose works we have scanned in search of the 'little epic' fall into line with the above four.

How can such a field be methodically and profitably explored? Shall we yield to the temptation to range this multitude of poets into two separate 'schools' according to whether Victor Hugo or Leconte de Lisle is their obvious master? François Coppée would easily fall into the first of these classes. His prosaic style, his facile local colour, his somewhat shallow stories and his cheaply sensational dénouements bespeak an imitative technique. *Les Orientales* and *la Légende des Siècles* provide him with practically all his models, and his melodramatic use of the supernatural, untransfigured by genius, is traceable to the same source. One poem—*le Jugement de l'Epée*[9]—amply illustrates this fact. A crusader suspecting his wife of infidelity, but not quite convinced of her guilt, consults his trusty sword:

> La généreuse épée, exempte de mensonge,
> Ne voulut pas que Guntz agît comme un
> bourreau,
> *Et, brusque, elle rentra d'elle-même au*
> *fourreau.*

Catulle Mendès would find himself in the uncomfortable posture of having a foot in either camp. If many of his *Contes épiques,* for example, savour strongly of Hugo in the latter's weaker moments, many also have their fount and origin in *les Poèmes barbares.* Mendès is at his best in this latter strain, for his artistry as a Parnassian can rise to great heights, whereas his rendering of the *Lion d'Androclès* theme is a masterpiece of bathos.[10] Nearly all the others, Louis Bouilhet, Anatole France, de Ricard, Louise Ackermann, Sully Prudhomme, would come under the aegis of the great Creole. But such a classification would be embarrassing and fruitless in the long run.

Nor would a review of each author in turn involve anything but repetition and monotony. A classification according to the scope and subject-matter of this bulk of poems offers greater advantages. In fact, the historical categories devised by Victor Hugo for *la Légende,* combined with that offered by the *Poèmes antiques* and the *Poèmes barbares,* provide a convenient framework for a rapid consideration of the 'little epic' during the Parnassian era, rapid because anything like an exhaustive survey would prove a waste of time.

No poets worth mentioning are preoccupied, like the author of *les Fossiles,* with the vision of Nature's procreative process revealed in a succession of prehistoric epochs.[11] But the metaphysic problem of Creation examined through the veil of biblical myths haunts the imagination of many. Hugo's cadre *d'Éve à Jésus* is therefore well-filled: Eden and the antediluvian world furnish favourable settings for the eternal Romantic theme of revolt. Naturally Jehovah and Lucifer, as symbols of contending forces or ideals, stand out in constant opposition: but nowhere more forcibly than in Léon Dierx' *l'Épreuve,*[12] where Satan the masterdialectician enjoys the last word in a debate over the quality of the Creator's work, or in Louise Ackermann's fragmentary *Satan,*[13] where the rebel archangel, typifying Justice in its struggle with tyrannical power, asserts himself as the real benefactor of man, having instilled the lust for knowledge in the latter—'mon *Fiat Lux* l'emporte sur le tien!' Catulle Mendès strikes a much weaker note in an attempt to portray the vanquished Satan's magnanimity,[14] and, in *l'Orgueil,* the base ingratitude of man.[15]

Poems enlarging on the primal bliss and ravishing beauty of Eve are quite frequent,[16] though Dierx characteristically imparts a foretaste of bitterness to the first transports of the mother of men.[17] Moore's *Loves of the Angels* gives Mendès an excuse for emphasizing the jealous propensities of the Male,[18] while Byron's *Heaven and Earth* provides Anatole France with a starting-point for yet another description of the Flood,[19] in which reminiscences of Vigny are also perceptible. But among all these poems one is outstanding, both for its vigour and originality—*la Révélation de Jubal,* by Léon Dierx.[20]

No doubt the material for it is mainly drawn from de Cailleux' *Monde antédiluvien,* whose combination of the grandiose and the gruesome it reproduces; but here all the taste and discretion of a born artist have given grace and proportion to a conception erstwhile crude and amorphous. *La Révélation de Jubal* invites comparison with de Lisle's *Qaïn,* though it should be remembered that it was published two years before the latter poem.[21] Again we are confronted with the spectacle of invincible human resentment against the capricious injustice or the malicious bungling of a despotic Creator. Like Leconte de Lisle, Dierx lacks the patience of a Vigny waiting with calm resignation for the day of final reckoning when God shall stand in the dock before accusing humanity.[22] With burning passion he arraigns him here and now, through the voice of the seer Jubal, 'le dernier chanteur . . . le dernier prophète des premiers temps,' at one with the race whose doom he is witnessing and 'jusqu'au bout pervers.'

The floods are mounting, and the last of the privileged children of Seth have been admitted to the security of the Ark. Above the seething waters swollen with tossing corpses Jubal, whom the seas cannot engulf—he represents the unquenchable fire of Promethean defiance which burns perpetual in the human breast—contemplates the execution of the Eternal's destructive decree. There bursts on his ear

> Un triple éclat de rire, effroyable dans l'ombre,
> Plein de haine et de joie, et tel, qu'horriblement
> S'ouvrirent les yeux blancs de tous les morts sans nombre.

And he sees looming overhead a Satan of gigantic proportions roaring out his contempt for the great experiment which its own author has been forced to bring to naught. Disdaining a wordy refutation, the destroying Angel points to the Ark laden with its precious content—the inheritors of a new covenant; but at this Satan's wrath only increases. The new race will be no more docile than the old; crime and blasphemy will reach new depths; and Babel, Sodom and Gomorrah, and Golgotha will be the lurid beacon-lights illuminating the path leading a second humanity to Hell. God will again repent Him of His sorry work:

> Tu diras: "Que la nuit se fasse!" Et, cette fois,
> Dans la flamme ou dans l'eau, pour jamais condamnées,
> Les générations périront sans appel.
> Mais le chemin, ô Maître, est ardu de ton ciel.
> Peu d'élus près de toi siègeront sous leurs nimbes,
> Tandis que mes états seront pleins jusqu'aux bords;
> Et l'éternel sanglot des enfers et des limbes,
> Montant vers toi, sera ton éternel remords!

As in *l'Épreuve,* Jehovah's spokesman has nothing to reply. Another poem in the same collection—*la Prière d'Adam*—furnishes a worthy pendant to this powerfully developed scene, though this time the debt to Leconte de Lisle is undeniable.[23] It conjures up the mournful figure of Adam counting the innumerable generations of his descendants, and crying out in tortured agony:

> "Seigneur! (murmurait-il), qu'il est long, ce supplice!
> Mes fils ont bien assez pullulé sous ta loi.
> N'entendrai-je jamais la nuit crier vers moi:
> "Le dernier homme est mort! Et que tout s'accomplisse!"

By such poems Léon Dierx puts his brother-poets in the shade. As for further scenes from Old and New Testament history—there are a few from the more facile pens of Coppée and Mendès, one also from Anatole France[24]—they are more or less original, and more or less effective in the concision of their ending, but do not demand more than a passing reference.[25]

We have already said that Jean Lahor (Henry Cazalis) makes much philosophical capital of Hinduism and Buddhism, though he only achieves epic style in *l'Enchantement de Siva,*[26] a new *Baghavat* relating the vain attempt of Maya, through the agency of a highly decorative *apsara,* to seduce the brahmanic deity from his nihilistic ataraxy. Coppée and Mendès occasionally exploit similar material, the former to sentimentalize the theme of *la Mort de Valmiki* in *l'Hirondelle du Bouddha,*[27] the latter to draw upon the *Rig-Veda* for his brilliant triad of poems entitled *Pagode,*[28] which is more of an exercise in erotic verse decked out with kaleidoscopic local colour than an occasion for metaphysical meditation. In actual fact, a less remote East inspires these lesser Parnassians to far better effect. Dierx' *Souré-ha*[29] unfolds a conflict between jealous rage and self-sacrificing love on a not-too-crowded Egyptian background; and along with Dierx the other three poets whose names must perforce be continually cropping up in a survey of the 'little epic'—Mendès, Coppée and France—produce a fair number of gems in the manner revealed in *les Orientales* and developed in *la Légende des Siècles.* Oriental ruthlessness, fanaticism, resignation and voluptuousness, in fact all the stock-in-trade of nineteenth-century French 'turquerie,' presented in lurid or sombre hues, set themes upon which these verse artists may expend their verve. Conspicuous among them is Dierx' *la Prophétie,*[30] which gives new vigour to the old tale of a tyrant's predestined assassination and at the same time furnishes proof of the author's psychological subtlety in tracing the progress of superstitious misgiving in the doomed man's mind. Mendès' *le Consentement*[31] is deservedly well-known for the perfection of its symmetry and concision as well as for the consummate ease with which it recaptures the authentic note of pastoral and patriarchal simplicity. France's *Homaï*[32] is well-conceived as a Mohammedan variant of the Judith and Holofernes theme. Coppée's *Pharaon* is only a miniature *Zim-Zizimi,* but his *Tête de la Sultane*[33] does stand out among these oriental tales as a grim picture of the traditional Turk in his cunning and callousness. In passing we may pause to mention a more genuinely historical though less artistically coruscating 'legend of the ages' in Louis de Ronchaud's *les Larmes de Xerxès,*[34] a semi-dramatic elegy whose evident source of inspiration is to be found in Aeschylus' *Persians.*

There is a striking amount of material inspired by classical themes, though not much of it is original in conception. Glatigny's triptych in *les Flèches d'Or*[35]—*Ariane, la Naissance de la Rose, Latone*—is merely the effusion of a personal sentimentalism. Louise Ackermann, in her *Premières Poésies,*[36] took the most beautiful legends of Hesiod as a starting-point for charming, discreet, though none the less personal reflections on human love and the suffering that goes with it. Armand Sylvestre's *Sonnets Païens*[37] and *Intermèdes Païens*[38] are exclusively erotic and sensual. Mendès contributes a Homeric pastiche in *Penthésilée,*[39] as well as paying his tribute in *Pantéleia*[40] to the same ideal worshipped by Baudelaire in *la Beauté* and by de Lisle in *la Vénus de Milo.* Here Mendès virtually dethrones the more palpable and less elusive Cypris in favour of a goddess 'born of the sky-foam,' the inaccessible personification of spiritual and physical beauty blended in a mystic union. De Ricard in his turn puts new meaning into the myth of the birth of Venus which he expounds by means of a phrase borrowed from Quinet: 'à la genèse de la matière a succédé la genèse de l'intelligence.'[41]

As a rule, however, the old myths are utilized less for the aesthetic than for the moral and social lessons that can be extracted from them. Sully Prudhomme makes Hercules the representative of active labour striving with parasitic capitalism—in *les Écuries d'Augias.*[42] Louise Ackermann interestingly revives the well-worn theme of Prometheus in order to extol the daring and inquisitive spirit of man gazing about him fearlessly, but resentfully, in a hostile universe.[43] Gobineau, as might be expected, finds in the legend of Achilles at Scyros material for a eulogy of martial heroism,[44] while Louis de Ronchaud, in *la Mort du Centaure,*[45] expands to the dimensions of a 'satiric drama' a theme already famous thanks to the prestige of Maurice de Guérin and Leconte de Lisle. Actually the satiric vein is slight in this poem, and the note of moral earnestness strong, for though, as in de Lisle's *Khirôn,* the texture of the plot is enriched with other mythological embroideries, the aged Centaur's, choice of death in preference to physical immortality serves to drive home the poet's conviction that man must look for the reward of his labours only in the deathless glory which attends their accomplishment.

To Louis Bouilhet belongs the distinction of having invented a new Hellenic myth, or at any rate of having grafted a new shoot on to an ancient stock. *L'Amour noir*[46] develops a conceit similar to that of Banville's *Éducation de l'Amour.*[47] But, while the latter poem, with its fiction of a hapless Eros exposed at Zeus' command to die in the wilds of the Indian forest yet surviving in order to learn from the animals the lesson of reckless cruelty, embodies Banville's conception of the destructive power of carnal passion, Bouilhet's piece stages a much more complicated action. *L'Amour noir* is a more regular attempt at an epic poem, ushered in moreover by the authentic invocation of the Muses. It recounts the adultery of Venus with Mars and the fortunes of their offspring Cupid. Hidden away from the jealous fury of the outraged Vulcan, he ventures innocently into the latter's forge and suffers cruel mutilation at his hands. Under Venus' passionate reproaches fury in Vulcan's heart gives place to remorse, and he laves Cupid's burns in the healing waters of Lethe. But at this treatment the infant god becomes a hideous monster, fully-grown, coal-black, leering, capable of inspiring terror in Vulcan himself, and fit only to carry the imperious law of Venus to the far-off Nubians and Ethiopians. So he becomes the barbaric god of the African jungle, and the poem winds up with a hymn to this as yet unsung deity. Bouilhet's intention was evidently to set in striking contrast to the graceful beauty of the Olympian gods the grotesque and terrible figments of the negroid imagination, whilst yet indicating that the same immeasurable and invincible forces lurk behind both conceptions.

This leaves us little else to glean in the Hellenic field, though of course the eclipse of classical paganism inspires a certain number of elegiac lamentations in the strain of *la Paix des Dieux.* Among them may well be cited another poem of Bouilhet: *la Colombe,*[48] where the poet follows Vigny[49] and Louis Ménard, and anticipates André de Guerne in sorrowfully contemplating the vain endeavour of Julian the Apostate to rehabilitate Olympus. The title of de Ricard's *Crépuscule des Dieux*[50] speaks for itself. That 'mystic paganism' whose echoes we find in Renan's *Prière sur l'Acropole*[51] dies hard, and almost all the few poems we have to consider having imperial or decadent Rome as their background are concerned with that wave of metaphysical and moral discontent and yearning, expressed often in addiction to strange cults or riots of voluptuous self-indulgence, which heralded and prepared the reign of—

> Ce Roi mystérieux qui console et qui pleure,
> Ce second Adonis et plus triste et plus pur. . . . [52]

Louis Bouilhet, who entrenched himself in the social study of imperial Rome, and added to his brilliant resuscitation *Mélaenis* a few additional satiric sketches such as *le danseur Bathylle* and *Cigognes et Turbots,*[53] pays no attention to the religious problem. His aim, like that of Flaubert, is to 'represent,' not to philosophize. In this connection Villiers de l'Isle-Adam and Anatole France come to the fore instead—Villiers with his *Chant du Calvaire,*[54] the latter with *Leuconoé,* from which the lines just quoted are taken, and *les Noces Corinthiennes.* This is a lyric drama, and not an epic poem, but its tone is so consonant with that of the 'little epics' of the period that I may perhaps be excused for quoting it here. It is the drama of Atala and Chactas re-enacted in an imperial setting, or perhaps it could be equally well qualified as a new *Romeo and Juliet,* a love tragedy whose dénouement is provoked, not by family feuds, but by the misguided zeal of a Christian mother trying to force her daughter to a monastic vocation.[55] *Leuconoé,* conceived in the best tradition of the *Poèmes antiques,* emphasizes the part played by cosmopolitan women in the religious transformation of the Roman world. To the *Weltschmerz* agitating their souls is attributed first the invasion of Rome by outlandish cults and then the triumph of the 'Galilaean.' André de Guerne himself, as we have seen, incorporated this theme into his *Orient chrétien.*

Given the Parnassian outlook, it is not surprising that the philosophic interest predominates when the poets of this generation are exploiting antique or early Christian subjects. Narrative for its own sake regains its rights when their attention is turned to Western 'barbarism,' to the 'dark ages,' and to medieval and modern times. Here indeed is the happy hunting-ground of Coppée, Mendès and Dierx in particular. Characteristic pieces are Glatigny's *Mort de Roland,*[56] similar in inspiration, but vastly inferior, to Vigny's *Cor;* Coppée's *Justicier*[57] and Mendès' *Landgrave de Fer,*[58] skilful stories after the mode of *Ratbert* or *Éviradnus.* But among many others which could be mentioned are two noteworthy specimens of the 'poèmes barbares' type deserving especial consideration. They are Léon Dierx' *Hemrick, le Veuf,*[59] and Mendès' *Soleil de Minuit.*[60]

The scene of *Hemrick* is laid in the bleak and rugged solitudes of Brittany at some indeterminate moment in history. The poem studies the ravages wrought by jealousy in the heart of a man who, having lost through death an adored wife and a trusted friend, has the conviction borne in upon him, as he watches the growth of his infant son, sees his features taking shape and notes the intonations of his voice, that the pair for whom he is mourning had betrayed him in guilty love. Full of anguish and delirious resentment, Hemrick hovers for some time on the brink of infanticide, before killing himself in the mad hope of pursuing his vengeance beyond the grave. This poem has one defect—its exposition halts a little at times and fringes on obscurity in the opening pages—but its force lies in the harmony its author has achieved between external setting and internal conflict; the Breton wastes are drenched with torrential rains and lit up with nocturnal thunder as lingering hope gives way to horrible certainty in Hemrick's harassed soul and his fury blazes out into madness. By comparison with de Lisle's *Jugement de Komor,* whose theme is a kindred one, *Hemrick, le Veuf* is extremely subtle and original; for whereas the author of *Poèmes barbares* had been content to clothe marital jealousy in a somewhat rigid, stylized medieval costume, Dierx has explored the innermost recesses of a mind confronted with a tragic and insoluble problem. That by virtue of this inward penetration the poem departs from one of the essential conditions of epic, which should transcribe internal conflict into visible action and graphic speech, is no doubt a regrettable but also an incontrovertible fact. Like other of Dierx' narrative poems, it borders on the domain of the verse *nouvelle.*

Le Soleil de Minuit attains greater heights of tragedy and stark horror, for it renders concrete and picturesque a similar spiritual drama, and shows inner reality transfusing itself into the sensible world which is at once its *décor* and the palpable symbol into which it is smitten. This poem is a sort of poetic *Thérèse Raquin* enacted amid arctic surroundings. The essential data are commonplace: an adulterous intrigue between the ruthless Snorra, linked in odious marriage to an aged seal-fisher 'visqueux d'eau marine, cassé sous le fardeau puant du poisson dépecé,' and a sturdy young huntsman Agnar who, after taking the initiative in seduction, becomes as putty in the hands of his mistress:

Ton choc fut rude, Agnar! sans prière ni
piège,
Soudain, hurlant, pareil à la trombe de neige
Qui frappe, emporte, abat le sapin résistant;
Et ma force, en tes bras sœur des joncs de
l'étang,
A subi ta rigueur redoutable, avec joie!

—With impatience as well as joy, for henceforth Snorra has but one ambition, to be rid of her unsavoury breadwinner. With a Cornelian briskness of riposte in argument—

AGNAR
Grâce! il est mon ami.
SNORRA
Frappe! il est mon époux,

and by dint of lashing taunts she brings her lover to the point of murder. While she is awaiting the consummation of her bloodthirsty desires, uncertain whether the deed is done or not, her hopes are dashed by her husband's return, and she is obliged to submit to his vinous and amorous attentions. At length she escapes from the nuptial couch, only to learn from her conscience-stricken accomplice that Snorro is indeed dead, that she has suffered the embraces of a spectre, intent on engendering his avenger in the womb of his murderer's instigator. This scene between a Scandinavian Lord and Lady Macbeth works up to a tirade which, were it not so redolent of Hugo, might almost be accounted Shakespearian:

Donc, les morts sont vivants, la mort est une
porte
Qui reste entrebaillée afin que l'on ressorte.
Hache de l'assassin, assaille l'homme! abats
Sa tête sur ses pieds, son bras après son bras,
Comme fait la cognée au sapin qu'elle
émonde,
Que le tronc reste en haut, festin de l'aigle
immonde,
Et que le crâne roule au fond du creux ravin,
La mort, calme, se dresse après le meurtre
vain,
Rattache ses deux bras, sans se hâter, rajuste
Sa tête dans le val ramassée, à son buste,
Rentre au logis, d'un pas ni trop lent ni trop
prompt,
Donne le gai bonsoir, baise sa femme au
front,
Parle, écoute un récit dont il rit ou se fâche,
N'en fait point de l'abîme effrayant qui le
lâche!
Et s'endort, souriant, les yeux clos à demi,
Comme s'il n'était pas pour toujours endormi.
L'étroit sépulcre même où le ver les travaille
Ne retient pas des morts la sourde relevaille.
L'être, sous les granits entassés, vains
fardeaux
Que disjoint la poussée horrible de son dos,
Reprend son crâne aux rats, ses os à la
belette,
Et, rassemblant sa chair autour de son
squelette,
Sans que l'odeur attire à son toit le corbeau,
Vient coucher dans son lit, étant las du
tombeau!

But this is only the kernel of Mendès' conception. This grim drama has for prologue and epilogue some pages of landscape-painting which are of the best that this poet ever achieved. They enclose the main theme in a secondary and descriptive one which brings the poem to perfection. The rising of the midnight sun in sinister redness is the harbinger of the crime about to be committed; its return to its wonted pallor is the sign whereby the poet hints at the retribution which awaits the guilty lovers. At the same time the sheer animality of their misdeed, dictated by the hard and rugged law of Nature which Snorra formulates in the following terms—

La louve concevra, mais d'un loup plein de
force . . .
Chasseur, c'est un scrupule où la crainte se
mêle
Que d'épargner le mâle, ayant pris la
femelle. . . .

is mirrored in the recurrent vision of a pair of wolves hunting and loving and killing in the baleful effulgence in which the arctic landscape is bathed.

Moving forward to modern times as reflected in these various collections of verse, we find less to attract attention, little but occasional pieces admirably fitted for inclusion within general anthologies, such as Coppée's *Bénédiction,*[61] a scene from the Peninsular Wars whose like Goya might have painted, the same poet's *Fils de l'Empereur,*[62] which evidently provided Edmond Rostand with a conclusion for the fourth Act of *l'Aiglon,* and his *Grève des Forgerons.*[63] What more need be said of these and kindred poems, except that they provide light, agreeable and often sentimental reading, by bringing a swiftly-told narrative to a more or less piquant climax; that they condense the technique of epic in a formula palatable to the crowd, but can only have a spasmodic appeal to the cultivated taste because, when all is said and done, the greater part of them are relatively meaningless as well as plagiaristic? More original productions in modern settings, such as Dierx' *Stella Vespera,*[64] where a Hoffmann-like fantasy embodies the by now threadbare truism that great art is the realization of the ideal, or Mendès' *Hespérus,*[65] a curious transcription of Swedenborgian doctrine that reads like a parody of Hugo's *Dieu,* have little or no epic flavour. We have seen that these poets, even when they are in a philosophic frame of mind, with the exception of Franòois Coppée whose *forte* lies in enveloping Sunday-School morality in fairly commonplace stories, have nothing new to say. The highest achievement they can hope to attain is to put old wine into new bottles. The pessimism which inspires Léon Dierx in *Marche funèbre*[66] or Catulle Mendès in *la dernière Âme*[67] is the same as that which informed *le Runoïa* and *Solvet Saeclum.* This fact would alone serve to prove that no advantage could be reaped by extending any further this survey of the last miscellaneous productions of a dying school.

Its members have no firm ground to stand on. Most of them have lost faith, that faith which permits some insight into the why and wherefore of an endless sequence of apparently meaningless phenomena. Life is

> . . . a tale
> Told by an idiot, full of sound and fury,
> Signifying nothing.

Religion is an empty dream, perfectibility a myth, the end cold darkness and annihilation. And once a few poets with original minds and a genius for artistic execution had rung the changes on this depressing theme, there was nothing fresh to look for from the Parnassian group.

Two generations of poets, donning the mantles of the seers, had set out to discover the secret linking together and making a coherent and rational whole of the bewildering succession of human vicissitudes. The second of these generations reached the conclusion that there was no secret to discover. A third generation, undeterred by this lamentable admission of failure, of inability to find motive and purpose behind the blind interaction of universal forces, was to abandon rational speculation in favour of intuitive surges towards the unknown; and thus 'Symbolisme' and 'Décadentisme' came into conscious existence, or rather emerged from the womb of Romanticism where they had been in process of gestation since the time of Ballanche and the Illuminists. It is not for us to enquire what these latest-comers have to say. . . .

Notes

[1] In *l'Aphroëssa* (1869). The 'Aphroëssa' is a ship carrying votive offerings sent from Athens to Delos, and the author gives it as the title to a collection of philosophic poems since the latter bears his tribute—not a very rich one—to the poetic Muse. See Rowbotham, p. 128.

[2] 1876.

[3] 1887.

[4] *Prométhée* (1878), *Orphée* (1883), *le Christ* (1892), *l'Empereur* (1893), etc.

[5] *Les Humbles* (1872), *Contes et Poésies* (1878-1885), *Contes en Vers* (1881).

[6] First edition 1875. I quote from Lemerre's edition of 1925, p. 1.

[7] Souriau III. p. 133.

[8] Gathered together under the title *En Orient* (1908).

[9] *Récits épiques.*

[10] *Le Lion* in *Contes épiques.* This hungry beast, waiting for his prey in the arena, is confronted by the disconcerting spectacle of a Christian virgin; he decides to forgo his anticipated repast:

> 'Lion!' dit la chrétienne.
> Alors, dans la poussière
> On le vit se coucher, doux et silencieux;
> *Et, comme elle était nue, il ferma les deux yeux.*

Cf. Soumet's gallant lion (supra, p. 192).

[11] Unless we count in Littré for his very prosy poem *la Terre* (*Revue de Philosophie positive,* 1867).

[12] *Poèmes et Poésies,* 1864.

[13] *Poésies philosophiques,* 1874.

[14] *Le Vaincu* in *Contes épiques,* 1872.

[15] Ibid.

[16] Grenier in *Éden* (1858), Coppée in *les Yeux de la Femme* (*Récits épiques,* 1878).

[17] *La Vision d'Ève* in *Poèmes et Poésies* (1864).

[18] *Les Fils des Anges* in *Contes épiques* (1872).

[19] *La Fille de Caïn,* dated July 1864, collected in *Idylles et Légendes,* 1896.

[20] *Les Lèvres Closes,* 1867.

[21] Cf. Souriau III, p. 282.

[22] *Journal d'un Poète* (edition Baldensperger, pp. 250 and 261).

[23] *La Fin de l'Homme (Poèmes barbares).*

[24] *La Part de Madeleine,* in *Idylles et Légendes.* The subject is reverently treated.

[25] Mendès: *Parvulus, la Femme adultère, la dernière Abeille* in *Contes épiques.* Coppée: *Blasphème et Prière, Sénachérib, Un Évangile* in *Récits épiques.*

[26] *La Gloire du Néant.*

[27] *Récits épiques.*

[28] Collected in *les Poésies de Catulle Mendès,* première série, 1876.

[29] *Poèmes et Poésies.*

[30] *Poèmes et Poésies.*

[31] *Contes épiques.*

[32] 1870. Collected in *Idylles et Légendes.*

[33] *Récits épiques.*

[34] 1886. Collected in *Poèmes de la Mort.*

[35] 1864.

[36] Written round about 1860, published in 1874.

[37] *Poésies,* 1860-1874.

[38] *Poésies,* 1872-1878.

[39] *Contes épiques.*

[40] 1861. Published with other poems in 1863 (by Hetzel).

[41] *Aphroditè-Anadyomenè* in *Ciel, Rue et Foyer.*

[42] *Les Épreuves,* 1866.

[43] *Poésies philosophiques,* 1874. The poem is dated 1865.

[44] *L'Achilléide* in *l'Aphroëssa.*

[45] *Poèmes de la Mort.*

[46] *Dernières Chansons,* 1872 (posthumous).

[47] In *les Exilés.* Banville dates his poem 1864. At what period did Bouilhet write *l'Amour noir?*

[48] *Dernières Chansons.*

[49] I am not suggesting that Bouilhet could have read *Daphné,* which remained unpublished until 1913. He could however have seen in Ratisbonne's edition of *le Journal d'un Poète* (1867) the references to the subject which are to be found there (years 1834-1836).

[50] *Ciel, Rue et Foyer.*

[51] First published in *la Revue des Deux Mondes,* 1876.

[52] Anatole France: *Leuconoé* (1876).

[53] Both from *Festons et Astragales* (1857).

[54] *Premières Poésies,* 1856-1858.

[55] As France's own notes show, the source is a tale of the supernatural by Phlegon of Tralles (*Poésies d'Anatole France,* 1896, pp. 267 sqq.).

[56] *Les Flèches d'Or* (1864).

[57] *Poèmes divers* (1866).

[58] *Contes épiques.*

[59] *Poèmes et Poésies.*

[60] *Poésies,* 1876.

[61] *Poèmes modernes.*

[62] *Récits épiques.*

[63] 1869.

[64] *Poèmes et Poésies.*

[65] 1871. *Poésies de Catulle Mendès,* première série.

[66] *Les Lèvres closes.*

[67] *Soirs moroses,* 1868.

PARNASSIANISM AND POSITIVISM

D. G. Charlton (essay date 1957)

SOURCE: "Positivism and Leconte de Lisle's Ideas on Poetry," in *French Studies,* Vol.II, No. 3, July, 1957, pp. 246-59.

[*In the following excerpt, Charlton discusses the Parnassian movement in relation to positivism, asserting that the connection is weaker than commonly thought.*]

It has been frequently alleged, especially in comparisons with the Symbolists, that the Parnassian poets are Positivistic in their attitude to life and poetry.[1] Van Tieghem, for example, comments: 'Ce que les purs artistes de 1830-35 refusèrent aux Saint-Simoniens, les poètes de 1850-60 l'accordèrent au positivisme', whilst Jasinski concludes: 'Accord du scientisme et de l'esprit «artiste», tel est bientôt le vif de l'inspiration parnassienne.' And of Symbolism by contrast he writes: 'A la certitude positiviste, qui prétendait chasser toutes les ombres, il oppose la perpétuelle énigme de l'indéfini, de l'insondable.'[2] Brunetière, Lanson, Thibaudet, Martino and many others all postulate or imply the same link: this generation, it is claimed, lives in the shadow of Auguste Comte.[3]

Such assertions need severe qualification for a number of reasons, and not least because the definition of Positivism they presuppose is often inexact or even erroneous. The term may be variously applied to the entirety of Comte's thought, or to his 'religion of Humanity', or to a fusion of philosophy of history and sociological theory of the kind which he first effected; but in its basic sense—upon which 'Comtian', 'religious' and 'sociological' Positivism build—it refers to a theory of knowledge. All we can know of reality is what we can observe or legitimately deduce from what we observe—namely, phenomena and the laws of relation and succession of phenomena; we cannot know what cannot be empirically verified. Hence, the spheres of logic and mathematics excepted, *a priori* knowledge is impossible. More broadly, Positivism may be interpreted as an *état d' esprit* in which confidence in science and the scientific methods is combined with religious and metaphysical agnosticism. Unfortunately, historians of literature have sometimes used the term much more loosely: impassibility, objectivity and impersonality in art, pessimism, opposition to Christianity, Republicanism, the use of scientific discoveries as the subject-matter of poetry—all these have been taken as evidence of 'Positivism', even though none of them, not even hostility to religion, is a necessary consequence of the Positivist philosophy. And such illegitimate definitions and criteria as these are in part responsible for the identification of the Parnassian outlook with Positivism. Nor, moreover, do Positivists claim (as Jasinski implies) to dispel 'toutes les ombres' or deny 'la perpétuelle énigme de l'indéfini, de l'insondable'. Indeed, the notion of *l'Inconnaissable* has a Positivist origin. Littré, no less than the Symbolists or the French admirers of Spencer (himself a Positivist), points us to the mysterious sea of the Unknowable—'dont la claire vision est aussi salutaire que formidable'—and he even adds: 'Rien n'élève plus l'âme que cette contemplation'.[4] But contemplation is not scientific verification and, for him at least, the Unknowable remains unknowable.[5] Similarly, one should not confuse the Parnassians' respect for science with acceptance of Positivism. A writer may admire the achievements of science and try to reconcile his own philosophy with its findings; he may borrow his subject-matter from it and imitate the scientific virtues of impersonality and objectivity—and yet not accept the distinctively Positivist view that the scientific methods represent man's only means of knowledge. Moreover, the Parnassian generation is attracted by science for reasons that are independent of the merits of its methods. Science is free of conventional morality and of any didactic motive: it is 'pure' in the sense in which they wished their art to be 'pure'. It is beyond the mental range of the vulgar crowd and the bourgeoisie and thus it appeals to their sense of isolated superiority. Its impartiality resembles their own determination to avoid sentimentality and an open display of personal feelings. Above all perhaps, and especially in the guise of *philologie,* it offers them a new source of poetic inspiration. But this ambiguously motivated cult of science is far from implying either Positivism or *scientisme,* its philosophical exaggeration. Poets like Leconte de Lisle and Ménard—in common with Flaubert or Baudelaire—still reject Du Camp's conception of a scientific poetry; to contrast them with a Zola is to realize how completely their cult of science is subordinated to their cult of art. As Cassagne concludes, minor exceptions apart, 'la devise l'art pour l'art ne s'est nullement changée en l'art pour la science'.[6]

Even more importantly, these equations disregard—or greatly underestimate—the intensity of anti-Positivist aspiration in the Parnassian poets and suggest that they are far less disturbed by religious and metaphysical longings than is the case. They neglect the eagerness with which Leconte de Lisle and Louis Ménard scrutinize the religions of the past to find a creed for the present, the heart-searchings of a Madame Ackermann as expressed in a poem like *Le Positivisme,* Sully Prudhomme's life-long, anxious preoccupation with the enigmas of God and immortality. Behind much of the Parnassian concern with *philologie,* for example, lies the belief that primitive mythology embodies a non-intellectual revelation of metaphysical truth to which our more sophisticated minds have been closed but which can be regained by sympathetic study. Following Creuzer, Constant and Quinet, this view is held above all by Louis Ménard—who, wishing to link poetic beauty and 'la recherche de l'idéal', cries in warning (not at all unlike the Symbolists whom he deplored):

> Pour tout ce qu'il y a encore dans l'humanité d'esprits jeunes et spontanés, il faut des symboles, c'est-à-dire sous des formes vivantes et palpables . . . un idéal mystérieux que nos rêves poursuivent toujours plus haut dans les profondeurs de l'inconnu.[7]

Nor is the intellectual background against which they lived as uniformly or even predominantly Positivist as is often declared. Christians, both Catholic and Protestant; Neo-Criticists like Renouvier, Cournot, Lequier and Pillon; Eclectics and Spiritualists like Ravaisson, Lachelier, Caro, Paul Janet, Saisset and Vacherot—all these, as well as the influence of foreign thinkers like Schelling, Fichte, Herder, Goethe and, more ambiguously, Kant and Hegel, are active at this time. There is also reason to think that the impact of Comte in France has been overrated, that only Littré amongst the thinkers of the age owes any major debt to him—and even he with many reservations. Above all, the leading Positivists themselves are divided in their allegiance: as witness not only Comte's 'religion of Humanity' but also Renan's 'religion of Science' and quasi-Bergsonian theory of knowledge, and Taine's method of metaphysical research. Renan erects the *Idéal* as God. Taine's faculty of abstraction leads him to moments of pantheistic vision in which the mind is overwhelmed by religious awe and 'elevated above the mortality and insignificance of the human condition': '[l'homme] jouit par sympathie de cette infinité qu'il pense, et participe à sa grandeur'.[8] Comte apart, these 'esprits mi-positifs et mi-méta-physiques' (in Littré's phrase) were always obsessed—unlike Bourget's Adrien Sixte—by 'le mystère impénétrable de la destinée'. Renan says even of Littré, the least troubled of them all: '[il] passa toute sa vie à s'interdire de penser aux problèmes supérieurs et à y penser toujours'.[9]

In short, close study of the outlook of Parnassian poets and Positivist thinkers alike would reveal many signs of a deep-seated desire to transcend the finite and the scientific, to penetrate to the 'Ideal', to a realm of spiritual meaningfulness. In this at least there may be a closer *philosophical* similarity between Parnassians and Symbolists than the wide differences in their poetic techniques might suggest. It is not without significance, for example, that Baudelaire can approvingly discern in Leconte de Lisle and Renan 'ce même esprit d'amour universel . . . pour les différentes formes, dont l'homme a, suivant les âges et les climats, revêtu la beauté et la vérité', that (as Peyre notes) Rimbaud's 'Lettre du Voyant' proclaims Leconte de Lisle, as well as Gautier and Banville, to be 'très voyant', and that Leconte de Lisle, in common with Baudelaire and Rimbaud, admires Hugo as a 'seer'.[10] This is not to imply that such elements in Symbolist poetry originate in Parnassianism: rather, both groups have a common intellectual and poetic ancestry in Romanticism, and it is this which in large measure accounts for the affinities between them. All are involved in a similar spiritual crisis, all are set in a similar social situation—hence their common pessimism, their withdrawal from the materialistic world around them, their cult of aristocratic superiority, their attempt to find refuge from a banal present in exotic or long-past cultures, in myth and legend, in flirtations with non-Christian religion or in contemplation of their personal sensibility. . . .

Notes

[1] Place of publication is Paris unless otherwise stated. References within the text to Leconte de Lisle's theoretical writings are to the Lemerre edition, 1926, of his *Derniers Poèmes*. To indicate the different works the following abbreviations are used: 1852 = 'Préface des Poèmes antiques'; 1855 = 'Préface des Poèmes et poésies'; 1861 = 'Charles Baudelaire' in *Les poètes contemporains;* 1864 = *Les poètes contemporains* (excepting 'Charles Baudelaire'); 1887 = 'Discours sur Victor Hugo'.

[2] Ph. Van Tieghem, *Petite histoire des grandes doctrines littéraires en France,* 1946, p. 242; and R. Jasinski, *Histoire de la littérature française,* 1947, vol. II, pp. 340 and 342.

[3] F. Brunetière, *Discours de combat,* 1900, pp. 4-5, and *L'évolution de la poésie lyrique au dix-neuvième siècle,* 9e éd., s.d., vol. II, pp. 114ff; G. Lanson, *Histoire de la littérature française,* 1906, p. 1014; A. Thibaudet, *Histoire de la littérature française de* 1789 *à nos jours,* 1936, pp. 404 and 409; and P. Martino, *Parnasse et Symbolisme,* 1947, p. 32. Cf. E. Estève, *Sully Prudhomme,* 1925, pp. 57-8; V. Giraud, *Essai sur Taine,* 6e éd., s.d., pp. 67, 182-3 and 185; P. Flottes, *Sully Prudhomme,* 1930, p. 38, amongst many variants on the same view.

[4] *Auguste Comte et la philosophie positive,* 1864, pp. 519 and 525.

[5] For his criticisms of Herbert Spencer's ideas on the 'Unknowable', see his 'Préface d'un disciple' in A. Comte, *Cours de philosophie positive,* 1864, vol. I, pp. xl-xliv.

[6] A. Cassagne, *La théorie de l'art pour l'art en France chez les derniers romantiques et les premiers réalistes,* 1906, p. 294.

[7] *Poèmes et rêveries d'un païen mystique,* 1895, p. 6 (normal spelling restored); and 'Les études d'histoire religieuse d'Ernest Renan', *Revue philosophique et religieuse,* VII (1857), pp. 184-5.

[8] *Les philosophes classiques du dix-neuvième siècle en France,* 13e éd., s.d., p. 371.

[9] *Discours et conférences,* 1928, p. 79.

[10] C. Baudelaire, *Œuvres* (éd. Le Dantec), 1954, p. 1124, 'Réflexions sur quelques-uns de mes contemporains-Leconte de Lisle'; and H. Peyre, 'The Literature of the

Second Empire: *La poésie*', *Symposium,* VII (Syracuse, N.Y., 1953), pp. 20 and 27. . . .

FURTHER READING

Brereton, Geoffrey. "Leconte de Lisle and Heredia." In *An Introduction to the French Poets: Villon to the Present Day*, pp. 166-77. London: Methuen & Co. Ltd., 1956.

Places the Parnassians between the Romantic poets of the early nineteenth century and the Symbolist movement which emerged in the 1880s. Identifies José-Maria de Heredia as the only "pure Parnassian" poet of note, and Leconte de Lisle as "the high priest of *La Parnasse*."

Denommé, Robert T. "The Elaboration of a Poetic Creed." In *Leconte de Lisle*, pp. 29-43. New York: Twayne Publishers, Inc., 1973.

Details Leconte de Lisle's support and defense of the "art for art's sake" philosophy and his incorporation of the classical aesthetic into the Parnassian movement.

Epstein, Edna. "Themes in Parnassian Poetry." *Modern Language Review* 65, No. 3 (July 1970): 541-51.

Describes the major ideological themes of the Parnassian movement, stressing the group's formal concerns and their placement of art in opposition to nature.

Harms, Alvin. "Heredia and the Parnassians." In *José-Maria de Heredia*, pp. 39-51. Boston, Mass.: Twayne Publishers, 1975.

Details Heredia's connection to the Parnassian movement, his literary salons, and his friendship with Leconte de Lisle.

Schaffer, Aaron. *The Genres of Parnassian Poetry: A Study of the Parnassian Minors*. Baltimore, Md.: The Johns Hopkins Press, 1944, 427 p.

Studies the Parnassian movement through the work of its principal figures, grouping them by thematic and philosophical concerns.

The Portrayal of Jews in Nineteenth-Century English Literature

INTRODUCTION

In nineteenth-century English literature, the most common portrayal of a Jew was a negative racial stereotype. In society, and thus in literature, Jews were often seen in terms of their "otherness"—their difference in appearance, social standing, religion and morality with respect to their non-Jewish counterparts. This is especially true of the fiction of the early nineteenth-century when the ghost of Shakespeare's greedy, evil Shylock still haunted English literature. However, even when Jews gained political equality in England with the passage of numerous reforms and a rise in realism in fiction caused novelists writing in the mid-1800s to look increasingly to real life rather than to established stereotypes as inspiration for their writing, Jews were (aside from a few more balanced portrayals) still depicted in extreme terms: as completely evil or as impossibly virtuous; as people seeking complete assimilation into English culture or as adamantly separatist; as wealthy politicians and international financiers or as lowly impoverished immigrants. And as interpretations of Jewish life and views regarding the appropriate role of the Jew in English society were set into fiction by both Jewish and non-Jewish novelists, an increasingly racial debate was also waged, both in and out of the realm of fiction, regarding the contributions of Hebraism to English culture.

Certain non-Jewish novelists are discussed below for their contribution to these trends in the portrayal of Jews in nineteenth-century English literature. Sir Walter Scott produced the first novel-length treatment of Jewish characters in *Ivanhoe* (1819). As Harold Fisch (1971) notes, Scott (who depicted the Jew in medieval society) defended the Jews by attacking some of the nineteenth-century prejudices against Jews and by attributing negative aspects of "Jewish character" to Christian oppression. But Scott also devoted much attention to the negative qualities of the Jew, Isaac of York, and made Isaac's daughter, Rebecca, the heroine of the story, represented as the height of beauty. Other non-Jewish writers treated Jews in similarly extreme terms. Some novelists, such as Amelia Bristow in *Sophia de Lissau* (1828), used their work as a platform to advocate the conversion of Jews to Christianity. But others, such as George Du Maurier in *Trilby* (1894) with the evil Jew Svengali, gave a portrayal of the Jew as wholly despicable that remained popular throughout the nineteenth-century. Charles Dickens produced one of the most famous examples of the stereotypical "evil Jew"—the character of Fagin in *Oliver Twist* (1838). Certain novelists attempted in later novels to "atone" for a negative portrayal of Jews in earlier novels. For example, Dickens portrayed the Jewish character Riah in *Our Mutual Friend* (1864-65) as a paragon of virtue compared to his earlier character Fagin. Similarly, Maria Edgeworth depicted the Jewish heroine in *Harrington* (1817) much more favorably than a Jewish character from her 1812 novel *The Absentee* (although, it has been pointed out that *Harrington*'s Jewish heroine also converts to Christianity). Against the backdrop of so many flawed portraits, George Eliot provided a portrait of the Jew in her novel *Daniel Deronda* (1876) that stands out as at least an honest effort at a more accurate portrayal of Judaism. And this portrait has been admired by many (including Jewish readers living at the time of the original publication of *Daniel Deronda*) for its faithful attempt at capturing the essence of Jewish life. As Rabbi David Philipson (1889) notes, *Daniel Deronda* can be identified as one of the few legitimate efforts at characterizing the Jew in fiction, in that it portrays the Jew as a follower of his religion rather than in racial terms. Yet the novel has also been criticized for the way in which the Jewish portions of the novel never fully integrate with the rest of its plot.

Nineteenth-century Jewish writers contributed to a more realistic representation of Jews in English literature. Jewish novelist Amy Levy (1886) took issue with Eliot's work, maintaining that, despite its "sincere and respectful attempt" at depicting the features of Judaism, the novel fails to genuinely reflect contemporary Jewish life. In Levy's own novel on middle-class Jewish life, *Reuben Sachs* (1889), Levy makes several direct criticisms of *Daniel Deronda*, including references to the Zionism of Eliot's Jewish characters. Levy defended her work as realistic, although some criticized her novel for presenting overly negative portrayals of Jewish life. Certain other British Jews, as Bryan Cheyette (1990) argues, felt compelled to "negotiate" between their cultural heritage and the English national culture. For example, Grace Aguilar, in *The Spirit of Judaism* (1842), adopted a form of "Christianized" or "Anglicanized" Judaism, in which she urged the acceptance of Jews and Judaism as an extension of Christian values. As Cheyette contends, other Anglo-Jewish novelists—such as Julia Frankau (Frank Danby), Benjamin Farjeon, and Israel Zangwill—attempted to revise prevalent Jewish stereotypes by making them more "acceptable" to the "majority values of English culture." However, Farjeon's novels (Cheyette notes) are similar to those of Benjamin Disraeli in their assumption of Jewish racial superiority. In such works as *Coningsby* (1844) and *Tancred* (1847), Disraeli (the Prime Minister of England [1867; 1874-80] who had been raised as a Jew until his father had a falling out with the synagogue and had subsequently been baptized as an adolescent) continually praised the Jewish race. As Rabbi Edward N. Calisch (1909) notes, Disraeli dubbed the Jewish race "the aristocracy of nature."

Disraeli was a prime contributor in the argument concerning the cultural ideals of Hebraism and Hellenism. According to Michael Ragussis (1995), Disraeli's beliefs on the significance of the Jewish race (expounded upon in novels such as *Tancred* and *Lothair* [1870]), appear to have influenced the poet Matthew Arnold. Disraeli maintained that English culture was based on Hebraism, but Arnold, while embracing the contributions of Hebraism (which Arnold equated with Jewish moral conduct and authority), argued in *Culture and Anarchy* (1869) that the overly Hebraic English culture needed to be balanced by Hellenism (Greek-inspired philosophy, culture, and art). In *Literature and Dogma* (1892), Arnold expressed his beliefs about Hebraism and Hellenism in terms of differentiation between the Aryan and Semitic races—with basic characteristics being assigned to each race. Arnold appeared to extoll the virtues of both races, on the one hand, but, on the other hand, to rely on the Aryan race to both respect the value of Hebraism and to balance the Hebraic with the Hellenic. Disraeli considered the ideology of Hellenism to be based on a racial criticism of the Jews.

Ninteenth-century novelists of Jewish and non-Jewish backgrounds fought, through their work, to make countless political, economic, racial, and religious statements about Jewish life, the "Jewish identity," and the role of the Jew in English society and culture. Many such arguments and portrayals have been characterized as negative, a few are arguably positive, and most continue to be evaluated in the twentieth-century. Yet students of this period and scholars alike might agree with critic Edgar Rosenberg (1960), who makes the following observation: "the image of the Jew in English literature has been a depressingly uniform and static phenomenon."

REPRESENTATIVE NOVELS

Grace Aguilar
The Spirit of Judaism 1842

Amelia Bristow
Sophia de Lissau 1828

Sir Edward Bulwer-Lytton
My Novel 1853

Hall Caine
The Scapegoat 1891

Charles Dickens
Oliver Twist 1838
Our Mutual Friend 1864-65

Benjamin Disraeli
Coningsby 1844
Tancred 1847
Lothair 1870

George Du Maurier
Trilby 1894

Maria Edgeworth
The Absentee 1812
Harrington 1817

George Eliot
Daniel Deronda 1876

Benjamin L. Farjeon
Solomon Isaacs 1877
Aaron the Jew 1894-95

Julia Frankau [Frank Danby]
Dr. Phillips; A Maida Vale Idyll 1887

Samuel Gordon
**Daughters of Shem* 1898

Amy Levy
Reuben Sachs 1889

George Meredith
The Tragic Comedians 1880

Charles Reade
It Is Never Too Late to Mend 1856

Sir Walter Scott
Ivanhoe 1819

William Makepeace Thackery
***Rebecca and Rowena* 1850
****Codlingsby* 1853

Anthony Trollope
Nina Balatka 1867

Israel Zangwill
Children of the Ghetto 1892
Ghetto Tragedies 1893
The King of Schnorrers 1894

*This work is a collection of short stories.
**This work is a parody of Scott's *Ivanhoe*.
***This work is a parody of Disraeli's *Coningsby*.

OVERVIEWS

George Eliot (essay date 1879)

SOURCE: "The Modern Hep! Hep! Hep!," in *Impressions of Theophrastus Such,* edited by Nancy Henry, William Pickering, 1994, pp. 143-65.

[*In the following essay, first published in 1879 and reprinted in 1994, Eliot (1) documents the negative stereotypes prevalent in nineteenth-century England, (2) argues that the "revived expression of old antipathies" had been stimulated by the fact that Jews had attained political power, and (3) defends Jews against the defamation that they continued to receive in her lifetime.*]

To discern likeness amidst diversity, it is well known, does not require so fine a mental edge as the discerning of diversity amidst general sameness.[1] The primary rough classification depends on the prominent resemblances of things: the progress is towards finer and finer discrimination according to minute differences.

Yet even at this stage of European culture one's attention is continually drawn to the prevalence of that grosser mental sloth which makes people dull to the most ordinary prompting of comparison—the bringing things together because of their likeness. The same motives, the same ideas, the same practices, are alternately admired and abhorred, lauded and denounced, according to their association with superficial differences, historical or actually social: even learned writers treating of great subjects often show an attitude of mind not greatly superior in its logic to that of the frivolous fine lady who is indignant at the frivolity of her maid.

To take only the subject of the Jews: it would be difficult to find a form of bad reasoning about them which has not been heard in conversation or been admitted to the dignity of print; but the neglect of resemblances is a common property of dulness which unites all the various points of view—the prejudiced, the puerile, the spiteful, and the abysmally ignorant.

That the preservation of national memories is an element and a means of national greatness, that their revival is a sign of reviving nationality, that every heroic defender, every patriotic restorer, has been inspired by such memories and has made them his watchword, that even such a corporate existence as that of a Roman legion or an English regiment has been made valorous by memorial standards,—these are the glorious commonplaces of historic teaching at our public schools and universities, being happily ingrained in Greek and Latin classics. They have also been impressed on the world by conspicuous modern instances. That there is a free modern Greece is due—through all infiltration of other than Greek blood—to the presence of ancient Greece in the consciousness of European men; and every speaker would feel his point safe if he were to praise Byron's devotion[2] to a cause made glorious by ideal identification with the past; hardly so, if he were to insist that the Greeks were not to be helped further because their history shows that they were anciently unsurpassed in treachery and lying, and that many modern Greeks are highly disreputable characters, while others are disposed to grasp too large a share of our commerce. The same with Italy: the pathos of his country's lot pierced the youthful soul of Mazzini,[3] because, like Dante's, his blood was fraught with the kinship of Italian greatness, his imagination filled with a majestic past that wrought itself into a majestic future. Half a century ago, what was Italy? An idling-place of dilettanteism or of itinerant motiveless wealth, a territory parcelled out for papal sustenance, dynastic convenience, and the profit of an alien Government.[4] What were the Italians? No people, no voice in European counsels, no massive power in European affairs: a race thought of in English and French society as chiefly adapted to the operatic stage, or to serve as models for painters; disposed to smile gratefully at the reception of half-pence; and by the more historical remembered to be rather polite than truthful, in all probability a combination of Machiavelli, Rubini, and Masaniello.[5] Thanks chiefly to the divine gift of a memory which inspires the moments with a past, a present, and a future, and gives the sense of corporate existence that raises man above the otherwise more respectable and innocent brute, all that, or most of it, is changed.

Again, one of our living historians[6] finds just sympathy in his vigorous insistance on our true ancestry, on our being the strongly marked heritors in language and genius of those old English seamen who, beholding a rich country with a most convenient seaboard, came, doubtless with a sense of divine warrant, and settled themselves on this or the other side of fertilising streams, gradually conquering more and more of the pleasant land from the natives who knew nothing of Odin,[7] and finally making unusually clean work in ridding themselves of those prior occupants. 'Let us,' he virtually says, 'let us know who were our forefathers, who it was that won the soil for us, and brought the good seed of those institutions through which we should not arrogantly but gratefully feel ourselves distinguished among the nations as possessors of long-inherited freedom; let us not keep up an ignorant kind of naming which disguises our true affinities of blood and language, but let us see thoroughly what sort of notions and traditions our forefathers had, and what sort of song inspired them. Let the poetic fragments which breathe forth their fierce bravery in battle and their trust in fierce gods who helped them, be treasured with affectionate reverence. These seafaring, invading, self-asserting men were the English of old time, and were our fathers who did rough work by which we are profiting. They had virtues which incorporated themselves in wholesome usages to which we trace our own political blessings. Let us know and acknowledge our common relationship to them, and be thankful that over and above the affections and duties which spring from our manhood, we have the closer and more constantly guiding duties which belong to us as Englishmen.'

To this view of our nationality most persons who have feeling and understanding enough to be conscious of the connection between the patriotic affection and every other affection which lifts us above emigrating rats and free-loving baboons, will be disposed to say Amen. True, we are not indebted to those ancestors for our religion: we are rather proud of having got that illumination from elsewhere. The men who planted our nation were not Christians, though they began their work centuries after Christ; and they had a decided objection to Christianity when it was first proposed to them: they were not monotheists, and their religion was the reverse of spiritual. But since we have been fortunate enough to keep the island-home they won for us, and have been on the whole a prosperous people, rather continuing the plan of invading and spoiling other lands than being forced to beg for shelter in them, nobody has reproached us because our fathers thirteen hundred years ago worshipped Odin, massacred Britons, and were with difficulty persuaded to accept Christianity, knowing nothing of Hebrew history and the reasons why Christ should be received as the Saviour of mankind. The Red Indians, not liking us when we settled among them, might have been willing to fling such facts in our faces, but they were too ignorant, and besides, their opinions did not signify, because we were able, if we liked, to exterminate them. The Hindoos also have doubtless had their rancours against us and still entertain enough ill-will to make unfavourable remarks on our character, especially as to our historic rapacity and arrogant notions of our own superiority; they perhaps do not admire the usual English profile, and they are not converted to our way of feeding: but though we are a small number of an alien race profiting by the territory and produce of these prejudiced people, they are unable to turn us out; at least, when they tried we showed them their mistake.[8] We do not call ourselves a dispersed and a punished people: we are a colonising people, and it is we who have punished others.

Still the historian guides us rightly in urging us to dwell on the virtues of our ancestors with emulation, and to cherish our sense of a common descent as a bond of obligation. The eminence, the nobleness of a people depends on its capability of being stirred by memories, and of striving for what we call spiritual ends—ends which consist not in immediate material possession, but in the satisfaction of a great feeling that animates the collective body as with one soul. A people having the seed of worthiness in it must feel an answering thrill when it is adjured by the deaths of its heroes who died to preserve its national existence; when it is reminded of its small beginnings and gradual growth through past labours and struggles, such as are still demanded of it in order that the freedom and wellbeing thus inherited may be transmitted unimpaired to children and children's children; when an appeal against the permission of injustice is made to great precedents in its history and to the better genius breathing in its institutions. It is this living force of sentiment in common which makes a national consciousness. Nations so moved will resist conquest with the very breasts of their women, will pay their millions and their blood to abolish slavery, will share privation in famine and all calamity, will produce poets to sing 'some great story of a man,' and thinkers whose theories will bear the test of action. An individual man, to be harmoniously great, must belong to a nation of this order, if not in actual existence yet existing in the past, in memory, as a departed, invisible, beloved ideal, once a reality, and perhaps to be restored. A common humanity is not yet enough to feed the rich blood of various activity which makes a complete man. The time is not come for cosmopolitanism to be highly virtuous, any more than for communism to suffice for social energy. I am not bound to feel for a Chinaman as I feel for my fellow-countryman: I am bound not to demoralise him with opium, not to compel him to my will by destroying or plundering the fruits of his labour on the alleged ground that he is not cosmopolitan enough, and not to insult him for his want of my tailoring and religion when he appears as a peaceable visitor on the London pavement. It is admirable in a Briton with a good purpose to learn Chinese, but it would not be a proof of fine intellect in him to taste Chinese poetry in the original more than he tastes the poetry of his own tongue. Affection, intelligence, duty, radiate from a centre, and nature has decided that for us English folk that centre can be neither China nor Peru. Most of us feel this unreflectingly; for the affectation of undervaluing everything native, and being too fine for one's own country, belongs only to a few minds of no dangerous leverage. What is wanting is, that we should recognise a corresponding attachment to nationality as legitimate in every other people, and understand that its absence is a privation of the greatest good.

For, to repeat, not only the nobleness of a nation depends on the presence of this national consciousness, but also the nobleness of each individual citizen. Our dignity and rectitude are proportioned to our sense of relationship with something great, admirable, pregnant with high possibilities, worthy of sacrifice, a continual inspiration to self-repression and discipline by the presentation of aims larger and more attractive to our generous part than the securing of personal ease or prosperity. And a people possessing this good should surely feel not only a ready sympathy with the effort of those who, having lost the good, strive to regain it, but a profound pity for any degradation resulting from its loss; nay, something more than pity when happier nationalities have made victims of the unfortunate whose memories nevertheless are the very fountain to which the persecutors trace their most vaunted blessings.

These notions are familiar: few will deny them in the abstract, and many are found loudly asserting them in relation to this or the other particular case. But here as elsewhere, in the ardent application of ideas, there is a notable lack of simple comparison or sensibility to resemblance. The European world has long been used to consider the Jews as altogether exceptional, and it has followed naturally enough that they have been excepted from the rules of justice and mercy, which are based on human likeness. But to consider a people whose ideas have determined the religion of half the world, and that the more cultivated half, and who made the most eminent struggle against the power of Rome, as a purely exceptional race, is a demoralising offence against rational knowledge, a stultifying inconsistency in historical interpretation. Every nation of forcible character—*i.e.,* of strongly marked characteristics, is so far exceptional. The distinctive note of each bird-species is in this sense exceptional, but the necessary ground of such distinction is a deeper likeness. The superlative peculiarity in the Jews admitted, our afffinity with them is only the more apparent when the elements of their peculiarity are discerned.

From whatever point of view the writings of the Old Testament may be regarded, the picture they present of a national development is of high interest and speciality, nor can their historic momentousness be much affected by any varieties of theory as to the relation they bear to the New Testament or to the rise and constitution of Christianity. Whether we accept the canonical Hebrew books as a revelation or simply as part of an ancient literature, makes no difference to the fact that we find there the strongly characterised portraiture of a people educated from an earlier or later period to a sense of separateness unique in its intensity, a people taught by many concurrent influences to identify faithfulness to its national traditions with the highest social and religious blessings. Our too scanty sources of Jewish history, from the return under Ezra to the beginning of the desperate resistance against Rome,[9] show us the heroic and triumphant struggle of the Maccabees, which rescued the religion and independence of the nation from the corrupting sway of the Syrian Greeks,[10] adding to the glorious sum of its memorials, and stimulating continuous efforts of a more peaceful sort to maintain and develop that national life which the heroes had fought and died for, by internal measures of legal administration and public teaching. Thenceforth the virtuous elements of the Jewish life were engaged, as they had been with varying aspects during the long and changeful prophetic period and the restoration under Ezra, on the side of preserving the specific national character against a demoralising fusion with that of foreigners whose religion and ritual were idolatrous and often obscene. There was always a Foreign party reviling the National party as narrow, and sometimes manifesting their own breadth in extensive views of advancement or profit to themselves by flattery of a foreign power. Such internal conflict naturally tightened the bands of conservatism, which needed to be strong if it were to rescue the sacred ark, the vital spirit of a small nation—'the smallest of the nations'—whose territory lay on the highway between three continents; and when the dread and hatred of foreign sway had condensed itself into dread and hatred of the Romans, many Conservatives became Zealots,[11] whose chief mark was that they advocated resistance to the death against the submergence of their nationality. Much might be said on this point towards distinguishing the desperate struggle against a conquest which is regarded as degradation and corruption, from rash, hopeless insurrection against an established native government; and for my part (if that were of any consequence) I share the spirit of the Zealots. I take the spectacle of the Jewish people defying the Roman edict, and preferring death by starvation or the sword to the introduction of Caligula's deified statue[12] into the temple, as a sublime type of steadfastness. But all that need be noticed here is the continuity of that national education (by outward and inward circumstance) which created in the Jews a feeling of race, a sense of corporate existence, unique in its intensity.

But not, before the dispersion, unique in essential qualities. There is more likeness than contrast between the way we English got our island and the way the Israelites got Canaan. We have not been noted for forming a low estimate of ourselves in comparison with foreigners, or for admitting that our institutions are equalled by those of any other people under the sun. Many of us have thought that our sea-wall is a specially divine arrangement to make and keep us a nation of sea-kings after the manner of our forefathers, secure against invasion and able to invade other lands when we need them, though they may lie on the other side of the ocean. Again, it has been held that we have a peculiar destiny as a Protestant people, not only able to bruise the head of an idolatrous Christianity in the midst of us, but fitted as possessors of the most truth and the most tonnage to carry our purer religion over the world and convert mankind to our way of thinking. The Puritans, asserting their liberty to restrain tyrants, found the Hebrew history closely symbolical of their feelings and purpose; and it can hardly be correct to cast the blame of their less laudable doings on the writings they invoked, since their opponents made use of the same writings for different ends, finding there a strong warrant for the divine right of kings[13] and the denunciation of those who, like Korah, Dathan, and Abiram,[14] took on themselves the office of the priesthood which belonged of right solely to Aaron and his sons, or, in other words, to men ordained by the English bishops. We must rather refer the passionate use of the Hebrew writings to affinities of disposition between our own race and the Jewish. Is it true that the arrogance of a Jew was so immeasurably beyond that of a Calvinist? And the just sympathy and admiration which we give to the ancestors who resisted the oppressive acts of our native kings, and by resisting rescued or won for us the best part of our civil and religious liberties—is it justly to be withheld from those brave and steadfast men of Jewish race who fought and died, or strove by wise administration to resist, the oppression and corrupting influences of foreign tyrants, and by resisting rescued the nationality which was the very hearth of our own religion? At any rate, seeing that the Jews were more specifically than any other nation educated into a sense of their supreme moral value, the chief matter of surprise is that any other nation is found to rival them in this form of self-confidence.

More exceptional—less like the course of our own history—has been their dispersion and their subsistence as a separate people through ages in which for the most part they were regarded and treated very much as beasts hunted for the sake of their skins, or of a valuable secretion peculiar to their species. The Jews showed a talent for accumulating what was an object of more immediate desire to Christians than animal oils or well-furred skins, and their cupidity and avarice were found at once particularly hateful and particularly useful: hateful when seen as a reason for punishing them by mulcting[15] or robbery, useful when this retributive process could be successfully carried forward. Kings and emperors naturally were more alive to the usefulness of subjects who could gather and yield money; but edicts issued to protect 'the King's Jews'[16] equally with the King's game from being harassed and hunted by the commonalty were only slight mitigations to the deplorable lot of a race held to be under the divine curse, and had little force after the Crusades began. As the slave-holders in the United States counted the curse on Ham[17] a justification of negro slavery, so the curse on the Jews was counted a justification for hindering them from pursuing agriculture and handicrafts; for marking them out as execrable figures by a peculiar dress; for torturing them to make them part with their gains, or for more gratuitously spitting at them and pelting them; for taking it as certain that they killed and ate babies, poisoned the wells, and took pains to spread the plague; for putting it to them whether they would be baptised or burned, and not failing to burn and massacre them when they were obstinate; but also for suspecting them of disliking the baptism when they had got it, and then burning them in punishment of their insincerity; finally, for hounding them by tens on tens of thousands from the homes where they had found shelter for centuries, and inflicting on them the horrors of a new exile and a new dispersion. All this to avenge the Saviour of mankind, or else to compel these stiff-necked people to acknowledge a Master whose servants showed such beneficent effects of His teaching.

With a people so treated one of two issues was possible: either from being of feebler nature than their persecutors, and caring more for ease than for the sentiments and ideas which constituted their distinctive character, they would everywhere give way to pressure and get rapidly merged in the populations around them; or, being endowed with uncommon tenacity, physical and mental, feeling peculiarly the ties of inheritance both in blood and faith, remembering national glories, trusting in their recovery, abhorring apostasy, able to bear all things and hope all things with the consciousness of being steadfast to spiritual obligations, the kernel of their number would harden into an inflexibility more and more insured by motive and habit. They would cherish all differences that marked them off from their hated oppressors, all memories that consoled them with a sense of virtual though unrecognised superiority; and the separateness which was made their badge of ignominy would be their inward pride, their source of fortifying defiance. Doubtless such a people would get confirmed in vices. An oppressive government and a persecuting religion, while breeding vices in those who hold power, are well known to breed answering vices in those who are powerless and suffering. What more direct plan than the course presented by European history could have been pursued in order to give the Jews a spirit of bitter isolation, of scorn for the wolfish hypocrisy that made victims of them, of triumph in prospering at the expense of the blunderers who stoned them away from the open paths of industry?—or, on the other hand, to encourage in the less defiant a lying conformity, a pretence of conversion for the sake of the social advantages attached to baptism, an outward renunciation of their hereditary ties with the lack of real love towards the society and creed which exacted this galling tribute?—or again, in the most unhappy specimens of the race, to rear transcendent examples of odious vice, reckless instruments of rich men with bad propensities, unscrupulous grinders of the alien people who wanted to grind *them?*

No wonder the Jews have their vices: no wonder if it were proved (which it has not hitherto appeared to be) that some of them have a bad pre-eminence in evil, an unrivalled superfluity of naughtiness. It would be more plausible to make a wonder of the virtues which have prospered among them under the shadow of oppression. But instead of dwelling on these, or treating as admitted what any hardy or ignorant person may deny, let us found simply on the loud assertions of the hostile. The Jews, it is said, resisted the expansion of their own religion into Christianity; they were in the habit of spitting on the cross; they have held the name of Christ to be *Anathema*. Who taught them that? The men who made Christianity a curse to them: the men who made the name of Christ a symbol for the spirit of vengeance, and, what was worse, made the execution of the vengeance a pretext for satisfying their own savageness, greed, and envy: the men who sanctioned with the name of Christ a barbaric and blundering copy of pagan fatalism in taking the words 'His blood be upon us and on our children'[18] as a divinely appointed verbal warrant for wreaking cruelty from generation to generation on the people from whose sacred writings Christ drew His teaching. Strange retrogression in the professors of an expanded religion, boasting an illumination beyond the spiritual doctrine of Hebrew prophets! For Hebrew prophets proclaimed a God who demanded mercy rather than sacrifices. The Christians also believed that God delighted not in the blood of rams and of bulls, but they apparently conceived Him as requiring for His satisfaction the sighs and groans, the blood and roasted flesh of men whose forefathers had misunderstood the metaphorical character of prophecies which spoke of spiritual pre-eminence under the figure of a material kingdom. Was this the method by which Christ desired His title to the Messiahship to be commended to the hearts and understandings of the nation in which He was born? Many of His sayings bear the stamp of that patriotism which places fellow-countrymen in the inner circle of affection and duty. And did the words 'Father, forgive them, they know not what they do,'[19] refer only to the centurion and his band, a tacit exception being made of every Hebrew there present from the mercy of the Father and the compassion of the Son?—nay, more, of every Hebrew yet to come who remained unconverted after hearing of His claim to the Messiahship, not from His own lips or those of His native apostles, but from the lips of alien men whom cross, creed, and baptism had left cruel, rapacious, and debauched? It is more reverent to Christ to believe that He must have approved the Jewish martyrs who deliberately chose to be burned or massacred rather than be guilty of a blaspheming lie, more than He approved the rabble of crusaders who robbed and murdered them in His name.

But these remonstrances seem to have no direct application to personages who take up the attitude of philosophic thinkers and discriminating critics, professedly accepting Christianity from a rational point of view as a vehicle of the highest religious and moral truth, and condemning the Jews on the ground that they are obstinate adherents of an outworn creed, maintain themselves in moral alienation from the peoples with whom they share citizenship, and are destitute of real interest in the welfare of the community and state with which they are thus identified. These anti-Judaic advocates usually belong to a party[20] which has felt itself glorified in winning for Jews, as well as Dissenters and Catholics, the full privileges of citizenship, laying open to them every path to distinction. At one time the voice of this party urged that differences of creed were made dangerous only by the denial of citizenship—that you must make a man a citizen before he could feel like one. At present, apparently, this confidence has been succeeded by a sense of mistake: there is a regret that no limiting clauses were insisted on, such as would have hindered the Jews from coming too far and in too large proportion along those opened pathways; and the Roumanians are thought to have shown an enviable wisdom in giving them as little chance as possible.[21] But then, the reflection occurring that some of the most objectionable Jews are baptised Christians, it is obvious that such clauses would have been insufficient, and the doctrine that you can turn a Jew into a good Christian is emphatically retracted. But clearly, these liberal gentlemen, too late enlightened by disagreeable events, must yield the palm of wise foresight to those who argued against them long ago; and it is a striking spectacle to witness minds so panting for advancement in some directions that they are ready to force it on an unwilling society, in this instance despairingly recurring to mediæval types of thinking—insisting that the Jews are made viciously cosmopolitan by holding the world's money-bag, that for them all national interests are resolved into the algebra of loans, that they have suffered an inward degradation stamping them as morally inferior, and—'serve them right,' since they rejected Christianity. All which is mirrored in an analogy, namely, that of the Irish, also a servile race, who have rejected Protestantism though it has been repeatedly urged on them by fire and sword and penal laws, and whose place in the moral scale may be judged by our advertisements, where the clause, 'No Irish need apply,' parallels the sentence which for many polite persons sums up the question of Judaism—'I never *did* like the Jews.'

It is certainly worth considering whether an expatriated, denationalised race, used for ages to live among antipathetic populations, must not inevitably lack some conditions of nobleness. If they drop that separateness which is made their reproach, they may be in danger of lapsing into a cosmopolitan indifference equivalent to cynicism, and of missing that inward identification with the nationality immediately around them which might make some amends for their inherited privation. No dispassionate observer can deny this danger. Why, our own countrymen who take to living abroad without purpose or function to keep up their sense of fellowship in the affairs of their own land are rarely good specimens of moral healthiness; still, the consciousness of having a native country, the birthplace of common memories and habits of mind, existing like a parental hearth quitted but beloved; the dignity of being included in a people which has a part in the comity of nations and the growing federation of the world; that sense of special belonging which is the root of human virtues, both public and private,—all these spiritual links may preserve migratory Englishmen from the worst consequences of their voluntary dispersion. Unquestionably the Jews, having been more than any other race exposed to the adverse moral influences of alienism, must, both in individuals and in groups, have suffered some corresponding moral degradation; but in fact they have escaped with less of abjectness and less of hard hostility towards the nations whose hand has been against them, than could have happened in the case of a people who had neither their adhesion to a separate religion founded on historic memories, nor their characteristic family affectionateness. Tortured, flogged, spit upon, the *corpus vile*[22] on which rage or wantonness vented themselves with impunity, their name flung at them as an opprobrium by superstition, hatred, and contempt, they have remained proud of their origin. Does any one call this an evil pride? Perhaps he belongs to that order of man who, while he has a democratic dislike to dukes and earls, wants to make believe that his father was an idle gentleman, when in fact he was an honourable artisan, or who would feel flattered to be taken for other than an Englishman. It is possible to be too arrogant about our blood or our calling, but that arrogance is virtue compared with such mean pretence. The pride which identifies us with a great historic body is a humanising, elevating habit of mind, inspiring sacrifices of individual comfort, gain, or other selfish ambition, for the sake of that ideal whole; and no man swayed by such a sentiment can become completely abject. That a Jew of Smyrna,[23] where a whip is carried by passengers ready to flog off the too officious specimens of his race, can still be proud to say, 'I am a Jew,' is surely a fact to awaken admiration in a mind capable of understanding what we may call the ideal forces in human history. And again, a varied, impartial observation of the Jews in different countries tends to the impression that they have a predominant kindliness which must have been deeply ingrained in the constitution of their race to have outlasted the ages of persecution and oppression. The concentration of their joys in domestic life has kept up in them the capacity of tenderness: the pity for the fatherless and the widow, the care for the women and the little ones, blent intimately with their religion, is a well of mercy that cannot long or widely be pent up by exclusiveness. And the kindliness of the Jew overflows the line of division between him and the Gentile. On the whole, one of the most remarkable phenomena in the history of this scattered people, made for ages 'a scorn and a hissing' is, that after being subjected to this process, which might have been expected to be in every sense deteriorating and vitiating, they have come out of it (in any estimate which allows for numerical proportion) rivalling the nations of all European countries in healthiness and beauty of *physique,* in practical ability, in scientific and artistic aptitude, and in some forms of ethical value. A significant indication of their natural rank is seen in the fact that at this moment, the leader of the Liberal party in Germany is a Jew, the leader of the Republican party in France is a Jew, and the head of the Conservative ministry in England is a Jew.[24]

And here it is that we find the ground for the obvious jealousy which is now stimulating the revived expression of old antipathies. 'The Jews,' it is felt, 'have a dangerous tendency to get the uppermost places not only in commerce but in political life. Their monetary hold on governments is tending to perpetuate in leading Jews a spirit of universal alienism (euphemistically called cosmopolitanism), even where the West has given them a full share in civil and political rights. A people with oriental sunlight in their blood, yet capable of being everywhere acclimatised, they have a force and toughness which enables them to carry off the best prizes; and their wealth is likely to put half the seats in Parliament at their disposal.'

There is truth in these views of Jewish social and political relations. But it is rather too late for liberal pleaders to urge them in a merely vituperative sense. Do they propose as a remedy for the impending danger of our healthier national influences getting overridden by Jewish predominance, that we should repeal our emancipatory laws? Not all the Germanic immigrants who have been settling among us for generations, and are still pouring in to settle, are Jews, but thoroughly Teutonic and more or less Christian craftsmen, mechanicians, or skilled and erudite functionaries; and the Semitic Christians who swarm among us are dangerously like their unconverted brethren in complexion, persistence, and wealth. Then there are the Greeks who, by the help of Phœnician blood or otherwise, are objectionably strong in the city. Some judges think that the Scotch are more numerous and prosperous here in the South than is quite for the good of us Southerners; and the early inconvenience felt under the Stuarts[25] of being quartered upon by a hungry, hard-working people with a distinctive accent and form of religion, and higher cheek-bones than English taste requires, has not yet been quite neutralised. As for the Irish, it is felt in high quarters that we have always been too lenient towards them;—at least, if they had been harried a little more there might not have been so many of them on the English press, of which they divide the power with the Scotch, thus driving many Englishmen to honest and ineloquent labour.

So far shall we be carried if we go in search of devices to hinder people of other blood than our own from getting the advantage of dwelling among us.

Let it be admitted that it is a calamity to the English, as to any other great historic people, to undergo a premature fusion with immigrants of alien blood; that its distinctive national characteristics should be in danger of obliteration by the predominating quality of foreign settlers. I not only admit this, I am ready to unite in groaning over the threatened danger. To one who loves his native language, who would delight to keep our rich and harmonious English undefiled by foreign accent, foreign intonation, and those foreign tinctures of verbal meaning which tend to confuse all writing and discourse, it is an affliction as harassing as the climate, that on our stage, in our studios, at our public and private gatherings, in our offices, warehouses, and workshops, we must expect to hear our beloved English with its words clipped, its vowels stretched and twisted, its phrases of acquiescence and politeness, of cordiality, dissidence or argument, delivered always in the wrong tones, like ill-rendered melodies, marred beyond recognition; that there should be a general ambition to speak every language except our mother English, which persons 'of style' are not ashamed of corrupting with slang, false foreign equivalents, and a pronunciation that crushes out all colour from the vowels and jams them between jostling consonants. An ancient Greek might not like to be resuscitated for the sake of hearing Homer read in our universities, still he would at least find more instructive marvels in other developments to be witnessed at those institutions; but a modern Englishman is invited from his after-dinner repose to hear Shakspere delivered under circumstances which offer no other novelty than some novelty of false intonation, some new distribution of strong emphasis on prepositions, some new misconception of a familiar idiom. Well! it is our inertness that is in fault, our carelessness of excellence, our willing ignorance of the treasures that lie in our national heritage, while we are agape after what is foreign, though it may be only a vile imitation of what is native.

This marring of our speech, however, is a minor evil compared with what must follow from the predominance of wealth-acquiring immigrants, whose appreciation of our political and social life must often be as approximative or fatally erroneous as their delivery of our language. But take the worst issues—what can we do to hinder them? Are we to adopt the exclusiveness for which we have punished the Chinese? Are we to tear the glorious flag of hospitality which has made our freedom the world-wide blessing of the oppressed? It is not agreeable to find foreign accents and stumbling locutions passing from the piquant exception to the general rule of discourse. But to urge on that account that we should spike away the peaceful foreigner, would be a view of international relations not in the long-run favourable to the interests of our fellow-countrymen; for we are at least equal to the races we call obtrusive in the disposition to settle wherever money is to be made and cheaply idle living to be found. In meeting the national evils which are brought upon us by the onward course of the world, there is often no more immediate hope or resource than that of striving after fuller national excellence, which must consist in the moulding of more excellent individual natives. The tendency of things is towards the quicker or slower fusion of races. It is impossible to arrest this tendency: all we can do is to moderate its course so as to hinder it from degrading the moral status of societies by a too rapid effacement of those national traditions and customs which are the language of the national genius—the deep suckers of healthy sentiment. Such moderating and guidance of inevitable movement is worthy of all effort. And it is in this sense that the modern insistance on the idea of Nationalities has value. That any people at once distinct and coherent enough to form a state should be held in subjection by an alien antipathetic government has been becoming more and more a ground of sympathetic indignation; and in virtue of this, at least one great State has been added to European councils.[26] Nobody now complains of the result in this case, though far-sighted persons see the need to limit analogy by discrimination. We have to consider who are the stifled people and who the stiflers before we can be sure of our ground. The only point in this connection on which Englishmen are agreed is, that England itself shall not be subject to foreign rule. The fiery resolve to resist invasion, though with an improvised array of pitchforks, is felt to be virtuous, and to be worthy of a historic people. Why? Because there is a national life in our veins. Because there is something specifically English which we feel to be supremely worth striving for, worth dying for, rather than living to renounce it. Because we too have our share—perhaps a principal share—in that spirit of separateness which has not yet done its work in the education of mankind, which has created the varying genius of nations, and, like the Muses, is the offspring of memory.

Here, as everywhere else, the human task seems to be the discerning and adjustment of opposite claims. But the end can hardly be achieved by urging contradictory reproaches, and instead of labouring after discernment as a preliminary to intervention, letting our zeal burst forth according to a capricious selection, first determined accidentally and afterwards justified by personal predilection. Not only John Gilpin and his wife, or Edwin and Angelina,[27] seem to be of opinion that their preference or dislike of Russians, Servians, or Greeks, consequent, perhaps, on hotel adventures, has something to do with the merits of the Eastern Question;[28] even in a higher range of intellect and enthusiasm we find a distribution of sympathy or pity for sufferers of different blood or votaries of differing religions, strangely unaccountable on any other ground than a fortuitous direction of study or trivial circumstances of travel. With some even admirable persons, one is never quite sure of any particular being included under a general term. A provincial physician, it is said, once ordering a lady patient not to eat salad, was asked pleadingly by the affectionate husband whether she might eat lettuce, or cresses, or radishes. The physician had too rashly believed in the comprehensiveness of the word 'salad,' just as we, if not enlightened by experience, might believe in the all-embracing breadth of 'sympathy with the injured and oppressed.' What mind can exhaust the grounds of exception which lie in each particular case? There is understood to be a peculiar odour from the negro body, and we know that some persons, too rationalistic to feel bound by the curse on Ham, used to hint very strongly that this odour determined the question on the side of negro slavery.

And this is the usual level of thinking in polite society concerning the Jews. Apart from theological purposes, it seems to be held surprising that anybody should take an interest in the history of a people whose literature has furnished all our devotional language; and if any reference is made to their past or future destinies some hearer is sure to state as a relevant fact which may assist our judgment, that she, for her part, is not fond of them, having known a Mr Jacobson who was very unpleasant, or that he, for his part, thinks meanly of them as a race, though on inquiry you find that he is so little acquainted with their characteristics that he is astonished to learn how many persons whom he has blindly admired and applauded are Jews to the backbone. Again, men who consider themselves in the very van of modern advancement, knowing history and the latest philosophies of history, indicate their contemptuous surprise that any one should entertain the destiny of the Jews as a worthy subject, by referring to Moloch and their own agreement with the theory that the religion of Jehovah was merely a transformed Moloch-worship,[29] while in the same breath they are glorifying 'civilisation' as a transformed tribal existence of which some lineaments are traceable in grim marriage customs of the native Australians. Are these erudite persons prepared to insist that the name 'Father' should no longer have any sanctity for us, because in their view of likelihood our Aryan ancestors were mere improvers on a state of things in which nobody knew his own father?[30]

For less theoretic men, ambitious to be regarded as practical politicians, the value of the Hebrew race has been measured by their unfavourable opinion of a prime minister who is a Jew by lineage. But it is possible to form a very ugly opinion as to the scrupulousness of Walpole or of Chatham;[31] and in any case I think Englishmen would refuse to accept the character and doings of those eighteenth century statesman as the standard of value for the English people and the part they have to play in the fortunes of mankind.

If we are to consider the future of the Jews at all, it seems reasonable to take as a preliminary question: Are they destined to complete fusion with the peoples among whom they are dispersed, losing every remnant of a distinctive consciousness as Jews; or, are there in the breadth and intensity with which the feeling of separateness, or what we may call the organised memory of a national consciousness, actually exists in the world-wide Jewish communities—the seven millions scattered from east to west—and again, are there in the political relations of the world, the conditions present or approaching for the restoration of a Jewish state planted on the old ground as a centre of national feeling, a source of dignifying protection, a special channel for special energies which may contribute some added form of national genius, and an added voice in the councils of the world?

They are among us everywhere: it is useless to say we are not fond of them. Perhaps we are not fond of proletaries and their tendency to form Unions, but the world is not therefore to be rid of them. If we wish to free ourselves from the inconveniences that we have to complain of, whether in proletaries or in Jews, our best course is to encourage all means of improving these neighbours who elbow us in a thickening crowd, and of sending their incommodious energies into beneficent channels. Why are we so eager for the dignity of certain populations of whom perhaps we have never seen a single specimen, and of whose history, legend, or literature we have been contentedly ignorant for ages, while we sneer at the notion of a renovated national dignity for the Jews, whose ways of thinking and whose very verbal forms are on our lips in every prayer which we end with an Amen? Some of us consider this question dismissed when they have said that the wealthiest Jews have no desire to forsake their European palaces, and go to live in Jerusalem. But in a return from exile, in the restoration of a people, the question is not whether certain rich men will choose to remain behind, but whether there will be found worthy men who will choose to lead the return. Plenty of prosperous Jews remained in Babylon when Ezra marshalled his band of forty thousand and began a new glorious epoch in the history of his race, making the preparation for that epoch in the history of the world which has been held glorious enough to be dated from for evermore. The hinge of possibility is simply the existence of an adequate community of feeling as well as widespread need in the Jewish race, and the hope that among its finer specimens there may arise some men of instruction and ardent public spirit, some new Ezras, some modern Maccabees, who will know how to use all favouring outward conditions, how to triumph by heroic example, over the indifference of their fellows and the scorn of their foes, and will steadfastly set their faces towards making their people once more one among the nations.

Formerly, evangelical orthodoxy was prone to dwell on the fulfilment of prophecy in the 'restoration of the Jews.' Such interpretation of the prophets is less in vogue now. The dominant mode is to insist on a Christianity that disowns its origin, that is not a substantial growth having a genealogy, but is a vaporous reflex of modern notions. The Christ of Matthew had the heart of a Jew—'Go ye first to the lost sheep of the house of Israel.'[32] The Apostle of the Gentiles had the heart of a Jew: 'For I could wish that myself were accursed from Christ for my brethren, my kinsmen according to the flesh: who are Israelites; to whom pertaineth the adoption, and the glory, and the covenants, and the giving of the law, and the service of God, and the promises; whose are the fathers, and of whom as concerning the flesh Christ came.'[33] Modern apostles, extolling Christianity, are found using a different tone: they prefer the mediæval cry translated into modern phrase. But the mediæval cry too was in substance very ancient—more ancient than the days of Augustus.[34] Pagans in successive ages said, 'These people are unlike us, and refuse to be made like us: let us punish them.' The Jews were steadfast in their separateness, and through that separateness Christianity was born. A modern book on Liberty[35] has maintained that from the freedom of individual men to persist in idiosyncrasies the world may be enriched. Why should we not apply this argument to the idiosyncrasy of a nation, and pause in our haste to hoot it down? There is still a great function for the steadfastness of the Jew: not that he should shut out the utmost illumination which knowledge can throw on his national history, but that he should cherish the store of inheritance which that history has left him. Every Jew should be conscious that he is one of a multitude possessing common objects of piety in the immortal achievements and immortal sorrows of ancestors who have transmitted to them a physical and mental type strong enough, eminent enough in faculties, pregnant enough with peculiar promise, to constitute a new beneficent individuality among the nations, and, by confuting the traditions of scorn, nobly avenge the wrongs done to their Fathers.

There is a sense in which the worthy child of a nation that has brought forth illustrious prophets, high and unique among the poets of the world, is bound by their visions.

Is bound?

Yes, for the effective bond of human action is feeling, and the worthy child of a people owning the triple name of Hebrew, Israelite, and Jew, feels his kinship with the glories and the sorrows, the degradation and the possible renovation of his national family.

Will any one teach the nullification of this feeling and call his doctrine a philosophy? He will teach a blinding superstition—the superstition that a theory of human wellbeing can be constructed in disregard of the influences which have made us human.

Notes

[1] The phrase 'Hep! Hep! Hep!' is an anti-Semitic cry which may have originated during the Crusades as an abbreviation of *'Hierosolyma est perdita'* (Jerusalem is lost), or perhaps as a cry used for driving herds of animals. It is the name given to a series of anti-Jewish riots which broke out in Germany in 1819.

[2] Byron died in 1824 in Missolonghi, where he had gone to help train Greek nationalists fighting against Turkish rule. Greek independence was achieved in 1830.

[3] Italian patriot and republican Giuseppe Mazzini (1805-72) who was instrumental in the unification of Italy, which was achieved in 1870.

[4] In the 1820's, Austria was an 'alien government' present in some Italian states.

[5] Italian political philosopher Niccolo Machiavelli (1469-1527), Giulio Rubini (c. 1845-1917), patriot who fought with Garibaldi in the campaign to unite Italy, and Neapolitan insurrectionist Tomasso Aniello Mansaniello (1620-47).

[6] Probably J. R. Green, author of *The History of the English People* (1878).

[7] Scandinavian name of Anglo-Saxon god Woden (one-eyed).

[8] Probably a reference to the Indian Mutiny of 1857.

[9] King Nebuchadnezzar of Babylonia captured Judah in 586 BC, destroyed the Temple, and exiled most of the Jews to Babylon. After the defeat of the Babylonians by Cyrus the Great of Persia, the Jews were allowed to return to Judah and Jerusalem. The return to Jerusalem was spread out over decades. Ezra describes the return of the Jews (c. 397) BC to a country in which the Temple had been rebuilt, but which was still dominated by pagan tribes. In addition to the Zealots (see note 12 below), there were a number of factions described by Josephus Flavius (c. AD 37-95) as fighting with the Romans between 63 BC-AD 70. His *The Jewish War* was a primary source of George Eliot's knowledge of Jewish history.

[10] The Seleucids were a Hellenistic dynasty established in Syria in 312 BC by Seleuces I. The Seleucids were an important power in the region and played a primary role in the Hellenisation of the Middle East. In 168 BC, Antiochus IV invaded Jerusalem and, in the following year, rededicated the Temple to Zeus and outlawed the Jewish religion. In 166 BC, Mattathias, a high priest, fled to the countryside with his five sons and began guerrilla war with the Seleucid conquerors. Mattathias died in 166 BC and Judas Maccabaeus took over leadership, reconquering Jerusalem in 164 BC, and rededicating the Temple. This is still marked by Chanukah. The family maintained control over the country until 63 BC when Pompey conquered it for Rome.

[11] The Zealots were a sect of Jews, driven by religious ardor and hatred of foreign occupation and paganism. Organised as a political party during the reign of Herod

the Great (37-4 BC), they conducted a campaign of violence against Roman occupation, ultimately leading to the revolt in AD 66 and the destruction of Jerusalem and the Diaspora in AD 70.

[12] The reference is to the Roman desecration of the Temple in Jerusalem by the placement of a statue of the deified emperor, Caligula, in the most sacred part of the building.

[13] The reference is to the English Civil War (1642-8) when both Puritans and Anglicans invoked biblical texts to justify opposing doctrines. James I, Stuart King of England (1603-25), was a proponent of the doctrine that kings drew their authority from God.

[14] Leaders of a rebellion against Moses and Aaron (Numbers 16:13).

[15] Extracting large sums of money on fraudulent, questionable, or arbitrary grounds. The reference is to the medieval, princely practice of forcing Jewish communities to pay large amounts of money to the local prince or King when money got tight in the royal household. These levies were not assessed against Christians.

[16] For nearly a millennium, beginning in the eighth century AD, Jews were considered unwelcome resident aliens in most European countries. Generally, they were not allowed to own land, or exercise most property rights granted to Christians. Moreover, Jews were not protected from attacks by their Christian neighbours. Some European kings and princes invited wealthy Jews, known for their commercial sagacity, to establish communities in their countries for the purpose of stimulating the economy. These Jews were given diplomas by the king, granting protection from attack, certain property rights, and often, the right to hire Christian workmen.

[17] Noah curses his son Ham (for seeing his father's nakedness) to be 'a slave of slaves' (Genesis 9:25).

[18] Matthew 27:25. The words of Jewish observers at the crucifixion of Jesus, taken as a sanction to persecute Jews for the death of Jesus.

[19] Words spoken by Jesus on the cross (Luke 23:34).

[20] Catholic Emancipation was achieved in 1829. Jews were admitted to the House of Commons in 1858.

[21] In 1866, the government of the newly united Rumania, under Alexander Cuza, enacted a constitution specifically excluding suffrage to non-Christians. This was followed by other legal restrictions on Jews and by years of anti-Semitic riots, in which many Jews were killed annually.

[22] Literally 'common body'. From the phrase: *Fiat experimentum in corpore vili* (Let the experiment be made on some common body). The phrase derives from a quotation in Antoine du Verdier's *Prosopographie . . . des hommes illustre* (Lyon, 1603) 3:2542-43.

[23] Throughout the nineteenth century, Jews living in the Turkish seaport of Smyrna were accused of the ritual murder of Christian children. The most well known of these accusations were brought in 1872, 1874, and 1876, and the cases received worldwide attention in the press.

[24] The leader of the Liberal party in Germany in 1878 was Eduard Lasker (1829-84). The leader of the Republican party in France may refer to Léon Gambetta (1804-81), who was reported to be Jewish. The head of the conservative ministry in England was Benjamin Disraeli (1804-81).

[25] The Scottish Stuarts ruled between 1603 and 1649 and were restored to the throne after the Civil War and English Commonwealth, ruling again between 1660 and 1714.

[26] Germany, which achieved total unification in 1871.

[27] See Cowper's ballad 'John Gilpin' (1782) and 'Edwin and Angelina, or the Hermit' (1764) by Goldsmith (included in *The Vicar of Wakefield*).

[28] 'The Eastern Question' was the term used in Western Europe to refer to a host of political-territorial problems related to the slow dissolution of the Ottoman Empire. The European provinces of the Empire, including Bulgaria, Bosnia, Serbia and Hercegovina were in constant turmoil beginning in the 1850s. British and French politicians were particularly concerned that the Russians would overrun these provinces and upset the carefully worked out balance of power that had been established in Europe during the first part of the century.

[29] The worship of Moloch, a Canaanite God, was distinguished by sacrifices of the first-born. The Mosaic law specifically prohibits such sacrifice: 'And thou shalt not give any of thy seed to set them apart to Moloch.' Leviticus 18:21.

[30] Cf. Ch. II, n. 23. Some anthropological theories of the late nineteenth century saw Aryan civilisation as superior to those 'less civilised' cultures, which were organised matrilineally, inheritances being established through the male relatives of the mother, rather than through the father.

[31] Benjamin Disraeli was a Jewish convert to Christianity. Robert Walpole (see Ch. XVI, n. 7) and William Pitt, First Earl of Chatham (see Ch. II, n. 2).

[32] Jesus to his disciples (Matthew 10:6).

[33] Letter of Paul to the Romans (9:3-5).

[34] 27 BC-14 AD.

[35] John Stuart Mill's *On Liberty* (1859).

Amy Levy (essay date 1886)

SOURCE: "The Jew in Fiction," in *The Jewish Chronicle,* June 4, 1886, p. 13.

[*In the following essay, Levy contends that, although Jews have secured a "prominent position" in English society, they have not been fairly represented in English novels—particularly George Eliot's novel* Daniel Deronda, *which, according to Levy, makes a "sincere and respectful attempt" at portraying Judaism but does not genuinely reflect contemporary Jewish life.*]

It is curious, that, while the prominent position of the Jew is recognised as one of the characteristic features of English social life of the present day, so small a place should be allotted him in contemporary fiction.

In finance, in politics, in society; in every branch of art and science the English Jew is to be found in a position of more or less distinction. It is only in the novel, with one notable exception, that his claims to consideration have been almost entirely overlooked. Rebecca, of York, with her hopeless love for the Gentile knight, and Isaac of York, divided, like Shylock, between his ducats and his daughter, remain to day the typical Hebrews of fiction. Dickens, as might be expected, places himself on the crudely popular side, but tries to compensate for his having affixed the label "Jew" to one of his bad fairies by creating the good fairy Riah. Thackeray has reproduced Jews in less romantic guise, as Mr. and Miss Moss of the sponging houses, and today Mr. Baring-Gould (a clergyman of the Church of England) slavishly follows the old Jew-baiting traditions in his absurd portrait of Emanuel Lazarus in *Court Royal.*

In *Daniel Deronda,* it is true, a sincere and respectful attempt was made to portray the features of modern Judaism. But which of us will not acknowledge with a sigh, that the noble spirit which conceived Mirah, Daniel and Ezra, was more royal than the king? It was, alas! no picture of Jewish contemporary life, that of the little group of enthusiasts, with their yearnings after the Holy Land and dreams of a separate nation. Nor can we derive much satisfaction from the superficial smartness of such sketches as that of Jacob Alexander Cohen and his family. As a novel treating of modern Jews, *Daniel Deronda* cannot be regarded as a success; although every Jew must be touched by, and feel

DANIEL DERONDA.

BY

GEORGE ELIOT.

IN TWO VOLUMES.

VOL. I.

HARPER'S LIBRARY EDITION.

NEW YORK:
HARPER & BROTHERS, PUBLISHERS,
FRANKLIN SQUARE.
1876.

grateful for the spirit which breathes throughout the book; perhaps, even be spurred by its influence to nobler effort, and taught a lesson, sadly needed, to hold himself and his people in greater respect.

As for Lord Beaconsfield's grandiloquent attempts in this direction, is not *Coningsby* forgotten in *Codlingsbey,* and which of us remembers the original of Raphael Mendoza?

In that clever, vulgar, unpleasant novel *Mrs. Keith's Crime* we are presented with several specimens of Jewish portraiture, which at least make some attempt at realism. Perhaps, however, no outspoken picture of Jewish vice could be so offensive as the author's condescending acknowledgement of Jewish virtue. "The Sardine," (as, with characteristic refinement, he is called throughout the book) is an impossibly slangy Jew of wealth and position, who spends his time in doing good to ungrateful Gentiles. The patronising reception of his kindness on the part of the extremely unpleasant heroine, is enough to fill with wrath the honest Semitic bosom. However, as a concession, no doubt, to modern feeling, the despised Sardine is allowed to be happy with a woman of his own race and is not, as we had expected, left forlorn at the last; a male and modern Rebecca of York. There is far more cleverness in the sketch of the elderly Jewess in the same book, with her indolence and persistence; her indifference and tenacity of purpose; a sketch which for once shows real insight into Jewish character, not mere observation of outward peculiarities.

But these and kindred efforts are, when all is said, of the slightest nature. There has been no serious attempt at serious treatment of the subject; at grappling in its entirely with the complex problem of Jewish life and Jewish character. The Jew, as we know him to-day, with his curious mingling of diametrically opposed qualities; his surprising virtues and no less surprising vices; leading his eager, intricate life, living, moving, and having his being both within and without the tribal limits; this deeply interesting product of our civilisation has been found worthy of none but the most superficial observation.

There is yet to be done for him, the comparison inevitably suggests itself, what M. Daudet has done for the inhabitants of Southern France. No picture of English 19th century life and manners can be considered complete without an adequate representation of the modern son of Shem.

While writers and readers of fiction complain that *tout est dit,* producers and consumers, alike, sending forth an Athenian cry for something new, it is strange that a field at once so rich and so untrodden, should have been almost entirely overlooked.

We have, alas! no M. Daudet among us. His mingled brilliance and solidity; his wonderful blending of picturesqueness and fidelity, have no counterparts among our own contemporary novel-writers. It is in the throng of aspirants to fame that must be sought a writer able and willing to do justice to the Jewish question in its social and psychological aspects.

Harold Fisch (essay date 1971)

SOURCE: "The Romantic Movement and Beyond," in *The Dual Image: The Figure of the Jew in English and American Literature,* KTAV Publishing House, 1971, pp. 53-79.

[*In the following essay, Fisch argues that the literature of the nineteenth-century typically portrayed Jews as evil rather than good, as representing one extreme or the other, and as not being fully integrated with the world of non-Jews.*]

The Poets

The Romantic Movement continued much of the inspiration of late eighteenth century benevolence and tolerance. Wordsworth had felt the thrill of the French Revolution and had responded to the new climate of universal brotherhood. It is not surprising therefore that his poems of humble folk, celebrating the sanctities of hearth and home, should have included one or two of Jewish interest. His *A Jewish Family* (1828) is a descriptive lyric in which the dark-brown curls of the Jewish child more or less exhaust the specifically Jewish character of the poem. His conclusion expresses a certain veneration for the unseen Guardian who has preserved Israel through history:

> Mysterious safeguard, that, in spite
> Of poverty and wrong,
> Doth here preserve a living light,
> From Hebrew fountains sprung;
> That gives this ragged group to cast
> Around the dell a gleam
> Of Palestine, of glory past,
> And proud Jerusalem!

But we should remind ourselves of a new kind of literary anti-semitism which arose as a by-product of the Enlightenment. (Among Jews also at this period and later the literary movement of Enlightenment (*Haskalah*) produced a strong anti-religious reaction.) We find in Blake as in Voltaire a hatred of the God of the Old Testament as the author of the moral law. In Blake's *Everlasting Gospel* (approx. 1818), the true Jesus is the protagonist of free-love who "lays his hand on Moses' law" and defies the God of Sinai by "putting back the bloody shrine" wherein his moral restrictions are inscribed. This mood is also exemplified by Shelley. In his early poem *Queen Mab* (1813), the free progress of mankind towards the possession of knowledge, love, and beauty in their ideal manifestations are shown to be impeded by the decrees of "tyrannous omnipotence" and his servant Moses whose history is characterised as follows:

> A Murderer heard
> His voice in Egypt, one whose gifts and arts
> Had raised him to his eminence in power,
> Accomplice of omnipotence in crime,
> And confidant of the all-knowing one.

And later, in Shelley's most mature verse-drama, *Prometheus Unbound,* the tyrant-god and enemy of the human race is Jupiter, who reveals no slight imaginative connexion with the God of the Hebrews. Clearly this ideological anti-semitism springs not so much out of a direct reaction to Jews or Judaism as out of the current revolt against evangelical orthodoxy and its negative *Christian* ethic, and also in particular it arose from the Romantic poets' hatred of the ugliness and illiberalism of the Industrial Revolution which was felt (rightly) to be associated with the religion of the nonconformist Middle Classes. This moral revolt in Blake and Shelley is thus in origin a Christian affair; it takes on an anti-semitic character through the false identification of Pauline Christianity—at war always with the World, the Flesh and the Devil—with Hebraism! (Matthew Arnold was later on guilty of the same false identification.) That anti-semitism should be produced as an extension of, and substitute for, anti-Christianity and, in particular, anti-Puritanism, is another example of that unfortunate confusion of values which we are constantly encountering in our discussion of this subject.

In Shelley's case confusion is made more confounded by the fact that in the very poem in which he first issues his defiance to the God of Israel, *viz., Queen Mab,* he also introduces as perhaps the most positive character in the poem, a character no other than Ahasuerus, the Wandering Jew. It is he who, as the author's mouthpiece, expresses the above-quoted blasphemies against the Old Testament God. Yet in contrast to the Wandering Jew as he figures in the ballads, there is here in Shelley no trace of anti-semitic feeling attaching to the Jew himself: he is rather a symbol of endurance "peaceful, and serene, and self-enshrined."

There is no doubt that the Wandering Jew exercised a peculiar compulsion over the romantic imagination. Both Wordsworth and Shelley were deeply impressed by the legend (though Wordsworth's *Song* for the Wandering Jew could equally well have been a song for the Wandering Indian or even for the Leech-gatherer). Shelley treated the subject five times. In his dramatic poem *Hellas,* Ahasuerus appears to reveal to Mahmud the secrets of the past and future:

> What has thought
> To do with time, or place, or circumstance,
> Wouldst thou behold the future? ask and have!
> Knock and it shall be opened—look, and lo!
> The coming age is shadowed on the past
> As on a glass.

Ahasuerus has insight into those truths which remain unchanged in a world of mutability. This positive approach to the legendary Ahasuerus is, however, only made possible by the weakening of the hold of Christian dogma which had earlier served to emphasise the disagreeable traits of the Wandering Jew. Thus we see how the processes of the Enlightenment served at the same time to promote a higher anti-semitism and to make possible a noble and tragic portrayal of the Jew of legend! The interest of the Ahasuerus story for Shelley and Wordsworth had nothing to do with its earlier use as an expression of Christian apologetics: indeed, insofar as the Wandering Jew was a recipient of the Divine curse, he was a figure to be pitied and admired. One could go further and say that the poets tended to identify themselves with the awesome and tragic figure of the Jew: this was especially the case with Shelley, who was an outcast, or at least a voluntary exile, and a rebel against the existing order. The romantic poet liked to think of himself as "a man of sorrows" elected for peculiar privilege and peculiar sufferings, and in the Wandering Jew he found the true model for such a self-portrait.

Coleridge's celebrated poem *The Ancient Mariner,* provides another example of the influence of the Wandering Jew story. There is good evidence that many touches in the mariner's guilt, his expiation, and his extraordinary sub-reading of the legend in M. G. Lewis's fantastic novel *The Monk* (1796) where the Wandering Jew specializes in exorcism and the uncovering of guilty secrets. The mariner's guilt, his expiation, and his extraordinary subsequent relation to society as well as the extent of his travels and his experience of life, all are features belonging to the legend; at the same time they reflect the peculiar burdens, obsessions, and intensities of the *poète maudit* of later romanticism.

All this suggests that the romantic poets were interested in Ahasuerus as a projection of themselves rather than in bestowing upon him a distinctive Jewish conscience or colouring. On the other hand, he does signify for them something which belongs essentially to the *rôle* of the Jew among the nations—he signifies the historical consciousness and memory of Man. The Jew, bringing with him, as it were about his person, the records and recollections of antiquity, is the supreme symbol of race-memory. He walks through history from the beginning to the end: he endures whilst the nations come and go, and therefore he stirs both awe and terror in the beholder. Part of the terror which the Jew inspires is due to the ancestral guilt which the beholder seeks to hide from himself and which the Jew as it were inevitably brings back to remembrance. In the medieval period, that very guilt is transferred by subsitution to the Wandering Jew himself: but the awe remains, investing the figure of Ahasuerus with sombre dignity.

In the late nineteenth century, Robert Buchanan wrote a poem of *The Wandering Jew,* which completely reverses the tradition. In it, the Jew is identified with the Christian Messiah still trying to save the world—but failing because the world's sinfulness, evidenced by its maltreatment of the Jew, is still too great. This comes near to the underlying psychological motive behind the medieval legend.

A more Hebraic tone than Shelley achieves and a more direct delineation of the Jew in history is introduced in Byron's *Hebrew Melodies.* Again the approach to the Jew is positive, even enthusiastically positive. Byron's Biblical drama *Cain,* whilst raising moral issues which one might suspect belong more to Byron's personal history than to an exegesis of the book of *Genesis,* likewise bespeaks a keen and vivid sense of the dramatic power of the Hebrew oracles. The Cain figure also, as G. K. Anderson has shown, embodies many features of the Wandering Jew. Both Cain and the Wandering Jew (in Lewis's *The Monk,* for instance) bear a mark on their forehead. Byron is here again seeking to exhibit his Romantic sense of guilt. The Jew is seen—like the poet—to bear both curse and blessing. But the brighter side of romanticism is also, for Byron, to be found in the Jew. He finds in him a national pride and a love of freedom with which he readily sympathizes. Had the issue of a Jewish national renaissance arisen in his day, we may be sure he would have sacrificed himself as readily for it as he did in the cause of Greek independence.

It seems that the new spirit of tolerance, combined with a general weakening of Christian orthodoxy as a compelling force in poetry, resulted in a presentation of the Jew in poetry which had all the compassion we noticed in Herbert and Vaughan in the seventeenth century but none of their theological questionings and rebukes. Byron's well-known stanza exemplifies the romantic poet's feeling for those who suffer from man's inhumanity to man:

> Tribes of the wandering foot and weary breast,
> How shall ye flee away and be at rest!
> The wild-dove hath her nest, the fox his cave,
> Mankind their country—Israel but the grave!

There is no difficulty now in the poet's identifying himself with suffering Israel, for he is not troubled by any conflicting loyalty. Indeed the romantic poet is himself in revolt against the constricting and stultifying forces (as he conceives them) of Christian morality and Christian institutions, and the Jew may become for him a symbol of a more liberal spirituality, and the Hebraism of the Old Testament may become on some occasions a source of moral and literary inspiration more human and realistic than the austere creed of Puritanism could afford. A line may be traced from Bishop Lowth's *Lectures on the Sacred Poetry of the Hebrews* (1753), through Bishop Percy's prose translation of the *Song of Songs* (1764), to Blake's *Jerusalem* (1804) and Byron's *Hebrew Melodies* (1815).

Browning, later in the nineteenth century, does not find his inspiration in the Old Testament, but he can find no better mouthpiece for his own liberal this-worldly, life-affirming ethical philosophy than the medieval Rabbi Ben Ezra (R. Abraham Ibn Ezra, 1093-1167). His acute understanding of human nature, and his psychological interests, lead him to sympathise with odd people in odd situations. In *Holy Cross Day,* he imagines what the Jews really said to one another when they were driven to Church to hear a compulsory sermon in Rome. The poem reveals a certain insight into Jewish psychology: but more than that it reveals a sardonic humour, and a satirical enjoyment of the hypocrisies of the Roman Catholic hierarchy. But this comic vein gives way at the end to a sombre note of religious meditation and hope, in what he calls "Ben Ezra's Song of Death":

> The Lord will have mercy on Jacob yet,
> And again in his border see Israel set.
> When Judah beholds Jerusalem,
> The stranger-seed shall be joined to them:
> To Jacob's House shall the Gentiles cleave.
> So the prophet saith and his sons believe.

Examples of sympathetic treatments of Jewish types and of a sympathetic handling of the Jewish problem can be multiplied from the minor poetry of the nineteenth century. But we should remind ourselves that the romantic poets and their followers represented, not the practical sentiment of the century, so much as the fine flower of its idealism. They spoke and sang as the heralds of truths which mankind had not yet achieved and (so the poet sometimes hints) of truths never likely to be achieved. For the poet in his own private world the Messiah has already come and the lion may forthwith lie down with the lamb. But as far as the social order is concerned, the ugliness of the Industrial Revolution and the desperate poverty and inhumanity which it brought in its wake suggest a world in which romantic sentiment has very little part to play. The poet with his sense of compassion, and his sense of beauty both in nature and in human relationships, is henceforward something of an outcast and exile from "the darkling plain" where as Matthew Arnold said, "ignorant armies clash by night." And because he is fundamentally an exile and outcast he sympathises with the nation of exiles and outcasts—the Jews. But in the world of hard realities, of hatreds, of new and old antagonisms, the bright flower of romantic love and sentiment blooms rarely, and for this harsher world it is the novelist rather than the poet who speaks.

The Novelists

Our attention is first drawn to Scott's *Ivanhoe* (1819) as the first full-length treatment of the Jewish character in nineteenth century English fiction. Scott was himself a romantic poet, and much of the sentiment of benevolence as well as the idealism which we have noted in the previous chapter clings to his picture of Isaac of York and his daughter Rebecca. Scott's medieval tale is a serious effort to visualise the Jew in medieval society and to combat as soberly as possible the prejudices he there aroused. But Scott tries to preserve a balance, and whilst attributing the disagreeable aspects of the Jewish character to the effects of Christian oppression, he nevertheless gives considerable weight to them in his description of Isaac:

> Introduced with little ceremony, and advancing with fear and hesitation, and many a bow of deep humility, a tall thin old man, who, however, had lost by the habit of stooping much of his actual height, approached the lower end of the board. His features, keen and regular, with an aquiline nose, and piercing black eyes; his high and wrinkled forehead, and long grey hair and beard, would have been considered as handsome, had they not been the marks of a physiognomy peculiar to a race, which during those dark ages, was alike detested by the credulous and prejudiced vulgar, and persecuted by the greedy and rapacious nobility, and who, perhaps, owing to that very hatred and persecution, had adopted a national character, in which there was much, to say the least, mean and unamiable.

Isaac is a usurer, and the various epigraphs to the chapters in which he appears indicate his lineage from Shylock. But Scott's enlightened understanding forbids him to see Isaac at any time as a bloodthirsty villain: a materialist and coward, yes, but a villain, no. Scott's picture of the medieval usurer is, in short, humanised to the point of making him, if not a sympathetic picture, at any rate an understandable one.

With Issac's daughter Rebecca it is different. On her the author lavishes all the beauty and goodness which his romantic imagination could conceive. We note again the black and white, or at any rate, grey and white, contrast between the Jew and his daughter, as in Shakespeare. Rebecca is the true heroine of the novel, endearing herself to the reader even more than the nominal heroine Rowena, because, as a Jewess, she has to suffer from undeserved discrimination. The hero, Ivanhoe, rescues her from death, but the reader is deprived of the normal romantic ending in which the beautiful lady and her rescuer proceed to nuptualities, because of the insurmountable racial and religious barriers between them. Her sad plight as the beatiful and tragically lonely Jewess is sufficient to arouse the tender emotions, but she is also meant to inspire admiration and respect through her wisdom and her well-aimed criticism of medieval society. In her speeches, the novelist voices his opinions on the bloodthirstiness of the tourney and the moral emptiness of the code of chivalry as a whole. The Jew may be unduly preoccupied with money but he no longer carries blood-guiltiness; that is squarely placed to the account of the Jew's enemies. Nor indeed is Israel in its historical ancestry and origin a nation of misers and usurers. In her final debate with her would-be seducer, the villainous Knight Templar, Bois-Guilbert, Rebecca eloquently and proudly describes the past glories of her people (in this of course very unlike the apostate type of good Jewess in Marlowe and Shakespeare) and recommends the knight to read in the Old Testament of the ancient Israelite stock of noblemen and heroes:

> Such were the princes of Judah, now such no more!—They are trampled down like the shorn grass, and mixed with the mire of the ways. Yet there are those among them who shame not such high descent, and of such shall be the daughter of Isaac the son of Adonikam! Farewell! I envy not thy blood-won honours—I envy not thy barbarous descent from northern heathens—I envy thee not thy faith, which is ever in thy mouth, but never in thy heart nor in thy practice.

That is the high water-mark of moral passion as expressed in this novel, and it is significant that such idealistic utterances are given to the Jewess rather than to any other character.

It is notable that the Jew is here used to shoot the arrows of bourgeois realism and bourgeois morality against the false values of the aristocracy. This is the inner meaning of the debate between Rebecca and Bois-Guilbert. In a sense this is already anticipated in Shakespeare who sets off Shylock and his world against the tinsel landscape of Belmont. The novel as it developed in the seventeenth and eighteenth centuries developed this confrontation as a major theme. For the novel was the literary medium of the rising middle class. Rebecca has the same lesson to teach Bois-Guilbert as Fanny has for the impudent Squire Didapper in Fielding's *Joseph Andrews.* The Jew with his sturdy respectability and family loyalty has become the hero of a middle class fable. And this aspect will reappear again in numerous authors down to E. M. Forster and C. P. Snow in our own century.

The mere fact that the Jew has become the hero of a realistic work of fiction is significant. In the Middle Ages such Jewish characters are represented only by the Israelites of Old Testament antiquity: from Judas onward it is felt that the character of the Jew has somehow radically changed for the worse—that is, unless he adopts Christianity. The fact that favourable, even ecstatically favourable, portraits of *post-Biblical* Jews can now appear in literature shows that this theological distinction has now no meaning for the romantic writer. But that does not mean that the dual image has been abolished. It is simply that the dividing line has shifted. There is Rebecca, but there is also Isaac. Earlier on, Maria Edgeworth had produced two contrasting types, the bad Jew Mordecai in *The Absentee* (1812) and the white Jew Mr. Montenero in *Harrington* (1817).

Scott, towards the end of his life, drew a further set of Jewish characters in *The Surgeon's Daughter* (1827). These are far less sympathetic than the Jews of *Ivanhoe.* Richard Middlemas, the half-Jewish rogue, is in particular ambitious, violent, and treacherous. The novel ends somewhat extravagantly with Richard being crushed to death by an elephant in India.

In realistic fiction, the Jew is more likely to be a figure of evil than a figure of good. We may instance Charles Kingsley's *Alton Locke* (1850) in which Jews are mentioned exclusively in connexion with the evils of the new sweat-shops in the tailoring industry. Thackeray very often turns his attention (in a rather incidental way) to Jews, and invariably treats them to a little pleasant sarcasm on the score of their supposed deceits and malpractices. His keen powers of social satire likewise find an easy target in the *nouveau riche* type of Jew trying to get on in gentile society. Such references in his novels tend to be merely incidental: in his journalistic work, as for instance in his account of his trip to Palestine (*From Cornhill to Cairo,* 1846), he reveals a more vicious strain of anti-semitism.

The most celebrated treatment of the Jew in Victorian fiction is of course to be found in Dickens. In the character of Fagin, the receiver of stolen goods, as presented in *Oliver Twist* (1837-8), Dickens has given a caricature portrait of the evil Jew of legend. The medieval details are curiously correct: his red hair, his blasphemies, his penchant for drugs and poisoning, his blood-guiltiness, and his grotesque humour. But the figure is secularised. He is not the enemy of Christianity, so much as the enemy of all good folk with kindly souls. He is simply the villain writ large, and more disagreeable even than Bill Sykes because his villainy is of the cunning and calculating kind rather than simply a matter of brutishness. Fagin is always "The Jew," and Dickens is here clearly not so much exploring a contemporary type as working on a stock figure associated in the public imagination with the word 'Jew.' Thus his character of Fagin testifies to the continuing vitality of the Judas-Devil myth in spite of the new liberal atmosphere which, as it happens, Dickens himself in other respects helped so much to diffuse.

Dickens was rebuked by a Jewish lady, Mrs. Eliza Davis for his injustice to the Jewish race in *Oliver Twist,* and perhaps this prompted him to balance the portrait some years later in *Our Mutual Friend* (1864-5). There he gives us Mr. Riah, the Jewish agent, who is as good and well-meaning as Fagin was crafty and villainous. Fascination Fledgeby, Riah's gentile employer, is now the crafty unscrupulous and avaricious wretch of the Fagin type! The *rôles* have been exactly reversed:

> "Now, you sir!" cried Fledgeby. "These are nice games!"
>
> He addressed an old Jewish man in an ancient coat, long of skirt, and wide of pocket. A venerable man, bald and shining at the top of his head, and with long grey hair flowing down at its sides and mingling with his beard. A man who, with a graceful Eastern action of homage, bent his head and stretched out his hands with the palms downwards, as if to deprecate the wrath of a superior.
>
> "What have you been up to?" said Fledgeby, storming at him.
>
> "Generous Christian master," urged the Jewish man, "it being holiday, I looked for no one."
>
> "Holiday be blowed!" said Fledgeby, entering. "What have you got to do with holidays? Shut the door." . . .
>
> Perched on the stool, with his hat cocked on his head, and one of his legs dangling, the youth of Fledgeby hardly contrasted to advantage with the age of the Jewish man as he stood with his bare head bowed, and his eyes (which he only raised in speaking) on the ground. His clothing was worn down to the rusty hue of the hat in the entry, but though he looked shabby, he did not look mean. Now, Fledgeby, though not shabby, did look mean.
>
> "You have not told me what you were up to, you sir," said Fledgeby, scratching his head with the brim of his hat.
>
> "Sir, I was breathing the air."
>
> "In the cellar, that you didn't hear?"
>
> "On the house-top."
>
> "Upon my soul! That's a way of doing business."
>
> "Sir," the old man represented with a grave and patient air, "there must be two parties to the transaction of business, and the holiday has left me alone." . . .
>
> "Your people need speak the truth sometimes, for they lie enough," remarked Fascination Fledgeby.
>
> "Sir, there is," returned the old man with quiet emphasis, "too much untruth among all denominations of men."
>
> Rather dashed, Fascination Fledgeby took another scratch at his intellectual head with his hat, to gain time for rallying.
>
> "For instance," he resumed, as though it were he who had spoken last, "who but you and I ever heard of a poor Jew?"
>
> "The Jews," said the old man, raising his eyes from the ground with his former smile. "They hear of poor Jews often, and are very good to them."

Here then is Dickens's contribution to the formulation of the dual image. He gives us the figure of the Jew who preys upon all good folk, corrupts youth and compasses every sort of crime; and he gives us the Jew who protects the weak and fatherless and humbly submits to calumny and ill-treatment. But in a way both are neutral portraits—they have neither of them much specific Jewish quality. Fagin with few alterations could be interchanged with some other particularly detestable villain in the Dickens canon; Mr. Riah has little to distinguish him from the hundred other kindly old gentlemen in humble occupations invented by the same author. The identification of them as Jews simply gives them extra piquancy by drawing upon a well-established and colourful convention which would help to control the audience's reaction to their characters.

On the whole, the Victorian novelists stick to the stereotyped figure of the Jew. Charles Reade presents as a central character in his novel *It Is Never Too Late to Mend* (1856) a Jew, Isaac Levi, who starts out by being more sinned against than sinning, but ends by taking a terrible revenge on his foe, the rascally John Meadows. Reade's point seems to be, as Rosenberg points out, that "behind every Sheva lurks a Shylock." Anthony Trollope gives us in *The Way We Live Now* (1875) the fantastically wicked Jew Augustus Melmotte drawn on the gigantic scale of melodrama and with no attempt at verisimilitude. But the most grotesquely infamous Jew of all is that of George Du Maurier in *Trilby* (1894). Here the traditional stereotypes are made more sinister by the influence of late nineteenth century philosophies of race. Svengali, the villain of that novel, is the evil Jew of tradition, a mixture of Shylock and the Wandering Jew: he is also the eternal alien, mysterious and dark. Du Maurier makes no claim to realism. He is writing a kind of Gothic thriller in which much of the audience's interest is focused on the occult powers of Svengali. Svengali is a preternatural genius in two senses: first, he has an incredible musical ability, transporting his hearers into heaven with holy raptures; second, he is a mesmerist having occult powers which he exercises over the heroine, Trilby. He is able to convert her very ordinary nondescript voice into that of a nightingale. But the dominant reaction that he arouses in the audience is that of loathing and fear. He belongs to an inferior race, and his courting of the heroine is evidently intended to symbolize the corruption of the pure white races by the leering and evil Semite.

But nineteenth century theories of race did not always work to the detriment of the Jews. George Eliot (*alias* Mary Ann Evans) wrote her famous last novel *Daniel Deronda* (1875) largely under the impact of the new interest in nationalism and ethnology. Differences of nationality are important and should be respected. Moreover, the acknowledgment of this leads her (as it led Disraeli earlier in the century) to a high estimation of the function of the Jews in the economy of mankind. For her the Jewish nation was by no means inferior to the rest. The opposite was the case. Instead of Svengali, the Jewish oriental, levelling his evil charm against the representative of the purer white races, we have the high-minded Jew, Deronda, seeking to help the erring British maiden, Gwendolen Harleth who, throughout the novel, is suffering rather severe domestic troubles. Deronda also (like Svengali) exercises a kind of mesmeric charm over the English maiden (this is stressed in the first Chapter of *Daniel Deronda*) but there is not the least trace of sexual exploitation on the part of Deronda. If anything, it is Gwendolen who allows herself to become attracted to Deronda. She would have liked to marry him, but she must learn by the end of the novel to keep her distance, whilst Deronda devotes himself to the solution of problems far transcending her little sphere.

As a study of the Jewish problem George Eliot's novel does not lack comprehensiveness. She is capable of drawing the unprepossessing Jewish *petit-bourgeois* in the person of Ezra Cohen, who passes from his Friday night sanctities to his pawnbroking business, and drives a hard bargain with Deronda over a diamond ring. But this character of "oily cheerfulness" represents only a marginal example of Jewish psychology—the real duality which confronts the serious students of Jewry is formed by the Jew who accepts and acknowledges his Jewish identity on the one hand, and the Jew who tries to escape from it on the other. The former is, in Sartre's terms, the authentic Jew: the latter is the inauthentic. George Eliot has got near enough to Jewish life to discover this crucial determinant of Jewish character. The inauthentic Jew yields a psychology marked by evasiveness, self-contempt, and weakness; the authentic Jew bears the burden of the exile with a certain pride, nourishes the promises of the past and the hope of the future, and lives his real life inwardly rather than in a vain attempt to "normalize" his status in the gentile world. Deronda who discovers his Jewish parentage in the course of the book is such a person: the discovery leads to new self-respect, new and galvanizing life-aims, and a sense of high purpose shared with the collectivity of Israel. But in the Philosophers' Club, the group of Jews to whom he resorts for enlightenment on matters Jewish, Daniel meets both types of Jews. On the one hand, there is Gideon, who believed in a reformed Judaism (like so many nineteenth century emancipated Jews whom George Eliot would have met). He wanted a faith adapted to a non-Jewish environment with all the stress removed from nationality and exclusiveness:

> I'm a rational Jew myself. I stand by my people as a sort of family relations, and I am for keeping up my worship in a rational way. I don't approve of our people being baptised . . . But I am for getting rid of our superstitions and exclusiveness. There's no reason now why we shouldn't melt gradually into the populations we live among.

Mordecai, on the other hand, is the Jewish sage and intellectual, knowing too much of the history and wisdom of Israel to overvalue the benefits of Western liberalism and of the new, shallow rationalism and egalitarianism which had seduced his brethren. He declares:

> Each nation has its own work, and is a member of the world, enriched by the work of each. But it is true, as Jehuda-ha-Levi first said, that Israel is the heart of mankind, if we mean by heart the core of affections which binds a race and its families in dutiful love, and the reverence for the human body which lifts the needs of our animal life into religion. . . . Where else is there a nation of whom it may be as truly said that their religion and law and moral life mingled as the stream in the heart and made one growth . . . ?

Mordecai's religious Zionism, his demand to "Revive the organic centre," gives the book, in its historical context, an oddly prophetic character, but even in the generation before Herzl, Zionist sentiments were in the air (witness the work of Rabbi Zwi Hirsch Kalischer and Moses Hess), and George Eliot's intuition of this was part of her general understanding for contemporary ideological trends shown in her work as a whole. In this case, her book even helped to stimulate the Zionist renaissance through its impact on men like Eliezer ben Yehudah, the restorer of the Hebrew language, as well as on writers such as Peretz Smolenskin. She had shown that she had more than an intelligent sympathy for Jews; she had a real and detailed knowledge of Jewish thought and tradition of a kind unprecedented in Christian writers in this country, at any rate in the field of *belles lettres.* And she sets a high standard in this respect for her successors.

Nevertheless, it should be added that literary critics from Henry James to F. R. Leavis have criticized this novel in comparison with other works of Eliot. They have complained that the whole Zionist part is inflated and rhetorical, and they have focused attention rather on the English upper middle-class characters, Gwendolen and Henleigh Grandcourt, whose domestic drama of tragic misalliance occupies much of the forefront of attention. This side of the novel, it is claimed, is marked by a closer attention to psychological realism and a more minute study of social manners. Leavis has even suggested cutting out the Zionist side by a kind of critical surgery and renaming the novel *Gwendolen Harleth!*

It is true that there are stylistic and tonal differences between the two halves of the book, but George Eliot was herself aware of this and yet claimed very emphatically that "everything in the book is to be related to everything else there." She intended the contrast between the English upper class world and its values on the one hand, and the world of the Jew carrying his historic burden on the other. The one is marked by minute observation of manners and morals, the other by the grander gestures of the epic, by a more eloquent style and a more Gothic tone. It is the conjunction of romance and realism that she is aiming it. The Jew seeking his historical destiny is the Romantic—she says so in Chapter XLI—whilst Gwendolen weighing her marriage prospects and making her small social calculations is the heroine of a drama of manners.

> Could there be a slenderer, more insignificant thread in human history than this consciousness of a girl, busy with her small inferences of the way in which she could make her life pleasant?—in a time too when ideas were with fresh vigour making armies of themselves, and the universal kinship was declaring itself fiercely. (Chapter XI.)

In putting side by side the universal stream of ideas represented by Deronda, and the private *Biedermeier* world of Gwendolen, and in allowing the two characters to come together for discussion and mutual aid, Eliot has a definite purpose. It is to provide an ironical perspective, a contrast. She is trying to show the limitations of the English upper middle class. In much the same way, Meredith in *The Tragic Comedians* (1880) had introduced the romantic revolutionary figure Alvan (a *persona* for the Jewish socialist leader Ferdinand Lassalle) into a circle of German provincial aristocracy. George Eliot and Meredith are trying to show what happens when genius irrupts into provincial decorum, when dramatically and unpredictably,

> After the cups the marmalade, the tea,
> Among the porcelain, among some talk of you
> and me—

someone appears who dares to disturb the universe and roll it towards some overwhelming question.

Eliot's aim is to create something like Tolstoy's *War and Peace,* where the doings of the characters, their loves and disappointments are set off against the august backdrop of the Napoleonic invasion of Russia. She is seeking to give to the everyday doings of the English middle classes the same Tolstoyan range and depth. She had achieved something like this some years earlier in *Middlemarch* (1871), introducing a St. Theresa figure into an English country town. But Dorothea finally abandons her exalted destiny and relapses into mere provinciality. She hoped to do even better by introducing the Jew as the connecting link between the quotidian and the sublime in *Daniel Deronda.* Eliot had noticed that among the Jews it was possible for the ordinary to co-exist with the extraordinary, the visionary gleam with the materialism of everyday, as in Rembrandt's Jewish portraiture. What she found in the household of Ezra Cohen was a huckster and a prophet (Mordecai) sharing the same roof:

> It was an unaccountable conjunction—the presence among these common prosperous, shopkeeping types,

of a man who in emaciated threadbare condition, imposed a certain awe on Deronda. (Chapter XXXIV.)

It was an "unaccountable conjunction" in general, but accountable she hints in terms of the special conditions of Jewish existence. Here messianic zeal can function against a background of the tawdry and the humdrum. George Eliot had an intuition of the peculiar exposure of Jews to world history. The grander movements of ideas, the history of nations is very much her theme. And the Jew is here peculiarly in place, for he lives in the glare of world history: the destiny of nations is his private destiny. He may try to retire from history into some domestic Dutch interior—and no-one knows better than he how to contrive such domesticity—but in the end (as the twentieth century has taught us) history will find him out. The introduction of the Jew into the setting of the English middle class as represented by Grandcourt, Gwendolen, and Mr. Bult thus enabled Eliot to operate with two time-schemes, the time of personal living and the time of nations, of historic epochs, and to somehow relate the two together.

This was her aim. Yet it must be admitted that the attempt does not wholly succeed. The Jewish part of the book is not fully integrated with the rest. To that extent the disjunctive critics are right. Perhaps the basic difficulty is that George Eliot, in spite of her great sympathy with the Jewish characters, is really observing them from the outside, from a standpoint within the Gwendolen-Grandcourt world. She does not achieve a sufficiently massive realization of Jewish experience from within. Her Jewish characters, especially Daniel and Mordecai, take on an etherealized pre-Raphaelite quality which is never wholly dispelled. They do not achieve the same substantiality as Mr. Bult and the Rev. Gascoigne belonging as they do to a circle whom George Eliot knew so much better. Thus the two images never really coincide. The Jew, as so often in history itself, refuses to assimilate and the non-Jew refuses to assimilate him.

The problem of focusing the novel (which is what finally defeats the author) is at bottom the problem of producing a coherent image of the Jew and his relation to the non-Jew. The dual image haunts the novelist's work at the technical level when it has been banished from his consciousness and moral outlook, creating distance where he requires proximity, strangeness where he requires intimacy, shrillness where he requires quiet persuasiveness. And we may suspect that the same dual image will remain—for the non-Jewish writer at any rate—until such time as Jew and gentile have found some common basis from which to view their respective destinies in the world.

The Jewish Contribution

One great and important change which took place in the course of the nineteenth century was that Jews themselves were emerging on the scene as writers of novels and plays, and a considerable Anglo-Jewish reading public had formed itself. One senses that Eliot's *Daniel Deronda* was written very much with an eye for Jewish readers, and perhaps this led to a greater sense of responsibility in the handling of Jewish characters. On the whole, the portrait of the Jew becomes more charitable, for this reason. A conversionist novel such as Charlotte Elizabeth Phelan's *Judah's Lion* (1843), breathes a strain of love and admiration for Jewry and preaches Israel regenerate and revived upon his own soil:

> I speak of Israel as a nation, now a sapless trunk indeed, blighted and naked, and to all appearance dead: but for the sake of the root, which was holy before God, he will once more cause life to circulate, and the old tree to put forth leaves and branches yet again: ay, and such branches too shall overshadow the whole earth.

Here is once again the parable of the good olive tree as in George Herbert's poem, *The Jews,* and in this novel too the chief Jewish characters are eventually converted to Christianity so ushering in the dawn of a new and blissful era for mankind. The novel is, from a literary point of view, not particularly important but shows a certain interest in contemporary Jewry and in the Jewish political future in the Holy Land.

The most illustrious Jewish convert to Christianity in the nineteenth century, Benjamin Disraeli, also wrote novels in which both the People and the Land of Israel figure, but they never seem to carry that powerful Christian message that Miss Phelan addressed to her readers. Sometimes one thinks that Disraeli was less interested in converting his Jewish friends to Christianity than in bringing the gentiles to a proper appreciation of Judaism, "What, I convert to Christianity?", he once said, "Why it is the Gentiles who are converts to Judaism!" His first novel, *David Alroy,* (1832), is an historical extravaganza set in the twelfth century in which the chief characters, Alroy, the legendary descendant of the House of David, and Jabaster, the High Priest, conspire to lead the Jews of Azerbaijan back to Palestine, there to restore the Jewish kingdom. The plan comes to nothing, but Alroy triumphs as a tragic hero by preferring death to apostasy. All Disraeli's novels are autobiographical, and here there is no doubt that he has dreamed himself into the heroism of Alroy on the one hand, and the priestly piety of Jabaster on the other. The novel thus tells us a great deal about Disraeli's subconscious (and perhaps not only subconscious) self-identification with Jewry and Judaism. On the other hand it is not so well informed in matters of Jewish literature and history as, say, George Eliot's *Daniel Deronda,* and his Jewish characters fail to convince as objective portraits.

In his more mature novels, Disraeli constantly reverts to Jews, Jerusalem, and the Jewish question. In *Coningsby* (1844), he gives us the character of Sidonia (again a subjective fantasy), whose superhuman gifts of wisdom and knowledge are placed at the disposal of the hero in his attempts to revitalise English political life:

> Sidonia had exhausted all the sources of human knowledge; he was master of the learning of every nation, of all tongues dead or living, of every literature, Western and Oriental. He had pursued the speculations of science to their last term, and had himself illustrated them by observation and experiment. He had lived in all orders of society, had viewed every combination of Nature and of Art, and had observed man under every phasis of civilisation. He had even studied him in the wilderness. The influence of creeds and laws, manners, customs, traditions, in all their diversities, had been subjected to his personal scrutiny . . .
>
> One source of interest Sidonia found in his descent and in the fortunes of his race. As firm in his adherence to the code of the great Legislator as if the trumpet still sounded on Sinai, he might have received in the conviction of divine favour an adequate compensation for human persecution. But there were other and more terrestrial considerations that made Sidonia proud of his origin, and confident in the future of his kind. Sidonia was a great philosopher, who took comprehensive views of human affairs, and surveyed every fact in its relative position to other facts, the only mode of obtaining truth.

Israel Zangwill (1864-1926)

Here is the omnicompetent and omniscient Jew of Disraeli's imagination. He appears again in *Tancred* (1847) guiding in some mysterious way the destinies of Tancred, the hero whose self-appointed task it is to revive the power and influence of the Church of England! There is clearly some psychological confusion here. The form that the dual image takes in Disraeli is a product of the peculiar distortions of his Judeo-Christian mentality. On the one hand, he celebrates Jews like Sidonia, Besso, and Eva (another perfect and beautiful Jewess of the Rebecca-Mirah family whom his hero meets in Jerusalem); on the other hand, his hero is committed to the doctrine of salvation through the universal reign of the Christian King and Saviour. If Disraeli distributed part of himself (or at least part of his imagined self) to Sidonia, he also distributed part of himself to Tancred, the young Anglican apostle, to Contarini Fleming, the outsider trying to get on in an alien environment, and to Vivian Grey, the rather precocious and ineffectual aspirant to fame. On the one hand, Disraeli spends his life in trying to establish himself successfully in the world of British politics by making himself into the most perfect English aristocrat; on the other hand, he makes satirical fun in *Tancred* of the "Mesdemoiselles Laurella" who were "ashamed of their race and not fanatically devoted to their religion" and in the perfect style of the assimilated Jewess of English society, he makes Sophonisbe declare that "the Jews would not be so much disliked if they were better known; that all they had to do was to imitate as closely as possible the habits and customs of the nation among whom they chanced to live . . ." On the one hand, Disraeli constantly declares his belief in the principle of race, maintaining that the Jews were the purest race in the world; and yet his efforts are devoted to the greater glory of England, and of the English Church and Nation as the New Israel destined to govern an Empire in which all the dreams of the prophets of Israel are to be fulfilled! It is no wonder that Disraeli's romantic ideas were received with some uneasiness both by Jew and Gentile. He represents, both in his life and in his work, a peculiar and complex example of the dual image.

However much Disraeli may have been preoccupied by Jews and the Jewish Question (his full-scale treatment of the latter is contained in his *Life of Lord Bentinck,* 1852) his novels were primarily addressed to, and read by, the Great British Public as a whole. Literature more exclusively aimed at the Anglo-Jewish reader becomes more important as the century proceeds. One begins with such a pious and well-intentioned novelist as Grace Aguilar (1816-1847), whose *Characters and Sketches from the Holy Scriptures and Jewish History,* represented the kind of domestic literature of edification for the Anglo-Jewish family in the earlier nineteenth century. A franker and more critical exposition of the life of the Jewish middle-class is provided by Amy Levy, author of *Reuben Sachs* (1889). And by the end of the century, we come upon Israel Zangwill producing a body of work of rich variety and literary significance. His is a unique contribution to Anglo-Jewish letters, and his portrait of the Jew represents a gallery of types of the first importance for the understanding of our subject.

Zangwill achieved that specifically Jewish combination of comedy and pathos which we recognise in Peretz and Sholom Aleichem on the continent. He first appears on the Anglo-Jewish literary scene as a writer of humorous short stories rather in the manner of his friend Jerome K. Jerome, with a dash of rich caricature reminiscent of Dickens. His *King of Schnorrers* (1894) is a good example of his early style with its truly great comic figure, Manasseh Bueno Barzilai Azavedo da Costa. Laughter is the medium through which we view him, but it is a laughter which holds in solution the two parts of his character; the Schnorrer (professional beggar) with his home-made turban, his grotesque overcoat, his deceits, his sloth, his roguery; and the king, with his pride, his consciousness of his Sephardi superiority his unfailing dignity, his resourcefulness, and his apt quotations from the Talmud. In his meeting with the financier, Grobstock, he is described as "towering above the unhappy capitalist, like an ancient prophet denouncing a swollen monarch"—and the situation that unfolds when Grobstock is caught out by the Schnorrer is richly entertaining. The highlight of the book is reached when we see Manasseh in the synagogue on the Sabbath preceding his daughter's marriage loudly offering great donations to charity to the astonishment of the beholders! The following day we see him visiting the congregants to raise the necessary £100 so as to prevent the synagogue having a bad debt! This contrast between the hero's Sabbath magnificence and his Sunday morning beggary is, in comic form, the version of the dual image which we get in the literature of Jewry itself. The ambiguity is the result of the conditions of life of a Covenant People which is nevertheless cast among the nations to beg a livelihood. Zangwill illustrates this situation by opposed groups of characters; on the one hand we have many staunch self-respecting characters; on the other hand we have the cringing, the broken-spirited, and the vicious. But Zangwill is also capable of illustrating the situation as the double psychological aspect of one and the same character! This is perhaps the subtlest difference between the dual image as it appears to the Jew and as it appears to the non-Jew. The Jew knows that until he has come to terms with his destiny he is an ambiguous figure harbouring within himself strengths and weaknesses, glory and reproach. The dual image is interiorised. On the one hand, there is the centripetal pull of the Covenant demanding loyalty, integrity and an adherence to Jewish spiritual values; on the other hand, there is the centrifugal force of assimilation, weakness, the abandonment of self-respect and the pursuit of purely material or temporal ends. This is the central conflict of all Zangwill's serious writing. It is the theme of his *Children of the Ghetto* (1892), where the important characters are seen to live what he calls "double lives," from the heroine Esther who is torn between life in the ghetto with her pious father and grandmother, and emancipation in the world outside with its secular values—to the Hebrew poet Melchitzedek Pinchas (evidently a rather unflattering caricature of N. H. Imber, author of the Hebrew national anthem *Hatikvah*) who writes lyrics of Zion in the style of Judah Halevi but supplements his income by producing Hebrew propaganda for the missionaries in the East End of London. The same theme may be discovered in practically all the characters described in his *Dreamers of the Ghetto* (1896)—Heine, Lassalle, Disraeli, and others. They too are torn between apostasy and the ghetto forms of life. In *Children of the Ghetto,* the characters generally remained in, or went back to, the ghetto; in *Dreamers of the Ghetto,* they generally chose the road of apostasy; but in both, the essential experiential reality on which this reading of Jewish life is based is the duality itself, the unresolved problem of dual loyalty.

Israel Zangwill in fact could tell us most of what we need to know about our subject, but we must content ourselves here with referring in conclusion to one of his short stories collected under the title of *Ghetto Tragedies* (1899). The story in question is entitled *Diary of a Meshummad* (i.e., Apostate). In it, he portrays the dual attitude of the Jew who is trying to bury his Jewish past, whilst at the same time, he is secretly trying to relive it. We may quote two entries in the diary. Both refer to Jews and Judaism:

> The thought of the men, of their gaberdines and their pious ringlets, of their studious dronings and their devout quiverings and wailings, of the women with their coarse figures and their unsightly wigs; the remembrance of their vulgar dialect, and their shuffling ways, and their accommodating morality, filled me with repulsion.

> . . . my heart faints within me for the simple, sublime faith of my people. Behind all the tangled network of ceremony and ritual, the larger mind of the man who has lived and loved sees the outlines of a creed grand in its simplicity, sublime in its persistence. The spirit has clothed itself with flesh, as it must do for human eyes to gaze on it and live with it . . .

What makes Zangwill so important a writer is the fundamental seriousness of his writing in relation to Jews and Judaism. In this he is in contrast to Disraeli, for whom one often feels that this subject (like so many others) is no life and death matter. His approach is basically fantastic, whereas for Zangwill the problem of double-lives is his own problem. For him, it is a crisis of identity. A ghetto-Jew himself, he had a strong sense of the values which stemmed from the ghetto, its warmth and vitality. At the same time he was on his way out (he turned from Jewish themes to a great extent later on) intoxicated by the opportunities of the great world. His failure was that he could not rise above his generation and see the possibility of a stable and significant Jewish existence outside the ghetto. But to achieve this, he would have had to achieve, in place of the dual image, a unified image of Jewish life, in which the Jewish past and the Jewish future find real expression in the Jewish present. It is doubtful whether any Jewish writer has ever to date achieved more than a trembling intuition of such a possibility. In general, the *Diaspora* Jew is committed, like his non-Jewish colleague, to a version of the dual image. It is a different version from that of the non-Jewish writer, of course: its negative component is less grotesque; its positive component is less unrealistic and remote from life. But it issues from a similar region of spiritual conflict. The non-Jewish world, we may say, is in revolt against the Jewish God, and this explains the peculiar virulence of its attack upon His witnesses, namely the Jews. But the non-Jewish world has also inherited the God of the Jews, and cannot wholly escape Him: this dual situation is clearly discernible in the Christian gospels and in the literary examples we have been discussing. But the Jew is likewise placed in an existential dilemma with regard to his obedience to the Jewish God. On the one hand, He is the God of Israel to whom the Jew is bound by love, obedience and by ancestral memories of the most sacred and intimate kind. On the other hand, He is the God who has laid upon the Jew the burden of exile, of the noon-tide arrow, and the terror by night. When the Jew seeks to escape from the awful challenge of Jewish history, he sees in the face of his People and in his own image, not majesty and greatness, but ugliness, pusillanimity, self-contempt, and all the moral and physical ills that flesh is heir to.

Anne Aresty Naman (essay date 1980)

SOURCE: "The Jew and His Image," in *The Jew in the Victorian Novel: Some Relationships between Prejudice and Art*, AMS Press, 1980, pp. 31-56.

[*In the following essay, Naman, focusing on the history of the Jew in England, discusses the history of the persecution of the Jew and the historical basis for some Jewish stereotypes.*]

Any history of the Jew must be concerned with the history of the Jew's image, for once the Jew becomes associated with certain physical features or with a particular socio-economic function, then these images become an influential factor in Jewish history in their own right, apart from the historical situation in which they originated.[1]

The history of the image is one of development and evolution rather than of radical change from one period to the next. The images that originated with the attitude of the medieval Church towards Jews may be termed the archetypal images: The moneylender, the murderer, the devil converged to form the image of the pariah—an outcast from society, a being separate from other beings.

The gravitation of Jews towards moneylending was caused by the Church's power over the occupations of its own followers, and by the dominant position of the guilds, which admitted only Christians. Jews were originally agriculturalists, although after the uprooting from Judea and subsequent migrations, they began to engage in occupations that did not require protracted settlement.[2] Jews were the first merchants, and were active in the retail trade of Europe.[3] It was only when the practice of usury became a reason for excommunication from the Church that the Jews, recognizing that it was economically necessary for someone to lend money at interest and that there would be an advantage in having little competition, took up the occupation on a large scale. Jews were also channelled towards moneylending as it became the only aspect of commercial enterprise in which the guilds would allow them to participate. Furthermore, moneylending was well-suited to the precarious position of the Jew, for it did not require the risk of travel and if forced to flee the Jew could easily carry his monetary property with him.[4]

The exclusive policy of the guilds also drove Jews from handicrafts towards retail trade in second-hand goods and peddling. Thus, the Jewish stereotypes of the old-clothes man and the peddler have a common history with that of the moneylender.

As a result of engaging in these occupations, the Jew came to be associated with some criminal practices. Of course, at this time usury, by its very definition, was considered a crime. There is evidence that some Jews were guilty of clipping coinage and receiving stolen goods.[5] The further charge that Jews demanded exorbitant interest must be placed within the context of the relationship between the Jews and the nobility. To a large extent, Jews were middlemen; they took money from other subjects in order to meet the heavy taxes imposed on them, and to pay the special fines which were the means of obtaining privileges and protection.[6]

The relationship between the rulers and the Jews had additional social ramifications. Resentment towards the Jew increased because he was considered to be in a privileged position with respect to the king or prince who was the source of oppression to many Christian subjects. However cordial his relationship with the nobility, the Jew was in truth paying dearly for rights that were given freely to others.

The image of murderer developed from the accusation by the Church that the Jews had committed deicide—that is, that they had killed Jesus Christ.[7] The dispersion of the Jews from Palestine that followed Roman invasions and wars of rebellion (the first few centuries, A.D.) was viewed as a punishment for this crime; consequently, this belief in the Jews' guilt would support the belief that the Jews were a nation who had no right either to their own homeland or to be a part of other nations.

The charge of deicide can be linked to the completely false accusation that Jews practised ritual murder. Originally, Christians believed that such murders were a mockery of the Passion of Jesus and that the blood of the victim was used for various magical ends. This developed into a belief that the Christian child was murdered by Jews in order that his blood could be used for making the unleavened bread which was essential to the celebration of Passover.[8]

The case of William of Norwich demonstrates how the myth of ritual murder became the motive for very real persecution. On the eve of Good Friday, 1144, the body of a young apprentice named William was discovered in a woods near Norwich in England. Riots were precipitated by the rumor that the murder was a mockery of the Passion. Although authorities attempted to protect the Jews, a prominent Jew was murdered by a zealous knight, who happened to be in debt to the Jew. William was made a saint, and his relics became the goal of pilgrims.[9] Recalling "The Prioress's Tale," one realizes that such incidents perpetuated prejudiced attitudes long after the cessation of initial violence.

The uprisings caused by the myth of ritual murder were minimal compared to the persecution that resulted from the religious enthusiasm of the Crusades. In the summer of 1096, the Crusaders, on their way to the Holy Land to cleanse it of infidels, made the Jewish infidels living in Christian countries their fist victims. In fairness, the massacres were for the most part the work of the mobs that formed around the organized armies, and the clergy and nobility of the countries through which the Crusaders swept tried to protect the Jews.[10] It is possible that the religious zeal of the Crusaders would not have in itself led to persecution if anti-Semitic attitudes had not already prevailed in those countries.

The images of criminal, murderer, and religious deviant are of course compatible with that of the devil. During the fourteenth century, the devil was undergoing a change in image from an abstract principle of evil to "a strongly individualized personality, horned and hairy, who infested the earth."[11] The image of the Jew and the devil merged in that the Jew was thought to be not only in league with the devil, but an actual personification of the principle of evil. Physical traits of the devil—horns, tail, talons, goat's beard, black coloring, a unique odor—became stereotypes of the Jew as well. The Jew also began to assume, in some minds, the attributes of the witch; in this way, he came to manifest the whole range of evil traits and occult practices.

Specific Church legislation made the pariah image of the Jew into a concrete reality. In 1215, under Pope Innocent III, a decree was issued which required both Jews and Moslems to wear some form of identifying badge. According to the historian Léon Poliakov, the badge not only facilitated the social isolation of the Jews, but also "impressed on men's minds the notion that the Jew was a man of another physical aspect, radically different from other men."[12] Social ostracism became inevitable with the institution of the ghetto. Venice created the first ghetto in 1516; Rome's was established in 1555, and the trend followed the Jews through Europe. Thus, physical reality supported the social and moral implications of the Jewish pariah.

Some aspects of the Jewish religion contributed both to the perception of the Jew as different and to his actual social isolation. It was expedient for Jews to live in close proximity to one another so that communal organizations could aid them in carrying out the Jewish law; dietary laws required special butchers, for example, and the study of Talmud required special schools. At the same time, the rigidity with which all the minutiae of Orthodox ritual were observed as well as particular practices, such as circumcision, which seemed barbaric,[13] and the dietary laws, which made Christian hospitality to a Jew problematical, contributed to the sense that the Jews were irrevocably different, exclusive, abhorrent.

Certain changes in the values to which Jews adhered can be traced to the position of the medieval Jewish community within the Christian one. While a high status was still accorded to learned Jews, wealth became another means of gaining prominence within the Jewish community. For it was the wealthy who met the heavy burden of taxation and who were able to obtain special privileges. This respect for wealth contributed to the stereotype of the greedy Jew, but one must remember that the pursuit of money sprung from a desire to survive, not from an inherent love of gleaming gold. Apart from the effect of communal organization, the enforced isolation of the Jews made them a more closely knit community. Certain traditional values such as the right to maintain their own internal government and the importance of education became accentuated in importance, for they were a means of asserting solidarity and individual strength.

From the time of the dispersion, Jews could not be identified by the country in which they lived. Others might still regard the Jewish people as a nation, but there were no geographical boundaries which would define the natives within those boundaries and their ancestors as Jews. In most of medieval Europe, ghetto walls (helped by the badge) replaced national boundaries as an aid to identification. At the same time, the Jews could still be defined as the group who practiced the Jewish religion. In medieval Spain, however, conditions were different, and this unique episode in Jewish history marks one of the first divisions within the Jewish group on the basis of different religious practices.

The Jews of medieval Spain were not ghetto Jews. They had gained important economic, cultural, and social positions during Spain's Golden Age, and had reaped the benefits of their importance. Consequently, when anti-Semitism increased in the fourteenth century it was neither an attractive solution nor a natural reaction to become a more closely knit, more religiously observant group as was the case in other parts of Europe. Poliakov explains: "The deep roots the Jews had put down in Spain, their familiarity with the local customs and culture, plus the latent skepticism of many intellectuals for whom security was well worth a Mass, all converged to orient them toward the convenient solution of baptism."[14]

Marranos, sometimes called New Christians or *conversos,* were Jews who had chosen baptism as an alternative to persecution, but who maintained some ties with Judaism, varying from spiritual allegiance to as strict an observance of religious practices as was clandestinely possible. The Marranos were considered by King Ferdinand and Queen Isabella to be a serious impediment to their ambition to rule a unified, Catholic Spain. In order to ferret out and destroy this and other kinds of heresy, the Spanish Inquisition was established. In 1478, a papal bull instituted the Castilian Inquisition; in 1480, the first tribunal came into operation in Seville. Not until 1834 was the Inquisition formally abolished.

At the time of the Inquisition, then, one could find at least three different groups of Jews: those who were of Jewish ancestry but had been sincere converts to Christianity, the Marranos, and those who still openly claimed to be Jewish. In other words, there was a difference between the group of people who had Jewish origins and the group of people who practiced Judaism, with further variations regarding religious observance. One might regard the Inquisition as an institution which attempted to define a Jew as one who practiced Judaism after it was no longer a good working definition. For eventually, avowed Jews as well as Marranos—in fact, anyone for whom a suspicion of practicing Judaism could be fabricated—became victims of the Inquisition. Finally, identification and punishment were no longer considered adequate means of keeping Catholicism (and Spain) safe from the threat of Jewish belief. On 31 March 1492, Ferdinand and Isabella signed the Edict of Expulsion to drive all Jews from Spain.

If the history of Jews in Spain virtually ends here, the history of Spanish Jews does not. The exiles spread to Turkey, Portugal, and the major European and overseas ports. They became involved in international trade, returning to an occupation that gradually had been closed to Jews in many places during the Middle Ages. They were often assimilated by the cultures in which they located, as had occurred in Spain.

In Germany, political and economic conditions seem more important than religious enthusiasm as causes of the rise and decline of the Jews' position. Poliakov cautions one, however, against ignoring the religious basis for persecution:

Historically, the Jew's theological function preceded and determined his economic specialization, and it is the composite image resulting from these two functions which continued to single him out as a Jew within the new bourgeois society. . . . That is why a history of anti-Semitism is first and foremost a theological history, however entangled it may be with economic history.[15]

The Jews were the backbone of Germany's financial structure from the medieval period until the end of the nineteenth century. As Court Jews, they performed a variety of duties besides that of financial administration with a combination of humility and dexterity which made for an influential and cordial relationship with the princes they served.[16] Their prominence continued with the rise of the nation-state since they were the only group prepared to grant credit to the state, and to be active in state business. Not until the rise of imperialism, when the expansion of capitalism depended on cooperation with the state, did others become interested in state finances, causing the Jews to lose their exclusive position.[17]

The political emancipation of the Jew in Germany resulted from his important role in the financial development of the nation-state. Prior to an edict of emancipation on 11 March 1812, it had been necessary to grant special privileges to more and more Jews who were becoming involved in state business to enable them to carry out financial transactions. The edict itself, however, was actually another extension of special privileges; since it contained an article that restricted Jews from state service, they did not attain complete political freedom.

It is not surprising that a political act which retained an element of separation did not curb prejudice. In 1819, anti-Jewish riots broke out in Würzburg and spread throughout Germany (with the exception of

Prussia) and into Bohemia, Alsace, the Netherlands and Denmark. New riots broke out in 1830, 1834, 1844, and 1848, resulting in Jewish emigration. The edict actually became a tool of anti-Semitism, for that one restrictive clause enabled several discriminatory measures to be taken against the Jews.

Because the definition of the Jew as one who adhered to Judaism still determined whether or not a Jew should be restricted from certain occupations, numerous Jews were converted to Christianity in order to remove this obstacle. A well-known example is Heinrich Heine, who was baptized in order that he might obtain a law degree. At the time, the action was performed with reluctance. He wrote to a friend, " 'I should regret deeply if my baptism should appear in any favourable light. I assure you that, if the law had permitted me to steal silver spoons, I should never have become converted.' "[18] Later as Christians became less devoted to their religion, an area of society developed into which assimilation was not checked by religious scruples, a fact which enabled Jews to move away from their religion as well without having to adopt another.

Those Jews who adhered to their religious beliefs and thus remained subject to restrictions had two areas of economic activity from which to choose. Some continued the occupations with which they were familiar; others benefitted from the increased activity brought by the Industrial Revolution. The areas of trade and finance and the liberal professions offered new possibilities for success.

Some perceived the combination of Jews entering into German society and keeping pace with commercial trends to be an undermining of the social, economic, and religious stability of the country. Resentment came primarily from those who had most to lose from new developments, namely, the landed aristocrats and the clergy concerned about the position of the Church: "They hated the entry of the Jews into their 'Christian' society; they hated the democratic, urban, commercial and secular civilisation in which the emancipated Jews found themselves at home."[19] For these people the Jews became a symbol of destructive change, when actually many groups had initiated changes.

Because so much criticism and envy was directed towards the Jewish businessman in Germany, and because there are still many negative stereotypes surrounding the Jewish businessman, it would be helpful to focus on the germ of truth behind the stereotypes and attempt to understand why many Jews did have an aptitude for business.

The modern business practices of the Jews which differed from that of non-Jews were extensions of their medieval practices. For example, specialization in pawnbroking developed into a tendency to deal in all types of merchandise. In addition, Jews had learned from lending money at interest that having a rapid turnover of stock by selling at low prices eventually offered a greater profit. Jews still had an incentive to work harder and take risks because money continued to be regarded as a means of obtaining security and status; success could make a vital difference in one's life, but one lost little by failure. Although Christians followed rigid rules of conduct in business, the Jews did not feel bound by such restrictions because their exclusion from the guilds had oriented them to work outside the Christian framework. Some practices that went against these rules included advertising, selling goods of inferior quality such as renovated old clothes, and disposing of war plunder, contraband, and stolen goods. In these activities the Jews were at times useful to the Christians as cover-ups, enabling the Christians to make a profit without losing their respectability.[20]

Just as modern practices descended from medieval ones, so did the image of the Jewish businessman which supported negative feelings descend from that of the medieval money-lender. The Jewish businessman appeared overly-aggressive and money-minded. The fact that he seemed to make a profit out of nothing added a touch of deviltry to his success; that he went beyond the confines of what was considered morally acceptable in business practices added a touch of criminality.

One might consider for a moment the elements of continuity and the elements of change in the Jews' role of scapegoat. Gordon Allport explains the presence of the Jews in this role by the fact that they represent the "fringe of conservative values":

> The expression . . . must be understood to cover not only deviance in religion, occupation, nationhood, but likewise departure from conservative mediocrity: conscience pricking, intellectual aspiration, spiritual ferment. . . . the Jews are regarded as just far enough *off center* (slightly above, slightly below, slightly outside) to disturb non-Jews in many different ways.[21]

The slight degree by which the Jew deviates from the status quo is itself disturbing and threatening to others. At the same time, the difference between the practices of the Jew and those who maintain the status quo is great enough to serve the scapegoating process. Since the Jew is already a cause for anxiety, it would be easy to rationalize blaming him for a variety of anxieties and frustrations. The deviancy is thus exaggerated by the scapegoating process in an attempt to alleviate anxiety.

With regard to the concept of the "fringe of conservative values," a distinction may be drawn between the marginal position of the Jew in medieval and in modern times. As long as the Jew remained in the ghetto and observed his religion, there was no difficulty in identifying the scapegoat. By the nineteenth century, as has been seen, the Jew could not always be identified by where he lived, what he wore, his occupation, or his religious practices. The degree of deviancy had become hazier, as many Jews had taken on more of the attributes of the society towards which they were supposed to stand in opposition.[22] A sense of difference was rendered more problematical by the Christians who also could no longer be identified by their religious practices.

Only a reliable means of defining the Jew would enable the Jew to continue to function as a scapegoat in the nineteenth century and as an out-group in contrast to which the dominant groups could define themselves. Consequently, the criterion for differentiation was taken away from the realm of religion and brought into the realm of race. As ethnocentrism increased during the eras of romanticism and nationalism, the basic theory that evolved was that of a tripartition: "the Aryan, or real man, was defined by comparison with both brother Shem, the Jews, half-man, half-demon, and brother Ham, the black, half-animal, half-man."[23] It was no longer necessary to base a belief in the evil nature of the Jew on his economic deviance or on religious myths of deicide. The Jew was evil because he was a Jew; it was an inherent part of his biological make-up. Furthermore, because the Jew was totally responsible for his own evil, no blame was cast on anyone else. The moral separation was clear, and the Jew, as evil, could once again be used by others to define their own goodness.

One of the myths that became more prominent in the nineteenth century was that of the Wandering Jew. The roots of the myth lie in the legend of Cartaphilus, who struck Christ as He was on His way to the cross, and in consequence was condemned by Christ to wander until His second coming.[24] Poliakov describes how the figure of the Wandering Jew was perceived:

> . . . no special laws, no theologically motivated punishment, no crime committed with deliberate intent, but a Jewish guilt which continued to exist, a mysterious and diffuse guilt, an even more tragic condition, an implacable curse, which it might be said no longer depended on what the Jew *did* but on what he *was,* on his very essence, his *nature.*[25]

It is clear why this myth became popular alongside the growth of racial anti-Semitism. Despite its origins in the story of Christ, the image of the Wandering Jew was not linked to theology or economy. As did the racial theory, it suggested that evil was inherent in all Jews; the person who adopted this image could ignore the variations in the socio-economic positions, religious practices, and morals among actual Jews in society.

Several images combined to create a new myth in the nineteenth century—that of a Jewish world conspiracy. The rootlessness of the Wandering Jew seemed to justify the feeling that the Jews dispersed over the globe were really a nation unto themselves whose loyalty to any particular country could be doubted. Supported by the old image of the devil Jew and the perceptions of the Jew at the front of change and in the center of finance, the belief developed that the Jews, through a secret government with a network of international connections, controlled government and politics, public opinion, the press, banks, and economic trends. The supposed goal of the Jews was no less than to have absolute power over the world, and the danger that they would achieve this goal seemed imminent.[26]

One sees in the nineteenth century a greater divergence than ever between the real Jew and his image. The "Jew on the street" continued to become more varied while the image of the Jew was clarified in order that the Jew could continue to function as a scapegoat.[27] This was achieved, paradoxically, by removing this image farther from the spheres of real conflict and making it more amorphous, more fluid, more pervasive.

The fact that England was the first country to expel the Jews and the last to give them political rights does not initially suggest a very flattering comparison with the rest of Europe. And yet, the reaction of the Englishman to the Jew was certainly milder, for prejudiced feelings in England did not culminate in violent expressions of anti-Semitism as they did in Europe.

The one period during which Jews have had a financial monopoly in a particular country was the twelfth century in England. However, the establishment of the Exchequer of the Jews at the end of the century restricted this economic freedom. Thereafter, every financial transaction took place in a central office under the close scrutiny of royal officials. At the same time, the Jews were subject to arbitrary, and often heavy, taxes. They were exploited by King John beyond their ability to comply, causing their status to decline in the thirteenth century.

The expulsion of the Jews from England was the result of an economically impractical piece of legislation that necessitated further legislation. In 1275, the *Statutum de Judeismo* forbad Jews to lend money at interest. In order for the Jews to survive economically, other trades had to be opened up to them, but the country was not ready to establish the social equality that was necessary in order to make this economic equality productive. The other alternatives open to Edward I were to legitimize moneylending again or to get rid of the problem by getting rid of the Jews.[28] Whether or not it was because the religious pressures were greater than economic ones, on 18 July 1290, the Jews were ordered to leave England by the first of November.

The critical situation of continental Jews in the seventeenth century motivated Manasseh ben Israel to appeal to Cromwell to change the role of England from a land of oppression to a haven of refuge. Although he failed to gain readmission on ideological grounds as he desired, his goal was eventually achieved through a casual motion in favor of a specific, practical issue. In 1655, the Marrano community in London declared themselves to be Jewish and petitioned Cromwell to provide "written permission to meet for private devotion according to Jewish rites in their houses without fear of molestation, as they had hitherto done, and to have a burial place for their dead."[29] The petition was considered favorably. Without having formally opened her doors, England now acknowledged that entrance by the Jews was legitimate.

Ironically, a more formal declaration based on the ideal of religious freedom might have been reversed along with most of Cromwell's measures by Charles II. Instead, the right of the Jews to reside in England was authorized in writing in August 1664. Another advantage to the lack of formal agreement was that no special clauses could be used to differentiate the privilege of the Jews from the freedom of the Christians.

The religious and economic atmosphere of England in the eighteenth century was conducive to a tolerant attitude towards Jews. The Puritan branch of Christianity was favorably disposed towards the Jews, partly because of the renewed interest in the Old Testament resulting from Calvinist doctrine. Poliakov suggests the reasons behind the greater tolerance for Jewish businessmen: "Because of the flexibility, or perhaps the 'modernity' of English trade, it could face Jewish competition without excessive fear. Moreover, in the event, this competition came primarily from the so-called Portuguese Jews, who . . . troubled the Christian imagination much less than their German and Polish brethren."[30]

However, the relatively congenial atmosphere of the eighteenth century did not mean that England was ready to grant political equality to her Jews. The passing of the Naturalization Bill of 1753, which allowed Jews who had been residents in Great Britain or Ireland for three years to be naturalized upon application to Parliament without having to take the Sacrament, precipitated a negative reaction throughout the country. Old tools of prejudice such as the myth of ritual murder were used to increase anxiety, and hence, further agitation. Pressured by such a clear indication of the wishes of the constituents, Parliament repealed the bill.

The reaction to this bill suggests a fundamental difference between modern anti-Semitism in England and on the Continent. Certainly, this isolated event indicates that there were latent feelings of prejudice not far beneath the tolerant surface. Yet, while under the circumstances a massacre would not have been surprising, the violence of the reaction was primarily verbal. Thus, in England, prejudice finds expression through, and is "satisfied" by, words; on the Continent, words are the precursors of action.

The failure of the first attempts to grant political emancipation to the Jews in the nineteenth century showed once more that an appeal to principle was not the most effective method in England. The struggle moved on to a series of test cases. Lionel de Rothschild, elected to Parliament by Westminster, could not take his seat because he was required to take an oath that ended with the phrase "on the true faith of a Christian"; the Lords refused to waive that phrase, and Rothschild resigned his seat. This pattern was repeated several times, a slight variation being provided by David Salomons in 1851; elected for Greenwich, he dispensed with the formality of the oath and took his seat, to the general disruption of the House.

Finally, that same year, Lord Lucan suggested that if the House of Lords refused to reword the oath, each House should be allowed to determine its own formula for the oath. This practical suggestion was accepted in the form of a resolution, and in 1858, Rothschild became an M.P.

Legislation soon followed. The resolution was made a standing order in an Act of 1860, so that it became a right rather than a privilege. In the Parliamentary Oaths Act of 1866, a new oath was issued for both Houses which contained no words to impede the Jew from exercising his rights.

Both the method and results of granting freedom to Jews in England clearly differed from the Continent. In Europe, Jewish emancipation came on the wave of the ideology of the French Revolution and the restructuring of nations on the premise of equality. In England, there was no great change of principle but rather, a gradual recognition of equality through Reform Bills. The granting of civil liberties to the Jews involved the recognition of one more group who had a rightful claim to political freedom. Even though emancipation was achieved through individual cases, legislation itself recognized that every member of the group, Jews, was entitled to political rights. In contrast, on the Continent a gap remained between principle and practice; the application to actual Jews involved restrictions. One might note, too, that the civil disabilities of the Jews in England were slight; emancipation was a matter of the final step being taken.

By the beginning of the nineteenth century, the Anglo-Jewish population contained much diversification. For one thing, Jews claimed allegiance to one of two groups, the Sephardim or the Ashkenazim. The former name designates the Spanish-Mediterranean-Levantine Jews while the latter refers to the Franco-German-Polish group. There were marked religious and cultural differences between these two groups, resulting in feelings of rivalry. The Sephardim had been settled for a longer period in England, and they did not want their status undermined by the influx of Ashkenazim that occurred at the end of the eighteenth century. At that time, most Ashkenazim belonged to a lower social and economic class than did the Sephardim, and their isolated life in the ghetto was not a good foundation for adaptation to a new country. The Sephardim also prided themselves on being descended from a superior Jewish lineage.[31] For these reasons, intermarriage between Ashkenazim and Sephardim was as much of an issue for the Jew as was intermarriage between Jew and Christian.

By 1850, the immigrants of the turn of the century had become a stable part of the community. There certainly could be no correlation between rich and Sephardim, poor and Ashkenazim. The socio-economic structure of Anglo-Jewry at this time was another element of diversity which cross-cut cultural differences.[32]

In England in 1850, the wealthier Jews were financiers, merchants, merchant bankers, and stockholders. There were relatively few Jews in the professions until later in the century.

Many of the occupations of the upper middle-class involved dealing with miscellaneous goods. There were manufacturers of umbrellas, shoes, pins and needles, cigars and pencils. Wholesale merchants and warehousemen imported luxury items such as oranges, lemons, nuts, furs, and jewelry, as well as a variety of "curios." These occupations reflect the tendency of the Jew to engage in a trade in which he might be able to use international connections and which was not already dominated by non-Jewish businessmen. They also reflect the willingness of the Jew to engage in speculation and take risks. In this same class one also found a stable retail trade. Jews owned ready-made clothing firms and stores which dealt in precious stones and jewelry.

Below this, one found the same tendencies on a smaller scale. There were manufacturers and traders who provisioned the hawkers, so that again the trade was in miscellaneous goods. There were also watchmakers, jewellers, and traders who had their own shops.

Finally, there was the beginning of an industrial working class, including cigar-makers, and workers in the tailoring and furniture trades. One also found the familiar street-sellers and street-traders with fixed stalls, peddlers, and old-clothes men. Actually, by this period the number of Jewish old-clothes men and peddlers had decreased due to competition and a reduced demand. The Irish immigrants in London were willing to work for less than were the Jews; cheap, ready-made clothing began to replace second-hand clothing for the poor, and the railways, by making it easier to reach market centers, lessened the necessity for itinerant traders.

The density of the Anglo-Jewish population in each class changed during the century. As the population increased from 25,000 in 1815 to 35,000 in 1851 to 60,000 in 1880, it changed from a population in which the majority were poor and only a small minority belonged to the middle class to a predominantly middle-class population with a minority of poor.[33]

By 1880, the term Anglo-Jewry was indeed appropriate; the Jews did have an English character, and they were anxious to maintain this character as a community, partly to ensure their acceptance by their Christian fellow-countrymen.[34] But at this time, the community suffered a much greater disruption than had been caused by the influx of Ashkenazim a century earlier. Disasters in Eastern Europe and Russia—disease, famine, pogroms, oppressive legislation—led to mass emigration from those countries. This created serious problems in England such as over-crowding, and adaptation was necessarily a slow process. At least the problems could be rectified by the concerted efforts of the Jews themselves—a different situation from that of persecution, over which there could be little control.

In trying to locate circumstances that prevented violent anti-Semitism in nineteenth century England, one might consider the similarities that existed between Jewish and Victorian values. The importance of the family, an emphasis on morality, a reverence for tradition—these earmarks of the Victorian Age were also integral to the Jewish way of life. Furthermore, this was the age of Samuel Smiles's *Self-Help,* when social mobility was possible if one worked hard to get ahead. Chaim Bermant, in speaking of the prominent Jewish families which he refers to as the "Cousinhood," draws the parallel between Smiles's precepts and Jewish values:

> It is part of traditional Jewish teaching and confirmed by everything in Jewish experience. The Cousinhood were thus Smilesian before Smiles and Victorian before Victoria. They could perhaps even be called super-Smilesians, for where others needed that extra effort to get ahead, the Jew required it to arrive at all.[35]

In themselves, these similarities do not explain the absence of overt acts of prejudice. More elusive factors such as the temperament of the English, whether society was perceived to be stable or unstable, and how much anxiety was generated by social mobility, must also have played a role.

Even though the Victorian Age was not prone to anti-Semitic violence, prejudice continued to be expressed.

At the same time that more liberal attitudes towards Jews could be detected in both social values and political legislation, the images that the Victorian had of the Jew reflected prejudicial thinking, both in adhering to traditional myths and in developing new stereotypes.

The prominent Jewish figures during the Victorian Age must have influenced the Victorians' conception of the group, Jews. At the same time, figures such as Benjamin Disraeli and the Rothschild family were themselves perceived through distorted images.

Benjamin Disraeli exemplifies the ironies that may arise from there being more than one way to define a Jew. Born a Jew, Disraeli received some religious education along with his secular studies. When he was thirteen, his father, Isaac D'Israeli, had a dispute with the synagogue and subsequently withdrew from the congregation. Persuaded that his children must be brought up in some religion, Isaac D'Israeli had them baptized in the Anglican Church. Because Benjamin Disraeli had ceased to be a Jew in religious terms, he was able to enter Parliament before Jews had the legal right to do so. Yet, in racial terms, it was a Jew, not an Anglo-Saxon, who eventually became Prime Minister.

Disraeli was a controversial, conspicuous figure in both society and politics. In the words of his biographer, Robert Blake, "His extravagant appearance, his mordant wit, his arrogant demeanour and his flamboyant conversation made Disraeli far from popular in some quarters."[36] Predictably, men who did not like him did not fail to remember that he was Jewish.[37]

Disraeli's theories, as well as his looks and manner, caused people to be wary of his Jewish background. As one of the Tories who supported the Jews' fight for civil liberties in Parliament, he argued that Christians were greatly indebted to the Jewish race and should consequently treat that race with more humanity. It must be realized that Disraeli always spoke as a Christian. He regarded Christianity as completed Judaism and hoped that eventually Jews would be converted to Christianity; but, he was quick to remind Christians that this would not occur unless Jews were treated more favorably.[38]

Behind these arguments is Disraeli's belief in the superiority of the pure Jewish race. In his novel, *Coningsby* (1844), Sidonia serves as spokesman for this theory: " 'the mixed persecuting races disappear; the pure persecuted race remains. And at this moment, in spite of centuries, of tens of centuries, of degradation, the Jewish mind exercises a vast influence on the affairs of Europe.' "[39] With the memory of Nazi Germany still fresh, one realizes that so much of the "evidence" used by Disraeli to assert the superiority of the Jew could also be used by those concerned with maintaining the purity of another race to assert that the Jew is too greedy and too powerful.

Such twisting occurs in *Punch.* In a mock preface to its sixth volume, this evidence is offered to prove that the world is "governed by the Hebrew mind": "Once PUNCH wanted money. Who lent it him at sixty per cent?—a Jew. Who sued him on the bill?—a Jew! Who arrested him?—a Jew. Who sold him up?—a Jew! . . ."[40] *Punch* used considerable space for satirizing Disraeli, making fun of his verbosity and criticizing his policies. Sometimes the link with his Jewishness was made, sometimes not. All this exposure would have exaggerated and distorted the reader's perception of Disraeli and encouraged a negative attitude towards the man.

This same process of distortion, although not always inviting a negative attitude, can be traced with respect to the Rothschild family. Nathan Mayer Rothschild, one of four sons of the Frankfort banker, Mayer Amschel Rothschild, was sent to England during the last decade of the eighteenth century. One of the primary ways by which he made his fortune was raising loans for the government. Bermant describes the elaborate intelligence system upon which his financial transactions depended:

> There were, first of all, the brothers themselves scattered across Europe. Nathan had agents and couriers all over the south coast and the facing ports in Holland, and his servants swarmed over the battlefields of Europe. The captains of many of the packet boats were also in his pay, and he was often better informed about events on the Continent than the Government itself.[41]

The immense wealth, the international family network, the relation between political and financial transactions, are all "facts" about the Rothschilds.

Nathan Mayer and his son, Lionel, had very different physical appearances and social positions. Nathan could be caricatured as the vulgar immigrant; he could only claim prestige on the basis of his wealth, for he strikingly lacked social graces and cultural awareness.[42] Lionel, on the other hand, combined financial genius with the manners of an English gentleman.[43] That he was anything but offensive to English sensibilities is suggested by the way in which Westminster championed his cause in the fight for emancipation.

The image that *Punch* creates of the Rothschilds is primarily based on the great wealth of the family. A short quip entitled "Generous Sympathy" informs the reader: "It seems, from an account in the French newspapers, that the interest upon Louis Philippe's fortune is only 55 francs a minute! We understand that Rothschild, when he read this, was so moved that he actually shed tears, 'as he never could have believed there was such destitution in the world.' "[44] The wealth of the Rothschilds here carries negative associations in that it has caused Rothschild to lose a realistic sense of what constitutes real suffering in the world.

But *Punch* also creates a more positive attitude towards this wealth in supporting Lionel Rothschild's fight to gain a seat in Parliament. This is part of a speech which *Punch* would have liked Rothschild to give to "The Misrepresented City": " 'You associate with me, foreign States deal with me, kings have been my clients, every capital in Europe puts confidence in me, *you* with the same confidence elect me your Member; but the House of Lords says, that confidence is grossly misplaced, because I am a Jew.' "[45] Here, Rothschild is presented as a man to be respected; his international business dealings are proof that he is a man to be trusted. The implication is that the fact that he is a Jew should not deprive him of a position for which he, as an individual, has proven worthy.

A brief survey of writing about Jews, focusing on other classes and on the group as a whole, will provide an awareness of more general images and attitudes which were perpetuated in Victorian England through the written word.

Punch provides this description of Hollywell Street, the location of a preponderance of shops run by Jews dealing in old clothes:

> "Do you vant a coat?"—"a vaistcoat?"—"a cloak, better as new?" . . . There stands IKEY LEVY, glancing mildly from his doorway as a jackal from his tomb! There watches SOLOMON SOLOMONS. with drooping lip (as though heavy with a weight of honey!), asking the wants of passing bipeds. And there, too, MIRIAM JONAS, a mother in Israel, the parent of eighteen JONASES—(poor pilgrims, vending the apocryphal fruit of Seville and Teneriffe, and selling black-lead pencils, never made to mark—scattered, it may be, about the town with nets of lemons to catch a customer)—there she stands, with the oil of new-fried flounders lustrous on her face and balmy on her lip![46]

This is rather a crude form of entertaining through prejudice, as the humor is primarily based on the unappealing characteristics of the Jews. Physically, the Jews are depicted as disgustingly vulgar. Miriam's greasiness is associated with the Jewish habit of frying fish for the Sabbath dinner. The Jewish men are pushy and money-minded. Together, their names form that of Ikey Solomons, a Jewish receiver of stolen goods whose name had become as synonymous with his trade as that of Rothschild had with banking. This hint of dishonest dealings also applies to the children who perpetuate the stereotype of the Jewish street-seller of inferior, exotic items.

The vulgarity of the Jews is closely linked to their ostentatious display of wealth in Thackeray's portrait of Jews as "Continental Snobs":

> Look at honest Nathan Houndsditch and his lady, and their little son. What a noble pair of blazing contentment illuminates the features of those Snobs of Eastern races! . . . As for the lady, she is all the colours of the rainbow! She has a pink parasol, with a white lining, and a yellow bonnet, and an emerald green shawl, and a shot-silk pelisse; and drab boots and rhubarb-coloured gloves; and parti-coloured glass buttons, expanding from the size of a fourpenny piece to a crown, glitter and twiddle all down the front of her gorgeous costume. . . . [47]

Thackeray is ambiguous about the social class of the Jewish family whose dress is sumptuous to the point of bad taste. The name Nathan and the fact that the family is on the Continent suggests that this is a portrait of the Rothschilds. The surname Houndsditch, however, implies that this is a portrait of an old-clothes man who dresses his family much better than he does his customers. Because of this ambiguity, the image of ostentatious vulgarity is applicable to all Jews.

In articles in which *Punch* denounces the atrocities of Moses and Son, the moral end of prejudice is in evidence along with the entertainment function. *Punch* sides with a woman who was charged with pawning clothes she had been commissioned to make for this retail establishment; that she only received seven shillings a week for her work produces this outcry:

> What is the cannibal to such money-spinning knaves? The savage slays his victim before he commences his revolting feast, the slop-seller refines upon such cruelty, and banquets day by day upon some throbbing nerve, or wasting muscle—"the pound of flesh nearest the heart"—until Death, more merciful than Mammon, closes the wretch's sufferings, . . . [48]

The emotional outcry of indignation is intensified by drawing upon negative Jewish stereotypes in order to characterize the proprietors of Moses and Son. They are grouped with Jews who murder innocent Christians; greed is the only code which governs action. With the reference to "the pound of flesh," *Punch* utilizes all the associations surrounding Shylock—revengeful, devil, murderer, dog, un-Christian—to give support to its own assertions.

Charles Lamb's essay, "Imperfect Sympathies," is perhaps one of the most honest, penetrating defenses of prejudice. What most disturbs Lamb about attempts to overcome the separation between Christian and Jew is the ambiguity of the resulting situation: "If *they* are converted, why do they not come over to us altogether? Why keep up a form of separation, when the life of it is fled? If they can sit with us at table, why do they keck at our cookery? I do not understand these half convertites."[49] One senses that Lamb desires to maintain intolerance because stable and clear social structures are necessary to him. Perhaps he does not need to actively hate the Jew, but he does need to know who is a Jew and who is a Christian.

Some details of the physical and moral image that Lamb has of Jews are given in this essay. Jews, he says,

> have not over-sensible countenances. How should they?—but you seldom see a silly expression among them.—Gain, and the pursuit of gain, sharpen a man's visage. I never heard of an idiot being born among them.—Some admire the Jewish female-physiognomy. I admire it—but with trembling. Jael had those full dark inscrutable eyes.[50]

Lamb draws a connection between features and moral values in both Jewish men and women. The sharp visage of a Jew is the mark of shrewdness, not of reassuring good sense. Jael killed a Canaanite captain with a tent pin when he took refuge in her tent; her eyes should be admired from afar, and their impenetrability taken as a warning.

T. B. Macaulay was an early champion of the Jews in their struggle for political freedom. His speech in Parliament in 1833 is based on the technique of historical explanations:

> . . . We drive them to mean occupations, and then reproach them for not embracing honourable professions. We long forbade them to possess land; and we complain that they chiefly occupy themselves in trade. We shut them out from all the paths of ambition; and then we despise them for taking refuge in avarice. During many ages we have, in all our dealings with them, abused our immense superiority of force; and then we are disgusted because they have recourse to that cunning which is the natural and universal defence of the weak against the violence of the strong.[51]

Macaulay presents all of the characteristics of a Jew that make him different and worthy of contempt; yet, to Macaulay these traits are not a justification of prejudice, but rather cause for self-blame on the part of the English. In this way, Macaulay undermines the very image that he presents in a way that Scott does not, for the implication is that if England's treatment of the Jews changed, then the Jews would lose their despicable traits.

In *The History of the Jews,* H. H. Milman seems much less objective than did Macaulay in his piece of political persuasion. In certain passages, it is clear that Milman's point of view is that of a Christian who feels that Christianity is the only "right" religion. While he does not defend the prejudices of the Christian, he does regard the despicable traits of the Jew to be inherent: " . . . Christianity, to work any change on the hereditary religious pride of the Jew, on his inflexible confidence in his inalienable privileges, must put off the hostile and repulsive aspect which it has too long worn. . . ."[52] Furthermore, Milman seems too ready to think the worst of the Jews: " . . . probably in England as in other countries, their sordid spirit, ever watchful to make reprisals on society, might give countenance to many scarcely perhaps exaggerated stories of their usurious extortions."[53]

As this chapter began with a discussion of the basis for prejudice in Christian beliefs, it may be appropriate to end with an indication that in Victorian England the Jew remained a religious problem for some Christians, and that there was still a religious basis for prejudice. This becomes evident in reading conversionist literature explicitly directed towards Jews.

In her novel *Sophia de Lissau,* Amelia Bristow describes the degraded state of Anglo-Jewry:

> The English Jews (generally speaking), unite in a singular degree, religious superstitution and bigotry, with the most careless apathy and levity, completely immersed in traffic and commercial speculations, and quitting business only to relax their minds, by entering on all the fashionable amusements of the day; the theatre, the ball-room, the card-table, nay even the prize ring, by turns, attract their attention, unchecked by any prohibition in their easy creed; . . . [54]

There is an inherent contradiction in such conversionist arguments. The immorality of the Jews is attributed to their disregard for their religion. But as the religion itself is narrow and bigoted—the Talmud is particularly reprehensible to the conversionists—stricter observance would really only cast more blame on the Jew.

For the most part, this literature strictly adheres to stereotypes. An article in a collection of *Gospel Triumphs* informs the reader that "Their very features are alike, and that in all climates. None can mistake the aquiline nose, dark eyes, pale forehead, and raven locks; they all bespeak the Jew. Their very habits seem stereotyped; their nationality cleaves to them always and everywhere."[55] There are, however, moments in which conversionists attempt to break down some stereotypes:

> They are far from being what we are accustomed to think them, a nation of pedlars and stockjobbers. Even those whom we are in the habit of beating down in their prices often put us to shame; for Christians sometimes obtain articles which Jews are enabled to sell below their real worth, because the charity of the rich has furnished the poorer brethren with the stock in which they trade.[56]

The Jews are here represented as engaging in a greater variety of activities than one normally associates with them, and in being generous towards the poor rather than greedy for themselves. Such passages remind one that the end towards which conversionists are working is to make Christians out of Jews, not to disseminate prejudiced attitudes. If negative stereotypes do not serve this purpose, they are not used.

If any generalization can be abstracted from this overview of Victorian conceptions of the Jew, it is that the image of the Jew has greater consistency than do the attitudes which accompany that image. The old clothes seller, Moses and Son, the Rothschilds, and Nathan Houndsditch all could be examples of Lamb's Jew who is marked by the pursuit of gain or Macaulay's Jew who is forced into avarice. The idea of identifiable physical traits and foreign customs is still prevalent, as is that of a Jewish nation. And yet, the attitudes pervading this image include contempt and sympathy, criticism and tolerance, blame and self-blame. Furthermore, a variety of intentions motivated writers to focus on Jews. Stereotypes do not necessarily serve the scapegoating process in these written accounts.

In turning to the Jew in the Victorian novel, one will want to keep in mind first, that one is confronting images, and secondly, that the attitudes towards an image and its function in the novel may be additional factors to be weighed separately in determining the relationship between the artistic portrait and the elements of prejudice contained in it.

Notes

[1] The term "image" is used to refer both to a mental conception held by an individual or a group and to a conception created by words. Image is a broader term than stereotype in that it involves the process of generalization but need not entail exaggeration or distortion; it also does not necessarily imply that it is used to justify a prejudiced attitude.

[2] Israel Abrahams, *Jewish Life in the Middle Ages,* Temple Books (New York: Atheneum, 1973), p. 240.

[3] *Ibid.,* p. 216.

[4] Léon Poliakov, *The History of Anti-Semitism,* Vol. I: *From the Time of Christ to the Court Jews,* trans. from the French by Richard Howard (London: Elek Books, 1966), p. 75.

[5] Abrahams, *op.cit.,* p. 104.

[6] *Ibid.,* p. 40.

[7] Anyone with a tendency towards Freudian psychology must consider whether ambivalent feelings are the basis for the anti-Semitism arising from the charge of deicide. From this point of view, the Jew has done what the Christian would have liked to have done—i.e., kill the Being (Father in Son) whose power engenders hatred as well as love. The Christian feels guilty for the vicarious satisfaction he gets from the Jew's crime; he then uses the scapegoat mechanism of alleviating guilt through displacement.

[8] Poliakov, *op.cit.,* I, p. 57.

[9] *Ibid.,* p. 58.

[10] *Ibid.,* p. 41f.

[11] *Ibid.,* p. 141ff.

[12] *Ibid.,* p. 67.

[13] A Freudian explanation would use the theory of the castration complex to explain the particular horror with which circumcision was regarded.

[14] Léon Poliakov, *The History of Anti-Semitism,* Vol. II: *From Mohammed to the Marranos,* trans. from the French by Natali Gerardi (London: Routledge and Kegan Paul, 1974), p. 154.

[15] Léon Poliakov, *The History of Anti-Semitism,* Vol. III: *From Voltaire to Wagner,* trans. from the French by Miriam Kochan (London: Routledge and Kegan Paul, 1975), p. 397.

[16] Poliakov, *op.cit.,* I, pp. 229-230.

[17] Hannah Arendt, *The Origins of Totalitarianism* (3rd ed.; London: George Allen and Unwin, Ltd., 1967), chap. 2.

[18] Antonina Vallentin, *Heine: Poet in Exile,* trans. by Harrison Brown (Garden City, New York: Doubleday and Co., Inc., 1956), p. 121.

[19] Parkes, *Antisemitism,* p. 22.

[20] Poliakov, *op.cit.,* III, pp. 7ff.

[21] Allport, *The Nature of Prejudice,* p. 243.

[22] There has always, of course, been a belief that the Jew can be identified by his physical characteristics. Even before the nineteenth century, this would have ceased to be true in reality. Allport suggests that the idea that the Jews have identifiable physical characteristics stems from the fact that a Semitic type was common in the region where Jews originated. While marriages between Jews of this type have perpetuated the myth of physical identification, this Semitic type actually included many non-Jews, and intermar-

riage has caused many divergences from this type among Jews. *Ibid.,* pp. 117-118.

[23] Poliakov, *op.cit.,* III, p. 319. Shem and Ham refer back to two of Noah's sons. Rather than choosing the name of the third son, Japheth, the self-designated superior race chose a name that represented a break from biblical authority. This at once denied church-controlled theories of origin and divided the race from any traces of a Jewish origin.

[24] Edgar Rosenberg, *From Shylock to [Svengali: Jewish Stereotypes in English Fiction* (Stanford, Calif.: Stanford University Press, 1960)], p. 188.

[25] Poliakov, *op.cit.,* III, p. 353.

[26] Norman Cohn, *Warrant for Genocide: The Myth of the Jewish World-Conspiracy and the Protocols of the Elders of Zion* (London: Eyre and Spottiswoode, 1967), pp. 22-23.

[27] Of course, for purposes of discrimination and extermination some means of categorizing real Jews is needed. In the cases of medieval Spain and Nazi Germany, the broadest definitions of birth and ancestry were adopted.

[28] Cecil Roth, *A History of the Jews in England* (3rd ed.; Oxford: Clarendon Press, 1964), pp. 80-81.

[29] *Ibid.,* p. 165.

[30] Poliakov, *op.cit.,* III, pp. 34-35.

[31] Poliakov, *op.cit.,* II, p. 133.

[32] The following discussion is drawn from V.D. Lipman, *Social History of the Jews in England 1850-1950* (London: Watts and Co., 1954), pp. 27ff.

[33] V.D. Lipman, "The Age of Emancipation 1815-1880" in *Three Centuries of Anglo-Jewish History, A Volume of Essays,* ed. by V. D. Lipman (Cambridge: W. Heffer and Sons, Ltd., 1961), pp. 70, 74.

[34] Lucien Wolf, "The Queen's Jewry" in *Essays in Jewish History,* ed. by Cecil Roth (London: The Jewish Historical Society of England; 1934), p. 359.

[35] Chaim Bermant, *The Cousinhood* (New York: The Macmillan Co., 1971), p. 425.

[36] Robert Blake, *Disraeli,* University Paperbacks (London: Methuen and Co., Ltd., 1969), p. 80.

[37] For example, he was referred to by some as the "Jew d'esprit." *Ibid.,* p. 81.

[38] Benjamin Disraeli, *Lord George Bentinck: A Political Biography,* (London: Archibald Constable and Co., Ltd., 1905), chap. 24, "The Jewish Question," esp. p. 329.

[39] Benjamin Disraeli, *Coningsby or The New Generation,* Everyman's Library (London: J. M. Dent and Sons, Ltd., 1911), Bk. IV, chap. 15, p. 208.

[40] *Punch,* VI (Jan.-June, 1844), p. v.

[41] Bermant, *op.cit.,* p. 30.

[42] *Ibid.,* p. 35.

[43] *Ibid.,* p. 92.

[44] "Generous Sympathy," *Punch,* VII (July-Dec., 1844), p. 54. One cannot be sure if the reference is to Nathan or Lionel Rothschild.

[45] "The Misrepresented City," *Punch,* XV (July-Dec., 1848), p. 214.

[46] "Holywell Street," *Punch,* II (Jan.-June, 1842), p. 179.

[47] W. M. Thackeray, *The Book of Snobs* (London: Smith, Elder and Co., 1869), p. 93. *The Book of Snobs* first appeared in *Punch.*

[48] "Famine and Fashion," *Punch,* V (July-Dec., 1843), p. 203.

[49] Charles Lamb, "Imperfect Sympathies" in *The Essays of Elia* (London: J. M. Dent and Co., 1897), p. 111.

[50] *Ibid.,* p. 112.

[51] T. B. Macaulay, "Jewish Disabilities" in *Selected Writings,* ed. by John Clive and Thomas Pinney, Classics of British Historical Literature (Chicago: The University of Chicago Press, 1972), p. 190.

[52] H. H. Milman, *The History of the Jews,* II, Everyman's Library (London: J. M. Dent and Sons, Ltd., 1909), p. 485. First published in 1830; fourth edition in 1866.

[53] *Ibid.,* p. 355.

[54] [Amelia Bristow], *Sophia de Lissau or A Portrait of the Jews of the Nineteenth Century: Being an Outline of the Religious and Domestic Habits of this Most Interesting Nation, with Explanatory Notes* (London: Gardner and Sons, 1826), p. 3.

[55] Rev. John Dunlop, ed. *Memories of Gospel Triumphs among the Jews during the Victorian Era* (London: S. W. Partridge and Co., 1894), p. 344.

[56] *Ibid.,* pp. 160-161.

ANGLO-JEWISH NOVELS

Rabbi Edward N. Calisch (essay date 1909)

SOURCE: "From 1800 to Date—" in *The Jew in English Literature: As Author and As Subject,* Bell Book and Stationary Co., 1909, pp. 161-82.

[*In the following excerpt, Calisch assesses the novels written during the nineteenth-century by Jews about Jewish life, and identifies novelist Israel Zangwill as "the foremost Jewish literary figure" of his time.*]

In the realm of fiction, Jewish literary genius finds large representation. There appears a number of names that will survive more than their own generation. A pioneer of the century was Grace Aguilar, 1816-1847. Her history is pathetically interesting. She was born of a Portuguese family of Maranos, who had fled to England for refuge in the eighteenth century. The family lived secluded, and Miss Aguilar's education was undertaken by her parents. She was frail from birth and in order to strengthen her constitution she was often taken to the seaside and into the country. Thus her companionship with her people was practically cut off. Yet she had an intense religious feeling and a deep sense of Jewish comradeship. In spite of her physical weakness she was very industrious and began writing as a child. By the time she was twelve she had written a drama, *Gustavus Vasa,* and two years later wrote a collection of verse. Her first publication, made anonymously, was in 1835, a book of poems, called *The Magic Wreath.* She continued to write mostly stories, and works dealing with Jewish topics. The most widely known of tales are "The Vale of Cedars," a story of Spain in the fifteenth century, and "Days of Bruce," a romance founded on Scottish history. She wrote a series of domestic stories, "Home Influence," "Mother's Recompense," and "Woman's Friendship," and a number of Jewish tales that were issued under the titles *Home Scenes and Heart Studies,* and *The Perez Family.* Two short volumes were separately published as *The Escape* and *The Edict.* She was also the author of a number of religious works, among which were *The Spirit of Judaism, The Women of Israel,* and *The Jewish Faith, Its Spiritual Consolation, Moral Guidance and Immortal Hope.* Her last work was a small *History of English Jews,* for Chamber's Miscellanies. Her works had considerable vogue a generation ago, and new editions of some of them appear now and then to-day. Her style is pleasing, though somewhat sentimental and diffuse. Her weaknesses, however, may be attributed to youth. She died when she was scarcely thirty-one years of age. Her whole life was practically a struggle against bodily weakness and illness, and she had to endure much family care and trial. One feels a sense of admiration for her brave spirit and her untiring industry, that in spite of such heavy hindrances, produced in the few years given her, so large a number of excellent volumes. Her religious feeling was strong and deep. She had been taken to a European cure, but this failing, she was removed to Frankfort, where she died. The last message she gave with her fingers, being unable to speak, was "Though He slay me yet do I trust in Him."

A contemporary of Grace Aguilar was Charlotte Montefiore, 1818-1854, and she, too, wrote for the uplifting of her people. Among her productions are *The Way to Get Rich, The Birthday, Caleb Asher,* and *A Few Words to Jews.* They are all pervaded with a moral atmosphere and are intended to form an ethical appeal to her coreligionists. She was an active philanthropist, and was interested in many educational and benevolent institutions. Another work, *The Jeweled Isle,* has been ascribed to her, but her authorship of it has been disputed.[1] Katie, now Lady, Magnus, born 1844, is another gifted Jewish writer who appeared a little later in the century. She, too, like her other talented sisters, has given much thought to Jewish topics. Her attention was directed to history as well as fiction. She wrote *Holiday Stories* and *Little Miriam's Bible Stories,* which have a charm for juvenile readers. Her historical efforts embrace two Jewish and one general topic. They are, *About the Jews Since Bible Times, Outlines of Jewish History,* and *First Makers of England.* A number of essays and papers, that had appeared in various periodicals, were collectively issued in a volume, called *Salvage.* Another volume of seven essays of particular Jewish interest was published under the name *Jewish Portraits.* In this there is a review of Dr. Kaufmann's *George Eliot and Judaism.*[2] Lady Magnus is an interesting writer, who displays much reading. Some of her best work is seen in her poems, which have appeared in 1905 in a *Book of Verse.*

Among the novelists of the first half of the century was Samuel Phillips, 1815-1854. Starting as an actor at the age of fifteen he turned his attention to journalism and literature. Through the kindness of friends he was enabled to take a course at Cambridge. His first work was a romance, *Caleb Stukely,* which was first printed in Blackwood's Magazine and later reprinted. Its success led to other tales, a number of which was issued in a volume called *We Are All Low People There.* He published two volumes of literary essays, 1852 and 1854, and served as literary critic on the Times staff. At the formation of the Society of the Crystal Palace he became secretary and literary director, and in connection with it wrote *The Guide* and the *Portrait Gallery.* He was a vigorous and fluent writer and his works commanded much attention, not merely for their intrinsic worth, but for the boldness with which he criticised the leading writers of the day, such as Dickens and Carlyle.

Benjamin L. Farjeon, 1833-1903, was a successful and prolific novelist. His first work, *Grif,* 1870, created a place for him in English letters. It attracted the favorable notice of Dickens. He wrote some forty odd novels, of which a number have Jewish characters and deal with things of Jewish interest. Among these latter are *Salomon Isaacs,* 1877, *Aaron the Jew,* 1894, *Miriam Rozella,* 1897, and *Pride of Race,* 1901. These novels deal very sympathetically with their Jewish themes and characters. Farjeon was an amiable writer, whose style was patterned after that of Dickens, but it is a rather weak imitation.

Julia Frankau, born 1864, writing at times under the pseudonym Frank Danby, was a writer of successful stories. Her first novel, *Dr. Phillips, A Maida Vale Idyll,* 1887, is a story of Jewish life in the West End of London. The work created a sensation by its realistic treatment, and doubtless paved the way for the later school of novelists, both Jewish and Christian, in England and America, who have made much of scenes of Jewish life. It was followed by *Babes in Bohemia,* 1890, *Pigs in Clover,* also with Jewish characters, and *Baccarat,* 1904. Under her own name she published a treatise on *Eighteenth Century Artists and Engravers,* 1901, and *Eighteenth Century Color Plates,* 1906, also the *Life and Works of John Raphael Smith,* 1902. She published other novels, *A Coquette in Crape,* 1907, and *The Sphinx's Lawyer,* 1906, and has been a frequent contributor of articles and essays to the press and reviews.

The elder D'Israeli, Isaac, the father of the famous premier, 1766-1848, tried his hand at novel-writing, and wrote at least four. They are *Vaurien, a Sketch of the Times, Flim Flams, or the Life of My Uncle, Mejnoun and Leila, the Arabian Petrarch and Laura,* and *Despotism, or the Fall of the Jesuits.* The first three appeared in 1797, the last named in 1811. His literary fame, however, does not rest on these novels, for they were not successful. He is better known through his essays, criticisms and miscellaneous writings. He was the son of a wealthy man, and could follow to the full his literary bent. He first appeared in print in the *Gentleman's Magazine,* December, 1786, with a defense of Dr. Johnson. A few years later he published a volume of verse with the title *A Defense of Poetry,* 1790. His best known work is *Curiosities of Literature,* in six volumes, at intervals from 1791 to 1823. There were numerous other productions of the character of the *Curiosities,* and an historical work, *Commentary on the Life and Reign of Charles II* about 1829. This last was a very scholarly work, based on original documents and it earned for him the degree of D. C. L., honoris causa, at Oxford, 1832.

While Mr. D'Israeli possessed abundantly the poetic temperament, his was not a creative talent. He was a gatherer, rather than a producer. He wandered to and fro over the fields of literature and culled many flowers which he wove into bouquets and gave unto the world. His works display a wonderful range of reading and contain a vast amount of interesting matter, interestingly put together. His stories and anecdotes about the lives of authors have become a fund that has been freely drawn upon, though on occasions he makes mistakes. The great success of his literary compilations may be attributed in measure to a peculiar public taste of the time, which retained enough of the passing period of classicism to delight in the small talk of literary gossip.

The incident that occasioned his withdrawal from the synagogue is of interest, not only on his account, but because of its influence on the subsequent career of his famous son. Mr. D'Israeli belonged to the Bevis Marks Synagogue, the house of worship of the Spanish-Portuguese Jews. The Spanish-Portuguese Jews may be said to have been, on the whole, the highest class of the Jewish people. They have been the most adventurous, the most enterprising, the wealthiest and the most intellectual. They were, so to say, the aristocracy of the Jewish race and until at least the middle of the nineteenth century, exercised a spiritual hegemony over the Jewry of London, though their spiritual and economic leadership has since passed into the hands of the German Jews so-called. They, the Spanish-Portuguese Jews, were the creators of the golden age of Jewish literature during the Moorish occupation of Spain, and they were the ones who felt the heavy hand of the infamous inquisition. Their religious loyalty was intense and profound, a loyalty whose soil has been enriched by the blood of many a martyr. But they are, withal, stalwart sticklers for form. So, when having elected Mr. D'Israeli to the position of warden in the synagogue, and he having politely declined to serve, they took no notice of his declination, because their custom demanded that he who was honored with office must serve. When he persisted in his declination, they fined him forty pounds. Mr. D'Israeli demurred against paying the fine, but they would hear no excuse, and he wrote finally saying, "I am under the painful necessity of wishing that my name be erased from the list of your members." This occurred in 1813.

It cannot be said that Isaac D'Israeli abandoned the religion of his fathers. His views were far in advance of his coreligionists of his day, but not such as to lead him to abjure his ancestral faith and to separate formally from them. His withdrawal from membership in the synagogue was for no subjective cause, but the result of external occasion. Twenty years after this incident, in 1833, he wrote his *Genius of Judaism,* in which he speaks enthusiastically of the Jewish religion and people, of their glorious and heroic past. He deplored only what he termed the spirit of exclusiveness. He had expressed these same views in his novel *Vaurien* and in an article on Moses Mendelsohn, written for the *Monthly Review* of July 1798, both of these publica-

Benjamin Disraeli (1804-1881)

tions appearing more than a decade and a half before the episode that led to his action. He attended the inauguration of the Reform Synagogue, at Burton Crescent in 1841, and his views were doubtless in accord with its platform. There is reason to suppose that had this synagogue existed earlier in his life he would have remained a worshipping member of it. He never expressed any wish to exchange Judaism for Christianity, nor did he submit to baptism. His son Benjamin, the future Premier, was baptized at the instance of Rogers, the poet, who represented that the future career of the boy, who was then about thirteen years of age and who appeared to be highly gifted, "might be compromised by connection with a race laboring under social and civic disabilities, and the entrance to the road to success might be irrevocably closed to him." This baptism took place in 1817.

Benjamin D'Israeli, 1804-1881, like his people in the history of nations, occupies a unique place in literature. Though the baptismal drops widened his material opportunities, they did not create his genius. They made it possible for him to become the Premier of England and to crown Victoria Empress of India, but they did not increase his abilities or enhance his brilliant mental gifts. Lord Beaconsfield remained intensely Jewish in spirit, and loyal to the house of David all his life. He was a firm believer in the power of race, and much of his writing is filled with a defense and exaltation of the Jewish race, which he named the "aristocracy of nature."

At the age of twenty-two he published his first novel, *Vivian Grey.* He was then an assistant in a solicitor's office, but this take-off on London's highest society was startingly realistic. The novel created a sensation and gained instant notoriety. Its magniloquent style, its veracious descriptions and caricatures of persons high in social and political life, amazed the haute monde when they came to learn that its author was merely an office boy. D'Israeli, falling sick, left England to travel in Egypt and Palestine. This trip did much to influence his whole future. The visit to the ancestral home of his people made an impression on him that is evident in all his subsequent career. It appeared in *Contarini Fleming,* in his *Letters to his Sister,* in *Coningsby,* in the *Life of Lord George Bentinck,* but most of all in *Tancred.* Tancred goes to the East for inspiration; ex oriente lux. He seeks to solve the great mystery of life and inspiration, and looks for it in the home of inspiration, as though inspiration were local and confined to any quarter of the earth. George Eliot likewise sends Daniel Deronda on a honeymoon trip to the East to begin the undefined mission which he is to accomplish. At Bethany, Tancred meets Eva, the Jewess, and in the discussion between these two, D'Israeli gives his ideas on the relations between Judaism and Christianity. He regards Christianity as the Judaism of the multitude, the flowering of the mother faith. But its substantial greatness, its morals and its ethical beauty are all Jewish, for Judaism was "the church in which Jesus was born and which he never quitted." It is in this work that he puts in the mouth of Eva that celebrated epigram, "One half the world worships a Jewess, and the other half a Jew," and then asks, "Which is the greater, the worshipped or the worshippers?"

In *Coningsby,* the Jewish character Sidonia is a somewhat mystical figure, a philosopher, a financier, a diplomat, a power in continental cabinets, a native of England, and yet an alien, for its laws prevent his becoming a citizen. It was with this character, Sidonia, that D'Israeli fought for his people in their political struggle. In Parliament his vote and his energy were constantly employed in their behalf, and he had their interests in mind when, in the making of the Treaty of Berlin, he insisted that Roumania, to have her independence guaranteed, should guarantee the civil rights of the Jews. It is a promise that, to the shame of the signatory powers to the treaty, has been wantonly violated. Sidonia was evidently a favorite character with his creator, for in his mouth D'Israeli places many of his finest defences of the Jewish race. "The Jews," for example, he says,[3] "independently of the capital qualities for citizenship which they possess in their industry, temperance and energy and vivacity of mind, are a race essentially monarchical, deeply religious, and shrinking themselves from converts as from a calamity, are ever anxious to see the religious systems of the countries in which they live flourish. Do you think that the quiet humdrum persecution of a decorous representative of an English university can crush those who have successfully baffled the Pharoahs, Nebuchadnezzar, Rome, and the feudal ages? The fact is, you cannot destroy a pure race from the Caucasian organisation. It is a physiological fact; a simple law of nature, which has baffled Egyptian and Assyrian kings, Roman emperors, and Christian inquisitors. No penal laws, no physical tortures, can effect that a superior race should be absorbed in an inferior, or be destroyed by it. The mixed, persecuting races disappear; the pure, persecuted race remains. And at this moment, in spite of centuries or tens of centuries, of degradation, the Jewish mind exercises a vast influence on the affairs of Europe. I speak not of their laws, which you still obey; of their literature, with which your minds are saturated; but of the living Hebrew intellect."

David Alroy is another Jewish novel in which D'Israeli rhapsodizes about the greatness of the Jewish people and the powerful incentive to sentiment which one finds in the East. The novel is based on the tale of a pseudo-messiah of the Jews, one David Alroy, or Alrui, who appeared in Turkey in the twelfth century as a saviour of the Jews.

D'Israeli's literary labors are closely identified with his political life. He began his political career with a defeat, but he established a name for pluck and perseverance. In his quarrel with O'Connell, the latter had said that "the impenitent thief on the cross must have been named D'Israeli." But this did him so little harm that the next year he was returned to Parliament. His parliamentary experience began with a rebuff. His maiden speech was howled down so that it could not be heard. When he sat down he cried, "I sit now, but time will come when you will hear me." The time did come. Interesting, too, is the incident when, being taunted with the fact he was a Jew, he flung back the taunt with the proud declaration of his joy in his ancestry. There is no question but that these episodes had much to do with the character of D'Israeli's writing. His Jewishness was intensified by the opposition that it inspired. He was the more insistent champion of his race because his opponents endeavored to discredit him on account of his race.

He was an anomaly in English political life, as he was in its literature. He combined the imagination of the Orient with the practical sagacity of western civilization. He was a "statesman-novelist," who "introduced the novelist's imagination into his statesmanship and the statesman's foresight into his novels." His novels were written with the purpose of promulgating his ideas. With his practical vision he saw that he could reach a wider constituency in his writings and that he could perhaps better convince them by picturing the ideals in concrete form. Herein is the psychology that characterizes him as it does his people. The Jews combine the spirit of idealism with intense practical energy. They are philosophers in action, dreamers awake. The Jewish strain is perceptible in D'Israeli in both his political and literary activities. In politics it gave him imagination, patience in waiting, tenacity in purpose. In literature it gave him this same imaginative faculty, brilliance of intellect, sustained power of effort, and analytical keenness. What if the brilliance on occasions had the effect of the bizarre, or that pride of race sometime ran to racial chauvinism? These are not inherent faults, they are the vices of exaggerated virtues. The exuberance of oriental imagery as manifest in dress, debate or diction of speech or book, were perhaps studied for effect. D'Israeli has been characterized as a brilliant poseur. Perhaps the exuberance seemed the greater by contrast with the sedate and sober excellence of his contemporaries, as the vivid sunshine of Judea might contrast with the gray fog of London.

The centenary of Mr. D'Israeli's birth was observed, in 1904, by a reawakened interest in the man and his achievements. Many articles and essays were contributed to magazines and periodicals reviewing his life and labors and his place in English literature. Two volumes of some pretentions appeared, *An Unconventional Biography,* by Wilfred Megnell, and *Beaconsfield,* by Walter Sichel. The latter has also published an elaborate character sketch, "D'Israeli." Two new editions of his works appeared. Though much of his writing deals with things of temporary interest, such as political views and conditions, yet much is destined to a permanent place in literature. *Lothair* and *Coningsby* may be considered as representative of his diction, his method, and his ideas. He is a satirist and a sentimentalist, and one is not always sure when he is in earnest. He revelled in material opulence, yet he unflaggingly pursues an ideal. In two things was he consistently steadfast, in his loyalty to his people, the "aristocracy of nature," and in profound respect for another aristocracy, that of talent.

Within the past two decades there has come into vogue a class of stories dealing with scenes of Jewish life. The century-long segregation of the Jews from the communal life of the peoples, among whom they dwell, has developed naturally social customs and conditions peculiar to themselves. Even though the barriers of physical ghettoes have been demolished, there is a certain social aloofness, partly objective, partly subjective, in which the Jews live. The inherited traditions and customs of centuries are not uprooted in a generation. The renewed persecutions during the past twenty-five years in Russia and southeastern Europe drove many Jews to take refuge in the more enlightened countries of the west, mostly in England and America, whose policy has been the most liberal and just. They have congregated in the large cities, especially of the seaboard, like London, Liverpool, New York, Philadelphia, Baltimore and Chicago. Naturally flocking together, they have established Jewish centers in these cities. The conditions created by these centers are fertile fields for literary harvests, which have been gathered by many writers both Jewish and Christian, and both in England and America. There is a powerful and tragic struggle constantly going on in the newly formed Ghettoes of these English and American cities. It is the conflict between isolation and assimilation. The tragedy of it lies in the intellectual and spiritual gulf that inevitably ensues between parents and children. Though some Christian writers can enter into an understanding of this tragedy and write of it with feeling and sympathy, its best interpreters are naturally Jews themselves. Of these English Jewish writers, in the realm of fiction, the foremost are Israel Zangwill and Samuel Gordon, the former being by far the more widely known, and easily the first.

Israel Zangwill was born in London in 1864, and, excepting a few years' residence at Bristol, his life has been spent in the metropolis. He was educated at the Jews Free School and at the University of London. For a while he was a teacher at the Free School, but resigned his position to devote himself to literature. He showed his literary proclivity at an early age. While at school he edited and helped to write an annual called *Purim.* His first novel was *The Premier and the Painter,* 1888. It was written in conjunction with Lewis Cowen and published under the pseudonym of "J. Freeman Bell." There are in it traces of the influence of D'Israeli and Dickens, but also the distinctive tone of Zangwill's peculiar style. The plot is unconventional, and the treatment bold and free. The keen sense of humor, the apt turning of a phrase, the brilliant epigram and the power of analysis, which have distinguished his writing, all make their appearance. He became one of a coterie of young literary aspirants, such as Jerome K. Jerome and Robert Barr and others. The predominance of the humorous element was made evident in his following works, *Bachelors' Club* and *The Old Maids Club,* both being a collection of sketches of fantastic and prankish humor.

The reputation gained from these works brought him a commission from the Jewish Publication Society of America to write a novel about Jewish life. The result was the *Children of the Ghetto, being Pen Pictures of a Peculiar People.* The work was published simultaneously in London and Philadelphia, 1892. It gave him international renown, and has been translated into a number of languages. In this Zangwill found himself. He had come into his own. His perfect understanding of the conditions which he pictured, his complete comprehension of their psychological background, his faculty of analysis, his power of pathos and humor, combined with his brilliant style, produced a remarkable work that commanded the attention of the literary world and declared the new star that illumined its horizon. The first volume pictures the Ghetto of London, with its perplexities and problems of adjustment. In the second volume, called *The Grandchildren of the Ghetto,* is described the change wrought by a generation, the evolution from Petticoat Lane to the West End. Like all progress, this, too, had its penalties. Zangwill's study is picturesque and true, and caused a commotion among some of the more supersensitive members of the community, who were not pleased to see their foibles and peculiarities thus laid bare to the gaze of the Gentile world. But the hand that exposed them was withal a kindly one and just. If it exhibited some superficial weaknesses, it also revealed to a world that had not credited them, an inherent moral strength and a beautiful spirituality, which underlie the crust of the sordid exterior compelled by the pressure of age-long persecution.

Following this line, Zangwill wrote a number of volumes dealing with Jewish life and characters. *The King of Schnorrers,* 1894, *The Dreamers of the Ghetto,* 1898, *They That Walk in Darkness,* 1899. *Ghetto Tragedies,* are sketches that give an accurate insight into conditions peculiar to the Jewish people. *The Dreamers of the Ghetto* are a number of historic Jewish personages, who have achieved fame in the world, such as Lasalle, Beaconsfield, Heine, etc.

In these, Zangwill's power is well displayed, as also in *They That Walk in Darkness.* The minor key, to which the note of continental Jewish life is too often attuned, is struck, but without monotony or lack of skill. The pathos is natural and unstrained. His latest publication in this direction is "Ghetto Comedies," 1906. In it he returns again to the Jews of the still submerged class. The stories are not all comedies, as in the prefatory note Mr. Zangwill states that he disregards the conventional distinction between comedy and tragedy. The flowering of his art is visible. Other sketches have been published under the titles *Without Prejudice,* 1896, and *The Gray Wig,* 1903.

His two novels of general interest, *The Master* and *The Mantle of Elijah,* have been widely read and were very successful from the point of view of popularity. But not so with regard to art. Zangwill is at his best in the short story. This is his metier. His genius in this direction rivals that of Poe and De Maupassant, and is unrivalled in England. In the longer novel his power flags, the excellence is not sustained. A master of epigram, he often sacrifices much for the sake of an epigram. He excels as a painter of miniatures. He fails with the larger canvas. This is true likewise of his dramatic efforts. These are sketches, not sustained dramas. *Six Persons, Three Penny Bits, The Revolting Daughter, The Moment of Death,* are all of them clever pieces, the last named especially is a strikingly original study, but they are curtain-raisers. The *Children of the Ghetto* was dramatized. In the United States it ran for some months with a fair degree of success. The theme of the play did not, however, appeal to the average non-Jewish auditor, and the somewhat abstruse Talmudical law regarding the validity of betrothals, upon which the climax of the play depended, was not wholly understood. It was put on in London, but soon withdrawn. His most successful venture in this direction was the dramatization of a Christmas tale, *Merely Mary Ann.* It is a sweet, clean story of a London "slavey," who falls in love with a man far above her station in life and who, with many pathetic little subterfuges, attempts to lessen the wide gulf between them. His latest drama is *The Melting Pot,* wherein he pictures the assimilative powers of the American Republic, and attacks, though not with conspicuous success, the inter-marriage problem. He has also been the author of many poems and verses, some of them being exquisite renderings of the synagogal liturgy and the medieval Jewish poets. Many of these poems have been published in a volume *Blind Children,* 1903.

From the standpoint of pure literature, Mr. Zangwill is doubtless the foremost Jewish literary figure of this generation, which is saying much, for there are many splendid scholars and writers, who grace this generation of English Jews. He has identified himself with the large communal activities of the Jewish people. At one time a strong Zionist, he has broken away from the older society because of the refusal of the Zionistic Congress to consider favorably the offers of the British Government of a tract of land in East Africa for colonization purposes, with an autonomous government under British sovereignty. He formed the "Jewish Territorial Organization," and has spent much time and effort advocating its cause. His heart is in full sympathy with his people, and though he does not hesitate to condemn what he disapproves, he never writes to wound. He is a brilliant, versatile and picturesque writer, a novelist, poet, essayist, dramatist, and critic, and his place in English literature is assured for all time.

As a successful novelist, both in general themes and on those of specific Jewish interest, Samuel Gordon is pressing Zangwill as a fairly good second. Born in Prussia, 1871, he came to London at the age of thirteen. A scholar of considerable classical attainment, even at that young age, Gordon soon won recognition in the City of London School and Cambridge University. Like Zangwill, he knows whereof he writes. His pictures are the result of practical experience and knowledge and not of academic study. His chief novels of Jewish life are *A Handful of Exotics,* 1897, *Daughters of Shem,* 1898, *Lesser Destinies,* 1899, *Sons of the Convenant,* 1900, *Strangers at the Gate,* 1902, and *Unto Each Man His Own,* 1904. *Sons of the Covenant* is a sustained novel, containing the story of two young boys, who are said to have been Gordon himself and his brother, who are very much in earnest about the welfare of their people, and who devise a decentralizing scheme for the amelioration of the conditions of the Jews of London's East End. His other stories of Jewish life are short tales, which are marked by a vivid realism. Gordon travelled extensively on the continent and gained at first hand a thorough knowledge of the unhappy conditions under which the Jews in the Pale of Settlement are condemned to live. These are pictured in *The Ferry of Fate,* 1906, a novel of intense interest, which gained for him the sobriquet of the *Jewish Maxim Gorki. Unto Each Man His Own* deals with the insistent inter-marriage problem, and in it Gordon found occasion to speak rather boldly. *In Years of Transition,* 1897, is a novel dealing with life in the Latin quarter of Paris. *The Queen's Quandary,* 1903, is a work of romantic character. Several of his short stories have been dramatized and produced with success. His first dramatic venture was somewhat unfortunate. It was a play based on the Captain Dreyfus episode in France. Its production was prohibited by the Lord Chamberlin's censor. Gordon is a fascinating writer. His style is lucid, easy and attractive. He has the faculty of seeing his problems from a detached view-point, and this has served him well, especially in his stories of Jewish life.

Other novelists of the period may be mentioned, Mrs. Alfred Sidgwick, Louis Zangwill, Bella Sidney Woolf, Lily Montagu and Violet Guttenburg. Mrs. Sidgwick also deals with stories of Jewish interest, though she writes of a higher social and more prosperous class. She evidences that religious loyalty is not necessarily concomitant with poverty only, but that refined, wealthy and successful Jews are no less imbued with the spirit of devotion to the faith of their fathers. *Scenes of Jewish Life, Lesser's Daughter, Isaac Eller's Money,* are among her Jewish works. She also wrote *The Beryl Stones, The Thousand Eugenias, The Inner Shrine, The Grasshoppers, A Woman with a Future* and *Mrs. Finch-Brassey.* Louis Zangwill is an author whose fame is handicapped by his "big brother's" greater fame. He is a brother of Israel Zangwill and he has written some volumes that have won recognition from the discerning. Among them are *A Drama in Dutch,* 1896, *A Nineteenth Century Miracle,* 1896, *The World and a Man,* 1896, *The Beautiful Miss Brook,* 1897, *Cleo the Magnificent,* 1899, *One's Womankind,* 1903, and *An Engagement of Convenience,* 1908. The last named treats a conventional theme in an unconventional way. An artist of genius marries beneath him at a critical moment to save his career. Later the more brilliant affinity makes her appearance. Usually the inferior woman is painted in crude colors in order to palliate the hero's inclination toward the affinity. Mr. Zangwill reverses the usual procedure to make a finer and more sympathetic presentation of the less brilliant wife.

Lily Montagu in *Naomi's Exodus,* 1901, tells the story of a clever young Jewess, who seeks a more congenial sphere outside of her own people and finds much trouble and trial. She also wrote *Broken Stalks,* 1902, and *Thoughts on Judaism,* 1904. Bella Sidney Woolf as a writer for young people, of young people, has achieved success, through a simple and charming style. Among her productions are *Jerry's Joe,* 1897, *My Nightingale,* 1897, *All in a Castle Fair,* 1900, *Dear Sweet Anne,* 1906, *Harry and Herodotus,* and *Little Miss Prue,* 1907. Violet Guttenberg was stirred by the controversy that raged in connection with the passage of the Alien Immigration Act. She wrote *Neither Jew nor Greek,* 1902, as a sort of warning though she herself says it is a novel of the impossible. She describes the expulsion of the Jews from England under the oppression of a hostile Home Secretary, and their return, because England could not prosper without them. She has also written *Modern Exodus,* 1904, and *The Power of the Psalmist,* 1903. . . .

Notes

[1] *Die Jüdischen Frauen in der Geschichte,*" etc., by M. Kayserling, p. 276.

[2] This was an appreciation of "Daniel Deronda," by Prof Kaufmann, of Buda Pesth. It was translated into English by J. W. Ferrier, and published by Blackwood & Sons, London.

[3] *Coningsby,* Vol. I., pp. 331-2.

Bryan Cheyette (essay date 1990)

SOURCE: "The Other Self: Anglo-Jewish Fiction and the Representation of Jews in England, 1875-1905," in *The Making of Modern Anglo-Jewry,* edited by David Cesarani, Basil Blackwell, 1990, pp. 97-111.

[*In the following essay, Cheyette examines the ways in which Victorian Jewish novelists were forced to "negotiate" or "reconcile" their own particular cultural heritage with the national culture of England.*]

In a recent study of minorities in an 'open society', Geoff Dench has argued that:

> Members of national minorities in modern states are subject to powerful contradictions. On the one hand they are regaled with promises of free and equal participation in society for all individuals—if not perhaps at once, then in a little while. On the other they are faced with a continuing reality of communalism, among themselves as well as in national minorities, whereby groups identifying themselves in terms of common origin, race or culture tend to stick together. This discrepancy creates tremendous dilemmas for them, and throws up moral and political issues for society as a whole.[1]

Whilst this basic contradiction between a particularist 'communalism' and a universalist promise of 'equal participation in society' is apparent in all aspects of British-Jewish life, it is nowhere more apparent than in the evolution of the Victorian Jewish novel.

Jewish novelists, like Jews in general, had to negotiate between the national culture of their host society and their own cultural heritage. By straying too far along the particularist road, Jews were always open to charges of 'clannishness'.[2] Writing in English, for a predominantly non-Jewish audience, the Jewish writer was especially sensitive to the mediating role in which he or she attempted to reconcile the universalist values of British liberal culture with particularist Jewish experience. This mediating position arose historically with the publication of the earliest Anglo-Jewish novels in the first half of the nineteenth century, all of which represented virtuous Jewish characters in their fiction during the campaign lasting three decades for Jewish political and civil rights.[3] This campaign centred around the debate over whether England was to remain a particularist 'Christian nation' or adopt the universalist liberal principle of 'liberty of conscience'.[4] The best-known early Anglo-Jewish novelist, Grace Aguilar, in her *History of the Jews in England* (1847), mediated between these two positions by arguing that:

> In externals and in all secular thoughts and actions, the English naturalised Jew is an Englishman, and his family is reared with the education and accomplishments of other members of the [English middle class] community. Only in some private and personal characteristics and in religious belief, does the Jew differ from his neighbour.[5]

In this account, Aguilar emphasizes the liberal construction in which Jews were turned into 'Englishmen of the mosaic persuasion' by relocating Judaism in the private sphere and making it merely a matter of personal 'conscience'. But Aguilar could also highlight the Christological defence of Judaism, especially in *The Spirit of Judaism* (1842) and 'The Perez Family' (1850), a short story set in Liverpool. In these works, Aguilar developed a form of 'Jewish Protestantism' or 'Christianized Judaism' and stressed the toleration of Jews and Judaism not for its own sake but as an extension of Christian values.[6]

Yet even such an Anglicized Judaism, which accorded with English culture, could not eschew its communal function and operate purely as a non-conformist, privatized religion. By the same token, English liberal values were also 'communalist' and were not entirely emptied of their particularist 'Christian' content. The still dominant Christian discourse of 'transcending' Judaism was reflected in the liberal *quid pro quo* of Jewish 'emancipation'—the idea that Jews would eventually adopt the dominant values of society after they had become citizens—which was made with some urgency in Victorian Britain.[7] Thus, when William Hazlitt typically identified Jewish emancipation with a Whiggish 'progress of civilization', this universalist position could just as easily be read in particularist terms by linking the 'progress of civilization' with a specific Jewish messianic purpose within Christendom.[8] Homi Bhabha has labelled this ambivalence as the '*double* vision' of racial discourse which constructs 'a subject of difference that is almost the same, but not quite . . . in which to be Anglicized, is *emphatically* not to be English'.[9] That is, behind an idealized Jewish Self—which represented the potentialities for liberal progress—is a particularist Other which, by its very presence, contradicts the promise of 'emancipation'.

Sander Gilman, from a social psychological perspective, has illustrated the mechanisms by which this discourse of difference is internalized by Jews. He argues that a minority community tends to accept the 'mirage of themselves' generated by the majority culture which necessarily results in a form of 'self-hatred'. That is, in Gilman's terms, an 'illusionary definition of the self' is caused by minorities accepting the dominant image of the Other. This ambiguity, according to Gilman, results in two common definitions of racial difference which are internalized by Jews. The first definition of racial difference he has called the 'liberal fantasy', where 'anyone is welcome to share the power of the [majority culture] *if* he abides by the rules that define that [culture]'. The second, contradictory definition of racial difference, however, excludes participation in the dominant culture. This Gilman has called the 'conservative curse':

> On the other hand is the hidden qualification of the internalized reference group, the conservative curse: The more you are like me, the more I know the true value of my power, which you wish to share, and the more I am aware that you are but a shoddy counterfeit, an outsider. All of this plays itself out within the fantasy of the outsider.[10]

It is this 'double vision' that 'plays itself out' in the Anglo-Jewish novelist. This was especially apparent by the 1870s since mass Jewish immigration—with an identifiable Yiddish sub-culture—had by this time begun to establish large Jewish populations which were seriously to challenge the 'liberal fantasy' of a Jew 'differing from his neighbour' purely in terms of his private religious beliefs.[11] It is in this context that I will now turn to three novelists—Benjamin Farjeon, Julia Frankau and Israel Zangwill—who, from differing perspectives, all attempted to transcend the Jewish Other in their fiction and replace it with an idealized image of selfhood. This resulted, inevitably, in a radically ambivalent construction of Jewishness.[12]

To some extent, Benjamin Farjeon can be said to be the first novelist to have brought the apologetic tradition of early Anglo-Jewish fiction into the twentieth century.[13] In a letter to the *Jewish Chronicle* he quotes, with some satisfaction, a reader's response to the *The Pride of Race* (1900): 'This work of yours is more than any novel; it is the lifting of a great people in the eyes of those who depreciate them; it is teaching them how good and kind and unselfish poor Jews are and can be.'[14] Significantly, *Solomon Isaacs* (1877), Farjeon's first novel concerning Anglo-Jewry, was read in periodical form to 'Jewish working people' as part of the Association for Free Lectures to Jewish Working Men and their Families. Most of Farjeon's forty novels, not just the four dealing with Jewish themes, were part of the 'massive flood of printed matter poured out upon [the lower classes]' which was designed 'to improve their minds and souls'.[15] Like Aguilar, who constructed Jews in liberal terms in the context of the campaign for Jewish emancipation, Farjeon 'moralized' the working-class Jewish immigrant in a bid to lessen the 'fear' caused by mass Jewish immigration into England.[16]

Where Farjeon differs from his mid-Victorian counterparts, however, is in the Disraelian construction of Jewish identity based on a belief in Jewish racial superiority. Aaron Cohen, the idealized central character of *Aaron the Jew* (1894) is, like his author, 'deeply interested' in 'the Jewish Working Men's Clubs in the East End'.[17] During one of his lectures to them Cohen argues that:

> there is no historic family in England or elsewhere the record of whose deeds can vie in splendour with the record of the Jew. His history is at once a triumph of brain power and spiritual vitality, and the proudest boast a Jew can make is that he is a Jew. (vol. III, p. 6)

Farjeon reflected this form of chauvinism throughout *Aaron the Jew,* stating at one point that 'nations that oppress the Jew' will necessarily 'fall into decay' (vol. III, p. 190) and making out a case for a special Jewish racial ability with regard to music (vol. I, pp. 57-8). Just as 'all is race' for Disraeli,[18] Farjeon notes that: 'as a rule, vices, virtues and all classes of the affections are hereditary, and the religious sentiments are not an exception. Aaron had studied the subject, and was conscious of the solemn issues dependent upon it' (vol. III, p. 15). This position is diametrically opposed to Aguilar's liberal construction of Jews as being 'Jews only in their religion—Englishmen in everything else'.[19] In fact, unlike the 'Jewish Protestantism' of a Grace Aguilar or Benjamin Disraeli, Farjeon is at pains in *Aaron the Jew* to differentiate between 'Christian' and 'Jew' in primarily racial terms.[20] Aaron adopts a 'Christian' daughter and her refusal to accept Judaism and marry a Jew is said to provide incontrovertible 'proof' of Jewish difference:

> Once a Jew, always a Jew, whether he follows the Mosaic laws or disregards them. So powerful is the

> seed of Judaism that it can never be entirely destroyed in the heart of one born in the ancient faith. We who are Jews know this to be incontrovertible; you who are Christians may not be able to understand it. (vol. II, pp. 194-5)

The construction of Jews as a separate 'historic family' was seen by Farjeon as a positive act, a means of representing cultural difference in Disraelian terms as a mirror image of 'religion, property and natural aristocracy'.[21] By the 1870s, in fact, with the universalist mid-Victorian liberal consensus under threat, particularist racial explanations of social questions were increasingly widespread. 'Englishness', in particular, was constructed as a 'completed' identity which was rigidly fixed in the past.[22] The rhetorical equivalent of this increasingly powerful representation was an emphasis on the deeds of 'historic Judaism' which similarly highlighted Jewishness as a 'completed' identity rooted in past glory and the 'pride of race.'

As Martin Weiner has shown, the construction of 'Englishness' in terms of the 'aristocratic' values of stability, tranquillity and spirituality countered the bourgeois ideals of economic and technical innovation. After the 1850s, the 'emotions laden onto the cultural symbol of England as a garden' made many Victorians uneasy about an increasingly 'modern'—urban, industrial and democratic—Britain. For this reason, the new dominant bourgeois culture in England adopted many of the values of the old aristocracy.[23] This general cultural ambivalence towards the modernization of England meant that the emancipation and acculturation of the Jewish upper and middle classes was perceived as peculiarly double-edged. The progressive liberal, on the one hand, might well have viewed the shedding of a particularist Jewishness as a symbol of the 'modernity' of a future England. However, an exclusivist conservative could just as easily understand Jewish assimilation as a denial of the cultural values and past history which was said to constitute 'Englishness'. This doubleness was reflected in both Disraeli and Farjeon—and many members of Anglo-Jewry's elite—who represented their own material progress as the natural ascent of a racial aristocracy.[24]

In fact, in his speech to the East End 'Jewish working men and their families', Farjeon articulates the beliefs and values of rural England:

> In the country men were brought into closer contact with nature, while in the town one moved in an atmosphere of mammon, of deceit, of fashion, false feeling and conventional ties and one is compelled to bring into play the meanest portion of oneself. In the country there is more simplicity, less humbug.[25]

Farjeon defines 'humbug' in his talk as 'assuming a superiority to which we are not entitled' and echoes the common unease, in late Victorian England, at the rise of a new elite based not on 'blood' and land but on money alone.[26] Continuing this theme of 'prosperous knavery', Farjeon argues that 'in receiving more than our due, we commit a kind of moral larceny' which reemphasizes the fixed place of his working-class audience within an already 'completed' social hierarchy.[27] The distinction between 'good' and 'bad' ways of making money is especially important in these terms as it associates 'good' money with the rural values of the English upper classes.

Farjeon's *The Pride of Race* is an extended illustration of this theme as the novel distinguishes between the unacculturated first-generation Jewish immigrant and the second-generation English-born 'Jewish gentleman'. The alliance between Jews and the English upper classes is complete in this novel and is confirmed by the sympathetic gentlemanly narrator who tells us that 'a man may be both a Jew and a gentleman; I have met with many such and have learned from them much that is worth learning' (p. 3). To be sure, the reader soon 'learns' that it is now 'common' for 'a member of [the] English aristocracy and of the Church of England [to] marry a Jew' as 'the Jews, who have the reputation of being an exclusive race, are broadening out and becoming assimilative' (p. 89). Raphael Mendoza, the son of the self-made millionaire Moses Mendoza, is the prime example of this 'assimilative' spirit as he marries into an impoverished English aristocratic family and becomes a Member of Parliament. Once again, a Disraelian construction of Jewishness prevails in Farjeon's novel. In the words of a fictional British Cabinet Minister, the ancestry of 'indigent Jews living in the poorest quarters of the city . . . outvies the noblest of ours' (p. 62). Moreover, even though Moses Mendoza makes his wealth the 'wrong' way on the Stock Exchange, he diverts it all, by the end of the novel, into the impoverished English aristocracy. In this way, Farjeon legitimizes both new wealth and the moral worth of the Jewish immigrant who, instead of disrupting the established social hierarchies, even donates a battleship to the nation (p. 71).

It is interesting to see the extent to which a Disraelian construction of Jewishness pervaded late Victorian English culture. This was, however, only one way of rewriting the mid-Victorian liberal consensus concerning Jews. Other less paternalistic forms of rewriting this consensus were especially apparent in the Anglo-Jewish novel of the 1880s. Julia Frankau, writing under the pseudonym 'Frank Danby', published four novels on Jewish themes, beginning with *Dr Phillips: A Maida Vale Idyll* (1887), which departed radically from the Victorian apologetic tradition. Frankau was particularly influenced by French naturalism. In her view, 'the realistic representation of life was the only desideratum of novel writing, the only consideration that would make it worth while'.[28] As P.J. Keating has demonstrated, a naturalistic focus on 'the realistic representation of life' helped introduce greater freedom in both subject matter and style in depicting the working classes in fiction at the turn of the century. And, just as this freedom was to eventually spill over into the English novel as a whole, it also broadened the concerns of the Victorian Anglo-Jewish novel.[29] Julia Frankau was especially friendly with George Moore who, in the 1880s, was one of the main proponents of French naturalism in England.[30] Significantly, Moore dedicated his first novel, *A Mummer's Wife* to James Davis, Julia Frankau's brother. Like George Moore, Frankau published her novel with Henry Vizetelly, who had been jailed for three months for publishing Zola's *L'Assommoir* and *Nana* in English translation in 1885. *Nana,* in particular, had a direct impact on both Moore's *Esther Waters* (1894) and Frankau's *Dr Phillips.* As with Moore's novels, *Dr Phillips* was suppressed in England and the United States on 'account of its realistic treatment', as it was part of a wider attack on the conventions and sexual mores of Victorian fiction.[31] It is in the context of this new freedom that Frankau's early fiction, along with Amy Levy's *Reuben Sachs* (1888), can be said to have rewritten the apologist Anglo-Jewish novel.[32]

Dr Phillips concerns the degeneracy of a talented Jewish doctor who gives up the 'pure' world of science for the world of Mammon. As part of his decline, Benjamin Phillips marries for money and has a Gentile mistress, Mary Cameron, around whom the novel largely revolves. It is the view of Anglo-Jewry through Mary Cameron's eyes that indicates the novel's main debt to *Nana.* In Zola's Rougon-Macquart saga, Nana, the prostitute, is the symbolic centre of the corrupt French Second Empire. In particular, she 'devours' Steiner, a 'terrible' Jewish plutocrat who is 'noted for his sudden passions' and whose 'furious appetite for women' ruins him.[33] Phillips is similarly characterized by 'an Eastern virility that brooked no denial' (p. 94) and, like Steiner, Phillips squanders his fortune because of his uncontrollable appetite for Mrs Cameron. However, the sexual explicitness of Frankau's novel resulted in a general outcry against *Dr Phillips. Punch,* for instance, commented that Frankau's 'advanced' book 'should never have been written. Having been written, it should never have been published. Having been published, it should not be read.'[34] The moral looseness of *Dr Phillips* undoubtedly contributed to the 'storm of indignation' which it caused within Anglo-Jewry.[35]

Nevertheless, it was Frankau's claim, in the novel, that large sections of the Jewish middle classes in Britain are 'entirely unemancipated' (p. 192) which was specifically noted by the established Jewish community. In her Preface to the second edition of *Dr Phillips,* Frankau directly addressed the question of 'unemancipated' Anglo-Jewry and argued that her novel was not an attack on all Jews but on a 'small and little known section of [Jewish] society before it yields to the influences of advanced civilization and education'.[36] In a bid to show the consequences of a particularist Anglo-Jewry which has not 'progressed' since its emancipation, Frankau focuses on a section of London Jewry whose 'Deity is Gain' (p. 15). Here is Frankau's equivalent of Zola's corrupt Second Empire—a 'decaying' society whose only value is the 'acquisition of wealth':

> It is a fact little understood that here, in the heart of a great cosmopolitan city . . . there is a whole nation dwelling apart in an inviolable seclusion, which they at once cultivate, boast of, and are ashamed at. There are houses upon houses in the West Central districts in Maida Vale, in the City, which are barred to Christians, to which the very name of Jew is an open sesame.

> All the burning questions of the hour are to them a dead letter; art, literature and politics exist not for them. They have but one aim, the acquisition of wealth. Playing cards at each other's houses is their sole experience of the charms of social intercourse; their interests are bounded by their homes and those of their neighbouring brethren. (p. 168)

And, just as Nana becomes the moral yardstick in Zola's novel, Mary Cameron becomes 'splendid' (p. 114) besides the degeneracy that surrounds her: 'It was strange to see this beautiful woman of loose morals accepted and moving among these heavy, coarse-featured narrow-minded Jewesses' (p. 168). Clearly, Frankau internalized a racial discourse about Jews. This is particularly apparent with reference to the influence of Zola's fiction in which semitic motifs appeared frequently.[37]

Frankau, however, differs from her non-Jewish counterparts in her recognition of the complexities of Jewish self-hatred in *Dr Phillips.* Thus, she notes that 'socially ambitious' Jews belong to a class of people who 'see in every Christian a probable "swell", in every Jew a direct descendant of an old clothesman or a hawker' (p. 9). By the end of the novel, after causing the death of his wife, Phillips leaves a Jewish milieu and 'became in time the Jew-hater . . . It irritated him to see [Jews] walking about the neighbourhood, that new Jerusalem which they have appropriated with their slow and characteristic walk' (p. 337). Moreover, one need only compare *Dr Phillips* with H. G. Well's *Marriage* (1912)—which also centred around the common theme of the corruption of 'pure' science by 'Jewish materialism'—to see the relative ambivalence of Frankau's treatment of this subject matter compared to Wells's outright hostility.[38] For Wells, that is, 'Jewish materialism' symbolized the degeneration of England as a whole, whereas, for Frankau, it applied only to one 'bad' section of Anglo-Jewry. This section would disappear in time, according to Frankau, and, presumably, assimilate into a relatively healthy English culture.

The naivety of Frankau's radical assimilationism becomes apparent when we learn of the use that Arnold White made of *Dr Phillips* in his anti-semitic *The Modern Jew* (1889). This work examines the 'fatal' domination of the 'English nation' by 'cosmopolitan and materialist influences'. In this context, White describes *Dr Phillips* as a 'brilliant but sinister' novel which demonstrates the 'aloofness of Israel' and the inability of Jews in general to lose their racial particularity.[39] Frankau herself, after writing *Dr Phillips,* was the victim of a number of anti-semitic attacks and, by 1900, distanced herself—through her sister, Eliza Aria—from any misinterpretation of her early novel:

> *Dr Phillips* was written in extreme youth; it is crude and harsh with immature judgement, but ['Frank Danby'] was bitterly hurt at the use Arnold White made of his boyish generalisations . . . One day I think Frank Danby will write another Jewish story, but he will write now in a different spirit—in one that will be worthy of the race that he loves.[40]

Aria's article in the *Jewish Chronicle* signalled the publication of *Pigs in Clover* (1903), which resisted exploitation by British anti-semites by reverting back to the Disraelian Jewish stereotype in Farjeon's *The Pride of Race.* Unlike the unremitting 'naturalism' of *Dr Phillips, Pigs in Clover* explicitly identifies elements of the 'Jewish plutocracy' with the good of the nation as a whole.[41]

Written in the wake of the anti-semitic outbursts which accompanied the Boer War (1899-1902), *Pigs in Clover,* Frankau's second major novel on a Jewish theme, is at pains to differentiate between the moral and immoral aspects of 'Jewish Finance' in England. To this end, Frankau rather crudely identifies two half-brothers, Karl and Louis Althaus, who symbolize the 'good' and 'bad' aspects of Jewish financial involvement in South Africa during the Boer War. Karl Althaus is, in fact, a thinly disguised amalgam of Alfred Beit and Barney Barnato, who both became millionaires in South Africa. Like Barnato, Karl was born in the Whitechapel slums of London and, like Beit, he wished to use the diamond mines in South Africa for the good of the British Empire.[42] By the end of the novel Karl learns of 'patriotism' under the acculturating influences of a woman novelist, an English aristocrat and the imperialist Cecil Rhodes (who appears as himself in the book). Karl's racial financial 'instinct' (p. 71) is reined in by these benign figures and he eventually refuses to 'love money, money only, but to his surprise, now, at the root of his heart, pulling at it, he found England' (p. 181). Rather like Farjeon's Moses Mendoza, Karl grows 'beyond money' (p. 253) and, confirming this, the aristocratic Stephen Hayward argues that Karl is 'a thorough good fellow, a gentleman too, for all his want of a coat of arms' (p. 327). By contrast, Louis Althaus, Karl's Polish half-brother, remains 'the descendant of that wheedling ringleted son of a weak race that is no longer a nation' (p. 131) who is without 'a drop of good blood in his veins' (p. 210). Instead of growing 'beyond money', Louis uses his power traitorously and thereby threatens British interests in South Africa. What finally differentiates Karl from Louis, however, is Karl's longing 'for Christianity and its early lessons, for himself and for his people' (p. 97). The logic of Frankau's radical assimilationism was such that only Christianity was able to ensure the necessary transcendence of a 'Maida Vale' Jewish particularity. Clearly, there is a thin line, in these terms, between mediating the dominant culture and being absorbed by it.[43]

By the 1890s, a spate of Anglo-Jewish novels emulated *Dr Phillips* and *Reuben Sachs* by portraying a particularist Anglo-Jewry which either was encouraged to improve itself by marrying into the English upper classes or which was rigidly demarcated into those Jews who were 'coarse and loud' compared to the 'gentle people of their persuasion'.[44] The *Jewish Chronicle* in May 1892 reacted to this shift away from the Victorian apologetic tradition by editorializing that:

> In England, Jewish writers have usually felt themselves called upon to portray the seamy side of Jewish life . . . It is hard that the Jewish novelist in England should have a keener vision for defects than for beauties, should show on the whole less sympathy with Jews than do those who accept an absurd convention and can at least plead ignorance in justification. Perhaps Mr Zangwill's forthcoming novel, 'Children of the Ghetto', will prove the long-awaited antidote to the literary poison that has been poured in the public ear by several clever and unsympathetic writers.[45]

The *Jewish Chronicle*'s focus on Zangwill was significant since, by the 1890s, he had a national reputation as the editor of *Ariel*—a journal of New Humour—and as the author of *The Bachelor's Club* (1891). In 1889, Zangwill had also published an article in the first volume of *The Jewish Quarterly Review* entitled 'English Judaism: A Criticism and a Classification', which brought him to the attention of Judge Mayer Sulzberger, the head of the recently formed Jewish Publication Society of America (JPSA). Judge Sulzberger, on the basis of this article and two published short stories on Jewish themes, commissioned Zangwill to write a major Jewish novel for the JPSA. After protracted negotiation, Zangwill was given '*carte blanche* to write exactly what I pleased' and in 1891 began what was subsequently to be known as *Children of the Ghetto: A Story of a Peculiar People* (1892).[46] It was in this context that the *Jewish Chronicle* projected Zangwill as a 'sympathetic' novelist who would act as an 'antidote' to the 'literary poison' of his 'unsympathetic' predecessors. This communal representation of Zangwill as a Jewish novelist who, in the words of a later critic, had 'advanced the cause of the Jew throughout the world', remains to this day.[47] Thus, in a recent edition of *Children of the Ghetto,* it is argued that:

> In 1891 a young Anglo-Jewish writer commissioned to write about the London ghetto would wish to demonstrate to the non-Jewish world the problems and virtues of the immigrants, their relationship to the previously established Jews in London, and their aspirations to become accepted into English society.[48]

To be sure, Zangwill was the first writer in England to represent the Jewish immigrants in fiction. His was a unique task, yet it would be wrong to separate Zangwill completely from the Anglo-Jewish novels that preceded him. Zangwill, in particular, fitted uneasily into the apologist tradition of Anglo-Jewish fiction. Whilst negotiating with Judge Sulzberger, he made it clear that he 'could not undertake for any amount of dollars to write a novel that would appeal exclusively to a section' and, a year after publishing *Children of the Ghetto,* he wrote to Clement Shorter, editor of the *Illustrated London News,* saying: 'I must resist the solicitations of editors to shut myself up in the Ghetto.'[49] This ambivalence towards becoming a particularist Jewish writer stems from similar premises to those which underpinned the 'unsympathetic' novelists identified by the *Jewish Chronicle* for its opprobium. This can be seen, especially, in Zangwill's regular column (1888-91) in the short-lived *Jewish Standard* edited by Harry S. Lewis, where he often benignly referred to the fiction of Amy Levy and Julia Frankau. Using the pen-name 'Marshallik', Zangwill, for instance, devoted a large part of one of his columns 'Morour and Charouseth' (Bitter and Sweet) to a satirical ballad entitled ' "Dr Reuben Green: A Study of the Maida Vale Jewish Colony" by Amy Danby', an obvious reference to *Reuben Sachs* and *Dr Phillips.*[50] This ballad resulted in what the *Jewish Standard,* in its subsequent editorial, called 'some little sensation'. Whilst condemning the anti-semites' use of Frankau's and Levy's fiction, the *Jewish Standard* differed from the *Jewish Chronicle* in arguing that 'we are not of those who think that a Jewish writer dealing with his own people is bound to paint everything in a glowing rose colour and to give us a picture suffused with light and no shade.'[51] Six months after this editorial, the *Jewish Standard* argued that *Reuben Sachs* was 'an acute diagnosis of the spiritual blight that has come over well-fed Judaism' and Zangwill, in his column, similarly noted with reference to *Dr Phillips* that 'it's no use blackguarding the mirror because it reflects such evil features'.[52] Zangwill's column, moreover, also satirized Mrs Mark Herbert's *Mrs Danby Kaufman of Bayswater* (1890), an apologist riposte to *Dr Phillips.*[53]

In general, the *Jewish Standard,* known as 'the organ of English Orthodoxy', represented the views of a group of Anglo-Jewish intellectuals who, influenced by the impact of modern German-Jewish philosophy on traditional thought, were in self-proclaimed 'rebellion' against an 'official Judaism' which they dubbed 'flunkey Judaism' because of 'its deference to a wealthy oligarchy'.[54] It is not surprising, therefore, that their newspaper should show some 'sympathy' for novels that criticized the materialism of the Jewish middle classes. Zangwill, in particular, in his article in the *Jewish Quarterly Review,* had argued that 'all over the world the old Judaism is breaking down' and, in 1888, he was forced to resign his post as a student-teacher at the Jewish Free School because of the publication of a satirical ballad on Anglo-Jewry.[55] Furthermore, Zangwill's earliest stories, 'Motsa Kleis' (1880) and 'Under Sentence of Marriage' (1888), had specifically poked fun at what he called 'Anglo-Jewish bourgeois life'. Such satire characterized 'Morour and Charouseth' and this column has been accurately described as 'the very breath which gives life to *Children of the Ghetto*'.[56] To be sure, many of the central concerns of Zangwill's fiction can be found in his column. This includes the opening scene in the novel where poor and hungry East Enders are forced to wait in a soup kitchen before

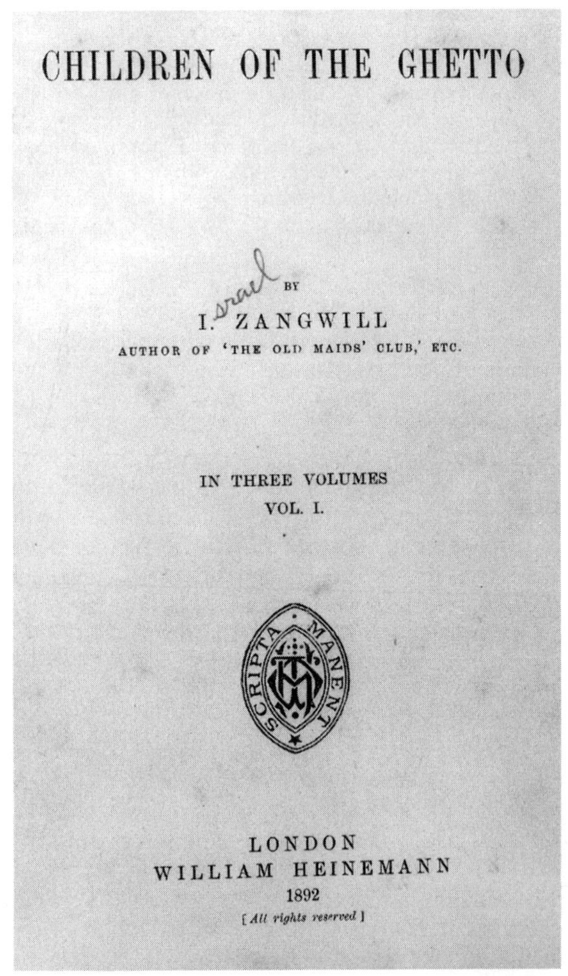
CHILDREN OF THE GHETTO

BY

I. ZANGWILL

AUTHOR OF 'THE OLD MAIDS' CLUB,' ETC.

IN THREE VOLUMES

VOL. I.

SCRIPTA MANENT

LONDON

WILLIAM HEINEMANN

1892

[*All rights reserved*]

they can eat, while their West End brethren make pompous speeches. Generally speaking, the attack on Anglo-Jewry's wealthy elite in 'Grandchildren of the Ghetto', the second half of the novel, is anticipated in much of 'Morour and Charouseth'. In 'Grandchildren', the satiric poem 'Reuben Green', for instance, reappears as the fictive 'Mordecai Josephs' by the heroine, Esther Ansell, exemplifying the generic novel of 'revolt'.

Children of the Ghetto can be especially linked to the fiction of Julia Frankau and Amy Levy because, like them, it centres around the conflict between Jewish particularity and what Esther Ansell, at the end of Book, I, calls 'the larger life' (p. 237). This conflict is usually played out in Zangwill's novel in generational terms and is reflected, at its most extreme, in the antipathy of the Anglicized Louis James towards his Orthodox father, whom he publicly rejects as 'an old Jew who supplies me with cash' (p. 324). A more optimistic, but short-lived, encounter between an Anglicized son and his Orthodox father can be seen in the death-bed reconciliation of Benjamin and Moses Ansell. As Harold Fisch has noted, Zangwill's Anglicized 'children' are desperately in need of self-improvement and, unlike the 'emancipated' second generation in Farjeon's novels, do not yet represent the 'progress of civilization'. The main thrust of *Children of the Ghetto* is, therefore, towards the transfiguration of its central characters who try and resolve the 'double lives' which they lead.[58]

Whilst Zangwill is clearly emulating the Anglo-Jewish novel of the 1880s, he was not simply a 'naturalist' writer.[59] In particular, Zangwill's explicit universalizing in *Children of the Ghetto* distinguishes his work from the Anglo-Jewish novel of the 1880s. By the end of the novel, for instance, Esther Ansell is openly described as 'an allegory of Judaism' (p. 398) which would not have been possible in the naturalist novel of the 1880s. The book's documentary realism—covering the widest range of subject matter and living individuals—can, like its central characters, be said to have been transcended by Zangwill's universalizing vision. This vision is implied in Esther's rejection of the 'ghetto' for a life in America, and it is also reflected in her reading of the New Testament and her wish that she had 'lived in the past, when Religion was happening' (p. 135). As the Proem to the novel makes clear, Zangwill locates Jewish spirituality in a historic 'ghetto' which has long since disappeared. Zangwill's characters, in these terms, are but 'vestiges of the old gaiety and brotherhood . . . the full *al-fresco* flavour [has] evaporated' (p. 7). This view, at its most extreme, results in a Christological construction of contemporary Judaism as an outmoded religion, an 'endless coil of laws' (p. 230). Because of this view of Judaism, the main thrust of Zangwill's art and politics after *Children of the Ghetto* was an attempt to transcend Jewish particularity.

In his article on 'English Judaism' Zangwill not only anticipated the 'break down' of the 'old Judaism' but also hinted at a grand synthesis of 'the scientific morality of Moses and the emotional morality of Christ'.[60] By the time of *Dreamers of the Ghetto* (1898), this synthesis is brought to fruition in a poem at the beginning of the book entitled 'Moses and Jesus'. Ten years later, Zangwill's play *The Melting Pot* (1908) articulated a view of America as the universalist ideal which was implicit in the end of *Children of the Ghetto*. In these terms, America is 'God's Crucible, the great Melting Pot, where all the races of Europe are melting and reforming'.[61] In particular, the intermarriage between David Quixano, a Jewish immigrant who came to the United States after his family was slaughtered in a Russian pogrom, and Vera Revendal, a Russian Christian aristocrat, illustrates the transcending powers of the 'melting pot'.[62] Zangwill's view of the 'melting pot' in fact complemented his political Zionism, which has recently been described by David Vital as a means of creating a non-particularist 'Jewish' nation.[63] It was according to these notions that Zangwill justified to Theodore Herzl, leader of the Zionist movement, his own intermarriage:

> Jews must become a people like any other. It is a positive duty to 'marry out'. Much as I value my Zionist activity, I cannot allow it to dwarf my larger sense of what the world needs, and what perhaps I exist to help to teach . . . I do not care to help [Zionism] except as a political movement . . . I am not sure, however, that the movement did not make a mistake in allowing itself almost to be captured by the religious party—you lose thousands of the most intelligent men in Judea, who are frightened away by the idea that Zionism is a movement of fanatics.[64]

Zangwill had also written to Herzl, regarding the possibility of his wife's conversion to Judaism, that 'the gates of Judaism are kept by clericism and she could no more become a Jewess than I could become a Jew.'[65] For Zangwill, Zionism would radically eliminate Jewish difference and would construct a nation state that would be 'Jewish only through the preponderance of its Jewish population'.[66] The mirror image of Zangwill's politics was his view of the 'melting pot', which can be similarly interpreted as a belief in a universalized Judaism as 'the future religion of all Americans'.[67] *Dreamers of the Ghetto,* Zangwill's collection of fictional portraits of the most famous Jewish apostates—including Christ, Spinoza, Heine and Disraeli—is a paradoxical expression of this universalized particularism. Zangwill intended his collection of stories to be a grand Arnoldian synthesis of 'Hebraism and Hellenism' where the 'most intelligent' non-particularist Jews can, finally, resolve the ambivalence of their own 'double lives'.[68]

Geoff Dench has rightly argued that the modern state has a 'dual character'. Formally, 'it is committed to progressive "universalist" values' but it still operates 'through traditional "national" vehicles tied to the destiny of particular communities'. Whereas the dominant national majority can interpret 'universalist prescriptions in partisan ways', this is not possible for weaker minority communities who lack 'the power to turn [these] contradictions in their favour'.[69] This results, according to Dench, in minority behaviour which, he states, 'can best be understood as attempts to minimize punishment for the majority. They need to act in ways which satisfy both communalist demands from the masses as well as the integrationist expectations of the national *elite*.'[70]

This describes well the project of the novelists that have been discussed in this essay. The fiction of all three writers 'minimizes punishment from the majority' by taking prevalent Jewish representations—such as the Jewish financier or, in Zangwill's case, the Jewish alien—which are then re-written in terms which make them 'acceptable' to the majority values of English culture. At the same time, Frankau and Zangwill, to some extent, resist the apologetic imperative of the Jewish community and, instead, radically conform to the 'integrationist expectations of the national elite'. And yet, the very construction of a 'Jewish novel' in Britain which differs in style and subject matter from its 'non-Jewish' counterparts signifies the very otherness which the 'universalist' writer would wish to transcend. Caught in this 'double bind', many Anglo-Jewish novelists before 1945 constructed a particularist novel with a universalist message, whether it be the plea to 'intermarry', as in the novels by Louis Golding, or, in the case of Samuel Gordon's *Sons of the Covenant* (1900), the need to 'decentralize' the Jewish East End so that it would, supposedly, no longer be a source of anti-semitism.[71] These contradictions were most clearly articulated by Israel Zangwill, who attempted to reconcile his Zionism, radical assimilationism and international reputation as a 'ghetto' novelist. To varying degrees, such contradictions were inevitable in a society which both promoted and denied racial difference as a means of constructing a particularist national identity which could not, by definition, be synonymous with its 'Anglicized' Other.

Notes

[1] Geoff Dench, *Minorities in the Open Society: Prisoners of Ambivalence* (London, 1985), p. 1.

[2] Ibid., p. 10.

[3] For these novelists see Linda Zatlin, *The Nineteenth-Century Anglo-Jewish Novel* (Boston, 1981), p. 30 and *passim.*

[4] Richard Davis, *The English Rothschilds* (London, 1983), pp. 81-4. See also M. C. N. Salbstein, *The Emancipation of the Jews in Britain* (London, 1982).

[5] Cited in Israel Finestein, 'Some Modern Themes in the Emancipation Debate in Early Victorian England', in ed. Jonathan Sacks, *Tradition and Transition: Essays Presented to Chief Rabbi Sir Immanuel Jakobovits* (London, 1986), p. 144.

[6] Beth-Zion Lask Abrahams, 'Grace Aguilar: A Centenary Tribute', *Transactions of the Jewish Historical Society of England,* 16 (1945-51), p. 142 and Zatlin, *Nineteenth-Century Anglo-Jewish Novel,* p. 39.

[7] For a recent discussion of this point see Andrew Benjamin, 'Kitaj and the Question of Jewish Identity', *Art and Design,* Winter 1988, p. 61.

[8] *Tatler,* March 1831. For the prevalence of these beliefs in early nineteenth-century Britain see W. H. Oliver, *Prophets and Millennialists: The Users of Biblical Prophecy in England from the 1790s to the 1840s* (Oxford and Auckland, 1978), *passim.* See also Finestein, 'Some Modern Themes', pp. 131-46.

[9] Homi Bhabha, 'Of Mimicry and Man: The Ambivalence of Colonial Discourse', *October,* 28 (1984), pp. 126-8.

[10] Sander Gilman, *Jewish Self-Hatred: Anti-Semitism and the Hidden Language of the Jews* (Baltimore, 1986), p. 2.

[11] For a detailed account of this racial discourse, see my forthcoming *Jewish Representations in English Literature and Society, 1875-1925: A Study in Semitism.*

[12] For a recent theoretical discussion of ambivalence, see Homi Bhabha, 'The Other Question . . .', *Screen,* 24 (November-December 1983).

[13] B. Cheyette, 'From Apology to Revolt: Benjamin Farjeon, Amy Levy and the Post-Emancipation Anglo-Jewish Novel, 1880-1990', *Transactions of the Jewish Historical Society of England,* 29 (1982-6) makes out this case, pp. 257-60.

[14] [*Jewish Chronicle*], 8 February 1901, [p.8, hereafter cited as *JC*].

[15] Louis James, *Fiction for the Working Man, 1830-1850* (Oxford, 1963), p. 135. See also *Jewish Chronicle,* 7 May 1875, p. 95 and 23 November 1877, p. 12.

[16] Gareth Stedman Jones, *Outcast London: A Study in the Relationship between Classes in Victorian Society* (Oxford, 1971), ch. 15 is the best account of this 'moralizing'.

[17] Benjamin Farjeon, *Aaron the Jew* (3 vols; London, 1894), volume III, p. 4. Page numbers of this novel

and subsequent fiction will be cited in the body of the text. Unless indicated otherwise, quotations will be from first editions.

[18] Benjamin Disraeli, *Tancred* (London, 1927 edn), p. 153.

[19] Cited in Abrahams, 'Grace Aguilar', p. 145.

[20] Ibid., for Aguilar's 'Jewish Protestantism' and for Disraeli see Todd Endelman, 'Disraeli's Jewishness Reconsidered', *Modern Judaism,* 5 (1985), pp. 109-23.

[21] Benjamin Disraeli, *Lord George Bentinck: A Political Biography* (London, 1905 edn), p. 323 and ch. 24 *passim.*

[22] For this construction of 'Englishness' in the late 1870s, see eds Robert Colls and Philip Dodd, *Englishness: Politics and Culture 1880-1920* (London, 1986), p. 22 and ch. 1 *passim.*

[23] Martin Weiner, *English Culture and the Decline of the Industrial Spirit 1850-1980* (Cambridge, 1981), p. 10 and ch. 1 *passim.*

[24] For examples of this see Robert Huttenback, 'The Patrician Jew and the British Ethos in the Nineteenth and Early Twentieth Centuries', *Jewish Social Studies,* 40 (Winter 1978), pp. 49-62.

[25] 'Mr B. L. Farjeon on "Humbug" ' *JC,* 7 May 1875, p. 95.

[26] Ibid. For examples of this unease see Ruth Roberts, *Trollope: Artist and Moralist* (London, 1971), pp. 166-7.

[27] 'Mr B. L. Farjeon on "Humbug" ', p. 95.

[28] 'Death of "Frank Danby" ', *JC,* 24 March 1916, p. 22.

[29] P.J. Keating, *The Working Classes in Victorian Fiction* (London, 1971), pp. 125-38.

[30] W. C. Frierson, 'The English Controversy over Realism in Fiction, 1885-1895', *PMLA* (June 1928).

[31] R. Schneider, *Bibliography of Jewish Life in the Fiction of England* (New York, 1916), p. 6. For the Vizetelly trials see ed. George Becker, *Documents of Modern Literary Realism* (NJ, New Jersey, 1963), pp. 350-5 and 369-82.

[32] For a discussion of Amy Levy's *Reuben Sachs* in this context, see Cheyette, 'From Apology to Revolt', pp. 260-3.

[33] G. Holden (ed.), *Nana* (1972, Penguin translation), p. 116.

[34] Cited in Gilbert Frankau, *Self-Portrait* (London, 1944), p. 22.

[35] Montague Frank Modder, *The Jew in the Literature of England* (Philadelphia, 1944 edn), p. 325.

[36] Cited in Zatlin, *Nineteenth-Century Anglo-Jewish Novel,* p. 98.

[37] For a useful discussion of this subject see E. F. Randell, 'The Jewish Character in the French Novel, 1870-1914', unpublished Ph.D. thesis, (Harvard University, 1940), pp. 20-51.

[38] For an analysis of H. G. Wells's *Marriage* in these terms, see Bryan Cheyette, 'H. G. Wells and the Jews; Antisemitism, Socialism and English Culture', *Patterns of Prejudice,* 3 (Winter 1988), pp. 22-35.

[39] Arnold White, *The Modern Jew* (London, 1899), pp. xi-xii and 145-7.

[40] *JC,* 4 May 1900, p. 22. For an example of an antisemitic attack on Julia Frankau see ed. D. H. Laurence, *George Bernard Shaw: Collected Letters, 1898-1910* (London, 1972), pp. 609-11.

[41] Zatlin, *Nineteenth-Century Anglo-Jewish Novel,* p. 113 is wrong to argue that 'all Jews receive Frankau's hostility' in *Pigs in Clover.*

[42] For biographical details of Barney Barnato and Alfred Beit, see Jamie Camplin, *The Rise of the Plutocrats* (London, 1978), ch. 3.

[43] For a recent account of the radical assimilation of the Frankaus see Aryeh Newman, 'From Exile to Exit: The Frankau Jewish Connection', *Jewish Quarterly,* 34:4 (1987), pp. 49-52.

[44] Leonard Merrick, *Violet Moses* (3 vols; London, 1891), vol. II, pp. 79 and 235. For an implicitly conversionist novel see Cecilly Sidgwick's *Isaac Eller's Money* (London, 1889).

[45] 'The Jew of Fiction, and the Jewess', *JC,* 20 May 1892, p. 9.

[46] Bernard Winehouse, 'Israel Zangwill's *Children of the Ghetto:* A Literary History of the First Anglo-Jewish Best-Seller', *English Literature in Transition,* 16 (1973), p. 95 and pp. 93-117 *passim.*

[47] Modder, *The Jew in the Literature of England,* p. 341.

[48] V. D. Lipman (ed.), Introduction to I. Zangwill,

Children of the Ghetto (Leicester, 1977) p. 13. References to this edition will be cited in the body of the text.

[49] Cited in Winehouse, 'Israel Zangwill's *Children of the Ghetto'*, p. 94 and Harold Fisch, 'Israel Zangwill: Prophet of the Ghetto', *Judaism,* 13:4 (1964), p. 414.

[50] *Jewish Standard,* 1 March 1889, pp. 9-10. See also 9 Oc'ober 1889, p. 14.

[51] Ibid., 'A Misunderstood Marshallik', 8 March 1889, Editorial.

[52] Ibid., 25 September 1889, p. 9 and 13 December 1889, p. 10.

[53] Ibid., 28 February 1890, p. 9.

[54] Norman Bentwich, 'The Wanderers and Other Jewish Scholars of My Youth', *Transactions of the Jewish Historical Society of England,* 20, (1959-61), p. 54.

[55] Israel Zangwill, 'English Judaism: A Criticism and a Classification', *Jewish Quarterly Review,* 1 (1889), p. 398 and idem, 'My First Book', *The Idler,* 2 (1893), p. 632.

[56] Bernard Winehouse, 'The Literary Career of Israel Zangwill from its Beginnings until 1898', unpublished Ph.D. Thesis (University of London, 1970), p. 55 and *Jewish Standard,* 30 November 1888, p. 9, for 'Marshallik's' comment on 'Under Sentence of Marriage'. This story is collected in *The Jewish Calendar* (1888-9), pp. 54-79.

[57] *Jewish Standard,* 'Opening of the Soup Kitchen—Wednesday Evening', 21 December 1888, p. 10. See also ibid., 22 June 1888, p. 10.

[58] Fisch, 'Israel Zangwill: Prophet of the Ghetto', pp. 415-16 to which I am indebted for my analysis of Zangwill.

[59] Ibid., pp. 407-8 for Zangwill's rejection of naturalism.

[60] Israel Zangwill, 'English Judaism', p. 403.

[61] Israel Zangwill, *The Melting Pot* (London, 1925 ed), p. 33.

[62] For a useful analysis of Zangwill's play see Neil Larry Shumsky, 'Zangwill's *The Melting Pot:* Ethnic Tensions on Stage', *American Quarterly,* 27:1 (March 1975), pp. 29-41.

[63] David Vital, *Zionism: The Formative Years* (Oxford, 1982), pp. 356 and 438.

[64] Ibid., p. 354, citing letter to Herzl, 21 December 1903.

[65] Ibid.: 5 November 1903.

[66] *Jewish Territorial Organization,* ITO Pamphlet Number One (London, 1905), cited in Vital, *Zionism,* p. 438.

[67] Shumsky, 'Zangwill's *The Melting Pot*', p. 31.

[68] For this argument see Maurice Wohlgelernter, *Israel Zangwill: A Study* (New York, 1964), ch. 7.

[69] Dench, *Minorities in the Open Society,* p. 8.

[70] Ibid.

[71] *JC,* 4 January 1901, p. 8, and 26 July 1901, p. 6, for this interpretation of the novel.

Linda Hunt (essay date 1994)

SOURCE: "Amy Levy and the 'Jewish Novel': Representing Jewish Life in the Victorian Period," in *Studies in the Novel,* Vol. 26, No. 3, Fall, 1994, pp. 235-53.

[*In the following essay, Hunt compares Amy Levy's first novel on Jewish life,* Reuben Sachs, *to George Eliot's novel* Daniel Deronda, *and demonstrates that, despite Levy's disparagement of Eliot's novel in* Reuben Sachs *and elsewhere, the novels are similar in that they both may be placed within the tradition of nineteenth-century British fiction due to their attacks on materialism and the "exaggerated individualism" of society.*]

In the last month of 1888 Macmillan brought out what was to become a controversial novel within the Jewish community on both sides of the Atlantic. Amy Levy, a twenty-seven-year-old Jewish woman who had already made something of a name for herself as a writer of poetry, non-fictional prose, and fiction, was the author of this book, *Reuben Sachs.* It was her first published work of fiction about Jewish life. The question of how to represent Jews in fiction had evidently been on her mind for a long time, for in 1886 Levy had published in the weekly *Jewish Chronicle* an article, "The Jew in Fiction," in which she had criticized the treatment of Jewish characters by a number of different novelists.

In this article Levy takes jabs at Dickens' unpleasant Fagin but is no more pleased by his idealized Jew, Riah (in *Our Mutual Friend*); she reminds us that Thackeray too has Jewish characters who are entirely negative; and she speaks disparagingly of a now-forgotten novelist, a Mr. Baring-Gould, who, she charges, "follows the old Jew-baiting traditions" in his novel *Court Royal.* She dismisses Lord Beaconfield's (Disraeli's) idealized Jewish characters as unmemorable, and, with considerable emotion, complains that another novel of the day, L.L. Clifford's *Mrs. Keith's Crime* (1885), is "offensive" in its "condescending" depiction of Jewish people (a reading of this book reveals that its Jewish characters, while likeable, are minor and used only for comic relief).[1] What is perhaps surprising is that Amy Levy includes in her critique the Jews in George Eliot's "Jewish novel" *Daniel Deronda* (1876); Eliot's book had been hailed by most literary Jews of the time and many since, as a model for how to treat Jewish people in fiction.[2]

In *Reuben Sachs,* Levy followed up on her 1886 critique of George Eliot by explicity satirizing the idealized depiction of Jews in *Daniel Deronda,* and, in doing so, rejected a way of representing Jewish life that had become one of the conventions for treating Jews available to the Victorian novelist, especially the Anglo-Jewish novelist. Dispensing with this convention allows her to raise the question of what it means to be a Jew and to probe the moral nature of the Anglo-Jewish community. At the same time, she uses George Eliot's last book to widen the significance of her own Jewish novel, and she relies on the resonance created by the intertextual relationship between the two books to make the novel accessible to the mostly gentile reading public. Moreover, as we shall see, Levy's dissatisfaction with George Eliot's approach to the representation of Jews in fiction, together with her criticisms of other novels with Jewish characters, may have led her to depart in *Reuben Sachs* from what is now often called "classic realism."

In "The Jew in Fiction," Levy had called for a serious treatment of Jewish life and character. Like most literary critics today, she admires the impulse behind the idealized portraits of the important Jewish characters in Eliot's novel but finds them impossibly virtuous; therefore she asks rhetorically. "[W]hich of us will not acknowledge with a sigh, that the noble spirit which conceived Mirah, Daniel, and Ezra, was more royal than the king?"

Toward the end of her article Levy asserts, "No picture of English 19th century life could be considered complete without an adequate representation of the modern son of Shem." The point which emerges (albeit implicitly) is that the Jews are an intrinsic part of British society and must therefore be neither romanticized nor trivialized in British fiction. Seeing the Jews as thoroughly English although singular in many ways, she dismisses *Daniel Deronda* as "no picture of Jewish life, that of the little group of enthusiasts, with their yearnings after the Holy Land and dreams of a *separate nation*" (emphasis mine).[3]

George Eliot's saintly Jews are in tune with what British critic Bryan Cheyette calls the "apologetic" tradition of nineteenth-century fiction about Jews. He uses this term to refer to novels written by British Jews who, he explains, throughout the nineteenth century, particularly in the years preceding the appearance of *Reuben Sachs,* tended to write fiction in which Jewish characters were pictures of perfection. These Anglo-Jewish novelists first chose "to portray Jews as particularly moral in character so that they could be considered 'deserving' of emancipation"[4] (Jews, that is, of course, Jewish men, were emancipated—given full political rights—in 1859) and later created idealized portraits in order to show that England need not fear the flood of Eastern European Jewish immigrants coming to its shores.[5]

Cheyette gives Levy credit for transforming the Victorian Anglo-Jewish novel in the direction of "revolt" while acknowledging that Levy was not the only Anglo-Jewish writer to eschew apology in the late 1880's. He points out that Julia Frankau's *Dr. Phillips: A Maida Vale Idyll* (1887) offered "a negative discussion of Jewish 'realities'" and that Cicely Ullman Sidgewick's (Mrs. Andrew Dean's) *Isaac Eller's Money* (1889) "had an explicitly conversionist message" which concludes that Jews could only become "good citizens by marrying into the English upper classes." His description of *Dr. Phillips* does not convey the virulence of Frankau's portrait of Jewish life.[6]

As in *Isaac Eller's Money* (and in *Reuben Sachs,* as we will see), the Jewish community in *Dr. Phillips* is crude and materialistic, but Frankau's protagonist, a Jewish physician, is a monster who ends by experimenting with his patients, "maiming men and unsexing women." Because his qualities of character are explicitly linked to his "Hebraism," the novel is a demonizing fable which belongs in the long tradition of anti-Semitic writing.

The Jewish Chronicle lumped the work of Frankau, Sidgewick, and Levy together, complaining in its review of *Isaac Eller's Money* (the last of the three novels just mentioned to appear), that "the clever ill-natured fiction of Jewish life has now reached a high stage of development. Can nothing be said in favour of Jews that is not hard fact?" It is surprising—given that, among other things, Levy does not recommend the demise of the Jewish community—that the unsigned reviewer asserts that Sidgwick's novel is "less intentionally offensive" than *Reuben Sachs.*"[7] In fact, in *Reuben Sachs* Levy paints a much more balanced picture of the life of her people than do the other two women writers under discussion. It is true that her Jews like money and things, and they are people who value, to an unhealthy degree, individualistic competition, yet she is attempting to do what her article, "The Jew in Fiction" had asked for: to represent the "Jew . . . with his curious mingling of diametrically opposed qualities, his surprising virtues and no less surprising vices."

There is no denying that the overall impression of life within the Anglo-Jewish community that one gets from this novel is not pretty. When the story opens, Reuben, a rising young lawyer with political ambitions, has just returned from the antipodes where he had gone to recover from a nervous breakdown. His father, we are told, died years before, and the narrator makes it clear that his death was premature since longevity runs in this family. In fact, as the various characters are introduced, the Jewish ones all being members of Reuben's extended family, we find that nearly all the men are defective, sick, or nervous. His brother, "a hopeless n'er-do-weel . . . had . . . been relegated to an obscure colony,"[8] and his cousin Esther's father is in a madhouse.

Ernest Leuniger, Reuben's cousin, is an important example: "[I]t would be unfair to say that he was an idiot. He was nervous, delicate; had a rooted aversion to society" (p. 204). He spends his time obsessively playing a game of solitaire, which involves a board, marbles, and a little glass ball. Near the end of the novel, he finally is triumphant at this game, the meaninglessness of which is signified by the condescension of Judith, the female protagonist, who is "vaguely" kind but unimpressed by his success.

Even though the game is solitary, it symbolically represents the competitive individualism to which Reuben, and, to a lesser extent, nearly all of the male Jewish characters in this novel, dedicate their lives and to which Reuben ultimately sacrifices so much. Reuben betrays his love for his cousin Judith because his ambition requires that he marry a wealthy woman; the night after he rejects her "there was a withered, yellow look about him," and his mother thinks, "He is not well" (p. 264). By the novel's end, he is dead. Judith is told by Bertie Lee-Harrison, a convert to Judaism, "It seems that his heart was weak; he had been overdoing himself terribly, and cardiac disease was the immediate cause of his death—cardiac disease" (p. 290). The redundancy of Bertie's wording emphasizes the metaphoric significance of how Reuben died. In *Reuben Sachs,* the Jewish way of life, with the drive that it requires and its false values, takes a severe toll.

The Jewish women are ambitious in a different way, involved in a different form of competition: Judith sees "herself merely as one of a vast crowd of girls awaiting their promotion by marriage" (p. 209). Such marriages are not love matches; indeed, Judith's mother says quite frankly, "No girl likes her intended—at first" (p. 279). Conventional to the core, though passionately in love with Reuben, Judith obediently makes a socially-advantageous marriage to Bertie for whom she feels no love, and in the novel's last pages we are told "she knew now more clearly than before . . . the nature and extent of the wrong which had been perpetrated; which had been dealt her; which she in her turn had dealt herself and another person" (p. 288). The language here—the use of the passive voice, except when describing Judith's own behavior—emphasizes Judith's victimization while acknowledging she was not without agency.

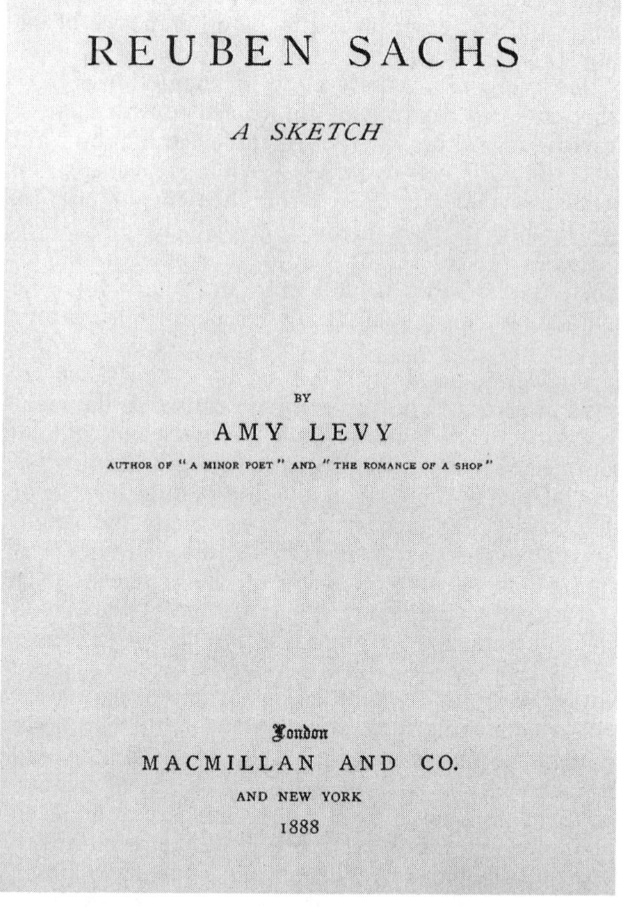
REUBEN SACHS

A SKETCH

BY

AMY LEVY

AUTHOR OF "A MINOR POET" AND "THE ROMANCE OF A SHOP"

London

MACMILLAN AND CO.

AND NEW YORK

1888

The other women in the novel, Reuben's sister and his Aunt Ada, for example, do not, in fact, give the impression that their affection for their husbands has grown over time. His mother and aunt are described in such a way that their very appearance speaks of the price they have paid for material wealth: we read of Mrs. Sachs's "wide, yellow expanse of . . . face, with its unwholesome, yet undying air, lighted up by the twinkling diamonds on either side of it, looking agitated and alarmed" (p. 242) and of Aunt Ada's "dejected, untidy figure, with the load of diamonds on the fingers, the rich lace round neck and wrists, the crumpled gown of costly silk" (p. 279). Levy makes the ubiquitous diamonds worn by the matrons an emblem of their pathos, and she reinforces the sense that the female characters have little control over their lives by associating the women with a pattern of drug imagery:. for instance, Judith in love is "like a hashish-eater" (p. 222); having lost Reuben, she has "the false calmness which narcotic drugs bestow" (p. 262); and Esther, one of the cousins, likes to say that "marriage was an opiate" (p. 284).

Finally, the narrator makes overt Levy's belief that the women of the Jewish community have the worst share of existence by having the narrator comment that for Jewish men "pride of sex is a characteristic quality" and quote the notorious Judaic daily prayer, " 'Blessed art Thou, O Lord my God, who hast not made me a woman' " (p. 214); Esther, who is rich, ugly, bitter, and cynical, tells Judith that as a child she revised that prayer, writing, " 'Cursed art Thou, O Lord my God, Who hast had the cruelty to make me a woman' " (p. 265).

But Levy said in her 1886 article that fiction should write of the Jew's virtues as well as of his vices, and she does. There can be little question that Reuben has an attractive vitality, which we see in the following portrait:

> He was back again; back to the old, full, strenuous life which was so dear to him; to the din and rush and struggle of the London which he loved with a passion that had something of poetry in it.
>
> With the eager curiosity, the vivid interest in life, which underlay his rather impassive bearing . . . he returned with unmixed delight to his own haunts; to the work and the play; the market-place and the greetings in the marketplace. (p. 200)

Reuben Sachs' extraordinary energy, if not his joy, is matched by that of his mother, who is described as having an "air of intense, but subdued vitality"; the narrator also tells us she is "an old lady it would be difficult to kill" (p. 198). His cousin Leo, a Cambridge student, is almost equally passionate in his commitment to music and in his romanticization of university life and the aristocratic friends he has made there; his youthful condemnation of his own people is also ardent.

In comparison, the only two gentiles whom Levy characterizes (others are mentioned) are conspicuously lacking in fire. We are given a brief sketch of Lord Norwood, Leo's friend, as possessing a "refinement of mind and soul and body, and . . . delicate strength of . . . character" (p. 246). The other gentile is Bertie, whose desire to convert seems ludicrous at least in part because he is too polite and vapid to seem capable of an intense spiritual quest.[9]

The most attractive thing about the members of Reuben and Judith's extended family is that they love each other to an almost remarkable, though always credible, degree. When Reuben returns from his sea voyage at the novel's opening, he can hardly wait to see his cousins, the Leunigers, and the other kin that live with them or frequent their home. When he enters, his little cousins throw themselves at him adoringly, and he responds to them with affection. When Judith is tossed aside by Reuben, her cousin Rose, a "good natured, high spirited" girl, gives her advice and affection which, if restrained, is nonetheless sincere.

Reuben's mother, whom we might expect to dislike Judith out of fear that Reuben would make a materially disadvantageous marriage to her, feels just the opposite: "She admired the girl immensely, and at the bottom of her heart was fond of her" (p. 215). Reuben feels tender towards his cousin Leo even though they disagree on everything and even though Reuben recognizes that Leo "regards me at present as an incarnation of the sevenSachs deadly sins" (p. 219). Of old Solomon, the family patriarch, we are told that "the ties of race, of family, were strong with him. His love for his children had been the romance of an eminently unromantic career" (p. 215). Amy Levy is able to evoke all this familial affection without ever slipping into sentimentality, truly an achievement in a Victorian novel.

Indeed, the way in which Jews are drawn toward one another is a major part of the substance of Reuben's moving attempt to answer his cousin Leo's attack on Jews and Judaism. Reuben refers with pride to "our love of race, home, and kindred, and regard for their ties," and goes on to say about his people:

> "[I]f we are to die as a race, we shall die harder than you think . . . That strange strong instinct which has held us so long together is not a thing easily eradicated . . . Jew will gravitate to Jew, though each may call himself by another name . . . If all the world, metaphorically speaking, thought one thought and spoke one language, there would still remain unspeakable mysteries, affinity and—love." (p. 240)

As if in proof of Reuben's prophecy, at the end of the book, Judith, married to the convert (who remains an outsider), feels "a strange fit of homesickness, an inrushing sense of exile." Her inner life is evoked powerfully by the narrator who speaks for her in the third person: "Her people—oh, her people!—to be back once more among them!" (p. 289). No longer part of the Jewish community, she is in alien space, and this is rendered emblematically by the fact that the scene is almost entirely framed by two references to the gold cross above the Albert Memorial outside her window.

What then does Levy suggest as possible answers to the questions: What does it mean to be a Jew? What is the moral nature of the Anglo-Jewish community? It would seem that, for her, some Jews and "Jewesses" possess a unusually powerful appetite for life. Even more important, the novel posits the idea that to be

Jewish is to be a communal creature, part of a people. The Jewish community represented in *Reuben Sachs* is corrupt, however, and the novel is in a sense a jeremiad, a lamentation for a people that has sold its soul for money and power, that has maltreated its women, that demands from its men a diseased and even suicidal style of life. These people love each other for the most part, but, as we have seen, that does not keep Reuben from betraying Judith—and himself. His treachery becomes a figure for a disturbing strain in Jewish life, seriously dimming, without entirely erasing, the hypothesis that the affection which holds these people together is enough to be redemptive.

The Jewish press on both sides of the Atlantic, responded, for the most part, negatively. The review in the *American Hebrew* is revealing:

> The story [*Reuben Sachs*] tells is that of an Englishman who is in love with a poor girl. His political ambition is about to be crowned with success in the shape of a seat in Parliament. The necessities of the situation require that he marry a rich woman, and renders [sic] it necessary that he give up the poor girl. Now the fatal blunder that Amy Levy makes is that she makes this Englishman a Jew as well, for no earthly reason whatsoever. She must know of course that there are Episcopalians and Dissenters in England who would have acted exactly as Sachs did and with as little, if not with less compunction. In fact, there are a number of other people in the book called Jews, for no evident reason than to say ill-natured things about them. It is a Jewish novel only in that sense that the characters are ostentatiously labelled with the name of their race.

It goes on to say, "An antipodal ethnological student reading Miss Levy's novel . . . would think that Thackeray and Dickens had either maligned the English people or that they had all since then become transformed perfect angels compared with the Jews."[10]

This reviewer makes a good point in recognizing that Levy's plot and the values which it attacks are squarely in the tradition of the English novel. One need only think of Thackeray and Dickens, as he does, and remember that, in *Vanity Fair,* George Osborne brings on his father's wrath by marrying poor Amelia Sedley, or that in, *Great Expectations,* Pip humiliates and rejects Jo, the good simple man who has been a father to him, because he is now higher than Jo in the class hierarchy. He would have been even more on target if he had thought of George Eliot's *Daniel Deronda,* as Levy asks her readers to do by twice referring to Eliot's novel in *Reuben Sachs.*

Toward the end of a dinner party that takes place at the home of the family patriarch on the Day of Atonement, the younger members of Reuben's extended family jokingly wonder about what the (at that point) would-be convert, Bertie, thought of the religious service he had attended and the dinner that broke the day's fast. Leo says, " 'I think . . . that he was shocked at finding us so little like the people in *Daniel Deronda.*' " His cousin Esther replies, " 'Did he expect . . . to see our boxes in the hall ready packed and labelled *Palestine?*' " Leo replies ironically, " 'I have always been touched . . . at the immense good faith with which George Eliot carried out that elaborate misconception of hers' " (p. 238).

This exchange serves several purposes. It reminds us that Levy does not believe Jews should be represented as paragons of virtue—she rejects the "apologetic" tradition that the *American Hebrew* reviewer would prefer—and that she regards England's Jews as natives who will remain in what is their own country. And, as indicated above, these remarks, together with a later allusion to George Eliot's Gwendolen Harleth and Grandcourt, signal the reader to bear *Daniel Deronda* in mind.

Two recent commentators on *Reuben Sachs,* Bryan Cheyette and Deborah Nord,[11] do exactly that although only Cheyette indicates an awareness that he is responding to Amy Levy's cue.[12] Both Cheyette and Nord recognize the many parallels between Levy's novel about Jewish life and the "English part" of *Daniel Deronda,* understanding that Levy's Jews, with their corrupt values and way of life, are a microcosm of the larger society (Cheyette, more than Nord, grasps that what is distinct about them is also the subject of the novel).

Both books attack a society given over to materialism and exaggerated individualism expressed through an obsession with competition. Again, this situates them squarely in the tradition of nineteenth-century British fiction, but the societies that George Eliot and Levy evoke are especially brutal. Levy uses two symbols that correspond to the gambling den depicted at the beginning of *Daniel Deronda.* We have already taken note of the game of solitaire that Ernest pursues so relentlessly, and another of Levy's symbols is the cardplaying that goes on whenever the Leuniger-Sachs clan gathers.

In developing the character and the plight of Judith Quixano, the character whose story rather surprisingly comes to dominate *Reuben Sachs,* Levy gestures to the narrative of Gwendolen Harleth repeatedly and with force. It is not that the two young women resemble each other in personality. Gwendolen is arrogant, narcissistic, and, at least superficially, daring; Judith is unassuming, not particularly self-absorbed, and conventional. Also, Gwendolen has a peculiar propensity for extreme nervousness in certain situations while Judith is distinguished by her calm demeanor (even if this composure comes to be questioned as a kind of narcotic).

Amy Levy (1861-1889)

Nevertheless, what the two female protagonists have in common is noteworthy. For one thing, each is the heroine of a novel named after the male protagonist, yet (in different ways) each takes over the narrative. Most readers find the story of Gwendolen Harleth more artistically satisfying and therefore more emotionally powerful than the Daniel Deronda narrative;[13] as for *Reuben Sachs,* about two-thirds of the way through the novel it shifts its focus to Judith Quixano, and the previously secondary feminist theme becomes prominent.

Both Gwendolen and Judith are poor relations living close to or with affluent kin: Gwendolen was not cast in this dependent role until her stepfather died, and even then does not feel its full force until her mother's money is lost through reckless financial speculation, while Judith, the daughter of an unworldly Sephardic scholar, came to live with her affluent relatives at an early age and grew up knowing she must marry expediently because she would have only a small dowry. These diverse histories explain Gwendolen's sense of entitlement and Judith's relative diffidence.

After Reuben's rejection, Judith sees no option other than marrying upper-class Bertie Lee-Harrison even though he is culturally alien to her and she is emotionally indifferent to him. After she accepts his proposal, Levy's narrator says, "Bertie, as Gwendolen Harleth said of Grandcourt, was not disgusting. He took his love, as he took his religion, very theoretically" (p. 282). This remark is surely intended to strike fear in the heart of Levy's readers because Grandcourt's cold and distant manner, which allows Gwendolen to think she will be able to tolerate him, turns into psychological sadism after the wedding. In fact, Bertie never does display any behavior more chilling than emotional remoteness and excessive politeness, but Amy Levy apparently wants the reader to link Judith with Gwendolen and be afraid for her.

One of Levy's major themes in *Reuben Sachs* is the vulnerability of women to commodification by the marriage market, particularly when their families are not financially sound. Gwendolen's uncle, a clergyman, makes no pretense about why he wants her to marry Grandcourt: "You are quite capable of reflecting, Gwendolen . . . You have a duty both to yourself and your family."[14] He goes on to say that she holds in her hands "a fortune . . . which almost takes the question out of the range of mere personal feeling, and makes your acceptance of it a duty."[15] Levy's Judith, in contrast, does not require such overt pressure; once Reuben is lost to her, she knows the script and performs her role. But Levy's explicit and implicit allusions to *Daniel Deronda* seem intended to remind us that women in British society, whether Jewish or gentile, are often sold to (and are expected to sell themselves to) the highest bidder.

Of course, the commodification of young women had been a theme in the British novel from the inception of the genre; a moment's reflection will bring to mind Richardson's *Clarissa,* the fate of Charlotte Lucas in Austen's *Pride and Prejudice,* and the pitiful ironmonger's daughter, whose misfortune it was to be married off to Crawley the baronet in *Vanity Fair.* Levy wants her reading public to place her novel in this context, and, like George Eliot in *Daniel Deronda,* gives this theme an even more central position than it has in most Victorian novels.

To make sure the reader notices the intertextual relationship she has created, Levy not only cites George Eliot directly; she also makes the analogues to *Daniel Deronda* particularly evident and numerous, and occasionally she allows herself to echo specific words and phrases. For example, the narrator of *Daniel Deronda* observes that "Of course, marriage was social promotion"[16] while Judith is said to be "awaiting promotion by marriage" (p. 209)

Perhaps the most important similarity between the two women is their narrowness of vision both in relation to their own possibilities and in regard to the world outside of themselves. Gwendolen Harleth's narrowness, as so many critics have noted, is her most distinguishing characteristic. George Eliot evokes it powerfully through her brilliant use of imagery, perhaps most memorably by Gwendolen's dread of wide spaces: "Solitude in any wide scene impressed her with an undefined feeling of immeasurable existence aloof from her, in the midst of which she was helplessly incapable of asserting herself."[17] The result is a crippling of the imagination, a total blindness to the needs of the world outside herself, so that while she has the desire to play a leading role and win the admiration of others, "such passions . . . dwelt among strictly feminine furniture, and had no disturbing reference to the advancement of learning or the balance of the constitution."[18]

Levy's Judith inhabits a world so limited that the perimeters of her imagination do not even permit an exaggerated sense of her own importance. The blinders that society has imposed on her make her unaware of her own uniqueness and value: "This woman, with her beauty, her intelligence, her power of feeling, saw herself merely as one of a vast crowd of girls" (p. 35). Amy Levy wants the reader to see the resemblance to Gwendolen but also to recognize a unique human being, one who, she believes, could only be produced by the particularities of Anglo-Jewish attitudes toward women which, *Reuben Sachs* suggests, are even more repressive than those of the larger society.[19]

The narrator says that Judith's "outlook on life was of the narrowest; of the world, of London, of society beyond her own set, it may be said she had seen nothing at first hand" (p. 210). The lack of a sufficiently wide view of existence is a major element in the oppression Gwendolen and Judith have experienced as women: both George Eliot and Amy Levy acknowledge that society's devaluation of women not only unfairly restricts them but also inhibits their potential, stunting their development as full human beings.

Another link between Gwendolen Harleth and Judith Quixano is that both are, to an important degree, constructed by the men with whom they are in love (but cannot marry) and by whom they are mentored. In many respects, George Eliot is using a convention in women's fiction that goes back to the eighteenth century: Fanny Burney's Camilla, for example, must undergo a painful reeducation under the guidance of her male mentor.[20] Gwendolen goes to Daniel for spiritual guidance after her marriage, and he counsels her patiently, trying to widen her horizons. Finally in her last note to him, she paraphrases his advice: "I have remembered your words—that I may live to be one of the best of women, who make others glad that they are born."[21] By allowing her heroine to accept a direction for her life that is highly conventional—these words could be the motto of Coventry Patmore's paradigmatic "angel in the house"—and by allowing a man who is much wiser than she to define that direction, George Eliot can hardly be said to be a feminist.

The relationship between Judith and Reuben can be seen as a bow to the young woman/male mentor convention, but Levy departs from Eliot and other predecessors by taking a negative attitude toward the role of the mentor. In significant counterpoint, Reuben does not provide an antidote to Judith's narrowness. Instead, his relationship with her is understood to be one of the reasons for her limitations. The paragraph quoted above about Judith's narrowness concludes: "[I]t may be said that she had seen nothing at first hand; had looked at it all, not with her own eyes, but with the eyes of Reuben Sachs" (p. 210). Levy shows us that Reuben has not done Judith a favor by shaping her development through directing her reading, lending her books, and exposing her to his ideas.

It is only after she has lost him that she begins to think for herself (even if she never is able to *act* unconventionally), coming to understand that, regardless of what Reuben and nearly everyone else in her world believes, "there was something to be said for feelings which had not their basis in material relationships. They were not mere phantasmagoria conjured up by silly people, by sentimental people, by women" (p. 269). After being prodded to think about *Daniel Deronda* throughout the reading of *Reuben Sachs,* readers are likely to note the contrast when Levy strikes out on her own in a more feminist direction.

Some of the reviews of *Reuben Sachs,* together with the Macmillan reader's report on the novel, enable us to see why Amy Levy needed the relationship her book bore to *Daniel Deronda* in order to expand its implications and make its themes more resonant for the gentile reader. The Jews in late-Victorian England were marginalized in the sense that even though they were tolerated and many doors were open to them[22] they were thought of as alien and, by many, repugnant.

We see this in George S. Street's turn-of-the-century "Essay on Jews," which focuses on *Reuben Sachs* and some other fiction, and concludes in response to their representation of Jewish life: "I am left partly in the accounts of these books repelled, partly attracted, but wholly baffled by a mystery."[23] The reviewer for *The Academy* says the Jews "are a people of whom the outside world knows but little."[24] The sense of Otherness that the Macmillan reader feels in relation to the life Levy represents is revealed by his opening remark: "A rather curious little book." It has "cleverness," but his lack of confidence in it—"I don't suppose the little book would achieve much popularity"—seems to stem from concern that the material is *outre* and distasteful.

His confidence that Levy's portrait of Jewish life is a "most effective bit of narrow and close photography" reflects an assumption, shared by other reviewers, that the novel exposes only negative truths about Jewish life and that this bleak portrait is the result of Levy's verisimilitude and not an interpretation on her part. He says that "The people are not made at all *excessively* [emphasis mine] disagreeable; but are painted just (I should think) as they really are in the synagogue, shopping at Whitely's, dining, and so on."[25] His parenthetical remark indicates his own lack of sufficient first-hand knowledge, but this does not shake his confidence in his convictions.

The reviewer for the *Academy*, who asserts that the majority population is not familiar with Jewish life, seems unfamiliar with the less attractive aspects of gentile society and the vast body of fiction which represents Englishmen engaged in a race for worldly goods and prestige. He states matter-of-factly and, one feels, smugly, "Miss Levy is apparently conscious of a certain soullessness and absence of ennobling ideals in the national character and deplores her kinsmen's sordid devotion to material interests and lack of any yearning for a higher life."[26] He also ignores everything in the novel that does not fit in with his preconceptions about Jewish people, the most obvious omission being Leo Leuniger's idealistic yearnings for transcendence.

Deborah Heller, in "Jews and Women in *Daniel Deronda,*" shows that George Henry Lewes and George Eliot herself were concerned that the Jewish dimension of *Daniel Deronda* would not be well-received, hurting the acceptance of the novel as a whole. Heller cites in evidence letters to Eliot's publisher, John Blackwood, written both before and after *Daniel Deronda* came out, and Blackwood's replies. The letters written after the novel was published reveal that their anxiety was well-founded. One could argue that the gentile reading public did not respond well to the Jewish half for aesthetic reasons, but both the Leweses and Blackwood assume a lack of sympathy on the part of the public toward Jews. In one letter, dated November 22, 1876, Blackwood remarks: " 'The Jews should be the most interesting people in the world, but even *her* [George Eliot's] magic pen cannot *at once* make them a popular element in a Novel.' "[27]

This correspondence about *Daniel Deronda* provides some possible insight into why Amy Levy was slow to publish fiction dealing with Jews and Jewish themes even though she had written at least one fine story about a Jew at Cambridge while still a Cambridge student herself between 1879 and 1881. This unpublished story, scribbled in a school notebook, is about a Leo Leuniger who is very much the same person he is in *Reuben Sachs,* and it includes two other characters who play a minor role in that book.[28] The appearance of these characters seven or eight years later in her published novel suggests a long preoccupation with them, together with a hesitancy to bring this material to the public eye.

Perhaps Levy needed artistic maturity to figure out how to amplify her Jewish material so that the public would want to hear it and would be able to understand its implications for Jewish life and for the society as a whole. Apparently she was more successful with her Christian audience than her Jewish one, the gentile reviews being quite favorable despite the fixation on the strangeness of Jewish society of some of the reviewers and the inability of many of them to see parallels with gentile life.

It is true that most non-Jewish reviewers saw the novel as a harsh condemnation of Jews and Judaism. Yet the reviewer for the *Literary World* is not alone in being able to recognize that the Jewish world of *Reuben Sachs* is no worse than the larger society which contains it. He writes that "*Reuben Sachs* is not a pleasant book to read; it has too much of the bitterness of reality in it. But we should advise Christians to be slow in reproaching Jewish society because of it; Mammon is a very popular god in all civilized lands."[29] One feels that Levy, in referring to *Daniel Deronda* in a variety of ways, hopes to legitimize the concern her novel has with questions pertaining to the Anglo-Jewish community and to enable her readers to receive *Reuben Sachs* as more than a foreign curiosity; her method relies in large part on triggering just such a recognition of how much Jews and gentiles have in common.

Daniel Deronda may have been useful to Levy in another and rather paradoxical way too; the presence of Jewish characters who are *not* nobleminded and handsome—who are unappealing in ways conventionally associated with Jews—may have prompted her to create a novel which suggests a range of responses to sensitive questions regarding Jewish matters but which offers them in an unresolved, polyphonic way.

Deborah Heller is one of the few critics who takes note of the fact that George Eliot's last novel contains some unfavorable "representatives of Judaism whose unattractiveness is inextricably tied to their conformity to familiar Jewish stereotypes."[30]

In this regard, she mentions or discusses several figures: the vulgar Jewish pawnbroker, Ezra Cohen, and his young son;[31] Mr. Wiener, the Leubrun dealer, to whom Gwendolen sells her turquoise necklace at the novel's start; Daniel's long-lost father, a moneylender and banker; and Lapidoth, Mirah and Mordecai's detestable thief of a father who was planning to sell his own daughter into concubinage for profit. She realizes that "the evident purpose of these unattractive Jews is to balance and therefore give credibility to the more ideal Jews" but remains troubled because "their unattractiveness is automatically presented as having a particularly Jewish flavour."[32]

Levy's unpublished story about Leo Leuniger at Cambridge indicates a pained awareness of anti-Semitism, as does one of her letters written when she was in high school[33]: she is unlikely to have missed the kind of negative stereotyping (in the case of Lapidoth, even demonization) Heller talks about. An article Levy wrote for the *Jewish Chronicle,* "Jewish Children," provides evidence that she was indeed disturbed by the minor Jewish characters in *Daniel Deronda.* Levy reminds us that young Jacob Alexander Cohen, the pawnbroker's son, wears "red stockings and velveteen knickerbockers," and she quotes a passage (which Heller also cites) that describes his voice as " 'hoarse in its glibness, as if it belonged to an aged commercial soul, fatigued with bargaining for many generations.' "

In her article, Levy also calls our attention to the way that George Eliot describes the remaining progeny of Ezra Cohen, thus revealing her sensitivity to nuances of stereotyping that Heller ignores. Jacob's sister, Adelaide Rebekah, has " 'monumental features,' " a " 'miniature crinoline,' " and, Levy paraphrases, a "Sabbath frock of braided amber." The baby, Eugenie Esther, " 'carries on her teething intelligently' " and "looks about her with such precocious interest." Levy's choice of these remarks indicates an understanding that George Eliot's Jews, when they are not poetic, are drawn from a received stock of ideas which include lack of physical charm, preternatural intelligence, and a penchant for overdressing and loud colors.

Levy registers her discomfort when she comments, "[T]hese three little persons are drawn . . . with an absence of tenderness which we should hardly have expected from the creator of Tottie, of Eppie, of Tom and Maggie Tulliver," and goes on to say, "The rather laboured jocoseness . . . seem[s] singularly out of place in her description of the young Cohens".[34]

Levy's recognition that stereotyping of Jews abounds even in a novel which was written in part to counter anti-Semitic ideas[35] may have led her to an important apprehension. *Reuben Sachs* can be read as suggesting that Levy had come to grasp that however well-intentioned and "realistic" a writer tried to be, British culture harbored so many deeply-held notions about Jews—so many unexamined ideological assumptions—that even the most gifted and serious of writers could only produce an interpretation built, at least for the most part, on received ideas. Such insights seem to have prompted her to depart from classic realism: *Reuben Sachs* shows Levy's recognition that the language of fiction has a complex and problematic relationship to any preexisting referents.

Aware that a writer's ability, including her own, to imagine the world and produce meaning is limited and defined by the belief-system which she receives from the systems of representation that the society makes available. Levy writes her Jewish novel in such a way that "truth" is hard to pin down. *Reuben Sachs* is a text whose stance toward the sector of Jewish society it seeks to represent is far from resolved. Epistemologically experimental, it lacks what Penny Boumelha, in a theoretical discussion of classic realism, calls "a controlling 'truth voice.' "[36]

Levy makes her novel polyphonic in the Bakhtinian sense by experimenting with narrative technique. It is important to note that the narrative voice functions inconsistently, sometimes calling attention to its omniscience and at other times undercutting its own authority. We see the former when the narrator shows off by predicting the future, telling us about young Leo, so eloquent in his hostility to his own people: "The time was yet to come when he should acknowledge to himself the depth of tribal feeling, of love for his race, which lay at the root of his nature" (p. 229).

At other moments, the narrator distances herself (assuming it is a she) from authority, as in the conclusion when, instead of closure, she offers a question: "Is life indeed over for Judith, or at least all that makes life beautiful, worthy—a thing in any way tolerable?" (p. 292). The chill of this possibility is only slightly mitigated by the news that Judith, unbeknownst to herself, is with child. The novel's last sentence predicting that the child shall bring both sorrow and happiness and a "quickening of purpose" still leaves the reader feeling that Judith's future is indeterminate.

Even when the narrator confidently predicts the future, as with Leo in the passage quoted above, the effect is to emphasize the fluidity of truth because the glimpse we get of a more mature Leo undermines the notion of a unitary self. The notion of a coherent self is subverted specifically in relation to attitudes towards the Jews and Judaism. Similarly, when the narrator tells us that Reuben "understood perhaps more of Leopold's state of mind than any one suspected, of the struggles with himself, the revolt against his surroundings which the lad was undergoing" (p. 219), the hint of a different, younger Reuben who felt negatively about being a Jew suggests that the reliably correct stance on what might be called the "Jewish Question" is not easily arrived at.

The authority of the narrator is again called into question by a remark she makes in the chapter about Yom Kippur, the Day of Atonement. Esther, Reuben's highly sarcastic cousin, does not go to synagogue, having had a fight with her mother. We are told: "She, poor soul, was of those who deny utterly the existence of the Friend of whom she stood so sorely in need" (p. 230). At this point the reader is likely to wonder: just who is this voice telling the story?

There has been no previous indication that the universe is watched over by a caring, or indeed, any other kind of God. In fact, religion has been devalued as when the narrator speaks mockingly of Yom Kippur, a day when observant Jews fast and spend the entire day in the synagogue:

> [F]rom an early hour, in all quarters of the town,
> the Chosen People—a breakfastless band—might have
> been seen making their way to the synagogues
> . . . if traces of depression were discernible on many
> faces, in view of the long day before them, it is
> scarcely to be wondered at. (p. 228)

Given this satiric attitude toward Judaism, who is this "Friend" the narrator is talking about? It doesn't seem likely that this God is a Jewish deity. Is Levy suggesting Judaism is an inadequate religion? Another thought comes to mind: is the narrator a gentile? Then one wonders about certain observations of the narrative voice which link the physical unattractiveness of the characters to their Jewishness and other remarks that make a connection between the fact that they are Jews and their materialism and obsession with success.

Reuben is described early on: "He wore good clothes, but they could not disguise the fact that his figure was bad, and his movements awkward; unmistakeably the figure and movements of a Jew" (p. 201). Another illustration of the narrator's assumption that Jews are unpleasant to look at should suffice: at a party in the home of the Leunigers, the narrator remarks that "some quite commonplace English girls and men who were here tonight looked positively beautiful as they moved about among the ill-made sons and daughters of Shem" (p. 251). Among the many statements made by the narrative voice which assume that Jews are excessively worldly in their values is the following: "[T]he Jewish people, so eager to crown success in any form, so determined to lay claim to the successful among their number, have scant love for those unfortunates who have dropped behind in the race" (p. 235).

One wonders if comments of this sort are not made from the perspective of an outsider, a non-Jew, who is simply revealing her own anti-Semitism. This hypothesis is supported by the fact that sometimes what the characters say and do undercuts the narrator's negative generalizations about Jews. The most dramatic illustration of this is the narrator's statement: "If there is a strong family feeling among the children of Israel, it often takes the form of acute family jealousy" (p. 249). The tone here is snide, suggesting that the narrator is not friendly toward the Jewish people; moreover, we see no signs of the jealousy of which she speaks. Instead, her generalization is patently belied by the close and loving ties which bind the Leunigers, the Sachses, and the Quixanos (the only exception would been the sneering attitude Reuben's relatives have toward the less assimilated and less affluent Samuel Sachses, from vulgar Maida Vale).

The relationship between narrator and narrative is certainly unstable. In some important respects, the characters do confirm remarks made by the narrator that strike the reader as anti-Semitic. Reuben himself acts, speaks, and thinks at times in ways that compel one to see Jewish life as oriented toward the single-minded pursuit of self-interest and ambition.

On the other hand, while he sometimes brings to mind stereotyped notions about Jews, most notably when he puts ambition ahead of his love for Judith, he is rendered with so much specific and contradictory detail—through what he does, what he says, and the access we are given to his inner life (by means of free indirect style)—that he never *becomes* a stereotype. When Leo charges that one doesn't find idealists among Jews, using the mythic King Cophetua as an example, Reuben responds with acute perception: "King Cophetua had an assured position. It isn't everyone that can afford to marry beggar-maids" (p. 237).

Reuben's self-conscious ability to understand the relationship between his values and his status as an outsider in English society enhances his three-dimensionality. It also provides motivation for his later decision to put ambition ahead of love, suggesting that his behavior is more than a reflex resulting from something innate in Jewishness. Finally, the many reminders of the corrupt gentile world of *Daniel Deronda* create a context that makes the negative side of Jewish life in *Reuben Sachs* look ordinary instead of appalling.

The result is a novel whose stance is so slippery—the relationship between narrator and narrative so shifting—the reliability of the narrative voice so questionable—the stereotypical ways in which some of the characters act maybe only a representation of the culturally dominant image of the Jew (or perhaps merely of late-Victorian bourgeois manhood)—that the reader is not at all sure where Levy stands.

Levy's use of narrative technique in *Reuben Sachs* allows her to tell a story, the meaning of which is unstable but suggestive of multiple possibilities. Read carefully, *Reuben Sachs* offers such a hotly contested ideological terrain that it becomes evident that Levy understood that "a serious attempt at serious treatment" of "the complex problem of Jewish life and Jewish character"[37] required going beyond apology, demonization, or "laboured jocoseness" in the direction of epistemological innovation.

Notes

[1] George Eliot's effort to write a book sympathetic to the Jews has been appreciated by them; in 1948 she had a street named after her in Tel Aviv, and there are now streets named after her in all of Israel's major cities. See Edgar Rosenberg, *From Shylock to Svengali: Jewish Stereotypes in English Fiction* (Stanford, CA: Stanford Univ. Press, 1960), p. 184; for a study of the Jewish response to *Daniel Deronda* see Shmuel Werses, "The Jewish Reception of *Daniel Deronda,*" *Daniel Deronda: A Centenary Symposium,* ed. Alice Shalvi (Jerusalem: Jerusalem Academic Press, 1976), pp. 11-47.

[2] It is interesting to note that not all Jews found the treatment of Jews in *Mrs. Keith's Crime* objectionable. An anonymous columnist praises it while glancing at a number of recent novels which have Jewish characters. See *The American Hebrew* (23 Aug. 1889): 36; Levy's standards were evidently higher or at least different.

[3] Amy Levy, "The Jew in Fiction," *The Jewish Chronicle* (4 June 1886): 13.

[4] Bryan Cheyette, "From Apology to Revolt: Benjamin Farjeon, Amy Levy and the Post Emancipation Anglo-Jewish Novel," *Jewish Historical Society of England Transactions* (Jan. 1985): 253-65. During the Victorian period gentile novelists faced with the task of creating Jewish characters tended either toward one-dimensional demonization or idealization (what Cheyettte calls "apology").

[5] Cheyette, " 'from Apology to Revolt,' " p. 256.

[6] *Ibid.,* p. 262. In a more recent essay Cheyette explains that in writing *Dr Phillips* Frankau was influenced by French naturalism, observing that she "internalized a racial discourse about Jews" and that in Zola's fiction "semitic motifs appeared frequently": see "The Other Self: Anglo-Jewish Fiction and the Representation of Jews in England, 1875-1905," *The Making of Modern Anglo-Jewry,* ed. David Cesarani (Oxford: Basil Blackwell, 1990), pp. 103-04.

[7] Review of Mrs. Andrew Dean's *Isaac Eller's Money, Jewish Chronicle* (2 August 1889): 12.

[8] Amy Levy, *Reuben Sachs, A Sketch* (London and New York: Macmillan and Co., 1888) rpt. *The Complete Novels and Selected Writings of Amy Levy,* 1861-1889, ed. Melvyn New (Gainesville: Univ. Press of Florida, 1993), p. 199; (all further page references to *Reuben Sachs* will be cited within the text).

[9] Reuben's family does not take Bertie's conversion seriously for other reasons as well: as Reuben says "he has a taste for religion," having started out High Church, "flirted with the Holy Mother" and "joined a set of mystics . . . somewhere in Asia Minor" before getting interested in Judaism (p. 205). Also, the younger members of this family are not themselves interested in the religious dimension of their Judaism.

[10] Review of *Reuben Sachs, The American Hebrew* (5 April 1889): 142.

[11] See Deborah Epstein Nord, " 'Neither Pairs Nor Odd': Female Community in Late-Nineteenth Century London," *Signs: A Journal of Women in Culture and Society* 15 (1990): 733-54, for an interesting discussion of three late-Victorian "New Women," one of them Amy Levy.

[12] Cheyette, p. 261.

[13] For the most famous devaluation of the "Jewish part" of *Daniel Deronda* see Frank R. Leavis, "George Eliot's Zionist Novel," *Commentary* XXX (1960): 317-25.

[14] George Eliot, *Daniel Deronda* (Great Britain: Penguin Books, Ltd., 1973), p. 178.

[15] *Ibid.,* p. 179.

[16] *Ibid.,* p. 68.

[17] *Ibid.,* pp. 94-95.

[18] *Ibid.,* p. 69.

[19] Levy's narrator refers to Jewish "orientalism" as an explanation for the inferior position of women within Jewish society on p. 210. Levy develops this idea in interesting detail in her article, "Middle-Class Jewish Women of Today," *The Complete Novels and Selected Writings of Amy Levy, 1861-1889,* pp. 525-27.

[20] For a discussion of the young woman/male mentor motif in eighteenth- and nineteenth-century British women's literature, see Linda Hunt, *A Woman's Portion: Ideology, Culture, and the British Female Novel Tradition* (New York & London: Garland, 1988), p. 43.

[21] Eliot, p. 882.

[22] For a discussion of the position of Jews in late- Victorian England see Todd Endelman. *Radical Assimilation in English Jewish History 1656-1945* (Bloomington: Univ. of Indiana Press, 1990), pp. 97-99.

[23] G. S. Street, "An Essay on Jews," *Pall Mall Magazine* 21 (1900): 288.

[24] Review of *Reuben Sachs, Academy* (16 February 1889): 109.

[25] Macmillan reader's report, British Library, BM Add.ms. 5541; pp. 146-47.

[26] Review of *Reuben Sachs, Academy* (16 Feb. 1889): 109.

[27] Deborah Heller, "Jews and Women in *Daniel Deronda,*" *Jewish Presences in English Literature,* eds. Derek Cohen and Deborah Heller (Montreal & Kingston: McGill-Queen's Univ. Press, 1990), p. 78.

[28] Amy Levy's unpublished story about a Jew at Cambridge is entitled "Leo Leuniger: a Study," and it is part of the collection of Amy Levy papers owned by Camellia Plc., London, England.

[29] Review of *Reuben Sachs, Literary World* (13 April 1889): 123.

[30] Heller, p. 85.

[31] Deborah Heller, in her essay cited above, finds Ezra Cohen a stereotype, describing him as "a mildly repulsive portrait of Jewish vulgarity and self-satisfaction" (p. 85). William Baker, in contrast, appears quite satisfied with the way his character is drawn; see William Baker, *George Eliot and Judaism* (Salzburg: Austria: Institut fur Englische Sprache und Literatur, 1975), pp. 223-26.

[32] Heller, p. 86.

[33] "Leopold Leuniger: A Study," cited above, is about Leo's deep sense of social inferiority in relation to the aristocratic friends he has made at Cambridge; the climax comes when he overhears them making anti-Semitic remarks. Levy's undated letter to her sister Katie was written when she was a student at the Brighton High School for Girls (between 1876-1879); she reports on the anti-Semitic remarks made by a classmate, expressing hurt and dismay.

[34] Amy Levy, "Jewish Children," *The Complete Novels and Selected Writings of Amy Levy, 1861-1889,* p. 528.

[35] Heller, p. 81.

[36] Penny Boumelha, "On Realism and Feminism," *Realism,* ed. Lilian R. Furst (London and New York: Longman, 1992), p. 320: this essay provides a good discussion of what is meant by the term "classic realism." For the most explicit explanation of the concept, see Catherine Belsey, *Critical Practice* (London, 1980), pp. 67-84, 112-17.

[37] Amy Levy, "The Jew in Fiction."

DEPICTIONS BY NON-JEWISH WRITERS

Rachel Mordecai Lazarus and Maria Edgeworth (correspondence dates 1815-1817)

SOURCE: "The Correspondence," in *The Education of the Heart: The Correspondence of Rachel Mordecai Lazarus and Maria Edgeworth,* University of North Carolina Press, 1977, pp. 3-18.

[*In the following correspondence, Lazarus (who helped her father—an American Jewish merchant—run a school for girls, and who read the educational treatises by Maria Edgeworth and her father, Richard Lovell Edgeworth) writes to Maria Edgeworth, politely condemning Edgeworth's portrayal of a Jewish character (in her 1812 novel,* The Absentee) *in a stereotypical, derogatory manner; then Richard Lovell Edgeworth and his daughter Maria reply; and finally Lazarus writes again regarding Edgeworth's later novel,* Harrington *(1817).*]

Warrenton, North Carolina
U.S. of America
August 7th, 1815

[*Original*]

A young American lady who has long felt towards Miss Edgeworth those sentiments of respect and admiration which superior talents exerted in the cause of virtue and morality never fail to excite, ventures, not without hesitation, to indulge a wish formed many months since of addressing her. If such temerity require more than an ordinary apology, it is to *Practical Education*[1] she must appeal as her intercessor; it is that, which by lately making her acquainted with the Edgeworth family, has gradually eradicated fear and in its stead implanted confidence.

With how much interest have I perused and re-perused the useful observations which those volumes contain. With what pleasure have I dwelt on the "anecdotes of the nursery," tho' it was a pleasure which on several accounts was tinctured with regret. First, as reminding me of deficiencies in my own mind and education, next, of my incapacity to impart lessons of equal utility, and lastly, I lamented that there were no more of them. But while reluctantly submitting to evils which are unavoidable, offered benefits should not be rejected; and I have resolved, that as far as my poor capacity will admit, these admirable lessons shall answer the benevolent intention of their authors and serve as models in the important business of education.

The eldest female of a numerous family, I find many claims on my diligence and exertion, and truly grateful am I to those who thus guide and direct me, in a course, by pursuing which, those who share my cares and my affections "may become good and wise and may enjoy the greatest possible share of happiness both here and hereafter."

To me the authors of Practical Education appear almost as individual friends, and friends the most disinterested; since, without knowing, they have assisted and encouraged me. I say *encouraged,* for I found both encouragement and comfort from the words, "A fond mother will tremble at the idea that so much depends on her own care in the early education of her children; but even tho' she may be unexperienced in the art, she may be persuaded that patience and perseverance will ensure her success; even from her timidity we may prophesy favorably, for, in education, to know the danger is often to a [*void it.*"]

True, I am *not* a mother, but if I were, I could hardly be more deeply interested; and with the consciousness of my deficiency, constantly rising in array before me, such an assurance came seasonably to my aid and encouraged me to *persevere.* In many of the opinions advanced, I found myself flattered, as they coincided perfectly with what had before been my own: of a far greater number which were new to me, I at once acknowledged the justness, and could not doubt the practical utility. May I not add, that the air of truth and candour which characterizes the whole work gave it in my estimation a value which without them, all its other excellencies would have failed to create.

How highly should I be gratified to know that the amiable and deserving family of Mr. Edgeworth are still as happy as they were, at the time that Practical Education was concluded; so far as depends on themselves, I think they must always be so.

The little volumes containing *Early Lessons,* the *Parents Assistant,* and *Moral Tales,*[2] I have read with pleasure, I trust with advantage, and am very certain they have contributed much to the improvement of the children in whose hands they have been placed. More of such works as the two first mentioned are much wanted; I seek in vain for successors of equal utility and merit. If I dared venture, I would ask if Laura, and my little friend Rosamond, are not real characters; and if the gentle, sensible Laura and the amiable Caroline Percy[3] are not drawn from the same individual. Such as the Caroline and Rosamond of *Patronage*[4] I should have supposed would be the characters of Laura and Rosamond when their minds had reached maturity.

With all my confidence in the benignant goodness of Miss Edgeworth I tremble at having said so much, and trespassed so very greatly on her patience and indulgence; still must I entreat that they may be extended to me yet a little longer.

Relying on the good sense and candour of Miss Edgeworth I would ask, how it can be that she, who on all other subjects shows such justice and liberality, should on one alone appear biased by prejudice: should even instill that prejudice into the minds of youth! Can my allusion be mistaken? It is to the species of character which wherever a *Jew* is introduced is invariably attached to him. Can it be believed that this race of men are by nature mean, avaricious, and unprincipled? Forbid it, mercy. Yet this is more than insinuated by the stigma usually affixed to the *name.* In those parts of the world where these people are oppressed and made continually the subject of scorn and derision, they may in many instances deserve censure; but in this happy country, where religious distinctions are scarcely known, where character and talents are all sufficient to attain advancement, we find the Jews to form a respectable part of the community. They are in most instances liberally educated, many following the honourable professions of the Law, and Physick, with credit and ability, and associating with the best society our country affords. The penetration of Miss Edgeworth has already conjectured that it is a Jewess who addresses her; it is so, but one who thinks she does not flatter herself in believing that were she not, her opinion on this subject would be exactly what it is now. Living in a small village, her father's the only family of Israelites who reside in or near it, all her juvenile friendships and attachments have been formed with those of persuasions different from her own; yet each has looked upon the variations of the other as things of course—differences which take place in every society. Again and again I beg pardon for thus intruding myself on Miss Edgeworth's notice; yet even now is my temerity about to appear in a new form while I give utterance to a very imperfect hope, that these lines may be honoured with a reply, and their author thus taught to believe herself not wholly unpardonable, in the liberty she takes in writing them. Should she be thus highly favoured, Miss Edgeworth will have the goodness to direct the letter according to the address, which a brother of the writer's, now in England, will annex.

With sentiments of admiration, esteem, and gratitude, Miss Edgeworth's

most respectful and obedient servant
Rachel Mordecai

Edgeworthstown, Ireland, August 4th, 1816

Whether I am addressing a real or an assumed character is more than I am able to determine; but the sentiments which your letter contained do honor to the understanding and to the feelings of the writer.

I have not seen the answer which my daughter sends to you with this, but I am certain that she felt real pleasure from the whole of your letter. We are used to receive compliments, but we have learned how to distinguish the value of the coin, by which we are repaid for our endeavours to be useful. I can assure you with great truth that we have steadily practised the precepts which we have published and that success has uniformly attended our exertions.

To praise my own is forbidden by the wise customs of society, but to acknowledge with gratitude the solace and delight which my declining health and age enjoy from the society and conduct of my numerous family may be permitted, as it holds out an encouragement to such generous minds as yours to persevere in the arduous task which you have begun.

If these letters reach you, pray make us better acquainted with your real self.

I have just heard that Miss Edgeworth has not mentioned to you the subject on which she is now employed; it will I hope be an *amende honorable* for former misrepresentation.

I am Madam,
Your Obed. Servant
Richard Lovell Edgeworth

Edgeworthstown, Ireland

Dear Madam,

Your polite, benevolent and touching letter has given me much pleasure, and much pain. As to the pain I hope you will sometime see that it has excited me to make all the atonement and reparation in my power for the past. It was impossible to remonstrate with more gentleness or in a more convincing as well as persuasive manner than you have done. Your own letter is the very best evidence that could have been offered of the truth of all you urge in favor of those of your own religious persuasion. And the candor and spirit of tolerance and benevolence you shew, you have a right to expect from others.

Will you be so kind to tell me how I can send you what I am now preparing for the press? It probably will not be published till the end of the year, so that I shall have time for your answer. Is there any person in London to whom I can consign the book? Though you did not sign any name to your letter and though it seems an extraordinary coincidence that your brother's name should happen to be *Mordecai* (absentee),[5] yet I am persuaded from the tone of truth throughout the letter that you are a real living person and that you think and feel all you say. Perhaps I am credulously vain in believing all the gratifying things you say about Practical Education, but I own that they have given me great pleasure. Nothing can be more agreeable to my father and to me than to think that what we have written on education has been practically useful, especially to one so amiably intent upon the education of a family as you appear to be. I should tell you that tho' for convenience the word *WE* is used all through Practical Education, yet I did nothing in the education of the family of whom I there gave the history.

In answer to your very kind inquiry about the happiness of this family I can assure you that we enjoy perfect domestic happiness and except from anxiety about my father's health we have scarcely anything in this world to wish for.

I am Dear Madam
Your obliged and grateful
Maria Edgeworth

[*Addressed: To the care of Samuel Mordecai,*[6] *Richimond, Virginia, North-Carolina.*]

[*Original*]

Warrenton, North Carolina, 25 September 1816

The twenty-fifth of September, if I kept a diary, should be noted as one of the most agreeable days I have ever known, and for its pleasurable sensations I am indebted to Mr. and Miss Edgeworth.

To express with simple truth the gratification derived from your letter, this morning received, would require terms which might appear exaggerated; I will therefore only acknowledge its politeness, its candour, may I not add, its friendliness, and return many thanks for a favor which I had scarcely permitted myself to think would be conferred. To those who, like you, delight in scenes of domestick unity, it would have been pleasing to see the animated countenances of my parents, brothers and sisters, as they witnessed and participated in my gratification; fortunately for us, the joy of one is the joy of all.

With Mr. Edgeworth's flattering request that I will make you better acquainted with my real self, I readily comply. It was not indeed in the first instance my intention to conceal my name, and it was signed at full length to my letter* but Rachel, as well as Mordecai, formed so striking a coincidence, that believing it would give an idea of my character being an assumed one, my brother erased both. [* That letter thrice crossed the Atlantic. My brother returning to America sooner than was expected and without visiting England, this letter was sent back and enclosed by him from Richmond. (*Miss Mordecai's note on the left margin of first sheet.*)]

Will you be interested to hear of one who, deprived of maternal care ere its value or its loss could be known or lamented, was for years dependent on nature and chance for the cultivation of her understanding and the forming of her heart and principles? To whom a second mother proved a blessing, and who in riper years learned patience, perseverance and cheerfulness in the school of adversity? My father, formerly a merchant, was in 1799 involved in the general ruin which attended the shippers of American produce, and after struggling under difficulties for several years, was prevailed on by many who had known him in better days to open an academy for young ladies. But just turned nineteen, I was sensible rather of requiring a governess myself than of possessing the capacity to become one, but the case was urgent, the best of fathers sought to encourage me, the confidence reposed by others inspired me with zeal, and with the commencement of the year 1808 we engaged in the all important business of education. A brother six years younger than myself,[7] but possessing information and steadiness far beyond his years, after the first six months became our assistant, and the eighth year will now soon close on our labours. Labours they are indeed, attended with fatigue, anxiety and care. Yet have we abundant cause for thankfulness, since they have been uniformly successful. In the improvement of our pupils, acknowledged by their parents, we often receive a reward the most grateful, and the number of applicants constantly exceeding that to which we have limited ourselves gives a satisfactory proof of publick approbation.[8]

I should perhaps have been less minute in relating these particulars did they not tend still further to prove the estimation in which persons of our persuasion are held in this country. A charge of the most sacred nature would scarcely be committed for years to any who could not be regarded with entire confidence. I might add that my father has been for more than twenty years in the commission of the peace for the town and county in which we live. Two sisters younger than myself are employed in attending to domestick arrangements,[9] our mother having a young family that has generally occupied her time and attention. It is the improvement of these children which forms my principal pleasure, as well as my greatest anxiety. Four young brothers and sisters share the attention of us all and are, thank Heaven, good and promising children.[10] Eliza, a child of seven years has always been particularly my charge. She possesses an excellent disposition and a degree of intelligence which, while it delights, often causes me to sigh, at my incapacity to cultivate it as it deserves. I seek by fixing your principles and precepts in my mind and making them as far as I can my guides, to supply in part my own deficiency.

What does Miss Edgeworth say of being "credulously vain" in believing all that I said about "Practical Education"? In acknowledging it my guide and director I shall gratify her less than by asserting, as I truly may, that to her and her excellent father *many children* are in a great degree indebted for their own happiness and their power of communicating it to those most dear to them. Since I last wrote I have met with the continuation of "Early Lessons," of which I had not before heard. I wish I could form a juvenile library of such books. It is principally by discovering how books ought to be written that we find the imperfections of such as we had before approved.

I must confess that I was rather gratified than surprised at Miss Edgeworth's frank admission of my charge (shall I call it) against her. It was my conviction of her being capable of a conduct so noble that first encouraged me to touch on so delicate a subject, but that she should immediately set about making what she calls 'atonement and reparation' was more than I could have hoped. Still do I rejoice at it, as it raises her character still higher in my estimation. We are told that authors at home and authors on our shelves are quite different persons; this assertion has often been a source of mortification to me, and I rejoice to find that in some instances at least it is erroneous. Your flattering attention in proposing to send me the book which you are now preparing for the press receives my warm acknowledgements. One of my brothers, who resides in Richmond, Virginia, and who forwards this will give a direction where it can be left so that (without accident) I shall receive it.

A tedious correspondent! am I not? And yet I cannot conclude without expressing a wish that the pleasure I have this day enjoyed may be repeated. A better feeling, I trust, than vanity gives rise to the wish of being allowed all the intercourse which a separation of three thousand miles will permit with such a family as the Edgeworths. Will you not let me know *you* better?

That Mr. Edgeworth's restoration to health may remove from his estimable family every cause of anxiety and that they may long live to improve mankind and to bless each other is the sincere wish of Mr. and Miss Edgeworths' obliged and grateful

R. Mordecai

[*Note at bottom of page*]

The original was sent to London by the ship Prince of Waterloo, under cover to Mr. Johnson, Bookseller, St. Paul's Church yard.

Any packet addressed to Samuel Mordecai, Richmond, Virginia, and left with Messrs. Marx and Wheattall, Merchants (Lime Street Square, near the India house, London) will be forwarded by those gentlemen.

[*Copy*]

Warrenton, October 28th, 1817

A few days since I had the pleasure of receiving the packet of books, for which I am indebted to the attentive kindness of Miss Edgeworth. Simple thanks are all the return that I can make for so great a favour, and I have to regret that I cannot to my own satisfaction express how much I am obliged. The publick papers had some weeks before given the melancholy information, which a note at the end of the preface to *Harrington* too surely confirmed, that the touching farewell was prophetick;[11] that the friend, the instructor, the benefactor of mankind was no longer permitted to dwell among us; he was summoned to receive his reward. None read or heard without emotion, for it was the concern of all; it seemed as if a luminary, which had shed its benignant influence over the world, was suddenly extinguished. I would not, dear and amiable Miss Edgeworth, probe the wound which filial affection united with confidence and tender friendship must too keenly feel, but I would convey that melancholy satisfaction which must arise from the assurance that in a foreign and far distant land, the worth of those we loved is known and felt, and that the tear of the stranger falls alike in sympathy with us, and in sorrow for his own individual misfortune. The last hours of the venerable and excellent Mr. Edgeworth must awaken, even in those most deeply afflicted, consolatory feelings: so calm, so collected, so amiable. What heart but must raise itself in the supplication, "May my end be like his." I fear to dwell longer on this painful subject. Miss E. requires not to be exhorted to submission and humble resignation to the Divine Will; and even while nature demands its tribute, she yields without repining, to the dispensations of the "Orderer of the Universe."

We have read both *Harrington* and *Ormond*[12] with much satisfaction; the former will, I hope by asserting the cause of toleration, reward the benevolent intentions of its author. In England, where from circumstances related in that work, we must believe prejudices carried to an excess, hardly conceivable by us in America, it will doubtless be productive of much good. If by scrutinizing the conduct of Jews, they are proved to fulfill in common with other men every moral and social duty, it is to be hoped that the stigma which habit has associated with the name will lose its influence. The eagerness with which Miss Edgeworth has sought for such characters, and such incidents, as were honourable to our unfortunate nation, evinces the sincerity with which she undertook their defence. It is impossible to feel otherwise than gratified by the confidence so strongly, yet so delicately manifested, by the insertion of a passage from the letter in which I had endeavoured to give an idea of their general standing in this country.[13] I say *in this country,* tho' I acknowledge myself but imperfectly acquainted with the opinions entertained in some parts of it. So far as regards some of the Southern States, I speak with confidence. The Northern might, I think, be included; the Eastern[14] are perhaps somewhat less liberal, but of this, I am not certain; and as for the Western they are yet in their infancy and have no determinate character.

To return to *Harrington.* The portrait of Mr. Montenero is rendered the more gratifying by its contrast with even the very few of those Israelites who have, in fictitious writings, been represented as estimable. I have met with none, that I recollect, but Cumberland's Shever.[15] And in Shever, tho' we find much to approve, there is still a want of respectability. He was a benevolent man; but in the profession of a *userer,* there is something against which correct principle revolts. Mr. Montenero is a good man, a man of science, and a gentleman whose acquaintance and intimacy anyone may covet. It is difficult duly to appreciate the greatness of mind which can relinquish opinions long indulged and avowed, and which has courage to recant when convinced that justice calls for recantation. The passage, page 30, beginning, "I have met with authors, professing candour and toleration, etc.," I read with peculiar satisfaction; such an instance of the candour, the superiority of Miss Edgeworth's mind and heart, I dwell on with a degree of pleasure, I may venture to say it, nearly equal to that which the reflection of having written it must yield herself. Many other remarks on this volume present themselves, but if I attempt to tell of all I found in it to give me pleasure, I shall say both too much and too little. Let me therefore, without dwelling longer on its many excellences, confess with frankness that in one event I was disappointed. Berenice was not a Jewess. I have endeavoured to discover Miss Edgeworth's motive for not suffering her to remain such; it appeared that there must be another, besides that of the obstacle it presented to her union with Harrington; and I have at length adopted an opinion suggested by my dear father, that this circumstance was intended as an additional proof of the united liberality and firmness of Mr. Montenero's principles. He had married a lady of different religious persuasion, without being inclined to swerve in the least from his own; and he had brought up his daughter in the belief of her mother, but with an equal regard for both religions; inculcating thereby the principle that, provided the heart is sincere in its adoration, the conduct governed by justice, benevolence, and morality, the modes of faith and forms of worship are immaterial; all equally acceptable to that Almighty Being, who looks down on all his creatures with an eye of mercy and forgiveness. It is not wonderful that I should, in the present instance, have adopted this opinion, for it is that in which all my father's children have been educated: we regard our own faith as sacred, but we respect that of others, and believe it equally capable of conducting them to the Throne of Grace. It would be gratifying to us to know how far our impressions respecting Berenice are correct.

In the character of Ormond, we found much to interest: its gradual development and formation, by casual circumstances, sometimes apparently adverse to its improvement, are happily delineated. This work forms a satisfactory contrast to "Vivian,"[16] a portrait, which tho' capable of proving eminently useful, leaves on the mind those unpleasant feelings which the view of such instability of character, whether real or fictitious, must always excite; while the firmness and decision of Ormond, united with good sense and nobleness of mind, promise every thing that we desire for our hero's happiness and respectability.

Miss Edgeworth will, I think, believe me when I say that I pause and hesitate, wondering at my own presumption in thus venturing, unasked, to offer my crude opinions; the confidence created by past indulgence alone encourages me to proceed. Still let me add, that I could not have ventured to trespass further than with acknowledgments on the receipt of the books, had I not been assured that Miss Edgeworth honoured my second letter with a reply, which unfortunately, I have never received.

The circumstance of my having addressed you, and obtained an answer, we had never mentioned, and we believed the secret confined to our family circle, till one of my brothers, travelling last summer to the northward, was astonished at being questioned respecting the letter mentioned in *Harrington,* just then published in New York. The ladies who enquired perceived his unfeigned surprise and told him they had heard from Mrs. Griffith[17] of Burlington, a correspondent of Miss Edgeworth's, that his sister was the lady alluded to. They had also heard from Mrs. Griffith that Miss E. had again written to his sister. The last pleasing, and encouraging piece of information came very seasonably to divert my thoughts from the formidable idea of being an object of general conversation. I forgave Mrs. Griffith the pain in consideration of the pleasure. But what can have become of this much desired letter? By what conveyance was it sent, and could the direction be mistaken?

I will not abandon the hope of receiving a reply to these enquiries, and I ask yet more, to know the contents of that letter, which I fear will not reach me. While complying with this request, Miss Edgeworth will have the goodness to say, if in seeking an occasional intercourse with her, I have exceeded the limits of her indulgence. Sensible as I am of the selfishness of this wish, and that I can offer no equivalent for the gift to my individual self of moments so precious and so worthily devoted to the general benefit, I cannot prevail on myself to suppress it; yet I should be unworthy of the lessons I have received from Miss Edgeworth were I unable to submit to a disappointment, severe as this would be, without murmuring. I cannot conclude without repeating assurances of esteem and admiration; yet even these words do not express all I feel.

With every wish for Miss Edgeworth's prosperity and happiness, I have the honour of subscribing myself,

her very grateful friend and servant
R. Mordecai . . .

Notes

[1] *Practical Education* by Maria Edgeworth . . . and Richard Lovell Edgeworth, 2 vols. (London, 1798); 3 vols. (London, 1801); 2 vols. (New York, 1801); 2 vols. (Providence and Boston, 1815); later editions not listed. *Practical Education* grew out of RLE's interest in his own children's education. He raised his eldest son, Richard, according to the tenets of Rousseau. Richard grew into an undisciplined youth, and as a child of nature he emigrated to America. Disillusioned, RLE tried other approaches with his younger children. In 1778 he and his second wife, Honora Edgeworth, began to keep notes of circumstances in the development of their children that they felt were worth recording. He continued this practice with his third wife, Elizabeth Edgeworth. Maria was drawn into the education of her younger brothers and sisters, and she studied the theories of Rousseau and Madame de Genlis. The work finally published in 1798 was the result of the collaboration of the whole Edgeworth family, from the recorded infant responses, the notes of the parents (the chapter "Obedience" woven around Elizabeth Edgeworth's notes), the chapter "Chemistry" by second son Lovell, to the general rounding out by Maria.

The word *practical* in the title can be understood to stand in opposition to *classical* with its emphasis on the memorization of arbitrarily chosen facts. The Edgeworths would eschew the prescriptive, and through sympathy and encouragement, they would stress the utilitarian and experimental.

The publication of *Practical Education* created a sensation in England, as well as on the Continent and in America. Not since Locke's *Thoughts* in 1693 had such a systematic treatment of education appeared. While widely admired, it was also condemned for its silence regarding religious education. It embodied the basis for modern education, and it made Maria and her father famous in their day.

[2] *Harry and Lucy, Part 1: Being the first part of Early Lessons, By the Author of the Parent's Assistant* (London 1801). *The Parent's Assistant: or Stories for Children,* 3 vols. (London, 1795). *Moral Tales for Young People,* 5 vols. (London, 1801).

[3] Laura and Rosamond are characters in ME's stories for children. Laura is sensible and Rosamond romantic. Caroline and Rosamond Percy are characters in *Patronage.*

[4] *Patronage,* 4 vols. (London, 1814); 3 vols. (Philadelphia, 1814).

[5] As indicated in her next letter, Miss Mordecai's brother had erased her name. "Mr. Mordecai, a famous London coachmaker," plays a villain's role in ME's *The Absentee.* Her other Jewish characters are in the vein of Shakespeare's Shylock.

[6] Samuel Mordecai, Rachel's brother. . . .

[7] Solomon Mordecai. . . .

[8] Accounts of the Mordecai School in Warrenton are given in: Gratz Mordecai, *Notice of Jacob Mordecai, Founder and Proprietor from 1809 to 1819, of the Warrenton (N.C.) Female Seminary,* Publications of the American Jewish Historical Society, No. 6, 1897; Caroline Cohen, *Records of the Myers, Hays, and Mordecai Families from 1707 to 1913* (Washington, D.C.: Published for the family, n.d.); Lizzie Wilson Montgomery, *Sketches of Old Warrenton, North Carolina* (Raleigh: Edwards and Broughton Printing Company, 1924).

[9] Two younger sisters, Ellen Mordecai and Caroline Mordecai. . . .

[10] The four youngest of Jacob Mordecai's children at the time of the writing of this letter were Alfred, Augustus, Eliza, and Emma. . . .

[11] Two weeks before his death, Richard Lovell Edgeworth wrote a preface for *Harrington* in which he made a public farewell to his daughter's readers: "I have been reprehended by some of the public critics for the notices which I have annexed to my daughter's works. As I do not know their reasons for their reprehension, I cannot submit even to their respectable authority. I trust however that the British public will sympathize with what a father feels for a daugher's literary success, particularly as this father and daughter have written various works in partnership. . . . And now, indulgent reader, I beg you to pardon this intrusion, and with the most grateful acknowledgements, I bid you farewell for ever. Richard Lovell Edgeworth. May 31, 1817." He died two weeks later on 13 June.

[12] *Harrington: A Tale;* and *Ormond: A Tale,* 3 vols. (London, 1817).

[13] In the novel *Harrington,* the father of the heroine, Berenice, is discussing with the hero his daughter's shock in experiencing anti-Semitic prejudices in England. In this passage Maria Edgeworth borrows directly from Rachel Mordecai's first letter to her: " 'Till she came to Europe—to England—she was not aware, at least not practically aware, of the strong prepossessions which still prevail against us Jews.' He then told me that his daughter had passed her childhood chiefly in America, 'in a happy part of that country where religious distinctions are scarcely known—where character and talents are all sufficient to attain advancement—where the Jews form a respectable part of the community—where, in most instances, they are liberally educated, many following the honourable professions of law and physic with credit and ability, and associating with the best society that country affords. Living in a retired village [*Warrenton, N.C.*], her father's the only family of Israelites who resided in or near it, all her juvenile friendships and attachments had been formed with those of different persuasions; yet each had looked upon the variations of the other as things of course, or rather as things which do not affect the moral character—differences which take place in every society' " (chapter 8).

[14] By Eastern states, Miss Mordecai refers to New England.

[15] Richard Cumberland (1732-1811), English dramatist; Sheva is a character in his play *The Jew,* first performed in 1794. The author was praised for his intention to defend the Jewish character.

[16] One of the *Tales of Fashionable Life* (London, 1812), "Vivian," according to RLE's prefatory note, "exposes one of the most common defects of mankind. To be 'infirm of purpose' is to be at the mercy of the artful, or at the disposal of accident."

[17] Mrs. Mary Griffith (d. 1877), American writer. She published two works anonymously, *Our Neighborhood* and *Camperdown: or News from Our Neighborhood* (Philadelphia, 1836). Widowed, she supported herself and her children on a farm in Charles Hope, New Jersey. Little is known of her, but her utopian story, "Three Hundred Years Hence," the first story in *Camperdown,* is the subject of an extended analysis by Vernon Louis Parrington, Jr., *American Dreams: A Study of American Utopias* (Providence: Brown University Press, 1947).

James Picciotto (essay date 1876)

SOURCE: "James Picciotto, Review, *Gentleman's Magazine*", 1876. Reprinted in *George Eliot: The Critical Heritage,* edited by David Carroll, Routledge and Kegan Paul, 1971, pp. 406-17.

[*In the following review, first published in 1876 and reprinted in 1971, Picciotto discusses the typical negative portrayal of Jews in literature, and then praises George Eliot's* Daniel Deronda, *arguing that Eliot "acquired an extended and profound knowledge of the rites, aspirations, hopes, flaws, and desires of the Israelites of the day."*]

Picciotto (1830-97) was a historian, the author of *Sketches of Anglo-Jewish History*. This review, entitled 'Deronda the Jew', is characteristic of the Jewish defence of the neglected half of the novel. . . .

Formerly the Israelite in novels was as accurate a representative of his race, as was the frog-eating French dancing master or the howling wild Irishman of ancient farces. He was a coiner, a buyer of stolen goods, a trainer of young thieves, a pettifogging attorney, a sheriff's officer, a money-lender, a swindling financier. He was a Jew, a man with no other thought than greed for money, no other sense of honour than that which is said to exist among the class to which he was compared, and with scarcely a soul to save. If old, he was hawk-eyed, hook-nosed, or with ferrety eyes. If young, he was red-lipped, with greasy ringlets, and wore showy jewellery. But young or old he was coarse, vulgar, the embodiment of covetousness and rapacity, with seldom one ennobling trait to redeem the repulsive picture. The delineation was as truthful as if a Whitechapel costermonger had been held out as the type of British merchants. To make a Jew the hero of a story, or even to endeavour to enlist the sympathies of the reader in his favour, was contrary to the canons of fiction.

The noble example of Sir Walter Scott has been forgotten by more recent novelists. Thackeray seldom had a kindly word for the Hebrew, though I believe that private representations made to him induced him to refrain from continuing to caricature the Jews in a story which he was publishing at the time in the pages of *Fraser's Magazine.*[1] Charles Dickens, it is true, made *amende honorable* before the world for the villanies of Fagin, in the virtues of Riah;[2] but the wrong he had committed was serious, and the effect of twenty years of misrepresentation by the most popular novelist of the day could be wiped out by no retractation.

The race is accustomed to hard knocks. It is difficult to know whether to admire most the tender feeling and good taste which induce Miss Rhoda Broughton[3] to regret that 'those oily, greasy Jews' can no longer be beaten to death with impunity, or the mental constitution of 'Ouida,'[4] according to whom a Jew who claimed payment for a bill he had discounted, was only spared from instant death for his presumption, by the rare magnanimity of the hero.

George Eliot (1819-1880)

At the same time, in some few instances, the Jew in fiction was a being endowed with almost supernatural gifts, an intellectual hero, a transcendent genius. Mr. Disraeli in his earlier works glorified beyond all things the Semitic race. A love for his lineage and a romantic disposition betrayed him occasionally into extravagance and exaggeration. The supremacy of the world belonged to the Jews, who reigned paramount everywhere by their wealth and intellect. The author of *Lothair,* however, seems to have modified his opinions, since in that work it is the Aryan race which contains the salt of the earth.

Alroy and *Tancred* were followed by some imitators, who ended by throwing ridicule upon the cause they intended to advance. No Erckmann-Chatrian[5] arose in England, like the Alsatian pair, to draw the foibles of the Jewish character, to delineate its virtues and faults with delicate humour and with deep pathos, with a keen and masterly pen freely wielded by a friendly hand. Nevertheless much has been written of late concerning the Jews, and a truer estimate is being formed of the Hebrew mind. The Jew is perceived to be neither a Sidonia[6] nor a Fagin; neither a Shylock nor a Riah. The mission of the Israelite is neither to govern the universe nor to discount suspicious little bills at 60 per cent. All the celebrated personages in the world are not Jews, nor all the millionaires; neither does the race absorb every old clothesman or money-lender or rogue.

A great novelist of non-Jewish extraction has now turned towards the comparatively uncultivated field. The first living artist in fiction in the English language has thought the modern Jews worthy of special study, the results of which have been given to the world in a highly-interesting form. Here we have what goes a considerable way towards filling an intellectual void—faithful pictures of modern Anglo-Jewish domestic life. But the author in some respects proceeds further, and evidently possesses loftier and wider aims than the mere exercise of the romance-writer's skill among new scenes. George Eliot has thrown no hasty or superficial glance over the externals of Judaism. She has acquired an extended and profound knowledge of the rites, aspirations, hopes, fears, and desires of the Israelites of the day. She has read their books, inquired into their modes of thought, searched their traditions, accompanied them to the synagogue; nay, she has taken their very words from their lips, and, like Asmodeus,[7] has unroofed their houses. To say that some slight errors have crept into *Daniel Deronda* is to say that no human work is perfect; and these inaccuracies are singularly few and unimportant. To Christians it is really of no consequence to know that the *kaddish* or prayer for the dead is recited by children only for their parents, and for the period of eleven months, and not eleven years, as Daniel Deronda's mother believes. Nor does it signify much that men repeat daily their thanks to God for not having been created females, instead of on the Sabbath only, as it is stated in the book. The author must have devoted much time and labour to the acquisition of the particular knowledge she has mastered; and these trifling blemishes do not detract from the general marvellous accuracy and vividness of the scenes depicted.

Curiously enough the Jewish episodes in *Daniel Deronda* have been barely adverted to by the reviewers. Most of these gentlemen have slurred over some of the finest and most characteristic passages in the book, with the remark that they possessed no general interest. Possibly the critics were unable to appreciate the beauty of the scenes they deemed unworthy of attention, or perhaps they considered the Jewish body too insignificant to be worth much discussion. However, it appears that the general public is not so indifferent to Jewish affairs as it is represented; and the periodical press of late has entered keenly enough into many details of Hebrew life and customs. Jewish thought is not entirely without influence in Gentile circles; and though the Hebrew personages in *Daniel Deronda* more immediately concern Israelites, yet there are several points and issues raised which more or less directly affect Christians and Christianity.

The aspirations of the hero of the book, it must be admitted, can scarcely enlist the warm sympathy of the general reader. Few of the novel-reading public are likely to have thought much about the restoration of Israel or to be aroused to any especial enthusiasm in its favour. Nevertheless many persons in all probability will peruse with curiosity descriptions of the habits and mode of life of the Jews. George Eliot's works are intended for people who possess intellectual faculties and know how to exercise them, and this class will find food for reflection in following the career of Daniel Deronda. The hero is seen under different lights, as various phases of his character are rendered apparent. At first we meet Deronda as one of those ideal men, drawn by feminine hands, who are happily impossible in real life, and whose very perfections would render them almost intolerable bores. In the hands of a less consummate artist he would have been one of those impeccable youths whose mission is to set himself up above the rest of mankind, and to preach morals by the yard, until his best friends must secretly dread his advent. In French novels this type of hero ordinarily becomes a mentor to beautiful young married women, whose education he completes by leading them into an infraction of the Seventh Commandment.

Fortunately, Daniel Deronda soon emerges from his shadowy superiority to show himself not absolutely above human weaknesses. He is fond of boating and cricketing, and his temper is not always angelic. He is a warm-hearted, romantic young man, with a feeling of intense sympathy for all kinds of suffering. His mental disposition inclines him to take up passionately the cause of wronged individuals as of oppressed races. Many of his actions are the result of pure impulse. He interferes to save from a dangerous indulgence in gambling propensities a young woman he had never seen before, and for whom he certainly felt no admiration; and he rescues another from drowning—a complete stranger—of whom he constitutes himself the guardian. In early youth all his associations were Christian, and his knowledge of Jews and Judaism must have been derived from books or hearsay. Nevertheless he enthusiastically accepts the mission bequeathed to him by Mordecai, however incongruous it may appear to an individual brought up in fashionable circles. How singular are, or at least were, popular notions on these subjects the reader can judge for himself. Mirah's question to Daniel, when she announces her faith—'Do you despise me for it?'—is a good test of the estimation in which her people were held.

How far a young man of good social position is likely to break with his former ties to embrace ancient religious forms which must, to say the least, expose him to the ridicule of his late companions, and cause him considerable embarrassment, must be determined by the amount of sacrifice each person is disposed to make on behalf of his convictions.

There is nothing inherently improbable in the fact of any given individual returning to the creed of his ancestors, especially in the case of descendants of a race who cling obstinately to their traditions. Moreover, with regard to Daniel Deronda, the impulses of his conscience are quickened by the contagious enthusiasm of a poetical dreamer, and by the love of a tender, bright pure face. In recent years, the well-known case has occurred in the Jewish community of an officer in the army, the grandson of an Israelite, albeit himself born a Christian, who returned spontaneously to the religion of his ancestors. In this instance no worldly circumstances to influence his conduct were visible, and certainly the change of faith of the convert could not have rendered his regimental position more agreeable.

The transformation of the *fat* Deronda, as Grandcourt calls him, into Deronda the Jew, is not then an astonishing event. The readiness of the supposed son of Sir Hugo Mallinger to undertake a national mission of the most improbable realisation, only proves an amount of belief in possibilities which all great men who have achieved difficult enterprises must have shared. The unity of Italy half a century since appeared as idle a dream as may now seem the reassembling of Israel in its own kingdom. Garibaldi and Mazzini were regarded as fanatics and visionaries, yet the leader of the thousand of Marsala has sat in the Parliament of United Italy which holds its meetings in the Eternal City. Daniel Deronda has never breathed, and may never live, but Jews have arisen and will again rise, who, if not resembling him in his perfections, will at least equal him in love of race and in ardour for the national cause.

The book is a romance. Artistic truth in literature, as in painting, is always sought for by great workmen in preference to mere realistic truth. In Daniel Deronda, George Eliot has created a type which, though scarcely likely to appeal to the masses, ought to teach more than one lesson to serious thinkers. Here is a man who lays aside entirely all purely personal considerations, all feelings of ambition or aggrandisement, to devote the best years of his existence to the loftiest national aims. True the Jews of England now possess a splendid example of high philanthropism in the person of a well-known benefactor of his race, who has repeatedly undertaken distant and perilous expeditions merely to help distressed mankind. Unfortunately illustrations derived from actual life frequently exercise little influence. It is possible that parallels drawn from fiction may prove more impressive.

The Princesss Halm-Eberstein forms a complete contrast to her son Daniel. He is emotional, sympathetic, affectionate, and tender-hearted. She is cold, calculating, ambitious, and of an unloving disposition. A mother who entrusts her only child to strangers for questionable reasons, is scarcely likely to inspire much sympathy or attachment. After remaining for nearly a quarter of a century without seeing her offspring, she might very well have gone to the end of her days without embracing a son for whom she did not pretend to feel any great solicitude. Why, indeed, she met him at that particular juncture is not explained. The secret of his birth might have been communicated by Sir Hugo Mallinger, and any one year would have served the purpose as well as another. In religious matters, too, the contrast between mother and son is very marked. While he is imbued with sincere belief in the principles of Judaism, she denounces that faith as too narrow, formal, and rigid; as a creed which places woman in an inferior position and limits her sphere to her domestic duties. The truth is the Princess is a bold ambitious woman who declines to be bound by the trammels of religion, just as she despises family ties. However, when she deserted her son she did not rob him of his due. She carefully placed his father's fortune under the guardianship of Sir Hugo Mallinger, who had formerly been an admirer of the lady, and who fulfils his trust with considerable kindness. Having once parted from her son and deprived him of maternal love, the Princess doubtless thought sincerely that she acted for his interest when she caused him to be brought up in ignorance of his origin, as a Christian gentleman. If in a particular country red-haired men laboured under any especial disqualification, a mother might be justified in having the hair of her child dyed of the hue affected by the inhabitants. Many others besides Princess Halm-Eberstein have preferred expediency to principle; and the forms of a religion which hangs rather loosely round the wearer may be easily thrown aside altogether in obedience to worldly considerations.

The sneers of the Princess with reference to the facility with which some Jews change their family names as they would an old garment, are not entirely undeserved. There is a growing tendency in this country among a certain class of the Jewish community to adopt strange patronymics as if they were desirous of concealing their Semitic origin. It must be stated at the same time that the Israelites of Spanish and Portuguese descent are above this weakness; they have carefully preserved through generations and ages their ancient family names, and are proud of them.

The Princess feels evident twinges of conscience concerning her conduct towards Daniel Deronda, and her misgivings and doubts are finely expressed. The Alcharisi, the greatest singer of the day, is no common personage. She is endowed with a strong masculine mind and with the musical genius undoubtedly possessed by the Hebrew race; and she displays acuteness of perception in resigning her stage royalty when she foresees the impending loss of her supremacy. It is to be regretted that she disappears as fitfully as she appears, and that a character which might have served as an interesting study, slips away from the reader and melts into thin air.

Had not Daniel Deronda formed casually an acquaintance with Mirah and Mordecai, it is very questionable whether his Jewish aspirations would ever have been developed. Of course chance is a most important element in human combinations, especially in fiction. His mother's revelations, but for his preceding adventures, might not altogether have delighted him. At the same time it is singular that he should never have suspected his origin, which ought to have left visible traces.

The influence exercised by Mirah seems to steal gradually and gently upon him, and, as usually happens in the case of women of her type, the power she acquires proves irresistible. Mirah is not a favourite character with the reviewers, who, whilst busy in following the fortunes of the grand Gwendolen and in attentively watching the evolution of her soul, lose sight of the unpretending little Jewess. Mirah is a typical daughter of Israel, simple and childlike, unambitious and unpretending, undervaluing her own talents, warm in affections, and above all profoundly attached to her family and race. It is astonishing of what deep heroism those quiet little women are capable. The serpent-like beauty of Gwendolen, her grand airs, her sharp tongue, would probably cause men to flock to her side in a drawing-room, leaving Mirah scarcely noticed until she began to discourse divine music. Nevertheless Mirah Cohen, with a San Benito over her lovely head, standing in the midst of roaring flames lighted by fierce fanaticism, would sing a hymn to the Lord of Israel; whilst in all human probability Gwendolen Harleth would readily embrace any faith that offered her wealth and a well-appointed establishment. Some critics cannot forgive the author for having made Daniel Deronda prefer the 'insignificant' Mirah to the stately and chastened Gwendolen. It may be suspected that some of the dissatisfaction expressed by those gentlemen arises from the fact that Daniel Deronda has become Deronda the Jew. Gwendolen Harleth, thoroughly selfish and detestable as she appears in the beginning of the book, succeeds by her misfortunes and by the better feelings which are evidently aroused in her, in enlisting the full sympathy of the reader. But a man in England is not yet permitted to marry two wives at the same time, and had Daniel Deronda selected Gwendolen, the author would have assuredly committed an artistic error. We must lament Gwendolen Grandcourt's trials, and regret to leave her a disconsolate widow. She is still young, and it is reasonable to suppose that she will find some heart-free individual who can make her drink the waters of Lethe.

Lapidoth forms a foil to the virtues of his daughter, and the author skilfully introduces the gambler and reprobate by the side of the pure-minded child. Lapidoth is a thief, Mirah is the soul of honour. George Eliot has studied nature too well not to divide her lights and shadows. No race monopolises moral excellence or villany, and unprincipled scoundrels unfortunately flourish among all nations and religions.

In addition to a wide range of reading in Jewish books, the author of *Daniel Deronda* must have had especial opportunities of personally observing Hebrew customs and manners and of speaking with intelligent Israelites. The portrait of the Cohen family is a photographic likeness which has probably been taken from life. Ezra Cohen is a pawnbroker in Holborn, a real embodiment of the qualities, good and indifferent, that make up the Jewish tradesman. The business of a pawnbroker is certainly not ennobling, but it may be carried on as honestly as any other. The small Jewish tradesman, keen as he usually is in the pursuit of gain, hard as he may seem in driving a bargain, is ordinarily an excellent father and husband and a strict follower of the practices of his faith. It is only some of the great families that find it convenient to drop troublesome ceremonies. Daniel Deronda's visit to the pawnbroker on imaginary business naturally affords an occasion for an insight into the ways of the family. Here we may admire the business aptitude of the youthful Jacob and the mixture of childish vanity and adult carefulness of his youngest sister when she asks whether she should wear her 'Shabbesfyock' before the strange gentleman. The shrewdness, vulgarity, and kindness of heart which combine to constitute the man Ezra Cohen are amusingly illustrated in his parting speech to Mordecai, which is an odd compound of calculation and sentiment. It seems singular, however, that the cautious pawnbroker should at first sight ask a complete stranger to share the Sabbath evening meal with his own family; and it is even more astonishing that Ezra Cohen, who is intended to be a strict Jew, should be described as transacting business on Friday evening, a proceeding which according to Jewish ideas would be deemed a desecration of the Sabbath.

The dreams and inspirations of Mordecai naturally chiefly concern Israelites. He is a prophet, a seer, but far from being the absolutely impossible character he has been considered by some critics. Anciently the most eloquent and learned rabbis among the Jews practised trades or handicrafts. Who shall say that among the immigrants from distant climes or among the Jews of Great Britain there is no workman whose whole heart is wrapped up in visions of the future greatness of his race? Indeed, it appears that Mr. G. H. Lewes, in an article on Spinoza, published in the *Fortnightly Review* of the 1st April, 1866, described a club which was wont to meet at a tavern in Red Lion Square about a generation since, and wherein the discussion of philosophical topics was carried on. The president of this club was a highly intelligent German named Kohn, Cohn, or Cohen, and probably he was the prototype of Mordecai.

The Jews, notwithstanding their ardour in mercantile pursuits, have always produced thinkers and philosophers.

Mordecai had long been seeking a co-religionist to whom he could confide the mission which fate would not permit him even to attempt to accomplish himself. He introduces Daniel Deronda to the philosopher's club, and the arguments therein brought to light, though possibly uninteresting to general readers, are deserving of close attention by Israelites. On the one hand, we have Gideon and Pash, who desire that the Jews should merge into the Christian population in the midst of which they dwell; and their opinion will be echoed by not a few of their co-religionists who care for naught but ease and self-indulgence.

On the other hand, Mordecai, with a loftier vision, expounds the mission of Israël. The poetry of Mordecai will prove *caviare* to the multitude. He is one of those pure abstractions such as all nations have produced—a man of dreams rather than a man of actions—and yet what could a poor Jew have accomplished? Even had the 'Ruach Hakodesh,' the breath of divine thought, entered that poor diseased body of his, not even his own co-religionists would have listened to its manifestations. George Eliot has studied Hebrew poetry, and the touching verses which she places in Mordecai's lips are not unlike those Hebrew poems recited by the Ashkenazim, and called 'Peyutim.' When Mordecai goes to his long sleep he is at all events happy, for he has bequeathed his mission to a trusty successor, and ere his breath leaves him the start is already made towards the East.

The author does not enter into the nice distinctions between the Sephardim or Spanish and Portuguese Jews, and the Ashkenazim or German and Polish Jews. Daniel Deronda appertains to the former class, which once contained the *sangre azul*[8] of the nation; whilst Mirah Cohen or Lapidoth, as coming from Poland, would naturally belong to the latter. To the present day these sections of the Hebrew race form in England and in most other countries distinct communities; but practically all difference between them has ceased to exist.

It is not necessary here to express any opinion on the merits of *Daniel Deronda* in its entirety as a work of fiction. George Eliot has passed from the realism of *Middlemarch* to the idealism of her present work. We cannot judge of Daniel Deronda and of Mordecai from the matter-of-fact surroundings of prosaic every-day life—albeit neither of these two characters is so totally imaginary and so far removed from actual truth as has been asserted. *Daniel Deronda* is no light novel to while away idle hours. It is a book full of deep thoughts, seeking to convey high lessons. It is scarcely a story in the ordinary sense of the word; the thread of the narrative is frequently disconnected and interrupted by reflections and disquisitions revealing a thinker and student of psychology of unusual faculties. The analysis of a difficult problem in human nature, the transformation of Gwendolen, is undoubtedly one of the aims of the book. But there is a far greater purpose in *Daniel Deronda* than the tale of a woman's life and the development of her soul. It is the vindication of a long maligned race against ignorant misrepresentation or wilful aspersion, the defence of Jews and Judaism against fanaticism and prejudice. George Eliot has laid open before a larger audience than had ever before been summoned for a similar purpose, the aims and scope and innermost thoughts of Judaism, and she has accomplished more for the cause of toleration and enlightenment than could have been achieved by any amount of legislation.

Two questions are raised in *Daniel Deronda* which concern principally, but not exclusively, the Jewish race. The object of Deronda, expressed in his own words, 'To bind our race together in spite of heresy,' is one of the aspirations that must be felt by every Israelite whilst admitting the difficulty of the solution. To bring the Judaism that was regarded 'as a sort of eccentric fossilised form which an accomplished man might dispense with studying and leave to specialists,' into consonance with modern ideas, is a task which only Daniel Deronda can effect. To maintain intact the spirit of Judaism, to preserve in pristine purity the faith and traditions of Israel, without keeping up the inflexible rigidity which opposes every improvement, and which drove out of the community an Isaac Disraeli, forms one of those problems which are still awaiting a satisfactory solution.

The political future of the Hebrew race may become more important to the world at large than its religious future. The reassembling of the Jews into a separate State, if such an event ever happen, must obviously affect more or less all Europe in addition to the provinces occupied. The influence possessed by the Jews in the financial world would certainly make itself felt on their withdrawal to distant lands. However, the dreams of Mordecai and Daniel Deronda are likely to remain dreams for the present. Not only are there no signs of their speedy realisation, but it is not at all sure that such a consummation is desired by the bulk of the Hebrew nation. The Israelites have become too firmly attached to the countries of western Europe, which have given them shelter, to be easily induced to abandon them *en masse,* and their magnates are scarcely likely to exchange the splendour and luxury they enjoy in the European capitals, for a residence in an arid and semi-civilised land. It is to be feared that notwithstanding all the efforts of Daniel Deronda and of real living philanthropists, it will be long before Palestine will cease to be, in the passionate language of Mordecai, 'a place for saintly beggary to await death in loathsome idleness.'

To have broached these questions before the popular mind is already to have obtained a great gain, and George Eliot has thus earned the gratitude, not only of her countrymen of the Jewish race, but of all thinkers and friends of progress.

Notes

[1] Two of the sketches which formed part of the 'Confessions of George Fitz-Boodle' in *Fraser's Magazine:* 'Miss Lowe' (October 1842), xxvi, 395-405, and 'Dorothea' (January 1843), xxvii, 76-84.

[2] In *Our Mutual Friend* (1864-5).

[3] Rhoda Broughton (1840-1920), novelist.

[4] Pseudonym of Marie Louise de la Ramée (1839-1908), romantic novelist.

[5] Compound name of two French writers: Émile Erckmann (1822-99) and Alexandre Chatrian (1826-90).

[6] Character in Disraeli's novels, *Coningsby* (1844) and *Tancred* (1847).

[7] *Tobit,* iii, 8.

[8] The 'blue blood', nobility.

Rabbi David Philipson (essay date 1889)

SOURCE: "Introduction to *The Jew in English Fiction,*" Robert Clarke, 1889, pp. 5-18.

[*In the following essay, Philipson examines the legitimacy of including the Jew as a character in fictional works, and argues that the only context in which "the Jew can be truthfully represented in the modern work of fiction . . . is as the follower and confessor of his religion." Philipson goes on to state that George Eliot has presented the Jew appropriately in* Daniel Deronda, *that is, as a follower of Judaism, rather than in racial terms.*]

As portrayed in English fiction from the time of Elizabeth to our day, the Jew is almost Protean in his character, if we may judge from the various guises he has been made to assume, running the whole length from the villainy of Barabbas to the ideal nobleness of Mordecai. So remarkable a phenomenon is well worthy of investigation. The theme is of sufficient importance to demand earnest, careful, and unprejudiced consideration. The influence of these productions in shaping the popular conception of the Jew can not be overestimated, since the fascinating form wherein the matter is presented is particularly effective in leaving a deep and lasting impression on the mind of the reader.

Where philosophy, with its investigations into the cause, aim, and effect of existence, with its far-reaching inquiries and conclusions, attracts but the few eager and restless minds who would delve into the very mystery of things; where theology, the philosophy of the highest, requires a depth and breadth of comprehension far above the ordinary; where positive science is an exacting mistress, demanding that exclusive devotion which only some choice spirits can or are willing to give; where historical investigation expects that search into past doings, customs, and thoughts, which can be satisfactorily accomplished only with the greatest labor and skill; where thus the pursuit of truth in any branch demands the discipleship of a lifetime and must be content with the least results, the many, impatient to be amused, not desirous of exerting the brain overmuch, have found in the novel, "the modern epic," as Fielding terms it, and in the drama, the novel presented to the eye, their chief mental excitement and amusement. Where one will find delight in any of the heavier products of thought, a thousand will eagerly quaff of the waters which flow from the fountain-head of fiction.

The ordinary reader is carried along, adopts the conclusions offered, has his opinions shaped and modeled by the writer of fiction. How many are there whose whole knowledge of history, for example, has been derived from this source. There are historical, scientific, philosophical, theological, and political novels, and great is the influence they exert. They are mighty factors in modern culture and modern life. Their power is great for good or for evil, as their producers will. Of many minds they are the only pabulum. It is not our object to decry the trash which passes to-day under the name of fiction, nor yet to extol the many productions of true genius which, presenting the phases of the development of the human life in this attractive form, have been among the benefactions of mankind, for there is scarcely one who has not been held as by a charm in the power of "the Wizard of the North," or has not laughed and wept and pitied and grown indignant with Dickens, or has not marveled at the biting scorn and sarcasm, and been startled at the deep insight into human nature of Thackeray, or has not stood amazed at the minute investigation of the broad, deep, philosophical mind of the greatest of the female novelists, the representative par excellence of psychological analysis in fiction, or has not drunk in and pondered and studied, and pondered again o'er the lines of the myriad-minded dramatist, England's first genius, and of the many lesser lights that revolve about this sun.

To these the greatest license is given; they touch upon any and every subject, whether legitimate or otherwise; none can bound the domain they may enter, none has yet attempted to define the proper province wherein fiction shall move. And yet there are but too evident instances that fiction, by offering a misrepresentation, has inflicted on innocent victims the greatest harm. Passion and prejudice readily communicate themselves from the page to the reader. Then ignorance, too, has impressed its seal on many a work whose influence all argument and all proof have in vain attempted to counteract. And that the Jew has suffered in this respect can not be denied. He has been a favorite character in fiction, treated with all the prejudice and ill-feeling which characterized the sentiments of the multitude, until the appearance of Lessing's "Die Juden" and "Nathan der Weise." How he suffered from the evil effects which these works of the imagination produced may be gathered from the following instance; whenever in the last century Shylock was performed, the passions of the multitude were excited to such a pitch that it was found necessary to produce, immediately thereafter, "Nathan the Wise," that this might act as an antidote towards quieting the aroused passions which might have culminated in excesses involving great danger to the unfortunate Jews.

Two questions present themselves for solution in this introduction: First. Was and is it legitimate to introduce the Jew into works of fiction? And, secondly, if so, to what extent can this be carried? Before answering the first question a few remarks will be necessary. Fiction is a compound of truth and imagination; its lasting power lies in the correct blending of these two factors. Exaggeration makes it bizarre and grotesque. Discerning minds will readily discover its weakness and its strength, and, according to the predominance of either, it will stand among the imperishable works of genius or disappear among the fleeting productions of the moment. Now, the truths which it lies within the province of the writer of fiction to touch, belong either to the inner world of human thought and emotion, the elaboration and development of which, in character, forms what we may term the analytical, psychological novel, or, if the novelist or the dramatist wishes to treat of external life—that is of real life, and desires to present his tale as containing elements thereof—he can employ only such characters and scenes which possess something strange, something different from that to which his readers are accustomed, and which can give a tangible hold to imaginative descriptions and events. This is what gives Scott his great and undying power; his Scotch descriptions and scenes came as a revelation to the reading world. They contain the element of truth and are drawn by a master hand. That is why Auerbach's *Dorfgeschichten* met with so generous a reception, because they dealt with scenes that had peculiarities sufficient to give them separate treatment. Therefore, too, the modern Russian, Swedish, and Norwegian works and tales attract so many intelligent readers, because competent minds have grasped upon that which is peculiar, and blending this truth with their imagination's fancies, produce these works, if not of genius, at least of great worth, in enabling us to understand the lives and incidents they portray.

Does Jewish life present these peculiar features, or any peculiar features which make it proper material for the novelist, so that the Jew, being introduced into the work of fiction, may be a truthful picture, and not a caricature? This question we ask regarding Jewish life, as not included in the Jewish religion; this point will be touched further on. Here, in the portrayal of Jewish life, it is that we must distinguish between past and present. We will not for a moment deny that in the past, and in those instances of the present which strictly follow the traditional lines set by the past—as is the case in the communities of Eastern and South-eastern Europe—the Jew, as man, apart from the Jew in religion, was and is a legitimate character to be introduced into fiction. His strict exclusiveness, his many peculiar habits, his (to the community) inexplicable customs, marked him off, as belonging to a nationality with peculiarities all its own. As, inclosed within the Ghetto he was cut off from all communication, except such as occasional business transactions required, so was he seemingly devoid of all sympathy with his surroundings. He had a national ideal; he regarded his present residence merely as a resting place in exile from the Holy Land. In many instances, he wore a costume by which he was distinguished. In short, his appearance, habits, customs, desires, inclinations, longings, hopes, were different from those of his neighbors. All things conspired to keep him thus; he was oppressed, jeered at—the butt of ridicule and cruelty. A character so strange, so readily distinguishable, with manners and habits so marked, became, as may be expected, popular with writers and authors; especially as by exaggeration and falsification they could delight and please their hearers and readers. Had the writers of these mediæval and later tales kept within the bounds of truth and reason, none could object to their introducing the Jew into their works. There are tales of this very Jewish life, portraying the peculiarities and strangenesses of the Ghetto-existence, giving pictures of every phase and every custom of this life, which are truly delightful and instructive reading. They were inspired, however, by friendship, or, at least, by impartiality, instead of by ignorance, hatred, and malice. The charming tales of past Jewish life of Kompert, Franzos, Sacher-Masoch, Baernstein, and Kohn, as tales of the past, although containing so much that is strange and idiosyncratic, we feel to be perfectly proper, although they are often concerned with non-religious doings; and why? Because they portray what was once a true state of affairs. Even should they contain passages unfavorable to the Jews, such as some chapters of Auerbach's

Spinoza, which tell of bigotry and intolerance, yet, knowing them to be true, none can object; none who would have the virtues appear would attempt to veil the failings and the errors.

This was; it belongs to history; and the fiction that would treat thereof must belong to historical fiction. Now, however, when the Jew has laid off all these peculiar customs; when he has stepped out of the Ghetto into the free light and air; when he has dropped his traditional distinguishing marks; when he in all has become like his neighbor—thinking like thoughts, indulging the same ideals, no longer a stranger in a strange land, nor looking upon his habitation as temporary, but filled with patriotic feeling for the welfare of whatever country he may inhabit; when, in all but religion, he is like unto all—every representation of the modern Jew, except in the religious light, in novel or in drama, in play or in tale, is a mark of gross ignorance, and, through ignorance, of gross evil and injustice. The prejudices of an early day have not yet died out, and this, coupled with the dense ignorance characterizing otherwise cultured people regarding Jews and Judaism, give these latter-day productions a truly pernicious power. From them many obtain their only knowledge of the Jews. The old thought of peculiarity and isolation is revived, if it ever had disappeared. Many who derive their knowledge from this literature never come into contact with the misrepresented character; and if they should, and would find him or her different from the presentation, they would not regard the portrayal incorrect, but only look upon their new acquaintance as a *rara avis*—a different somebody from the usual class; for had they not been informed by their author that the Jews speak differently, that they act differently, than their Christian neighbors?

All such works written and published add but another layer to the dividing line already existing. They are unjust to the Jew; they are but new antagonistic elements with which he is forced to combat. Even if written without prejudicial intent, they contain the insidious seed which sinks deeply and produces poisonous and noxious weeds. An author has a superficial acquaintance, we will say, with some Jews; he has picked up, here and there, some Hebrew phrases; he has noted a few distinguishing customs among some classes of Jews; he has also met with some loud, uncultured characters among them. Without any knowledge of true Judaism whatsoever, he will now set himself up as a teacher, to inform, through the pages of a novel, the general public what the Jews are, how they live, how they act, how they speak. He commits an injustice of the greatest character; he makes them speak a frightful jargon; he does more to increase the already existing prejudice than many a better book can undo; he gives them sentiments which are a disgrace to honest men; he at times tries to glaze over things by a kind word, or a pat on the back, as it were, but this is only the treacherous device that strengthens the wrong view presented. No worse enemy of the Jews exists; these novels are hidden thrusts; they are but tracts, as pernicious in their tendency as any anti-Semitic sheet ever published; they rest on a little superficial knowledge; they present, not the Jew, but a caricature; they introduce to us some coarse, loud individuals as Jews, and hence, as will be inferred from this, as types; they strengthen that widely prevalent notion of a peculiar people, and are to be denounced as falsities, as misrepresentations, as calumnies.

Because there are some vulgar, uncultured people among the Jews, is this a reason that such are to be specially represented as Jews? Because some Jews have grown suddenly rich, and are loudly ostentatious, is this a cause that the flagrant injustice be done, that they, with these characteristics, be held up by the name of their religion? 'T is time that this should cease; 't is time that those maligned and slandered should speak their word and counteract this dangerous and insidious influence; 't is time at last that Jews altogether be not characterized and represented by the few who are what they are, not as Jews, but as men. Any man, be he Jew or Christian, Mohammedan or heathen, who has been bred in ignorance, and has suddenly acquired a fortune, will be shoddy, for thus he thinks to air his importance, as his money is the only claim he has thereto, will be vulgar and loud, and generally disgusting to cultured people; but his religion has nought to do therewith. That is the trait in human nature which makes the parvenu, who has been a favorite character for ridicule from ancient days to our time, made typical by Molière's famous presentation of Jourdain in *Le Bourgeois Gentilhomme.* But Molière speaks not of his parvenu's religion; he presents him as a type, that can be met with every day. How would not a book be decried, or else considered beneath notice, that would introduce an Episcopalian, or a Methodist, or a Presbyterian, as the representative of shoddyism, of vulgarity, of loudness! We can readily imagine what a reception such a work would receive. The author would be ridiculed, the statements made be denounced as false, or it might become a curiosity illustrative of the strange perversion of a mind that could couple Christianity with qualities with which that religion, as well as no other, has any thing to do. And yet there is as much shoddyism among all those classes as among the Jews; as much glitter and tinsel, as much parvenuism and loudness.

Culture takes time. The children of the upstart will be more cultured and refined than he; his grandchildren still more so. Among us surely, in this land, there is no cause for any casting of stones; for the great and small fortunes have been acquired only comparatively lately, and the earliest ancestor of families which make even the greatest pretensions to culture is a very small distance of time off, when compared with that length of years back when the ancestors of the Jews, with the

Greeks, comprised the culture of the world. In discussing any of these books, it is not apposite to adduce the fact that we all enjoy the broad humor and strange characteristics of the Irish, as presented in works of fiction; that Hugo employs the French character in its distinctiveness; that Stinde seizes upon the peculiarities of Berlin life; that Howells sets forth the traits of American society—that all means something different—those are national peculiarities, which characterize only those depicted; but the qualities which are given the Jew in these works are those which can belong to any man. Further, it is neither legitimate nor truthful to treat the Jews as nationalities are treated. There are no Jewish national traits; as Englishmen, they have the qualities of Englishmen, and so with every nation among whom they may dwell. Among one nation, and one only, has this truth come home, and that is the French—due, perhaps, to the fact that the government supports the three religions, and makes no distinction in favor of any. Elsewhere the lesson must still be learned that Jews are to be contrasted with Christians, not with Englishmen, Germans, or Americans.

Following this line of thought, there is but one manner in which the Jew can be truthfully represented in the modern work of fiction, and that is as the follower and confessor of his religion; and that only by such as have made a long and exhaustive study of the same. Whether the presentation offered be true or false, favorable or unfavorable, is another question; but as long as the fictionist keeps within these lines, he is at least faithful unto the feelings and sentiments of the Jews themselves in this respect. Then it becomes the province of the critic to determine whether the writer has given a true statement of the religious acts and customs or not. As George Eliot, with perfect propriety, introduced into her earlier tales the Dissenters, and gave a vivid picture of their religious manners, habits, and customs; as Scott portrays the Scotch Covenanters, with all their fire, their obstinacy, their dogged determination, and their habit of introducing religious discussions at all times, so that Mause Headrigg, for example, has become a character fixed and typical; as Hawthorne now and then discourses on the religious customs of the New England Puritans; so, too, and so only, are the Jew and the Jewish religion to be employed for fiction's purposes, if they are to be employed at all, in novels and plays representing modern life. One great novelist of our days alone has done this, the writer of *Daniel Deronda;* if correct or not in her presentation, is a question to be discussed later on.

The name Jew is the proud cognomen of the confessors of that parent religion, through whose medium the truth of the one God was divulged to the world. However, ere they are Jews they are men. As Jews, they stand a distinctive religious community; as men, they are as their neighbors, one with them in all else. If they are to be distinguished from them, it is only in this; in all else there is nothing peculiar. Every representation as aught else is false. Christian and Jew are lost in that wider relationship of man, as Lessing's Nathan so well says to the Templar: "Are Christian and Jew such before they are men? Oh! would that I had found in you one whom it sufficed to be called man!"

Montagu Frank Modder (essay date 1939)

SOURCE: "Conclusion to *The Jew in the Literature of England—To the End of the 19th Century,*" Meridian Books and The Jewish Publication Society of America, 1960, pp. 347-64.

[*In the following excerpt, first published in 1939 and reprinted in 1960, Modder contrasts the portrayal of Jews in early nineteenth-century literature with their portrayal in late nineteenth-century literature. Modder argues that during the nineteenth-century the development of realism in literature and certain political developments brought about changes in the drawing of literary characters in regard to the use of real life rather than of literary stereotypes for inspiration, and in regard to the depiction of new types of literary characters including the "old-clothes man" (following new waves of Eastern European Jewish immigration) as well as Jewish heroes based on political leaders and wealthy, cultured men.*]

[A]s the Jewish communities in England advanced in numbers and in prestige, they attracted the notice, sometimes of the liberal forces, and at other times of the reactionary groups in English society. Eventually, late in the nineteenth century, through the influence of the liberal and more tolerant elements among both Jews and gentiles, the English Jews emerged into political emancipation and social acceptance.

In 1800 there were about 8,000 Jews in England; in 1900 there were about 160,000 in London alone, and at least 270,000 in the British Isles. At the beginning of the century the Sephardim, or Spanish-Portuguese community, was still predominant, and the Ashkenazim, or German community, constituted the bulk of the "ghetto" Jews of the industrial centers. But, by the end of the century, the character of English Jewry had been considerably changed by the fresh arrivals from Germany, Russia, Poland and other parts of Europe. At the beginning of the century, the English Jews were excluded from the learned professions, and labored under severe political and social disabilities; by the end of the century, they achieved equality with other Englishmen in the professions and governmental service, and manifested an astonishing aptitude for identifying themselves with the nation in which they cast their fortunes. Dean Milman, in the 1870 edition of his *History of the Jews,* comments on the change as follows:

> In 1829, I wrote thus: 'They (the Jews) are excluded from the higher branches of the learned professions . . . from the lower chiefly by popular opinion of their own habits. In the city of London they are prevented by municipal regulations from exercising their freedom'. Since that time, all the higher offices of the city of London have been filled by Jews. A Jew, Mr. Salomons, has been Lord Mayor; it may be said that few have maintained the office with greater dignity, liberality or popularity.

In the course of the years the English Jews passed from a position of insecurity to one of security and influence in the British Empire, and were transformed from an immured community of aliens into an integral part of the body politic. The attitude of the English people in general towards the Jews changed with all these changes. "It is difficult to realize," says the *Westminster Review,* "that barely half a century ago, the Jews as a people were denounced by members of the House of Commons—Cobbett among them—as nothing more than a miserable set of grovelling money-grabbers." At the end of the century, it was acknowledged that the alliance of Jew and gentile in England was "based upon an identity of interests; it was cemented by similarity of tastes, pursuits and needs; it was confirmed by reciprocal obligations." As early as 1868, the *Spectator* made the observation:

> We call them (the Jews) the "unchangeable people," but did any other people change so quickly, has any other or could any other remain as separate, yet be more English than the English? So far from being the unchangeable, they are the most adaptable of mankind; and as persecution ceases everywhere, this very quality will tend to merge them in the people among whom they live and with whom they have at last found that they have sympathies . . . Day by day families drop away, inter-marry, subside, often half consciously, into the mass, and we see no guarantee that in a couple of centuries more, if the world advances on its course, the Jews will be in any way a separate or a noticeable people, more distinct than Unitarians among ourselves, or Protestants in France, or Catholics in America . . .

Whether or not this expression can be substantiated by fact, does not concern us here any more than the question whether or not the Jews would welcome such complete assimilation. What we are interested in is the attitude of a section of the English public toward the change in the status of the English Jews. The same journal observes that the Hebrew community is at last able to take a part, and a leading part, in the general interests of humanity, in politics, in social life, and the great sequence of movements which we term the progress of civilization.

Side by side with the liberalizing and humanizing spirit from the outside, we have observed the growth of liberalization among the younger members of the Jewish community within the ghetto. Jewish youth at the close of the century is seen occupying a more formidable and strategic position than in former years. In the struggle between fathers and sons, the latter are gradually cutting themselves loose from the anchor of their religious heritage and centuries-old tradition, and drifting towards the new educational centers, where they are becoming imbued with foreign ideas of social relationships, art and literature. "These young men and women," observes a Jewish critic, "whether they stayed abroad and remained outside the ghetto, or returned to their native heath as spiritual guides and instructors, became the apostles of a new era."

We have already seen that, with the development of the realistic school, nineteenth century literature began to mirror with increasing truth and accuracy the circumstances and attitudes of English society; and we have studied in detail the many and varied portraits of the Jew reflected in the stream of this literature, observing the changes in color and form made by the shifting currents of thought. Now, as we look back on these studies in the mass, it is apparent that certain well-defined types emerge, and we may, perhaps, observe, in a final examination of these types as they shift and alter with the changes in contemporary thought, even more clearly than can be done in the study of individual cases, the close interrelation between literary and social trends.

Among the Jewish types which stand out conspicuously in English literature of the nineteenth century, there naturally appear those modeled on the conventional patterns inherited from earlier times. The Shylock tradition had persisted since the Tudor age, and it still admirably met the demand of the early nineteenth century reader for the exotic and the unusual. The Jew of this type was a swarthy, hook-nosed merchant, money-lender and usurer, always gesticulating, bowing and fawning; he was versed in mystic lore, magic, sorcery, and the healing art; in learning, he was usually somewhat in advance of the rest of the community. Almost invariably, he was a widower, and fond of an only daughter. If old, he was shriveled and hawk-eyed; if young, he was red-lipped and showy. Young or old, he was coarse, vulgar, rapacious, with seldom an ennobling trait to redeem the repulsive picture. No attempt was made, of course, to model such characters from life. "The delineation," says James Picciotto, "was as faithful as if a Whitechapel costermonger had been held out as a type of British merchant."

In what ways was this pattern altered by the changing currents of nineteenth century thought? As the century progressed, writers began, as we have seen, to turn to life itself for their models, and swayed, sometimes consciously, sometimes unconsciously, by the liberal spirit of the age, to inject something of real humanity into these lay figures, to allow them even some virtues, and to view their faults with some degree of tolerance. There is a world of difference between Maria Edgeworth's presentation of Solomon, the rapacious money-lender in *Belinda* (1801), Solomon, the art-dealer in *The Prussian Vase* (1801), and Mr. Carat, the jeweler, in *The Good Aunt* (1801)—to cite typical examples of the old pattern—and the same author's portrayal of the Jewish man of business who is also a philosopher and a gentleman, in her later novel, *Harrington* (1816). Likewise, Charles Lever's presentation of Ignaz Oppovich in *That Boy of Norcott's* (1869), a Jew of whom it was said that he could teach many a Christian the virtues of his own faith, and Charles Dickens's portrait of Mr. Riah in *Our Mutual Friend* (1864), a Jew who, though a man of business, is benevolent and gentle,—reveal a tendency to humanize the traditional stage-Jew of the seventeenth and eighteenth centuries. In the *Rebel Queen,* Sir Walter Besant adds another of this type in the character of Emanuel Elveda, a man of intellect, for whom the things of the spirit are more important than the possession of money or power. These examples suggest what happened in the course of the nineteenth century to the Shylock type which was reproduced so faithfully according to the old pattern at the beginning of the period.

Sir Hall Caine, in an address in 1892, stated that, if the Shylock and Fagin types continued to prevail in literature, it was because writers copied each other, having no knowledge of better types. The novelist continued:

> And, if so, is their ignorance altogether their fault, or partly their misfortune? Do the Jews in their old inveterate distrust of the imaginative writer, in their dislike and fear of the novelist or dramatist who has pursued them through centuries with odium and ridicule, shut themselves up from him, and so make it difficult to see the nobler qualities which no man carries on his sleeve? . . . May I dare to say that it would be well if the Jews came oftener into the light and free air of the world that is common to all men. The Jew is notoriously assimilative and clubable, and it would be easy for him—in England at least—to laugh the grotesque Jew out of all claim to be regarded as a Jew.

Another type of Jewish character which curiously persisted in English literature from an early age was that of the Wandering Jew. He had his appeal to early nineteenth century readers whose prejudices were perhaps nourished by contemporary discussions on "the conversion of the Jews," "the mission to the Jews," "the Jews as objects of divine wrath," and the like. The image of the doomed wanderer, kept alive by William Godwin's version of the legend in *St. Leon* (1779) and by M. G. Lewis's *The Monk* (1795), was implanted more firmly in the public mind by John Galt's popular romance, *The Story of the Wandering Jew* (1818), and George Croly's lengthy tale of *Salathiel* (1828). In the middle years of the century, the hoary legend was still further popularized by the translation into English of Eugene Sue's *Wandering Jew,* after which, according to Landa, "there was a glut of wandering Jews on the English stage." However, this type, too, was altered under the inspiration of the new humanitarian and evangelical movements. We find that this nineteenth century Wandering Jew is wont to do good as he passes along the way, and that it is possible for human compassion to proffer some light mitigation of the divine sentence. Eventually, after the removal of civil disabilities in England, when the Jews are permitted to become fixed members of society and occupy public office and a seat in Parliament, the tragic wanderer of tradition seems more or less of an anomaly in modern life and in current fiction.

So much for the nineteenth century treatment of the time-honored Jewish types. We have already had occasion to observe that new social, economic and political developments during the century gave rise to new literary characters. The old-clothes-man and the itinerant peddler, for instance, appeared in English fiction as the direct result of the presence of thousands of Jewish immigrants from the Rhine districts and Russia. These fresh arrivals from continental ghettos, outlandishly dressed, speaking a strange gibberish, and resorting to every available means of earning a penny or two until they could find their place in the land of their adoption, became a familiar sight in every English town and hamlet. Writers of fiction were quick to recognize their literary possibilities and to make use of them in the creation of two new types. By some writers these uncouth aliens were depicted as beings of a different world, to be viewed with distrust and fear. The *London Mirror* in 1827 described one of these unfortunates as possessing "the head of a fox on the body of a mastiff," and living a life which was "a long game of verbal and periodical lies, of substitution and sycophancy . . . a vile slinking principle curling about his lips, a fitful puckering-up of his eyes, a thrilling of chicane at the very tip of his nose." Little actually was known by English writers about these ghetto Jews in the early years of the century, and therefore much villainy was attributed to their mysterious appearance and uncouth ways. It was customary, as we are told by Maria Edgeworth in *Harrington,* to make use of them in literature as "bogies", to scare children and to make the adult flesh creep. Also, according to Besant, it was the usual thing for school boys to run out on the streets and pelt these tragic-looking creatures whenever they passed by. On the other hand, this same class of Jews appealed to the comic spirit in other writers. The strange lisp, the long beard, the gesticulations struck many as being grotesque. For purposes of comic relief, they were soon introduced into the music-hall skits and fiction, their success as mirth-provokers being increased by an exaggeration of the incongruous elements of their speech, manner and dress. The comic type persisted throughout the century with little change, except that, as the ghetto Jew became more "anglicized" and lost his peculiarities of dress and manner, the comedy which he afforded became predominantly psychological rather than sartorial. The "bogey" type, on the other hand, was inevitably softened and modified, as, with the passage of years, ignorance gave place to knowledge, and fear and distrust to familiarity and human understanding. The Jewish peddlers of Captain Marryat's stories and those of Israel Zangwill's ghetto stand worlds apart, but the nineteenth century covered the distance in its stride.

Another new Jewish type which the portrait gallery of the period offers is that of the Jewish hero. The Jewish group in England proved itself worthy of recognition by producing leaders of the type of Sir Moses Montefiore, Sir David Salomons, Baron Lionel de Rothschild, and Sir Francis Henry Goldsmid, men of wealth, culture and character. Now a literary champion appeared on the scene to glorify the Jewish race and to champion the Jewish cause. It was the part of Benjamin Disraeli to set forth with magnificent courage and eloquence his declaration of faith in the destinies of his race. In *Alroy* (1833), he conceived what novelists up to this time had refused to conceive—a noble Jewish character, far removed from the Shylocks and Isaacs of romantic fiction. In *Coningsby* (1844) and *Tancred* (1847), he presented the Jewish Sidonia, a fine gentleman, adroit in politics, profound in scholarship, and gifted with the wisdom of his race. Through Sidonia, the novelist pictured the industry, temperance, energy and vivacity of the Jewish mind. He showed that in every great intellectual movement in Europe the Jews had played leading parts; that they were of the true nobility of the earth, possessing a lineage so splendid and so ancient that, in comparison, the oldest English families were but of yesterday.

Beside these portraits we may set Grace Aguilar's heroic pictures of the little understood and persecuted leaders of medieval and Renaissance Jewry in Spain and England, of the ghetto dreamers and scholars of the historic past.

But the Jew was not portrayed as a hero only by writers of his own blood. In *Daniel Deronda,* George Eliot presented Mordecai, whose dreams and aspirations were all for his people, and Daniel himself, who, although brought up as a gentile, was prepared, on discovering that he was a Jew, to lay aside every personal consideration, all feelings of selfishness and aggrandizement, and to devote the rest of his life to the loftiest national aims of Israel.

Alongside the portraits of the Jew as a hero, we may place the more conventionalized pictures of the Jewess as heroine. It may be set down as a general rule that the Jewish woman in fiction is almost invariably treated with a sense of chivalry by English writers. The Abigails, Nerissas, Rachels and Miriams, are all of one type—they are all endowed with beauty, grace and charm. Be she angel of purity or courtesan, the Jewess retains her fascinating and almost magical loveliness of face and form. Paying tribute to the charm of Scott's Jewess, Thackeray in his *Roundabout Papers* says:

> Rebecca, daughter of Isaac of York, I have loved thee faithfully for forty years! Thou wast twenty years old (say) but I was twelve, when I knew thee. At sixty odd, love, most of the ladies of thy orient race have lost the bloom of youth, and bulged beyond the line of beauty; but to me thou art ever young and fair, and I will do battle with any felon Templar who assails thy fair name.

As a rule too, the Jew's daughter is accomplished; she is well read in the Hebrew scriptures, acquainted with magic and the art of healing, and able to sing and play on some instrument of music. She is loyal to her faith, and, if she becomes a Christian, it is for deeply religious reasons, and not for any social benefits that she may derive from the change.

There are of course some departures from the traditional delineation of the Jewess, especially in the latter part of the century when realistic portraiture became more the fashion. For example, in George Eliot's *Daniel Deronda* (1876), the Princess Alcharisi, and in Sir Walter Besant's *Rebel Queen* (1893), Madame Elveda, are as worldly as their masculine prototypes. In the pages of Amy Levy's *Reuben Sachs* (1888), the English reader is given a close view of other Jewesses who are "sad-eyed elderly women, unsatisfied and heart-hungry amid the wealth and gorgeousness which are esteemed as the chief good in existence." In the stories of Frank Danby and Mrs. Andrew Dean too we found others of this type, a pathetic and futile group, so unlike the Rebeccas and the Miriams of the romantic tale. These modern Jewesses are pledged to the pursuit of fashion and fortune and manifest as little interest in the traditions of Israel as possible.

The unbelieving and worldly Jew and Jewess are new types in English fiction, appearing for the first time in this period. That there were certain Jews who protested against the intolerance and the rigidity of the Jewish system of conduct and ceremonial was a fact well-known to the Jewish and and the gentile world for many centuries, but this rebel Jew was not presented as a character in English fiction before the nineteenth century. In Kingsley's *Hypatia,* there is a suggestion of rebelliousness in the character of Miriam, the Jewish procuress. She is an apostate to her faith, fallen and vile, but she does not openly rebel against Judaism as does Deronda's mother, whose desire to spare her son the miseries of her race and religion lead her to have him brought up as a Christian. The Princess Alcharisi protests against the forms and "oppressive burdens" of her stern father's faith, and, once free of husband and father, she resolves to have no more to do with Jews and Judaism. Similarly, the sole object of Madame Elveda is to renounce her people. "Your old traditions," she says to her husband, "your jumble, and jargon of ceremonies and superstitions, I will follow no longer. I throw them off." To these individuals, as to Heine, Judaism is a misfortune. They are so mortified by their social position as Jews that they resent the humiliations brought upon them by their faith.

In the nineteenth century gallery of masculine portraits there are figures like Baron Levi, in Bulwer Lytton's *My Novel,* who, straying further and further away from Jewish associations, belong in fact among the modern "emancipated" Jews who are ready to break old home ties and forget their Jewishness. Pash, in *Daniel Deronda,* is perhaps a fair representative of this new class of un-Jewish Jew. He declares that he is not in sympathy with the "rubbish" in Judaism and is not interested in the future of Israel. He is on good terms with both Jews and gentiles. With him stands Gideon, who believes that it is time to get rid of "superstitions and exclusiveness." These characters represent the assimilationists who are willing to melt into the population. "A man's country is where he is well off," sums up Gideon's philosophy of living. A typical example of the Jew who completely throws aside his Jewish interests and becomes a law unto himself is given in the character of the plutocrat, David Jost, in *Temporal Power.* Jost is described as a Jew by birth but not by temperament. "He kept his Hebraic colors flying for the King," says the novelist, "judging that to flatter royalty was always a safe course for Jews."

The process of transition from orthodoxy to rebellion is best illustrated in the pictures of Jewish life in *Reuben Sachs.* The white-haired, shrewd, prosperous grandfather Sachs, who, his fortune won, fills up his leisure hours with constant, mechanical muttering of Hebrew prayers, belongs to the passing order. His grandchildren still conform outwardly to the exactions of the old religion, but in devious ways; some ignorantly and unthinkingly, some with reverent mockery, and some with practical philosophy, holding the Jewish religion in affection for the sake of the Jewish group, but none with deep, intelligent conviction of the heart. Material success becomes the real god of Reuben Sachs, and he deliberately breaks away from the grand passion of his life from mercenary and ambitious motives.

In Israel Zangwill's pictures of the talmudic Judaism crumbling under the pressure of modern culture, we find almost every type represented, from the *schnorrer* to the rich merchant, from the pious peddler to the radical who shares Heine's belief that "Judaism is a misfortune." Under the sway of centrifugal impulses, we see the more progressive characters move out of the ghetto to form new colonies, moulting their old feathers, and replacing them by finer. Zangwill describes the various stages of transition, as only one who has watched the process with an intimate knowledge of the Jewish heart could describe it. In the work of Samuel Gordon, also, we find a sympathetic and vivid portrayal of these same types of a transitional period.

In this study of the presentation of Jewish characters in English literature, it is of passing interest to note the type of English characters who are opposed to the Jew, and to observe the novelist's attitude toward them. In the historical romances, the traditional enemies of the Jews in England are members of the established Church. For example, in *Ivanhoe,* Christian society as a whole resents the presence of "the unbelieving Jew." The Abbot feels free to insult Isaac of York, and the Templar will not tolerate "a dog Jew" under any circumstances. The Pilgrim and the Palmer and all the servants of Cedric's Saxon household oppose the Jew on religious grounds. For his part, the Jew realizes the danger of living in the domains of Philip de Malvoisin and Reginald Front de Boeuf, and knows perfectly well that from these Christians he can expect no sympathy and protection.

This attitude of medieval Christian society towards Jews is carried into nineteenth century society by certain representatives of the church-going classes. "These Christians," says Imlah Durvan to his daughter, "have been taught to dread the contamination of a Jew . . . and we walk in a strange land, the very scoff of mankind." Another Jewish character, Joseph Perez, tells his sister, "Henry Stevens said the other day that Jews have no faith, and how can we trust them?" In *Fair Jewess* by Farjeon, the medieval Christian attitude is clearly shown by Mr. Pointer, "the true Christian, regular in his attendances at church," who hates Aaron Cohen because he is an unbeliever. Manifestly the novelist has very little sympathy for these un-Christian Christians and invariably shows them up as hypocrites and fanatics. In the case of Mr. Poynter, Farjeon does not hesitate to reveal the fact that this man who sought to "find something in the Jew's past that would bring shame upon him," is the man who betrayed the mother of Ruth Cohen.

A second type of English character expresses hate for the Jew because he is a foreigner. The turn of the head, the carriage of the back, the glance of the eye, the oriental coloring, the Jewish nose; these are the unmistakable signs in the Jew that are resented. Not even an English hat, coat or manner can disguise these foreign characteristics. Concealment is useless; the Jew's very being breathes another race. And so, although Harrington's father cannot explain his anti-Semitic feelings, he simply opposes the Jew Bill in Parliament and warns his son to keep away from the Jews. Similarly, in *Fair Jewess,* the chief objection to the Jew, as expressed in the speech of Mr. Whimpole, is "There is a prejudice against your race."

> "Am I not aware of it?" says Aaron. "Is not every Jew aware of it? . . . Your use of the word 'prejudice' is appropriate, for, as I understand its meaning, it represents a judgment formed without proper knowledge. Yes, sir, it is not to be disputed that there exists a prejudice against our race."
>
> "Which, without putting any false meaning upon it, will make this ancient and respectable town—too hot to hold you," said Mr. Whimpole.

In *The Tragic Comedians,* Meredith makes it clear that the only reason why the von Rudiger family are opposed to the marriage of their daughter to Alvan is the young man's origin. When the story opens, we are informed that Clotilde herself shared her family's "abhorrence of Jewry." "The Jew was to Clotilde as flesh of swine to the Jew . . . One of the favorite similes of the family for whatever grunted in grossness, wiggled with meanness, was a Jew."

In the majority of the novels, however, as far as we are able to determine, the chief objection to the Jew in England seems to be the notion that he is a usurer, an unscrupulous man in business and given to driving a hard bargain against the natives who are unfortunate enough to get into his clutches. It has been a strangely persistent notion, carried on from generation to generation until long after money-lending had ceased to be a fairly common Jewish occupation. John Meadows, in *It is Never Too Late to Mend,* evicts old Isaac Levi from his house, for just that reason.

> "What have I done to gain your enmity, sir?" asks the Jew.
>
> "You lend money."
>
> "A little, sir, now and then—a very little."
>
> "That is to say, when the security is bad you have no money in hand; but when the security is good nobody has ever found the bottom of Isaac Levi's purse."

Perhaps the chief objection Fledgeby, in *Our Mutual Friend,* has to Mr. Riah is that the Jew is in business. "Now, Judah," says the Englishman, "What are you up to there? . . . You mean mischief, Jerusalem, yes, you do. Oh, you sinner, Oh, you Jew." And so, the gentle Mr. Riah is believed to be "the bitingest and tightest screw in London."

It is significant to note that in whatever form they may appear, these English characters who obstruct the progress of the Jew in England and in one way and another insult, injure or show resentment against Israelites are in general represented by the novelist (with the possible exception of Charles Dickens in *Oliver Twist* and Anthony Trollope in *The Way We Live Now*) as belonging to an ignorant, or cowardly or even degraded class of citizen.

In concluding this study of the Jew in the literature of England, it may seem appropriate to add a word of final comment on the work of the Jewish writers of the period. What the Jew has to say about his own people is obviously of great significance. "Perhaps it is only today," says the *London Quarterly Review* (1897), "when some children of Israel have taken the pen and written true words of their people, that the English Jew is beginning to be rightly understood by his neighbor, the English Gentile." In the Jewish fiction of later years we see the reaction of the individual Jew towards the problems which the question of emancipation raise and answer, as well as towards those more persistent problems which only the passage of time and perhaps countless generations in the future can solve. All these writers show an interest in the difficulties facing the contemporary Jew and seek to find a way out. All points of view are represented in their work. We have the sugared sentimentality of a Grace Aguilar and a Farjeon, in whose representations nearly every Jewish character is made to figure as a peaceful, unoffending saint, with hardly any blemish to mar his character or to explain his maltreatment. We have the passionate cry against materialism of an Amy Levy, a Frank Danby or a Mrs. Andrew Dean, who, as severe critics of their people, deal with the local history of their day. We have the eloquent presentation of the political situation and a remarkable championship of the glory of Israel in the studies of a Disraeli. We have the understanding compassion of a Zangwill, whose profound pessimism sees in Zionism a possible way out, and the optimism of a Samuel Gordon, who hopefully turns to the saving grace of orthodox Judaism for the future happiness of Israel. Which is right, which is wrong? Only the future can answer.

"The Jew is now a great figure in literature," says an English novelist, "both as creator and the subject of it. No base tyranny can be perpetrated on the Jews with the old impunity. The pen is the sword of modern warfare, and it is the friend and champion of the Jew."

Notes

Every Parliament since the time of Baron Lionel Rothschild and Sir David Salomons has had its professing Jewish members; Sir George Jessel, Solicitor General and Master of the Rolls, Lord Pirbright, Parliamentary Undersecretary of the Board of Trade, Sir Julian Goldsmid, deputy speaker of the House of Commons, Sir Herbert Samuel, Undersecretary of The Home Department, being among the most conspicuous Jewish leaders.

Edgar Rosenberg (essay date 1960)

SOURCE: "What News on the Rialto," in *From Shylock to Svengali: Jewish Stereotypes in English Fiction,* Stanford University Press, 1960, pp. 262-304.

[*In the following excerpt, Rosenberg investigates the variety of ways in which non-Jewish writers portrayed Jews in their novels, and observes that nineteenth-century novelists depicted Jews only in extreme terms (for example, either as the exploited or the exploiter), and always as a foreigner or outsider.*]

In looking back on the portrayal of the Jew in the nineteenth-century novel, one is likely to be struck first by the novelist's dependence on traditional types, and by his failure to do something with the Jew in literature that had not already been done in the sixteenth and again in the eighteenth century. The major novelists with whom this essay has dealt took over their opposing types almost ready made: one, a monster of cupidity, fundamentally anti-realistic in conception, functioning as a caricature in comedy, satire, and melodrama; the other, a paragon of economic probity, equally (but dissimilarly) unrealistic, treated as an idealized figure in didactic literature and commissioned explicitly to argue his antipode out of existence. For the novelists from Edgeworth to Trollope, the basic facts about the wicked Jew were his commercial rascality and a bottomless egoism which led him to trample over human lives and thus placed him beyond the social and moral pale; and the basic facts about the good Jew after Smollett and Cumberland were his commercial probity and his insistence, in the name of humanitarianism, that he had been placed beyond the social pale unfairly, that he suffered guiltlessly and deserved better treatment.

Good Jew or bad, rich Jew or poor, tyrant or slave, money was almost bound to be at the root of his problem. The referent being one and the same, the character of the good Jew in one novel by Author X usually turned out to be as nearly as possible the strict antithesis of the bad Jew in X's previous (or next) novel. Since the Jews in Maria Edgeworth's early stories are commercial scoundrels, Montenero in *Harrington* has got to be a model of generosity. Scott's Isaac is a frightened tightwad; old Moncada a baronial coin-flinger. Dickens's Fagin is an agent of economic exploitation, and so Dickens's Riah must be a victim of economic pressures. Trollope's Melmotte commits fraud on a grand scale; hence Trendelssohn in *Nina Balatka* must stand up for the principle, afterward propounded in one of Bernard Shaw's paradoxes, that in money matters irresponsibility is more often to be found among Christians than among Jews.[1] Brehgert is a greasily honest and plain-speaking Jew; Father Joseph Emilius, the Mayfair convert of *The Eustace Diamonds,* is an unctuous hypocrite. Whether Smollett calls his Jew a "compassionating Israelite" in *Ferdinand Count Fathom,* or a "cent per cent. fornicator" in *Roderick Random,* the yardstick remains strictly one of economic decorum. A compassionate Israelite differs principally from his antipode in that he dispenses with the interest: compassion in the Jew is embarrassingly apt to exhaust itself in financial aid—although it is also likely to be attended by gestures of philanthropy in a wider sense. Even a figure like Riah the synagogue-mouse, who is exempted by his poverty from "doing good by stealth" in the Sheva meaning of the term, is so transparently contrasted with the greed of his overseer that his goodness is all the more plainly brought into direct relation with the cash nexus. Had Riah money to spend, so runs the implication, he would spend it all—on the Jenny Wrens of the world and the Lizzie Hexams—and on the odious Fledgebys, too, who have kept him in bondage.

If Author X could not make up his mind whether to present his Jew as exploiter or exploited, the logical compromise was to present him as both. This is what happens, for example, in Charles Reade's "matter-of-fact romance" *It Is Never Too Late to Mend.* Reade's solution is simply to split his Jew down the middle, let him have the best of two worlds, and make the public a present of two clichés instead of one. Reade's Jew, Isaac Levi, is ushered into the novel as a gentle and pathetic old soul, "an aged and lonely man," who has buried two children and his wife Leah, who supports himself in his Berkshire cottage by lending money at a perfectly respectable rate; he has been a model resident among the native farmers as well as a devoutly religious Hebrew, with some traits of the Wandering Jew in his make-up, having "sojourned in Madras and Benares, in Bagdad, Ispahan, Mecca, and Bassora, and found no rest." In the opening chapters of the novel, Levi's cutthroat landlord, the villain of the book, expels him, without notice and without explanation, from the cottage in which Levi has passed his declining years, and, with a few savage comments on usurious Jews in general, sets him adrift on the world. Levi naturally trots out all the Sheva-clichés in an effort to placate his enemy, reels them off as though he had been wound up directly before he came onstage, reminds the landlord of his widowerhood, his piety, his industry, his trustworthiness, points to his grey hairs as numerical indices to his sorrows, and makes the speech about the oppressed people: to no avail. And then the Sheva-half of him is dropped and the Shylock-half mobilized. With the ominous constatation that "a Jew knows how to revenge himself," Levi follows the landlord to Australia, "resolving Oriental vengeance" and "feeding fat the ancient grudge." Positively rejuvenated by the landlord's call to action, he makes his fortune in gold-prospecting, spends the rest of the novel in grandiose exploitation schemes with the object of gaining a stranglehold on the landlord and sending him to jail, and even cheats his partners a little. He hatches plots "worthy of Machiavel," "patient as a cat, keen as a lynx," "an Oriental spider . . . the threads of which were so subtle as to be altogether invisible." When his patience forsakes him, he experiences diabolic twitches. " 'A tooth for a tooth!' And the old man ground his teeth, which were white as ivory, and his fist clenched itself, while his eye glittered, and he swelled from the chair, and literally bristled with hate—'A tooth for a tooth!' "[2]

Reade manages the difficult transition from Philip Sober to Philip Drunk by pretending that none is needed, and that behind every Sheva lurks a Shylock; and in this, at least, he has literary history to back him up. But if you turn your character upside down in the first place, you virtually owe it to him to stand him right side up again in the sequel. Accordingly, on page 582, with little to prepare us except the title of the novel, we are told that Isaac has "softened." Back in the Berkshires, the title deeds to his home restored to him, he writes out a cheque to the bankrupt landlord, urges him "to repent and prosper," and assures him that "Isaac Levi wishes you no ill from this day, but rather good." Evidently, it is never too late to mend. In the novel of the nineteenth century, Reade's Jew remains a kind of final exemplar, a product of Reade's arid persuasion that there are only two sides to the Jewish question, and that gold is at the bottom of both. "What news on the Rialto?" Shylock kept asking, after turning down Bassanio's dinner invitation; his question is still, among his Victorian relations, the basic one.

Would Riah have embraced Fagin in his sympathies, too, in the great sentimental, private welfare state established by the dynasty of Nathan the Wise? Yes, definitely, and—though Fagin would have rejected the offer—with the greatest pleasure. First, because there were no limits to Riah's mercy (a quality, it will be remembered, whose properties were originally defined for Shylock's personal benefit), and second, because the Jew in literature is never really at ease except in Zion. "True friendship between Jew and Christian is impossible," remarks one of the Jewish characters in Walter Besant's novel *The Rebel Queen* as late as 1893. Whether the Jew placed himself beyond the social limits by his baroque criminality, or whether he was crowded out by the hostile mass of men, he continued to be treated as an alien, a thing apart, an object of awe or hatred or contempt, to be vilified as a monster or patronized as an oddity. In either case, he existed apart from the body politic, to which he stood in the relation of parasite or benefactor. Whether he was Shylock or Sheva, Isaac or Trendelssohn, Montenero or Melmotte, the Jew enjoyed prominent standing in a separatist community, acting as spokesman for its moral code, the key inside-figure in an outside group, the center of a dim little planet on the periphery of the universe. His separatism defined him; it explained (at worst) his unnatural will to evil and (at best) his outward eccentricities, his antique garb, his queer habits—his rationalized will to good.

His desire for social acceptance by the Gentiles did not necessarily imply a desire to share their religion. In Shakespeare's day, the gesture of apostasy from the tribe might have been the means of his salvation, but he did not care to be saved, a job his daughter performed much better; in George Eliot's day, apostasy no longer meant salvation but disloyalty, desertion, flight; and so he knew better than to cast off his faith. His refusal to convert thus cuts across moral stratifications: it was held against him when the Jew was by definition odious, one of the "phrentic and lunatic" people in the Tudor medical texts, the denizen of Satan's heart, the "foreskin-clipper" in Nashe's surreal atmosphere; it was held in his favor when it no longer mattered so much what you were as long as you knew what you were and lived up to your racial and religious identity. This is merely another way of saying that what defines the Jew in literature is his exclusive Jewishness, which may be a good or a bad thing, but in any case freezes him in the role of outsider. The pious Riah, padding down the London alleys in his Oriental costume, is as much "out of it" as the blaspheming Shylock, dragged to the baptismal font. The Jew in literature remains on the whole obstinately Jewish. At once rejecting the majority and rejected by them, he elects to display the proverbial badge of all his tribe with tenacity and a certain ostentatiousness. Even when Meredith's socialist-hero boasts, "I am for the world, for man!" one detects behind the boast not only the conventionally philanthropic motive but the gesture of the self-conscious Jew who *feels* himself playing the role assigned to him by tradition, the part of the Tragic Comedian who, while he is himself in fetters, dreams of setting his jailers free.

But there are also those few, the professional murderers, the hallucinations we thought we left in the backroom, the sensation-Jews of Dickens and Ainsworth, who are irretrievable even to their own tribe, the final infidels who elude all social meaning, for whom the profit motive is a cover-up to mask their madness, for whom gold is the least thing that glitters. "You cannot take from me," reads Fagin's exit line, "anything I will not willingly part withal—except my knife, except my knife, except my knife."

Business: Nathanheimer versus Oppovich

Other times, same manners? Not quite. The market analyst on the Rialto reveals some new alignments.

Until the nineteenth century, and well into it, the conflict in the novels we have discussed was provided by a clear-cut economic antagonism between the Christian and the Jew: the one exploited the other. Through the latter part of the eighteenth century, all the thievery was axiomatically charged to the Jews; thereafter, Gentile and Jew enjoyed a roughly equal chance of cheating the other. The importance lies in the division itself, which was either taken for granted or unmistakably spelled out down to about 1850. The good Jew, naturally, held out his hand to the Christians, but chiefly from a sense of having himself been exploited by them. This entitled him to deliver a good-natured and mildly self-righteous homily on the exploitation of the Jews, which always came round to the prayer that Heaven preserve the Jews from doing unto the Christians as the Christians have done unto the Jews, and which merely underlined the fundamental enmity between the races. One is struck by the moral strategy behind all this: in subsidizing his Christian exploiters, the Jew is so obviously intended to be moved by a policy of turning the other cheek, of engaging in what Nietzsche, in his sour and succinct way, calls the "inhuman" gesture of blessing those by whom one is being cursed, that the Jewish paragon—no matter how fiercely loyal he may remain to his tribe—is in effect made to assimilate a morality which the novelist regarded as peculiarly and definitively Christian. For the student of ethics, the implications of this sort of moral kidnaping present a rather mordant irony of their own. They suggest that the nineteenth-century novelist still has to "disinfect" his Jews with the baptismal sprinkler before the public can be brought to keep company with them. Were one to look for a slogan, it would read: Make the Jews Safe for Christianity. The decent Jew, in other words, is decent in so far as he acts out and (to keep misunderstandings at a minimum) in so far as he pays lip-service to all the specifically New Testament virtues.

Occasionally, the novelist makes a special point of stressing the incongruity which this kind of transference is apt to involve on a purely lexical level. In Reade's book, for example, one of the Gentile prospectors, who has been selling his gold dust to the Jew Isaac, worries about finding a market for his produce once Isaac has left the campsite. On being reassured by the Jew that "the Christian merchants" will continue to patronize his gold dust, the Christian automatically bursts out that "they are such—Jews." Similar verbal ambiguities are found in novels in which the morally sound Jew at the center of the story is surrounded by lesser Jewish lickspittles and parasites. In Hall Caine's *The Scapegoat,* for example, a product of the 1890's, the self-righteous Jewish hero instinctively falls into the stance of the Gentile antagonist by calling his fellow Jews Shylocks and Bildads to their faces. There is not a trace of cynicism in his outburst, and certainly no assimilationism; the man is convinced of his Judaic mission and is full of passionate intensity in carrying it through. But he has projected his own situation to the point at which he can look at "the Jew" from the outside and regard the whole notion of the Jew in the popular—that is, hostile—meaning of the term; he momentarily assumes Antonio's view of Shylock, the view of the "inauthentic" Jew. The tension so far is interracial all the way. It is Jew against Christian, or Jew against Gentile.[3]

To keep this conflict sharply in focus, the novelists, down to about the middle of the century, did not bother to distinguish among kinds and varieties of Jews, beyond observing the conventional clash between the heavy father and the romantic daughter, or between the greedy Jewish master and the starved comic underling. To do more than this would have blurred the issue. The major Jewish figures came equipped with one or two Jewish cronies—their Tubals and Kirjaths and Cohenlupes—who were not, however, notably discriminated from the principals. They merely enjoyed a little less status, less wealth, less influence. In their bearing toward the chief they generally imitated the chief's own bearing toward the Gentile: the picture is that of the spaniel fawning on the big cur who elects to fawn on *homo sapiens.* With Edgeworth's *Harrington* the novelist begins to recognize the possibilities for stratifying the Jews more distinctly along economic lines, from the peddler to the millionaire, and to individualize them accordingly. Still, Edgeworth's Jews are all—necessarily and *a priori*—cut from the same moral pattern; since they all alike spend themselves in hortatory paragraphs, delivered in flawless English, they appear to be intellectual equals as well, so that one is left with the impression of a merely fortuitous distinction among them, a sense that the indigent Jacob needed only to be treated to some of Montenero's unique opportunities on the Rialto to become indistinguishable from him.

By the middle of the century, the novelist had begun to take an interest in the dramatic conflicts among the Jews themselves. As his samples from among English and continental Jewry accumulated, it became possible to deal with intramural rivalries and competitions, sometimes (though infrequently) without emphatic reference to the Gentiles beyond the wall. As a result, what we often find among the late Victorians is the novelist's concern with the exploitation of the Jew by the Jew. The theme emerges, directly or obliquely, in novels like *The Newcomes, Hypatia, Daniel Deronda, The Rebel Queen,* and *That Boy of Norcott's;* and it is formulated with a certain Machiavellian backhandedness both in Reade's novel and in Dickens's *Our Mutual Friend,* in which the Veneerings, the Lammles, and their sort, who have adopted all the sordid upstart traits associated with "Jewish capitalism" and who are probably themselves thinly veiled portraits of Jews, personify the very vices that elsewhere in the same novel the cloddish Riah is explicitly made to repudiate. Since Dickens's parvenus are far more cunningly drawn than Riah, one not only takes more interest in them but is apt to believe in the Veneering-reality long after the Riah-artifice has become drearily transparent. By and large, it is the small-time Jew who is unfavorably contrasted with his more amply endowed coreligionists, the men of culture, wealth, and knowledge, whom he tries, in a greasy way, to hoodwink: Lapidoth robbing Deronda, Besant's Mr. Angelo scheming to attach the Elveda fortune, the transparently named Abraham Pigman in Hall Caine's novel conspiring against the heroic Israel-ben-Oliel, the mercenary procuress Miriam in Kingsley's book acting as a foil to her unacknowledged son Raphael-Aben-Ezra, the gifted and civilized man. But the exploitation could also work the other way. If the novelist liked on the whole to depict the Jewish man of property in the image of the racially unexceptionable Sephardim on whom the poor Jew sponges, he could also typecast him in the role of the robber-baron of the Melmotte variety who no longer cares whether he pauperizes Gentile or fellow Jew.

To observe how the novelist deals with the exploitation of the Jewish merchant class by the international Jewish financier, one can go to Charles Lever's interesting story *That Boy of Norcott's,* the minor production of a minor novelist whom Bernard Shaw, in his quixotic way, cited (at Ibsen's expense) as one of his countless forgotten literary divinities.[4] Like most of his stories, Lever's novel (novella really) is made up of some loosely connected episodes in the life of its Irish narrator, a romantically disinherited and as it were misfiled young nobleman whose adventures bring him to Austria-Hungary and a secretarial job with the export house of Hodnig & Oppovich, late of Fiume, specialists in "grain trade from Russia, rags from Transylvania, staves from Hungary, fruit from the Levant, cotton from Egypt, minerals from Lower Austria, and woollen fabrics from Bohemia . . . besides a fair share in oak bark and hemp." Hodnig, the senior partner, is out of the picture, having some time ago "overspeculated and died of a broken heart," with the result that he has ruined the firm and left it to the surviving partner, the patriarchal Ignaz Oppovich, "after years of patient toil and thrift" to restore the credit of the house.

Oppovich is up to a point depicted as the conventionally good Jew and treated to the understandably tired phrases: "a Jew that could teach many a Christian the virtues of his own faith," "a Jew that never refused an alms to the poor, no matter of what belief, and that never spoke ill of his neighbour," a Jew who inspires in his townsmen the rhetorical surmise "what would become of the hospital, or the poorhouse, or the asylum for the orphans here, but for him?"—in other words, the Jew as samaritan, the Jew as John the Baptist, the Jew as Florence Nightingale. But Lever, who is something of a romantic realist, a lesser English Daudet or Berthold Auerbach, is by no means unqualified in his approval of the Oppoviches: if it may be said of them that they bring "to the battle of trade resolution and boldness and persistence and daring not a whit inferior to what their ancestors had carried into personal conflict," it must also be admitted that they have left the social graces behind with the Maccabees. Lever's young hero, who is in love with the Jewish daughter and is therefore motivated to look only on the bright side, cannot help noticing the "coarseness," "unculture and roughness" he finds in both the Oppovich home and the Oppovich countinghouse: indeed, the thing that keeps appalling him is the failure to distinguish between the two, and the monomania for trade which makes Profit and Loss a subject for discussion at high table. "So unlike was all this to the tone of dinner conversation I was used to, that I listened in wonderment how they could devote the hour of social enjoyment and relaxation to details so perplexing and vulgar." For all that, Lever leaves no doubt that he wants you to admire the Oppoviches, who, in a way, constitute the commercial "yeomanry" of their age, besides being the chief benefactors to their community; they are a strong-willed as well as soft-hearted clan, traits which commend them to Lever's Irish bias.

But as the novel bounces along toward its premature ending (Lever's bookseller wanted the novel for the Christmas trade, possibly because it contains a seasonable sleighride), it becomes clear that the Oppovich economy, through no real fault of Oppovich's own, is rotten at the center, that the firm has been conducted in continual fear of being wiped out, and that if the Oppoviches talk so obsessively about money, they do so with the partly realistic obsessiveness of people who stand to lose all their financial safeguards at any moment. The maintenance of Hodnig & Oppovich has been for years at the mercy of a massive Jewish combine which controls the smaller Jewish businesses, of "the great Jew House of 'Nathanheimer' of Paris"—and Nathanheimer of Paris, by any other name, is

Rothschild, with or without Lever's pointed quotation marks. "It's all Nathanheimer! If a man prospers and shows that he has skill in business, they'll stand by him, even to millions. If he blunders, they sweep him away." One of Oppovich's salesmen enlarges on the Nathanheimer policy and machinery for conquest, enslavement, and elimination; the policy is absolutist and dynastic, though Lever (and this is where he parts company from his friend Trollope) allows his tycoons a certain element of "sportsmanship," and never leaves one with the sense of purely inflating the Melmotte issue. The employee describes

> how these great potentates of finance and trade had agencies in every great centre of Europe, who reported to them everything that went on, who flourished, and who foundered; how, when enterprises that promised well, presented themselves, Nathanheimer would advance any sum, no matter how great, that was wanted. If a country needed a railroad, if a city required a boulevard, if a seaport wanted a dock, they were ready to furnish each and all of them. The conditions, too, were never unfair, never ungenerous, but still they bargained always for something besides money. They desired that this man would aid such projects here, or oppose that other there. Their interests were so various and widespread that they needed political power everywhere, and they had it.
>
> One offence they never pardoned, never condoned, which was any, the slightest, insubordination amongst those they supported and maintained. Marsac [the speaker] ran over a catalogue of those they had ruined in London, Amsterdam, Paris, Frankfort, and Vienna, simply because they had attempted to emancipate themselves from the serfdom imposed upon them. Let one of the subordinate firms branch out into an enterprise unauthorised by the great house, and straightway their acceptances become dishonored, and their credit assailed. In one word, he made it appear that from one end of Europe to the other the whole financial system was in the hands of a few crafty men of immense wealth, who unthroned dynasties, and controlled the fate of nations, with a word.
>
> He went on to show that Oppovich had somehow fallen into disgrace with these mighty patrons.

By the end of the book the Nathanheimers have taken their business away from Oppovich and so ruined him. Just why and how he has incurred their displeasure is not clear. There is a suggestion that he may have become too independent in his methods to suit his principals and begun to speculate without their consent; more likely, he became too soft and feeble with age to keep up with the Nathanheimer tempo. Having outlasted his usefulness to them, he goes the way of his senior partner and dies of a broken heart. The thing is virtually and emblematically a suicide: the end of business, the vital activity, is the end of life for these people. The job in life is to stay ahead; the disgrace is in falling behind. Oppovich dies a superannuated man. But with another page to fill up after Oppovich's death and in line with his aesthetic, to give his readers "a laugh without much trouble for going in search of it," Lever brings matters to an optimistic conclusion by arranging for a marriage between his hero, who has just then come into his title and his fortune, and Oppovich's capable daughter, a girl who is transformed from a ruggedly unique Rebecca—a conceited and insolent female, with a head full of business facts and figures—into a merely conventional one, "a pale Jewish girl, silent and half sad-looking, but whose low soft voice still echoed in my heart." *Abie's Irish Rose,* more or less, with the sexes and nationalities transposed.[5] But in the story of old Ignaz Oppovich, Lever has written a pathetic, often touching, very slight, *Death of a Salesman.*

The likeness of the Nathanheimers to the Rothschilds differs from other Rothschild portraits in literature only in being more patent and literal than most. It must be remembered that in their portrayals of the great Jewish entrepreneurs, the bankers and philanthropists and big businessmen alike, the Victorian writers were largely drawing on historical models, who became blurred in the novelists' imaginations with the inherited stereotype of the Jew, so that it is often difficult, from the point of confluence, to track down the separate sources. How much of Trollope's Daubeny goes back to Shylock; and how much of him is Beaconsfield? What part of Melmotte comes out of Barabas; and what part of him is Gottheimer? By 1869, when Lever wrote about them, the Rothschilds alone could mean whatever the novelist (or anybody else) wanted them to mean. Disraeli and Balzac both wrote about them in the 'forties; to Disraeli, they meant Sidonia (or rather that part of Sidonia which Disraeli had not preempted for purposes of auto-mythology), champion and purifier of the race, lonely overlord of a fabulous family combine; to Balzac, they meant Nucingen, the big Alsatian manipulator with the vulgar accent, the degenerate Goriot's aggressive son-in-law. Dostoyevski and Trollope both wrote about the Rothschilds in the 1870's; for Dostoyevski, they furnished the Jews with a convenient blind ("wasn't the late James Rothschild of Paris a good man?") to the real fiasco, the Jews' "carnivorous craving for personal material welfare," the threat of "their complete reign," when "there would ensue such an era as could be compared not only with the era of serfdom but even with that of the Tartar yoke"; Trollope, writing about them in *The Eustace Diamonds* five years before Dostoyevski, sourly regards their installation in political life as a dreary *fait accompli,* not an apocalyptic probability: "all the Directors of the Bank of England were in the gallery of [the House of Lords], and every chairman of a great banking company, and every Baring and every Rothschild, if there be Barings and Rothschilds who have not been returned by constituencies, and have no seats in the House by right." And as late as 1893, Henry Adams pined for the day of wrath which should find him at the barricades, "helping the London mob pull up Harcourt and Rothschild on a lamppost in Piccadilly." In this, too, his education turned out, as regards himself, a thing of nought; naturally the Rothschilds survived the holocausts and, for the purposes of literature, they were still in circulation at least as late as 1940, when Franz Werfel's Jacobowsky, expert in the techniques of flight, talked or bribed the Rothschild chauffeur into selling him the family limousine, the last operating motor-vehicle left in occupied Paris and the last means of escape from the current lamppost law.[6]

Family: Fathers, Sons, Lovers

The Jewish paragon, like the criminal, has some new features to register, though the animus behind his conception—to talk Shylock out of our system—has changed little. A few of his latter-day poses have already defined themselves in the foregoing remarks. He is a little more complicated than he used to be, which is to his credit. For example, he is no longer necessarily in business, though he still meets us in this guise three-fourths of the time. "It is just as well that some of our ability should show itself in other than business lines," one of Besant's Jewish characters remarks with a certain cynical satisfaction, speaking of his cousin, who is both a scientist of genius and a talented woodcarver. Whether he is nominally in business or not, the good Jew has been spiritualized in the past hundred years. Like Eliot's Daniel Deronda, Kingsley's Raphael, Besant's Emanuel Elveda, or Hale White's Baruch Cohen, he is often an essentially meditative human being, who has swapped the soul of a shopkeeper for the sensibilities of an artist, who feels himself doubly isolated in a nation—supposedly—of shopkeepers, and who thus points forward to the twentieth-century cliché of the Jew as well as back to the eighteenth-century stereotype. If he still sounds a little bombastic at times, at least he has stopped being the clown, the "little Jew" with the droll inflections, on whom Cumberland and his generation practiced their tolerance. He has grown in inches as well as inwardness; he is taller and deeper than his grandfathers were. The Jew's wisdom has always been the better part of his valor, but where his wisdom spent itself wickedly in necromancy, it now presumes a scrupulous and humane application to science and philosophy, religion, art, scholarship. Of the introspective middle-aged Baruch Cohen of *Clara Hopgood,* a mathematical instrument maker by profession, we are told that

> his features were Jewish, his thinking was Jewish, and he believed after a fashion in the Jewish sacred books, or, at any rate, read them continuously, although he had added to his armoury defensive weapons of another type. In nothing was he more Jewish than in a tendency to dwell upon the One, or what he called God, clinging still to the expression of his forefathers, although departing so widely from them. In his ethics and system of life, as well as in his religion, there was the same intolerance of multiplicity which was not reducible to unity. He seldom explained his theory, but everybody who knew him recognised the difference which it wrought between him and other men. There was a certain concord in everything he said and did, as if it were directed by some enthroned but secret principle.[7]

In a passage like this, one is struck by the apparent paradox that although the author goes out of his way to emphasize Cohen's typically Jewish qualities, the result is not really a type, and scarcely a stereotype at all, except in the limited sense that one is apt to find, after George Eliot, a tendency to identify the thoughful Jew with Spinoza, often physically as well as intellectually. Cohen's first name is pointedly the same as the philosopher's; his family is Dutch on the father's side; the father's break with orthodox Judaism suggests, of course, Spinoza's expulsion from the synagogue; and Cohen's own nominal half-Jewishness (the mother is a Gentile) symbolically recalls Spinoza's schismatic role, Talmudic and secular both. But all this really tells us more about Hale White's personal interest in Spinoza (whose *Ethics* he translated) than about anything "typed" in Cohen, who is, among other things, a substantial, serious, rather unhappy human being, whose problems connect up with the problems of other human beings, Gentile or Jew.

If the Jew has gained in spiritual depth, in "character," he has also become more public-minded. Often, as we saw, he has translated his grievances as a Jew and his defense of the Jew's private status in a hostile society into a positive creed for political action. Mordecai, Raphael, Daniel, Alroy, Sigismund Alvan, are exemplars of the Jewish activist who emerges in the course of the century as Zionist, socialist, or positivist, but always as a good soldier in the civil war of mankind. A figure like Alvan no longer practices charity privately and domestically, after the fashion of Sheva and Manasseh, doing good by stealth to a half-dozen near acquaintances, but performs on the public stage, doing good arrogantly and with a certain hard defiance. Meredith evidently enjoys the irony of a situation in which the world's great humanitarian tragically mismanages his private life by his overbearing egoism; but such a view itself suggests a degree of sophistication in the portrayal of the Jew which would have been inconceivable in Lessing's day.

The benevolent Jew, in short, has become both more extraverted and more introverted in the course of the century: the fact is that he has become some thirty years younger than we knew him to be. Down to about 1820, the paragon might have been mistaken from a distance for his cousin Shylock himself, since they were roughly contemporary—both in their fifties or sixties, say, bearded, and done up in the vestments of orthodoxy. Sheva and Isaac and the elderly cabbalistic gentlemen in Godwin and Maturin (I mean the "real" Jews who appear in their novels, not the Wandering) are well past the meridian of life, physically beyond the point where they can be expected to exert themselves aggressively *in coram publico*. Even someone like Mr. Montenero, who is still in his prime and cuts rather a dashing figure, seems to be comfortably ensconced in the part of elder statesman, not active politician. Near relations of Nathan the Wise, all of them, they are defined by their patriarchal qualities; they are fathers, not sons; widowers, not suitors. If they are all a little New Testamental in their meekness, they are at least gotten up to look like Abraham and Isaac, by whom they are always made to swear and after whom half of them are named.

By contrast, Disraeli's Alroy and Trollope's Trendelsshon, Besant's Elveda and Hale White's Cohen, Scott's Middlemas and Bulwer's Levy (these last-named bad Jews, however, not good), as well as the Jews in Eliot, Kingsley, and Meredith, are young enough to serve the purposes of romance. The interesting thing about all these figures is that each of them at some point during his courtship has to face the question of intermarriage—as if the author had a difficult time in conceiving anything romantic about intramural marriages among the Israelites, or could not expect the public to buy so dreary an article. The general idea is that if Jews can never be friends with Gentiles, the least they can do is to marry them. "Nina Balatka," Trollope opens his novel, "was a maiden of Prague, born of Christian parents, and herself a Christian—but she loved a Jew; and this is her story"; and by the time the story is over, young Trendelssohn has been allowed to keep both his girl and his Judaism. Daniel Deronda is, in a sense, "converted" to Judaism and alerted to an awareness of Mirah's availability by discovering that he is a Jew on prior grounds; Alvan and Alroy both, though for vastly different reasons, come to grief by seeking their partners among the Gentiles. In Besant's *Rebel Queen* and Hall Caine's *Scapegoat*—both products of the 'nineties—Jew is mated with Jewess, but the results do not warrant optimism: in Besant's novel, the marriage is dissolved almost immediately, and in Caine's novel the Jewess dies with similar promptitude, leaving the husband in charge of their sole daughter after the fashion of the earlier elderly paragon. In their sonship, almost all these figures revolt, tacitly or openly, against the parent: the emancipated Trendelssohn Junior against the stiff-necked Trendelssohn Senior; the pious scholar Mordecai against the pious fraud Lapidoth; the convert Daniel against the apostate Charisi; the enlightened Raphael-Aben-Ezra against the superstitious mother figure of Miriam; Alroy, conqueror and captive audience of the caliphs, against the parent-body of the rabbinate; Caine's Israel-ben-Oliel, the idealist, against Oliel the mercenary father, who enters on matrimony as on "another business transaction," and whose dying summons the son obeys "without a throb of filial affection," not because he is wicked but because the father has relinquished all claims to his affection.

In other words, the young Jew has taken on some of the plot-functions that it was customary heretofore to assign to his counterpart, the Jewess—though the Abigail-Jessica problem, in so far as it involves marrying outside the clan, continues at least to be touched on, in one form or another, in connection with the daughter. Thus we have the examples of Berenice Montenero (who providentially turns out not to be a Jewess); Mirah Lapidoth (whose boy friend providentially turns out to be a Jew); Sarah Oppovich (whose intermarriage proves little either way, since it seems not to have been foreseen by the author); Scott's Rebecca (who renounces the Gentile, and is renounced by him, as a matter of course and of historical necessity); Marie Melmotte and the title-heroine of Bulwer's *Leila* (both of whom aspire to the hand of the non-Jew and are punished for their efforts by the father, one by being "whipped within one inch of her life," the other by sacrificing that final inch as well); Sherrick's daughter in *The Newcomes* (who goes needlessly far afield by marrying a Protestant clergyman, an insufferable hypocrite, whose hypocrisy extends precisely to marrying a Jewess); and, finally, Leah Gibson in Du Maurier's last novel (the course of whose true love runs relatively smooth, though it takes a Martian resident to get it going to begin with).

Since he functions, within the tradition, as something of a daughter-surrogate, we must not be surprised to find the Jewish son frequently retaining a certain quantum of girlishness, often in conjunction with a lot of voluble and heroic derring-do. An idealist first and a realist second, in the course of the century he has shed some of the common sense that used to safeguard his purse-proud ancestors; he is definitely a third-generation Buddenbrook. "What with making their way and enjoying what they have won, heroes have no time to think. But the sons of heroes—ah, they have all the necessary leisure."[8] The romantic young Jew is still terribly involved in the ethics of an acquisitive society, but half the time in order to repudiate them: either endeavoring, like Raphael-Aben-Ezra, to find the *via media* between the meaningless dog-eat-dog materialism of the Hebraic, and the spineless abstract formalism of the Hellenic world; or, like Daniel and Mordecai, deliberately standing Shylock upside down. The second-generation Jews are not notably interested in making a fortune. Anton Trendelssohn, the hero of Trollope's

Nina Balatka, is something of an exception—and even Trendelssohn, like a smaller and saner Sidonia, endows money with a certain liturgical quality by which it is brought into relation with his other articles of faith and ultimately divested of its purely commercial function:

> To go forth and be great in commerce by deserting his creed would have been nothing to him. His ambition did not desire wealth so much as the enjoyment of wealth in Jewish hands, without those restrictions upon its enjoyment to which Jews under his own eyes had ever been subjected. It would have delighted him to think that, by means of his work, there should no longer be a Jews' quarter in Prague, but that all Prague should be ennobled and civilised and made beautiful by the wealth of Jews.

There is something of the same detached quality in this as in Barabas's greed, but the argosies plainly sail in opposite directions: for Barabas the point is to have his infinite riches piled up in front of him, where he can see, smell and touch them in the manner of the old-fashioned miser; for Trendelssohn the idea of wealth is both deprived of its personal function and transformed to mean "Jewish wealth"—though without any of the obnoxious associations elsewhere attached to the phrase.

In the strictly practical aspects of the economy the young Jew is not vastly interested—but the young Jewess is, very much so. Some of the Rialto values, without the attendant brutality, have suddenly developed on the modern Jessica—without the attendant frivolity. It is not among people like Daniel and Raphael or even Anton that we may look for solid common sense, but among people like Marie Melmotte, educating herself to the world of stocks and bonds, or Sarah Oppovich, who replies to her lover's romantic effusions with a laconic business letter, full of freight rates, bank drafts, and discounts.

In rebelling against the parent, the Jewish son or daughter, of course, re-enacts an ancient literary ritual. Long before the Jews began to cut each others' throats commercially, conflicts within the family had become an essential feature of the myth. The economic rivalry among the Jews in literature is an emphatically Victorian phenomenon, but the clash between the generations is as old as Marlowe. In the Tudor prototypes, the daughter initiates at best a secondary conflict; and she provides the old Jew with the one foil from within the tribe—a notoriously stiff-necked and clannish community, in which such defections counted for a good deal. In the nineteenth century, the tensions between Barabas and Abigail no longer require the presence of Ferneze: what used to be sub-plot stands now on its own. By and large, the novelist continues to side with the younger generation against the old, with Abigail (or the male surrogate) against Barabas; but the alignment is not a rigid one, and occasionally the formula may be reversed. In *Clara Hopgood* and *The Rebel Queen,* for example, the fathers, Baruch and Emanuel, are sympathetically contrasted with the children, who are a little too ready to make snide comments about Jews; young Adolph Oppovich in Lever's story is simply a ne'er-do-well in a family that takes its civic and commercial responsibilities most seriously; and in a novel like Trollope's *Nina Balatka,* in which the conflict between the generations and the ancillary problem of intermarriage spell out the dominant themes of the book, the issue all but ends in a draw.

On the whole, Trollope is all with Anton Trendelssohn in his battle for emancipation, his struggle to break out of the bohemian ghetto environment in which he has been raised, to intermarry with a Catholic girl, and book passage on the next train heading west. "To crush the prejudice which had dealt so hardly with his people—to make a Jew equal in all things to a Christian—this was his desire; and how could this better be fulfilled than by his union with a Christian?" But Trendelssohn himself is presented as a terribly gloomy, sullen, and saturnine person, while the father, the orthodox ghetto-Jew, not only is free from any of the fanatic bigotry that marks his Catholic opposites, but faces the question of intermarriage with admirable restraint and common sense. By allying himself with a Christian, he cautions his son, Anton is simply going to create impossible social barriers for the girl as well as for himself. " 'You will live to rue the day in which you first saw her,' said the elder Jew. 'She will be a bone of contention in your way that will separate you from all your friends. You will become neither Jew nor Christian, and will be odious alike to both. And she will be the same.' " Trollope's understanding, as evidenced in a passage like this, is remarkably in advance of his day (*Nina Balatka* was published in 1867); the viewpoint expressed here by the old ghetto-merchant is precisely that of Mr. Leonard March, the retired banker in C. P. Snow's novel ninety years later, and the conflict suggests something of the same inevitability in both books, though Trollope's is infinitely more trivial. Still, equivocal as he is in his presentation of Anton, Trollope ends by taking his stand with him, both because the attitude of the elders strikes him as reactionary and inhibiting, and because he seems to resent parental interference on principle—it will be remembered that in *The Way We Live Now* he flourishes Marie Melmotte's opposition to her parents and her insistence on marrying a Gentile as a point greatly in her favor.[9]

Considering some of the interesting moral implications Trollope has raised in that novel, it is a pity that *Nina Balatka* never rises much above the patronizing tone of its opening sentence. Trollope's latest interpreter, Bradford Booth, has called his characterization of Anton "a remarkably acute study in racial history":

> In a more ambitious and infinitely more difficult psychological portrait than he usually attempted, Trollope develops in Anton the disabling experiences of ghetto segregation and persecution. . . . In him Trollope traces the disintegration of European ghetto society and the emergence of a more self-reliant Jewish individualist who can escape environmental neuroses.[10]

And his treatment of Anton the lover is remarkably unromantic and balanced. Trollope shows him to be a fallible human being who, for all his idealism, retains a good many elements of the disreputable merchant. He does not look the part of a lover, really: "his eyes were somewhat too close together in his face, and the bridge of his aquiline nose was not sharply cut, as is mostly the case with such a nose on a Christian face. The olive oval face was without doubt the face of a Jew, and the mouth was greedy . . ." And if Anton is, at bottom, like Daniel Deronda after him, something of a visionary, going forth to forge in the West the uncreated conscience of his race, he does not talk about it like a promotional dust-jacket. The prophet is also a shrewd businessman.

The opening sentence of *Nina Balatka* states the theme of intermarriage, of Gentile versus Jew; the closing sentence resolves the conflict between parent and son, East and West, ghetto and freedom: "Early in the following year, while the ground was yet bound with frost, and the great plains of Bohemia were still covered with snow, a Jew and his wife took their leave of Prague, and started for one of the great cities of the West." Throughout the story proper, Anton remains safely insulated in Prague; and if one comes upon *Nina Balatka* after reading *The Way We Live Now,* one is apt to be nervous about Trendelssohn's reception in Paris or London. The uncomfortable suspicion urges itself that he will be as unwelcome to Trollope as Melmotte and Brehgert and Joseph Emilius and Daubeny and Cohenlupe. By ringing down the curtain the moment Trendelssohn's train crosses the border, Trollope avoids meeting head-on the problem of a Jew in his own backyard. While in Prague, Trendelssohn remains virtuous, because "contained"—a relatively complex bundle of loyalties and hostilities. In view of Trollope's effort to deepen for once the Semitic caricatures and gargoyles with which he peopled three or four very good novels afterward, it is doubly regrettable that *Nina Balatka* should be one of his worst—thin, humorless, badly underplotted, soap-opera in tone and incident, as though Trollope were bent on warning potentially anti-Semitic teenagers to be guided by the sterling example of Nina Balatka, Maiden of Prague, who dared marry a Jew, got away with him, and lived happily ever after.

Race: Svengali Adler

Anton is an Easterner, an Ashkenazi among Jews—not, on the whole, the best sort of catch from the racial point of view, if one is to trust the evidence of Victorian fictionists; Nina Balatka could have done better. To a girl of marriageable age, Jewess or Gentile, who is desirous of finding a partner for life among the Jews, a member of the Sephardic race from the southern countries is to be most warmly recommended. She is likely to find him, in comparison with his English or Middle- and Eastern-European cousins, richer, better looking, more creative, more intelligent, and better groomed for society; and his pedigree stretches back (though uncertainly) to Solomon and his seven hundred concubines. He may well be an issue of some one of the seven hundred, considering the mysterious wealth of possibilities in which his antecedents remain poised, the genius he has for turning out to be somebody else's descendant than his or hers he has been tricked into believing himself. It is all part and parcel of his exotic make-up. The Sephardic Jew is to be found among the upper crust and he has an excellent chance of being famous. He has (ideally) wealth, knowledge, culture, leisure, and, though he may not wish to take advantage of it, the right of political power; he retains strong traces of his Spanish or Portuguese or Italian or Near-Eastern ancestry; and the very euphony of his name, with the romantic associations it evokes, serves as a certificate of moral beauty: Montenero, Elveda, Deronda, Sidonia, Mendoza, Moncada, Baroni, Baruch [Spinoza] Cohen, Alcharisi, Oriel-ben-Israel, Joshua Manasseh. Nina (or Mirah) ought to be cautioned, however, that the Sephardic Jew is also more apt than his Eastern relative to tax her patience by his bookishness, his bias toward cabbalistic hocus-pocus, his assumption that she would rather serve as a sounding board for his metaphysics than engage in gossip, and his tendency to brood about the nature of the world instead of scheming to get the better of it. But then there is an even chance of his having the better of it already by right of inheritance—assuming that his heredity has been established.

What does he look like? Well, like Daniel Deronda; like the youthful Emanuel Elveda. His features are not picturesque so much as they are evocative; what they add up to is less the portrait of an individual than the history of a race.

> When in your walks abroad you pass such a young man . . . you begin to think of a street in a Spanish city—narrow, with lofty houses, windows with balconies, women leaning over the balconies, bits of bright people down below showing just such faces. Then the word Sephardim comes back to your memory. This face, you say, belongs to the Children of the Dispersion; they were in Spain long before the legions of Titus completed that Scattering; they are of the ancient people, whose

lineage is so long that, compared with them, the Bourbons are mushrooms and the Hapsburgs are of yesterday.

In this face there was something of the eagle, the nose was narrow and slightly aquiline, the nostrils were finely cut and delicate, the eyes keen and clear, deep-set, under straight and well-marked eyebrows, and in color blue as the finest steel of Damascus; the lips were firm, the mouth finely curved; there was a rich, deep coloring of the cheek; the forehead was broad and white, the clustering hair was chestnut; the sun had touched that face with a glow which lingered on it. Surely the Rabbi Akiba, or Gamaliel, or even Onkelos himself, must have had such a face. Surely this was the face which belonged to the illustrious Maccabaean house. Surely this was the face at sight of which Joshua's enemies turned and fled. Such a face . . . may serve for [the portrait of] the Prophet Elisha when he was still young and had just received the cloak of his Master and Forerunner. Such a face . . . is always striking and always handsome.[11]

The homegrown what-have-you London Jew, as well as the Ashkenazi to the East—Oppovich, Trendelssohn, Brehgert, Lucas, Max Goesler, Melyius, Shedrick alias Shadrach—is not so distinguished as his southern relative in either his looks or his outlook. His outlook is businesslike, solidly or shadily. His face, too, is both plainer and less sunny than the Sephardic, identified in a glance and exhausted in a glance. It does not, like Elveda's, connect up with anything behind it; it suggests nothing except that the trunk which holds it up is a Jew's. But the trunk has no roots in Spain, let alone in Joshua's Lebanon; neither is it crowned by the crown of Akiba or Onkelos. The genealogy of Elveda's Eastern antitype is lost in the obscurity of the ghetto; he gives you the impression of having sprung directly from the gutters of the metropolis and gone on from there to bigger, if not better, things. His history is clinched in the notation that he has been spawned in some estaminet of Antwerp, blistered in Brussels, patched and peeled in London—patched by Old-Clothes Levi and peeled by Nathanheimer's London agent or by Melmotte, whose name is no more Melmotte than Gottheimer's is Grant. These last gentlemen notwithstanding, we may expect to see the Eastern- and Central-European Jew assigned to a relatively modest income-group, to the distinctly non-U middle classes made up of the shopkeeping and small trading interests, or he may even be dumped to the bottom layer of peddlers, fences, and thieves. His name (if he is middle-class) is apt to be nothing more exciting than Cohen (or Cohenlupe, Cohen in Wolf's Furs) or Levy or Levi—names which in effect reveal their bearers to be primates in the Jewish hierarchy, but which encourage the uninformed common reader to take a common view of them. But if the Jew is quite needy, the novelist thinks nothing of compounding his indigence by peeling him of his Christian name, too, and sending him out into the streets as Jacob or Isaac or Rachub or Fagin.

Since the Sephardic Jew tends to social exclusiveness within his own venerable community, encounters between him and the merchant-upstart are rare. Instead of consorting with Cohens and Levis, the ideally constructed Deronda talks only to Mordecai, and Mordecai talks only to God. When the mushroom-Cohen does find himself by the side of the Hidalgo, the contrast does not, as has been suggested, accrue to his advantage. In Meredith's *Tragic Comedians,* the Christian heroine, Clotilde von Ruediger, is about to meet the Jewish hero, Sigismund Alvan—factually a German Jew (the Lassalles were Silesians named Wolfssohn until the 1812 Emancipation Laws) but affectively the purest-bred Castilian. Clotilde knows that Alvan is a Jew but she has not seen him before. Meredith places her in a room with three men—her host, who looks "mildly Jewish"; a caricature of a Semite; and a tall demigod of a man—and puts her through a guessing game: which of the three Jews is Alvan? Naturally Clotilde, who has definite ideas about what definitive Jews look like, assumes him to be the caricature. (Naturally he turns out to be the demigod.) The passage, interesting for the contrast Meredith establishes by placing the two racial antitypes side by side, gains added interest from the character of Clotilde's preconceptions. Writing in 1880, Meredith already views the stereotype as an object for parody. The result is not so much a stereotyped Jew as a stereotyped Christian viewpoint. The three of them are as it were lined up for the guessing game like so many caskets labeled Gold, Silver, and Sampson Brass; to them, Portia.

They were indistinct; she could see that one of them was of good stature. One she knew; he was the master of the house, mildly Jewish. The third was distressingly branded with the slum and gutter signs of the Ahasuerus race. Three hats on his head could not have done it more effectively. The vindictive caricatures of the God Pan, executed by priests of the later religion burning to haunt him out of worship in the semblance of the hairy, hoofy, snouty Evil One, were not more loathsome. She sank on a sofa. That the man? Oh! Jew, and fifty times over Jew! nothing but Jew!

The three stepped into the long saloon, and she saw how veritably magnificent was the first whom she had noticed. . . . This man's face was the born orator's, with the light-giving eyes, the forward nose, the animated mouth, all stamped for speechfulness and enterprise, of Cicero's rival in the forum before he took the headship of armies and marched to empire. . . . Alas, he could not be other than Christian, so glorious was he in build! One could vision an eagle swooping to his helm by divine election. . . .

> Then again, could that face be the face of a Jew? She feasted. It was a noble profile, an ivory skin, most lustrous eyes. Perchance a Jew of the Spanish branch of the exodus, not the Polish. There is the noble Jew as well as the bestial Gentile. . . . The noble Jew is grave in age, but in his youth he is the arrow to the bow of his fiery eastern blood, and in his manhood he is—ay, what you see there! a figure of easy and superb preponderance, whose fire has mounted to inspirit and been tempered by the intellect.[12]

It will be observed that the Italianate quality of the Jew, once so inseparably linked up with the Jew's fiendishness, has come to suggest three hundred years after Shakespeare an aura of good breeding, of social and intellectual unction, a relaxed sense of one's historical moorings, and an aristocratic view of one's wealth. Though the same quality also continues to throw into sharp relief the Jew's alien features, the important thing, after all, is that they are handsomely alien, issuing the good-natured reminder that it will never do to cry "Money-bags!" after someone, "compared with whom, the Bourbons are mushrooms and the Hapsburgs are of yesterday." The Italianate Jewish villain of the old school, who represents a direct sexual threat to the Gentiles, has to all intents gone the way of the religious ogre. He already looks a little threadbare by 1838, the year Fagin died, when Mrs. Trollope tried to give him another run in her slickly venial three-volume *A Romance of Vienna,* where he appears as Imla Balthazar, the repulsive castellan of a stout-hearted English girl, whom he feebly endeavors to ravish from time to time; and even Balthazar, though his tactics recall the prototypical Machiavel, is nominally a German Jew. Though Shylock's literary offspring has grown younger with the years, along with the antipode, the old Shylock remains more important than the son. Shylock Junior is far less dangerous than his parent used to be, and correspondingly more ludicrous. Since he is bound to fail in his one vital scheme, to seduce the Christian girl, he stands a much better chance of making a fool of himself than his father, whose failure to carry out his Oriental vengeance came so close to success as to excite terror; and besides he used to be a public menace, where the son is merely a domestic nuisance. Thanks to his Italianate coloring, the younger Shylock, like the younger Sheva, is defined more by his amorous desires (one cannot really call them erotic) than by his businesses, and as he has it not in him to be either a capable villain, like his father, or a capable hero, like his antipode, his importance for literature is relatively negligible. There is no wicked (or silly) young Jew in Victorian fiction comparable with the tame young lions in *Daniel Deronda, Hypatia, The Tragic Comedians.* He is a born minor character.

Shylock Junior may be recognized by his swarthy complexion, his oily black hair, which he is fond of wearing in curls and ringlets, his fleshy red lips and his flashy clothes, his name-dropping, and his maladroit efforts to look smooth. A portrait of Mrs. Trollope's man—Shylock at thirty-five—may be hung beside those of Trendelssohn and Elveda to complete the tryptich of racial types: solid middle-grade Eastern, top-grade Sephardic, low-grade Austrian, compounded of Eastern vulgarity and Italianate malice.

> His person was . . . very short and plump; and his nether lip, too, was so untowardly large and thickset, that, notwithstanding its being richly red, it could hardly escape being considered by most people, and by all Christian ladies in particular, as singularly disagreeable. . . . His nose was large, high and arched; and there are advocates for such noses who would have declared it a very handsome nose: but all who look at expression rather than outline in a face, must decidedly have voted against the nose as well as the lip; for, if the latter spoke of coarse and vulgar voluptuousness, the former . . . gave notice of a keen and wary spirit that might come in contact with many varieties of human acuteness, and delude them all. In complexion the gentleman was of a sallow white, and not a few deep marks of the smallpox were visible in various parts of his large face; though, perhaps, more still were concealed by the careful cultivation of his black favourites, which were trained and trimmed with such happy skill as to leave that portion of his visage between them very nearly of an oval form. . . . This personage extended a short-fingered thick white hand to lead the trembling Countess to a seat.[13]

Mrs. Trollope's laboriously burlesqued vocabulary makes it fairly plain that the Countess has nothing to fear from an Israelite who, as a specimen of comic horror, is three parts comedy to one part horror, and that if she nonetheless trembles, it is merely because that is what Countesses automatically do in the presence of Jews. But it is difficult to think Balthazar capable of rape, let alone slaughter, though Mrs. Trollope, whose perceptions are unbelievably crude and infantile, apparently meant him to be capable of both. Elsewhere the youthful Jew's basic harmlessness is underlined by droll externals. Occasionally (like Dickens's Barney) he lisps. At other times (like young Moss, Clive Newcome's companion) he speaks through his nose. Instead of saying "Step in, Mr. Newcome, any day you are passing down Wardour Street," he says, "Step id, Bister Doocob, ady day idto Vordor Street," which presents difficulties to the reader, who is thus apt to be more exasperated with Thackeray than with young Moss.[14] There is no physical menace in any of this. The hopeful seducer may get as far as the Gentile's drawing room, and usually he does, but it takes no great vigilance to keep him out of the bedroom—unless, like Joseph Emilius, he comes as father-confessor to Lady Eustace's bedside, reading her first a chapter from the Bible in his celestial capacity, and after that the first half of the fourth canto of *Childe Harold* in his terrestrial one. Balthazars and Baron

Levys may ogle their Mary Ringolds and Nora Avenels all they want, but that is as far as they get. Brehgert could have Georgina Longestaffe if he wanted her, but the prospect of their union merely proves that the Genteel Tradition is about to declare its bankruptcy; and besides, Brehgert, though very greasy, is relatively sound. Of the remaining boudoir-Machiavels—the antitypes to Alvans and Derondas—Scott's Middlemas scores high as a seducer, but he is only half a Jew in fact and barely more than a quadroon to look at. Toward the end of the century, of course, there is Svengali, whose real name, however, is Adler, which is hardly better than Cohen.

It is in our own century rather than in the last that the Jew once more affronts us as an object of quasi-religious as well as sexual horror: he reappears, sponsored by T. S. Eliot and the protégés of Eliot, the by-product of an aesthetic impulse which has rejected, as being somehow too thin, the socio-economic basis of the nineteenth-century novel, and has propped it up with religious and mythological materials, and which has sacrificed realistic techniques of fiction to surreal and symbolistic ones. The ghastly figure of Clerk Simon in Charles Williams's eerie novel *All Hallows' Eve,* for example—a combination of Svengali, Black Priest, and Eternal Jew—is a creature at once so acutely horrible, so minutely and graphically defined, and at the same time so vastly distorted by the totemic and symbolic uses to which Williams puts him, that in reading the book one has the impression of dreaming the whole thing, an impression Williams controls by resorting to frequently monotonous and oddly mesmeric sentence rhythms.[15]

A creature who is at home among both the living and the dead, Simon Magus (to stay with the book for a moment) endeavors not simply to "murder Progress" in the slick sense in which an anti-Semitic crank of John Jay Chapman's ilk uses the phrase, but literally to remand the universe to its prerational phase, part *Urschleim* and part kingdom of the dead, to be dominated absolutely by his own sinister Messianic powers; his is going to be the "final miracle" of Kazanzakis's sentence, the miracle of turning civilized life back into a fairy tale. Before he walks into the story in person, his appearance is foreshadowed in the appropriate frame of a surreal painting, in which both his sacerdotal and primitivistic features define themselves:

> The extended hand [of the priest] was no longer a motion of exposition or of convincing energy, holding the congregation attentive, but drawing the congregation after it, a summons and a physical enchantment. . . . A crowd of winged beetles, their wings yet folded but at the very instant of loosening, was about to rise into the air and disappear into that crevice and away down the prolonged corridor. And the staring emaciated face that looked out at them and over them was the face of an imbecile. . . . Blatant and blank in the gray twilight, where only a reflection of the sun shone from the beetles' coats, the face hung receding; blank and blatant, the thousand insects rose toward it.

When in England, Clerk Simon rents a meeting hall in Holborn, where he performs ghastly sexual rites, works at the manufacture of homunculi, and drains his auditors of all rational energies; the place furnishes the background for a periodical lecture in which the elements of a Black Mass are fused with those of a massive brainwashing:

> The Clerk sat and spoke. His hands rested on the arms of his chair; his body was quite still; except that his head turned slightly as he surveyed the half-moon of his audience. The Jewish traits in his face were more marked. The language in which he spoke was ancient Hebrew, but he was pronouncing it in a way not common among men. . . . A curious flatness was in his voice. He was practicing and increasing this, denying accents and stresses to his speech. . . . The Clerk was going farther yet. He was removing meaning itself from the words. They fought against him; man's vocabulary fought against him. Man's art is perhaps worth little in the end, but it is at least worth its own present communication. . . . It was this that the Clerk was removing; he turned, or sought to turn, words into mere vibrations.

Simon, as Eliot notes in his introductory comments to the novel, "is defined by his function of representing the single-minded lust for unlawful and unlimited power"; and the attainment of power, on the theological level on which Simon seeks it, involves not only the denial of human freedom by the anaesthetizing of the will (of transforming men into vermin), but the Clerk's own withdrawal into a preconscious arena, sacramental and bestial, shrouded in secrecy and hemmed in by power taboos. In process of setting himself up as God-surrogate, for example, Simon begets a child who is eventually to negotiate his incursions into the Christian world; and the scene of begetting is itself dense with fear, a rite in which Simon reverts to the role of the Jew who is both demiurge and beast, Anti-Christ as well as satyr.

> He was standing between [the woman's] bed and the great mirror. They had had that mirror put there for exactly such operations, and however dark the room there always seemed to be a faint gray light within the mirror, so that when she saw him in it, it was as if he himself and no mere image lived and moved there. He had put off his clothes, and he stood looking into the mirror, and suddenly the light in it disappeared and she could see nothing. But she could hear a heavy breathing, almost a panting, and almost animal, had it not been so measured and at times changed in measure. It grew and deepened, and presently it became so low a moan that the sweat broke out on her forehead and she bit her hand as she lay. But even that moan was not so

> much of pain as of compulsion. The temperature of the room grew hotter; a uterine warmth oppressed her. She sighed and threw the blankets back. And she prayed—to God? not to God; to him? certainly to him. She had given herself to his will to be the mother of the instrument of his dominion; she prayed to him now to be successful in this other act.

In passages like these, Williams has recaptured some of the primitive sensations of religious fright that the Jew must have inspired in his early sub-literary manifestations, before he passed from the literal fact into the metaphorical extension, midway in his journey from the cave into the ghetto. Williams's appeal is direct, instinctive; the nineteenth century had nothing like it to offer. Svengali, compared with Simon Magus, is a silly man who plays the flageolet; even Fagin momentarily slides back into a relatively consoling perspective, from which it is possible to view him as the poor old Jew, the fence, a man who has his feet solidly on the ground, teaching little boys the useful craft of stealing watches and handkerchiefs. In the nineteenth-century portrayal of the Jew, sacerdotalism is likely to look for its priests among the multimillionaires; the high-priest is Melmotte, turning his banquets into affairs of liturgical magnificence in the absence of other powers and dominations.

History: Coleridge and Mrs. Disraeli

All the same, the nineteenth century, too, had its genuine Jewish Priests and Prophets—or had had them, rather, in the pluperfect, for they had passed from the scene of action so long ago that one could only toast them *in absentia,* sigh for their restoration, and—pending their return—put them to rhetorical uses, teaching aids by which to measure the distance between the Jewish ideality and the Jewish reality. Throughout the century we encounter this insistence on the ambivalent character of the Jew—the ambivalence Coleridge rhetorically formulated when he opposed the thunder of the Prophet Isaiah to the nasal twang of old Levi of Hollywell Street. Some years after Coleridge's pronouncement, the Baroness Lionel de Rothschild gave birth to a son and received a visit from Mary Anne Disraeli who, in her scatterbrained way, is supposed to have said to her: "My dear, that beautiful baby may be the future Messiah, whom we are led to expect. Who knows? And you will be the most favored of women!" A wife to Disraeli, with his singular ideas of the Jews' world mission, may be expected to mix up her mythologies and think of the Messiah as coming in a general Nativity setting, in a manger as it were, on Christmas, more or less immaculately conceived by the Baroness de Rothschild. But at any rate Mrs. Disraeli managed to reconcile the discrepant images of prophet and businessman which drew from Coleridge his pious disapproval. "For the Messiah to be the son of the world's wealthiest Jewish bankers," Cecil Roth annotates the story, "is a curiously nineteenth-century conception."[16] (Mrs. Disraeli, of course, may have remembered that the Merchant-Prophet already enjoyed literary currency in the superb Sidonia, an invention of her husband's, who combines the features of Disraeli's optimistic image of himself with traits taken from his friend Lionel, the parent of the future Messiah, God the Father of God the Son.)

But in this, as in most other matters, Disraeli remained the maverick; other writers subscribed to Coleridge's antithesis, opposing the prophet to the merchant, the visionary to the materialist, the ugly present to the glorious past; and more often than not Disraeli himself furnished them with a point of reference. "After reading his last work, *Tancred*"—a contributor to *Punch* maliciously formulated the contrast—"we took quite a fresh view of all the itinerant sons of Israel, whom we met in the streets of the great Metropolis. 'Look at that Old Clothes Man,' said we to ourselves. 'Who would think that the unmixed blood of the Caucasus runs through the veins of that individual who has just offered his nine-pence for our penultimate hat?' " The same juxtaposition (and rather the same malice) is at the bottom of countless parodies. There is Thomas Ingoldsby's vicious critique of *Alroy* under the title of *The Wondrous Tale of Ikey Solomons;* the brief and witless take-off on *Tancred* which Trollope wrote into *Barchester Towers,* in which Bertie Stanhope, on a mission to convert the Jews, runs into "one of the family of Sidonia," "a dirty little man," who converts Stanhope to Judaism instead, robs him of his money, and installs himself indefinitely in the Stanhope villa; and there is Thackeray's famous parody of the same personage:

> The occupants of the London Ghetto sat at their porches basking in the summer sunshine. . . . Ringlets glossy, and curly, and jetty—mid-summer night, when it lightens . . . every man or maiden, every babe or matron in that English Jewry bore in his countenance one or more of the characteristics of his peerless Arab race.
>
> "How beautiful they are!" mused Codlingsby, as he surveyed these placid groups calmly taking their pleasure in the sunset.
>
> "D'you vant to look at a nishe coat?" a voice said, which made him start.[17]

Naturally the lines between Alroy and Ikey, Coningsby and Codlingsby, are not quite so clear cut in the novel as Coleridge drew them in epigram or Thackeray in parody, so that we are apt to find among the Hollywell-Street Levis a few (Isaac Levi comes to mind, but Scott's Isaac, too) whose mercenary features shade off into a quality which, remotely and intermittently, betray the angry prophet in the cheap jack, in whose eyes the fire has not quite gone out, and whose wrath is as the wrath of Isaiah when it does not trail off into the empty fulminations of the ragman. All the same, Scott, Dickens, Eliot, Reade, Bulwer, get round sooner or later to the reflection that if the Jews are a race of hucksters now, at least they can console themselves with the knowledge of having once been a race of warrior-prophets. The *ubi sunt* motif haunts nineteenth-century literature about the Jew—*ubi sumus,* rather, since the point is always made by the Jews themselves, by Riah and Mirah and Mordecai. The dominant note is one of defeatism as much as defiance, of apology as well as accusation, as if they chiefly blamed themselves for having fallen so on evil days since the generations of Joshua and of David and of the Hasmoneans; and indeed the Dispersion is often experienced by the Jews as a just punishment for their ante-exilic crimes. Rebecca may be very resonant in telling the Templar "thou art the man," but behind the reproach one detects the sense of an historic self-destruction, a comprehensive national eclipse, in course of which Maccabaeus went underground and re-emerged two thousand years later, looking either like Lapidoth, the small-time thief, like Riah, the walking archaism, or like Mordecai, the consumptive. The *ubi-sumus* motif is always sounded by the sentimentally good Jews, never by the bad, for the wicked have no genealogy, and besides they never apologize; they merely say "I am not well"—not from a sense of their racial decline but from a sense of the opportunism of being unwell.

"In the meantime," writes Edmund Wilson, "for the Jew—or for many Jews—it must become almost as embarrassing to be taken for a Hebrew prophet on confidential terms with God as for a diabolical demiurge who is out to 'murder Progress' [in John Jay Chapman's phrase]." Wilson, to back this up, tells an amusing story about Dr. Paul Tillich: Dr. Tillich, the story goes, used to dislike the idea of Zionism on the grounds that the Jews as a group demonstrated the possibility of survival in the modern world by a common religious faith independent of patriotic ties. But it was then "pointed out to him by a Jewish friend that he was being quite unfair to the 'petty bourgeois Cohens and Levis,' who could hardly be expected to be Moseses and Isaiahs," and who, without a national homeland to fall back on, had no choice but to acquiesce in the role of aliens in countries to which they were not really assimilable. "Dr. Tillich was so struck by the justice of this that he at once joined a Zionist organization."[18] Disraeli would no doubt have ridden roughshod over this argument with one of his Arabian steeds and claimed that the burden of assimilating rested, not with the Jews, but with everybody else (I take this to be the point of Trollope's parody, in so far as it has a point); and George Eliot might have accepted it with some tentative reservations, either claiming the advent of an occasional Moses or Isaiah from "among the finer elements" of the bourgeois Cohens, "some men of instruction and ardent public spirit, some new Ezras, some modern Maccabees, who will know . . . how to triumph by heroic example over the indifference of their fellows"; or arguing that the bourgeois Cohens (as long as they did not become too depressingly bourgeois) could display their integrity just as well in the Diaspora as in Zion, and that Dr. Tillich should not have allowed himself to be outmaneuvered but stuck to his original proposition. For the majority of the novelists, however, the Jew remains a king of shreds and patches, a symbol of lost grandeur, who gave up his heroic status at about the time Judas rose to point the way toward a different iconography.

For the novelists who disliked either the Jewish reality around them or the dualism implied in the foregoing remarks, two solutions were possible. One has been mentioned: to idealize the contemporary Jew by exaggerating his Sephardic qualities. Someone like Walter Besant's hero in a way begins to reconcile (though inadequately) the extreme alternatives by evoking the memory of Kings and of Prophets in his own character and conduct, and thus establishing a direct link with the heroic past instead of merely making it an object of polemic (though he does that too). The second solution is to ignore the Jew's present vices and humiliations altogether, to turn one's back on the current Rialto-facts, and to deal with the Jew entirely in the context of an exotic and idealized past by writing historical romances about him. The logical answer to Ikey Alroy is David Alroy, Ikey's sponsor. This solution was offered by a number of famous novelists, whom I have neglected throughout this essay as being ancillary to Scott and the purveyors of the paragon, and whom I salute belatedly: the young Disraeli, Croly, Kingsley, Bulwer, and a dozen largely forgotten novelists in the 'nineties: Rider Haggard, Marie Corelli, Hall Caine, Charlotte Yonge.

Kingsley's *Hypatia,* much the most thoughtful of these novels, has been mentioned: it is set in fifth-century Alexandria and has for its hero a young Jewish intellectual who both observes and later on engages in the conflict between the expiring paganism of the Greeks and the growing spirit of Christianity. Dissatisfied with the doctrines prevailing among Hebraists and Hellenists alike, he converts to Christianity at the end of the novel.[19] Bulwer's *Leila, or the Siege of Granada* hinges on a similar question of conscience, presents a corresponding conflict, and urges a similar conclusion: the story, put in a nutshell, is about a Spanish Jewess who loved a Moor and became a Christian.[20] Leila the Jewess (*floruit* 1491) is not much more than a rather anemic and flattened-out combination of Rebecca (in her looks) and Abigail (in her plot-function), who moves a little dazedly between two worlds, both of them overfurnished with ottomans, lords, and liveries—

between the "Egyptian gorgeousness" of her father's establishment and the "light pavilions of the graceful Moors." Before she has a chance to install herself in the mansions of Christ by way of logical compromise, her father Almamen, a hot-tempered Jew as well as a practicing sorcerer, settles the issue by stabbing her under the cool gaze of Torquemada, just as Leila is on the point of taking the veil. ("Thus—thus—thus—Almamen the Jew delivers the last of his house from the curse of the Galilee!") Bulwer pushes the issue beyond Scott back to Marlowe not only in allowing the girl to convert but in presenting her as a Christian affectively even before she turns into one factually: "Leila was a Christian, while she still believed herself a Jewess"; but that is old hat. The story is silly enough and not even Bulwer specialists like to talk about it; the conversation, measured even by Bulwer's dreary standards, is hopeless ("My soul wants a bath of music; these journeys into a pathless realm have wearied it, and the streams of sound supple and relax the travailed pilgrims"); and, boring as it is, the plot is wrapped up with unseemly haste; thus: "Book V, Chapter IV. The Return. The Riot. The Treachery. And the Death." But the novel derives a certain strategic usefulness from the figure of Almamen who stands before us, an amalgam of so many bromidic Jewish stock-traits, that he commands at least the secondary importance that attaches to a composite and exemplary cliché.

Leila appeared in the same year as *Oliver Twist* and Mrs. Trollope's light-weight triple-decker, and by then Bulwer already had enough models to be as eclectic as he liked. Almamen thus serves the purposes of autopsy. To anatomize him is to lay bare, for the last time, the separate mechanisms, the rusty and inelastic springs, that compelled the Jew in English literature to act the way he acted over a period of five centuries. What roles could he play? Seven or eight, hardly more, and he played those without finesse. But at least he knew the script by rote and could reel off his lines in his sleep. Almamen has his choice of sounding

(I) like Sheva:

> " . . . while my lord the king rejects the fanaticism of belief, doth he reject the fanaticism of persecution? You disbelieve the stories of the Hebrews; yet you suffer the Hebrews themselves, that ancient and kindred . . . race, to be ground to the dust . . ."

(2) or like Isaac, with Sir Walter in the prompter's box:

> "Your laws leave [the Jews] no ambition but that of avarice, and as the plant will crook and distort its trunk, to raise its head through every obstacle to the sun, so the mind of man twists and perverts itself, if legitimate openings are denied it, to find its natural element in the gale of power or the sunshine of esteem."

(3) He may look like Shylock in his Satanic role:

> The dark face . . . became terrible in its wrath and passion: his brow and lip worked convulsively . . . Amidst the infidels . . . at a little distance he gazed for a few moments upon the fierce and relentless slaughter of Moor and Christian with a smile of stern and complacent delight . . .

(4) or in his parasitic role:

> the art with which the Jews concealed their wealth, scattering it over various cities, had secured to Almamen the treasures the tyrant of Granada had failed to grasp . . .

(5) though the metaphor may also relate him to Fagin:

> Serpent as he was, he cared not through what mire of treachery and fraud he trailed his baleful folds, so that at last he could spring upon his prey. . . . He had the crawl of the reptile,—he had also its poison and its fangs.

(6) He has his choice of playing the Wandering Jew in his harmless dromomaniac phase:

> . . . the youth of that remarkable man had been spent, not in traffic and merchandise, but travel and study. . . . He had visited the greater part of the world then known; and resided for many years in the court of the sultan of that hoary Egypt which still retained its fame for abstruse science and magic lore . . .

(7) unless he prefers to feature himself as Black Magician:

> A wonderful change had come over [Almamen]; he seemed to stand amongst [the Christians] literally wrapped in fire; flames burst from his lip, and played with his long locks, as, catching the glowing hue, they curled over his shoulders, like serpents of burning light. . . . He seemed indeed to verify all the superstitions of the time,—no longer the trembling, but the mighty demon or the terrible magician. . . . There was a dead silence, broken by a cry and groan; and when, after some minutes, the darkness gradually dispersed, Almamen was gone. One of the guards lay bathed in blood upon the ground . . .

(8) By concealing his wizard's costume, he may even revert to the role of the medieval Judas:

> Ferdinand beheld opposite to him a strange form, that seemed . . . rather fiend than man; his raven hair and beard, clotted with blood, hung like snakes about a countenance whose features, naturally formed to give expression to the darkest passions, were distorted with the madness of despairing rage.

(9) If he plays the evil prophet among Moors and Christians, he sets himself up as the prophet militant among the "tribe of Moisa":

> "What matters who the instrument that would have restored thee thy throne? Yes! I who have ruled thy councils, who have led thine armies, I am of the race of Joshua and of Samuel, and the Lord of Hosts is the God of Almamen!"

(10) And though he may bicker like Shylock, he barters like George Eliot:

> "I demand for the people of Israel free leave to trade and abide within the city, and follow their callings subjected only to the same laws and the same imposts as the Christian population."

Almamen, in the course of the book, avails himself of all these roles. The result is neither depth nor complexity, but the exhaustion of banality, the complete coverage of the surface.

Shylock and Out

For this, surely, is the conclusion which urges itself upon us at the end of this study: that the image of the Jew in English literature has been a depressingly uniform and static phenomenon, and that the changes and variations which were struck upon it in the course of the centuries fade into relative insignificance in the face of its monumental durability. The obtrusive presence in literature of such a thing as a Jewish stereotype reduces such a conclusion to something of a tautology, for it is in the nature of stereotype to be an oversimplified and persistent image; it conforms to a fixed pattern, the reflection, in art or what passes for art, of a popular idée fixe. "A type," to return to the sentence by Praz that stands at the head of this study, "is like a neuralgic area. Some chronic ailment has created a zone of weakened resistance, and whenever an analogous phenomenon makes itself felt it immediately confines itself to this predisposed area, until the process becomes a matter of mechanical monotony." At the heart of the problem is the comic Shylock, not simply an Elizabethan stage-figure called "Shylock," but a figure who is, as it were congenitally, "*a* Shylock," the member of a species: a type. There are other comic types who are identified with a single literary referent—Pecksniffs, Tartuffes, Babbitts, Quixotes, Don Juans—but offhand I should say that the Jews are one of the few peoples on earth, in the recent history of culture, to have one all to themselves.

Of the two conventions I have tried to describe, the convention of the Jew-villain has no doubt been the more successful and the more persistent, and we have not seen the last of it yet. The benevolent Jew was perhaps too much the creature of a single historical impulse to survive the exhaustion of that impulse: a product of humanitarian and sentimental doctrines, he has little to say to an age which is not notably humanitarian and prides itself on being unsentimental. As to the deeper question, why the novelists failed on the whole to produce a decent Jew who had other claims on our attention than his decency, the answer has been suggested: he had only Shylock to fall back on. Sheva, like Shylock, ends by making one uncomfortable, not because he is so embarrassingly kind, but because he is so embarrassingly careful to be kind. His presence points at an element in our moral blood stream which is in its way as disturbing as the presence of his opposite number, though it will not lead to massacre. Both stereotypes are finally "inauthentic," but Sheva is inauthentic in the special modern sense of Sartre's "inauthentic Jews," who "have allowed themselves to be poisoned by the stereotype that others have of them and live in fear that their acts will correspond to this stereotype," whose conduct, like Sheva's, is "perpetually overdetermined from the inside," and whose generosity is vitiated "by the decision to be generous."[21] An earlier, more notorious philo-Semite assigned all absolutes to the domain of pathology, and the Sheva-type is no less suspect for posing as the absolute denial of an absolute. The generosity is too patent, and so is the self-consciousness, and behind the self-consciousness, the anger. Sheva, too, is one of our "terrible simplifiers." Indeed, his proper métier is not literature but journalism. He does not figure in sensational trials such as sent Shylock to the baptismal font and Fagin to the scaffold, but he may well be found in the gallery—among the sea of faces at which Fagin "wistfully" glanced from the dock—stoking up fuel for an editorial in the liberal press.

For there is, it seems to me, another way of looking at the caricature of the good Jew in English literature, the Fagin-view of Sheva, and it suggests some family likeness between them. Sheva's whole history in the literature of the West (it is his whole point) has been a history of martyrdom, an interminable atonement for the guilt of Judas, and there clings to him a vague and remote suggestion of horror of which not even his most enlightened interpreters—a Lessing or a George Eliot—quite succeed in depriving him. In this connection, another phrase of Nietzsche's comes to mind: that dreadful experiences suggest something dreadful in him who experiences them. There is a point at which figures like Riah and Mordecai and Isaac cease to be papier-mâché agents of pathos and turn under one's eyes into terrible grotesques, as though they were engaged in living down some primitive shock. They remind one of those types of lunacy with which Dickens peopled his world, harmless and engaging creatures, who received some fright in the past, in their anterior existence, before the curtain went up on the farce, which permanently stunted their growth and froze them in the role of eccentrics—benevolent and funny people, but mad. Their motions are a source of laughter, but their history—their case-history, abstracted from the absurd consequences—is instinct with anguish. Sometimes Dickens, with an astonishing sense of timing, rends the veil between past and present, and at those moments he reaches the heights of his genius: in the scene, for example, in which Copperfield's aunt, Betsey Trotwood, is startled out of her permanent amazement to confront, with sad and sudden insight, the whole meaning and ruin of her life. " 'Six-and-thirty years ago, this day, my dear,' said my aunt, as we walked back to the chariot, 'I was married. God forgive us all!'" And there comes a moment when even the most insipid Jew in fiction (and often precisely the most insipid) retraces this process—when he reveals himself, the more one looks at him, as some such monumental oddity, and one is made to feel that it cannot be for nothing he has turned out the way he has. At some point in the history of the race, he must have incurred some appalling affront, which paralyzed his reflexes and immobilized him in a single gesture, a monotonous refrain. Beneath the bleak pages of his Vindication of the Rights of Man there lies, like a palimpsest, the illustrated diary of his martyrdom. This kept him relatively infantile. He acted out his eccentricities with a certain strident aplomb. Like a child, he gave you the appearance of taking himself very seriously; but he was not serious. He must have looked with amazement at the "holy mirth" that inspired young Ben Disraeli to take the part of Gratiano, the Jew-baiter, in a schoolboy performance of *The Merchant of Venice.* It is recorded, however, that he played the part badly, and the chances are anyhow that the Shylock he scorned was already being played for all the sympathy one could put into him.[22]

Meanwhile old Shylock our Heavy Father lives, though nervously. In the verse of T. S. Eliot he continues to figure in the traditional images of the toad, squatting on the window-sill; of the vulture, murderously tearing at the grapes; of the rat beneath the piles; or in the image of the simian Bleistein: "a saggy bending of the knees / And elbows, with the palms turned out, / Chicago Semite Viennese." In the fiction of Evelyn Waugh we meet him as Augustus Fagan, Esquire, Ph.D., of *Decline and Fall,* director of a unique boys' academy, who combines the professional gesture of Augustus Melmotte ("his fingers crooked like claws") with the professional substance of his other namesake; in the greasy trader Youkoumian of *Black Mischief* and "Father Rothschild," S.J., the Jesuit impostor in the crazy society of *Vile Bodies.* In the novels of Graham Greene, the Jewish criminal persists in the functions of the mutilator, the alien upstart, and the usurer; he lives on in the gangster Colleoni of *Brighton Rock,* the small Jew with the neat round belly, who has swapped the old knife for a razor blade; in the vulgar parvenu Myatt of *Stamboul Train,* the little Jew in the big fur coat with "the too familiar features, the small eyes, the large nose, the black oiled hair"; or in the sinister magnate Sir Marcus of *This Gun for Hire,* whose "lip was like a badge of class—his great white open face was like a curtain on which you can throw grotesque images: a rabbit, a man with horns." To the Mrs. Davises, the position of a writer like Greene, who publicly defends the Jews in his radio broadcasts while peopling his novels with odious Jewish caricatures, may be dishonest or disgraceful—doubly disgraceful in a writer who no longer has the excuse of writing down to the Victorians. But whether the nauseating figures and allusions which Greene or Waugh or Eliot have taken over from the old conventions are the hallmarks of the anti-Semite must remain for the moment a moot point; they prove chiefly a point about the old conventions.[23]

There are also in our own day the conscious anti-Semites, writers on the order of Lawrence, Wyndham Lewis, and Ezra Pound, whose versified insults of the Jews are confirmed by his extra-literary statements in prose. When, in *The Pisan Cantos,* Pound notes that "the goyim go to saleable slaughter" for "David rex the prime s.o.b.," it is evidently no longer possible to explain away Pound's lines exclusively on the grounds of literary convention, in view of his statements elsewhere that the Jews started the Second World War. The man who described Geneva as "the usurers' dunghill / Frogs, brits with a few dutch pimps"; who claims that "Pétain defended Verdun while Blum was defending a bidet," and jokingly refers to mass murder as "fresh meat on the Russian steppes" is clearly the same man who on the Rome radio approved the massacre of the Eastern European Jews and warned American Jews that it was their turn next. For writers like Eliot and Greene—this is the distinction to be made—the Jew operates as a metaphor, and it is with fictional metaphors that this study has concerned itself, with the "prosaic statement of a poetic truth" or a "poetic lie," not with statements of abuse. "Moving from the cliché to the theatrical personification," Harold Rosenberg notes, "art does no harm. What does the harm is the movement in the opposite direction, from the personification to the cliché. This second movement is made by the propagandist and the sociological critic. With these, the personifications made by artists for pleasure become descriptions of 'reality.' "[24]

Still, one cannot ignore the personification either, and in the long run the Fagin-issue ceases to be a literary sport and raises some serious problems in the modern world. The trouble is that the cliché is embarrassingly apt to create the "zone of weakened resistance" in which the play-figure secures and consolidates its hold on the public imagination. (To say, with Harold Rosenberg, that "Shylock is not my brother, but brother to those other Shakespearean pigstickers, Iago, Claudius, Macbeth" on the grounds that "one is labeled a Jew, the others Italian, Dane, Scot," is not really meeting the issue head-on either, in so far as Iago, Claudius, and Macbeth have a good many more strings to their bows than their Italian, Danish, and Scottish strings, whereas Shylock is entirely the slave of his Jewishness.) Effects have a way of being anyhow confused with causes; and a literary stereotype, which is up to a point almost prescriptively a distortion, no matter how stupendous, of the observed reality, ends by persuading the superstitious mass of men to mistake the genuine article for the fabulous imitation. Such a state of affairs is an appalling convenience to propaganda machines the world over. From this point of view, the stereotype of the Jew is doubly vulnerable since it has been, from the first, a physically repulsive type, accessible to the crudest kind of caricature. In *My Life as German and Jew,* the novelist Wassermann, observing that as a child he escaped the customary brow-beating of Jews because of his un-Jewish features, writes:

> This argument sounds primitive; but people who have not had this experience cannot imagine how primitive non-Jews are in their estimation of what is Jewish or in their idea of Jewish characteristics. Their instinct is silent when it is not confronted by a caricature. I have always found that the race prejudice into which they talk themselves, or of which they let themselves be convinced, is fed by the most external things.[25]

For the gratification of the less primitive, the physical caricatures can be dressed up with sophistic race-theories; the cartoon can be filled in with pretentious pseudo-scientific jargon; and the mischief is done.

In the meantime, too, the myth of Shylock has, as it has once before, given rise to the countermyth: the myth of the Jew as artist, as aesthete, as hypersensitive and anxious man; and in this mask he has engaged the attention of the great novelists of our century. For the creators of Swann (but also Bloch), of Leopold Bloom, Joseph K, as well as the recreator of the Biblical Joseph, the Jew has come to reflect increasingly the problems and pressures of Western man. If he is still (or more than ever) the Outsider, he knows that he has been cast in a role that symbolically identifies him with a world of Ishmaels—viewed no longer from the historical perspective of a Scott, but solidly within the framework of his own generation. In the Age of Anxiety, as Leslie Fiedler has reminded us, the Jew as symbol in literature has moved from the periphery to the center—but by remaining, as ever, on the periphery of the active social and moral world. His weapon is no longer the aggressive cunning of a Machiavel but the melancholy cunning of the ironic man: the irony of Swann, who squints at the world by negotiating his view of it in quotation marks, as much as to say: I don't really mean it that way; of Joseph, the beautiful boy in the pit, supercessor of Hugh of Lincoln in his sewer, who needs to console himself with the quixotic reminder that he is only living in a story-world after all; of Joseph K, the *eiron* who submits to the knife which has been torn from his hands and who dies—*ganz wie ein Hund.* "Under our very eyes," Diana Trilling writes, "we see the Wandering Jew become wandering man, the alien Jew generalizing into the alienated human being. We would do well to transfer some of our anxiety about the anti-Jewish myth to all the anti-human myths which contemporary culture is so self-destructively bent upon creating.[26]

How, finally, is one to get around the stereotype—any stereotype? It is idle to pretend that, for the purposes of literature, Jews share all qualities with all men, and that therefore whatever is peculiar, eccentric, individual about them ought to be suppressed. Unless the Jew in fiction is in some sense recognizably Jewish (he need not either have a long nose or parade his cosmic fatigue), the writer ought not to have bothered to make him one. (I may as well confess that the Jewishness of Joyce's Bloom has always struck me as erring on this side of the picture. The intention is there; the symbolization points to the Jewish qualities; Bloom's reveries are there to confirm it all, but, substantial human being though he is, the Jewishness remains oddly extraneous, unassimilated, to be taken on faith and Joyce's say-so.) How is one to supersede intelligently the Meyer Wolfsheims and the Myatts, the Bleisteins and Youkoumians, short of waiting for them to die of attrition and short of coming up with merely another stereotype?

It is easier, after all, to answer with an example than a prescription. Such an example, it seems to me, and a very recent one, is provided by C. P. Snow's novel *The Conscience of the Rich.*[27] It deals with its Jewish characters in such a way that they are both unmistakable Jews as well as ordinary sensual men, whose perplexities and well-being are at once rooted in their Jewish make-up and in the wider social context of their times. Sir Charles is too scrupulous a novelist simply to call his characters Jews and then deprive them of their Jewish qualities merely in order to repudiate an antique image, to take the sting out of Shylock. His Jews happen to be exceedingly rich; they gesticulate enormously; they frown on intermarriage; some of them are odiously confused in their politics; naturally they are very conscious of being Jews. But they are a good deal else; they suffer the domestic shocks and public calamities of other men; they go about their businesses; they know as well as most people that everything is necessary under the sun, and everything is dangerous. Since Sir Charles also treats them in the spirit of comedy and critique which have been the intellectual props of the novelist in all ages, one feels that justice has been done.

Notes

[1] *Saint Joan,* iv.

[2] *It Is Never Too Late to Mend: A Matter-of-Fact Romance* [1856], Library Ed. (London, 1913). Modder's discussion of Reade (*The Jew in the Literature of England* [[Philadelphia, 1944]], pp. 229-31) presents Levi virtually as another paragon, a bias similarly apparent in his comments on Borrow, Lever, Caine, and others. Hilaire Belloc's sour remark that "with writers as different as Charles Reade and George Eliot we reach a time when the Jew is impeccable" (*The Jews,* p. 225) is nonsense not only with respect to Reade. A brief, perceptive critique of Reade by the late George Orwell may be found in "Books in General," *New Statesman,* Aug. 17, 1940; Reade's literary technique is comprehensively analyzed in Walter C. Phillips, *Dickens, Reade and Collins: Sensation Novelists* (New York, 1919).

[3] In Caine's novel, the antagonists of the Jewish hero are described almost as though they were a Shylock-collective, who propose not only to rob the leader of the tribe but to exercise something very like ritual murder on him. Similar displays of fanaticism within the tribe can be found, earlier in the century, in Croly's Wandering-Jew romance *Salathiel,* in which the hero keeps running up against the contrast between Hebrew feuding and Christian forbearance, until he gets the point and flirts with the prospect of converting. See Hall Caine, *The Scapegoat* [1891, 1899], Manx Ed. (New York, 1899); and Rev. George Croly, *Salathiel: A Story of the Past, the Present and the Future* (New York, 1828). The author of *Ben-Hur* has cited *Salathiel* as "one of the six greatest novels ever written," an opinion to be seriously credited by readers who agree with him on any one of the other five.

[4] *That Boy of Norcott's* [1869], Copyright Ed. (London, 1897-99), XXXV, 1-222. Shaw's debt is recorded in the Preface to *Major Barbara.*

[5] In the Palliser novels, Trollope handles the same relationship—Irish lover, continental Jewess—with incomparably greater sophistication and insight in describing the amour between Phineas and "Madame Max," the widow of a German banker. It may be noted that in *Phineas Redux,* Trollope plays the same game of mixed doubles with his Jews and Jewesses that he repeats in *The Way We Live Now:* A courtship involving a Jew (Emilius-Lizzie, Brehgert-Longstaffe) is played off against one involving a Jewess (Madame Max-Phineas, Marie Melmotte-Felix). Naturally, the rules are flexible. Besant, for example, sets up two parallel romances—Gentile lovers, Jewish girls—and achieves his contrast in other ways: one of the Jewesses turns down a Gentile who is much too good for her; the other runs after a Gentile who is a cad and an imbecile. In Snow's *Conscience of the Rich* we get still another configuration: Leonard March's daughter intermarries with a Gentile whereas his son marries a Jewess. The permanent breach, however, is not with the daughter for marrying the Gentile (much as this revolts the father *prima facie*) but with the son for marrying a Jewess whose political radicalism undermines the stability of the March family a lot more than a good middle-class intermarriage does.

[6] Dostoyevski, "The Jewish Question," *Diary of a Writer* [1873-80] (New York, 1949), II, 637-53; Trollope, *The Eustace Diamonds* [1872], Oxford Trollope (London, 1950), II, 130; Henry Adams, *Letters* (Boston, 1938), II, 33 (to Elizabeth Cameron, Aug. 8, 1893); Werfel, *Jacobowsky and the Colonel* (New York, 1944). Disraeli drew on the Rothschilds both for his portrayal of Sidonia and for his group picture of the Neufchatels in *Endymion* [1880]; and Sidonia himself, it has been suggested, derives from two separate Rothschilds: Alfred, the head of the Neapolitan branch, who furnished the prototype for the Sidonia of *Coningsby,* and Lionel, who figures as Sidonia in *Tancred.* Balzac's De Nucingen, modeled on the Parisian principal James R., turns up throughout the *Comédie. La maison de Nucingen* [1838] describes his financial ascendancy; *Splendeurs et misères des courtisanes* [1838-47] his erotomania for Esther Gobseck; but he may also be tracked down to *Le père Goriot* [1835], *César Birotteau* [1837], *Un grand homme de province* [1839], *Pierrette* [1840], and *La cousine Bette* [1847].

[7] *Clara Hopgood* [1896] (London, 1923). Rutherford's debt to Spinoza is intensively analyzed in the standard work on the subject: Wilfred Stone, *Religion and Art of William Hale White* (Stanford, 1954), pp. 101-21; *vide* also Basil Willey, *More Nineteenth Century Studies* (London, 1956), pp. 186-247. For a discussion of *Clara Hopgood,* see pp. 159-73 of the study by Stone, who elaborates the parallel of Spinoza and Baruch Cohen, pp. 161-64. White, like Eliot, translated Spinoza's *Ethics.*

[8] Aldous Huxley, *Vulgarity in Literature* (London, 1930), p. 10.

[9] *Nina Balatka: The Story of a Maiden of Prague* [1867] (Edinburgh, 1879). L. P. and R. P. Stebbins, *The Trollopes,* p. 270, discuss Trollope's views on parental interventionism; see *supra,* Chap. VI.

[10] Bradford A. Booth, *Anthony Trollope: Aspects of His Life and Art* (Bloomington, 1958), pp. 30-31. Booth's critical work, the finest book on Trollope since Sadleir's biography, is also the one which analyzes Trollope's portrayals of Jews most astutely and thoroughly.

[11] Walter Besant, *The Rebel Queen* (New York, 1893).

[12] *The Tragic Comedians: A Study in a Well-Known Story,* Memorial Ed. (1909-12), XV. For the prototypes of these people, see the works listed *supra,* Chap. I, n.3.

[13] *A Romance of Vienna* (London, 1838), I, 96-98. Mrs. Trollope heads this "A Portrait from the Life." Her novel may be read as a counterirritant to *Salathiel* as one of the six worst novels ever written. Mrs. Trollope's primitive attitude toward Jews supposedly stemmed in part from her contact with them in Vienna, where she spent some months of social-climbing in 1836, getting as high up as the Metternichs, who dined and entertained her. In her book of travels *Vienna and the Austrians* (London, 1838), which came out the same year as the *Romance* and forms a companion volume to it, she writes: "The love of this stiff-necked race for gold is so well known and so universally acknowledged in every land into which their active service has found entrance, that it will appear little better than a paradox to say that it is the excess of this eagerly-sought gold which generates the canker so evidently destroying the heart's ease of all the Israelitish tribes in Vienna. . . . Do not believe that these observations arise from intolerance; they arise solely from observation" (II, 5). Eileen Bigland, *The Indomitable Mrs. Trollope* (London, 1953), pp. 176-88, deals with Mrs. T.'s Austrian experiences.

[14] *The Newcomes: Memoirs of a Most Respectable Family* [1855] (London, 1911), XII-XIII; XII, 231.

[15] *All Hallows' Eve* (New York, 1948).

[16] Roth, *Benjamin Disraeli, Earl of Beaconsfield* (New York, 1951), p. 83. The other way of reconciling the discrepancy is James Russell Lowell's. In his review of *Tancred* in the *North American Review* (LXV [1847], 201-24), Lowell wrote: "Seldom has the inner life been so aptly symbolized in the outward as in the case of the Jews. That the idolaters of ceremony and tradition should become the venders of old clothes, that the descendants of those who, within earshot of the thunders of Sinai, could kneel before the golden calf, should be the money-changers of Europe, has in it something of syllogistic completeness. The work by which the elder D'Israeli will be remembered is the old curiosity shop of literature. He is merely a cast-off-clothes-dealer in an aesthetic sense. The son, with his trumpery of the past, is clearly a vender of the same wares, and an offshoot from the same stock."

[17] The lines from *Punch* are cited by Modder, p. 209; on Ingoldsby's "Ikey Solomons," which came out in *Blackwood's* in 1832, see Philip Rieff, "Disraeli: The Chosen of History," p. 29. Trollope's Sidonia appears in Chaps. IX and XIX of *Barchester Towers* [1857]; Trollope also uses the name in a kidding allusion to Disraeli's politics in *Framley Parsonage* [1861]. Thackeray's burlesque, of course, is "Codlingsby," second in the book *Notes by Eminent Hands* [1847], in *Works,* VI, 478-88. Disraeli returned the favor by caricaturing Thackeray as the envious and conceited minor novelist St. Barbe in *Endymion.* Two notes by C. L. Cline clarify these little lrterary feuds: "Disraeli and Thackeray," *Review of English Studies,* XIX (1943), 404-8, and " 'Coningsby' and Three Victorian Novelists," *Notes and Queries,* CLXXXVI (1944), 41-42.

Rather more amiable fictional versions of Disraeli are found in Anthony Hope's *Quisanté* [1900] and in two novels by Mrs. Craigie: *The School for Saints* [1897] and its sequel *Robert Orange* [1899]. In *School for Saints,* Disraeli merely has a walk-on part, but in the later novels Mrs. Craigie uses the Disraeli-myth for all she can get out of it: Orange, himself an idealized portrait of Disraeli, at the same time functions as a political adherent of the historical one, with the result that Disraeli, on one level of reality, walks into the novel every so often to encounter himself on another level, and Disraeli finds himself writing letters to Disraeli. This is quixotic but humorless. Cf. the author's comments in *The Life of John Oliver Hobbes ("Mrs. Craigie")* (London, 1911), pp. 107 ff. Roland Grey, "Disraeli in Fancy Street," *Cornhill,* LXVI (1929), 102-10, gives a run-down of Disraeli portrayals in English fiction and drama.

[18] *A Piece of My Mind,* pp. 102-3.

[19] *Hypatia, or New Foes with an Old Face* [1852], Westminster Ed. (New York, 1899). Discussions of the novel and its Jewish characters appear in W. F. Lord, "The Kingsley Novels," *Nineteenth Century,* LV (1904), 996-1004; Stanley E. Baldwin, *Charles Kingsley* (Ithaca, 1934), pp. 126-34; Margaret Farrand Thorp, *Charles Kingsley* (Princeton, 1937), pp. 108-16; W. M. Conacher, "Charles Kingsley," *Queens Quarterly,* XLV (1938), 503-11; and Una Pope-Hennessy, *Canon Charles Kingsley* (London, 1948).

[20] *Leila, or The Siege of Granada,* Knebworth Limited Ed. (Boston, 1891-92), XXI, 1-175.

[21] *Anti-Semite and Jew* (New York, 1948), pp. 95-96.

[22] W. F. Monypenny and G. E. Buckle, *Life of Benjamin Disraeli,* rev. ed. (New York, 1929), I, 24.

[23] The foregoing summary comes out of Leslie Fiedler's brilliant piece, "What Can We Do About Fagin?" *Commentary,* VII (1949), 411-18. His article should be read in conjunction with the symposium in *Commentary* which it provoked: "The Jewish Writer and the

English Literary Tradition," VIII, 209-19 and 361-70, with contributions by David Daiches, Alfred Kazin, Harry Levin, Lionel Trilling, *et al.;* and Milton Hindus, "F. Scott Fitzgerald and Literary Anti-Semitism," *Commentary,* III (1947), 508-16, which contains pertinent material on Eliot. Josef Rischik, *Graham Greene und sein Werk* (Berne, 1951), pp. 84-87, reviews Greene's Jewish personnel. The dates of Greene's novels are: *Stamboul Train,* 1932; *This Gun for Hire,* 1936; and *Brighton Rock,* 1938; Waugh's appeared as follows: *Decline and Fall,* 1928; *Vile Bodies,* 1930; *Black Mischief,* 1932. The usual unflattering allusions to "the whores and the Jews" and to the young girls who deserve something better in life than "a Jew called Furstein who kept a girl in Shepherd's Market" may be spotted in Greene's *It's a Battlefield* [1934] and *The Confidential Agent* [1939]. To Waugh's gallery of miniature monsters should be added his portrait of Ambrose Silk, the half-Jewish homosexual littérateur of *Put Out More Flags* [1942], editor of the aesthetic journal *The Ivory Tower,* who sits out the Second World War in the Ministry of Information (Department of Religion, Desk: Atheism) and ends up in Ireland as Fr. Flanagan, S.J.: a combination of Fr. Rothschild and Youkoumian, the squalid Financial Secretary to the Azanian Minister of Modernization.

[24] "The Jewish Writer and the English Literary Tradition," p. 218. On Pound, see Peter Viereck, "Pure Poetry, Impure Politics, and Ezra Pound," *Commentary,* XI (1951), 340-46, to which I am indebted for the quoted matter from the *Pisan Cantos.* To restore the balance, see Archibald MacLeish, *Poetry and Opinion* (Urbana, 1950). William Van O'Connor and Edward Stone have put the much publicized Bollingen Award to pedagogic uses in freshman themes by anthologizing the pertinent journalistic, critical, and legal documents in *A Casebook on Ezra Pound* (New York, 1959), including reprinted pieces by George Orwell, Dwight Macdonald, and others. Eliot's position cannot perhaps be so neatly divorced from Pound's as the above remarks suggest, in so far as his cultural program calls for a certain amount of religious discrimination which gets itself into his polemical utterances. (Conversely, one often hears it alleged that Pound is the one who speaks in symbol and metaphor, who, when he says "Jew," means USURA, whether he says it in verse or in prose.) The text which it is customary to cite against Eliot is: *After Strange Gods* (New York, 1934), page 20: "reasons of race and religion combine to make any large number of free-thinking Jews undesirable." But that was in 1934. Hindus ("Literary Anti-Semitism," p. 518) draws the line by noting that anti-Semitism is "central, philosophical, obsessive" for Pound (or Céline, whose *Trifles for a Massacre* struck Gide as so vehemently exaggerated that, in his review, he mistook it for a satire on anti-Semitism) and "decorative, fashionable, literary," for Eliot (or Gide), whose anti-Jewishness, on the level of explicit prose statement, "as its explosive social qualities were revealed was completely and silently dropped."

[25] *My Life as German and Jew* (New York, 1933), pp. 11-12.

[26] "The Jewish Writer and the English Literary Tradition," p. 216.

[27] *The Conscience of the Rich* (New York, 1958). Snow's novel is the latest in the sequence collectively entitled *Strangers and Brothers.* The structure of this work and Snow's literary techniques generally have been analyzed by Pamela Hansford Johnson, "Three Novelists and the Drawing of Character," *Essays and Studies,* N.S. III (1950), 82-99, and, most recently, by William Cooper, *C. P. Snow,* "Bibliographical Series" (London, 1959), pp. 15-29.

HEBRAISM VERSUS HELLENISM

G. L. Hersey (essay date 1976)

SOURCE: "Aryanism in Victorian England," in *Yale Review,* Vol. 66, Autumn, 1976, pp. 104-13.

[*In the following essay, Hersey notes that the novel* Lothair *of Benjamin Disraeli (Prime Minister [1867; 1874-80] as well as novelist) "gently mocked" the views on Aryanism of Lord Leighton (painter), and that Leighton's positioning of Aryanism against Semitism resembled the construction of Matthew Arnold's arguments on Hellenism versus Hebraism.*]

The cult, or philosophy, of Aryanism has flourished at various times and in various places during the past 150 years. In Britain from the late 1860's through at least the early 1890's it manifested itself both in art and politics; and the appearance last year of these two books [*Lord Leighton,* by Leonée and Richard Ormond; and *Lothair,* by Benjamin Disraeli, edited by Vernon Bogdanor] raises the question of Aryanism's effect on two key Victorians: Frederick, Lord Leighton, the greatest "classical" painter of the period, and Benjamin Disraeli, who, after temporarily relinquishing the prime ministership, in 1870 wrote a novel in which Leighton and his Aryan beliefs were gently mocked. Though William Gaunt alluded to these matters in *Victorian Olympus* (1952) they have never received the study they deserve. Victorian Aryanism was a fascinating business—an episode of philosophical racism done up in imperialistic and neopagan trappings.

However neither Mr. Bogdanor in his introduction to *Lothair* nor the Ormonds in their monograph on

Leighton take the opportunity to discuss the subject. Otherwise, I must immediately add, they have done well. Mr. Bogdanor's introduction and notes to the novel usefully identify the real-life characters who sat for Disraeli's portrayals—they range from Cardinal Manning to Bishop Wilberforce—though it is perhaps less essential to be told by Mr. Bogdanor who St. Michael is, or what happens when someone's face "mantles with emotion." Mr. Bogdanor also supplies a bibliography and a chronology of Disraeli's life. The book is well produced and a pleasure to read. *Lord Leighton,* meanwhile, is a typical Mellon Centre book—sumptuous in appearance if somewhat shallow in substance. Yet it should be warmly welcomed. It contains a large amount of new, or newly accessible, information about this interesting man, his work, and his circle. It sets the scene for further research, one aspect of which, surely, will deal with Leighton's Aryanism.

Aryanism was of the greatest fascination both to Disraeli and Leighton. Indeed to the latter it was, for a time, of overwhelming importance and explains much about his art. The concept of an "Aryan" art seems to have come into Victorian culture mainly via the writings of Friedrich Max Müller, the Oxford philologist, and Ernest Renan. The word really meant much the same thing as "Indo-European." Except for this: the propounders of the Aryan doctrine believed that the speakers of the Indo-European languages belonged to a single race or group of races which had arisen in Northern India and which had traditionally ruled the great empires of the world. The more extreme Aryanists believed that it was the destiny of this race eventually to destroy all other human strains. Sir Charles Dilke, in his famous polemic *Greater Britain,* published two years before *Lothair,* claimed that the Anglo-Saxons were nothing more nor less than the latest and most powerful of the Aryans. "In essentials the race was always one," he wrote, adding, "the Anglo-Saxon is the only extirpating race on earth." Dilke sees it "ever pushing with burning energy towards the setting sun." Among the lesser breeds which he singles out for "extirpation" are the populations of China, Chile, Peru, Japan, and the African tablelands.

Dilke was a friend and patron of the Aryan artists in Leighton's circle. But these artists were very far from depicting scenes of Anglo-Saxons extirpating Chinese or Chileans. Their subject matter was ancient Greece and Rome. The new art began in about 1867 and at first caused considerable shock. For one thing the nude, after a mid-Victorian eclipse, reappeared and with a frequency and dominance it had never before achieved in British art. These "classical" nudes, furthermore, possessed a monumentality that had been found in earlier British art only in the field of portraiture. In gestural language and body rhetoric the new Aryan personages could reflect a variety of sources ranging from the Elgin Marbles to Pre-Raphaelitism. Most of the paintings were genre scenes; but, as I am suggesting, it was genre of a stately sort. And the air of pride and sensuous power in these figures is often mixed with a curious sleepiness, or at least languor, that has few precedents in British painting. Meanwhile the backgrounds often consist of fresh, cold, Poussinesque skies and mountains. The rich colors of foreground fabric and foliage play against the sugary marble of temples, palaces, and pools. The most prominent of the artists were Albert Moore, E. J. Poynter, Alma-Tadema, Burne-Jones and Watts in special and limited ways, and of course Leighton. The Continental parallels were Gérôme, Cabanel (the genre was known in France as Néogrec), and Böcklin.

What is the connection between this sort of painting and Dilke's Anglo-Saxon extirpators? *Lothair* tells us. Disraeli's novel is a *Bildungsroman* in which the young English nobleman Lothair is tempted by, and then ultimately rejects, various false religions and ideologies. One of these is preached by a painter called Gaston Phoebus (whose name, Mr. Bogdanor ought to have told us, is taken from a famous fifteenth-century Gascon knight). Mr. Phoebus is the Apollo of English Aryanism. He is, we are told, brilliant, brave, boastful, vain, arrogant, eccentric, "accomplished in all the graceful pursuits of man." He is also tall, lithe, athletic, "aquiline," and possessed of a countenance remarkable for its radiance. So fiery is his eye, indeed, and so lustrous are his complexion and his chestnut curls, that onlookers are positively dazzled. But Mr. Phoebus is no mere mannequin. He is "nursed in the philosophy of our times," and his face is weighted with deep and haughty thought.

Mr. Phoebus's theory of art requires not the study of Nature and of Man, but rather that of beautiful Nature and beautiful Man only. Nature and Art must be studied exclusively as they are found in countries inhabited by first-rate races "and where the laws, the manners, the customs, are calculated to maintain the health and beauty of a first-rate race." These conditions existed in Periclean Athens, in Hadrian's Rome, and in Renaissance Italy. Otherwise, Aryanism's archenemy in thought, law, art, and race has fully or partially prevailed. This enemy is Semitism. Semitism, which includes Christianity, especially the Protestant kind, destroys art and teaches man to despise his body.

Lothair, hearing Mr. Phoebus expound all this, regrets that he has for so long been ignorant of it. " 'Do not regret it,' said Mr. Phoebus, 'What you call ignorance is your strength. By ignorance you mean a want of knowledge of books. Books are fatal.' " And he goes on to deplore the invention of the printing press, which has interfered with the truer, nobler instruction obtained via the hand, voice, ear, and eye of a living teacher. " 'The essence of education,' continued Mr. Phoebus, 'is the education of the body.' " Physical exercise, knowledge of no more than one language, no books: these principles, which have been happily practiced for generations by the British landed gentry, are the best and highest that there are. They are those of classical Greece. If Britain continues to apply them, and at the same time administers them eugenically, prohibiting armaments to all lesser races, she will extricate herself from the morass of Semitism in which she still lies. Inspired by painted and sculptured specimens of Aryan physical perfection—"Phidian types"—a new Aryan era, comparable to those of Greece, Rome, and the Renaissance, will come about in Britain.

Looking forward to this achievement, Mr. Phoebus and his circle bring elements from the more important Aryan epochs into their lives. Madame Phoebus, for instance, is a Cantacuzene—a descendant of the Byzantine Emperors. To Mr. Phoebus she thereby represents Aryanism's Greek patrimony. But she adds details from other parts of the tradition:

> Madame Phoebus and her sister Euphrosyne welcomed Lothair in maritime costumes which were absolutely bewitching; wondrous jackets with loops of pearls, girdles defended by dirks with handles of turquoises, and tilted hats that, while they screened their long eyelashes from the sun, crowned the longer braids of their never-ending hair.

This picture is quintessentially Victorian-Aryan: Greek ladies welcoming a Saxon nobleman, the ladies in costumes that sound part Byzantine mosaic, part Paolo Veronese, part James Tissot.

They are all on board Mr. Phoebus's yacht, the *Pan,* en route to the painter's private Aegean island where he maintains "an Aryan clime, an Aryan landscape, and an Aryan race. It will," adds Lothair's host, "do you good after your Semitic hallucinations." (This refers to Lothair's recent abortive reception into the Roman Catholic Church.) Mr. Phoebus's enchanted isle possesses an academy of fine arts, gymnasia, and schools of music and dance. These are the only forms of education. The religion of the upper classes is classical paganism; only the poor are literate, apparently, or Christian. But even they, and even their priests, are unconscious pagans. Here, Semitic culture is a melting mask. Christ and his saints fade out as, behind them, Diana and Venus, Jupiter and Mercury—not to mention Narcissus—shine through.

But suddenly the plot of *Lothair* takes a surprising turn. Mr. Phoebus is seduced from Aryanism. He is asked to become court painter to the Czar, and President of the Russian Academy. He accepts. Worse, he is to begin this new career with a series of scenes executed in Semitism's very epicenter: Jerusalem. Thus does an Aryan Leighton suddenly turn into a super-Semite, a veritable Holman Hunt. As the novelist remarks:

> Considering that the great objects in life with Mr. Phoebus were to live in an Aryan country, amid an Aryan race, and produce works which should revive for the benefit of human nature Aryan creeds, a proposition to pass some of the prime years of his life among the mongolian race, and at the same time devote his pencil to the celebration of Semitic subjects, was startling.

But if Mr. Phoebus thus ingloriously goes off the rails Frederick Leighton did not. In the years following the appearance of Disraeli's novel, Leighton's Aryanism only rang out the more loudly. Actually, his paintings had been pronouncedly panathenaic for years; but in 1879, nine years after Disraeli's delicately derisive portrayal, he began giving his *Royal Academy Addresses,* which were published as a book in 1893. These are the most definitive Victorian expression of the Aryan philosophy of art that I have come across. Leighton does not go to Mr. Phoebus's extremes. He never advises his listeners—students at the RA Schools—to leave off reading books, to be content with one language only, to advocate eugenics, or to deny arms to lesser races. He does not even advise his listeners to take up body culture, though he often praises athletics. But Leighton certainly does celebrate, if not advocate, paganism as a religion; he does trace the principles of Aryan art through history, separating on this basis the "first-rate" from the lesser races; and he does advocate a recurring Phidian racial type as the model for his students' pictures. Leighton also makes much of the fact that Semitism has always been inimical to good art. Thus he teaches what we might call artistic eugenics—the creation of an ideal, purpose-bred population. In artistic eugenics that population lives in the world of paintings rather than in the real world.

Indeed Leighton in some respects is more extreme than Mr. Phoebus. He sees Aryanism and Semitism as two great contraposed principles, the one of intellect and beauty, the other of conscience and will. These two principles have guided not just the history of art but that of civilization. In this, of course, he is echoing the Matthew Arnold of *Culture and Anarchy* (1869), whose oppositions between Hellenism and Hebraism amount to much the same thing.

Leighton's theories may have had Arnold as one immediate inspiration, and they also grew out of Möller and Renan, as I have said; but that is only their anthropological side. On the artistic side they link up with the associationism of Archibald Alison, Hazlitt, and Ruskin. Like Ruskin's, Leighton's theory was at its core narcissistic. An individual stands before Nature as before a looking glass, and translates what he sees into images of himself. This vision provokes a powerful reaction, and art begins when that observer utters or moves his body in response to his recognition of himself in the looking glass of Nature. The response is elaborated by what Leighton calls "the anthropomorphic impulse," which is the continual humanizing and personalizing of the world, the making of it into a perfected reflection of the self. This happens through the ever more far-reaching identification of Nature with the self.

The same thing happens before a transcription of Nature, that is, a work of art. Even in a landscape painting we ultimately see ourselves: mountains and clouds are personifications, anthropomorphic shapes and fragments, heroic encounters between personages who can ultimately all be reduced to self-images. Leighton uses the word "metaphor" to describe this reductive faculty. This sort of virtuoso self-seeing is the most primitive as well as the most central form of aesthesis. Man's earliest artistic act, says Leighton, was to freeze a self-image, for the oldest works of art are the "exact images" and "doubles" that the ancient Egyptians made of themselves. These visible egos, or *eidoloi* as Leighton calls them, survive death. In this way they are more powerful and more permanent than their makers. They are also more beautiful, and the rest of the history of art is simply an elaboration of this original self-portraiture. The historiography of art, in turn, chronicles man's increasing ability to discern himself in whatever images he sees—his increasing powers of anthropomorphic or even automorphic metaphor. Indeed one gets the impression, though this is never actually claimed, that in Leighton's system this is pretty much all there is not only to art but to the whole of seeing: when one does not see one's self, in short, one sees nothing.

The basic vision of the self is split into a multitude of sensations, connected into groups by the association of ideas. In their truest and best manifestation these groups constitute "that joyous fellowship of gods and goddesses, loving and hating, scheming and boasting, founders of dynasties on earth"—the gods of Greek popular religion. Phidias's sculpture records the appearance and actions of these divinities, and we sense their power still in his art; indeed it is not too much to say that Greek religion is derived from Greek art rather than the other way round; in this view pagan art prefigures and brings about religion.

In short, once one has penetrated the gaudy clouds of Leighton's rhetoric one arrives at the following bizarre proposition: the highest artistic experience is to contemplate the self in Nature, or in a transcription of Nature, as that self is sensed through Greek divinities portrayed by Phidias. In this manner the human sensibility can reach out, says Leighton in a Paterian passage, into the furthest realms of experience. The associated divinity-sensations

> come fraught with dim complex memories of all the ever-shifting spectacle of inanimate Creation, and of the more deeply-stirring phenomena of Life; of the storm and the lull, the splendour and the darkness of the outer world; of the storm and the lull, the splendour and the darkness of the changeful and transitory lives of men. Nay, so closely overlaid is the simple aesthetic sensation with elements of ethic or intellectual emotion by these constant and manifold accretions of associated ideas, that it is difficult to conceive of it independently of this precious outgrowth.

Because the Greek gods have best embodied these sensations they are the first and best of all races. They are a sort of ur-Aryan race. And, among humans, Athens in the Age of Pericles most directly imitated the actions and forms of these gods, producing the purest form of Aryanism among humans. It is only at this point in history, at the Periclean point, that the "sluggish stream" of earlier civilizations gives way to the "upleaping of a living source, reflecting and scattering abroad the light of a new and more joyous day; a spring at which men shall drink to the end of all days and not be sated." The only modern parallel to this ancient, purest Aryanism is "sometimes found in the women of another Aryan race—your own." With this sudden apostrophe to the listeners before him Leighton bestows on Victorian womanhood the marks of its Aryan heritage. One assumes that here, if anywhere, is the starting-point for any new racial radiance, or upleaping living source, in Britain.

The theory of Aryanism continues. In the period between the decline of Pericles and the rise of Victoria the cultures of man were still deeply tinged with Semitism. Leighton chronicles the ups and downs of these lesser breeds and their lesser arts. Before Greece, the Egyptian *eidoloi* though beautiful in their Aryan properties were Semitic in their "peculiarity and inertness." They expressed the Semitized Egyptian race's "narrow but tenacious spirit." The Chaldeans and Assyrians were even more Semitic and hence had worse art. The Jews of course were the most Semitic of all. They were utterly "void of the artistic impulse." This was partly because of the second commandment and partly because, living in the level and monotonous desert, they were without the vivid landscape features, the hills, brooks, and trees that the Greeks transformed into anthropomorphic beings—"the joyous fellowship of gods and goddesses." Polytheism is the archfriend, as monotheism is the archenemy, of Beauty. Leighton quotes Renan to the effect that, in Palestine, the very desert itself is monotheistic.

Another Semitic race, more hybrid than the Jews, did succeed in creating an art. But it was the bad art of a bad people: "the obese and unattractive male personages who take their ease and toy with their prodigious necklaces, and not less the lolling ladies who lie lazily curled in their last slumber on the sepulchral urns . . . by no means belie in their suggestiveness the character bestowed on their prototypes by Greeks and Romans alike—the character of gluttons and of sluggards." So much for the Etruscans.

If the Etruscans were less than purely Semitic the Christians have been almost more than that. For Leighton, Christianity is not merely a branch of Semitism, it is Semitism's most potent form. Christianity teaches that the enjoyment of beauty is the enjoyment of a mirage and a snare. Christianity is indeed a reversal of paganism; the gods of the Greeks became Christianity's devils. Pan kept his historicity along with his horns and hooves, and turned into Satan. Similarly were standards of bodily beauty turned upside down. The era of the Man of Sorrows ushered in the worship of "gaunt ungainliness" in art, says Leighton. Early Italian painting, for example, though expressive in line, is ignorant of Nature, empty and inaccurate in drawing. (The thought comes amiss from an artist whose reputation had been made with a picture entitled *Cimabue's Madonna is Carried in Procession through the Streets of Florence.*) Only with the revival of humanism, and with the restudy of Nature, of the human physique, and of classical art, was Aryanism again to triumph. The Italian Renaissance was thus a recrudescence of essentially Greek racial qualities, a "strange mixture of Attic subtlety and exquisiteness of taste, with a sombre fervour and a rude Pelasgic strength." But this brief revival was swept away (and here Leighton sounds more than ever like Arnold) by the Semitic wing of the Renaissance—the Reformation.

Leighton's theory of art, as published, is thus by no means antithetical to Disraeli's earlier parodistic version of it, a version which would have been based on Leighton's conversations rather than on his lectures. The only thing lacking in the *Addresses* is something comparable to Mr. Phoebus's program for artistic eugenics. Leighton did not discuss the art of his own time. But one can take his pictures and those of his "classical" contemporaries as contributions to such a program. Today, for example, we often criticize these Late Victorian artists because their figures, while pretending to be Greek or Roman, are so obviously Victorian and Anglo-Saxon. It seems absurd, as William Gaunt has said, to rebaptize these Daisys and Mary Annes as so many Euphrosynes and Psyches. Modern critics go on to say that the Victorian artists have "failed" for, setting out to imitate Greek art, they have been unconsciously betrayed by the visual flavor of their own time. They have in fact doubly failed, for they ought never to have tried to paint Greek and Roman scenes at all. They should instead have been Realists or Impressionists.

If we abandon these critical assumptions—and they really have no justification—and if instead we turn to Leighton's *Addresses* as the proper text for Leighton's art, then we find that his Victorian goddesses and nymphs are in all probability intentionally Victorian. His purpose was to *conflate* the Daisys and Mary Annes of Victorian England with their "Phidian" prototypes, just as Madame Phoebus was part Greek, part Venetian, and part British. It was with this "bewitching" combination of Byzantine pearls, Renaissance daggers, and Victorian hats that Mr. Phoebus's wife and sister-in-law were able to carry Lothair off to their enchanted island.

I noted that Leighton's Aryanism seemed to expand rather than contract after *Lothair,* and that in places the *Addresses* seem almost to have been inspired by Disraeli's novel. There is another occasion on which Leighton seems to have been influenced by *Lothair.* In that book, at the end of Chapter 35, Disraeli describes one of Mr. Phoebus's paintings, *Hero and Leander.* It was in his studio covered by a curtain. A group of visitors entered and

> when the curtain was withdrawn, they beheld a figure of life-like size, exhibiting in undisguised completeness the perfection of the female form, and yet the painter had so skilfully availed himself of the shadowy and mystic hour and of some gauzelike drapery, which veiled without concealing his design, that the chastest eye might gaze on his heroine with impunity. The splendour of her upstretched arms held high the beacon light, which threw a glare upon the sublime anxiety of her countenance, while all the tumult of the Hellespont, the waves, the scudding sky, the opposite shore revealed by a blood red flash, were touched by the hand of a master who had never failed.

Many years later, in 1887, while he was delivering his addresses on Aryan art, Leighton painted such a picture. It is now in the City Museum and Art Gallery, Manchester, and is very much what Disraeli describes except that the curtain is an actual part of the scene, and Hero holds this rather than a lantern. Leighton has also—and here he may more pointedly be making fun of, while drawing inspiration from, Disraeli's description—supplied a glaring lack in Disraeli's imagined picture. For, though Mr. Phoebus's painting was entitled *Hero and Leander,* there is no mention of the latter. And in Leighton's painting Leander occupies a predella under the main scene, like an afterthought or footnote.

Do such things constitute some sort of self-parody? A similar joke shows up in Leighton's famous 1880 self-portrait in the Uffizi, painted for that gallery's collection of self-portraits of the members of various European academies. Leighton, who was at the time President of *his* academy, portrays himself in his brilliant scarlet Oxford University gown. Reynolds had done the same for himself in his own day; but Leighton is not really coming on as successor to the Royal Academy's first and greatest president. Rather, behind his head is a detail from the Parthenon frieze, a part of the Panathenaic procession: Aryanism's apogee. Posing before these "Phidian types," with his curly hair, burnished beard, and brilliant eyes, Leighton assimilates, if ever such assimilation took place, a classical divinity to a modern face. He is Jupiter Olympus. It is an extraordinary exercise in comic arrogance. It illuminates that side of Leighton and his philosophy that appealed to Disraeli's affectionate wit. As a "Phidian" self seen in Nature, Leighton's picture shows the genial, even the playful, aspect that Aryanism could have before the Germans, inspired by Houston Stewart Chamberlain and other late Victorians, turned it into a deadly serious matter.

Vassillis Lambroupoulos (essay date 1989)

SOURCE: "Violence and the Liberal Imagination: The Representation of Hellenism in Matthew Arnold," in *The Violence of Representation: The Literature and the History of Violence,* ed. Nancy Armstrong and Leonard Tennenhouse, Routledge, 1989, pp. 180-93.

[*In the following excerpt, Lambroupoulos explains that, in the dialectical scheme of Hellenism and Hebraism, Arnold identifies conduct and authority with Hebraism and culture with Hellenism, and that Arnold argues for the synthesis and balance of these forces in order to preserve the stability of the state.*]

IV

For almost three centuries, since it first posited itself as an essence, a problem, and a quest, western thought has conceived of the world in terms of an all-encompassing polarity: the Hebraic vs. the Hellenic. In literature, art, criticism, scholarship, epistemology, and metaphysics, in different forms and manifestations, whenever thought has portrayed itself (as conscience, subconscious, inspiration, knowledge, talent, language, Being, writing, subjectivity, fragmentariness, or gender) and has inquired after non-thought (the negative, God, difference, otherness, alienation, silence, lack, absence), it has always operated on the basis of this antithesis, where the Hebraic is the positive term—the depth, the horizon, and the meaning—while the Hellenic is the opposite—the surface, the moment, and the message. Thought thematizes and articulates itself as the Hebraic, the dark silence of the ontic; and it questions its materiality, its fleeting presence in this Greek world of blinding light and deceptive form. Ever since the western mind asked the question of identity, from Spinoza to Derrida, it has been searching for the different—because the question of identity is the search for the secular transcendence of difference. And the different is always Hebraic—muted, strange, exilic, always already chosen and punished: chosen to sin and punished to be chosen; while identity is the source and the cause of guilt—the material, the profane, the present, the temporary, the exchange value of the sign, the never before or again. The Hebraic stands for the transcendent: thought about itself and man against his (and lately her) self; while the Greek stands for the worldly, the earthly, the limited, the finitude of use. Ultimately, the distinction is between the Old Athens and the New Jerusalem, the Acropolis and the Temple, the philosopher and the prophet, beauty and faith, perfection and salvation. But as in every dialectical scheme, the two need, define, verify, support, reinforce each other: for thought to seek its other it must posit a self, to find salvation it must indulge in sin, to find meaning it must create form.

If [Matthew] Arnold's treatment of the polarity has been the most popular, this may be attributed partly to two reasons: his strong identification of the Hebraic with authority, and his vision of a possible reconciliation of the opposite forces. According to his program of national rejuvenation, the role of culture will be to renew and strengthen authority by preparing and cultivating individuals for a new national consensus to be expressed and monumentalized in the state. The old order will not be destroyed (let alone allowed to collapse) but rather supplemented by a new force, so that eventually a reconciliation of classes, religions, denominations, individual interests, and political goals will be implemented. In this scheme, the two forces of order and renovation are represented (and allegorized) respectively by Hebraism and Hellenism; and the remedy for the national malady is rational, orderly, educated, and informed Hellenization of the Hebraic order that has grown old, fanatic, and exclusive.

Arnold endorses the traditional absolute distinction between them: "Hebraism and Hellenism—between these two points of influence moves our world" (1971: 107). But he is careful not to accept their opposition as necessary: "And these two forces we may regard as in some sense rivals,—rivals not by the necessity of their own nature, but as exhibited in man and his history,—and rivals dividing the empire of the world between them" (ibid.). On the other hand, this situation should not continue, since the two trends have a major element in common: "The final aim of both Hebraism and Hellenism, as of all great spiritual disciplines, is no doubt the same: man's perfection or salvation" (1971: 108). In this sentence, especially the last parallelism, Arnold may have captured the essence of the whole dichotomy in its fundamental isomorphism: profane and divine, secular and holy, art and religion, beauty and faith—the equation of the two shows their ideological roots in the search for transcendence in both worlds, this and the other (—any other). Salvation and perfection, the Hebraic and the Hellenic, are the two sides of the dialectic coin. "At the bottom of both the Greek and the Hebrew notion [of felicity] is the desire, native in man, for reason and the will of God, the feeling after the universal order,—in a word, the love of God" (1971: 109). The forces may be radically different but they are isomorphically parallel, and their efforts converge in the search for God's love as the law of universal order. If we can work toward making them converge on this earth and in this life, Arnold suggests, we shall establish, in the absolute, all-embracing institution of the state, the law of worldly order. And the model of perfection provided by art, as encoded in culture, will help us achieve secular salvation in the balanced, total order of communal will, reason, and desire—the state.

Distinctions between the trends are not and cannot, of course, be eliminated. "They are, truly, borne towards the same goal; but the currents which bear them are infinitely different" (1971: 110). Their approaches differ greatly. This, however, makes them complementary rather than antithetical:

> their single history is not the whole history of man; whereas their admirers are always apt to make it stand for the whole history. Hebraism and Hellenism are, neither of them, the *law* of human development, as their admirers are prone to make them; they are, each of them, *contributions* to human development,—august contributions, invaluable contributions. (1971: 115)

But Arnold urges his audience to work toward reconciliation and combination, a final, stable synthesis. He envisions a world where "man's two great natural forces, Hebraism and Hellenism, will no longer be dissociated and rival, but will be a joint force of right thinking and strong doing to carry him on towards perfection" (1971: 173). This is his dream of totality and integration of the two elemental forces, after their conflicts in history have been overcome: reconciliation and transcendence, because man needs them both. The spread of culture will help this happen, and it will take place in/as the institution of state. But before we elaborate on that, we ought to explain his conception of the two powers.

The Hebraic belongs to, and expresses, the realm of the moral: it represents doing, acting, and believing. It provides principles of behavior and rules of conduct, and commands obedience to them. The Hellenic belongs to, and expresses, the realm of the intellectual: it represents thinking, knowing, and exploring. It provides light and beauty, and inspires spontaneity. The first emanates from the social and the public, while the other from the personal and the private. Therefore the two define different spheres of experience, both basic and important. To generalize further, the Hebraic deals with issues of the soul, and the Hellenic with issues of the mind. And they find their most paradigmatic expression and systematization in religion and art respectively. This is in fact what each civilization contributed to humanity: our religion and faith are Jewish, our art and beauty Greek; we owe salvation to the former, perfection to the latter. Undoubtedly, religion is the more important experience; yet it is often stark, unsettling, demanding—it may even lead, in its fanatic expressions, to hostility to man, because self-conquest requires severe moral strictness. That is why it needs the clarity, simplicity, and freedom of art provided by Hellenism in the comprehensive expressions of culture. Virtue needs to be balanced with disinterestedness, obedience must be sweetened with play. Extremes should meet, negotiate, and merge harmoniously according to the laws of their nature.

Hebraism and Hellenism, then, must be properly combined and balanced. That is not the case today, though, and the resulting disequilibrium has allowed anarchy to develop into a real threat. Authority, Arnold suggests, must again be balanced and its exclusiveness tempered. Historical developments, he proposes, have led to too much Hebraization. In his general view of history,

> by alternations of Hebraism and Hellenism, of a man's intellectual and moral impulses, of the effort to see things as they really are, and the effort to win peace by self-conquest, the human spirit proceeds; and each of these two forces has its appointed hour of culmination and seasons of rule (1971: 116)

Thus in the sixteenth century Hellenism re-entered the world with the Renaissance after centuries of disappearance following the Hebraic triumph of Christianity. Then came a Hebraizing revival, the Reformation and the return to the Bible, which culminated in Puritanism. Arnold finds that this stage persists. "Obviously, with us, it is usually Hellenism which is thus reduced to minister to the triumph of Hebraism" (1971: 108). He agrees with Ernest Renan (1868) that this phenomenon has reached its extremest form with American Puritanism. "From Maine to Florida, and back again, all America Hebraises" (1971: 15). Therefore the current neglect of Hellenism may be attributed to "the long exclusive predominance of Hebraism" (1971: 130), which accounts for the loss of balance in the exercises of authority. Now it is deemed necessary to cure Puritanism of its excesses and redress the balance. Moral and religious feelings will not survive the onslaught of skepticism unless buttressed with the intellectual pursuits of culture. Faith must be fortified with knowledge and cultivated as an art.

Arnold's vision of an enlightened religiosity directly addresses this pressing issue, the rejuvenation of Hebraic authority with Hellenic culture. The roots of Christianity, he argues, are both Jewish and Greek. Therefore, a Christian nation should be organized as a system that draws from these two sources. In the present stage, Hellenism should receive more attention and encouragement. "Now, and for us, it is time to Hellenise, and to praise knowing; for we have Hebraised too much, and have over-valued doing" (1971: 27). Arnold is not, of course, advocating complete Hellenization, but only a minor (yet indispensable) adjustment of the existing system.

> And when, by our Hebraising, we neither do what the better mind of statesmen prompted them to do, nor win the affections of the people we want to conciliate, nor yet reduce the opposition of our adversaries but rather heighten it, surely it may not be unreasonable to Hellenise a little, to let our thought and consciousness play freely about our proposed operation and its motives, dissolve these motives if they are unsound,—which certainly they have some appearance, at any rate, of being,—and create in their stead, if they are, a set of sounder and more persuasive motives conducing to a more solid operation (1971: 145-6)

This is the gospel of Arnold's liberalism: if authority is losing ground, if division and animosity divide people and nations, then some freeplay, some informed rethinking, and some flexibility may help the reinforcement of law and order. Let us be more open-minded about administration and government, Arnold advises: when he defends the idea "to Hellenise, as we say, a little" (1971: 167), he simply means "the habit of fixing our mind upon the intelligible law of things" (1971: 166), of supporting religion with evidence and argument now that faith is far from able to guarantee the old habits of obedience. He is essentially defending the right of the new individual, the subject, to entertain his own thoughts at leisure and free of interest, when properly trained and informed: "Plain thoughts of this kind are surely the spontaneous product of our consciousness, when it is allowed to play freely and disinterestedly upon the actual facts of our social condition, and upon our stock notions and stock habits in respect to it" (ibid.). His principal concern is how the aesthetic attitude and behavior will be integrated in bourgeois life, at the same time fulfilling and justifying it. For this purpose, and for the ultimate task of the preservation of authority in mind, it would suffice to effect a "fruitful Hellenising within the limits of Hebraism itself" (1971: 154). Thus Hellenism will supplement, temper, and balance the excesses of Hebraism, and will preserve its essence intact.

Arnold makes an intense plea for "mutual understanding and balance" (1971: 122) between the two supreme forces. Still, throughout his discussion and his defense of Hellenism, he leaves no doubt about its subservient role and the superiority of Hebraism. Notice how he does not lose sight of his priorities when he admonishes that "we are to join Hebraism, strictures of the moral conscience, and manful walking by the best light we have, together with Hellenism, inculcate both, and rehearse the praises of both. Or, rather, we may praise both in conjunction, but we must be careful to praise Hebraism most" (1971: 123). This is an explicit warning: the Hellenic spirit in itself is unimportant, knowledge, culture, and the disinterested pleasures of subjectivity are meaningless, unless they serve the Hebraic establishment. Hellenism, through culture, will help "the diseased spirit of our time" (1971: 137) survive, and explore new ground for, and forms of, authority. "Hellenism may thus actually serve to further the designs of Hebraism" (1971: 133). Culture is necessary only to the extent that it protects and advances the causes of authority, whose foundations lie in the Jewish faith.

V

In writing *Culture and Anarchy,* Arnold is presenting a concrete political project: he is outlining a method for salvaging the existing modes of authority from the danger of anarchy by renewing order. He realizes that the old order has lost its credibility; he therefore looks for means of overcoming the rigidity and suffocation, and inspiring again confidence and obedience. Faced with voices publicly demanding change, exercising criticism, and claiming rights, he counter-argues by shifting the terms of the debate. For him the problem is not one of structure but of arrangement; not of default but of balance; not of power but of authority; not of politics but of science; not of religion but of culture; not of failure but of efficiency. His main aim is to fight the modern, the revisionary, the radical; he fights the combative with the dialectic. The main strategy consists in presenting the new, the unknown, the critical, as non-new, in fact as only the other, neglected half of the old. Religion and culture, he argues, together form the basis of our civilization: they represent faith and intellect respectively, and they need and entail each other. Naturally, the one is more basic and important than the other; but both are by definition implicated in a good and balanced society. The authority of religion needs the enlightenment of culture. When either predominates, the seeds of anarchy are sown. For Arnold, then, the contemporary problem is not the establishment but its excesses and abuses. He believes that cultivated, right reason may prevent them. For this reason, he seeks a strategic adjustment of power, one that will allow more individuals—namely, the participants of culture—to take part in its administration by volunteering their grateful submission. The liberalization of power will protect it from libertarian demands, and the modernization of authority will guard it against the modern. More power will not help establishments achieve subjection; instead, culture will cultivate subjects—disciplinary topics made for knowledge will educate disciplined individuals for authority.

The distinction between authority and culture is allegorized by Arnold in the Hebraic-Hellenic dichotomy. Hebraism represents authority at its best, most meaningful, and most enduring—religion. It gives it an apocryphal background, a timeless relevance, a transhistorical validity, and a prophetic power. Hellenism, on the other hand, represents enlightenment at its most comprehensive and consummate—culture. It gives authority a sense of tradition, a continuous past, a glorious history. The problem facing Arnold is how to protect religion from political criticism, and politics from individual intervention. To the threat of this problem he gives the name of anarchy, or lack of authority. His solution is to endow authority with the prestige of culture, religion with the wisdom of right knowledge, and to transform the esoteric, exclusive system of the establishment into the public, panoptically present institution of the state. The concrete suggestion, in terms of cultural enrichment, is to look at the "best art and poetry of the Greeks, in which religion and poetry are one, in which the idea of beauty and of a human nature perfect on all sides adds to itself a religious and devout energy" (1971: 43), and to imitate that model, to try to reach again that harmonious fusion. He observes that, in the modern world, literature, religion, and politics suffer from a severe "absence of any authoritative centre" (1971: 91). Religion and art/poetry have been of course separated, and the former is losing its justification while the latter is gaining in both independence and respect. But the center does not hold, and perfection is growing into an isolated aesthetic pursuit. "We have most of us little idea of a high standard to choose our guides by, of a great and profound spirit which is an authority while inferior spirits are none" (1971: 92). We should therefore look to art for a model and aspire to a broad culture which will provide "a certain ideal centre of correct information, taste, and intelligence" (1971: 91).

Culture is called upon to support, enlighten, and justify authority—not in its old form, though, the religion of authority, but in a new one: the art of authority. Until now, religion and its strict principles of conduct was the model of authority, as encapsulated in the Hebraic; but now, for the survival of the power of the establishment, a new model is needed, that of culture-as-art exemplified by the Hellenic. The Hebraic authority of religion, based on rules of obedience and belief, ought to be supplemented by the Hellenic authority of culture, which invites obedience as disinterested knowledge. Although authority and culture, religion and art, have so far been rivals and antagonistic forces, it is now time to be reconciled, because they can beneficially complement each other. Culture informs, enlightens, and serves authority, but without its grounding it is meaningless, if not impossible; religion, on the other hand, needs the sweetness and light of art. Culture is an auxiliary yet indispensable instrument of power, and this holds true for the Hellenic in its relationship with the Hebraic. Arnold argues that authority needs culture, religion art, virtue beauty, consciousness thought, the tyrant the poet, and power truth. In his vision of the new, all-embracing, benevolent establishment of democratic administration, the state, art will be the new faith and culture its religion: culture, as the religion of the state, will be the first secular dogma for all people, in which everybody can play freely and spontaneously. Culture will be the religion, the dogma, and the morality of the bourgeoisie.

Arnold's conception of culture-as-art, as the religion of the modern era, the cult of the dominant middle class, dictates two major principles and requires two corresponding socio-historical developments. The first is the state as the supreme form of political authority. Building it is an urgent priority because

> a State in which law is authoriative and sovereign, a firm and settled course of public order, is requisite if man is to bring to maturity anything precious and lasting now, or to found anything precious and lasting for the future. Thus, in our eyes, the very framework and exterior order of the State, whoever may administer the State, is sacred; and culture is the most resolute enemy of anarchy, because of the great hopes and designs for the State which culture teaches us to nourish. (1971: 170)

The state, then, is Hebraic authority fortified with Hellenic culture. It is characterized by sovereignty, order, direction, maturity, permanence, but above all a sacred form. In its case, the content or the agent of power are not as important as its surface and appearance as authorized by culture, because the state is pure form and total signification: authority as art. The state of culture is a product of the art, not the religion, of authority: it commands by soliciting perfection. The order of the state is sacred because it is the order of culture, of art, of form, of harmony, of the independent signifier, of the naturalized language, of pure writing, of the disinterested play with difference.

The second major principle and requirement dictated by Arnold's conception of culture is perfect individuality, the best self the bourgeois may submit for the approval of his rights. As he states in detail,

> what we seek is the Philistine's [the middle class's] perfection, the development of his best self, not mere liberty for his ordinary self. And we no more allow absolute validity to his stock maxim, *Liberty is the law of human life,* than we allow it to the opposite maxim, which is just as true, *Renouncement*

> *is the law of human life.* For we know that the only perfect freedom is, as our religion says, a service; not a service to any stock maxim, but an elevation for our best self, and a harmonising in subordination to this, and to the idea of a perfected humanity, all the multitudinous, turbulent, and blind impulses of our ordinary selves. (1971: 153)

The crucial terms in this passage form a recognizable set (renouncement, subordination, service) and are together opposed to liberty. The task of the bourgeois is to improve and perfect his self, and that, as we saw before, he is encouraged to perform in the most disinterested way. But the outcome must serve the interests of a perfect, harmonious humanity. As with art, interest is no longer part of the process but a component of the result. Thus perfection is an aesthetic, private procedure that produces a political, public result. The Philistine bourgeois must mould himself into an artwork—perfect, total, autonomous, independent, fulfilled, asocial, transhistorical. But this perfect self must submit his harmonious independence to a social service. Perfection, as an aesthetic goal, justifies itself, but liberty, as a political one, does not. As Hebrew religion has taught, freedom is submission; and as Hellenic art has shown, freedom is perfection. The modern individual, then, as an independent subject, should be willing to perfect and submit himself for voluntary service. His freedom requires (and is based on) renouncement—of the ordinary, the everyday, the commonplace, the non-artistic in general.

The individual self, the absolute expression of the middle class, is the common man purged of all commonness, absolved of all interests, who elevates himself to the level of art and serves the order of the state. His secular faith in culture generates his trust in worldly authority. The more independent and perfect he is, the better servant of the state he may become. His harmony with his self faciliates the harmonization of his pursuits with those of the state in that, through perfection, he subjects himself willingly. His highest ideals are a life of art and a state of culture. In Arnold's vision, the individual as artwork is the masterpiece of culture, and the state as site its museum, which succeeds the institution of the Church. From a matter of taste, the canon becomes a guide to good conduct. In this universe of decorated exteriors, natural signs, and self-conscious enjoyments, control reaches an incomparable purity as it turns into the sheer formalism of administration. The self at its best, a law of art unto himself, has been prepared to serve the rule of the state. Independence will cost him individuality, his rights will cost him his protests, and his culture his liberty. Art will administer his pleasure, culture his desire, science his thought, and the state his salvation. Selves are for service, subjects for subjection. Those who cannot be served by religion alone any more will be given another chance, this time on the personal level, to atone by/in/as art: they may renounce life and redeem the ordinary in beauty.

The Hebraism-Hellenism dichotomy that Arnold employs helps him dramatize the conflict between authority and dissent, and show a path toward reconciliation. The dramatization is effected through an opposition and allegorization of the two forces which are hypostasized as two natural powers, unraveling in (and constituting through their competition) western history. The Hebraic represents the dark kingdom of religion, while the Hellenic the radiant presence of art. In Arnold's scheme, the former stands for the moral austerity of order and authority, and the latter for the disinterested knowledge of harmony and culture. Culture is of course the first word in the title of the book. But as we noted earlier, the other basic notion, authority, appears in the title only through its semantic opposite, anarchy, and thus it is obscured—"made dark", i.e., Hebraic. The effect of this choice of words may be explained in two ways. One is to say that Arnold introduces a new polarity, implying that anarchy actually opposes culture and that, conversely, only culture can save us from anarchy. This view is partly corroborated by the original title of the book's first chapter, "Sweetness and Light," which, when the text was presented as a lecture, was "Culture and its Enemies." There is another possible reading, though, which may not be incompatible with this one. Let us again recall that the Hellenic represents mind, thought, exploration, spontaneity, and independence, and not soul, faith, morality, obedience, proper conduct, and strictness. As these polar distinctions imply, the Hellenic is not only what generates culture, but also what makes anarchy possible. If the Hebraic is order and the Hellenic play; if order requires faith and play facilitates inquiry; if the faith in order produces obedience and the play of inquiry advances knowledge (whose consequence is sin)—then the power of the Hellenic is truly ambiguous and ambivalent: it may lead to either renewed or to overturned order, it may strengthen authority or engineer anarchy, it may release either the beneficial or the eruptive power of culture. Anarchy, then, is part of the Hellenic potential—it is the uncontrolled, untamed, free, skeptical, and irreverent Hellenic.

Arnold seems to realize that exclusive, static, coercive power provokes extreme critiques of authority, and invites disobedience with its traditionalism. His method of defense includes three tactics: first, to allegorize the two forces by branding them with the names and emblems of two ancient civilizations; second, to integrate dissent into the second, and depict it only as its worst potential, an irregularity, a disease of culture; and, third, to advocate the reconciliation of the two forces, provided that the Hellenic remains healthy and reasonable. The title *Culture and Anarchy,* then, reflects the two possibilities and faces, the double potential of

Hellenism, and the book outlines the benefits of its positive version for authority, the secularization of religion through/as art by culture. When uncontrolled, Arnold implies, culture may lead and turn into anarchy: today, for example, its unrestrained exercise threatens the foundations of old authority. Instead of letting the rivalry grow by fighting against culture, we should graft it onto authority; instead of rejecting and suppressing it, we should bring it to contribute to the creation of a new establishment. Because of its earthiness, inquisitiveness, and irreverence, the Hellenic is the real threat. It must be properly controlled by being fashioned after art and by being given the administration of science. Its role and territory, then, will be the construction of a national tradition and of a canon of perfection. It will thus serve and grace authority by making training mandatory and coercion redundant. Arnold's approach to the world of craft, custom, and festival is wholly aesthetic and allegorical, and intends to avert its politicization. The praise of culture and of the Hellenic advocates the former as the religion of the state and the latter as the supplementary beauty and supporting knowledge of the Hebraic. In his method of argumentation, there is no Hebraic without the Hellenic, and no defence of authority without both. To invoke the two is to distinguish the two and thus to hierarchize them, all in order to justify the rights and exercises of authority by the middle class. In all cases, the Hebraic is the modern—the modernist, the middle class, the moral, soul, progress, utopia, God; and the Hellenic is its different—its negative, its other, its supplement, its plenitude, its waste; its debauchery, its debasement, its debacle; its dis-interest, its dis-sent, its dis-sonance. The polarity reveals the aesthetic fashioning of man in the construction of bourgeois identity.

VI

Arnold kept the Hebraism-Hellenism distinction alive and graphic in all his work. But the most important return to it took place a few years after *Culture and Anarchy*, in *Literature and Dogma. An Essay Towards a Better Apprehension of the Bible* ([1873] 1892). The title of the former contains the two sides of the Hellenic; the new one contains both the Hellenic and the Hebraic. The first attempts to counter anarchy with culture, and combine the latter with authority; the latter tries to reconcile the two paradigmatic expressions of Hellenism and Hebraism, and show how they can work together. The opening sentence of its "Preface" sets the context unequivocally: "An inevitable revolution, of which we all recognise the beginnings and signs, but which has already spread, perhaps, farther than most of us think, is befalling the religion in which we have been brought up" (1892: v). Arnold worries about the "spread of scepticism" among the *"lapsed masses"* (1892: vi). People question the Bible and even reject it, while the churches can do nothing because theology is false and does not speak a relevant language. "Our mechanical and materializing theology, with its insane licence of affirmation about God, its insane licence of affirmation about a future state, is really the result of the poverty and inanition of our minds" (1892: xii). It excludes people by only confirming truth and power, without allowing them to participate through knowledge and understanding in faith. "Here, then, is the problem: to find, for the Bible, a basis in something which can be verified, instead of something which has to be assumed" (1892: ix-x). The old religious institutions and their practices cannot protect the faith from its corruption and the imminent collapse under the critique of dissent. A radical change is necessary, a broad revision. "The thing is, to recast religion. If this is done, the new religion will be the national one" (1892: x). A national religion is needed to unite all people—one respecting the rights and expectations of the middle class.

Arnold's aim is "to show that, when we come to put the right construction on the Bible, we give to the Bible a real experimental basis, and keep on this basis throughout" (1892: xi). His concern is the preservation of and correct approach to the Bible, so that a national religion may be built. And to this end he has again one remedy to recommend: "*culture,* the acquainting ourselves with the best that has been known and said in the world, and thus with the history of the human spirit" (ibid.). In regard to the question how can culture help our understanding of the Bible, this means *"getting the power, through reading, to estimate the proportion and relation in what we read"* (1892: xiv). Thus again he insists that culture, the secular religion, can help build the national religion. But, as we see, faith has been replaced by correct reading, believing by interpreting. Now the Bible is a text. His specific suggestion, as indicated in the title of the book, is that we read the Bible as literature, the Book as a book. We are not to take theological explanations for granted; we are rather to read and interpret. We do not necessarily need the mediation of the Church, since we can develop a direct, personal relationship with the text. Culture will help our interpretation, interpretation our religion, religion our nation. As Heinrich Heine would say, it is time to exercise our basic civil right, interpretation, and advance our collective interests.

It comes as a surprise to see literary reading invoked as an aid to understanding the Bible (and recasting religion). Only a century ago, it was biblical criticism that gave birth to literary criticism and gave it its first credibility by letting it use other texts as scriptures. But it is a sure sign of literary criticism's great success that it can now lend its power to revive the authority of the Bible. Arnold admits that the canon does not hold (1892: xxiv, xxvi). Reading-as-interpretation, which was generated by biblical studies, must now contribute to the study of the Bible, and return to its original model. This will be done through culture. In a major aphorism, Arnold states that "culture is *reading*" (1892: xxvii). The statement ought to be amplified: bourgeois culture is literary reading; the bourgeois religion of the state (=culture) is reading of the literary scriptures (=interpretation). Literary interpretation is the consummate experience of the bourgeois, his supreme and purest civil right: it is private, domestic, silent, passive, faithful. It is what culture teaches the middle class to do, how culture trains people in subjectivity, how it accommodates their libertarian claims in the privacy of beauty. That is why the topic of Arnold's book is "the relation of letters to religion," "their effect upon dogma," and "the consequences of this to religion" (1892: 5). Letters and religion, literature and dogma, culture and authority—we are back again in the realm of the secularized Hebraic.

Close to the end of his book, Arnold returns explicitly to the Hebraism-Hellenism dichotomy, using now the more specific terms "Greece" and "Israel." The former, he argues, gave to the world art and science, the latter conduct and righteousness. All these elements are important for a full life. "But conduct, plain matter as it is, is six-eighths of life, while art and science are only two-eighths. And this brilliant Greece perished for lack of attention enough to *conduct;* for want of conduct, steadiness, character" (1892: 320). Anxious to disperse any lingering misunderstandings of his earlier position, Arnold repeats himself in the "Conclusion" to explain that he never questioned the supremacy of Hebraism. Even when he praised culture, the importance of righteousness was paramount in his mind and taken for granted:

> And, certainly, if we had ever said that Hellenism was three-fourths of human life, a palinode, as well as an unmusical man may, we would sing. But we never said it. In praising culture, we have never denied that conduct, not culture, is three-fourths of human life. (1892: 345)

The awkward quantification highlights his despair about keeping the correct balance between the two forces. And his preference is strongly expressed, as when he states that "the revelation which rules the world, even now, is not Greece's revelation but Judaea's" (1892: 320). Of course it is true that the historical Israel perished too; but its lesson will never disappear.

> Thus, therefore, the ideal Israel for ever lives and prospers; and its city is the city whereto all nations and languages, after endless trials of everything else except conduct, after incessantly attempting to do without righteousness and failing, are slowly but surely gathered. (1892: 318)

The Hebraic moral revelation rules the world, and culture is called to serve its ultimate victory. It is also true that "conduct comes to have relations of a very close kind with culture" (1892: 345) and that it is "impaired by the want of science and culture" (1892: 347). But authority belongs to the rules of conduct, not the laws of art and science.

Culture, however, is necessary in its subservient role as a defense against skepticism and dissent that question authority. "And therefore, simple as the Bible and conduct are, still culture seems to be required for them,—required to prevent our mis-handling and sophisticating them" (1892: 348). In recognition of the fundamental law of our human being, which is both "aesthetic and intellective" and "moral" (1892: 349), we should accept that "even for apprehending this God of the Bible rightly and not wrongly, letters, which so many people now disparage, and what we call, in general, *culture,* seems to be necessary" (1892: 350). Aesthetics and literary criticism will repay a debt to theology and biblical interpretation, from which they arose, and will secularize their book, make it a literary text, translate it in terms the middle class understands and in situations it cherishes. Since reading/interpreting has become the fundamental experience, let us finally integrate it with its original subject, the Bible. Arnold seems to argue: if the bourgeois reads, give him the Bible to read, since you cannot expect him any longer to believe in it; now that he has no interest in the holy, give him the Bible for a truly disinterested experience.

In order to defend religion, the Bible, his class, and the nation, Arnold has to rehearse the Hebraism-Hellenism dichotomy. This thesis-antithesis rules his world, helps him make sense out of its divisions. It was also an integral part of his vision for the future. At the end of *Literature and Dogma,* he sees the possibility for a religious art that will only aspire to please God: "For, the clearer our conceptions in art and science become, the more they will assimilate themselves to the conceptions of duty in conduct, will become practically stringent like rules of conduct, and will invite the same sort of language in dealing with them" (1892: 349). But he does not stop here. He ventures into anthropological theories of race and, elaborating on the positions of Emil Burnouf, proceeds

> to talk about the Aryan genius, as to say, that the lore of *science,* and the energy and honesty in the pursuit of *science,* in the best of the Aryan races, do seem to correspond in a remarkable way to the love of *conduct,* and the energy and honesty in the pursuit of *conduct,* in the best of the Semitic. To treat science with the same kind of seriousness as conduct, does seem, therefore, to be a not impossible thing for the Aryan genius to come to. (1892: 349)

Here the Hebraism-Hellenism dichotomy culminates in a radical differentiation between the Aryan and the Semitic races, and their respective basic characteristics. The suggestion is one of conciliation, of possible combination of science and religion. Arnold always cared deeply about a natural religion that would express the race naturally, utilize the resources of culture (i.e., art and science), and unite all people in the community of a national state. His advice to his nation was to support and propagate the Hebraic religion with Hellenic art, authority and culture. From our historical perspective, it may seem strange to see him putting so much trust in the Aryan race. When he used his basic dichotomy to divide people in two races, so that the institutions of the new national reality could be justified, he was unable to predict the war of Aryan religion and culture that was to follow later. But by that time bourgeois authority was too fortified with culture to be stopped from barbarism. Apparently all that its early advocates, like Matthew Arnold, knew how to worry about was just anarchy.

References

Arnold, Matthew (1892) *Literature and Dogma. An Essay Towards a Better Apprehension of the Bible* [1873]. London: Macmillan.

———. (1971) *Culture and Anarchy. An Essay in Political and Social Criticism* [1869]. Ed. Ian Gregor. Indianapolis/New York: Bobbs-Merrill.

Renan, Ernest (1868) *Questions Contemporaines*. Paris.

Michael Ragussis (essay date 1995)

SOURCE: "Arnold's Hebraism and the *Science of Origins*," in *Figures of Conversion: "The Jewish Question" and English National Identity,* Duke University Press, 1995, pp. 211-33.

[*In the following excerpt, Ragussis compares Matthew Arnold's arguments on Hellenism and Hebraism with those of Benjamin Disraeli, and maintains that Arnold argued for the preservation of cultural diversity and the need for Hellenism to balance an overly Hebraic English culture, while Disraeli stressed the Hebraic foundation of English culture and exposed the ideology of Hellenism as based on a racial criticism of Jews.*]

Arnold's Hebraism and the "Science of Origins"

Disraeli's location of English Protestant culture within the context of the cultural history of the Jews should not be seen as a personal eccentricity, outside the mainstream of nineteenth-century English discourse. First, Disraeli's trilogy was a direct response to a kind of discourse about race and culture already in place by the early 1840's; and second, the trilogy was to have a profound influence on one of the most famous representations of English culture later in the century, Matthew Arnold's celebrated formulation of the Hebraic foundation of English national life.

The rhetoric of Saxon, Norman, and Jew in Disraeli's trilogy is best understood as a reaction against a kind of revolution in English racial and cultural discourse that was occurring in the early Victorian period. Under the influence of the developing ideologies of nationalism, imperialism, and colonialism, the discourse about the Anglo-Saxons underwent two critical changes between the late eighteenth century and the early 1840s. First, as scholars have noted, this discourse more and more became based not simply on cultural institutions, but on race.[54] Second, it is my claim that this discourse became diffused in a much broader kind of terminology, focusing no longer simply on the composition of the British people (that is, on the relative merits of Britons, Picts, Celts, Normans, Saxons, etc.), but on the position of the Anglo-Saxons in such larger racial "families" as the Caucasian and the Aryan. By the time Disraeli came to write his trilogy, the flowering of Anglo-Saxon historiography, the development of comparative philology, but most of all, the birth of the new discipline of ethnology—what Arnold called the "science of origins"[55]—had already begun to crystallize the idea of the superiority of the Anglo-Saxon race and its place in the Caucasian or Aryan racial family.

In an influential work, *The Races of Men* (1850), Robert Knox referred directly to Disraeli's novels, arguing "that the real Jew has no ear for music as a race, no love of science or literature; that he invents nothing, pursues no inquiry; that the theory of 'Coningsby' is not merely a fable as applied to the real and undoubted Jew, but is absolutely refuted by all history." Knox's work was not unlike many of the other racialist works that passed for science in the mid-nineteenth century. Knox found it easy to use the name of science to invalidate the mere novels that Disraeli produced: "A respect for scientific truth forbids me refuting the romances of Disraeli; it is sufficient merely to observe that, in the long list of names of distinguished persons whom Mr. Disraeli has described as of Jewish descent, I have not met with a single Jewish trait in their countenance, in so far as I can discover; *and, therefore, they are not Jews,* nor of Jewish origin."[56] So much for the penetrating empiricism of the "science" of origins, a science that writers such as Arnold were too willing to believe without question.

Criticizing Disraeli as the great popularizer of the word "Caucasian," the ethnologist offers no scientific argument, only anti-Semitic stereotypes. Using the "cast-off" speculations of Blumenbach's racial categories, Disraeli, "true to *his race,* . . . picks up the worn-out, threadbare rag, and *declares* it to be a sound and excellent garment—'as good as new.' " Here, "the bold and chivalrous author of 'Tancred' and 'Coningsby' "[57] is revealed as no more than an old-clothes man, the same anti-Semitic stereotype that Thackeray used in *Codlingsby* to mock Disraeli's Sidonia and that the crowds used to mock Disraeli during his early election campaigns.[58] The detection of Jewish identity in nineteenth-century England seems always to require the same unveiling: in the socially mobile world of the time, the Jew's racial origins, masked behind the powers and achievements he has won, can be exposed by revealing him to be no more than a dealer in rags—and for Knox, "Caucasian" is no more than an invention, in Disraeli's hands, used to whitewash that reality.

What we call the prejudice of stereotyping, Knox called the science of ethnology: the Jew is always reducible to a certain set of marked characteristics. . . . It is no accident that Knox at the same time refuses to believe in the power of conversion, for the unconvertibility of the Jew is a boon to the racial doctrine that attempts to fix—permanently—each person in his or her racial category. Hence Knox's apparently gratuitous reflections on the conversion of the Jews: "Societies are got up for their conversion! Be it so. Nothing can be said against them; but in one hundred years they will not convert one hundred Jews—not even one real Jew. . . . Nature alters not."[59] Knox calls into question the work of the conversionist societies, not because of the questionable ethics of their procedures, but because of the Jew's unchangeable racial nature. In so doing, Knox comes dangerously close to the ideology of fifteenth-century Spain, where religious affiliation became a matter of biological filiation, a matter of race. In establishing the power of race, the new science of ethnology enters the debate over the conversion of the Jews by placing the barrier of "Nature" in the way.

It was such an idea that Arnold encountered when, in a series of works written during the 1860s and 1870s, he followed Disraeli in defining the basis of English culture as Hebraic. While it has been a critical commonplace to claim that Arnold borrowed the ideas of "Hellenism" and "Hebraism" from Heine, I wish to argue that Arnold's use of these terms more urgently reflects his response to Disraeli's view of the Hebraic foundation of English culture.[60] But first I would claim that Arnold's cultural criticism is descended not only from Disraeli, but from Scott. At a pivotal point in *On the Study of Celtic Literature* (1866) Arnold attempts to dislodge the English from a conception of themselves as a unicultural and uniracial nation. Like Scott, who insisted on the mutuality of the Norman and Saxon contributions to the English nation, and like Disraeli, who insisted on the Hebraic contribution to English life, Arnold sets out to prove the value of the Celtic genius and its place in "English" culture. He rejects the myth of national unity, of England's cultural and racial "purity," but unlike Scott and Disraeli, he is able to do so from the inside, as an Englishman whose heritage is unquestioned: "But true Anglo-Saxons, simply and sincerely rooted in the German nature, we are not and cannot be" (*CP,* 3.383 [See note 55]), Arnold argued, despite his father's claim in 1841, "Our English race is the German race."[61] Like Scott and Disraeli, Arnold refuses the equation between England and Anglo-Saxon Teutonism, an idea that had continued to grow in the decades that led up to the period of his cultural criticism.

Arnold uses a concept very much like Scott's idea of conversion as racial annihilation to frame the ongoing Victorian debate over the value of Celtic culture. With sharp mockery, he poses the rhetorical question: "Might not these divine English gifts, and the English language in which they are preached, have a better chance of making their way among the poor Celtic heathen, if the English apostle delivered his message a little more agreeably?" (*CP,* 3.392)—a suggestion that had been traditionally made, from the time of the Reformation, about the Christian proselytization of the Jews. Arnold uses this figure of conversion to expose England's goal as the utter erasure of Celtic culture. In this text on the survival of the Welsh language and culture, he criticizes the characteristic English claim that the successful colonization of the world by the language and culture of England was proof of Anglo-Saxon superiority. This was the view that his father propounded when he characterized England as "this great English nation, whose race and language are now overrunning the earth from one end of it to the other"—the same view that, later in the century, Freeman, like so many other Victorian intellectuals, continued to propound.[62] But according to Arnold, the English are in danger of committing the crime of racial extermination—no crime, of course, within the perspective of the hegemonic ideology of conquest and conversion: "we [Saxons] have plenty of strength for swallowing up and absorbing as much as we choose; there is nothing to hinder us from effacing the last poor material remains of that Celtic power which once was everywhere, but has long since, in the race of civilisation, fallen out of sight. We may threaten them with extinction if we will" (*CP,* 3.298). The conversion of the Celts into the English, the extermination of the inferior race in the ever-forward-moving "race of civilisation," is part of that ideology which Scott, and after him Thierry, anatomized.

Like Scott and Thierry, Arnold philosophically accepts the inevitability of the assimilation of races as part of modern civilization: "The fusion of all the inhabitants of these islands into one homogeneous, English-speaking whole, the breaking down of barriers between us, the swallowing up of separate provincial nationalities, is a consummation to which the natural course of things irresistibly tends" (*CP,* 3.296-97). Almost no nineteenth-century writer withstands this idea of the exigencies of "modern civilisation" (*CP*, 3.297), but like Scott and Thierry, Arnold argues for the preservation of cultural diversity. Such a position, in all three writers, sometimes seems like no more than a cultural archaeology in which a politically disenfranchised people is preserved simply through its artifacts in a kind of museum of cultural diversity. Nonetheless, it is important to recognize that even such a view was a minority position increasingly difficult to maintain as the century progressed and as the ideology of cultural and national homogeneity, based on the notion of the superiority of some races, became more and more popular. Arnold's writings, we must remember, have been criticized as "anti-patriotic" from the time of their appearance through the beginning of the twentieth century, with the claim that Arnold was in fact "a stranger," an alien, failing to understand the English character.[63]

Moreover, the concrete political contexts and consequences of such arguments about cultural diversity should not be minimized, for even an argument about the value of medieval Celtic literature could be used in contemporary political debate. In the manner of Thierry's idea of the two nations, Arnold explodes the myth of the one nation: "in England the Englishman proper is in union of spirit with no one except other Englishmen proper like himself. His Welsh and Irish fellow-citizens are hardly more amalgamated with him now than they were when Wales and Ireland were first conquered, and the true unity of even these small islands has yet to be achieved" (*CP*, 3.393). Arnold shows that the ideology of conquest and racial absorption does not lead to national unity (as historians like Prescott and Freeman claimed) but to a nation that remains divided on the basis of race. In such a light, *On the Study of Celtic Literature* becomes no mere literary project; behind it stands the entire parliamentary debate on Home Rule for Ireland, since the argument about the racial inferiority of the Celts (which Arnold claims to have learned at his father's knee) was an argument about the way in which the Irish (Celts), unlike the English (Saxons), have no gift for self-government[64]—an argument that the president of the Anthropological Society of London supported by using the racial theories of Robert Knox.[65] Similarly, Disraeli's argument about the Hebraic basis of English culture was an argument for enfranchising the Jews as English citizens. So, such topics as ancient Hebrew culture and medieval Celtic literature had in Victorian England a shared political goal in helping to determine what role to assign the modern representatives of such races in English government and culture.

A critical moment in *On the Study of Celtic Literature* occurs when a specifically racial argument emerges. Both here and in succeeding texts, Arnold highlights the moment in the history of English cultural discourse when ethnology becomes accepted as a science empowered to revise not only the place of the Celts but that of the Hebrews. This crucial moment is given special power by being at once a turning point in English cultural discourse and in Arnold's personal life.

Arnold recollects his youth by recalling the way in which the English were raised with an antipathy to the Celts and an affinity to the Hebrews. He begins with a picture of his father's influence on him in the matter of race: "I remember, when I was young, I was taught to think of Celt as separated by an impassable gulf from Teuton; my father, in particular, was never weary of contrasting them; he insisted much oftener on the separation between us and them than on the separation between us and any other race in the world; in the same way Lord Lyndhurst, in words long famous, called the Irish, 'aliens in speech, in religion, in blood' " (*CP*, 3.299-300). Arnold goes on to use the Jew as a figure to measure varying degrees of foreignness, but in Arnold's example the Jew is conceived as the cultural brother of the Teuton! "Certainly the Jew,—the Jew of ancient times, at least,—then seemed a thousand degrees nearer than the Celt to us," he explains. "Puritanism has so assimilated Bible ideas and phraseology; names like Ebenezer, and notions like that of hewing Agag in pieces, came so natural to us, that the sense of affinity between the Teutonic and the Hebrew nature was quite strong" (*CP*, 3.300). In such a passage we see the beginning of Arnold's more famous and elaborate articulation of the Hebraic foundation of English life a few years later in *Culture and Anarchy* (1869). But we also notice what I might term the negative historicization of the Jews, by means of which they are fictionalized and figuralized as no more than an ancient race, divorced from the living Jews of contemporary England—a process of historical distancing that writers such as Grace Aguilar and George Eliot critiqued.

But Arnold's depiction of the English affinity for the Jew over the Celt suddenly turns into a way of recording a radical revolution in such cultural representations. This revolution is caused by the institutionalization of the science of ethnology from the 1840s to the 1860s in England: "But meanwhile, the pregnant and striking ideas of the ethnologists about the true natural grouping of the human race, the doctrine of a great Indo-European unity, comprising Hindoos, Persians, Greeks, Latins, Celts, Teutons, Slavonians, on the one hand, and, on the other hand, of a Semitic unity and of a Mongolian unity, separated by profound distinguishing marks from the Indo-European unity and from one another, was slowly acquiring consistency and popularising itself" (*CP*, 3.300-301). While ethnology made the Celts "our brothers in the great Indo-European family" (*CP*, 3.302)—an idea that Arnold eagerly embraces, in support of his claims for the Celtic genius—ethnology at the same time, on the basis of race, upset a profound cultural affinity between the English and the Hebrews.

Arnold accepts the argument about race as a profound chasm in the continuity of English and Hebrew cultural traditions. He echoes Knox's remarks about the barrier of Nature: "we are none the better for trying to make ourselves Semitic, when Nature has made us Indo-European" (*CP,* 3.369). He accepts the modern tendency "to establish a sense of native diversity between our European bent and the Semitic bent, and to eliminate, even in our religion, certain elements as purely and excessively Semitic, and therefore, in right, not combinable with our European nature, not assimilable by it" (*CP,* 3.301). Such passages certainly seem to close the door on Disraeli's Hebraic project, and, in what shortly will be articulated as a call for the Hellenic over the Hebraic in *Culture and Anarchy,* Disraeli's project is seen as increasingly suspect. In the following pages I suggest, first, that Arnold's famous formulation of Hellenism and Hebraism in the 1860s and early 1870s is a complicated double movement in relationship to Disraeli—an endorsement and elaboration of Disraeli's formulation of the historical basis of Hebraic England, and a critique and revision of the powerful role of Hebraism in present-day England—and, second, that the new racialism of ethnology becomes an especially powerful tool in this revisionary process.

Because Arnold refused to give up the more broadly based notion of the importance of cultural traditions (as opposed to racial categories), he does not restrict himself in *Culture and Anarchy* to reiterating the racial differences between the Semite and the Indo-European. He characterizes Hebraism in ways that Disraeli would have approved—in ways, in fact, that copy Disraeli's formulations in *Coningsby, Tancred,* and elsewhere. When Arnold sent a copy of *Culture and Anarchy* to Disraeli, perhaps he had in mind not simply influencing a member of Parliament on certain political issues of the day, but also acknowledging this text as a sequel to, and revision of, Disraeli's attempt to Hebraize England. Disraeli certainly would have approved of many of Arnold's remarks, especially those in which Christianity and Hebraism seem interchangeable terms: "Christianity changed nothing in this essential bent of Hebraism to set doing above knowing" (*CP,* 5.165); "the great movement of Christianity was a triumph of Hebraism" (*CP,* 5.172). When Arnold calls Christianity "the later, the more spiritual, the more attractive development of Hebraism," and speaks of Christianity's "deeper effectiveness" and "wider influence" (*CP,* 5.169-70), he sounds like Tancred claiming that "Christianity is Judaism for the multitude, but still it is Judaism"—or even like the elder D'Israeli, who claimed in *Vaurien* that "Christianity is nothing but improved Judaism"; or, in *Genius of Judaism,* that "in Judaism we trace our Christianity, and in Christianity we are reminded of our Judaism."[66]

In such passages in *Culture and Anarchy* Arnold attempts to use Hebraism in the same way that he used the Celtic genius in *On the Study of Celtic Literature.* We have a striking explanation of this goal in a letter he wrote to Louisa de Rothschild, an intimate Jewish friend in whom he often confided about his work. While acknowledging the idea of racial difference, he explains at least one critical function that Hebraic culture holds for his English audience: "It is curious that, though Indo-European, the English people is so constituted and trained that there is a thousand times more chance of bringing it to a more philosophical conception of religion than its present conception of Christianity as something utterly unique, isolated, and self-subsistent, through Judaism and its phenomena, than through Hellenism and its phenomena."[67] As usual, what Arnold regularly called the Philistinism of the English is their failure to recognize the cultural diversity that stands behind their most prized institutions, so that, just as the proper valuation of the Celtic genius can show the English the varied origins of their national culture and history, an understanding of Judaism can expand their narrow view of Christianity as unique, isolated, and self-subsistent.

Only one month later, in a letter written to another woman who exerted an even more powerful influence on Arnold's life, especially insofar as she was the guardian of Thomas Arnold's memory, Arnold writes to his mother about not the Hebraic but the Hellenic origins of Christianity—with the added notion of devaluing the Hebraic contribution to Christianity:

> I have been reading this year in connexion with the New Testament a good deal of Aristotle and Plato, and this has brought papa very much to my mind. Bunsen used to say that our great business was to get rid of all that was purely Semitic in Christianity, and to make it Indo-Germanic, and Schleiermacher that in the Christianity of us Western nations there was really much more of Plato and Socrates than of Joshua and David; and, on the whole, papa worked in the direction of these ideas of Bunsen and Schleiermacher, and was perhaps the only powerful Englishman of his day who did so.[68]

So, while in his letter to Lady de Rothschild, Arnold thinks that the English need to comprehend the Judaic origins of their Christianity, in his letter to his mother, his classical reading—especially as a reminder of his dead father—seems to function as a vehicle to reinstate the connection of the English to the Hellenic by means of the racial category of the Indo-Germanic, recalling both the classical learning and the long-prized

Teutonism of his father. Suddenly, what seems called for is "to get rid of all that was purely Semitic in Christianity"—as if, while Arnold's theoretical project might be to establish the historical origins of Christianity in Judaism, his practical goal was to purge, for the contemporary Englishman, the Semitic element in Christianity.

In trying to specify the nature and extent of the Jewish influence on *Culture and Anarchy,* we must understand Lady de Rothschild's role both in her direct relationship with Arnold and in her function as the mediator of Arnold's relationship with Disraeli, setting up meetings, carrying messages between them, sending Arnold's work to Disraeli, and so on. It is more than fitting that she is the recipient of the letter in which Arnold (like Disraeli) seems to take as his goal the attempt to demonstrate to the English the Judaic roots of Christianity. For Arnold began to use Lady de Rothschild as a sounding board for such an idea in the time leading up to the writing of *Culture and Anarchy,* just as he used her as a go-between in his relationship with Disraeli. Arnold's biographer even suggests her influence on his book on Celtic literature: "Cultivated, learned, realistic, she had a sense of impermanence and change, of the suffering of her race, of the pathos of the historic past," that contributed to Arnold's sympathy for the downtrodden Celts.[69] Finding the power of Jewish women captivating, Arnold seems to bring alive that long line of fictional English heroes (including Harrington, Ivanhoe, Arthur Stanley, and Tancred) who find their Anglo-Saxon sympathies broadened in the encounter with Jewish women. Arnold wrote to his mother: "What women these Jewesses are! with a *force* which seems triple that of the women of our Western and Northern races."[70] Perhaps Arnold even imagined himself a kind of heroic champion of the Jews—certainly his flirtation with Lady de Rothschild, and their long and intimate relationship, leads one to believe that she was not without her influence in the formulation of the idea of the Hebraic roots of Christianity. Her influence on *Culture and Anarchy* was perhaps most fully acknowledged when Arnold, having completed the book, assigned her the role of messenger: "I hope a copy of my book has to-day gone to you; and I have also sent a copy of it to Mr. Disraeli, as I told you I should. It will be very kind of you if you will tell him that it needs no acknowledgment."[71] Not only is she the recipient of the book—she is the recipient of a message for Disraeli. And as their go-between, she carries a curiously suggestive message from Arnold, the new purveyor of the Hebraic, to Disraeli, the man who decades earlier had been a kind of prophet for the idea of Hebraism: "no acknowledgment" is necessary—on Disraeli's part, or on Arnold's?

Disraeli would have approved of the view of Christianity as an extension of Judaism in *Culture and Anarchy.* And he did, on more than one occasion, find himself in a position to approve of Arnold's work, just as Arnold flattered Disraeli on the score of his literary accomplishments. Arnold told Disraeli of mentioning "to Gladstone some of the epigrammatic things in *Endymion,*" Disraeli's last novel—an anecdote that must have delighted Disraeli, especially since the old political rivals had been cast as well in the role of literary rivals. Disraeli in turn responded with a compliment that Arnold was happy to record in a letter to his sister: "He went on to say that he read me with delight, that I was doing very great good, and ended by declaring that I was the only living Englishman who had become a classic in his own lifetime." Arnold realized that "what I have done in establishing a number of current phrases—such as Philistinism, sweetness and light, and all that—is just the sort of thing to strike him."[72] This similarity between the two writers did not go unnoticed by the public when, as early as 1869, a reviewer of *Culture and Anarchy* made a telling comparison between them: "Mr. Arnold's phrases are themselves a possession. He has all Mr. Disraeli's knack *plus* a sincerity which Mr. Disraeli has not, and grafted on a poetic and intellectual temperament of a transcendently higher stamp."[73]

When Arnold and Disraeli shared the podium in 1875 at the Royal Academy, Arnold used his speech to refer directly to Disraeli, who, as prime minister, was one of the honored guests and scheduled speakers. Arnold told a fascinating anecdote about a colony of Greeks settled in Italy, "who retained for an extraordinary length of time their Greek language and civilization" (*CP,* 8.374)—a figure, in Arnold's speech, for the way in which the artist (as statesman) strives to keep alive the Greek ideal of art, even amid the demands of state. Disraeli was the central example. After all, Arnold continued, "the brilliant statesman at the Head of Her Majesty's Government, to whom we shall listen with so much admiration by-and-by, may even boast that he was born in Arcadia" (*CP,* 8.374). The remark is a subtle attempt to convert by flattery the man whom Arnold had called, only two years earlier, a Hebrew who disparaged the Greek genius (*CP,* 6.164). Now, at the Royal Academy, he suggests that if Disraeli, sitting among the artists present, wished to be a member of the community, he would have to see himself as a Greek, a remarkable realization of Arnold's desire to Hellenize Hebraic England by calling on the Hebrew prime minister to convert. Arnold seems not to recognize that his story of the Greek colony could be read as a figure of Disraeli's fondness not for his figurative past as an artist (or Greek), but for his literal ancestry, for the glory of his Hebrew past. Arnold concludes by calling on everyone present (including Disraeli) "to confess that we were once Greeks" (*CP,* 8.375), a subtle pressure on the man who was for Arnold the leading exponent of Hebraism as opposed to Hellenism.

Arnold's apparently playful attempt to acknowledge Disraeli as an artist while attempting to de-Hebraize him and his value system is, I would argue, the key to the uneasy relationship that existed below the surface of their public encounters. It is of course Arnold's literary relationship to Disraeli that lies at the center of this uneasiness. The literary anxiety Arnold felt in relation to Disraeli is most openly expressed in the essay "Equality" (1878) when Arnold explains his motive in writing: "About four years ago Lord Beaconsfield held it [equality] up to reprobation in a speech to the students at Glasgow;—a speech so interesting, that being asked soon afterwards to hold a discussion at Glasgow, I said that if one spoke there at all at that time it would be impossible to speak on any other subject but equality. . . . I never yet have been able to go and speak there. But the testimonies against equality have been steadily accumulating from the date of Lord Beaconsfield's Glasgow speech" (*CP,* 8.278). Arnold's analysis of his intentions here represents, on a broader level, the literary relationship he shared with Disraeli. First, Arnold characterizes Disraeli as setting the literary agenda—as Disraeli did in the case of Hebraism, placing it at the center of discussions of English national identity. Next, Arnold characterizes his own belated text, "Equality" (or, I would argue, *Culture and Anarchy*), as a corrective, at once borrowing Disraeli's subject and revising the terms of that subject—only in *Culture and Anarchy* Arnold was far less open in his acknowledgment of Disraeli's influence. Even when Arnold came to announce writing a series of religious works immediately after *Culture and Anarchy,* taking up once again the idea of Hebraism, he seems to mock Disraeli as a potential model: "And this we propose to do in three or four attempts, attempts which, perhaps, if they were novels and we were Mr. Disraeli, we should call a trilogy or tetralogy; but which, they and we being what we are, we shall call simply three or four essays" (*CP,* 6.537-38). On the one hand, these words are excised from the fuller book-length version of *Literature and Dogma* because they were no longer true of the form that Arnold's work took. On the other hand, the deleted words remain a clue to the way in which Disraeli's trilogy exists as a kind of erased, or sublimated, or parodied precursor of Arnold's cultural criticism.

In *Culture and Anarchy* Arnold borrows not only Disraeli's formulations of the Hebraic basis of Christianity, but his central idea that the English owe a debt to the Hebrews. In an elaborate reformulation of that debt, Arnold sets out to show its limits:

> And, immense as is our debt to the Hebrew race and its genius, incomparable as is its authority on certain profoundly important sides of our human nature, worthy as it is to be described as having uttered, for those sides, the voice of the deepest necessities of our nature, the statutes of the divine and eternal order of things, the law of God—who, that is not manacled and hoodwinked by his Hebraism, can believe that, as to love and marriage, our reason and the necessities of our humanity have their true, sufficient, and divine law expressed for them by the voice of any Oriental and polygamous nation like the Hebrews? (*CP,* 5.208)

In this passage Arnold is demonstrating the political urgency of the otherwise apparently neutral and transhistorical terminology of Hebraism and Hellenism by speaking against a bill that, on the authority of Hebrew Scripture, would allow a man to marry the sister of his deceased wife. By calling the Jews an "Oriental" nation, he falls back on that series of references to race that seals his argument for Hellenism and against Hebraism; he asks if an "Indo-European race, the race which invented the Muses, and chivalry, and the Madonna, is to find its last word on this question in the institutions of a Semitic people, whose wisest king had seven hundred wives and three hundred concubines?" (*CP,* 5.208). In the end, Arnold uses the authority of ethnology to frame his argument that in England the corrective influence of Hellenism (against Hebraism) is needed: "Science has now made visible to everybody the great and pregnant elements of difference which lie in race, and in how signal a manner they make the genius and history of an Indo-European people vary from those of a Semitic people. Hellenism is of Indo-European growth, Hebraism is of Semitic growth; and we English, a nation of Indo-European stock, seem to belong naturally to the movement of Hellenism" (*CP,* 5.173). By using what I earlier called a consolidating pronoun of national identity ("we English"), Arnold reconstructs the English nation as the "natural" home of one "race" (Indo-European) and not another (Semitic). In short, he uses race as the final arbiter in a debate about cultural diversity and national identity. In a profound act of renaming, Arnold now seems to renounce the name that demonstrated "that peculiar Semitico-Saxon mixture which makes the typical Englishman" in favor of a name that excludes the Semitic from the national community consolidated in "we English"—excluding, in some sense, the Jews even from the readership of *Culture and Anarchy.* Finally, while I have been arguing that Arnold performs an act of authorial appropriation on Disraeli's work, here Arnold seems to perform an act of cultural appropriation. He absorbs Hebraic culture in English culture (like the absorption of Judaism in Christianity, or Hebrew Scripture in the Christian Bible), authorizing himself to limit and even to eradicate the elements of difference by which Hebraism undermines his definition of what is English—here, a racially pure definition of the English nation.

In attempting to convert Disraeli the Hebrew to Hellenism, and to absorb Hebrew culture in English culture by performing the same kind of conversion, Arnold returns to what he announced as the controlling metaphor for his work early in his career. In the early 1860s he styled himself as a kind of cosmopolitan apostle to the Philistines, "with the risk always before me, if I cannot charm the wild beast of Philistinism while I am trying to convert him, of being torn in pieces by him; and, even if I succeed to the utmost and convert him, of dying in a ditch or a workhouse at the end of it all."[74] Nor should we forget that he framed *Culture and Anarchy,* in his Preface, with the figure of conversion: "For our part, we rejoice to see our dear old friends, the Hebraising Philistines, gathered in force in the Valley of Jehoshaphat previous to their final conversion, which will certainly come" (*CP,* 5.254). Arnold's contemporary critics were quick to chastise him for his proselytizing tone in *Culture and Anarchy,* for his tendency "to preach the gospel of urbanity."[75] Moreover, we cannot neglect to notice that his attempt to convert the Philistines uses the Jew as the model of the convert. He attempts to bring the gospel of culture to "born Hebraisers" (*CP,* 5.199), to "rigid Hebraisers" (*CP,* 5.208), to those who follow "the stiff and stark notions of Hebraism" (*CP,* 5.208). Finally, the Preface to *Culture and Anarchy* endorses an ideology of assimilation that bears directly on Jewish identity: "it would still have been better for a man, during the last eighteen hundred years, to have been a Christian and a member of one of the great Christian communities, than to have been a Jew or a Socinian; because the being in contact with the main stream of human life is of more moment for a man's total spiritual growth" (*CP,* 5.251).

If *Culture and Anarchy* can be seen as an attempt to absorb, revise, and even undermine the Hebraism of Disraeli's project, it should come as no surprise that, with the publication of his first novel since *Tancred,* after a twenty-three-year hiatus, Disraeli entered the latest battle in the race wars of Victorian England by acknowledging the presence of a new participant. Disraeli's *Lothair,* published in 1870 immediately after *Culture and Anarchy,* makes direct reference to Arnold's famous formulation of Hellenism and Hebraism, and even tentatively endorses it, though not without producing a striking critique of the extremes of Hellenism, since what Arnold had done was to critique the extremes of Hebraism. And Disraeli's critique of Arnold's formulation of Hellenism did not go unnoticed by the younger author, for it was to *Lothair* that Arnold referred in *Literature and Dogma* (1873) when he spoke of Disraeli as "Lord Beaconsfield, treating Hellenic things with the scornful negligence natural to a Hebrew" (*CP,* 6.164). But, while Arnold here is referring to a passage in *Lothair,* Disraeli had already worked the ground of Hebraism and Hellenism as early as 1852, long before Arnold: "The Greek nevertheless appears exhausted. The creative genius of Israel, on the contrary, never shone so bright."[76] In *Lothair,* Disraeli's critique of Hellenism is aimed at the extreme Aryanist, Mr. Phoebus, an artist who represents pure Hellenism, or the kind of "worship of the beautiful"[77] for which Arnold was publicly taken to task in his formulation of Hellenism in *Culture and Anarchy.*[78] Mr. Phoebus attempts to (mis)educate Lothair:

> so strong and perfect a type as the original Aryan must be yet abundant among the millions, and may be developed. But for this you want great changes in your laws. It is the first duty of a state to attend to the frame and health of the subject. The Spartans understood this. They permitted no marriage the probable consequences of which might be a feeble progeny; they even took measures to secure a vigorous one. The Romans doomed the deformed to immediate destruction. The union of the races concerns the welfare of the commonwealth much too nearly to be entrusted to individual arrangement. The fate of a nation will ultimately depend upon the strength and health of the population. . . . Laws should be passed to secure all this, and some day they will be. But nothing can be done until the Aryan races are extricated from Semitism.[79]

Disraeli shrewdly exposes the ideology of Hellenism as based on a racial critique of the Jews, chillingly anticipating the consequences of such an ideology in the Nazism of the Third Reich.

Elsewhere in *Lothair,* however, Disraeli was willing to give some ground to Arnold's celebrated formulation of Hebraism and Hellenism. Modeled on the earlier mentorship between Sidonia and Tancred, the Syrian Paraclete instructs Lothair, a young English nobleman who is on a pilgrimage to the Holy Land:

> "In My Father's house are many mansions," and by the various families of nations the designs of the Creator are accomplished. God works by races, and one was appointed in due season and after many developments to reveal and expound in this land the spiritual nature of man. The Aryan and the Semite are of the same blood and origin, but when they quitted their central land they were ordained to follow opposite courses. Each division of the great race has developed one portion of the double nature of humanity, till after all their wanderings they met again, and, represented by their two choicest families, *the Hellenes and the Hebrews,* brought together the treasures of their accumulated wisdom and secured the civilisation of man (emphasis added).[80]

This speech, while not neglecting the Semitic genius for spirituality, focuses on the racial kinship of Aryan and Semite, an idea that Arnold had disputed not only in *Culture and Anarchy* but also in *On the Study of Celtic Literature* on the basis of the recent claims of ethnology. Disraeli gives Arnold his due by citing his famous formulation, but refuses to submit to the racial argument to which Arnold yields: "Hellenes" and "Hebrews" are related "families" that descend from the same "great race," and hence they are conceived as collaborators in the great work of civilization.

Just as Disraeli seemed willing to yield some ground to Hellenism, Arnold followed *Culture and Anarchy* (and Disraeli's *Lothair,* I would add) with the publication of *Literature and Dogma,* in which he defines the limits of his acceptance of racial theories for his interpretation of Hebraism. He responds to the work of Emile Burnouf, who argues that "the oracles of God were not committed to a Semitic race at all, but to the Aryan; that the true God is not Israel's God at all, but is 'the idea of the absolute' which Israel could never properly master" (*CP,* 6.239). Arnold's reaction to Burnouf's claim is an ironic remark that baits the Philistine self-congratulation that he so often associates with the largest part of his fellow countrymen: "So that we Christians, who are Aryas, may have the satisfaction of thinking that 'the religion of Christ has not come to us from the Semites' " (*CP,* 6.239). Burnouf argues that what we traditionally have taken to be Israel's original position in relation to God is historically untrue; in fact, Israel represents only a kind of bastardization of the original divine message, based on the inferiority of the Semitic races. Arnold quotes Burnouf: " 'in passing from the Aryan race to the inferior races, religion underwent a deterioration due to the physical and moral constitution of these races' " (*CP,* 6.239-40). Again, Arnold's double-edged barb is aimed at once at Burnouf and those Englishmen who will gladly rejoice in another sign of Indo-European superiority: "As Aryas or Aryans, then, we ought to be pleased at having vindicated the greatness of our race" (*CP,* 6.240). In such remarks the seeds of a full-fledged critique of the science of racialism appear, but Arnold never develops them, though he does mock the extremes of racial discourse: "Israel, therefore, instead of being a light of the Gentiles and a salvation to the ends of the earth, falls to a place in the world's religious history behind the Arya. He is dismissed as ranking anthropologically between the Aryas and the yellow men; as having frizzled hair, thick lips, small calves, flat feet, and belonging, above all, to those 'occipital races' whose brain cannot grow above the age of sixteen; whereas the brain of a theological Arya, such as one of our bishops, may go on growing all his life" (*CP,* 6.240).

This documentation of Burnouf's theories is another pivotal moment in Arnold's own personal history and the history of cultural discourse in England and Europe generally. Burnouf's *La Science des Religions,* published serially between 1864 and 1869 and in book form in 1872, marks the point when the science of race becomes empowered not simply to claim the inferiority of the Jews (as in Knox's ethnology), but to displace them from what Burnouf calls the "foremost" position in the history of religion and morals often accorded them. This is the critical moment when the ideology of race becomes empowered to disauthorize religious affiliations and to rewrite the history of religions, arguing, for example, that the Semites as a race are incapable of producing the religion of Christianity. The science of race has become, as the title of Burnouf's book proclaims, the basis for a science of religion. Burnouf's kind of racial theory found numerous proponents at the turn of the century, when, for example, Houston Stewart Chamberlain argued that the Teutons, not the Jews, were the great religious race, and that Christ, a member of the Galilean people (who had Aryan blood in them), was not a Jew.[81] Chamberlain's view develops from Burnouf's taking to its racial extreme Ernest Renan's division between Galilee and Jerusalem. We have seen how racial conflict became in nineteenth-century historiography the central historical background to the foundation of the modern nation-state. Now Burnouf imagines a kind of race war at the foundation of the religion of Christianity: "The more or less modified Mosaic doctrines of Israel only suited people of mixed races whose capital was Jerusalem; it had not the universality which characterizes a common religion, nor the transcendent metaphysics demanded by the Aryan genius. This is why, when the new religion was first preached, its earliest enemies were the Semites of Judaea; they killed Jesus."[82] The nineteenth century's racial rereadings of medieval history—produced by such writers as Scott, Thierry, Prescott, and Freeman—function as the ideological context for a racial rereading of biblical history. The Jews are reinvented as the murderers of Christ in a kind of modern-day race war that pits Semites against the Aryan Christ.

Such ideas reinvent in the late nineteenth century the kind of argument made by the Church fathers in their formulation of early Christianity. Eusebius argued that Abraham and other famous Jews were not Jews at all, but Hebrews, a code word for proto-Christians. Eusebius even argued that Christianity in its primordial form predated the religion of the Jews. In the nineteenth century such arguments are fueled by the science of race. Burnouf argues that Aryan religious doctrines predate the religion of the Semites, which is no more than a corruption of the purer, earlier religion. His explanation makes racial history the frame for understanding the history of religions: "every religion which is conveyed into the midst of an inferior race must there undergo decay."[83] Such an idea widens the gulf that we saw Disraeli closing. What he had argued was the historical continuity between two creeds, one developing out of the other, now has become a kind of racial impossibility, opening ever more widely the avenue for anti-Semitism by disinheriting the Jews, on the basis of race, from their position as the ancestors of Christianity.

Disquieted at the rising stakes in such racial arguments, Arnold retreats by taking up his position in support of Hebrew Scripture and the legitimacy of the claim that makes the Jews our first and foremost teachers in the sphere of conduct: "But we, who think that the Old Testament leads surely up to the New, who believe that, indeed, 'salvation is of the Jews,' and that, for what concerns conduct or righteousness (that is, for what concerns three-fourths of human life), they and their documents can no more be neglected by whoever would make proficiency in it, than Greece can be neglected by anyone who would make proficiency in art . . . —*we* are naturally not satisfied with this treatment of Israel and the Bible" (*CP*, 6.240-41). But such a judgment on the side of Israel, the Bible, and Hebraism comes not without its own anxieties, sounded in the elaborate statement that, as a kind of safety net, allows Arnold to speak in favor of Israel only when speaking in the same breath in favor of Greece.

Such anxieties are expressed most tellingly in Arnold's dissociation of himself from Disraeli at the beginning of *Literature and Dogma,* a fascinating maneuver in the text that is perhaps Arnold's most Hebraic. It is in the opening sentence of the Introduction that Arnold characterizes Disraeli as "Lord Beaconsfield, treating Hellenic things with the scornful negligence natural to a Hebrew" (*CP,* 6.164). But I am suggesting that we read this criticism of the Hebraic Disraeli as a sign of Arnold's own anxiety over what may be seen as an equivocation on his part, as if, renegade-like, he has suddenly turned his back on his great Hellenic, Indo-European heritage, failing to follow the advice he himself set forth in *Culture and Anarchy* by uncritically embracing Hebraism. Arnold publicly discloses this anxiety when he confesses in his Conclusion to *Literature and Dogma:* "But now, after all we have been saying of the pre-eminency of righteousness, we remember what we have said formerly in praise of culture and of Hellenism, and against too much Hebraism. . . . And we cannot wonder whether we shall not be reproached with inconsistency" (*CP,* 6.407). The text ends in a gesture of reconciliation that does not refuse the terms of race and that even takes a tentative step toward Burnouf's theories: "And so far let us venture to poach on M. Emile Burnouf's manor, and to talk about the Aryan genius, as to say, that the love of art and science, and the energy and honesty in the pursuit of art and science, in the best of the Aryan races, do seem to correspond in a remarkable way to the love of conduct, and the energy and honesty in the pursuit of conduct, in the best of the Semitic" (*CP,* 6.410). *Literature and Dogma,* then, begins by setting up Disraeli as the Hebrew who undermines the Hellenic genius—lest Arnold himself, in this newly Hebraic work that mocks Aryan pride, be so accused—and it ends by anticipating that the charge of Hebraism may now be leveled against Arnold himself and by seeking to reestablish the difficult balance between Hebraism and Hellenism.

While he tried to dissociate himself from Disraeli's project, Arnold found himself in the 1870s defending Hebraism against the specific kinds of attacks that Disraeli himself had described earlier in the century. Disraeli had recorded a series of historical events and cultural developments that attempted to undermine the significance of Semitic culture: the French Enlightenment and the French Revolution, or more recently, the German school of biblical criticism, or more recently still, the science of ethnology. Disraeli located such developments within a highly ordered series of historical alternations that anticipate Arnold's conception of the alternation between Hebraism and Hellenism, but Disraeli named them differently—"a continual struggle between Asia and the North" (*T,* 217). Disraeli placed side by side, for example, the German school of biblical criticism and the French Enlightenment as parallel, but ultimately doomed, critiques of Semitic power: "But there is no reason to believe that the Teutonic rebellion of this century against the Divine truths entrusted to the Semites will ultimately meet with more success than the Celtic insurrection of the preceding age."[84] Disraeli understood these "rebellions" as part of a cyclical pattern that was perpetually fated to fail: "I believe the state of affairs is only one of the periodical revolts of the Northern races against Semitic truth, influenced mainly by mortified vanity in never having been the medium of direct communication with the Almighty."[85] He recorded periodic disruptions, from the North, of the bedrock of Semitic truth, a view that Arnold, to his own surprise, inched towards in the 1870s.

In Disraeli's General Preface to his works, published in 1870, we find an extraordinarily accurate history of the religious doubts and attacks on the Church of England against which Arnold found himself fighting more and more after *Culture and Anarchy.* In fact, Disraeli's 1870 picture in many ways could serve as an introduction to *Literature and Dogma,* which started appearing serially in 1871. Disraeli begins with a characterization of the origins of the Church of England—"Resting on the Church of Jerusalem, modified by the divine school of Galilee, it would have found that rock of truth which Providence, by the instrumentality of the Semitic race, had promised to St. Peter"—and proceeds to characterize the enemies of religion that Arnold will come to face: "This disturbance in the mind of nations has been occasioned by two causes; first, by the powerful assault on the divinity of the Semitic literature by the Germans, and secondly, by recent discoveries of science, which are hastily supposed to be inconsistent with our long-received convictions as to the relations between the creator and the created." In the midst of this description of the causes of doubt in Victorian England, Disraeli subtly criticizes Arnold's recent stance in *Culture and Anarchy,* a stance Arnold himself goes on to critique in *Literature and Dogma* because of his renewed faith in Hebraism: "To those who believe that an atheistical society, though it may be polished and amiable, involves the seeds of anarchy, the prospect is full of gloom."[86] In such a statement Disraeli ironically inverts Arnold's famous formulation: "anarchy" proceeds from a society that has turned its back on Hebraism, a Hellenic society that is "polished and amiable" but morally empty.

Such a view is the basis of the kind of prognosis that Arnold began to make from 1870 on, with the fall of France:

> her fall is mainly due to that want of a serious conception of righteousness and the need of it, the consequences of which so often show themselves in the world's history, and in regard to the Graeco-Latin nations more particularly. The fall of Greece, the fall of Rome, the fall of the brilliant Italy of the fifteenth century, and now the fall of France, are all examples. Nothing gives more freshness and depth to one's reading of the Bible than the sense that this is so, and that this testimony is perpetually being borne to the book of righteousness, though the nation out of which it came was itself a political failure so utter and miserable.[87]

Disraeli had already made this point, using the conventional distinction between (godless) France and (Christian) England, while representing England as the land of Hebraism: "Since the great revolt of the Celts against the first and second testament, at the close of the last century, France has been alternately in a state of collapse or convulsion. Throughout the awful trials of the last sixty years, England, notwithstanding her deficient and meagre theology, has always remembered Sion."[88] The same idea, without the compliment to England, was to work its way into Arnold's rereading of the Bible in *Literature and Dogma:* "Down they come, one after another; Assyria falls, Babylon, Greece, Rome; they all fall for want of *conduct,* righteousness" (*CP,* 6.387). Disraeli made the point in this way, some two decades earlier: establishing that "The Jews represent the Semitic principle; all that is spiritual in our nature," he claims, "It may be observed that the decline and disasters of modern communities have generally been relative to their degree of sedition against the Semitic principle."[89]

Time and again cast in the role of the defender of Israel in the 1870s, Arnold sounds more and more like Disraeli. Both men produced encapsulated world histories in which the degeneration and fall of nations and empires depended on a failure in morals, that is, on a failure in upholding the Semitic principle of moral conduct. I locate such histories within the context of an emerging debate on Teutonism, articulated (for instance) by Thomas Arnold when he defined the Teutonic race as "the regenerating element in modern Europe,"[90] a view Disraeli's Tancred answered: "It is Arabia alone that can regenerate the world" (*T,* 465). In such a vein Arnold responded to one of his critics in a book entitled *God and the Bible* (1875): "And although we may willingly allow . . . that the mind and life of our Aryan race has deeply modified the religion of Semitic Israel already, and will yet modify it much more, still that cannot prevent the root of the matter for us, in this immense concern of religion, being in the Israel of the Bible, and he is our spiritual progenitor—*A Syrian ready to perish was thy father*" (*CP,* 7.395). Arnold's quotation, taken from Deuteronomy 26:5, is worthy of Disraeli's *Tancred,* with its Syrian settings and its melancholy protest against the failure of Europe to remember the Asian beginnings of its faith. Conceived in this way, Disraeli and Arnold here can be seen as revising the work of the patriotic nineteenth-century historiographers of the Middle Ages, who ask the modern Englishman to recall his early Teutonic ancestors, or the work of Arnold's own father, who spoke of "our Saxon and Teutonic forefathers."[91] Both Disraeli and Arnold became enlisted in the same battle to save the dying Syrian father in a genealogy of morals that sought the origins of modern Christian England in Israel, "our spiritual progenitor." In his religious studies of the 1870s, then, Arnold shared with Disraeli the strategy of asking his readers to see the way in which the moral genealogy of the English people was as important as their racial genealogy.

Notes

. . .[54] For a history of this development, see Reginald Horsman, "Origins of Racial Anglo-Saxonism in Great Britain Before 1850," *Journal of the History of Ideas* 37, no. 3 (July-Sept. 1976): 387-410. For an analysis of the development of a specifically "scientific" discourse about race during this period, see Nancy Stepan, *The Idea of Race in Science: Great Britain, 1800-1960* (Hamden, Conn.: Archon Books, 1982), chaps. 1 and 2.

[55] Matthew Arnold, *On the Study of Celtic Literature,* in *Complete Prose Works,* ed. Super, 3.299; hereafter abbreviated *CP.*

[56] See Robert Knox, M.D., *The Races of Men: A Philosophical Enquiry into the Influence of Race over the Destinies of Nations,* 2nd ed. (London: Henry Renshaw, 1862), pp. 193, 208. On the "pivotal" importance of Knox's work in nineteenth-century racialism in England, see Stepan, *The Idea of Race in Science,* pp. 41-45. On Knox's influence on the founder and president of the Anthropological Society of London, James Hunt, who spoke of having "imbibed [my views] from the late Dr. Knox," see Ronald Rainger, "Race, Politics, and Science: The Anthropological Society of London in the 1860s," *Victorian Studies* 22 (Autumn 1978): 51-70, esp. 55-64.

[57] See Henry Lonsdale, *A Sketch of the Life and Writings of Robert Knox* (London: Macmillan, 1870), p. 380.

[58] See Monypenny and Buckle, *The Life of Benjamin Disraeli,* 1.375, on the cries of "Old clothes!" and "Shylock" that met Disraeli for nearly an hour when he electioneered in 1837.

[59] Knox, *The Races of Men,* p. 206. Henry Lonsdale, Knox's biographer, who styles himself Knox's "Pupil and Colleague," takes a swipe—in the manner of his mentor—at Disraeli's conversion in particular, and at Jewish conversions in general, in *A Sketch of the Life and Writings of Robert Knox,* p. 249n.

[60] See Joseph Carroll, *The Cultural Theory of Matthew Arnold* (Berkeley: University of California Press, 1982), pp. 231-56, for the most comprehensive view of Arnold's debt to Heine; no mention is made, however, of Arnold's debt to Disraeli. Noting that Arnold was "steeped in the novels of Disraeli," Park Honan nonetheless does not explore the way in which Disraeli's novels influenced Arnold. *Matthew Arnold: A Life* (New York: McGraw-Hill, 1981), p. 130. Ruth apRoberts tentatively begins to suggest the effect of Arnold's reading of Disraeli. *Arnold and God* (Berkeley: University of California Press, 1983), pp. 171-75.

[61] Thomas Arnold, "Inaugural Lecture" (delivered at Oxford in 1841) in *Introductory Lectures on Modern History* (New York: D. Appleton, 1845), p. 44.

[62] See Thomas Arnold, "Inaugural Lecture," p. 42. On Freeman's presence at Thomas Arnold's inaugural lecture and reverence for him as "that great teacher of historic truth," see W. R. W. Stephens, *The Life and Letters of Edward A. Freeman,* 2 vols. (London and New York: Macmillan, 1895), 1.66. Matthew Arnold's conflict with the Anglo-Saxonism and Teutonism of the middle decades of the nineteenth century (and with Freeman in particular) is discussed by Frederic E. Faverty, *Matthew Arnold the Ethnologist* (1951; New York: AMS Press, 1968), chap. 2.

[63] See Faverty, *Matthew Arnold the Ethnologist,* pp. 4-7, on the history of the charge of antipatriotism against Arnold.

[64] See L. P. Curtis, Jr., *Anglo-Saxons and Celts: A Study of Anti-Irish Prejudice in Victorian England* (Bridgeport, Conn.: University of Bridgeport Press, 1968).

[65] See Rainger, "Race, Politics, and Science: The Anthropological Society of London in the 1860s": "In two articles published in 1868, Hunt outlined Knoxian theory on the Saxon and the Celt, insisting that the majority of Irish were Celtic and thus any question relative to their government must be settled in terms of race ('Knox on the Celtic Race')," p. 64.

[66] D'Israeli, *Vaurien,* 2.219; *The Genius of Judaism,* p. 14.

[67] *Letters of Matthew Arnold, 1848-1888,* ed. George W. E. Russell, 2 vols. (New York and London: Macmillan, 1895), 1.434.

[68] *Letters of Matthew Arnold, 1848-1888,* 1.442.

[69] See Honan, *Matthew Arnold,* p. 318.

[70] *Letters of Matthew Arnold, 1848-1888,* 1.234.

[71] *Letters of Matthew Arnold, 1848-1888,* 2.1.

[72] *Letters of Matthew Arnold, 1848-1888,* 2.218-19.

[73] *Matthew Arnold, Prose Writings: The Critical Heritage,* ed. Carl Dawson and John Pfordresher (London and Boston: Routledge and Kegan Paul, 1970), p. 246 (unsigned review of *Culture and Anarchy, Spectator,* Mar. 6, 1869).

[74] *Letters of Matthew Arnold, 1848-1888,* 1.240.

[75] See Arnold, *Complete Prose,* ed. Super, 5.638.

[76] Benjamin Disraeli, *Lord George Bentinck: A Political Biography* (1852; London: Longmans, Green, 1872), p. 354.

[77] Benjamin Disraeli, *Lothair* (London: Oxford University Press, 1975), p. 315.

[78] See Sidney M. B. Coulling, "The Evolution of CULTURE AND ANARCHY," *Studies in Philology* 60 (Oct. 1963): 637-68, who explains the way in which Arnold in response to his critics adds the category of intelligence to his definition of culture as beauty in the second article of *Culture and Anarchy* (pp. 650-51).

[79] Disraeli, *Lothair,* p. 108.

[80] Disraeli, *Lothair,* p. 316.

[81] On Chamberlain's race theories, see Frank H. Hankins, *The Racial Basis of Civilization: A Critique of the Nordic Doctrine* (New York: Alfred A. Knopf, 1931), pp. 86-88.

[82] Emile Burnouf, *The Science of Religions,* trans. Julie Liebe (London: Swan Sonnenschein, Lowrey, 1888), p. 196. On the influence of both Renan and Burnouf on Arnold, see Faverty, *Matthew Arnold the Ethnologist,* pp. 178-81.

[83] Burnouf, *The Science of Religions,* p. 190.

[84] Benjamin Disraeli, General Preface, p. xvi, in *Lothair* (Westport, Conn.: Greenwood Press, 1970).

[85] Monypenny and Buckle, *The Life of Benjamin Disraeli,* 4.350.

[86] Disraeli, General Preface, pp. xv-xvi.

[87] *Letters of Matthew Arnold, 1848-1888,* 2.55-56.

[88] Disraeli, *Lord George Bentinck,* p. 365.

[89] Disraeli, *Lord George Bentinck,* p. 365.

[90] Arthur Penrhyn Stanley, *The Life and Correspondence of Thomas Arnold, D.D.,* 2 vols. in 1 (New York: Charles Scribner's Sons, 1910), 2.328.

[91] See chap. 3 for a discussion of the way in which such historians as Sharon Turner and Edward Augustus Freeman formulate the bond between the modern Englishman and his Anglo-Saxon ancestors. See Thomas Arnold's claim that "the land of our Saxon and Teutonic forefathers" was "the birthplace of the most moral races of men that the world has yet seen" (Stanley, *The Life and Correspondence of Thomas Arnold,* 2.328), as opposed to the claim of Disraeli and Matthew Arnold that Israel was the center of the moral universe.

FURTHER READING

Baker, William. Introduction to *George Eliot and Judaism*, pp. 1-10. Salzburg, Austria: Institut für Englische Sprache und Literatur, Universität Salzburg, 1975.

Discusses the critical response to the Jewish content of *Daniel Deronda.*

Braude, Benjamin. "The Heine-Disraeli Syndrome among the Palgraves of Victorian England." In *Jewish Apostasy in the Modern World*, edited by Todd M. Endelman, pp. 108-41. New York: Holmes and Meier, 1987.

Compares the "well-known obsessions with their Jewish pasts" of Benjamin Disraeli and Heinrich Heine with similar "obsessions" of lesser known converts, such as the Palgraves, a prominent Victorian family, headed by Francis Ephraim Cohen.

Cohen, Derek, and Deborah Heller, eds. *Jewish Presences in English Literature*. Montreal: McGill-Queen's University Press, 1990, 143 p.

Traces the depiction of Jews throughout English literature, including chapters on the works of Charles Dickens, Anthony Trollope, and George Eliot.

Cowen, Anne, and Roger Cowen. *Victorian Jews through British Eyes*. Oxford: Oxford University Press, 1986, 196 p.

Discusses the perceptions prevalent among Victorians regarding Jews and the historical basis for such perceptions.

Endelman, Todd M. "Native Jews in the Victorian Age." In *Radical Assimilation in English Jewish History, 1656-1945*, pp. 73-113. Bloomington: Indiana University Press, 1990.

Explores the historical and economic developments in the nineteenth-century that affected English Jews and the perceptions about Jews. Analyzes the impact of such developments and perceptions on nineteenth-century literature.

Gallagher, Catherine. "George Eliot and *Daniel Deronda*: The Prostitute and the Jewish Question." In *Sex, Politics, and Science in the Nineteenth-Century Novel*, edited by Ruth Bernard Yeazell, pp. 39-62. Baltimore: Johns Hopkins University Press, 1986.

Discusses the "specific historical associations confronting professional women writers in the nineteenth century, when the metaphor of the author as a whore was commonplace," and uses this discussion as a basis for understanding Eliot's last novel. Links the prostitute and the stereotypical Jewish usurer as representatives of those "divorced from production" in England's developing market economy and argues that this sense of alienation is reflected in the literature of the time.

Henriques, U. R. Q. "The Jewish Emancipation Controversy in Nineteenth-Century Britain." *Past and Present* 40 (July 1968): 126-46.

Studies the history of the thirty-year struggle of Jews for political equality in England.

Jenkyns, Richard. "Change and Decay." In *The Victorians and Ancient Greece*, pp. 264-97. Cambridge, Mass.: Harvard University Press, 1980.

A portion of this chapter addresses Matthew Arnold's views of Hellenism and Hebraism as he expressed them in *Culture and Anarchy*. Jenkyns examines the various "historical and symbolic" meanings and implications of the terms "Hellenism" and "Hebraism."

Johnson, Edgar. "Dickens, Fagin, and Mr. Riah: The Intention of the Novelist." *Commentary* IX (January-June 1950): 47-50.

Defends Dickens against charges of anti-Semitism, accusations of which stem from his portrayal of Fagin in *Oliver Twist*.

Kaufmann, David. *George Eliot and Judaism: An Attempt to Appreciate "Daniel Deronda."* Translated by J. W. Ferrier. 2nd ed. New York: Haskell House Publishers, 1888, 95 p. Reprint, 1970.

Argues that *Daniel Deronda* "is a Jewish book not only in the sense of its treatment of Jews, but also in the sense that it is pre-eminently fitted for being understood and appreciated by Jews. . . ."

Knoepflmacher, U. C. "*Daniel Deronda*: Tradition as Synthesis and Salvation." In *Religious Humanism and the Victorian Novel: George Eliot, Walter Pater, and Samuel Butler*, pp. 116-48. Princeton, N.J.: Princeton University Press, 1965.

Provides a detailed study of the novel, including a section contrasting the relative "purposelessness" of the English nation with the Zionism of the novel's Jewish characters.

Landa, M. J. *The Jew in Drama*. London: P. S. King & Son, 1926, 340 p.

Traces the history of the appearance of Jewish characters in dramatic works, from a tradition of ancient Greek anti-Semitism through the Victorian period and beyond.

Lane, Lauriat, Jr. "Dickens: Archetypal Jew." *PMLA: Publications of the Modern Language Association of America* LXXIII, No. 1 (March 1958): 94-100.

Examines the stereotypical aspects of two of Dickens's Jewish characters (Fagin in *Oliver Twist*, and Riah in *Our Mutual Friend*).

Leavis, F. R. "George Eliot's Zionist Novel." *Commentary* 30, No. 4 (October 1960): 317-25.

Reverses his earlier suggestion that the Jewish portion of *Daniel Deronda* be excised from the novel, leaving only the English portion to be published as *Gwendolen Harleth*.

Naman, Anne Aresty. *The Jew in the Victorian Novel: Some Relationships between Prejudice and Art*. New York: AMS Press, 1980, 238 p.

Contains chapters discussing the prejudice regarding Jews represented in the writings of Charles Dickens, Anthony Trollope, and George Eliot.

Ragussis, Michael. *Figures of Conversion: "The Jewish Question" and English National Identity*. Durham, N.C.: Duke University Press, 1995, 340 p.

Studies the history of English views regarding tolerance and conversion of English Jews, and the role of the novel in "the public controversy over the missions to the Jews." Argues that "a particular tradition of the novel attempted to secularize this notion of tolerance toward the Jews" by "reinvent[ing] the representation of Jewish identity. . . ."

Shaffer, E. S. "*Daniel Deronda* and the Conventions of Fiction." In *"Kubla Khan" and "The Fall of Jerusalem": The Mythological School in Biblical Criticism and Secular Literature, 1770-1880*, pp. 225-91. Cambridge: Cambridge University Press, 1975.

Gives a detailed examination of George Eliot's novel, including an analysis of the novel's comparison of English identity and Jewish identity.

Stone, Harry. "Dickens and the Jews." *Victorian Studies* 11, No. 3 (March 1959): 223-53.

Studies the apparent change in Dickens's attitude toward Jews as exemplified by the characters Fagin (*Oliver Twist*) and Riah (*Our Mutual Friend*).

Tyrwhitt, R. St. John. "The Greek Spirit in Modern Literature." *The Contemporary Review* XXIX (18 March 1877): 552-66.

Reviews the nineteenth-century debate regarding Hellenism and Hebraism, as discussed by Matthew Arnold and John Addington Symonds.

Vreté, Mayir. "The Restoration of the Jews in English Protestant Thought, 1790-1840." *Middle Eastern Studies* 8, No. 1 (January 1972): 3-50.

Discusses the development of the "Jewish question" in England in Protestant writings, identifying this issue as concern regarding "the conversion of the Jews and their restoration to the land of their forefathers."

Werses, Shmuel. "The Jewish Reception of *Daniel Deronda*." In *Daniel Deronda: A Centenary Symposium*, edited by Alice Shalvi, pp. 11-43. Jerusalem: Jerusalem Academic Press, 1976.

Surveys the critical and popular Jewish reaction to Eliot's novel at the time of the novel's publication.

West, Shearer. "The Construction of Racial Type: Caricature, Ethnography, and Jewish Physiognomy in Fin-de-Siècle Melodrama." *Nineteenth-Century Theatre* 21, No. 1 (Summer 1993): 5-40.

Examines the movement of Jewish characters in melodrama from stock characters to more prominent roles, and links this development with the rise in immigration of Eastern European Jews to Britain in the 1890s.

Zatlin, Linda Gertner. *The Nineteenth-Century Anglo-Jewish Novel*. Boston: Twayne Publishers, 1981, 157 p.

Discusses the influence of politics, religion, and history on the development of the Anglo-Jewish novel.

Nineteenth-Century Literature Criticism

Topics Volume
Cumulative Indexes

Volumes 1-72

How to Use This Index

The main references

Calvino, Italo   1923–1985 .... **CLC 5, 8, 11, 22, 33, 39, 73; SSC 3**

list all author entries in the following Gale Literary Criticism series:

BLC = *Black Literature Criticism*
CLC = *Contemporary Literary Criticism*
CLR = *Children's Literature Review*
CMLC = *Classical and Medieval Literature Criticism*
DA = *DISCovering Authors*
DAB = *DISCovering Authors: British*
DAC = *DISCovering Authors: Canadian*
DAM = *DISCovering Authors: Modules*
DRAM: *Dramatists Module;* ***MST***: *Most-Studied Authors Module;*
MULT: *Multicultural Authors Module;* ***NOV***: *Novelists Module;*
POET: *Poets Module;* ***POP***: *Popular Fiction and Genre Authors Module*
DC = *Drama Criticism*
HLC = *Hispanic Literature Criticism*
LC = *Literature Criticism from 1400 to 1800*
NCLC = *Nineteenth-Century Literature Criticism*
PC = *Poetry Criticism*
SSC = *Short Story Criticism*
TCLC = *Twentieth-Century Literary Criticism*
WLC = *World Literature Criticism, 1500 to the Present*

The cross-references

See also CANR 23; CA 85-88;   obituary CA116

list all author entries in the following Gale biographical and literary sources:

AAYA = *Authors & Artists for Young Adults*
AITN = *Authors in the News*
BEST = *Bestsellers*
BW = *Black Writers*
CA = *Contemporary Authors*
CAAS = *Contemporary Authors Autobiography Series*
CABS = *Contemporary Authors Bibliographical Series*
CANR = *Contemporary Authors New Revision Series*
CAP = *Contemporary Authors Permanent Series*
CDALB = *Concise Dictionary of American Literary Biography*
CDBLB = *Concise Dictionary of British Literary Biography*
DLB = *Dictionary of Literary Biography*
DLBD = *Dictionary of Literary Biography Documentary Series*
DLBY = *Dictionary of Literary Biography Yearbook*
HW = *Hispanic Writers*
JRDA = *Junior DISCovering Authors*
MAICYA = *Major Authors and Illustrators for Children and Young Adults*
MTCW = *Major 20th-Century Writers*
NNAL = *Native North American Literature*
SAAS = *Something about the Author Autobiography Series*
SATA = *Something about the Author*
YABC = *Yesterday's Authors of Books for Children*

Literary Criticism Series Cumulative Author Index

Author Index

Author Index

Literary Criticism Series Cumulative Topic Index

This index lists all topic entries in Gale's *Classical and Medieval Literature Criticism, Contemporary Literary Criticism, Literature Criticism from 1400 to 1800, Nineteenth-Century Literature Criticism,* and *Twentieth-Century Literary Criticism.*

NCLC Cumulative Nationality Index